Child Psychology

Development in a Changing Society

BICENTENNIAL
1807
WILEY
2007
BICENTENNIAL

THE WILEY BICENTENNIAL—KNOWLEDGE FOR GENERATIONS

$\mathcal{E}$ach generation has its unique needs and aspirations. When Charles Wiley first opened his small printing shop in lower Manhattan in 1807, it was a generation of boundless potential searching for an identity. And we were there, helping to define a new American literary tradition. Over half a century later, in the midst of the Second Industrial Revolution, it was a generation focused on building the future. Once again, we were there, supplying the critical scientific, technical, and engineering knowledge that helped frame the world. Throughout the 20th Century, and into the new millennium, nations began to reach out beyond their own borders and a new international community was born. Wiley was there, expanding its operations around the world to enable a global exchange of ideas, opinions, and know-how.

For 200 years, Wiley has been an integral part of each generation's journey, enabling the flow of information and understanding necessary to meet their needs and fulfill their aspirations. Today, bold new technologies are changing the way we live and learn. Wiley will be there, providing you the must-have knowledge you need to imagine new worlds, new possibilities, and new opportunities.

Generations come and go, but you can always count on Wiley to provide you the knowledge you need, when and where you need it!

WILLIAM J. PESCE
PRESIDENT AND CHIEF EXECUTIVE OFFICER

PETER BOOTH WILEY
CHAIRMAN OF THE BOARD

Child Psychology

Development in a Changing Society

Fifth Edition

Robin Harwood

University of Connecticut

Scott A. Miller

University of Florida

Ross Vasta

State University of New York at Brockport

John Wiley & Sons, Inc.

Vice President and Publisher	Jay O'Callaghan
Executive Editor	Christopher T. Johnson
Assistant Editor	Eileen McKeever
Editorial Assistant	Carrie Tupa
Developmental Editor	Mary Ellen Lepionka
Executive Marketing Manager	Jeffrey Rucker
Senior Production Editor	William A. Murray
Senior Designer	Kevin Murphy
Senior Illustration Editor	Anna Melhorn
Senior Photo Editor	Jennifer MacMillan
Photo Researcher	Elyse Rieder
Cover and Interior Design	Amy Rosen
Cover Photo	Masterfile
Bicentennial Logo Design	Richard J. Pacifico

This book was typeset in 10.5/12.5 Adobe Caslon Regular by Preparé and printed and bound by R. R. Donnelley, Inc. The cover was printed by R. R. Donnelley, Inc.

This book is printed on acid free paper.⊗

To order books or for customer service please call 1-800-CALL WILEY (225-5945).

Library of Congress Cataloging-in-Publication Data

Harwood, Robin L.
    Child psychology: development in a changing society / Robin Harwood,
Scott A. Miller, Ross Vasta. — 5th ed.
        p. cm.
    ISBN 978-0-471-70649-6 (cloth)
1. Child psychology—Textbooks.   I. Miller, Scott A.   II. Vasta, Ross.   III. Title.
    BF721.V345 2008
    155.4—dc22
                                                                                2007031695

Printed in the United States of America

10 9 8 7 6 5 4 3 2 1

Preface

The major goals of the first four editions of *Child Psychology* (Vasta) were to serve instructors' needs, maximize student learning, and reflect accurately and comprehensively the present-day discipline of child psychology. These goals have remained central as we prepared a 5th edition. We also, however, have substantively expanded and reworked the coverage in ways that make this edition a truly new version of the textbook, one that captures the excitement and relevance of child psychology at the beginning of the 21st century. This is exemplified in the text's new subtitle: *Development in a Changing Society*. This new edition places children, child development, and the contexts in which development occurs at the center of the discourse.

• This new edition uses a contextual model as its integrative theme. This is visible in every chapter throughout the book through headings, text, features, chapter sequence, and design. For example, the chapter sequence is structured to move from the microsystem to the macrosystem. Also, every chapter has a concept map that takes a main idea from the chapter and expresses it using the framework of Bronfenbrenner's ecological systems model.

• The chapters themselves have been restructured for greater ease of presentation. Prenatal Development and Birth have now been combined so that they are included in the same chapter. The Piagetian and Vygotskian approaches to cognitive development are now presented in a single chapter, while two separate chapters are now devoted to Relationships with Peers and to Families and Society, allowing for expanded coverage of these topics.

• In addition to these broad organizational changes, we have expanded coverage of numerous topics, including development of the brain, physical health in childhood, cultural perspectives on cognition and schooling, core knowledge approaches, social problem solving, intrinsic motivation and mastery learning, development of ethnic identity, alternative family structures, and the impact of mass media and technology.

• In addition, in every chapter we have added a section that relates the chapter subject to (1) social and cultural contexts, or (2) implications of research for social policy, public practice, or societal change. Thus, *Child Psychology: Development in a Changing Society* has a strong balance of theory, research, and real-world application.

• The new edition retains its commitment to research, evident in a separate chapter on research methods and by featuring research in every chapter in a Research and Society box as well as in narrative context. However, in this new edition the focus has shifted from researchers to readers. The "Classics of Research" and "Cutting Edge Research" boxes in the 4th edition have been selectively reintegrated into the new edition's text narrative, retained as boxes, or moved to the companion web site with added pedagogy.

• At the same time that it represents research in the field of child development, the new edition focuses more on social relevance and practical application. The 4th edition was praised for its Applications boxes, and this feature has been retained in the new edition. New Applications features focus on research-based practical advice on topics of importance to parents and caregivers. In addition, each chapter has a subtitled feature, called Conversations, showcasing actual professionals in diverse fields related to child development, who talk about the families and children they serve. In Conversations, these professionals explain, for example, how knowledge of child development helps them in the challenges and rewards of working with infants and children.

• Finally, we have streamlined and integrated the pedagogical features for the fifth edition. Each chapter outlines several learning objectives which appear at the top of major sections. These learning objectives are then linked to Test Your Mastery Questions at the end of each major section. Finally, the Summary at the end of every chapter provides students with an outline to the learning objectives and mastery questions, and their answers.

MAJOR FEATURES OF CHILD PSYCHOLOGY: CHILD DEVELOPMENT IN A CHANGING SOCIETY

Several important features have characterized *Child Psychology* throughout each of its editions: an emphasis on a contextualist view of human development, a concern with cultural context and cultural diversity, and an emphasis on state-of-the-art coverage. In addition, *Child Psychology* has always featured topical organization, and a focus on readability and accessibility to students.

A Contextualist Approach

The most important and distinctive feature of *Child Psychology: Development in a Changing Society* remains its emphasis on the contextualist view of human development. Inspired by Urie Bronfenbrenner's seminal work and fueled by the rediscovery of Lev Vygotsky's writings, modern child psychology has increasingly adopted a contextualist perspective. The child is not viewed as a passive recipient of environmental influences but as an active producer of those influences. From the very beginning, the infant engages in a transactional "dance" with the caregiver, each regulating the behavior of the other. As the child grows, development interacts in critical ways with the social contexts in which it occurs, some of the most important being the family system, the peer group, the school, and the cultural environment.

As in previous editions, *Child Psychology* integrates relevant contextual material throughout the text. Thus, in addition to discussing the effects of schools, families, and peers in separate chapters, we consider such influences for each of the topics for which they are relevant. For example, Chapter 11 examines the impact of adverse social circumstances on the development of attachment, Chapter 12 discusses the ways in which schools can affect self-esteem, and Chapter 14 considers the impact of both parents and peers on moral development. This approach allows the course to move from one area of development to another in a topical manner, while including the broad tapestry of variables that affect each area.

We have made three major changes to the present edition that we believe result in an even stronger presentation of contextual influences. First, we have made the contextual perspective a guiding model throughout the text, with structural reorganization and a conceptual map at the end of every chapter demonstrating key elements of the child's ecosystem that influence development according to each chapter topic. Second, we have reworked the "Families and Peers" chapter into two separate chapters: Relationships with Peers, and Families and Society. Discussions of peer and family influences still occur throughout the book. The new organization, however, permits a fuller consideration of general issues in the study of peers and the family (e.g., parenting styles, the family as a system), and the expanded coverage in the final chapter on Families and Society allows for a deeper examination of the influence of the exosystem and macrosystem on child development.

Cultural Diversity

Each edition of this book has seen expanded coverage of research in diverse communities in North America and in cultures around the world. This remains true for the fifth edition. Discussions of development in different cultures are woven throughout the text. For example, we describe how different cultures foster different approaches to language learning (Chapter 10), we discuss different conceptions of the self and morality across different cultures (Chapters 12 and 14), and we consider cultural variations in childrearing practices (Chapter 16).

In addition, the inclusion of the contextual model as a guiding perspective has allowed us to provide a conceptual framework within which students can interpret such work. We believe that this change makes our treatment of development in cultural context exceptionally strong.

State-of-the-Art Coverage

Information is being generated in the field of child development at a staggering rate. To prepare a textbook of manageable proportions, authors must make some tough decisions. We have chosen to balance seminal and classical studies in the field with up-to-date references of articles published in the last few years.

In addition to such general updating, every chapter includes a feature entitled Research and Society. These sections permit a fuller discussion of some especially interesting recent research developments that have high real-world relevance, such as the mapping of the genome or the latest brain imaging techniques. Although our focus is on current work, we recognize that some truly classic studies should be known by every student of human development. This material has been integrated into the text.

Topical Organization

We have chosen to organize the book topically. By considering each topic area in a single chapter, we believe we can most effectively present and critique the full body of research and theorizing relevant to that area. The 16 chapters can be grouped into five general parts, integrated thematically according to an ecological model:
• Understanding the Contexts of Child Development: Chapters 1, 2, and 3 provide the foundation of the discipline, covering theoretical and historical frameworks for child development, studying child development in context, and the biological context of development.
• Contexts of Physical Development: Chapters 4-6 focus on aspects of physical development, such as prenatal development and birth; the early capacities of infancy, including motor, sensory, and perceptual development; and physical growth and health.

• Contexts of Cognitive Development: Chapters 7-10 cover Piagetian and Vygotskian approaches to cognitive development; information processing and the core knowledge approach; intelligence and schooling; and language and communciation.

• Contexts of Social and Emotional Development: Chapters 11-14 describe social and emotional development, including emotional development, attachment, the self-system, moral reasoning, prosocial and antisocial behavior, and gender role development.

• Peer, Family, and Community Contexts: Chapters 15-16 focus on peer relations, families, and influences of the larger society.

Although the overall organization is topical, the internal presentation of Chapters 4-16 is developmental. The topic area—be it language, gender roles, or whatever—begins with the newborn and describes development through adolescence. This approach helps the student to appreciate the continuity of growth within each area and also to understand the ongoing interactions between biological processes and contextual influences. In addition, a new feature highlights content links between chapters in the margins of the text.

Readability and Accessibility

We have worked hard to make our text above all interesting and accessible to the student reader. We believe that the text's comfortable writing style and the clarity with which concepts are introduced, discussed, and interrelated will enable students to read and understand a rigorous treatment of the issues. Users of previous editions have consistently praised the text's accessibility.

In addition, we have focused throughout the text on real-world relevance and application. This is particularly evident in our use of the Applications and Conversations features in every chapter.

PEDAGOGICAL FEATURES

In our effort to be complete and up to date, we have not forgotten that this is a textbook whose audience includes college sophomores. We have designed into the book a number of features to maximize the likelihood that students will learn the material.

Chapter-Opening Vignettes

Each of the chapters begins with a brief story designed to capture the student's interest and to introduce the topic under consideration. In Chapter 3, for example, we open with the story of Carbon Copy, the cloned kitten, and we consider some of the intriguing ethical questions posed by the research. In Chapter 8 we preview the discussion of information processing with the true story of Josh Waitzkin, child chess champion, and ask students to consider what types of thinking might distinguish a novice from an expert in a given domain.

Research & Society Feature

The Research and Society Feature, which appears in every chapter, is designed to make students aware of recent and exciting research findings that have high real-world relevance and application. Among the topics singled out for such coverage are the Human Genome Project (Chapter 3), Technology and Gender Selection (Chapter 4), Imaging the Brain (Chapter 6), Bilingual Education (Chapter 10), and Bullying and Victimization (Chapter 15).

Conversations Feature

• This feature, appearing in every chapter, showcases actual professionals in diverse fields related to child development, who talk about the families and children they serve. In Conversations, these professionals explain, for example, how knowledge of child development helps them in the challenges and rewards of working with infants and children. Examples include conversations with an adoption social worker (Chapter 3), a pediatric physical therapist (Chapter 5), a speech-language pathologist (Chapter 10), and men in nontraditional roles (Chapter 13).

Applications Feature

This feature appears in every chapter and presents examples of research programs and findings that have been applied to the solution of practical problems in schools, homes, hospitals, and other real-world settings. Examples include Society, Teens and Sexuality (Chapter 6), Brains in a Box: Do New Age Toys Deliver on the Promise? (Chapter 8), and Reducing Stereotype Threat in Minority Populations (Chapter 9).

Test Your Mastery Sections

At the end of each major section in a chapter, questions are presented that link to the learning objective for that section. This organization encourages students to pause and reflect on what they have just read and helps set the stage for the sections that follow. Learning is reinforced when the answers to the Test Your Mastery sections are provided in the Chapter Summary.

Chapter Summaries

Each chapter ends with a summary of the major points and issues to help students organize and review the chapter's material. These summaries are designed to facilitate learning by linking clearly to the learning objectives and Test Your Mastery sections for each chapter.

Running Glossary

Boldfaced glossary items in the text highlight terms of continuing importance to students. These items are defined in the margin on the same page, as well as at the end of the book, providing a convenient guide for reviewing the material.

For Discussion Questions

Included in each chapter are a set of questions designed to foster critical thinking. Each question notes a finding or principle from the chapter and asks the student to apply it to an issue of real-world or personal relevance.

Margin Links to Related Content

Each chapter features links to related content in other chapters, provided in the margins. This gives students a greater appreciation for the ways in which development in one domain relates to development in other domains.

Illustration Program

We reworked many of the figures and drawings from the previous edition to create new, effective illustrations in a full-color format. We also carefully selected many new color photos that depict situations and events described in the text, along with some that illustrate laboratory techniques and other research methods.

SUPPLEMENTARY MATERIALS

Accompanying the text is a full package of materials to support student learning and classroom teaching. The package includes the following.

Student Study Guide

The study guide for students contains chapter outlines, learning objectives, key terms, application exercises, critical thinking exercises, self-test questions, and practice exams. This guide was prepared by Claire Novosad of Southern Connecticut State University.

Instructor's Resource Manual

The Instructor's Resource Manual contains guidelines for the first-time instructor, chapter outlines, learning objectives, key terms, lecture topics, discussion questions, in-class and out-of-class activities, supplemental readings, video guide, and media materials. The guide was prepared by Joyce Hemphill of the University of Wisconsin, Madison, and is available on-line at www.wiley.com/college/harwood.

Test Bank

The test bank provides approximately 120 questions for each chapter, keyed to the text in multiple-choice and essay formats. Each question notes the text page on which the answer can be found and whether the question is factual or conceptual. The test bank was prepared by Susan Siaw of the California State Polytechnic University, Pomona and is available on-line at www.wiley.com/college/harwood.

POWERPOINT FILES

A set of files with accompanying lecture notes is available on-line at www.wiley.com/college/harwood for instructor use. The PowerPoint slides were prepared by Jennifer Lindner.

Video Library

Instructors can choose from a variety of videos and clips for class presentation from the Child Psychology Video Library. Please contact your local Wiley representative for more details about the different video options.

Web Site

Using the Vasta Web site, located at http://www.wiley.com/college/harwood, students can take practice quizzes for each chapter, and instructors can download the text supplements directly to their computers.

Acknowledgments

A project of this size requires the participation of many people. We thank Lisa Comparini for her work on Chapter 7; Gretchen Van de Walle for her work on Chapters 7 and 8; Stephen Burgess for his work on Chapters 9, 10, and 12; and Kathryn Jtineant and Gozde Demir for their work on the reference list. We are grateful to Alastair Younger for his contributions to the third and current editions of the text, especially Chapter 2, and to Marshall Haith and Shari Ellis, who were coauthors of earlier editions of the book. Finally, we are grateful to our colleagues who supplied material for the Culture and Society, Conversations, and Applications features: Frances Waksler, Lisa Comparini, Vivian Carlson, Jeannine Pinto, Patricia Greenfield, Caroline Johnston, Gail Rollins, Amy Miller, Kathy Hirsh-Pasek, Chloe Bland, Joan Miller, Ronald Rohner, and Abdul Khaleque.

This book is about children, and we never would have entered the field of child psychology—let alone have pursued its study with such pleasure—without the inspiration of our own wonderful children. They always have our deepest gratitude.

We owe special thanks to our Developmental Editor, Mary Ellen Lepionka. This book could not have been completed without her assistance and dedication.

We would also like to acknowledge the contributions of the many colleagues who have provided reviews or suggestions that have helped to strengthen the various editions of this text. The following individuals served as reviewers or provided other forms of input for the current edition.

Mary Beth Ahlum *Nebraska Wesleyan University*
Daisuke Akiba *Queens College of the City University of New York*
Dana Albright *Clovis Community College*
Maria Bravo *Central Texas College*
Nancy Budwig *Clark University*
Bruce Carter *Syracuse University*
Juan F. Casas *University of Nebraska, Omaha*
Dionne Clabaugh *Gavilon College*
Robert Cohen *University of Memphis*
Donna Couchenour *Shippensburg University of Pennsylvania*
Bill Curry *Wesleyan College*
Shawn E. Davis *University of Houston-Downtown*
Melanie Deckert-Pelton *University of West Florida*
John Dilworth *Kellogg Community College*
Janet DiPietro *Johns Hopkins University*
Rosanne K. Dlugosz *Scottsdale Community College*
Ken Dobush *Bridgewater State College*
Gina Annunziato Dow *Denisen University*
Jerome B. Dusek *Syracuse University*
Anne O. Eisbach *Quinnipiac University*
Khaya Novick Eisenberg *University of Detroit-Mercy*
David Estell *Indiana University*
S. A. Fenwick *Augustana College*
Donna Fisher-Thompson *Niagara University*
William Franklin *California State University*
Harvey J. Ginsburg *Southwest Texas State University*
Dennis M. Goff *Randolph-Macon Woman's College*
Allen Gottfried *California State University*
Elizabeth K. Gray *North Park University*
Joelle K. Greene *Pomona College*
Jiansheng Guo *California State University*

Rob Guttentag *University of North Carolina-Greensboro*
Dorathea Halpert *Brooklyn College, City University of New York*
Steven J. Hayduk *Southern Wesleyan University*
Beth Hentges *University of Houston-Clear Lake*
Jennifer M. Hill *City University of New York Graduate Center*
Jeffrey A. Howard *Eckerd College*
Margaret Hellie Huyck *Illinois Institute of Technology*
Marsha Ironsmith *East Carolina University*
Elaine M. Justice *Old Dominion University*
Kathleen N. Kannass *University of Kansas*
Kevin Keating *Broward Community College-North Campus*
Cheri L. Kittrell *University of Tampa*
Paul Klaczynski *Pennsylvania State University*
Kathy F. Kufskie *Florissant Valley Community College*
Lloyd Lorin La Rouge *The University of Wisconsin, Whitewater*
Lana Larsen *University of Maryland, University College*
Cynthia Legin-Bucell *Edinboro University of Pennsylvania*
Angeline Lillard *University of Virginia*
Wendy M. Little *Westmont College*
Glenn Lowery *Springfield College*
Arlene R. Lundquist *Utica College*
Saramma T. Mathew *Troy State University*
Jessica Miller *Mesa State College*
Terry C. Miller *Wilmington College of Ohio*
Mary Mindess *Lesley University*
Elizabeth A. Mosco *University of Nevada, Reno*
Ron Mulson *Hudson Valley Community College*
Robin Musselman *Lehigh Carbon Community College*
Jeffrey Nagelbush *Ferris State University*

Dawn Niedner *Purdue University Calumet*
Sonia Nieves *Broward Community College*
Claire Novosad *Southern Connecticut State University*
Alan Y. Oda *Azusa Pacific University*
Rose R. Oliver *Amherst College*
Leanne Olson *Wisconsin Lutheran College*
Robert Pasternak *George Mason University*
Margarita Pérez *Worcester State College*
Wayne J. Robinson *Monroe Community College*
Stephanie Rowley *University of Michigan*
Claire Rubman *Suffolk County Community College*
Larissa Samuelson *University of Iowa*
Nicholas R. Santilli *John Carroll University*
Pamela Braverman Schmidt *Salem State College*
Billy M. Seay *Louisiana State University*
Tam Spitzer *St. John Fisher College*
Richard A. Sprott *California State University-Hayward*
Ric Steele *University of Kansas*
Mary Steir *University of Hartford*
Margaret Szweczyk *University of Illinois, Urbana-Champaign*
Francis Terrell *University of North Texas*
David G. Thomas *Oklahoma State University*
Lesa Rae Vartanian *Indiana University—Purdue University Fort Wayne*
Amy Wagenfeld *Lasell College*
Alida Westman *Eastern Michigan University*
Matthew Westra *Longview Community College*
Colin William *Columbus State Community College*
Herkie Lee Williams *Compton Community College*
Laurie A. Wolfe *Raritan Valley Community College*
Gretchen Miller Wrobel *Bethel College*

We are also grateful to colleagues who provided reviews of the earlier editions of the book.

Brian P. Ackerman *University of Delaware*

Linda Baker *University of Maryland, Baltimore County*

Marie T. Balaban *Eastern Oregon University*

Byron Barrington *University of Wisconsin-Marathon County*

Karen Bauer *University of Delaware*

Dan Bellack *College of Charleston*

Sarah Bengston *Augustana College*

Cynthia Berg *University of Utah*

Rebecca Bigler *University of Texas, Austin*

Dana Birnbaum *University of Maine*

Fredda Blanchard-Fields *Georgia Institute of Technology*

Cathryn L. Booth *University of Washington*

Theodore Bosack *Providence College*

Michelle Boyer-Pennington *Middle Tennessee State University*

Kristine Brady *Rider University*

Gordon F. Brown *Pasadena City College*

Harriet Budd Roger V. Burton *SUNY at Buffalo*

Bruce D. Carter *Syracuse University*

Stephen J. Ceci *Cornell University*

Xinyin Chen *University of Western Ontario*

Stewart Cohen *University of Rhode Island*

Jodi Compton *Framingham State University*

Ed Cornell *University of Alberta*

James Dannemiller *University of Wisconsin-Madison*

K. Laurie Dickson *Northern Arizona University*

Janet DiPietro *Johns Hopkins University*

Shelly Drazen *SUNY Albany*

Beverly D. Eckhardt *Albuquerque Vocational-Technical Institute*

Melissa Faber *University of Toledo*

Beverly I. Fagot *University of Oregon*

Shirlee Fenwick *Augustana College*

Mary Ann Fischer *Indiana University-Northwest*

William Franklin *California State University, Los Angeles*

Barry Ghoulson *University of Memphis*

Katherine W. Gibbs *University of California, Riverside*

Gail S. Goodman *University of California, Davis*

Allen Gottfried *California State University, Fullerton*

Terry R. Greene *Franklin & Marshall College*

Vernon Hall *Syracuse University*

William S. Hall *University of Maryland at College Park*

Yolanda Harper *University of Tulsa*

Yvette R. Harris *Miami University*

Vernon Haynes *Youngstown University*

Melissa Heston *University of Northern Iowa*

Erika Hoff *Florida Atlantic University*

Kenneth I. Hoving *University of Oklahoma*

Marsha Ironsmith *East Carolina University*

Jane Jakoubek *Luther College*

Boaz Kahana *Cleveland State University*

Kenneth Kallio *SUNY Geneseo*

Christine Kenitzer *Texas Tech University*

Janice Kennedy *Georgia Southern University*

Wallace Kennedy *Florida State University*

Marguerite D. Kermis *Canisius College*

Katherine Kipp *University of Georgia*

Paul Klaczynski *Pennsylvania State University*

Gerald Larson *Kent State University*

Elizabeth Lemerise *Western Kentucky University*

Gary Levy *University of Utah*

Angeline Lillard *University of Virginia*

Pamela Ludeman *Framingham State University*

Kevin MacDonald *California State University, Long Beach*

Barbara Manning *University of Nebraska-Omaha*

Tammy A. Marche *St. Thomas More College*

John C. Masters *Vanderbilt University*

Robert G. McGinnis *Ancilla College*

Patricia McKane *Augustana College*

Margie McMahan *Cameron University*

Carolyn Mebert *University of New Hampshire*

Morton J. Mendelson *McGill University*

Richard Metzger *University of Tennessee at Chattanooga*

Barbara Moely *Tulane University*

Ernst L. Moerk *California State University, Fresno*

Derek Montgomery *Bradley University*

Lisa Oakes *University of Iowa*

Cynthia O'Dell *Indiana University-Northwest*

Lynn Okagaki *Purdue University*

Jeff Parker *Pennsylvania State University*

Vicky Phares *University of South Florida*

Harvey A. Pines *Canisius College*

Catherine Raeff *Indiana University of Pennsylvania*

Dina Raval *Towson State University*

D. Dean Richards *University of California, Los Angeles*

William L. Roberts *York University*

Marite Rodriguez-Haynes *Clarion University*

Karl Rosengren *University of Illinois*

Jane Rysberg *California State University, Chico*

Nicholas R. Santilli *John Carroll University*

Ellin Scholnick *University of Maryland*

Frederick M. Schwantes *Northern Illinois University*

Gayle Scroggs *Cayuga Community College*

Kathleen Sexton-Radek *Elmhurst College*

Harriet Shaklee *University of Iowa*

Cecilia Shore *Miami University*

Susan Siaw *California Polytechnic State University*

Robert S. Siegler *Carnegie Mellon University*

Gregory Simpson *University of Kansas*

Frank J. Sinkavich *York College of Pennsylvania*

Rita Smith *Millersville University of Pennsylvania*

Thomas R. Sommerkamp *Central Missouri State University*

Kathy Stansbury *Mount Holyoke College*

Debra Cowart Steckler *Mary Washington University*

Ric G. Steele *University of Kansas*

Margaret Szewczyk *University of Illinois at Urbana-Champaign*

Francis Terrell *University of North Texas*

David G. Thomas *Oklahoma State University*

Laura Thompson *New Mexico State University*

Katherin Van Giffen *California State University, Long Beach*

Lesa Rae Vartanian *Indiana Purdue University, Fort Wayne*

Diane N. Villwock *Moorehead State University*

Leonard Volenski *Seton Hall University*

Amye Warren *University of Tennessee at Chattanooga*

Beth Wildman *Kent State University*

Nanci Stewart Woods *Austin Peay State University*

Alastair Younger *University of Ottawa*

Martha Zlokovich *Southeast Missouri State University*

About the Authors

Robin L. Harwood

Robin Harwood is a Research Scientist at the University of Connecticut, Department of Anthropology, and a Visiting Professor at the Ruhr University, Bochum, Germany. She received her Ph.D. in developmental psychology from Yale University in 1991. She has previously authored (with Joan Miller and Nydia Lucca Irizarry) *Culture and Attachment: Perceptions of the Child in Context*. Her research has focused on cultural influences on parenting and early socioemotional development.

Scott A. Miller

Scott Miller is Professor of Psychology at the University of Florida. After completing his undergraduate work at Stanford University in 1966, he entered the Institute of Child Development at the University of Minnesota, where he earned his Ph.D. in 1971. His initial appointment was at the University of Michigan. He is a Fellow in the American Psychological Association (Division 7). He has previously authored *Developmental Research Methods*, second edition, and coauthored (with John Flavell and Patricia Miller) *Cognitive Development*, fourth edition. His research has been in the cognitive area, focusing on Piaget's work, children's understanding of logical necessity, theory of mind, and parents' beliefs about children.

Ross Vasta

Before his death in 2000, Ross Vasta was Distinguished Professor of Psychology at the State University of New York at Brockport. He received his undergraduate degree from Dartmouth College in 1969 and his Ph.D. in clinical and developmental psychology from the State University of New York at Stony Brook in 1974. He was a Fellow in the American Psychological Society and the American Psychological Association (Division 7). In 1987 he was awarded the SUNY Chancellor's Award for Excellence in Teaching. His previous books include *Studying Children: An Introduction to Research Methods, Strategies and Techniques of Child Study*, and *Six Theories of Child Development*. He also edited the annual series *Annals of Child Development*.

Brief Contents

Contents

3 The Biological Context of Development

PART II CONTEXTS OF PHYSICAL DEVELOPMENT

4 Prenatal Development, Birth, and the Newborn

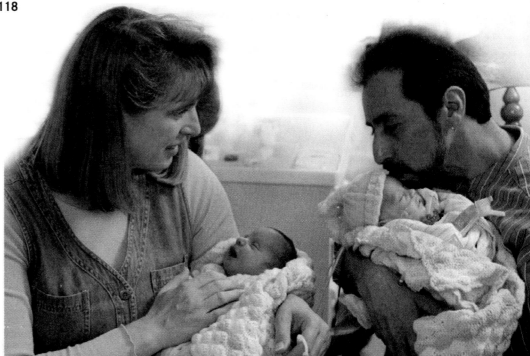

7 Piaget and Vygotsky

8 Information Processing and Core Knowledge Approaches

13 Sex Differences and Gender Role Development

14 Moral Development

Frameworks
for Development

In what ways does this child's cultural & historical contexts shape his development?

(John Warburton-Lee/Danita Delimont)

The [Gusii of] Nyansongo [Kenya] had the largest number of children (50 percent) involved in the herding of animals. The young boys took the cattle, sheep, and goats to the homestead pastures or drove them along the sides of the road where there was grass. They were responsible for seeing that the animals did not get into the gardens and ruin their own or someone else's food supply. They drove the cattle, sheep, and goats to the river to drink and took care that they returned home with the proper number of animals. (Whiting & Whiting, 1975, p. 90)

[In] Orchard Town [New England, USA] the tasks assigned to children are less clearly related to the economy and welfare of the child or the child's family and probably seem more arbitrary to the child. . . . The need for having clothes hung up, bureau drawers tidy, or the bed smoothed out neatly is probably not immediately clear, nor are the consequences of negligence obviously serious. (Whiting & Whiting, 1975, p. 106)

These paragraphs describe children who are growing up in two very different contexts. The first context is a small village in Kenya populated by subsistence farmers. Children help with chores that are essential to survival. Through their daily involvement with these tasks, they learn the skills necessary to become productive farmers themselves someday. The second context is a small town in the northeastern United States. Children grow up in home settings and go to schools that are typically separated from adult work environments. School usually focuses on acquiring skills that children may not easily associate with the adult roles they will someday assume.

How might growing up in these two very different contexts affect a child's development? For example, what skills and abilities are likely to be practiced and acquired by a child who is contributing to daily subsistence through herding animals or watching younger siblings while parents work in the fields, as compared to a child who spends a great deal of after-school time in leisure activities such as play and TV? ■

Child Development in Space and Time

Developmental psychology
The branch of psychology devoted to the study of changes in behavior and abilities over the course of development.

The study of child development, also known as **developmental psychology**, is one of the largest of psychology's many subfields. It is concerned with the changes in behavior and abilities that occur over time as development proceeds. Developmental researchers examine what the changes are and why they occur.

The field of child development consists of five major topics or dimensions of development that researchers focus on in their studies: physical, cognitive, linguistic, emotional, and social. In this book, we will discuss child development as it occurs within each of these broad domains.

- A researcher who studies the *physical* domain will examine topics such as development's genetic foundations, physical growth, motor development, health, or sensory and perceptual development.
- Someone who studies *cognitive* development will focus on questions such as how children think, learn, remember, and solve problems.
- *Linguistic* development is concerned with how children acquire speech and learn to communicate using language.
- Studies of *emotional* development examine topics such as children's temperament, or styles of responding to the environment, the quality of their attachments, and the development of emotions and self-concept.
- Researchers who are interested in children's *social* development will study topics such as peer and family relationships, moral development, aggression, and prosocial behavior.

In addition, the field of child development is usually broken down into specific age periods. These are:

- *Prenatal*, or conception to birth
- *Infancy/toddlerhood* (birth to 36 months)
- *Preschool or early childhood* years (3–5 years)
- *Middle childhood or school age* (6–12 years)
- *Adolescence* (ages 13–18)

When we study children's development over time, we are looking at how children change in their physical, cognitive, linguistic, emotional, and social development across these age periods.

Finally, child development researchers recognize that children are born into families—typically, families that hope the best for them. These families live within neighborhoods, which exist within communities, that in turn are part of larger societies and cultures. As children develop, their lives are influenced by each of these contexts: families and the love and types of resources they bring; neighborhoods and the educational settings they provide; communities and the peers and activities they offer for play and enrichment. Societies provide laws and institutions that guide childrearing, whereas cultures shape the beliefs and values that permeate the lives of children and their parents at all levels. In addition, societies and cultures change over time in some ways, while staying the same in other ways. These conditions and changes are the contexts of child development.

Many aspects of child development reflect our biological heritage as human beings and so are universal across cultures and societies. This textbook traces the growing child's biological development from the embryo's earliest beginnings to the child's eventual adolescence. Many other aspects of development, however, are shaped by children's families, neighborhoods, communities, and cultures. In addition to paying attention to the influence of biology on child development, this textbook focuses on the larger environmental context in which child development takes place. Thus, this textbook presents child development within a contextual framework.

Questions for Thought
    and Discussion
In what ways has your development been shaped by your time and place?

Questions for Thought
    and Discussion
What behaviors or aspects of children's development are you particularly interested in learning about in this course?

Contexts of Child Development

Traditionally, scientific research on children's development has taken place in laboratory settings, and for many good reasons. The most important reason is that scientific investigation demands careful experimental control, and the laboratory has traditionally afforded the only setting in which such control can be achieved. However, children's development does not take place in laboratories. It takes place at home, with the family; at school, with classmates and teachers; in the park, with neighbors and peers; and within a larger social and cultural environment. In short, *development always occurs in a context, and the context often influences the course of development.*

An Ecological Model The contexts of child development can be understood as a kind of ecological system. Urie Bronfenbrenner's **ecological systems model** is based on the idea that we can understand development completely by considering how the unique characteristics of a child interact with that child's surroundings (1979, 1992; Bronfenbrenner & Morris, 1998; Pinquart & Silbereisen, 2004). The child possesses a variety of personal characteristics, such as personality traits, physical appearance, and intellectual abilities. Bronfenbrenner described the most important characteristics as (1) *developmentally generative*—capable of influencing other people in ways that are important to the child; and (2) *developmentally disruptive*—capable of causing problems in the environment with corresponding negative effects on the child.

For example, suppose 2-year-old Avery has the developmentally generative characteristic of being highly verbal for her age. This affects her environment, for example, by

Ecological systems model
Brofenbrenner's model of development, which focuses on individuals and their relationships and interactions within their environmental contexts.

encouraging her parents to spend more time reading to her, which in turn encourages Avery to further expand her vocabulary. Avery's preschool teachers also respond to her verbal behavior by providing additional reading materials and speaking to her using more complex sentence structure and a greater variety of vocabulary words. Her teachers' response to her verbal skills leads to a further increase in her verbal skills relative to other children her age, which in turn affects her environment when she is placed in an advanced reading group in first grade. Developmentally disruptive characteristics affect the interactions between the child and his or her environment in similar ways. For example, a child who is highly active and distractible may be born to parents whose own temperaments are more sedate. The parents may be at a loss as to how to respond to their child's personality and may become frustrated. Their frustration may result in poor discipline strategies, which may end up increasing rather than decreasing the child's undesirable behaviors. When he brings these behaviors to school, teachers may also respond negatively, and, in the absence of effective strategies for modifying his behavior, his disruptive behavior may worsen. Thus, a child's own personality characteristics may initiate positive or negative feedback loops with parents, teachers, and other adults.

As you can see, by eliciting various responses and reactions from others, children in a sense become "producers" and "shapers" of their own environments. In Bronfenbrenner's ecological model, shown in Figure 1.1, the child and the environment continually influence one another in a bidirectional, or transactional, manner. At the center of the model is the child and his or her physical and personal attributes. Around the child is the environment, viewed as a series of interrelated concentric layers or rings. Environmental influences that are closest to the child have the most direct impact and those farther away influence the child's development more indirectly.

Nearest the child is the **microsystem**—settings that influence the child directly through the child's immediate participation. For most children, the microsystem includes home, school, church, playground, and so forth, along with the relationships that the child forms within these settings. The microsystem possesses physical characteristics, such as the size of the child's house, the amount of nearby playground equipment, and the number of books in the child's day care center. It also consists of people, including family members, the child's teachers, and other children. These people, in turn, possess characteristics that may be relevant to the child's development, such as the socioeconomic status of the peer group, the educational background of the parents, and the political attitudes of the

Questions for Thought
and Discussion

In your development, how have you influenced the environment that influences you? What desirable and undesirable aspects of your environment have you produced?

Microsystem
The environmental system closest to the child, such as the family or school, the first layer of context in the ecological systems model.

FIGURE 1.1

Bronfenbrenner's ecological model of the environment.

Source: U. Bronfenbrenner, from T. Berndt. (1997). *Child Development*, 2nd ed. (p. 35). New York: McGraw-Hill.

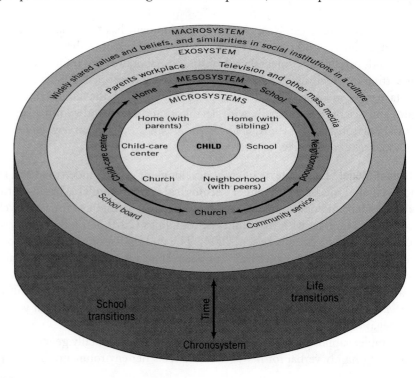

teacher. The microsystem is not constant but changes as the child grows and moves into different types of physical settings with different people. For example, a 3-year-old who spends much of the day interacting with her family members and preschool teachers and friends may grow into a 9-year-old who also plays soccer and takes dance lessons. Her microsystems have changed as she has grown older.

The **mesosystem** refers to the system of relationships among the child's microsystems. This might include the parents' relationships with the child's teachers and the relationship between the child's siblings and neighborhood friends. In general, the more interconnected these systems are, the more the child's development is likely to be supported in a clear and consistent way. For example, Michelle, the mother of 3-year-old twins Josh and Jayden, has a friendly and mutually supportive relationship with their preschool teacher, Miss Stephanie. Michelle and Stephanie discuss the twins' activities both at home and at school, and agree about important developmental goals and ways to achieve them. Michelle is also good friends with the mother of the twins' best friend at school, and the two families get together regularly on the weekends. Sometimes when they are on a play date at the park, the two families bump into Miss Stephanie and her own children, where they will socialize together briefly. These kinds of positive interconnections among the people in a child's life—the mesosystem—provide a supportive context for that child's development.

The **exosystem** refers to social settings that can affect the child but in which the child does not participate directly. Some examples are the local government, which decides how strictly air pollution standards will be enforced or which families will be eligible for welfare payments; the school board, which sets teachers' salaries and recommends the budget for new textbooks and equipment; and the parents' places of employment, which determine work hours, health care benefits, and the satisfaction or stress that a parent brings home each day.

The **macrosystem**, which involves the culture and subculture in which the child lives, affects the child through beliefs, values, and traditions. Children living in the United States may be influenced, for example, by beliefs regarding individualism and perhaps the virtues of capitalism and free enterprise. Children also may be affected by religious beliefs or political attitudes about, say, the importance of recycling or the role of guns in everyday life.

The values and cultural traditions of a particular geographic region or a particular ethnic group are also part of the macrosystem. For example, 18-year-old Bernadette lives in a tight-knit family in a northeastern suburban setting. Her grandparents immigrated to

Mesosystem
The interrelationships among the child's microsystems, the second layer of context in the ecological systems model.

Exosystem
Social systems that can affect children but in which they do not participate directly, the third layer of context in the ecological systems model.

Macrosystem
The culture and subcultures in which the child lives, the fourth layer of context in the ecological systems model.

Warm, positive interconnections between the different settings and individuals of a child's microsystem, called the mesosystem, provide a supportive context for child development. The children in this photo are interacting in a home setting with people whom they also see at church and at school. What might be some examples of influences of a child's mesosystem on the child's development? (Ariel Skelley/Corbis)

the United States from Italy. She grew up with the expectation that her closest relationships would be within the family with her cousins and not with unrelated friends from school. She also grew up with the family expectation that she would live at home with her parents until she married. However, messages from the larger U.S. society, as well as from her peers, influenced Bernadette to believe that getting her own apartment after graduating from high school was a desirable goal. She and one of her cousins responded to these conflicting cultural messages by each renting an apartment in a duplex just down the street from their families. That way, they could each live with family while still satisfying expectations of independence through having one's own apartment.

The macrosystem tends to be more stable than the other systems, but it, too, can change as a society adapts to historical and geopolitical changes—for example, from a liberal political era to a conservative one, from economic prosperity to depression, or from peace to war (Elder & Caspi, 1988; Pinquart & Silbereisen, 2004).

An additional factor that must be considered when studying human development is the passage of time, or the chronosystem, depicted as the arrow shown at the bottom of Figure 1.1. The interactions that take place among the various systems in the child's world gradually change over time and as the child grows. This historical and chronological context—the **chronosystem**—adds even more complexity and richness to the challenge of understanding children's development.

The Developmental Niche of Childhood In addition to an ecological perspective, a **cultural perspective** is essential for understanding the influence of culture on children's lives. Super and Harkness (1986) describe the **developmental niche**, which consists of three interconnected dimensions of culture that shape children's lives, thus affecting physical, cognitive, linguistic, social, and emotional development in childhood. First, culture has an impact on the *physical settings and conditions* of daily life, such as quality of diet, type of housing, available activities, and opportunities for interaction. For example, in many parts of middle-class America a three-bedroom house in the suburbs is common. In cities or in other countries where the population is denser, apartments, subdivided houses, or smaller detached homes may represent a more typical home.

Culture also influences the activities that parents choose for their children. In middle-class America, children may be placed from very young ages in specialized activity groups such as gymnastics, dance, or soccer. In these groups, children are exposed weekly to many other same-age peers engaged in a specific activity. In many other countries, mixed-age, unstructured neighborhood playgroups are a more common activity setting. Similarly, cultures differ in the extent to which children experience contact with extended family members. For example, many middle-class European American infants are likely to have fewer face-to-face contacts with extended family, whereas middle-class infants in Puerto Rico are likely to spend more time interacting with relatives (Miller & Harwood, 2001).

Second, culture affects the *childcare customs* that children are exposed to. For example, researcher Rebecca New studied infants in the United States and Italy. She found that in the United States, parents dealt with potential hazards in the child's environment through "childproofing" (e.g., locks on cabinet doors containing chemical cleaning solutions, plastic stops in electrical outlets) and through restricting access to certain areas (e.g., through the use of baby gates). The end result was that, within specifically defined spaces, the infant was free to explore. In contrast, in Italian families these same potential hazards were dealt with by containing the baby (e.g., in a walker, stroller, high chair, playpen, or on someone's lap). They spent relatively little time crawling around on the floor exploring, but a great deal of time in direct social interaction with others (New & Richman, 1996). Similarly, in many cultures around the world, it is common for infants to co-sleep with their parents, whereas in middle-class America it is preferred that infants sleep in their own rooms from very early on (Shweder, Jensen, & Goldstein, 1995).

Chronosystem
Bronfenbrenner's term for historical contexts and the passage of time as a context for studying human development.

Cultural perspective
Researchers' attempts to understand the ways in which culture influences child development.

Developmental niche
Three interconnected dimensions of culture that shape children's lives, thus affecting physical, cognitive, linguistic, social, and emotional development in childhood.

Questions for Thought
and Discussion
How would you describe your developmental niche at this time in your life? How does this niche affect your development?

Third, culture influences parents' *childrearing beliefs and goals*, as well as the meanings that they give to different types of behaviors. In the past, much of the research on child development was conducted using middle-class, European American families. This over-reliance on a single population led many psychologists to assume that what was true of parenting practices and child development among middle-class, European American families must be true of everyone else as well. In recent years, researchers have become more aware of the fact that parents' childrearing beliefs and goals are not the same around the world. For example, in a study that compared middle-class, European American mothers living in Connecticut with middle-class Puerto Rican mothers living in Puerto Rico, the European American mothers were more likely to state that they wanted their children to become self-confident and independent. In contrast, the Puerto Rican mothers were more likely to express the desire that their children treat others with respect and fulfill inter-personal obligations. These cultural ideals influence the types of behaviors that parents encourage as well as the way that different behaviors are interpreted and responded to (Harwood, Miller, & Lucca Irizarry, 1995; Harwood, Schoelmerich, Ventura-Cook, Schulze, & Wilson, 1996; Miller & Harwood, 2002).

The Child's Developmental Niche Includes:
- Physical settings and conditions
- Childcare customs
- Childrearing beliefs and goals

Parents in different cultures also have different expectations for the rate at which their children should meet certain developmental milestones, such as self-feeding, sleeping through the night, and self-toileting. For example, middle-class European American families often have expectations for early self-feeding, the early ability to sleep through the night, but late self-toileting. These expectations are not always shared by others. In many groups, both within the United States and in other societies around the world, children

An 18th century American primer warned children, "Consider you may perish as young as you are; there are small Chips as well as great Logs, in the Fire of Hell." Children were seen as inherently or naturally bad, made good through education and discipline. In the 19th century, the poet Wordsworth wrote, "Heaven lies about us in our infancy!" The view of children had softened and refocused on their innocence, which parents were supposed to preserve and protect until it was inevitably lost in the general corruption of adulthood. What construction of childhood do you think might be represented in the photograph of 20th century U.S. parents with their infants in a Gymboree play session? (*Left*, Hulton Archive/Getty Images; *right*, courtesy of D'Arcy Norman)

often learn to self-feed at a later age but may learn self-toileting skills at a younger age (Pachter & Harwood, 1996; Schulze, Harwood, & Schoelmerich, 2001; Schulze, Harwood, Schoelmerich, & Leyendecker, 2002).

"Culture" has many dimensions and may be understood as a shared set of beliefs, meanings, and behaviors (D'Andrade, 1984; LeVine, 1984). Dimensions along which cultural groups vary may include such things as place of origin, ethnic background, and socioeconomic status. Culture thus influences the lives of children by affecting the physical settings, childcare customs, and childrearing beliefs that parents bring to parenting. It should be kept in mind that many aspects of children's lives that have often been considered typical, such as sleeping in one's own room at night, might reflect the overreliance on research done only with middle-class, European American families. Today, researchers have a better understanding that children's lives around the world are shaped in ways that reflect the settings, customs, and beliefs of different cultural groups.

Perceptions of Children Across Time

Cultural beliefs and values regarding childrearing have varied not only across societies, but also over time. As scientists, child development researchers hope to find information that will withstand the changing winds of time, that will be true for children everywhere and in all times. However, many of the topics that child development research has focused on reflect the social concerns of a given time period.

For example, beginning in the 1970s, there began to be greater public recognition and acceptance in U.S. society of a variety of family structures, including families headed by a single parent, either through divorce or through choice, families "blended" together through divorce and remarriage, families formed through adoption or assisted reproduction, as well as families headed by same-sex couples. In addition, since the 1970s, a greater percentage of women in the United States, including mothers of young children, have entered the paid labor force. These societal changes have altered the ways that researchers choose to study child development. Prior to the 1970s, maternal employment and alternative family structures, whether they arose through divorce or lifestyle choices, were seen as social problems, and research reflected this view. For example, many studies focused on problems that children from single-parent families were presumed to have. Today, however, as maternal employment and alternative family structures have become more common in our increasingly diverse society, researchers no longer begin by "problematizing" different family structures as contexts of child development.

In addition to mirroring the changing concerns and conditions of society over time, child development research also reflects prevailing cultural norms regarding what are viewed as desirable outcomes of development. For example, consider the families of 3-year-old Avery and Natalie. Avery's family places great emphasis on her learning through logical consequences. When Avery refused to bring her sidewalk chalk in from outside, her parents decided to let it remain there overnight. When it rained, the chalk became soggy and unusable. When queried about this strategy, Avery's parents stated that, left to learn in this way, Avery will be more likely to internalize the reasoning behind such rules as bringing her chalk in at night. She will then pick up after herself due to internal motivation rather than simply out of compliance to parental expectations. Her parents believe that, in this way, Avery will learn what they consider to be desirable qualities of initiative and independence.

In contrast, Natalie's family emphasizes mutual obligations and interdependence within the family, with Natalie's respect for their authority as parents complementing their greater wisdom and experience. As her parents, their responsibility is to care for her, including making sure that she brings her toys in at night. As the child, her responsibility is to comply. In this way, Natalie's parents believe she will learn the behaviors and habits that

Questions for Thought and Discussion

Do you think children are inherently good or evil? Why or why not? Is this a question that developmental psychologists should study?

will make her a well-socialized adult who knows how to behave appropriately and respectfully in a variety of circumstances.

Students who read through child development research and expert advice over the past 30 years will notice that it tends to reflect more closely the model followed by Avery's parents. Emphasis is placed on childrearing strategies that are said to optimize the development of independence, self-confidence, and personal fulfillment. However, researchers who have studied cultural influences on children and their families have noted that these particular goals and strategies do not represent universal goals of development. That is, a belief in their primacy is not shared by families everywhere or across time. Instead, they represent the unique cultural concerns arising in the latter part of the 20th century among the population most often studied by development psychologists: middle-class, European Americans. Different cultural groups, as well as European Americans from a different time period, may place greater emphasis on other developmental goals, such as respectfulness or the ability to fulfill interpersonal obligations—in short, interdependence rather than psychological independence may be viewed as the most desirable outcome of development (Harwood, Miller, & Lucca Irizarry, 1995; Kessen, 1979; Markus & Kitayama, 1991; Miller, Mintz, Hoogstra, Fung, & Potts, 1992; Ochs & Schieffelin, 1984; Shweder & Bourne, 1984; Sorkhabi, 2005; Tobin, Wu, & Davidson, 1989).

In 1999, the self-expressive individualism of U.S. culture was examined in a special issue of the *New York Times Magazine* called "The Me Millennium." It featured articles such as: "On Language" (subtitled "Me, Myself, and I"); "I'm Okay, You're Selfish"; "In the Age of Radical Selfishness" (subtitled, "What it's like being 30-something, overpaid and totally disconnected"); and "Be Different! (Like Everyone Else!)." In her book, *The Me Generation*, psychologist Jean Twenge considers the benefits and costs of America's radical individualism. (Photo by Nelson Cepeda and Cristina Martinez Byvik/Zuma Press. Courtesy The Free Press.)

Other cultural psychologists have described the long-term costs of placing too much emphasis on psychological independence as a primary goal of development, at the expense of recognizing our fundamental relatedness to others (Cushman, 1991; Kessen, 1979; Le & Stockdale, 2005; Sampson, 1989). In an important article, Kessen (1979) criticized child psychologists for mindlessly reflecting a culturally embedded view of the child as "a free-standing isolable being who moves through development as a self-contained and complete individual. Other similarly self-contained people—parents and teachers—may influence the development of children, to be sure, but the proper unit of cultural analysis and the proper unit of developmental study is the child alone. The ubiquity of such radical individualism in our lives makes the consideration of alternative images of childhood extraordinarily difficult" (p. 7).

Cultural beliefs in the importance of psychological independence, as opposed to interdependence, have led many developmental researchers within the United States to focus on issues such as the achievement of self-esteem, the self-construction of a positive identity, the attainment of psychological independence, and the construction of social networks that will buffer against personal loneliness. As stated concisely by the editors of the *New York Times Magazine* special issue, "We put the self at the center of the universe. Now, for better or worse, we are on our own." Today, researchers must consider "alternative images of childhood" that go beyond the unreflective individualism that characterized much of U.S. culture—and psychological research— in the 20th century. In this text, it is our hope that, by focusing on childhood's contexts both within our society and across cultures, we will introduce you to broader and more durable visions of childhood.

Learning Objective 1.1: *Describe ways that cultural and historical contexts have influenced our understanding of child development.*

1. What are the parts of Bronfenbrenner's ecological model? How does the model help us understand child development?
2. What is meant by the cultural niche of childhood? What are its three major components?
3. What are some examples of the cultural contexts of child development?
4. How does history affect our study and understanding of child development?
5. How can it be said that childhood is a social construction?

Key Issues In Child Development

Researchers have wrestled with several key issues in our efforts to understand child development. Four issues in particular have emerged as major themes: (1) nature and nurture as sources of influence; (2) stability and change in development across childhood; (3) "typical" development versus individual variation; and (4) "universal" development versus cultural variation.

Nature and Nurture as Sources of Influence

A long-standing issue in child development is the relative influence of inborn, biological factors (nature) and environmental, experiential factors (nurture). Today, virtually all child researchers assume that both nature and nurture contribute to human development. However, despite general agreement that both nature and nurture play some role in development, researchers continue to debate their exact relationship. Some believe that nature plays a primary role, with the environment simply modifying to a greater or lesser extent what nature provides. Others think that biology lays a foundation for development, but that significant differences in outcomes are determined by experience. **Nature versus nurture** questions underlie almost every topic in this text. Questions such as heredity

---

Q**uestions for Thought and Discussion**
What are some common characterizations of children and childhood in American culture today?

Test Your Mastery...

Learning Objective 1.2
How can we understand the influences of nature and nurture, stability and change, and uniformity and variation on child development?

Nature versus nurture
A scientific controversy about the main causes of developmental change as biological and genetic (nature) or environmental and experiential (nurture)

BOX 1.1 **The Social Construction of Childhood**

Is childhood a universal, natural, biological category? Or is childhood an idea that is created in the social world—and created differently by different societies and social groups? The theoretical perspective called "the social construction of childhood" explores the different ways that children are described and defined throughout the world by specific societies and social groups as well as by scientists. The perspective draws on Berger and Luckmann's classic work, *The Social Construction of Reality* (1966), in which they argue that reality is not given but is constructed by people as they live and work in the world. The authors speak not of "reality" but of "realities," recognizing that different societies and groups view "reality" in different ways.

What is childhood? What is a child? From the perspective of the social construction of childhood, the answer depends on the social context in which the questions are asked and answered. In the United States 13-year-old girls who give birth may be described as "children having children." In other societies, 13-year-old girls may be seen as simply wives and mothers—no longer children. The competence or incompetence attributed to children varies throughout the world. In some societies children do productive work (carrying water, doing housework, working in the fields, doing factory work) from a very young age, whereas in other societies they are kept from such work until they are much older.

Different constructions emerge in relation to regional culture, ethnicity, social class, and a wide range of other variables. Moreover, these constructions often relate to broad social needs. In a subsistence economy where workers are scarce, young children may be seen as able workers. In societies where adult workers are readily available, children may be kept out of the workforce, defined as incapable, "too young," innocent, and needing to be protected from the adult world. Whether or not one thinks that young children ought to work and in what capacities, that they can and do work suggests their competence and the different ways that childhood can be defined.

Some sociologists (for example, Atkinson, 1980; Mackay, 1973) suggest that a certain amount of what passes for expert information about childhood may simply be culturally specific, "common-sense," untested views about children. Thus people engaged in scientific activity, like other adults, may construct *versions* of childhood, based on those views. Some formulations of childhood are ideological rather than scientific. In some theories, adults are viewed as deity-like figures, concerned solely with the welfare of their charges, sacrificing their own needs to those of children, kindly and loving, and both motivated to prepare children for adult society and equal to that task. Children, on the other hand, may be viewed in opposite terms or in terms of lacks, faults, or inabilities. They are taken to be passive recipients of socialization rather than active participants in the world and active seekers of knowledge of how that world works.

Adults' versions of childhood may be very different from children's ideas of what it is to be a child. Children may see themselves as having rich social lives, lived in part in relation to adults and in part in relation to other children. By exploring children's views of childhood and of their lives as children, researchers gain access to a very different view of childhood, one that is at odds with adults' ideas of children's perspectives. Children who are afraid of monsters, for example, may not be comforted by adults' claims that monsters do not exist; to the contrary, they may decide that monsters do exist but adults do not care that they, the children, are in danger (Waksler, 1996). If childhood is socially constructed, then it is possible to see adults as *teaching* children how to be children. Adults may criticize children for "acting like babies," urge them to "act like a big boy/girl," or fault them for acting "too grown up." They instruct them about when they are "too young" or "too old" for certain activities.

The social construction of childhood provides a new and different perspective on both adults and children. If childhood is viewed as a social construction, it becomes possible to ask: How is childhood constructed? Who constructs childhood? How do they do so? Why do they do so? What are the consequences of those constructions for children? How do children view them? How do children act to support or refute these views of them? The social construction of childhood opens up many kinds of questions for empirical investigation.

versus environment, maturation versus learning, and emergent abilities versus acquired skills all relate to this fundamental issue.

Consider, for example, 4-year-old Neema, who demonstrates a keen ability in music. He is already taking piano lessons and doing well with them. His parents have placed him in a special music class for children who show similar skills. Some researchers studying this group of children might highlight the role that genetics has played and examine the extent to which parents or other family members display similar musical talent. Other researchers might pay more attention to environmental factors, investigating, for example, the opportunities that children such as Neema have had to acquire and practice their musical skills and abilities.

Another example can be found in the development of aggressive behavior. Some researchers explain aggressive behavior in terms of environmental factors, such as exposure to violent models or ineffective parenting that rewards aggression. Others might offer a biological account that focuses on an inherited disposition that makes it difficult for the child to regulate his or her emotions or perhaps neurological problems that interfere with the processing of social cues.

In reality, of course, both giftedness and aggressive behavior are best understood in terms of a combination of biological and experiential factors. Children who excel in a domain, such as music or sports, are born with a unique combination of characteristics that increases their likelihood of success in those domains. In turn, their early success leads to increased opportunities and rewards. Similarly, some children who exhibit anti-social behavior may have a biologically based propensity to respond aggressively to frustrating situations. Nevertheless, the way that they act on their aggressive impulses is the result of learning.

There is still much to learn about the processes by which biological and environmental factors work together over the course of development. Recent advances in the fields of behavioral genetics and the brain sciences suggest that these processes may be even more complex than previously thought. We now know, for example, that genes and basic brain chemistry, once thought to be unchanging, are as responsive to environmental influence as the behaviors they help to regulate (Plomin & Rutter, 1998; Shonkoff & Phillips, 2000). Chapter 3 and Chapter 6 give more detail on theories that describe how our genes and environment may work together to guide our behavior.

Stability and Change in Developmental Pathways

A second long-standing issue in the field of child development is how to characterize the developmental process (Caspi, 1998; Emde & Harmon, 1984). Are patterns of development smooth and stable, with new abilities, skills, and knowledge gradually and continuously added at a relatively uniform pace? Or does development occur discontinuously and at different rates, alternating between periods of little change and periods of abrupt, rapid change? And how do patterns of development shape individuals over time? In terms of **continuity versus discontinuity**, some theorists emphasize continuity and stability, showing how the behaviors and abilities of adolescents and adults can be traced back directly to individual development early in life. Other theorists emphasize discontinuity and change, suggesting that some aspects of development emerge independently of prior experience and cannot be predicted from the child's previous behavior (Clarke & Clarke, 1976; Withnall, 2006).

The continuity model often is associated with the belief that human behavior consists of many individual skills that are added one at a time, usually through learning and experience. As children acquire more skills, they combine and recombine them to produce increasingly complex behaviors. Neema, for example, who began playing the piano at age 4, was able by age 5 to play simple pieces requiring the use of both hands. By the age of 7, he was able to play a variety of pieces, and the complexity and sophistication of the music he plays continues to grow over time. Here, change is quantitative, as the skills acquired in playing the simplest pieces are added to produce more advanced capabilities. Experience drives this development, as Neema continues to take lessons and practice his skills at home.

In the discontinuity model, in contrast, development occurs in stages, guided primarily by internal biological factors. Stage theorists, for example, point out the unevenness of children's development—relatively stable periods followed by abrupt changes, reflecting the discontinuousness of the changes taking place in the body and brain. Two examples of developmental benchmarks widely recognized as discontinuous are the attainment of the ability to walk at roughly 1 year of age and the physical changes associated with puberty. In this model, development involves qualitative changes in previous abilities and behaviors. Like the nature-versus-nurture issue, the question of continuity versus discontinuity is not all-or-nothing. Psychologists on both sides of the debate agree that some developmental processes are described more accurately by one model, and others by a competing

---

Links to Related Material
Chapters 3 and 6 explore the interaction of biology and environment more fully.

Continuity versus discontinuity
A scientific controversy about the process of development as constant and connected (continuous) or uneven and disconnected (discontinuous).

Questions for Thought and Discussion
How predictable are you? Which aspects of your personality have remained the same since you were a young child and which have changed?

How might the development of this child's skill reflect both stability and change across time? How might drawing involve both continuous and discontinuous development? How might both inheritance and learning be involved in the development of this skill? What social and cultural contexts might influence this child's drawing experiences? (Laura Dwight Photography)

model (Bjorklund, 1997; Rutter, 1987). In addition, developments such as learning to walk and sleep consolidation in infancy clearly involve both quantitative and qualitative changes (Scher, Epstein, & Tirosh, 2004).

Typical Development and Individual Variation

In **normative versus idiographic development**, some child development researchers are concerned with typical or normative development—aspects of development that are similar for all children. Others focus on individual variations, or idiographic development—the differences in development from one child to the next (Caspi, 1998).

Normative research focuses on the statistically "average" child, with the primary goal of identifying and describing how normal development proceeds from step to step. Parenting books that describe the average ages at which young children typically attain specific motor development milestones—such as rolling over, sitting up unaided, and walking—represent a normative perspective. Idiographic research, in contrast, centers on the individual child and the factors that produce human diversity.

As another example, researchers interested in normative language development may search for common patterns in children who speak the same language, while those interested in idiographic language development may focus on the individual differences that become evident as children master language skills. Individual differences might result from differences in experience, such as the type of verbal environment that adults provide, or from biological factors, such as the presence of a brain injury or cognitive disorders.

Normative versus idiographic development
A research choice between identifying commonalities in typical human development (normative) or the causes of individual differences (idiographic).

Cultural Differences and Similarities in Development

A related issue involves searching for **universals of development**—behaviors or patterns of development that characterize all children everywhere versus recognizing that some developmental pathways may be specific to certain cultures. For example, around the world, children of our species begin to babble using the sounds of their native language at around 6 months of age, take their first unassisted steps at roughly the age of 1 year, and show the same sequence of physical changes associated with puberty. Such universals are deeply rooted in our biology as human beings.

Universals of development
Aspects of development or behavior that are common to children everywhere.

In contrast, other behaviors or patterns of development show significant cultural differences. For example, in the United States today, infants typically begin self-feeding before the age of 1 year, often as young as 9 or 10 months. This self-feeding is encouraged through the use of finger foods, such as cheerios and other small portions of adult foods that are easy for young hands to grasp and transport into the mouth. At well-child visits, pediatricians often encourage parents to facilitate the move toward self-feeding at a young age, and parenting books offer similar advice. In many other cultural groups, however, early self-feeding is not a priority. It is expected that parents will spoon-feed children until the children old enough to handle eating utensils properly (Miller & Harwood, 2002). In all cultural groups, most children eventually become adept at self-feeding and learn to follow culturally appropriate practices. However, the path toward independent feeding varies culturally, such that expert advice for one cultural group may not be suitable for another.

Cultural variability also occurs in beliefs about the ultimate goals of socialization. What behaviors, traits, and personality characteristics are considered most desirable for children to cultivate? In some cultural groups, qualities such as self-confidence and psychological independence are considered most desirable, whereas other groups may place more emphasis on qualities such as respectfulness or the ability to fulfill family obligations (Harwood, Miller, & Lucca Irizarry, 1995; Kohn, 1977). Specific long-term socialization goals such as these influence childrearing practices. For example, for Eileen and Kevin, it is paramount that their 3-year-old daughter, Avery, develop self-confidence and curiosity. They take a democratic approach in their childrearing style, offering Avery a variety of choices in her everyday life, soliciting her opinion regarding family activities, and offering explanations for many of their parenting decisions. When Avery refused to dress herself one morning, her mother let her wear her pajamas to school, knowing that Avery would choose to dress herself after experiencing the natural consequence of embarrassment. Eileen and Kevin have also allowed Avery to wear diapers past her third birthday, preferring that their daughter potty train herself when she is ready.

In contrast, for Rosa and Luis, it is most important that their daughter, Natalie, learn to be respectful and engage in socially appropriate behavior. They are firm with her and, although they are nurturing and listen to her feelings, they are clear that she must respect their authority as parents. When Natalie refused to dress herself one morning for preschool, Rosa placed her in a time-out until she cooperated so that her daughter would learn that there are some things she simply must do in the morning—going to school in her pajamas was not socially appropriate and was not an option. In addition, Rosa and Luis made certain that Natalie was potty-trained around the age of 2, when they saw signs that she was physiologically ready. It did not occur to them that their young child should decide for herself when to take this developmentally necessary step.

Such culture-based differences in childrearing can cause conflict when families, teachers, and other professionals with different goals and practices come into contact with one another. People have different expectations about what constitutes a "good" parenting style or desirable child behavior. Thus, cultural differences affect both childrearing and the development of the child.

Questions for Thought and Discussion

What were your family's long-term socialization goals for you? How were those goals influenced by your culture or subculture? What attitudes and behaviors did your family regard as most important to inculcate in you?

✔ *Test Your Mastery...*

Learning Objective 1.2: *How can we understand the influences of nature and nurture, stability and change, and uniformity and variation on child development?*

1. How do nature and nurture jointly contribute to child development?
2. Why might some researchers focus on stability or continuity in development, while others focus on discontinuity or change?
3. Why might some researchers focus on typical or normal development, while others focus on individual variation?
4. What are some examples of universals of development compared to culturally different pathways?

Child Development Research in Applied Contexts

How does research translate into real-life situations? Child development researchers often consider this question, because their work may be relevant for practical considerations in a variety of applied contexts, such as parenting, schooling, and childcare settings. Research on development also may have an impact on social policy.

Learning Objective 1.3
Describe how research-based knowledge of child development is applied in real-life contexts.

Parenting

Parents have access to a variety of resources related to child development and childrearing, including books, magazines, newspaper columns, the Internet, and TV and radio shows. At best, these resources are scientifically informed and offer parents encouragement and ideas for handling issues that arise in the course of their child's development. At worst, these resources elevate personal opinion to expert status, are judgmental about parents who make childrearing choices that differ from those offered by the expert, and leave parents feeling worried about their own child's developmental progress or their own adequacy. Consider, for example, the proliferation of early learning devices, such as electronic toys that purport to teach the alphabet to children as young as 9 months. Such toys are often accompanied by advertisements and endorsements regarding the importance of early learning in a child's development, which may leave parents feeling that they need to supply children with toys such as these in order to stimulate cognitive development.

Where possible, this text examines the implications of research for parenting and identifies some misinformation that has become popularized through the media, such as the proliferation of heavily promoted electronic toys purportedly designed to stimulate cognitive development in very young children. Should parents invest in such devices? Other questions will be considered as well: Does it matter in the long run that young children vary widely in their attainment of developmental milestones, such as walking or uttering two-word sentences? What early intervention services are available to parents, and when should parents contact service agencies? What effect does television programming have on young children's development? How do children's sleep needs change over the years? What might parents keep in mind when choosing discipline strategies? Child development research provides information that can help parents answer these questions.

Questions for Thought
    and Discussion
What are some examples of popular childrearing advice given in print and broadcast media today? How would you decide what advice to follow?

Schools and Child Care

Most children spend a major portion of their lives in school settings, sometimes beginning formal care shortly after birth. Research in child development has had clear practical implications for schools and other educational and caregiving settings. Numerous studies have focused on questions about the benefits and risks of day care for infants and young children, for example. Other research questions ask, What factors correlate with success in school and academic achievement? What types of home activities best prepare a child for school? What is important for teachers and parents to know about peer aggression? What constitutes a high-quality preschool environment? What effects do tracking versus mainstreaming have on children's development? How do children develop the ability to read? This text highlights child development research that has contributed to educational and childcare settings and practices.

Social Policy

Another arena in which child development research has clear practical implications is social policy. *Social policy* refers to governmental decisions about the regulation of people's behavior, including decisions that affect public health and welfare, public education, and public access to social programs. In the United States, federal, state, and local policies relating to children—such as vaccination, health care, parental leave, custody issues, preschool certification, and even the question of who may become a parent and by what

BOX 1.2   Conversations with an Outreach Liaison

Amy Miller, 31, grew up in Slidell, Louisiana. Here, she speaks about her experiences as an Outreach Liaison for the National Institutes of Mental Health (NIMH) in Bethesda, Maryland.

While I was in college majoring in psychology at the University of New Orleans, I worked in four different research labs on a variety of topics, including culture and child development. Having spent my entire life up till that point in just one small town, I didn't realize the variations in making families and raising children that exist around the world, and learning about this fascinated me. I ultimately decided to go to graduate school in Connecticut to study culture and child development.

After finishing graduate school, I moved to the D.C. area to do a postdoctoral fellowship at the National Institutes of Health (NIH). During my postdoc, I realized that we were doing a lot of research that the American people know nothing about, so I wanted to be in a position where I could disseminate the information that we learn through research.

I then took a fellowship through the American Psychological Association, the APA Congressional Fellowship. This was an exciting opportunity that allowed me to work in Congress for a year. I worked for Senator Rockefeller from West Virginia. I advised him on child and family policy issues, such as welfare reform, as well as on adoption and foster care issues. When my fellowship wrapped up, I did a lot of informational interviews with a variety of groups, including advocacy groups, lobby shops, and executive branch agencies. I selected my current job because it allowed me to take science-based information and disseminate it around the country. I work for the NIMH Outreach Partnership Program, which is a nationwide effort to disseminate science-based mental health information across the nation.

NIMH funds a lot of research that goes on across the country. My program is housed in the Office of the Director of NIMH in Bethesda, MD, right outside of D.C. We do two basic things. We take our science and translate it for public consumption, through publications, Web sites, and other public forums. We have representative organizations in all 50 states plus the District of Columbia. We tell them when there are new publications, and send them press releases on new mental health updates so they are prepared to answer

means—are strongly influenced by research in child development. For example, in the 1980s child development researchers recommended the establishment of a national policy regarding the provision of parental leave by employers following the birth or adoption of an infant (Frank & Zigler, 1989). These recommendations were instrumental in the establishment in 1993 of the Family and Medical Leave Act (FMLA), which guaranteed

Teachers in this preschool took child development courses as part of their training. Continuing knowledge of child development research also helps them improve their practice. How, for example, could they improve their practice through information about nature and nurture in child development, about continuity and discontinuity, typical development and individual variation, or universalities of development and culturally diverse developmental pathways? (Blend Images/Alamy Images)

questions from the media. We also hold an annual meeting where we have NIMH-funded scientists give scientific updates. We have forums on information dissemination techniques and workshops on techniques for public education. We have a Web site at *http://www.nimh.nih.gov/outreach/partners/index.cfm.*

We also have a national network of partners, which consists of professional groups, advocacy groups, and education groups, such as NAMI (National Alliance for Mentally Ill), NMHA (National Mental Health Association), and the APAs (American Psychological Association and American Psychiatric Association). We send our partners research updates and ask them to be available to our outreach partners. E.g., when one of our outreach partners has a question about eating disorders, we refer them to one of our partner professional organizations that does public education on eating disorders.

My role is outreach liaison, so I am a conduit between NIMH and the outreach partners, who provide information to the American public about mental health issues. For example, I am in charge of planning the program for the annual meeting, which includes picking speakers, workshop topics, and poster session participants. Our annual meeting has two parts: a science update and a more practical how-to component for educators. Our audience is an educated lay population, which means they know about mental health issues, but aren't trained specifically in scientific methods. They want to know why the study was done and what was found, and how it is directly relevant to mental health issues in their state. They use this information to educate families and consumers in their state.

I do a lot of behind the scenes stuff. For example, mental illness is still stigmatized in our culture. Recently some new data came out about the prevalence of different kinds of mental illnesses in our country, including among children. So, we sent information about this to our partners, so that they are ready and able to answer questions from the public about it. The prevalence data indicated that something like 20 to 25 percent of Americans have mental health problems. If we explain to people that these are common, treatable, and the result of a medical condition, then having a mental health problem will be less stigmatized. That is our hope. We also hope that if people know they are not alone, they will be more likely to seek treatment.

I think there is a lot of potential for child development majors in the public arena, but they have to be open to a lot of possibilities. Sometimes opportunities are in government (e.g., NIMH), or the private sector (e.g., nonprofit organizations such as advocacy groups like NAMI). Students can search the Web sites of different organizations for potential employment opportunities.

families meeting certain criteria at least 6 weeks of paid leave following the birth of a child. This textbook points out how research in child development has affected social policy in the United States and in other countries, and how social policy changes have affected child development.

Learning Objective 1.3: *Describe how research-based knowledge of child development is applied in real-life contexts.*

1. In what real-life contexts is child development research applied?
2. What are some examples of applied research in child development?
3. How do the contexts of development described in this section relate to Bronfenbrenner's ecological model, described earlier in this chapter?

✔ *Test Your Mastery...*

Theoretical Perspectives—An Overview

Most child development researchers have a particular theoretical orientation that underlies their view of how development occurs and which factors are most important for explaining changes in children's behavior. Today, the majority of researchers identify themselves with one of four general theoretical perspectives: behavioral or social learning approaches, cognitive-developmental approaches, evolutionary or biological approaches, and sociocultural approaches. In addition, psychoanalytic approaches remain popular with many people who study, work with, or write about young children. This final part of this chapter outlines the principal ideas and underlying assumptions of these five broad theoretical approaches.

Learning Objective 1.4
What are the five major theoretical perspectives in the field of child development?

As you read, keep in mind that while each major developmental approach has its own ideas, philosophy, and methods, theorists also accept many ideas from other models. As research continues to add to our knowledge of child development, overlaps among the approaches will undoubtedly grow. In addition, today's theorists no longer attempt to explain human development with only a few principles or processes. Behavior has many causes, and the mechanisms through which those causes operate are intricate and often interrelated. Modern theoretical explanations reflect this increasing complexity.

Today's models are based on scientific data. Early theories of human development were mostly the products of philosophical debates and logical deductions. Modern explanations, in contrast, have grown out of research findings, which are continually being modified and revised in response to new observations and data. A particular child psychologist or child development researcher may prefer one theoretical approach to another, but the evidence provided by research will determine which theories will survive and which will be abandoned.

Psychoanalytic Approaches

A theoretical approach that has had considerable influence on a variety of disciplines over the last century is based on the writings of Sigmund Freud (1856–1939). Freud's greatest impact was in the area of clinical psychology, where his model of personality and techniques of psychoanalysis continue to represent a major school of thought in psychotherapy. Although he spent little time observing children directly, he used his patients' and his own recollections of childhood experiences to construct a comprehensive model of child development.

Psychosexual development
Freud's theory that people progress through stages of personality development based on the strength and location of sexual pleasure (libido) in the body (oral, anal, phallic, latent, genital).

Freud's contribution to our understanding of child development was his stage theory of **psychosexual development**. The central theme of this theory is that each child is born with a certain amount of sexual energy, called *libido*, which is biologically guided to certain locations on the body, called the *erogenous zones*, as the child grows. "Sexual energy" refers simply to the ability to experience physical pleasure. The arrival of the libido at each location marks a new stage in the child's psychosexual development, and during that stage the child receives the greatest physical pleasure in that erogenous zone. Freud identified five stages, beginning at birth and ending in late adolescence (see Table 1.1). Successful movement from stage to stage requires that children receive the proper amount of physical pleasure from each erogenous zone.

Freud's theory of child development is actually a theory of personality formation. It assumes that many aspects of the adult personality result from events during the childhood psychosexual stages. If the child's experiences during a stage are not what they should be, some portion of the libido will remain *fixated* in that erogenous zone, rather than moving on to the next one. For example, if a child is not given the appropriate amount of oral gratification during the first stage, the libido will remain partially fixated at the mouth. Later in life, this fixation will be manifested in the adult's continually seeking physical pleasure in this erogenous zone—perhaps by smoking or chewing gum.

During the phallic stage, according to Freud, children fall in love with the parent of the opposite sex, often expressing a desire to marry him or her, a situation referred to as the *Oedipus complex*. But they soon experience feelings of conflict as they realize that the same-sex parent is a powerful rival. Children presumably resolve this conflict in two ways. First, they force their desires into the unconscious, a process called **repression**, which also wipes out conscious memories of these feelings. Then, they compensate for this loss by making a determined effort to adopt the characteristics of the same-sex parent, a process called **identification**.

Repression
Freud's term for the process through which desires or motivations are driven into the unconscious, associated with the phallic stage of psychosexual development.

Identification
The Freudian process through which the child adopts the characteristics of the same-sex parent during the phallic stage.

Although Freud's theory had some influence on American developmentalists, they never fully accepted it, for several reasons. First, its key elements cannot be scientifically verified or disproved. In addition, Freud relied heavily on unobservable mechanisms, such as unconscious motives, which makes scientific inquiry difficult. Science is based on measurable and verifiable observations.

TABLE 1.1 Stages of Development: Erikson and Freud

ERIKSON'S PSYCHOSOCIAL STAGES

AGES (YRS)	NAME	CHARACTERISTICS
Birth–1.5	Basic Trust vs. Mistrust	Infants must form trusting relationships with caregivers. If care is inadequate, mistrust develops instead.
1.5–3	Autonomy vs. Shame	As they master various skills—walking, toileting, and so forth—children begin to develop feelings of autonomy and self-control. Failure to meet expectations can lead to shame and doubt.
3–6	Initiative vs. Guilt	Children take more initiative in dealing with their environments but may experience guilt as a result of conflicts with caregivers.
6–12	Industry vs. Inferiority	School-age children develop industry by successfully dealing with demands to learn new skills; failure leads to feelings of inferiority.
12–18	Identity vs. Role Confusion	Teenagers must develop a sense of identity in various areas, such as occupation and gender, or risk role confusion in adulthood.
Young adult	Intimacy vs. Isolation	Young adults must form intimate relationships or suffer from loneliness and isolation.
Adult	Generativity vs. Stagnation	Adults must find ways to support future generations, through childrearing or other productive activities, or come to a standstill in their lives.
Older adult	Ego Integrity vs. Despair	Older adults must come to feel a sense of fulfillment in life or experience despair as they face death.

FREUD'S PSYCHOSEXUAL STAGES

AGES (YRS)	NAME	CHARACTERISTICS
Birth–1.5	Oral	Libido is located at the mouth; principal source of physical pleasure is sucking.
1.5–3	Anal	Child attains physical pleasure first from having bowel movements and later from withholding them.
3–6	Phallic	Libido moves to the genital area. Children fall in love with the parent of the opposite sex but experience conflict as they realize the same-sex parent is a powerful rival. Resolving this conflict involves forcing the libido into the unconscious and trying to adopt the characteristics of the same-sex parent.
6–12	Latency	Libido remains repressed and inactive.
12–18	Genital	Libido reemerges in the genital area; child again develops attraction toward opposite sex—this time directed toward peers.

In spite of its failings, Freud's theory of child development includes two fundamental concepts that are generally accepted today. Freud was the first major developmental psychologist to argue that nature and nurture interact as significant contributors to the child's development. Today almost all child development researchers take this interactionist position, accepting the role of both inborn processes and environmental factors in child development. Second, Freud suggested that early experiences could have important effects on behavior in later life. Most people in child development today agree with this idea, and many researchers look to early childhood experiences, particularly relationships with parents, as a way to understand outcomes later in life (Beier, 1991; Emde, 1992).

Freud's theory inspired other models of development that have achieved somewhat greater acceptance, such as Erik Erikson's theory of **psychosocial development**. Erik Erikson (1902–1994), a psychoanalyst, grew up in Germany but practiced primarily in the United States. His model of development is based on the idea that social and emotional development continue throughout life. He thus replaced Freud's five stages of development with an eight-stage model that continues into old age. Erikson also believed that we could not understand personality development without considering the environment in which it occurs. After studying a number of diverse cultures—including Native American tribes in

Psychosocial development
Erikson's theory that people progress through stages of personality development based on their resolution of conflicts between potentially positive or negative outcomes of behavioral changes.

California and South Dakota, inner-city youth, and the people of India—Erikson developed a *psychosocial* model (in contrast to Freud's psychosexual model) of personality that included a major role for social and cultural influences. Finally, Erikson's model was based on the study of normal individuals and emphasized the positive, healthy aspects of personality, whereas Freud's model drew heavily on his work with patients in psychoanalysis.

Identity
In Erikson's theory, the component of personality that develops across the eight stages of life and that motivates progress through the stages.

Like Freud, Erikson believed that all children progress through a predictable series of stages (see Table 1.1). This progression, he argued, is not random but follows a blueprint or timetable built into our genes. According to Erikson, each individual's ultimate goal is the quest for **identity**, which develops gradually across the eight stages. But at each stage, the individual must resolve a conflict. A positive personality characteristic associated with the search for identity conflicts with a negative one resulting from interaction with the social world. For example, in Erikson's second stage, a toddler's newfound physical abilities—such as walking and controlling bladder and bowel functions—lead to the positive feelings of *autonomy* as the child begins to exert more control over his or her life. But these new abilities also tend to cause conflict in the child's social world—with parents, for instance—leading to feelings of *shame* and *doubt*. According to Erikson, a successful resolution of this conflict would leave the child with a stronger sense of autonomy than of shame and doubt. This resolution would then contribute to the child's adaptation to another conflict in the next stage of psychosocial development.

Evolutionary and Biological Approaches

Evolutionary-biological approach
Viewing development principally as a product of evolutionary adaptation and biological processes.

Ethology
The study of animal behavior in its natural environment from an evolutionary perspective.

Another major theoretical perspective among child development researchers is the **evolutionary-biological approach**. The historical roots of this tradition can be traced to the work of Charles Darwin. The modern version of the approach is based on **ethology,** the study of animal behavior in its natural habitat from an evolutionary perspective. Our species, like others, is the product of millions of years of change. What we are today represents a small part of an enormous process, and we are only one of the 5 million or so species that presently inhabit the earth. Ethology considers human development within the context of the entire animal kingdom. It should not be surprising, then, that much of the research in ethology has involved nonhuman species.

According to ethological theorists, developmental changes have both immediate and evolutionary determinants. Immediate determinants include the environment in which the behavior occurs, the animal's recent experiences, and the state or condition of the animal—whether it is hungry, tired, or angry, for example. The evolutionary determinants of behavior are inherited behaviors or characteristics that have become part of a species through natural selection or mechanisms of population genetics. These characteristics have in some way contributed to the survival of the species. For example, some animals live in social groups, procreate promiscuously, cooperatively hunt for food, and use tools. Others live separately, mate for life, feed independently, and cooperatively build and guard nests. To explain behaviors relating to these characteristics, ethologists consider both the immediate circumstances of the animals under observation and factors in the animal's evolutionary past.

Ethology In 1973 Konrad Lorenz and Niko Tinbergen were jointly awarded a Nobel Prize for their pioneering research, begun in the 1930s, on animal behavior. This research laid the groundwork for the application of ethological principles to child development. They identified four *innate mechanisms*, or qualities that characterize virtually all innate, or inborn, behaviors (Eibl-Eibesfeldt, 1989).

1. These behaviors are *universal* to all members of the species.
2. The behaviors are biologically programmed responses to very specific stimuli, and thus *require no learning or experience.*
3. The behaviors become *stereotyped*, meaning that they occur in precisely the same way every time they are displayed.
4. They are only *minimally affected by short-term environmental influences.*

Examples of such behaviors are many, including, for example, the nest-building of ants, migration of geese, pecking order of chickens, herding of antelope, and mutual grooming among primates. In humans, innate behaviors are most evident during infancy. An inborn response such as sucking, for example, is found in all newborns, does not need to be learned, occurs in a stereotyped pattern (the same way every time), and is influenced very little by the environment.

Some of these behaviors, such as grooming, are complex sequences of innate behaviors, which ethologists call *modal action patterns*. These are the chains of responses that occur, for example, when spiders spin webs, squirrels store food for the winter, birds build nests, or bears care for newborn cubs. A modal action pattern is triggered by a specific stimulus in the animal's environment—such as temperature, length of day, hormonal or pheromonal changes—what Lorenz called an *innate releasing mechanism*. Ethologists believe that many response patterns in humans are also triggered by very specific stimuli. Maternal breastfeeding behavior, for example, may begin as a response to hearing a newborn baby's cry and is reinforced by the baby's sucking behavior. Thus, many basic aspects of human behavior are controlled by innate evolutionary processes.

Ethologists also study how an animal's genetic or biological makeup can influence the learning process—that is, how nature and nurture work together to change behavior. Animals are biologically programmed so that some behaviors are learned most easily during certain periods of development, called **sensitive periods**. A dramatic example is *imprinting*, the process by which newborns of some species form an emotional bond with their mothers. Among bird species whose young can walk almost immediately after hatching, for example, baby birds soon begin to follow the mother as she moves about. This simple act of following is responsible for the strong social bond that develops between the newborn and the parent (Lorenz, 1937).

Lorenz further discovered that the age of the chicks influenced imprinting. If the chicks followed during the first two days, the attachment bond reliably developed. When the following behavior occurred only before or after this period, however, little or no imprinting resulted, suggesting the existence of sensitive periods, when learning a particular behavior is easiest. Child researchers have also applied the concept of sensitive periods to language acquisition (Newport, 1991) and gender-role development (Money & Annecillo, 1987). Modern researchers are finding many other areas of development in which ethological and evolutionary processes may be important (Archer, 1992; Geary & Bjorklund, 2000; Scarr, 1993).

Questions for Thought and Discussion
What other kinds of human behaviors do you think would have aided survival or reproductive advantage?

Sensitive period
A period of development during which certain behaviors are more easily or quickly learned.

To confirm his idea of imprinting, Lorenz removed just-hatched goslings from their mother and had them follow another animal, or various nonliving objects that he pulled along, or even himself. As he predicted, the young birds quickly imprinted to whatever they followed and thereafter treated it as their mother. (Nina Leen/Time Inc. Picture Collection)

Attachment
The emotional bond between infants and their parents or other caregivers.

Evolutionary developmental psychology
A theoretical approach that emphasizes the evolutionary origins of human thought patterns, emotions, and cognitive abilities.

Behavioral and social learning approaches
Perspectives on development that give greatest importance to environmental influences and learning experiences as sources of development.

John Bowlby's Attachment Theory A scientific application of the ethological model to child development is reflected in the work of an English physician and psychoanalyst, John Bowlby (Bowlby, 1969/1982, 1973, 1980). In his work Bowlby witnessed the emotional problems of children who had been reared in institutions. Such children often have difficulty forming and maintaining close relationships. Bowlby attributed this problem to the children's lack of primary attachment to a caregiver during infancy. His interest in this area led him to a theory of how and why the mother-infant bond is established (Bretherton, 1995; Holmes, 1995; Sroufe, 1986).

Bowlby's theory is an interesting mix of ethology and psychoanalytic theory (Holmes, 1995; Sroufe, 1986). Like Freud, Bowlby believed that the quality of the early mother-infant relationship is critical to later development and that early experiences are carried forward in the unconscious mind. Like the ethologists, Bowlby also understood that in humans a close mother-infant bond is crucial for the survival of the young. Infants who remain near the mother can be fed, protected, trained, and transported more effectively than can infants who stray from her side. Bowlby's work has encouraged much research on attachment and bonding in humans and other aspects of child development that operate within an evolutionary context. Psychologists have since investigated children's aggression, peer interactions, and cognitive development, for example.

Evolutionary Developmental Psychology A more recent development is the emergence of evolutionary developmental psychology (Bjorklund & Pellegrini, 2000, 2002), a subdivision of *evolutionary psychology* (Buss, 1999). **Evolutionary developmental psychology** shares the general ethological emphases on evolution and the selection of adaptive behavior. Its scope, however, is broader. In particular, it encompasses the evolutionary origins of human thought patterns, emotions, and cognitive abilities as well as basic processes that underlie social relations and social interactions. This emphasis is reflected in books such as *The Evolution of Cognition* (Heyes & Huber, 2000), *The Adapted Mind* (Barkow, Cosmides, & Tooby, 1992), and *The New Science of the Mind* (Buss, 1999).

Evolutionary developmental psychologists point out that adaptations characteristic of our species may or may not fit well with present-day adaptive challenges. Many behavioral characteristics that evolved over hundreds of thousands of years still serve us well today. Examples are the formation of an attachment bond in infancy and the ability to master a language. New behavioral challenges have arisen since the last significant evolutionary change in our species, however, such as learning to perform complex mathematical operations and many other skills transmitted through formal education. Evolutionary psychologists accurately predict that culturally derived skills such as higher mathematics will be more difficult to attain and more variable across children than developments such as attachment or language. However, because the ability to solve complex math problems usually does not affect survival or the ability to transmit genes, this behavior is unlikely to affect human evolution.

Evolutionary developmental psychology also provides a framework for making sense of the attributes and developmental tasks that characterize different periods of childhood. As you saw, for example, certain characteristics of babies promote caregiving and thus survival. Bjorklund and Pellegrini (2002) offer another example. They suggest that the rough-and-tumble play that is common among boys may help boys learn forms of social behavior that will be beneficial to them at later ages. Rough-and-tumble play also provides exercise that is important for skeletal and muscular development.

Behavioral and Social Learning Approaches

Behavioral and social learning approaches focus on the fact that much of human behavior, especially social behavior, is acquired rather than inborn. Biological factors make important contributions to human development, but learned behavior may be more important for understanding human development. Behavioral psychology is based on the belief that the changes in behavior that occur as children develop often are *learned*. They result from conditioning and the operation of other learning principles. *Learning* does not refer simply to what goes on in a classroom. It is any potentially long-lasting behavior that results from practice or experience or interaction with the environment.

A simple type of learned behavior that has been researched in child development is **habituation**, or learning through repetition. For example, infants learn to sleep through routine household noises. If given enough exposure, babies very quickly get used to slamming doors, ringing phones, and similar sounds that might otherwise wake them. Unfortunately, many parents, unaware of this fact, try to keep everyone very quiet during nap times. The absence of typical household sounds, however, may prevent the infant from becoming accustomed to them and make her or him more likely to awaken at the first bark of the family dog.

If you clap your hands loudly near an infant, initially the infant will display a full-body startle *reflex*. If you continue to clap your hands at frequent intervals (say, every 15 seconds), the size of the startle response will decrease steadily until it cannot be detected. This simple change in behavior caused by repeatedly presenting a stimulus illustrates learning through habituation. Habituation has proved to be a useful method for studying infants' early perceptual abilities, examined in Chapter 5.

Classical Conditioning Sometimes called *respondent conditioning*, **classical conditioning** was developed by Russian physiologist Ivan Pavlov (1849–1936). It involves learning through association, as reflexes or other respondent behaviors are paired with other stimuli. In this type of learning, the stimulus is termed the *unconditioned stimulus (UCS)*, and the response to this stimulus is called the *unconditioned response (UCR)*. In Pavlov's experiments, for example, dogs salivated (UCR) when presented with food (UCS). Then the stimulus is "conditioned"; that is, another stimulus is presented along with the UCS, with the result that the new stimulus elicits the same response as the original stimulus. For example, Pavlov's dogs salivated (UCR) when presented with the sound of a chime, which had been repeatedly associated with the UCS (food). The sound of the chime, previously neutral, became a conditioned stimulus (CS).

Children's emotional responses often are a result of this kind of conditioning. Fear responses, for instance, are naturally elicited by stimuli such as pain. Consider a child visiting the dentist for the first time. The stimuli in that environment—the dentist, the office, the instruments, and so forth—are neutral to the child and so have no particular effect on emotional behavior. A child's experience of pain (UCS) during the visit, however, may elicit fear (UCR). The various neutral stimuli in the dentist's office may then become conditioned stimuli (CS) through association with the UCS. After that, the sight of the dentist or sound of the drill, for example, may also elicit the fear response. In the same way, many common fears of childhood can be learned responses to places or objects that previously were not frightening.

Classical conditioning often produces *stimulus generalization*, which means that stimuli similar to the CS also become conditioned. For example, a child may come to fear all dentists, or even all people wearing a white lab coat. Fortunately, conditioned responses also can be unlearned, a process called *extinction*. If the child returns to the dentist often without experiencing more pain, the conditioned stimuli will no longer elicit fear.

B. F. Skinner's Operant Conditioning Pavlov's experiments concerned respondent behavior, but B. F. Skinner was interested in the effects of conditioning on operant behavior. In humans, *respondent behaviors* include reflexes, such as sucking in response to contact with a nipple and grasping in response to touching of the palm. Older children and adults also display respondent behaviors—physiological responses (blinking and sneezing) and emotional responses (some aspects of fear, anger, and sexual arousal).

Operant behaviors, however, are very different. Generally, they are responses that people produce voluntarily—for example, saying "thank you," or asking, "Please can I have a cookie?" rather than simply grabbing the cookie from another child. Operant behaviors,

Habituation
A type of learning in which a behavioral response decreases or disappears as a result of repeated exposure to a stimulus.

Links to Related Material
Habituation-dishabituation, a procedure based on behavioral principles, has been useful for studying infants' early perceptual abilities, examined in Chapter 5.

Classical conditioning
A pattern of learned response involving reflexes, in which a neutral stimulus acquires the power to elicit the same response as an unconditioned stimulus through association or pairing. The neutral stimulus becomes conditioned. Through this process an organism learns to respond to conditioned stimuli in the same way that it responds to unconditioned stimuli.

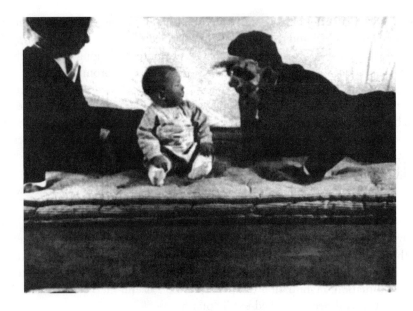

In the 1920s, psychologist John Watson demonstrated that he could condition a child (his son, "Little Albert") to fear a white rat, by associating the presence of the animal with a loud noise, and that he could also make the child generalize his fear to other white furry objects, such as the experimenter's beard in this picture. Such an experiment would never be allowed today. Why? (Watson & Raynor)

which include the vast majority of human behaviors, are controlled by their effects—their consequences. Pleasant consequences make the behaviors more likely to be repeated, whereas unpleasant consequences have the opposite result (Skinner, 1953). These changes in behavior are called **operant conditioning**.

Many of the everyday behaviors of children recur simply because they resulted in desirable consequences in the past. Any consequence that makes a behavior more likely to recur is called a *reinforcer*. Consider the following examples. Four-year-old Keshia may (1) share her toys with a friend because doing so often produces similar sharing by the other child; (2) throw a temper tantrum in the supermarket because this sometimes results in getting candy from her parent; (3) twist and shake the knob of the playroom door because this behavior is effective in getting it open; (4) work hard at dance lessons because the teacher praises her when she performs well; and (5) block her ears when her baby brother is crying because this behavior helps reduce the unpleasant sound.

As you can see, **reinforcement** can take many forms. Nevertheless, they all fall into one of two categories: Those that involve getting something good are called *positive reinforcers*, and those that involve getting rid of something aversive are called *negative reinforcers*.

The above examples also show that the reinforcement process is not confined only to desirable or beneficial responses. Reinforcement increases the likelihood of any behavior that leads to a pleasant consequence, whether that behavior is viewed as appropriate (sharing toys), inappropriate (throwing a tantrum in a supermarket), or neutral (opening a door).

Not all consequences are reinforcing, however. Behavior sometimes produces effects that are unpleasant, and these *reduce* the likelihood that the behavior will recur. Such consequences are called *punishers*. You may think of punishment as something unpleasant that is delivered by parents or teachers for misbehavior, but the principle of punishment, like the principle of reinforcement, is simply part of nature's learning process. **Punishment** teaches organisms which responses are wise to repeat and which are better to avoid. Punishment can entail either getting something bad (such as a time-out, a failing grade, or a scraped knee) or losing something good (such as a favored stuffed animal, a chance to sit by a friend at lunch, or TV privileges for a week). Either way, behaviors that lead to punishing consequences naturally decrease.

Social Learning Theory Another approach that emphasizes the role of environmental influences in child development is **social learning theory**, represented by the work of Albert Bandura (1986, 1992, 2001). Bandura's contributions are based on his observation that children sometimes acquire new behaviors simply by seeing someone else perform

Operant conditioning
A pattern of learned response involving voluntary behavior, in which the consequences of the behavior (reinforcement or punishment) strongly influence whether the organism will repeat the behavior.

Reinforcement
Any consequence that increases the occurrence of a behavior. Reinforcement may be positive (something pleasant happens) or negative (something unpleasant stops happening).

Punishment
Any consequence that decreases the occurrence of a behavior. Punishment may be positive (something unpleasant happens) or negative (something pleasant is removed).

Social learning theory
Any theory that adds observational learning to classical and operant learning as a process through which children's behavior changes.

them. In addition, children sometimes become more or less likely to perform a behavior after seeing another person experience consequences that are reinforcing or punishing for that behavior. In these situations children learn vicariously and acquire new behaviors through imitation.

According to Bandura, as children grow, their development is increasingly based on **observational learning**. Learning by observation occurs when the behavior of an observer is affected by witnessing the behavior of a model (and often the consequences of that behavior). Children are the observers, and the models on which they base their behavior include parents, teachers, siblings, peers, sports celebrities, TV personalities, fictional heroes, even cartoon characters—just about anyone in the child's world.

Bandura and other researchers have studied three important questions about the **modeling** process:

1. Which models are most likely to influence a child's behavior?

2. Under what circumstances is this influence most likely to occur?

3. How does the child's behavior change as a result of observational learning?

The simple answer to the first question is that a model who possesses a characteristic that the child finds attractive or desirable—such as talent, intelligence, power, good looks, or popularity—is most likely to be imitated. Other issues can sometimes come into play, however, including the child's level of development and the types of behaviors being modeled.

The circumstances under which *modeling* is most effective also can vary, but one of the most important factors is whether the model receives reinforcing or punishing consequences for the behavior. One of Bandura's most significant contributions to social learning theory was his demonstration that the consequences of a model's behavior can affect the behavior of an observer. When a child sees a model receive reinforcement for a response, the child receives vicarious reinforcement and, like the model, becomes more likely to produce that same response. The opposite is true when the child receives vicarious punishment as a result of witnessing a model being punished. Thus, observational learning is like operant conditioning, except that the child experiences the consequences vicariously rather than directly.

An important result of modeling is *imitation*, which occurs when children copy what they have seen. Imitation can take such varied forms as adopting the clothing style of a popular professional athlete, climbing on a chair to steal a cookie from the shelf after

Observational learning
A pattern of learning based on vicarious reinforcement in which an observer's behavior changes as a result of observing and imitating a model.

Modeling
Changes in behavior as a result of observing the behavior of a model, usually through imitation.

Q**uestions for Thought and Discussion**
What three persons or characters most influenced your behavior through your observational learning during childhood?

Albert Bandura's early research showed that children who observed adults behaving violently towards an inflated "Bobo" doll were capable of very accurately imitating the model's aggressive acts when given the opportunity to reproduce them. The children's behavior was a consequence of social, or observational, learning. Through the same type of learning, young children will "feed" a baby doll, or "make dinner" in a toy microwave. (Courtesy of Albert Bandora, Stanford University)

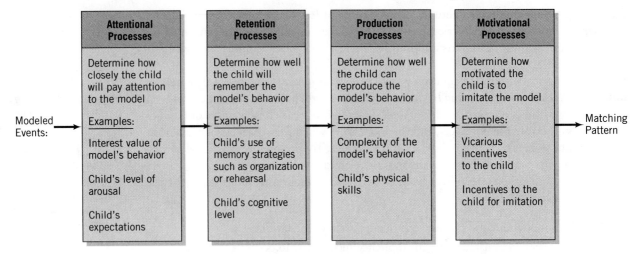

FIGURE 1.2   Factors Involved in Observational Learning

In learning from observation, children are exposed to a modeling event, pay attention to it, remember it, imitate it, and continue to direct their behavior to match it.

SOURCE: Adapted from Albert Bandura, *Social Learning Theory*, 1977, p. 23. Reprinted by permission of Prentice-Hall, Inc., Upper Saddle River, New Jersey.

seeing an older sibling do it, or choosing to draw pictures of space aliens after observing a classmate draw similar pictures. A second result of modeling occurs when the observer becomes less likely to perform a behavior that has just been modeled. This effect, known as *response inhibition*, is a common result of vicarious punishment. The teacher who publicly disciplines an unruly child to set an example for the rest of the class is counting on observational learning to inhibit similar behaviors in the other children.

Children do not always immediately display behavior learned from models. A striking illustration of this point occurred in one of Bandura's early studies, in which one group of youngsters observed a model rewarded for displaying new aggressive behaviors toward an inflated toy clown, and a second group saw those same behaviors punished. When given an opportunity to play with the doll, the children who witnessed the reinforcement imitated many of the model's aggressive acts toward the doll, whereas the group that observed punishment did not. But later, when offered rewards for reproducing the aggressive behaviors, both groups were able to perform them quite accurately (Bandura, 1965). All of the children had acquired (learned) the new behaviors, even though the vicariously experienced punishment had inhibited some children from performing them. This distinction between acquisition and performance has been of particular interest to researchers studying the potential effects of viewing television violence on children's aggressive behavior, discussed in Chapters 10 and 15.

Bandura's theory also suggests why, in everyday life, children do not imitate everything they see. As Figure 1.2 shows, a child may fail to imitate an observed behavior because he or she did not pay attention to what the model was doing, does not recall the model's responses or consequences of modeling, does not possess the physical skills to repeat the model's behavior, or simply feels little motivation to do what the model did. Bandura's addition of observational learning to the behavioral approach, along with his incorporation of cognitive aspects of development, has greatly increased the explanatory power of social learning theory.

Cognitive-Developmental Approaches

Another theoretical perspective of child development emphasizes cognition, or activities of the mind, and **cognitive development**, or developmental changes in the way children think. According to cognitive-developmental approaches, the changes we witness in children's behaviors and abilities arise largely from changes in their knowledge and intellec-

Links to Related Material
Bandura's social learning theory has been of particular interest to researchers studying the potential effects of viewing television violence on children's aggressive behavior, discussed in Chapters 10 and 15.

Cognitive development
Changes in the ways that children think about and make sense of the world and solve problems.

tual skills. The major goals of these approaches, therefore, are to specify what children know, how this knowledge is organized, and how it changes or develops. The work of Jean Piaget (1896–1980) revolutionized thinking about children and their behavior. Piaget was interested not in the precise knowledge and facts that children possess—for example, *what* children know when they enter school—but rather in how they go about acquiring and using that knowledge—that is, *how* children think.

Piaget's Theory of Cognitive Development

Piaget's research technique was to challenge children with simple tasks and verbal problems that required solutions and explanations. He asked a question or posed a problem and then, depending on the child's response, followed up with other questions that might reveal the child's reasoning or problem-solving approach. Beginning in the late 1950s, American psychologists began to discover Piaget's work, and his studies were replicated through controlled experiments (Flavell, 1963). His theory generated many new questions about children's cognitive development, such as their understanding of time, logic, and causality. Piaget's many books on child development remain one of the greatest contributions to the field by a single scholar (Beilin, 1992).

The most fundamental aspect of Piaget's theory, and often the most difficult to understand, is the belief that intelligence is a process—not something that a child *has* but something that a child *does*. Piaget's child understands the world by acting or operating on it. Through this process, a child's *cognitive structures* continually change.

For example, Piaget would describe an infant's knowledge of a ball in terms of the various actions the infant can perform with it—pushing the ball, grasping it, mouthing it, and so on. These actions are a reflection of the cognitive structures of infancy, called *schemes*. *Schemes* are mental structures for "knowing" objects (such as a ball) and for interacting with objects. A young infant has comparatively few schemes, which are interrelated in very simple ways. As development proceeds, however, schemes increase in both number and complexity of organization. These two characteristics of children's cognitive structures— number and complexity—define the child's intelligence at any point in development.

Schemes and other cognitive structures are flexible in the way they are expressed by individual infants and also in the way that they change over time. A particular scheme, such as grasping, reflects more and more skill as the infant applies it to more and more objects. In this way, schemes eventually become more individualized, or *differentiated*, so that a ball becomes primarily an object to be thrown, a rattle primarily an object to be shaken, and a nipple primarily an object to be sucked.

Beyond these simple schemes of infancy, new and higher-level cognitive structures gradually emerge. An 8-year-old with a ball, for example, still has all the earlier schemes available (although sucking the ball is not a very likely response). At the same time the older child can understand the ball by assigning it certain properties (color, size), acting

In Piaget's theory, children act upon the world at every stage of development. The schemes with which they do so, however, change as the child develops. How do these pictures illustrate developmental differences in children's use of schemes? (*Left*, Elizabeth Crews/The Image Works; *right*, ©David Young-Wolff/PhotoEdit)

Links to Related Material
Piaget's influence on our understanding of cognitive development is examined in more depth in Chapter 7.

Adaptation
An organism's attempt to fit with its environment in ways that promote survival.

Assimilation
Adaptation through interpreting new experiences in terms of existing cognitive structures.

Accommodation
Adaptation through changing existing cognitive structures to fit with new experiences.

Stages of cognitive development
Piaget's four stages or periods of development, based on the means by which children know the world, from sensorimotor and preoperational intelligence to concrete operational intelligence and formal operations.

on it (bouncing, hitting), or classifying it (as a member of the class "round things"). For Piaget, *development* referred to this continual reorganization of knowledge into new and more complex structures, discussed in more detail in Chapter 7.

Piaget identified two general functions that guide cognitive development. One is *organization*. Because an individual's cognitive structures are interrelated, any new knowledge must be fitted into the existing system. According to Piaget, it is this need for integrating new information, rather than simply adding it on, that forces our cognitive structures to become ever more elaborately organized.

The second function is **adaptation**, an organism's attempt to fit with its environment in ways that promote survival. In Piaget's model, cognitive adaptation involves two processes. **Assimilation** entails trying to make sense of new experiences in terms of our existing cognitive structures. The infant who brings everything to his or her mouth to suck is demonstrating assimilation, as is the toddler who calls all men "Daddy." Assimilation may require some distortion of the new information to make it fit into the child's existing schemes. Trying to fit new things into what we already know is one way we adapt to the world.

When new information is too different or too complex, **accommodation** occurs. Here, our cognitive structures change to integrate the new experiences. For example, the infant eventually learns that not all objects are to be sucked, just as the toddler learns that different labels or names need to be applied to different men. It is primarily through accommodation that the number and complexity of children's cognitive structures increase—that is, that intelligence grows.

Piaget assumed that assimilation and accommodation operate closely together. A growing child is continually making slight distortions of information to assimilate it into existing structures while at the same time also making slight modifications in these structures to accommodate new objects or events. The interplay of these two functions illustrates another important aspect of Piaget's theory, the concept of *constructivism*. Children's knowledge of events in their environment is not an exact reproduction of those events—it is not like a perfect photograph of what they have seen or a precise recording of what they have heard. Rather, children take information from the environment and bend, shape, or distort it until it fits comfortably into their existing cognitive organization. Even when they accommodate structures to allow for new experiences, the accommodation is seldom complete, and some distortion of the information remains. Thus, when children 6, 8, and 10 years old watch a movie or hear a lecture, they come away with somewhat different messages, even though they may have seen or heard the same input. In addition, each child acts on the information somewhat differently, fitting it into his or her own existing set of structures. In this sense, the child constructs knowledge about the world, rather than simply receiving it.

The functions of assimilation and accommodation make the child's cognitive system increasingly more powerful and adaptive. However, these processes produce only small-scale changes. At certain points in development, Piaget argued, more major adjustments are required. At these points, the cognitive system, because of both biological maturation and past experiences, has completely mastered one level of functioning and is ready for new, qualitatively different challenges—challenges that go beyond what the current set of structures can handle. At such points, the child moves to a new stage of development.

Piaget believed that all children move through the same **stages of cognitive development** in the same order. At each stage, the child's cognitive functioning is qualitatively different and affects the child's performance in a wide range of situations. There are four such general stages, or periods, in Piaget's model.

- The *sensorimotor period* represents the first 2 years of life. The infant's initial schemes are simple reflexes, and knowledge of the world is limited to physical interactions with people and objects.
- During the *preoperational period*, from roughly 2 to 6 years, the child begins to use symbols, such as words and numbers, to represent the world cognitively.

- The period of *concrete operations* lasts approximately from age 6 to age 11. Children in this stage are able to perform mental operations on the pieces of knowledge they possess, permitting a kind of logical problem solving that was not possible during the preoperational period.
- The final stage, the period of *formal operations*, extends from about age 12 through adulthood. This period includes all the higher-level abstract operations, enabling the child to deal with events or relations that are only possible, as opposed to those that actually exist.

The accuracy of Piaget's theory has been studied extensively over the years. In Chapter 7 we consider the four stages in detail and describe the evidence psychologists have gathered that both supports and questions various aspects of this theory.

Information Processing Model

A second cognitive-developmental approach is **information processing**, described in more detail in Chapter 8. Information processing theorists view cognition as a system composed of three parts.

1. Information in the world provides input to the system, when it enters our senses in the form of sights, sounds, tastes, and so on.

2. Processes in the brain act on and transform the information in a variety of ways, including encoding it into symbolic forms, comparing it with previously acquired information, storing it in memory, and retrieving it from memory when necessary.

3. The third part of the system is the output, which is our behavior—speech, social interactions, writing, and so on.

As an input-output model, the information processing approach to cognition resembles the operation of a computer. Some researchers make this connection very strongly. Their goal is to construct computer programs that create artificial intelligence and simulate human behavior, so that ultimately we will be able to specify our cognitive processes in precise mathematical and logical terms. More often, however, researchers use the *computer analogy* simply as a way of thinking about information flowing through a system, where it is processed and then reemerges in a different form. Information processing models have been used in research on children's problem solving, memory, reading, and other cognitive processes (Kail & Bisanz, 1992; Klahr & MacWhinney, 1998).

In recent years, the information processing view has emerged as a leading approach in the study of human cognition. Its popularity reflects in part the growing interest in *cognitive science*, an interdisciplinary field in which researchers in biology, mathematics, philosophy, neuroscience, and other disciplines are attempting to understand the workings of the human mind (e.g., Keil, 1998; Osherson, 1990; Siegler & Alibali, 2005).

Information processing
A way of viewing cognition, memory, and intelligence as neurophysiological processes or by analogy with the structures and functions of the computer.

Questions for Thought and Discussion
What are some advantages and disadvantages of conceptualizing the mind in terms of computer operations?

Links to Related Material
The influence of information processing models on our understanding of children's cognitive development will be discussed in further detail in Chapter 8.

Sociocultural Approach: The Work of Vygotsky

Cognitive-developmental researchers typically investigate children's thinking by asking them to reason about problems in settings far removed from the daily situations in which children usually apply their cognitive skills. Furthermore, cognitive-developmental theories locate the sources of cognitive change primarily in the heads of individual children. The **sociocultural approach,** which we describe in greater detail in Chapter 7, offers a very different perspective that views development as occurring in social, cultural, and historical contexts. These contexts include other people, such as parents and teachers, who support and guide children's cognitive activities, as well as the cultural tools and traditions that shape mental processes. Defining features of the sociocultural approach, then, include an emphasis on social processes, cultural practices, and the everyday contexts of development.

Contemporary theory in the sociocultural tradition is based largely on the work of the Russian psychologist Lev Vygotsky (Glassman, 1994; Kozulin, 1990). Vygotsky's model

Sociocultural approach
Theoretical perspective expressed by Vygotsky, emphasizing children's learning through interaction with others and problem solving within the context of society and culture.

of human development holds that the individual's development is a product of his or her culture. In this theory, development refers largely to mental development, such as thought, language, and reasoning processes. Vygotsky assumed that these abilities develop through social interactions with others (especially parents) and thus represent the shared knowledge of the culture. Whereas Piaget believed that all children's cognitive development follows a very similar pattern of stages, Vygotsky saw intellectual abilities as much more specific to the culture in which the child was reared (Kozulin, 1990; Wertsch & Tulviste, 1992).

Culture makes two sorts of contributions to the child's intellectual development.

1. Children acquire much of the content of their thinking—that is, their knowledge—from the culture around them.

2. Children acquire their thinking and reasoning processes—what Vygotskians call the *tools of intellectual adaptation*—from their culture. In short, culture teaches children both what to think and how to think.

How does culture exert its influences? Vygotsky believed that cognitive development results from a process in which the child learns through shared problem-solving experiences with someone else, usually a parent or teacher (Greenfield, 2004; Rogoff, 1998). For example, consider a Mayan child learning to weave, a skill essential to the economy of the Central American village where she lives. Her mother or another skilled adult may demonstrate a complex weaving pattern for her. She will then reproduce the pattern to the best of her ability, asking for direction again when the task becomes too complex for her. From Vygotsky's point of view, they are together solving a problem, "How do we weave this sweater for sale to tourists at the local market?" In the United States, a group of Girl Scouts might be given the complex task of selling cookies in their neighborhood. Adult advisers and older, more experienced girls in their troop will guide them through the process of solving the problem, "How do we sell our cookies?" Initially, the adult assumes most of the responsibility for guiding the problem solving. Gradually, however, the responsibility shifts partly and then completely to the child. Language plays a central role in this process in two ways. First, language describes and transmits to children the rich body of knowledge that exists in the culture. Second, it provides the means, or method, of problem solving, which is demonstrated by the adult and then adopted by the child.

This transfer of control from adult to child reflects Vygotsky's idea that development is a process of **internalization** (Cox & Lightfoot, 1997). Bodies of knowledge and thinking tools at first exist outside the child, in the surrounding culture. Development, according to Vygotsky, consists of gradually internalizing them. This is what Vygotskians mean when they say that children's cognitive abilities grow directly out of their interactions with others in culturally meaningful settings.

Links to Related Material
The influence of the sociocultural approach on our understanding of children's cognitive development will be discussed in greater depth in Chapter 7.

Questions for Thought and Discussion
Which approach to explaining human development—psychoanalytic, evolutionary, environmental-learning, cognitive, or sociocultural—best fits with your own thinking about how we develop? Why?

Internalization
Vygotsky's term for the child's incorporation of culturally meaningful information, primarily through language and interactions with others in culturally meaningful settings.

 **Test Your Mastery...**

Learning Objective 1.4: *What are five major theoretical perspectives in the field of child development?*

1. What assumptions and beliefs underlie the psychoanalytic approaches of Freud and Erikson?
2. What aspects of child development do ethology and evolutionary psychology help us understand?
3. How are classical conditioning, operant conditioning, and social learning alike and different?
4. How are Piaget's theory of cognitive development and information processing theory alike and different?
5. What assumptions and beliefs characterize Vygotsky's sociocultural approach?
6. Where would you place Bronfenbrenner's ecological-environmental model and contextual perspective in this array of theoretical approaches to child development?

BOX 1.3   Theories as Everyday Explanations for Behavior

Often, people think of theories as abstractions that are removed from everyday life. However, many theories of child development have entered mainstream thinking in the United States and are regularly used as everyday explanations for behavior.

For example, in 1999 (August 16), *Time Magazine* published an article titled, "Is This the Meanest Kid in All of Alabama?" It tells the story of a 15-year-old boy named Lance Landers, who had been barred by a state judge from all Alabama public schools after assaulting a teacher's aide on a school bus and threatening to grab the steering wheel and cause a wreck. Some of Lance's other school behaviors included hurling batteries at other students, spitting into trays of food in the cafeteria, drawing pictures of him beating other kids with a baseball bat, and greeting the principal with obscenities.

Where does Lance's behavior come from? Ask this question of a roomful of adults in the United States and you will get a variety of answers, including:

- Lance has ADHD or some other disorder and should be placed on medication.

- Lance did not form a supportive, loving bond with his parents when he was young, leaving him insecure and mistrustful of others.

- Lance's parents have not provided proper supervision, discipline, or guidance:
  - They might have modeled aggressive behavior.
  - They might have rewarded or failed to punish their son's aggressive behavior.

- Lance is modeling violence from other sources in his environment, such as:
  - TV
  - Computer or video games
  - His neighborhood or peers

- Lance may not have a good understanding of how to solve and respond to social problems; he may believe that violence or aggression is the only answer.

- Lance's behavior reflects larger influences in our society, such as:
  - Permissive behavioral standards in our families and schools, making it more difficult for parents and other caretakers to know when and how to discipline effectively;
  - Breakdown of extended family and community ties, which have traditionally provided children with social and emotional buffers from personal and familial stress;

- Media saturated with violent models that glorify physical violence, often equating it with masculinity, and that may not provide alternate models for problem solving, or send clear messages regarding the negative consequences of physically violent behavior; and

- A health insurance system that for monetary purposes too often reduces complex social and emotional problems to chemical imbalances that can be treated only with pills.

All these answers reflect theories of child development, described in this chapter, used as everyday explanations of behavior. As you can see, psychological explanations of human behavior have permeated our society and culture.

The first type of response—that Lance has some kind of disorder requiring medication—clearly reflects a biological model of development. Behavioral problems are viewed as having their primary roots in genetics or physiology. The second explanation—that Lance did not form a good relationship with his parents—echoes John Bowlby's work on attachment, and the primacy of early attachment bonds for later social and emotional development. The next two types of answers—that Lance's parents did not provide proper guidance or that he has learned violent behavior from other sources—mirror behavioral and social learning approaches to development through their emphasis on the concepts of reinforcement and observational learning.

The idea that Lance may not have a good understanding of how to solve and respond to social problems reflects cognitive-developmental perspectives on human behavior. Lance, like all human beings, has over the years built mental models for understanding and responding to others. Research supports the view that highly aggressive children tend to have cognitive models of others as highly aggressive in their intents and motives (Rubin, Bukowski, & Parker, 1998). The final explanation—that Lance's behavior reflects larger problems in our society—is consistent with the contextual and sociocultural views, which consider development within the larger framework. From this perspective, explanations that look for answers only within Lance (his biology or his cognitive abilities or his early relationships or his responses to environmental reinforcers) are missing a large part of the picture. Each of these things may contribute, but we will completely understand Lance's behavior—and others like him—only when we place it within the context of larger societal and cultural forces.

Learning Objective 1.1
Describe ways that cultural and historical contexts have influenced our understanding of child development.

1. What are the parts of Bronfenbrenner's ecological model? How does the model help us understand child development?	There are four parts to Bronfenbrenner's ecological model. The *microsystem* consists of the settings that influence the child directly through the child's immediate participation. The *mesosystem* refers to the system of relationships among the child's microsystems. The *exosystem* refers to the social settings that can affect the child in which the child does not participate directly. The *macrosystem*, which involves the culture and subculture in which the child lives, affects the child through beliefs, values, and tradition. Bronfenbrenner's model helps us to understand child development by considering how the unique characteristics of the child (personality traits, physical appearance, and intellectual abilities) interact with that child's surroundings.
2. What is meant by the cultural niche of childhood? What are its three major components?	The cultural niche of childhood refers to the idea that cultural influence is an integral aspect of a child's development. The three major components are the child's *physical settings* and conditions of daily life, *childcare customs*, and *childrearing beliefs and goals*.
3. What are some examples of the cultural contexts of child development?	Middle-class American children are often placed from very young age in specialized activity groups such as gymnastics, dance, or soccer. This allows them weekly exposure to same-age peers. This is an example of the cultural context of daily life activities. Allowing young children to explore in "childproofed" areas is an example of a childcare custom that many American parents follow. Parental expectations of when a child should meet a certain developmental milestone, such as self-feeding, is an example of a culturally influenced childrearing goal.
4. How does history affect our study and understanding of child development?	Although child development researchers strive to find information that will withstand time and be true for children everywhere, many topics that are addressed reflect the *social concerns* of a *given time period*. For example, over the last few decades, there has been increased recognition and acceptance of changes in family structure, families headed by same-sex couples, and the increased numbers of women in the paid labor force. Prior to 1970, these issues may have been seen as social "problems." Similarly, researchers have become more aware of the idea that the experiences of middle-class European Americans in the 20th century cannot be generalized to those individuals living in other cultures or time periods.
5. How can it be said that childhood is a social construction?	The theoretical perspective called "the social construction of childhood" explores the *different ways that children are described and defined* throughout the world by specific societies and social groups as well as by scientists. Different constructions of childhood emerge in relation to regional culture, ethnicity, social class, and a wide range of other variables. Moreover, these constructions often relate to broad social needs. In addition, adults' versions of childhood may be very different from children's ideas of what it is to be a child. By exploring children's views of childhood and of their lives as children, researchers gain access to a very different view of childhood.

Learning Objective 1.2

How can we understand the influences of nature and nurture, stability and change, and uniformity and variation in child development?

1. How do nature and nurture jointly contribute to child development?	Researchers generally agree that both nature and nurture play some role in development. However, the exact relationship is cause for continued debate. Some researchers believe that biological factors (*nature*) play a primary role, with the environment modifying inherent characteristics. Others believe that while biology lays a foundation for development, significant differences in outcomes are determined by experience (*nurture*).
2. Why might some researchers focus on stability or continuity of development, while others focus on discontinuity or change?	A particular focus of a researcher is related to a belief about how development occurs. The *continuity model* assumes that human behavior consists of many individual skills that are added one at a time, producing increasingly complex behaviors indicative of quantitative change. In the *discontinuity model*, development occurs in stages with relatively stable periods of development interrupted by abrupt changes. In this model development involves qualitative changes in previous abilities and behaviors. Researchers agree that some developmental processes are described more accurately by one model and others by the competing model.
3. Why might some researchers focus on typical or normal development, while others focus on individual variation?	*Normative* research focuses on the statistically "average" child with the goal of identifying and describing how normal development proceeds from step to step. Research on *idiographic* development centers on the individual child and the factors that produce human diversity. In addition, research on individual variation allows researchers to more accurately pinpoint the origin of atypical development.
4. What are some examples of universals of development compared to culturally different pathways?	*Universals of development* are behaviors or patterns of development that characterize all children everywhere. These universals are deeply rooted in our biology as human beings. Examples of universal development are children babbling in their native language around 6 months of age, taking their first unassisted steps at roughly one year, and experiencing the sequence of physical changes at puberty. Other childhood milestones may be *culturally influenced*—for example, the age of self-feeding, self-toileting, and engagement in socially appropriate behavior.

Learning Objective 1.3

Describe how research-based knowledge of child development is applied in real-life contexts.

1. In what real-life contexts is child development research applied?	Child development research can be applied to a variety of contexts, including parenting, school, and childcare settings, and may also have an impact on the development of social policy.
2. What are some examples of applied research in child development?	Child development research informs parents in the areas of early learning, television programming, sleep patterns, and discipline strategies. Schools and childcare agencies benefit from research on academic research, school readiness, and peer aggression. Vaccinations, healthcare, parental leave, and custody issues are some of the social policy issues that child development research addresses.
3. How do the contexts of development described in this section relate to Bronfenbrenner's ecological model, described earlier in this chapter?	According to Bronfenbrenner's model, parents are a child's microsystem, the primary level of influence on a child's development. The parents' relationships with teachers and care providers from the mesosystem, those areas in a child's life that interact with the home environment. Social policy is an example of the macrosystem, which represents the values and ideals of society.

Learning Objective 1.4

What are the five major theoretical perspectives in the field of child development?

1. What assumptions and beliefs underlie the psychoanalytic approaches of Freud and Erikson?	The basic assumptions are that nature and nurture interact as significant contributors to a child's development; and that early childhood experiences, particularly relationships with parents, influence outcomes later in life. While *Freud's psychosexual model* ends in adolescence, *Erikson's psychosocial model* suggests that emotional and social development continue throughout life. Both models hold the belief that all children progress through a predictable series of stages. Movement through each stage is contingent on the successful completion of the prior stage.

2. What aspects of child development do ethology and evolutionary psychology help us understand?

According to these theorists, development changes have both immediate and evolutionary determinants. Immediate determinants include environment and experiences. *Evolutionary determinants* are inherited behaviors that have become a part of the species due to natural selection. In humans, innate behaviors are most evident during infancy and are evidenced by the infant's inborn sucking mechanism. An innate evolutionary process may control the response pattern between mother and infant during breastfeeding.

3. How are classical conditioning, operant conditioning, and social learning alike and different?

The similarity of these models is that they all focus on how a child learns. Learning is defined as a change in behavior due to experience or interaction with the environment. In all of the models, some type of stimulus is the catalyst for learning. In *classical conditioning* the learned behavior is an involuntary response. Conversely, *operant behavior* is a voluntary response. A child's behavior is more likely to be repeated if a pleasant consequence is experienced. In *social learning*, the child learns by observing the behavior of others as well as the consequence of that behavior.

4. How are Piaget's theory of cognitive development and information processing alike and different?

Both Piaget's theory and the information processing model are cognitive-developmental approaches, viewing information from the world as the stimulus for development. In both models, individuals actively process this information. In the information processing model, knowledge is built up in domain-specific ways. In Piaget's model, as more complex structures for knowledge are developed, children's cognitive capacities are viewed as shifting qualitatively.

5. What assumptions and beliefs characterize Vygotsky's sociocultural approach?

The defining features of the sociocultural approach are an emphasis on *social process, cultural practices*, and the *everyday contexts of development*. Vygotsky assumed that a child's mental development, such as thought, language, and reasoning processes, develop through social interactions with others, especially parents. According to Vygotsky, intellectual abilities are specific to the culture in which the child is reared.

6. Where would you place Bronfenbrenner's ecological-environmental model and contextual perspective in this array of theoretical approaches to child development?

All of the theories that are discussed in this chapter allow for the idea that our experiences and the environment in which we are raised have at least some influence on a child's development. For Freud, Erikson, and Piaget, drive for development comes from the individual. In classical and operant conditioning, the environment is the catalyst for a change in behavior. In the evolutionary perspective, the environment influences individual development by evolving innate or inborn behaviors. One of the main components of the contextual perspective on development is the idea that an interaction process exists between the individual and the environment. It is this interaction that is a catalyst for development. Vygotsky's sociocultural approach states that a child's intelligence is formed through culture. Bronfenbrenner's model fits best with contextual approaches such as Vygotsky's.

Studying Child Development
and Its Contexts

Candlelight vigil for slain Virginia Tech students and professors.
(Win McNamee/Getty Images/NewsCom)

STUDYING CHILDREN
Learning Objective 2.1
EXPLAIN THE PROCESS BY WHICH RESEARCHERS GENERATE HYPOTHESES AND ENSURE OBJECTIVITY.
From Observation and Theory to Hypothesis
Ensuring Objectivity

METHODS USED TO STUDY CHILDREN
Learning Objective 2.2
COMPARE AND CONTRAST THE RESEARCH METHODS COMMONLY USED TO STUDY CHILDREN.
Descriptive Methods
- Observation • Interview Methods • Case Studies

CONVERSATIONS with a Cross-Cultural Psychologist
Correlational Research
Experimental Research

APPLICATIONS Wise Consumers of Research on Development

STUDYING DEVELOPMENT
Learning Objective 2.3
ANALYZE THE STRENGTHS AND LIMITATIONS OF THE FOUR BASIC METHODS FOR STUDYING CHILD DEVELOPMENT AS A PROCESS.
Longitudinal Research
Cross-Sectional Research
Cross-Sequential Design
Microgenetic Method

ISSUES IN THE STUDY OF CHILDREN
Learning Objective 2.4
UNDERSTAND SPECIAL ISSUES INVOLVED IN STUDYING CHILDREN.
Ethical Considerations in Child Development Research
Cultural Considerations in Child Development Research

RESEARCH & SOCIETY Studying AIDS Orphans in Africa

On April 16, 2007, gunman Seung-Hui Cho murdered 32 of his fellow students and professors when he opened fire in a dormitory and a classroom building at Virginia Tech in Blacksburg, Virginia. In the aftermath that followed this deadliest of mass shootings in U.S. history, people asked themselves over and over again, "Why?" What would cause a young college student to commit such a deadly and violent act? Child development research attempts to answer questions such as these ■

Studying Children

Learning Objective 2.1
Explain the process by which researchers generate hypotheses and ensure objectivity.

Links to Related Material
In Chapter 1 you saw that explanations of children's behavior are common in everyday life and that these explanations often reflect theoretical approaches to understanding child behavior. Research methods are strategies that researchers use to try to understand which possible explanation for a given behavior is the best or right one.

Theory
A broad set of statements describing the relation between a phenomenon and the factors assumed to affect it.

Hypothesis
A predicted relation between a phenomenon and a factor assumed to affect it that is not yet supported by a great deal of evidence. Hypotheses are tested in experimental investigations.

Questions for Thought and Discussion
How might you design a study to test this hypothesis?

Objectivity
A characteristic of scientific research; it requires that the procedures and subject matter of investigations should be formulated so that everyone, in principle, could agree on them.

In Chapter 1 you saw that explanations of children's behavior are common in everyday life and that these explanations often reflect theoretical approaches to understanding child behavior. For example, many explanations were offered for Seung-Hui Cho's violent rampage at Virginia Tech, including mental illness, social isolation, easy access to guns, personal obsession with violent material, and a troubled family life. But how do you know if a given explanation for children's behavior is actually true? When trying to understand the reasons for a child's aggressive behavior, how do we know which explanation is the "right" one? Moreover, thinking beyond individual instances such as the massacre at Virginia Tech, how do we explain aggression in children in general? What causes children to be aggressive? Is it biology? Parents? Too much violence on television?

Researchers make use of research methods to try to understand which possible explanation for a given behavior is the best or right one. This chapter examines some of those strategies and how they might be used to help us better understand children's development.

From Observation and Theory to Hypothesis

When studying children's development, researchers do not randomly study any question that pops into their heads. Most research is guided by an underlying theory of child development. Thus, cognitive-developmentalists tend to investigate characteristics of children's knowledge, whereas environmental-learning theorists are more likely to study ways in which behavior is acquired through experience. Similarly, sociocultural theorists focus on the social and cultural bases for development, whereas ethologists are more likely to search for biological explanations for behavior.

In the study of child development, a **theory** is an integrated set of statements that explain and predict behavior. Researchers draw explanatory statements directly from a theory (for example, "Johnny is aggressive because he has modeled aggression from his environment, particularly the violence that he views on TV"). On the basis of this statement, researchers then generate a **hypothesis** or prediction (for example, "Watching violent television programming will increase children's tendency to behave aggressively"). The hypothesis is thus a statement that proposes a relationship between factors, or variables. The variables would be (1) television viewing of violent programming, and (2) childhood aggression. The proposed relationship would be that increased viewing of violent television programming increases aggressive behavior in children who view it. An investigator would then design a study to test this hypothesis.

Ensuring Objectivity

In conducting research on child development, one major concern is ensuring **objectivity.** That is, any researcher conducting the same study in the same manner should arrive at the same results. Attention to objectivity helps reduce potential sources of bias that may enter into the research, such as the researcher's personal beliefs or preferences regarding what the results should be.

Objectivity is achieved in a number of ways. One way is to focus on characteristics and behaviors that are directly *observable*. It is difficult, if not impossible, to study something if we cannot observe it. Physical characteristics such as height and weight can be observed and measured as children grow, but other kinds of characteristics are more difficult to observe directly. In this case researchers must find ways to observe the actions or effects of those behaviors. We usually cannot know, for example, what a person is thinking, though we can examine his or her behavior as an expression of those thoughts. Also, we usually cannot directly observe abstract entities, such as children's friendships, but we may observe how a child interacts with peers or we may ask children questions about their views on friendship.

A second requirement for ensuring objectivity is that we must be able to measure what we observe. Behavior must be measurable to give us confidence in our observations. When did it occur? How do we know it occurred? Researchers achieve confidence by precisely defining and describing what they are studying, so that independent observers would have no trouble agreeing on what happened in a given situation. For example, to study aggressive behavior in children, a researcher must first define clearly what actions on the child's part constitute aggression—for example, hitting or name-calling. Similarly, suppose you are interested in studying children's altruism—their willingness to help someone else without expectation of reward. You might first define altruism in terms of helping behaviors and then develop a procedure for observing and measuring those behaviors. In this way, abstract concepts such as "aggression" and "altruism" become measurable in an objective, scientific way.

A third way to achieve objectivity—a further aspect of measurement—is to make everything in the study *quantifiable*, that is, able to be counted. In quantitative research, the researcher counts not only children's behaviors but also the factors that the researcher hypothesizes may be affecting the behaviors. Physical factors, such as the number of hours spent watching TV each day, as well as the types of programs watched, are relatively easy to quantify. Factors that involve the behaviors of others—social approval, peer interactions, or modeling, for instance—are more difficult to deal with, but they, too, must be carefully defined and quantified so that they can be measured and counted.

How Do Researchers Increase Objectivity and Reduce Sources of Bias?
- Focus on characteristics and behaviors that are directly *observable*.
- Be able to define and measure what is observed.
- Make everything in the study quantifiable, or able to be counted.

One special type of quantitative research is called meta-analysis. In **meta-analysis**, researchers compare different studies on a particular topic using a set of *quantitative* rules for analyzing and interpreting the body of data (Hunt, 1997; Rosenthal & DiMatteo, 2001). For example, you could determine whether there is a statistically significant difference in aggression between boys and girls by performing a meta-analysis of all relevant studies. After defining observable and measurable variables, the researcher must decide how to collect the relevant data. Suppose, for example, that you decide to measure attachment through behaviors that infants exhibit when interacting with their parents. How can you determine which behaviors a particular baby shows? One way would be to observe the baby and his or her mother in their home environment. Another way might be to bring them into a laboratory setting to observe their behavior. You might also gather the information from someone who is knowledgeable about the baby's typical behavior. Thus, there is no one single way to study children. There are many ways, each of which has advantages and shortcomings.

Scientific method
The system of rules used by scientists to conduct and evaluate their research.

Meta-analysis
A method of reviewing the research literature on a given topic that uses statistical procedures to establish the existence and size of effects.

Questions for Thought and Discussion
*Can we use the **scientific method** to study everything about child development? Are there aspects of children's lives that we might not be able to study using methods that are objective and quantifiable?*

For a scientific study on children's toy preferences in relation to age and gender, how might you define "toy preference"? What specific characteristics and behaviors might you choose to observe? How might you count, or measure, those characteristics and behaviors? (Digital Vision Ltd./SUPERSTOCK)

✔ *Test Your Mastery...*

Learning Objective 2.1: *Explain the process by which researchers generate hypotheses and ensure objectivity.*

1. What is the relationship between theories and observations?
2. What is the relationship between theories and hypotheses?
3. How do researchers seek to ensure objectivity in their studies of children?
4. What is the research value of quantitative data?

Methods Used to Study Children

Research generally falls into one of three broad categories: descriptive, correlational, or experimental. Here we briefly discuss each of these approaches as they apply to the study of children, and then in a table we compare the various descriptive, correlational, and experimental methods used in the study of children.

Descriptive Methods

The oldest form of research is the descriptive approach. When applied to children, **descriptive research** involves observing or interviewing children or their parents or other significant people in their lives and recording information of interest. The researcher typically makes no attempt to manipulate variables and observe consequences, but rather describes things as objectively as possible the way they are. Child development researchers have used descriptive research to document the amount of time children of different ages devote to TV viewing and other leisure activities, the content of children's disputes with friends and family, and how adolescents distribute their time among friends, family, and peers. Descriptive methods take various forms, such as observation, interviews, and - in-depth case studies.

Observation One descriptive method employed in the study of children is **naturalistic observation,** which entails carefully observing children's behavior in natural settings. Researchers watch children interacting, playing, solving problems, and so on. Many people

Learning Objective 2.2
Compare and contrast the research methods commonly used to study children.

Descriptive research
Research based solely on observations, with no attempt to determine systematic relations among the variables.

Naturalistic observation
Systematic observation of behavior in natural settings.

In this study, researchers are examining the quality of infants' attachment to their mothers through a standardized laboratory situation called the Strange Situation. What steps should they take to design their study? What steps should they take to increase objectivity? (Courtesy of Jennie Noll)

enjoy watching children at play or at work and may have spent periods of time simply observing them. What differentiates scientific observation as a method for studying children is that, unlike casual observations, it stresses objectivity and purposefully addresses specific questions about children.

Because naturalistic observations may be influenced by the observer's expectations, beliefs, and values, researchers take steps to minimize these potential sources of bias. First, they identify clearly what behaviors are to be recorded, and they define clearly what constitutes an instance of the behavior. Then, observers are given training using this *observational protocol*. Having two observers watch the same episode of behavior and independently record their observations assesses the accuracy of observations. If there is good agreement between observers in their independent observations, then you can be confident in the *reliability* of the observations. Today observational studies are usually videotaped, and observers are trained to record observable discrete behaviors rather than interpretations of behavior. Videotapes can be viewed repeatedly to test the reliability of observers' data. *Microanalysis* of videotaped interactions between parents and infants have yielded valuable conclusions.

Simply knowing that you are being observed can affect your behavior. It is important to minimize such ***observer effects***—the effects of knowing that you are being observed— so that you can have confidence that your observations are valid. One way to minimize observer effects is to make the observer's presence as inconspicuous as possible. The observer or video camera may be placed discreetly in a corner of the playground or classroom, or may perhaps be placed behind a window overlooking the playground. Another way is to habituate participants to the presence of an observer prior to the actual study. For example, the video camera can be placed in the corner of the playground for a few days prior to the beginning of the actual study. Although children's behavior may initially be influenced by the camera's presence, children quickly forget that the camera is there and their behavior returns to normal.

Sometimes researchers using an observational approach find that the behaviors they want to study do not occur frequently or consistently in the naturalistic setting and may therefore be difficult to study. Moreover, because the investigator has no control over what takes place in the naturalistic setting, the situation may not be identical for each child, making it difficult to compare one child's behavior to that of another. For these reasons,

Questions for Thought
    and Discussion
What are some examples of research questions that you think could be studied using naturalistic observation? How would you go about studying them?

Structured observation
Observation of behavior in settings that are controlled by the investigator.

Interview method
Collecting information through verbal reports gathered via interviews or questionnaires.

researchers may choose to observe children in settings that the researchers control. Such **structured observations** may take place in a laboratory setting, where researchers can control the physical aspects of the environment in which the child is being observed, such as the presence of certain toys or certain individuals. In such a setting researchers can also control the events that occur. Standardization of the setting allows the study of children's reactions to experiences that might occur only rarely in the natural environment. In addition, researchers can compare children in terms of how each responds to the same event. However, because the structured setting of the lab differs from real-life settings, observations made in the lab may not be completely generalizable to other settings.

Interview Methods Another descriptive method used in the study of children is the **interview method**, whereby researchers talk with children about aspects of their lives. Interviews can be *open-ended*, with children responding freely and in a conversational way on a given topic, or they can be *structured*, with the interviewer asking a specific set of questions. Open-ended interviews can gather a wealth of information about children's knowledge, opinions, feelings, beliefs, and values, and that information can be used to generate hypotheses for further study. Open-ended interviews can be studied *qualitatively* for themes that emerge, thus increasing our understanding of particular meanings that children themselves may give to events or activities. Alternatively, many researchers create a standardized *interview protocol*, or *questionnaire* in which every child is asked the exact same questions in the same order. This facilitates quantification of the information gathered.

The interview method is not restricted to children. Researchers often ask questions of other knowledgeable informants. Parents or teachers, for example, often are good sources of information about children, and are frequently asked about children's behavior and performance. In studies of children's social relationships, classmates or other peers may be knowledgeable informants who can offer insights on behavior.

Interviews and questionnaires can be valuable sources of information about how the person interviewed feels and thinks. However, interviews rely on the informant's knowledge, memory, and ability or willingness to communicate information. As such, they may

What do you observe happening in this picture? In a study of peer relations, one observer wrote, "playfully and affectionately pats another child on his back." Another observer wrote, "aggressively swats the other child on his back." How do you know which observation is correct? What could the researchers do to make their observations more useful for a scientific study of child development? (Photoalto/Inmagine Corporation LLC)

not always accurately reflect actual behavior. For example, asking a child why it is important not to hit other children can yield interesting information on children's perceptions of morality. However, asking the child how many times in the past week he or she has actually hit another child may not yield an accurate answer.

Case Studies Sometimes descriptive research involves only a single individual who becomes the subject of a **case study**. Often these studies are concerned with clinical issues, such as when a child displays a rare disorder or when a new treatment approach is applied to a developmental problem. Occasionally, a child has encountered experiences so unusual as to attract the interest of psychologists for theoretical reasons.

A dramatic example of such a situation is the case of "Genie," a child who was kept isolated by her parents and was never spoken to until she was 13 years old (Curtiss, 1977; Rymer, 1994). Genie presented language researchers with a unique opportunity to investigate whether being deprived of exposure to language at a young age can affect a child's ability to acquire verbal skills at an advanced age. Such a question, of course, could never have been studied in any conventional experimental way.

The major limitation of using only a single research participant is that the researcher must be very cautious about drawing conclusions from the case. Genie, for example, was not only deprived of language but also experienced an extremely harsh and unusual childhood because of her parents. Whether the data regarding her language abilities can be generalized to other children thus remains unclear. Despite limitations, case studies are an important resource with regard to clinical intervention. They can also be valuable in the research process by raising new questions or issues that can be studied using more carefully controlled research methods. Case studies, like data collected using other methods, also guide applications of research to issues in child development.

Correlational Research

Other research methods focus on identifying systematic relationships, or **correlations**, in the data derived from observations, interviews, cases, or experiments. Specifically, researchers attempt to identify correlations among variables. A **variable** is any quantifiable factor that may influence the characteristic or behavior under study. Examples of variables are physical characteristics such as height, weight, and age; or aspects of the environment, such as temperature, room size, distance to the nearest library, and number of people in a family. Behaviors, if carefully defined and measured, are also variables—for example, how many times a child asks the teacher for help (*frequency*), how loudly a baby cries (*intensity*), or how long a child practices the piano (*duration*).

Questions for Thought and Discussion
Why might interviews and observations concerning children's behavior yield contradictory data? What questions might be interesting to ask children and other knowledgeable informants in their lives?

Case study
A research method that involves only a single individual, often with a focus on a clinical issue.

Correlation
The relation between two variables, described in terms of direction and strength.

Variable
Any factor that can take on different values along a dimension.

Naturalistic observation allows researchers to study the behavior of children in real-life settings. What could be some drawbacks of observing in this naturalistic setting? What information might interviews provide that observation alone could not? Whom might you interview for a study of the formation of playmate groupings in this playground setting? What potential drawbacks of the interview approach would you need to consider? (Sally and Richard Greenhill/Alamy Images)

Positive correlation
A correlation in which two variables change in the same direction.

Negative correlation
A correlation in which two variables change in opposite directions.

Scatter plot
A graphic illustration of a correlation between two variables.

A correlation is a statement that describes how two variables are related. Perhaps you would like to know whether children's ages are correlated with—systematically related to—their heights. You might observe and record the heights of 100 randomly selected children, ages 2 to 12, and examine whether changes in the one variable correspond to changes in the other. In this case, you would find a clear relationship between the variables of age and height—that is, as children increase in age, they normally increase in height as well. This type of relationship, in which two variables change together in the same direction, is a **positive correlation.**

What about the relationship between a child's age and the number of hours each day that the child spends at home? In this case you also would discover a systematic relationship, but the variables would change in opposite directions—that is, as a child's age increases, the amount of time the child spends at home usually decreases. This relationship is called a **negative correlation** because the variables are changing in opposite directions; as one increases, the other decreases.

In many cases, researchers find no correlation between variables, such as the relationship between a child's height and the number of others in the child's classroom. Correlations can be described in terms not only of their direction (positive or negative) but also their strength. A strong correlation means that two variables are closely related. In such cases, knowing the value of one gives us a good indication of the value of the second. As a correlation grows weaker, the amount of predictability between the two variables decreases. When the variables become completely unrelated, knowledge of the value of one gives us no clue as to the value of the other.

Correlations can be presented visually with a **scatter plot**, such as the one shown in Figure 2.1, where one variable is plotted on the vertical axis and the other on the horizontal axis. Each dot in this hypothetical study represents one child and shows the child's values for the two variables: (1) reading readiness as measured on a test of reading level and (2) number of hours spent watching TV each day.

For such a study you would need to select randomly a number of children and measure each child's reading ability and the number of hours each week that the child watches television. Then you would calculate the correlation between the two sets of scores. According to the scatter plot in Figure 2.1, would you find a negative or positive correlation? Would you describe the correlation as strong or weak?

What would you conclude from these data? You perhaps concluded from Figure 2.1 that TV watching interferes with the development of the skills children need to learn to read. People often assume that a change in one variable causes change in the other. But—and herein lies a major limitation of correlational research—*a correlation is not the same thing as a cause. Correlations cannot be used to show causality between variables.* The correlation in the example may accurately reveal the pattern and strength of the

The New Haven, Connecticut, Child Development-Community Policing (CD-CP) program applies knowledge from case studies in its efforts to help children exposed to domestic violence. The case studies are gathered at the Yale University Child Study Center in collaboration with the National Center for Children Exposed to Violence. The CD-CP program uses case studies to understand the child's perspective and plan appropriate shared interventions to break the cycle of family violence. (Omni Photo Communications/© Index Stock Imagery)

reading–viewing relationship, but it cannot reveal cause and effect between the variables. Why not?

If you think carefully about the findings, you will realize that some other conclusions cannot be ruled out. For example, rather than TV viewing having an effect on reading readiness, the reverse is equally plausible. That is, children whose prereading skills are less advanced may be less interested in reading as an activity and so may spend more time watching TV than children with better prereading skills. Another possibility is that the two variables are both influenced by some third variable that you have not measured. For instance, the educational background of the child's parents may affect both variables. There is a good chance that the better educated a child's parents are, the more likely they are to engage in activities that promote prereading skills, such as reading books with their children, and the less likely they are to rely on the television to entertain their child. Thus, although correlational research is a valuable tool for identifying and measuring systematic relationships among variables, it cannot be used to explain them. Explanation requires further research.

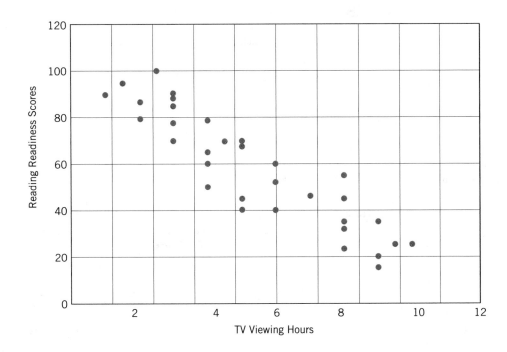

FIGURE 2.1 Example of a Scatter Plot

What is the relationship between reading readiness and TV viewing?

BOX 2.1 Conversations with a Cross-Cultural Psychologist

Catherine Tamis-LeMonda, 46, is a professor of developmental psychology at New York University, in the Department of Applied Psychology. A native New Yorker, she grew up in Queens, and currently lives on Long Island with her husband and three children.

When I began college, I wanted to become a teacher in theater arts, so I started out as an educational theater major. I took a psychology course to fulfill one of my social science requirements. One psychology course led to another until, as a junior in college, I took a course in developmental psychology with Professor Marc Bornstein, and became completely captivated with the material. I was especially intrigued with questions pertaining to stability and change in behavior and thinking over developmental time, particularly during early childhood. I ended up majoring in psychology and finally decided to pursue a Ph.D. in developmental psychology: Thus, although my pathway to developmental psychology was not direct, I knew it was the right one for me.

My situation is unique in that I have stayed at the same institution, New York University, for many years—from my undergraduate days until today. As a professor, the vast majority of my time is dedicated to engaging in research and mentoring both graduate and undergraduate students in research. For example, I work with students on creating and generating ideas, and help them to come up with their own research questions and studies. Much of my day is spent with students, but not in a traditional classroom. Of course, I do classroom teaching as well, teaching courses in infancy, cognitive development, and developmental psychology, but I would say that most of the teaching I engage in occurs outside the classroom, where I seek to equip students with the tools and skills that are necessary to successful collaborative and independent research.

I am primarily interested in field-based research—that is, how behavior unfolds and what babies experience in naturalistic settings. Thus, I conduct my research in the homes of participating families, schools, and other everyday settings. Currently, I am the director of the NYU Center for Research on Culture, Development, and Education. The Center's research focuses on understanding pathways of development in different ethnic groups including African Americans, Mexican Americans, Dominicans, Puerto Ricans, and European Americans. Our goal is to better understand the diverse experiences of young babies and youth from ethnically and racially diverse families. Much of what we know has been based on European American populations. However, at this point in the history of developmental psychology, researchers are seeking to expand knowledge on human development to encompass different groups within and outside the United States, not just European Americans. So that is the primary mission of our Center.

The major studies that we are currently pursuing at the Center are based on two major age emphases. There is an early childhood cohort, which involves recruiting several hundred

Catherine Tamis-LeMonda (Courtesy Catherine Tamis-LeMonda)

Questions for Thought and Discussion
What are some aspects of children's behavior that might correlate with their viewing of violence on TV? Can you think of some possible explanations for these correlations?

Experimental Research

An important research method that allows us to understand causal relations between variables is the experiment. A simple experiment often involves investigating the relation between just two variables, but, unlike correlational research, experimental studies can lead to scientific conclusions about cause and effect.

Much of the experimentation conducted by child development researchers takes place in laboratories or child study centers, where researchers can control testing conditions. Experimental studies can also be conducted in field settings—playgrounds, classrooms, or children's homes, for example—to study the child's behavior under more natural conditions.

In an experiment, you systematically change one variable to observe its effect on a second variable. In developmental research, the dependent variable is typically some aspect of behavior, whereas the independent variable is a factor the researcher suspects may families from diverse backgrounds at the time of their infants' births and following them through entry into school and beyond. We want to understand their experiences at home, school, and child care, and how those experiences shape development. In addition, we hope to better understand not only what parents *do* but why they engage in the activities that they do. Therefore, through in-depth interviews with parents we probe their motives, goals, value systems, and beliefs in efforts to examine how these views shape parenting.

Faculty members of the Center at NYU are also studying an early adolescent cohort, where young adolescents are followed as they transition to middle school, and then later into high school. In this study, parents are being interviewed about their monitoring of their adolescents' behavior, routines of family life, and their views about adolescent development and their role as parents.

In all of these studies we are employing longitudinal designs, in which we follow children over time to examine continuity in development and to examine the predictive power of early experiences on later outcomes. In addition, our two different age groups require us to adopt different types of methods that are suitable to the age being studied. For the early ages, we rely on direct observations that involve videotaping of infants as well as direct assessments of infants. With the adolescent group, we rely much more heavily on direct interviews, something that we are unable to do with the infants! Studying two different age groups also gives us the opportunity to ask similar questions at two different developmental stages. Our hope is that the project will shed light on families, parenting, and child development in different ethnic groups at different ages.

One thing I find extremely satisfying about my profession is the creativity that is involved in generating exciting, new ideas. Being an academic is a generative profession. We are responsible for creating new knowledge, designing new studies, and figuring out the best ways to ask new questions, and we are ultimately the originators of new knowledge. For example, I might wonder to myself, "Do mothers talk to boys and girls differently? Do they have different expectations of their boys versus girls?" Well, I can go and find out the answer to these questions through my research! Mentoring students is also satisfying. A common concern of Ph.D. students is whether and how they will ever find a dissertation topic, but by the time we get to that point in their schooling, there is never trouble finding a question. Rather, the hardest part is trying to figure out which of the so many exciting questions to devote energy to!

For me, one of the most memorable experiences was attending my first national conference, and having a chance to actually meet in person the researchers who had written the studies I had found so interesting to read. I was so appreciative of the opportunities to engage in conversations with these experts and was so impressed that they would actually want to talk to me for hours about ideas. I have been impressed with how much senior researchers really enjoy talking to a variety of students, postdoctoral fellows, and junior faculty. I particularly appreciate the generosity of senior scholars who can recognize newer, younger talent and are eager to accommodate new ways of thinking in flexible ways. I aspire to ultimately be the kind of faculty member who will pass the torch to the younger generation so that they might shed new light on developmental processes.

I've known so many students who, when they begin a psychology major, have a narrow idea of the field. They may think only of clinical work or of wanting to become a therapist, and may actually be intimidated by the word "research." Students often conclude that research is not for them, for the idea of engaging in research can be daunting at first. However, our entire lives and worlds are shaped and informed by knowledge. Anyone who can ask a question like, "I wonder why that child just hit/bullied/helped that other child?" has within themselves the ability to do research. I truly believe that the capacity for engaging in research is in everyone. College students should knock on the door of faculty members in their department—after all, so much exciting research goes on in universities—and get involved. I would love to see more students get excited about research earlier in their undergraduate careers, and not be intimidated by the idea of working directly with a faculty member on a project. The sooner you can learn about the tools of research, the better. It opens so many doors for you! It's addicting!

influence or cause that behavior. For example, if we want to understand the effects of TV viewing on prereading skills among preschoolers, then an experiment constructed to test this relationship would systematically manipulate TV viewing, called the **independent variable**. In this instance, the variable affected (at least potentially) by this manipulation would be prereading skills, also called the **dependent variable**.

As in correlational research, you would select a number of children. Unlike correlational research, however, it is important to randomly divide the children into several groups. Randomly dividing the participants into groups minimizes the possibility that there might be other differences between the groups that could affect the result of the experiment. Let's say the children are randomly divided into four groups. The first group is instructed to watch 30 minutes of TV each day; the second group, 1 hour; the third group, 2 hours; and the fourth group, 3 hours a day, or 21 hours a week. After several weeks or months, you would then administer the reading test to all the children and compare the

Independent variable
The variable in an experiment that is systematically manipulated.

Dependent variable
The variable that is predicted to be affected by an experimental manipulation. In psychology, usually some aspect of behavior.

In photographs taken during U.S. deployment of troops in Vietnam (roughly 1959 to 1975), you would find a positive correlation between the number of years that the war went on and the average length of young men's hair in the United States. That is, as the number of years of fighting increased, so did the average length of young men's hair. However, knowing this tells you nothing about why it exists, or if one variable caused the other. Surely the Vietnam War alone did not cause young men to grow their hair longer, nor did the length of male hair cause the war. Instead, it is likely that a third factor was involved. Another possibility, for example, is that young men who were against the war were more likely to grow their hair long in protest against authority. Attitudes toward the war and toward U.S. government authorities clearly mediated the relationship between the two variables, length of Vietnam War and average length of young men's hair. (© Underwood Archives)

results. See possible results in the bar graph in Figure 2.2. If the differences in performance between, say, the first group and the last group are significantly large, then not only can you conclude that the two variables are systematically related but you also can say that spending time watching TV interferes with the development of prereading skills. In this case, your hypothesis would be supported by experimental data.

Not all variables can be experimentally manipulated. For example, researchers interested in how children react to divorce cannot realistically conduct experimental research. Imagine the ethical implications if a researcher were to assign families randomly to two groups and subsequently require the parents in one group to divorce while keeping those in the other group together. How many parents would go along with such a manipulation, even in the interests of science? Moreover, some independent variables cannot be manipulated, such as gender, age, and linguistic background. Researchers must study participants as they find them.

FIGURE 2.2 TV Viewing and Prereading Skills

Does watching TV affect the acquisition of prereading skills? Each bar shows the average reading test score for all the children in each of four experimental groups, differentiated in terms of the amount of time they spent watching TV each day. Why can you say from these findings that TV viewing negatively affects prereading skills?

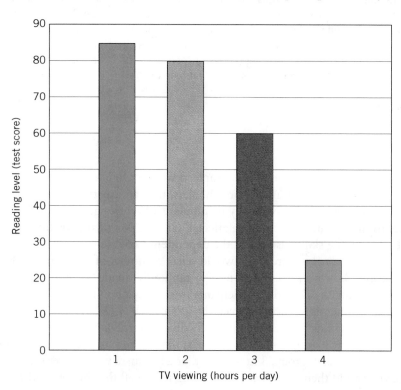

In these **quasi-experimental** studies, the groups to be compared are determined on the basis of an existing characteristic of the participants. A study looking at divorce compares groups of parents who are divorced and those who are nondivorced. A study looking at gender differences compares boys and girls. Researchers can talk about differences between groups, but they cannot make statements about cause and effect as in experimental studies.

Table 2.1 summarizes the descriptive, correlational, and experimental methods used in the study of children.

Quasi-experiment
Comparison of groups differing on some important characteristic.

TABLE 2.1 Types of Research Used in the Study of Children				
TYPE OF RESEARCH	**METHOD**	**DESCRIPTION**	**ADVANTAGES**	**LIMITATIONS**
Descriptive	Naturalistic Observation	Children's behavior is observed in real-life settings.	Direct source of information for how children behave in the natural setting.	Presence of observers may alter the setting and thus the behavior.
				Some behaviors may be difficult to observe in the natural setting.
				Setting may not be the same for all children, making it difficult to compare between participants.
	Structured Observation	Children's behavior is observed in a structured laboratory environment.	Controlled laboratory environment ensures that the behaviors of interest will occur. Allows for comparisons across participants.	Setting is not real life, which can reduce the generalizability of the findings.
	Interview	Children or other knowledgeable informants are asked to provide verbal reports via interview or questionnaire.	Can provide valuable information about what informants think or feel.	Not all behaviors are accessible to verbal report. Concerns about what the interviewer wants to hear or about portraying oneself positively may influence the accuracy of reports.
	Case Study	Detailed descriptive study of a single individual.	Allows the study of specific or unusual situations, thus aiding clinical intervention. Can raise questions for further study using other research methods.	Because only one child is studied, findings may not be generalizable to other children.
Correlational	Correlational Study	Examines how two or more variables are related.	Allows researchers to quantify relationships between variables and make predictions about one variable based on the other.	Cannot be used to show causality.
Experimental	Experiment	Researcher manipulates independent variable and looks for corresponding changes in dependent variable.	Shows the effects of one variable on another.	It is not always possible or ethical to manipulate certain types of variables.
	Quasi-experimental	Groups that differ on some important characteristic are compared.	Allows researchers to examine variables that cannot be experimentally manipulated.	Cannot be used to show causality.

✔ *Test Your*
M a s t e r y . . .

Learning Objective 2.2: *Compare and contrast the research methods commonly used to study children.*

1. What are observational research, the interview method, and the case study method? What are the advantages and disadvantages of each of these methods?
2. What is correlational research? What does it tell us about causal relations between variables?
3. What elements comprise an experiment? What are the advantages and disadvantages of the experimental method in research with children?

Learning Objective 2.3
Analyze the strengths and limitations of the four basic methods for studying child development as a process.

Studying Development

Development, as you have seen, involves changes in behavior over time. Many questions focus on how children's behavior at one age differs from their behavior at another age. How does a child's speech progress from the one-word utterances of the toddler to the complex and grammatical sentences of the school-age child? What are the possible effects of full-time day care on children's later social adjustment? For either type of question, you will need a research method that will allow the comparison of behaviors at different ages. Four methods are available for this purpose: the longitudinal design, the cross-sectional design, a method that combines the two called the cross-sequential design, and the microgenetic technique (see Table 2.2).

TABLE 2.2 Methods of Studying the Process of Development			
METHOD	**DESCRIPTION**	**USEFULNESS**	**DRAWBACKS**
Longitudinal	Studies the same group of children repeatedly at different ages.	Allows the researcher to study changes as children age. Can be used to examine the stability of behavior as well as effects of early experiences.	Attrition. Repeated testing can influence results. Issues and instruments may become outdated. Time-consuming and expensive.
Cross-sectional	Compares groups of children of different ages at one point in time.	Relatively quick and low cost. No problems of attrition or repeated testing.	Cannot be used to examine stability and change. Cohort effects can influence findings.
Cross-sequential	Combines cross-sectional and longitudinal research. Children of different age groups are followed longitudinally.	Allows both cross-sectional and longitudinal comparisons to be made. Allows researchers to examine for effects of cohort effects.	Time consuming and costly.
Microgenetic	Intensive study of a small number of children over a brief period of time.	Allows examination of developmental changes that are discontinuous.	Repeated testing can influence results.

An example of a longitudinal study is the U.S. government's Early Childhood Longitudinal Study, which is designed to provide decision makers, researchers, childcare providers, teachers, and parents with detailed information about children's early life experiences. The birth cohort of the Early Childhood Longitudinal Study (ECLS-B) looks at children's health, development, care, and education during the formative years from birth through first grade. The birth cohort consists of a nationally representative sample of more than 10,600 children born in in the United States in 2001. (© LOOK Die Bildagentur der Fotografen GmbH/Alamy Images)

Longitudinal Research

In the **longitudinal design**, the behaviors of interest are measured first at one point in development and then again at various intervals as the child grows. The main advantage of this method is that you can study directly how each behavior changes as the child gets older (Menard, 1991).

The number of years required for a longitudinal study varies. Some questions can be explored within a brief time frame, for example, determining whether different techniques of caring for premature infants have different effects on the age at which the babies begin to walk and talk. This question could be answered within two years of observation. Other questions, such as determining to what extent a child's early disciplinary experiences influence his or her own disciplinary strategies as a parent, may extend over decades.

Longitudinal studies can be descriptive, correlational, or experimental. Two types of research questions are particularly well suited to the longitudinal approach (Magnusson et al., 1994). The first concerns the *stability*, or persistence, of behaviors. For instance, if you wish to determine the extent to which a child's temperament (an aspect of personality) remains constant throughout life, the best approach is to observe and measure this characteristic in the same children periodically as they develop. The second type of question concerns the *effects of early experiences* on later behavior. If you wish to determine the long-term effects of certain events or conditions during a child's early years—divorce, an infant stimulation program, or the quality of diet, for instance—you will use an experimental longitudinal approach. For example, you might identify children who have participated in an early stimulation program and children who have not and then follow both groups for a number of years to see if differences emerge over time in their success in school.

The longitudinal approach does have certain disadvantages. One is the problem of *attrition*—the loss of individuals under study as families move away, children become ill or develop other problems that interfere with participation in the study, or parents may simply lose interest and withdraw from the project. Another problem is that scores or test results can become skewed because children learn to perform better on tests through repeated administration. Sometimes, over a long period of time, the research questions or the instruments used to measure them may become outdated. Finally, there is a practical disadvantage. Because it often requires a large research staff and many hours of observation or testing, longitudinal research can be very expensive.

Longitudinal design
A research method in which the same individuals are studied repeatedly over time.

Questions for Thought and Discussion
Why is longitudinal research used to study development?

BOX 2.2 Wise Consumers of Research on Development

Why is it important to study research methods in a course on child development? Understanding how research is conducted is valuable because it is from research that we gain information about children and their behavior. We act on that information, and social policy is based on it. You are exposed to the results of research every day in the news media, and as a parent, teacher, or another professional working with children, you are exposed to research-based advice or training. Knowledge about research methods can make you a wiser consumer of information. Being a wise consumer of research means using what you have learned to think critically about research and its applications. When evaluating research, consider the following six areas.

The Theory and Hypotheses

Is it clear in the study what researchers were looking at? Is the rationale of the study—why the researchers conducted the study—clear? What is the theoretical basis for the study? Are the researchers' hypotheses well defined, and is it apparent where they come from? Does the study "make sense" in view of what you know about child development? Although some findings can be surprising, does the researcher explain things in a way that makes good theoretical sense?

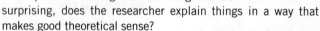

The Participants

Who participated in the study, and how were they recruited? Knowing the answers to these questions can help determine how much weight to place on the findings of the study. Was the population of children who participated sufficiently diverse for us to generalize our findings to all children? Alternatively, did the strategies for recruiting children limit the study's generalizability? For example, magazines sometimes report results of surveys they conduct of their readers. Although the results may seem very interesting, it is important to ask: Who responded to this survey? Is it a sample of the population in general, or is it a select group of readers that the magazine is marketed towards who felt the inclination to respond? In other words, do these findings reflect the views of people in general or simply those of motivated magazine readers?

The Method

Is it clear that objectivity was stressed in the study? Objectivity helps reduce bias that could have entered into the research. Is

the research descriptive, correlational, or experimental, and were the researchers alert to the limitations of the type of study they used? Being aware of the method used and its limitations is important in the interpretation of the results.

The Findings

Although a reader rarely has actual access to the individual scores of each participant, studies usually report summaries of their findings. When you look at the findings, do they seem to support the researchers' conclusions? Can you think of other possible explanations for these results? How might the findings affect what you believe or what you choose to do?

An especially important question is whether cause-and-effect conclusions are reported and whether they are warranted. For example, a few years ago findings were reported in the media linking overall performance of particular school districts to the number of computers each school possessed. In particular, it was found that school districts that possessed a larger number of computers also had students who were scoring higher on standardized tests. Many politicians misinterpreted this finding to mean that the presence of computers in the schools was causing the higher test scores. Can you think of another explanation for the relation between these two variables?

The Implications

An important question to ask is what the findings of this particular study tell us about the bigger picture of children and their development. What do the findings really mean, and where do the findings apply? How might the findings affect public policy or medical practice or parenting behavior?

The Ethics of the Research

Does the study appear to be ethical? This question is important because it reflects on the quality and integrity of the research. The rights of children and the obligations of researchers to protect those rights are fundamental components of good research. Did an institutional review board examine this research? Was informed consent obtained? Were steps taken to minimize risk of harm? If these criteria do not appear to have been satisfied, could the researchers have examined the same question using some alternative procedure?

Cross-Sectional Research

Cross-sectional design
A research method in which people of different ages are studied simultaneously to examine the effects of age on some aspect of behavior.

An alternative to longitudinal research is the **cross-sectional design**, which allows researchers to examine developmental differences in behavior by studying children of different ages at the same point in time. In this type of research, the age of the children becomes an independent variable. This approach is less time-consuming than the longitudinal method. Rather than waiting five years to determine, say, how memory processes in 3-year-olds differ from memory processes in 8-year-olds, we can study a group of 3-year-olds and a group of 8-year-olds at the same time.

People of a given generation may be affected by factors unique to their generation, such as growing up during the Great Depression. How can such cohort effects influence the findings of cross-sectional designs? (Topham/The Image Works)

The cross-sectional approach has two significant disadvantages. First, this method cannot be used to investigate questions about the stability of behavior over time or about the effects of early experience. The second disadvantage is a problem known as the **cohort effect**, a result of the fact that some aspects of behavior are influenced by the unique events and conditions you experience as a member of your generation (called a cohort). The cohort effect can be seen when comparing the cognitive skills of people of different ages. People in their 50s, 60s, and 70s, for example, have had different educational experiences, which affect their performance on tests of cognitive ability. For example, people currently in their 70s were in school during World War II, when progressive ideas and nationalistic ideals shaped the curriculum. People in their 60s started school after 1950, when sweeping postwar changes stimulated an emphasis on teaching science, mathematics, and technology. And people in their 50s started school in the early 1960s, when greater emphasis began to be placed on children's social and emotional development. The different experiences of these three cohorts may affect their cognitive performance independently of the differences in their ages alone.

Cohort effect
A problem sometimes found in cross-sectional research in which people of a given age are affected by factors unique to their generation.

Cross-Sequential Design

Researchers sometimes combine the longitudinal and cross-sectional methods into a **cross-sequential design**. This approach begins with a cross-sectional study involving groups of children of different ages simultaneously. The same groups are then studied again at later times to provide a longitudinal perspective on the question.

For instance, you might begin by measuring the amount of competitiveness displayed by 4-year-olds, 7-year-olds, and 10-year-olds playing a game. Three years later, you would retest the children, who are now 7, 10, and 13 (Figure 2.3). This cross-sequential proce-

Cross-sequential design
A research method combining longitudinal and cross-sectional designs.

	TIME 1	TIME 2,3 YEARS LATER
Group 1	4 years	7 years
Group 2	7 years	10 years
Group 3	10 years	13 years

FIGURE 2.3   A Cross-Sequential Design
Children ages 4, 7, and 10 years are compared cross-sectionally at Time 1 to reveal age differences. Three years later, at Time 2, another cross-sectional study is conducted comparing these children, who are now ages 7, 10, and 13. How might cohort effects play a role in any differences found? To examine the stability of competitiveness, each of the three groups is then examined longitudinally, comparing their scores at Time 2 to those at Time 1.

Questions for Thought and Discussion

What events have affected the life course of people your age? How might your life have been different if those events had not occurred?

Microgenetic method
A research method in which a small number of individuals are observed repeatedly in order to study an expected change in a developmental process.

Links to Related Material
In Chapter 1, you read that some aspects of human development are thought to be discontinuous—that is, they are stable for a period of time but then change abruptly to another level. You can use the microgenetic approach to examine the particular developmental process as it goes from one level to the next.

✓ *Test Your Mastery...*

Learning Objective 2.4
Understand special issues involved in studying children.

dure makes a number of comparisons possible. For example, cross-sectional comparisons at both the initial testing and the later testing can show if children at the different ages have different levels of competitiveness. In addition, longitudinal comparisons can show the stability of each child's competitiveness at two different ages. This combined design also provides a basis for having more or less confidence in the results, depending on how similar the data are both within and between the groups.

Microgenetic Method

A different approach to the study of developmental change involves the intensive study of a small number of children over a brief period of time. The purpose of this **microgenetic method** is to investigate changes in important developmental processes as they are occurring (Flynn, O'Malley, & Wood, 2004; Kuhn, 1995; Kwong & Varnhagen, 2005; Miller & Coyle, 1999; Pressley, 1992; Siegler, 1995).

As you read in Chapter 1, some aspects of human development are thought to be discontinuous—that is, they are stable for a period of time but then change abruptly to another level. You can use the microgenetic approach to examine the particular developmental process as it goes from one level to the next. Much of children's cognitive development appears to be discontinuous, for example. At some point, an infant either understands or does not understand that objects continue to exist when they are out of sight. At some point, a child is or is not able to see a situation from another's point of view. The concept of discontinuous change is an outgrowth of the work of Piaget and other cognitive-developmental psychologists.

A microgenetic study begins with several children around the age at which a developmental change is expected to occur. You repeatedly observe and measure the behavior of interest in these children. For example, if you were interested in children's use of cognitive strategies for solving problems, you would ask the children to problem-solve over a period of time. In this type of study, you would not only note the correctness of the children's solutions but also how they approach each problem, perhaps by asking them to describe what they are doing. In this way, you can identify when a child moves from a simpler cognitive strategy to a more sophisticated one. Teachers often perform microgenetic studies informally in their classrooms.

Learning Objective 2.3: *Analyze the strengths and limitations of the four basic methods for studying child development as a process.*

1. What are the strengths and limitations of longitudinal research?
2. What are the strengths and lmitations of a cross-sectional research design?
3. What are the strengths and limitations of a cross-sequential research design?
4. What are the strengths and limitations of microgenetic research?

Issues in the Study of Children

So far, you have read about the major methods used in studying children and their development. However, research often involves challenges that go beyond deciding which method to employ. There are ethical considerations, for example. Some research questions might entail discomfort or even risk to the participants. What options and responsibilities do researchers have toward participants? No one would question that research often produces findings that benefit children, adults, and society as a whole. Nevertheless, almost any research involving humans can pose a variety of risks. Investigators have an obligation to determine exactly what potentially negative effects may result from their studies and to consider whether these risks outweigh the potential value of the findings (Fisher & Tryon, 1990; Kodish, 2005; Thompson, 1990).

Ethical Considerations in Child Development Research

Concern over ethical issues has not always been as great as it is today. Early investigators had few restrictions on their research, as evidenced by such questionable experiments as Watson's conditioning of 11-month-old Little Albert, mentioned in Chapter 1. Today, attention is increasingly focused on safeguarding children's rights and well-being (Kodish, 2005; Sieber, 1992).

A concern in any research is the possibility of physical injury to the child, although this problem is relatively rare in developmental research. A more common, and often more subtle, issue involves potential psychological harm to the child. For example, a strictly experimental approach to the question of whether viewing violence on television leads to an increase in violent behavior would require that children be placed into control and experimental groups, with the experimental group of children exposed to large amounts of violence on TV for a given period of time. Such an experimental manipulation would answer our questions regarding causality, but it would raise serious concerns regarding ethics. If viewing violence on television is psychologically harmful to a child, then it would be unethical to deliberately expose children to it. Other, less obvious concerns arise. For example, an experiment may require observing how children respond when they cannot solve a problem, or are prohibited from playing with an attractive toy. These procedures may produce various negative emotions, such as feelings of failure, frustration, or stress. The concern is that the children may continue to experience these emotions for some time after leaving the experimental situation.

A less obvious category of problems involves violations of privacy. If a researcher secretly gains access to a child's school records, if observations are conducted without a child's knowledge, or if data regarding a child or a family become public knowledge, the legal and ethical rights of these individuals may be violated.

The concern for ethical research practices has led to the development of safeguards to avoid or eliminate potential risks. These safeguards have become a routine part of modern research procedures. In addition, professional scientific organizations have developed codes of ethical standards to guide their members. *Ethical Principles of Psychologists and Code of Conduct* (2002), published by the American Psychological Association, and *SRCD Ethical Standards for Research with Children* (Committee for Ethical Conduct in Child Development Research, 1990), published by the Society for Research in Child Development, are two important examples.

An important way of ensuring that research is conducted ethically is *peer review*. Before beginning a research study, investigators are in most situations required to submit the research plan to an *Institutional Review Board* in the setting where the research will be conducted. The Institutional Review Board weighs the possible value of the research findings against the potential risks. Sometimes members of the Review Board offer suggestions as to how negative effects may be prevented or minimized, and sometimes they may even reject the proposed research. Almost all research carried out in institutional settings such as colleges, universities, hospitals, and school boards in North America must first be carefully evaluated by the institution's review board. Virtually all government agencies that provide funding for research require ethical compliance, as do the scientific and professional journals that publish the research.

An important requirement of ethical compliance is that researchers obtain the *informed consent* of the participants in the study. When children are the participants, researchers must first obtain the written permission of the child's parents. In addition, each child must be made aware of the general procedures of the study. Most importantly, the child has the right to refuse to participate or to withdraw from the study at any time, even though the parents have given their permission. Ensuring that children understand their rights as research participants can be an especially challenging task (Abramovitch et al., 1991; Hurley & Underwood, 2002).

If the research procedures may produce negative feelings in the child, the investigator must provide some means of reducing those feelings before the child leaves. For example,

Links to Related Material
In Chapter 1, you read about early investigations, such as Watson's conditioning of Little Albert, that would not be permitted today. Researchers today focus on safeguarding children's rights and well-being in the procedures they use.

Questions for Thought and Discussion
Do you think 3-year-olds can give informed consent for research participation? How can the principle of informed consent be satisfied in research with young children?

if a child is participating in an experiment in which he or she experiences failure, the investigator might end the research session by having the child perform an easier task that will ensure success. Also, to whatever extent seems reasonable, the investigator should at some point explain to the child the purpose of the study and the child's role in it, a procedure called *debriefing*.

Maintaining *confidentiality* is also a crucial aspect of ethical research. Whenever possible, the identities of the participants and information about their individual performances should be concealed from anyone not directly connected with the research. Often, anonymity is achieved by assigning numbers to the participants and then using these numbers instead of names during the analysis of the data.

Finally, all researchers have some ethical responsibilities that go beyond the protection of the individuals participating in the research. For example, scientists who report data that may be controversial or that may affect social policy decisions have an obligation to describe the limitations and degree of confidence they have in their findings. In addition, investigators should give participants information about the final results of the research, as an acknowledgment of the importance of their contribution to answering the research question.

Cultural Considerations in Child Development Research

Research on child development also involves questions of cross-cultural validity. Some research questions may have very different answers if studied in another culture or in culturally different groups within a society. As you read in Chapter 1, an emphasis on the social and cultural contexts for development is a defining feature of the sociocultural approach to children's development. How can we determine the role culture plays in particular aspects of behavior or development?

The most common approach is to study the same behavior in different cultures. In **cross-cultural studies**, researchers may use culture as an independent variable in a quasi-experimental design and examine how it is related to the dependent variable(s) of interest. Cross-cultural psychologists use a variety of methods, including interviews, observations of everyday activities, and archived reports of early travelers and anthropologists, as well as laboratory tasks and psychological tests.

One important use of cross-cultural studies is to test the universality of a phenomenon. Motor development serves as a good example. Although there are significant individual differences in the ages at which infants acquire motor skills, such as crawling and walking, differences between cultures are far smaller than one might expect given the large variations in the amount of time and encouragement children are given to practice those skills from culture to culture.

Cross-cultural studies are also useful for documenting variations in child development across cultures. As we will see throughout this text, cross-cultural studies have revealed impressive variability across a wide range of behaviors and abilities, including parenting, moral reasoning, mathematical reasoning, and memory (Berry, 1997; Monzó & Rueda, 2006).

Cross-cultural psychologists face a number of methodological challenges. One is the difficulty of devising experiments that measure the "same" behavior in different cultural contexts. Experimental tasks and situations that are common or sensible in one culture often seem strange to children living elsewhere. When experimental procedures differ markedly from a child's everyday experience, it is hard to know whether psychologists are tapping into the same behavior observed under conditions that more closely resemble the child's daily life.

A second approach to the study of culture and development has emerged, partly in response to the methodological problems of cross-cultural research. This approach, known as

Cross-cultural studies
Research designed to determine the influence of culture on some aspect of development and in which culture typically serves as an independent variable.

Links to Related Material
As you read in Chapter 1, an emphasis on the social and cultural contexts for development is a defining feature of the sociocultural approach to children's development. How can researchers determine the role that culture plays in particular aspects of behavior or development?

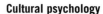

cultural psychology, favors studying a single culture or a small number of cultures in depth. The aim of this approach is to understand as fully as possible the different aspects of culture and how they are interrelated (Cole, 1996; Jessor, Colby, & Shweder, 1996; Shweder, 2003). The starting point, therefore, is not some set of measures developed by Western researchers (as is true in most cross-cultural research) but rather lengthy immersion in the culture or cultures of interest. The researcher might live for months or even years as a member of a culture, during which time he or she will use various **ethnographic methods** (observations, informal conversations, structured interviews) to gather as much information as possible about cultural practices and values. Cultural psychologists may use standardized psychological instruments, but they derive these procedures from practices in the cultures under study instead of importing established instruments from outside.

Cultural psychologists and cross-cultural psychologies study many of the same issues, including childrearing, reasoning, and basic cognitive processes. However, both their methods and their goals differ. Specifically, cross-cultural psychologists attempt to test all groups under similar conditions, ideally using identical tasks and procedures. Cross-cultural psychologists have the goal of integrating the results of studies from a variety of cultures to create a more universal theory of human development. Cultural psychologists, in contrast, may vary their methods from culture to culture, adapting their methods to existing cultural practices. Cultural psychologists believe this approach is best suited to understanding development within cultural context.

Cultural psychology reflects the fact that past research on child development has been criticized for cultural bias—the assumption that the ideas that define one's own group apply to the whole world. European American middle-class researchers have tended to study European American middle-class children or to impose their cultural and class values on groups that were not European American or middle class. Sometimes researchers have erred in attempting to generalize their findings to children in "other" societies or even to all children. Today, understanding cultural differences has become an important focus of study, in addition to validating universals in child development cross-culturally. Qualitative research contributes to understanding different cultural groups from their own positions and perspectives—from within rather than from the outside. Such understanding may make developmental research more valid and useful.

Cultural psychology
Study of a single culture from the perspective of members of that culture, the goal being to identify the values and practices important to the culture.

Ethnographic methods
Methods of study employed in cultural psychology, in which the researcher lives as a member of a culture and gathers information about the culture through various techniques (e.g., observations, interviews) over an extended period of time.

Questions for Thought and Discussion
What kinds of factors do you think need to be taken into account by researchers studying the impact of natural disasters, such as Hurricane Katrina, on children's lives?

Why would differences in the social and cultural contexts of these children's development be of interest to child development researchers? Cultural psychologists and cross-cultural psychologists also study the effects of ethnic and class differences on child development within a society or nation. Cultural and family expectations, childrearing practices, participation in religions, and conditions such as poverty or war can influence development in profound ways. (Ellen Senisi/The Image Works)

BOX 2.3 Studying AIDS Orphans in Africa

The spread and endemic nature of HIV/AIDS in Africa has resulted in growing populations of orphans—children whose parent(s) have died of the disease. In southern Africa alone, the number of orphans who have lost both parents is expected to rise to 2.6 million children by 2010 (Foster, 2004). Many of these children are themselves infected, although massive international efforts to prevent pediatric AIDS and to treat children with HIV are becoming successful. Nevertheless, a World Bank study in Tanzania suggested that HIV/AIDS may reduce the number of primary school children by as much as 22 percent as a result of increased child mortality (Richter, 2004). What happens to AIDS orphans, and how does their status affect their development? Researchers studying this phenomenon have learned that they must take so-cioeconomic and cultural factors into account in answering this question.

The safety net for orphans in African societies is the extended family network, defined by the kinship system. In most African cultures, the concept of adoption does not exist, even with parental death, because a child is seen as "belonging to" the extended family and not just the parents. Fostering, however, is a tradition, and it is not uncommon for parents to send a child to be raised by relatives, usually aunts or uncles, through mutually beneficial economic arrangements. Problems arise, therefore, when fosterage entails no mutual benefits and when continuing mortality leaves no hope of restoring the balance of family reciprocity (Foster, 2004).

Who will care for these AIDS orphans in Swaziland, Africa? How will growing numbers of orphaned children affect African societies and children's development? (Peter Mckenzie/ Panapress/Getty Images News and Sport Services)

Test Your Mastery...

Learning Objective 2.4: *Understand special issues involved in studying children*

1. What ethical considerations must be addressed when studying children?
2. How does culture influence child development?
3. What is the goal of cross-cultural research?
4. How do the questions and methods asked by cultural psychologists and cross-cultural psychologists differ?
5. Why is it important to account for cultural differences in child development research?

According to one researcher (Foster, 2004, p. 67), children are affected long before they become orphans, along with the kin groups and local communities to whom they belong.

Many children are first affected during the terminal illnesses of their parents, when they shoulder new responsibilities such as additional domestic chores, taking care of sick parents, income-generating activities and childcare duties for younger siblings. Indeed, it is now recognised that educational, social, economic and psychological problems may be more severe before, as opposed to after, children become orphans. In addition, AIDS increasingly affects almost everyone in severely affected communities, even households without HIV-infected members. Children may thus be affected when families provide money to support sick relatives and mothers leave home to provide care for AIDS-affected relatives, or when their children's standard of living deteriorates when cousins move in after the deaths of aunts and uncles.

In addition, as a consequence of AIDS deaths among aunts and uncles, many orphans find they must migrate to live with distant relatives they do not know in remote areas or in rural households already stressed by poverty (Baylies, 2002). Studies show that children find their migration experiences traumatic in the short term but that their natural resilience enables most to adapt successfully. Failed fosterage, which may lead to multiple migrations, may result from a foster family's ill treatment of the orphan or the orphan's impact on further reducing the economic circumstances of the foster household (Ansell and Young, 2004). Selective deprivation may increase as poverty deepens.

Studies of child development in rural Lesotho and Malawi suggest that public policies should aim to reduce families' burden of care for orphaned children, give orphans a greater voice in what happens to them, and place children with relatives who can best meet their nonmaterial as well as material needs (Young and Ansell, 2003). Studies of orphaned children in Dar-es-Salaam suggest that public policies should focus on supporting their school attendance as well (Makame and Grantham-Mcgreggor

2002). Orphans are less likely than nonorphans to be enrolled in school, partly because school attendance represents an additional financial burden on foster families. In addition, a longitudinal study in rural Kenya showed a substantial decrease in school attendance just before and following a parent death. Effects were largest for children whose mothers died, for girls under age 12, and for children with lower academic performance (Evans and Miguel, 2004).

A child's social status as an orphan, lack of school attendance, and the stress of coping with day-to-day hunger were found to be associated with mental health problems during childhood (Makame and Grantham-Mcgreggor, 2002). Thus, just as extended families may need socioeconomic and financial support to care for AIDS orphans, for healthy development the orphans themselves may also need psychosocial support, counseling services, and job training.

African governments, foreign aid programs, and international nongovernmental organizations struggle to provide these supports, but time and resources are limited. Signs of failure in the traditional system of fosterage include increases in the number of child-headed households. As their foster parents die of AIDS or their grandparents die of old age, children as young as 10 or 12 are left to care for surviving assortments of younger siblings and cousins. Children living in child-headed households face routine food and shelter insecurity, lack of access to health care and education, and vulnerability to abuse and exploitation (Foster, 2004). When these survivor families fail, the children may disperse to other inadequate homes or public institutions, enter the world of child labor, or become street children.

The impacts of HIV/AIDS on societies include economic deprivation; population dislocation; changes in family composition; loss of income, homes, and assets; decline in education; threats to public health and nutrition; and increased vulnerability to HIV infection. Impacts on AIDS orphans involve multiple domains of child development—an interaction of biological, sociocultural, and psychosocial factors that creates a major challenge to humanity in our times (Richter, 2004). Researchers studying this phenomenon, and others like it, must attend to the multiple contexts that influence children's lives in a variety of settings around the world.

To Do Research that Takes Seriously the Contexts of Child Development, Researchers Must Consider:

- Child's own biological contributions
- Family characteristics, such as family composition, cultural background, parenting style, marital satisfaction, social networks, and socioeconomic status
- Characteristics of the child's other settings, such as school or day care
- Neighborhood characteristics that influence quality of life
- Characteristics of parents' work setting, such as stress and satisfaction
- Influence of the media in the home
- Larger cultural values that influence childrearing goals, strategies, and experiences

Summary for Chapter 2

Learning Objective 2.1
Explain the process by which researchers generate hypotheses and ensure objectivity.

1. What is the relationship between theories and observations?

Each theory investigates child development from a different viewpoint. For example, cognitive developmentalists focus on how children acquire knowledge, whereas environmental learning theorists are more likely to study ways in which behavior is acquired through experience. A *theory* is an integrated set of statements that explain and predict behavior. Statements are formulated from observations of behavior.

2. What is the relationship between theories and hypotheses?

Hypotheses are derived from explanatory statements that are drawn directly from a theory. An example of a statement might be, "Watching violent television programming will increase children's tendency to behave aggressively." The *hypothesis* proposes a relationship between factors or variables. In this example, the variables are television viewing of violent programming and childhood aggression. An example of a hypothesis might be, "Children who watch violent television programs will act more aggressively than those children who do not."

3. How do researchers seek to ensure objectivity in their studies of children?

Objectivity is achieved in a number of ways. One way is to focus only on behaviors that are directly observable. It is very difficult to study something that we cannot observe. If a characteristic is not directly observable, then an attempt is made to examine the actions or effects of those behaviors. Second, researchers must be able to measure what is observed. Confidence is gained by precisely defining and describing what is being studied, so that independent observers would have no trouble agreeing on what happened in a given situation. Third, everything in the study must be quantifiable. That is, everything must be able to be counted, including the behaviors and the factors that affect the behaviors.

4. What is the value of quantitative data?

Quantitative data provides a researcher with the opportunity to run sophisticated analyses of the behaviors that are being studied. One special type of analysis is called meta-analysis in which researchers compare different studies on a particular topic using a set of quantitative rules for analyses and interpretation.

Learning Objective 2.2

Compare and contrast the research methods commonly used
to study children.

1. What are observational research, the interview method, and the case study method? What are the advantages and disadvantages of each of these methods?	There are two types of observational research, *naturalistic* and *structured*. In naturalistic observation, children's behaviors are carefully observed in settings that are natural to the child such as their home or school. In structured observation, which may take place in a laboratory setting, researchers can control the physical environment as well as the events that occur. The advantage of naturalistic observation is that the child is already comfortable in the environment. However, it is important for researchers to follow an observational protocol so that the reliability of the observations is maintained. Similarly, observer effects must be minimized, either by having the observer remain hidden or by using a video camera. In structured observations, the standardization of the setting allows the study of children's reactions to experiences that might not occur in a natural environment. However, observations made in the lab may not be generalizable to other settings.

In the *interview method*, researchers talk with children about aspects of their lives. Interviews can be conversational, where children respond freely (open-ended), or standardized, meaning a standardized protocol or questionnaire is used. In addition, researchers often ask questions of other knowledgeable informants such as parents, teachers, classmates, or peers. Interviews can be a valuable source of information on how a person thinks and feels. However, since interviews rely on the informant's knowledge, memory, and ability or willingness to communicate information, they may not always accurately reflect actual behavior.

In the *case study method*, the research involves only a single individual. Often these studies are concerned with clinical issues, or if a child has experienced something so unusual as to attract the interest of psychologists for theoretical reasons. In these instances case studies are a valuable research tool. The major limitation of using only a single research participant is that the researcher must be very cautious about drawing conclusions from the case.

2. What is correlational research? What does it tell us about causal relations between variables?	Correlational research identifies systematic relationships between variables. A *correlation* is a statement that describes how two variables are related. If two variables change together in the same direction, it is a positive correlation. If the variables change in opposite directions, it is a negative correlation. Correlations can also be described in terms of their strength. A strong correlation means that two variables are closely related. As a correlation grows weaker, the amount of predictability between the two variables decreases. A major limitation in correlational research is that a correlation is not the same thing as a cause. Correlations cannot be used to show causality between variables, but only to show the nature and strength of the relationship between two variables.

3. What elements comprise an experiment? What are advantages and disadvantages of the experimental method in research with children?	In an *experiment* you systematically change one variable to observe its effect on a second variable. The dependent variable is generally some aspect of behavior. The researcher manipulates the independent variable in order to observe its influence on the dependent variable. In a quasi-experimental study, groups that differ on some important characteristic are compared. This type of experiment is used when it is not possible to manipulate the independent variable (e.g., age or gender) or when the dependent variable cannot be reasonably studied by using an experimental design. The advantage of experiments is that causality can be determined between two variables. The disadvantage is that it is not always possible or ethical to manipulate certain types of variables. The advantage of the quasi-experimental method is that it allows researchers the ability to examine variables that cannot be experimentally manipulated. The disadvantage is that this type of research cannot be used to show causality.

Learning Objective 2.3

Analyze the strengths and limitations of the four basic methods for studying child development as a process.

1. **What are the strengths and limitations of longitudinal research?**

In *longitudinal research* the same group of children is studied repeatedly at different ages. The strengths of longitudinal research are that it allows researchers to study changes as children age, as well as to examine the stability of behavior over time and the effects of early experiences. There are certain limitations to longitudinal research. First is the problem of attrition—the loss of individuals under study as families move away and as children become ill or develop other problems that interfere with participation in the study. Or loss of interest may occur, and the parents may simply withdraw from the study. Another problem is that scores or test results can become skewed as children learn to perform better on tests through repeated administration (practice effect). In addition, over a long period of time, the instruments used for measurement may become outdated. Finally, longitudinal studies can be time-consuming and expensive.

2. **What are the strengths and limitations of cross-sectional research design?**

In *cross-sectional research*, groups of children of different ages are compared at one time. The strengths of this type of research are that it is relatively quick and low cost, and there are no problems with attrition or repeated testing. The drawback to cross-sectional design is that it cannot be used to examine stability and change. In addition, cohort effects (unique events experienced by a particular generation) can influence the findings.

3. **What are the strengths and limitations of cross-sequential research design?**

Cross-sequential research combines cross-sectional and longitudinal research. Children of different age groups are followed longitudinally. The advantages of this type of design are that it permits both cross-sectional and longitudinal comparisons to be made. It also permits researchers to examine cohort effects. The disadvantages are that it is time consuming and costly.

4. **What are the strengths and limitations of microgenetic research?**

Microgenetic research is an intensive study of a small number of children over a brief period of time. The strength of this research design is that it allows examination of developmental changes that are discontinuous, that is, an abrupt change from one level of development to another. The limitation of this type of research is that repeated testing can influence results.

Learning Objective 2.4
Understand special issues involved in studying children.

1. What ethical considerations must be addressed when studying children?	Physical injury to the child is always a concern in any research; however, this problem is relatively rare in developmental research. *Potential psychological harm*, such as producing feelings of failure, frustration, or stress must be considered. Similarly, a child's privacy must be considered when designing experiments that involve children.
2. How does culture influence child development?	*Culture* influences child development in the way that a child experiences activities of daily life, the childcare practices that a specific culture employs, and the goals those parents of a particular culture have for their children.
3. What is the goal of cross-cultural research?	One important goal of *cross-cultural studies* is to test the universality of a phenomenon, such as motor development. Although there are significant individual differences in the ages at which infants crawl and walk, differences between cultures are far smaller than one might expect. Cross-cultural psychologists also have the goal of integrating the results of studies from a variety of cultures to create a more universal theory of human development.
4. How do the questions and methods asked by cultural psychologists and cross-cultural psychologists differ?	Cross-cultural psychologists attempt to test all groups under similar conditions, ideally using identical tasks and procedures. *Cultural psychologists* may vary their methods from culture to culture, adapting their methods to existing cultural practices.
5. Why is it important to account for cultural differences in child development research?	Past research on child development has been criticized for cultural bias—the assumption that the ideas that define one's own group apply to the whole world. European American middle-class researchers have tended to study European American middle-class children, imposing cultural and class values on groups that were not European American or middle class. Understanding cultural differences is an integral part of research in child development today.

The Biological Context
of Development

"CC" (Carbon Copy, left) is a clone of "Rainbow" (right) but does not look exactly like her. How can the kitten be a clone but not be identical?

(Courtesy College of Veterinary Medicine Texas A&M University)

"Copy cat" aptly describes the calico kitten peering out from the photo. The kitten is the result of the first-ever cloning of a household pet, according to researchers at Texas A&M University, where she was born in December 2001. Scientists at the university performed the cloning procedure by inserting the nucleus of a cell from a genetic donor cat, Rainbow, into an egg cell in another cat, Allie. Because the kitten grew from this nucleus, her genetic makeup is identical to the genetic makeup of the donor. In contrast, a kitten produced in the ordinary way would receive half its genes from the mother and half from the father.

Successful cloning of mammals dates back to February 1997, when scientists in Scotland announced the birth of Dolly, a cloned lamb. Since then, researchers have produced sheep, cattle, goats, pigs, rabbits, and mice through cloning, and efforts are reportedly under way to clone humans. Needless to say, this research has generated a great deal of controversy, both for practical reasons (the success rate is less than 10 percent, and cloned animals are often sickly) and for ethical reasons (many say life shouldn't be created in a laboratory). In fact, the U.S. Congress has considered banning human cloning experiments.

Amid the controversy, it's useful to think more closely about what cloning is. Is a clone a sort of photocopy, identical in every way to the original? That's what might be expected based on the identical genetic makeup of the clone and the donor. But according to Dr. Duane Kraemer, one of the Texas A&M researchers, the cloning of Rainbow the cat "is a reproduction, not a resurrection."

For one thing, of course, Rainbow has had unique life experiences—and learning and experience are not inherited. What the new kitten learns as she develops may make her different from Rainbow in many ways.

That's not all. Take another look at the photo of the kitten—whose name is "CC," for "carbon copy"—and then look at Rainbow, the donor, shown in the photo. You can see that, in spite of her name, CC's coloration isn't exactly like Rainbow's. "The pattern of pigmentation in multicolored animals is the result of genetic factors as well as developmental factors that are not controlled by genotype," explains Dr. Mark Westhusin, the lead investigator in the cloning project. As the embryo of a calico cat develops, chromosomes that determine fur color are randomly turned on or off in millions of cells. Even identical genes will not necessarily produce identical results. The basic elements—a mix of white, orange, and black or brown—will be present, but the pattern is unpredictable. Interestingly, environment plays a role in the switching on and switching off of chromosomes.

You learned in Chapter 1 that one of the enduring issues in developmental psychology concerns the relative importance of biological (nature) factors and environmental (nurture) factors. You learned also that most child researchers today favor an interactionist perspective. Environmental effects played out at the chromosomal level offer an insight into how complex and subtle these interactions can be. This chapter delves more deeply into the fascinating world of genetics, considering both the biological starting point for development and the ways in which nurture then works with nature to sculpt the mature human. ■

Links to Related Material
As you saw in Chapter 1, the interaction of nature and nurture is an enduring issue in developmental psychology. This chapter delves more deeply into how genes and the environment interact to influence child development.

Learning Objective 3.1
Identify and describe the mechanisms and processes by which physical and behavioral characteristics are inherited.

Chromosomes
Chemical strands in the cell nucleus that contain the genes. The nucleus of each human cell has 46 chromosomes, with the exception of the gametes, which have 23.

Mechanisms of Inheritance

How does a baby inherit the characteristics of his or her parents—skin color, hair color, stature, and so on? How does a fertilized human egg know to develop into a person rather than a chimpanzee? How does a single cell give rise to trillions of other cells that become different parts of the body—the fingers, the heart, the brain, and so on? Such questions lie at the heart of the puzzle of inheritance, a mystery that scientists are now slowly beginning to solve.

Cell Division

All living things are composed of cells. Adult humans, on average, possess about 10 trillion of them. Cells have three major subdivisions: the nucleus; the cytoplasm, which surrounds the nucleus; and the cell membrane, which encases the cell.

Inside the nucleus lies the body's genetic material, DNA, which is organized into chemical strands called **chromosomes**. In humans, each cell nucleus contains 23 pairs of chromosomes, 46 in all. For each pair, one chromosome came from the father, the other from the mother. Twenty-two of the pairs are called **autosomes**. The members of these pairs are similar to one another and carry the same genes in the same locations. The 23rd pair makes up the **sex chromosomes**, X and Y. The X chromosome carries a good deal of genetic material, whereas the Y chromosome is much smaller and has many fewer genes. When the pair consists of two X chromosomes (XX), the person is female. When it consists of one of each type (XY), the person is male.

Cells constantly reproduce. Their reproduction is probably the most fundamental genetic process that takes place in our bodies. In the time it takes you to read this sentence, more than 100 million cells in your body will have reproduced. *Body cells*, by far the most numerous, reproduce by a process called mitosis, whereas *germ or sex cells* reproduce by a process called meiosis.

In **mitosis**, diagrammed on the left-hand side of Figure 3.1, each parent cell produces two identical child cells through a series of three phases. In the first phase (Figure 3.1*a*), each of the 46 chromosomes in the cell duplicates itself, producing two identical strands connected near their centers, like an X. Next, these joined strands line up at the cell's midline (Figure 3.1*b*). Each X splits and the two identical chromosomal strands move to opposite sides of the cell, a nucleus forms around each set of chromosomes, and the cell itself divides in two (Figure 3.1*c*). With mitosis complete, each new cell contains 46 chromosomes and is genetically identical to the parent cell.

Autosomes
The 22 pairs of human chromosomes, other than the sex chromosomes.

Sex chromosomes
The pair of human chromosomes that determines one's sex. Females have two X chromosomes; males have an X and a Y.

Mitosis
The process by which body cells reproduce, resulting in two identical cells.

FIGURE 3.1   Mitosis and Meiosis

Mitosis results in two cells identical with the parent cell and with each other. Meiosis results in four cells different from the parent cell and from each other.

SOURCE: Adapted from G.D. Brum & L.K. McKane, (1989). *Biology: Exploring Life* (p. 152). New York: John Wiley & Sons. Adapted by permission of the authors.

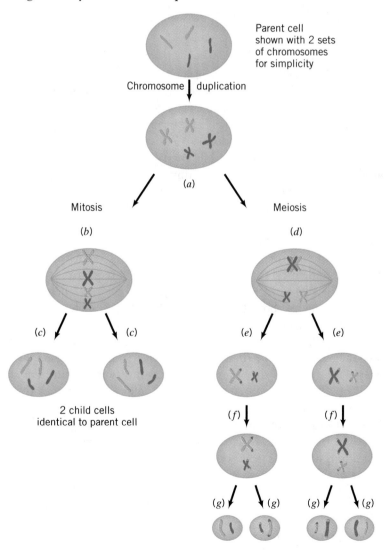

Parent cell shown with 2 sets of chromosomes for simplicity

Chromosome | duplication

(a)

Mitosis   Meiosis

(b)   *(d)*

(c)   *(c)*   *(e)*   *(e)*

2 child cells identical to parent cell

(f)   *(f)*

(g)   *(g)*   *(g)*   *(g)*

4 child cells with half the number of chromosomes as parent cell

Meiosis

The process by which germ cells produce four gametes (sperm or ova), each with half the number of chromosomes of the parent cell.

Crossing over

The exchange of genetic material between pairs of chromosomes during meiosis.

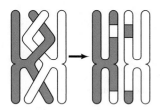

FIGURE 3.2   Crossing Over

Crossing over results in the exchange of genetic material. After the crossover, all four strands are different.

Source: Adapted from G.D. Brum and L.K. McKane. (1989). *Biology: Exploring Life* (p. 44). New York: John Wiley & Sons.

Deoxyribonucleic acid (DNA)

A stair-like, double-helix molecule that carries genetic information on chromosomes.

Questions for Thought and Discussion

If crossing over did not occur, would children look more similar or less similar to their siblings and parents? Why?

Gene

A segment of DNA on the chromosome that codes for the production of proteins; the basic unit of inheritance.

Alleles

Genes for the same trait located in the same place on a pair of chromosomes.

In **meiosis**, the process by which germ or sex cells reproduce, four child cells are produced that are all different from one another and that contain only 23 chromosomes each. These child cells, called *gametes*, are the sperm or the ova that will combine at conception to form a new individual with the full complement of 46 chromosomes. Meiosis, diagrammed on the right side of Figure 3.1, requires several additional phases. The 46 chromosomes of the cell similarly duplicate themselves into two identical strands that remain attached like an X (Figure 3.1*a*). Then an important new process occurs. The X-shaped chromosomes pair up with their partners (remember, the 46 chromosomes are arranged in 23 pairs) and the strands of one X exchange pieces with the strands of the partner X (Figure 3.1*d*). This process, called **crossing over**, means that the two strands that form each X are no longer identical.(Figure 3.2 offers a greatly simplified representation of such an exchange.) The X's then line up at the midline of the cell. One X from each pair moves to one end of the cell, a nucleus forms around each half, and the cell divides (Figure 3.1*e*). This process is then repeated (Figures 3.1*f* and 3.1*g*). Thus, when meiosis is complete, the resulting four gametes possess 23 chromosomes each and are genetically unique.

If you consider that every one of the 23 chromosomes in a gamete now represents a one-of-a-kind combination of genetic material and that these 23 chromosomes must combine with another set of original chromosomes from a gamete of the other parent, it should become clear why people come in so many sizes, colors, and shapes. Crossing over virtually ensures that no two people (except identical twins, produced from the same fertilized egg) will ever have exactly the same genes.

Inside the Chromosome

Deoxyribonucleic acid (DNA) is the carrier of genetic information inside the chromosome (Watson & Crick, 1953). In 1953 James Watson and Francis Crick found that the DNA molecule has the structure of a double helix, much like the sides of a spiral staircase joined by rungs, as shown in Figure 3.3. These rungs are composed of four bases: adenine (A), thymine (T), guanine (G), and cytosine (C). Each rung, called a *nucleotide*, consists of a pair of these bases linked together. Only two types of pairings occur, A–T and G–C. The sequence of these base pairs (rungs) determines the coded information carried by the gene. Nucleotides are the mechanism for the replication of DNA (see Figure 3.3).

Because each nucleotide base can link to only one other base, each half-rung of the DNA molecule can serve as a blueprint for the other half. Thus, during cell division, the chromosome "unzips" down the length of the staircase, breaking the links that connect the bases at the middle of each rung. The half-rungs then pair, base by base, with new material to form two new, identical copies of the original DNA sequence

A **gene** is just a section of the DNA strand containing some set of these nucleotide rungs. On average, a gene contains about 1,000 nucleotides, although some contain as many as 2 million. Again, when you consider that the chromosomes in a human body cell together contain about 25,000 or 30,000 genes, and that each chromosome underwent the crossing-over process during meiosis, it is easy to understand why each individual person is truly unique.

The location of genes on the chromosome is also very important. For each pair of chromosomes, the genes for the same trait (e.g., eye color or nose shape) are in the same locations and are called **alleles**. Both genes are involved in how the trait is expressed, but because the two alleles are not always the same, many different combinations of characteristics can result. In recent years scientists have made remarkable progress in mapping the precise locations of various genes on the human chromosomes, which will give them a clearer picture of the human genome.

Mendel's Studies

In the mid-1800s, an Austrian monk named Gregor Mendel studied the process of hereditary transmission. He wondered how pea plants passed on characteristics such as seed texture and flower color to the next generation. People believed at the time that when a mother and father had different traits, the traits blended in the child. But Mendel knew that the

FIGURE 3.3 Structure and Replication of DNA

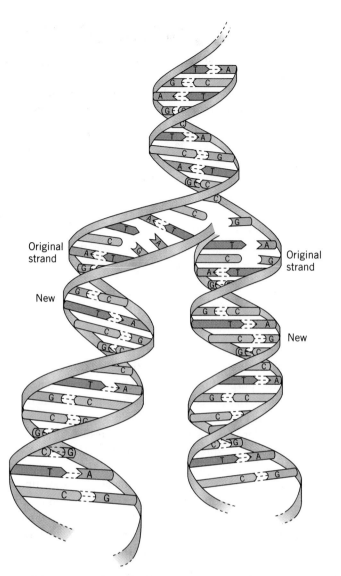

process had to work in some other way because crossing plants with purple flowers and plants with white flowers did not produce offspring with lavender flowers. In the first-generation, all the offspring had purple flowers. But when Mendel mated the first-generation plants with each other, one out of every four of their offspring had white flowers.

Mendel developed the theory that each observable trait, such as color, requires two elements, one inherited from each parent. We now know that these two elements are a pair of genes (alleles). Today, we call the expressed or observable trait the **phenotype** and the underlying genes the **genotype**.

Phenotype
The characteristic of a trait that is expressed or observable. The phenotype results from an interaction of genotype and environment.

Genotype
The arrangement of genes underlying a trait.

The number and precise sequence of nucleotides in the genes answers the question of how cells know to develop into a human rather than a chimpanzee. The sequence is especially critical because approximately 98 percent of human DNA is also found in the DNA of the chimpanzee. (H.S. Terrace/Animals Animals/Earth Scenes)

SOURCE: Biological Systems. (1988, June 10). *Science*, 240, p. 1383.

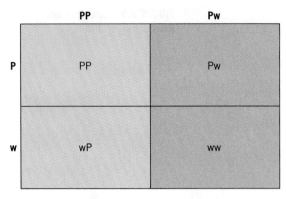

FIGURE 3.4 Mendel's Principles of Genetic Transmission

If the color trait in the pea plant involves purple (P, dominant trait) or white (w, recessive trait) genes, then plants with the genotype PP, Pw, or wP will have purple flowers, and only those with the genotype ww will have white flowers. Plants thus can have the same phenotype (purple flowers) with different genotypes (PP, Pw, or wP).

TABLE 3.1 Some Common Dominant and Recessive Traits	
Mendel's principles have proved to be accurate, not just for pea plants but also throughout the huge variety of life forms. His discovery of dominant and recessive traits applies to many human characteristics, as shown in this table. Do you have any recessive traits?	
DOMINANT	**RECESSIVE**
Normal hair	Baldness (in men)
Dark hair	Blond hair
Type A or B blood	Type O blood
Freckles	No freckles
Dimples	No dimples
Free earlobes	Attached earlobes
Double-jointed thumbs	Tight thumb ligaments

Dominant gene

A relatively powerful allele whose characteristics are expressed in the phenotype regardless of the allele with which it is paired.

Recessive gene

A relatively weak allele whose characteristics are expressed in the phenotype only when it is paired with another recessive gene.

Polygenic inheritance

The case in which a trait is determined by a number of genes.

Principles of Genetic Transmission Mendel's theory included the *principle of dominance*—the alleles of a trait (for example, purple-flower gene and white-flower gene) are not equal, and one often dominates the other. In pea plants the gene for purple flowers is a **dominant gene**, and the gene for white flowers is a **recessive gene** (Table 3.1). Mendel discovered that when either gene is dominant, the dominant characteristic is expressed. Only when both genes are recessive is the other characteristic expressed (Figure 3.4).

Mendel's theory included other principles as well. The *principle of segregation* states that each inheritable trait is passed on to the offspring as a separate unit (the alleles that produce flower color are separate from one another and are passed on that way, which is why the blending idea was incorrect). The *principle of independent assortment* states that traits are passed on independently of one another (for example, which flower-color trait is passed on has no bearing on which seed-texture or stem-length trait is passed on).

Principles of Inheritance Since Mendel Years of research have supported Mendel's basic ideas but have also uncovered other processes involved in hereditary transmission. For instance, single traits are often the product of more than one pair of genes—a process known as **polygenic inheritance**. In humans, height, weight, and skin color are all the product of polygenic inheritance. Most behavioral traits—for example, temperament and intelligence—are also affected by multiple genes.

A second modification is that some traits result from genes that display *incomplete dominance;* that is, they are neither entirely dominant nor entirely recessive. For example, sickle-cell anemia is passed on through a recessive gene. However, the blood of people who have this recessive gene along with a dominant normal gene will show some mild characteristics of the disease.

A third addition to Mendel's principles involves *codominance,* in which both genes of a trait are dominant and so both characteristics are expressed completely. For example, the genes for A and B blood types are codominant, so a person who inherits one from each parent will have blood type AB.

In some instances a trait does not follow any of the usual laws of inheritance because it has *genomic imprinting.* The alleles for the trait are biochemically marked such that one of them is "imprinted" or silenced and only the other allele affects the phenotype. In this case, it matters whether the mother or father provides the imprinted gene. For example, diabetes is more likely to be inherited from the father, whereas the mother is a more likely source of asthma. It is estimated that the human genome contains between 100 and 200 imprinted genes (Davies, Isles, & Wilkinson, 2001).

Learning Objective 3.1: *Identify and describe the mechanisms and processes by which physical and behavioral characteristics are inherited.*

1. What are genes, where are they in the body, and what do they do?
2. How do cells reproduce in a way that makes every individual genetically unique?
3. What is DNA, and how does it combine to create genes?
4. What facts and principles of inheritance did Mendel discover?
5. What are some principles of inheritance that researchers have uncovered since Mendel?

Genes and Behavior

Genes affect every aspect of our development from blood type to fingerprints to hair color. Genes also affect behavior. The goal of research in **behavior genetics** is to determine the contribution that genes make to individual differences in behavior and development. This research is done through family studies, adoption studies, and twin studies.

Family Studies

Children inherit 50 percent of their genes from each parent. Siblings, on average, share 50 percent of their genes. Grandparent and grandchild share 25 percent, as do aunts and uncles with their nieces and nephews. The family study approach asks whether the phenotypic similarity on some trait follows from the genotypic similarity among the people being compared. If it does, then you should be more similar to your parents or siblings than you are to an uncle or cousin, and more similar to the uncle or cousin than you are to people with whom you share no genes.

Family studies have shown that a number of traits do follow the pattern that would be expected if genes are important—that is, close relatives are most similar, and the degree of similarity drops off as the degree of genetic overlap drops. Table 3.2 shows typical correlations among family members for intelligence as measured by performance on IQ tests. Similar results have been obtained for behavioral traits such as sociability and aggression (Bouchard, 2004; Loehlin, 1992).

Family studies also suggest that there is a genetic basis for various forms of psychopathology. Children of mothers who have schizophrenia, for example, are about 13 times as likely as children of normal mothers to develop the disorder. Children who have siblings with schizophrenia are 9 times as likely to become schizophrenic as children in the general population (Plomin et al., 1997a). Genetic processes reach into many more areas of development than was once believed. One researcher summarizes this conclusion

Learning Objective 3.2
Describe the influence that genes have on the development of psychological abilities and traits.

Behavior genetics
The field of study that explores the role of genes in producing individual differences in behavior and development.

TABLE 3.2 Correlations in IQ as a Function of Degree of Genetic Relation	
Correlations measure the relation between two sets of scores. A correlation of .50 (as is found for parents and children) is a moderately strong relation, indicating that intelligent parents tend to have intelligent children but also that there are exceptions to this pattern. Lower values (such as those for cousins) indicate a weaker relation.	
RELATION	**CORRELATION**
Siblings	.55
Parent-child	.50
Grandparent-grandchild	.27
First cousins	.26
Second cousins	.16

SOURCE: Adapted from S. Scarr-Salapatek. (1975). Genetics and the development of intelligence. In F. D. Horowitz (Ed.), *Review of Child Development Research* (Vol. 4, p. 33). Chicago: University of Chicago Press. Copyright (c) by the University of Chicago Press.

Why do the people in this family resemble one another? According to research in behavior genetics, what other kinds of characteristics might these family members share? Which of your family members, past and present, do you most resemble? Who do you take after in your personality? (PhotosIndia/Age Fotostock America, Inc.)

Links to Related Material
In Chapter 9, you will learn more about how the genetic foundations of intelligence interact with environment to influence children's cognitive development.

succinctly: "Everything is heritable" (Turkheimer, 2000, p. 160). This statement certainly does not mean that any human psychological or behavioral trait is totally genetic in origin. But it does mean that genes have been shown to play some role in virtually every psychological and developmental outcome that has been the subject of behavior genetics research. These outcomes include, for example, cognitive abilities, skill levels in other abilities, personality attributes, and psychiatric problems.

Adoption Studies

A limitation of family studies is that patterns of family resemblance also can be explained through similarities in environment. That is, children may be similar to their parents and their siblings not only because they share genes, but also because they share a family environment. Adoption studies help to distinguish the degree of genetic overlap from the degree of environmental overlap among different family members.

In adoption studies, children who are living in adoptive homes are compared with their biological parents (who share their genes but not their environments) and with their adoptive parents (who share their environments but not their genes). If the correlation with one set of parents is stronger than that with the other, researchers have a good idea whether biological or environmental factors are making the greater contribution to individual differences in the trait they are measuring.

Sometimes the method includes siblings, because many adoptive families go on to adopt a second child. These two children share a similar environment but none of the same genes. Their similarity in behavior thus can be compared with that of biological siblings in families used for comparison. Again, differences in the correlations between the two sets of siblings can shed light on whether environment or heredity has the greater influence.

The Colorado Adoption Project, for example, is a longitudinal study begun in 1975 (DeFries, Plomin, & Fulker, 1994; Petrill et al., 2003). It involves about 250 families with adopted children and, for comparison, 250 families with biological children. The children were first studied when they were infants and preschoolers, and they have been followed and studied ever since. More than 90 percent of the original participants remain in the study 30 years after it began.

The Colorado study has supported findings from earlier adoption studies (e.g., Loehlin, Horn, & Willerman, 1997), as well as findings from family studies. The children have been tested for both general intelligence and specific cognitive skills (such as memory, vocabulary, spatial relations, and reading). Results have shown that biological siblings are much more similar to each other in these abilities than are adoptive siblings, and that despite being raised apart from their biological parents, adopted children are more similar to their biological parents than to their adoptive parents. These findings indicate that to some degree children inherit their intellectual abilities (Cardon, 1994; Cherny & Cardon, 1994; Wadsworth et al., 2001).

Adoption studies also help explain the origins of problems in development. For example, one study sought to explain the hostile and antisocial behaviors of a group of adolescents who had been adopted at birth (Ge et al., 1996). It was found that these adolescents were more likely to have biological parents with psychiatric disorders, suggesting that some problem behaviors can be inherited. Second, the troubled adolescents also were more likely to have adoptive parents who used harsh and inconsistent punishment. This is an environmental influence. Furthermore, children of parents with psychiatric problems were more likely to encounter harsh discipline from their adoptive parents, linking the genetic and environmental influences. That is, the link between the biological and adoptive parents was the children's genes. First, the children inherited their behavior problems from their biological parents, and then these problem behaviors led to the harsh discipline they received from their adoptive parents. Thus, children's genes can influence the environments they encounter.

Adoption studies have also addressed the issue of schizophrenia, described earlier. Children of schizophrenic mothers who are placed in adoptive homes are around 10 times as likely to develop schizophrenia as are either the biological children of the adoptive parents or adopted children of normal mothers (Plomin et al., 1997b). This finding suggests a major role for heredity in the development of the disease and is consistent with other research showing that psychological disorders can be inherited (Plomin & McGuffin, 2003).

Twin Studies

Twins provide an interesting opportunity to study the role of genetic similarity in development. Twins come in two varieties. **Identical twins** develop from the same fertilized egg and are called **monozygotic twins (MZ)** (mono meaning "one" and zygote, "fertilized egg"). They have exactly the same genes. Identical twins occur once in approximately every 300 births. **Fraternal twins** develop from two different eggs and are called **dizygotic twins (DZ)** (di, "two"). Their genetic makeup is the same as that for any children who have the same parents. On average, 50 percent of the genes of fraternal twins are the same, just as for any siblings. Fraternal twins occur more frequently than do identicals; the exact likelihood varies, however, as a function of a number of factors, including the age and ethnicity of the mother.

The logic of the twin-study approach begins with the assumption that fraternal twins share an environment that is as similar as the environment shared by identical twins. Researchers then look at a particular trait or behavior displayed by the sets of twins. If the trait is more similar in the identical twins than in the fraternal twins, the usual conclusion is that the greater similarity results from the greater similarity of their genes.

Researchers take twin studies one step further. As we mentioned earlier, studying the similarity of siblings reared in the same household confuses shared genes with shared environment. In addition, how do we know that a family treats a set of fraternal twins as similarly as a set of identical twins? Because identical twins look more alike, and perhaps because they know they are identical, parents and others may expect them to act the same. These expectations may influence how people behave toward the children and, as a result, may affect how the children themselves behave.

To better separate out the influence of genes and environment, researchers have chosen to study twins who were separated early in life and reared in different adoptive homes. If genes play a role in creating individual differences in behavior, then identical twins reared apart should still be more alike than are fraternal twins reared apart.

The best-known research project of this type is the Minnesota Study of Twins Reared Apart (Bouchard, 1997, 2004; Bouchard et al., 1990; Bouchard & McGue, 2003; Segal, 1999). The study involves 135 pairs of twins who are currently in their mid-to-late 50s.

Identical (monozygotic twins)
Twins who develop from a single fertilized ovum and thus inherit identical genetic material.

Fraternal (dizygotic) twins
Twins who develop from separately fertilized ova and who thus are no more genetically similar than are other siblings.

Questions for Thought and Discussion
Do genes or environmental factors play the larger role in musical ability? What about athletic skill? Interpersonal skills? Why do you think so? How could you study these questions?

TABLE 3.3 Average Heritability Coefficients of Various Psychological Traits from Several Twin Studies	
Verbal Ability	.48
Spatial Ability	.60
Extraversion	.54
Negative Emotionality (Neuroticism)	.44
Social Potency	.54
Traditionalism	.52

SOURCE: Drawn from T. J. Bouchard, Jr., & M. McGue. (2003). Genetic and environmental influences on human psychological differences. *Journal of Neurobiology, 54,* 4–45.

This project and others like it have yielded important information on the heritability of a variety of abilities, traits, and behaviors. Table 3.3 presents heritability coefficients that researchers have derived based on examining the results of multiple studies of monozygotic and dizygotic twins reared together and reared apart (Bouchard, 2004; Bouchard & McGue, 2003; Devlin, Daniels, & Roeder, 1997).

As you can see in Table 3.3, researchers have found that genes exert a moderate to strong influence on a wide range of psychological abilities and traits, including personality characteristics such as extraversion and neuroticism (Bouchard, 2004; Loehlin, 1992). Genetic heritability even extends to some outcomes (such as religious attitudes and social conservatism) that otherwise seem unlikely to be affected by genes (Bouchard, 2004; Bouchard & McGue, 2003).

In addition, twin studies have also been used to understand personality traits in infancy, such as *temperament*. Babies come into the world with a particular style of responding. Some are irritable and cry frequently; some are easygoing and smile a lot; some are active; some are cuddly; and so forth. Aspects of temperament, discussed further in Chapter 11, sometimes persist well into the early school years and may eventually form the basis for adult personality. Do genes influence temperament? Apparently they do to some extent. As early as 3 months of age, and throughout the first years of life, identical twins are more similar than fraternal twins on a variety of measures, including ability to pay attention, activity level, and shyness (Cherny et al., 1994; Emde et al., 1992; Manke, Saudino, & Grant, 2001).

Researchers have noted one important limitation regarding twin and adoption studies as a means of determining the heritability of psychological abilities and traits. The major limitation is that, because of the adoption practices followed by most agencies, the homes in which adopted children are placed tend to be relatively homogeneous. For example, adopted children are generally placed in middle-class or high-income families, and so the environmental effects associated with being reared in poverty are not typically included in adoption studies of twins reared apart. This fact suggests that adoption studies may underestimate environmental influences, simply by holding socioeconomic factors relatively constant across adoptive homes (Bouchard & McGue, 2003).

Links to Related Material
In Chapter 11, you will learn more about temperament, a genetically based dimension of personality evident in infancy.

Test Your Mastery...

Learning Objective 3.2: *Describe the influence that genes have on the development of psychological abilities and traits.*

1. What are family, adoption, and twin studies?
2. What does each of these types of studies tell us about the heritability of psychological abilities and traits?
3. What are some examples of behavioral characteristics that are affected by genetic endowment?
4. What major limitation do researchers point to regarding adoption studies?

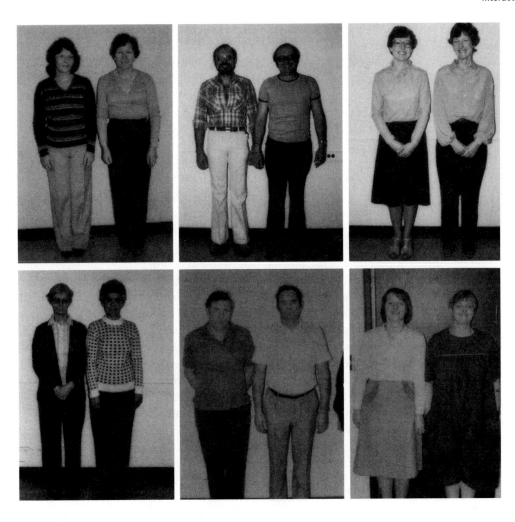

These photos are of twins who participated in the Minnesota Study of Twins Reared Apart. The top row includes three pairs of identical twins, and the bottom row includes three pairs of fraternal twins. These unposed photographs suggest genetic influence on body posture because the identical twins are standing in more similar positions than are the fraternal twins. (Courtesy Dr. Thomas J. Bouchard Jr.)

Interaction of Genes and Environment

As you have seen, family, adoption, and twin studies all suggest that genes make an important contribution to a wide range of outcomes in child development. Genes can account at best for only half of the variation we see in phenotypes, however, meaning that environment accounts for at least half. Furthermore, many behavioral and developmental traits are not determined by single genes but by multiple genes, perhaps as many as thousands of genes in a complex trait such as intelligence. The effect of any gene depends on the genotype as a whole, and the expression of the genes depends on the environmental context. The phenotype—whether height, weight, intelligence, or personality—always depends on environmental factors as well as on genetic endowment. Thus, at every point in development genes and environment work together to determine every aspect of who we are and how we behave. Even identical twins are not identical in behavior, for example, and any differences between identical twins must be environmental in origin. Clearly, genes (nature) and environment (nurture) interact to determine human behavior. But how?

Reaction Range

An influential model proposed by Irving Gottesman (1974) suggests that genes interact with the environment by setting the upper and lower limits of our development. Our environment and experiences then determine where we fall within this **reaction range**. One way to visualize this concept is to imagine a handful of sunflower seeds planted in soil. If the seeds are planted well spaced in fertile soil at the right time of year, and if the seedbed is then watered appropriately and receives adequate sunlight, we will expect that the

Learning Objective 3.3
How do genes and environment interact to influence the development of behavior?

Reaction range
The term for the range of ability or skill that genes set. The value achieved within this range is determined by the environment.

differences we see in the mature plants will reflect differences in the genetic potential of individual seeds. However, if these conditions fail—if the soil lacks necessary nutrients, water, and sunlight—then although we would still find that some plants manage to survive better than others, we would nonetheless expect dramatic stunting in the growth of all the plants, regardless of their individual potential.

A similar example drawn from the lives of people might be athletic prowess. Assuming that all the boys who try out for the local Little League team are adequately nourished, in good physical health, and have had similar opportunities to practice relevant baseball skills, then we might expect that the boys who end up making the team have more individual athletic potential than boys who try out for the team but do not make it. However, to the extent that these conditions do not prevail—in other words, to the extent that limitations in the environment limit individual potential—we would expect that making the team or not making the team would reflect those environmental limitations as much as it would differences in individual potential.

The concept of the range of reaction has helped researchers understand how genes and environment might interact to produce individual differences in IQ. Figure 3.5 illustrates this model by showing the ranges of possible IQs that might exist for groups of children born with different genetic potential for intelligence. Group A consists of children whose genetic potential is the lowest, Groups B and C represent variations within a more typical range, and Group D represents children who have exceptional genetic potential for intelligence. The graph also includes three levels of environment: restricted (an environment that provides minimal intellectual stimulation), natural (Gottesman idealized this as the environment of a youngster growing up in a "typical" U.S. town), and enriched (an environment that provides an exceptional degree of intellectual stimulation).

This model suggests how genes and environment interact. The genes have set the upper limits on potential intelligence, such that Group A children cannot become as intelligent as Group D children, for example, regardless of the quality of their environment. At the same time, Group D children, with the broadest reaction range, have the greatest opportunity to benefit from environmental enrichment.

Note, too, that the reaction ranges overlap. This means that genotypes or environments can have a stronger effect over the other. It also means that knowing the phenotypes (in this case I.Q. scores) does not tell us why two children differ in that trait. The differences could be genetic in origin (assuming that the children experienced equally supportive environments), they could be environmental in origin (if children with similar

FIGURE 3.5 Reaction Range

In this model, RR stands for reaction range. Children with each genotype for intelligence (as measured by I.Q. tests) achieve fuller potential as the favorableness of the environment increases for the development of this trait.

SOURCE Adapted from I.I. Gottesman. (1974). Developmental genetics and ontogenetic psychology: Overdue détente and propositions from a matchmaker. In A. Pick (Ed.), *Minnesota Symposia on Child Psychology* (Vol. 8, p. 60). Minneapolis: University of Minnesota Press.

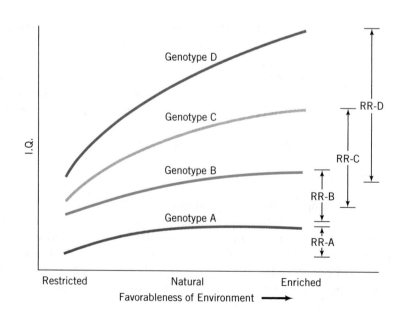

genotypes grew up in different environments), or they could be a combination of both. Whatever the outcome, development is always a function of both genes and environment, and differences among people can result from either or both of these sources.

Gene–Environment Correlations

The reaction range model is a useful way to convey the dual importance of genes and environments, but it does not go far enough. It assumes that the pairing of genotypes and environments is random, such that children with different genetic potentials are equally likely to experience the full range of different environments. This is not the case, however. The genes children inherit and the environments they experience are often correlated in that they act together to push development in the same direction. In the case of intelligence, for example, children with a high genetic potential (Group D) are likely to have parents who are themselves more intelligent, and such parents are more likely to provide an intellectually stimulating environment. Such children therefore receive a double boost: Both genes and environment promote the development of intellectual skills.

This **gene–environment correlation** can be passive, evocative, or active (Scarr, 1992, 1993; Scarr & McCartney, 1983). The example just discussed is passive in the sense that the child does nothing to bring it about; rather, parents provide both the genes and the environment. As another example, consider the child of parents who both love music. The parents will pass along both the genes that contribute to a love of music and an environment (e.g., music playing in the home, provision of music lessons and musical instruments) that nurtures an appreciation for music.

As children get older, the gene–environment correlation changes. Children now do things that evoke certain responses from their parents and others. For example, a child who speaks and reads early—behaviors that likely have some genetic basis—may prompt parents to provide a rich language environment, including books, storytelling, and educational games. The child's genetic predispositions help create a compatible environment.

Finally, as children gain more independence, they actively participate in producing environments that suit them. That is, children, on their own, can seek out the particular environments that best fit their interests and talents—such as the library, gym, or rock concert. They can engage in what Scarr labels *niche-picking*—finding the niches that fit their genetic predispositions.

The notion of active gene–environment correlations leads to an interesting prediction. In the traditional view, genes are most important early in development, with the environment assuming an increasingly greater role as experience has more chance to operate. In contrast, the active-correlation model suggests that genetic influences might actually grow stronger with age, as children become better able to recruit the environments their genes bias them toward.

Two findings from adoption studies provide support for this prediction (Turkheimer & Waldron, 2000; Bouchard & McGue, 2003). First, adoptive siblings (that is, unrelated children growing up in the same home) are more similar to one another in early childhood than they are by the time they reach adolescence, even though by adolescence they have had many more years of living together in the same home. Second, with age, the psychological characteristics of an adopted child become increasingly similar to those of the biological mother and less similar to those of the adoptive mother, again despite the fact that the older child has spent more time in the environment of the adoptive home. These findings do not mean that by adolescence the environment has become unimportant and everything is genetic. Rather, these findings presumably occur because parents generally control children's environments at younger ages, but as children grow older they are increasingly able to choose their own environments and experiences, thus permitting their genes to operate in a more active way to influence their development. Because adoptive siblings have different genes, they seek out and are influenced by different environments.

Gene–environment correlation
Situation in which genes and environment affect development similarly because the genes the child receives from the parents are compatible with the environment the parents provide (passive); because the child evokes environmental effects consistent with genetic predispositions (evocative); or because children seek out experiences and shape their environments that suit them (active).

Questions for Thought and Discussion
Are you aware of "niche-picking" during your childhood or in your life now? To what extent do you seek out environments that best fit your genetic predispositions?

How could we determine the roles of genetic and environmental influences in this child's gift? How would the reaction range model explain it? How would gene–environment correlation models explain it? What role might the child play in this behavioral development? (CAMERA PRESS/Retna)

Nonshared Environment

Siblings, of course, are similar in many ways, as the results from family studies consistently show. These similarities are not surprising, given that siblings share both many of the same genes (50 percent) and the same family environment. But family studies also confirm what any parent of two or more children has probably always known: Siblings are not identical, and in some instances they are very different. How can this be, given that siblings share both nature and nurture?

Part of the answer is that siblings share only part of their nature. Although 50 percent of siblings' genes are the same, 50 percent are different, and these genetic differences contribute to differences in development. The rest of the answer is that most siblings apparently experience surprisingly different environments—their nurture.

Environment operates primarily to make the children within a family *different*. This model of gene–environment interaction emphasizes the **nonshared environment** as the source of developmental differences among children (Loehlin, Neiderhiser, & Reiss, 2005; Plomin, 2000; Reiss et al., 2000). Children experience their environment differently, and parents treat children differently in the family. Children also interpret and react to the same family events differently. These differences arise in part from children's different genetic predispositions. In addition, the effects of the nonshared environment are stronger in higher risk environments, that is, families with lower socioeconomic status, greater family chaos, or greater maternal depression (Asbury, Dunn, Pike, & Plomin, 2003). Thus, once again, we

Nonshared environment
A concept used in behavior genetics to refer to aspects of the environment that children experience differently, leading to individual differences.

Q**uestions for Thought and Discussion**
In what ways did you and your siblings live in a nonshared environment? How do you think your own and your siblings' experiences contributed to differences in your development? How might the experiences you provide your children lead them down different life paths?

Siblings growing up in the same household often have very different personalities and interests. How does the nonshared environment model help to explain this phenomenon? (Radius Images/Alamy Images)

TABLE 3.4 A Contextual Model for Gene–Environment Interaction

Child inherits a gene for musical talent from parents

Family and school settings
- Child observes and models parents' musical ability.
- Child's musical abilities are also encouraged in the music classes that the parents find for the child, beginning in the toddler years.
- Parents interact with child's music teachers and supports at home those musical activities learned in school settings.

Socioeconomic status
- Parents' work environment influences child's experience through:
  - Living in an affluent neighborhood that offers multiple opportunities for exposure to and participation in musical resources within the community.
  - Time and availability that parent has to spend with child in musical activities each day.
- Larger cultural and societal influences
  - Child is exposed to a variety of musical activities valued in the larger culture, with different groups valuing different activities; for example, playing in a rock band is more highly valued by peers, whereas the child's parents and music teachers more highly value classical music and orchestras.

see that children's genes influence the environments they receive, just as the environment itself affects how those genes are expressed. Nature and nurture interact with one another.

Table 3.4 suggests how the relationships between genetic and environmental factors might be conceptualized in terms of an ecological or contextual model.

Learning Objective 3.3: *How do genes and environment interact to influence the development of behavior?*

1. What is meant by the range of reaction? What does it tell us about the interaction of genes and environment?
2. What are gene–environment correlations? How do they help us understand the interaction of genes and environment?
3. What is meant by nonshared environment?

✔ *Test Your Mastery...*

Genetic Disorders

Given the billions of sperm cells generated by the male and the 2 million or so ova generated by the female, it is not surprising that genetic imperfections sometimes occur. These variations, or **mutations**, are the driving force behind evolution. When the "errors" turn out to be adaptive, they result in improvements in the species or the creation of a new species. The overwhelming majority of mutations, however, are maladaptive. Through a natural screening process in humans, about 90 percent of all genetic abnormalities result in miscarriage rather than live births. So although more than 10,000 single-gene disorders have been identified in humans (McKusick, 1998), only about 1 percent of all babies have detectable chromosomal abnormalities.

Some abnormalities are entirely hereditary and are passed along according to the same principles of inheritance that determine eye color and nose shape. Other genetic disorders are not inherited but may result from errors during cell division in meiosis. Chromosomes and the genes they carry can also be made abnormal by radiation, drugs, viruses, chemicals, and perhaps even the aging process. Table 3.5 presents some examples of genetic disorders.

Learning Objective 3.4
Describe different types of genetic disorders and their impact on child development.

Mutations
Sudden and permanent changes in genetic material.

TABLE 3.5 Examples of Genetic Disorders

DISORDER	CAUSE	INCIDENCE (U.S.)	DESCRIPTION
Huntington's disease	Dominant gene on chromosome 4	1 in 18,000 to 25,000	Deterioration of the nervous system, uncontrollable muscular movements, disordered brain function, death
Neurofibromatosis (Type 1)	Dominant gene on chromosome 17	1 in 3,000	Discoloration and tumors of the skin, heightened probability of learning difficulties and mild retardation
Tay-Sachs disease	Recessive gene on chromosome 15	1 in 3,600 for Ashkenazi Jews	Nervous system deterioration, blindness, paralysis, early death
Phenylketonuria	Recessive gene on chromosome 12	1 in 10,000	If untreated, severe mental retardation, hyperactivity, convulsions
Sickle-cell anemia	Recessive gene on chromosome 11	1 in 500 for African Americans	Oxygen deprivation, severe pain, tissue damage, early death
Cystic fibrosis	Recessive gene on chromosome 7	1 in 2,500	Breathing and digestive problems, infection of lungs, early death
Hemophilia	Recessive gene on X chromosome	1 in 4,000 to 7,000 males	Blood does not clot normally. Can result in severe internal bleeding
Duchenne muscular dystrophy	Recessive gene on X chromosome	1 in 3,000 to 5,000 males	Degenerative muscle disease, resulting in balance problems and loss of ability to walk, usually during middle childhood
Red-green color blindness	Recessive gene on X chromosome	8 in 100 males	Inability to distinguish shades of red and green
Down syndrome	Extra chromosome at pair 21	1 in 1,000	Moderate to severe mental retardation, distinctive physical features, immune deficiencies, heart defects

Hereditary Autosomal Disorders

Just as a child may inherit genes for straight or curly hair, abnormal genes can be passed along to offspring according to Mendel's principles. Whether defective genes are expressed in the phenotype depends on whether they are dominant or recessive.

Dominant Traits Dominant genes that cause severe problems typically disappear from the species, because the affected people usually do not live to reproduce. In a few cases, however, severely disabling dominant genes are passed on because they do not become active until relatively late in life. People with these genes may reproduce before they know that they have inherited the disease. An example is *Huntington's disease*. The age of onset of this disease varies, but it typically strikes people between about 30 and 40 years of age. Quite suddenly, the nervous system begins to deteriorate, resulting in uncontrollable muscular movements and disordered brain function. Until recently, the children of a person stricken with Huntington's had no way of knowing whether they also carried the gene and could pass it on to their offspring. Late in 1983, scientists discovered which chromosome carries the gene for Huntington's, and 10 years later they located the exact gene responsible for the disease and learned how to tell whether a person has inherited it, thus allowing families and individuals to evaluate their risk for transmitting the disease to their own children (Morell, 1993; Taylor, 2004). About 30,000 Americans have been diagnosed with this genetic disorder, which can be traced back to a dominant mutation in a Venezuelan woman in the 1800s.

Recessive Traits Like Mendel's purple flowers, which did not reveal the white flower gene they carried, parents can carry problem recessive genes that have no effect on them. If both parents carry such a gene, they can combine in the offspring to produce the disorder (just as two dark-haired parents can produce a blond child). It has been estimated that on average, each of us carries four potentially lethal genes as recessive traits (Scarr & Kidd,

1983), but because most of these dangerous genes are rare, it is unlikely that we will mate with someone who has a matching recessive gene. Even then, the probability of a child's receiving both recessive genes is only one in four.

Some diseases carried by recessive genes produce errors of metabolism, which cause the body to mismanage sugars, fats, proteins, or carbohydrates. With *Tay-Sachs disease*, the nervous system disintegrates because of the lack of an enzyme that breaks down fats in brain cells. The fatty deposits swell, and the brain cells die. Tay-Sachs disease is rare in the general population, occurring in only 1 in 300,000 births. However, among Ashkenazi Jews, who account for more than 90 percent of the Jewish population of the United States, it occurs in 1 in every 3,600 births. Infants afflicted with the disease appear normal at birth and through their first half-year. Then, at about 8 months of age, they usually become extremely listless, and often by the end of their first year, they are blind. Most stricken children die by the age of 4. At present, there is no treatment for the disorder.

A more encouraging story is that of *phenylketonuria* (PKU), a problem involving the body's management of protein. This disease occurs when the body fails to produce an enzyme that breaks down phenylalanine, an amino acid. As a result, abnormal amounts of the substance accumulate in the blood and harm the developing brain cells. Infants with PKU are typically healthy at birth but, if untreated, begin to deteriorate after a few months of life as the blood's phenylalanine level mounts. Periodic convulsions and seizures may occur, and the children usually become severely retarded.

The understanding of how PKU disrupts normal metabolism resulted in one of the early victories of science over genetic abnormalities. Discovery of the mechanism of the disease led to the development of special diets, which are low in phenylalanine and thus prevent its accumulation in the bloodstream. Children placed on these special diets shortly after birth remain at risk for some cognitive deficits (Diamond et al., 1997). Most, however, achieve at least close to normal intellectual functioning, in marked contrast to the devastating effects in the absence of treatment. Because of the dramatic results of timely intervention in this disease, newborn babies are now routinely tested for PKU through a simple blood-test procedure. The lesson in the PKU story is that genes are not necessarily destiny. How or whether a gene's influence is played out can depend on interactions with the environment.

A recessive genetic abnormality that does not involve metabolism is *sickle-cell anemia* (SCA). People who have inherited a gene for this recessive trait from both parents have

These scanning electron micrographs show red blood cells from normal individuals (left) and from individuals with sickle-cell anemia (right). An African American newborn has a 1 in 12 chance of being a carrier of the disease, and a 1 in 500 chance of developing the disease. In most states babies are automatically screened for SCA at birth. Today in many cases serious illness or death can be prevented through treatments ranging from antibiotics to blood transfusions. (Bill Longcore/Science Source/Photo Researchers)

red blood cells that do not contain normal hemoglobin, a protein that carries oxygen throughout the body. Instead, abnormal hemoglobin causes their red blood cells to thicken and elongate. These "sickled" cells tend to clog small blood vessels instead of easily passing through them as normal cells do, thus preventing blood from reaching parts of the body. An unusual oxygen demand, such as that brought on by physical exertion, may cause the sufferer to experience severe pain, tissue damage, and even death because of the inadequate supply of oxygen.

About 8 percent of African Americans carry the recessive gene for SCA. Among the Bamba, a tribe in Africa, the incidence has been reported to be as high as 39 percent. Such a high rate of occurrence seems surprising from a Darwinian perspective, which holds that nonadaptive traits are weeded out through natural selection, because individuals who have two genes for SCA frequently die young and produce few children. How, then, could such a characteristic be preserved through evolution? The answer reveals a rare instance in which a gene is maladaptive for one purpose but adaptive for another.

Scientists have noted that the Bamba live in areas where the incidence of malaria is high, but Bamba children who carry the SCA gene are resistant to malaria. This resistance allows more carriers of SCA to grow up and have children, even though one in four will have SCA. Apparently, the negative effects of malaria on reproduction are greater than the negative effects of carrying the SCA gene.

The Old Order Amish and Mennonite communities of Pennsylvania, Ohio, and Indiana provide an interesting case study in population genetics. The Old Order communities in this region were originally settled in the early 1700s by a relatively small number (about 250) of Swiss families. In the roughly 14 generations since then, there has been relatively little movement of newcomers into these communities. Growth has occurred primarily through large family sizes, in conjunction with relatively high rates of intermarriage among Old Order families. One result of this genetic homogeneity has been the emergence of high incidences of otherwise rare genetic disorders. Between 1988 and 2002, researchers identified 39 heritable disorders among the Old Order Amish and 23 among the Mennonites (Morton, Morton, Strauss, et al., 2003). These include two forms of dwarfism and several metabolic disorders. For 18 disorders regularly seen at an area clinic, incidences are quite high: 1 in 250 or 1 in 500 births compared to 1 out of several thousand in the general population. Researchers and physicians who work in these communities emphasize that "the burden of genetic disease is high and the need for specialized and comprehensive care is essential to the health community" (Morton et al., 2003, p. 7). Populations such as the Old Order Amish and Mennonites provide a unique opportunity to study the biology of rare genetic disorders and also point to the importance of genetic diversity in maintaining the health of a population.

Many new findings are on the horizon of genetic research. Within the last few years, investigators have discovered the gene for a type of Alzheimer's disease that runs in families. They also have located the genes for cystic fibrosis and for amyotrophic lateral sclerosis (ALS), also known as Lou Gehrig's disease. The genetic locus of many other diseases may soon be discovered as part of the Human Genome Project, discussed in the Research & Society box.

X-Linked Disorders

As can be seen in the photograph, the Y chromosome is only about a third the size of the X chromosome. This size difference between the chromosomes has implications for the transmission of certain kinds of disorders called **x-linked disorders**. One result of the larger X is that it contains more genetic information. As a consequence, some genes that travel on the X chromosome do not have a corresponding allele on the Y chromosome. In a female, if there is a recessive allele on one X chromosome, there is a good chance that the corresponding allele on her other X chromosome will override its expression. Males

X-linked disorders

Disorders that travel on the X chromosome, leaving males more vulnerable to their expression.

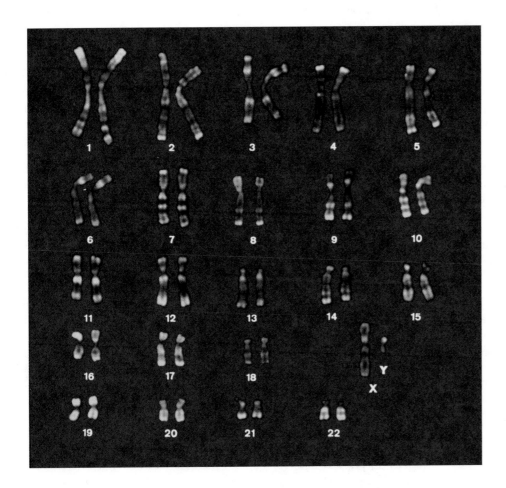

Karyotyping is a process that allows researchers and doctors to take pictures of the 23 pairs of human chromosomes. The 23rd pair consists of the chromosomes that determine a person's sex. As you can see here, the X chromosome is two to three times larger than the Y chromosome. What implications does this have? (Phototake Inc./ Phototake)

have no such protection and are thus more vulnerable than females to recessive disorders that travel only on the X chromosome.

An example of an x-linked disorder is the allele responsible for normal blood clotting. A recessive version of this allele causes *hemophilia*, a serious bleeding disorder caused by low levels or complete absence of a blood protein essential for clotting. Women, who are likely to have a normal version of this allele on their other X chromosome, are less likely to have the disorder, although they can pass the defective allele on to their own children (see Figures 3.6 and 3.7). Men, who do not have a second protective allele, will have the disorder if they inherit the recessive allele from their mother. Other x-linked disorders include *Duchenne muscular dystrophy* and *red-green color blindness*.

Questions for Thought
and Discussion

What do you think are some possible future outcomes of the Human Genome Project? What ethical issues might the new knowledge and associated technology raise?

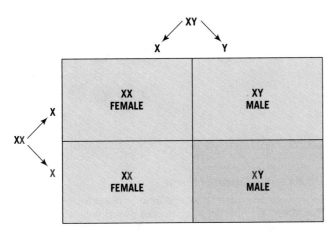

FIGURE 3.6 Transmission of Hemophilia through Carrier Mother and Normal Father

The transmission of hemophilia is a classic example of the x-linked inheritance pattern.

XY = Affected Male
XY = Normal Male
XX = Carrier Female

X = Normal Allele from Mother
X = Affected Allele from Mother

BOX 3.1 The Human Genome Project

If scientists knew where each of the genes was on the 46 human chromosomes, they would be in a better position to learn what each of these genes does. The potential benefits would be enormous. Health scientists, for example, would possess the tools to identify defective genes that produce many inherited diseases. In some cases, these defects could be detected even before people showed their effects, and preventive treatment might be possible. Locating the genes on the chromosomes is referred to as *mapping the genome.*

But such mapping is only one step toward understanding. If scientists knew the exact sequence of nucleotides in each gene, they would be able to specify how the gene is defective. This knowledge might, in turn, make it possible to correct the defective sequence. Identifying the sequence of the 3 billion nucleotides in the DNA molecule is called *sequencing the genome.*

In 1989 the United States launched the Human Genome Project, headed by James Watson, one of the discoverers of the DNA molecule. The purpose of the research was to achieve the dual aims just described: to map and sequence human DNA.

This effort has been likened to the Manhattan Project, which produced the atomic bomb, or the Apollo program, which placed the first human being on the moon (Watson, 1990). Like these predecessors, the Human Genome Project ranks as both one of the most challenging and most important scientific efforts ever undertaken.

It also ranks as one of the most successful. Initially, progress was slow, and midway through the intended time period only 2 percent of the sequence had been completed. Two developments, however, resulted in a remarkable scientific success story. One was that the publicly funded effort was joined by work in private laboratories, most notably Celera Genomics. The second was the development of new technologies for sequencing large amounts of DNA rapidly and automatically. As a result, a "working draft" of the genome, approximately 90 percent complete, was published in February 2001 (Genome International Sequencing Consortium, 2001; Human Genome Project, 2001). Publication of the complete sequence followed in 2003, two years ahead of the original schedule.

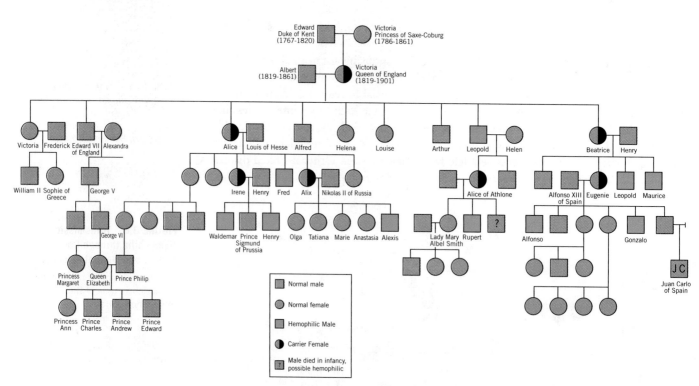

FIGURE 3.7 Transmission of Hemophilia across Thrones of Europe

In the 19th century, thrones across Europe were devastated by hemophilia when Queen Victoria of Britain turned out to be a carrier of the disorder. When her carrier daughters married princes in other countries, the result was hemophilia among several European royal families, including Russia, Spain, and Prussia (Kimball, 1983).

The Human Genome Project is already yielding many of the benefits for the treatment and prevention of genetically related problems. It is now possible to screen for the presence of genes associated with hundreds of different diseases or disorders. Such genetic testing can occur at various points in life, ranging from prenatal screening of newborns to tests for susceptibility to late-onset diseases in middle-aged or elderly adults. Such testing can also inform prospective parents of possible genetic problems in their offspring (Khoury, McCabe, & McCabe, 2003). In many instances, necessary treatment can begin earlier than was formerly the case, and treatment can benefit from greater understanding of underlying causes. Although *gene therapy—* that is, surgical correction of defective genes—is still limited, some successes have been reported, and it seems likely that major advances will soon be forthcoming. The project is also yielding some surprises for scientists. Perhaps the most surprising finding is that we have far fewer genes than was once believed—perhaps only 25,000 to 30,000, in contrast to previous estimates of as many as 140,000. This number is about the same as that for the mouse, and only about twice that for the fruit fly.

Clearly, it is not the sheer number of genes that defines a species, but rather their specific nature and specific combination. Today, for example, research on the human genome has identified specific genes for other diverse phenotypic outcomes in human development, such as intelligence, language, aggression, neuroticism, dyslexia, homosexuality, and sensation seeking. Because of the implications for understanding our species, comparative work is essential to the Human Genome Project, mapping not only the human genome but the genomes of other organisms as well. Discovering the 2 percent of our DNA that we do not share with chimpanzees will tell us something about what it means to be human.

Structural Defects in the Chromosome

Genetic abnormalities such as Tay-Sachs disease and PKU are passed along according to the regular principles of inheritance. But genetically based problems also may result from physical changes in chromosomes. These changes can occur during meiosis in one of the parents, and they can involve any of the 22 autosomes or the sex chromosome. As mentioned, environmental hazards can also damage chromosomes.

Down syndrome occurs in about one in 1,000 live births. Individuals with Down syndrome have 47 chromosomes instead of 46. In addition to their distinctive appearance, children with Down syndrome often have congenital heart defects and other medical problems. Today their average life expectancy in the United States is 55. (Bill Aaron/PhotoEdit)

Autosomal Defects One of the most frequently observed effects of structural abnormality is *Down syndrome*, named after John Langdon H. Down, the physician who first described it. In Down syndrome, one of the pairs of chromosomes has a third member. Children born with this disorder typically have cheerful dispositions and are friendly and outgoing. They also, however, are moderately to severely retarded; they tend to have poor muscle tone and problems with expressive language; and they have a distinctive appearance that includes a flattened face and folded eyelids. The cause of Down syndrome was identified in 1957, marking the first time a human disease had been directly linked to a chromosomal disorder.

The likelihood that a couple will produce a child with Down syndrome increases dramatically with the age of the mother. Fewer than 1 in 1,000 babies of mothers under age 30 have Down syndrome. The risk rises to about 1 in 350–400 live births at age 35 and to about 1 in 100 at age 40 (Hook & Lindsjo, 1978).

Disorders of the Sex Chromosomes Normally, a child receives either two X chromosomes or one X and one Y. Occasionally, the process does not work as it should. When this happens, the embryo may have an unusual arrangement of sex chromosomes.

One such abnormality occurs when an ovum is fertilized by a sperm that carries no sex chromosome at all, or when the sperm provides an X and the ovum has no sex chromosome. In either case, the resulting embryo has only an X. In the few cases in which the fetus survives and develops completely, the child displays an array of abnormalities referred to as *Turner's syndrome*. At birth, the baby is female in appearance, but the ovaries have already disappeared and do not produce the hormones necessary for the sex differentiation process to continue. As a result, women with Turner's syndrome do not develop breasts or menstruate unless they are given hormone therapy (El Abd, Turk, & Hill, 1995; Ross, Zinn, & McCauley, 2000).

Another chromosomal problem occurs when an egg carrying two X chromosomes is fertilized by a sperm carrying a Y chromosome, producing *Klinefelter's syndrome*. The presence of the Y chromosome causes the child to have a male appearance, but he is somewhat feminized because his male hormone levels are low. Men with Klinefelter's syndrome have long arms, very little body hair, an underdeveloped penis, and sometimes overdeveloped breasts (Mandoki et al., 1991).

Disorders of the Sex Chromosomes			
Turner's Syndrome	XO, Female Affects 1 out of 2,500 women.	No ovaries, short stature, may have heart, kidney, thyroid, or skeletal problems.	Normal life with growth hormone and estrogen replacement therapy. Fertility specialists can help with bearing children.
Klinefelter's Syndrome	XXY, Male Affects 1 out of 700 men.	Underdeveloped penis and testicles, low testosterone levels, enlarged breasts, increased risk of learning disabilities.	Normal life with hormone therapy (testosterone). Fertility specialists can help with fathering children.
XYY Syndrome	XYY, Male Affects 1 out of 1,000 men.	Tall stature, learning problems.	Normal life. Able to conceive children.
Fragile X Syndrome	XY or XX Population estimates vary.	Mental retardation and social anxiety problems, with males more severely affected than females.	Impaired functioning.

A third chromosomal abnormality occurs when the sperm provides two Y chromosomes. The males produced when this occurs have large body builds and often have learning disabilities, or delayed speech and language skills (Owen, 1979). It was once thought that these men were more likely than others to become criminals or to display antisocial behavior. More recent research, however, has not supported this contention (Ike, 2000).

A fourth disorder of the sex chromosomes is *fragile X syndrome*, a condition caused by an abnormal gene on the X chromosome (Hagerman, 1996). Fragile X syndrome is second only to Down syndrome as a genetically based cause of mental retardation. Boys are more likely to be affected than are girls. The majority of males who inherit the gene display retardation and other physical and behavioral symptoms.

Genetic Counseling

Rapid progress in genetics research has made it possible for people to exert some control over the incidence of genetic disorders. **Genetic counseling** involves a range of activities focused on determining the likelihood that a couple will give birth to a child with a genetic disorder. This section considers the kinds of counseling available to prospective parents prior to pregnancy. Chapter 4 discusses the further kinds of information that become available once a pregnancy has occurred.

Any couple or prospective parent can consult with a genetic counselor. Having a family history of some genetic disease is a reason to seek counseling. In some instances, a prospective parent may already know that he or she is a carrier for a disease. More commonly, one or more relatives is known or suspected to have had a genetic disorder. The more closely related the relative, the more serious are the implications for a couple considering parenthood. Most serious of all is having already given birth to a child or children who were born with a genetic disease.

Another risk factor for genetic disorders is membership in an ethnic group that is known to have a heightened probability of inheriting a specific disorder. As mentioned earlier, for example, Tay-Sachs disease is considerably more common among Ashkenazi Jews than it is among other ethnic groups, and sickle-cell anemia is more prevalent among African Americans than other groups. If only one parent is a member of the group in question, the increased risk is not necessarily great: Because these are recessive disorders, the child must inherit the problematic gene from both parents. If both parents are members of the ethnic group, the risk increases substantially.

Genetic counseling
The practice of advising prospective parents about genetic diseases and the likelihood that they might pass on defective genetic traits to their offspring.

Links to Related Material
In Chapter 4, you will learn more about genetic testing that is available once a woman has become pregnant.

What various reasons might this couple have for seeking genetic counseling? If you intend to become a parent, do you plan to be screened before trying to conceive? Why or why not? (Michelle Del Guercio/Photo Researchers, Inc.)

Advanced age is a third possible reason to seek genetic counseling (see Table 3.5). Down syndrome is not the only condition related to parental age, however. Most chromosomal defects become more likely as the parents of either sex grow older (Snidjers & Nicolaides, 1996). The father's age is indicated in the genetic disorder *achondroplasia*, which is characterized by bone defects and dwarfism. The probability of achondroplasia increases tenfold when the father is in his 40s or older at the time of conception (Friedman, 1981).

A Counseling Session Genetic counseling can take many forms, depending on the specific situation under discussion. Generally, however, discussions with a counselor proceed through four phases (Croyle, 2000; Shiloh, 1996): history taking, genetic testing, discussion, and decision making.

1. *Collection of the relevant family history.* The counselor will attempt to obtain as detailed a medical history as possible, concentrating especially on disorders that are known to have a genetic basis.

2. *Genetic testing of the prospective parents.* Whether testing occurs depends on what the family history suggests and also, of course, on the wishes of the couple. If the decision is made to test, then samples of DNA will be obtained from bodily tissues or blood and will be tested for the presence of defective genes. It is now possible to identify the genes for more than 900 genetic diseases, including all those listed in Table 3.5.

3. *Discussion of results of testing.* In most cases, the counselor will convey probabilities rather than certainties. Even if no problems are detected in the genetic testing, current technology cannot guarantee that the baby will be disease- or defect-free. And if problems *are* detected, there is still a chance that the baby will be born without problems. As you have seen, the probability that the baby will inherit the disorder when parents are carriers of a defective gene depends on the type of gene involved. If one parent is a carrier of a defective dominant gene that is autosomal, the chances are one in two that their baby will inherit the disorder. If both parents are carriers of the same defective recessive gene, the chances are one in four that their baby will be affected.

4. *Decisions about how to proceed.* Although the counselor may assist in this process, he or she will not make the decision or argue for a particular course of action. The counselor's role is to ensure that all of the relevant information has been made available. The couple must decide what to do.

Population Screening

Population screening efforts have been directed at ethnic groups known to be at heightened risk for a genetic disorder, such as African Americans and sickle-cell disease. The goal is to identify and to counsel as many carriers of the disease gene as possible, and thus to reduce the incidence of the disorder in future generations (Khoury, McCabe, & McCabe, 2003). Other groups and disorders that have been screened for in this fashion include Tay-Sach disease among Ashkenazi Jews; thalassemia, a blood disorder, among people of Mediterranean descent; and cystic fibrosis among whites of northern European origin.

In some cases, population screening has produced dramatic effects. A widespread screening program initiated in 1970 eventually identified more than 50,000 carriers of the Tay-Sachs gene, including 1,400 couples in which both partners were carriers (Kaback, 2000). Counseling and (in cases of pregnancy) prenatal screening followed, and it is estimated that the births of over 600 infants with the fatal disease were prevented. Overall, the incidence of the disease was reduced by 90 percent.

Questions for Thought and Discussion

Who should have access to or control genetic information about individuals? families, physicians, employers, insurance companies? To what uses should genetic information be put? Do you think there should be limits to those uses?

✔ *Test Your Mastery...*

Learning Objective 3.4: *Describe different types of genetic disorders and their impact on child development.*

1. How are genetic autosomal disorders transmitted?
2. What are some examples of dominant and recessive autosomal disorders?
3. How are x-linked disorders transmitted, and why do they affect males more than females?

4. What are some examples of x-linked disorders?
5. What are some examples of disorders caused by defects of the autosomes?
6. What are some examples of disorders caused by defects of the sex chromosomes?
7. What are genetic counseling and population screening?

Pathways to Parenthood

One important biological context to consider with regard to child development is parental age, particularly the age of the mother. In the past decade, births to older women have increased dramatically, owing in part to societal changes that have led many women to delay childbearing until their careers are established. In 2002, nearly 40 percent of live births were to women over the age of 30, and births to women age 35 and older continue to rise (U.S. Department of Health and Human Services, 2004). Because fertility in women drops dramatically after the age of 35, this demographic trend in delayed childbearing is associated with an increase in women seeking alternative paths to parenthood. What are some of these pathways, and what effect do they have on child development? In addition, how do they challenge traditional assumptions regarding the centrality of genetic relatedness to family membership? In this next section, we will consider some of the different ways that families today are created. In some of these methods, a genetic connection between parent and child is present; in others, it is not. The prevalence of alternative paths to parenthood has created a variety of family contexts in which children today may grow up. Awareness of the variety of these contexts, and the ways in which they may challenge traditional assumptions regarding genetic relatedness between parents and children, is essential to all who will be working with children and their families.

Assisted Reproduction

Beginning with the birth of the first "test-tube baby" in 1978, a variety of technologies have been developed to assist couples or individuals to achieve parenthood in ways other than the traditional approach. Such techniques are referred to as **assisted reproductive technologies (ARTs)** (Pasch, 2001). These new technologies have proved a blessing for millions of people who would once have remained childless. But their use also raises a number of difficult questions.

A variety of reasons may underlie the decision of a couple or an individual to seek out an assisted reproductive technology. A woman may wish to conceive a baby without a male partner, for example, or a woman's health may prevent her from going through pregnancy herself. By far the most common candidates for ART, however, are couples who are experiencing infertility. The definition of **infertility** used by health care professionals is failure to conceive after a year of sexual intercourse without the use of contraceptives (Office of Technology Assessment, 1988). In the United States, about 10 percent of couples experience infertility (Diamond et al., 1999; Fishell, Dow, & Thornton, 2000). What are some of the reproductive technologies available to parents, and what effect, if any, do they have on child development?

Louise Brown, the world's first test-tube baby, was conceived by a process known as *in vitro* **fertilization (IVF)**. Approximately 1 percent of births in Western societies now occur through IVF, accounting for more than a million births since the inception of the procedure (Van Balen, 1998). A 1995 article in *Scientific American* identified *in vitro* fertilization as one of the most important discoveries of the last 150 years, putting it on the same list with polio vaccine, radiography, cars, and computers (Rennie, 1995).

With IVF, the woman first receives fertility drugs to increase the production of ova, after which mature eggs are removed and fertilized in a laboratory dish. In the majority of instances, the sperm is provided by her husband or male partner, although this is not always the case. Within 24 hours one or more fertilized ova are inserted into the womb. If the procedure is successful, the result is a normal pregnancy. The average success rate

Learning Objective 3.5
Describe alternative paths to parenthood.

Assisted reproductive technologies (ARTs)
Techniques, such as *in vitro* fertilization or donor insemination, intended to help couples or individuals achieve a pregnancy through means other than sexual intercourse.

Infertility
Difficulty in achieving a pregnancy, defined in medicine as failure to conceive after a year of sexual intercourse without the use of contraceptives.

***In vitro* fertilization**
An assisted reproductive technology in which a mature ovum is removed and fertilized by sperm in a laboratory dish.

These children were born as an outcome of *in vitro* fertilization. What is the IVF procedure? How does IVF compare with other assisted reproduction procedures? (John Howard/Photo Researchers, Inc.)

for IVF is 29 percent (ASRM, 2005). Although this figure might seem disappointing, especially in light of the cost (typically about $12,000), it is higher than the 20 percent probability of conception in any given month with sexual intercourse.

In vitro fertilization is just one of a number of ART options. When male infertility is the problem (or when the woman does not have a male partner), *donor insemination* is sometimes used: insemination of the woman with sperm from a donor male. In such cases, the child is genetically related to the mother only. With *egg donation* (a less common procedure), a donor female is used, and the child is not genetically related to the mother but may be related to the father. With *surrogacy*, another woman bears the child for the eventual parents; the child may be related to both parents (if both eggs and sperm were donated) or only the father (if insemination was used).

As you can see, the genetic relation between parent and child varies across different ARTs, and it can also vary across different uses of a particular technology. With *in vitro* fertilization, for example, it is possible for the child to have just two parents with whom he or she has the usual genetic relationship: half the genes from the father (because he provided the sperm) and half the genes from the mother (because she provided the ovum). It is also possible (though certainly rare) to have six potential parents: the man and woman who donate the sperm and egg, the surrogate mother in whom they are implanted and who gives birth to the child, the surrogate's husband, and the parents who then rear the child.

In an unusual case in California, this is exactly what happened. In this case, John and Luanne Buzzanca entered into a surrogacy agreement with another married couple, Pamela and Randy. Pamela was to be implanted with an embryo created with anonymously donated sperm and ovum. John and Luanne were the intended parents, who were to assume responsibility for the child's care from birth. However, approximately one month before the child, named Jaycee, was born, John petitioned for divorce. Although Luanne claimed she was the lawful mother, John refused to pay child support, asserting that he was not genetically related to Jaycee and therefore was not responsible in any way toward her. In a complicated history, Pamela and Randy at one time considered filing for custody but ultimately disclaimed any legal rights to Jaycee. In 1997 the California court that heard the case decided that none of the six people who participated in Jaycee's creation were in fact her legal parents, including John and Luanne Buzzanca.

Who are Jaycee's parents? In 1998, when Jaycee was three years old, a California court finally ruled that John and Luanne Buzzanca were her legal parents. This case provided

Some Methods of Assisted Reproduction
- IVF or *in vitro* fertilization
- Insemination of the mother with donor sperm
- Implantation with a donor egg or embryo
- Use of a surrogate mother to carry the developing child to term

important precedent regarding the legal status of children born through donor sperm, eggs, embryos, or surrogacy arrangements. In this case, it was decided that the intention to parent is an important legal factor that carries with it rights and obligations when donors or surrogates are used to help create a family.

Effects of ART on Child Development Do these new methods of conception have any negative effects? Concerns have been of two sorts. One concern has been with possible physical effects. Before Louise Brown was born, there was no way to know for certain whether babies conceived in nontraditional ways would develop normally. In fact they do, a conclusion that applies not only to IVF births but also to ART births more generally. Such babies, however, are at greater than average risk for preterm birth and low birth weight. Use of ARTs also increases the likelihood of multiple births. *In vitro* fertilization results in twins in almost a third of the cases and in triplets 5 percent of the time (ASRM, 2005).

What about possible psychological effects? Concerns here have revolved around the unusual nature of the family composition in many ART families. In some instances, only one parent is genetically related to the child, and in some instances neither is. These children are sometimes told about the circumstances of their birth, and sometimes they are not. Will normal parent-child relations and normal child development occur under such circumstances?

Most of the available evidence concerns IVF families, and conclusions about other ARTs must therefore be made with caution (Golombok & MacCallum, 2003). To date, however, there is no evidence that conception through assisted reproduction is associated with any negative outcomes in child development. Indeed, when differences between ART families and comparison families are found, they tend to be in the other direction. In some instances, for example, IVF parents have been found to be warmer and more emotionally involved with their children (Golombok et al., 1995).

This conclusion is perhaps not surprising. It seems likely that parents who must seek special methods of conception will be heavily invested in the job of parenting. Genetic ties between parents and children may not be as important as the parents' strong commitment to parenthood.

Adoption

In contrast to assisted reproduction, adoption is an option that has long been available to couples wanting a child, although its frequency and form have varied across time periods and cultural settings. It is, of course, an option that fulfills two needs: that of adults who wish to have a child and that of children who would otherwise grow up without parents. Until recently, the United States government did not keep official statistics on adoption. The 2000 Census was the first to include questions directed to the frequency and nature of adoptions (U.S. Census Bureau, 2003). At that time there were 2.1 million adopted children in the United States who were still living at home, accounting for 2.5 percent of children under 18. The annual rate of adoption in the years immediately preceding the census was 127,000, a figure that reflects a slight upward trend throughout the decade of the 1990s. The census did not distinguish kinship adoptions (i.e., instances in which a relative adopts the child) from other forms; other sources estimate that 40 to 50 percent of adoptions in the United States are by relatives.

The census revealed that slightly more than 15 percent of adopted children were from other countries, with Asian countries accounting for about half of that total. This percentage

Links to Related Material
In Chapter 11, we will consider how emotional attachment to a parent may become a factor in complex custody disputes.

Questions for Thought and Discussion
Methods of alternative reproduction, such as donor sperm, eggs, and embryos, as well as surrogacy agreements, have raised complex legal questions when children created through these means find themselves in the center of custody disputes. How do you think the factors of genetic relatedness, giving birth, and the intention to parent should be weighed when considering cases such as these?

Questions for Thought and Discussion
Why has international adoption increased in popularity in the United States in recent decades?

BOX 3.2 Journey to Parenthood

Lisa and Bob Cody live in Stamford, Connecticut, with their daughters Katelyn, 7, and Claire, 12 months. Lisa is an elementary school teacher and Bob is a military technician. They adopted Claire from Taipei, Taiwan, in January 2005, when she was 9 months old.

We always knew we wanted to have more than one child. When I was pregnant with Katelyn, I had medical complications related to a rare combination of genetic factors that affect blood clotting. I almost died in childbirth. Afterwards, we researched what had happened to see if it could be prevented from happening in a second pregnancy. It couldn't. We decided that for us adoption was the only safe route to a second child.

We knew a couple of families who had adopted through Family & Children's Agency (FCA) in Connecticut, and they recommended the agency highly. We then went to an informational session there and decided to look no further. We started out in the domestic program but became disillusioned. Birth parents would look at our portfolio, but they didn't choose us as the family they wanted to place their child with. Nothing seemed to be happening for us in the domestic program, so after a year and a half we decided to switch to international adoption.

My sister had adopted a daughter from China a few months after Katelyn was born. Through our niece we became immersed in Chinese culture, and so it made sense for us to go with an Asian nation. FCA's Taiwan program had just opened up. We liked that travel to Taiwan was not required, as Bob was in Iraq by then. So we went with it!

Taiwan's adoption procedure is different from most other international programs. In Taiwan, birth mothers look through portfolios and choose the family they want to place their child with, just as they do in domestic adoptions here in the U.S. We did not specify a gender—we reasoned that we would not have been able to specify if I had been pregnant a second time—but the birth mother who chose us had had a girl, and so that's how we ended up with a second daughter.

What we did not know is that the birth mother can request that the adoptive family she chooses travel to Taiwan for the baby, and this is what happened to us. So I ended up traveling to Taiwan in January 2005, with my mother-in-law, while Katelyn stayed in Connecticut with my mother. Jennifer Yang from FCA also traveled with us.

We arrived in Taipei on January 7 at about 9:30 A.M. We stopped briefly at the hotel, then went straight to the orphanage to get Claire. Her Chinese name was Jing-Miao. Jennifer told us that the first part of her Chinese name meant "clear and bright." Katelyn had kept saying she wanted to name her new baby sister "Claire," which lo and behold had very much the same meaning as our baby's Chinese name! So, her name was a natural choice for us—she became "Claire Jing."

Lisa Cody bringing home her daughter Claire. (Courtesy of Lisa & Claire Cody)

has gone steadily up in recent years. Approximately 53 percent of adopted children were girls, a disparity resulting at least in part from the greater availability of girls in Asian adoptions. In China, for example, 95 percent of the children available for adoption are girls; with the government's "one-child policy," parents are much more likely to give up daughters than sons. In 17 percent of adoptions, the race of the child and the race of the parents differed. Adoptions from Asian countries account for part of this figure; so-called transracial adoptions (primarily adoptions of African American children by white parents) also contribute.

Adoptions—like births from ARTs—come in many forms. The common element is that in adoption the child always has two distinct sets of parents: the genetic parents and the parents who rear the child. One of the difficult questions that has always faced parents of adoptive children is whether to tell the child that he or she is adopted, and if so, when and how to do it. Those opposed to telling adopted children about their origins argue that the perception of genetic relatedness, and of being "wanted" by the genetic parent, is crucial to the child's sense of self as well as to others' acceptance. Proponents of the view that children should know of their origins from early on point to the harm of secrecy, the im-

Questions for Thought and Discussion

Do you think you would enjoy being an adoption social worker? What might you find difficult about Jennifer's job? What might you find rewarding?

Claire cried inconsolably the first day while we were with her at the orphanage. She finally cried herself to sleep on my shoulder. Then when she woke up she kind of looked at me like, "Oh you're still here," and since then it's been amazingly seamless. We expected she would grieve her nannies at the orphanage, but the connection formed so quickly, and aside from that first day she did not. It's been a smooth adjustment.

We spent six days in Taipei. Being in Taiwan was an eye-opener for me. I had never traveled out of the U.S. before, and it was very different from what I expected. I am very glad now that I went and have that connection to her birth country. What struck me most was how very helpful everyone was. Whatever need Claire had, people went out of their way to help us—water for her bottle, a place to change her—one lady we met in a mall even sent us some relaxing naptime music for Claire to listen to!

Claire spent time in both foster care and in the orphanage. When we got her, it was clear she had been well-loved and taken care of. She had no physical or motor delays at all. In fact, she was walking at 9 months! I think this was due to the six months she spent in the foster home. Her language development seems right on target, too.

It means a lot to me that we have a connection to her birth mother. We know that she placed Claire for adoption because she was single, and in Taiwan the social stigma of being a single parent is so great—it was definitely the most loving, caring thing she could do for her baby. I'm glad that we can keep contact with her, that Claire can know about her beginnings, and also about her medical history. I'm glad that we have this tie.

The entire process, from the time we sent our dossier [paperwork] over to Taiwan to the time we brought Claire home, took about 14 months. On the whole, people have responded to her presence in our family very positively. I did get some wicked stares once from a stranger in a store, but aside from that it has been very positive. Our family has also been very supportive. My sister is in the process of adopting a second daughter from China, so my mother now will have four grandchildren—three of them from Asia! To all the aunts and uncles and cousins, Claire is the new baby in the family, and they love her just as she is.

We will do what we can to maintain Claire's connection to Chinese culture. While I was in Taiwan, I bought her a present from her birth country for every year until she is 18. I got her traditional clothing, items made of jade, even a Dr. Seuss book that is written in both English and Chinese, to help her feel a special connection to her birth country. We also plan to attend activities through the Connecticut chapter of Families with Children from China [a national organization for children adopted from China; children from Taiwan and Vietnam are also welcomed in many chapters]. We will see about things like culture camp and Chinese language lessons when she is older. It will depend in part on Claire's own interests and preferences.

For us, this was definitely the right decision. There was never any doubt in my mind that Claire was the baby intended for us. When I saw her referral picture, I finally knew why nothing else had worked out—the baby meant for us wasn't born yet! As soon as I looked at her picture, I fell head over heels in love. When I held her for the first time, I felt an immediate and profound connection.

With many international programs, the adoption is completed in the country where you get your baby. With the Taiwan program, we needed to file to formalize the adoption in the U.S. after our return. We are still working on that. I think we would adopt again. Sometimes I think about it, but I don't know if we actually will.

One morning in the hotel in Taipei, I was still half-asleep. I had the crib next to the bed and I must have rolled over with my hand hanging over into crib. In my half-asleep, half-awake state I felt this little hand reaching out for mine. She put her hand in my hand, and I thought, "This is so right, this is how it's meant to be."

portance of knowing one's true family medical history, and also to the disruption in identity that revelation of adoption can cause if it happens when a child is older or even grown (Carp, 1998). Currently, best practice favors telling children the truth of their genetic origins from an early age.

Another question that has assumed increasing prominence in recent years as adoption policies have changed is whether the child should have knowledge of and contact with the birth parents. As the adopted child matures, this issue becomes one not just for the parents but also for the child to decide. One of the most comprehensive examinations of this question is the Minnesota-Texas Adoption Research Project (Grotevant, Perry, & McRoy, 2005). This study has followed 190 adoptive families and 169 biological mothers since the mid-1980s. Of particular interest have been the various degrees of "openness" with regard to the adoption—that is, the extent to which there is contact and sharing of information between the adoptive family and the birth mothers. The extremes vary from no sharing of information at all to frequent face-to-face meetings involving not just the adoptive parents but the children as well.

BOX 3.3 Conversations with an Adoption Social Worker

Jennifer Yang-Kwait, 31, was born in Taipei, Taiwan. At the age of 12, she moved with her family to the United States. She currently lives in Fairfield, Connecticut, with her husband and son, Nathaniel, age 10 months. Jennifer works for the Adoption Center at Family & Children's Agency, Inc. (FCA), a private nonprofit agency in Norwalk, Connecticut. FCA provides a variety of services to families, including relief for seniors, mental health counseling, family support and foster care, youth development, support for working parents, pregnancy counseling, and international and domestic adoption. Jennifer serves as a birth parent counselor and is also the coordinator of the Taiwan/Vietnam International Adoption Program. Jennifer is a social worker. After double majoring in Psychology and Fine Arts at the University of Denver, she received a master's degree in Social Service Administration from the University of Chicago. She joined FCA in 2001.

I find my work with FCA's international and domestic adoption programs very satisfying. I love helping clients complete or

Jennifer Yang-Kwait in Taiwan with adoptee Claire Cody.
(Courtesy of Jennifer Yang-Kwait)

expand their families. The best part is seeing families happily adjusted and bonded with their children at postplacement visits and FCA events. It is also rewarding to receive notes, e-mails, letters, and photos from families over the years.

Through FCA, prospective parents can adopt children internationally through Russia, Korea, China, the Ukraine, and Taiwan. FCA's most popular international program is currently Korea, due to a relatively short wait time. The children are usually about six months old at the time of arrival. In addition, FCA has a Vietnam program, which, however, is currently on hold due to major restructuring of the adoption process in that country.

In recent years, families have been favoring international over domestic adoptions for a variety of reasons. First, in most international programs there is no involvement from the birth parent. Many people are apprehensive of birth parents. There have been cases handled by unethical or inadequate facilitators in the U.S., highly publicized by the media, where birth parents have come back to reclaim a child after placement in the adoptive parents' home. Because of fears surrounding cases such as these, international adoption may seem safer to a lot of prospective parents.

Second, in international programs the adoption process itself may be shorter, with more predictability and structure. If you adopt in China or Korea, you have a pretty good idea what the timeline is, and how long the wait will be for a referral. And you know how long after your referral it will be before you travel to receive your child. It is often more predictable than many domestic adoptions.

In the U.S. today, people are comfortable and open with the idea of adoption, and transracial adoption is not an issue in the way it might have been in the past. It isn't as important anymore to a lot of parents to find a child who "looks" like them, or who can "pass" as their biological child. People are more open and accepting of adoption as a way to create families, including adoption across racial lines. All of these reasons make international adoption today an appealing option for many parents. At the same time, domestic adoption remains a viable and important choice for many prospective parents.

Links to Related Material

In Chapter 11, you will read about the psychological effects of early emotional deprivation that some internationally adopted children have experienced. In Chapter 16, you will learn more about outcomes among children adopted through the U.S. foster care system. In both chapters, you will learn more about the critical role that age of adoption can play in children's lives.

One basic message from this study is that there is no simple or single answer to the challenges of adoption; in the words of the researchers, there is no "one size fits all" conclusion. In general, however, when differences have emerged on either parent or child measures of psychological functioning, they have tended to favor the families with relatively open arrangements. Such findings cannot tell any family how to handle the situation themselves. They do suggest, however, that contact with the birth mother is not necessarily harmful and may in some instances be beneficial.

Finally, the importance of nurture over nature is evident in research showing that the age at which a child is adopted is an important factor in the long-term psychological outcomes of adopted children. In particular, the older a child is when adopted, the greater the risk becomes that he or she will manifest a variety of behavioral and psychological prob-

I love counseling birth mothers and helping them arrive at the best solution for themselves and their child—that is, whether to raise the child with family and friends' support, or to find a suitable, loving adoptive home for the child. Placing a child for adoption means only that you cannot parent at this time, and you are mature enough to recognize what it takes to raise a child. It is just a matter of right timing.

In an open or semi-open adoption process, it is possible for the child to know his or her birth parents. Different families have different agreements about the birth parents' involvement in the child's life. In a semi-open arrangement, the adoptive parents would have access to information about the birth parents—for example, first names, medical history, and personal circumstances. They would then decide how much of this information to disclose to the child and when. In a semi-open arrangement, the adoptive parents might also provide the birth family with photos and updated information over the years. At the other extreme, in a really open arrangement, the birth parents might be actively involved in the child's life. But it's more common that people just exchange letters and photos. Often, this is done through the adopting agency. Sometimes families start out communicating only through the agency, but after a few years may renegotiate their contract and have more direct communication.

When a semi-open or open adoption is done right, it benefits the adoption triad—child, adoptive family, and birth parents. For adopted children, one of the issues they face growing up is wondering why they were placed for adoption in the first place. With a semi-open or open adoption, the child can know the whole story—"your birth mom was a student, and too young to raise a child on her own." It helps the child to know what happened. It may also benefit the child just to know that his or her adoptive placement was arranged in an open and honest fashion.

An open or semi-open adoption can benefit the birth parents and adoptive families as well. The birth mother might be active in choosing the family she will place her baby with, making her more comfortable with the placement. She also can get updates about the child over the years and feel satisfied that the child is doing well. In addition, adopted children often have questions such as: "why do I like art when no one else in our family does? Why do I have this nose?" With open or semi-open arrangements, the adoptive parents have the information they need to answer the child's questions, plus it is possible for them to obtain updated medical information from the birth parents in the future.

In international adoptions, with the exception of Taiwan and Korea, information about the birth parents is rarely available. Sometimes, international adoptive families travel back to the birth country with the child when the child is older. Sometimes knowing and feeling connected to the birth country takes the place of the birth family for the internationally adopted child. Every child is different, though. Some feel this hunger to know about their past, but others do not feel it the same way.

Adoption is a beautiful way to expand a family. It can also be a solution for an unplanned or untimely pregnancy. It works out both ways when all parties involved have received proper education and counseling. There are all different families—families with stepchildren, biological children, adopted children, grandparents. It can take a lot of hard work, learning, understanding, and compromises to create that special family bond.

But it's worth it. It's particularly moving when parents adopt special needs kids. One adoptive mother I know was encouraged by an orphanage director to take a different baby than the one she had received her referral for, because that baby was sick and developmentally delayed. But to the mother this was already her baby. She had been carrying her picture around with her, and she had bonded to her. She knew that if she left the baby behind she would probably not live very long. So she went ahead and brought the baby home. When I saw her a couple years later, I couldn't even tell it was the same child. She was bright, beautiful, and healthy. The mom said she couldn't imagine what would have happened to her child if she had left her behind, and she could not imagine having a different daughter. The first year was very hard, but she bonded to that little photo she had received in the mail, and now her daughter is a beautiful, healthy child. I have had so many memorable experiences working in this field. It is very satisfying and rewarding.

lems (Rutter, Kreppner & O'Connor, 2001). You will learn more about age as a risk factor in adoption in Chapters 11 and 16.

Learning Objective 3.5: *Describe alternative paths to parenthood.*

1. What is infertility, and what are some of its common causes?
2. How does *in vitro* fertilization work?
3. What are some other common types of assisted reproductive technologies (ARTs) that families can use?
4. What are some current national trends in adoption in the United States?

✔ *Test Your*
M a s t e r y . . .

Learning Objective 3.1

Identify and describe the mechanisms and processes by which physical and behavioral characteristics are inherited.

1. What are genes, where are they in the body, and what do they do?

Inside the cell's nucleus, the *genes,* which are composed of DNA, carry genetic information. *DNA* is organized into chemical strands called chromosomes. In humans, each cell nucleus contains 23 pairs of chromosomes, one from the father and the other from the mother. The members of these pairs are similar to one another and carry the same genes in the same location. The 23rd pair makes up the sex chromosomes. When the pair consists of two X chromosomes (XX), the person is female. When it consists of one of each type (XY), the person is male.

2. How do cells reproduce in a way that makes every individual genetically unique?

Cell reproduction is the most fundamental genetic process that takes place in our bodies. Through a process called *meiosis,* sex cells reproduce to form gametes, the sperm or the ova that will combine at conception to form a new individual. In an additional process called crossing-over, the X partners share genetic material. When the entire process is complete, the resulting four gametes possess 23 chromosomes each and are genetically unique. The gamete now represents a one-of-a-kind combination of genetic material. When combined with 23 original chromosomes from the other parent, it is clear why people come in so many shapes and sizes.

3. What is DNA, and how does it combine to create genes?

Deoxyribonucleic acid (DNA) is the carrier of genetic information inside the chromosome. The *DNA* molecule has the structure of a double helix, much like the sides of a spiral staircase joined by rungs. The rungs consist of four bases (nucleotides): adenine (A), thymine (T), guanine (G), and cytosine (C). The sequence of how these rungs link together determines the coded information carried by the gene.

4. What facts and principles of inheritance did Mendel discover?

From experimenting with pea plants, Mendel developed a theory that each observable trait, such as color, requires two elements, one inherited from each parent. These two elements are a pair of genes (*alleles*). The expressed trait is called the phenotype and the underlying genes, the genotype. Mendel's theory included the principle of dominance. This principle states that when either gene is *dominant*, the dominant characteristic is expressed. Only when both genes are *recessive* is the other characteristic expressed. The principle of segregation states that each inheritable trait is passed on to the offspring as a separate unit. The principle of independent assortment states that traits are passed on independently on one another.

| 5. What are some principles of inheritance that researchers have uncovered since Mendel? | First, single traits are often the product of more than one pair of genes. This process is known as *polygenic inheritance*. Second, behavioral traits, such as temperament and intelligence, are also affected by *multiple genes*. Third, some traits result from genes that display *incomplete dominance*; they are neither entirely dominant nor entirely recessive. Fourth, *codominance* occurs when both genes of a trait are dominant; therefore, both characteristics are expressed completely. Finally, in some instances a trait does not follow any of the usual laws of inheritance because it has genomic imprinting. The alleles for the trait are biochemically marked such that one of them is "imprinted" or silenced and only the other allele affects the phenotype. |

Learning Objective 3.2

Describe the influence of genes on the development of psychological abilities and traits.

| 1. What are family, adoption, and twin studies? | The *family study* approach asks whether the phenotypic similarity on some trait follows from the genotypic similarity among the people being compared. That is, close relatives are most similar, and the degree of similarity drops off as the degree of genetic overlap drops. Therefore, you should be more similar to your parents or siblings than you are to an uncle or cousin. In *adoption studies*, children who are living in adoptive homes are compared with their biological parents and with their adoptive parents. These studies help distinguish the degree of genetic overlap from the degree of environment overlap among different family members. Sometimes this method includes siblings because many adoptive families go on to adopt a second child. Again, differences between adoptive siblings and biological siblings can shed light on whether environment or heredity has the greater influence. Adoption studies also explain the origins of problems in development as well as the heritability of psychological disorders. The logic of the *twin study* approach begins with the assumption that fraternal twins share an environment that is similar to the environment shared by identical twins. If a trait is more similar in the identical twins than the fraternal twins, the usual conclusion is that the great similarity results from similar genes. Twin studies have also examined the differences between identical and fraternal twins reared apart. In addition, the personality trait of temperament has also been studied. |

| 2. What does each of these types of studies tell us about the heritability of psychological abilities and traits? | They all suggest that *genes* make an important contribution to a wide range of outcomes in child development. However, genes are never all-important; the *environment* also plays a role. |

3. What are some examples of behavioral characteristics that are affected by genetic endowment?

Researchers have found, for example, that the characteristics of *sociability* and *aggression* are genetically influenced.

4. What major limitation do researchers point to regarding adoption studies?

The major limitation is that, because of the adoption practices of most agencies, the homes in which adopted children are placed are relatively *homogeneous*. Adopted children are generally placed in middle-class or high-income families, and so the environmental effects associated with being reared in poverty are not typically included in adoption studies.

Learning Objective 3.3
How do genes and environment interact to influence the development of behavior?

1. What is meant by range of reaction? What does it tell us about the interaction of genes and environment?

This model (Gottesman, 1974) suggests that genes interact with the environment by setting the *upper and lower limits* of our development. Our environment and experiences then determine where we fall within this reaction range. In other words, our genes have set the upper limits on our potential, whereas our environment and experience may or may not provide us with the opportunity to achieve that potential.

2. What are gene–environment correlations? How do they help us to understand the interaction of genes and environment?

The genes children inherit and the environments they experience are often correlated in that they act together to push development in the same direction. For example, in the case of intelligence, children with a high genetic potential for intelligence are more likely to have parents who are more intelligent, and such parents are more likely to provide an intellectually stimulating environment. Such children therefore receive a *double boost* in that both genes and environment promote the development of intellectual skills.

3. What is meant by nonshared environment?	The nonshared environment model emphasizes how the environment operates primarily to make the children within a family *different*. Children experience their environment differently, and parents treat children differently in the family. The child also interprets and reacts to the same family events differently than a sibling might. These differences arise in part from children's different genetic predispositions. Therefore, a child's genes act as an influence on the environment he or she receives.

Learning Objective 3.4

Describe different types of genetic disorders and their impact on child development.

1. How are genetic autosomal disorders transmitted?	Whether or not defective genes are expressed in the phenotype depends on whether they are *dominant* or *recessive*. If a defective gene inherited from the parent is recessive, the dominant (and usually normal) allele from the other parent can prevent the problem from happening. However, the problem gene still exists in the genotype and will be transmitted to approximately half of the person's offspring. Most of the offspring will be unaffected, but those who receive the defective gene from both parents will develop the disorder.
2. What are some examples of dominant and recessive autosomal disorders?	Dominant genes that cause severe problems typically disappear from the species, because the affected people usually do not live to reproduce. In some cases, severely disabling dominant genes are passed on because they do not become active until relatively late in life, and people with these genes may reproduce before they know that they have inherited the disease. Examples of disorders from *dominant* genes are Huntington's disease and neurofibromatosis. It is also possible to carry potential lethal genes as recessive traits, but because most of these dangerous genes are rare, it is unlikely that we will mate with someone who has a matching recessive gene. Even then, the possibility of a child's receiving both recessive genes is only one in four. Examples of disorders from *recessive* genes are Tay-Sachs disease, sickle-cell anemia, and cystic fibrosis.
3. How are x-linked disorders transmitted, and why do they affect males more than females?	The Y chromosome is only about a third of the size of the X chromosome. One result of the larger X is that it contains more genetic information. Consequently, some genes that travel on the X chromosome do not have a *corresponding allele* on the Y chromosome. For a female, if there is a recessive allele on one X chromosome, there is a good chance that the corresponding allele on the other X chromosome will override its expression. Males have no such protection, and are more vulnerable than females to recessive disorders that travel only on the X chromosome.

4. What are some examples of x-linked disorders?

Hemophilia, Duchenne muscular dystrophy, and red-green color blindness are examples of *x-linked disorders*.

5. What are some examples of disorders caused by defects of the autosomes?

Genetically based problems may result from physical changes in chromosomes. These changes occur during meiosis in one of the parents, and they can involve any of the 22 autosomes. Down syndrome is an example of a disorder caused by an *autosomal defect*. Children born with this disorder typically have cheerful dispositions and are friendly and outgoing. They also, however, are moderately to severely retarded, tend to have poor muscle tone, and have problems with expressive language.

6. What are some examples of disorders caused by defects of the sex chromosomes?

In *Turner's syndrome* the child has only one X chromosome. While the child looks female at birth, her ovaries will not produce the hormones necessary for the sex differentiation process to continue. She will not develop breasts or menstruate. In *Klinefelter's syndrome*, an egg carrying two X chromosomes is fertilized by a sperm carrying a Y chromosome. The presence of the Y chromosome causes the child to have a male appearance; however, male hormone levels are low. A third chromosomal abnormality occurs when the sperm provides two Y chromosomes. The males produced when this occurs have large body builds and masculine personality characteristics. The most common disorder of the sex chromosomes is *fragile X syndrome*, caused by an abnormal gene on the X chromosome, causing mental retardation.

7. What are genetic counseling and population screening?

Genetic counseling involves a range of activities focused on determining the likelihood that a couple will give birth to a child with a genetic disorder. Couples may seek genetic counseling if there is a family history of some genetic disease. The more closely related the relative, the more serious are the implications for a couple considering parenthood. Most serious of all is having already given birth to a child or children who were born with a genetic disease. Other risk factors are membership in an ethnic group that is known to have a heightened probability of inheriting a specific disorder (Tay-Sachs, sickle-cell anemia) or advanced age of the parents. In *population screening*, the goal is to identify and counsel as many carriers of the disease gene as possible in an attempt to reduce the incidence of the disorder in future generations. These efforts are directed at ethnic groups known to be at increased risk for a genetic disorder such as African Americans and sickle-cell disease, or Ashkenazi Jews and Tay-Sachs disease.

Learning Objective 3.5
Describe alternative paths to parenthood.

1. What is infertility, and what are some of its common causes?

Infertility is defined as a failure to conceive after a year of sexual intercourse without the use of contraceptives. One common female source of infertility is blockage of the fallopian tubes. Deterioration in the quality of the ova (usually due to maternal age) is another common cause. The most common cause of male infertility is low sperm count, which itself can occur for various reasons.

2. How does *in vitro* fertilization work?

With *in vitro* fertilization (*IVF*) the mother first receives fertility drugs to increase the production of ova, after which a mature ovum is removed and fertilized in a laboratory dish. In most instances, the sperm is provided by her husband or male partner, although this is not always the case. Within 24 hours the fertilized ovum is inserted into the womb. If the procedure is successful, the result is a normal pregnancy.

3. What are some other common types of assisted reproductive technologies (ARTs) that families can use?

When male infertility is the problem, *donor insemination* is sometimes used. In this process, the woman is inseminated with sperm from a donor male. In such cases, the child is genetically related to the mother but not the father. With *egg donation*, a donor female is used, and the child is genetically related only to the father. With *surrogacy*, another woman bears the child for the eventual parents; the child may be related to both parents (if both eggs and sperm were donated) or only the father (if insemination was used).

4. What are some current national trends in adoption in the United States?

The *2000 Census* was the first to include questions directed to the frequency and nature of adoption. At that time there were 2.1 million adopted children in the United States, accounting for 2.5 percent of children under 18. There was a slight upward trend in adoptions during the decade of the 1990s. The census did not distinguish kinship adoptions from other forms; other sources estimate that 40 to 50 percent of adoptions in the United States are by relatives. The census revealed that slightly more than 15 percent of adopted children were from other countries, with Asian countries accounting for about half of that total. This percentage has risen in recent years. Approximately 53 percent of adopted children were girls, due in part to China's "one-child policy."

Prenatal Development, Birth, *and* the Newborn

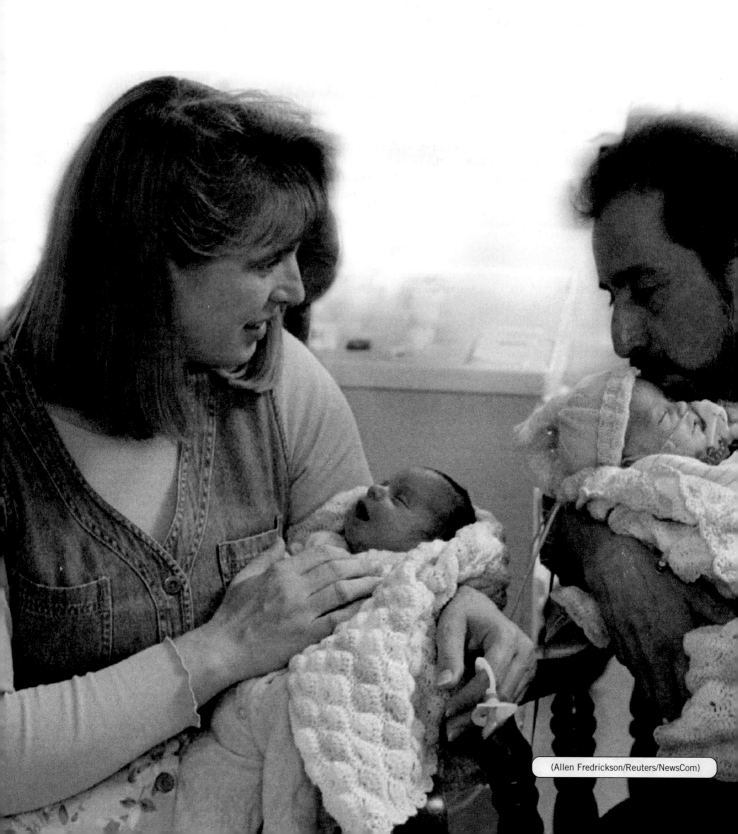

After over a year of trying to conceive their first child without success, 35-year-old Michelle and her husband Robert went to see an infertility specialist. The doctor placed Michelle on a fertility medication, which helped stimulate egg production. Michelle's menstrual cycle was then tracked carefully, and, just prior to ovulation, the doctor performed an office procedure called donor insemination. In this procedure, Robert's sperm was placed directly in Michelle's uterus using a thin catheter. Michelle was then instructed to go home, eat well, and take it easy.

The first two cycles of fertility treatment were unsuccessful. Michelle became concerned that she herself was doing something that was preventing a successful pregnancy. She learned from her doctor that contact with a variety of external agents could affect pregnancy, including bacteria sometimes found in feta cheese and deli meat. She added these to her list of items to avoid, which already included second-hand smoke, alcohol, and caffeine. She also learned from her doctor that wearing boxer shorts rather than briefs can facilitate sperm production in men by helping to maintain a slightly lower body temperature in the scrotum. Accordingly, she purchased several pairs for Robert and urged him to wear them.

Michelle and Robert were overjoyed when, after the third cycle of fertility treatment, her home pregnancy test came back positive. Michelle ate well, took her vitamins, saw her obstetrician for prenatal checkups, and continued to avoid harmful substances. During her sixteenth week of pregnancy, she went for an ultrasound and a prenatal screening blood test. The blood test came back normal, but the ultrasound showed that she had twins! Her doctor told her that multiple births were a frequent result of fertility medications.

By her fifth month of pregnancy, Michelle was beginning to have premature contractions called Braxton-Hicks contractions. Her doctor ordered her on complete bedrest for the remainder of her pregnancy, and was very concerned that she complete at least 26 weeks of gestation and preferably, the doctor said, 32 weeks. At 34 weeks, Michelle gave birth to twin boys. The boys were six weeks premature and weighed around 5 pounds each. After several days in the hospital, the boys were sent home with their new parents, in good health.

Technological advances have altered the face of pregnancy and childbirth today. We have increased our understanding of all aspects of the birth process as well as our capacity to intervene effectively—from conception and prenatal screening and health to methods of childbirth and the diagnosis and treatment of birth complications. In this chapter we examine the child's development from conception to birth. In the process, we consider the influences of the larger familial, societal, and cultural contexts on development from the very beginning. ■

Pregnancy

Learning Objective 4.1
Discuss factors that influence conception and evaluate types of screening performed during pregnancy.

Much happens in a child's development during the nine months from conception to birth. Genetic influences are realized, including the presence or absence of inherited disorders or structural defects. Gender is determined and sex differentiation occurs. The embryo and later the fetus grow in a prenatal environment that promotes or inhibits optimal health. In addition, familial and societal attitudes shape childbirth choices and practices, thus influencing the child's earliest moments. Before any of this occurs, however, a series of events must happen that result in a viable pregnancy. What are those events, and how do they influence the child's development?

Factors that Influence Conception

Development begins at **conception,** or fertilization, which occurs when a sperm unites with an ovum (egg) to form a single cell, called a **zygote.** The zygote receives 23 chromosomes from the mother and 23 from the father, to form a new and genetically unique person. Several factors influence whether conception will occur. The first is timing. The man's sperm, typically deposited in the woman's vagina, will survive for about three days. The woman's ovum, released each month by her ovaries, will live for 12 to 24 hours. Conception is most likely to occur when the sperm, which have a long journey through the cervix and the uterus, are already in the fallopian tube when the egg is released by the ovary (see Figure 4.1). Because of this time window, conception is most likely to occur when intercourse occurs in the four days prior to and including the woman's ovulation.

On average, a woman's menstrual cycle lasts 28 days, with ovulation on day 14. However, many women have longer or shorter cycles than this, and ovulation can occur as early as day 6 or as late as day 30 of the cycle. In addition, factors such as stress and illness can delay ovulation. Timing, based on each woman's individual cycle, thus becomes critical for understanding when conception is most likely to occur.

Another influence on conception is the reproductive health of both prospective parents. The woman's reproductive system must be free of disorders that might prevent ovulation, or prevent the movement of the egg through the fallopian tubes to the uterus. It is also critical that the woman's hormones are adequate to produce the mucus that enables the sperm to travel through the cervix and uterus and into the fallopian tubes. The woman's hormones must also be sufficient to make the thick endometrial lining that will allow the fertilized zygote to implant in the uterine wall and be nourished there. Also, the man must have a sufficient quantity of normal, actively moving sperm to withstand the long journey from the vagina into the fallopian tubes. Of the several million sperm that are typically deposited, only 100 to 200 of the strongest and healthiest make it all the way to the ovum, where only one will actually penetrate the wall to fertilize the ovum.

A third factor that greatly influences the likelihood of conception is the woman's age. Each woman is born with a unique lifetime number of eggs. As she ages, her eggs age as

Conception
The combining of the genetic material from a male gamete (sperm) and a female gamete (ovum); fertilization.

Zygote
A fertilized ovum.

Millions of sperm from the father enter the vagina of the mother, but only several hundred reach the ovum and only one actually fertilizes it. What conditions determine if conception will occur? (Petit Format/Photo Researchers, Inc.)

FIGURE 4.1 Events of the First Week of Human Development

The period of the zygote lasts about two weeks, from conception to the completion of implantation in the uterus.

Fertilization
12–24 hours later

Two-cell stage at approximately 30 hours

Fallopian tube

Multicell stages at 3 and 4 days

Uterus

Implantation begins at about 6 days

Ovulation

Ovary

Links to Related Material

In Chapter 3, you read about different assisted reproduction technologies. Here, you learn how the fertility drugs often used with these therapies increase the likelihood of giving birth to twins, triplets, or higher order multiples.

Questions for Thought
and Discussion:
How did the age, reproductive health, and genetic endowments of your parents affect your existence?

Links to Related Material

In Chapter 3, you read that the risk of Down syndrome increases with maternal age. Here, you learn more about how the biology of aging affects a woman's chances of conceiving and giving birth to a healthy infant.

well. Conception rates for young healthy couples are, at best, 20 to 25 percent per menstrual cycle. As a woman grows older, particularly after the age of 35, her fertility begins to decline. By age 40, it is estimated that a woman's likelihood of conceiving is in the range of 8 to 10 percent per month, and by age 43, a woman's chance of conceiving each month may be as low as 1 to 3 percent.

As women grow older, there is not only a reduced chance of becoming pregnant; there is also a significant increase in the risk of chromosomal abnormalities in the embryo and miscarriage. As a woman's eggs age, they become increasingly fragile and subject to chromosomal error during cell division. As you read in Chapter 3, the risk of Down syndrome increases from roughly 1 in 900 live births at age 30, to about 1 in 100 at age 40. Considering all types of chromosomal abnormalities, the risk increases from 1 in 385 at age 30 to 1 in 66 at age 40 (Creasy & Resnick, 1999). In one large-scale study of maternal age and miscarriage in Denmark, researchers found that, of a total of 1,221,546 birth outcomes in that country between 1978 and 1992, the risk of miscarriage was 8.9 percent in women aged 20–24 years and 74.7 percent in women aged 45 years or more (Nyobo, Andersen, et al., 2000).

Impacts of Parental Age

The typical age at which a woman gives birth to her first child has risen dramatically in the United States since the 1970s. Between 1978 and 2002 the rate of births to mothers between the ages of 35 and 39 rose by more than 100 percent, and the increase for mothers 40 or older was almost as great (Martin et al., 2002). In contrast, births to teenagers have declined in recent years. From 1991 to 2002, the rate of births to teenage mothers in the United States declined dramatically from 61.3 to 23.9 per 1,000 female teenagers aged 10–17 (Sutton & Mathews, 2004). Nevertheless, almost 500,000 teenagers give birth in the United States each year.

The father's age also carries a risk for the fetus, because the frequency of mutation in the father's sperm increases with age. A genetic disorder related to the father's age is *achondroplasia*, a dominant mutation that causes bone deformities. The most obvious characteristics are dwarfism and a large head with a prominent forehead and a depressed bridge of the nose. The likelihood that a child will inherit achondroplasia increases with the father's age, just as the likelihood of Down syndrome increases with the mother's age (Tiemann-Boege, Navidi, Grewal, et al., 2002). Genetic disorders are not the only risk that older parents face. Older parents are more likely to face problems with infertility, and thus they are more likely to use assisted reproductive therapy.

Nearly all types of assisted reproduction, described in Chapter 3, include placing the mother on fertility drugs that stimulate the ovaries to produce multiple eggs each menstrual cycle. One result of the increased use of fertility drugs has been a dramatic increase in multiple births. Between 1980 and 2002, the number of twin births in the United States increased by 65 percent, and the number of births involving three or more babies quadrupled (Martin, Kochanek, Strobino, Guyer, & MacDorman, 2005). Much of this increase is directly related to delayed childbearing among many women in the United States.

Women who are pregnant with multiples are at greater risk for preterm birth, with twins arriving on average three weeks and higher-order multiples on average six weeks preterm (Martin et al., 2005). In addition, older mothers are often at higher risk for pregnancy-related medical conditions such as gestational diabetes and hypertension (Gilbert, Nesbitt, & Danielsen, 1999). However, many pregnancy-related medical conditions can be managed with appropriate prenatal care. When the mother's health is good, pregnancy past the age of 35 appears to carry only minimal risks.

At the other end of the parental age spectrum, babies who are born to mothers in their teens are also frequently considered to be at greater than average risk. These risks include complications during pregnancy, preterm birth, and low birthweight (Moore & Brooks-Gunn, 2002). Here, too, however, factors associated with pregnancy during a particular age period appear to be more important than maternal age per se. In particular, teen mothers are less likely than mothers in general to receive adequate prenatal care and more likely to engage in behaviors that pose risks for both their own and their fetuses' health, such as smoking, drinking, or use of illegal drugs during pregnancy. When these factors are addressed, the problems associated with teen pregnancy are greatly reduced.

Prenatal Screening

Because of increased pregnancy risks associated with parental age, physicians generally recommend that pregnant women over the age of 35 receive prenatal screening. Many tests for genetic abnormalities are now available for both women and men. Also, advances in medical technology have provided prospective parents with several screening tools that can be used to assess the health of the developing fetus.

Ultrasound One of the least invasive prenatal screening tools available to parents is the ultrasound. **Ultrasound imaging** is a technique for looking inside the body by using sound waves to create images of the fetus and its environment. A device that produces sound waves is moved over the pregnant woman's abdomen, and reflections of these waves form images of the contents of the uterus. The image permits an assessment of fetal age and identification of the sex of the fetus by 16 to 20 weeks. The ultrasound also shows if there is more than one fetus. Although many potential problems are not detectable with ultrasound, the procedure can reveal some disorders, including abnormal head growth; defects of the heart, bladder, and kidneys; some chromosomal anomalies; and neural tube defects (Anderson & Allison, 1990; Stoll et al., 1993).

Amniocentesis An especially important tool for prenatal assessment is **amniocentesis**, because it provides samples of both the amniotic fluid and the fetal cells within it. With amniocentesis, a needle is passed through the mother's abdomen and into the amniotic cavity to collect the fluid. Analysis of the fluid can reveal abnormalities. For example, alpha-feto protein (FEP), a substance the fetus produces, circulates in the amniotic fluid. Abnormally high levels of FEP occur when the fetus has certain types of damage to the brain, the central nervous system, or the liver and kidneys. Chromosomal analysis of the fetal cells can also detect a variety of disorders. Fetal cells also can be tested for genetic disorders. With the success of the Human Genome Project, the list of detectable diseases has grown dramatically in recent years, with more than 6,000 different single gene disorders

Ultrasound imaging
A noninvasive procedure for detecting physical defects in the fetus. A device that produces sound waves is moved over the pregnant woman's abdomen, and reflections of these waves form an image of the fetus.

Amniocentesis
A procedure for collecting cells that lie in the amniotic fluid surrounding the fetus. A needle is passed through the mother's abdominal wall into the amniotic sac to gather discarded fetal cells. These cells can be examined for chromosomal and genetic defects.

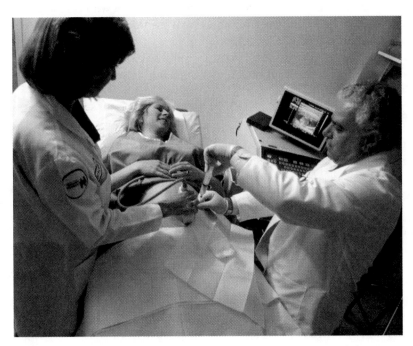

With modern diagnostic techniques, many potential problems can be detected prenatally. With amniocentesis, a needle is passed through the mother's abdomen to collect amniotic fluid and fetal cells. What information can an analysis of amniotic fluid and fetal cells provide? (Yoav Levy/Phototake)

identified, including achondroplasia, cystic fibrosis, Duchenne muscular dystrophy, and Tay-Sachs disease (Steele, Stockley, & Ray, 2000).

Chorionic Villus Sampling Amniocentesis is most effective after the period during which abortion is safest for the mother. **Chorionic villus sampling (CVS)** can make information about the fetus available much earlier. In this procedure cells are collected from the chorion, a part of the placenta. A small tube is inserted through the cervix and into the fetal placenta to collect a sample of fetal cells. These cells reveal large-scale defects of the chromosomes as well as more minute defects in the DNA. CVS is possible as early as 9 to 11 weeks, with results available in a few days. Both amniocentesis and CVS carry a slight risk (ranging from 1 to 2 percent) of miscarriage following the procedure (Cavallotti, Casilla, Verrotti, Fieni, & Gramellini, 2004; Scott, Boogert, Robertson, et al., 2002).

Endoscopic Fetoscopy A relatively new procedure available to parents for prenatal screening is endoscopic fetoscopy. In this procedure, a fiber-optic endoscope is inserted into the uterus either through the abdomen or the cervix. The endoscope allows the health care provider to visualize the fetus, obtain fetal tissue samples, or even perform fetal surgery. Some of the fetal abnormalities that may be treated by endoscopic fetoscopy are congenital diaphragmatic hernia and urinary tract obstruction. Diagnosing and treating these defects prenatally can prevent serious complications that may arise during and following birth.

Test-tube Screening Scientists have succeeded in screening embryos in the test tube before they are implanted in the mother's uterus. Egg cells are collected from the mother and then fertilized in a petri dish through *in vitro* fertilization. One cell is removed from each embryo when it reaches the eight-cell stage. From this one cell, the sex of the embryo can be determined, and, within a few hours, the DNA of the cell can be checked for suspected anomalies.

Chloe O'Brien, born in the United Kingdom in April 1992, was the first baby to be born after *in vitro* fertilization following DNA analysis before implantation. Her parents were carriers of the cystic fibrosis gene. If they had conceived in the normal fashion and had discovered that their fetus had cystic fibrosis by the other techniques described, they would have faced a decision on abortion. Using test-tube screening, they were assured that the embryo that was implanted was free of this disease.

It is possible to detect several hundred disorders through various screening techniques. However, only a small minority of women who have at-risk pregnancies participate in prenatal screening. The risk of problem pregnancy is higher for a woman who (1) has a history of miscarriages or has had children with congenital disorders, (2) is outside the optimal childbearing age range, (3) has relatives (or is carrying a child whose biological father has relatives) with genetic abnormalities, (4) is poor and has inadequate medical supervision and nutrition, or (5) takes drugs or abuses alcohol during pregnancy.

Prenatal Treatment

But what happens when parents discover that their fetus is developing abnormally? The parents may decide to terminate the pregnancy, but there may also be treatment alternatives they may wish to consider. Current approaches to prenatal treatment include medical therapy, surgery, and genetic engineering.

Medical Therapy Medical therapy is the most common prenatal treatment. An example is providing extra vitamins to the mother when enzyme deficiencies are discovered in the blood of the fetus. Similarly, drug treatment of pregnant women with HIV has markedly reduced the incidence of babies who are born infected with the virus.

It is also possible to provide therapy directly to the fetus. One of the first such cases was reported in mid-1989. Parents in Lyons, France, whose first child had died in infancy of a hereditary disorder, learned that the fetus the mother was carrying had the same disorder, involving an immune deficiency that leaves the infant open to almost any infection.

Chorionic villus sampling (CVS) A procedure for gathering fetal cells earlier in pregnancy than is possible through amniocentesis. A tube is passed through the vagina and cervix so that fetal cells can be gathered at the site of the developing placenta.

Links to Related Material
In Chapter 3, you learned about genetic counseling, which provides parents with information on genetic risk. Here, you learn about different screening methods for prenatal detection of genetic or chromosomal abnormalities.

Questions for Thought and Discussion
Which types of prenatal screening might you choose, and why?

Doctors decided to try to treat the fetus in the mother's womb. They injected immune cells from the thymus and liver of two aborted fetuses into the umbilical cord; this was the first time this procedure had been done. After the baby was born, the injected cells multiplied, as the doctors had hoped (Elmer-DeWitt, 1994), and the hereditary immune deficiency did not develop.

Surgery   The use of fetal surgery is illustrated by the experience of a pregnant woman who had earlier given birth to an infant with hydrocephaly, an abnormal accumulation of fluid inside the skull that results in brain damage. An ultrasound diagnosis showed that her fetus was accumulating fluid on the brain and would likely suffer brain damage if treatment was delayed until birth. Surgeons at the University of Colorado Medical School, working through a long, hollow tube inserted through the mother's abdomen and the amniotic sac, installed a small valve in the back of the fetus's head to permit the excess fluid to drain, thereby relieving pressure on the brain. The fetus survived the surgery and at 16 months of age appeared to be normal (Clewell et al., 1982).

Physicians are now able to carry out surgery on fetuses to address life-threatening problems and conditions that will result in severe damage if not corrected early in development. For example, fetal surgery is used for blockage of the urinary tract, congenital diaphragmatic hernia (a condition in which the diaphragm does not fully form, allowing organs to enter the chest cavity and affect lung growth), and spina bifida and other neural tube defects.

Genetic Engineering   Probably the greatest promise for prenatal treatment is in genetic engineering. Suppose we could detect, say, the lack of an enzyme in a fetus's blood and could identify the specific gene that caused the defect. Working in the laboratory with a blood sample from the fetus, we would clip out the defective gene and insert a synthetic replacement gene. After producing many copies of the blood cells containing the repaired chromosome, we would inject them into the fetus, where they would survive and replicate and provide sufficient amounts of the enzyme for normal development.

In September 1990, scientists undertook the first federally approved attempt at human **gene therapy** of this kind. It involved a 4-year-old girl named Ashanti who suffered from ADA deficiency, a severe and incurable disease of the immune system. Cells were extracted from the girl, and harmless viruses were used to carry the needed ADA gene into the cells. The cells—a billion or so—were then reinjected into the child's bloodstream. The cells produced the needed ADA, and Ashanti has now survived to adolescence, although she does need repeated treatments.

Ethical Considerations

The ability to diagnose abnormal prenatal development raises innumerable ethical questions—questions that people may find difficult to answer. Today's fetal-screening techniques can detect the presence of sickle-cell anemia, Huntington's disease, Down syndrome, cystic fibrosis, and numerous other life-threatening maladies. What are the consequences of this knowledge? If no treatment is possible, the options are to terminate the pregnancy or to bring a child with a serious disorder into the world. Should fetuses with serious genetic or chromosomal disorders be aborted? If so, how serious or disabling must the genetic disorder be? If a fetus is diagnosed with a genetic disorder, should insurance companies be able to deny the child insurance at birth, considering that the health expenses of that child will be exorbitant compared with those of other children?

The treatment of disorders while babies are still in the mother's womb also raises difficult ethical questions. Procedures such as fetal surgery and gene repair are expensive, and not all families have the resources to benefit from them. Who would have access to such procedures, and who would not? In addition, many such procedures are still in the experimental phase, and they carry risks for both the baby and the mother (American College of Obstetricians and Gynecologists, 2001). Still further issues arise when babies are born with severe disorders, as in the case of Baby Jane Doe. Baby Jane Doe was born with

Questions for Thought and Discussion
Why is stem cell research so controversial? What is your stand on the issues?

Ashanti was the first recipient of human gene therapy to prevent the development of an inherited severe immune deficiency. At age 15 Ashanti is still doing well. What criteria would you adopt for undertaking prenatal gene therapy? (Courtesy of Van De Silva)

Questions for Thought and Discussion
Do you think it should be public policy for a population to be genetically screened? What might be some potential dangers in such a policy?

Questions for Thought and Discussion
What are some advantages and disadvantges of knowing many months before birth whether a fetus is male or female? Would you want to know? Why, or why not?

BOX 4.1 Technology and Gender Selection

Research & Society

Prenatal screening and treatment options also potentially permit parents to select, even alter, the sex of their offspring. Throughout history, sages and quacks have offered couples advice on how to influence the sex of their offspring. Aristotle counseled ancient Greek males desirous of a son to tie off their left testicles. Since the 13th century, Chinese women have consulted an astrology chart to determine when they are most likely to conceive a boy or a girl.

German folklore recommends that couples hoping for a daughter place a wooden spoon under the mattress before intercourse. And, in recent decades, books and magazines describing low-tech sex selection methods (e.g., manipulating the timing of intercourse) have become best-sellers. Now, with the discovery of new sperm-sorting technologies, we are about to embark on an era in which prospective parents will be able to determine with 100 percent certainty whether they have a baby boy or baby girl.

Would you take advantage of this emerging technology? The medical body that oversees physicians involved in reproductive health—the American Society of Reproductive Medicine (ASRM)—expects that many people will. Anticipating growing demand for this procedure, the ASRM has declared it ethical to offer sex selection to parents for reasons unrelated to the health of the baby or the mother (Ethics Committee of the ASRM, 2001).

Critics have raised numerous objections to the ASRM's decision. Some fear that sex selection will lead to a preponderance of one gender, a fear that has become a reality in some countries where male infants have greater societal value than female infants, or a particular type of family configuration (e.g., older brother–younger sister sibling pairs). Others worry about the possibility of psychological harm to sex-selected offspring in cases where the child's behavior fails to meet parents' gender-specific expectations. And still other opponents argue that the opportunity to choose the sex of children focuses undue attention on a nonessential human characteristic and will ultimately promote and reinforce gender bias.

Currently, the ASRM proposes to offer nonmedical sex selection only to parents who already have offspring of one gender and wish to have a child of the opposite sex. They note that most parents interested in sex selection do not favor one sex over another but are hoping for a "balanced" family that includes at least one child of each gender. According to the ASRM, this preference for children of each gender reflects a basic truth about human nature—that there are well-established physical and psychological differences between male and female children. These differences, the doctors assert, shape parents' childrearing experiences. Raising boys is simply different from raising girls, they argue, and parents who wish to have both kinds of experience have the right to use available technologies to make that desire a reality.

---

hydrocephalus, spina bifida, and microcephaly. Her parents had two options. They could approve two operations, after which it was likely that she would live past age 20 but be paralyzed, severely retarded, and in pain; or they could refuse to permit surgery, in which case she would likely die before the age of 3. They chose not to allow surgery, but others felt it was not the parents' choice to make alone. Most significantly, the U.S. Justice Department for the first time sued on behalf of the medical rights of an infant with a disability. Ultimately, the U.S. Supreme Court ruled against the government and upheld the parents' right to choose (Holden, 1986).

Decisions regarding the health and life of a fetus or infant are intensely emotional and deeply embedded in social, political, ethical, and moral convictions. They are also very personal. As new technologies are developed, the fine line that separates these personal beliefs and feelings on the one side, and the government's role in protecting the rights of fetuses and infants on the other, may become increasingly blurred.

✔ *Test Your Mastery...*

Learning Objective 4.1: *Discuss factors that influence conception and evaluate types of screening performed during pregnancy.*

1. How does conception occur? What factors strongly influence conception?
2. What role does parental age play in fetal health?
3. What prenatal screening tests are available to women during pregnancy?
4. How and when can prenatal treatments best be used to improve fetal health?
5. What ethical issues must be taken into consideration when considering prenatal screening and treatment options?

Stages of Prenatal Development

Although it is the largest cell in the body, the ovum is no larger than the period at the end of this sentence, and the sperm cell that fertilizes it weighs less than 1/30,000 as much. In only 9 months, this tiny genetic package nevertheless grows into a baby whose mass is billions of times greater. Every stage of development from conception to birth represents a mix of the influences of nature and nurture. Even the genetic material that the mother and father contribute to the offspring can be affected by environmental factors, such as exposure to chemicals or radiation. Other environmental factors, such as maternal nutrition, infections, and drug abuse, can also influence development. In this section, we follow the baby's prenatal development through three stages, or periods—the period of the zygote, the period of the embryo, and the period of the fetus.

As you learned in the previous section, prenatal development begins at conception, when a sperm unites with an ovum (egg) to form a single cell, the zygote. Within about an hour of penetration by the fertilizing sperm, the genetic material from the sperm and the ovum have completely merged to form a zygote, and development of the embryo begins. **Gestation**, or the length of time from conception to birth, is technically 38 weeks. However, parents typically do not know the exact date of conception, so physicians use the date of the woman's last menstrual period as a way to calculate gestational age and to estimate a baby's due date. This estimate is not exact, because women's menstrual cycles vary. Two weeks (the amount of time assumed to pass from the date of the last menstrual period to the date of ovulation) usually is added to the calculation for a total gestation time of 40 weeks.

Period of the Zygote (First Two Weeks)

The period of the zygote comprises the period of time from conception until implantation in the uterine wall, typically two weeks. After conception, the zygote multiplies rapidly as it continues its 4-day, 4-inch journey through the fallopian tube to the uterus. At first the zygote is a solid mass of cells, but it gradually changes into a hollow sphere as it prepares to implant into the wall of the uterus. Now the cells begin to specialize, some forming an inner cell mass, which will become the embryo, and others forming important structures that will support the embryo's development.

Implantation takes about a week. During this time, the zygote settles into the blood-enriched lining of the uterus, where it will remain attached for the duration of the pregnancy. The period of the zygote ends about 2 weeks after fertilization, which corresponds to the woman's first missed menstrual period. By the time a woman suspects she may be pregnant, prenatal development is well under way.

Learning Objective 4.2
Trace the changes that occur in the three stages of prenatal development.

Gestation
The length of time from conception to birth, typically calculated from the date of a woman's last menstrual period.

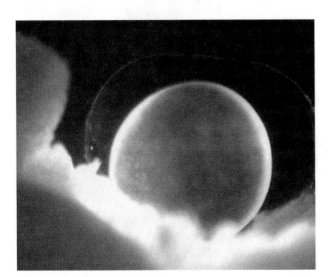

This image shows a zygote implanted in the uterine wall. To gradually and firmly embed itself, the developing zygote secretes enzymes that erode the cells of the wall of the uterus. If implantation is not successful for any reason, the menstrual cycle resumes without the mother ever realizing she was pregnant. (Lookat Sciences/Phototake)

Period of the Embryo (3rd to 8th Week)

Embryo
The developing organism from the third week, when implantation is complete, through the eighth week after conception.

In this photo, you can see the head, development of the spine, and location for eye development. The bump below the head is the primitive heart, and the upper and lower limbs have just begun to form as tiny buds. (Image provided by Anatomical Travelogue, www.anatomicaltravel.com. From the book *Conception to Birth: A Life Unfolds*, authored by Alexander Tsiaras.)

Links to Related Material
In Chapter 13, you will learn more about how gender daifferentiation occurs prenatally, and the effects that exposure to hormones prenatally has on gender development.

FIGURE 4.2 Human ova and embryos from 3 to 8 weeks

The sequence of images in this figure shows the rapid growth in body size and differentiation of body form that develops between the third and eighth weeks of pregnancy.

Source: Adapted from H.E. Jordan and J.E. Kindred (1948). *Textbook of Embryology*, 5th ed. (p. 87). New York: Appleton-Century-Crofts. Copyright © 1948 by Appleton-Century-Crofts. Adapted by permission.

The period of the **embryo** begins when implantation is complete and lasts for around 6 weeks. Although the embryo at first is only the size of an apple seed, all major internal and external structures form during this period. For that reason, these weeks are the most delicate of the pregnancy and the time when the growing embryo is most vulnerable to threats from internal and external environments.

In the third week, the inner cell mass differentiates into three layers, from which all body structures will emerge. Two layers form first—the *endodermal* layer and the *ectodermal* layer. The endodermal cells will develop into internal organs and glands. The ectodermal cells become the parts of the body that maintain contact with the outside world—the nervous system; the sensory parts of the eyes, nose, and ears; skin; and hair. The third cell layer then appears between the endodermal and ectodermal layers. This is the *mesodermal* layer, which will give rise to muscles, cartilage, bone, sex organs, and the heart. The heart is beating by the end of the third week.

Around the beginning of the fourth week, the embryo looks something like a tiny tube. The shape of the embryo gradually changes, however, because cell multiplication is more rapid in some locations than in others. By the end of the fourth week, the embryo assumes a curved bumpy form, as shown in the photograph.

The embryo's body changes less in the fifth week, but the head and brain develop rapidly. The upper limbs form, and the lower limbs appear, looking like small paddles. In the sixth week, the head continues to grow rapidly, and differentiation of the limbs occurs as elbows, fingers, and wrists become recognizable. It is now possible to discern the ears and eyes. The limbs develop rapidly in the seventh week, and stumps appear that will form fingers and toes.

By the end of the eighth week, the embryo has distinctly human features. Almost half of the embryo consists of the head. The eyes, ears, toes, and fingers are easily distinguishable. All internal and external structures have formed. Thus, in 8 weeks, a single, tiny, undifferentiated cell has proliferated into a remarkably complex organism consisting of millions of cells differentiated into heart, kidneys, eyes, ears, nervous system, brain, and other structures. Its mass has increased a staggering 2 million percent. Figure 4.2 gives some indication of the magnitude of this change.

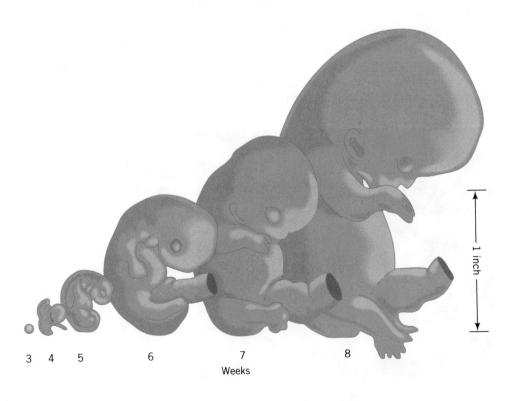

1 inch

3   4   5   6   7   8
Weeks

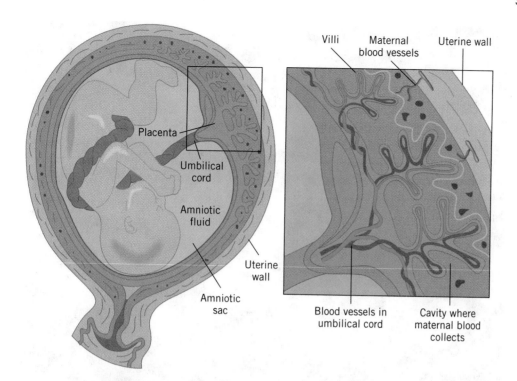

FIGURE 4.3   Development of the prenatal environment
Maternal structures that support the embryo and fetus include the placental villi, amniotic sac, placenta, and umbilical cord.

Just as the embryo's inner cell mass changes rapidly in the early weeks of development, so do its other cells linking it to its prenatal environment. Three major structures arising from these cells develop by the end of the embryonic period: the amniotic sac, the placenta, and the umbilical cord (see Figure 4.3).

The **amniotic sac** is a watertight membrane filled with fluid. As the embryo grows, the amniotic sac surrounds it, cushioning and supporting it within the uterus and providing an environment with a constant temperature. The **placenta**, formed from both the mother's tissue and the embryo's tissue, is a remarkable organ through which the mother and the embryo (later the fetus) exchange materials, such as oxygen, nutrients, and fetal waste. Linking the embryo to the placenta is the **umbilical cord**, which houses the blood vessels that carry these materials.

The exchange of materials takes place in the *placental villi*. These ornate-looking structures (shown in Figure 4.3) are small blood vessels immersed in the mother's blood but separated from it by a very thin membrane. The membrane serves as a filter—nature's way of keeping many diseases, germs, and impurities in the mother's blood from reaching the baby. Unfortunately, as you will see, it is not a perfect filter. Blood itself does not pass between the mother and the fetus (which is why the mother and baby can have different blood types). However, oxygen and nutrients do pass from the mother's blood through the placenta to the fetus, and waste products of the fetus pass into the mother's blood to be carried away and excreted.

Period of the Fetus (9th to 38th Week)

At the end of the eighth week, the period of the **fetus** begins. The principal changes for the fetus are to develop further the already formed organ structures and to increase in size and weight. Beginning its third month weighing less than an ounce and measuring 2 inches in length, the average fetus will be born 266 days after conception weighing about 7 to 8 pounds and measuring about 20 inches in length. Fetal growth begins to slow around the eighth month—which is good for both the mother and the fetus because at that rate, if it did not, the fetus would weigh 200 pounds at birth!

During this period, the fetus's appearance changes drastically. The head grows less than do other parts of the body, so that its ratio decreases from 50 percent of the body mass

Amniotic sac
A fluid-containing watertight membrane that surrounds and protects the embryo and fetus.

Placenta
An organ that forms where the embryo attaches to the uterus. This organ exchanges nutrients, oxygen, and wastes between the embryo or fetus and the mother through a very thin membrane that does not allow the passage of blood.

Umbilical cord
A soft cable of tissue and blood vessels that connects the fetus to the placenta.

Questions for Thought and Discussion
The embryo stage is the most vulnerable time for prenatal development, but this is 3 to 8 weeks after conception when many women do not even realize they are pregnant. What are the implications of this fact for sexually active women?

Fetus
The developing organism from the 9th week to the 38th week after conception.

At 12 weeks, a fetus's head is 50 percent of its body mass. (Image provided by Anatomical Travelogue, www.anatomicaltravel.com. From the book *Conception to Birth: A Life Unfolds*, authored by Alexander Tsiaras.)

at 12 weeks to 25 percent at birth. The skin, which has been transparent, begins to thicken during the third month. Facial features, which appeared almost extraterrestrial at 6 weeks, become more human looking as the eyes move from the sides of the head to the front.

The eyelids seal shut near the beginning of the third month and remain that way for the next 3 months. Nails appear on fingers and toes by the fourth month, and pads appear at the ends of the fingers that will uniquely identify the individual for life. Head hair also begins to grow. Bone structure begins to support a more erect posture by 6 months.

Changes in external appearance are accompanied by equally striking internal changes. By 3 months, the brain has organized into functional subdivisions—seeing, hearing, thinking, and so on. Most of the 100 billion cells that make up the adult brain are already present in the fetus by the fifth month, but the 14 trillion connections they will make between themselves and incoming and outgoing nerve cells will not be completed until well after birth. Other nerve cells grow and establish connections throughout fetal development.

A major mystery facing scientists is how the single, undifferentiated zygote cell can give rise to billions of fibers that properly connect eyes, ears, touch sensors, muscles, and the parts of the brain. Part of this answer lies in what are known as *regulator genes*. From the moment of conception, this subset of genes directs the activity of other genes, causing some to form arms, some legs, and so forth. It is also clear, however, that environmental factors and interactions between nerve cells play a role, as no two brains are wired identically, not even those of identical twins, who have exactly the same genetic material (Edelman, 1993; Rakic, 1988).

Other internal organs continue to develop. Sexual differentiation begins to occur by the end of the third month. In females, the precursors of ova, or *oocytes*, form on the outer covering of the ovaries. All the oocytes the female will ever possess will be present at birth. The fallopian tubes, uterus, and vagina develop, and the external labia become discernible. In the male, the scrotum, testes, and penis develop.

Fetal activity begins in the third month, when the fetus is capable of forming a fist and wiggling toes. The mother, however, does not feel this activity until around the fourth or fifth month of pregnancy. The fetus also appears to become sensitive to environmental stimulation, moving its whole body in response to a touch stimulus.

By the fourth month the eyes are sensitive to light through the lids, and by the fifth month a loud noise may activate the fetus. During this same month, the fetus swims effortlessly, a luxury gradually lost later as quarters become increasingly cramped. The fetus is now capable of kicking and turning and may begin to display rhythms of sleep and activity. By the seventh month, brain connections are sufficient for the fetus to exhibit a sucking reflex when the lips are touched.

The later stages of prenatal development ready the fetus to live outside the mother's body. Although separate from the mother in many ways during development, the fetus is nevertheless completely dependent on her for survival during most of the prenatal period. Recall that the support system in the uterus provides oxygen, nutrients, waste disposal, and a constant temperature for the developing baby. The **age of viability**, or the age at which the developing baby can survive outside the womb, occurs sometime between the 22nd and 26th weeks, usually when the fetus reaches a weight of 500 grams or about 1.1 pounds. The chances of survival for babies who are born weighing less than 500 grams remain very slim (Martin et al., 2005).

The major obstacle to independent life for a fetus born prematurely is the immaturity of the air sacs of the lungs, which have to exchange carbon dioxide for oxygen. The fetus's inability to digest food or control body temperature is also a problem, and fat has not yet formed under the skin to assist in temperature regulation.

By 6 to 7 months of age, the fetus has a chance of survival outside the mother's body. The brain is sufficiently developed to provide at least partial regulation of breathing, swallowing, and body temperature. However, a baby born after only 7 months of development needs extra oxygen, can take food only in very small amounts, and must live for several weeks in an incubator for temperature control.

In the eighth month, fat appears under the skin, and although the digestive system is still too immature to extract nutrients from food adequately, the fetus begins to store maternal nutrients in its body. Even then, a baby born at 8 months is susceptible to infection. Beginning in the eighth month, the mother's body gives the developing baby disease-fighting antibodies, which she has developed through her own exposure to foreign bodies. This process is not complete until 9 months of fetal age. It is an important process because the antibodies help protect newborn babies from infection until they are around 6 months of age, when they can produce their own antibodies in substantial amounts.

Some individual differences become evident during the last weeks of prenatal life. Fetuses differ, for example, in how much they move around in the womb, and these differences relate to individual differences children show in both activity level and

Age of viability
The age (presently around 23 or 24 weeks) at which the infant has a chance to survive if born prematurely.

This couple celebrates the growth of their 8-month-old fetus. What changes have occurred during this long period of the fetus? What challenges would they face if their baby were born now? (Anne Ackermann/Digital Vision/Getty Images, Inc.)

temperament at 2 years of age (DiPietro et al., 2002). Similarly, fetuses vary in their patterns of heart rate change, and these variations have been shown to correlate with some aspects of both temperament and cognitive development in early childhood (Bornstein et al., 2002; DiPietro et al., 1996). Nevertheless, individual temperament and behavioral characteristics cannot be predicted accurately from measures during the prenatal period. Thus, parents should not anticipate a challenging toddler just because their fetus seems to kick more than the average baby.

✔ *Test Your Mastery...*

Learning Objective 4.2: *Trace the changes that occur in the three stages of prenatal development.*

1. What is the period of gestation in humans, and how is it calculated?
2. What changes occur during the period of the zygote between conception and the end of the second week of development?
3. What changes occur during the period of the embryo between weeks 3 and 8?
4. What changes occur during the period of the fetus between the 9th week and birth?

Prenatal Environmental Influences

Learning Objective 4.3
Describe the impacts of teratogens and maternal health as environmental influences that affect prenatal development.

The baby's earliest development is influenced not only by genetic heritage, but also by the environment in the only home the embryo and fetus know: the mother's uterus. A number of factors affect the quality of this early home and determine whether or not development is optimal—even if development can occur at all. Some factors are external agents, acting on the baby through the mother. Others involve the health of the mother herself.

Teratogens

Approximately 3 to 4 percent of all babies born alive are identified as having a birth defect (National Center on Birth Defects and Developmental Disabilities, 2005). In addition to genetic causes, malformations may result from prenatal exposure to infectious diseases, drugs, harmful chemicals, and other environmental hazards. External agents that can cause malformation in the embryo and fetus and are not genetic in origin are referred to as **teratogens** (from a Greek word, *teras*, meaning "monster").

Teratogen
An agent that can cause abnormal development in the fetus.

Teratogens are defined in terms of their physical effects, although teratogens can have psychological and behavioral effects as well. Many researchers use behavior as well as physical outcomes to study the potentially damaging effects of teratogens. For many years in the United States, people believed that the embryo and fetus lived in a privileged environment, protected against harm by the placenta and its amniotic world. By 1930, however, people discovered that X-rays could retard prenatal growth and cause microcephaly (an abnormally small head and brain) and small eyes. By the mid-1940s, it was clear that a pregnant mother who contracted rubella (German measles) during the early months of pregnancy had a good chance of producing a baby with congenital abnormalities of the eye, ear, heart, and brain. Thus, it is important to be immunized against German measles prior to pregnancy.

In the early 1960s, a major disaster finally shook people's faith in the privileged-environment belief. A mild and seemingly harmless sedative, thalidomide, was marketed in the late 1950s, and many pregnant women took it for morning sickness. Physicians soon noticed a sharp increase in the number of babies born with defective limbs. Research showed that thalidomide was the culprit. Since that time many more teratogens have been identified as causing birth defects in people.

The following principles explain how teratogens work (Hogge, 1990).

1. *A teratogen's effect depends on the genetic makeup of the organism exposed to it.* A prime example is thalidomide. The human fetus is extremely sensitive to this substance, but rabbits and rats are not. One reason thalidomide was not initially suspected to be a teratogen was that testing on these animals revealed no ill effects.

2. *The effect of a teratogen on development depends partly on timing.* Even before conception, teratogens can affect the formation of the parents' germ cells. Formation of female germ cells begins during fetal life, and formation of sperm can occur up to 64 days before the sperm are expelled. Thus, a fetus can be affected by drugs that the pregnant grandmother took decades earlier or by X-ray exposure that the father experienced many weeks before conception.

For 2 to 3 weeks after conception, the zygote's fluids do not mix with those of the mother, so the zygote is relatively impervious to some teratogens. After the zygote has attached to the uterus, however, substances in the mother's bloodstream can pass through the placental barrier and mix with the blood of the embryo, and the embryo enters a particularly sensitive period. As can be seen in Figure 4.4, teratogens can produce organ malformation from 2 to 8 weeks because this is a time when organs are forming. After the organs have formed, teratogens primarily produce growth retardation or tissue damage (Goldman, 1980).

Which organ is affected by a teratogen depends in part on which organ is forming. Rubella is an example of how crucial timing can be. Rubella affects only 2 to 3 percent of the offspring of mothers infected within 2 weeks after their last period, whereas it affects 50 percent of offspring when infection occurs during the first month following conception, 22 percent during the second month, and 6 to 8 percent during the third month. Whether

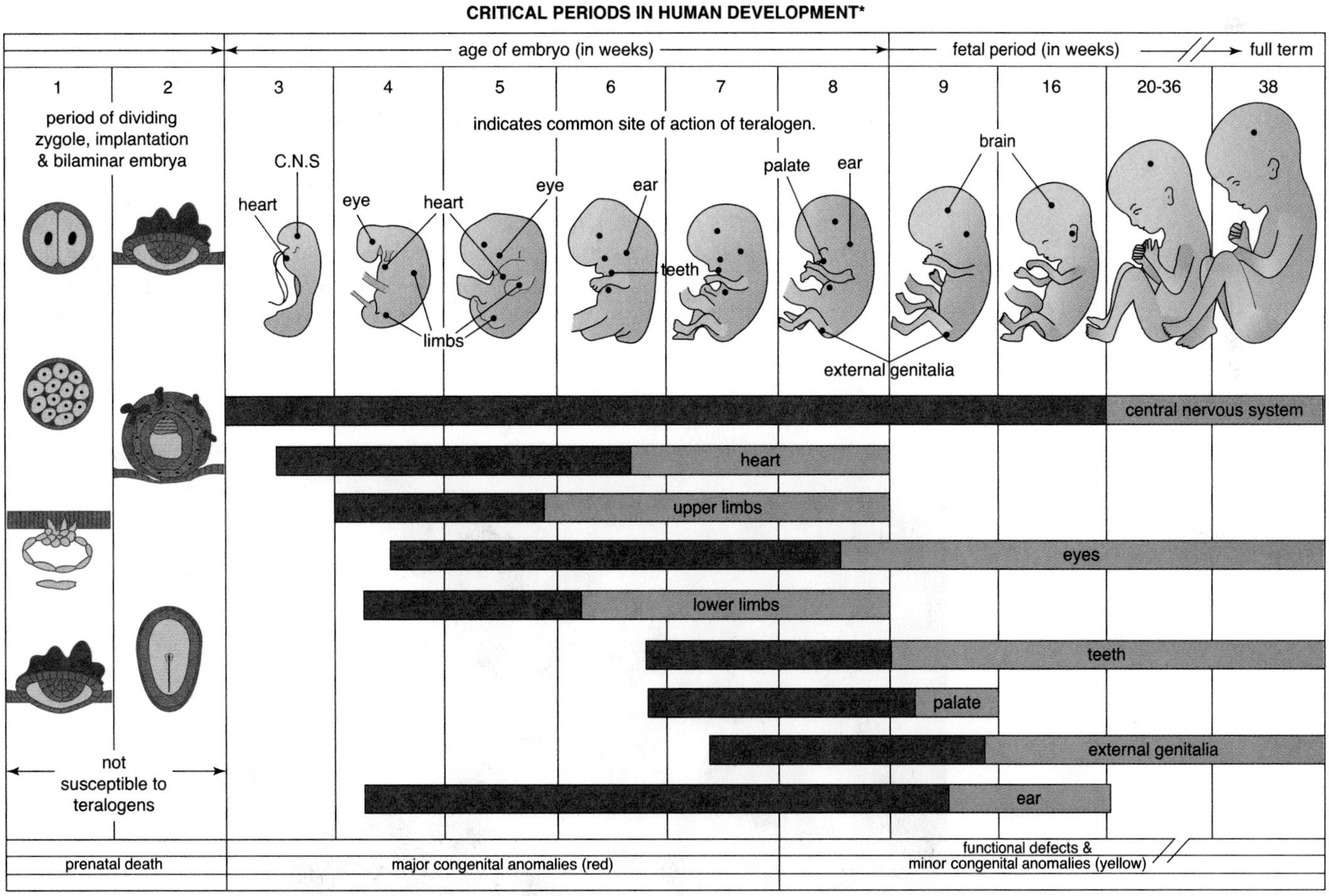

CRITICAL PERIODS IN HUMAN DEVELOPMENT*

*Red indicates highly sensitive periods when teratogens may induce major anomalies.

FIGURE 4.4   Sensitive periods in prenatal development

The effect of a teratogen depends in part on its timing during prenatal development. Sensitivity to teratogens is greatest from 3 to 9 weeks after conception, the period when organ formation occurs. The most critical age period of vulnerability for each organ is shown in green and continuing periods where the likelihood of damage declines is shown in yellow.

SOURCE: Adapted from K.L. Moore. (1989). *Before We Are Born*, 3rd ed. (p. 118). Philadelphia: Saunders.

ear, eye, heart, or brain damage occurs depends on the stage of the formation of each organ when the mother is infected (Murata et al., 1992; Whitley & Goldenberg, 1990).

3. *The effect of a teratogen may be unique and severe.* For example, thalidomide produces gross limb defects (sometimes limbs fail to form at all), whereas rubella primarily affects sensory and internal organs. In addition to malformations, teratogenic effects may include growth retardation, functional and behavioral disorders, or even death.

4. *Teratogens differ in how they gain access to the fetus.* Radiation passes to the fetus directly through the mother's body, for example, whereas chemicals usually travel to the fetus through the blood and across the placental membrane. The mother's blood may be able to filter some potentially harmful chemicals to protect the fetus. The placenta serves as a filter, but not as a complete barrier; materials may be slowed but not stopped.

5. *The likelihood and degree of abnormal development increase with the fetus's dosage of the harmful agent.* Depending on the amount of the teratogen to which the fetus is exposed, the outcome can range from no effect at all to death.

Teratogens can be drugs—either illegal drugs, such as heroin or cocaine; controlled substances that are easily available, such as alcohol or tobacco; therapeutic drugs, including prescription drugs like thalidomide, as well as over-the-counter medications. Teratogens can be hazards from the external environment, such as radiation or mercury or lead poisoning. Or they can be diseases contracted by the mother that cross the placental barrier and affect the fetus. Common teratogens and their effects are listed in Table 4.1.

Illegal and Harmful Drugs

The increasing availability of powerful mood- and mind-altering illegal drugs since the 1960s has been a major health concern in the United States and, unfortunately, has provided substantial evidence about the dangers of drug intake by pregnant women, both to themselves and to their fetuses. Addictive drugs have attracted the most attention.

Heroin addicts, for example, are more likely to have medical complications during pregnancy and labor, and their newborn babies are likely to undergo drug-withdrawal symptoms (Sprauve, 1996). Frequently, addiction to heroin is compounded by poor nutrition and inadequate health care. As many as half of all babies born to mothers who use heroin during

Newborn babies who have been exposed to cocaine as fetuses are more likely to be premature and irritable and to have disrupted sleep patterns. (Mark Richards/PhotoEdit)

TABLE 4.1 Some Teratogens and Conditions That May Harm the Fetus

TERATOGEN	POTENTIAL EFFECT
ILLEGAL DRUGS	
Cocaine and crack	Growth retardation, premature birth, irritability in the newborn, withdrawal symptoms
Heroin and methadone	Growth retardation, premature birth, irritability in the newborn, withdrawal symptoms, SIDS
LSD and marijuana	Probable cause of premature birth and growth retardation when used heavily; possible chromosomal breakage
TOBACCO, ALCOHOL, AND CAFFEINE	
Smoking	Growth retardation, prematurity
Alcohol use	Brain and heart damage, growth retardation, mental retardation, fetal alcohol syndrome
Caffeine	Miscarriage, premature birth, and lower birth weight
THERAPEUTIC DRUGS	
Aspirin	In large quantities, miscarriage, bleeding, newborn respiratory problems
Barbiturates	Newborn respiratory problems
Diethylstilbestrol (DES)	Genital abnormalities in both sexes, vaginal and cervical cancer in adolescent females
Phenytoin (an anticonvulsant drug)	Threefold increase in likelihood of heart defects and growth retardation
Streptomycin	Hearing loss
Tetracycline	Most commonly, staining of teeth; can also affect bone growth
Thalidomide	Deformed limbs, sensory deficits, defects in internal organs, death
ENVIRONMENTAL HAZARDS	
Lead	Miscarriage, anemia, mental retardation
Mercury	Abnormal head and brain growth, motor incoordination, mental retardation
PCBs	Growth retardation
Radiation	Leukemia, abnormal brain and body growth, cancer, genetic alterations, miscarriage, stillbirth
Dioxin	Leukemia and other cancers
Pesticides	Leukemia and other cancers, abnormal reproductive development
INFECTIOUS DISEASES	
AIDS	Congenital malformations; leaves infant vulnerable to infections of all types
Cytomegalovirus	Deafness, blindness, abnormal head and brain growth, mental retardation
Herpes	Mental retardation, eye damage, death
Rubella	Mental retardation, eye damage, deafness, heart defects
Syphilis	Mental retardation, miscarriage, blindness, deafness, death
Toxoplasmosis	Abnormalities in brain and head growth, mental retardation

pregnancy are low birthweight, and many are also preterm. Medical complications include placental abruption (when the placenta pulls away from the wall of the uterus, causing extensive bleeding), poor fetal growth, and preterm delivery. These babies are also more likely to suffer health problems related to preterm birth, including brain bleeds and problems with lung development. In addition, babies born to heroin users are likely to suffer withdrawal symptoms after birth, such as trembling, irritability, vomiting, and continual crying. Infants exposed to heroin prenatally are also ten times more likely to die of sudden infant death syndrome (SIDS) than other infants (March of Dimes, 2005).

Another illegal drug that has received a lot of attention is cocaine. A conservative estimate is that at least 45,000 cocaine-exposed infants are born each year (Lester, Boukydis, & Twomey, 2000). The ready availability of cocaine, especially in the much cheaper form of crack, has increased use of the drug to epidemic proportions.

Cocaine affects the fetus indirectly through reduced maternal blood flow to the uterus, limiting the fetus's supply of nutrients and oxygen. In addition, cocaine passes through the placenta and enters the fetus's bloodstream, where it gains direct access to the brain in as little as 3 minutes. In the brain, cocaine affects chemical nerve transmitters in addition to increasing heart rate and blood pressure.

Cocaine-exposed babies are more likely to be miscarried or stillborn. If they are born alive, they are more likely to be preterm or low birthweight. They also are more likely to be difficult to arouse and more irritable. They may have difficulty regulating their level of alertness as well as their sleep patterns (DiPietro et al., 1995; March of Dimes, 2005; Phillips et al., 1996).

Despite these problems, studies have turned up conflicting findings as to how babies exposed to cocaine turn out. Some studies have reported that exposed babies later are more impulsive than nonexposed babies and have greater difficulty regulating their attention. Other studies report few or no long-term effects that can be attributed to cocaine exposure alone. Cocaine research shares the same difficulties as research on many other teratogens. Mothers who use cocaine are more likely to use other drugs and to smoke and drink. They are also more likely to live in chaotic environments, to experience poverty, to be undernourished and in poor health, and to be depressed. Given this complex of factors, which often exist both before and after a child is born, it is difficult to pinpoint the precise role of prenatal cocaine exposure in the child's development (Lester, 2000; Mayes & Fahy, 2001; Stanwood & Levitt, 2001).

The use of marijuana and hallucinogens accelerated rapidly in the 1960s and 1970s, and today marijuana remains the most often used illicit drug. As with other drugs, the effects of marijuana are difficult to separate from other environmental effects and health care practices. However, useful findings have been obtained from one major longitudinal study by Peter Fried in Ottawa, Canada. Fried and his colleagues followed a group of children who were exposed prenatally to marijuana smoke (Fried, 1989). The study initially involved 682 women in the Ottawa region. A subsample of 180 children was selected for follow-up into childhood and adolescence (Fried, 2000b). The researchers interviewed participating mothers-to-be once during each trimester of their pregnancy and collected information about their backgrounds, diet, and health, as well as their cigarette, alcohol, and marijuana use.

From these interviews, Fried (1989) observed that many mothers reduced or stopped their use of alcohol and cigarettes. It seemed that the message from health authorities concerning the harmful effects of prenatal alcohol and tobacco use was getting across. However, a similar reduction was not seen for marijuana use. Prenatal marijuana exposure affects the developing baby in several ways. First, abnormalities in the spacing of the eyes and the shape of the eyelids was observed in infants whose mothers had been heavy marijuana users (those who smoked more than six times per week) (Fried, 1989, 2002b). In addition, newborns exposed prenatally to marijuana tended to display neurological consequences, such as increased fine motor tremors, exaggerated and prolonged startle responses, and poorer habituation to visual stimuli (Fried, 1989, 2002b).

Fried and colleagues followed up with their sample, repeatedly testing them throughout childhood and into adolescence (Fried, 2002b). There seemed to be little evidence for any effects during the toddler period, but as the children grew, signs of mild cognitive effects became apparent that continued into adolescence. Prenatal marijuana exposure seemed to have no effect on children's overall IQ, but did affect children's "executive function"—cognitive abilities and behaviors that affect motivation and are critical in effortful, goal-oriented situations (Fried 2000a, 2000b). Children exposed to marijuana showed problems in executive functions such as paying attention, controlling impulses, problem solving, and persisting in visual-perceptual tasks such as reading. Thus, there is some evidence for long-term negative consequences of prenatal exposure to marijuana.

Tobacco About one-fourth of the women of childbearing age in North America smoke. Although many quit at the time they become pregnant, 11 percent continue to smoke throughout pregnancy (Martin, et al., 2005). The effects of nicotine and cigarette smoke on the fetus have been well investigated (Cornelius & Day, 2000). Smoking is known to impair the functioning of the placenta, especially oxygen exchange. The following are some risks to women who smoke while they are pregnant:

- On average, their babies weigh less. According to some estimates, smoking during pregnancy is responsible for as many as 20 percent of the low-birthweight infants born each year in the United States (American Cancer Society, 2004).
- The likelihood of premature delivery and related complications increases with the number of cigarettes they smoke per day (Cornelius et al., 1995).
- Their babies are 25 to 56 percent more likely to die at birth or soon thereafter (Murata et al., 1992).
- Their babies are as much as 50 percent more likely to develop cancer (Stjernfeldt et al., 1986).
- Their babies, particularly if they smoke both before and after pregnancy, are two to three times more likely to die of SIDS than the babies of mothers who do not smoke (American Cancer Society, 2004).

As children, their babies are at heightened risk for social and behavioral problems (Day et al., 2000; Wasserman et al., 2001) and for poor performance on measures of language and cognitive development (Cornelius et al., 2001; Fried et al., 1992). Even passive exposure to second-hand smoke has been shown to affect the growth of the fetus (Dejin-Karlsson et al., 1998).

Alcohol In the United States, alcohol is the most widely used drug that is known to harm the fetus (Olson, 1994). It is the leading cause of preventable mental retardation (Alexander, 1998; American Association on Mental Retardation, 2002). Alcohol withdrawal effects in newborns of mothers who drink heavily can mimic those of drug addiction (Abel, 1980, 1981). In 1973 investigators studying chronic maternal alcoholism first described **fetal alcohol syndrome (FAS)**, a unique set of problems for the fetus caused by the mother's alcohol consumption (Jones et al., 1973).

FAS may lead to limb and facial malformations, congenital heart disease, failure to thrive, anomalies of the external genitalia, growth retardation, mental retardation, and learning disabilities. Behavior problems compound these difficulties, as infants with FAS are irritable, do not sleep well, and are difficult to feed (Wekselman et al., 1995). By school age, these children are more likely to have difficulty sustaining effort and attention and to have language problems and motor-performance deficits (Larsson, Bohlin, & Tunell, 1985; Schonfeld et al., 2001; Streissguth & Connor, 2001).

The incidence of fetal alcohol syndrome is 1 to 2 per 1,000 live births. Among samples of alcoholic women, it rises to as high as 10 percent (Mayes & Fahy, 2001). CDC studies show FAS rates ranging from 0.2 to 1.5 per 1,000 live births in different areas of the United States (2005, http://www.cdc.gov/ncbddd/fas/fasask.htm#how). Native North Americans in Canada and the United States appear to be at greater risk. Some children exposed to alcohol during the prenatal period demonstrate some but not all of the characteristics of FAS. Such children are said to suffer from *fetal alcohol effects (FAE)*, which is two to three times more common than FAS (Streissguth & Connor, 2001).

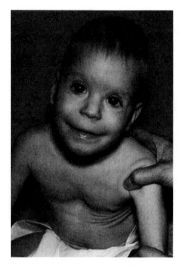

This infant was born with fetal alcohol syndrome. What health risks and life challenges will this child likely face? How could these problems be prevented? (©James W. Hanson)

Fetal alcohol syndrome (FAS)
A set of features in the infant and child caused by the mother's use of alcohol during pregnancy; typically includes facial malformations and other physical and mental disabilities.

Questions for Thought and Discussion
Should pregnant mothers who knowingly ingest teratogens be prosecuted for child abuse? What might be some drawbacks of such a public policy?

Therapeutic Drugs

Many pregnant women take prescribed drugs as part of a continuing regimen of health care—for example, to treat diabetes or reduce risk of stroke—or as treatments for health problems brought on by the pregnancy. Some of these drugs may increase risk for the fetus, and that risk needs to be weighed against the risk to the mother if she does not take the drug.

Anticoagulants (blood thinners), anticonvulsants (for epileptics), antibiotics, and even heavy use of over-the-counter medications such as aspirin have been implicated in fetal growth retardation, malformations, and death, especially when taken during the first three months of pregnancy. In addition, drugs may interact in harmful ways. For example, aspirin, which is harmless at a particular dosage in rats, can be teratogenic if administered with benzoic acid, a widely used food preservative. Sex hormones, such as estrogen and progesterone, are sometimes used to treat breast cancer in women and to reduce the likelihood of miscarriage. However, the use of sex hormones in early pregnancy has been associated with central nervous system malformations in offspring and, more frequently, with masculinization of the external genitalia of females.

In the early 1950s and 1960s some pregnant women took a damaging synthetic hormone, diethylstilbestrol (DES) to reduce the likelihood of miscarriage. Much later, physicians discovered that a high percentage of the female children of these women developed vaginal and cervical problems when they reached adolescence, and some of these young women (known as "DES daughters") developed cancer of the cervix (Giusti, Iwamoto, & Hatch, 1995). Recently, evidence has accumulated that the male offspring ("DES sons") of mothers who took DES are more likely to develop testicular cancer and to have a lowered sperm count (Sharpe & Skakkebaek, 1993; Wilcox et al., 1995). The studies of sex hormones illustrate yet another problem in detecting teratogenic agents—the possible delay by many years of any observable effect. The teratogenic effects of thalidomide, mentioned earlier in this chapter, is another example. Around 15,000 children in 46 countries were born with birth defects caused by prenatal exposure to thalidomide, with only 8,000 of them surviving past the first year of life. Clearly, we had a lot to learn about how different chemicals affect the fetus, and we still do. This incomplete knowledge makes it all the more unwise for pregnant women to ingest drugs that they can avoid.

Environmental Hazards

The number and amount of chemicals in our environment have increased explosively since the beginning of the Industrial Revolution. Insecticides, herbicides, fungicides, solvents, detergents, food additives, and miscellaneous other chemicals have become common in our daily existence. Approximately 70,000 chemicals are presently in use (Bellinger & Adams, 2001). Only a small fraction of these chemicals have been tested as potential teratogens in pregnant laboratory animals.

Researchers often find that chemicals are potentially teratogenic in animals, but at doses much larger than people normally are exposed to. Exceptions are rare industrial accidents or concentrated dumping of hazardous waste (for example, in Love Canal, a former chemical dumping ground near Niagara Falls). Rates of defective births and spontaneous abortions are monitored routinely in many hospitals in the United States, providing a measure of protection against long-term chronic exposure to undiscovered teratogens. However, as you have seen, complex interactions among chemicals and delayed effects can often make detection difficult.

A clear example of the effects of environmental pollution comes from Cubatão, a small town in an industrial valley in Brazil that manufactures petrochemicals. Cubatão was slowly choking through pollution of its streams, air, and countryside. Thousands of tons of particulate matter were being discharged into the air from smokestacks, and huge amounts of organic matter and heavy metals were being dumped into the streams. These conditions caused high rates of cancer, stillbirths, and birth defects. At times children and the aged had to be supplied with emergency oxygen. Through an ambitious cleanup program the town reduced discharges of particulate matter by 72 percent, organic waste into rivers by 93 percent, and heavy metals by 97 percent. The infant mortality rate in Cubatão dropped to one-half the 1984 rate (Brooke, 1991).

Heavy metals are particularly harmful. Mercury and lead, for example, have been suspected teratogens for many years. A disaster comparable to that caused by thalidomide occurred in Japan between 1954 and 1960, when people ate fish from a bay that had been contaminated with mercury from industrial dumping. Soon after the contamination, the proportion of miscarriages and stillbirths rose to 43 percent (Bellinger & Adams, 2001). Many mothers who ate the fish gave birth to infants with mental retardation and neurological symptoms resembling cerebral palsy. Autopsies of those who died revealed severe brain damage (Dietrich, 1999).

Prenatal exposure to lead from automobile exhausts and lead-base paints has been implicated in miscarriages, neuromuscular problems, and mental retardation (Bellinger et al., 1986). Follow-ups of children who experienced high lead exposure as babies reveal negative effects even after 11 years on a variety of measures, including vocabulary, motor coordination, reading ability, and higher-level thinking (Needleman et al., 1990).

Another group of environmental chemicals that can harm fetuses consists of polychlorinated biphenyls (PCBs), widely used as lubricants, insulators, and ingredients in electrical equipment, paints, plastics, varnishes, rubber products, waxes, dyes, and carbonless copy paper. According to the Environmental Protection Agency, more than 1.5 billion pounds of PCBs were manufactured in the United States prior to cessation of production in 1977. Cooking oil used in Japan in 1968 and in Taiwan in 1979 was accidentally contaminated by PCBs, and pregnant women who used the oil were more likely to have stillborn infants and infants with darkly pigmented skin.

In the United States, PCB levels were relatively high in fish taken from Lake Michigan. Offspring of mothers who ate these fish were smaller at birth, had somewhat smaller heads, and were more likely to startle and be irritable. Babies with detectable PCB levels in their blood at birth performed more poorly on various visual measures at both 7 months and 4 years of age (Jacobson & Jacobson, 1988; Jacobson et al., 1992). It is partly for these reasons that PCBs are no longer produced or imported in the United States.

Infectious Diseases

As mentioned previously, several viral and bacterial infections and sexually transmitted diseases that might be present in the mother during pregnancy can damage the fetus. For example, if the mother contracts rubella (German measles) during her first trimester of pregnancy, it can have devastating effects on the developing baby. The virus can damage the central nervous system of the embryo or fetus, resulting in blindness, deafness, and mental retardation. The heart, liver, and bone structure may also be damaged, depending on the timing of infection.

Herpes Two viruses in the herpes group can produce central nervous system damage. Cytomegalovirus (CMV), the most common intrauterine viral infection, may cause birth defects such as hearing loss, vision impairment, and varying degrees of mental retardation. In addition, mothers who contract CMV during pregnancy are likely to have infants who are born already infected with the virus. CMV can be transmitted by sexual contact, breast milk, transplanted organs, and rarely from blood transfusions (CDC National Center for Infectious Disease, 2002, http://www.cdc.gov/ncidod/diseases/cmv.htm).

Another herpes virus, herpes virus type 2, infects the genitals of adults. This virus had reached epidemic levels in the United States by the early 1980s. In the infant, herpes 2 can cause encephalitis, central nervous system damage, and blood-clotting problems. Most herpes 2 infections of newborns occur from direct contamination by contact with the mother's infected birth canal (Murata et al., 1992; Whitley & Goldenberg, 1990).

HIV Another virus that reached epidemic levels in the 1980s and continues to ravage populations today is the human immunodeficiency virus (HIV), which causes acquired immunodeficiency syndrome (AIDS). The virus is transmitted from one person to another exclusively through body fluids. It can be transmitted from mother to infant through breast milk following birth. It can also be transmitted from mother to fetus through the placenta prior to birth, as well as through contact with the mother's blood in the birth canal.

In addition to causing AIDS, HIV can act as a teratogen. Some infected babies are born with facial deformities—larger-than-normal eye separation, boxlike foreheads, flattened nose bridges, and misshapen eye openings. Until recently, approximately 25 percent of infants with HIV-infected mothers acquired the virus, and most died in early childhood. Fortunately, the development of new forms of drug treatment has substantially reduced the prenatal transmission of HIV, as well as lengthened the period before disease onset for children who are infected (Culhane et al., 1999; Hutton, 1996).

Syphilis and Gonorrhea Syphilis and gonorrhea are sexually transmitted diseases with teratogenic effects. After declining for several years, the incidence of syphilis began to increase in the late 1980s. This disease is caused by a spirochete, a type of bacteria, which can infect the fetus and cause central nervous system damage, deformities of the teeth and skeleton, and even death. The fetus is relatively resistant to infection from the syphilis spirochete until the fourth or fifth month.

Gonorrhea is also caused by a bacterial agent. Its incidence has been reported to be as high as 30 percent in some populations. In 2002, a total of 351,852 cases of gonorrhea were reported to CDC, or 125 per 100,000 persons (http://www.cdc.gov/std/Gonorrhea/STD-Fact-Gonorrhea.htm#common, 2005). Premature birth, premature rupture of membranes, and spontaneous abortion are associated with gonorrhea. The fetus is affected in about 30 percent of cases. The most common problem is eye infection, which can lead to blindness if untreated. Fortunately, almost all newborns are treated with silver nitrate eyedrops at birth to prevent this problem (Murata et al., 1992; Whitley & Goldenberg, 1990).

Maternal Health

Much current media attention focuses on potential teratogens that mothers voluntarily consume or to which mothers are exposed in the modern industrial environment. Yet mothers and their developing babies have always faced natural challenges from the environment. The quality of the mother's nutrition and overall health is an important determinant of how the fetus develops. Maternal experiences and stress may also have an effect.

The original fertilized egg must multiply into trillions of cells to form a fully developed fetus. During prenatal development, cells increase not only in number but also in size. As Table 4.2 illustrates, the baby and its accompanying support system within the

TABLE 4.2 Weight Gain during Pregnancy	
DEVELOPMENT	**WEIGHT GAIN (LB)**
Infant at birth	7 1/2
Placenta	1 1/2
Increase in blood supply to the placenta	4
Increase in mother's fluid volume	4
Increase in size of uterus and supporting muscles	2
Increase in breast size	2
Amniotic fluid	2
Mother's fat stores	7
Total	30

SOURCE: Reprinted by permission from E.N. Whitney and S.R. Rolfes. (2002). *Understanding Nutrition*, 9th ed. (p. 507). Copyright (c) 2002 by Wadsworth Publishing Co.

mother's uterus will weigh 25 to 30 pounds by the ninth month of pregnancy, billions of times the weight of the fertilized egg.

Where does all of this mass come from? The mother! Thinking about the issue this way brings home the importance of maternal nutrition. The quality of the fetus's cells can be no better than that of the nutrients the mother supplies through the placental circulation system. This simple fact is often not fully appreciated. Particularly in the early stages of development, the functioning of cells depends on their environment. The quality of the mother's nutrition is probably the most important environmental influence on the fetus and newborn baby (Morgane et al., 1993).

Nutrition The prospective mother, then, must supply nutrients for the developing baby and its support system within her uterus. In part, her ability to do this depends on her nutrition during pregnancy. But it also depends to a great extent on her nutritional status *before* pregnancy. Both the mothers and their fetuses fare more poorly when the mother has had long-term malnutrition than when the mother has had good nutrition prior to pregnancy (Rosso, 1990). Maternal malnutrition is associated with increased rates of spontaneous abortion, infant death, and congenital defects. Pregnant women who have inadequate diets are also more likely to have small and premature babies (Bauerfeld & Lachenmeyer, 1992).

As is sometimes the case with teratogens, however, it can be difficult to isolate the effects of malnourishment from other factors. Malnutrition is often accompanied by inadequate housing, health care, sanitation, and education, as well as the daily stress of poverty. Catastrophes sometimes provide a means for separating out the influences of at least some of these factors. During World War II, for example, the entire populations of many countries had severely limited food supplies not associated with the other factors. In the Netherlands, for example, scarce food supplies caused a decline in conceptions and a substantial increase in miscarriages, stillbirths, and congenital malformations.

Food quantity is not the only issue in maternal nutrition. A pregnant woman and her fetus have special dietary needs for proteins, vitamins, and minerals. Animal studies reveal that protein deficits produce damage to the kidneys and intestines and disrupt skeletal growth in the fetus. Low intake of certain vitamins can affect the eyes and internal organs and increase the number of malformations (Rosso, 1990).

Trace elements in the diet are also important. An absence of iron in the mother's blood can produce anemia in her baby. Diets lacking iodine are associated with an increased likelihood of cretinism, a severe thyroid deficiency that causes physical stunting and mental deficiency. Deficits of copper, manganese, and zinc produce central nervous system damage and other negative effects in rats, and zinc deficiency has been implicated in the occurrence of anencephaly (absence of the cortex of the brain). Deficits of folic acid in pregnant mothers have been associated with neural tube defects—anencephaly and nonclosure of the spinal cord (spina bifida)—in babies (Grantham-McGregor, Ani, & Fernald, 2001; Rosso, 1990).

Outcomes after birth depend to a large extent on children's postnatal environments. For example, children who were malnourished as fetuses because of World War II but had adequate diet and stimulation as infants and children showed no long-term intellectual deficit. Many Korean orphans suffered malnutrition during the Korean War but were later adopted by families who provided them with good nutrition and education. These children later performed as well on intelligence and achievement tests as children who had not suffered early deprivation. Thus, an enriched home environment may compensate for many of the cognitive effects of early malnutrition, but the outcome also depends on when during pregnancy the malnutrition occurred and how severe it was (Morgane et al., 1993; Vietze & Vaughan, 1988; Zeskind & Ramey, 1981).

Babies who are malnourished both as fetuses and after birth are more likely to experience developmental delays. They may remain inattentive, unresponsive, and apathetic (Bauerfeld & Lachenmeyer, 1992). Health organizations worldwide have recognized the lasting consequences of early nutritional deficits and have initiated attempts to supplement

Questions for Thought
and Discussion
How might problems of impoverished developing nations relate to problems of prenatal development in their populations?

the diets of pregnant women and infants. Babies with supplemented diets are more advanced in motor development, have better cognitive outcomes, and are more socially interactive and energetic, an encouraging sign that the consequences of bad nutrition may be avoided (Grantham-McGregor et al., 2001; Joos et al., 1983).

Excesses of nutrients can also be damaging. For example, a fetus may suffer brain damage from intrauterine exposure to the amino acid phenylalanine, present in mothers with the disease phenylketouria. Pregnant women can protect the fetus by maintaining a restricted diet during pregnancy (NIH, 2000). Excesses of the sugar galactose in diabetic mothers may cause cataracts and other physical problems, even death, in fetuses. Babies of diabetics at birth may have passive muscle tone and be less attentive (Langer, 1990). Just as deficits in iodine can cause problems, excess iodine can have a detrimental effect on thyroid function. Excesses of vitamin A can cause damage to the eyes, brain, and spinal cord of the developing fetus (Ogle & Mazzullo, 2002).

Stress Researchers have become increasingly interested in the potential effects of maternal stress on the developing baby. It is well known that when a person experiences psychological stress, the activity of the adrenal glands increases. Secretions from the adrenal glands may enter the mother's blood and be transmitted to the fetus through the placenta, thus affecting the baby's developing nervous system. In addition, hormones released during stress can reduce the blood flow and oxygen available to the fetus. Thus, a mother's emotional states can affect her unborn child.

Research reveals that high levels of anxiety are associated, for example, with newborn irritability, with feeding and sleep problems during infancy, and with behavioral problems at age 4 (O'Connor et al., 2002; Van Den Bergh, 1992). Maternal anxiety may also be associated with higher probability of congenital physical anomalies, such as heart defects and cleft palate (Carmichael & Shaw, 2000). Some animal studies found that the chemical effects of maternal stress can essentially reprogram fetal development, leading to irreversible malfunctions of the brain even in adulthood.

Again, it is difficult to control for all the potentially important variables in these relationships, and it is hard to separate prenatal and postnatal influences on the human infant. A mother who has reported a great deal of prenatal anxiety may handle her infant differently, for example, and it may be this handling that makes her baby irritable. Also, the genetic relationship between the mother and her baby, rather than the prenatal experience, may be the cause. That is, a mother who is genetically predisposed to anxiety could pass on this trait to her offspring.

High levels of prenatal stress increase the probability of preterm birth, as well as low birthweight and problems during delivery (Lobel, Dunkel-Schetter, & Scrimshaw, 1992; Paarlberg et al., 1995). Chronic maternal stress can be decreased, however, through social services and social support. When emotional support is available—for example, a supportive spouse or readily available family members—then negative outcomes for the baby become less likely (Dunkel-Schetter et al., 1996; Feldman et al., 2000).

Prenatal Care Prenatal care is medical attention designed specifically for a pregnant woman and her developing baby. Women who receive prenatal care are counseled regarding diet, exercise, prenatal testing, and substances to avoid. They are given medical advice regarding warning signs such as vaginal bleeding or cessation of fetal movement. In addition, screening procedures are performed for a variety of maternal medical conditions that can affect the developing baby, including anemia, sexually transmitted diseases, rubella, RH factor, hepatitis, HIV, gestational diabetes, hypertension, and cervical cancer. Finally, prospective mothers who receive prenatal care have access to a knowledgeable and supportive person with whom they can discuss common pregnancy-related concerns and issues.

Typically, prenatal visits are scheduled once each month until about the 28th week, when the visits might increase to every 2 to 3 weeks. After 36 weeks, pregnant women are usually seen every week until delivery. Compared to women who receive prenatal care, women who do not receive this care are more likely to have underweight and/or preterm

Babies born to women who receive early and adequate prenatal care weigh more and are healthier at birth. What specifically will this mother-to-be gain from attending scheduled prenatal consultations? (Andersen Ross/Getty Images, Inc.)

babies, and those babies are four times more likely to die following birth. One of the objectives of the Healthy People 2010 initiative, set by the U.S. Department of Health and Human Services, is to increase the proportion of pregnant women who receive prenatal care in the first trimester to 90 percent, up from its 1990 level of about 75 percent and its 2003 level of about 84 percent (Hamilton, Martin, & Sutton, 2004).

As can be seen in Figure 4.5, ethnic differences have been found in the utilization of early prenatal care. In 2003, although the overall rate was around 84 percent, only about 76 percent of African Americans, 77 percent of Hispanics, and 71 percent of Native Americans received early and adequate prenatal care, compared to nearly 90 percent of European Americans.

Why would obtaining early and adequate prenatal care differ by the mother's ethnicity? One answer is provided by looking at the relationship between socioeconomic status and health care. Differences in education, income, and occupation account for some of the differences in prenatal care. For example, in 1996, among women with at least 16 years of education, 95 percent of European American women and nearly 90 percent of African American women received prenatal care during the first trimester of pregnancy. However, among women in both groups with less than a high school education, fewer than 70 percent received prenatal care. Similar disparities in health care access and use are found based on income and occupational status. At the same time, society constrains and differentially distributes opportunities based on race or ethnicity, creating a situation in which socioeconomic status and race are often intertwined (Williams & Johnson, 2002). Unfortunately, then, inadequate prenatal care for women in poverty too often translates into inadequate prenatal care for a disproportionate number of minority women.

European American	89%
African American	77%
Hispanic	78%
Native American	70%
Asian American/Pacific Islander	86%

FIGURE 4.5 Pregnant women receiving early and adequate prenatal care by ethnicity of mother

SOURCE: Adapted from Martin, J.A., Hamilton, B.E., Sutton, P.D, Ventura, S.J., Menacker, F., & Kirmeyer, S. (2006). *Births: Final data for 2004.* National Vital Statistics Report, 55(1), p. 16.

✔ *Test Your Mastery...*

1. What are the different types of teratogens that can affect prenatal development?
2. How do teratogens work?
3. What are some effects of teratogenic substances?
4. What are some examples of environmental factors and diseases that have teratogenic effects?
5. At what stages of prenatal development do different teratogens have their most potent effect?
6. What conditions of maternal health can influence prenatal development?
7. Why is prenatal care important to the developing baby?

Birth

Learning Objective 4.4
Discuss the stages of labor and the social and cultural factors that influence childbirth.

Birth is truly a momentous event as the baby moves from the relatively sheltered and protected environment of the mother's womb to the busy and much less predictable outside world. Typically, the birth process proceeds smoothly. In this technological age, we sometimes forget that women have given birth for millennia without hospitals, doctors, or elaborate equipment. In fact, as we shall see, one decision that women and their partners must make in today's society involves the level of medical intervention that they wish to plan for during the birth process.

Labor and Delivery

Typically, around 38 weeks after fertilization, or at what is considered 40 weeks gestation, a pregnant woman will go into labor, the first step in the birth process. Labor appears to be initiated by changes in the fetal brain (Nathanielsz, 1995). Chemicals are released that signal the muscles of the mother's uterus to start contracting rhythmically, initially every 15 to 20 minutes and then at shorter intervals. The complete birth process requires, on average, about 8 to 16 hours for the first baby and about half as much time for later babies.

Labor consists of three stages, shown in Figure 4.6. The first and longest stage begins when the early contractions start to dilate or widen the cervical opening, through which the baby will pass. This stage ends when the cervix, ordinarily about the size of a pencil lead, is fully dilated to about 10 centimeters or 4 inches. By the end of this stage, the contractions are very intense, occurring every 2 to 3 minutes. The second stage begins when the fetus starts to pass through the cervix and ends when the baby has been completely delivered into the world. During this stage, the contractions are long and closely spaced,

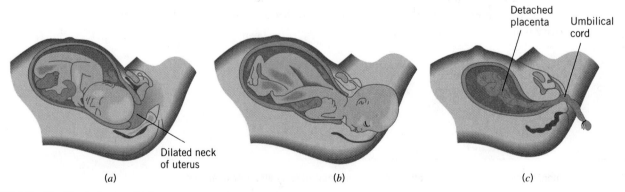

FIGURE 4.6   The three stages of labor
During labor (*a*) the neck of the uterus dilates, (b) the baby is delivered, and (c) the placenta is expelled.

and the mother is encouraged to assist the process by pushing with each contraction. The third stage, which often lasts only minutes, involves the delivery of the placenta and related other membranes, referred to as the *afterbirth*.

Childbirth and Society

Childbirth, and society's attitudes toward it, have changed dramatically over the past 125 years. In late-19th-century Europe and North America, maternal mortality rates were high. Beginning in the 1930s, thanks in large part to improved health technologies such as antibiotics, blood transfusion, and safe anesthesia and surgery, maternal deaths during childbirth in Western, industrialized countries dropped to their present rate of around 1 or 2 in 10,000 births. One objective of the Healthy People 2010 program is to further reduce the maternal mortality rate within the United States to 3.3 deaths out of 100,000 live births (Horon, 2005; Loudon, 1993).

In many countries around the world, particularly in rural settings where access to basic health care is extremely limited, maternal mortality during childbirth remains high. The World Health Organization estimates that 515,000 women die each year from pregnancy-related causes, with nearly all of these deaths occurring in developing countries. For example, in Africa the maternal mortality rate is about 1,000 out of 100,000 live births. Researchers emphasize that only widespread access to emergency obstetric care, as well as to community-based, hospital maternity care services, can lessen maternal mortality in developing countries (Mavalankar & Rosenfield, 2005).

In Europe and North America, the relative availability of high-quality health care, combined with a dramatic reduction in maternal mortality over the past 80 years, has paved the way for a different kind of debate surrounding childbirth. In particular, one long-term result of childbirth's dramatically increased safety has been what many have called the "over-medicalization" of childbirth (Davis-Floyd, 1992, 1994) in Europe and North America. Some researchers are concerned that medical intervention has sometimes gone beyond the level of ensuring safety to the level of interfering with a woman's control over her natural birth processes (Esposito, 1999). For example, many hospitals have come to apply a wide range of medical practices to all women in labor, regardless of whether such practices are clinically indicated in individual women. These practices have included the supine birth position (on the back), pubic shaving, enemas, artificial rupture of the amniotic membrane, continuous electronic fetal monitoring, episiotomies (cuts to make the vaginal opening larger), and withholding of food and water in the event that general anesthesia will be required (DeJonge & Lagro-Janssen, 2004; Saunders, 1997).

Birthing centers, typically managed by nurse-midwives, were developed in the 1970s as a safe alternative for women with low-risk pregnancies who wished to avoid the "high-tech" obstetrics of what had become the traditional hospital childbirth setting. A **certified nurse-midwife** is a health care provider who has been trained in both nursing and midwifery, and who provides a full range of gynecological and obstetric primary care services to women. Studies have demonstrated that, for low-risk women, giving birth in a birthing center is at least as safe as birthing in-hospital (Esposito, 1999; Rooks, Weatherby, Ernst, et al., 1989). Women who are experiencing high-risk pregnancies are advised to give birth in the hospital.

Birthing centers typically offer a relaxed, home-like atmosphere where nurse-midwives view themselves as "facilitating birth" rather than "delivering a baby," and working with the woman rather than performing procedures on her. Birthing centers have been predominantly a middle-class phenomenon in the United States. However, in one study that examined low-income women from diverse backgrounds who used a midwife-managed birth center in the inner city, researchers found that these women expressed a greater sense of control over their own bodies, and felt they were treated with greater dignity and respect in the birthing center compared to their experiences giving birth in-hospital (Esposito, 1999).

Certified nurse-midwife
A health care provider who has been trained in both nursing and midwifery, and who provides a full range of gynecological and obstetric primary care services to women.

Doula

A woman who has been trained to provide a woman with continuous one-on-one support during child-birth, primarily in the form of nonmedical physical and emotional care

In addition to the potential benefits of birthing centers for women experiencing low-risk pregnancies, several researchers have argued that doulas can benefit all women in labor. A **doula** is a woman who has been trained to provide a woman with continuous one-on-one support during childbirth, primarily in the form of nonmedical physical and emotional care. In addition, many doulas are trained to help with breastfeeding and are available for lactation assistance for several days after delivery (Stein, Kennell, & Fulcher, 2004). Because the doula has no other responsibilities, no other patients, and does not work on a shift, she can devote herself fully to just one woman and stay with her continuously throughout the labor until the baby is born.

Some researchers speculate that just knowing that the doula will be there throughout the birth process helps to reduce anxiety in both the laboring woman and her family. "It is possible that the enhancement of feeling safe and confident, a key to a woman's ability to labor effectively, leads to suppression of anxiety-produced" hormones that can inhibit labor (Stein, Kennell, & Fulcher, 2004, p. 1490). Meta-analytic studies support this

BOX 4.2   Conversations with a Certified Professional Midwife

Erika Beecher is a certified professional midwife (CPM), who lives in Worcester, Massachusetts, with her husband and four children. In the United States, there are two broad categories of midwives, nurse-midwives and direct-entry midwives. Nurse-midwives are trained in nursing and midwifery, and usually practice in hospitals and birth centers. Direct-entry midwives focus their training on midwifery alone, not on nursing, and are particularly prepared to attend homebirths and births at free-standing birth centers. Direct-entry midwives have varied educational backgrounds, including apprenticeship with a senior midwife or doctor, or attendance at a Direct-Entry Midwifery Training Program. Some choose to obtain the title of certified professional midwife (CPM), a credential that recognizes multiple routes of education.

Erika Beecher is a CPM, certified through the North American Registry of Midwives. She has worked in cooperation with two other midwives for about 10 years and opened her own private practice in Massachusetts 5 years ago. Erika *has a B.S. in biology, and experience as a U.S. Peace Corps volunteer in Papua, New Guinea, where she helped run a rural development center and gained extensive midwifery experience in the local clinic. Back in the United States, she began assisting a senior midwife in Massachusetts, with whom she completed a formal apprenticeship. She then completed a midwifery internship in Jamaica before becoming a CPM in Massachusetts.*

Erika has a home office where she conducts prenatal visits with women who have chosen to have homebirths. She describes her daily work as part of the Midwives Model of Care (http://www.cfmidwifery.org/mmoc/define.aspx), which rests on the premise that pregnancy and birth are normal life processes.

We are experts in normal birth with healthy women. During an initial consultation I ask questions about lifestyle and health, and discuss my training, style of practice, safety concerns, and any other personal concerns that a woman might have. It is during this visit that we determine whether a woman is a good candidate for a potential homebirth. Women with a prior history of diabetes, heart disease, or other chronic conditions are not good candidates for homebirth and should seek the care of a physician in a hospital setting.

Prenatal care is such a big part of our work, and I allocate an hour for each visit in order that I might treat each woman and her family holistically. I spend a lot of time on education, relationship development, monitoring the pregnancy, routine lab work, and also refer women to other practitioners or specialists as needed. Nutrition and a healthy lifestyle are essential for maintaining a healthy pregnancy and low-risk status for homebirth. The prenatal period is also a time during which we develop a closeness, which ultimately allows us to relax into a woman's individual labor and birth process.

Once labor begins, I go to the house first. I listen to the baby, take the mother's vitals, set up a birth and resuscitation station with a warming pad, and homeopathic remedies that might be used. When labor becomes active, I call the other two

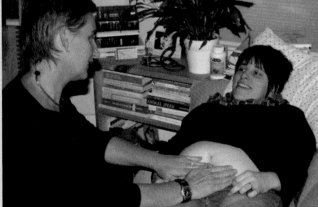

Erika Beecher (Courtesy of Erika Beecher)

hypothesis, finding that births assisted by doulas had 50 percent fewer **cesarean sections** (also called *c-sections*), in which the baby is surgically removed directly from the uterus; 40 percent less forceps use; 60 percent fewer requests for epidurals; and a 25 percent decrease in labor length (Stein, Kennell, & Fulcher, 2004).

Other changes in childbirth practices have been evident in the United States, and also reflect a trend toward making the birth process less medicalized and shifting more control to the individual woman and her family. For example, as recently as 1972, only 27 percent of U.S. hospitals permitted fathers or other family members in the delivery room. By 1980, 80 percent of U.S. hospitals had an open policy; today very few do not allow the fathers to be present. In 1944, English obstetrician Grantly Dick-Read wrote a book called *Child-birth Without Fear*, in which he put forth the view that Western societies had created an association between childbirth and pain. Fear of pain, he said, actually created tension and muscle cramping that produced pain unnecessarily. These ideas were reinforced by Dr. F. Lamaze in *Painless Childbirth* (1970). Lamaze's popular method of preparation for

Cesarean section
Surgical delivery of the fetus directly from the uterus; performed when normal delivery is prohibited.

midwives. It has been our experience that having three midwives present enables us to work calmly and efficiently, ensuring that we have the appropriate hands and experience available to monitor the baby and mother, and to handle variations and complications should they arise.

A big part of our model of care includes continuous hands-on assistance during labor and delivery. One of my favorite parts of the job is labor support. As birth attendants we are well-versed in touch techniques, breath work, and other comfort measures (massage, aromatherapy, homeopathy, herbal preparations, ice packs, suggestions for positional changes), including laboring in water, as the value of water (the "midwife's epidural") in labor is well known. A woman having a home birth is free to assume any position that seems right for her at different stages, is free to eat and drink, and is allowed to find her own way through the birthing process. If this means she roars like a lion and gives birth on all-fours, so be it. There are times when we have to intervene, to suggest or alter a woman's chosen position for birth, but we explain our reasons to her.

When the baby is born, the mother lifts her baby to her breast and we cover the little one with a blanket. Newborns need to bond and connect, to touch, hear, smell, and nuzzle with their parents. We leave the cord uncut until it stops pulsing, as this provides the baby with oxygen as they make the transition to air breathing. The midwife responsible for the baby does any necessary suctioning and the initial APGAR at one minute of age. The baby is gently stimulated, if needed, by rubbing with a warmed blanket. At five minutes, we do the second APGAR.

The initial newborn period of adjustment is closely observed, watching for signs of respiratory difficulty, poor color, or obvious congenital problems. Oxygen and a resuscitation station are always set up at the bedside to use if needed. We also evaluate the perineum, suture if necessary, perform a thorough newborn exam, get the woman up to go to the bathroom, and settle her back in a fresh bed. We then make sure the baby has a good nursing session. We stay at least 3 hours or more after the birth. When we are satisfied that the baby's vitals are within normal range and that the baby has attempted to breastfeed, we leave postpartum instructions and discuss situations in which to call us with concerns.

I return to the home again at 24 hours and at 3 days postpartum. This enables mother and baby to stay cozy in their bed and develop the nursing relationship without interruption. I monitor the mother for any signs of infection, check her uterus, inspect the perineum if she had tearing or sutures, and provide suggestions for assisting the healing process using hot herbal compresses or other natural measures. We discuss the baby's initial attempts at breastfeeding, and I give assistance as needed. I measure the baby, check the cord, make sure that any weight loss is within normal range, and do the newborn screening. We discuss diet, rest, sleep, and family adjustments. We discuss and are supportive of the emotional feelings that can come up at this time, as the mother's body goes through massive hormonal changes. I then see mother and baby in two weeks back at the office, and again at 6 weeks.

Although the vast majority of homebirths occur without complications, emergency situations can occur in which the mother and baby would need to be transported to a hospital. Failure to progress, desire for pain relief (usually epidural), unsatisfactory fetal heart tones, exhaustion or dehydration, rising blood pressure, or other undesirable trends with the mother's vital signs, are all reasons to do a nonemergency transport. We feel it is crucial to make an emergency plan in advance, something we do at the 36-week visit. We always carry necessary supplies like oxygen and medications for bleeding, and we maintain certifications for Neonatal Resuscitation and Healthcare Provider CPR.

I work with healthy, low-risk women who choose to take greater responsibility for their birthing experience. What these women give me is a huge advantage: their confidence, health, and willingness to participate and accept responsibility are a leg up in terms of outcomes. While obstetrical care is appropriate for high-risk women and as backup when complications arise, more cooperation between obstetricians and midwives would result in the best possible care for all women.

Birthing centers typically offer a relaxed, home-like atmosphere for labor and delivery. They are geared toward women who are experiencing low-risk pregnancies, and a nurse-midwife and doula, or birthing coach, may be present. What practices led to the development of birthing centers in the United States? What role will the doula play? (Brand X Pictures/Images)

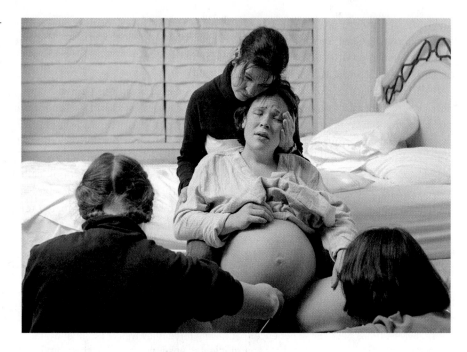

childbirth is based on reducing pain during childbirth through breathing and muscle exercises, as well as on educating women and their partners about pregnancy and labor. Other researchers have found that women with a lower fear of and sense of personal control over childbirth were less likely to use epidural anesthesia during labor (Heinze & Sleigh, 2003). *Epidurals* block sensation in the lower part of the body, thus reducing pain; however, they can also reduce a woman's ability to push during labor and so significantly increase the risk of delivery by Cesarean (c-section).

Other, related childbirth practices have emerged in recent years. One involves having the woman's partner present during the birth process, sometimes serving as the breathing coach. Another is a return to giving birth at home, often with the assistance of a trained midwife. Although the number of homebirths in the United States has increased in recent years, the percentage remains low, about 1 percent (Curtin & Park, 1999). In many European countries, however, births at home, as well as births attended by nurse-midwives, have long been a popular alternative to the hospital setting. In Scandinavia, the use of highly trained midwives was associated with relatively low maternal mortality rates beginning in the 19th century. In the early 20th century, Sweden's maternal mortality rate was roughly half that of the United States (Chamberlain, McDonagh, Lalonde, & Arulkumaran, 2003; Hogberg, Wall, & Brostrom, 1986). Many researchers today emphasize the complementary health care roles that can be played by physicians, who are qualified to intervene in high-risk obstetric cases and emergencies, and nurse-midwives, who are trained to manage and assist with low-risk births.

CHILDBIRTH PREPARATION METHODS

Lamaze: Teaches the mother relaxation and breathing techniques to reduce pain, and emphasizes the importance of entering the birth process ready to make informed decisions.

Bradley: Also known as "Coached Childbirth"; instructors teach mothers natural breathing techniques and encourage spouse or partner support through the labor and delivery process.

LeBoyer: Advocates easing the newborn gently through the delivery process using such techniques as giving birth in a quiet, dimly lit room; gently massaging the newborn; placing the newborn on the mother's stomach to encourage bonding; and placing the baby in a warm bath shortly after birth in an attempt to re-create the uterine environment.

Learning Objective 4.4: *Discuss the stages of labor and the social and cultural factors that influence childbirth.*

1. What happens during the three stages of childbirth?
2. What societal attitudes influence the experience of chilbirth in the United States today?
3. What complementary roles might physicians, nurse-midwives, and doulas play in delivery?

✔ *Test Your Mastery...*

The Newborn

The average newborn is about 20 inches long and weighs about 7.5 pounds. Parents may initially be surprised at their newborn's appearance. When first born, the baby is covered in a white, cheesy-like substance called the *vernix*, and the head, quite large relative to the rest of the body, may look somewhat elongated following its trip through the birth canal. Fortunately, most babies are born not only beautiful to their new parents, but healthy as well.

Learning Objective 5
Analyze the factors that indicate newborn health.

Assessing the Newborn's Health

Perhaps as a sign of things to come, almost all babies born in the United States begin life with a test. Tests are used to screen babies for disorders, to determine whether a baby's nervous system is intact, and to characterize how a newborn responds to social and physical stimuli. Even though newborns are new to the external world, they possess a surprising range of behaviors and physiological functions. Newborn tests can assess more than 85 percent of these behaviors and functions (Francis, Self, & Horowitz, 1987). Here we consider the two most often used tests: the Apgar exam and the Brazelton Neonatal Behavioral Assessment Scale.

In 1953, Dr. Virginia Apgar introduced a test that permitted obstetricians to record objectively the newborn's health status. This test has become the standard for the baby's first assessment, and it is typically administered at one minute and five minutes following birth. The **Apgar exam** focuses on five of the newborn's vital physiological functions: heart rate, respiration, muscle tone, response to a mildly painful stimulus, and skin color. As can be seen in Figure 4.7, the newborn receives a score from 0 to 2 on each of these items. The highest possible score on the Apgar is 10. An Apgar of 7 or above indicates that the newborn is healthy. Infants with Apgar scores between 4 and 6 need special help to establish their breathing and stabilize their vital signs. Infants with an Apgar score of 3 or below are

Apgar exam
An exam administered immediately after birth that assesses vital functions, such as heart rate and respiration.

	SCORE		
SIGN	**0**	**1**	**2**
Heart rate	No heartbeat	Under 100 beats/min	100–140 beats/min
Respiratory effort	None for 60 secs	Irregular, shallow breathing	Strong breathing and crying
Reflex irritability	No response	Weak reflexive response	Strong reflexive response
Muscle tone	Completely limp	Weak movements of limbs	Strong movements of limbs
Color	Blue	Body pink with blue limbs	Body, arms, legs pink

FIGURE 4.7   The Apgar Scale

SOURCE: Adapted from V. Apgar. (1953). A proposal for a new method of evaluation of the newborn infant. *Current Researches in Anesthesia and Analgesia, 32,* 260–267.

in medical danger and require immediate intervention. Among newborns, 77 percent have Apgars of 8 or above (Apgar, 1953). Many factors can lower an infant's Apgar score, including maternal smoking, drinking, and labor medication.

The Apgar exam assesses vital life processes and can be quickly administered, but the results provide only limited information. The newborn possesses a wealth of behavioral tools that cannot be captured in a brief exam that focuses on physiological functioning. Moreover, newborn babies differ substantially in how they behave, and these differences may affect how parents and others treat them. For these reasons, investigators have focused increasingly on tests of how well the newborn's behavior is organized.

The **Brazelton Neonatal Behavioral Assessment Scale** (Brazelton & Nugent, 1995) is the most comprehensive of the newborn assessment tools. The main idea underlying this scale is that the seemingly helpless newborn actually possesses organized behaviors for dealing with both attractive stimuli—such as pleasant sights, sounds, and tastes—and offensive stimuli—such as loud noises and pinpricks. Assessors observe the baby in a number of states, or levels of alertness, to obtain a sense of the baby's style and temperament. An important feature of the exam is that it evaluates the newborn's ability to habituate. Recall from Chapter 1 that habituation is a simple form of learning in which a reflex response to a stimulus declines or disappears when the stimulus repeatedly occurs.

The exam includes items in four categories: attention and social responsiveness; muscle tone and physical movement; control of alertness (habituation, irritability, and excitability); and physiological response to stress. The baby's performance on these measures provides indicators of well-being and risk. For example, a baby who is unable to habituate to a repeated stimulus or to remain alert may fall into a higher risk category. Figure 4.8 provides some sample items from the Brazelton Scale.

The Brazelton Scale does a fairly good job of characterizing how a baby is doing in the first month of life. It is helpful, for example, in identifying problems in babies who have been subjected to conditions that put them at risk, such as low birthweight or prenatal drug exposure. It is not a good predictor, however, of development beyond the early infancy period (Lester & Tronick, 2001). The same conclusion applies to other early assessment instruments.

Birth Complications

Technological advances permit continuous monitoring of the baby's state during birth. Physicians can visualize the fetus, the umbilical cord, and the placenta by ultrasound to determine, for example, whether there is a danger that the umbilical cord will wrap around

Brazelton Neonatal Behavioral Assessment Scale
The most comprehensive of newborn assessment instruments; assesses attention and social responsiveness, muscle tone and physical movement, control of alertness, and physiological response to stress.

Links to Related Material
In Chapter 1, you read that habituation is a simple form of learning. Here, you see how habituation is used to evaluate a newborn's health.

---

1. While infant is asleep, shine light in eyes and observe response; after response disappears, wait 5 seconds and re-present; continue for either 10 trials or until habituation occurs.
2. While infant is asleep, shake rattle near ear and observe response; continue for either 10 trials or until habituation occurs.
3. Slowly move a red ball across the infant's field of vision; record ability to track both horizontally and vertically.
4. Have examiner slowly move his or her face across the infant's field of vision; record ability to track both horizontally and vertically.
5. While out of the infant's line of sight, have examiner speak softly into baby's ear; record ability to localize on each side.
6. With infant in supine position, hold cloth over eyes for 30 seconds; record defensive responses (e.g., swipes at cloth).

FIGURE 4.8 **Examples of items from the Brazelton Neonatal Behavioral Assessment Scale**
Source: Adapted from T. Berry Brazelton and J.K. Nugent. (1995). *Neonatal Behavioral Assessment Scale*, 3rd ed., London: Mac Keith Press. Copyright © 1995 by Mac Keith Press. Adapted by permission.

the fetus's neck (which can cause strangulation). They also can record electronically the heart rate and activity of the fetus through the mother's abdomen to determine whether there are signs of **fetal distress**, which would be indicated by an abnormally high or low heart rate (Anderson & Allison, 1990).

Sometimes birth cannot proceed according to nature's plan because, for example, the baby is lying in an unusual position in the uterus (that is, sideways or buttocks down, also called the *breech* position). In other cases, the delivery is proceeding too slowly, or the baby's head is too large to pass through the cervical opening. In such cases, the doctor often elects to perform a cesarean section. The rate of cesarean deliveries has risen across the last several decades. In the United States the percentage of cesarean births increased from 5 percent in 1969 to 29.1 percent in 2004. One goal of the Healthy People 2010 program is to reduce the U.S. c-section rate to 15 percent. This percentage is consistent with the worldwide guidelines for c-section rates offered by the World Health Organization.

Why are c-section rates higher than desirable in the United States today? Some reasons cited by researchers have included fear of medical liability among physicians, over-reliance on continuous electronic fetal monitoring, and increased use of epidurals (Guillemin, 1993; Van Tuinen & Wolfe, 1993). In addition, many c-sections are performed automatically on women who have had previous c-sections, based on the fear that the uterine scar could rupture in an attempted vaginal delivery following a c-section. However, researchers have found that vaginal birth following a c-section was successful in 87 percent of women laboring at birth centers and in about 70 percent of women laboring in hospitals. Actual uterine rupture was rare, around 0.4 percent (Lieberman, Ernst, Rooks, Stapleton, & Flamm, 2004; Windrim, 2005).

Birthweight and Gestational Age

In 2003, 7.9 percent of the babies born in the United States were low birthweight (Hamilton, Martin, & Sutton, 2004) or below 2,500 grams (about 5.5 pounds). Low-birthweight babies are about 40 times more likely to die in the first month of life than are babies with normal birthweight (Paneth, 1995). They also are at greater risk for many problems, large and small (Hack, Klein, & Taylor, 1995). Why is this so?

The newborn must make a number of adaptations to the outside world. Temperature control and nutrition are no longer provided by the mother's body, but these needs are rather easily met by the parents or other providers. Breathing, however, is a different story. After living in a water world for almost 9 months, the baby must draw the first breath of air within seconds after birth. Babies with low birthweight are more likely to have difficulty initiating or maintaining breathing. Failure to breathe prevents the delivery of oxygen to cells—a condition called **anoxia**—which can cause the cells to die. The brain cells are especially sensitive to oxygen deficits. Severe anoxia, for example, may damage the brain area that controls movement of the limbs, resulting in a spastic-type movement referred to as cerebral palsy (Behrman, Kliegman, & Jenson, 2000).

Low-birthweight babies may be placed in two groups. One comprises babies whose birthweights are low because they were born **preterm**, meaning before 38 weeks gestation. Preterm babies often have the breathing problems just described. In many, tiny blood vessels in the brain burst, causing bleeding and contributing to the infant's risk.

Even disregarding these physical challenges, development in a preterm baby may lag behind that in a full-term baby, at least for a time. Although we would expect the preterm infant, who is comparable to a fetus still in the womb, to be less advanced than the full-term baby, even when matched for the number of days following fertilization, the preterm infant usually has less mature brain patterns and is more disorganized and difficult to soothe (Als, Duffy, & McAnulty, 1988; Duffy, Als, & McAnulty, 1990). In the long term, these babies can be expected to have more frequent problems with growth and overall health issues (Saigal et al., 2000). They also are at greater risk for cognitive and behavioral problems in later childhood (Taylor et al., 2000).

Fetal distress
A condition of abnormal stress in the fetus, reflected during the birth process in an abnormal fetal heart rate.

Anoxia
A deficit of oxygen to the cells, which can produce brain or other tissue damage.

Preterm
Describes babies born before 38 weeks gestation.

BOX 4.3   Caring for Preterm and Low-Birthweight Infants in the NICU

Preterm and low-birthweight babies are typically cared for in neonatal intensive care units (NICUs). Babies in the NICU receive various forms of stimulation—rocking, sound recordings of the mother's heartbeat, high-contrast mobiles, gentle massage, and the like—which appear to assist their early development (Field, 2001; Mueller, 1996). One consequence of these interventions is that very tiny babies who would once have died at birth are now kept alive. These babies, however, face strong challenges to life and later well-being; the lighter the baby, the higher the risks.

Some babies who are born at risk have suffered brain or central nervous system damage that affects their functioning throughout life. However, in many cases, whether babies born at risk achieve normal development appears to depend largely on the context in which they are reared. Because most of the research supporting this finding has been carried out with preterm infants, we focus on that work, but many of these factors play a role in determining the outcome of any baby at risk.

One factor in a baby's developmental progress is the quality of the relationship that forms between the parents and the baby (Mangelsdorf et al., 1996). At-risk babies often pose special challenges to this relationship. For example, a preterm baby may spend weeks in a plastic enclosure in a special-care hospital nursery that affords the parents little opportunity to hold and cuddle the baby. When finally at home, the baby is likely to have an irritating cry, be difficult to soothe, and have irregular patterns of sleep and wakefulness (Parmelee & Garbanati, 1987). Such babies also smile less when interacting with adults and are more likely to turn away and avoid eye-to-eye contact (Eckerman et al., 1999).

These real problems are aggravated by people's reactions to preterm babies. In one study, several sets of parents were shown a film of a 5-month-old baby after they had been told that the baby was either normal, difficult, or premature (a term the researchers used for both SGA and preterm babies). Those who were told that the baby was premature judged crying segments of the film as more negative than did other parents, and physiological measures indicated that they experienced the baby's cries as more stressful (Frodi et al., 1978).

Other investigators have observed that parents treat their preterm children differently even after apparent differences between them and full-term babies have disappeared (Barnard, Bee, & Hammond, 1984; Beckwith & Parmelee, 1986). The tendency to expect negative behavior from premature infants is referred to as *prematurity stereotyping* (Stern & Karraker, 1992). Such stereo-

types increase the possibility that a negative cycle between parent and infant will be set in motion. Of course, the degree to which this occurs depends in part on the tolerance and flexibility of the caregivers, which is often related to their accurate understanding of the infant's needs (Benasich & Brooks-Gunn, 1996). The resources available to the family can also be important. By 2 to 3 years of age, children born preterm into families that have strong financial resources seem indistinguishable from children born at term. Conversely, the presence of financial and other stresses reduces the emotional availability of the parents and makes it less likely that they will adapt successfully to the challenges of the preterm infant (Hoy, Bill, & Sykes, 1988).

A contributor to disruption of the parent-infant relationship in the past was the hospital's policy of not permitting the parents to hold or touch their infant in the special-care nursery because of the fear of infection. We can easily imagine how a parent's confidence in caring for his or her newborn might be jeopardized after being limited for 6 to 8 weeks to watching the baby through a transparent incubator shield. As investigators began to recognize the importance of the very earliest social interactions between parent and infant, the situation changed. A group at Stanford University took the daring step of permitting parents to handle their infants in the special-care nursery and demonstrated that no increased danger of infection resulted (Barnett et al., 1970). Subsequent work demonstrated that handling enhanced mothers' self-confidence in responding to their babies (Leiderman & Seashore, 1975; Seashore et al., 1973).

A related factor is the lack of stimulation that infants often experience when they must spend time in the hospital. The temperature-controlled, patternless plastic chambers in which they are placed deprive them not only of human physical contact but of sensory input as well. As we have seen, intervention procedures introduced by NICUs have begun to address this problem.

There is concern, however, that for some premature babies added stimulation becomes overstimulation and has a negative rather than positive effect. One creative idea is to provide stimulation that the babies themselves can decide to experience or avoid. For example, one investigator placed a "breathing" teddy bear in the baby's bed, which the baby could either contact or avoid. Premature babies who had the breathing bear tended to stay near it more than those who had a nonbreathing bear, and they spent a longer amount of time in quiet sleep (Thoman, 1993).

Small for gestational age (SGA)
Describes babies born at a weight in the bottom 10 percent of babies of a particular gestational age.

The other group of babies born with a low birthweight are those whose fetal growth was retarded. These babies are considered **small for gestational age (SGA)**. They may be born at the expected gestational age of 40 weeks, or they may be born earlier (and so be both SGA and preterm), but they are in this category because their weight places them among the bottom 10 percent of babies born at that particular gestational age. Although

BOX 4.4   Contextual Model of Prenatal Development and Birth

Infant is conceived with a specific set of genetic characteristics that may influence the health of the fetus.

Family setting

- Parental age and health affect factors such as ease of conception and financial resources available for parenting, as well as decisions regarding the need for prenatal screening.
- Mother's physical health and exposure to teratogens influence the health of the fetus.
- Social support available to mother during her pregnancy affects her health.

Socioeconomic status and work setting

- Parental education, as well as economic and community resources, influence the quality of prenatal care that a mother receives. Better prenatal care leads to a healthier newborn.
- Good health benefits offered by employers lead to better use of prenatal care as well as to better parental leave options following birth.
- A more satisfying, less stressful work environment influences the health of the mother and her unborn child.

Larger societal and cultural influences

- Childbirth settings, including use of hospitals, doulas, birth centers, and professional midwives, as well as likelihood of cesarean sections and other medical interventions, are influenced by cultural models regarding what constitutes a "normal" birth process.

the cause is frequently unknown, several factors appear to increase the likelihood that a baby's prenatal growth will be delayed, including chromosomal abnormalities, infections, poor maternal nutrition, and maternal substance abuse.

SGA babies also face developmental risks (Goldenberg, 1995). For example, these infants do not arouse easily, and they tend to have poor muscle tone, appearing limp when held. They also are disadvantaged beyond the newborn period; for example, they show poorer recognition memory than do babies born at normal weight (Gotlieb, Baisini, & Bray, 1988). SGA babies who are preterm perform more poorly on verbal tests of IQ as preschoolers than do preterm babies whose weights were appropriate for their ages, although their eventual developmental course depends heavily on the quality of their post-birth environment (Dowling & Bendell, 1988; Gorman & Pollitt, 1992).

Steady improvement in technology has produced a dramatic decline in deaths resulting from low birthweight. Although a birthweight below 2,500 g (5.5 lb) is classified as low, babies weighing only 500 g (a little more than 1 lb) have at least a 25 percent chance of living, and the odds rise to more than 90 percent for babies who weigh at least 1,000 g (about 2.2 lb) (Minde, 1993). The tiniest babies, those who weigh less than 1,000 g, are 50 to 60 times more likely to survive today than was the case 35 years ago (Minde, 2000).

Learning Objective 4.5: *Analyze the factors that indicate newborn health.*

1. What common procedures are used to assess the newborn's health?
2. What are some common birth complications?
3. What is a c-section, and what contributes to the high c-section rates in the United States today?
4. Discuss the reasons for low birthweight in infants.
5. What interventions can be used to care for low-birthweight and preterm infants?

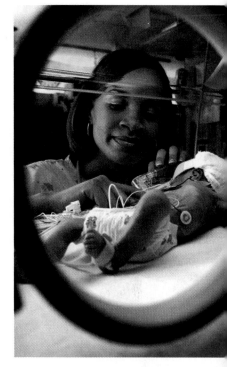

This baby was born two months premature and needs special care in the Neonatal Intensive Care Unit (NICU). What special challenges do preterm and low-birthweight infants face? (David Joel/Photographer's Choice/Getty Images, Inc.)

✔ *Test Your Mastery...*

Summary for Chapter 4

Learning Objective 4.1
Discuss factors that influence conception and evaluate types of screening performed during pregnancy.

1. How does conception occur? What factors strongly influence conception?

Conception occurs when a sperm unites with an ovum (egg) to form a single cell, called a zygote. The *zygote* receives 23 chromosomes from the mother and 23 from the father, to form a new and genetically unique person. The first factor to influence conception is timing. The man's sperm, typically deposited in the woman's vagina, will survive for about three days. The woman's ovum, released each month by her ovaries, will live for 12 to 24 hours. Another influence on conception is the *reproductive health* of both prospective parents. For women, this means having no disorders that might prevent ovulation and sufficient hormones to produce mucus to enable the sperm to travel through the reproductive tract as well as to build the endometrial lining in the uterine wall. For men, a sufficient quantity of normal, actively moving sperm are required to withstand the long journey from the vagina to the fallopian tubes. Finally, a woman's *age* can greatly influence the likelihood of conception. A woman's eggs age as she does, which may lead to difficulty conceiving.

2. What role does parental age play in fetal health?

For older men, sperm can mutate, causing increased risk of the genetic disorder achondroplasia. Older women are at an increased risk of having a child with Down syndrome. Similarly, older parents are more likely to face problems with *infertility* and thus are more likely to use *assisted reproductive therapies*. One result of increased use of fertility drugs has been a dramatic increase in multiple births. Women who are pregnant with multiples are at greater risk for preterm birth. Conversely, teenage mothers are more likely to receive limited prenatal care, have complications during pregnancy, and are at risk for preterm births. Teenage mothers may also engage in risky behaviors such as smoking, drinking, or the use of illegal drugs during pregnancy.

3. What prenatal screening tests are available to women during pregnancy?

Prenatal screening is recommended for pregnant women over the age of 35. These tests include *ultrasound* imaging, which is a way to look inside the body using sound waves. *Amniocentesis* tests amniotic fluid for abnormalities. *Chorionic villus* sampling samples cells from part of the placenta, which can reveal chromosomal defects. Test-tube screening allows the screening of embryos before they are implanted in the mother's uterus. It is possible to detect several hundred disorders through these various screening techniques.

4. How and when can prenatal treatments be used to improve fetal health?

Current approaches to prenatal treatment include medical therapy, surgery, and genetic engineering. *Medical therapy* is the most common prenatal treatment. Two common prenatal medical treatments are the provision of extra vitamins for women who are deficient and drug treatment for HIV positive women. Physicians are now able to carry out surgery on fetuses to address life-threatening problems and conditions that will result in severe damage if not corrected early in development. Surgery may be used for blockage of the urinary tract, congenital diaphragmatic hernia, spina bifida, and other neural tube defects. Perhaps the greatest promise for prenatal treatment is genetic engineering. Working in the laboratory with a blood sample from the fetus, doctors can clip out the defective gene and insert a synthetic replacement gene.

5. What ethical issues must be taken into consideration when considering prenatal screening and treatment options?

Today's *fetal-screening techniques* can detect the presence of many genetic disorders and life-threatening maladies. If no treatment is possible, the options are to terminate the pregnancy or to bring a child with a serious disorder into the world. If a fetus is diagnosed with a genetic disorder, should insurance companies be able to deny the child insurance at birth, considering that the health expenses will be exorbitant compared with those of other children? Fetal surgery and gene repair are expensive, and not all families have the resources to benefit from them. Who would have access to such procedures and who would not? Further issues arise when babies are born with severe disorders. Decisions regarding the health and life of a fetus or infant are intensely emotional and deeply embedded in social, political, ethical, and moral convictions. Most of all, they are very personal. There is a fine line between personal beliefs and feelings and the government's role in protecting the right of fetuses and infants.

Learning Objective 4.2
Trace the changes that occur in the three stages of prenatal development.

1. What is the period of gestation in humans, and how is it calculated?

Gestation, or the length of time from conception to birth, is technically 38 weeks. However, since parents don't always know the exact date of conception, physicians use the date of the woman's *last menstrual period* as a way to calculate gestational age and to estimate a baby's due date. This estimate is not exact because women's menstrual cycles vary. Two weeks is usually added to the calculation for a total gestation time of 40 weeks.

2. What changes occur during the period of the zygote between conception and the end of the second week of development?

After conception, the *zygote* multiplies rapidly as it continues its 4-day, 4-inch journey through the fallopian tube to the uterus. At first, the zygote is a solid mass of cells, but it gradually changes into a hollow sphere as it prepares to implant into the wall of the uterus. Cells begin to specialize, some forming an inner cell mass, which will become the embryo, and some forming important structures that will support the embryo's development. Implantation takes about a week, as the zygote settles into the blood-enriched lining of the uterus.

3. What changes occur during the period of the embryo between weeks 3 and 8?

All major internal and external structures form during this period; thus, these weeks are the most delicate of the pregnancy and the time when the growing *embryo* is most vulnerable to threats from both internal and external environments. In the third week, the inner cell mass differentiates into three layers, from which all body structures will emerge. Endodermal cells develop into internal organs and glands, while ectodermal cells become the parts of the body that maintain contact with the outside world—the nervous system; the sensory parts of the eyes, nose, ears; skin; and hair. Mesodermal cells give rise to muscles, cartilage, bone, sex organs, and the heart. The heart is beating by the end of the third week. By the end of the fourth week, the embryo assumes a curved, bumpy form. Head and brain development occur in the fifth week, along with the formation of upper and lower limbs. Week 6 sees the continuation of the growth of the head, differentiation of the limbs into elbows, finger, and wrists, and the discernment of eyes and ears. Limbs develop rapidly in week 7, and stumps appear that will form fingers and toes. By the end of the eighth week, the embryo has distinctly human features. All internal and external structures have formed.

4. What changes occur during the period of the fetus between the ninth week and birth?

The principal changes for the *fetus* are further development of the already formed organ structures and increases in size and weight. External changes, such as thickening of the skin, and the development of more human-looking facial features occur. The eyelids seal shut near the beginning of the third month, and nails appear on fingers and toes by the fourth month. Head hair begins to grow, and bone structure begins to support a more erect posture by 6 months. By 3 months, the brain has organized into the functional subdivisions of seeing, hearing, and thinking. Nerve cells grow and establish connections throughout fetal development. Sexual differentiation begins to occur by the end of the third month. Fetal activity begins in the third month, though the mother may not feel it until around the fourth or fifth month of pregnancy. In the fourth month, light sensitivity occurs, and the fetus is now able to kick and turn and may begin to display rhythms of sleep and activity. By the seventh month, brain connections are sufficient for the fetus to exhibit a sucking reflex when the lips are touched. The later stages of prenatal development ready the fetus to live outside the mother's body. By six or seven months of age, the fetus has a chance of survival outside the mother's body. In the eighth month, fat appears under the skin, and the fetus begins to store maternal nutrients in its body. Individual differences become apparent during the last weeks of prenatal life.

Learning Objective 4.3
Describe the impacts of teratogens and maternal health as environmental influences that affect prenatal development.

1. What are the different types of teratogens that can affect prenatal development?	*Teratogens* are external agents that can cause malformation in the embryo and fetus and are not genetic in origin. These include infectious diseases, drugs, harmful chemicals, and other environmental hazards. Teratogens can have physical, psychological, and behavioral effects. X-rays can retard prenatal growth and cause the birth defects of microcephaly and small eyes. A pregnant mother who contracts rubella during the early months of pregnancy can produce a baby with congenital abnormalities of the eye, ear, heart, and brain. Thalidomide, marketed for morning sickness in the 1950s, was discovered to be the cause of a sharp increase in the number of babies born with defective limbs.
2. How do teratogens work?	Some teratogens gain access to the fetus directly through the mother's body, whereas others travel through the blood and across the placental membrane. The likelihood and degree of abnormal development increase with the fetus's dosage of the harmful agent.
3. What are some effects of teratogenic substances?	A teratogen's effect depends on the genetic makeup of the organism exposed to it. A human fetus may be more sensitive to a substance than an animal would be. In addition, the effect of a teratogen on development depends partly on timing. Teratogens can affect a fetus by drugs that the pregnant grandmother took decades earlier or by X-ray exposure the father experienced many weeks before conception. A zygote is more sensitive to teratogens after week 3 of gestation when substances in the mother's bloodstream can pass through the placental barrier. Similarly, the zygote is vulnerable during weeks 2 through 8 when organs are forming. Teratogens' effects may be unique and severe. Some cause gross limb defects, whereas others cause growth retardation and even death.

4. What are some examples of environmental factors and diseases that have teratogenic effects?

Environmental factors such as lead, mercury, radiation, and pesticides can produce miscarriages, anemia, mental retardation, leukemia, and abnormal brain growth. *Infectious diseases* such as AIDS, herpes, rubella, and syphilis can cause congenital malformations, mental retardation, eye damage, deafness, heart defects, miscarriage, and death.

5. At what stages of prenatal development do different teratogens have their most potent effect?

There are *sensitive periods* in prenatal development when a teratogen may have a more devastating effect. In the case of rubella, only 2 to 3 percent of offspring are likely to be affected if the mother is infected within two weeks of her last period, whereas 50 percent of offspring are affected when infection occurs during the first month following conception. Whether ear, eye, heart or brain damage occurs depends on the stage of formation of each organ when the mother is infected.

6. What conditions of maternal health can influence prenatal development?

The quality of the mother's nutrition and her *overall health* are important determinants of how the fetus develops. Maternal experiences and stress may also have an effect. Maternal malnutrition is associated with increased rates of spontaneous abortion, infant death, and congenital defects. However, an enriched home environment may compensate for many of the effects of early malnutrition, but the outcome depends on when during pregnancy the malnutrition occurred and how severe it was. Similarly, high levels of maternal anxiety are associated with newborn irritability, feeding and sleep problems during infancy, and subsequent behavioral problems.

7. Why is prenatal care important to the developing baby?

Prenatal care consists of medical attention designed specifically for a pregnant woman and her developing baby. Counseling on diet, exercise, prenatal testing, and medical advice regarding warning signals are provided. In addition, screening procedures are performed for a variety of maternal medical conditions that can affect the developing baby. Finally, prospective mothers who receive prenatal care have access to a knowledgeable and supportive person with whom they can discuss common pregnancy-related concerns and issues.

Learning Objective 4.4

Discuss the stages of labor and the social and cultural factors that influence childbirth.

1. What happens during the three stages of childbirth?

The first and longest stage of *labor* begins when the early contractions start to dilate or widen the cervical opening. This stage ends when the cervix is fully dilated to about 10 centimeters or 4 inches. By the end of this stage, the contractions are very intense, occuring every 2 to 3 minutes. The second stage begins when the fetus starts to pass through the cervix, and it ends when the baby is completely delivered into the world. During this stage, the contractions are long and closely spaced, and the mother is encouraged to push with each contraction. The third stage lasts only a few minutes and involves the delivery of the placenta and related membranes, referred to as the afterbirth.

2. What societal attitudes influence the experience of childbirth in the United States today?

In Europe and North America, the relative availability of high-quality health care, combined with a dramatic reduction in maternal mortality over the past 80 years, has resulted in dramatically increased safety. Some researchers have therefore questioned the *"overmedicalization"* of childbirth. For example, many hospitals have come to apply a wide range of medical practices to all women in labor, whether or not they are clinically indicated for individual women. These practices include supine birth position, pubic shaving, enemas, artificial rupture of the amniotic membrane, continuous electronic fetal monitoring, episiotomies, and withholding food and water in the event general anesthesia will be required.

3. What complementary roles might physicians, nurse-midwives, and doulas play in delivery?

Physicians can encourage women to explore *alternative childbirth options*, such as the use of a birthing center. Nurse-midwives provide a wide range of gynecological and obstetric primary care services to women, and they "facilitate birth" rather than "deliver a baby." A doula is a woman who has been trained to provide continuous one-on-one support during childbirth. This level of support reduces the anxiety of the laboring woman and her family, and so decreases the incidence of c-sections.

Learning Objective 4.5
Analyze the factors that indicate
newborn health.

1. What common procedures are used to assess the newborn's health?	The *Apgar* exam has become the standard for the baby's first assessment, and it is typically administered one minute and five minutes following birth. This exam focuses on five vital physiological functions: heart rate, respiration, muscle tone, response to a mildly painful stimulus, and skin color. The *Brazelton Neonatal Behavioral Assessment Scale* evaluates the newborn's ability to habituate. The exam includes items in four categories: attention and social responsiveness; muscle tone and physical movement; control of alertness; and physiological response to stress.
2. What are some common birth complications?	Common *complications* include the umbilical cord wrapping around the fetus's neck, fetal distress, which is indicated by an abnormally high or low heart rate, and the baby lying in an unusual position such as buttocks down (breech).
3. What is a c-section, and what contributes to the high c-section rate in the United States today?	In a *cesarean section*, the baby is surgically removed directly from the uterus. Fear of medical liability among physicians, overreliance on continuous electronic fetal monitoring, and increased use of epidurals are all reasons that the U.S. c-section rate is high. In addition, many c-sections are performed automatically on women who have had previous c-sections, based on the fear that the uterine scar could rupture in an attempted vaginal delivery following c-section.

4. Discuss the reasons for low birthweight in infants.

Low-birthweight babies may be placed in two groups: (1) babies whose birthweights are low because they were born preterm (before 38 weeks gestation); and (2) those whose fetal growth was retarded. These babies are considered small for gestational age (SGA). They may be born at the expected gestational age of 40 weeks, or they may be born earlier, but they are in this category because their weight places them among the bottom 10 percent of babies born at that particular gestational age. The cause is frequently unknown, though chromosomal abnormalities, infections, poor maternal nutrition, and maternal substance abuse are factors that appear to be influential.

5. What interventions can be used to care for low-birthweight and preterm infants?

Preterm and low-birthweight babies are typically cared for in neonatal intensive care units (*NICUs*), where they receive various forms of stimulation—rocking, sound recordings of the mother's heartbeat, high-contrast mobiles, and gentle massage. At-risk babies often pose special challenges to establishing the parent-infant bond. These challenges include the inability to cuddle the infant due to the baby spending weeks in a plastic enclosure. Therefore, every effort should be made to allow parents to have as much contact with their infants as is medically indicated.

Early Capacities in Infancy

THE ORGANIZED INFANT
Learning Objective 5.1
DESCRIBE WAYS IN WHICH THE INFANT'S BEHAVIOR APPEARS TO BE ORGANIZED AT BIRTH.
States of Arousal
Changing Sleep Patterns

APPLICATIONS Sleep in Cultural Perspective
Reflexes
Congenitally Organized Behaviors
• Looking • Sucking • Crying

MOTOR DEVELOPMENT
Learning Objective 5.2
TRACE THE DEVELOPMENT OF MOTOR SKILLS IN INFANCY AND CHILDHOOD.
Development of Motor Skills in Infancy
Motor Development in Cultural Context
Dynamic Systems Approach to Motor Development
Motor Development in Childhood

CONVERSATIONS with an Infant Physical Therapist

PERCEPTUAL DEVELOPMENT
Learning Objective 5.3
OUTLINE THE AREAS OF PERCEPTUAL DEVELOPMENT DURING INFANCY.
Studying Perceptual Development
Touch, Smell, Taste, and Vestibular Sensitivity
• Touch • Smell and Taste • Vestibular Sensitivity
Hearing
• Prenatal Hearing • Sound Localization
Vision
• Visual Acuity • Color Vision • Visual Pattern and Contrast • Visual Organization
• Face Perception • Can Newborns Recognize Their Mothers' Faces?

RESEARCH & SOCIETY Infants' Perception of Motion
Perception of Objects and Their Properties
• Size Constancy • Seeing Objects as Continuous • Perception of Depth
The Integrated Senses
• Exploration • Representation
Attention and Action
• Development of Attention • Helping Children with Attentional Problems

When Emily and David brought newborn Zachary home, they were surprised at how much he slept—about 16 hours out of each 24. Unfortunately, however, his 16 hours of sleeptime were not distributed in a way that fit naturally with their own night-time sleep needs. Instead, he woke up every few hours, crying. Emily and David began to wonder what they had heard many new parents ask: "When is he going to sleep through the night?"

Most children and adults have regular patterns of daily activity. For the most part, they sleep at night, are awake during the day, and eat at fairly predictable times. We can say that their daily patterns follow a repeating rhythm. On the other hand, one need only look at the red, tired eyes of new parents like Emily and David to know that the newborn baby's habits are not so regular. Can we conclude, then, that the baby enters the world with no rhythms at all and must be taught by the parents when to eat, when to sleep, and when to wake? Not at all. Newborn babies are rhythmic creatures. The newborn's biological clock just seems to tick at a different rate than ours, and it gradually shifts into synchrony with ours as the baby develops. ■

The Organized Infant

Learning Objective 5.1
Describe ways in which the infant's behavior appears to be organized at birth.

Often, people's perceptions of newborn infants are that they are passive bundles of helplessness who come into the world unable to do things on their own. In recent decades, however, child psychologists have emphasized the extent to which infants are born with capacities and competencies that enable them to get what they need from their environments. In other words, their behaviors appear organized at birth in a way that leaves them well adapted to the family lives they are usually part of. What are babies' biological rhythms and how do babies become integrated into family life?

States of Arousal

When LaShawn watched newborn Kiaree sleeping in her infant seat, she was struck by the different behaviors her baby displayed. Sometimes she was in a very quiet, deep sleep; other times, she thrashed her arms and legs jerkily while asleep. Still other times, Kiaree's eyes were partially open even while she gazed drowsily straight ahead; then, Kiaree's eyes would open wide with alertness, and she was clearly ready to interact with her mother. These behaviors are examples of different **states of arousal**.

States of arousal
The states of alertness that infants display, from deep sleep to alert activity and crying.

LaShawn's observations are similar to those made 40 years ago by researcher Peter Wolff. Wolff carefully watched several newborn babies for many hours and was struck by the different levels of sleep and wakefulness he observed in them (Wolff, 1959, 1966). He captured these observations by defining six states of infant arousal or alertness: (1) quiet, or deep, sleep; (2) active, or light, sleep; (3) drowsiness; (4) alert inactivity; (5) alert activity; and (6) crying. These states are described in Table 5.1.

Several aspects of these states and how they change with age make them useful for understanding early development, for assessing the effects of various factors—such as teratogens—on development, and for comparing one infant with another. Recordings of brain activity by an **electroencephalograph (EEG)** reveal that arousal states become increasingly distinct with age. Investigators believe this change reflects how the baby's brain matures (Colombo, 2001). Similar information can be obtained by examining the ease with which babies move from one state to the next (Halpern, MacLean, & Baumeister, 1995).

Electroencephalograph (EEG)
An instrument that measures brain activity by sensing minute electrical changes at the top of the skull.

Because the organization of sleep states—their differentiation and timing—reflects brain maturation, preterm and other at-risk babies are less organized in their states of

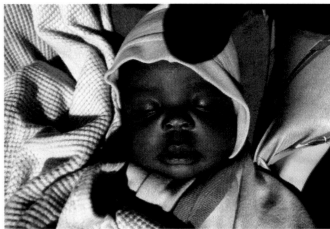

These pictures demonstrate two states of arousal in infancy: (a) alert activity, and (b) quiet or deep sleep. (Photri-Microstock)

TABLE 5.1 States of Arousal	
STATE	**CHARACTERISTICS**
Deep sleep	Regular breathing; eyes closed with no eye movements; no activity except for occasional jerky movements
Light sleep	Eyes closed but rapid eye movements can be observed; activity level low; movements are smoother than in deep sleep; breathing may be irregular
Drowsiness	Eyes may open and close but look dull when open; responses to stimulation are delayed, but stimulation may cause state to change; activity level varies
Alert inactivity	Eyes open and bright; attention focused on stimuli; activity level relatively low
Alert activity	Eyes open; activity level high; may show brief fussiness; reacts to stimulation with increases in startles and motor activity
Crying	Intense crying that is difficult to stop; high level of motor activity

arousal than other infants, especially when they are exposed to alcohol and drugs prenatally. Also, babies who are more unstable than others in the time they spend in various states between 2 and 5 weeks of life are more likely to have medical and behavioral problems later (Cohen, Roux, Grailhe, et al., 2005; Halpern et al., 1995; Tuladhar, Harding, Adamson, & Horne, 2005).

Arousal states also play an important role in infants' interactions with the environment. When babies are in states of alertness—rather than crying, asleep, or drowsy—they are more receptive to stimuli, learn more readily, and are better prepared for social interaction (Berg & Berg, 1987; Feldman, 2006; Thoman, 1990). Thus, states can affect the impact of external events on a baby. External events, in turn, can affect an infant's state. For example, a crying baby will often shift to a quiet, alert state if picked up by an adult and gently rocked up and down on the adult's shoulder (Karp, 2002; Korner & Thoman, 1970; Pederson & Ter Vrugt, 1973). Swaddling, or wrapping an infant tightly, can also soothe an infant's cries and improve the quality of sleep (Franco, Seret, Van Hees, et al., 2005).

Changing Sleep Patterns

The newborn's rhythmic states are especially apparent in the pattern of sleep–wake cycles. The baby engages in a cycle of active and quiet sleep that repeats each 50 to 60 minutes. This cycle is coordinated with a cycle of wakefulness that occurs once every 3 to 4 hours (Parmelee & Sigman, 1983; Scher, Epstein, & Tirosh, 2004). What produces this behavior?

BOX 5.1   Sleep in Cultural Perspective

Sharing the parental bed with an infant or young child—*cosleeping*—is a practice that arouses strong emotions among many parents. Some families assume that infants and young children should sleep in their own cribs or beds from as young an age as possible. This practice may begin at birth in many American hospital nurseries, with each child placed in a separate isolette. However, parents in many societies are puzzled by the idea that a young child would be left alone in a bed. Some child development experts support cosleeping, whereas others advocate individual sleeping arrangements for all family members. Developmental risks and benefits are cited for both types of arrangements. Controversies regarding cosleeping have led to the popularization of two opposing viewpoints: the Ferber "cry-it-out" behavioral approach to sleep training and the Sears "attachment parenting" approach.

Pediatrican Richard Ferber's "cry-it-out" sleep training approach encourages parents to increase the child's tolerance for sleeping alone in his or her crib by gradually increasing the time that the child is permitted to cry each night, with parental support offered through touch and verbal interactions, but without removal from the crib. Advocates of this approach cite increased safety for infants in cribs, more positive marital relationships, and increased self-reliance and independence for the growing child.

In contrast, pediatrician William Sears has popularized the "family bed" as a primary component of what he calls "attachment parenting" (Sears & Sears, 2001). According to this approach, cosleeping enhances mother-child bonding, promotes breastfeeding, and increases sleep quality for both mother and infant. These benefits are part of a philosophy that encourages close physical contact and loving responsiveness to the infant's needs as a means of establishing secure parent-child attachment relationships.

Which of these approaches is "best"? The answer to this question may depend on parents' own beliefs, which are influenced by the larger culture. For example, families that strongly emphasize the importance of early independence may be more likely to advocate individualized sleeping arrangements. On the other hand, parents whose socialization goals emphasize the primacy of interdependence and close interpersonal relationships may be more likely to encourage cosleeping among family members. Family sleeping arrangements may also reflect the sleeping patterns familiar to parents from their own childhoods. Finally, some parents may choose a particular approach based on expert opinions from popular literature.

Some research has found that cosleeping among European Americans is associated with ambivalent mother-child relationships (Lozoff, Wolf, & Davis, 1984). However, these findings may be true for parents who cosleep in response to child sleep problems or parental anxiety, rather than for parents who consciously choose cosleeping as part of a parenting philosophy. Among African and Appalachian Americans whose cultural values include traditions of cosleeping, associations between cosleeping practices and negative developmental outcomes are not found (Harkness & Super, 2002; Lozoff et al., 1984).

The "cry-it-out" behavioral training approach to promoting independent sleep views cosleeping as a problem behavior that interferes with the development of independence and results when parents do not set limits well (Ferber, 1995). Other objections concern sexual stimulation, relationship difficulties, and possible suffocation among cosleeping families (Madansky, &

Links to Related Material

In this chapter, you learn about the development of the sleep–wake cycle during infancy. In Chapter 6, you will learn more about how sleep patterns develop, and the ways in which cultural settings structure sleep–wake patterns throughout childhood.

You might think that the sleep–wake cycle reflects a cycle of hunger or environmental events that disrupt sleep. However, the cycle, evident from the first days of life, seems to be controlled internally as a result of brain maturation and is evident prenatally (Rivkees, 2003; Thoman & McDowell, 1989).

Much to the relief of their parents, infants gradually adapt to the 24-hour light–dark cycle. Sleep periods become longer at night, usually around 5 or 6 weeks of age, as awake periods lengthen during the day. By 12 to 16 weeks, the pattern of sleeping at night and being awake during the day is fairly well established, even though the baby still sleeps about the same amount as the newborn (Berg & Berg, 1987).

Although the rhythms of the newborn seem to be biologically programmed, they are not free from environmental influences. For example, newborn babies who stay in their mothers' rooms in the hospital begin to display day–night differences in their sleep cycles earlier than babies who stay in the hospital nursery. Babies who room with their mothers also spend more time in quiet sleep and less time crying than do babies in nursery groups (Keefe, 1987). Finally, exposure to low-intensity cycled lighting appears to help infants establish a healthy circadian rhythm (Rivkees, 2003).

Another external factor is where the baby sleeps. In the United States, most middle-class families have babies sleep by themselves in their own beds. Among many other groups both in the United States and in countries around the world, babies are more likely to sleep with their parents and siblings. The most common reasons given by middle-

Edelbrock, 1990; Morelli, Rogoff, Oppenheim, & Goldsmith, 1992). On the other hand, countries where parent-child cosleeping is the norm have the lowest rates of Sudden Infant Death Syndrome (SIDS), which is thought to occur when infants are unable to arouse themselves after they briefly stop breathing during sleep. McKenna (1996) concluded that cosleeping could possibly reduce SIDS rates by promoting breastfeeding, increasing infant arousal, and allowing mothers to be more aware of their infant's breathing.

Some themes emerge from these contradictory findings. Families whose own shared values and family experiences include cosleeping are likely to continue this practice with their own children. Among these families, cosleeping is not seen as a problem and is unlikely to result in any negative developmental consequences. Families that cosleep in response to

child sleep problems may be uncomfortable or ambivalent about this practice, and thus it may disrupt family relationships. Children from families that choose parent-child cosleeping in infancy and early childhood have been found to have somewhat higher cognitive outcomes at 6 years of age. However, at age 18 these children did not show any negative or positive consequences of cosleeping (Okami, Weisner, & Olmstead, 2002).

When working with families around the issue of cosleeping, it is important to respect family values and parenting decisions. Sleeping arrangements among families vary across cultures, are often related to parents' own childhood experiences, and may involve conscious philosophical choices. Professionals should be careful that they do not impose their own cultural assumptions on family sleep practices.

In many cultures around the world, and many groups within the United States it is common and considered desirable for infants and young children to share the parents' bed. Other cultural groups think infants should learn to sleep on their own from an early age. What factors contribute to childrearing decisions such as where children should sleep? (Eisenhut & Mayer/Jupiter Images)

U.S. mothers for the separate sleeping arrangements are the desire to build the infant's independence, and to better meet their own needs for sleep and privacy. The most common reasons given by mothers who prefer sharing a bed are the desire to develop a closeness with the infant as well as the ease of feeding and caregiving (Kawasaki et al., 1994; Morelli et al., 1992). Researchers have found that infants who cosleep have more awakenings each night than infants who sleep alone, but these awakenings are briefer. Thus, cosleeping does not affect overall quality of infant sleep (Mao, Burnham, Goodlin-Jones, Gaylor, & Anders, 2004). Having the infant share a bed or a room with the parents—**cosleeping**—is a common practice in many of the world's cultures (Nelson, Schiefenhoevel, & Haimerl, 2000).

Reflexes

In addition to having rhythmic states of arousal, newborns are also equipped with a number of innate behaviors and behavior patterns called reflexes (defined in Chapter 1). Many reflexes, such as breathing and blinking, are essential to survival, whereas others, such as grasping, may have served important survival functions sometime in our evolutionary past. The presence or absence of a reflex provides information about the baby's brain and nervous system. For example, an infant should reflexively bend to the left when you run your thumb along the left side of the baby's spinal column. If this reflex occurs on one side but not the other, it may indicate damage to nerves on the other side.

Links to Related Material
In Chapter 11, you will learn more about parenting behaviors that lead to a secure attachment relationship in infants and children.

Cosleeping A practice in which babies and young children sleep in the same bed or room with one or both parents.

Questions for Thought and Discussion
What sleeping arrangements were preferred in your family? Which view of cosleeping do you or would you favor as a parent?

Some reflexes last throughout life, but the reflexes of most interest here are those that disappear in the first year of life, because their disappearance indicates the development of more advanced brain functions. Table 5.2 lists some common reflexes as well as the stimuli that produce them and their developmental course.

The *rooting reflex* is one of the most evident to new parents. If you stroke a newborn's cheek near the mouth, the baby will turn the head to that side and search with the mouth. This reflex is adaptive in an evolutionary sense because it helps the baby find the nipple of the mother's breast for feeding. This reflex appears as early as 2 to 3 months after conception and represents the first indication that the fetus can respond to touch. Rooting generally disappears in infants around 3 to 4 months of age (Peiper, 1963).

The *palmar reflex* is elicited by pressure against the palm of a newborn's hand, which causes the baby to grasp the source of that pressure. Tightly grasping your fingers, for example, a newborn is capable of supporting his or her own weight. This trait was adaptive for babies of our evolutionary ancestors, who needed to cling tightly to their

TABLE 5.2 Newborn Reflexes

Name	Testing Method	Response	Developmental Course	Significance
Blink	Flash a light in infant's eyes	Closes both eyes	Permanent	Protects eyes from strong stimuli
Rooting reflex	Stroke cheek of infant lightly with finger or nipple	Turns head toward finger, opens mouth, and tries to suck finger	Disappears at approximately 3 to 4 months	Absent in depressed infants; appears in adults with severe cerebral palsy
Babinski	Gently stroke the side of the infant's foot	Flexes the big toe dorsally; fans out the other toes; twists foot inward from heel to toes	Usually disappears near the end of the 1st year	Absent in infants with defects of the lower spine
Tonic neck Lay reflex	baby down on back	Turns head to one side; baby assumes fencing position, extending arm and leg on this side	Found as early as 28th prenatal week; frequently present in first weeks, disappears by 3 or 4 months	Paves way for eye–hand coordination
Palmar or hand grasp	Press rod or finger against the infant's palm	Grasps object with fingers; can suspend own weight for brief period of time	Increases during the 1st month and then gradually declines and is gone by 3 or 4 months	Weak or absent in depressed babies
Moro reflex (embracing reflex)	Make a sudden loud sound; let the baby's head drop back a few inches; or suspend baby horizontally, then lower hands rapidly about six inches and stop abruptly	Extends arms and legs and then brings arms toward each other in a convulsive manner; fans hands out at first, clenches them slightly	Begins to decline in 3rd month, generally gone by 5th month	Absent or constantly weak Moro indicates serious disturbance of the central nervous system; may have originated with primate clinging
Stepping or automatic walking reflex	Support baby in upright position with bare feet on flat surface; move the infant forward and tilt him slightly from side to side	Makes rhythmic stepping movements	Disappears in 2 to 3 months	Absent in depressed infants

SOURCE: Excerpted from E.M. Hetherington and R.D. Parke. (1979). *Child Psychology: A Contemporary Viewpoint*, 2nd ed. (Table 4.1). New York: McGraw-Hill. Copyright ©1979 by McGraw-Hill, Inc. Excerpted by permission of the McGraw-Hill Company.

mothers as they moved along. This reflex disappears at 3 to 4 months of age, and children do not regain the ability to support their own weight until around 4 or 5 years of age (McGraw, 1940).

The *Moro reflex* consists of a series of reactions to sudden noises or the sudden loss of head support. The infant first thrusts his arms outward, opens his hands, arches his back, and stretches his legs outward. Then the infant brings his arms inward in an embracing motion with fingers formed into fists. The absence of a Moro reflex is a sign of brain damage, and its failure to disappear after 6 or 7 months of age is also cause for concern. Ernest Moro, who first described this startle reflex (Moro, 1918), suggested that it was an adaptive reaction of primates to threat stimuli such as sudden falling or sudden attack.

When pressure is applied to the soles of the feet, the baby will flex her legs up and down in the *stepping reflex*. This reflex, which mimics the motions later used in upright walking, usually disappears by around 3 months of age. The disappearance of the stepping reflex at this time seems to result from the increasing weight of the baby's legs. Research has shown that if the legs are supported in water, the reflex can be demonstrated in older infants (Thelen & Fisher, 1983). Similarly, if the reflex is practiced, it can become stronger (Zelazo et al., 1993).

Although there is an automatic quality to reflexes, environmental factors do affect them. For example, a baby who has just nursed may not show a rooting response, and most other reflexes are also somewhat sensitive to the baby's biological state. Still, reflexes are generally tied to specific stimuli and are rarely seen in their absence. This is not the case for the behaviors known as congenitally organized behaviors.

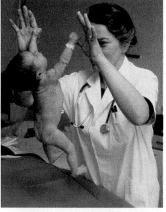

Newborn reflexes include the palmar reflex and stepping. What adaptive value might these automatic behaviors have for human evolution? What other reflexes are present at birth? (*Top*, Petit Format/Photo Researchers, Inc.; *bottom*, Elizabeth Crews/The Image Works)

Congenitally Organized Behaviors

Not all early behaviors are responses to stimulation. The newborn also initiates activities and is capable of sustaining them over considerable periods of time. Such activities are called **congenitally organized behaviors**. Looking, sucking, and crying are three well-organized behaviors that, unlike reflexes, are often not elicited by a discrete, identifiable stimulus. These behaviors provide infants with means to get nourishment and to control and explore their environments.

Looking The keenness of an alert newborn's gaze is often unexpected (Crouchman, 1985). New parents may be amazed when their baby, even in the first moments of life, will lie with eyes wide open, seemingly examining them and other objects in the room. In a room that is dimly lit, the light coming through the window may be an especially attractive target. Yet looking is not simply a reflexive response to light. As early as 8 hours after birth, in complete darkness, babies open their eyes wide and look around, as if they are searching for something to explore (Haith, 1991). Looking behavior shows that newborns possess tools for acting on their world, not just for reacting to it.

Sucking In some ways, sucking seems to fit the definition of a reflex, because it is easily elicited by oral stimulation, especially when the newborn is hungry. In other ways, however, it is not reflex-like. Babies may suck spontaneously without stimulation, even during sleep. The sucking act also is not stereotyped but adapts to different conditions, such as how much fluid can be obtained with each suck. In addition, sucking behavior responds to sensory events. Babies who are sucking tend to stop when they see something start to move or when they hear a voice (Haith, 1966). These characteristics set sucking apart from simpler reflexes.

Sucking is a marvelously coordinated act. Babies suck one to two times each second, and each suck requires an orchestration of actions. Milk is extracted from the nipple both by suction (as with a straw) and by a squeezing action, and these actions must be coordinated with both breathing and swallowing. Some babies show excellent sucking coordination from birth, whereas others may require a week or so of practice. Preterm infants may have more difficulty with sucking than full-term infants (Medoff-Cooper & Ratcliffe, 2005; Peiper, 1963).

Links to Related Material
In this chapter, you learn about reflexes as part of a newborn's early capacities. In Chapter 7, you will read about how Piaget viewed reflexes as the first stage in his theory of cognitive development in infancy.

Congenitally organized behaviors
Early behaviors of newborns that do not require specific external stimulation and that show more adaptability than simple reflexes.

Infants are born with many capacities, including the ability to engage with the world. What three congenitally organized behaviors are described in this chapter? (Jeff Greenberg/Age Fotostock America, Inc.)

Links to Related Material
In Chapter 11, you will learn more about how parents' responses to early infant cries help to shape the parent–child relationship.

No other newborn behavior seems to serve quite as many purposes as sucking. It is a way to get nourishment, but it is also a primary means by which babies begin to explore the world. Even at birth, many babies suck their fingers and thumbs, and it appears that some newborns have even practiced this as fetuses. Later, they will continue to explore with their mouths as they become better able to grasp and find new objects (Rochat, 1989). Sucking also seems to buffer the infant against pain and overstimulation. Agitated babies quiet when they suck on a pacifier, especially when it contains a sweet substance (Smith & Blass, 1996).

Crying A third organized behavior of the newborn is crying. Like sucking, crying coordinates various components of behavior, such as breathing, vocalizing, and muscular tensing, in a rhythmic pattern. Researchers have been interested in crying both as a diagnostic tool and for its social role as a critically important form of communication for the newborn infant. Crying is one of the baby's strongest and clearest responses, and caregivers appear to be especially responsive to it (Demos, 1986; Soltis, 2004).

Charles Darwin believed that crying in newborns evolved as a means of providing the mother with information about the baby's state or condition (Darwin, 1872). For crying to serve as a form of communication, two conditions are necessary. First, different types of cries should communicate different messages. And they do; infants' pain cries differ in pitch and intensity from hunger cries (Soltis, 2004; Wasz-Hockert, Michelsson, & Lind, 1985). In addition, variations in cries can convey other information. For example, as the pitch of crying increases, adult listeners tend to perceive the baby's problem as becoming more serious and urgent (Leger et al., 1996; Zeskind & Marshall, 1988).

Second, for crying to be communicative, listeners must be able to discriminate one type from another. Caregivers must understand whether the baby is saying, for example, "I'm hungry," "I'm wet," or "I'm frightened." Studies have reported that adults can be quite good at interpreting babies' cries (Soltis, 2004), an ability based in part on experience. In general, parents and other adults who have spent time around newborns are better at decoding infant crying than are adults with little experience (Green, Jones, & Gustafson, 1987; Gustafson & Harris, 1990). Similarly, parents of 4-month-olds are better skilled in this area than are parents of 1-month-olds (Freeburg & Lippman, 1986).

The communication role of crying thus has elements of both nature and nurture. At first, crying is innately elicited by internal stimuli (such as hunger) and external stimuli (such as chafing from a soiled diaper). Such crying serves primarily to draw the parent near. As parents become more accurate at reading the information in these signals, babies learn to use the crying response as a means of controlling the parent's attention and care.

Researchers distinguish three types of cries in the very young infant: a basic or hungry cry, a mad or angry cry, and a fear or pain cry (Wasz-Hockert, Michelsson, & Lind, 1985; Wolff, 1969). The first two differ in that the mad cry forces more air through the vocal cords, producing more variation. The pain cry has a more sudden onset with a much longer initial burst and a longer period of breath holding between cries. Adults can distinguish among cries based on intensity and are more likely to respond as the cry becomes more intense (Gustafson, Wood, & Green, 2000; Soltis, 2004). Contextual cues then aid in determining the meaning of the cry.

The crying of healthy, newborn infants is fairly characteristic in both pitch and rhythm. An unusual cry, therefore, can signal problems. Babies who are immature or brain damaged produce higher-frequency cries with abnormal timing patterns (Zeskind & Lester, 2001). Babies who are malnourished or preterm at birth often also have higher-pitched cries. Infants with genetic anomalies, such as *cri du chat* syndrome (in which the infant's cry sounds like that of a cat) and Down syndrome, have atypical cries as well.

Some investigators have speculated that babies influence early social relationships with their caregivers by the nature of their cries (Lester, 1984). Cries of at-risk babies are perceived as more grating, piercing, and aversive than the cries of other babies, and "difficult" babies seem to have more aversive cries than "easy" babies (Lester, 1984; Pinyerd, 1994; Soltis, 2004). As noted earlier, cries experienced as aversive may set in motion a negative cycle between baby and caregiver. Crying is a major factor in early social interaction because it is one of the infant's basic tools for getting the caregiver to come closer. Because adults dislike hearing babies cry, they typically do something to quiet the crying baby. Parents may try various techniques for soothing a baby who fusses for no apparent reason. Picking the baby up, swaddling (or wrapping a baby snugly in a blanket), rocking, or offering a pacifier to suck on may be effective (Campos, 1989; Carp, 2002). In the first month of life, infants often stop crying if they have interesting things to watch or sounds to listen to (Wolff, 1969).

Learning Objective 5.1: *Describe ways in which the infant's behavior appears to be organized at birth.*

Test Your Mastery...

1. What states of arousal does the infant demonstrate?
2. How does the newborn's sleep–wake cycle change in the early months of life?
3. How does culture shape our expectations regarding where infants should sleep?
4. What is a reflex? What are some of the newborn's reflexes?
5. How are congenitally organized behaviors different from reflexes?
6. What roles do looking, sucking, and crying play in an infant's development?

Motor Development

The acquisition of motor skills is a key feature of development in human infancy, in effect giving the baby power tools for acquiring knowledge and gaining competence and self-control. These skills continue to develop well into the childhood years, when they play important roles in other aspects of development—for example, time spent with peers and adults in organized activities such as dance or karate lessons, soccer, and the swim team, or more informally playing jump rope or kickball on the school playground.

Motor development concerns both **postural development** and **locomotion**, which involve control of the trunk of the body and coordination of the arms and legs for moving around. Motor development also involves **prehension**, the ability to use the hands as tools for such purposes as eating, building, and exploring. The development of motor skills tends to follow two general principles. The first principle is that control over the body develops in a **cephalocaudal**, or head-to-foot, direction. The progression of early postural and locomotor skills illustrates this principle. The second principle is that development proceeds in a **proximodistal** direction—that is, body parts closest to the center of the body come under control before parts farther away from the center. The acquisition of fine motor skills such as reaching and grasping illustrates this principle.

Development of Motor Skills in Infancy

Newborn Natalie is placed on her back on a blanket on the living room floor, where she can move her head from side to side and look around. However, her head must be supported when she is lifted to someone's shoulder. At 6 weeks, she is able to hold her head up, erect and steady, when in her mother's arms. At 2 months, she lies on her stomach and pushes off the mattress with her hands to lift her head and shoulders and look around. When she is four and a half months old, her mother can no longer leave her lying on her back in her baby gym because she has learned to roll over! At 7 months, Natalie is able to sit on the quilt on the floor without support, ready to play with the stacking cubes next to her. When she is 8 months old, her parents find her standing in the crib, rattling the bars and uncertain about how to sit down again! Around her first birthday, Natalie is able to control her legs and balance sufficiently to take her first unassisted steps.

Table 5.3 presents some milestones of motor-skill acquisition, showing the proximodistal and cephalocaudal principles in action. The majority of babies follow these general sequences. It is important to note, however, that the **average age** for attaining a

Learning Objective 5.2
Trace the development of motor skills in infancy and childhood.

Postural development
The increasing ability of the baby to control parts of his or her body, especially the head and trunk.

Locomotion
The movement of a person through space, such as walking and crawling.

Prehension
The ability to grasp and manipulate objects with the hands.

Cephalocaudal
Literally, head to tail. This principle of development refers to the tendency of body parts to mature in a head-to-foot progression.

Proximodistal
Literally, near to far. This principle of development refers to the tendency of body parts to develop in a trunk-to-extremities direction.

Average age
The average age for attaining a motor milestone is the age at which 50% of babies in a population have mastered that skill.

An infant's first steps are a major milestone of development and are often a joyous event for their families. What developmental changes enabled this baby to walk? How does walking illustrate the cephalocaudal and proximal principles of development? (David Young-Wolff/Stone/ Getty Images)

Prereaching
Early direction of arm movements toward an object.

Ulnar grasp
An early grasp using the whole palm.

Pincer grasp
Grasping an object between the thumb or forefinger.

Links to Related Material
In this chapter, you learn about the sequence and timing that most infants exhibit in their development of motor skills. In Chapter 7, you will read about how Piaget linked developing motor skills to the infant's growing understanding of the world. In Chapter 11, you will learn more about how an infant's increased motor skills leads to the growth of separation anxiety and the display of attachment behaviors, such as the ability to follow a departing parent.

particular motor milestone represents the age at which 50 percent of babies in a population have mastered that particular skill. This means that many babies will master that skill at a younger age than the average, and many will master it at an older age, as can be seen by the age ranges given in the third column of Table 5.3. This individual variation in the age of attainment for motor skills is significant in light of the recent discovery that infants also vary in how they develop specific skills.

Proximodistal development is evident in the case of Masami. In the first weeks of life, newborn Masami can position herself toward the colorful fabric animals hanging from her mobile, but she cannot reach them. Although her arm movements seem almost random to her carefully watching mother, Masami does direct some movements, called **prereaching**, toward the giraffe. In the second month of life, Masami sweeps her hand more deliberately near the giraffe and begins to make contact with it and other animals in the mobile more consistently. By 4 months of age, she can often grab at the animals and pull them toward her in a way that looks quite deliberate, but she uses her whole hand in what is called the **ulnar grasp**, with as yet little individual finger control. Nevertheless, her parents decide it is time to remove the mobile from the crib.

Gradually, Masami coordinates her fingers, so that at 4 months of age, she may reach with one hand for a stacking cube with all fingers extended; once the cube is in her hand, she is able to transfer it from one hand to the other, and also to rotate her wrist so that she can see the cube from various perspectives. By 9 months, Masami can grasp a raisin neatly between forefinger and thumb in a fine movement called the **pincer grasp**. By one year, she can hold a crayon to make marks on paper.

Learning to move around is not only a motor accomplishment for babies; it also helps them organize their world (Bertenthal, Campos, & Kermoian, 1994). For example, babies' self-produced locomotion seems to contribute to their spatial understanding. In one study, a toy was hidden in one of two colored containers placed in front of an infant. Infants with crawling experience were better able to find the toy under a variety of conditions—such as when the babies were placed on the opposite side of the table (thereby reversing the location of the toy from the baby's perspective)—than were babies of the same age who had not yet mastered crawling (Benson & Uzgiris, 1985).

As babies gain greater control over their body movements, they also become better able to gauge distance and height. For example, Josh began crawling a couple of weeks

TABLE 5.3 Motor Skill Development		
SKILL	**AVERAGE AGE OF ATTAINMENT**	**AGE RANGE IN WHICH 90% OF INFANTS ACHIEVE THIS SKILL**
Holds head erect and steady in upright position	6 weeks	3 weeks–4 months
Pushes self up with arms when lying on stomach	2 months	3 weeks–4 months
Grasps cube	3 months, 3 weeks	2–7 months
Rolls over from back to side	4.5 months	2–7 months
Sits unsupported	7 months	5–9 months
Crawls	7 months	5–11 months
Pulls self to standing position	8 months	5–12 months
Walks unassisted	11 months, 3 weeks	9–17 months
Builds tower with two cubes	13 months, 3 weeks	10–19 months
Walks up stairs with help	16 months	12–23 months
Jumps	23 months, 2 weeks	17–30 months

SOURCES: Based on information from N. Bayley. (1969). *Manual for the Bayley Scales of Infant Development.* New York: Psychological Corporation; and N. Bayley. (1993). *Bayley Scales of Infant Development* (2nd ed.). New York: Psychological Corporation.

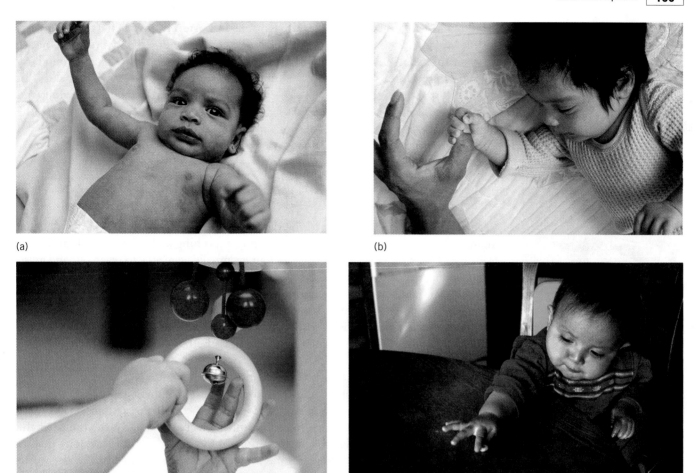

(a)

(b)

(c)

(d)

Milestones in the development of voluntary reaching include (a) prereaching, (b) using the ulnar grasp, (c) transferring an object from hand to hand, and (d) using the pincer grasp. (*Top left*, Corbis Premium Collection/Alamy Images; *top right*, Omni-Photo Communications; *bottom left*, Peter Usbeck/Alamy Images; *bottom right*, Elizabeth Crews/The Images Works)

before his twin brother Jayden. Their mother noticed that, after Josh began crawling, he seemed much more watchful of the stairs whenever she carried him up or down them. Jayden, on the other hand, continued to look around rather than down at her feet when going up and down the stairs, until he began crawling a couple weeks later. Indeed, researchers have found that fear of heights emerges shortly after infants learn to crawl. Thus, the act of crawling gives the infant an opportunity to learn more about visual cues regarding depth and distance (Campos, Bertenthal, & Kermoian, 1992).

Motor Development in Cultural Context

Motor skills appear in a fairly predictable sequence and at similar times for infants everywhere. Does this mean that sitting, crawling, reaching, and so forth are genetically programmed and simply emerge according to a biological set of instructions within the child? More and more, psychologists are answering this question No.

For one thing, different childrearing experiences—often associated with different cultural practices—can affect the timing of motor skill development. For example, African infants generally sit, stand, and walk from one to several weeks earlier than do American infants (Konner, 1976; Super, 1981), and in some environments may not be encouraged to crawl. Childrearing practices and other environmental factors, not heredity, seem to account for such differences.

Kipsigis (in Kenya, Africa) believe that their infants need practice to learn certain postural skills, such as sitting. In what other ways can cultural attitudes and practices influence motor development? (Photo used by permission of Dr. Charles Super, Pennsylvania State University)

Questions for Thought and Discussion
How have cultural expectations affected your motor development and motor skills?

Dynamic systems approach
Thelen's model of the development of motor skills, in which infants who are motivated to accomplish a task create a new motor behavior from their available physical abilities.

One investigator reported that the Kipsigis in western Kenya believe their infants will not sit, stand, or walk without practice. Thus, they energetically provide practice for their infants in these skills. For example, they dig a special hole in the ground using sand to reinforce their infants' postures so they can practice their sitting skills. In the development of skills that are not encouraged in this way, such as crawling and rolling over, Kenyan babies do not differ from American babies (Super, 1981). Mothers in Jamaica provide their babies with similar types of early physical stimulation, and these babies, too, develop motor skills earlier than do infants in many other cultures (Hopkins, 1991).

Dynamic Systems Approach to Motor Development

Researchers have carefully charted the development of motor skills in many individual infants. One study examined the development of reaching and grasping in four infants from ages 3 weeks to 1 year. Although all four eventually were able to reach out and grasp a toy, the manner in which they achieved this goal varied considerably from one child to the next (Thelen, Corbetta, & Spencer, 1996). These sorts of findings have prompted researchers to think about motor development in a new way. The **dynamic systems approach**, originally developed in the field of physics, has been applied to children's motor development by developmental psychologist Esther Thelen and others (Thelen, 1995, 2000; Thelen & Smith, 1998).

Thelen proposes that both nature and nurture contribute to the development of motor skills, and that developmentalists need a model to help them understand the combined contributions of these two factors. According to her dynamic systems analysis, the crucial element that unites the nature and nurture contributions, and that stimulates the development of any particular skill, is the nature of the infant's "task." As babies mature biologically and cognitively, they become motivated to accomplish tasks in the world around them. They seek to reach things, to grasp things, to move or shake things, to move themselves closer to things, and so on. These are the tasks of infancy. To accomplish such tasks, babies learn that various motor behaviors—such as those involving the arms, fingers, head, shoulders, and so on—can be useful.

When the task requires a behavior that the child does not possess, the infant must create such a behavior. To do this, infants draw on the physical responses and abilities already available to them—what they can already do with arms, legs, hands, and fingers; muscle strength; balance and coordination; and so on. These abilities depend largely on age and biological maturation, but they also depend on the abilities a baby has created up to that point. A 9-month-old, therefore, should have many more physical responses and abilities on which to draw than would, say, a 4-month-old. As a result, even when faced with the same task, the two children will likely create different new motor behaviors and so accomplish the task or solve the problem in different ways. Note that this is true not just for babies of different ages; any two children, even of the same age, will have different physical resources available to them as a result of both genetic differences and different experiences up to that point.

Thelen has found that as infants try to assemble a new motor behavior from the abilities currently available to them, they go through two stages. The first stage involves *exploration*, as the baby tries many different responses in a relatively random and uncoordinated fashion. In the second stage, *selection*, the baby learns exactly what works and what doesn't work and fine-tunes the many responses into an efficient package.

In short, the dynamic systems approach predicts that the motor skill a particular child develops at any given time will depend on (a) the task at hand, including how difficult it is and how motivated the child is to accomplish it, and (b) the physical abilities the child already possesses that form the starting point for creating the new behavior. The first of these (the task) is obviously very much influenced by the baby's environment and experiences; the second (the infant's physical abilities) is strongly influenced by the baby's biological maturation as well as prior experiences.

Thelen demonstrated these principles in a clever laboratory study. Three-month-old infants were placed in cribs on their backs, where they could see a mobile suspended above them. Each baby's foot was attached to the mobile with a ribbon, so that single kicks or alternating kicking movements were both effective in making the mobile move. At first the babies explored different leg movements, but after a short while they learned to produce the necessary kicking behaviors, presumably because they were motivated to accomplish the task of moving the mobile. Thelen next tied each baby's feet together loosely, so that the motor behavior that would best move the mobile was a combined two-foot kick. Again the infants explored various leg movements before finally selecting a coordinated leg action that was effective in achieving their purpose (Thelen, 1994).

Another example involves locomotion. Researchers at the University of Denver videotaped the motions of babies' body parts as they learned to creep across the floor to reach an object. The babies wore black bodysuits that had small reflective markers (the kind bicyclists wear at night) at the shoulder, elbow, and other joints. Reflections from these markers were read by a computer and analyzed to determine the path, velocity, and timing of the children's movements.

The researchers found that once babies have the physical strength to move along with their bodies held above the floor, they begin to explore different patterns of arm-and-leg coordination and eventually settle on a diagonal pattern (right hand and left leg, then left hand and right leg) as the most efficient and stable way of locomoting along and thus reaching the object (Benson, 1990; Freedland & Bertenthal, 1994).

The essence of the dynamic systems approach, then, is that an infant does not simply wake up one morning with a new motor skill that has emerged spontaneously from his or her genetic code. Instead, a new skill is developed only when the infant is motivated to accomplish a task and has sufficient physical abilities to assemble into the necessary motor behavior.

Why, then, do most babies follow the same general sequence of motor development? The answer is probably that the infants' physical resources at the same points in development are similar, and infants' tasks in any given culture tend also to be similar. Thelen's dynamic systems analysis also shows why it should not be surprising that babies differ in the timing of their motor-skill development and in the manner in which they may acquire these skills.

In Esther Thelen's experiment, babies developed specific new motor skills to accomplish a particular task. What two steps did they take in learning how to make the mobile move? How does this experiment illustrate the dynamic systems model? (Michael Newman/PhotoEdit)

Motor Development in Childhood

Motor skills continue to develop during the childhood years. By the second birthday, most children have overcome their battle with gravity and balance and are able to move about and handle objects fairly efficiently. Their early abilities form the basis for skills that appear between 2 and 7 years of age. Three sets of fundamental movement skills emerge: locomotor movements, manipulative movements, and stability movements (Gallahue & Ozmun, 1995).

Locomotor movements include walking, running, jumping, hopping, skipping, and climbing. *Manipulative movements* include throwing, catching, kicking, and dribbling. *Stability movements* involve body control relative to gravity and include bending, turning, swinging, rolling, head standing, and beam walking. These fundamental skills typically appear in all children and can be further refined in older children and adolescents, who may develop exceptional skills as skaters, dancers, and gymnasts.

The refinement of motor skills depends a great deal on the development of the muscles and the nerve pathways that control them, but other factors are important as well. Motor skills depend in part on sensory and perceptual skills, for example, and children acquire many of their motor skills in play, which involves social and physical interaction.

One important aspect of motor skills is reaction time—the time required for the external stimulus to trigger the ingoing nerve pathways, for the individual to make a decision, and for the brain to activate the muscles through the outgoing nerve pathways.

BOX 5.2   Conversation with an Infant Physical Therapist

MaryAnn Delaney-Tuttle is a pediatric physical therapist. She grew up in upstate New York. For the past 18 years she has lived in Tolland, Connecticut, with her husband and their two sons.

When I was very young, I used to spend Sundays visiting the elderly at a county nursing home with my sister. I decided that I would like to do something with older people, so I got a B.S. in physical therapy at Russell Sage College in Troy, New York. I worked in adult rehabilitation for five years. I had always liked children, but it wasn't until I had some nieces of my own that I really began to watch how they learned to play and move. I then thought about how I might integrate my physical therapy training with my love for children. I ended up doing my Masters in physical therapy at Boston University.

When my husband took a new job and we moved our young family to Connecticut, I decided to start a private practice specializing exclusively in the physical therapy needs of children. Initially, my practice grew by word of mouth and by introducing myself to pediatricians. I built a reputation as being family-focused and as working with families who had children with severe medical needs. When Connecticut began its early intervention program, Birth to Three, in the early 1990s, I began to receive referrals from the statewide network because of the reputation I had built up. I became a contractor with Birth to Three regional networks in eastern Connecticut. Currently, I work almost exclusively for a Connecticut Birth to Three agency that is an association of occupational therapists, physical therapists, speech therapists, and professional educators.

Birth to Three, or early intervention, is a federally funded, mandated program through the Department of Education. The goal of the Birth to Three program is to remediate developmental problems before the child enters the school system. Developmental delays are usually more effectively remediated when intervention occurs at an early age. Early intervention also promotes better family interactions and is less expensive in the long run than it would be to wait until the child is older before intervening. Children are eligible for early intervention services if they are between the ages of birth and 36 months, and if they have a significant developmental delay in one of five domains: social-emotional, communication, self-help/adaptive, cognitive, and motor. In the past, the services

have been free, but due to recent budget cuts, families in many states are now being charged fees, but these are still typically low.

Any professional or layperson concerned about a child's development, including parents, can call early intervention services in their state to have a child evaluated. All intervention services, including the initial evaluation, are performed in the child's home or other natural environment, such as day care. The initial evaluation is done using a standardized test, such as the Battelle Developmental Inventory. To be eligible for services in Connecticut, a child must exhibit a significant developmental delay, meaning he or she must be at least 2 standardized deviations below the norm in one domain, or 1.5 standard deviations below in two or more domains, or have a categorical disability, such as Down syndrome, spina bifida, cerebral palsy, or cleft palate.

A report of the initial evaluation is written and presented to the family. If the child meets eligibility criteria, then an individual family service plan (IFSP) is developed. The IFSP is the contract between the agency and the family, focusing on the family's strengths and perceived needs, to help the child achieve specific developmental goals, such as sitting up, walking, or talking. My job is to help the family to help the child meet the developmental goals specified in the IFSP. The IFSP is reviewed every 6 months and revised if necessary, or more often if the family requests.

I generally see 4 or 5 children a day in their homes. All of the interventions that I do are home-based and family-centered. I go to the child's home and will work on general development, focusing on the child's movement and gross motor skills. I do that through play, working always with the parent or other primary caretaker in the child's natural environment, either at home or at day care, teaching them ways to enhance the child's development. Sometimes I'll do joint visits with other therapists, like an occupational or speech therapist, in order to be sure that my interventions are addressing the whole child. The frequency of visits is based on the child's needs and the family's ability to carry out the program and to schedule having people in their homes. Visits are scheduled around the parent and child's schedules—nap, school, work. I sometimes will bring special therapy equipment with me, such as therapy balls or bolsters or

Reaction time improves substantially through the preschool and elementary school years, even for simple motor movements (Bard, Hay, & Fleury, 1990; Dougherty & Haith, 1993).

✔ *Test Your Mastery...*

Learning Objective 5.2: *Trace the development of motor skills in infancy and childhood.*

1. What general patterned sequences do most infants show in their acquisition of motor skills?
2. What are examples of milestones in a sequence of motor development?
3. How does cultural context shape early motor development?
4. What is the dynamic systems approach to motor development?
5. How do motor skills continue to develop in childhood?

standers, and sometimes even novel toys to engage the child's interest. I also try to use what's available in the child's home.

Many of the children that I work with have special health care needs, such as feeding tubes, tracheostomies, and oxygen support, and so my experience and training as a physical therapist allows me to work with the family with positioning the child and helping the child to move under those circumstances. I also identify needs for special equipment that will better help the child explore his or her environment, such as braces, scooters, wheelchairs, and mobile standing frames.

What I find particularly satisfying is the joy in a family and child's eyes when I help the child do something that they've dreamed of, but never thought was going to happen. For example, recently I procured for an 18-month-old girl with spina bifida a mobile standing device that allows her to be upright and move around, playing with her siblings at eye level. Also satisfying is a child with Down syndrome who cruises along the furniture for the first time or climbs up on mommy's lap.

Some of the children I work with are very fragile medically. For instance, there is a rare neurological condition called holoprosencephaly, in which an infant has had severely abnormal brain development in utero. Typically, the child survives for only a few months. In those cases, the challenge is to make the baby comfortable, as responsive to his environment as his development allows, and to give the family as much joy in the child as we possibly can for the few months that the child is alive. But this is a small minority of cases. In most cases, the children turn three and move into the school system, sometimes needing continued services, and sometimes having caught up with their peers.

It's hard to say goodbye to them after working with them intensively for as long as three years, but it's satisfying knowing that they can function better at home and at school and in their communities, than if they hadn't received the early intervention services. It's also nice to know that the family has a better understanding of the child's strengths and needs.

For example, there was one situation where I met a child and her family when she was only a few months old, and she was very floppy and low-tone. Over the course of the three years, I helped the family discover her diagnosis (myotonic dystrophy, which is a congenital muscular dystrophy), and realize that the baby's three and a half year old sibling and several other family members also had this disorder and had never realized it. This is a disease that gets worse with subsequent generations and the parent's case was much milder. The little girl learned to

walk by herself by the time she was two and a half. Just getting to know this family and helping them through everything, as well as helping the little girl learn to move was very gratifying. If I had seen her in a hospital clinic, I wouldn't have had the same connection with the family. That was very meaningful, very rewarding. There were a lot of sad times and tears with them, too, but to be able to help the family go forward with more information and skills was the best part of it.

I think what isn't always evident when you start out as a physical therapist is the impact that you have on the whole person and their extended family. It is a tremendous responsibility, yet it is rewarding to know that maybe in some small way each day you make a difference in a family's life. Early intervention, with its family focus, really allows me to do more than just physical therapy. It really enables me to change lives holistically.

This 11-month-old boy practices his sitting, balance, and prewalking skills with his physical therapist, MaryAnn Delaney-Tuttle. By having him use his own toys in his home, where he and his family are most comfortable, therapeutic activities can be integrated into the family's daily routine, thus extending his learning beyond the weekly therapy session. (Mary Ann Delaney-Tuttle)

Perceptual Development

To talk about perceptual development, we must first distinguish among three processes: sensation, perception, and attention. **Sensation** refers to the detection and discrimination of sensory information—for example, hearing and distinguishing high and low tones. **Perception** refers to the interpretation of sensations and involves recognition ("I've heard that song before") and identification ("That was thunder"). **Attention** refers to the selectivity of perception, as when a child fails to hear a parent calling because he or she is watching television.

Whether the focus is on sensation, perception, or attention, research on perceptual development addresses the same two general questions that underlie all research in child

Learning Objective 5.3
Outline the areas of perceptual development during infancy.

Sensation
The experience resulting from the stimulation of a sense organ.

Perception
The interpretation of sensory stimulation based on experience.

Attention
The selection of particular sensory input for perceptual and cognitive processing and the exclusion of competing input.

Questions for Thought and Discussion
Why is it important to distinguish behaviors that mainly result from "nurture" from those that mainly result from "nature"?

Habituation–dishabituation
A method commonly used by researchers to study infants' early perceptual abilities that relies on babies' natural responses to changes in stimulation.

development: What are the most important changes that occur across the course of development, and how can we explain these changes? All the sensory systems are working at birth, and all achieve close to adult-level functioning by the end of infancy. In the development of perception, therefore, infancy, in the words of Bornstein and Arterberry (1999, p. 244), is where "most of the 'action' . . . takes place." The question of how to explain perceptual development, like other domains of development, can be answered only by considering the interaction between nature and nurture.

A "nurture" perspective is that the child begins life with only minimal ability to take in and make sense of sensory input. The emphasis is on the role of experience in perceptual development.

Research on the central nervous system illustrates how experience can affect even single sensory cells—both their survival and the connections that form among them. Many of the neurons we are born with die early in life. Researchers believe that visual experience activates some cells, which survive, but that other cells are not activated, and these die or their synapses are trimmed back (Greenough & Black, 1999).

For example, each brain cell (neuron) in the visual area of the brain is stimulated by one visual quality, such as vertical edges, but not by other qualities, such as horizontal edges. Other brain cells respond to horizontal edges but are insensitive to vertical edges. Still other cells respond specifically to angles, or diagonal lines, or other visual qualities. Researchers believe that when a stimulus repeatedly activates combinations of such cells—as when a baby looks at a square—the connections among these cells grow stronger. Eventually, the cells fire together in synchrony, and a child sees a whole square rather than a combination of visual qualities such as lines and intersections (Hebb, 1949). Thus, these cells are sensitive to experience at a very early age (Antonini & Stryker, 1993).

Other theorists believe that the biological contribution to perceptual development is greater than that of experience (Spelke & Newport, 1998). This "nature" view emphasizes the natural equipment that organisms have evolved for gathering information about their world, equipment that is either present from the start of life or emerges in the course of biological maturation.

Theorists James and Eleanor Gibson, for example, do not believe that perception involves combining pieces of input through experience, as in the traditional environmental/learning view (Gibson, 1966, 1969; Gibson & Pick, 2000). Instead, they argue, objects in the world give off physical energy that is already organized and can be perceived in its entirety. Perceptual development is defined as a child's increasing sensitivity to the organization of this energy and the properties of objects and people that remain stable and that change. An example is the ability of young infants to sense the synchrony of visual and auditory events. When young babies watch people speak, they can detect when speakers' lip movements are not synchronized with the sounds that they hear (Kuhl & Meltzoff, 1988). This natural ability is difficult to account for using a nurture perspective alone. In general, the earlier in development a perceptual skill emerges, the less likely it is that it has been acquired by experience. Nevertheless, even in approaches that stress the biological bases for perceptual development, the emphasis is not solely on nature. Nurture always plays an important role as well (Gibson 1969). With experience, infants and children become increasingly skilled at detecting the information available in sensory stimulation and thus at perceiving the world accurately.

What capacities do babies have for learning about the objects and people in their world? How do these capacities develop? How do children coordinate information from different perceptual modes and integrate perception and attention with action in the smooth flow of behavior?

Studying Perceptual Development

How do we know what a newborn baby can hear, see, smell, taste, or feel? One method commonly used by researchers is called the **habituation–dishabituation** procedure,

Babies' ability to perceive interesting objects, such as Mom's face, is a result of both nature and nurture. How do both nature and nurture contribute to what this baby sees? What other perceptual abilities do babies develop early in their infancy? (Penny Gentieu/Stone/Getty Images)

described in Chapter 1. In this procedure, researchers use babies' naturally occurring responses to changes in stimulation. The baby may tighten his eyelids, for example, in response to a sound, or turn his head and eyes toward the source of the sound, or perhaps become quiet. Changes in the baby's heart rate and breathing also occur in response to sounds (Aslin, Pisoni, & Jusczyk, 1983).

Imagine that we are interested not just in whether babies can detect sounds but in their ability to discriminate among different sounds. In the habituation–dishabituation procedure, we might first present a particular sound (for instance, an alarm clock ringing) repeatedly until the baby habituates to it—that is, no longer shows much (if any) response. Then we present sound B (for instance, a kitchen timer buzzing). If the baby dishabituates in response to this change in stimulus—that is, if the baby again reacts as though it is a new sound—then we have good evidence that she can hear a difference between these two sounds.

The habituation technique is a general methodology that has been applied to each of the sensory modes. It has provided the basis for several of the conclusions about infants' early capacities with regard to touch, smell, taste, hearing, and vision.

Touch, Smell, Taste, and Vestibular Sensitivity

Infants develop capacities for knowing the world through touch, smell, taste, and vestibular sensitivity. Anyone who wonders whether the newborn baby senses touch or experiences pain should watch the baby's reaction to a heel prick for a blood sample (Hadjistavropoulos et al., 1994). The angry cry that follows the prick of the needle is a clear sign that the baby can feel pain, as are the physiological changes—for example, changes in blood cortisol level—that follow a medical procedure such as circumcision (Gunnar et al., 1985). Furthermore, the effects of early exposure to pain may be long lasting. Newborns who receive repeated needle pricks as part of a screening test for diabetes react more strongly against subsequent blood tests than do other newborns (Taddio et al., 2002). Male babies who are circumcised without anesthesia are more sensitive to pain during vaccinations 4 to 6 months later (Taddio et al., 1997). For years, standard medical practice was to perform neonatal surgical procedures without anesthesia, both because of doubts about whether newborns experience pain and because of concerns about the safety of anesthesia for the tiny neonate. Fortunately, advances in knowledge about the newborn have spurred the search for effective forms of pain relief for this age group (Zempsky & Cravero, 2004).

Touch Newborn babies also show touch reflexes. Even the fetus displays the first signs of sensitivity to external stimulation through reactions to touch, and touch sensitivity increases over the first several days of life (Haith, 1986).

Haptic perception
The perceptual experience that results from active exploration of objects by touch.

Touching is important for relationships between children and adults. Placing a hand on a newborn's chest can quiet a crying episode, and gentle stroking can soothe even premature babies (Oehler & Eckerman, 1988). For older infants, touching increases positive emotion and visual attention during interactions between infant and caregiver (Stack & Muir, 1992). The active, exploratory use of touch is called **haptic perception**. Neonates' ability to acquire information about objects through touch is shown by their tendency to habituate when the same object is placed in their hand repeatedly and to dishabituate when the shape of the object is changed (Streri, Lhote, & Dutilleul, 2000). By the end of the first year of life, infants can recognize a familiar object through exploration with the hand alone (Rose, Gottfried, & Bridger, 1981). Haptic perception continues to improve throughout the childhood years (Morrongiello et al., 1994b).

Smell and Taste When can babies smell odors? How might we be able to tell? Researchers have examined this question by presenting babies with a smell and observing if they make a face, turn their heads, or do not respond at all. Even newborns turn their heads away from a cotton swab that smells bad (Rieser, Yonas, & Wikner, 1976). Babies produce positive facial expressions in response to banana, strawberry, and vanilla smells and negative expressions in response to smells of rotten eggs and fish (Crook, 1979; Steiner, 1979). Thus, the newborn's sense of smell is keen, and it improves over the first few days of life (Lipsitt, Engen, & Kaye, 1963).

The infant uses this ability as early as the first week of life to distinguish the mother's smell. Three-day-old infants orient more toward a pad moistened with the mother's amniotic fluid than to a pad moistened with the fluid of another woman (Marlier, Schaal, & Soussingham, 1998). Six-day-olds turn more frequently toward the mother's breast pad than toward the pad of another woman (MacFarlane, 1975). Parents make use of sensory cues as well. For instance, parents can recognize their infant from touch or smell alone within the first few days of life (Kaitz et al., 1993; Porter, Balogh, & Makin, 1988).

Babies are also sensitive to taste at birth. As the fluid that a baby sucks is sweetened, the baby sucks harder, consumes more, and tends to quiet faster from crying episodes (Blass & Smith, 1992; Smith et al., 1992). Even preterm neonates prefer a sweetened solution, which shows that taste receptors are functioning before the normal term for birth (Smith & Blass, 1996).

As illustrated in Figure 5.1, newborn babies can distinguish among different tastes. At 2 hours of age, babies make different facial expressions when they taste sweet and nonsweet solutions, and they also differentiate sour, bitter, and salty tastes (Rosenstein & Oster, 1988). At around 4 months of age, they begin to prefer salty tastes, which they found aversive as newborns (Beauchamp et al., 1994).

Vestibular sensitivity
The perceptual experience that results from motion of the body and the pull of gravity.

Vestibular Sensitivity **Vestibular sensitivity** refers to our ability to detect gravity and the motion of our bodies, which helps us maintain body posture and balance. In adults, disturbance of the vestibular sense causes dizziness and an inability to remain standing in the dark.

Newborns are sensitive to vestibular stimulation along all three axes of motion—front to back, up and down, and side to side (Reisman, 1987). The soothing properties of rocking and jiggling for crying babies clearly demonstrate this sensitivity. Postural adjustments can also affect a baby's alertness. For instance, babies are often more alert when in a vertical than when in a horizontal position (Korner & Thoman, 1970).

Hearing

Hearing is one of our most important senses, because a great deal of information about the world comes to us from sound alone. How do we know that a newborn baby can hear? As with smell and taste, we can exploit babies' naturally occurring responses to changes in stimulation. Newborn Neema can tighten his eyelids, for example, in response to a sound, or turn his head and eyes toward the source of the sound, or perhaps become quiet.

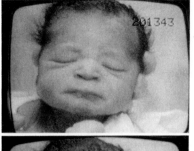
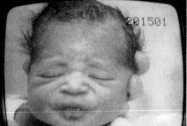
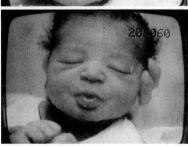

(a)

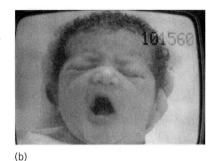

(b)

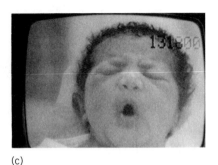

(c)

FIGURE 5.1   Infant responses to taste.

A newborn tasting (a) sweet, (b) bitter, and (c) sour solutions. The fact that newborns reject certain fluids and grimace in response to negative odors and tastes indicates that they come into the world with likes and dislikes.

Source: From D. Rosenstein and H. Oster. (1988). Differential facial responses to four basic tastes in newborns. *Child Development, 59,* 1561–1563. Copyright © 1988 by the Society for Research in Child Development, Inc. Reprinted by permission.

Changes in the baby's heart rate and breathing also occur in response to sounds (Aslin, Pisoni, & Jusczyk, 1983).

Prenatal Hearing   Even the fetus can hear. Electrical recordings of brain responses demonstrate sound reception in fetuses as early as the 25th week after conception, about 3.5 months before full-term birth (Lecanuet, 1998; Parmelee & Sigman, 1983). These findings indicate that fetuses receive sound impulses, but how do they respond to sound? Studies using ultrasound images of fetuses responding to auditory stimuli indicate that, after 28 weeks gestation, virtually all fetuses clamped their eyelids in response to sound. The fetuses that did not respond after this age (1 to 2 percent) were born with hearing deficits or serious impairments (Birnholz & Benacerraf, 1983).

Are babies affected by what they hear prenatally? The answer appears to be Yes. DeCasper & Fifer (1980) found that babies less than 4 days old can discriminate their mothers' voices from strangers' voices. Discrimination was shown by the fact that the babies altered their sucking rhythms more readily when their own mother's voice served as a reinforcer than they did when the reinforcer was the voice of a stranger.

One possible explanation for such early discrimination and preference for the mother is that the babies had become familiar with their mothers' voices in the womb. If this explanation is correct, we would expect no early preference for the father's voice, despite the fact that babies often hear the father in the days following birth. This, in fact, is the case: 4-day-old babies show no preference for their father's voice over that of a male stranger (DeCasper & Prescott, 1984).

The case for learning through prenatal hearing would be strengthened further if the infant could recognize a particular event that he or she experienced before birth. DeCasper and Spence (1986) asked pregnant women to read aloud one of three stories each day in the last six weeks of pregnancy. When tested at 3 days of age, their babies showed a preference for the familiar story over a new story, whether it was the mother's voice reading the story or that of a stranger. This finding demonstrates a clear effect of prenatal experience, and it tells us as well that the fetus can learn not only the mother's voice but also specific sound patterns that the mother produces.

Babies are especially sensitive to the characteristics of sound that will be important for language perception. Young infants prefer to listen to sounds that fall within the frequency range of the human voice, and they can distinguish different speech sounds as early as 1 month of age (Aslin, Jusczyk, & Pisoni, 1998).

Sound Localization An important property of sounds is the direction from which they come. Even newborns distinguish general sound location (Morrongiello et al., 1994a). They turn their eyes and heads toward a sound source to the left or right, if the sound is continuous. In one experiment, carried out in the delivery room by a scientist-parent, some ability to localize sounds was evident within 10 minutes of birth (Wertheimer, 1961).

Research indicates that the localization response disappears around the second month of life and reappears in the third or fourth month in a more vigorous form. The response is faster and more skilled, suggesting that a different brain center has taken control of this ability (Muir & Clifton, 1985). Localization is one of several behavioral systems that show this pattern of development in early infancy (Bever, 1982).

Vision

Take a moment to look around and appreciate the richness and complexity of your visual environment. You can see variations in brightness and color and texture, and you can tell which surfaces are hard and which are soft. You can see dozens of objects and their functions—light switches that can be flicked, containers that hold objects, shelves that support books, chairs that support people. Vision provides an immense amount of information about the world, and you know how to interpret this information easily.

Now, consider what this world must look like to a newborn baby. First, can the newborn see? If so, how well? When the baby can see well enough to make out objects, how does he or she know that one object is in front of another, that an object can serve as a container, or even that the container—say, a cup—is separate from the table on which it rests? How does the baby know that a tree seen through a window is outside the room rather than part of the glass? From this small sample of questions, you can see how much the baby must come to understand. We know that newborns can see. New parents notice their baby often turns her head toward a source of light, such as a window. In the first days of life, awake babies also distinguish light intensity. They open their eyes widely in dark-

Babies are better at discriminating complex sounds than we think. Infants as young as 4 months are sensitive to various properties of music, such as rhythm. Like most adults they prefer harmony (consonant musical inputs) to noise (dissonant musical inputs) (Trainor & Heinmiller, 1998; Zentner & Kagan, 1998). By the middle of the first year, babies can pick out melodies, even when the key changes (Trehub & Schellenberg, 1995). Babies can also tell the difference between a lullaby and an adult-directed song, even when the song and lullaby are from a foreign culture (Trehub & Henderson, 1994). From birth infants show a preference for lullaby-type input over adult songs (Masataka, 1999). (Camille Tokerud/The Image Bank/Getty Images, Inc.)

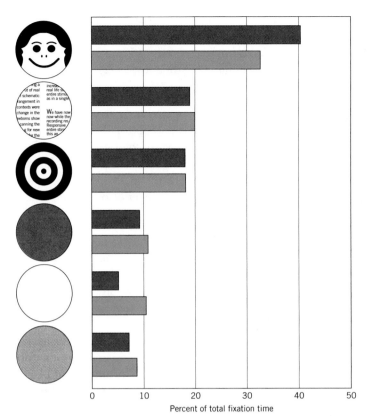

FIGURE 5.2 Stimuli that Robert Fantz showed to infants.
In this figure, the length of the bars indicates the average time that younger (2- to 3-month old) and older (3- to 6-month old) infants looked at each stimulus. Robert Fantz found that both younger and older infants enjoyed looking at complex patterns more than simple patterns. How would you describe the stimuli that infants prefer most of all?

Source: From R. Fantz. (1961). The origin of form perception. *Scientific American, 204*, 72. Copyright © 1961 by Scientific American. Reprinted by permission.

ness and close them in bright light; typically, they choose to look at moderate light levels (Haith, 1980). But it is hard to know what babies see, because we cannot easily communicate with infants. However, a researcher named Robert Fantz observed that babies look at different things for different periods of time (Fantz, 1961). He suggested that we could measure the amount of time babies look at one display rather than another to determine what babies can see and discriminate.

The procedure for measuring where babies look is straightforward. The researcher shows the baby two displays, side by side. With properly adjusted lighting, the researcher can see the reflection of these displays on the surface of the baby's eye, much as you can see the reflection of a window in daylight in the eyes of a person to whom you are talking. When the baby looks at one of the displays, that display is reflected from the surface of the eye. The researcher, using two stopwatches, can record how long the baby looks at each display. This is the **preference method**, because it shows if the infant has a preference—that is, looks longer at one stimulus than at the other. If the infant does show a preference, we conclude that he or she can discriminate between the stimuli.

Figure 5.2 shows some of the viewing preferences demonstrated by infants in Fantz's early studies. Researchers have used this powerful technique to study aspects of infant vision, including visual acuity, color perception, form perception, face recognition, and picture perception. The preference method is also used to study the development of memory, because an infant's interest in a particular visual display decreases over time but increases in the presence of novel stimuli. Researchers also can study how developmental problems such as Down syndrome or prematurity affect perceptual processing and memory (Bornstein & Sigman, 1986).

Visual Acuity Using the techniques developed by Fantz, researchers have estimated that the newborn's **visual acuity** is about 20/400 to 20/800 (meaning that a normal-vision adult sees at 400 to 800 feet what the newborn sees at 20 feet), compared with normal adult acuity of 20/20 (Kellman & Banks, 1998; Maurer & Lewis, 2001). By 3 months of age, acuity improves to around 20/100; by 6 months, it approximates that of the adult (Hainline, 1998; Nelson 1987).

Preference method
A research method for the study of visual ability in infancy. Two visual stimuli are presented simultaneously, and the amount of time the infant looks at each is measured.

Visual acuity
The clarity with which visual images can be perceived.

Visual acuity improves dramatically during the first months of life. Why do younger infants have poorer vision? One possibility is that the brain circuits that are responsible for focusing are not mature yet. The ability to focus improves between 1 and 3 months of age and is almost adult-like by 6 months of age (Hainline & Abramov, 1992).

Color Vision When can babies see color? The answer is: In a limited way, from birth, but much better by 4 months. Babies tend to look at colored objects, and newborns can make some color discriminations—red from green, for example, and both red and green from white (Adams, 1989; Adams & Courage, 1998). Otherwise, early color perception is limited, and newborns are unable to see many of the contrasts that adults can see (Adams, 1995). Color perception improves rapidly, however, and by 4 months infants' ability to perceive color appears equivalent to that of an adult (Teller & Bornstein, 1987).

Visual Pattern and Contrast What patterns do infants enjoy looking at? Researchers have discovered that newborns look primarily at high-contrast edges—for example, where black and white meet—and move their eyes back and forth over those contrast edges (Haith, 1980, 1991). As babies get older, they prefer patterns that are more densely packed. Three-week-olds look longer at a small checkerboard, whereas 6-week-olds are more likely to look longest at a midsized checkerboard and 3-month-olds at the most complex display (Karmel & Maisel, 1975).

An early theory held that babies prefer increasing complexity (that is, more checks) as they get older and become more complex themselves. However, several investigators have pointed out that as the number of checks increases, so does the amount of black-white edge in the display. Most investigators now believe that babies are attracted to the displays that offer the most edge contrasts that they can see at a particular age (Banks & Ginsburg, 1985). Why?

When babies move their eyes over edges, they activate cells of the visual areas of the brain. The strongest brain activity occurs when the baby adjusts the eye so that images of the edges fall near the center of the eye—that is, when the baby looks straight at the edges. Also, the more detail the baby can see, the stronger the activation. Haith (1980) has suggested that the baby's visual activity in early infancy reflects a biological "agenda" for the baby to keep brain-cell firing at a high level. This agenda makes sense because cells in the brain compete to establish connections to other cells. Activity tends to stabilize the required connections, while inactive pathways deteriorate (Greenough & Black, 1999). Fortunately, this agenda brings the baby to areas of the visual display that are also psychologically meaningful. Edges provide information about the boundaries of objects, their relationship in depth of field, and the location where they can be grasped.

Thus, the baby appears biologically prepared to engage in visual activity that is very adaptive. This activity produces the sensory input needed to maintain and tune the neural apparatus and also focuses the baby's attention on the most informative parts of the visual world. You can see that the young infant is anything but passive. Even the newborn possesses tools to get necessary experience for normal development.

Visual Organization Growing babies must move beyond simply exciting their own brains and begin to perceive organization in the visual world. Mother's face, for example, needs to be seen as a whole meaningful object rather than simply as eyebrows, eyes, ears, a nose, and so on.

Evidence suggests that babies really begin to "put things together" between 1 and 3 months of age (Cohen, 1998; Haith, 1990). One experiment is pictured in Figure 5.3. Infants were shown an arrangement of bars that formed a circular or square pattern. In some patterns, one bar was misaligned. To an adult, the one misaligned bar seems strange, because the adult sees all the other bars as going together. The misalignment had no effect on the visual fixations of 1-month-olds, but 3-month-olds looked longer around the displaced bar (Van Giffen & Haith, 1984). Thus, between 1 and 3 months of age, babies begin to see the organization in visual displays rather than only the details.

Links to Related Material

In Chapter 6, you will learn more about the effects of environmental stimulation on the development of synaptic connections in the brain.

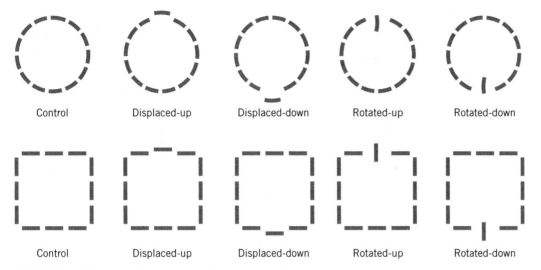

FIGURE 5.3   Stimuli used in a study of visual organization.

At 1 month of age, babies did not attend to the misaligned bars in the squares and circles above. By 3 months of age, they did, indicating that they were responding to the overall organization of the visual display and not just its details.

Source: From K. Van Giffen and M.M. Haith. (1984). Infant visual response to gestalt geometric forms. *Infant Behavior and Development, 7,* Figure 1, 338. Copyright © 1984 by Ablex Publishing Corp. Reprinted by permission.

Of course, babies do not appreciate all possible visual relations by 3 months of age. As you can demonstrate to yourself by walking into a modern art gallery, the perception of organization takes time and effort and knowledge. Consider the display shown in Figure 5.4. Adults report perceiving a square overlaying full circles at each corner in this display. They also report faint edges that connect the corners of the square, even though no such edges exist. Researchers who have examined infant responses to this illusion have found that by 7 months, babies are able to perceive it reliably as well (Ghim, 1990).

Studies show that the perception of visual organization, like most developmental phenomena, is not something that happens all at once for all displays. The ability to appreciate visual organization begins between 1 and 3 months of age, but this ability continues to improve and is affected by knowledge and the cues the environment provides (Condry, Smith, & Spelke, 2001; Kavsek, 2002; Needham, 2001).

Face Perception Babies show an interest in faces or face-like stimuli from birth. As with perception of patterned stimuli in general, however, it is hard to tell if the infant is responding to the face per se or simply to the interesting parts that make up the face. As Figure 5.5 shows, young infants' processing of faces is limited—they tend to look near the high-contrast borders of the face, and they pay relatively little attention to interior detail. In addition, a number of studies with infants in the first two or three months of life have failed to find a preference for faces over nonface stimuli with similar contrast, brightness, and shape (Maurer, 1985).

Nevertheless, as can be seen in the experiment depicted in Figure 5.6, newborns are most interested in faces (Johnson et al., 1991). Since this research, there have been several other demonstrations that newborn babies respond differentially to faces (Cassia, Simion, & Umilta, 2001; Mondloch et al., 1999). There is also increasing evidence that it is really faceness and not other aspects of the stimulation that attract newborn attention (de Haan, 2001; Johnson & de Haan, 2001).

By about 3 months of age, the preference for faces over comparable nonface stimuli is clearly established (Dannemiller & Stephens, 1988). By this age most babies also show a preference for a familiar face (typically mother's) over an unfamiliar one (Barrera & Maurer, 1981). Interestingly, babies also show a preference for relatively attractive faces (as determined by adult ratings) over relatively unattractive ones (Langlois et al., 1987), a preference seen even in newborns (Slater et al., 1998). One possible explanation for this finding

*Q**uestions for Thought and Discussion***

To stimulate development of the visual system, how might you design a nursery for an infant 1 to 6 months of age?

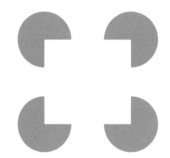

FIGURE 5.4

Adults perceive a square in the middle of the figure above. By 7 months, infants reliably perceive it as well.

Source: From B.I. Bertenthal, J.J. Campos, and M.M. Haith. (1980). Development of visual organization: The perception of subjective contours. *Child Development, 51,* Figure 1, 1073. Copyright © 1980 by the Society for Research in Child Development, Inc. Reprinted by permission.

FIGURE 5.5 What babies look at when viewing a face

A computer reconstruction shows babies' visual fixations on a face when (a) the adult is quiet and (b) the adult is talking. Babies in this study tended to look near the high-contrast borders of the face. What changes in the computer reconstruction would you predict for older infants, and why?

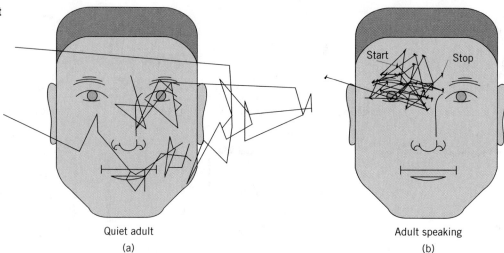

Quiet adult
(a)

Adult speaking
(b)

Questions for Thought and Discussion:

What criteria would you use to identify an "attractive" face? Which of those criteria might an infant possess innately? Why do you think infants prefer "attractive" faces?

is that attractive faces resemble composites of all faces, an averaging of a range of human features. Perhaps babies pay more attention to these faces than to those that deviate from the average (Rubenstein, Kalakanis, & Langlois, 1999).

After 6 months of age, infants become capable of recognizing a face as the same despite changes in expression or orientation (Cohen & Strauss, 1979). They also show an ability to classify faces as male or female (Fagan, 1976), and they can differentiate their own familiar face from others'. Infants tend to look more at the moving faces of other infants than at their own (Legerstee, Anderson, & Schaffer, 1998). In addition, by 6 months of age, infants, like older children and adults, show different forms of brain activity when processing faces than when responding to other sorts of stimuli (de Haan & Nelson, 1999).

Faces are also sources of social information. The sensitivity of babies to emotional expressions in faces grows slowly over the first two years of life (de Haan & Nelson, 1998; Walker-Andrews, 1997). Even 3-month-olds, however, may look longer at faces as the intensity of the smile increases. This tendency appears to depend on experience. Babies whose mothers call attention to themselves and smile when their babies look at them are the babies who show the strongest preferences for smiling faces (Kuchuk, Vibbert, & Bornstein, 1986).

Can Newborns Recognize Their Mothers' Faces? One of the important tasks of infancy is to learn to recognize and to prefer the primary caregiver, who in most instances is the

FIGURE 5.6 Stimuli and results from the Johnson et al. study of newborn's tendency to track moving objects.

Infants were shown a face-like pattern, a "scrambled" face, and a blank drawing. These were shown not statically but in motion across the infant's visual field. The question was whether the face-like pattern would prove more interesting than the other targets. The answer was Yes: Newborn babies, including some just a few minutes old, tracked the face more than they did the other stimuli (Johnson et al., 1991).

SOURCE: Reprinted from M.H. Johnson, S. Ddziurawiec, H. Ellis, and J. Morton. (1991). 'Newborns' preferential tracking of facelike stimuli and its subsequent decline. *Cognition, 40.* With permission from Elsevier Science Publishers.

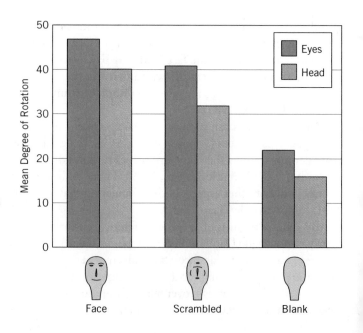

baby's mother. As you have read, a preference for the mother's voice or the mother's odor emerges in the first few days of life. Might a preference for the mother's face also be present this early?

Recent research suggests that newborns *do* recognize their mothers' faces. Babies as young as 2 days old have been shown to look more at their mothers' faces than at the face of a stranger (Bushnell, Sai, & Mullin, 1989; Pascalis et al., 1995). Newborn babies also alter their sucking patterns more readily for a chance to see their mother's face than a stranger's (Walton, Bower, & Bower, 1992). How could a baby with such a limited visual system and such limited visual experience recognize the mother? The study by Pascalis et al. (1995) suggests an answer. After demonstrating the preference for the mother's face, the researchers repeated the experiment, but with one difference: Now the women wore scarves that covered their hair and part of their foreheads. With the scarves in place, newborns could no longer distinguish their mother from a stranger. A subsequent study demonstrated that it is not until about 5 weeks of age that infants can recognize the mother when she is wearing a scarf (Bartrip, Morton, & de Schonen, 2001).

This research suggests that newborn recognition of the mother is not based on attention to the inner details of her face. Newborns seem to rely instead on more peripheral information, such as hairline and shape of head. Early recognition of the mother, like the early interest in face-like stimuli, is therefore limited compared to the face perception of older infants. Nevertheless, early responsiveness to faces contributes to the important task of forming emotional ties with others.

Perception of Objects and Their Properties

The ability of babies to appreciate the relationships among visual elements—for example, lines, angles, and edges—is important for their perception of the objects that populate the world. But knowledge of objects involves more than the ability to perceive how the parts fit together to make a whole. Knowledge of objects includes perception of the constancy of size, the continuity of objects, brightness, and color.

Size Constancy As an object moves farther away from us, its image on the eye shrinks. Yet the object continues to appear to be the same size, at least up to a point. For example, a child standing in front of you seems shorter than an adult standing across the street, even though the child casts a larger image on your eyes than does the adult. This phenomenon is called **size constancy.**

One approach to testing size constancy in very young infants is shown in Figure 5.7 (Slater, Mattock, & Brown, 1990). The stimuli are two cubes, one twice as large as the other. The baby first receives a series of familiarization trials in which one of the cubes is presented at different distances. For example, a baby might see the small cube at a distance of 23 cm, then at 53 cm, then at 38 cm, and so forth. Because both the distance and the size of the retinal image vary from trial to trial, the only constant element is the actual size of the cube. The test trials follow the familiarization phase. Now both cubes are presented simultaneously, but at different distances, with the larger cube twice as far away as the smaller one. The question of interest is whether the baby will show a preference by looking longer at one of the two cubes. The answer is Yes, infants show that they are able to perceive that the cube farther away from them is larger, even though it produces the same size retinal image as the smaller cube. This demonstrates that young infants perceive size constancy among objects in their visual world.

Seeing Objects as Continuous Our knowledge of objects extends beyond size constancy. We understand principles of solidity and continuity, and therefore we see objects as continuous and whole even when our view is partially blocked. For example, when a person stands in front of a table, blocking the midsection of the table from our view, we naturally infer that the two ends of the table are connected. In a sense, we perceive a whole table even when we don't see one. Do young infants also perceive objects as continuous and whole when they are partially blocked by other objects? In a series of experiments

Size constancy
The experience that the physical size of an object remains the same even though the size of its projected image on the eye varies.

BOX 5.3 Infants' Perception of Motion

As social beings, we must perceive and interpret the actions of other people and of animals. To function well in a social environment, we need to be able to distinguish between Auntie Em coming toward us with open arms and the Wicked Witch coming toward us shaking her pointy finger. Most adults are adept at these tasks, yet it is not clear how we do this. Researchers are combining information from studies of human adults and children as well as studies of animals in their efforts to understand this important capacity and its development. Research on the perception of human movement is helping us understand how we grow into socially adept adults.

Studies of the visual perception of human movement typically employ "biological motion displays" in which the human figure is represented by a set of "point-lights" attached to the head and major joints of the body (see Photo a, p. 175). The human form is not recognizable in any single static frame of a biological motion display, but when the elements move, adults can identify the figure and action in less than 200 ms (Johansson, 1973). This is amazing because the point-light elements could be grouped or organized in hundreds of millions of different ways. It is unlikely that adults consider and reject all of the other groupings possible in order to reach an interpretation. Moreover, adult observers perceive not just the organization of the elements but also more subtle information such as emotional state or gender of the actor (Brownlow et al., 1997; Dittrich et al., 1996; Kozlowski & Cutting, 1977, 1978; MacArthur & Baron, 1983).

Given the social importance of human movement and the ease with which adults interpret it, some researchers have speculated that the visual system may have specialized mechanisms for perceiving the movements of other people and, perhaps, animals more generally. This hypothesis is plausible. Many animals are sensitive to the form and motion characteristics of members of their own species as well as of predators and prey. Although the human visual system may have evolved more flexible processing capacities than our nonhuman ancestors, we appear to share some nervous system mechanisms as well. We may share a specialized sensitivity to animal movement.

Some of the available evidence is consistent with this speculation. Electrophysiological studies (in which electrodes are used to monitor the activity of individual neurons) show that single brain cells in macaque monkeys responded preferentially to point-light displays of human movement (Oram & Perrett, 1996). Emily Grossman has demonstrated that analogous areas in the human cortex respond when people view biological motion displays (Grossman, Donnelly, Price, et al., 2000). Children with autism (a disorder characterized by a selective impairment in the ability to perceive others' mental states) show impairments in the perception of human movements in biological motion displays (Blake, Turner, Smoski, et al., 2003).

When mature capacities suggest a plausible evolutionary influence and a specialized mechanism, researchers once assumed that the underlying mechanisms were innate (Fodor, 1986). Studies of development are essential to critically examining such assumptions. Indeed, studies of infants' perceptions of human movement suggest that specialized mechanisms in the perception of biological motion are not (wholly) innate, but may arise in part through experience.

Systematic studies of infants' ability to discriminate point-light displays provide a complex picture of capacities and limitations during the first year of life. Infants as young as 3 months of age can discriminate coherent point-light displays of human movement from randomly moving dots (e.g.,

investigating this topic, it was found that infants even as young as 1 month apparently can perceive partially obscured objects as wholes (Kawabata et al., 1999; Kellman, 1996; Spelke, 1988; Johnson, 1997; Johnson & Aslin, 1995). Newborns cannot, however, which suggests that some experience may be necessary for this accomplishment (Slater et al., 1994, 1996).

Perception of Depth As babies acquire the ability to move around, they also develop the capacity to get into trouble. One potential danger is falling over edges if they cannot perceive that a surface that supports them drops off. Eleanor Gibson and Richard Walk (1960) first tested infants' perception of depth by using a unique device called a **visual cliff.**

The visual cliff consists of a sheet of Plexiglas on which the infant can crawl. A patterned cloth lies just beneath the clear surface on one side. Under the other side is the same cloth pattern, but it lies several feet below the clear surface. Infants able to crawl were placed on a small platform just at the edge of the boundary between "safe" and "deep." Although their mothers called to them from across the deep side, most infants were unwilling to cross, apparently because they perceived the depth and danger. Subsequent research has confirmed the pattern identified by Gibson and Walk. Most babies old enough to be tested avoid the deep side of the cliff, and by 9 or 10 months this avoidance response is quite strong (Bertenthal, Campos, & Kermoian, 1994).

Visual cliff

A research method for the study of depth perception in infancy. The infant is placed on a glass-covered table near an apparent drop-off, and perception of depth is inferred if the infant avoids the drop.

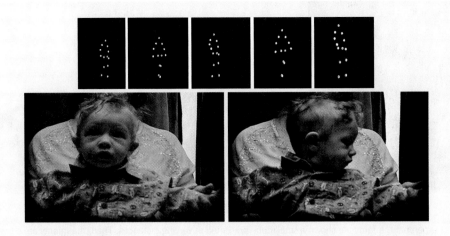

(a) Five static frames from an animated "point-light" or "biological motion" display depicting a normal human figure walking. Although the figure is comprised of merely 12 dots, adults effortlessly recognize the figure and its activity as it moves. (b) During a visual habituation procedure, this 6-month-old infant watches the point-light display from his mother's lap, until he gets bored and turns away. (Courtesy of Jeannine Pinto)

Bertenthal, Proffitt, & Kramer, 1987a, 1987b; Bertenthal, Proffitt, Kramer, & Spetner, 1987; Fox & McDaniel, 1982), suggesting that the capacity to perceive some organization among the elements is present or acquired very early in life. Nonetheless, 3-month-old infants do not appear to be sensitive to the whole constellation that comprises the human body. Instead, they appear to be sensitive to relatively limited areas of the displays such as the angle made by the wrist, elbow, and shoulder as the arm moves (Booth, Pinto, & Bertenthal, 2004). As a result of this localized attention, 3-month-old infants respond similarly to point-light figures depicting cats, spiders, and people. By 5 months, and more so by 7 months, infants respond differently to human and nonhuman figures. These findings suggest that their responses have become attuned to the features that distinguish human forms from other four-legged figures (Pinto, 2005).

How might an infant learn quickly about the structure of a human form? How can the infant apply that knowledge to abstract point-light displays? Although knowledge of human form may not be innate, the learning process may be guided by inherent preferences. For example, infants attend preferentially to face-like stimuli over other stimuli. Since faces recruit infants' attention, facial information may be more quickly learned than other classes of stimuli. Knowledge of human form may operate similarly, guided by a preference for configurations that are part of the human body. Alternatively, motion itself may tutor the visual system. Motion recruits attention. When something moves in your visual periphery, you tend to turn toward it to find out more about it. The movements of a person therefore would be an attractive stimulus to an infant. By orienting to such a stimulus, the infant creates opportunities to learn from it, and therefore to acquire some expertise in the visual appearance of human bodies in motion. Finally, infants' mental representation of human bodies may arise from proprioceptive information provided by their neuromuscular system. We cannot be confident of the relative importance of nurture and nature until we can specify what experience shapes the visual system and how.

Around the time that babies develop skill in crawling they become fearful of heights, as they display in their reluctance to cross a visual cliff. What perceptual ability does this fear signify? (Mark Richard/PhotoEdit)

When does the ability to perceive the depth of the deep side develop? An ingenious approach to this question, one that can be used with infants too young to crawl, involves measuring infants' heart rates as the experimenter lowers them to the clear surface of the visual cliff on both the deep and the safe sides. The heart rates of infants as young as 2 months of

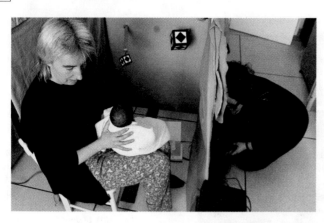

FIGURE 5.7 **Procedure for testing size constancy in newborns.**

In this experiment, infants are shown a small cube presented at varying distances. Then, the infants are shown the small cube again, at the same time that they are shown a larger cube that is identically marked but twice as large. The larger cube is placed twice as far away as the smaller one, thus producing identical retinal images on the infant's eyes. Will infants recognize that the cubes are different sizes? The answer is Yes, demonstrating that young infants perceive size constancy among objects in their visual world.

All the newborn babies tested looked significantly longer at the larger cube. This means that they could see a difference between the two cubes, despite the equivalent retinal images. Their preference for the novel stimulus suggests that the small cube was familiar to them and therefore less interesting, which also shows the perception of size constancy. Size constancy is stronger by 3 or 4 months of age and improves up to at least 10 or 11 years of age (Day, 1987).

Source: From A. Slater, A. Mattock, and E. Brown. (1990). Size constancy at birth: Newborn infants' responses to retinal and real size. *Journal of Experimental Child Psychology, 49*, 317, 318. Copyright © 1990 by Academic Press. Reprinted by permission.

age slow when the infants are lowered to the deep side. This finding tells us that the babies notice the difference and are interested in it; there is no evidence, however, that they fear the depth. By 9 months the response is quite different. Now heart rate increases over the drop-off, suggesting that babies are afraid, and now most infants are also unwilling to cross over to the deep side (Campos, Bertenthal, & Kermoian, 1992; Campos et al., 1978).

The shift from interest to fear in response to drop-offs occurs after about 7 months of age. This is also the time when babies begin to take responsibility for their own movements—for instance, by crawling or by pushing themselves around in walkers. Might the two developments be related? Various kinds of evidence suggest that they are (Campos, Bertenthal, & Kermoian, 1992). For example, there is a correlation between crawling experience and fear of depth: Babies who have been crawling the longest are most likely to show the fear response on the visual cliff. When infants begin to move around by themselves, links between perception and action become even stronger. Self-produced movement produces new experiences and sometimes new understandings—such as the onset of fear of heights (Campos et al., 1992). Moving around independently also requires new perceptual learning. This is so because babies in the first year of life have difficulty separating their perception of space from the actions they perform. For example, babies who are able to reach around a barrier for a hidden object have to relearn the task when they are required to crawl around the barrier to get it (Lockman, 1984; Lockman & Adams, 2001). Similarly, infants who can perceive and avoid a drop-off while in a sitting posture may respond differently when put in the posture for crawling (Adolph, 2000). Thus, what seem like very similar tasks to an adult do not at first seem similar to the baby. As infants gain more experience with the effects of their own movements, they gradually develop a more unified understanding of space.

The Integrated Senses

Our experience of people and objects in the world actually involves more than one perceptual mode simultaneously. A dog, for example, provides visual information. It also provides auditory information by barking, panting, and moving around. Touch may provide another cue as the dog brushes against you. Finally, its odor may stimulate your sense of smell. Alone and in combination, these perceptual cues tell you that a dog is nearby. How does the child come to realize that cues from different senses "go together"? Jean Piaget (1952) argued that the sensory modes are largely separate at birth and that the baby integrates them only through experience. For example, the baby can relate touch and vision only when he learns to look at objects as his hand grasps them. Other theorists have argued that some coordination of the senses is present from the start (e.g., Gibson, 1988). As it turns out, there is evidence for both claims (Lewkowicz, 2000; Lickliter & Bahrick, 2000; Rose & Ruff, 1987).

Some studies focus on how exploring in one perceptual mode (such as reaching out to touch a stuffed bear) triggers exploration in a different mode (bringing the bear to the mouth and tasting it). Other studies focus on how input from different senses comes to indicate a single mental representation—how we know, for example, that a particular sight, touch, and smell all come from the same dog. Exploration and representation are two ways that babies integrate sensory input. Babies come into the world with a number of inborn relations among sensory modes, which they elaborate through exploration. Forming mental representations of objects by integrating the inputs of many perceptual modes requires experience. As always, nature and nurture work together to guide development.

Exploration Will a newborn baby, who has had no opportunity yet to make associations between an object's sights and sounds, recognize that these are related? The answer is Yes. The newborn turns his or her eyes and head toward the sound of a voice or a rattle if the sound continues for several seconds (Ennouri & Bloch, 1996; Morrongiello et al., 1994a). Recall, too, that one of the infant's earliest reflexes involves turning the head toward the cheek being stroked, an exploratory action that helps the newborn find the nipple. Similar relations exist between smell and vision, as when a 6-day-old baby will turn toward the smell of his or her mother's milk (MacFarlane, 1975).

The relationship between vision and reaching is important for perceptual integration. Infants' reaching for a rattle that they see illustrates how vision can trigger tactile exploration. Babies do not reach and grasp objects accurately before 4 or 5 months of age, but shortly after birth they move their arms in the right direction (Hofsten, 1982; White, Castle, & Held, 1964). Thus, some sensory integration is present at birth, presumably because this has evolutionary value. Do babies realize they are exploring the same object in different perceptual modes? This question raises the issue of mental representation.

Representation Two kinds of evidence show us how infants can use different perceptual modes to form a single mental representation of an object. First, we can see if babies can transfer the benefit of experience from one mode to another. Second, we can determine if babies know that the same object—such as a music box or a nipple—is stimulating two modes (vision and hearing or touch and vision, respectively).

As noted earlier, babies use haptic perception, such as grasping and sucking, to explore by touch. Some experiments have shown, for example, that even very young infants can transfer information gained from sucking to visual perception of the same object. Meltzoff and Borton (1979) provided 1-month-old infants with an opportunity to suck on either a nubby (bumpy) nipple or a smooth nipple. They then presented the infants pictures of the nubby and smooth nipples, side by side. Infants looked longer at the nipple they had sucked. This finding suggests that cross-modal cues can specify the same object for infants at an amazingly early age, but we should be careful in reaching conclusions. Although some experimenters have reported similar findings (Gibson & Walker, 1984; Pecheux, Lepecq, & Salzarulo, 1988), others have been unable to replicate the results (Brown & Gottfried, 1986; Maurer, Stager, & Mondloch, 1999), and thus at present it is not clear how early such oral-visual matching is possible.

Similarly, babies can detect a correspondence between a sound and a visual event and naturally look at visual events that correspond to the sounds they hear. For example, Spelke (1976) showed 4-month-old infants two films, side by side. (Figure 5.8 shows the typical experimental arrangement in research of this sort.) One film showed a person playing peekaboo, and the other showed a hand hitting a wooden block and a tambourine. A soundtrack was played that was appropriate to one of the films. Babies looked more at the film that matched the soundtrack, suggesting that they recognized the sight–sound correspondence.

FIGURE 5.8 Intermodal perception.

In this experiment, infants are shown two videotapes. In each is a face that is talking. However, the soundtrack that the infant hears corresponds to the lip movements of only one of the speakers. How will researchers determine if infants are capable of integrating auditory and visual sensory input from the same stimulus? Which face will infants prefer?

SOURCE: From P.K. Kuhl and A.N. Meltzoff. (1982). The bimodal perception of speech in infancy. *Science, 218,* 1139. Copyright © 1982 by the AAAS. Reprinted by permission.

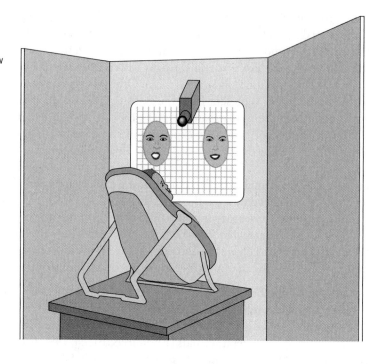

Through what perceptual modes is this toddler exploring the pet rabbit? What needed to happen before the child could form a mental representation for "rabbit"?

Babies also can match auditory and visual events when the matching involves tempo (sound) and rhythm (sight) (Bahrick & Lickliter, 2000; Bahrick & Pickens, 1994). And by 4 months of age, babies have some idea about the types of sounds new objects will make when they bang together, a feat that requires knowledge of several properties of objects—for example, their hardness and whether one item or several items are involved in the action (Bahrick, 1983, 1992).

Babies appreciate auditory-visual relations involving people. By 4 months of age, babies look more at a male face when they hear a male voice and more at a female face when they hear a female voice, even when the faces and voices are unfamiliar (Walker-Andrews et al., 1991). Four-month-olds also can match on the basis of age, directing attention to either an adult or a child speaker, depending on whether the voice they hear is adult-like or childlike (Bahrick, Netto, & Hernandez-Reif, 1998).

Infants, then, are surprisingly good at *intermodal perception*—picking up the commonality in cues from different senses. The baby's awareness that different cues from the same objects are coordinated greatly simplifies the task of organizing the overwhelming number of stimuli in the world into more manageable chunks. Intermodal capabilities emerge at different times. At first, infants simply appreciate that synchrony exists between visual and auditory events, while more subtle forms of intermodal perception appear in steps as the baby matures (Lewkowicz & Lickliter, 1994).

Attention and Action

The perceptual modes are the mind's tools for gathering information about the environment, and the mind uses these tools actively. *Attention* is the active, selective taking in of some but not all information available in a situation. Perception is mediated by attention. In addition, perception guides action, because perception is a means toward the goal of operating on the world effectively: "We perceive in order to act and we act to perceive" (Pick, 1992, p. 791). How does action affect perception, and how does perception guide action?

Development of Attention Even newborn infants attend to sounds and sights. Their bodies become quieter, they stop what they are doing (such as sucking), they widen their eyes, and their heart rates slow. These changes in behavior appear to optimize the baby's readiness to receive stimuli. First described by Sokolov (1960) as the **orienting reflex**, these changes can be observed, for example, when newborns attend to moving lights, to sounds

Questions for Thought and Discussion

Research suggests that we perceive in order to act. Does this generalization apply to you in your daily activities? How might it apply to the life of an infant?

Orienting reflex

A natural reaction to novel stimuli that enhances stimulus processing and includes orientation of the eyes and ears to optimize stimulus reception, inhibition of ongoing activity, and a variety of physiological changes.

that change gradually, or to sounds of low frequency (Haith, 1966). However, if the physical stimuli are too intense or the changes too abrupt, infants close their eyes and become agitated and their heart rates increase—a protective reaction called the **defensive reflex** (Graham & Clifton, 1966). The orienting and defensive reflexes may be the baby's earliest forms of positive and negative attention.

Infants also develop **selective attention**—the ability to focus on one stimulus rather than another. Even newborns have the capacity for selective attention, preferring displays of moderate brightness over very dim or very bright displays (Lewkowicz & Turkewitz, 1981) and patterned over plain displays (Fantz, 1963).

The looking activity of young infants is a good example of the role that action plays in perception. When alert and active, young infants make new visual fixations two or three times each second. Newborns even search actively with their eyes in darkness, indicating that their perceptual system is active even when there is no stimulus to produce a reaction. They continue to search when a light is turned on until they find light–dark edges. When they do, they look back and forth over those edges, adjusting their visual scanning. They seem to come into the world with a set of rules for acting:

1. If awake and the light is not too bright, open eyes.
2. If in darkness, search around.
3. If find light, search for contrasting edges.
4. If find edges, stay near them and look back and forth over them.
5. As the clustering of edges increases, scan the edges more minutely.

This inborn set of rules serves the biological function of activating visual cells in the brain and ensuring that cells form proper hookups with each other (Haith, 1980, 1991). Such rules also illustrate that from the earliest moments of a newborn's external life, action affects perception just as perception affects action.

Action can also anticipate perception. Recent research indicates that young infants can anticipate perceptual events before they occur, through the formation of expectations (Haith, 1994; Haith, Wentworth, & Canfield, 1993; Wentworth, Haith, & Hood, 2002). In these studies, infants see attractive pictures that flash in a preset pattern on a computer screen—for example, left-right-left-right. They can quickly learn the sequence and begin to look to the next location prior to the picture's appearance. After less than a minute of experience with such series, most infants move their eyes, during the delay period, to the place where the next picture will appear. By 2 months of age infants show such anticipatory behavior for a simple alternating pattern; by 3 months they can learn more complex sequences. The ability to anticipate future events is an important component of many kinds of cognitive activity throughout the lifespan (Haith et al., 1994). Apparently, such "future-oriented processing" begins very early. As children age, the source of control of attention shifts from external stimuli to self-regulation based on the individual's own goals and intentions. Flavell (1985) identified four important aspects of attention that develop with age.

1. *Control* of attention improves with age as attention span increases and distractibility decreases. For example, children under 2.5 years of age are easily distracted from watching TV programs by toys in the room and other events in the house. Soon enough, however, it may become difficult to pull them away from the set (Anderson et al., 1986; Ruff, Capozzoli, & Weissberg, 1998).

2. *Adaptability* of attention to the task also changes. When an experimenter tells children to pay attention to a particular task, older children do so and disregard things that are not central to it. Younger children, however, focus on many more irrelevant aspects and so do not perform as well on the main task (Hagen & Hale, 1973; Miller, 1990).

3. Another feature of attentional change is *planfulness*. When an experimenter asks children to judge whether two complex pictures are the same, younger children often use a haphazard comparison strategy, not examining all the details before making a judgment. Older children are more systematic, comparing each detail across pictures, one by one (Vurpillot, 1968).

Defensive reflex
A natural reaction to novel stimuli that tends to protect the organism from further stimulation and that may include orientation of the stimulus receptors away from the stimulus source and a variety of physiological changes.

Selective attention
Concentration on a stimulus or event with attendant disregard for other stimuli or events.

Questions for Thought
and Discussion

*Do you have strategies for paying
attention? Are the same strategies
generally available to infants and
young children? Why, or why not?*

4. Finally, children become better at *adjusting* their attentional strategies as they gather information from a task. For example, experienced readers change their reading speed as the difficulty of the text changes, whereas younger readers tend to maintain a fairly regular reading speed regardless of difficulty (Day, 1975).

The study of children's eye movements demonstrates the interplay of action and perception in the study of older children as well as of infants. In one experiment, children were shown pairs of houses, such as those in Figure 5.9, and were asked to judge whether the houses in each pair were identical or different. The experimenter recorded the children's eye fixations and movements as they looked at the two houses (Vurpillot et al., 1975). Each house had several windows of varying shapes with varying decorations. A thorough examination of the houses required comparing each window of the houses one by one.

Striking differences in efficiency were found between children 4 and 9 years of age. The younger children appeared to lack a plan or systematic approach for the task. Rather than comparing the corresponding features in a pair of houses, the younger children often looked at features in different locations, in a haphazard order, and did not check all features before deciding the houses were the same. In contrast, older children scanned comparable features, systematically checking each pair before making a "same" decision. They were also more efficient, ending their inspection as soon as a difference between windows permitted them to say "different" (Vurpillot & Ball, 1979).

In general, studies of visual scanning and other perceptual activities reveal that children are more careful in gathering information, more flexible in search, and less distractible as they move from the preschool to the middle-elementary school years (Ruff & Rothbart, 1996). Such studies also reveal clear links between attention and learning and problem solving. Individual differences in attention at any age are one reason some children learn more effectively than others.

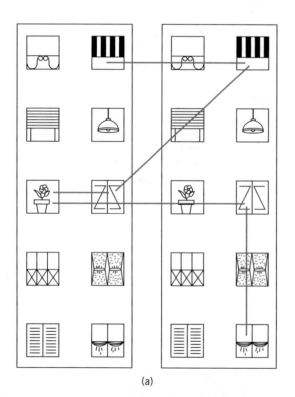

(a)

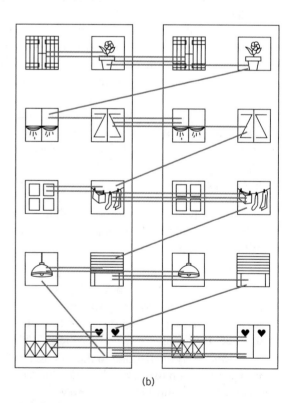

(b)

FIGURE 5.9 Eye movements and judgments of similarity.

Children were shown pairs of houses and asked to judge whether the windows in two houses were identical or different. The child who attends more efficiently scans the pairs of stimuli systematically for similarities and differences.

Source: From E. Vurpillot, R. Castelo, and C. Renard. (1975). Extent of visual exploration and number of elements present around the stimulus in a perceptual differentiation task. *Année Psychologique, 75,* Figure 2, 362–363. Reprinted by permission of Presses Universitaires de France.

Cultural differences also influence children's patterns of attention. Barbara Rogoff and colleagues (Chavajay & Rogoff, 1999; Rogoff et al., 1993) observed toddlers (children 12 to 24 months old) in the United States and Mayan toddlers in Guatemala in situations with many potential stimuli and events. The Mayan toddlers were more likely than their American counterparts to attend simultaneously to two or three on-going events rather than focus on a single event at a time. One 12-month-old, for example, "skillfully closed things in a jar with his older sister, whistled on his toy whistle that his mother had mischievously slipped into his mouth, and at the same time watched a passing truck with interest" (Chavajay & Rogoff, 1999, p. 1080). The basis for the differences among the toddlers became evident from observations of the mothers' behavior: Mayan mothers, like their children, were more likely than the American sample to attend simultaneously to multiple events. The children's attentional patterns, then, reflected those of their mothers. Thus, children are socialized for forms of activity—in this case, patterns of attention—that are valued in the culture in which they are developing.

Helping Children with Attentional Problems

An important developmental achievement is the capacity to control and direct attention effectively. Not all children, however, master the challenges of attentional control as quickly or as fully as others. You may have observed children who constantly fidget and talk out inappropriately, who seem unable to stay seated or to concentrate for more than brief periods of time, and whose uncontrolled behavior may detract from their own and others' activities and learning. **Attention-Deficit Hyperactivity Disorder (ADHD)** is a clinical syndrome characterized by these patterns of behavior. (Attention Deficit Disorder [ADD] is the same condition without the hyperactivity.)

Children with ADHD have great difficulty maintaining attention and often are hyperactive and impulsive in their behavior. Children with untreated ADHD are likely to perform poorly in school and may have difficulties in interpersonal relations as well. ADHD emerges early in childhood and can be a lifelong condition, with symptoms persisting into adulthood in up to 40 percent of childhood sufferers (Mannuzza & Klein, 2000). In addition, children with continued ADHD symptoms are at greater risk for the later development of antisocial behavior and substance use disorders. With appropriate treatment, however, most ADHD children are able to function adequately in adulthood, achieve gainful employment, attain higher educational and vocational goals, and show no evidence of emotional or behavioral disorder in adulthood (Mannuzza & Klein, 2000).

The diagnosis of ADHD has become increasingly common. Current estimates of the percentage of people with ADHD in the United States are 5 percent for school-age children and 3 percent for adults. Because complicating factors may be present, such as memory problems, conduct disorder, other learning disabilities, or depression, ADHD may be difficult to diagnose. For this reason percentages are sometimes given as a range from 4 to 12 percent (American Academy of Pediatrics, 2000). Boys are diagnosed with the disorder more often than are girls. It is unclear, however, whether this disparity reflects a genuine difference between the sexes or simply the fact that boys are more likely to show the disruptive behaviors that lead to clinical evaluation (Gaub & Carlson, 1997). Gender differences are especially marked when teacher reports are the basis for identifying children for evaluation (Campbell, 2000).

The precise cause of ADHD remains a source of controversy (Faraone & Biedermann, 2000; Joseph, 2000). The evidence suggests that in most cases both nature and nurture contribute. The fact that ADHD tends to run in families suggests a biological component. Approximately 50 percent of children with ADHD have a relative with ADHD, usually a parent (especially the father) or a sibling (Silver, 1999). In one study, 51 percent of identical twin pairs shared the disorder (Goodman & Stevenson, 1989).

Further evidence for the importance of biological factors comes from studies of genetics and brain structure and functioning. For example, a gene associated with ADHD is responsible for "novelty seeking." Scientists speculate that this trait may have conferred a selective advantage to carriers during human evolution, because novelty

Attention-Deficit Hyperactivity Disorder (ADHD)
A developmental disorder characterized by difficulty in sustaining attention, hyperactivity, and impulsive and uncontrolled behavior.

seeking would have aided in finding new ways to adapt to environmental challenges. About 50 percent of children with ADHD have the recessive form of this trait (*Proceedings of the National Academy of Sciences*, 2002). In addition, an immune system gene has been found to be linked to susceptibility to ADHD. The gene controls a protein used in coping with stress.

Individuals with ADHD often show abnormalities in the frontal lobe of the cortex—the part of the brain responsible for attention and inhibition of behavior (Riccio et al., 1993; Zametkin et al., 1990)—and in the limbic system—the part of the brain responsible for arousal. New brain imaging studies of blood flow to these areas permit diagnosis of different types of ADD/ADHD, permitting more effective treatment.

Experience also can be important. Children may be exposed to teratogens such as alcohol or drugs, which may mimic or exacerbate the characteristics of ADHD (Silver, 1999). Also, the home lives of children with ADHD may be characterized by high levels of stress and parental punitiveness (Bernier & Siegel, 1994; Jacobvitz & Sroufe, 1987). Thus, aspects of parenting may contribute to the child's problems. At the same time, the presence of a difficult child also creates stress for the parents, whose attempts to cope may then make the child's problems even greater (Campbell, 2000).

General advice to parents and teachers of children with ADD/ADHD includes:
- use structured environments and consistency in routines to help children deal with change;
- break down tasks into small components and provide strategies for organizing time;
- use colors, shapes, and textures, or other visual and tactile stimuli, to help children organize;
- reduce distractions and the number and intensity of sensory stimuli in the environment;
- engage the child in frequent changes of task to work within the child's attention span without repeatedly reaching frustration points.

Links to Related Material
In Chapter 10, you will read about how television viewing may influence the development of ADHD.

As you can see, just as both nature and nurture may contribute to the emergence of ADHD, attempts to help children with ADHD may take both biological and environmental routes. Stimulant drugs such as Ritalin have been used to treat ADHD since the 1930s. This treatment leads to improvement in approximately 80 percent of cases by decreasing activity levels and heightening attention (Silver, 1999). Negative side effects often can be controlled by reducing dosage or adding secondary drugs, such as antidepressants, although in 2004 clinical reports led the U.S. Food and Drug Administration (2004) to discourage their use in children and adolescents. New nonstimulant drugs for children over 6 have 70 percent effectiveness, while avoiding possible problems with treating overstimulated nervous systems with stimulants (*Journal of Clinical Psychiatry*, 2002). Although drug treatment can be an important part of a therapy program for ADHD, medication does not cure the condition, and medication alone is unlikely to give children with ADHD all the help they need. The most effective treatment programs combine medication with behavior therapy and changes in the child's environment. Environmental interventions that have proved beneficial are operant conditioning of appropriate behaviors, modeling, and family-oriented forms of therapy (Barkley, 1998; Pelham & Hinshaw, 1992). Interventions that involve both the school and the home tend to be most effective.

At present, there is no known cure for ADHD, and not even the best treatment programs can guarantee long-term success. Still, recent years have seen important advances in our ability to help children and families cope with a common and serious childhood disorder.

BOX 5.4   Contextual Model of Early Infant Capacities

Infant is born with biological capacities related to behavioral organization, development of motor milestones, and early perceptual abilities.

Family and school settings

- How do adults structure the wake–sleep schedule for infants and young children?
- Do parents cosleep with the infant?
- Is the infant or young child encouraged to practice certain motor skills?
- What sorts of perceptual experiences are young children provided with?
- Do infants and young children typically interact with adults in multiperson or dyadic settings? What effect might these have on how children learn to divide their attention?

Socioeconomic influences

- Do parents and schools have the resources to provide the infant and young child with a wide range of experiences that stimulate motor and perceptual development in a variety of ways?

Cultural influences

- What are larger cultural expectations regarding cosleeping, sleep–wake schedules for young children, development of motor skills, and perceptual experiences?

Learning Objective 5.3: *Outline the areas of perceptual development during infancy.*

1. How do biology and the environment interact to shape perceptual development?
2. What capacities does the newborn exhibit regarding touch, smell, taste, and vestibular sensitivity?
3. How, and what, do infants see and hear?
4. What do we know about the infant's ability to perceive objects?
5. How do infants develop an ability to integrate sensory inputs?
6. How does attention develop during infancy and childhood?
7. What are some causes and consequences of attentional disorders such as ADHD?

✔ *Test Your Mastery . . .*

Summary for Chapter 5

Learning Objective 5.1
Describe ways in which the infant's behavior appears to be organized at birth.

1. What states of arousal does the infant demonstrate?	There are six states of *infant arousal* or alertness: (1) quiet or deep sleep; (2) active or light sleep; (3) drowsiness; (4) alert inactivity; (5) alert activity; and (6) crying.
2. How does the newborn's sleep–wake cycle change in the early months of life?	Infants *gradually adapt* to the 24-hour light–dark cycle. Sleep periods become longer at night around 5 or 6 weeks of age as awake periods lengthen during the day. By 12 to 16 weeks the pattern of sleeping at night and being awake during the day is fully established.
3. How does culture shape our expectations regarding where infants should sleep?	Whether or not a baby shares the parental bed (*cosleeping*) evokes strong emotions. However, developmental risks and benefits are cited for both sleeping arrangements. Among middle-class American families, babies sleeping by themselves is the norm. This is seen as a way to build the infant's independence. For other groups of Americans and in countries around the world, babies are more likely to sleep with parents or siblings. Controversies regarding cosleeping have led to two opposing viewpoints: Ferber's "cry-it-out" behavioral approach and the Sears "attachment parenting" approach.
4. What is a reflex? What are some of the newborn's reflexes?	A reflex is an *innate behavior* or behavior pattern. Reflexes like breathing and blinking are essential to survival, while others may have served important survival functions sometime in our evolutionary past. For example, the rooting reflex, in which the baby turns the head to the side when the corresponding cheek is stroked, usually disappears around 3–4 months of age. Similarly, the palmar reflex, which causes the baby to grasp the source of pressure placed on the hand was adaptive for babies of our evolutionary ancestors, who needed to cling tightly to their mothers as they moved along. This reflex disappears at 3–4 months of age as well.
5. How are congenitally organized behaviors different from reflexes?	A reflex is a response to stimulation, whereas activities that are initiated by the newborn and sustained over a considerable period of time are *congenitally organized* behaviors. Examples of these behaviors are looking, sucking, and crying. All of them are well organized and are often not elicited by a discrete identifiable stimulus.

6. What roles do looking, sucking, and crying play in an infant's development?

As early as 8 hours after birth, even in the dark, babies open their eyes wide and explore their surroundings. The keenness of their gaze is often unexpected. However, this demonstrates that newborns have the *tools for acting on their world*, not just reacting to it. Sucking is an incredibly coordinated act. Babies suck 1 to 2 times each second, with each one requiring an orchestration of suction and squeezing to express milk. These actions must be coordinated with breathing and swallowing. Sucking is one of the primary ways that infants explore their world, especially as they become better able to grasp and find new objects. Sucking also acts as a buffer against pain and overstimulation. Crying coordinates breathing, vocalizing, and muscular tension in a rhythmic pattern. It is a critically important form of communication for the newborn. Different types of crying communicate different messages. Babies have separate cries for fear, hunger, and pain.

Learning Objective 5.2
Trace the development of motor skills in infancy and childhood.

1. What general patterned sequences do most infants show in their acquisition of motor skills?

Motor developments concern both postural development and locomotion, which involve control of the trunk of the body and coordination of arms and legs for moving around. It also involves the ability to use the hands as tools for eating, building, and exploring. Two principles guide our understanding of the development of motor skills. First, control over the body develops in a head to foot direction (*cephalocaudal*). Second, development proceeds in a *proximodistal* fashion; body parts closest to the center of the body come under control before parts further away from the body.

2. What are examples of milestones in a sequence of motor development?

A milestone is an *average age for attaining* a particular developmental skill. In voluntary reaching, developmental milestones are prereaching, using the ulnar grasp, transferring an object from hand to hand, and using the pincer grasp.

3. How does cultural context shape early motor development?

Different childrearing experiences, often associated with different cultural practices, can affect the *timing* of motor development. For example, African infants on average sit, stand, and walk from one to several weeks earlier than do American infants. This may be the result of African parents designing ways in which the infant can "practice" these developmental skills. Jamaican mothers provide similar types of early physical stimulation.

4. What is the dynamic systems approach to motor development?	The *dynamic systems* approach proposed that both nature and nurture contribute to the development of motor skills. According to this approach, the crucial element that unites the nature and nurture contributions, and that stimulates the development of any particular skill, is the nature of the infant's "task." In order to accomplish the tasks of infancy (e.g., seeking to reach, grasp, move, or shake things), babies learn various motor behaviors. Skills are accomplished depending on the task at hand, including how difficult it is and how motivated the child is to accomplish it, and the physical abilities the child already possesses that form the starting point for creating the new behaviors.
5. How do motor skills continue to develop in childhood?	A child's early abilities such as learning to walk and handle objects fairly efficiently, form the basis for skills that appear between 2 and 7 years of age. Three sets of fundamental movement skills emerge: *locomotor* movements, *manipulative* movements, and *stability* movements. Locomotor movements include walking, running, jumping, hopping, skipping, and climbing. Manipulative movements include throwing, catching, kicking, striking, and dribbling. Stability movements involve body control relative to gravity and include bending, turning, swinging, rolling, head standing, and beam walking. The refinement of motor skills depends a great deal on the development of the muscles and nerve pathways that control the body along with sensory and perceptual skills.

Learning Objective 5.3
Outline the areas of perceptual development during infancy.

1. How do biology and the environment interact to shape perceptual development?	From the "*nurture*" perspective, the child begins life with only minimal ability to take in and make sense of sensory input. Connections between neurons strengthen or die based on input from the environment. The "*nature*" view emphasizes the natural equipment that organisms have evolved for gathering information about their world. From this perspective, objects in the world give off physical energy that is already organized and can be perceived in its entirety. A child develops perceptually as an increasing sensitivity to the organization of this energy is achieved. In general, the earlier in development a perceptual skill emerges, the less likely it is that it has been acquired by experience. With experience, infants and children become skilled at detecting the information available in sensory stimulation and perceive the world accurately.

2. What capacities does the newborn exhibit regarding touch, smell, taste, and vestibular sensitivity?

Newborn babies show touch reflexes. Even the fetus is sensitive to touch, and touch sensitivity increases over the first several days of life. The sense of touch is called *haptic perception*. By the end of the first year of life, infants can recognize a familiar object through exploration with the hand alone. The newborn's sense of *smell* is keen, and it improves over the first few days of life. Babies use this ability as early as the first week of life to distinguish the mother's smell. *Taste* is also well developed by the time a baby is born. Even preterm neonates prefer a sweetened solution over an unsweetened one. Newborn babies can distinguish among sweet, sour, bitter, and salty tastes. *Vestibular sensitivity* refers to the ability to detect gravity and the motion of our bodies, which helps us maintain body posture and balance. Newborns are sensitive to vestibular stimulation from front to back, up and down, and side-to-side. The soothing properties of rocking and jiggling for crying babies clearly demonstrate this sensitivity.

3. How and what do infants see and hear?

It is hard to know what babies see because we cannot easily communicate with infants. However, by measuring the amount of time babies look at one display rather than another, researchers are able to record how long babies look at each display. If the infant shows a preference, we conclude that he or she can discriminate between the stimuli. Through use of this technique, *newborn visual acuity* has been estimated to be about 20/400 to 20/800 compared to normal adult acuity of 20/20. The ability to focus improves between 1 and 3 months of age and is almost adult-like by 6 months of age. *Color perception* is equivalent to an adult by four months. Babies prefer to look primarily at *high-contrast edges* (where black and white meet) because this stimulates the visual areas of the brain.

Researchers have found that after 28 weeks of gestation, virtually all fetuses clamped their eyelids in response to sound. Babies appear to be affected by what they *hear* prenatally. Days-old infants can discriminate their mothers' voices from strangers' voices. Babies are especially sensitive to the characteristics of sound that will be important for language perception, preferring to listen to sounds that fall within the frequency range of the human voice. Newborns are also able to distinguish general sound location, turning their eyes and heads toward a sound source.

4. What do we know about the infant's ability to perceive objects?

Infants are able to perceive *size constancy* among objects in their visual world. This means that the infant is able to recognize the difference in objects, even when researchers manipulate the objects so that they produce the identical retinal images on the infant's eyes. Infants are also able to perceive objects as continuous and whole even if the object is partially blocked from view. Similarly, infants are able to perceive *depth* and move from curiosity to fear of falling off a drop-off by the age of 7 months.

5. How do infants develop an ability to integrate sensory inputs?

According to Piaget, the sensory modes are largely separate at birth and the baby integrates them only through experience. Other theorists believe that some *coordination of the senses* are present from the start. Research supports both claims. Babies use exploration and representation to integrate sensory input.

6. How does attention develop during infancy and childhood?

The *orienting reflex*, where the baby responds to sounds and sights by quieting, readies the infant to receive stimuli. Infants also develop *selective attention*, the ability to focus on one stimulus rather than another. Four important aspects of attention that develop with age are: (1) control of attention, or attention span increases; (2) adaptability of attention to the task; (3) planfullness, a systematic comparison strategy; and (4) the adjusting of attentional strategies as information is gathered from the task.

7. What are some causes and consequences of attentional disorders such as ADHD?

The precise cause of *attentional disorders* such as ADHD remains a source of controversy. The evidence suggests that in most cases both nature and nurture contribute. ADHD tends to run in families, therefore suggesting a biological component. Experiences can also be important. Children may be exposed to teratogens such as alcohol or drugs, which may mimic or exacerbate the characteristics of ADHD. Children with attentional disorders have great difficulty maintaining attention and are often hyperactive and impulsive in their behavior. Children with untreated ADHD are likely to perform poorly in school and may have difficulties in interpersonal relations as well. In addition, children with continued ADHD symptoms are at greater risk for the later development of antisocial behavior and substance abuse disorders.

The Brain, Physical Growth, *and* Health

March of Dimes poster child, Justin Lamar Washington
(Courtesy of the March of Dimes)

THE BRAIN

Learning Objective 6.1

DESCRIBE THE STRUCTURE AND FUNCTIONS OF THE BRAIN AND TRACE THE DEVELOPMENT OF THE BRAIN DURING CHILDHOOD.

Structure of the Brain

Development of the Brain

Hemispheric Specialization

The Developing Brain and Early Experience

RESEARCH & SOCIETY Imaging the Brain

PHYSICAL GROWTH

Learning Objective 6.2

DESCRIBE THE PATTERNS OF GROWTH AND MATURATION IN DEVELOPMENT AND THE FACTORS THAT INFLUENCE THEM.

Changes in Physical Growth Across Time and Place

Individual Differences in Growth Rates

• Gender • Genetic Factors • Malnutrition and Illness

Changes in Body Proportion and Composition

Puberty Changes and Timing

Cultural and Social Attitudes toward Puberty

PHYSICAL HEALTH IN INFANCY

Learning Objective 6.3

ANALYZE IMPORTANT FACTORS THAT AFFECT PHYSICAL HEALTH IN INFANCY.

Infant Mortality

Nutrition

• Breastfeeding • Cultural Perspectives on Weaning and Feeding • Malnutrition

CONVERSATIONS with a Family Nutritionist

Sleep

Immunization and Child Health Care

Sudden Infant Death Syndrome (SIDS)

PHYSICAL HEALTH IN CHILDHOOD AND ADOLESCENCE

Learning Objective 6.4

IDENTIFY AND DESCRIBE SOME SIGNIFICANT HEALTH CONCERNS OF CHILDHOOD AND ADOLESCENCE TODAY.

Physical Activity and Sports Participation

Obesity

Eating Disorders

Substance Use and Abuse

APPLICATIONS Just Say No? Teens, Sexuality, and Society

Like most 8-year-old boys, Justin Lamar Washington loves to ride his bike, swim, and play with his friends. Justin has also just completed a second year as the March of Dimes National Ambassador. He was the first child to serve as ambassador for two years in a row.

By all indications, Justin is now a normal and healthy child. As his selection by the March of Dimes suggests, however, his childhood has by no means been typical or easy. Indeed, Justin has overcome obstacles that few children have ever had to face.

Because she had a history of miscarriages, Justin's mother took special precautions when she became pregnant with Justin, restricting her physical activity and seeing her doctor for weekly check-ups. Despite these precautions, she went into labor in her fifth month of pregnancy, and doctors were able to postpone the birth for only a brief period. Justin was born 4 months before the normal time period for birth. He weighed 1 pound, 8 ounces.

Until recently, babies as young and as tiny as Justin would not have survived. Justin's survival did not come easily. He spent the first 4 months of his life in the hospital, breathing with the aid of a ventilator for much of the time because his underdeveloped lungs could not function on their own. For 48 days he received intravenous feeding. He underwent intestinal, hernia, and laser eye surgery. He was treated for anemia and temporary liver malfunction. When he finally went home at 4 months, much of the medical equipment went with him. It was only very slowly that Justin grew strong enough to be weaned away from the supports and to assume a normal path of physical growth and development.

Clearly, Justin's case is a triumph of modern medical science. It is also a testimony to the strengths that even the tiniest babies—and their families—can summon in the face of physical adversity.

This chapter focuses on the child's physical growth and health and factors that affect this process. Because physical growth depends crucially on the maturation of the brain, we begin with how the brain develops and operates. We then consider not only physical growth and maturation, but issues related to health and wellness. In particular, we are concerned not just with the typical course of physical development, but also with factors that influence the child's overall health and well-being. In infancy, we give special attention to issues that dramatically impact the health of young children worldwide, such as nutrition, immunization, sleep patterns, and infant mortality. In childhood and adolescence, we focus on factors that are of particular concern to the overall health of children in the United States: physical activity, obesity, eating disorders, and substance use. By addressing these larger issues of health and well-being, we will gain a greater understanding of the extent to which the physical development of children is affected by the social and cultural worlds that they inhabit. ■

Learning Objective 6.1

Describe the structure and functions of the brain and trace the development of the brain during childhood.

Neuron

A nerve cell, consisting of a cell body, axon, and dendrites. Neurons transmit activity from one part of the nervous system to another.

The Brain

We begin our study of physical development with the brain. The development of the brain reflects the power of both biology and the environment. Central to every aspect of development and every sort of human function, the brain contains approximately 100 billion nerve cells, or **neurons**. Each cell has an average of around 3,000 connections with other cells, which adds up to several quadrillion message paths. The construction of these message paths is influenced by both genetic inheritance and individual experience.

Structure of the Brain

Like every other cell, each neuron has a nucleus and a cell body. But neurons are unique among cells in that they develop extensions on opposite sides, as shown in Figure 6.1. On the incoming side, the extensions, called **dendrites**, often form a tangle of short strands that look like the roots of plants. The outgoing extension, called an **axon**, is more like a long single strand. Axons often are covered with a sheath of fatty substance, **myelin**, which insulates them and speeds message transmission. Cells do not quite touch one another but are separated by fluid-filled gaps called **synapses**. Information is passed along a neuron as an electrical signal and crosses the synapse through the flow of chemicals called **neurotransmitters**.

Neurons are not the only brain cells. **Glial cells** bridge the gap between neurons and the blood that nourishes the nerve cells. Glial cells also form the myelin sheath around the axons. Glial cells greatly outnumber neurons, and their proliferation accounts for much of brain growth following the prenatal period.

The brain has three major parts. The **brain stem** includes the cerebellum, which controls balance and coordination. The **midbrain** serves as a relay station and controls breathing and swallowing. The **cerebrum**, the highest brain center, includes the left and right hemispheres and the bundle of nerves that connect them.

The thin shell of gray matter that covers the brain is called the **cerebral cortex**. This structure is the most recently evolved part of the brain and is crucial for the functioning of the senses, language, memory, thought, and decision making, as well as for the control of voluntary movement. Particular areas of the cerebral cortex govern specific functions, and some areas are more specialized than others (see Figure 6.2). Despite localization, however, most brain functions are distributed across different parts of the brain to some extent.

Development of the Brain

Scientists only partially understand how the brain develops in its amazing complexity. Genes clearly are important. Although the brain accounts for only 2 percent of adult body weight, estimates suggest that at least 50 percent of the human genome is devoted to making the brain (Pennington, 2001). The brain begins as a hollow tube. The neurons are generated along the inner walls of this tube and then travel to their proper locations (Kolb, 1989). The most prolific period for neuron generation is between 10 and 26 weeks

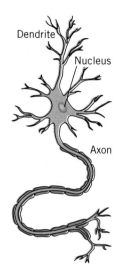

FIGURE 6.1
Nerve cells, or neurons.

Dendrite
One of a net of short fibers extending out from the cell body in a neuron; receives activity from nearby cells and conducts that activity to the cell body.

Axon
A long fiber extending from the cell body in a neuron; conducts activity from the cell.

Myelin
A sheath of fatty material that surrounds and insulates the axon, resulting in speedier transmission of neural activity.

Synapses
The small spaces between neurons, across which neural activity is communicated from one cell to another.

Neurotransmitter
A chemical that transmits electrical activity from one neuron across the synapse to another neuron.

Glial cells
Cells of the brain that support and nourish neurons (the other kind of brain cell) and form the myelin sheath around axons.

Brain stem
The lower part of the brain, closest to the spinal cord; includes the cerebellum, which is important for maintaining balance and coordination.

Midbrain
A part of the brain that lies above the brain stem; serves as a relay station and as a control area for breathing and swallowing and houses part of the auditory and visual systems.

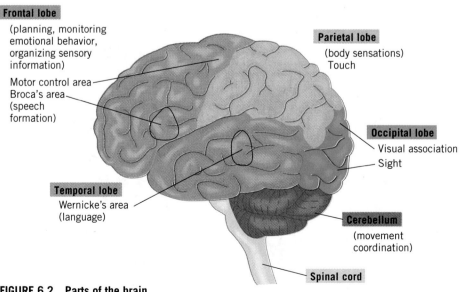

FIGURE 6.2 Parts of the brain
The four parts of the brain and some of the functions of the part known as the cerebral cortex.

Cerebrum
The highest brain center; includes both hemispheres of the brain and the interconnections between them.

Cerebral cortex
The thin sheet of gray matter that covers the brain.

Links to Related Material
In Chapter 4, you learned about how teratogens can harm the prenatal develoment of the fetus. Here, you read about the effect that teratogens can have on prenatal brain development.

following conception—a time during which the fetal brain generates neurons at a rate of 250,000 per minute! The brain actually overproduces neurons and later trims them back by as much as 50 percent, a process known as neural pruning (Barinaga, 1993). Some parts of the brain remain capable of generating neurons throughout adulthood (Tanapat, Hastings, & Gould, 2001).

After cells develop near the center of the brain, they must migrate outward to their proper locations. This *cell migration* is the second stage of early brain development and is complete by 7 months gestational age (Huttenlocher, 1990). This normal process can be disrupted by teratogens (Chapter 4). One way that prenatal teratogens exert their effects is by interfering with the movement of neurons to their expected destinations (Gressens, 2000).

When the neuron has found its home, the third stage, *cell elaboration*, begins. In this phase, axons and dendrites form synapses with other cells, a process that begins during prenatal development and continues for several years after birth. Just as the brain produces more neurons than it will need, the brain also generates many more synaptic connections than will survive—up to double the number in some areas of the brain. Thus infants and toddlers have far more synaptic connections than adults. Or, as one researcher put it, the 2-year-old's brain has about twice as many synapses as her pediatrician's (Shore, 1997). The rapid development of synaptic connections in the first two years of life is illustrated in Figure 6.3.

The fetus's brain grows faster than any other organ (except perhaps the eye), and this pace continues in infancy. At birth, the infant's body weight is only 5 percent of adult weight, but the brain weighs 25 percent of its adult equivalent. By 3 years of age, the brain has attained 80 percent of its ultimate weight, compared with only 20 percent for body weight, and by 6 years it has reached 90 percent (Kolb & Wishaw, 2003; Thatcher et al., 1996).

The brain does not mature uniformly. The first area to mature is the primary motor area, beginning with the locations that control activity near the head. Maturation proceeds downward, and this is the cephalocaudal direction in which motor control proceeds. Similarly, the areas that control the arms mature earlier than those that control the fingers, which corresponds to the proximodistal principle.

Not far behind the motor area in maturity are the major sensory areas—touch, vision, and hearing, in that order. Myelin formation, or *myelination*, indicates how mature an area is. For example, the areas that control fine-motor movement continue to myelinate until about age 4, whereas the areas associated with attention and consciousness continue to myelinate until puberty (Tanner, 1990).

FIGURE 6.3   Development of synaptic connections.

Source: J.L. Conel., *Postnatal Development of the Cerebral Cortex*, Vol. 1, 1939, Vol. 3, 1947, and *The Postnatal Development of the Human Cerebral Cortex*, vol. 4, 1951. Cambridge, MA: Harvard University Press.

(1) Newborn   (2) 3 months old   (3) 6 months old

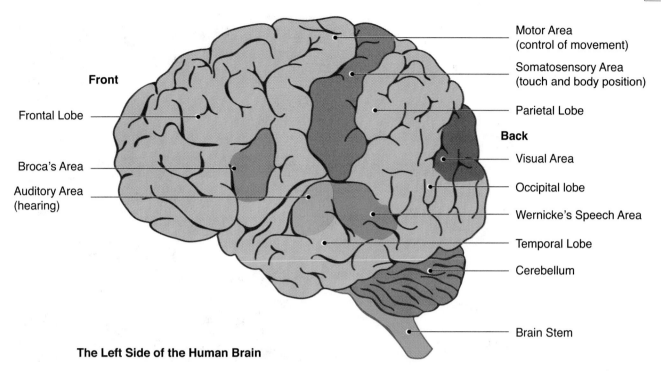

Front

Frontal Lobe

Broca's Area

Auditory Area
(hearing)

Motor Area
(control of movement)

Somatosensory Area
(touch and body position)

Parietal Lobe

Back

Visual Area

Occipital lobe

Wernicke's Speech Area

Temporal Lobe

Cerebellum

Brain Stem

The Left Side of the Human Brain

Hemispheric Specialization

The two hemispheres of the brain are not perfectly symmetrical but rather are *lateralized*—meaning that the left brain and the right brain are somewhat specialized (Figure 6.4). In general, the left side of the brain manages sensory input and motor movements on the right side of the body, while the right side of the brain controls input and movements on the left side. In addition, the left side of the brain usually is more specialized for language performance and the right side for spatial and mathematical tasks.

One kind of evidence for **hemispheric specialization** comes from cases of brain injury: Damage to the left hemisphere is more likely to result in language impairments than is damage to the right hemisphere (Bates & Roe, 2001). Another kind of evidence comes from imaging techniques for measuring brain activity (see Research & Society: Imaging the Brain). Such techniques reveal that the left side of the brain is typically more active during language tasks and the right side is more active during mathematical tasks. However, these techniques also show that brain function is not completely specialized: Most tasks, including language processing, involve areas on both sides of the brain (Scott & Wise, 2003). Hemispheric specialization also shows individual differences. That is, not everyone shows the typical left-brain dominance for language. Some people have right-brain dominance for language, and some people have mixed dominance. *Left-handers* more frequently have right-brain or mixed dominance. In addition, people who have problems with reading performance sometimes are associated with mixed or right-brain dominance for language. Children with *dyslexia*, for example, but with otherwise normal or superior intelligence, are more likely to lack strong left-brain dominance than are normal readers (Goswami, 2004).

Finally, as you will see further in Chapter 13, gender differences exist with regard to hemispheric specialization. In particular, males on average show greater specialization than females. For example, females are more likely to process language on both sides of the brain than males, who remain more strictly lateralized for language (Rosen, Galaburda, & Sherman, 1990).

The first signs of hemispheric specialization appear quite early. Electrical brain recordings in newborn infants reveal more activity in response to speech sounds on the left than on the right side (Molfese & Molfese, 1979), and some physical differences

FIGURE 6.4 Hemispheric specialization.

The two hemispheres of the brain are somewhat specialized in their functions. Here is shown specialization of speech production and comprehension, which for most people is in the left hemisphere.

Hemispheric specialization
The tendency of the right and left sides of the brain to specialize with regard to different functions skills.

Links to Related Material
In Chapter 13, you will read more about how gender relates to the hemispheric specialization of the brain.

Schools today are much more accepting of the biological basis of handedness than in years past. This student writes at a desk that accommodates lefties. In today's schools, accommodations large and small facilitate performance for many learners with individual differences in the structure and function of the brain. (Mary Kate Denny/PhotoEdit)

in size and shape between the hemispheres are already present at birth (Kosslyn et al., 1999). Nevertheless, newborns and infants do not show all the forms of lateralization that will eventually develop (Werker & Vouloumanos, 2001). The division of labor between the two hemispheres develops gradually during childhood.

The Developing Brain and Early Experience

As mentioned previously, much of brain development involves loss as neurons die and synaptic connections are pruned. These losses occur on a massive scale. At peak times, up to 100,000 synaptic connections may be lost per second (Kolb, 1995)! What determines which connections survive and which ones die out? Scientists believe that the answer lies in experience.

As you read earlier in this chapter, research has shown that there is a kind of Darwinian survival of the fittest among neurons and synaptic connections (Edelman, 1993). The critical determinant of success is use. That is, the connections that are used more often are more likely to survive than those that are not used (Greenough & Black, 1999; Johnson, 2001).

During prenatal development, neuronal firing probably is mostly under genetic control. After birth, however, an important factor in determining which connections get used is the environment the child encounters. Thus the ultimate form that the brain takes is only partly determined by the genes. Genes provide the starting-point possibilities, but experience then selects and extends these possibilities to shape the mature brain.

Plasticity
The capacity of the brain to be affected by experience as it develops.

The responsiveness of the brain to experience is known as **plasticity**. Because it is still developing and is not yet fully committed, the young, immature brain possesses greater plasticity than does the adult brain. This plasticity is implicated in skills that young children often acquire more easily than adults, such as learning multiple languages or learning to play a musical instrument. This greater plasticity is also the main reason that recovery from brain injury usually is greater the earlier in life the injury occurs (Kolb, 1989; Stiles, 2000). The importance of plasticity extends beyond recovery from trauma, however. Plasticity is central to normal brain development, for it reflects the brain's capacity to be affected by experience.

What sorts of experience are important? In one influential model, two kinds of experiences affect brain development: experience-expectant processes and experience-dependent processes (Greenough & Black, 1999; Greenough, Black, & Wallace, 1987). **Experience-expectant processes** relate to experiences available in any normal or expected environment that any child might encounter. For example, early visual input—seeing—is necessary for normal visual development. If such input is not available during the customary time period in development (because, for example, the individual was reared in the dark), then the visual cortex does not develop normally. Experience-expectant processes are available to all members of a species and operate to produce similarities rather than differences among them—to ensure, for example, that all members develop the same sort of visual system.

The second kind of experience, in contrast, is more likely to produce individual differences. **Experience-dependent processes** are based on specific experiences that are not shared by all and that therefore are more variable across individuals and groups. Living in a particular time or place with particular caregivers is an example, as is exposure to a particular language or training in a particular musical instrument.

What are the implications of the new brain science for children's development? Results have included numerous prescriptions for parents about the best ways to stimulate their child's brain growth during the critical early years by exposing them to specific experiences, such as a certain kind of music and early instruction in numbers and letters (Kotulak, 1996; Shore, 1997). To what extent are such practices effective?

Some scientists are skeptical about the effectiveness of special applications (Bruer, 1999; Thompson & Nelson, 2001). Most of what we know about early experience and brain development concerns conditions that are likely to occur in most families with adequate resources. According to Shonkoff and Phillips (2000), research in developmental neuroscience tells us more about what conditions pose threats to the developing brain than it does about what we can do to enhance or accelerate brain development. As you read in Chapter 4, environmental threats to the developing brain include prenatal teratogens such as rubella and alcohol, poor nutrition such as iron or protein deficiency, and chronic stress stemming from abuse and neglect. In contrast, the types of early experiences that are necessary for healthy brain development are present in the homes of

Experience-expectant processes
The preservation of important synaptic connections early in development through exposure to experiences in the expectable environment.

Experience-dependent processes
The creation of new synaptic connections through exposure to experiences specific to the individual.

L**inks to Related Material**
In Chapter 4, you learned about prenatal threats to the developing brain, such as alcohol and poor nutrition. Here, we consider the question of what is required for optimal brain development in normally developing children. In Chapter 8, you will read about the potential usefulness of educational materials designed to enhance cognitive growth in young children.

Synaptic connections between neurons are created and maintained through repeated exposures to certain events. In what areas of the brain are these children building synaptic connections through their experiences? (*Left,* John Dominis/©Index Stock Imagery; *right,* Detail Heritage/Alamy Images)

BOX 6.1 **Imaging the Brain**

Recent years have seen some exciting advances in techniques to study the brain (Casey & de Haan, 2002; Johnson, 2002; Nelson & Luciano, 2001). Such **functional imaging techniques** have allowed scientists for the first time to examine not only the anatomy of the brain but also brain *activity* as people perform different tasks (Casey & de Haan, 2002).

Recall that in hemispheric specialization the left side of the brain typically is more active in tasks that involve the processing of language. One kind of evidence for this conclusion came from a technique called *positive emission tomography*, or *PET*. The PET procedure measures metabolic activity in the brain through the injection of a radioactive isotope into the bloodstream. Brain areas that are especially active "light up" as the radiation is emitted, and the PET scanner provides pictures of the activation. In the language studies, for example, areas within the left hemisphere proved to be especially active when processing of language was required.

Because it requires the injection of a radioactive substance, PET is regarded as a relatively "invasive" procedure, and the U.S. Food and Drug Administration explicitly forbids its routine use in research with children. To date, PET studies with children have been limited to clinical cases in which diagnostic needs have justified use of the procedure.

A more widely applicable technique is *functional magnetic resonance imaging*, or *fMRI*. When a brain area is active, there is an increase in blood flow and blood oxygenation in that area, and the oxygenated blood is more magnetized than nonoxygenated blood. The fMRI procedure uses a powerful magnet to record the changes in oxygen level. Figure 6.5 shows the kind of images fMRI produces. The question under study was whether different parts of the brain were implicated in face perception and location matching. As the figure shows, these tasks did in fact involve different parts of the brain, and this was true in both children and adults. The research also revealed a developmental difference, however, in that adults showed a more focused pattern of activation than did children.

Although fMRI does not carry the potential hazards of PET, its use does require that the participant remain very still for an extended period, which is difficult for young children to do. For this reason, the procedure is seldom used for children below about age 5 or 6.

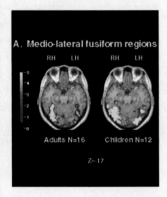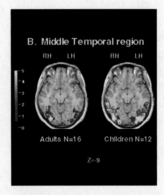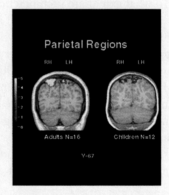

FIGURE 6.5 Examples of functional magnetic resonance imaging.
Radio waves and a strong magnetic field are used to provide pictures of blood flow and chemical changes in the brain as different cognitive tasks are performed. In both children and adults, different regions of the brain are activated for different tasks, such as face recognition and the processing of information about object location. (*Note:* RH = right hemisphere and LH = left hemisphere.)
Source: From A.M. Passarotti, B.M. Paul, J.R. Bussiere, R.B. Buxton, E.C. Wong, and J. Stiles. (2003). The development of face and location processing: An FMRI study. *Developmental Science, 6,* 108, 109.

most children: interactions with supportive parents and other family members, objects to manipulate and play with, and environments that provide stimulation and opportunities for learning and social communication.

Researchers also emphasize that the direct effects of experience on brain development are not limited to the first three years, but are evident throughout life (Goswami, 2004). For example, brain imaging studies have found that London taxi drivers show enlarged formation of the hippocampus, a small brain area involved in spatial represen-

Functional imaging techniques
Methods (such as PET, fMRI, and ERP) of measuring brain activity associated with behavior.

A third technique for imaging the brain is the measurement of *event-related potentials*, or *ERPs*. In this technique, electrodes attached to the scalp record the neuronal activity that follows presentation of a particular stimulus. Unlike either PET or fMRI, ERP measurement can be used with people of any age, even infants.

As can be seen in Figure 6.6, these new imaging techniques help us gain insight into the development of a variety of human abilities (Casey, Davidson, & Rosen, 2002; de Haan & Thomas, 2002; Taylor & Baldeweg, 2002). Much of what we have learned has implications for education (Goswami, 2004).

Language

ERP studies show that when a language is acquired late in life (as in the case of immigration), both hemispheres are used to process grammatical information. In contrast, early language learners rely primarily on the left hemisphere for grammatical processing (Weber-Fox & Neville, 1996). In addition, people who are born blind use both hemispheres for language, and also process speech more efficiently than the sighted do (Röder, Rösler, & Neville, 2000).

Reading

Imaging studies have shown that functions involved in reading alphabetic scripts are localized in the left hemisphere. The ability to recognize and manipulate the component sounds in words (*phonological awareness*), an ability that is necessary for successful reading acquisition, happens in the temporo-parietal junction in the left hemisphere. This site, also implicated in spelling disorders, may be the primary location in the brain that supports letter-to-sound recoding. Dyslexic children, who typically have phonological deficits, show reduced activity in this region during specific tasks requiring phonological awareness (Goswami, 2004). Interestingly, researchers have found that targeted reading remediation increases activation in this area (Simos et al., 2002). ERP studies also suggest that the phonological system of the dyslexic child is immature rather than deviant (Goswami, 2004). These findings emphasize the importance and efficacy of early intervention with children who have problems in this domain.

Mathematics

Multiple sites in the brain are important for processing different types of mathematical tasks. Some mathematics information, repeated so often that it is overlearned (such as $2 + 2$, 5×2), is stored verbally, in the language system, as "number facts." Other mathematics functions, such as calculations, take place in other areas of the brain, especially the parietal lobe. This location suggests a link between numeracy and the sense of touch, especially in the fingers. Disability in mathematics, called dyscalculia, makes mathematical calculation and problem solving more difficult and may also involve difficulty with time keeping and score keeping; remembering people's names, schedules, locations, directions, and formulas; using money and budgeting; and understanding layouts and mechanical processes. Researchers hope that brain imaging techniques will help us better understand the biological basis of dyscalculia and other mathematical difficulties (Goswami, 2004).

PET, fMRI, and ERPs help answer the following questions:

- What brain regions are involved in the performance of different activities, and to what extent?
- How does brain activity change across the lifespan from infant to child to adolescent to adult to elder?
- How do experience and maturation influence brain activity?
- What neuronal factors cause or contribute to individual differences in quality of performance?
- To what extent can brain measures distinguish or predict successful from less successful performance?
- How can knowledge about brain activity patterns help us treat individuals with clinical syndromes or developmental disorders, such as dyslexia, autism, and Attention-Deficit Hyperactivity Disorder (ADHD)?

FIGURE 6.6   What can task comparisons tell us?

---

tation and navigation (Maguire et al., 2000). Similarly, skilled violinists have enlarged neural representations for their left fingers, those most important for playing the violin (Elbert et al., 1995), while skilled Braille readers are more sensitive to tactile information across all fingers (Roder et al., 1997). Thus, brain plasticity is found in adults in response to direct experience. Specific types of stimulation from the environment cause the brain to form new synaptic connections. Although such plasticity is likely to be even greater for children, the capacity for learning is not limited to early childhood (Goswami, 2004).

Test Your Mastery...

In general, researchers emphasize that, for healthy brain development, young children need environments that support growth across all domains: physical health, social competence, and emotional well-being, as well as cognitive skills important to school success (Shonkoff & Phillips, 2000).

Learning Objective 6.1: *Describe the structure and functions of the brain and trace the development of the brain during childhood.*

1. What is the brain's structure?
2. Through what processes do the structure and functions of the brain develop?
3. What is hemispheric specialization? Which activities show such specialization?
4. What do brain imaging studies tell us about brain development?
5. What is the significance of brain plasticity for human development?
6. How do different kinds of experiences affect the development of the brain?
7. What environmental conditions are optimal for healthy brain development in children?

Physical Growth

Learning Objective 6.2
Describe the patterns of growth and maturation in development and the factors that influence them.

Physical growth is one of the most visible aspects of child development. It is continuous throughout childhood, but it does not happen uniformly. Rather, the overall rate of growth fluctuates over time. For example, in Chapter 4 you saw the fetus's dramatically rapid growth rate, which, however, necessarily slows as birth approaches. This general slowing trend continues up to adolescence. Moreover, physical growth is affected by resources available in the environment that promote good nutrition and lack of illness.

Changes in Physical Growth Across Time and Place

Links to Related Material
Environmental resources that promote good nutrition and lack of illness are important for optimal growth throughout childhood, just as they were in the prenatal period, as you read in Chapter 4.

Changes over time in adult height have been documented in many countries. One dramatic example comes from the Netherlands, where conscription records of the height of all adult males have been kept since 1851 (Fredriks et al., 2000; Van Wieringen, 1986). In 1863, a Dutch man 5′6″ tall was in the 76th percentile for height. By 1983, a man of this height was only in the 5th percentile (Cole, 2000). Among Dutch women, the average height since 1965 has risen from just over 5′5″ to about 5′7″. Similar rises in adult height have been documented elsewhere in the world. In recent years, gains of 10 millimeters per decade have been typical for males in Western European countries, while in Eastern Europe and Japan height gains have been even greater at about 30 millimeters per decade.

Secular trend
Changes over time in physical growth, such as adult height and age of menarche.

These changes over time in physical growth, called the **secular trend**, reflect societal changes in physical health and affluence—so much so that physical growth has been called "a mirror of conditions in society" (Tanner, 1990). Numerous factors affect the secular trend in height, including social class, income and education, family size, urban versus rural location, and geographic region. The secular trend has been observed most clearly in populations where, across generations, pregnant and lactating women and young children have access to highly nutritious diets, and where rates of infectious disease are relatively low (Cole, 2000). The most dramatic gains in adult height in recent decades are evident in societies that have shown the greatest improvement in these factors, such as Eastern Europe and parts of Asia. In populations with inadequate access to health care and nutrition, adult height remains limited.

Menarche
Onset of menstruation among girls.

The secular trend has also been observed in relation to age of **menarche**, or the onset of menstruation among girls. Although average age of menarche has fallen steeply in industrialized countries over the past 150 years, it appears to have stabilized to a worldwide average of about 13 years. Poor environmental conditions delay menarche, but there appears to be a physiological lower limit to its average age (Cole, 2000; Hauspie, Vercauteren, & Susanne, 1997).

In the United States, ethnic differences exist. Data from the Third National Health and Nutrition Examination Survey (Wu, Mendola, & Buck, 2002) indicate that in recent years, on average, African American girls have achieved menarche at age 12.1, Mexican American girls at 12.2, and European American girls at 12.7. These results were attained after adjusting for the influence of weight and various social and economic variables, all of which can affect age of menarche.

Individual Differences in Growth Rates

In addition to population-wide growth trends that are influenced by general access to health care and nutrition, we also observe individual variations in physical growth within populations. Such individual variation is caused by factors such as gender, genetics, and episodes of illness or malnutrition.

Gender Figure 6.7 shows an average growth curve for males and females in the United States. Boys and girls are about the same height until around 10 years of age. A *growth spurt*, or period of rapid growth, typically occurs between 10 and 12 years of age for girls and between 12 and 14 years of age for boys. This age difference in average growth spurt between boys and girls accounts for the common observation that girls are often taller than boys in middle school or junior high. This fact reverses itself a few years later, but not without producing some anxiety in many boys this age. In North America and northern and western Europe today, height increases are just about completed by 15.5 years of age in girls and 17.5 years in boys; less than 2 percent of growth is added afterward (Malina, 1990; Tanner, 1990).

As you can see, there is no one normal growth rate, only a normal range. And just as individuals reach different ultimate heights and weights, their rates of growth may also

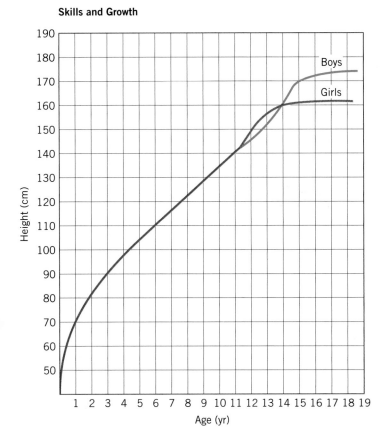

Skills and Growth

FIGURE 6.7   Typical male and female growth curves.

Birth length doubles by around the 4th year, but growth slows until puberty (Lowrey, 1978; Tanner, 1990). Girls' and boys' growth spurts normally occur at different ages.

Source: From J.M. Tanner, R.H. Whitehouse, and M. Takaishi. (1966). Standards for growth and growth velocities. *Archives of Disease in Childhood, 41,* 467.

FIGURE 6.8 Curves showing individual differences in growth in the heights of three girls over time.

This curve shows the heights of three girls over time. Age of menarche is indicated by an X. What conclusion can you draw about growth curves from this example?

Adapted from N. Bayley. (1956). Individual patterns of development. *Child Development, 27,* 52. Copyright © 1956 by The Society for Research in Child Development, Inc. Adapted by permission.

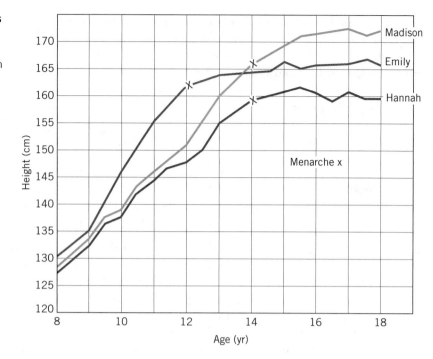

differ. To illustrate, Figure 6.8 shows a growth curve for three girls. Emily reached menarche before Madison and Hannah. She was taller than both other girls at age 12, but was ultimately shorter than Madison. Such differences in age of onset of the growth spurt are likely to accompany differences in age of puberty.

Genetic Factors Genes play a major part in our growth and physical maturation. Thus, children tend to resemble their parents—tall parents, for example, usually have taller children than do short parents. Genetic factors can be seen in which twin studies, in which similarities in identical twins are compared with similarities in fraternal twins to determine the extent to which genetic factors influence particular behaviors. Twin studies also yield information about the role of heredity in body structure and the onset and pace of puberty.

The adult height of identical twins shows a correlation of about .94, while the adult height of fraternal twins correlates at about .50, the same as for any pair of siblings. A similar pattern exists for weight (Wilson, 1986). In addition, identical twins are more similar than fraternal twins in their growth spurts and lags (Mueller, 1986).

Maturation
The process of attaining physical maturity.

Several other measures support the role of heredity in the rate of **maturation,** or the process of attaining physical maturity. Identical twins display much higher similarity in the age of eruption of their teeth than do fraternal twins, and they are more similar in the pace of bone development, as well as in breast development in girls and testicular development in boys. The age of onset of menarche differs by only a few months in identical twins. One study revealed that even when identical twins were reared apart, the onset of menarche differed by an average of only 2.8 months. In contrast, fraternal twins reared together typically differ by 6 to 12 months in the age of onset of menarche. Such findings imply that genes play a substantial role in maturation, a conclusion also supported by similarities in the age of onset of menarche between mothers and daughters (Bailey & Garn, 1986). Like every other aspect of human development, however, growth and maturation are also influenced by the larger context of development.

Skeletal maturity (bone age)
The degree of maturation of an individual as indicated by the extent of hardening of the bones.

Given adequate nutrition, how might we distinguish a child whose rate of maturation is slow from a child who is genetically targeted for relatively short adult stature? A technique for making this distinction uses the child's **skeletal maturity,** or **bone age,**

These identical twins not only are very similar in physical appearance, but also show similar rates of development. They have attained a milestone of development at the same time—the loss of their baby teeth. Genetic factors thus play a significant role in the timing of development as well as the outcomes. (Peter Cade/Getty Images, Inc.)

which may differ from the child's **chronological age**, or age as measured in years. Bones develop from the center and extend outward toward the bone ends, called the *epiphyses*. As a bone reaches its ultimate length, the epiphyses close, and no further growth is possible. Scientists can use X-rays to determine how a child's bone development compares with that of his or her peers and approximately how much more growth remains to occur (Tanner, 1990).

Malnutrition and Illness Another factor that may produce individual differences in growth rates includes episodes of malnutrition and illness. For example, researchers recorded the growth rate of a child who suffered from two episodes of inadequate nutrition (Prader, Tanner, & von Harnack, 1963). The child's growth was severely affected. After the episodes were over, the child did not simply return to his normal rate of growth. Rather, he experienced a remarkable acceleration in growth, which returned him to his expected growth path. This **catch-up growth** is relatively common during childhood in the aftermath of disease or limited malnutrition (Tanner, 1992). Children who have experienced early malnutrition can show catch-up growth throughout childhood (Adair, 1999). However, limited catch-up growth has been found among children who are born small for gestational age, particularly the very preterm (Hack, Weissman, & Borawski-Clark, 1996; Knops et al., 2005).

Changes in Body Proportion and Composition

Another aspect of growth concerns the rates at which different parts of the body develop. Most noticeably, the relative size of the head changes from 50 percent of total body length at 2 months fetal age to 25 percent at birth and to only about 10 percent by adulthood. This shift reflects the cephalocaudal, or top-down, sequence of development described in Chapter 5.

Internal organs also follow individual paths of growth. Up to about 6 to 8 years of age, the brain grows much faster than the body in general, and the reproductive organs grow much more slowly. Then the rate of brain growth slows, whereas the reproductive system reaches a plateau between 5 and 12 years of age and surges at around 14 years of age.

Chronological age
Age as measured in years.

Catch-up growth
Accelerated growth that follows a period of delayed or stunting growth resulting from disease or malnutrition. The pace of growth during childhood and adolescence is influenced by both nature and nurture factors.

Links to Related Material
Cephalocaudal development is reflected in the growth spurt in adolescence, just as it was in motor development in infancy, as you saw in Chapter 5.

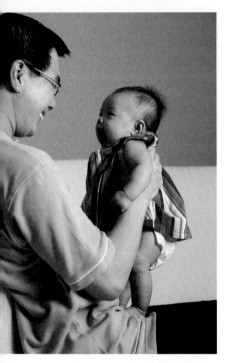

"Shaken baby syndrome" happens when a baby is shaken forcefully enough to cause the brain to bounce against the skull, causing significant brain injury or death. In this photo, you can see how large an infant's head is in proportion to the rest of the body, especially compared to the parent's. What do you think an infant's head to body proportions might tell us about the severe, often fatal, consequences that occur when a baby is shaken? (Marcus Mok/Asia Images/Getty Images, Inc.)

Puberty
The period in which chemical and physical changes in the body occur that enable sexual reproduction.

Primary sexual characteristics
Pubertal changes to the reproductive organs.

Secondary sexual characteristics
Other pubertal bodily changes, such as breast development in girls, voice change in boys, and the development of pubic hair in both sexes.

The proportion of fat to muscle also changes with age and differs for boys and girls. The fetus begins to accumulate fat in the weeks before birth. This process continues until around 9 months after birth. After that, fat gradually declines until around 6 to 8 years of age. Girls have a bit more fat than boys at birth. This difference increases gradually through childhood until about 8 years of age and then increases more rapidly (Siervogel et al., 2000).

During the adolescent growth spurt, girls continue to gain fat faster than males. Muscle growth also occurs during adolescence, more strikingly for boys than for girls (Malina, 1990). However, because girls reach their growth spurt before males, there is a two-year period in which girls, on average, have more muscle than boys. Changes in body proportions that occur in adolescence result in greater shoulder width and muscular development in males and broader hips and more fat in females.

Puberty Changes and Timing

Gender influences growth in several ways, other than body size and composition, especially in adolescence. Adolescence produces the greatest postnatal surge of differentiation between the two sexes. These changes occur when certain chemicals—hormones—provided by various endocrine glands are released into the bloodstream. Especially important glands for growth and sexual differentiation in adolescence are the gonads, the adrenals, and the thyroid. In addition, growth hormone, secreted by the pituitary gland, helps stimulate bone growth (Kulin, 1991; Paikoff & Brooks-Gunn, 1990).

The most significant aspect of development during adolescence is **puberty,** the series of changes that culminate in sexual maturity and the ability to reproduce. Some changes, called **primary sexual characteristics**, involve development of the reproductive organs—the vagina, uterus, and ovaries in girls, and the penis, scrotum, and testes in boys. Other changes, called **secondary sexual characteristics**, involve related body proportions, such as breast development in girls, voice change in boys, and the development of pubic hair in both sexes. Puberty usually begins between the ages of 10 and 14, and typically is earlier for girls than for boys.

In males, the first sign of puberty, which occurs at around age 11 on average, is an enlargement of the testes and a change in the texture and color of the scrotum. Later, the penis enlarges, pubic hair appears, and sperm production begins, followed by the appearance of hair under the arms and on the face. Near the end of puberty, the larynx lengthens, causing the male voice to become deeper. For females, the first sign of puberty is breast budding, followed by the appearance of pubic hair. Menarche occurs relatively late in puberty. Usually, ovulation follows the onset of menarche by one or two years. Ethnic differences have been found in the average onset of puberty, with African American girls showing the beginnings of pubic hair and breast development as early as age 9.5, Mexican American girls at around age 10, and European girls at around age 10.5. Menarche occurs up to two and a half years after a girl begins to get breast buds.

Variations among adolescents in the timing of puberty are caused by genes, nutrition, and general physical health. Even conditions in the home can affect the timing. In one study, girls whose home lives were characterized by high levels of stress (for example, discord between parents or an abusive or psychologically absent father) entered puberty earlier than girls who lived in less stressful home environments (Ellis & Garber, 2000). How fast adolescents move through puberty varies as widely as when they start. For example, it may take a girl as few as 1.5 years or as many as 5 years to complete puberty. If we were to study a single class of boys and girls in elementary school, beginning when the first student began puberty and following the group until the last student finished puberty, chances are we would have to follow the group for a full 10 years (Petersen, 1987). You can imagine how much variation in maturation there would be during those years and how it might play out in social relations, self-image, and confidence.

Cultural and Social Attitudes toward Puberty

Social and cultural factors are important in our understanding of puberty (Graber, Brooks-Gunn, & Petersen, 1996). In particular, social and cultural factors influence how adolescents feel about the changes in their bodies as well as when these changes occur relative to their peers. In the United States, the ideal female is thin, although females naturally add fat during puberty, and their hips broaden. In contrast, males add muscle and shoulder width, characteristics that better fit the preferred cultural image of males. Not surprisingly, then, early maturing females tend to be more dissatisfied with their bodies during puberty than late-maturing females, whereas the opposite is true for males (Crockett & Petersen, 1987; Graber et al., 1994; Ohring, Graber, & Brooks-Gunn, 2002). In addition, studies in both the United States and China have found that young girls who have either negative perceptions of menarche or inadequate preparation for menarche have more negative feelings about its onset (Yeung, So-kum Tang, & Lee, 2005). Later in life, these girls are also more negative about menstruation, report more severe symptoms, and are more self-conscious about it than are other girls (Brooks-Gunn, 1987, 1991).

A negative body image is not the only outcome linked to early or late maturity. Early maturity in girls is associated with a heightened probability of problems such as depression, eating disorders, delinquency, and substance abuse (Dick et al., 2000; Ge, Conger, & Elder, 2001a; Stice, Presnell, & Bearman, 2001). On average, however, most early maturing girls escape such outcomes. For boys it is late maturity that tends to carry problems, including heightened anxiety and lower popularity among peers (Jones, 1965; Petersen, 1988).

Only limited research exists on how early and late maturers succeed later in life. One longitudinal study indicates that the difficulties encountered by early maturing girls are not necessarily lasting; by early adulthood, the girls who had been early maturers were similar on most measures to their late maturing peers (Stattin & Magnusson, 1990). Another study reported that adolescent boys who had been early maturers had more stable careers than late maturers and that they scored higher on tests of sociability, dominance, self-control, and responsibility. On the positive side, late-maturing boys were more nurturant and seemed better able than earlier maturers to face their emotions and feelings (Brooks-Gunn & Reiter, 1990; Jones, 1965).

In middle school, boys are often dismayed when girls their age outperform them in tests of strength. This is a temporary reversal that reflects the earlier age at which girls, on average, achieve their growth spurt. (RF/Corbis)

Learning Objective 6.2: *Describe the patterns of growth and maturation in development and the factors that influence them.*

1. How can growth change over time in different populations?
2. What is the secular trend, and how is this a mirror of society?
3. How do genetics, gender, nutrition, and health affect individual differences in growth rates?
4. How do growth rates and body proportions change across childhood?
5. What physical changes occur with puberty for girls and boys?
6. How do cultural practices and social attitudes affect the experience of puberty?

✔ *Test Your Mastery...*

Physical Health in Infancy

One of the chief concerns that parents have for their children is providing the foundations for good physical health. The World Health Organization has defined **health** as a "state of complete physical, mental and social well-being and not merely the absence of disease or infirmity." Growing up in a state of health enables children to grow to their full potential physically, cognitively, emotionally, and socially. What factors contribute to physical health in infancy? What environmental factors may affect a child's ability to achieve and maintain a healthy state of physical well being?

Learning Objective 6.3
Analyze important factors that affect physical health in infancy.
Health
A state of complete physical, mental and social well-being and not merely the absence of disease or infirmity.

Infant Mortality

Infant mortality rate
The number of deaths in the first year of life per 1,000 live births.

The **infant mortality rate** is defined as the number of deaths in the first year of life per 1,000 live births. It is an important index of a society's health (U.S. Department of Health and Human Services, 2000). High rates of infant mortality may reflect poor maternal health, inadequate prenatal care, infant malnutrition, limited access to adequate health care, endemic disease, or other factors.

Across the world, infant mortality rates vary tremendously from a recent high of over 190 per 1,000 live births in Angola to a low of 3 in Sweden. Recent statistics on worldwide infant mortality rates consistently place the United States last among western, industrialized countries, and behind countries or regions such as Greece, the Czech Republic, and Hong Kong. In 2002, the U.S infant mortality rate, which had been declining, rose 3 percent to 7 deaths per 1,000 live births, the first increase in over four decades (MacDorman, Martin, Mathews, Hoyert, & Ventura, 2005).

Why is the U.S. infant mortality rate so high compared to that of other wealthy countries? To begin to answer this question, we must look at causes of infant mortality, as well as at differences based on the ethnic and racial background of the mother. In recent years, the three leading causes of infant mortality in the United States have been birth defects, low birthweight, and Sudden Infant Death Syndrome (SIDS). Together, these three causes account for about 45 percent of infant deaths in the first year of life (CDC National Center for Health Statistics, 2004).

The United States' relatively high infant mortality rate among wealthy countries relates to the proportion of deaths due to low birthweight and preterm birth (see Table 6.1). Because of their much higher risk for death, these infants contribute greatly to the total infant mortality rate. In 2002, 7.8 percent of infants were born at low birthweight, but they contributed to over two-thirds of deaths in the first month of life (MacDorman, 2005).

What are the causes of low birthweight leading to infant death in the United States? One cause, already discussed in Chapter 4, is lack of prenatal care. Group differences in access to early and adequate prenatal care are mirrored by group differences in the infant mortality rate. As can be seen in Table 6.1, in 2002 infant mortality rates ranged from 4.8 for Asian American mothers to 13.8 for African American mothers.

In addition to the risk factors outlined in Table 6.1, higher rates of infant mortality have also been reported (CDC National Center for Health Statistics, November 24, 2004) among women who are:

- Using assisted reproductive technologies, described in Chapter 3. These technologies lead to an increase in multiple births.

- Smokers. In 2002, infant mortality was 68 percent higher for these mothers than it was for women who did not smoke during pregnancy.

- Less educated and unmarried. These factors tend to be associated with low income, which is in turn associated with limited access to early and adequate prenatal care.

- Born in the United States, compared to women who were born outside the United States. The reason for this association remains unclear.

- Living in the South. Infant mortality rates are generally lower for states in the Northeast and on the West Coast than they are for southern states. Rates for 2000–2002 among states ranged from 10.5 for Mississippi to 4.8 for Massachusetts.

Globally, infant mortality rates are highest among nations in Southeast Asia and sub-Saharan Africa, where 1 out of 5 African women can expect to lose a baby in her lifetime, compared with just 1 in 125 in wealthy countries. Newborns account for about 40 percent of all deaths in children under five years of age and over half of infant mortality. According to the World Health Organization (World Health Report, 2005), nearly 75 percent of all neonatal deaths in these countries could be prevented if women were adequately nourished and received appropriate medical care during pregnancy, childbirth, and the postnatal period.

Links to Related Material
Infant mortality rates are affected by quality of prenatal care, discussed in Chapter 4.

Links to Related Material
Infant mortality is also affected by the use of assisted reproductive technologies, which lead to an increase in multiple births, as you saw in Chapter 3.

TABLE 6.1 U.S. Infant Mortality Rates, or Deaths in the First Year of Life per 1,000 Live Births, within Specific Populations, 2002

National Average	7.0
By Prenatal Care*	
Care initiated in 1st trimester	6.1
No care	33.8
By Mother's Ethnic Background	
European American	5.8
African American	13.8
American Indian	8.6
Asian or Pacific Islander	4.8
Hispanic	5.6
By Mother's Age	
Under 20	10.4
20–24	7.8
25–29	6.0
30–34	5.6
35–39	6.5
40–44	8.3
45–54	11.3
By Plurality	
Singletons	6.1
Twins	30.2
Triplets & higher order	67.5
By Birthweight	
Low birthweight (< 2,500 gm)	59.5
Very low birthweight (< 1,500 gm)	250.8
By Gestation	
Moderately preterm (32–36 weeks)	9.2
Very preterm (< 32 weeks)	186.4
By Gender**	
Boys	7.9
Girls	6.3

SOURCES: Adapted from *National Vital Statistics Reports, 53,* (12), January 2005.
*Figures for 2000, Centers for Disease Control & Prevention. (2000). Entry into Prenatal Care—United States, 1989–1997. *MMWR Weekly Report, 49*(18), 393–398.
**Figures for 2003: Hoyert, Kung, & Smith, Deaths: Preliminary data for 2003, *National Vital Statistics Reports, 53*(15), Table 1.

Nutrition

Nutrition is the process by which our bodies take in and use food. Children need energy and nutrients to support growth and activity. Adequate nutrition has strong links to a child's growth, well-being, and development.

Even before an infant is born, parents must begin making nutritional decisions for their child. Should they breast or bottle feed? When should they wean, and when should they begin to supplement the baby's diet with solid foods? What potential nutritional problems should they be concerned about?

Breastfeeding One of the earliest nutritional decisions parents must make is whether to breast or formula feed their infant. In a summary of research conducted on breastfeeding in

TABLE 6.2 Benefits of and Barriers to Breastfeeding

Benefits to the child include decreased rates of:
- Infectious diseases, including ear infections, respiratory tract infections, and diarrhea.
- Infant mortality (reduced by 21 percent in breastfed infants).
- Sudden Infant Death Syndrome (SIDS).
- Diabetes.
- Childhood cancer, including lymphoma, leukemia, and Hodgkin's disease.
- Childhood obesity.
- Asthma.
- Slightly enhanced performance on cognitive tests.

Benefits to the mother include:
- Decreased postpartum bleeding.
- More rapid return of uterus to prepregnancy size.
- Increased spacing of children due to lactational amenorrhea, the cessation of ovulation that often occurs while breastfeeding.
- Earlier return to prepregnancy weight.
- Decreased risk of ovarian and breast cancer.
- Reduced risk of osteoporosis in postmenopausal period.

Benefits to society include decreased:
- Annual health care costs of $3.6 billion in the United States alone.
- Employment absenteeism and associated loss of productivity incurred when parents need to miss work to care for sick children.
- Environmental waste.

Barriers to breastfeeding include:
- Insufficient prenatal education regarding its importance.
- Early hospital discharge combined with lack of timely routine follow-up care and postpartum home visits.
- Commercial promotion of infant formula through distribution of hospital discharge packs and formula coupons.
- Maternal employment in the absence of workplace facilities and support for breastfeeding.
- Lack of family support and broad societal support.
- Media portrayal of bottle feeding as normative.
- Misinformation about the nature of breastfeeding.
- Lack of guidance and encouragement from health care professionals.

SOURCE: American Academy of Pediatrics. (2005). Breastfeeding and the use of human milk, *Pediatrics, 115,* 496–506.

Only about a third of U.S. women continue to breastfeed until the infant is six months old, and fewer than 20 percent continue until 12 months, the minimum amount of time recommended by the AAP. Given its benefits, why don't more women in the United States today breastfeed? (Nancy Ney/Digital Vision RF/Getty Images, Inc.)

Question for Thought and Discussion

Should women be allowed to breastfeed in public?

the last 20 years, the American Academy of Pediatrics (AAP) calls human milk "uniquely superior for infant feeding," and recommends that infants be exclusively breastfed for the first six months of life. Moreover, the AAP recommends that breastfeeding continue with supplementation until at least the age of 12 months, and beyond for as long as desired by the mother and child. The AAP concludes its policy statement on breastfeeding with the assertion that "breastfeeding ensures the best possible health as well as the best developmental and psychosocial outcomes for the infant" (American Academy of Pediatrics, 2005, p. 501). Table 6.2 details some of the benefits of and barriers to breastfeeding.

In the United States today, 70 percent of all women initiate breastfeeding following birth (among African American women the figure is 53 percent; among Hispanic and European American women, the figure is about 73 percent). More highly educated women are more likely to breastfeed than women with less education (Celi, 2005).

Cultural Perspectives on Weaning and Feeding As mentioned earlier, the American Academy of Pediatrics recommends that children be breastfed for a minimum of one year, with supplementation from solids after the age of six months. No upper limit is given to the duration of breastfeeding, nor is there evidence of psychological or developmental harm from breastfeeding into the third year of life or longer (American Academy of Pediatrics, 2005).

In the United States, children are commonly bottle-fed from birth or weaned within a few months. However, in some societies, nursing may continue until the child is 4 or 5 years old (Stuart-Macadam & Dettwyler, 1995). In the United States, self-feeding with finger foods is encouraged in infants as young as 8 or 9 months of age. In other societies, it is expected that children will be primarily spoon-fed by parents until they are old enough to use utensils (Miller & Harwood, 2002). The emphasis placed in the United States on the early attainment of self-feeding appears to be related to cultural beliefs regarding the importance of giving young children as much control as possible over their own bodies from a very young age (Schulze, Harwood, Schoelmerich, & Leyendecker, 2002). In the long run, children who learn to self-feed at later ages show no disadvantages compared to children who begin to self-feed before the age of one year.

Malnutrition **Malnutrition** occurs when a child experiences a deficit of one or more essential nutrients needed by the body. About one in three of the world's children suffers from malnutrition before the age of 5 (State of the World's Children, 2006). The effects of malnutrition include growth delay or failure and lowered resistance to disease, as well as specific nutritional deficiencies such as anemia and rickets. Malnutrition also has behavioral consequences, such as lowered physical activity and cognitive performance.

The most common nutritional deficiency in children is *iron deficiency anemia*, a condition that occurs when the diet lacks enough iron to build an adequate supply of healthy red blood cells. Iron deficiency anemia (IDA) has negative effects on motor and mental development throughout childhood and adolescence. Studies using the Bayley Scales of Infant Development have found that infants with IDA score lower on a variety of mental and motor tests, effects that appear to persist long after the IDA has been corrected (Kazal, 2002). Results from the National Health and Nutrition Examination Survey, 1999–2000 (Centers for Disease Control and Prevention, 2002) estimated that, in the United States, 7 percent of toddlers ages 1 to 2 years, and 9–16 percent of adolescent females were iron deficient. Iron deficiency was also about two times higher among African American and Mexican American (19–22 percent) than among European American (10 percent) women. Common factors associated with IDA among infants and young children in the United States include:

- Maternal anemia or poorly controlled diabetes during pregnancy.
- Low birthweight and preterm birth.
- Ingestion of cow's milk, which is low in iron and also decreases the absorption of iron from other sources.
- Breastfeeding without iron supplementation.
- Use of low-iron formula.
- Low socioeconomic background.

In addition to iron, nutrients that appear particularly important for the development of the brain and emerging cognitive functions include iodine, folate, zinc, vitamin B-12, and omega-3 fatty acids (Bryan et al., 2004). Another nutritional disorder with serious developmental consequences is *rickets*. Caused by inadequate intake or absorption of calcium, vitamin D, or phosphate, rickets is characterized by a weakening and softening of the bones.

On a global scale, **protein energy malnutrition (PEM)** is a major health problem that affects about a quarter of the world's children and that contributes to one out of two deaths (53 percent) associated with infectious diseases among children under age 5 in developing countries (World Health Organization, 2006). PEM results from a diet that is chronically

In this family, early self-feeding is not emphasized. This child will be primarily spoon-fed until able to use eating utensils properly. (Brand X Pictures/Brand X/PictureArts)

Malnutrition
A deficit of one or more essential nutrients needed by the body.

Protein energy malnutrition (PEM)
Type of malnutrition that results from a diet that is chronically insufficient in protein and energy.

BOX 6.2 Conversations with a Family Nutritionist

Janet Scussel grew up in Stafford Springs, Connecticut, and is 56 years old, single, and has no children. She is a registered dietitian working as a WIC nutritionist at a health center in Springfield, Massachusetts. She loves her job in the Women, Infants, and Children (WIC) program.

WIC, a federal program administered through the U.S. Department of Agriculture, provides free food and counseling and referral services to low-income women and their infants and children under 5 years of age. Research suggests that women in the WIC program eat better, receive earlier prenatal care, and have healthier babies than their non-WIC peers. Infants born to WIC mothers tend to weigh more and grow and develop better. Children in WIC are more likely to eat foods with iron and vitamin C, visit their doctors more regularly, and receive immunizations.

Both education and experience were important in Janet's route to her present position. She became a registered nurse in 1970 and earned a bachelor of science degree in nursing in 1984.

I was a registered nurse for 20 years, when I did hospital nursing. I realized that for the most part I was treating the end stages of poor nutrition! My patients had cancer, heart disease, stroke, and kidney disease—all strongly influenced by lifelong diet. I was becoming dissatisfied with my role. I wanted to get at the causes of these health problems, so I decided to choose dietetics.

Janet had a goal! She learned that a professional nutritionist has a college degree with a major in nutrition, so she went on to earn another B.S. degree, this time in nutritional sciences (BSNS) at the University of Connecticut.

My BSNS allowed me to apply for a dietetic internship. After the nine-month internship, which included more classes and clinical experiences in the hospital food service and community programs, I took my exam and passed and became a registered dietitian.

As a registered dietitian, in 1997 Janet became a licensed dietitian/nutritionist in the Commonwealth of Massachusetts, where she chose to work in a community setting rather than in a hospital.

insufficient in protein and energy, and it can lead to a wasting of body tissues and increased susceptibility to infection. Two of the most serious forms of PEM are kwashiorkor and marasmus. *Kwashiorkor*, caused primarily by insufficient protein in the diet, is characterized by a severely swollen stomach, sparse hair, atrophy of the muscles, mental apathy, and generally retarded development. *Marasmus* is caused by insufficient caloric intake (starvation) and is characterized by stunted growth and wasting of muscle and tissue. Children with marasmus are small for their age, with weakened immune systems leading to frequent infections.

Although kwashiorkor and marasmus are uncommon in the United States, researchers have expressed concerns regarding *food-insecurity*, that is, homes that lack access to enough food at all times for active, healthy living (Nord, Andrews, & Carlson, 2004). In 2003, 11.2 percent of all U.S. households, but nearly 17 percent of households with children and over 31 percent of single-mother families, were defined as food-insecure. Studies with at-risk populations have verified the value of providing nutritional improvements during both pregnancy and the early childhood years as a way to promote health and optimal development for all children (Grantham-McGregor, Ani, & Fernald, 2001).

Sleep

Sleep, like food, is essential for survival, but researchers continue to debate exactly why sleep is important. Hypotheses about the physiological functions of sleep have focused on restoration of brain metabolism and recovery of body systems, as well as on memory consolidation and learning (Jenni & O'Connor, 2005; National Institute of Neurological Disorders & Stroke, 2005).

Sleep patterns change across childhood and through adulthood. The newborn infant sleeps on average 16 hours each day, 50 percent of which is spent in **rapid eye movement (REM) sleep**, the stage of sleep in which dreaming occurs. By age 3 to 5 years, total daily sleep decreases to an average of just under 12 hours per day, while the percentage of time spent in REM sleep each night declines to about 20 percent. Total daily sleep needed tends

Rapid eye movement (REM) sleep
A stage of light sleep, characterized by rapid moving of the eyes behind the closed eyelids, in which dreaming occurs.

When she decided to serve women and children as a WIC nutritionist, she found that her knowledge of prenatal, infant, and child growth and development became an important part of her work.

I work in an office, doing nutritional assessment and counseling for low-income pregnant women, women who breastfeed, and infants and children. I also work with nutritional assistants, paraprofessionals who may have education beyond high school but who have no advanced degrees. These program assistants are trained by WIC to deal with common problems in nutrition. They also are part of the team that assesses income eligibility for WIC services, does client scheduling, and prints the WIC food vouchers.

The most challenging part of my work is providing nutritional counseling to a diverse population of varying races, ethnicities, cultures, and religious and educational backgrounds. Besides individual counseling, I do group education, stressing the importance of breastfeeding for infants, addressing the problem of childhood obesity, and advising on the feeding of solid foods to younger and older infants.

To increase the motivation for change in parents, WIC has instituted "emotion-based" group education. In this model, WIC participants bring up issues they themselves are concerned about and help one another with advice. The nutritionist facilitates and guides the discussion. Another tool we use is showing posters of pictures with short captions linking success, health, and happiness with good nutrition. For example, one poster shows an older infant with a graduation cap. The caption reads, "Kids who take the full-year breast-feeding program graduate smart!" Mothers then show an increased desire to breastfeed and want more information.

Besides nutritional issues we assess children's immunization status and make referrals to other agencies as needed. Recently, we have been focusing especially on domestic violence and postpartum depression. Team members can serve on several WIC state task forces, including nutrition education, obesity prevention in children, and breastfeeding. As members of these task forces we can develop new educational materials and provide guidelines for WIC policies. As a result, I feel that I'm not just addressing problems; I'm contributing to solutions.

The satisfying aspect of my work is helping people and seeing results. When a mother has followed my recommendations and tells me that she was able to breastfeed successfully, I am satisfied. And I am satisfied when a mother's decision to decrease fried foods and give healthy snacks to her child results in a normal weight gain. It may not seem like much in the scheme of things, but those children likely will be healthier and will live longer lives. I'm making a difference.

to decline throughout the lifespan, with 8.5 hours the average among adults. REM sleep declines during childhood, increases again slightly during adolescence, and then decreases to as little as 15 percent among older adults (Roffwarg et al., 1966). REM sleep is thought to play a special role in memory consolidation and learning (Maquet, 2001). However, research is mixed regarding this idea (Siegel, 2001). As children grow older, their daily distribution of sleep also changes, with more sleep occurring during the night and less during the day (Howard & Wong, 2001).

Although sleep is clearly regulated by biological processes, it is also influenced in several ways by cultural standards (Jenni & O'Connor, 2005; Pachter & Harwood, 1996). First, culture influences the way in which daily sleep patterns are distributed throughout the night and day. For example, research conducted in the 1990s found that preschoolers in Italy went to bed later each night than American children and woke up earlier. This allowed the children to participate in late family meals and other social activities (Ottaviano, Giannotti, Cortesi, Bruni, & Ottaviano, 1996; New & Richman, 1996). In Holland, it was found that Dutch 3-month-old infants slept as much as two hours longer each night than their American counterparts (Super, Harkness, van Tijen et al., 1996). These differences across societies have been related to differences in cultural beliefs regarding the importance of child participation in family activities, even when they occur late at night, versus cultural beliefs in the importance of individual autonomy and regularity in the child's sleep patterns (Pachter & Harwood, 1996).

Cultural differences have also been found in the presence of elaborate bedtime routines, which are more common in societies in which children sleep separately in their own rooms than in societies in which children cosleep with other family members, particularly parents (Jenni & O'Connor, 2005). Recall from Chapter 5 that cosleeping shows wide cultural variability, regarded in some societies as normative and desirable but in others as an indicator of discipline problems or other family issues (Shweder, Jensen, & Goldstein, 1995). The boundaries between what is considered "normal" and what is considered "problem" sleep behavior also appear to be heavily influenced by cultural beliefs and practices (Jenni & O'Connor, 2005).

Links to Related Material
In Chapter 5, you read about cultural variability in cosleeping practices. Here, you read more about cultural influences on the development of sleep patterns.

Kwashiorkor, or protein deficiency, and marasmus, or wasting disease caused by starvation, are severe conditions that interfere with growth and development and may lead to death. Together these conditions are called protein energy malnutrition (PEM). PEM is a leading cause of death among children in developing countries, where it is typically caused by a diet that lacks adequate protein and energy. Geographically, over 70 percent of children suffering from PEM live in Asia, and another 26 percent in Africa (World Health Organization, 2003). In the United States, PEM more commonly occurs as a complication of AIDS, cancer, and other illnesses that impair the body's ability to absorb or use nutrients. (Natalie Behring/Getty Images News and Sport Services)

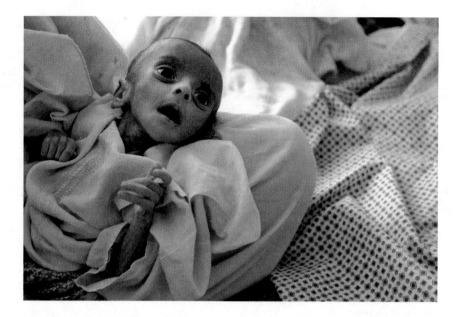

Clearly, sleep is heavily influenced by both biology and culture, highlighting the extent to which nature and nurture are intertwined in human development. This interaction also highlights the need for tolerance and open-mindedness when working with families with diverse childrearing beliefs and practices.

Immunization and Child Health Care

Rates of childhood immunization are considered one of the leading health indicators of a society (U.S. Department of Health and Human Services, 2000). Vaccines, which can prevent disability and death from a variety of infectious diseases, are recommended for universal administration to children on a set schedule during the first three years of life.

As can be seen in Table 6.3, in 2003, the percentage of children aged 19–35 months receiving the combined series of recommended vaccinations rose to 79.4 percent, a record high in the United States (Morbidity and Mortality Weekly Report, 2004). Statewide rates ranged from 94 percent in Connecticut to 67.5 percent in Colorado. Children who lived in major urban areas were less likely to receive the complete combined series.

Globally, about 78 percent of preschool children have received the DTP3 (three doses of the diphtheria-tetanus-pertussis combination) vaccination series, up from 20 percent in 1980 (World Health Organization, March 2005). Children in South Asia and sub-Saharan Africa show the lowest coverage, where as many as half of children do not receive the DPT vaccination in the first year of life (World Health Organization, 2006).

Closely related to the issue of childhood immunization is that of health insurance. Many children lack health insurance, either private or public, through Medicaid or through state children's health insurance programs. According to an Urban Institute Analysis of the CDC's 2002 National Health Interview Survey (August 2004), these children are:

- Less likely to receive proper medical care for childhood illnesses such as ear infections, tonsillitis, or asthma.
- Less likely to have received a well-child medical check-up in the past year.
- More likely to have an unmet or delayed medical need.
- More likely to lack a regular source of medical care.
- More likely to rely on hospital emergency rooms for routine care.

In the United States in 2003, 11.4 percent of all children under the age of 18 lacked health insurance. However, as can be seen in Table 6.4, differences arose by poverty status, age, and ethnic background.

TABLE 6.3 Vaccination Coverage among U.S. Children aged 19–25 Months, 2003

VACCINATION	% COVERAGE
DTP, 4 doses	84.8
(Diphtheria, Tetanus, Pertussis or Whooping Cough)	

Diphtheria is a bacterial infection that causes a thick gray coating at the back of the throat that makes it hard to breathe and swallow, and can result in suffocation, paralysis, and heart disease. One in 20 people who get the disease dies from it.

Tetanus is a bacterial infection that causes severe and painful muscle spasms, seizures, and paralysis. Tetanus can lead to locking of the jaw, making it impossible to open your mouth or swallow and causing death by suffocation in about 30 percent of the people who get the disease.

Pertussis is a bacterial infection that causes coughing spells so bad it's hard for children to eat, drink, or breathe for weeks at a time. It can lead to pneumonia, seizures, brain damage, and death.

Poliovirus, 3 doses	91.6

Polio is a serious disease that can cause paralysis and death

Hib, 3 doses	93.9
(Haemophilus influenzae type b)	

Hib is the leading cause of bacterial meningitis. Meningitis is an infection of the fluid of a person's spinal cord and the fluid that surrounds the brain. It can cause seizures and death.

MMR, 1 dose	93.0
(Measles, Mumps, Rubella)	

Measles is an acute, highly contagious infectious diseases. Measles causes a rash and high fever. About 1 child in every 1,000 who get measles will get encephalitis, an inflammation of the brain that can lead to convulsions and deafness. For every 1,000 children who get measles, 1 or 2 will die from it.

Mumps is a highly infectious disease that causes enlargement of the salivary glands at the side of the throat. It carries risks of partial deafness (1 in 25), meningitis (1 in 200), and encephalitis (1 in 5,000).

Rubella or German measles is caused by a virus. It is a mild disease in children, but it can lead to fetal death if contracted by a woman during pregnancy.

Hepatitis B, 3 doses	92.4

Hepatitis B is a serious disease caused by a virus that attacks the liver. It can cause lifelong infection, scarring of the liver, liver cancer, liver failure, and death.

Varicella, 1 dose	84.8
(Chickenpox)	

Chickenpox is typically mild illness, but certain groups of people who get chickenpox (including infants and people of any age with weakened immune systems) are at greater risk for severe complications, including widespread bacterial infection, pneumonia, and encephalitis. Also, anyone who has had chickenpox is at risk for a complication later in life called shingles, which is a painful, blister-like rash caused by a revitalization of the varicella virus in the nervous system later in life.

PCV, 4 doses	36.7
(Pneumococcal conjugate)	

A common bacterial cause of ear infections, pneumonia, sepsis, and meningitis.

Combined Series	79.4
(DPT, Polio, HIB, MMR, Hib, Hepatitis B)	

SOURCE: Centers for Disease Control, National, state, and urban area vaccination coverage among children aged 19–35 months, United States, 2003. *Morbidity and Mortality Weekly Report*, July 30, 2004/53(20): 658–661.

Globally, around 10.6 million children died in 2004 before reaching their fifth birthday. Most of these deaths are attributable to a handful of preventable conditions, such as acute respiratory infections (19 percent), diarrhea (18 percent), malaria (8 percent), measles (4 percent), HIV/AIDS (3 percent), and neonatal conditions resulting from

Since 1980, measles mortality around the world has declined by 80 percent, due in large part to sustained efforts to promote immunization (World Health Organization, 2005). (Kamran Jebreili/© AP/Wide World Photos)

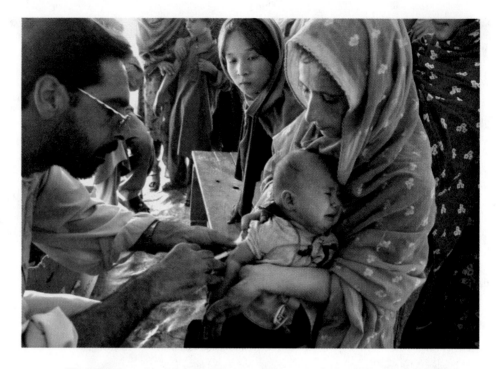

preterm birth, birth asphyxia, and infections (37 percent). According to the World Health Organization (2005), poor or delayed health care contributes to up to 70 percent of child deaths worldwide.

Sudden Infant Death Syndrome (SIDS)

Sudden Infant Death Syndrome (SIDS)
The sudden and unexpected death of an apparently healthy infant under the age of 1.

Each year in the United States approximately 3,000 babies go to sleep and never wake up. This tragic event, known as **Sudden Infant Death Syndrome**, or **(SIDS)**, is a significant concern to parents of young infants. SIDS, the sudden and unexpected death of an apparently healthy infant under the age of 1, is one of the most common causes of infant death in industrialized countries beyond the neonatal period. The most vulnerable period is between about 2 and 4 months of age.

Despite decades of concerted research effort, the causes of SIDS are still not fully understood. Researchers have succeeded, however, in identifying a number of risk

TABLE 6.4 Uninsured Children in the United States, by Poverty Status, Age, and Ethnic Background	
All Children	11.4%
Children in poverty	19.2%
Age	
Under 6 years	10.3%
6–11 years	11.0%
12–17 years	12.7%
Ethnic Background	
European American	7.4
African American	14.5
Asian American	12.4
Hispanic	21.0

SOURCE: C. DeNavas-Walt, B.D. Proctor, & R.J. Mills. (2004, August). Income, poverty, and health insurance coverage in the United States: 2003. *U.S. Census Bureau Current Population Reports.*

factors—that is, factors whose presence increases the likelihood of SIDS. Fortunately, many of these factors are conditions that are under the control of parents and other care providers.

One clearly important factor is the position in which the baby is placed for sleep. Sleeping in the prone, or on-the-stomach, position is associated with a heightened probability of SIDS (Simpson, 2001). Discovery of this association led to a "Back to Sleep" campaign in the United States, a campaign that encouraged parents to place babies on their backs rather than their stomachs. Within five years, the percentage of American babies who were placed on their stomachs had declined from 70 percent to 20 percent. The incidence of SIDS declined by 42 percent. Comparable declines occurred in other countries in which similar campaigns were initiated (American Academy of Pediatrics, 2000).

Other aspects of the sleep environment may also be important. Soft bedding is a risk factor, and so is overheating (Kleeman et al., 1999). It is perhaps natural for parents to bundle the baby up and keep the heat high during the winter months (the most common time period for SIDS); too much confinement and warmth, however, may be dangerous rather than beneficial.

Another risk factor that is clearly under the control of parents and other caretakers is second-hand smoking. Both smoking while pregnant and smoking in the vicinity of the infant are associated with an increased probability of SIDS. The association with SIDS is not the only reason to stop the practice—parental smoking has been linked to a number of health problems in infancy (Mannino et al., 2001).

Some of the predictors of SIDS reside more in the infant than in the immediate environment. Babies who were born preterm or at low birthweight, who were exposed to drugs prenatally, or who had low Apgar scores are at heightened risk for SIDS. More immediately, babies who are suffering from respiratory infections are more vulnerable to SIDS. There is also evidence that some victims of SIDS may have abnormalities in the portion of the brain that controls breathing and waking from sleep (Panigrahy et al., 1997). Particularly when other risk factors are operating (such as overheating or a respiratory infection), these babies may simply be unable to regulate breathing and rouse themselves from the sleep state. At present there is no certain prescription for guarding against SIDS. Nevertheless, it clearly makes sense for parents to do all that is under their control to try to prevent this most heartbreaking of family tragedies.

Learning Objective 6.3: *Analyze important factors that affect physical health in infancy.*

1. What is infant mortality, and what factors are associated with its increased risk?
2. What are the benefits of breastfeeding? What are some barriers to breastfeeding?
3. What are some cultural influences on feeding and weaning?
4. What are some leading forms of malnutrition, and how do they affect a child's physical growth and health?
5. How does sleep change across the life cycle? What are some cultural influences on sleeping?
6. Why are immunizations important for children, and what factors affect children's ability to receive appropriate immunizations and health care?
7. What is SIDS, and what can be done to prevent it?

✔ *Test Your*
Mastery...

Physical Health in Childhood and Adolescence

Challenges to health in childhood and adolescence may relate to accidents and risk-taking behavior. Trauma is the leading cause of injury and death in children over 1 year of age (Hsu & Slonim, 2006). Leading causes of injuries—other than child abuse—include dog bites and bicycle accidents. The leading causes of trauma death, in order of frequency, are motor-vehicle accidents, drowning, burns, poisonings, firearms, and falls. Other challenges to health may include lack of exercise, obesity, eating disorders, substance abuse, and sexually transmitted diseases.

Learning Objective 6.4
Identify and describe some significant health concerns of childhood and adolescence today.

TABLE 6.5 Physical Activity among Children and Youth in the United States

Factors Associated with Greater Activity in Childhood (ages 3–12)
    Male gender
    Healthy diet
    Access to sports programs & facilities
    Time spent outdoors
    Parental fitness status

Factors Associated with Greater Activity in Adolescence (ages 13–18)
    Male gender
    Perceived activity competence
    Access to community sports
    Support from others, including parents
    Sibling physical activity
    Opportunities to exercise

Factors Associated with Decreased Activity in Childhood and Adolescence
    Perceived barriers to activity
    Age
    Depression
    Sedentary activities at home, especially television and computer use

SOURCE: Adapted from J.F. Sallis, J.J. Prochaska, & W.C. Taylor. (2000). A review of correlates of physical activity of children and adolescents. *Medicine and Science in Sports and Exercise, 32*, 963–975.

Physical Activity and Sports Participation

Physical activity and sports participation are recognized as important contributors to physical and psychological well-being. The dramatic increase in the percentage of overweight children in the past 20 years, combined with findings that children tend to become less physically active as they grow older (Trost et al., 2002), has led researchers to wonder what factors may be influencing physical activity (or its lack) among youth today. In a review of 108 studies, Sallis, Prochaska, & Taylor (2000) found consistent associations between physical activity and the characteristics detailed in Table 6.5.

In a qualitative study of adolescent males' perceptions of perceived barriers to physical activity (Allison et al., 2005), both internal and external barriers were identified. Internal barriers included low perceived physical competence and lack of confidence; higher value placed on academics; and preference for technology-related activities such as television, computer use, and video games. External barriers that adolescents cited included the influence of peers and family; safety concerns; lack of time due to schoolwork and after-school jobs; and lack of accessible, affordable indoor facilities.

Obesity

Obesity, or excess fat storage, is an increasingly common nutritional disorder among children in the United States today. Obesity is measured using the **body mass index (BMI),** which is expressed as weight divided by height. Children with BMI at or above the 85th percentile for their age and gender are defined as overweight; children with BMI above the 95th percentile are considered obese. According to the 1999–2002 National Health and Nutrition Examination Survey (NHANES), 16 percent of U.S. children aged 6–19 years

Questions for Thought and Discussion
What is your fitness status? What is your profile for physical activity and sports participation?

Obesity
A condition of excess fat storage; often defined as body mass index above the 95th percentile.

Body mass index (BMI)
A measure of the person's weight in relation to height.

were currently overweight or obese. This represents a 45 percent increase over the NHANES estimate for 1988–1994 (CDC National Center for Health Statistics, 2005). These recent increases in childhood obesity have been linked in particular to decreased physical activity among children (Kimm & Obarzanek, 2002).

How can we better understand the effects of obesity on physical and psychological health and development. A study of 4,743 adolescents in grades 7–12 using data from the National Longitudinal Study of Adolescent Health (Swallen, Reither, Haas, & Meier, 2005) found that adolescents who were overweight or obese had significantly worse self-reported physical health, and also were more likely to experience functional limitations based on their weight. Interestingly, researchers found an association between being over-weight or obese and experiencing poorer emotional, school, or social functioning only among young adolescents (ages 12–14).

A few studies have demonstrated racial differences in measures of self-perception and perceived social acceptance based on weight. In particular, European American girls appear more likely than African American girls to be dissatisfied with their weight and body shape, despite the fact that African American girls are more likely to be identified as over-weight or obese (Kimm & Obarzanek, 2002). Lower parental education has also been linked to a greater likelihood of being overweight in childhood.

Eating Disorders

Eating disorders are a significant health issue facing young women in America today. It has been estimated that as many as 4 percent of women will suffer from an eating disorder in their lifetime (American Psychiatric Association Work Group on Eating Disorders, 2000). Eating disorders affect a young person's physical health, psychological well-being, and social life. Depression, anxiety, and substance use are also associated with eating disorders. Compared to other mental disorders, the death rate among individuals with eating disorders is high (U.S. Department of Health and Human Services, 1999).

There are three major types of clinically recognized eating disorders. **Anorexia nervosa** is characterized by excessive weight loss, fear of body fat and weight gain, and an inaccurate perception of one's own body weight or shape. Individuals suffering from anorexia believe they are fat even when they are severely underweight. They will strive to achieve an abnormally low body weight, typically through diet, fasting, or strenuous exercise. Induced vomiting after eating or laxatives may also be used. People with anorexic nervosa typically weigh less than 85 percent of their expected weight. The average age for onset of anorexia nervosa is 17 years (U.S. Department of Health and Human Services, 1999).

People with anorexia experience many of the same consequences that victims of starvation do, such as brittle hair and nails, cold intolerance, and loss of menstrual cycle. Long-term consequences of anorexia, even when treated, may include irregular heart rhythms and heart failure. The death rate among young women ages 15–24 with anorexia is estimated to be about 12 times higher than in the general population. Death may occur from starvation, cardiac arrest, other medical complications, or suicide (Sullivan, 1995).

Bulimia nervosa is charactized by binge eating (ingesting large amounts of food within a short period of time), followed by purging, or behaviors to rid the body of the food that was eaten. Purging may be accomplished through self-induced vomiting, laxatives, diet pills, diuretics (pills that rid the body of water), strenuous exercise, or fasting. Often, these behaviors are carried out in secret while the individual maintains an apparently normal body weight.

Bulimia has long-term health consequences, long after binging and purging behaviors have ceased. Repeated vomiting can cause inflammation of the esophagus and erosion of tooth enamel. The loss of potassium associated with repeated vomiting can damage the heart muscle and increase the risk for cardiac arrest.

Questions for Thought
    and Discussion
What is your BMI? BMI is your weight in kilograms divided by your height squared (in centimeters). You are overweight if your index is 25.0 to 29.9, and you are obese if it is 30.0 or above.

Anorexia nervosa
A severe eating disorder, usually involving excessive weight loss through self-starvation, most often found in teenage girls.

Bulimia nervosa
A disorder of food binging and sometimes purging by self-induced vomiting, typically observed in teenage girls.

Young girls in U.S. society receive multiple messages regarding unrealistic standards of physical beauty. In response to the civil rights and feminist movements, many doll manufacturers added new product lines to offer alternative standards for physical beauty. Although Mattell did not change Barbie's proportions, this popular doll has appeared as a doctor, astronaut, businesswoman, police officer, UNICEF volunteer, and athlete. (Rorke/The Image Works)

Binge-eating disorder
A condition characterized by episodes of uncontrolled eating.

Binge-eating disorder is a more recently recognized condition that is characterized by episodes of uncontrolled eating. Unlike anorexia and bulimia, however, binge-eating disorder typically occurs without compensatory activities, such as vomiting or laxative abuse, to avoid weight gain (U.S. Department of Health and Human Services, 1999).

Eating disorders are most likely to be treated successfully when they are diagnosed early. When abnormal eating behaviors continue over time, they are more difficult to overcome, and effects on physical health are more likely to be lasting. Presently, there is no universally accepted standard treatment for either anorexia or bulimia. Integrated approaches to treatment may include the cooperation of nutritionists, mental health professionals, and endocrinologists (U.S. Department of Health and Human Services, 2000).

The causes of eating disorders are not completely understood. Researchers have examined a variety of influences, including genetically related biochemistry, personality factors related to self-esteem and stress management, and social pressure from family and/or friends to be thin and control weight. In addition, researchers have noted the significant role played by our culture, which idealizes thinness, provides women with unrealistic standards of physical beauty, and places too much emphasis on women's appearances as opposed to their ideas or accomplishments (U.S. Department of Health and Human Services, 2000).

Eating disorders are about ten times more common in females than in males. However, there is evidence that rates are increasing among males and may be particularly high among selected groups of males, such as wrestlers, jockeys, and others who must meet weight limits to compete. Substance abuse, such as the illegal use of steroids, may also affect the health of young athletes. Eating disorders are found across all ethnic and racial groups. Their incidence peaks during adolescence and early adulthood, but these disorders are increasingly common in all age groups, particularly prepubertal girls ages 9–11 (Shisslak, Crago, McKnight, et al., 1998).

Links to Related Material
Exposure to media messages regarding unattainable standards of feminine beauty appear linked to the greater incidence of eating disorders in young women. In Chapter 13, you will learn more about societal influences on how we construct "feminine" and "masculine" behavior.

Substance Use and Abuse

Substance abuse has long been associated with problematic outcomes in adolescence, including academic failure, school dropout, delinquency, and unprotected sexual activity and its consequences. Smoking, drinking, and illicit drug use are also leading causes of injury and death among adolescents (Johnston et al., 2005). As a result, researchers have sought to understand what leads young people to use (and misuse) drugs.

Factors that increase the risk of substance abuse in adolescence include an individual's attitudes toward and early introduction to drugs and a tendency to antisocial behavior. Family factors include poor family supervision, conflict in the home, and parental attitudes toward drug use. Other factors include peer drug use, drug-related behaviors and rewards, and low degree of commitment to school. Larger community and societal factors include low neighborhood attachment, community disorganization, multiple transitions, high mobility, laws and norms favorable to drug use, and the perceived availability of drugs (Arthur & Blitz, 2000).

Since 1975, a nationwide survey has monitored attitudes toward and patterns of substance use among twelfth-grade students. In 1991, eighth and tenth graders were added to the annual survey. In 2003, the total sample included 48,500 students in 392 schools across the nation (Johnston et al., 2004). As you can see in Figure 6.9, long-term trends in substance use among adolescents in the United States indicate that overall usage reached a peak in the late 1970s, declined steadily through the 1980s, and then rose again in the 1990s. Overall rates have remained steady or declined slightly since about 1998. In 2003, lifetime use of any illicit drug among twelfth-graders stood at 51 percent; in 1975, when the survey began, lifetime use among this population was 55 percent.

Unlike trends for overall usage, use of most individual drugs has fluctuated widely over time. For example, recent changes include a drop in the use of ecstasy since 2002, and an increase in the use of inhalants since 2003. Drugs that have held fairly steady in recent years include heroin, cocaine, and crack. Drugs thus appear to wax and wane in their popularity, reflecting rapidly changing factors specific to each drug. These factors include availability, new information about a drug's effects and risks, and consequent acceptability within the peer group. More resistant to change has been the overall proportion of young people in any given year who appear willing to use drugs (Johnston et al., 2004).

Use of the legal drugs, cigarettes and alcohol, continues to pose considerable concern. In 2003, 24 percent of U.S. twelfth graders smoked tobacco on a regular basis, and over half (58 percent) reported having been drunk at least once in their life. Other recent trends of concern to researchers include rising rates of drug use among females, a phenomenon that is closing the long-standing gap between male and female substance use. The average age at which young people initiate drug use has declined as well, with an increase in the number of younger adolescents who report using drugs (Sloboda, 2002).

Trends: in Lifetime Prevalence of an illicit Drug Use Index for Twelfth Graders

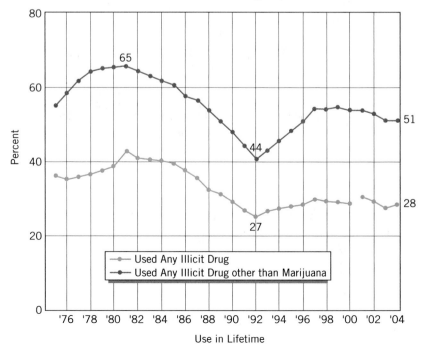

Use in Lifetime

FIGURE 6.9 Lifetime illicit use of any drug among twelfth-graders, 1976–2004

SOURCE: L.D. Johnston, P.M. O'Malley, J.G. Bachman, & J.E. Schulenberg. (2005). *Monitoring the Future National Survey Results on Drug Use, 1975–2004. Volume I: Secondary School Students* (NIH Publication No. 05-5727). Bethesda, MD: National Institute on Drug Abuse, 680 pp.

BOX 6.3 Just Say No? Teens, Sexuality, and Society

Government statistics show dramatic declines in pregnancy, birth, and abortion rates among teens between 1991 and 2003 (National Center for Health Statistics, 2006). For example, the teen birth rate declined by a third to 40.4 per 1,000 females 15 to 19 years of age, including a sharp drop for African American teens. There are significant differences in birth rates and contraceptive use by race/ethnicity. For example, Hispanic girls have the highest teen birth rates (81.5 per 1,000 versus 26 among European Americans and 60.9 among African Americans).

Nevertheless, U.S. rates are disproportionately high compared to those of other developed countries. Based on pre-1995 data, U.S. teen pregnancy rates were the second highest in the world, following the Russian Federation, and Japan and Italy had the lowest rates (Alan Guttmacher Institute, 2004). These data suggest the major role that society and culture play in people's sexual behavior.

Religion and education are major sociocultural factors in the expression of sexuality. Roman Catholic groups have traditionally prescribed premarital abstinence, a view that is increasingly shared by Christian fundamentalist groups. Recent "Just Say No" moral education programs, once geared toward drug and alcohol abuse prevention, strive to make it cool to refrain from sexual activity. In contrast, traditional sex education programs have sought instead to inform youths about pregnancy alternatives and sexually transmitted diseases and to promote contraception, such as the use of condoms.

What works? The CDC's National Center for Health Statistics reports that sexual activity has declined significantly among younger teenagers, showing that they are delaying sexual activity, and that contraceptive use has improved (2004). These results are interpreted as a sign that school sex education programs are effective. However, other analysts believe delayed sexual activity and declining birth and abortion rates are an outgrowth of the new teen abstinence programs, which are delivered through Christian church organizations and over the Internet. One nationwide mass media program is Silver Ring Thing (SRT), an organization in which teens make public declarations of virginity and wear a ring as a pledge of their sexual abstinence.

Abstinence can be defined liberally, however, as sexual activity that does not involve penetration. This may contribute to the fact that teens who make a one-time pledge to remain virgins are infected with sexually transmitted diseases about as often as whose who do not pledge abstinence. According to a study based on data from the National Longitudinal Study of Adolescent Health (Bruckner and Bearman, 2005), over time, teens who make a public pledge to delay sex have fewer sex partners, are less likely to use condoms, get married at younger ages, contract STDs just as often as other teens, and are less likely to seek testing or treatment for STDs. Thus, "Just Say No" may work in the short term but not in the long run, and so far no study has been able to show the effectiveness of abstinence-only curricula.

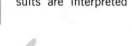

Evidence suggests that adolescent sexual behavior must be treated as a public health education matter and not as a morality issue alone. Even so, the federal government has poured millions of dollars into the development of abstinence programs, as much a reflection of the conservative political agenda and religious fundamentalism as of threats of HIV/AIDS and STDs in today's youth populations. In 2005, under threat of a "separation of church and state" lawsuit by the American Civil Liberties Union, the U.S. government formally withdrew its funding of the Moon Township-based Silver Ring Thing abstinence organization, because it is religion and faith based.

✔ *Test Your Mastery...*

Learning Objective 6.4: *Identify and describe some significant health concerns of childhood and adolescence today.*

Links to Related Material
Here, we consider adolescent sexuality and the use of contraception. In Chapter 13, you will learn about issues such as sexual orientation and gender identity.

1. What are some examples of the leading cause of injury and death to children over 1 year of age?
2. What factors affect young people's physical activity and sports participation?
3. Why is childhood obesity a growing health concern, and what factors place a child at risk for it?
4. What are some causes and consequences of the two leading eating disorders?
5. What factors are associated with substance abuse in adolescence?
6. What trends in substance use have been apparent over time?

BOX 6.4   Contextual Model for Physical Growth and Health

Infant is born in relative health or ill health, depending on genetic constitution and quality of prenatal care.

Family and School Settings

- Families with more education and more financial resources are more likely to provide optimal nutrition for physical growth, including breastfeeding.
- Schools with greater financial resources are more likely to provide and encourage a range of opportunities for participation in sports.
- Some families are more likely to model physical activity and sports participation than other families.

Socioeconomic Status

- Parents' access to quality health care through their employers affects child growth and health through preventive care, including regular check-ups, immunizations, and diagnosis and ongoing care of chronic and acute health problems.
- Workplace policies for sick leave affect the ability of parents to access health care for their children in a timely manner.
- More affluent neighborhoods and communities provide more opportunities for physical recreation and sports participation.

Larger Cultural and Societal Context

- Television greatly influences children's choices regarding nutrition and physical activity.
- Cultural values regarding femininity influence development of specific problems such as eating disorders.
- Availability of and attitudes toward the use and misuse of certain substances, such as alcohol, tobacco, and illegal drugs, affect likelihood of adolescent use.

Learning Objective 6.1
Describe the structure and functions of the brain and trace the development of the brain during childhood.

1. What is the brain's structure?

The brain operates through networks of communication that involve neurons and neuron pathways. Messages travel along *neurons* as electrical signals, which are picked up by the incoming dendrites and passed along by the outgoing axons. *Neurotransmitters* allow messages to travel across the synapses from cell to cell.

The brain has three major parts: the *brain stem*, the *midbrain*, and the *cerebrum*. Of most interest to psychologists is the cerebral cortex, which controls higher-level brain functions. Some areas of the cortex are specialized for various functions, including visual, auditory, and touch sensation.

2. Through what processes do the structure and functions of the brain develop?

Development of the fetal brain passes through three stages: *cell production*, *cell migration*, and *cell elaboration*. Although most neurons are present by around 26 weeks of fetal age, cell elaboration continues for years. Both neurons and synapses are overproduced and then cut back, and the cutting-back process continues into adolescence.

3. What is hemispheric specialization? Which activities show such specialization?

The *left and right hemispheres* of the brain are specialized to some extent. Evidence suggests that even at birth, the left side of the brain is usually prepared to control language functioning and the right side to control spatial and mathematical functioning.

4. What do brain imaging studies tell us about brain development?

Brain imaging techniques have allowed scientists to examine not only the anatomy of the brain but also brain *activity* as people perform different tasks. This permits us to understand which parts of the brain are used when people engage in different activities, such as language or spatial and mathematical reasoning.

5. What is the significance of brain plasticity for human development?	The responsiveness of the brain to experience is known as *plasticity*. This plasticity is implicated in skills that young children often acquire more easily than adults, such as learning multiple languages or learning to play a musical instrument. This greater plasticity is also the main reason that recovery from brain injury usually is greater the earlier in life the injury occurs. Plasticity is central to normal brain development, for it reflects the brain's capacity to be affected by experience.
6. How do different kinds of experiences affect the development of the brain?	An individual's daily, repeated experiences affect which *synaptic connections* will die. Neuronal pathways associated with repeated experiences are maintained, whereas other pathways are likely to be trimmed away.
7. What environmental conditions are optimal for healthy brain development in children?	For *healthy brain development*, young children need interactions with supportive parents and other family members, objects to manipulate and play with, and environments that provide stimulation and opportunities for learning and social communication.

Learning Objective 6.2
Describe the patterns of growth and maturation in development and the factors that influence them.

1. How can growth change over time in different populations?	Changes over time in physical growth, called the *secular trend*, reflect societal changes in physical health and affluence. Numerous factors affect the secular trend in height, including social class, income and education, family size, urban versus rural location, and geographic region. The secular trend has been observed most clearly in populations where, across generations, pregnant and lactating women and young children have access to highly nutritious diets, and where rates of infectious disease are relatively low.

2. How do genetics, gender, nutrition, and health affect individual differences in growth rates?	Many factors influence growth and maturation. *Genetic processes* are clearly important, but such *environmental factors* as nutrition and disease also come into play.
3. How do growth rates and body proportions change across childhood?	Growth is continuous through childhood but does not proceed uniformly. The rate of growth gradually slows, then experiences a *spurt* at adolescence, and stops soon afterward. Growth *rates* vary widely among children, as do the heights ultimately reached. Different parts of the body develop at different rates, following a *cephalocaudal* progression. Body organs also vary in rates of maturation; the brain, for example, develops very early.
4. What physical changes occur with puberty for girls and boys?	Boys and girls grow fairly similarly until adolescence. *Girls* typically experience the adolescent growth spurt and puberty earlier than do boys. *Boys* add more height once their growth spurt has begun, as well as more muscle mass and shoulder width. *Girls* add relatively more fat and hip width.
5. How do cultural practices and social attitudes affect the experience of puberty?	The adolescent's attitude toward these changes may reflect *social and cultural factors*, such as the amount of information he or she has about the changes and the body image that society holds up as ideal. On average, relatively early pubertal onset is a risk factor for girls, whereas relatively late onset is a risk factor for boys.

Learning Objective 6.3

Analyze important factors that affect physical health in infancy.

1. What is infant mortality, and what factors are associated with its increased risk?

Infant mortality refers to the number of deaths per 1,000 live births in a given country in a given year. In the United States, low birthweight and preterm birth are leading causes of infant mortality. Significant differences also appear by mother's ethnic background, highlighting the importance of adequate prenatal care for optimal infant health and survival.

2. What are the benefits of breastfeeding? What are some barriers to breastfeeding?

Infants who are breastfed are less likely to develop a variety of infectious illnesses. *Mothers* who breastfeed show lowered rates of breast cancer. A benefit to *society* is lowered worker absenteeism due to illness of a child. *Barriers* include unaccommodating workplaces and negative societal attitudes. The *AAP recommends* exclusive breastfeeding for the first six months of life, then breastfeeding supplemented with solids at least till one year, and thereafter for as long as is comfortable for the individual family.

3. What are some cultural influences evident with regard to feeding and weaning?

The attainment of *early self-feeding* milestones is valued in the contemporary United States. Early self-feeding is less important in many other societies, where children are likely to be spoon-fed until later ages.

4. What are some leading forms of malnutrition, and how do they affect a child's physical growth and health?

Iron deficiency anemia is a major form of malnutrition suffered by children around the world. *Kwashiorkor* or *protein malnutrition* is characterized by a severely distended abdomen. *Marasmus*, a condition associated with starvation, is a severe, wasting disease.

5. How does sleep change across the life cycle? What are some cultural influences on sleeping?	The average newborn sleeps about 16 hours per day. Roughly half of this sleep time is spent in REM or dream sleep. As children grow older, the amount of time spent in *REM sleep* decreases. Neurological maturation allows *sleep consolidation* after the age of 3–4 months. Culture influences patterns of sleep consolidation throughout the day. Cultures also vary widely with regard to attitudes toward *cosleeping*.
6. Why are immunizations important for children, and what factors affect children's ability to receive appropriate immunizations and health care?	Immunizations prevent a variety of serious diseases and medical complications associated with these diseases, including death. In the United States, children living in *major urban areas* are less likely to receive the complete series of immunizations. Children living in *poverty* are less likely to have adequate health care, to receive regular well-child check-ups, and to be treated for illnesses.
7. What is SIDS, and what can be done to prevent it?	SIDS is the sudden, unexplained death of a young infant, usually in the first 2–4 months of life. Measures that parents can take to reduce the risk of *SIDS* include placing the child on his or her back when sleeping; reducing the amount of bedding; and avoiding exposing the child to tobacco smoke, including second-hand smoke.

Learning Objective 6.4
Identify and describe some significant health concerns of childhood and adolescence today.

1. What are some examples of the leading causes of injury and death to children over 1 year of age?	Leading causes of *injuries*—other than child abuse—include dog bites and bicycle accidents. The leading causes of *trauma death*, in order of frequency, are motor-vehicle accidents, drowning, burns, poisonings, firearms, and falls.

2. What factors affect young people's physical activity and sports participation?

Male gender, access to sports facilities and opportunities to exercise, and family attitudes and health-related behaviors influence young people's *physical activity and sports participation*.

3. Why is childhood obesity a growing health concern, and what factors place a child at risk for it?

The percentage of children and adolescents who meet the criteria for being overweight or obese is growing in the United States today. Adolescents who are *overweight or obese* have significantly worse self-reported physical health and are also more likely to experience functional limitations based on their weight.

4. What are some causes and consequences of the two leading eating disorders?

Anorexia nervosa and *bulimia nervosa* are two leading eating disorders. Anorexia is characterized by a preoccupation with thinness, distorted body image, and behaviors that lead to abnormally low weight. Bulimia is characterized by binging and purging, often in secret. Both have serious long-term health consequences, including increased risk for heart failure and death. Women are more likely than men to suffer from eating disorders. Eating disorders appear to have multiple causes, including biological, personality, and family factors, as well as pressure from others and from society to maintain unrealistic standards of physical beauty.

5. What factors are associated with substance abuse in adolescence?

Substance abuse is associated with impairment in academic performance and increased risk for delinquency, school dropout, and unprotected sexual activity. Exposure to peer groups and parents who promote drug use, early initiation into antisocial behavior, and low attachment to schools and neighborhoods increase the risk for substance abuse.

6. What trends in substance use have been apparent over time?

Substance abuse *patterns over time* indicate relatively little change in the absolute number of adolescents who have ever used any substance. Individual drugs, however, have fluctuated considerably in popularity, depending on a variety of perceived costs and benefits. Alcohol and tobacco use remain of considerable concern to researchers.

Piaget *and* Vygotsky

5-year-old child asking questions of a parent
(Jose Luis Pelaiz/Getty Images, Inc.)

PIAGET'S COGNITIVE-DEVELOPMENTAL THEORY
Learning Objective 7.1
DEFINE THE CONCEPTS FROM BIOLOGY THAT PIAGET USED TO EXPLAIN
COGNITIVE DEVELOPMENT AND EVALUATE HIS THEORY OF STAGES.

Mechanisms of Cognitive Change

The Concept of Stages

COGNITION DURING INFANCY: THE SENSORIMOTOR PERIOD
Learning Objective 7.2
TRACE THE SUBSTAGES AND BENCHMARKS OF THE SENSORIMOTOR PERIOD IN CHILD DEVELOPMENT.

Six Substages of Sensorimotor Thought

Object Permanence

Testing Piaget: Recent Work on Infant Cognition
• Violation of Expectancy Method • Representing Hidden Objects • Deferred Imitation

THOUGHT IN THE PRESCHOOLER: THE PREOPERATIONAL PERIOD
Learning Objective 7.3
IDENTIFY SOME STRENGTHS AND LIMITATIONS OF PREOPERATIONAL THOUGHT IN CHILDREN'S COGNITIVE
DEVELOPMENT.

Symbolic Function
• Emergence of Symbolic Play • Symbolic Advances of Early Childhood

APPLICATIONS Selecting Developmentally Appropriate Play Materials

Strengths of Preoperational Thought

Limitations of Preoperational Thought
• Egocentrism • Perspective-Taking Abilities • Centration • Focus on Appearances

MIDDLE-CHILDHOOD: THE CONCRETE OPERATIONAL PERIOD
Learning Objective 7.4
ANALYZE THE COGNITIVE TASK MASTERIES THAT CHARACTERIZE CONCRETE OPERATIONAL THOUGHT.

The Concept of Operations

Conservation

Relational Reasoning: Class Inclusion and Seriation

Testing Piaget: Operational vs. Preoperational Differences
• Preoperational Perspective Taking • Preoperational Conservation

ADOLESCENT AND ADULT: THE FORMAL OPERATIONAL PERIOD
Learning Objective 7.5
EXPLAIN THE CHARACTERISTICS AND OUTCOMES OF FORMAL OPERATIONS COMPARED TO CONCRETE
OPERATIONS.

Hypothetical-Deductive Reasoning

Reasoning about Pendulums

Testing Piaget: Formal Operations vs. Concrete Operations

Evaluating Piaget's Theory
• The Issue of Stages • The Issue of Universality

VYGOTSKY AND THE SOCIOCULTURAL APPROACH
Learning Objective 7.6
ANALYZE THE THREE MAIN THEMES ON WHICH SOCIOCULTURAL APPROACHES TO DEVELOPMENT ARE BASED.
The Temporal Contexts of Development
The Social Origins of Thought

RESEARCH & SOCIETY Weaving Generations Together: Evolving Creativity in the Maya of Chiapas
The Use of Cultural Tools and Artifacts
• Interaction with Toys and Objects • Implications of Object Play for Development
The Role of Pretend Play

PIAGET AND VYGOTSKY ON LANGUAGE AND THOUGHT
Learning Objective 7.7
COMPARE AND CONTRAST THE THEORIES OF PIAGET AND VYGOTSKY ON THE ROLE OF LANGUAGE IN COGNITIVE DEVELOPMENT.

IMPACTS OF PIAGET AND VYGOTSKY ON EDUCATION
Learning Objective 7.8
EVALUATE THE CONTRIBUTIONS OF PIAGET AND VYGOTSKY TO EDUCATIONAL PRACTICE.

CONVERSATIONS with an Early Childhood Educator

COMPARING THE COGNITIVE-DEVELOPMENTAL AND SOCIOCULTURAL APPROACHES
Learning Objective 7.9
COMPARE AND CONTRAST THE SOCIOCULTURAL AND COGNITIVE-DEVELOPMENTAL APPROACHES TO CHILD DEVELOPMENT.

"Why can I put my hand through water and not through soap?"
"Why doesn't butter stay on top of hot toast?"
"When I mix red and orange it makes brown, why?"
"Where I was before I was born?"
"When are all the days going to end?"

As any parent knows, children frequently ask questions. Some of the earliest studies in child development have examined children's spontaneous questions. The examples above, which were collected by Paul Harris (2000), come from several of these pioneering studies, including the work of Jean Piaget.

As the examples make clear, children's questions come in many forms. Some concern mundane matters; others address issues of deep personal or scientific significance. Some questions are easily answerable; others pose issues that continue to challenge philosophers or scientists. The constant element is the search for understanding: in the journey from infancy to adulthood, children strive to make sense of literally thousands of topics. How can we make sense of children's sense-making efforts?

Sense-making is a function of cognitive development. **Cognition** refers to the higher-order mental processes—such as thinking, reasoning, learning, and problem solving—by which humans attempt to understand and adapt to their world. Infants and young children are often far more competent in these processes than we used to believe. Yet children's thinking differs from that of adults in many ways. These differences intrigue and baffle researchers and parents alike. What competencies and limitations characterize thought at different points in childhood? How do children discover how to overcome cognitive limitations and achieve new forms of competence? This chapter considers two general approaches to these questions. First is the cognitive-developmental approach, as represented by the work of Jean Piaget. We examine both Piaget's original theory and research and more recent studies that challenge, modify, or extend Piaget's findings. Second is the sociocultural approach, represented by the work of Lev Vygotsky. Although these two approaches have some important similarities, they differ in important ways as approaches to cognitive development. ■

Piaget's Cognitive-Developmental Theory

Piaget's goal was to answer basic philosophical questions about the nature and origins of knowledge by studying the growth of knowledge in children. His research focused on the child's understanding of basic concepts such as space and time, causality, number and quantity, classes (or categories), and relations between classes. He believed that, while children experience long periods of relative conceptual stability, these concepts also change dramatically over the course of development. Piaget claimed that these basic forms of knowledge develop throughout childhood.

The field of biology inspired Piaget's ideas about the structure and function of intelligence. A basic biological principle is that of *organization*. An organism is never simply a random collection of cells, tissues, and organs; rather, organisms are always highly organized systems. A biologist aims to discover the nature of that underlying organization. Piaget maintained that the same principle applies to human intelligence. For Piaget, the essence of intelligence does not lie in individually learned responses or isolated memories; the essence lies in the underlying organization. This organization takes the form of cognitive structures that the developing child constructs. *Cognitive structures* are ways to organize information to understand and remember it more effectively. The job of the cognitive psychologist is to discover what these structures are and how they change.

Mechanisms of Cognitive Change

Another basic biological principle is *adaptation*. All organisms adapt to the environment in which they must survive, often by means of complex mechanisms. The biologist tries to discover what these mechanisms of adaptation are. Human intelligence, according to Piaget, is an adaptive phenomenon—it is the primary means by which humans adapt to the environmental challenges they face.

Adaptation occurs through the complementary processes of **assimilation** and **accommodation**. In many of our interactions with the environment, we *assimilate* the environment into our current cognitive structures—that is, we interpret new experiences in terms of what we already understand. When children assimilate, they may distort reality to fit with the understanding they already possess. For example, a preschooler who is familiar with the category, "fish," may insist on her first visit to Sea World that dolphins and whales are also fish—she is assimilating these aquatic animals into her current understanding of what "fish" are. At the same time, we are continually changing our cognitive structures to *accommodate* or to better fit our knowledge to environmental realities. So, as a child learns more about the characteristics of fish and mammals, she changes her understanding of whales and dolphins to reflect their status as mammals. Through accommodation, children's understanding of the environment around them gradually becomes more accurate as they incorporate new information into their cognitive structures. It is through innumerable instances of assimilation and accommodation that cognitive development occurs.

Why, given that modifying one's thinking requires effort, would children ever engage in accommodation? Piaget believed that just as all organisms strive to maintain biological equilibrium or harmony with their environment, children, too, seek to achieve cognitive balance with the environment. Piaget referred to this as **equilibration**: a self-regulatory process that provides the motivation for cognitive change. When children become aware that their understanding is inadequate, they experience a feeling of cognitive discomfort, or *disequilibrium*. Cognitive *equilibrium* is restored when children modify their understanding to fit more adaptively with the cognitive challenge facing them. Equilibrium is

Cognition
Higher-order mental processes, such as reasoning and problem solving, through which humans attempt to understand the world.

Assimilation
In Piaget's theory, the fitting in or interpreting of new experiences in terms of what we already understand.

Accommodation
In Piaget's theory, changing our cognitive structures—what we understand—to fit in with environmental realities.

Questions for Thought and Discussion
The biological concepts that Piaget used apply throughout the lifespan. What are some examples from your life in which you responded to new experiences using assimilation and accommodation?

Equilibration
In Piaget's theory, the process of self-regulation in which individuals naturally seek to maintain or restore balance within their cognitive system.

achieved when the child's cognitive structures can respond to environmental challenges without either undue distortion or undue misunderstanding. Equilibration thus provides a means through which children can internally regulate the balance between leaving their understanding intact but potentially misinterpreting the environment (assimilation) and changing their understanding to better fit the environment (accommodation).

On hearing that dolphins and whales are not fish, the child may realize that her "fish" concept does not fit with her current experience. She may choose simply to disregard this new information and continue to assimilate dolphins into her concept of fish. However, she may experience disequilibrium arising from the conflict between her current concept and the new information. In this case, she engages in equilibration—struggling to change her concept to accommodate the fact that dolphins are not fish. When her understanding of fish and mammals is sufficient to accurately classify the animals that she encounters, including whales and dolphins, our preschooler has achieved equilibrium again. Equilibration thus explains how cognitive structures continually become more coordinated or organized, as individuals are naturally motivated to seek equilibrium. Ideally, each time cognitive equilibrium is restored as a result of satisfactorily resolving an intellectual conflict, the child achieves a better understanding, advancing cognitive development (Piaget, 1957, 1977). It is worth noting, however, that while the concept of equilibration makes a great deal of intuitive sense, it has been difficult to define, measure, and test scientifically (Chapman, 1992; Zimmerman & Blom, 1983).

Thus, Piaget characterized children as *active participants* in their own cognitive development. Children deliberately seek out new information about the environment. Piaget also characterized cognitive development as a *constructive process*. Children do not simply absorb incoming information as it is presented; rather, they interpret new information in light of their existing level of understanding. More advanced cognitive structures thus build on earlier, more primitive, structures—much as a car engine, for example, is constructed out of more elementary parts. One could not build a car engine without first having constructed a carburetor and gas tank. Similarly, a child could not engage in sophisticated cognitive processes like hypothesis testing without first having attained the ability to combine information logically. This **constructivism**—the idea that children actively construct their own knowledge—is one of Piaget's most lasting contributions to our understanding of cognitive development.

The Concept of Stages

In Piaget's theory, no single organization or set of cognitive structures defines childhood intelligence. Piaget believed that development progresses through a series of *stages*. Each stage involves a distinct set of mental structures that cause thinking at each stage to be qualitatively different from that of preceding or subsequent stages. The *qualitatively different* thinking of older children is not just better or faster than that of younger children; it differs in kind, much the way that a butterfly differs from a caterpillar. Furthermore, the specific ways of organizing experience at each stage should apply to every aspect of a child's thinking. That is, Piaget's stages are *global*. A child should reason in the same way regardless of the topic. Finally, because more advanced thinking builds on less advanced cognitive skills, every child must pass through the stages in precisely the same order. Thus, the stages are *order invariant*. Piaget divided cognitive development into four such stages: sensorimotor, preoperational, concrete operational, and formal operational. These periods were introduced in Chapter 1 and are summarized in Table 7.1.

Learning Objective 7.1: *Define the concepts from biology that Piaget used to explain cognitive development and evaluate his theory of stages.*

1. What is cognition?
2. What is the role of organization in the development of cognitive structures?
3. What are some forms of knowledge that children reorganize as they develop?
4. What three processes of adaptation are essential for cognitive change, and how do they work?
5. What four stages of cognitive development did Piaget propose, and how do they differ?

Questions for Thought and Discussion
What might be some real-life examples of events that cause disequilibrium and equilibration in the process of cognitive change?

Constructivism
The idea that children actively construct their knowledge of the world.

✔ *Test Your Mastery...*

TABLE 7.1	Piaget's Four Periods of Development	
PERIOD	**AGES (YRS)**	**DESCRIPTION**
Sensorimotor	0–2	Infants understand the world through the overt actions they perform on it. These actions reflect sensorimotor schemes. As the schemes become progressively more complex and interrelated, children gradually construct the ability to represent the world symbolically.
Preoperational	2–6	The child can now use mental representations rather than overt actions to solve problems. Thinking is consequently faster, more efficient, more mobile, and more socially sharable. Because children cannot operate logically on their mental representations, thinking is also egocentric and centered.
Concrete Operational	6–12	The advent of *mental operations* allows the child to overcome the limitations of preoperational thought. Mental operations are a system of internal mental actions that permit logical problem solving. The child comes to understand various forms of conservation, as well as classification and relational reasoning. Children's reasoning is limited, however, to concrete, tangible problems.
Formal Operational	12–adult	The acquisition of *hypothetical-deductive reasoning* enables children to generate and systematically test abstract hypotheses about things that do not currently exist. Thought begins with possibility and works systematically and logically back to reality. The prototype for such logical reasoning is scientific problem solving.

Cognition During Infancy: The Sensorimotor Period

The sensorimotor period extends from birth to about age 2. Infants make dramatic cognitive advances during this period. Piaget identified some of the most interesting and significant changes infants undergo and organized them into a coherent theory of infant development.

Piaget based his theory of infant development on his observations of his own three children from birth through the end of infancy (Piaget, 1951, 1952, 1954). His method of study combined naturalistic observation with experimental manipulation. Both Piaget and his wife, Valentine (herself a trained psychologist), spent many hours simply watching the everyday behavior of their babies. They supplemented these naturalistic observations with frequent, small-scale experiments. If, for example, Piaget was interested in his daughter's ability to cope with obstacles, he might place a barrier between her and her favorite toy and then record her response to this challenge.

Piaget's method has both strengths and weaknesses. On the positive side, the method combines observation of behavior in the natural setting and longitudinal study of the same children as they develop. This approach permitted insight into forms and sequences of development that could not have been gained solely from controlled laboratory study. One might worry, however, about the limited size of Piaget's sample. Three subjects is a small sample on which to base conclusions about universals of human development—especially when all three are from the same family and are being observed by their own parents! However, Piaget's observations are some of the most robust in all of developmental psychology. Many researchers have replicated Piaget's experiments with larger, more representative samples and more objective techniques of data collection. Despite its potential limitations, then, Piaget's picture of infant behavior was reasonably accurate (Haith & Benson, 1998).

Learning Objective 7.2
Trace the substages and benchmarks of the sensorimotor period in child development.

Six Substages of Sensorimotor Thought

Piaget divided the sensorimotor period into six substages. In the descriptions that follow, the ages should be taken simply as rough averages. What is important in a stage theory is not the age but the sequence—the order in which the stages come—which is assumed to be the same for all children.

Links to Related Material

In Chapter 5, you learned about some of the basic reflexes that infants are born with. Here, you read how Piaget's theory treats these reflexes as the first step in the infant's ability to understand the world.

Sensorimotor schemes
Skilled and generalizable action patterns by which infants act on and understand the world. In Piaget's theory, they are the cognitive structures of infancy.

Substage 1: Exercising Reflexes (Birth to 1 Month) In Piaget's view, the newborn's adaptive repertoire is limited to simple *reflexes*. Reflexes are innate, automatic motor responses that are triggered by specific environmental stimuli. Thus, the newborn sucks when a nipple rubs against the lips, grasps when an object grazes the palm, and orients when an appropriate visual stimulus appears. Even during the first weeks of life, reflexes undergo small, adaptive alterations. By the end of the first stage, reflexes have become the infant's first *sensorimotor schemes*.

In Piaget's theory, *schemes* are cognitive structures that allow children to make sense of their experience. **Sensorimotor schemes** are skilled and generalizable action patterns with which the infant acts on and makes sense of the world. The scheme concept emphasizes the role of action in intelligence. For Piaget, intelligence at every period of development involves some form of action on the world. During infancy, the actions are literal and overt, mediated through the senses and movement. The infant knows the world through behaviors such as sucking, grasping, looking, and manipulating.

These initial schemes are essential because they are the building blocks from which all future development proceeds. Development occurs as these initial schemes are modified through the processes of assimilation and accommodation. Infants apply their schemes to more objects and events—that is, they assimilate more things into their understandings of the world. They also modify their behavior in response to new experiences—that is, they accommodate their schemes in order to better fit the environment. As their initially automatic, inflexible action patterns begin to be modified by experience, infants enter the second of the sensorimotor substages.

Substage 2: Developing Schemes (1 to 4 Months) Schemes become more adaptive and more flexible during the second substage of development. First, schemes become more refined. A 1-month-old sucks on any object that contacts her lips in the same way, whether it is a nutritive nipple, a finger, the edge of a blanket, or even a stuffed toy. A 4-month-old, in contrast, has accommodated the sucking scheme to more appropriately fit these different items. She may suck fervently on a nipple when hungry, occasionally on a finger or blanket edge when bored, and may not suck a stuffed toy at all! Piaget observed that although infants initially discover the interesting effects of their actions by accident (e.g., sucking one's own thumb produces both a new oral and a new tactile sensation), they tend to repeat those actions to reproduce the effect. Such repetition is adaptive in that it allows infants to solidify newly established schemes.

The second change involves the coordination of schemes into larger units. Schemes involving the different sensory modes—sight, hearing, touch, taste, smell—begin to be brought together. Thus, infants may hear a sound and turn toward the source of the sound, coordinating hearing and vision. They may look at an object and then reach out to grasp and manipulate it, coordinating vision and touch.

Despite these advances, schemes continue to be fairly limited. Infants do not deliberately vary their schemes, but instead repeat only the precise action they originally produced. In addition, stage 2 schemes are oriented primarily toward the infant's own body—that is, infants focus on the effect of schemes on the *infant* rather than the effect they have on the *environment*. Infants use schemes for the pure pleasure of using them—grasping for the sake of grasping, sucking for the sake of sucking. At this stage, Piaget believed that infants are unaware of the external environment except insofar as it triggers the infant's action patterns.

Substage 3: Discovering Procedures (4 to 8 Months) In substage 3, the infant begins to show a clearer interest in the outer world. The baby begins to direct schemes away from his body and toward exploration of the environment. Thus, the substage 3 infant who manipulates a toy does so because of a real interest in exploring that object.

One manifestation of this greater awareness of the environment is that the infant discovers *procedures* for reproducing interesting events. For example, an infant lying in her baby gym might wave her arm about and accidentally knock one of the small stuffed animals suspended from the top of the gym, causing it to swing about. Delighted, the infant may then spend the next 10 minutes happily knocking the animal and laughing when it swings. Or the infant might happen to create an interesting sound by rubbing a toy against the side of the crib and then repeat the procedure to hear the sound again. The infant is beginning to develop knowledge of what he can do to produce desirable outcomes. At first this knowledge is obtained *accidentally*, after the fact. Once the infant has accidentally discovered an interesting or pleasing outcome, he or she may be able to reproduce it. What the infant cannot yet do, however, is figure out in advance how to produce that outcome.

Intentional behavior
In Piaget's theory, behavior in which the goal exists prior to the action selected to achieve it; it is made possible by the ability to separate means and end.

Substage 4: Intentional Behavior (8 to 12 Months) During substage 4 the infant begins to be able to predict outcomes. The infant first perceives some desirable goal and then figures out how to achieve it. In so doing, the infant demonstrates the first genuinely intentional behavior. In Piaget's analysis, **intentional behavior** involves an ability to separate *means* from *ends*. The infant uses a scheme as a means to lead to some other scheme, which becomes the goal, or end of the action. Researchers study intentional behavior by seeing how infants respond to obstacles. Suppose the baby is about to reach for a toy and you place a pillow between hand and toy. How does the baby respond? Simple though this problem may seem, prior to substage 4, the infant cannot solve it. The younger infant may "attack" the pillow or grab it instead of the toy. The substage 4 infant, in contrast, will first intentionally push the pillow aside and then reach for the toy. This sort of adaptive problem solving requires an understanding of the difference between means and ends. The infant must use the push-aside scheme as a means to get to the reach-and-play scheme.

Links to Related Material
How do you think that the infant's increasing motor skills, discussed in Chapter 5, might influence the kind of physical actions upon objects that Piaget's theory maintains is the hallmark of the sensorimotor period?

This infant intentionally strikes this object to produce sounds. Now he experiments with striking different keys. He also experiments with using the mallet to strike different objects to see what sounds they will make. According to Piaget, his ability to use tools intentionally to create new schemes indicates that he is operating in which substage of the sensorimotor period? (Corbis RF/Corbis)

Substage 5: Novelty and Exploration (12 to 18 Months) Piaget's name for substage 5 is "the discovery of new means through active exploration." The use of *new* schemes differentiates substage 5 from substage 4. The behavior of the substage 4 infant, though certainly intelligent, is conservative, because the infant uses familiar schemes to produce familiar effects. Substage 5 infants, in contrast, begin deliberately and systematically to vary their behaviors, creating both new schemes and new effects.

The advances of substage 5 are evident when the infant has a problem to solve. The infant now is not limited to reproducing variations of previously successful solutions. Instead, the infant can discover completely new solutions through an active process of trial and error. Piaget documented, for example, how substage 5 infants come to discover that a distant object can be retrieved by pulling a string and that a stick can be used as an extension of the arm to push, pull, or otherwise act on some distant object. These behaviors also represent the first instances of an important human capability—the ability to use tools (Flavell, Miller, & Miller, 2002).

The substage 5 infant also experiments for the pure pleasure of experimentation. An example familiar to many parents is the "high-chair behavior" of the 1-year-old. The baby leans over the edge of his high chair and drops her spoon to the floor, carefully noting how it bounces. The parent retrieves and returns the spoon, whereupon the baby leans over the other side of the chair and drops the spoon again, perhaps with a bit more force. The parent again returns the spoon, and this time the baby flings it across the room—whereupon the exasperated parent ends the scheme by removing either baby or spoon from the situation. It is through such active experimentation that infants learn about the world and about their own ability to affect objects in it.

Substage 6: Mental Representation (18 to 24 Months) The first five sensorimotor substages are a time of remarkable cognitive progress, but another important advance must be made. During the first five substages, the infant's adaptation to the world occurs entirely through overt behavior. Even the substage 5 infant's problem solving is based on trying out one behavior after another until a solution is found. At substage 6, however, the infant becomes capable for the first time of **mental representation**—of thinking about and acting on the world internally or mentally and not merely externally through behavior. It is this advance that brings the sensorimotor period to an end and inaugurates a new period of cognitive development.

An example of substage 6 behavior involves Piaget's daughter Jacqueline, who is carrying some blades of grass through the house.

> Jacqueline [at age 1 year, 8 months, 9 days] arrives at a closed door—with a blade of grass in each hand. She stretches out her right hand toward the knob but sees that she cannot turn it without letting go of the grass. She puts the grass on the floor, opens the door, picks up the grass again and enters. But when she wants to leave the room things become complicated. She puts the grass on the floor and grasps the doorknob. But then she perceives that in pulling the door toward her she will simultaneously chase away the grass which she placed between the door and the threshold. She therefore picks it up in order to put it outside the door's zone of movement. (Piaget, 1952, p. 339)

When Jacqueline pauses with her hand on the doorknob the second time, she is apparently doing two things. She is imagining the problem—the door sweeping over the grass. She is also imagining the solution—moving the grass beyond the sweep of the door. She is thus engaged in a kind of mental problem solving, based on an internal use of representations or symbols, which is not possible earlier in infancy.

Table 7.2 summarizes the six sensorimotor substages. For Piaget, the onset of representation defines the change in development from the sensorimotor period to the preoperational period.

Mental representation
The use of symbols to picture and act on the world internally.

TABLE 7.2 The Six Sensorimotor Substages

STAGE	AGES (MOS.)	DESCRIPTION
1. Exercising reflexes	0–1	The infant is limited to exercising inborn reflexes—for example, sucking and grasping—that evolve into the first adaptive schemes.
2. Developing schemes	1–4	Schemes begin to be refined and coordinated. They are focused, however, on the effects they have on the infant, rather than the effects they have on the environment.
3. Discovering procedures	4–8	Behavior becomes more outwardly oriented. The infant develops procedures for reproducing interesting events.
4. Intentional behavior	8–12	The first truly intentional behavior emerges. The infant can separate means and end in pursuit of a goal.
5. Novelty and exploration	12–18	The infant begins to vary the schemes systematically to produce new effects. Problems are solved through an active process of trial and error.
6. Mental representation	18–24	The capacity for representational or symbolic functioning emerges. Mental problem solving begins to replace overt trial and error.

Object Permanence

An important benchmark in infant development is the phenomenon of object permanence. **Object permanence** is the knowledge that objects continue to exist independent of our perception of them. For example, a toy or any other object does not cease to exist just because you can no longer see or feel or otherwise sense it. It is hard to imagine a more basic fact than this. Yet Piaget's research suggests that infants only gradually come to understand object permanence across the entire span of infancy.

Piaget described the development of object permanence in terms of the six-stage progression that characterize the sensorimotor period. During the first two substages—in the first 3 or 4 months—babies do not realize that objects exist apart from their own actions on those objects. If a toy drops out of sight, for example, the 4-month-old acts as though it no longer exists. The young infant will not search for a vanished object and turns instead to some other activity. At most, the baby may follow an object with her eyes or stare briefly at the place where an object has just disappeared.

It is only during the third substage, at about 4 to 8 months, that babies even begin to search for hidden objects. However, infants at this substage search only to the extent that part of the object remains visible. If only a small part of a sought-after toy is visible, the baby may sit perplexed. As soon as more of the object is revealed, however, the baby may happily reach out and retrieve it. Searching also is more likely if the infant's own action caused the object disappear. The baby who pushes a toy over the edge of the high chair may look down at the floor to find it, but if you do the pushing, the baby is less likely to search. For Piaget, this behavior is evidence that the infant's knowledge of the object still depends on his or her action on it.

Substage 4 marks an important step toward full object permanence. The infant now (at about 8 to 12 months) can search systematically and intelligently even for objects that are entirely hidden from view. The substage 4 infant also searches when the object disappears through some agency other than his or her own. Yet infants' understanding of permanence is still limited, especially when they must cope with more than one hiding place. Piaget might hide a toy under a pillow to his daughter's left two or three times, for

Object permanence

The knowledge that objects have a permanent existence that is independent of our perceptual contact with them; in Piaget's theory, a major achievement of the sensorimotor period.

This child is searching for a ball that her older sister rolled under the couch. Her behavior shows that she has mastered substage 5 of the phenomenon of object permanence. At that stage, how is the baby likely to respond if she sees her older sister hide the ball in a different location, and why? (©Myrleen Ferguson Cate/PhotoEdit)

A-not-B error
Infants' tendency to search in the original location in which an object was found rather than in its most recent hiding place; a characteristic of stage 4 of object permanence.

example, each time allowing her to retrieve it successfully. Then, with his daughter watching, he might hide the same toy under a blanket to her right. The baby would watch the toy disappear under the blanket and then turn and search under the pillow! What seemed to define the object was not its actual location, but the baby's previous success at finding it—it became "the thing that I found under the pillow." For Piaget, this behavior (called the **A-not-B error**) is evidence that even at substage 4, the baby's knowledge of objects is not freed from her own actions on them.

The infant eventually overcomes this limitation. The substage 5 infant (about 12 to 18 months) can handle the multiple-hiding-place problems that baffle a younger baby. But there is still one more limitation. The infant can handle these problems only if he or she can see the object's movements and disappearances in hiding places. If movements are not visible, the task involves what Piaget labeled *invisible displacements*, which substage 5 babies have difficulty solving. Piaget might hide a toy in his fist, for example, and then move his fist from one hiding place to another, and then show an empty fist. To infer the location of the hidden object, the infant must be able to represent the object when it is not visible. Solution of this problem is found only at substage 6, when infants develop the capacity for using *symbols*.

Decentering
Piaget's term for the gradual decline in egocentrism that occurs across development.

Egocentrism
In infancy, an inability to distinguish the self (e.g., one's actions or perceptions) from the outer world; in later childhood, an inability to distinguish one's own perspective (e.g., visual experience, thoughts, feelings) from that of others.

Invariants
Aspects of the world that remain the same even though other aspects have changed. In Piaget's theory, different forms of invariants are understood at different stages of development.

The work on object permanence illustrates two general themes in Piaget's approach to development. First, development is a process of progressive **decentering**—that is, infants gradually understand the world apart from themselves. According to Piaget, infants begin life in a state of profound **egocentrism;** that is, they cannot distinguish between themselves and the outer world. The newborn and the young infant simply do not know what is specific to the self (their own perceptions, actions, wishes, and so on) and what exists apart from the self. This egocentrism is seen in the first substages of object permanence, when objects exist for young babies only to the extent that they act on them. Only gradually does the infant decenter and grow more aware of both self and world.

The second theme in Piaget's approach is the importance of **invariants**—things that do not change—in development. We live in a world of constant flux, a world in which all sorts of things (what we can or cannot see, how things look, etc.) change from one moment to the next. Piaget maintained that one important kind of knowledge that the child must acquire is an understanding of what stays the same—remains constant or invariant—in the face of continual change. The first and most basic cognitive invariant, learned during the sensorimotor period, is object permanence—the realization that the existence of objects is invariant despite changes in our perceptual experience of them.

Testing Piaget: Recent Work on Infant Cognition

Piaget's studies continue to inspire much contemporary research on infant intelligence. Object permanence has been the most popular focus for such research, and replication studies have amply confirmed Piaget's claims about the kinds of errors infants make in searching for hidden objects (Harris, 1989). Nevertheless, many researchers have wondered if the infant's understanding is as limited as Piaget believed. For example, Piaget emphasized search behaviors in assessing object permanence—that is, behaviors such as lifting a cloth or pushing aside a screen. Might an infant know perfectly well that an object still exists but simply fail to show the kinds of active search behaviors that Piaget required? How else might we assess what infants know about objects?

Violation of Expectancy Method   The most informative approach has made use of a variation on the habituation phenomenon described in Chapter 1. *Habituation*, you may recall, refers to a decline in response to a repeated stimulus. Conversely, *dishabituation* refers to the recovery of response when the stimulus changes Think now of a magic show in which you watch the magician make a person disappear. Absolutely fascinating, right? Studies investigating infants' object knowledge have capitalized on the same tendency that causes you to watch every instant of a magic show. Infants, too, prefer to look not only at novel stimuli but at events that they do not expect to see, a method known as the *violation of expectancy* paradigm (Spelke, 1985). Researchers can observe infants' increased attention when their expectations of reality are violated and thus can gain insight into infants' knowledge of the world.

Representing Hidden Objects   A study by Renée Baillargeon (1987a) provides an example of infants' understanding of object permanence using the violation of expectancy method. In Baillargeon's study, babies first saw a screen that rotated, like a drawbridge, though a 180-degree arc (see Figure 7.1*a*). Although this event was initially quite interesting, after a number of repetitions the babies' attention dropped off, showing that they had habituated to the rotation. At this point researchers placed a wooden box directly in the path of the screen (see Figure 7.1*b*). Although the baby could see the box at the start of a trial, the box disappeared from view once the screen had rotated straight up. On some trials, babies saw a "possible event" (Figure 7.1*c*): the screen rotated to the point at which it should hit the box and then stopped—as indeed it should since a solid object was in its path. On other trials, babies saw an "impossible event" (Figure 7.1*b*): the screen rotated to the point of contact with the box and then kept going through its full 180-degree arc! (This outcome was made possible by a hidden platform that dropped the box out of the way.)

Any adult confronted with such an event would probably be quite surprised because he or she would know that the box still existed behind the screen, even though it could no longer be seen. Infants as young as 4.5 months apparently possess the same knowledge. Their attention did not increase when they viewed the possible event; looking times increased greatly, however, when the screen appeared to pass magically through a solid object. The most obvious explanation for such recovery of interest (dishabituation) is that the infants knew that the box must still exist and therefore expected the screen to stop.

Young infants may also know something about the properties of hidden objects. In a further experiment, Baillargeon (1987b) replaced the box with a squishy foam block. Infants did not recover interest in the continued rotation of the screen through the foam block, as they had with the hard box. Thus, they retained information not only about the presence of the hidden object but also about the fact that it was squishy and could thus be compressed by the rotating screen.

Not all researchers of infancy have been persuaded that studies such as Baillargeon's demonstrate object permanence months earlier than Piaget believed (Bogartz, Shinskey, & Schilling, 2000; Haith, 1998; Haith & Benson, 1998). Some have argued that correct responses may not really reflect knowledge of hidden objects. In the drawbridge study, for example, infants may look longer at the 180-degree screen rotation because they find the movement of the screen inherently interesting (Rivera, Wakeley, & Langer, 1999). Others suggest that infants retain a short-lived perceptual image of the vanished object rather than a full-blown object representation. Their increased attention thus comes from the mismatch between the perceptual image and the test event the infant is currently viewing rather than from a violation of the principle of object permanence (Meltzoff & Moore, 1999a). Though most would agree that Piaget underestimated infants' abilities to some degree, no study to date has contradicted his claim that active search behaviors for hidden objects do not

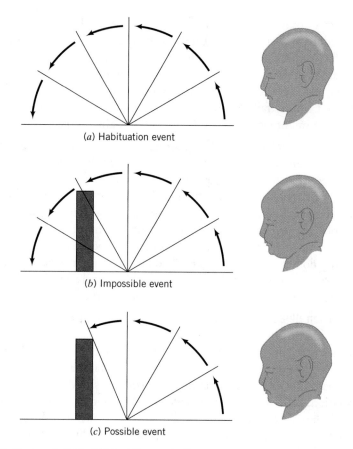

(a) Habituation event

(b) Impossible event

(c) Possible event

FIGURE 7.1   Baillargeon's Test of Object Permanence

Infants were first habituated to the event shown in (a), in which a screen rotates through a 180-degree arc. Then responses were measured to either the possible event (c), in which the screen stops where it hits an obstacle, or the impossible event (b), in which the screen appears to move through the area occupied by the box. At what age did infants respond to the impossible event?

Source: Adapted from R. Baillargeon. (1987). Object permanence in 3½-and 4½-month-old infants. *Developmental Psychology, 23*, 656. Copyright 1987 by the American Psychological Association. Adapted by permission.

appear until 8 or 9 months of age. Why babies' ability to organize intelligent behaviors lags so far behind its first appearance in violation of expectancy studies is one of the most intriguing questions in modern infancy research (Bertenthal, 1996; Munakata et al., 1997).

Deferred Imitation   In his sensorimotor studies Piaget also explored the development of imitation. He reported that imitation, like other sensorimotor accomplishments, begins with rudimentary and limited forms early in life and slowly progresses toward the skilled behavioral system of the toddler or preschool child. Imitative behavior in the first 6 or 8 months, according to Piaget, consists only of behaviors that infants already produce spontaneously and can see and hear themselves perform. Piaget argued that babies could not engage in **deferred imitation**—that is, imitating an action seen in the past—until well into the second year of life. This inability, he believed, was simply another manifestation of the sensorimotor child's inability to mentally represent objects and events in the absence of current sensory or motor input.

Recent research, however, reveals that infants' imitative abilities are substantially more sophisticated and emerge much earlier than Piaget believed. In one demonstration, Andrew Meltzoff and Keith Moore (1994) allowed babies only 6 weeks old to watch as an experimenter demonstrated a novel behavior: sticking his tongue out to the side. Infants not only imitated the action when they first viewed it, but also 24 hours later when they again viewed the (now still-faced) experimenter. Deferred imitation becomes rapidly more sophisticated. By 6 to 9 months, infants imitate not just facial gestures but also

Deferred imitation
Imitation of a model observed some time in the past.

simple actions on objects that they saw an adult perform a day earlier (Hayne, Boniface, & Barr, 2000). For example, Meltzoff (1988) allowed 9-month-old babies to watch as an adult pressed a button to sound a beeper, pushed an upright hinged board so that it folded flat, and rattled an orange plastic egg. Although the babies had never before played with these objects themselves, they nonetheless repeated the actions they had seen the day before. Babies even imitated the actions when they saw the adult model only on a TV monitor! Infants can imitate previously seen actions and must thus mentally represent those actions far earlier than Piaget suspected.

Learning Objective 7.2: *Trace the substages and benchmarks of the sensorimotor period in child development.*

1. What distinguishes the first two substages of Piaget's sensorimotor period of cognitive development?
2. What roles do schemes and procedures play in cognitive development?
3. When during infancy does intentional behavior develop?
4. What role do mental representations play in cognitive development?
5. What is object permanence, and how do infants develop this and other physical knowledge?
6. How do contemporary studies inform Piaget's classic work on cognitive development in infancy?

✔ *Test Your Mastery...*

Thought in the Preschooler: The Preoperational Period

The preoperational period extends from about age 2 to about age 6. Keep in mind that Piagetian age norms are always rough guidelines. Any individual child may develop more quickly or more slowly than the average. Keep in mind, too, that children's thinking is a mixture of competence and limitations, with surprisingly adult-like abilities on the one hand and glaring, hard-to-believe errors on the other. At no other time during development is this mixture quite so striking or so challenging to explain as during the preoperational period. Some of the most fascinating contemporary research in child psychology is directed at exploring the mysteries of the preoperational mind.

Learning Objective 7.3
Identify some strengths and limitations of preoperational thought in children's cognitive development.

Symbolic Function

The defining characteristic of the movement from the sensorimotor to the preoperational period is the onset of representational ability, or what Piaget called *symbolic function*. Piaget defined **symbolic function** as the ability to use one thing to represent something else—that is, to use one thing as a symbol to stand for some other thing, which is then symbolized. Symbols can take a variety of forms. They can be motor movements, or they can be mental images, as may have been the case when Jacqueline thought through the blades-of-grass door-opening problem. Symbols can be physical objects, as when a 3-year-old rides a broom as if it were a horse. And, of course, symbols can be words.

Piaget (1951) cited five kinds of behavior that become evident at the end of infancy, all of which seem to require representational ability and none of which he had observed earlier in infancy. Two of these behaviors are the internal problem solving of substage 6 in the sensorimotor period and the ability to handle invisible displacement versions of the object permanence problem. Perhaps the most striking evidence for representational functioning, discussed in Chapter 10, is the first appearance of words. Although children often say their first words well before the beginning of the preoperational period, Piaget stressed that words take on a truly symbolic function only when children can talk about objects and events even when they are not visible.

A fourth sign is the appearance of *deferred imitation*. Although babies imitate from early in life, they can at first imitate only models that are directly in front of them. Only near the end of infancy, according to Piaget, does the baby begin to imitate models from the past—for example, some behavior that an older sibling performed the week before.

Symbolic function
The ability to use one thing (such as a mental image or word) as a symbol to represent something else.

Links to Related Material
In Chapter 10, you will learn how children's increased representational abilities, which are a hallmark of preoperational thought, are tied to the explosion in language development that also occurs around this age.

The ability to imitate behavior from the past clearly implies the capacity to store memories of that behavior in some representational form, though as you have read, Piaget may have underestimated children's ability to engage in deferred imitation during the sensorimotor period.

Emergence of Symbolic Play Piaget's fifth hallmark of the symbolic function, familiar to any parent, is the emergence of *symbolic play*. The preoperational child can deliberately use one object as a stand-in for another. Sticks turn into boats, sand piles into cakes, cushions into castles, and brooms into horses. **Symbolic play** becomes rapidly more sophisticated during the preoperational period as children's symbolic function develops. At first, children can pretend only with objects that bear some resemblance to the actual thing—pretending that a toy phone is a real phone, for example. Later, physical resemblance becomes less important. A child might pretend a banana is a phone. Still later, the child needs no actual object at all—she can pretend to use a phone by simply enacting the gestures we use to pick up and speak into a telephone! Pretend play sequences become more sophisticated as well. A young preoperational child might simply pretend to eat a piece of toy food or put a doll to sleep. The older child can enact an entire sequence—feeding herself and the doll dinner, preparing the doll for a nap, reading the doll a story, and eventually tucking her into bed.

Symbolic Advances of Early Childhood Recent research on children's understanding of symbolic representation has confirmed that infants differ dramatically from young children in symbolic competence. For example, although infants can recognize the correspondence between object and picture, they apparently do not yet realize that a picture is simply a symbolic depiction of the real thing. A 9-month-old presented with a realistic color photograph of an object pats and rubs the photo as though it were the object itself (DeLoache et al., 1998). By 19 months this confusion has disappeared, and pointing and vocalizing replace manual exploration. Similarly, 18-month-olds do not care whether the picture they are viewing is right side up or upside down, but by 30 months a preference for upright orientation has emerged (DeLoache, Uttal, & Pierroutsakos, 2000).

Children who have just entered Piaget's preoperational period, in contrast to younger infants, have developed still more sophisticated understanding of symbols. They begin to appreciate that the person who creates a symbol determines its meaning. Three- and 4-year-old children take into account the artist's intent when identifying a picture (Bloom

Symbolic play
Form of play in which the child uses one thing in deliberate pretense to stand for something else.

Representational behavior, such as symbolic play, is a hallmark of the preoperational stage of cognitive development. The emergence of symbolic play is one of the clearest signs of the preoperational child's representational skills. What are some other examples of the role of representation in the development of cognitive abilities? (Ellen B. Senisi/The Image Works)

& Markson, 1998; Browne & Woolley, 2001). When presented, for example, with a drawing of a stick with an oval on top, they label it as either *lollipop* or *balloon*, depending on what they have been told the artist intended to draw, and they may vigorously object to the other (objectively equally valid) interpretation.

The preschool child also begins to master conventional symbol systems, such as maps and scale models (Huttenlocher, Newcombe, & Vasilyeva, 1999; Uttal, 2000). Consider an experiment involving a hide-and-seek game (DeLoache, 2000, 2002; DeLoache, Miller, & Rosengren, 1997; DeLoache & Smith, 1999). An experimenter hides a Snoopy doll somewhere in the room, and the child's job is to find Snoopy. As Figure 7.2 shows, the room offers a number of possible hiding places. The experimenter also shows the child a scale model of the room that reproduces all of its features in miniature, including a miniature Snoopy. The experimenter explains that the Little Snoopy will be hidden in the same place in his little room as Big Snoopy is hiding in his big room. Can children use this symbolic equivalence to solve the task? By 3 years of age they can: Once they see Little Snoopy disappear into his hiding place, they run immediately to the matching place in the real room to find Big Snoopy.

In contrast to the impressive symbolic competence of the 3-year-old, children just a few months younger are strikingly unable to solve the Snoopy task. Deloache suggests that younger children lack **dual representation**—the realization that an object can be represented in two ways simultaneously. In the find-Snoopy task, the model room and its miniature snoopy are symbols of the larger room, but they are also objects themselves. Two-year-olds apparently cannot appreciate this dual status. This current research thus illustrates the limitations of the newly preoperational child's symbol use.

Dual representation
The realization that an object can be represented in two ways simultaneously.

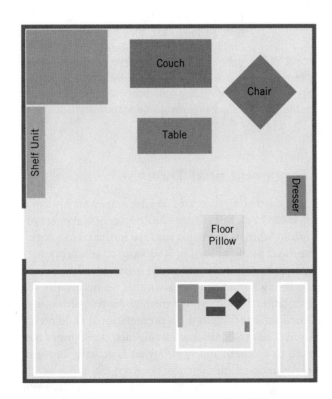

Figure 7.2   Where's Snoopy? Testing young children's symbolic abilities.

This is the experimental arrangement that the DeLoache research team used in their study of early symbolic ability. The colored areas in the scale model correspond to the labeled items of furniture in the room. By age 3, children shown on the scale model where a doll is hidden can find the doll in the equivalent place in the room.

SOURCE: From J. S. DeLoache. (1989). Young children's understanding of the correspondence between a scale model and a larger space. *Cognitive Development, 4,* 125. Copyright 1989 by Ablex Pubishing Company. Reprinted by permission.

BOX 7.1   Selecting Developmentally Appropriate Play Materials

What is a good toy? According to the American Academy of Pediatrics (Glassy & Romano, 2003), the best toys are safe, affordable, appeal over a period of time, and stimulate the young child's imagination. Good toys also bring children and parents together in play.

Consider two toys that a 1-year-old might receive for her birthday. One is a relatively expensive doll that lights up and makes dancing motions when the hand is squeezed. The other is a relatively inexpensive toy phone. Although both toys are safe, and relative expense is already clearly stated, which best meets the criteria of appealing over time and stimulating the imagination? The answer may be surprising. Although at first visually captivating, a pricey doll that lights up and dances when squeezed in fact has relatively little lasting appeal, and very little ability to stimulate the imagination. The toy phone, on the other hand, stimulates imitation, role-playing, and the beginnings of pretend play, and may be used effectively by infants and young children of different ages. Moreover, a toy phone can be used interactively with adults in a turn-taking game in which the adult scaffolds simple phone conversations for the child. Other examples of affordable toys for infants that are enduring and stimulate active exploration and imaginative play include a simple set of brightly colored stacking cups, plastic pop-beads, or a shape-sorter with a removable lid.

According to the American Academy of Pediatrics (Glassy & Romano, 2003), parents should be skeptical of toys that claim to enhance specific intellectual abilities. Toys that promote the use of the imagination and further development in a variety of ways are to be preferred. For example, versatile toys such as blocks, legos, a tambourine and maracas, play-doh, simple art supplies, plastic dishes, a tricycle, and dress-up clothes provide preschoolers with multiple opportunities for role-playing, exploration, and creativity.

Toys should not be used as a substitute for loving attention from parents and other adults. Learning through play materials is enhanced when adults join in play. Parents can observe the child's current skills and focus the interaction in such a way as to enhance those skills (Glassy & Romano, 2003). For example, while playing with blocks with their 18-month-old, parents can introduce the idea that blocks can be used not only to build towers, but also to represent a breakfast of toast and scrambled eggs.

The American Academy of Pediatrics also warns that some toys may pose social and emotional risks. Toys that encourage violence or aggression should be avoided, as should toys that promote negative racial, cultural, ethnic, or gender stereotypes. Parents should monitor and restrict the amount of time that children spend on computer and video games (which often contain interactive violence).

Finally, the American Academy of Pediatrics stresses that, despite the claims of some toy manufacturers, no toy is necessary or sufficient for optimal learning to occur (Glassy & Romano, 2003). Good toys do not have to be trendy or expensive. At their best, toys serve a supportive role in enhancing a child's development. Warm, loving interaction with attentive parents and other caretakers remains primary.

For a complete copy of the American Academy of Pediatrics' policy statement on selecting toys for young children, see *http://www.aappolicy.aappublications.org.*

Questions for Thought and Discussion
What were your favorite toys as a child? What made them developmentally appropriate for you?

Strengths of Preoperational Thought

In Piaget's theory, the cognitive structures of later stages are always more powerful and more adaptive than those of earlier stages. Consequently, the onset of symbolic function (or *representational thought*) marks a major advance in the child's cognitive abilities. Representational, in-the-head problem solving is superior to sensorimotor problem solving in a number of ways. Representational intelligence is considerably faster and more efficient. Rather than actually trying out all possible solutions—a necessarily slow and error-prone process—the representational child can try them out internally, using mental representations rather than literal actions. When the representational child acts, the solution can be immediate and adaptive. Representational intelligence is also more mobile. Sensorimotor intelligence is limited to the here and now—what is actually in front of the child to be acted on. With representational intelligence, however, the child can think about the past and imagine the future. The scope of cognitive activity is thus enormously expanded.

Representational thought is also socially sharable in a way that sensorimotor thought is not. With the acquisition of language, the child can communicate ideas to others and receive information from them in ways that are not possible without language. Piaget's theory does not place as much stress on either language or cultural transmission as do many other theories. Nevertheless, he consistently cited social experience as one of the factors that account for development (Piaget, 1983). And both the extent and the nature of social experience change greatly once the child has entered the preoperational period.

The preoperational period is also a time when children acquire new cognitive abilities. For example, the child develops a form of knowledge that Piaget labeled **qualitative identity** (Piaget, 1968). Qualitative identity refers to the realization that the basic nature of something is not changed by changes in its appearance. It is the realization, for example, that a wire remains the same wire even after it has been bent into a different shape, or that water remains the same water even though it may look different after being spilled from a glass. Qualitative identity, like object permanence, reflects a central Piagetian theme: the importance of mastering invariants in the environment.

Limitations of Preoperational Thought

Despite the positive features just noted, Piaget focused primarily on the limitations, rather than the strengths, of preoperational thought. The weaknesses all stem from the fact that the child is attempting to operate on a new plane of cognitive functioning, that of representational intelligence. Although young children can think symbolically, their abilities to logically manipulate these mental symbols are quite limited. Hence the term *preoperational*—to refer to the fact that the child lacks the mental "operations" that allow logical, effective representational problem solving.

Egocentrism **Egocentrism** and centration are two limitations in the thinking of the preoperational child. Recall that a major achievement of the sensorimotor period is the gradual decentering through which the infant distinguishes the self from material objects in the external world. The preoperational period begins in a state of mental egocentrism. In Piaget's view, the young preoperational child has only a limited ability to represent the psychological experiences of others—to break away from his or her own perspective to take the perspective or point of view of someone else. Instead, the young child often acts as though everyone shares his particular point of view—sees what he sees, feels what he feels, knows what he knows, and so on. Egocentrism thus means difficulty in taking the point of view of another (not egotism or selfishness).

Preoperational egocentrism is evident in children's speech. Piaget's first book, *The Language and Thought of the Child* (1926), examined both naturally occurring conversations between children and experimentally elicited speech of various sorts. Piaget found that children's speech was often jumbled and hard to decipher, even when they clearly were trying their best to communicate. Figure 7.3 presents some examples from an experiment in which children attempted to retell a story (the phrases in brackets are Piaget's comments on their efforts). Piaget attributed such **egocentric speech** to the young child's basic cognitive egocentrism. Young children often fail to assume the perspective of their listener, acting instead as though the listener already knows everything that they know. Certainly, anyone will agree who has listened to a 3-year-old relate the events of her day!

Perspective-Taking Abilities Piaget also studied the child's ability to assume the visual perspective of another (Piaget & Inhelder, 1956). The best-known task for studying such visual perspective taking is the *three-mountains problem* pictured in Figure 7.4. After walking around the display, the child sits on one side and the researchers then move a doll to various locations around the board. The child's task is to indicate what the doll would see from the different locations. For many young children, the answer is clear: The doll would see exactly what they see. Again, the young child acts as though his or her own perspective is the only one possible.

Centration Another limitation of preoperational thought is the young child's tendency to focus on only one aspect of a problem at a time. This tendency is called **centration**. As an example, consider a famous Piagetian task—the conservation of matter problem. **Conservation** is the realization that the basic quantitative properties of objects—their number, length, mass, weight, and so on—are not changed by changes in their appearance or location (see Figure 7.5).

Qualitative identity
The knowledge that the qualitative nature of something is not changed by a change in its appearance. In Piaget's theory, a preoperational achievement.

Egocentrism
A self-centered view of the world in which preoperational children have only a limited ability to represent the psychological experiences of others.

Egocentric speech
In Piaget's theory, the tendency for preoperational children to assume that listeners know everything that they know, revealing difficulty with perspective taking.

Centration
Piaget's term for the young child's tendency to focus on only one aspect of a problem at a time, a perceptually biased form of responding that often results in incorrect judgments.

Conservation
The knowledge that the quantitative properties of an object or collection of objects are not changed by a change in appearance; in Piaget's theory, a concrete operational achievement.

STORY PRESENTATION

Once upon a time, there was a lady who was called Niobe, and who had 12 sons and daughters. She met a fairy who had only one son and no daughter. Then the lady laughed at the fairy because the fairy only had one boy. Then the fairy was very angry and fastened the lady to a rock. The lady cried for 10 years. In the end she turned to a rock, and her tears made a stream which still runs today.

EXAMPLES OF CHILDREN'S REPRODUCTIONS

Met (6 years 4 months), talking of Niobe: "The lady laughed at this fairy because she [who?] only had one boy. The lady had 12 sons and 12 daughters. One day she [who?] laughed at her [at whom?]. She [who?] was angry and she [who?] fastened her beside a stream. She [?] cried for 50 months, and it made a great big stream." Impossible to tell who fastened, and who was fastened. Gio (8 years old): "Once upon a time there was a lady who had 12 boys and 12 girls, and then a fairy a boy and a girl. And then Niobe wanted to have some more sons [than the fairy. Gio means by this that Niobe competed with the fairy, as was told in the text. But it will be seen how elliptical is his way in expressing it]. Then she [who?] was angry. She [who?] fastened her [whom?] to a stone. He [who?] turned into a rock, and then his tears [whose?] made a stream which is still running today."

FIGURE 7.3   Children Retell a Story: Examples of Egocentric Speech

Source: Adapted from J. Piaget. (1926). *The Language and Thought of the Child*. New York: Harcourt Brace, pp. 99, 116, 121. Adapted by permission.

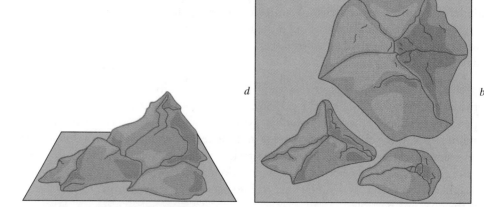

FIGURE 7.4   Piaget's Three Mountains Experiment

To assess children's ability to take the perspective of another, Piaget asked them to judge how this landscape would look to someone viewing it from another vantage point. What limitation of preoperational thought does this experiment address? What were the results? At about what age are children capable of perspective taking?

Source: Based on J. Piaget and B. Inhelder. (1956). *The Child's Conception of Space*. London: Routledge and Kegan Paul.

In the first example in Figure 7.5, the conservation of number problem, children view two rows of five chips (Piaget & Szeminska, 1952). As long as the chips are arranged in one-to-one correspondence, even a 3- or 4-year-old can tell us that the two rows have the same number of objects. But if, while the child watches, you spread out one of the rows so that it is longer than the other, virtually every 3- and 4-year old will say that the longer row now has more chips. Asked why, the child finds the answer obvious—because it is longer. In Piaget's terms, the child's attention is *centered* on the length of the row, leading to the failure to conserve the number.

Centration, then, is a perceptually biased form of responding characteristic of young children. For the preschooler, what seems critical is how things look at the moment. The child's attention is captured by the most salient, or noticeable, element of the display, which in the number task is the length of the rows. Once his or her attention has been captured, the child finds it difficult to take account of other information—for example, the fact that the rows differ not only in length but also in density. Thus the child is easily fooled by appearance and often, as in the conservation task, arrives at the wrong answer.

Focus on Appearances Centration also leads to another striking limitation in preoperational children's thought—the inability to dinstinguish appearance from reality. A striking example is found in Rhetta DeVries's "Maynard the Cat" study (1969). DeVries first introduced preschoolers to a friendly black cat named Maynard. She then transformed Maynard by putting a realistic and fierce-looking dog mask on him. When DeVries asked children what kind of animal Maynard was following the transformation, young children emphatically maintained that Maynard was now a dog, who would bark and eat dog food! Their centered thinking led them to focus exclusively on Maynard's current, dog-like perceptual features. Not until the end of the preoperational period around age 5 or 6 did children appreciate that although Maynard now *appeared* to be a dog, he was *really* still a cat.

According to Piaget, the surprising limitations in preschoolers' thinking stems from their inability to operate logically on their mental representations. They are unable, for example, to mentally reverse a transformation such as spreading out a row or coins or

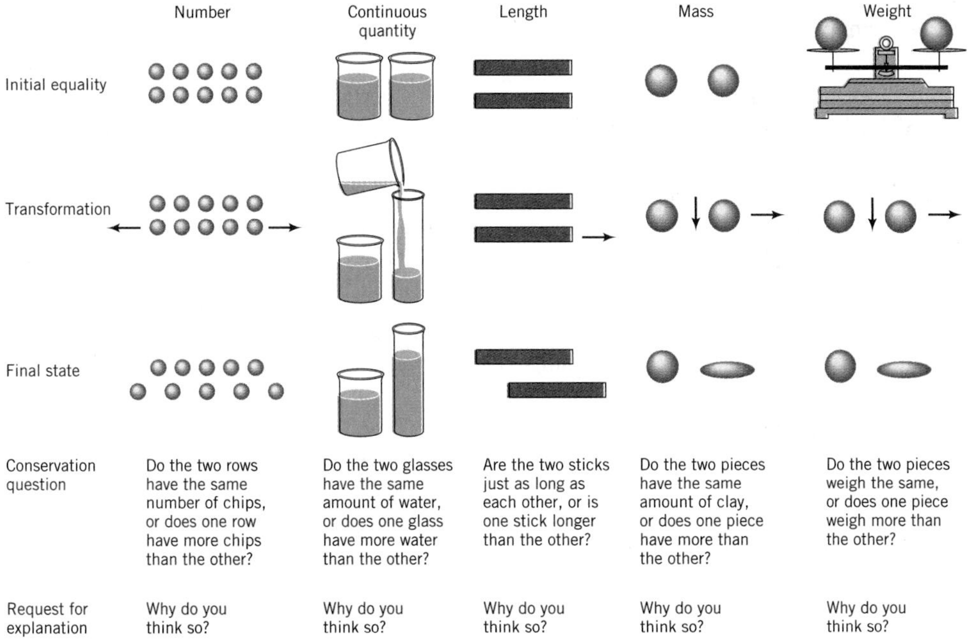

Questions for Thought
and Discussion
Are adults also sometimes egocentric and centered in their thinking? What are some examples from your own experience and observation?

FIGURE 7.5 Examples of Conservation Problems

These are some of Piaget's experiments to test children's ability to overcome centration as a limitation of preoperational thought. He found that children can solve conservation problems only toward the end of the preoperational stage of cognitive development at around age 5.

placing a dog mask on a cat to realize that these transformations do not affect numerical or biological identity. As we shall see, the transition into the next stage of thinking represents a major advance in the ability to engage in mental operations.

Test Your Mastery...

Learning Objective 7.3: *Identify some strengths and limitations of preoperational thought in children's cognitive development.*

1. How is preoperational thinking an advance over sensorimotor cognitive functioning?
2. What cognitive abilities does the child acquire during the preoperational stage?
3. What are two significant limitations of preoperational thinking?
4. What experiments did Piaget use to test the strengths and limitations of young children's thinking?

Middle-Childhood Intelligence: The Concrete Operational Period

Learning Objective 7.4
Analyze the cognitive task masteries that characterize concrete operational thought.

Operations
Piaget's term for the various forms of mental action through which older children solve problems and reason logically.

Decentration
The ability to keep in mind multiple aspects of a situation simultaneously.

Reversibility
Piaget's term for the power of operations to correct for potential disturbances and thus arrive at correct solutions to problems.

The concrete operational period spans middle childhood, from about age 6 to about age 11 or 12. The cognitive differences between preschoolers and grade-schoolers make up a long list of contrasts (Flavell et al., 2002; Ginsburg & Opper, 1988). To sum up these differences, however, the older child is more *logical*. This is not to say that preschoolers are totally illogical. Their attempts at logical reasoning are inconsistent, working impressively in some contexts but going badly astray in others. Preschoolers seem to lack an encompassing logical mental system that they can apply with confidence to a wide range of problems, particularly the kinds of scientific problems that Piaget stressed. The older child, in contrast, does possess such a system.

The Concept of Operations

Piaget's goal was to use children's overt performance as a guide to their underlying cognitive structures. During middle childhood, these structures are labeled *concrete operations*. By **operations**, Piaget meant mental activities such as reversing, combining, or separating information in a logical fashion. Children gradually organize these operations into larger systems of interrelated cognitive structures, which permits increasingly sophisticated thought. In this way the concept of operations is similar to Piaget's concept of sensorimotor schemes. However, whereas sensorimotor schemes are expressed in external actions—such as reaching, grasping, or manipulating—operations, in contrast, are a system of internal, mental actions that support logical thought.

A primary feature of concrete operational thought is **decentration**: the ability to keep in mind multiple aspects of a situation simultaneously. Children are now able to appreciate, for example, that while some features of a problem may change, others remain constant—that is, they appreciate the concept of *identity*. They can also mentally reverse transformations rather than focus exclusively on current appearances. Piaget referred to this mental operation as **reversibility**. These new mental skills permit the concrete operational child to successfully solve the problems that preoperational children fail.

One of the most basic forms of conservation is the conservation of quantity. To realize that the amount of liquid is the same in the two containers, the child must avoid centering on the misleading appearance caused by the different shapes of the containers. This concrete operational 6-year-old has no trouble with this conservation task. (©Elizabeth Crews)

Conservation

Recall the conservation of mass, weight, and volume; of length, area, and distance; and of time, speed, and movement illustrated in Figure 7.5 (Piaget, 1969, 1970; Piaget & Inhelder, 1974; Piaget, Inhelder, & Szeminska, 1960). In each case, to conserve the quantity, the child must be able to overcome the misleading, perceptual appearance. Preoperational children's centered thinking leads them to erroneously focus exclusively on salient, but misleading, perceptual appearances. As a result, they fail to conserve. Concrete operational children, in contrast, can accurately represent and operate on each aspect of the transformation. They appreciate, for example, that while the length of a row has increased, density has decreased, and the numerical identity remains constant as a result. School-age children also appeal to the fact that such transformations are reversible and thus do not affect identity.

Despite this qualitative improvement in children's thinking, Piaget appreciated that gradual improvements occur throughout the concrete operational period. Children master different forms of conservation at different times. Conservation of number is typically one of the first to be acquired, appearing by about age 5 or 6. Conservation of mass and conservation of continuous quantity are also relatively early achievements. Conservation of length and conservation of weight are more difficult, typically coming two or three years after the first conservations, and other forms of conservation emerge still later.

The transformations children confront in conservation tasks are examples of invariants; the quantities do not change. During the sensorimotor period, the infant masters the invariant of object permanence—the knowledge that existence is a given. During the preoperational period, the child comes to understand qualitative identity—the knowledge that the qualitative nature of objects remains the same. During the concrete operational period, the child masters the various forms of conservation—the knowledge that quantitative properties of objects are invariant.

Relational Reasoning: Class Inclusion and Seriation

The preoperational child can identify objects as instances of particular categories or classes. He or she can, for example, identify a never before seen dog as belonging to the category *dog*. Preoperational children do not, however, appreciate the hierarchical relationships among categories—that a poodle, for example, is a member not only of the category *dog*, but also the categories *poodle*, *mammal*, *animal*, and *object*. The best-known task for probing the child's understanding of categories is the **class inclusion** problem. Suppose that you present a child with 20 wooden beads, 17 red and 3 white. The child agrees that some of the beads are red, some are white, and all are wooden. Then ask the child if there are more red beads or more wooden beads. Or ask which would make a longer necklace, all the red beads or all the wooden beads?

However you word the question, the preoperational child will respond that there are more red beads than wooden beads. Young children apparently cannot think about a bead as belonging simultaneously to both a subclass (all the red ones) and a superordinate class (all the wooden ones). Instead, once the child has centered on the perceptually salient subclass—the many red beads—the only comparison left is with the other subclass—the few white beads. She cannot appreciate the *relation* between classes. The result is that the child makes a fundamental logical error and judges that a subclass is larger than its superordinate class. The concrete operational child, on the other hand, can solve this and other versions of the class inclusion problem. Furthermore, this child appreciates the logical necessity of the class inclusion answer. The child knows that it is logically impossible for a subclass to be larger than the superordinate class (Miller, 1986).

Another Piagetian task having to do with relational reasoning is the **seriation** task (Piaget & Szeminska, 1952). To study seriation, you might present 10 randomly assorted sticks of different lengths. The child's task is to order the sticks by length. You might expect that any persistent child eventually will solve the problem through trial and error. Yet most young children cannot do it. They may end up with two or three groups of "big" and "little" sticks, or they may line up the tops of the sticks but completely ignore the bottoms. They also cannot correctly insert new sticks into a completed array. Seriation requires that the child appreciate multiple relations among the sticks: each stick is simultaneously longer than the one that precedes it in seriation and shorter than the one that comes after it. The concrete operational child can hold these relationships in mind in a way that the preoperational child cannot.

Questions for Thought
and Discussion

What are some examples of real-life situations in which young children might make errors in conservation?

Class inclusion
The knowledge that a subclass cannot be larger than the superordinate class that includes it; in Piaget's theory, a concrete operational achievement.

In his sorting of similar objects, this 8-year-old enjoys solving problems of seriation and class inclusion. Understanding the nature of classes is an important achievement of the concrete operational period. (Michael Newman/PhotoEdit)

Seriation
The ability to order stimuli along some quantitative dimension, such as length; in Piaget's theory, a concrete operational achievement.

Transitivity
The ability to combine relations logically to deduce necessary conclusions—for example, if A > B and B > C, then A > C. In Piaget's theory, a concrete operational achievement.

Questions for Thought and Discussion
Children who solve problems quicker are generally viewed as more intelligent, but this value placed on speed is not universal. What other cognitive values may differ from culture to culture?

The operational child also appreciates the **transitivity** of quantitative relations (Piaget et al., 1960). Suppose you work with three sticks—A, B, and C—that differ only slightly in length. Show the child that A is longer than B (A > B) and that B is longer than C (B > C). Then ask about the relative lengths of A and C, but do not allow the child to compare them perceptually. Solving this task requires the ability to add together the two premises (A > B and B > C) to deduce the correct answer (A > C). By around age 7 or 8, the concrete operational child has this ability. In both transitivity and class inclusion, the correct answer follows as a logically necessary result of the information available.

These relational abilities are evidence of *operational* thought, a major advance of the concrete operational stage. As you have seen, the concrete operational child, in contrast to the preoperational child, operates cognitively by means of logical manipulation of mental representations. The term *concrete*, on the other hand, characterizes the basic limitation of concrete operational thought. Concrete operational children are limited to the representation of transformations and relations between objects that are directly in front of them—that which is concrete, tangible, real. What the child at this stage cannot yet do well is deal with the hypothetical—with the whole world of possibility rather than immediate reality. In the next stage of cognitive development, formal operational thinkers show no such limitation.

Testing Piaget: Operational vs. Preoperational Differences

Recent research suggests that young children's thinking is really more advanced than Piaget claimed and that the differences between early childhood and later childhood are not so great. Piaget frequently relied on unfamiliar, contrived tasks that are highly unfamiliar to most children. Furthermore, successful performance often requires sophisticated verbal competence—both to understand the problem and to provide the correct response—that most young children lack. In challenging Piaget, researchers have employed tasks that simplify the problem for children but nonetheless test the same cognitive skill that Piaget sought to target. Such strategies have revealed that young children are not as hopelessly illogical as Piaget once believed.

Preoperational Perspective Taking Children as young as 3 can predict the other's viewpoint when familiar toys rather than Piagetian mountains serve as landmarks (Borke, 1975). Even 2-year-olds can demonstrate some awareness of the other's viewpoint in very simple situations. When asked to show another person a picture, for example, 2-year-olds hold the picture vertically so that its face is toward the viewer rather than toward the self (Lempers, Flavell, & Flavell, 1977). Similarly, 2-year-olds realize (popular myth notwithstanding) that the fact that *their* eyes are closed does not mean that other people also cannot see (Flavell, Shipstead, & Croft, 1980). Even 18-month-olds will point to objects that they want an adult to notice, a behavior that suggests some realization that the adult does not necessarily see what they see (Rheingold, Hay, & West, 1976). Children's ability to tailor their speech to the needs of others also turns out to be more advanced than one would expect from Piaget's accounts of egocentric speech. Four-year-olds use simpler speech when talking to 2-year-olds than when talking either to other 4-year-olds or to adults (Shatz & Gelman, 1973). Thus, they adjust the level of their communication to the cognitive resources of the listener. Even 2-year-olds talk differently to their infant siblings than to adults (Dunn & Kendrick, 1982).

Children can also adjust to temporary variations in what the listener knows, as opposed to the general differences that exist between babies and adults. They describe an event differently, for example, depending on whether the adult to whom they are talking was present when the event occurred (Menig-Peterson, 1975). They also make different inferences about what listeners know, and they structure their communications differently in response to differences in listeners' past experiences (O'Neill, 1996).

Preoperational Conservation As with perspective taking, investigators have simplified the conservation task in various ways. They have reduced the usual verbal demands, for example, by allowing the child to pick candies to eat or juice to drink rather than answer questions about "same" or "more." Or they have made the context for the question more natural and familiar by embedding the task within an ongoing game. Although such changes do not eliminate the nonconservation error completely, they often result in improved performance by supposedly preoperational 4- and 5-year-olds (Donaldson, 1982; Miller, 1976, 1982). In simple situations, even 3-year-olds can demonstrate some knowledge of the invariance of number.

In one study (Gelman, 1972), the 3-year-old participants first played a game in which they learned, over a series of trials, that a plate with a row of three toy mice affixed to it was a "winner" and a plate with two toy mice was a "loser." Then, in a critical test trial, the three-mice plate was secretly transformed while hidden. In some cases the length of the row was changed; in other cases one of the mice was removed. The children were unfazed by the change in length, continuing to treat the plate as a winner. Any change in number, however, elicited surprise, search behaviors, and various attempts at an explanation. The children thus showed recognition that number, at least in this situation, should remain invariant.

Learning Objective 7.4: *Analyze the cognitive task masteries that characterize concrete operational thought.*

1. What did Piaget mean by operations?
2. How is operational thinking different from preoperational thinking?
3. How do concrete operational children perform on problems of conservation and classification?
4. How do seriation and transitivity tasks reveal the relational logic used by concrete operational thinkers?
5. What evidence suggests that Piaget underestimated the operational competence of preschool-age children on tasks involving perspective taking and conservation?

✔ *Test Your Mastery...*

Adolescent and Adult: The Formal Operational Period

Formal operations follows concrete operations and is the final period in Piaget's stage hierarchy. Piaget believed that individuals remain at this stage, once achieved, throughout their lives. Children enter formal operations around the age of 12 or 13, at the beginning of adolescence. Formal operations may emerge later than this, however, or not at all. Evidence suggests that not everyone achieves this level of cognitive development.

Learning Objective 7.5
Explain the characteristics and outcomes of formal operations compared to concrete operations.

Hypothetical-Deductive Reasoning

The distinguishing characteristic of the formal operational period is the capacity for **hypothetical-deductive reasoning**. The formal operational thinker moves easily and surely through the world of what-ifs, might-bes, and if-thens. Adolescents sometimes seem more at home with the hypothetical—with imagined worlds, counterfactual propositions, life dreams, and schemes—than in the world of mundane reality.

The *deductive* part of *hypothetical-deductive* is also important. To qualify as formal operational, thought must involve more than simply imagining possibilities. The formal operational thinker possesses a rigorous logical system for evaluating hypotheses and deducing necessary outcomes. As the term *operations* implies, this system again involves various forms of mental action.

Hypothetical-deductive reasoning
A form of problem solving characterized by the ability to generate and test hypotheses and draw logical conclusions from the results of the tests. In Piaget's theory, a formal operational achievement.

Piaget's favorite way of characterizing the difference between concrete operations and formal operations was to talk about a reversal in the relation between reality and possibility. For the concrete operational child, the starting point is always immediate reality. From this point, the child can make very limited extensions into the hypothetical. For the formal operational thinker, in contrast, the starting point is the world of possibility—whatever it is that might be true. From this starting point in the possible, the thinker works back to what happens to be true in the case.

Reasoning about Pendulums

Inhelder and Piaget's (1958) tasks for studying formal operations consist mostly of problems in scientific reasoning. In one task, for example, the participant must determine what factors (length, thickness, shape, and so on) influence the bending of a rod. In another, the task is to experiment with various chemical solutions to determine which combinations produce a specified outcome. Other content areas include the projection of shadows, determinants of floating, conservation of motion, and laws of centrifugal force.

The pendulum task is one of the most famous. In this task, the participant is shown a simple pendulum consisting of a weight hanging on a string. Other weights and lengths of string are also available for experimentation. The problem is to figure out what determines the frequency of oscillation of the pendulum—that is, how fast the pendulum swings back and forth. Is it the heaviness of the weight? the length of the string? the height from which the weight is dropped? the force with which it is pushed? or perhaps some combination of two or more of these factors?

It turns out that the only factor that really has an effect is the length of the string. But the point is not that the formal operational thinker knows this in advance, because he or she probably does not. The point is that the formal operational thinker possesses a set of cognitive structures that will allow systematic exploration of the problem. The solution requires first identifying each of the potentially important variables—weight, length, and so on—and then systematically testing them out, varying one factor at a time while holding other factors constant. The participant must be able to generate all the possible variables and combinations of variables, keep track of what has been done and what remains to be done, and must be able to draw logical conclusions from the overall pattern of results. In the case of the pendulum, the performance of all relevant tests will lead to the conclusion that if the string is short the pendulum swings fast, and only if the string is short does the pendulum swing fast.

As with all Piagetian stages, the achievements of formal operations are clearest when contrasted with the preceding period. The concrete operational child is unlikely to solve the pendulum problem. The 9- or 10-year-old faced with such a task will do some intelligent things, including accurately testing some of the possible variables. But the younger child is not able to generate and examine the full range of possibilities on which a logical conclusion depends. Instead, the child may find that a heavy weight on a short string swings fast and conclude that both the weight and length are important, a conclusion that is not valid in the absence of further tests.

Note that the formal operational approach to the problem embodies the kind of reversal between reality and possibility that Piaget stressed. The formal operational thinker begins by considering all the various possibilities—maybe the weight is important, maybe the length is important, and so on. At first, these are merely hypotheses; none of them has yet been observed, and most of them will turn out to be false. Yet it is only by systematically considering all the possibilities that the subject can determine what happens to be true. Thus, the movement of thought is from the possible to the real.

Testing Piaget: Formal Operations vs. Concrete Operations

Later studies using the Inhelder and Piaget tasks, such as the pendulum experiment, typically have found lower levels of performance than Inhelder and Piaget reported (Shayer, Kucheman, & Wylam, 1976; Shayer & Wylam, 1978). Some studies have even found substantial proportions of adults who fail at these tasks (Commons, Miller, & Kuhn, 1982). Just as Piaget may have underestimated the abilities of infants and young children, he may have underestimated the abilities of individuals in middle childhood while overestimating the competence of adolescents and adults!

The Inhelder and Piaget tasks are unfamiliar to most people, and the usual method of administering them may not elicit the individual's optimal performance. Studies have shown that the addition of a simple hint or prompt concerning the appropriate procedure can lead to a marked improvement on later trials (Danner & Day, 1977; Stone & Day, 1978). More extended training, as well as simpler procedures, have elicited formal operational performances in children as young as 9 or 10 (Fabricius & Steffe, 1989; Kuhn, Ho, & Adams, 1979).

Another possible approach is to vary the content of the tasks. Perhaps people use formal operations when reasoning about content that is interesting and familiar to them. For some people, the natural science problems used by Inhelder and Piaget may provide such content; others, however, may require comparable tasks in literary analysis, or auto mechanics, or cooking. Piaget himself suggested this possibility (Piaget, 1972). In one example, De Lisi and Staudt (1980) demonstrated that college students' ability to reason at a formal operational level depended on the fit between academic training and specific task: Physics majors did best on the Inhelder and Piaget pendulum task; English majors excelled on a task involving analysis of literary style; and political science majors earned their highest scores on a problem in political reasoning.

Findings from cross-cultural research confirm the importance of specific experience. People from non-Western cultures seldom do well on the Inhelder and Piaget problems, but they may have high levels of performance on culturally salient tasks involving hypothetical-deductive reasoning. Prior to the availability of magnetic compasses, for example, Micronesian navigators sailed their canoes for hundreds of miles from one island to another without the aid of instruments, an achievement few Western sailors would attempt to duplicate. The navigators' ability to maintain course depended on a complex, culturally transmitted, computational system in which star positions, rate of movement, and fixed reference points were systematically combined in ways that seem fully equivalent to the highest levels of performance shown by Inhelder and Piaget's participants (Hutchins, 1983).

Questions for Thought and Discussion
Are you a formal operational thinker? In what contexts or tasks are you most likely to function at this highest level of cognitive development?

Formal operational reasoning is a universal human capability and is not limited to the science laboratory. The navigational achievements of Micronesian sailors, for example, depend on a complex system of computations and logical deductions passed on through intergenerational teaching and learning. (Culver Pictures Inc.)

More indication of the importance of experience comes from across-time comparisons of performance on formal operational tasks. Adolescents tested in the 1990s earned higher scores on these tasks than did comparable samples from the 1960s and early 1970s (Flieller, 1999). The most plausible explanation for this rise in performance lies in changes in relevant experience across the 25-year span. Changes might include improvements in education that explicitly engage students in hypothetical-deductive reasoning and in metacognition—thinking about thinking. Nevertheless, debates about the best way to characterize this formal operational thinking continue (Braine & Rumaine, 1983; Byrnes, 1988; Eckstein & Shemesh, 1992; Ennis, 1976; Keating, 1988; Martorano, 1977; Moshman, 1998).

Evaluating Piaget's Theory

Other debates about Piaget's theory of cognitive development focus on the validity of stages and the question of whether Piaget's stages are valid cross-culturally. There is much debate about the validity of stages in theories like Piaget's that rely on a set progression of steps through which everyone passes.

The Issue of Stages As you read at the beginning of this chapter, a **stage theory** requires that changes be *qualitative* rather than *quantitative*. That is, stages must show changes in *how* the child thinks and not merely in how much the child knows or how quickly the child can do things. Piagetian theorists maintain that development does show qualitative change from one period to the next. Looking at Table 7.1, you can identify the qualitative changes that mark each stage. A second criterion is that stages must follow an *invariant sequence*—each stage builds on the one before, and no stage can be attained until the preceding one has been mastered. A child cannot become preoperational, for example, without first achieving the cognitive abilities of the sensorimotor period.

The third criterion for the validity of stage theories is that there should be *concurrences* in development. That is, once developed, the same cognitive structures should appear around the same time and be reflected consistently in a variety of cognitive tasks. Yet children's cognitive performances typically show a good deal of inconsistency. A child in the concrete operational stage of development may succeed on some concrete operational tasks, for example, but not on others. Piaget wrote that cognitive tasks may be mastered at different times, a concept he called *horizontal decalage*. Nevertheless, researchers have found great inconsistencies in developmental change (de Ribaupierre, Rieben, & Lautrey, 1991; Jamison, 1977; Kreitler & Kreitler, 1989) and continue to debate the validity of stage theories (Fischer & Bidell, 1998; Lourenco & Machado, 1996; Miller, 2001).

The Issue of Universality A second issue is the validity of ideas about development across cultures. In Piaget's view, all children all around the world pass through the same stages in the same order. And all children develop the same basic forms of knowledge, such as object permanence and conservation. The study of child development in other cultures thus provides a way to test the claim of universality. It has long been known that children growing up in the United States or Canada show the same basic patterns of development that Piaget first identified in children in Switzerland some 50 or 60 years ago. But does development in non-Western societies follow the same patterns?

Cross-cultural research confirms that the specific experiences available to children can affect their cognitive development (Laboratory of Comparative Human Cognition, 1983; Rogoff & Chavajay, 1995). And culture can affect both the rate of development and the final level of development. In societies without formal schooling, for example, few individuals attain formal operations, although humans everywhere generally are capable of logical thinking. Furthermore, the order in which certain abilities emerge may vary across cultures. For example, children from pottery-making families master conservation of matter earlier than other operations (Price-Williams, Gordon, & Ramirez, 1969). Similarly, children in nomadic societies develop spatial abilities sooner than children from other groups (Dasen, 1975).

Stage theory
Any theory in which qualitative change is said to occur across an invariant sequence of stages, leading to concurrences of behavior.

Questions for Thought and Discussion
On the basis of your observations, are children of the same age more similar or more different in their cognitive development? Is any one child more consistent or more inconsistent in their thinking? Are you and your peers all in the same stage of cognitive development?

No one, however, has ever found a culture in which children do not eventually acquire forms of knowledge such as object permanence and conservation, or in which children master conservation without going through an initial preoperational phase, or in which the order of the four general periods of development is reversed. Even some reported lags in rates of development disappear when the tests are made appropriate to the cultural setting—for example, when children are interviewed in their native language by a native speaker (Nyiti, 1982) or when the children themselves play an active role in the assessing cognitive tasks (Greenfield, 1966).

As you have read, Piaget often underestimated children's ability, especially during the infant and preschool years. And development is not as orderly and consistent as Piaget's stage model seems to imply. Significantly, Piaget did not offer a completely satisfactory explanation of cognitive change. Although the concepts of assimilation, accommodation, and equilibration provide a general model of how children's thought undergoes the kinds of changes Piaget described, they have been difficult to specify and to test in experimental settings. Also, while Piaget claimed that the stages he described are universal, some researchers have found variations in performance on Piagetian tasks when the children and adults studied are of different cultural backgrounds. This variation may arise simply because the experimental settings do not reflect cultural contexts or because some aspects of cognitive stages may not be universal. Nevertheless, Piaget's theory has played a central role in our understanding of child development and in the applications of that understanding to both parenting and schooling.

Learning Objective 7.5: *Explain the characteristics and outcomes of formal operations compared to concrete operations and evaluate Piaget's theory overall.*

Questions for Thought and Discussion
What aspects of cognitive development would you expect to stay the same across cultures, and why?

✔ *Test Your Mastery...*

1. What is the chief difference between formal operations and concrete operations?
2. How does the pendulum task test for the use of hypothetical-deductive reasoning?
3. Why is there debate about formal operations as a stage of cognitive development?
4. How do interest, experience, and culture influence performance on formal operational tasks?
5. On what key issues do evaluations of Piaget's stage theory focus?

Vygotsky and the Sociocultural Approach

Like Piaget's work, the Soviet scholar Lev Vygotsky's (1896–1934) ideas about cognitive development, referred to as the *sociocultural approach*, defined in Chapter 1, have also had a profound impact on the study of child development. Like cognitive-developmental theories, the sociocultural approach focuses on the development of intellectual skills and sees the child as an active participant in development. The approaches differ, however, in their views on how change occurs, the factors that influence the process, and the outcomes of development.

According to the sociocultural approach, cognitive development is fundamentally a social and cultural process. Hundreds of studies drawing on Vygotsky's work have been published in recent decades, reflecting growing interest in the cultural context of child development. What different developmental pathways can be observed among children of different cultures and of different ethnic groups within cultures?

The sociocultural approach answers this question in more than one way, as it is not a single theory but a family of theoretical frameworks. The common core that unites these theories is a focus on the social and cultural foundations of developmental processes. According to the sociocultural approach, individuals inherit their environments as much as they inherit their genes. These environments are organized by **culture**—the accumulated body of knowledge of a people encoded in language and embodied in the beliefs, values, norms, rituals, physical artifacts, institutions, and activities that are passed down from one generation to the next (Cole, 1996). Throughout the lifespan, biological and cultural aspects of development act in concert. Individual growth and development are the products of the coordination of these two organized, dynamic systems. Thus, socioculturalists

Learning objective 7.6
Analyze the three main themes on which sociocultural approaches to development are based.

Culture
The accumulated knowledge of a people encoded in their language and embodied in the physical artifacts, beliefs, values, customs, institutions, and activities passed down from one generation to the next.

believe that individual development must be understood in—and cannot be separated from—its social and cultural/historical context (Cole, 1996; Gauvain, 1998; Rogoff, 2003; Schweder et al., 1998; Valsiner, 1997).

Three themes in Vygotsky's writings have guided contemporary sociocultural theory and research (Wertsch, 1981). The first theme is that the study of mental functioning requires the study of change at all levels—from momentary learning to species history. This is the *cultural-historical context* of development. The second theme is that individual mental development and thought have *social origins*. The third is that human thought and action are mediated by *cultural tools and artifacts*.

The Temporal Contexts of Development

The first theme in Vygotsky's writing is that to understand human cognition, we need to understand its origins and the transitions it has undergone over time (Wertsch & Kanner, 1995). Vygotsky proposed the study of development over four interrelated temporal contexts, or time frames—ontogenetic, microgenetic, phylogenetic, and cultural/historical.

Ontogenetic development
Development across years of an individual's life, such as childhood.

Microgenetic development
Moment-to-moment learning of individuals as they work on specific problems.

Phylogenetic development
Development of the species.

Cultural/historical development
Development that occurs over decades and centuries and leaves a legacy of tools and artifacts, value systems, institutions, and practices.

- **Ontogenetic development** occurs across the years of an individual's life, such as infancy, childhood, and adolescence.
- **Microgenetic development** is moment-to-moment learning as individuals work on specific problems or tasks.
- **Phylogenetic development** is the development of the species. Existing human capacities for culture are products of biological evolution. Of particular interest to sociocultural theorists are the capabilities that distinguish humans from other animals. These capabilities include the use of tools such as language and other social-cognitive abilities that support learning in social contexts.
- **Cultural/historical development** occurs over decades and centuries in particular times and places and leaves a legacy of tools and artifacts, value systems, institutions, and practices.

In the cultural/historical context, individual development unfolds in a particular cultural and historical niche that itself is dynamic and changing. As noted earlier, socioculturalists believe that individual development must be studied in its cultural context. Moreover, socioculturalists study how changes in cultural practices and institutions (such as the introduction of formal schooling, move to a market economy, or invention of new technologies) shape the human mind.

The Social Origins of Thought

Questions for Thought and Discussion
Sociocultural theories emphasize that learning is inherently social. For example, how might a seemingly solitary activity—such as studying for a geography test—be considered a social activity?

In addition to emphasizing the cultural contexts of knowledge and intelligence, Vygotsky focused on the role of social interaction in learning. According to Vygotsky, children acquire knowledge and cognitive skills by participating in cultural activities with more experienced partners. By participating in culturally meaningful activities with more knowledgeable members of their society, children internalize the values, customs, beliefs, and skills of their culture and, over time, come to use them independently.

Vygotsky believed that the most productive interactions occur in what he termed "the zone of proximal (potential) development." The **zone of proximal development** is the distance between what a child can accomplish on his or her own and what the child can achieve under the guidance of an adult or in collaboration with a more capable peer. The zone of proximal development involves activities that are slightly beyond the child's current capabilities but can be accomplished with help. Interactions within the zone of proximal development promote cognitive development because the social support allows children to extend their current skills to a higher level of competence.

Zone of proximal development
The distance between what a child can accomplish independently and what the child can accomplish with the help of an adult or more capable peer.

Sociocultural researchers also study how other people support and encourage children's development. One way experienced partners assist children's learning is through a process known as scaffolding (Wood, Bruner, & Ross, 1976). During **scaffolding**, more capable partners adjust the level of help in response to the child's level of performance, moving to more direct, explicit forms of teaching if the child falters and to less direct, more demanding forms of teaching as the child moves closer to independent mastery. Scaffolding appears to be effective not only in producing immediate success but also in instilling the skills necessary for independent problem solving in the future.

Scaffolding best captures the processes involved in the deliberate instruction that characterizes formal education. Much of what children come to know is not the result of explicit teaching, however. Rather, it is a by-product of participating in routine cultural activities. These cultural activities—household chores, economic pursuits, religious practices, and so on—may serve as learning opportunities, but their primary function is social rather than instructional.

Barbara Rogoff (1990) coined the term **guided participation** to describe the process by which young children become competent by participating in everyday, purposeful activities under the guidance of more experienced partners. As in scaffolding, the more expert partner is sensitive to the capabilities of the learners and structures tasks accordingly. For example, the partner may assign simple chores and adapt tools to the child's abilities, even in situations where no deliberate instruction takes place. As children grow more competent, their roles and responsibilities change. In the process, their understanding of the task also changes, which is cognitive change.

Scaffolding
A method of teaching in which the adult adjusts the level of help provided in relation to the child's level of performance, the goal being to encourage independent performance.

Guided participation
The process by which young children become competent by participating in everyday, purposeful activities under the guidance of more experienced partners.

The Use of Cultural Tools and Artifacts

The third theme in Vygotsky's writings is that human thought and action can only be understood through an understanding of the tools and signs that mediate them (Vygotsky, 1981). *Tools*, in this context, refer to all the means that individuals have at their disposal to achieve desired goals. These means may range from simple objects (such as sticks and rope) to complex technological devices (such as telephones and calculators). Tools also include representations, such as maps; sign and symbol systems such as language; and social practices such as routines and rituals that organize and structure human activity.

Children learn how to use these cultural tools through interactions with parents, teachers, and more experienced peers. As a result of using these tools—first in cooperation with others and later independently—the child develops **higher mental functions**—complex mental processes that are intentional, self-regulated, and mediated by language and other sign systems. Examples of higher mental functions include focused attention, deliberate memory (consciously using strategies for remembering things), and verbal thinking (thought using words that denote abstract concepts).

Vygotsky believed that the particular structure and content of higher mental functions vary with social experience and cultural tools. Cultural tools for thinking both enhance and transform mental capabilities. Formal systems and implements for measuring time or distance, for example, enhance human thinking by improving accuracy. As children learn how to use these tools, their thinking is transformed, and they come to think about time and distance differently—that is, in units such as minutes, seconds, inches, or meters. Thus, children's thinking grows more sophisticated as they master the tools provided by their culture.

Questions for Thought and Discussion
Was early exposure to a variety of objects, especially toys, emphasized in your family? Why might object play be given less importance in other families, communities, or societies?

Higher mental functions
Complex mental processes that are intentional, self-regulated, and mediated by language and other sign systems.

Interacting with Toys and Objects Piaget viewed developmental differences in the ways infants use objects in play and problem solving as reflecting fundamental changes in underlying cognitive abilities. In contrast, sociocultural researchers focus on cultural practices that shape those encounters. Cultural practices dictate how much contact infants have with objects, which objects young children have access to, and whether they use the objects in work or play, in solitary activity or jointly with others.

BOX 7.2   Weaving Generations Together: Evolving Creativity in the Maya of Chiapas

Socialization is intrinsically oriented toward the future. It prepares children for an adulthood that has not yet arrived. It follows that changing socialization patterns should be a key component of the psychological adaptation to social change. However, in conditions of ecocultural change, an important question arises: do parents merely repeat the socializing process that they underwent as children? Or do parents develop new methods and processes as societal and economic conditions change? And what, if any, consequences do such changes in socialization have for the development of children?

The sociohistorical research tradition, derived from Vygotsky (1962, 1978), emphasizes that development is constructed through social interaction, cultural practices, and the internalization or cognitive appropriation of symbolic tools (Saxe, 1990). The historical dimension of cultural practices and symbolic tools is emphasized—that is, we understand how the practices and tools fit with the development of the culture itself over time. Yet, until the research of Patricia Greenfield and colleagues (Greenfield, Maynard, & Childs, 2003), the developmental implications of historical change for cultural practices and symbolic tools had never been studied directly. To do so, diachronic evidence comparing the development and socialization of one generation with that of the next is required. This is exactly the unique evidence that Patricia Greenfield presents in her book, *Weaving Generations Together: Evolving Creativity in the Maya of Chiapas* (Greenfield, 2004).

In 1970, during the first wave of Greenfield's studies, weaving instruction in the Zinacantec Maya hamlet of Nabenchauk was characterized by a relatively error-free, scaffolding process, based on observation of models, obedience to developmentally sensitive commands, and use of help when needed (Childs & Greenfield, 1980; Greenfield, 1984). This mode of formal instruction was well adapted to the Zinacantec goal of preserving the *baz'i* or "true" (i.e., traditional Zinacantec) way

of life (Greenfield & Lave, 1982). In terms of developmental theory, weaving apprenticeship followed a Vygotskian model of learning (Vygotsky, 1978).

In the two decades after the first weaving data were collected, profound social changes occurred in Nabenchauk and other Zinacantec communities. Patricia Marks Greenfield, her colleague Carla Childs, and her daughter, photographer Lauren Greenfield, went back in 1991, 21 years later, to document social change and how it had affected apprenticeship, creativity, and cognitive development.

When they returned in 1991, they found that Zinacantecs had become entrepreneurs, voluntarily joining the Mexican national economy for the first time. The community was in a process of transition from an agricultural, subsistence economy to commerce, entrepreneurship, and cash. Both men and women had become involved in the new cash economy. Some men who formerly farmed were now involved in the transport business. Many girls and women wove and embroidered for money, selling their textile products both to other community members and to outsiders.

Whereas the method of apprenticeship practiced in 1970 seemed adapted to transmitting a tradition intact, another method of apprenticeship, trial-and-error learning, with its emphasis on the learner's own discovery process, should foster the development of an ability to innovate. If innovation had in fact entered the culture as a value orientation in response to or as part of entrepreneurial commerce, Greenfield thought that weaving education would make a corresponding shift. Earlier, the teacher had carefully built a scaffold of help for the learner, providing help before the learner had an opportunity to make a serious error. Because the learner, in this situation, received very little opportunity to make a mistake, much less to explore, Greenfield predicted that the methods of teaching and learning would change to a more independent trial-and-error approach. From the

Girl weaving in 1970, by Patricia Greenfield, p. 70 *Weaving generations together* (Patricia & Lauren Greenfield/VII Photo Agency)

Girl weaving in 1991, by Patricia Greenfield, p. 74 *Weaving generations together* (Patricia & Lauren Greenfield/VII Photo Agency)

The number and types of objects infants and toddlers are allowed to explore vary widely among cultures. In wealthy, industrialized societies, caregivers provide infants with an abundant supply of specially manufactured toys and structure the infants' joint play episodes around these toys (Whiting & Edwards, 1988). For example, one study of native-born Canadian infants reported that babies had an average of 27 toys by the time they

Historical change in Mayan weaving patterns (Patricia & Lauren Greenfield/VII Photo Agency)

Novel striped patterns (Patricia & Lauren Greenfield/ VII Photo Agency)

point of view of developmental theory, this is the model of learning emphasized and valued by Piaget (1965).

Greenfield's study of the effects of cultural change on developmental processes had three parts. In the first part, she predicted and found that informal weaving apprenticeship at home was moving from a more controlled, interdependent style to a more independent, trial-and-error, "discovery" style across two generations of the same family. These findings were based on a systematic comparison of hour-long videos taken while girls were learning to weave. The first generation was videotaped in 1970; their daughters, nieces, and younger cousins were videotaped in the early 1990s. The photos show two generations of girls from the same family learning to weave. The girl in the black-and-white photo is learning to weave in 1970; the girl in the color photo is her daughter learning to weave in 1991, 21 years later. Both girls are the same age, about nine years old. Compare the closeness between learner and teacher (the mother) in 1970 with the distance between learner and teacher (a sister) in 1991. The 1991 learner is weaving more independently; she is also learning from a member of the peer generation, rather than a member of the older generation, an important part of the shift from authority to independence. Quantitative analysis derived from the whole sample of many families confirmed this qualitative portrait of intergenerational changes; these changes were concentrated in families where mother and daughter were more involved in weaving commerce.

In the second part, Greenfield predicted that the economic shift toward entrepreneurship, with its value of innovation, and the apprenticeship shift toward discovery-oriented learning would be accompanied by greater innovation in Zinacantec woven artifacts; this prediction was also confirmed. While Zinacantec weaving and embroidery still included the basic patterns as background, the textile design process had expanded beyond these patterns to incorporate constant innovation in both weaving and embroidery. For example, as can be seen in the photos, shawls that had earlier been woven in two basic color schemes now existed in a rainbow of colors. In 1969, the concept of creativity was a conservative, community model of creativity. Its ideal was to maintain traditions that identify a group of people

as a community. By 1991, this model had changed to include a model of individual creativity in which individual uniqueness and innovation are valued; this is creativity as we understand it in our culture.

In the third part, Greenfield used an experiment to understand the cognitive processes that underlay this shift from tradition to innovation in the domain of cultural artifacts. As part of the experiment, girls were asked to place wooden sticks in a frame to continue novel striped patterns, patterns that were not part of the culture in general or weaving in particular; these were patterns that the participants would never have seen before. With a total sample of 106 girls across both generations, Greenfield predicted and found that girls' skill in correctly continuing novel patterns increased from 1969 and 1970, when pattern innovation was absent from the culture, to 1991, when it was present. In addition, more independent weaving learners were significantly better at representing novel patterns. In other words, there was the predicted link between the cognitive representation of novelty in an experiment that required girls to embroider or weave novel patterns in the real world, and independent, trial-and-error learning,

What important lessons do we learn from Greenfield's *Weaving Generations Together?* We learn the following: First, learning processes are not stable over historical time. Thus, parents do not necessarily teach their children the way they were taught. Instead, under conditions of social transformation, parents make unconscious changes that help their children adapt to a changing world. Second, cognitive development is not stable over historical time; it, too, changes in response to changing economic conditions. Third, the definition of creativity is neither universal nor stable; what it means to create can be radically different in different times and different places. These studies and this book have implications beyond this one indigenous community in Mexico; these same changes, from subsistence and agriculture, to money and commerce are going on all over the world. We now know something about how they affect family processes of socialization and individual processes of development.

were 3 months of age. By 9 months, they averaged nearly 60 toys (Pomerleau, Malcuit, & Sabatier, 1991)!

Other communities, such as Mayan villages in rural Guatemala, provide infants with few toys and actively restrict exploration of other objects (Gaskins, 1999). Others, such as the !Kung (now Ju'/hoansi), a hunter-gatherer society of southern Africa, allow infants access to a variety of natural objects, including twigs, grass, and stones, in addition to household implements (Bakeman et al., 1990). In still other cultures, caregivers encourage infants to manipulate tools used by older children and adults in productive work or miniature versions of tools fashioned by adults for small hands (Lancy, 1996). The Aka, a hunter-gatherer group in the tropical rain forests of the Central African Republic, for example, begin to teach their infants how to use sharp objects, such as knives, digging sticks, and axes, before the children reach their first birthday (Hewlett, 1992).

In still other cultural communities, object play takes a back seat to social interaction. During their first year, infants spend their waking hours in the laps of adults or on the hips of older children; they have no occasions to sit alone and play with baby toys. As children become mobile and move about on their own, they are in demand by older children and adults of the community as toys themselves. They are looked on as entertainers, and all of their waking hours are spent in the company of others (Heath, 1983, pp. 76–77).

According to the sociocultural approach, these variations in children's early experiences with objects can only be understood within a broad cultural context that includes the physical environment (e.g., whether infants spend their time indoors or outdoors), social environment (e.g., whether the infants are usually in the company of other children or adults or are alone), and customs of child care (e.g., whether infants are free to move about or are physically restrained) (Super & Harkness, 1986). It may seem unwise, for example, to put potentially dangerous objects such as knives and axes in the hands of infants, but the practice is common in cultures where infants are rarely beyond arm's reach of a caregiver and have many opportunities to observe the tools being used by older children and adults (Rogoff, 2003).

Implications of Object Play for Development The differing cultural ideas about the role of object play in development lead to an obvious question: Do different cultural practices have different developmental results? Specifically, does toy play during the early years foster cognitive development? Evidence is mixed. Some studies suggest that early experience exploring objects may not be essential for normal cognitive development. Despite wide cultural differences in access to objects, infants the world over follow the same sequence (though not necessarily the same timing) of sensorimotor development and use the same procedures to manipulate and explore objects (e.g., mouthing, squeezing, dropping). Other studies, however, have shown a positive relationship between infants' access to toys and their performance on assessments of cognitive development during infancy and early childhood (Bradley et al., 1994; Yarrow, Rubenstein, & Pedersen, 1975). In addition, the amount and quality of infants' object play alone and with caregivers predicts children's current and subsequent performance on various measures of cognitive competence (Belsky, Goode, & Most, 1980; Tamis-LeMonda & Bornstein, 1991; van den Boom, 1994; Yarrow et al., 1983).

The link between the availability of toys and performance on measures of cognitive ability may also vary across cultural groups. Although the provision of toys during infancy is highly predictive of the intellectual capabilities of white North American children, for example, access to toys does not predict the intelligence test performance of Hispanic children (Bradley et al., 1994). Nonetheless, consistent with sociocultural theory, researchers have found that infants spend more time exploring objects and engage in more focused and complex exploration when interacting with caregivers than when playing alone (Hofsten & Siddiqui, 1993; Lockman & McHale, 1989; Tamis-LeMonda & Bornstein, 1991). Infants and toddlers are also far more likely to use objects as tools to solve problems (such as using a stick to retrieve an out-of-reach toy) by seeing others use them, rather than by discovering how to do so on their own (Chen & Siegler, 2000; Tomasello, Savage-Rumbaugh, & Kruger, 1993).

The Role of Pretend Play

Early encounters with objects are important opportunities for infants to learn about cultural tools and artifacts, particularly when those encounters involve other people. In addition to object play, pretend play also seems to develop within the context of joint action with caregivers or older children. Symbolic or **pretend play**—the "voluntary transformation of the here and now" (Garvey, 1990)—becomes more sophisticated during the preschool years. During this time, children's burgeoning symbolic skills support increasingly complex and abstract pretend or make-believe sequences. The role of symbolic function can be seen in **solitary pretense**, in which children pretend by themselves. Solitary pretense can be quite simple or very complex, as when a preschooler acts out a complicated drama with a collection of dolls and stuffed animals. Because of their interest in the cultural transmission of information, sociocultural theorists focus on **sociodramatic play** in which two or more people enact related roles (e.g., mother and baby, driver and passenger, pet and owner).

For Vygotsky, make-believe play is a unique activity in which children try out a number of different skills within their zone of proximal development. They exercise their budding representational abilities as they create imaginary situations, substituting objects for other objects within a play-frame (pretending that a block is a telephone, for example). In addition, they create scenes within which they enact certain social rules (pretending to be the daddy, for example, who helps the baby to put on her shoes). The particular themes enacted in such scenes vary, as one would expect, with the particular social activities the children engage in on a daily basis. Worldwide, the most common themes enacted in toddlers' pretense are those that center on domestic life (such as cooking, eating, and child care); adult work activities (such as hunting, planting, and fishing); and adult rituals (such as marriage and dancing) (Power, 2000).

The extent to which children engage in pretend play depends on an important aspect of a culture's organization: the significance caregivers place on play compared to other daily activities. Consequently, the prevalence of pretend play has been found to vary widely among families of different cultures. In societies such as the Mayan community described earlier (Gaskins, 1999), where caregivers depend on small children to perform important chores such as tending livestock or the garden and running errands, children's work responsibilities allow them little time for pretend play. In some areas of Mexico, mothers attach no particular value to play and rarely engage in pretense with their children (Farver & Howes, 1993). Similarly, Farver and her associates found that Korean American caregivers dismiss pretend play as mere amusement and do little to encourage it. Korean American children whose parents had recently immigrated to Los Angeles engaged in pretend play less often than European American children both at home and at school (Farver, 1999). These differences were traced to adult beliefs about the value of play. Whereas the European American parents and teachers valued the educational and cognitive benefits of play, the Korean American adults viewed memorization, hard work, and task persistence as a means to academic success. These beliefs were reflected in the ways adults structured children's activities.

In cultures where adults believe pretend play facilitates development, caregivers tend to view their own participation in play as both appropriate and desirable and to participate actively in children's pretending (Haight, Parke, & Black, 1997). Parent-child pretend play is common among middle-class families in a variety of countries (Bornstein et al., 1999; Göncü et al., 2000; Haight et al., 1999), where play is viewed as a type of instruction as well as a form of play. These findings show variation in the themes of pretend play, the importance placed on pretend play, and the particulars of who engages in pretend play with children.

Piaget viewed pretend play as a natural outcome of children's developing symbolic abilities, but Vygotsky claimed that pretend play grows out of the child's collaborations with others. Although early studies of pretend play tended to focus on solitary play, observational studies in everyday settings reveal that most pretend play takes place in a social context with other people acting as either spectators or partners. Studies also reveal that pretend-play partners often scaffold young children's pretense, thereby scaffolding the development of a wide variety of cognitive skills.

According to Vygotsky, the most powerful cultural tool is language. Language is the primary means by which members of a cultural community pass on knowledge and values

Pretend play
Symbolic play other than object play, solitary or with others, with or without props, involving pretense or make-believe.

Solitary pretense
Form of symbolic play in which children by themselves pretend.

Sociodramatic play
In sociocultural approaches to development, pretend play in which participants enact social roles and themes.

Links to Related Material
In Chapter 9, you will learn more about cultural differences in definitions of intelligence and parental involvement in schooling. You will also read about the value of so-called educational toys to accelerate children's cognitive development.

Questions for Thought and Discussion
What are some examples of other cultural tools or artifacts that change the way you reason or solve problems?

These children are being exposed to a critically important cultural tool in a formal social context: reading! As the children identify the letters and master the sounds they make, how will their thinking be transformed? (Ken Chernus/Taxi/Getty Images)

surrounding cultural practices to succeeding generations. Language also functions as a tool in its own right, shaping children's thinking and problem solving. Children's thinking is transformed as children master the language arts and symbol systems such as mathematics.

One way that researchers try to understand how tools shape children's intellectual development is to identify specific features of the tools that might be associated with different types of thinking. Studies of how children learn mathematics—with its rule-based structure—have been helpful for this kind of analysis, along with cross-cultural research comparing mathematical tools used in different language systems. For example, researchers have noted that Asian number systems are in some respects easier to master than the English-language system. In any case, children often use even complex tools effectively long before they fully understand them, through the guidance of more capable members of their communities and also because tools themselves often are designed in ways that scaffold their use.

Learning Objective 7.6: *Analyze the three main themes on which sociocultural approaches to development are based.*

1. What temporal and cultural contexts did Vygotsky identify, and why are they important in the study of development?
2. What applications based on Vygotsky's theory demonstrate how children learn through social interaction?
3. According to Vygotsky, what is the role of cultural tools and artifacts in cognitive development?
4. According to the sociocultural view, what is the significance of pretend play in cognitive development?

Piaget and Vygotsky on Language and Thought

Learning Objective 7.7
Compare and contrast the theories of Piaget and Vygotsky on the role of language in cognitive development.

Piaget believed that language is a verbal reflection of the individuals' conceptual understanding. Language reflects cognition. At the end of infancy and the sensorimotor period, children become capable of thinking symbolically. According to Piaget, the acquisition of language symbols speeds up thinking because a sequence of thoughts can usually be carried out more quickly than a sequence of actions. But because language reflects thought, language development cannot cause cognitive development. Rather, for Piaget, cognition determines language.

Piaget found support for this view in two different forms of speech often used by young children: *egocentric speech* and *collective monologues*. If you have had the chance to observe young children, you have seen how they often talk out loud to themselves when playing or trying to solve problems. Piaget referred to this kind of talk as *egocentric*

Test Your Mastery...

speech—"talk for self," defined earlier in this chapter. In Piaget's theory, this kind of speech is diagnostic of young children's inability to decenter, or to take the perspective of another.

Another form of speech used by young children is what Piaget termed a **collective monologue**, in which children use egocentric speech in play with other children. You may notice that while preschoolers often appear to be playing and conversing together, their remarks actually focus on what they themselves are doing by themselves, with no real regard for their partner and no apparent intention of communicating with anyone. There may be a turn-taking structure to their "conversations," with each child speaking after the other has finished, but the content of what each child contributes relates only to what she or he just said. Each child narrates an event to himself or herself without considering what the other child is talking about. Piaget believed that collective monologues give way to genuine dialogues as children develop the ability to adopt others' points of view.

Vygotsky had a completely different perspective on the relationship between language and thought. He believed that the onset of language is one of the most important events with the power to transform early abilities into a qualitatively new form of thinking. It is with the onset of language that "elementary mental functions" are transformed into "higher mental functions" (Wertsch, 1985). Although Piaget believed that language is a reflection of inner cognitive workings, Vygotsky maintained that language in a sense "precedes" thought. According to Vygotsky, language is social from the outset in that it is first used to communicate in interaction with others. Thus, language precedes thought in the sense that it is first experienced on the social plane and then is later internalized as individual thought.

Vygotsky pointed out that children's development always occurs in a context organized and watched over by adults, and thus that children's experience of language is social from the outset. Children's first words are communicative acts, mediating their interactions with the people around them. To Vygotsky, this sequence suggested a progression from social and communicative speech to internal dialogue, or inner, **private speech**, in which thought and language become intimately interconnected. Thus, language allows thought to be individual and social at the same time. It is the medium through which individual thought is communicated to others while at the same time it allows social reality to be converted into the idiosyncratic thought of the individual.

Vygotsky's private speech therefore differs from Piaget's egocentric speech (Vygotsky 1934, 1962). First, Vygotsky noted that egocentric speech occurs when the child is having difficulty or is doing a difficult task, suggesting that it serves a particular cognitive function, rather than simply reflecting a lack of cognitive ability for perspective taking. Thus, far from being nonsocial, Vygotsky (1934/1962) maintained that young children's private speech grows out of their interactions with parents and other more experienced others as they work together on various tasks. For example, much of a parent's speech involves guiding and regulating the child. Over the course of many interactions, children begin to use versions of their parents' instructional comments to direct their own behavior. Thus, according to Vygotsky, this kind of talk was a child's way of self-guiding or self-directing. Gradually, the controlling speech becomes internalized as thought, as children eventually produce "silent statements" (thoughts) similar to the verbal ones. Self-regulation thus develops out of the child's social interactions—a process Vygotsky called **sociogenesis** (Van der Veer & Valsiner, 1988).

Vygotsky also challenged Piaget's claim that the language in private speech and collective monologues is not intended to communicate anything. In one experiment, he placed preschoolers among deaf-mute children. He reasoned that if the preschoolers did not intend to communicate through private speech, their communication would not be affected by the discovery that their playmates could not hear them. This was not the case, however. Vygotsky found that the preschoolers' levels of egocentric speech declined, suggesting that they did intend to communicate.

Similarly, Vygotsky hypothesized that the same factors that encourage social speech would encourage greater amounts of private speech as well. To test this hypothesis, Vygotsky created a series of situations, similar to the one described earlier, that discouraged or prevented social interaction and then measured preschoolers' private speech. In one experiment, he placed children in a very noisy classroom. In others, he surrounded children with

Collective monologue
Piaget's term for young children's tendency to use egocentric speech with each other during play, resulting in noncommunication.

Private speech
In Vygotsky's theory, children's self-talk, speech that they produce and direct toward themselves during problem solving.

Sociogenesis
The process of acquiring knowledge or skills through social interactions.

peers who spoke a foreign language or who were deaf and had no oral language, or placed children in settings where they were isolated at a table by themselves or with unfamiliar peers. In each situation, self-talk declined significantly. Conversely, he found that private speech increased when children were in the presence of responsive social partners (Goudena, 1987). Thus, self-talk is not simply egocentric speech reflecting an inability to consider another's point of view.

Later research has identified other factors that affect the frequency with which children talk to themselves while solving problems. Private speech occurs most often on tasks that are challenging but not impossibly difficult (Behrend, Rosengren, & Perlmutter, 1989; Berk & Garvin, 1984; Kohlberg, Yaeger, & Hjertholm, 1968). It is most evident at the beginning of a new task and at times of difficulty, but it decreases (becomes internalized) as they master the task (Berk, 1994; Meichenbaum & Goodman, 1979).

Other evidence supporting the idea that private speech is used for self-guidance comes from research done with children who have learning and behavior problems. Such children tend to rely on private speech for a longer period of time than their peers, suggesting that such verbalizations are a way of compensating for impairments in certain cognitive functions (Berk & Landau, 1993; Winsler et al., 1999). Researchers also have found that in middle and later childhood private speech frequently takes the form of whispering, which may reflect the process of gradual internalization (Duncan & Pratt, 1997; Frauenglass & Diaz, 1985). These functions suggest that private speech is social in origin, as Vygotsky maintained is the case with all cognitive abilities, rather than a symptom of preoperational thought, as Piaget maintained. Thus, using cultural tools, children construct knowledge in social contexts. Their learning drives their development, just as language can drive thought.

Learning Objective 7.7: *Compare and contrast the theories of Piaget and Vygotsky on the role of language in cognitive development.*

1. How did Piaget and Vygotsky differ in their view of the relationships between language and thought?
2. How did Vygotsky's dynamics of private speech differ from Piaget's concept of egocentric speech?
3. How did Vygotsky interpret children's collective monologues differently than Piaget?
4. What did Vygotsky mean by his idea of the sociogenesis of cognitive development?

Impacts of Piaget and Vygotsky on Education

American child psychologists began to discover Piaget in the late 1950s and the early 1960s as translations and summaries of his books began to appear (Flavell, 1963). Since that time, Piaget's writings have inspired literally thousands of studies of children's thinking and extended his work as it applies to the field of education and other areas (Chapman, 1988; Ginsburg & Opper, 1988; Modgil & Modgil, 1976). Piaget wrote two books about education (Piaget, 1971, 1976), and others have written extensively about the educational implications of his work (Cowan, 1978; DeVries & Zan, 1994; Duckworth, 1987; Kamii & DeVries, 1993).

Three main principles underlie Piagetian approaches to education. One is an emphasis on **discovery learning**, or active learning. This emphasis relates to Piaget's belief that children learn by acting on the world, not by passively taking in information. Piaget distrusted educational methods that are too passive, rote, or verbal. In his view, education should build on the child's natural curiosity and natural tendency to act on the world to understand it. Knowledge is more meaningful when children construct it themselves rather than when it is imposed on them.

A second, related principle arises from Piaget's mechanisms of development—assimilation, accommodation, and equilibration—and their timing. Piaget believed that, while all children go through the same sequence of stages, they do so at their own pace. A child's *readiness to learn* depends on the child's current level of thinking. Experience—educational or otherwise—does not simply happen to the child; rather, the child must

---

✔ *Test Your Mastery...*

Learning Objective 7.8
Evaluate the contributions of Piaget and Vygotsky to educational practice.

Discovery learning
An educational approach based on Piaget's idea that children learn by acting on the world individually, not by passively taking in information.

always integrate it with existing cognitive structures through the processes of assimilation and accommodation. A new experience will be beneficial only if the child can make some sense of it. In addition, a child's *motivation to learn* depends on the timing of educational experiences. In order for children to move ahead in their cognitive development, they must experience disequilibrium, or a challenge to their thinking. Thus, development takes place when children are ready for an experience, and the experience provokes them to advance their level of thinking.

A third principle, based on the idea that children move through cognitive stages at different rates, is that teachers must be sensitive to *individual differences* among students in a classroom. Piaget's diagnostics about what a child does or does not know at different stages of development helps teachers to understand where the child is in development and what naturally comes next. Because children go through the same cognitive stages at different rates, however, learning must be based on the skill level and developmental pacing of individual children.

Based on these three principles, Piagetian-inspired classrooms are structured so that children have ample opportunities to learn through active exploration of their environment. Unlike traditional teacher-centered classrooms, Piagetian-inspired classrooms have activity centers in which children can engage in hands-on activities of their own choosing. Allowing children to select activities for themselves is also consistent with the idea that skills should not be imposed on children before they are ready. Thus, teachers in Piagetian-inspired classrooms introduce activities that appropriately challenge each child at his or her level of development. Teachers in Piagetian-inspired classrooms also evaluate children differently. Because children are expected to develop at their own pace according to their own readiness to learn, they are not evaluated against a set standard for the whole classroom. Rather, children are each evaluated in comparison with their own prior developmental achievements.

Vygotsky's work also has had an important influence on educational practices, seen, for example, in the use of scaffolding and cooperative learning. Vygotsky, like Piaget, recognized the importance of active learning of recognizing children's individual differences in cognitive development (Miller 2001). Where they diverge is in how they view the relationship between the classroom experience and cognitive development. For Piaget, the classroom exists to provide children with rich opportunities to explore and discover on their own. For Vygotsky, the emphasis is not on individual discovery, but rather on **assisted discovery** through interactions between teacher and student, as well as between students. The role of teacher is to carefully guide each child, according to his or her current ability level, to improve skills in using and manipulating the symbolic systems of their culture. The emphasis then, is on the child's interactions with others as the child participates in meaningful activities with others in the classroom.

Assisted discovery
An educational approach based on Vygotsky's idea that children learn through interactions between teachers and students as well as between students.

In one recent study, Kevin Crowley, Maureen Callanan, and their associates observed 4- to 8-year-old children at an interactive exhibit at the San Jose Children's Museum (Crowley et al., 2001). The exhibit was a zoetrope—a simple animation device that produces an illusion of motion when one looks through the slots of the spinning drum. Experimenting with this device, children can explore how cartoons, movies, and videos work. Of particular interest was whether and how parents would support their children's interactions with the zoetrope. According to the sociocultural approach, children as novices learn most effectively when their efforts are guided by more expert partners. Parents support children's learning by managing their attention, simplifying the task, regulating frustration, modeling appropriate action, offering useful hints, and helping the child interpret outcomes. The results of this study support the idea that working with an adult partner enhances children's performance.

Another important difference between Piagetian and Vygotskian approaches to education is in the role played by peers. An important aspect of children's play is that it usually takes place within the context of social interaction with other children. Research has suggested that play with peers may provide a richer context for the development of cognitive skills than play with adults (Farver, 1993; Farver & Wimbarti, 1995).

Sociocultural researchers interested in education have also found that interaction with peers plays a special role in cognitive development in the classroom. The traditional view of a typical classroom is one in which the teacher is the sole authority who

As used in classrooms today, cooperative learning and peer coaching are outgrowths of Piaget's and Vygotsky's contributions to education. Collaborative teaching and learning strategies have gained widespread acceptance as research has underscored the importance of social interaction with peers in cognitive development. (Jeffry Myers/©Index Stock Imagery)

Peer learning
In Piaget's view, the teaching and learning that take place between peers with lesser and greater knowledge or experience (novice and expert).

Sociocognitive conflict
Piaget's term for cognitive conflict that arises during social interaction, when one's way of thinking is challenged.

Questions for Thought and Discussion
Some students and their parents resent peer learning, arguing that it holds back the more capable students. What do you think? Under what conditions do you think peer learning works best?

Peer collaboration
In Vygotsky's view, the cooperative learning that takes place when peers of roughly equal cognitive ability work together to solve a problem.

Intersubjectivity
A commitment to find common ground on which to build shared understanding.

provides information to students who must passively listen and learn from the teacher, not from their fellow students. As we have seen, Piagetian approaches to schooling challenge this view, suggesting that children play a more active role. Piagetian approaches also emphasize the importance of peers in providing alternative perspectives that motivate students to reevaluate their own views. Vygotskian theory and research also challenge the view of the passive learner and point out the important role that peers play in student learning (Miller 2001). Beyond these points, however, Piagetian and Vygotskian views of *peer learning* differ.

Peer learning has been an active area of study in developmental psychology for nearly three decades (reviewed in Azmitia, 1996; De Lisi & Goldbeck, 1999; Garton, 1992; Hogan & Tudge, 1999; Webb & Palincsar, 1996; Rogoff, 1998). Interest in peer learning is fueled by a belief that group work often promotes greater understanding and higher levels of achievement than solitary efforts. In addition, there is a growing appreciation of the importance of collaborative skills in settings outside of school, such as research laboratories, government agencies, medical practices, manufacturing firms, and the corporate world (Hinds & Kiesler, 2002).

Initial interest in collaboration was based on Piaget's theory (Piaget, 1932). Recall that Piaget pointed out that during peer interaction children are challenged by different ways of thinking about problems or issues. Piagetians call this kind of experience **sociocognitive conflict** (Bearison, 1982; Doise & Mugny, 1984; Piaget, 1932). Cognitive change occurs when children work to reconcile this conflict or discrepancy between their views and views held by peers.

An assumption that underlies Piagetian studies of peer collaboration is that logical and cogent arguments will most likely persuade individuals to change their thinking, because these arguments are more likely to reflect correct understanding rather than flawed reasoning. Piaget was not suggesting that the social context was responsible for cognitive change. Rather, cognitive growth was fueled by the child's recognition that his or her views were different and perhaps less logical than those of peers. Thus, the experience and resolution of sociocognitive conflict push development forward.

In one study, for example, second-graders worked in pairs on Piagetian conservation tasks (Miller and Brownell, 1975). It was found that conservers and nonconservers asserted their views equally often but that conservers were able to offer a greater variety of arguments to support their answers. Consequently, nonconservers were more likely to be convinced by their conserving partners than the other way around. This pattern of change—nonconservers advancing through the influence of conservers—has been replicated many times (Murray, 1982).

In contrast to a cognitive-developmental explanation of the success of peer learning, such as Piaget's, a sociocultural or Vygotskian explanation focuses on the cooperation rather than on conflict resolution. Peer learning is best achieved when students cooperate to achieve a common learning objective. In **peer collaboration**, or cooperative learning, rather than placing one student in an authoritative role of "teacher," as is often done in tutoring or mentoring, the learning partners start out with roughly the same levels of competence and work together to create new knowledge.

Students sharing responsibility for a task are more likely to engage in cooperative dialogues to resolve differences of opinion actively (Forman & McPhail, 1993; Nastasi, Clements, & Battista, 1990; Tudge, 1992). In situations with more or less equal distribution of power and knowledge, children may feel more comfortable questioning others' ideas and more motivated to understand those ideas (Bearison & Dorval, 2002; Damon, 1984; Hatano & Iagnaki, 1991). Partners negotiate—or co-construct—new understandings as they clarify, refine, extend, and build on each other's reasoning (Forman & Cazden, 1985; Forman & McPhail, 1993). Success depends on the ability of the learning partners to establish **intersubjectivity**—a commitment to find common ground on which to build shared understanding (Rommetveit, 1979).

BOX 7.3   Conversations with an Early Childhood Educator

Today, at age 48, after a long career as an elementary and preschool educator, Stephanie Lynn Gaarde Deering teaches prospective teachers about early childhood development at South Plains College in Lubbock, Texas. A native of Ames, Iowa, Stephanie now lives in Lubbock with her husband and 16-year-old daughter. We asked her to reflect on her career path and professional life.

Growing up, I always knew I wanted to be a teacher. My father was a coach and a teacher, and I had an aunt who also influenced me. I briefly considered other, more financially lucrative careers, but none of those included children! Pursuing my dream, I earned a bachelor's degree from Iowa State University in Elementary Education, and then a master's degree from Texas Tech University in Special Education with Early Childhood certification. I have also pursued other professional development opportunities in a variety of areas, but my prime area of interest is children with special needs. The bulk of my career (13 years) has been spent teaching young children with special needs.

Stephanie's students today are adults! At South Plains College she is responsible for teaching a variety of college-level classes in the field of Child Development/Early Childhood. She also serves as adviser and practicum supervisor to a diverse, often nontraditional, group of students. In this context, Stephanie also works with the CD/EC program chairperson, who is her friend, colleague, and mentor in her new field of adult education. Stephanie had been teaching at South Plains as an adjunct, but took a full-time position there in January 2005. Her new job brings her full circle in her career as an early childhood educator.

I have always been in the field of education, but have worked in several different areas. I began in elementary school, teaching first, second, third, and fifth grades. Then I moved into the field of special education and then early childhood (ages 3–5). Most recently I taught 3-year-olds in a private early childhood program. At Early Odyssey Developmental School in Lubbock, I was responsible for the 3-year-olds' early childhood programming. I worked with many other early childhood teachers at Early Odyssey. I became a leader, educator, and mentor to many of them, and I like to believe that I had a positive impact on the direction of their careers in early childhood—on the path toward developmentally appropriate practice! I also worked with a wide variety of parents and family members and thoroughly enjoyed the partnerships we built.

The most satisfying aspect of my career right now is helping adults develop the perspectives and skills necessary to have a positive impact on the lives of young children. One of my most meaningful experiences, however, occurred in the preschool setting. It involved the opportunity to work with a 3-year-old boy who had "failed" in a number of other preschool settings. (He had been diagnosed with Attention-Deficit Hyperactivity Disorder and was not able to follow the traditional routines of those programs.) Later, after participating in our more developmentally appropriate setting, geared toward his individual strengths and needs, this young boy was able to successfully transition to kindergarten.

The chance to make a difference in the lives of others is what this field of education is all about. No matter the age, ability, or background of a student, teaching is the opportunity to recognize the unique potential of children (and adults) and to help them reach that goal. It's the opportunity, and the reward, of a lifetime!

Studies of collaboration on Piagetian tasks, mathematical problem solving, scientific reasoning, and even writing show that students who work on problems with partners of relatively equal ability often produce solutions superior to those of individuals working alone. In addition, collaboration can promote a deeper understanding of the problem or concept that lasts over time (Forman & McPhail, 1993; Levin & Druyan, 1993; Tudge, 1989, 1992).

Learning Objective 7.8: *Evaluate the contributions of Piaget and Vygotsky to educational practice.*

✔ *Test Your Mastery...*

1. On what three principles are Piagetian-inspired classrooms based?
2. What kinds of learning activities are you likely to find in a Vygotskian-inspired classroom?
3. How did Piaget's and Vygotsky's views differ on the role of peers in learning and development?

Comparing the Cognitive-Developmental and Sociocultural Approaches

As you have seen, the sociocultural approach is similar in several ways to the cognitive-developmental theories theory of Piaget. Socioculturalists and researchers working within a cognitive-developmental framework study the same aspects of mental functioning,

Learning Objective 7.9
Compare and contrast the sociocultural and cognitive-developmental approaches to child development.

including attention, memory, conceptual understanding, and academic skills such as mathematics, scientific reasoning, and literacy. Both approaches view the child as an active participant in his or her own development (as opposed to a passive recipient of environmental input), and both hold that the individual undergoes qualitative as well as quantitative change over the course of development (Miller, 2001).

The approaches differ, however, in explaining the mechanisms of change. Piagetians focus on processes internal to the individual child, such as the reorganization of cognitive structures, increased speed of task completion, and the child's individual attempts to understand the world. From this perspective, cognitive change takes place when children actively explore, manipulate, and experiment on their surroundings.

Sociocultural theorists, in contrast, believe that developmental change is socially mediated and takes place within the context of social interaction. According to this perspective, development is the direct result of interactions with other people and the tools and artifacts that are the products of human culture. The emphasis is on how children's actions are shaped not only by their own active attempts, but by participation in meaningful activities with others. In this view, both children and their caregivers are active participants in the process of development.

Cognitive-developmental theories view cognitive development as changes in internal mental capabilities. In contrast, sociocultural theories situate thinking in practice. That is, development takes place in the way a child participates in socially meaningful activities. Thus, the development of a particular skill cannot be isolated from the social and cultural purposes to which it is put. Children learn not only the skill but also the values surrounding its use. As Goodnow (1990) notes: "We do not simply learn to solve problems. We learn also what problems are worth solving, and what counts as an elegant rather than simply an acceptable solution" (p. 260). What develops, then, is a culturally constructed system of knowledge that includes goals, values, and motivation (Miller, 2001).

Another difference is in the degree of emphasis on stages and the gradualness and continuity of development from stage to stage. Piaget described a set of unique stages that a child must pass through in succession. Vygotsky also described development as a discontinuous process consisting of "revolutionary shifts, rather than steady quantitative increments" (Wertsch, 1985, p. 19). Vygotsky described language development as continuous, however. Language provides the foundation for all higher cognitive processes during early childhood, creating a qualitatively new means of thinking. Language development continues as a gradual process as adults and more knowledgeable peers scaffold the younger child's use of language.

Piaget believed that the stages through which children develop are consistent for children of every culture. Sociocultural theorists, on the other hand, anticipate variability in both performance content and the sequencing of cognitive abilities of children from different sociocultural communities. Socioculturalists accept the possibility that cognitive development could occur in stage-like fashion if cultures organized children's experiences in that way, but they do not believe that there are universal stages in children's cognitive development (Rogoff, 1998, 2003).

One final difference is in how the two approaches view the outcome or end point of development. In the cognitive-developmental view, the end point of development is the ability to think in highly abstract ways that follow rules of logic. As the individual passes through each successive stage, his or her thought becomes increasingly detached from material circumstances until as a young adult the individual is able to manipulate variables mentally in order to solve a problem. This, for Piaget, is a culmination of an individual human's cognitive capacity.

Sociocultural theorists, on the other hand, question whether there is some ideal end point of development (Rogoff, 1998, 2003). They maintain that the kind of abstract thought characterized by Piaget's final stage of development may itself be a product of culturally situated values. Instead, sociocultural theorists argue that sociocultural groups define the end point of development in accordance with the values and practices that have evolved in their particular communities. Thus, the hypothetico-deductive reasoning that Piaget found to characterize adult thought in his culture may not characterize the end point of development for other cultural groups in which abstract reasoning is not highly valued.

Sociocultural approaches also face challenges, however. Critics point out that those working within the sociocultural framework often idealize learning (Anderson, Reder, & Simon, 1996). As Goodnow (1996) observed, "one rarely finds, within Vygotskian-style analyses of learning, accounts of expert-novice interactions that depart from a picture of 'willing teachers/eager learners'" (p. 356). She points out that experts are not always so willing to give away all that they know. And novices are sometimes reluctant to take over responsibility for their own learning when they have the competence to do so. To better understand the social origins of thought (and to have broader application to real-world learning), researchers need to examine learning in these less-than-optimal situations.

Another challenge sociocultural researchers face is how to integrate data across multiple spheres of development. You may recall in Urie Bronfenbrenner's ecological systems model, for example, that social and cultural contexts of development include the microsystem, mesosystem, exosystem, macrosystem, and chronosystem. Without data from these multiple levels of development, although we may accumulate information about lives in different cultures and test the universality of psychological theories, we cannot really gain much insight into the dynamic processes of development in cultural context. As Bronfenbrenner pointed out, in the past too much research failed to consider development in context, but "we now have a surfeit of studies on 'context without development'" (1986, p. 288).

A related concern is that sociocultural approaches tend to neglect the role of basic cognitive skills such as memory, attention, and the acquisition of expertise in cognitive development. As Chapter 8 explains, these skills play a major role in children's increasing ability to solve problems and to think efficiently.

Learning Objective 7.9: *Compare and contrast the sociocultural and cognitive-developmental approaches to child development.*

1. In what core ways are the sociocultural and cognitive-developmental approaches alike?
2. How do the two approaches differ in both the means and the ends of cognitive development?
3. What challenges to their work do socioculturalists continue to face?

Links to Related Material
In Chapter 8, you will learn more about cognitive skills such as memory, attention, and the acquisition of expertise.

✔ *Test Your Mastery...*

BOX 7.4   Contextual Model of Cognitive Development

- Infant is born with human genetic capacity and inclination to seek and learn new information.
- Parents and teachers expose child to culturally appropriate knowledge. This differential exposure may shape the timing of the young child's achievement of concrete operations, or other types of knowledge, in different domains.
- Cultures and societies provide different opportunities to learn different kinds of knowledge. A child growing up in America is likely to learn how to operate a DVD player at a young age, but is unlikely to learn how to track animals in the wild.

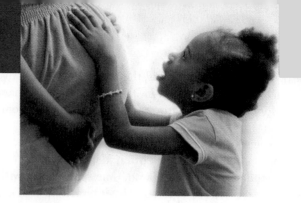

Learning Objective 7.1

Define the concepts from biology that Piaget used to explain cognitive development and evaluate his theory of stages.

1. What is cognition?	*Cognition* refers to higher-order mental processes, such as thinking, reasoning, learning, and problem solving, by which humans attempt to understand and adapt to their world.
2. What is the role of organization in the development of cognitive structures?	*Organization* is a basic biological principle in Piaget's theory of cognitive development. For Piaget, the essence of intelligence lies not in individually learned responses of isolated memories, but in the underlying organization. Cognitive structures are ways to organize information to understand and remember it more effectively.
3. What are some forms of knowledge that children reorganize as they develop?	Children reorganize *basic concepts* such as space and time, causality, number and quantity classes (or categories), and *relations between classes*. Piaget believed that while children experience long periods of relative conceptual stability, these concepts also change dramatically over the course of development.
4. What three processes of adaptation are essential for cognitive change, and how do they work?	Reorganization is accomplished through a process known as *adaptation*. Adaptation occurs through the complementary processes of *assimilation* and *accommodation*. As humans we assimilate our interactions with the environment; that is, we interpret new experiences in terms of what we already understand. At the same time, we are continually changing our cognitive structures to accommodate or fit in with environmental realities. Through accommodation, children's understanding of the environment around them becomes more accurate as they incorporate new information into their cognitive structures. When children become aware that their understanding is inadequate, they experience a feeling of cognitive discomfort (disequilbrium). Cognitive equilibrium is restored when children modify their understanding to fit more adaptively with cognitive challenges facing them. This self-regulatory process is called *equilibration*.

| 5. What four stages of cognitive development did Piaget propose, and how do they differ? | The four stages of cognitive development are sensorimotor, preoperational, concrete operational, and formal operational. In the *sensorimotor* stage (0–2 years) infants understand the world through the overt actions they perform on it. In this stage children gradually obtain the ability to construct the world symbolically. In the *preoperational* stage (2–6 years), the child now can use mental representations rather than overt actions to solve problems, resulting in faster and more efficient thinking. The *concrete operational* stage (6–12 years) bring the advent of mental operations, a system of logical problem solving. In the *formal operational* stage (12–adult), the acquisition of hypothetical-deductive reasoning enables children to generate and systematically test abstract hypotheses about things that do not currently exist. |

Learning Objective 7.2

Trace the substages and benchmarks of the sensorimotor period in child development.

| 1. What distinguishes the first two substages of Piaget's sensorimotor period of cognitive development? | In substage 1, *simple reflexes* (sucking, grasping) become the infant's first sensorimotor scheme. Sensorimotor schemes are skilled and generalizable action patterns with which the infant acts on and makes sense of the world. *Schemes* become more adaptive and more flexible during the second substage of development as schemes become more refined. An infant now has a more elaborate sucking scheme and is capable of distinguishing between a nipple, a finger, or the edge of a blanket. |

| 2. What role do schemes and procedures play in cognitive development? | *Schemes* are fairly limited. *Procedures* reflect the infant's developing knowledge of what he or she can do to produce desirable outcomes. At first this knowledge is obtained accidentally; eventually, however, it leads to intentional behavior. |

3. When during infancy does intentional behavior develop?	*Intentional behavior* involves the ability to separate means from ends. The infant uses a scheme as a means to lead to some other scheme, which becomes the goal or end of the action. The infant is capable of intentional behavior at 8–12 months of age.
4. What role do mental representations play in cognitive development?	*Mental representation* is thinking about and acting on the world internally and not merely externally through behavior. This advance brings the sensorimotor stage to an end and initiates a new period of cognitive development.
5. What is object permanence, and how do infants develop this and other physical knowledge?	*Object permanence* is the knowledge that objects continue to exist independent of our perception of them. Infants gradually come to understand object permanence across the entire span of infancy, which is comprised of six substages. It is only during the third substage (4–8 months) that babies even begin to search for hidden objects. Then, in substage four (8–12 months), the infant can search systematically and intelligently even for objects that are hidden entirely from view.
6. How do contemporary studies inform Piaget's classic work on cognitive development in infancy?	Contemporary researchers have explored Piaget's ideas about *object permanence*, and some have found that infant's concept of object permanence develops months earlier than Piaget believed. However, not all researchers agree with this finding. Conversely, recent research reveals that infants' *imitative abilities* are substantially more sophisticated than Piaget thought.

Learning Objective 7.3

Identify some strengths and weaknesses of preoperational thought in children's cognitive development.

1. How is preoperational thinking an advance over sensorimotor cognitive functioning?

The onset of symbolic function (representational thought) marks a major advance in the child's cognitive abilities. *Representational intelligence* is faster and more mobile than sensorimotor intelligence, and it is also socially sharable. With the acquisition of language, the child can communicate ideas to others and receive information from them in ways that is not possible without language.

2. What cognitive abilities does a child acquire during the preoperational stage?

During this stage the child develops *qualitative identity*, or the realization that the basic nature of something is not changed by changes in its appearances.

3. What are two significant limitations of preoperational thinking?

Egocentrism and *centration* are two limitations in thinking of the preoperational child. With egocentrism, the young child often acts as though everyone shares his or her particular point of view. Centration refers to the child's inability to distinguish appearance from reality and to focus only on one aspect of a problem at a time.

4. What experiments did Piaget use to test the strengths and limitations of young children's thinking?

The best-known task for studying *visual perspective taking* is the Three Mountains problem. In this experiment Piaget asks children to judge a landscape as someone viewing it from another vantage point. In addition, Piaget used various experiments to study children's realization that the basic quantitative properties of objects are not changed by changes in their appearance, for example, showing a child two rows of chips and asking if they are equal in number. Perhaps the most well-known *conservation experiment* is the conservation of liquid experiment, where children are asked to view water levels in different-sized containers.

Learning Objective 7.4

Analyze the cognitive task masteries that characterize concrete operational thought.

1. What did Piaget mean by operations?	*Operations* are mental activities such as reversing, combining, or separating information in a logical fashion. Children gradually organize these operations into larger systems of interrelated cognitive structures, which permits increasingly sophisticated thought.
2. How is operational thinking different from preoperational thinking?	*Operational thinking* is comprised of a system of internal mental activities that support logical thought. *Preoperational* children's centered thinking leads them to focus on salient but misleading perceptional appearances.
3. How do concrete operational children perform on problems of conservation and classification?	In conservation problems, *concrete operational* children can accurately represent and operate on each aspect of the transformation. They appreciate that while the length of a row has increased, so has its density, and the numerical identity remains constant as a result. In classification problems, the concrete preoperational child can solve class inclusion problems. Futhermore, this child appreciates the logical necessity of the class inclusion answer. The child knows that it is logically impossible for a subclass to be larger than a class.
4. How do seriation and transivity tasks reveal the relational logic used by concrete operational thinkers?	The concrete operational child can hold quantitative relationships in mind when solving both *seriation and transivity tasks*. Seriation requires that the child appreciates multiple relations among items; one item may be simultaneously longer than the one that precedes it in seriation and shorter than the one that comes after it. The concrete operational child can also appreciate that if item A is longer than item B and Item B is longer than Item C, then Item A is longer than Item C. This is known as transivity of quantitative relations.
5. What evidence suggests that Piaget underestimated the operational competence of preschool-age children on tasks involved in perspective taking and conservation?	In challenging Piaget, researchers have employed *tasks that simplify the problem* for children but nonetheless test the same cognitive skill that Piaget sought to target. These strategies have revealed that young children are not as illogical as Piaget once believed. Young children can predict the other's viewpoint when familiar toys rather than Piagetian mountains serve as landmarks. They also adjust their level of their communication to the cognitive resources of the listener, talking differently to their infant siblings than to adults. Children can also adjust to temporary variations in what the listener knows, as opposed to the general differences that exist between babies and adults. They describe an event differently depending on whether the adult to whom they are talking was present when the event occurred. Similarly, in simple situations even a 3-year-old can demonstrate some knowledge of invariance of number (conservation).

Learning Objective 7.5

Explain the characteristics and outcomes
of formal operations compared to
concrete operations.

1. What is the chief difference between formal operations and concrete operations?

The distinguishing characteristic of the formal operational period is the capacity for *hypothetical-deductive reasoning*. The formal operational thinker moves easily and surely through the world of what-ifs, might-bes, and if-thens.

2. How does the pendulum task test for the use of hypothetical-deductive reasoning?

The *pendulum task* challenges the individual to identify each of the potentially important variables—weight, length, and so on—and then to systematically test them out, varying one factor at a time while holding the other factors constant. The participant must be able to generate all the possible variables and combinations of variables, keep track of what has been done and what remains to be done, and be able to draw logical conclusions from the overall pattern of results.

3. Why is there debate about formal operations as a stage of cognitive development?

There is evidence that Piaget may have overestimated the competence of adolescents and adults. Researchers have found that extended training and simpler procedures have elicited formal operational performances in children as young as 9 or 10, much younger than Piaget would have suggested. Similarly, people may use formal operations when reasoning about content that is familiar to them. This reflects an *environmental influence* rather than a developmental change.

4. How do interest, experience, and culture influence performance on formal operational tasks?

Across-time comparisons of performance on formal operational tasks indicate that *experience* can play an important role in formal operational thought. Adolescents tested in the 1990s earn higher scores on these tasks than did comparable samples from the 1960s and early 1970s. These changes may be due to improvements in education that specifically engage students in hypothetical-deductive reasoning. Cross-cultural research confirms that the specific experiences available to children can affect both the rate of development and the final level of development. In societies without formal schooling, for example, few individuals attain formal operations.

| 5. On what key issues do evaluations of Piaget's stage theory focus? | Researchers have found *inconsistencies* in developmental change and continue to debate the validity of stage theories, as well as the question of whether Piaget's stages are *valid cross-culturally*. |

Learning Objective 7.6

Analyze the three main themes on which sociocultural approaches to development are based.

| 1. What temporal and cultural contexts did Vygotsky identify, and why are they important to the study of development? | Vygotsky proposed the study of development over four interrelated *temporal contexts*: ontogenetic, microgenetic, phylogenetic, and cultural/historical. Ontogenetic development occurs across the years of an individual's life. Microgenetic development is the individual's moment-to-moment learning. Phylogenetic development is the development of the species. Of particular interest to sociocultural theorists are the capabilities that distinguish humans from other animals. Cultural/historical development occurs over decades and centuries in particular times and places, leaving a legacy of tools, artifacts, value systems, institutions, and practices. |

| 2. What applications based on Vygotsky's theory demonstrate how children learn through social interaction? | By participating in culturally meaningful activities with more knowledgeable members of their society, children internalize the values, customs, beliefs, and skills of their culture, and over time, they come to use them independently. The *zone of proximal development* is when the most productive interactions occur. This involves activities that are slightly beyond the child's current capabilities but can be accomplished with help. Interactions within the zone of proximal development promote cognitive development because the social support allows children to extend their current skills to a higher level of competence. Similarly, scaffolding is a way that experienced partners can assist children's learning. During *scaffolding*, more capable partners adjust the level of help in response to the child's level of performance, moving to more direct, explicit forms of teaching if the child falters and to less direct, more demanding forms of teaching as the child moves closer to independent mastery. Finally, *guided participation* is the process by which young children become competent by participating in everyday, purposeful activities under the guidance of more experienced partners. |

| 3. According to Vygotsky, what is the role of cultural tools and artifacts in cognitive development? | Children learn how to use cultural tools through interactions with parents, teachers, and more advanced peers. *Cultural tools* for thinking both enhance and transform mental capabilities. Formal systems and implements for measuring time or distance, for example, enhance human thinking by improving accuracy. As children learn how to use these tools, their thinking is transformed, and they come to think about time and distance differently. Thus, children's thinking grows more sophisticated as they master the tools provided by their culture. According to Vygotsky, *language* is the most powerful cultural tool. Language is the primary means by which members of a cultural community pass on knowledge and values surrounding cultural practices to succeeding generations. |

| 4. According to the sociocultural view, what is the significance of pretend play in cognitive development? | For Vygotsky, *make-believe play* is a unique activity in which children try out a number of different skills in their zone of primal development. They exercise their budding representational abilities as they create imaginary situations, substituting objects for other objects within a play-frame. In addition, they create scenes within which they enact certain social rules and activities. |

Learning Objective 7.7

Compare and contrast the theories of Piaget and Vygotsky on the role of language in cognitive development.

| 1. How did Piaget and Vygotsky differ in their view of the relationships between language and thought? | Piaget believed that language is a verbal reflection of the individual's conceptual understanding, and the acquisition of language symbols speeds up thinking, because a sequence of thought can usually be carried out more quickly than a sequence of actions. For *Piaget*, cognition determines language. On the other hand, Vygotsky believed that the onset of language is one of the most important events, with the power to transform early abilities into a qualitatively new form of thinking. It is with the onset of language that "elementary mental functions" are transformed into "higher mental functions." For *Vygotsky*, language precedes thought. |

| 2. How did Vygotsky's dynamics of private speech differ from Piaget's concept of egocentric speech? | According to *Vygotsky*, children's experience of language is social from the outset. Their first words are communicative acts, mediating their interaction with the people around them. This sequence suggests a progression from social and communicative speech to internal dialogue (private speech). *Piaget* believed that children's egocentric speech ("talk for self") was the result of the inability to take the perspective of another. |

| 3. How did Vygotsky interpret children's collective monologues differently than Piaget? | *Vygotsky* believed that children use collective monologues in order to communicate with others, and he supported this claim with findings from his experiments. *Piaget* believed that while children will take turns in conversations, each child's contribution only relates to what she or he just said. Each child narrates an event to himself or herself without considering what the other child is talking about. Eventually, collective monologues give way to genuine dialogues as the child develops the ability to adopt others' points of view. |

4. What did Vygotsky mean by his idea of sociogenesis of cognitive development?

According to *Vygotsky*, far from being nonsocial, young children's private speech grows out of their interactions with parents and more experienced others as they work together on various tasks. During these tasks, children begin to use versions of their parents' instructional comments to direct their own behavior. This kind of talk is a child's way of *self-guiding* or self-directing. Gradually, the controlling speech becomes internalized as thought, as children eventually reproduce "silent statement" (thoughts) similar to the verbal ones. Self-regulations thus develop out of the child's social interactions. This process is what Vygotsky referred to as sociogenesis.

Learning Objective 7.8
Evaluate Piaget's and Vygotsky's contributions to educational practice.

1. On what three principles are Piagetian-inspired classrooms based?

The first principle is an emphasis on *discovery learning* or active learning. This emphasis relates to Piaget's belief that children learn by acting on the world, not by passively taking in information. A second related principle is a child's *readiness to learn* and depends on the child's current level of thinking. Experience, educational or otherwise, does not simply happen to the child; rather, the child must always integrate it with existing cognitive structures through the process of assimilation and accommodation. In addition a child's motivation to learn depends on the timing of educational experiences. A third principle is that teachers must be sensitive to *individual difference* among students in the classroom. Because children go through the same cognitive stages at different rates, however, learning must be based on the skill level and developmental pacing of individual children.

2. What kinds of learning activities are you likely to find in a Vygotskian-inspired classroom?

Vygotsky believed that children learned best through *assisted discovery* through interactions between teacher and student, as well as between students. The teacher's role is to carefully guide each child, according to his or her ability level, to improve skills in using and manipulating the symbolic systems of their culture. The emphasis is on the child's interactions with others as the child participates in meaningful activities with others in the classroom.

3. How did Piaget's and Vygotsky's views differ on the role of peers in learning and development?

For *Piaget*, cognitive growth is fueled by the child's recognition that his or her views are different and perhaps less logical than those of peers. Thus, the experience and resolution of sociocognitive conflict pushes development forward. *Vygotsky's* explanation of peer influence focuses on cooperation rather than conflict resolution. Peer learning is best achieved when students cooperate to achieve a common learning objective. Students sharing a responsibility for a task are more likely to engage in cooperative dialogues to resolve differences of opinion actively. Partners negotiate, or co-construct new understandings, and they clarify, refine, extend, and build on each other's reasoning.

Learning Objective 7.9

Compare and contrast the sociocultural and cognitive-developmental approaches to child development.

1. In what core ways are the sociocultural and cognitive-developmental approaches alike?	Both approaches view the child as an *active participant* in his or her own development, and both hold that the individual undergoes *qualitative as well as quantitative change* over the course of development.
2. How do the two approaches differ in both the means and the ends of cognitive development?	*Piagetians* focus on process internal to the individual child, such as the reorganization of cognitive structures, increased speed of task completion, and the child's individual attempts to understand the world. *Sociocultural theorists* believe that developmental change is socially mediated and takes place within the context of social interaction. Developmental is the direct result of interactions with other people and the tools and artifacts that are the products of human culture. In the *cognitive-developmental* view, the end point of development is the ability to think in highly abstract ways that follow rules of logic. *Sociocultural theorists*, on the other hand, question whether there is some ideal end point of development. They maintain that the kind of abstract thought characterized by Piaget's final stage of development may itself be a product of culturally situated values.
3. What challenges to their work do socioculturalists continue to face?	*Critics* point out that those working within the sociocultural framework often idealize learning. For example, not all experts are always willing to give away all they know to their students. And novices are sometimes reluctant to take over responsibility for their own learning even if they have the competence to do so. Another challenge is how to integrate data across multiple spheres of development. Without data from the multiple levels of development (e.g., microsystem, mesosystem, exosystem, macrosystem, and chronosystem), although we may accumulate information about lives in different cultures and test the universality of psychological theories, we cannot really gain much insight into the dynamic processes of development in context.

Information Processing *and* Core Knowledge Approaches

Josh Waitzkin draws a game with world chess champion Garry Kasparov at the age of 11. How does the chess knowledge of an expert like Josh differ from the knowledge of a novice learner? (Courtesy Bonnie Waitzkin)

CHAPTER

DEFINE THE INFORMATION PROCESSING APPROACH AND DESCRIBE THREE
METHODS OF STUDYING INFORMATION PROCESSING.

EXPLAIN THE INFORMATION PROCESSING MODEL OF MEMORY, AND TRACE DEVELOPMENTAL CHANGES
IN THE KINDS OF MEMORY.

• Recognition Memory • Recall Memory

RESEARCH & SOCIETY Children's Eyewitness Testimony

CONVERSATIONS with a Child Therapist

DESCRIBE THREE COGNITIVE TOOLS THAT CONTRIBUTE TO THE DEVELOPMENT OF MEMORY DURING
CHILDHOOD.

• Developmental Changes in Strategy Use • Variability in Strategy Use

• Developmental Changes in Metacognition • Effects of Metacognition on
Memory Performance

ANALYZE THE ABILITIES AND SKILLS CHILDREN USE TO SOLVE PROBLEMS, AND GIVE EXAMPLES OF HOW
RESEARCH ON PROBLEM SOLVING CAN BE APPLIED.

• Preschoolers' Rule-Based Reasoning • Developments in Rule-Based Reasoning

• Strategy Construction and Selection in Arithmetic • Development of a Conceptual
Knowledge Base in Physics • Metacognitive Awareness in Comprehension

The 1993 film, *Searching for Bobby Fischer,* is based on the true story of Josh Waitzkin. Josh first encountered chess at the age of 6 while walking with his mother in New York City's Washington Square Park, where he noticed street hustlers playing the game. At the age of 7, Josh began classical study of the game with his first formal teacher, Bruce Pandolfini. He won the National Primary Championship in 1986 at the age of 9. At the age of 11, he drew a game with World Champion Garry Kasparov. At age 13, Josh earned the title of National Master, and at age 16, he became an International Master.

Clearly, Josh excelled at the game of chess from a young age. Researchers who have studied children with special abilities like Josh have asked how young children who are experts in a field such as chess represent the game to themselves compared to children (and adults) who are not experts. That is, how does the knowledge of an expert differ from the knowledge of a novice learner? In the field of information processing, researchers study knowledge, how it is represented, and how it changes over time.

Chapter 7 described how Jean Piaget and Lev Vygotsky inspired two general theories of how children think and know—the cognitive-developmental approach and the sociocultural approach. These theories have had considerable impact on contemporary research in child development, and that research has gradually given rise to two alternative approaches to thinking about early cognitive development: information processing and core knowledge. ■

The Information Processing Approach to Cognition

Learning Objective 8.1
Define the information processing approach and describe three methods of studying information processing.

To think is to process information (Siegler & Alibali, 2005). This observation has led researchers to study how children's ability to encode, process, store, and retrieve information changes with age and experience (Kail & Miller, 2006; Klahr & MacWhinney, 1998; Miller, 2001; Siegler, 2005). The specific information to be processed varies as children encounter new challenges in different contexts, such as exploring a new toy, learning to play a new game, remembering the route to a friend's house, or following an instruction from the teacher. Children employ an arsenal of psychological processes in confronting and solving each new problem they encounter. Some tasks require careful attention to critical details, for example, whereas others require accurate comparison with information previously stored in memory. Still others require determining an appropriate sequence of steps to arrive at a solution. The goal of the information processing approach is to specify these underlying psychological processes—and the developmental changes they undergo.

Information processing approaches are based on a computer metaphor. Psychologists have observed that computers could systematically transform a variety of inputs into a variety of outputs. To do so, computers require precise programs that specify each step of the transformation. Information processing theorists saw in the digital computer a useful metaphor for the human mind. If scientists could specify the steps by which the mind transforms sensory inputs into cognitive or behavioral outputs, they would have a complete account of human thought. Methods of studying information processing include computer simulations, neural networks, and microgenetic studies.

Computer Simulations and Neural Networks

For many information processing theorists, the computer is not just a metaphor. It also provides a method—the computer simulation. In a **computer simulation**, the researcher attempts to program a computer in order to produce some aspect of intelligent behavior in the same way that humans produce the behavior. The idea is to build into the computer program whatever knowledge and computational abilities may be important for the human problem solver.

Suppose, for example, that you want to test a theory of how first graders solve simple addition problems. You might program the computer to apply the rules that you think children use and then see how the computer responds to the same tasks. The program's success in generating the target behavior—in this case, the pattern of first-grade responses—is a test of your theory of how children arrive at their answers.

Computer simulations can take the form of a set of rules children might use to solve a problem. For example, first graders' behavior might be captured in a rule such as: [IF addend #1 = addend #2 THEN retrieve sum from memory, ELSE count out the two addends on fingers.] Rule-based models have provided researchers with a rich understanding of cognitive development in several domains, but they have an important weakness: They provide only a static description of cognitive processing at one instant in development. They do not model developmental change.

Today, in an approach called **connectionism**, scientists attempt to construct computer simulations that more closely approximate the structure of neural connections within the human brain. Though human and computer have much in common, the brain is not built at all like a digital computer. As you read in Chapter 6, the brain is constructed of millions of interconnected neurons, the complexity of which cannot be duplicated (at least not now!) in a machine.

Connectionist computer programs seek to approximate the function of neural systems through **artificial neural networks**, rather than through strings of explicit rules like those used in conventional computer programs. Such networks consist of multiple interconnected processing units, just as the brain consists of multiple interconnected neurons. The units are arranged in layers, including an *input layer* that encodes information about a task and an *output layer* that represents an eventual response. Networks also often contain one or more sets of *hidden layers* representing the information used to execute the task. Like neurons in the brain, units "fire" or pass information along to units in the next layer when the amount of activation they are receiving reaches a certain threshold. Connections among units vary in strength, just as is true for connections among neurons in the brain. The pattern of activity that eventually reaches the set of output units determines the network's response to the task (Plunkett, Karmiloff-Smith, Bates, Elman, & Johnson, 1997).

Neural networks are programmed to change or "learn" with experience. The network uses feedback on the accuracy of each output to modify connection strengths among the units. When the response is correct, the connections that produced it are strengthened slightly; when the response is wrong, the connections are weakened. As a result, patterns of activation change throughout the network. This is how learning occurs and how new, more accurate responses

Computer simulation
Programming a computer to perform a cognitive task in the same way in which humans are thought to perform it; an information processing method for testing theories of underlying process.

Connectionism
Information processing approach using computer simulations that approximate the structure of neural connections within the human brain, enabling programs to solve cognitive tasks and modify their solutions in response to experience.

Links to Related Material
In Chapter 6, you read how the brain is constructed of millions of interconnected neurons. Here, you learn about computer models of cognitive development that attempt to simulate these neural networks.

Artificial neural networks
Multiple interconnected processing units arranged in layers in a computer, just as the brain consists of multiple interconnected neurons.

Questions for Thought
and Discussion

What might be some limitations of the computer metaphor for understanding cognitive development? What aspects of cognition are not now captured in a computer program?

gradually replace old, incorrect ones. Researchers can thus ask not only whether the model produces responses like a child at a given time, but also whether the model shows the same pattern of learning over time that real children demonstrate (Munakata & McClelland, 2003). When networks perform similarly to human children, researchers conclude that they have created a plausible model of how learning occurs in the task under investigation.

The connectionist approach has provided insight into a host of aspects of cognitive development. Some topics include infant perception (Mareschal & Johnson, 2002), object permanence (Munakata, 1998), Piagetian concrete operational concepts (Buckingham & Shultz, 2000), category learning (Mareschal, French, & Quinn, 2000), conceptual development (Rogers & McClelland, 2005), and language (MacWhinney & Chang, 1995).

Despite these successes, the use of connectionism as a tool for understanding cognition has also been criticized. Similarities between such networks and human brains often are exaggerated, and connectionist systems always require hundreds or even thousands of trials in order to learn simple tasks. Unlike humans, these models never experience the "aha moments" or "eurekas" of insight that humans often report, in which an answer simply becomes clear (Marcus, 2001). Furthermore, such models are never "aware" and cannot direct "attention" deliberately in the way young children can and do (Cowan, 2003). Finally, connectionist models cannot model the role of sociocultural interaction in promoting cognitive advances in young children.

Microgenetic Studies

Links to Related Material

In Chapter 2, you learned about the microgenetic method as a way to understand developmental changes. Here, you read about how this methodology has been used to study children's understanding of arithmetic.

This child has not yet discovered the min strategy for solving addition tasks. The min strategy involves counting up from the larger of two addends to arrive at a sum. For example, the problem 10 + 2 would be solved by thinking "10, 11, 12; the answer is 12." Microgenetic studies can capture the cognitive process of this discovery. What other kinds of things can microgenetic techniques tell us? (Lawrence Migdale/Stone/Getty Images)

Computer simulations typically complement studies of human performance, which often employ a microgenetic technique. As you may recall from Chapter 2, a microgenetic study begins with the selection of a sample of children who are thought to be in transition for the knowledge or ability being studied—that is, they are close to moving to a higher level of understanding. Researchers observe the children in several sessions over time as they attempt to solve a variety of problems that assess the ability of interest. The goal is to observe processes of change as the change occurs. While longitudinal research gives us snapshots—pictures of the cognitive system at different points in time—microgenetic research gives us a movie—a continuous record of change over time (Siegler, 2006).

An example of a microgenetic study is Siegler and Jenkins's (1989) investigation of children's learning of addition strategies. They selected 10 children who did not yet know how to count up from the larger addend when solving simple arithmetic problems (the *min strategy*). These children then participated in three experimental sessions per week across a period of 11 weeks. During each session they attempted to solve seven addition problems; across sessions the complexity of the problems gradually increased. Both videotapes of the children's performance and direct questioning were used to infer the strategies underlying their answers. Through this approach, Siegler and Jenkins were able to document the gradual discovery of the min strategy by seven of the eight children who made it through all 11 weeks. Because of their extensive observational records, they knew when and how the strategy first appeared, as well as what preceded it and to what it subsequently led. The examples in Table 8.1 include the first appearance of the strategy for one child, Brittany.

Siegler (1996) identifies five issues related to cognitive change for which microgenetic techniques can provide valuable data:

- The *path* of cognitive change: the sequences and levels through which children move in acquiring new knowledge.
- The *rate* of change: how quickly or slowly different forms of knowledge are mastered.
- *Breadth* of change: when a new competency (such as a particular arithmetical strategy) is acquired and how narrowly or broadly it is applied.
- *Variability* in the pattern of change: children often do not all follow the same route in mastering a new concept.
- The *sources* of change: the experiences and processes through which new knowledge is constructed.

TABLE 8.1 Children's Use of the Min Strategy for Solving Addition Problems

1. Experimenter (E): How much is 6 + 3?
   Lauren (L): (Long pause) Nine.
   - **E:** OK, how did you know that?
   - **L:** I think I said . . . I think I said . . . oops, um . . . I think he said . . . 8 was 1 and . . . um . . . I mean 7 was 1, 8 was 2, 9 was 3.
   - **E:** OK.
   - **L:** Six and three are nine.
   - **E:** How did you know to do that? Why didn't you count "1, 2, 3, 4, 5, 6, 7, 8, 9"? How come you did "6, 7, 8, 9"?
   - **L:** 'Cause then you have to count all those numbers.
   - **E:** OK, well how did you know you didn't have to count all of those numbers?
   - **L:** Why didn't . . . well I don't have to if I don't want to.

2. Experimenter (E): OK, Brittany, how much is 2 + 5?
   Brittany (B): 2 + 5—(whispers)—6, 7—it's 7.
   - **E:** How did you know that?
   - **B:** (excitedly) Never counted.
   - **E:** You didn't count?
   - **B:** Just said it—I just said after six something—seven—six, seven.
   - **E:** You did? Why did you say 6, 7?
   - **B:** 'Cause I wanted to see what it really was.
   - **E:** OK, well—so, did you—what—you didn't have to count at one, you didn't count, 1, 2, 3, you just said 6, 7?
   - **B:** Yeah—smart answer.

3. Experimenter (E): OK, Christian, How much is 1 + 24?
   Christian (C): 1 + 24!?
   - **E:** Yep.
   - **C:** Umm . . . 25.
   - **E:** How did you know that?
   - **C:** I . . . counted in my head.
   - **E:** How did you count it in your head?
   - **C:** What was it again?
   - **E:** 1 + 24
   - **C:** I went . . . 1, 2, 3, 4, 5, si . . . I went, 24 + 1, I, well. . . . I'll try to get you to understand, ok?
   - **E:** OK.
   - **C:** I went 24 + 1.. (whispers) 24 . . . (whispers) 25 . . . that's what I did.
   - **E:** OK, that's good, well, why didn't you count 1, 2, 3, 4, 5, 6, 7, 8, 9, 10, all the way to 24?
   - **C:** Aww, that would take too long . . . silly.

SOURCE: From R.S. Siegler and E. Jenkins (1989). *How Children Discover New Strategies*. Mahwah, NJ: Erlbaum, pp. 66, 80, 91. Copyright © 1989 by Lawrence Erlbaum Associates. Reprinted by permission.

Learning Objective 8.1: *Define the information processing approach and describe three methods of studying information processing.*

✔ *Test Your Mastery...*

1. What are the goals of the information processing approach to cognition?
2. How does the information processing approach reflect a computer metaphor?
3. What are the strengths and limitations of connectionism in the information processing approach?
4. What can we learn from microgenetic studies of cognition?

Memory

Learning Objective 8.2
Explain the information processing model of memory, and trace developmental changes in the kinds of memory.

Memory
In information processing theory, the proceses by which information is taken in, stored, and retrieved.

All information processing models rely on a theory of memory. Children can learn through their experiences only if they can somehow retain information from these experiences over time. To be learned at all, information must first enter the brain through the senses. Once there, the information may be lost and thus forgotten. Alternatively, the information may undergo further mental processing in which it is encoded and stored to be retrieved when needed at a later time.

Memory changes with development. Infants' and young children's memory capacity is quite limited in comparison to that of older children. Thus the development of **memory**—of how information is taken in, stored, and retrieved—and its effects on children's ability to process information have been a central focus for information processing theories. Figure 8.1 uses a flowchart to show memory as a system for processing information.

The information processing flowchart presents the *memory store model*. Imagine, for example, that a 6-year-old in a first-grade classroom has just heard a word for the first time. This word enters the *sensory register*, where a literal image of a stimulus can be held, but only for a matter of milliseconds. The word then moves to *short-term* or *working memory*, the center for active and conscious processing. Although information typically remains in short-term memory for only a few seconds, various strategies may prolong it. Finally, the word may be transferred to *long-term memory*, where it can exist indefinitely. Getting the word to long-term memory is the teacher's goal when presenting a new term to be learned. You have thousands of words stored in your permanent memory.

The information processing model also shows psychological processes involved in memory. *Control processes* affect the maintenance of information and its movement from one store to another. *Response-generating mechanisms* permit overt responses—for example, the child's ability to say a recently learned word. The memory store model illustrates two important aspects of the information processing approach. First, the flowchart structure defines precisely how information flows through the cognitive system. Second, information must be acted on or processed in various ways to continue its journey to the

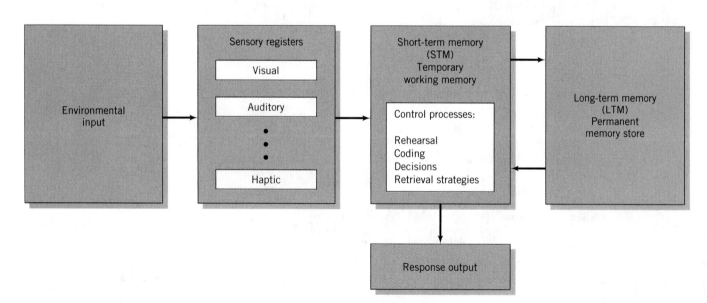

FIGURE 8.1   Information Processing Model of Memory
This diagram illustrates the kind of flowchart representation that information processing theorists use to describe the sequence of information processing. What roles do the senses and memory play in that sequence?

Source: From R.C. Atkinson and R.M. Shiffrin (1971). The control of short-term memory. *Scientific American, 225,* 82. Copyright credit Allen Beechel.

long-term memory store, where it becomes part of the child's permanent knowledge base. Understanding the processing steps that occur between the external stimulus and the child's behavioral response is the primary goal.

Basic Memory Processes in Infancy

In late infancy, children begin to construct their memories through social interaction and social mediation. In **event memory**, for example, children develop scripts for sequences of familiar actions or routine events in their daily world (Nelson, 1996). A **script** is a representation of the typical sequence of events in a familiar context. Children come to regard their scripts, such as the "birthday party" script or the "going to the store" or the "finding my way home" script—as natural and logical and may even resist attempts to change them. Scripts are both the product and the process of constructive memory and can lead to both improved memory and memory distortions. **Constructive memory** refers to the ways that individuals interpret the information they take in from the world in terms of their preexisting knowledge, which affects what they remember. Parents and teachers use prompts and cues during social interaction to help children develop event memory and constructive memory. **Autobiographical memory**, on the other hand, refers to specific, personal, and long-lasting memory about the self. Autobiographical memory contains information about unique events such as the first day of school or a vacation to the beach. These memories are part of one's life history and are culturally constructed through verbal and social interaction.

Event memory and autobiographical memory are of particular interest to sociocultural theorists. However, psychologists using the information processing approach focus on two other basic forms of memory that begin in infancy: recognition and recall. **Recognition memory** refers to the realization that some object you are currently perceiving or event has been encountered before. When you identify the correct answer on a multiple-choice test, for example, you rely on recognition memory. **Recall memory** refers to the retrieval of some past object or event when it is *not* perceptually present. Passing an essay test, for example, requires good recall memory. Much of the behavior that you produce as an adult would be impossible if you lacked the capacity to recognize and recall previously experienced stimuli.

Recognition Memory Can infants recognize previously experienced information? Yes indeed! Many of the findings from the study of infant perception discussed in Chapter 5 require recognition. For example, in order to prefer their mother's voice, infants must remember that voice. The most common method of studying recognition memory in infancy has been the habituation–dishabituation procedure, described in Chapter 7. *Habituation* occurs as a stimulus becomes familiar and the infant's response to it declines. This decline is possible only if the infant can recognize the stimulus from trial to trial. Without such memory, the infant would experience every appearance of the stimulus as a novel event. Similarly, *dishabituation* can occur only if the infant is able to compare the new stimulus to some memory of the original.

Recognition memory first emerges from birth and possibly even earlier. Thus even a newborn infant can show habituation across a range of modalities: visual (Slater et al., 1991; Turati et al., 2006), auditory (Zelazo, Weiss, & Tarquino, 1991), and tactile (Kisilevsky & Muir, 1984). Studies of recognition memory in infants demonstrate very short-term memory. As infants develop, the length of time during which they can remember their experiences steadily increases, soon reaching impressive levels. By 5 months of age, babies can recognize a photo of a face, initially viewed for only two minutes, after a delay of two weeks (Fagan, 1973). With a more dynamic, moving stimulus, recognition has been demonstrated across a three-month delay for babies who were only 3 months old at the time of initial exposure (Bahrick & Pickens, 1995). Newborns can remember speech stimuli across a period of at least 24 hours (Swain, Zelazo, & Clifton, 1993). And, as noted in Chapter 6, studies of

Event memory
Recall of things that have happened in experience.

Script
A representation of the typical sequence of actions and events in some familiar context.

Constructive memory
The ways that individuals interpret the information they take in from the world in terms of their preexisting knowledge, which affects what they remember.

Autobiographical memory
Specific, personal, long-lasting memory regarding the self.

Questions for Thought and Discussion
Autobiographical memory is constructed within the larger contexts of family and community history and biography. How did family photo albums influence your memories as a child?

Recognition memory
The realization that some perceptually present stimulus or event has been encountered before.

Recall memory
The retrieval of some past stimulus or event that is not perceptually present.

Links to Related Material
In Chapter 5, you read about studies of infant perception that require the infant to recognize objects that have been seen before. Here you learn more about the development of recognition memory in infants.

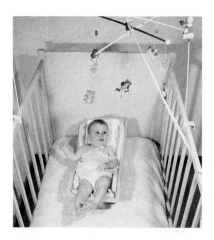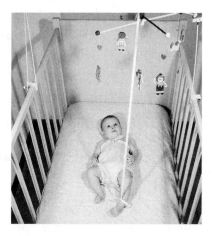

In this experiment on infants' ability to remember, babies learn that when the ribbon is attached to the ankle, kicking makes the mobile move. Infants as young as 2 months rapidly learn to make the mobile jump, rapidly increasing their kicking rate to earn the reward (Rovee-Collier, 1987; 1999). Two-month-olds can remember the association for 3 days, 3-month-olds for 8 days, and 6-month-olds for 21 days (Rovee-Collier & Shyi, 1992). In one study, 2-month-olds who received periodic reminders still remembered the kicking response 5 months after initial exposure to the mobile (Rovee-Collier, Hartshorn, & DiRubbo, 1999)! These photos were made available by Dr. C.K. Rovee-Collier.

The recall memory of this 2-year-old tells her what to do in what order in the "give baby a bath" event sequence. If she is following a socially transmitted or mediated script, this behavior will also become part of her event memory. How do we know that recall memory has its origins in infancy? How long would she remember this activity sequence as a 1-year-old? (Michael Newman/PhotoEdit)

Infantile amnesia
The inability to remember experiences from the first two or three years of life.

memory for prenatally experienced speech sounds have typically involved even longer intervals between the last prenatal exposure and the first postnatal test (DeCasper & Spence, 1991).

Recall Memory Can infants not only recognize familiar stimuli or events but also actively call such stimuli or events to mind? Recall memory is difficult to study in infancy because infants cannot produce verbal reports or drawings to show what they recall. Nonetheless, studies of deferred imitation provide compelling evidence of recall memory in infancy. As you read in Chapter 7, infants as young as 6 weeks demonstrate some degree of recall, reproducing a model's tongue protrusion 24 hours after they first saw it. By 14 months, infants can recall unusual actions like pressing one's forehead against a panel to turn on a light a full 4 months after they witnessed an adult doing this (Meltzoff, 1995).

Infants also can recall and imitate simple sequences of action (Bauer, 2002; Bauer et al., 2000). Thirteen-month-olds, for example, can reproduce three-action sequences for events such as giving a teddy bear a bath (first place in tub, then wash with sponge, then dry with towel) or constructing a simple rattle (place ball in large cup, invert small cup into large, shake) (Bauer & Mandler, 1992). By 24 months children can remember sequences of five actions (Bauer & Travis, 1993), and by 30 months children can retain as many as eight separate steps (Bauer & Fivush, 1992). Memory for the order in which events occur is an important form of knowledge, and studies indicate that such memory has its origins in infancy.

Early recall, like early recognition, also extends over a considerable time. Some memory for two-action sequences has been demonstrated after six months for infants who were only 10 months old at the time of initial learning (Carver & Bauer, 2001). Infants who are 16 months old at the time of learning show some recall of three-action sequences eight months later (Bauer, Hertsgaard, & Dow, 1994). In one study (McDonough and Mandler 1994), infants remembered sequences of actions, like the teddy bear and rattle tasks, a full year after these actions were modeled.

If infants are able to form long-term memories, how do we explain the phenomenon of **infantile amnesia**—the inability to remember experiences from the first two or three years of life? Sigmund Freud suggested that early memories are lost through repression of forbidden thoughts into the unconscious. Contemporary theorists, however, point to several contributing factors (Howe, 2000; Newcombe et al., 2000). Among these are

BOX 8.1 Children's Eyewitness Testimony

It has been estimated that at least 100,000 children testify in court cases in the United States every year (Ceci & Bruck, 1998). This figure does not include the much larger number of instances in which children provide depositions or other kinds of evidence outside court. The cases in which children testify span a range of topics, but the most frequent category among criminal trials, accounting for about 13,000 cases each year, is child sexual abuse. In most instances of alleged abuse, the child witness is also the target of the abuse. In many, the child is the only witness. Can the testimony of a young child be trusted? Should such testimony be admissible in court?

Questions like these can be critically important and are very difficult to answer. Researchers who study children's memory for abuse face some obvious challenges. Experiences of abuse are typically highly traumatic; they may continue for extended periods of time; and they often involve the child as a participant and not merely as a bystander. Furthermore, what children say about abuse may involve more than simply what they remember. Complex social and emotional factors may be important, such as the child's guilt about being a participant or reluctance to implicate a parent or friend. Questioning by a parent or an authority figure may lead the child to particular responses, especially if questioners believe they already know the truth or if, as advocates within the court system, they have an interest in a particular outcome. All these characteristics make memory for abuse different from the kinds of memory that psychologists usually study—or that they *can* easily study in an ethically acceptable way.

Researchers have tried in various ways to discover or devise memory tests that bear some similarity to the abuse situation. Some have created experimental settings that reproduce some elements of the real-life situations of interest—for example, a Simon Says game in which child and experimenter touch parts of each other's bodies (White, Leichtman, & Ceci, 1997). Others have focused on memory for naturally occurring traumatic experiences—for example, going to the dentist (Peters, 1991), receiving an injection (Goodman et al., 1991), or undergoing urinary catheterization (Quas et al., 1999). Still others have investigated children's long-term recall of highly traumatic, naturally occurring events that affected them directly, such as major hurricanes (Fivush, Sales, Goldberg, Bahrick, & Parker, 2004). Although such experiences can hardly equal the trauma of abuse, they do capture some of its characteristics.

In many studies, researchers have also attempted to simulate the types of questioning that suspected victims of abuse must undergo. A child may be questioned several times across a period of weeks, for example, or the interviewer may include some deliberately leading questions in an attempt to determine how suggestible the child is. Children may be told to "keep a secret" about what happened to them during the experimental session (Bottoms et al., 1990), or a police officer rather than research assistant may do the questioning (Tobey & Goodman, 1992).

Such studies suggest several conclusions about children as witnesses (Bjorklund, 2000; Bottoms & Goodman, 1996; Ceci & Bruck, 1995, 1998; Eisen, Quas, & Goodman, 2002). First, research verifies that recall memory improves with age and that older children typically report more of their experiences than do younger children (Ornstein et al., 2006). The memories of 3-year-olds (the youngest age group tested in such research) are especially shaky. Second, as the delay between an event and questioning about it increases, the completeness and accuracy of recall decline; this may be especially true for young children. In many real-life cases, there are delays, often substantial ones, before children are first questioned, and so this finding is a cause for concern. Third, in at least some cases, young children are more suggestible than are older children or adults—that is, they are more likely to be influenced by leading questions from an adult authority figure. This finding indicates the need for caution in accepting the reports of young children who have undergone repeated and leading questioning, as is often true in investigations of suspected abuse.

On the other hand, in many studies memory differences between younger and older children or between children and adults are not very great. Age differences, as well as memory inaccuracies in general, are most likely when specific questions are used. Conversely, they are minimized by the use of free recall measures that allow children to say what happened in their own words. Furthermore, the memory problems that children do show are mainly errors of omission rather than of commission—that is, they are more likely to fail to report certain details than they are to introduce false information. This finding suggests that any clearly spontaneous mentions of abuse by children should be taken very seriously.

Much controversy remains about exactly what the research shows and what the implications are for children's legal testimony. Fortunately, all researchers agree that more study is necessary, and the topic of eyewitness memory is currently the focus of a major research effort. Among the topics being explored in this research is the issue of how and when best to question children in order to meet two goals: maximizing the accuracy of testimony and minimizing stress to the child (Goodman et al., 1992; Lamb & Poole, 1998; Ornstein et al., 2006; Poole & Lindsay, 2002). Having to provide testimony can add to the trauma of an already traumatic situation. It is therefore important to devise procedures that protect the child from further harm.

---

immaturity of parts of the brain involved in memory (Nelson, 1995), differences in format between early and later memory systems (for example, nonverbal versus verbal), the lack of a sense of self in infancy, and the absence of a social system within which to share and rehearse memories.

Questions for Thought and Discussion

What is your first memory? How old were you? How might you explain your infantile amnesia?

BOX 8.2 Conversations with a Child Therapist

Understanding children's beliefs about their own and others' mental worlds—along with understanding children's feelings—is critically important in the work of child therapists. Here is the story of one child therapist, Cheryl Lynn Hall. She is 44 years old, was born in Chicago, and grew up in Illinois, Indiana, and Kentucky, graduating from high school in Lexington, Kentucky. She has been married since 1998 to John McCollum and they have one child, Molly Hall McCollum, age 4. Dr. Hall's occupation is clinical psychologist, and a substantial part of her private practice is children and adolescents.

I first became interested in psychology in high school. I had an excellent psychology teacher who was enthusiastic about and encouraged self-directed learning and exploration. I still remember writing a paper on autism; my curiosity was in motion regarding the whole area of personality development and intervention for emotional disorders.

As an undergraduate, I dabbled in other majors, trying to convince myself that other areas could be just as interesting. At that point in my life, a Ph.D. seemed too long of a journey! Nevertheless, I declared a psychology major at the beginning of my junior year. I had an opportunity to work in an adolescent ward of a state hospital during my senior year, which further solidified my desire to work with children and teens with psychiatric disorders.

I earned my B.A. in psychology from Hanover College in Indiana and immediately went on to pursue a master's degree in clinical psychology at Southern Illinois University at Edwardsville, Illinois. It was a terminal degree, designed for students who were not going on for a Ph.D. The master's would allow me to get some real-world experience, and I chose this program because it had a heavy emphasis on practicum. Then, after five years of work experience, I went back to school and pursued my Ph.D. at Texas Tech University. I did research on peer rejection and peer neglect in the schools and had several practicums, including one in the school district providing counseling for children with emotional disturbance.

I chose to take the elective child psychology courses along with the required adult coursework, to be better prepared to work with all ages. During my internship at the Oklahoma University Health Sciences Center, some of my rotations were with children. I worked in a hospital setting providing counseling and pain management for children with cancer and burns. I assessed children with emotional and learning problems and provided interventions for the children individually, as well as for their parents.

After my internship, my first job was as a staff psychologist working at a residential treatment center for emotionally disturbed children and adolescents. During my three years there, I gained tremendous depth and breadth of experience in

Developmental Changes in Memory

Older children remember better than younger children. This fact was undoubtedly apparent to parents, teachers, and test makers long before there was research to verify it. IQ tests, for example, include recall memory as one of their components. On average, the older the child, the better the performance on such memory measures. Developmental improvements in memory thus have practical importance because they influence what parents and teachers expect of children and how they treat children. A 10-year-old can be entrusted with a string of verbal instructions that would overtax the memory of a 4-year-old. How can we explain the fact that older children remember better than younger ones?

Learning Objective 8.2: *Explain the information processing model of memory, and trace developmental changes in the kinds of memory.*

1. What is the memory store model in the information processing approach?
2. What kinds of memory are present in infancy, and how are they different?
3. How do researchers study recognition and recall memory in infants and young children?
4. How does memory change as children develop?

 **Test Your Mastery...**

Cognitive Tools

Learning Objective 8.3

Describe three cognitive tools that contribute to the development of memory during childhood.

Three cognitive tools other than recognition memory and recall memory that contribute to developmental improvement in memory during childhood are greater use of memory strategies, greater knowledge about memory, and more powerful cognitive structures.

providing child therapy. Now that I am in private practice, I see fewer children with severe emotional problems, but my work at the treatment center prepared me well for working with any difficulty a child may present. I work in a private office setting and share a building with two other psychologists. We each have our own office and share general space and staff. I see children, teens, parents, and individual adults for therapy.

As part of my work with children, I interface with teachers, physicians, probation officers, child protective services caseworkers, and others. I must communicate with them to gain more knowledge about the child's life outside my office, so that therapy can be most effective. In turn, I provide information to these other caregivers, as appropriate, on how to understand and interact with the child, manage their behavior, and about what to expect realistically, given that child's circumstance. Sometimes, if a child's problem is prominent at school, I observe the child in the classroom. I conduct an in-depth interview with the parents and sometimes administer behavioral checklists to get a better understanding of what the adults who live with this child observe on a daily basis.

My role as child therapist is to listen to what children "say" through words, play, and art. I listen, draw, talk, and play with them. It is a child-directed approach. You can learn a lot about what a child is feeling through play, when they don't know what they are feeling or how to express it. One response to trauma, for example, is to role-play or draw what happened. As children use therapy in this way, the emotional intensity of the event lessens and they feel less helpless. They often project their need to feel mastery over the event by creating powerful characters that triumph over adversity. I do not have to verbally interpret their play, although

sometimes I do with older children, so we can process what is going on emotionally. Children work through memories, painful feelings, and loss, with the therapist acting as a helper and guide.

As a child therapist I can learn what a child's beliefs are about self, others, and the world, and I can decide where and how to intervene. Play therapy can be supplemented by more structured cognitive-behavioral therapy to change negative beliefs that are contributing to anxiety, depression, acting-out behaviors, or interpersonal conflicts. I give parents input on how best to help their children through difficult times. I also offer education on how to reward children's appropriate behaviors effectively and minimize negative behaviors. I help them understand their child's temperament and developmental stage, so they can adjust their expectations accordingly. It's important to remember that you do not work with the child in isolation, as you would an adult. The child is your client/patient, but you are working with parents, siblings, teachers, and other adults who are important in that child's life.

The most satisfying aspect of my profession is the joy of connecting with children and watching them improve through therapy. They are more flexible in their patterns of thinking and behavior, and they respond more quickly to therapy than adults do. I observe the positive change in their mood, and parents and teachers report the improvement in behavior. The most memorable experiences are those where a child is in emotional pain and his or her behavior, school performance, and socialization are negatively affected. Gradually, through therapy and support from the adults in their life, they overcome the effects of grief, divorce, trauma, or impairment from depression, anxiety, or behavioral disorders.

Imagine that you are confronted with the following task. A list of words, such as that in Table 8.2, is presented to you at the rate of one every 5 seconds. A 30-second delay follows the last word, and you must then recall as many of the words as possible. How might you proceed?

Adults faced with such a task are likely to do a variety of things to help themselves remember. They may say the words over and over as the list is presented and during the delay period. They may seek to make the list more memorable by grouping the words into categories—noting, for example, that several of the items name foods and several others name animals. Or they may attempt to create associations among the words by imagining a scenario in which several of the words are linked—for example, a mental image of a cow eating a banana while riding a bicycle.

TABLE 8.2 Items to Be Recalled on a Short-Term Memory Test	
Cow	Truck
Tree	Hat
Banana	Bear
Bicycle	Apple
Dog	Flag
Orange	Horse

What memory strategies might this child use to play this game? (Frank Siteman/Stone/Getty Images, Inc.)

The Role of Strategies

The alternatives for remembering the items in Table 8.2 are examples of *mnemonic strategies*. A **mnemonic strategy** is any technique that people use to help them remember something. The examples just given correspond to three well-studied strategies in research on memory: *rehearsal* of the items to be recalled (the saying-over-and-over technique), *organization* of the items into conceptual categories (grouping into foods, animals, and so on), and *elaboration* of the items by linkage in some more general image or story (the picture of the cow on the bicycle with the banana).

Developmental Changes in Strategy Use An increase in the use of strategies is a source of improvements in memory that come with age. Dozens of studies have demonstrated that older children are more likely than younger children to generate and employ a variety of mnemonic strategies (Bjorklund, 1990; Murphy, McKone, & Slee, 2003; Schneider & Bjorklund, 1998). This finding holds for rehearsal (Flavell, Beach, & Chinsky, 1966); organization (Hasselhorn, 1992); and elaboration (Kee & Guttentag, 1994). It also holds for other mnemonic strategies that develop across childhood—for example, the ability to direct one's attention and effort in optimal ways, such as by attending to central rather than irrelevant information (Miller, 1990) or by concentrating on difficult rather than easy items (Dufresne & Kobasigawa, 1989).

Children who use strategies show better recall than children who do not. Sometimes, however, children do not benefit from their initial attempts to employ a strategy, perhaps because executing the new strategy places too great a demand on their limited information processing resources (Woody-Dorning & Miller, 2001). In this case, there is a **utilization deficiency** (Bjorklund & Coyle, 1995; Miller & Seier, 1994). Also, young children do not generate strategies before about age 5 or 6, no doubt because they do not realize that their memories are limited. The failure to generate strategies spontaneously, even though the child is capable of executing and benefiting from a strategy, is referred to as a **production deficiency** (Flavell, 1970).

As children get older, strategies become more complex as well as more frequent. Rehearsal is a relatively simple strategy and one of the first to emerge, typically at about age 6 or 7. Organization appears somewhat later, and elaboration later still. In addition, each strategy changes in complexity. Younger children's rehearsal efforts, for example, tend to

---

Mnemonic strategies
Technique (such as rehearsal or organization) that people use in an attempt to remember something.

Questions for Thought and Discussion
What mnemonic strategies do you find most effective for you in your studies? How do those strategies work?

Utilization deficiency
The failure of a recently developed mnemonic strategy to facilitate recall.

Production deficiency
The failure to generate a mnemonic strategy spontaneously.

be limited to naming each item as it appears. Older children are more likely to repeat larger chunks of the list each time ("cow," "cow-tree," "cow-tree-banana," and so on) (Ornstein, Naus, & Liberty, 1975). In general, older children can generate more complex strategies than younger children, are better able to match a particular strategy to a particular task, and are more skilled at executing their strategies—all of which contribute to their superior memory performance.

Even very young children are capable of generating a mnemonic strategy. In one study, 3-year-olds played a game in which they had to keep track of a toy dog that had been hidden under one of several cups. During the delay between hiding and retrieval, many of the children sat with their eyes glued to the critical cup and a finger planted firmly on it (Wellman, Ritter, & Flavell, 1975). These are simple strategies, to be sure, but they *are* strategies, and they are available to even young children. Furthermore, they work. Children who produced such strategies showed better recall than children who did not. Other studies using a similar hide-and-seek procedure have demonstrated that children as young as 18 to 24 months can produce and benefit from simple memory strategies (Wellman, 1988).

Variability in Strategy Use Recent memory research highlights the surprising variability in children's strategy use. Rather than employ a single preferred strategy, many children try out and combine several different approaches, sometimes generating as many as three or four strategies even within a single trial (Coyle, 2001; Coyle & Bjorklund, 1997). A particular child, for example, might not only rehearse the items to be remembered but also name the categories to which they belong and perhaps sort them into groups as well. Such variability is adaptive in that it provides experience from which children can eventually determine the optimal strategy for a particular task (Siegler & Svetina, in press). According to this explanation, children learn to select the most effective mnemonic strategies from the many possibilities that they initially explore.

Research on strategies also illustrates an important theme of the information processing approach (Siegler, 1998). Information processing capacities are always limited. Only a limited amount of information can fit in short-term memory, for example, and this information typically can be held only briefly. If new information can be rehearsed, however, its lifetime can be extended considerably. If the child can think in terms of categories and not merely in terms of individual items, then much more can be retained. Much of development consists of the creation of techniques to overcome information processing limitations and thereby increase the power of the cognitive system (Siegler & Svetina, in press). Mnemonic strategies are a prime example of such techniques.

The Role of Knowledge: Experts and Novices

Cognitive processing—from the interpretation of speech sounds or the recognition of musical phrases to the retrieval of a phone number or the solution to a puzzle—involves knowledge acquired through previous experience. *Content knowledge* (or the *knowledge base*) refers to organized factual knowledge about some content domain—that is, what you know about some topic such as physics, human behavior, cooking, or cars. Clearly, knowledge changes as people develop. Adults know more than children and children know more than infants.

Knowledge is integral to information processing. Consider, for example, the influence of knowledge on the encoding and storage of new information. What we know about a topic is the information we have previously stored about that topic. This knowledge in turn determines how well we learn and remember new information about that topic (Bjorklund, 1987; Chi, Glaser, & Farr, 1988; Ornstein et al., 2006). Thus, the interaction between knowledge and information processing is bidirectional.

To the extent that domain-specific knowledge influences information processing, people vary in **expertise**—factual knowledge about a content domain. Researchers interested in the role of knowledge in developmental change, therefore, often compare experts and novices (e.g., Chase & Simon, 1973; McPherson & Thomas, 1989; Schneider, Gruber, Gold, & Opwis, 1993). One such study tested differences in the memory of expert and

Expertise
Organized factual knowledge regarding some content domain.

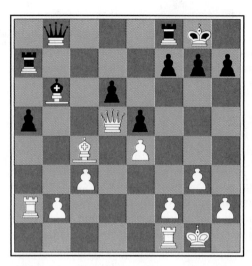 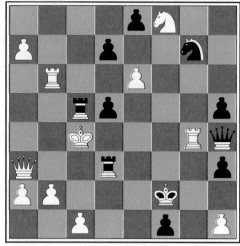

FIGURE 8.2 Chessboard arrays in a study of the effects of knowledge on memory.

Chess players show better memory for the chessboard on the left, which is a meaningful possibility in a game, than for the chessboard on the right, which shows a random configuration of pieces. As experts, players can use their knowledge of chess to remember.

Source: From W. Schneider, H. Gruber, A. Gold, and K. Opwis. (1993). Chess expertise and memory for chess positions in children and adults. *Journal of Experimental Child Psychology, 56,* p. 335. Copyright © 1993 by Academic Press. Reprinted by permission.

novice chess players for chessboard arrays (Schneider et al., 1993). Which array in Figure 8.2 do you think you could remember well enough to reproduce after viewing the arrays for 10 seconds?

If you do not play chess, the chances are that you would find the two arrays in Figure 8.2 equally difficult to recall. Both contain the same number and the same variety of stimuli. If you are a chess player, however, the top array would almost certainly be easier to remember. It would be easier because the pieces are in positions that might actually occur in a game, whereas those in the bottom array are randomly arranged. You could therefore draw on your knowledge of chess as you took in the information, stored it in memory, and retrieved it to reproduce the positions.

Expertise is content specific. Your expertise may be high in chess or dinosaurs or parenting but low when the topic turns to baseball or cooking or physics. Where expertise is high, so is memory, and variations in expertise contribute to variations in memory. Chess experts, for example, show better memory for chess positions and other chess-related information than they do for most other topics. Experts also remember more about the subject of expertise than do novices. Finally, variations in expertise contribute to developmental changes in memory across the span of childhood. Older children possess more expertise for most topics than do younger children, and this greater expertise is one reason they remember more (Murphy, McKone & Slee, 2003).

Experts have a greater quantity of knowledge. Expert chess players, for example, might represent as many as 50,000 board patterns in memory; a good player only perhaps 1,000 or so (Bedard & Chi, 1992). However, there are also qualitative differences, as knowledge is represented differently as expertise increases. Experts represent more than just individual bits of information in memory; they represent relationships among individual items. A novice chess player, for example, might know the starting positions of the pieces on the board and the positions that might follow from the first move or two of each piece. An expert chess player, on the other hand, not only knows more configurations, but he or she also knows the moves an opponent is likely to make and the most effective responses to those moves. An expert can also relate individual configurations to overall game strategies. Because their knowledge base is richly and meaningfully organized, experts can quickly make sense of incoming information (Schneider & Bjorkland, 1998).

What factors determine the rate and ease of information processing? With regard to these dinosaurs, the adult is the novice and the child is the expert. How do constructive memory and domain-specific knowledge contribute to the child's ability to develop expertise? (Jose Luis Pelaez, Inc./Blend/IPN Stock)

In addition to comparing experts and novices of the same age, Schneider et al. (1993) examined the effects of age on memory performance. Half the chess experts and half the novices were adults, and the other halves were 10- to 13-year-old children. On memory tasks that did not involve chess, the adults demonstrated better memory than the children. On the memory-for-chess measure, however, expertise, not age, proved critical. Thus, the 10-year-old experts outshone the adult novices in reproducing chess positions—despite the fact that the adults had more general knowledge and greater memory spans. Researchers have found that young participants in memory tasks can equal or even outperform older ones when the content is something they know well. Content areas for which child superiority has been demonstrated include dinosaurs (Chi & Koeske, 1983), cartoon figures (Lindberg, 1980), baseball (Recht & Leslie, 1988), and soccer (Schneider, Korkel, & Weinert, 1987).

Contemporary information processing theories of development stress the role of expertise not only in memory but also in reasoning and problem solving (DeLoache, Miller, & Pierroutsakos, 1998; Hmelo-Silver & Pfeffer, 2004). For example, expertise affects the speed of processing. When knowledge about some domain is great, information relevant to that domain can be taken in and processed more rapidly, thus freeing cognitive resources for other activities, such as generating strategies (Bjorklund & Schneider, 1996). Because they are better at distinguishing important from irrelevant information, children who know more also use cognitive strategies more effectively than children with less knowledge (Bjorklund, Muir-Broaddus, & Schneider 1990). Finally, because experts understand problems at a deeper, more conceptual level, they are better able to conceptualize both the problem and its likely solution (Chi, Feltovich, & Glaser, 1981; Slotta, Chi, & Joram, 1995).

Q**uestions for Thought and Discussion**
Are you an expert in something? What makes you an expert, and how did you become one?

The Role of Metacognition

How do you know when to employ a particular memory strategy? In part, you rely on your previous experience and current skill level in strategy use. You also appeal to what you already know about the content to be remembered to direct attention to the most relevant aspects of the problem—that is, you rely on your knowledge base. Finally, to select an appropriate strategy for a situation you use your understanding of your thought processes. What children know about thinking and memory—their *metacognition*—changes with age, and these changes in knowledge contribute to changes in memory (DeMarie & Ferron, 2003).

Metamemory
Knowledge about memory.

Metacognition refers to knowledge about thinking, while **metamemory** refers to knowledge about memory. It includes knowledge about thinking in general, for example, that we think all the time, not just when we have a problem to solve; that recognition is easier than recall; and that a short list of items is easier to memorize than a long list. Metacognition also includes knowledge about one's own thinking and memory—for example, the ability to judge whether you have studied long enough to do well on an exam. Children at first are novices in metacognitive knowledge, which is a powerful body of knowledge to acquire. Acquiring a metacognitive knowledge base affects children's performance on many other information processing tasks.

Developmental Changes in Metacognition J. Flavell (1971) was among the first child psychologists to focus explicitly on "thinking about thinking," and he coined the term *metacognition* to refer to thoughts that have mental or psychological phenomena as their target. Children's thinking about memory, for example, changes as they develop. Even young children realize that there is such a thing as memory. They may behave differently, for example, when told to remember something than when told simply to look, thus demonstrating some awareness that remembering may require special cognitive activities (Baker-Ward, Ornstein, & Holden, 1984). They also have some understanding of the relative difficulty of different memory tasks. By age 5 or 6, most children realize that familiar items are easier to remember than unfamiliar ones (Kreutzer, Leonard, & Flavell, 1975), that short lists are easier to learn than long ones (Wellman, 1977), that recognition is easier than recall (Speer & Flavell, 1979), and that forgetting becomes more likely over time (Lyon & Flavell, 1993).

In other ways, however, young children's metacognitive skill is limited. They do not always behave differently when faced with an explicit request to remember (Appel et al., 1972). They do not yet understand many phenomena of memory, such as the fact that related items are easier to recall than unrelated ones (Kreutzer et al., 1975) or that remembering the gist of a story is easier than remembering the exact words (Kurtz & Borkowski, 1987). Most significantly, young children's assessment of their own mnemonic abilities is far too optimistic. In one study, for example, over half of the preschool and kindergarten participants predicted that they would be able to recall all 10 items from a list of 10, a performance that no child in fact came close to achieving (Flavell, Friedrichs, & Hoyt, 1970). Furthermore, young children do not adjust their expectations readily in response to feedback. Even after recalling only two or three items on one trial, they may blithely assert that they will get all 10 on the next attempt (Yussen & Levy, 1975). Older children are both more modest and more realistic in assessing their own memories (Schneider & Pressley, 1997).

Effects of Metacognition on Memory Performance How does metacognition contribute to developmental changes in memory performance? It seems logical that knowing more about memory might be related to better remembering. Knowledge of the demands of different memory tasks should help the child select the best strategy for remembering. Knowledge of one's own thought processes should be helpful in deciding how to allocate attention, what material to study, and so on. However, this knowledge–behavior relationship has been difficult to demonstrate empirically (Cavanaugh & Perlmutter, 1982). Thus, knowledge about memory does not always relate clearly to performance on memory tasks. The following quotation, taken from one of the first metamemory studies, suggests a possible reason for this discrepancy. Here, a little girl describes a wonderfully complex procedure for memorizing phone numbers (her metaknowledge), but then suggests at the end that her actual behavior might be quite different.

> Say the number is 633–8854. Then what I'd do is—say that my number is 633, so I won't have to remember that, really. And then I would think now I've got to remember 88. Now I'm 8 years old, so I can remember, say my age two times. Then I say how old my brother is, and how old he was last year. And that's how I'd usually remember that phone number. [Is that how you would most often remember a phone number?] Well, usually I write it down. (Kreutzer et al., 1975, p. 11)

Questions for Thought
and Discussion
What other aspects of cognitive development might help account for changes in children's metacognitive awareness as they age?

More recent studies have been more successful in identifying relations between knowledge and behavior (Schneider, 1999). One promising approach has been to train children in various forms of metamemory and then look for possible effects on subsequent memory performance (Ghatala et al., 1985; Pressley, Borkowski, & O'Sullivan, 1985). Such training does improve memory. Thus, it may prove possible to help children with memory problems by teaching them about memory itself. Most successful strategy training programs include instruction in metacognition. Children benefit most from memory training if they learn both what to do and why to do it.

The information processing approach recognizes that the many different processes that go into intelligent behavior do not occur in isolation or without direction. The child must somehow select and coordinate specific cognitive activities, and a full model of intelligence must explain how this selection and coordination occur. For example, a mnemonic strategy such as rehearsal does not simply happen. The realization that rehearsal is an appropriate strategy, monitoring its execution, and evaluating its success are themselves cognitive processes. Metamemory—the child's knowledge of memory—is one sort of "executive control" that determines how the child goes about remembering.

Learning Objective 8.3: *Describe three cognitive tools that contribute to the development of memory during childhood.*

1. What are mnemonic strategies, and how do they contribute to memory development in children?
2. What does research on novices and experts tell us about the role of knowledge in cognitive development?
3. What is metacognition, and how does this ability contribute to memory development?

✔ *Test Your Mastery...*

Problem Solving

Children not only acquire more knowledge as they get older; they also acquire better, more sophisticated skills for solving problems. These changes are reflected in the expectations schools have of students as well as the ways that parents attempt to reason with and control their children. What are children's problem-solving skills, and how do those skills change (DeLoache, Miller, & Pierroutsakos, 1998; Ellis & Siegler, 1994)? Two kinds of problem-solving skills are (1) forming rules for combining information and making judgments; and (2) reasoning by analogy. Other factors that contribute to problem-solving ability include developmental changes in basic cognitive abilities affecting memory and knowledge.

Learning Objective 8.4
Analyze the abilities and skills children use to solve problems, and give examples of how research on problem solving can be applied.

Rule-Based Problem Solving

Robert Siegler (1978, 1981) has proposed that some important aspects of children's cognitive development can be characterized in terms of the construction of rules. **Rule-based strategies** are set procedures for acting on the environment and solving problems—for transforming input to output. They can be expressed as "if . . . then" statements. If A is the case, do X; if B is the case, do Y; and so forth. In the rules for behavior at traffic lights, for example, if the light is green (input), proceed (output); if the light is yellow, prepare to stop; if the light is red, stop. Rules for problem solving are more complex, however. While traffic rules are prescribed by law and taught to us explicitly, rules in human information processing systems—those guiding judgment and decision making, for example—are rarely taught explicitly. They remain below the level of conscious awareness, implicit in our thoughts and behavior.

Rule-based strategies
Set procedures for acting on the environment and solving problems.

Preschoolers' Rule-Based Reasoning Recent studies have found that preschoolers are capable of rule-based problem solving (Frye, 1999; Zelazo, 1999; Zelazo and Frye, 1998). The basic task in this research—labeled the *dimensional-change card sort*—is illustrated in

Q**uestions for Thought and Discussion**
How might Piaget's conservation tasks reflect the development of rule-based problem solving?

FIGURE 8.3 The Dimensional-Change Card Sort Task

Can children as young as age 3 sort cards like these by one criterion or rule (e.g., color or category)? What happens when they are asked to resort the same cards by another rule? What executive cognitive functions do children need for rule-based problem solving?

Source: From P.D. Zelazo and D. Frye. (1998). Cognitive complexity and control: II. The development of executive function in childhood. *Current Directions in Psychological Science, 7,* 122. Copyright © 1998 by Cambridge University Press. Reprinted by permission.

Target Cards

Test Cards

Figure 8.3. The child is given a series of cards that vary in both shape and color and is instructed to sort them by one of the two dimensions. If the task is the "color game," for example, then the instructions will be to put the red ones in the box with the red picture and the blue ones in the box with the blue picture. Most 3-year-olds readily learn this task. After several such trials, the rule changes: Now the task becomes the "shape game," and the instructions are to put the cars in one box and the flowers in the other. Most 4-year-olds easily make the switch. Most 3-year-olds do not. Even when they receive the new instructions at the start of every trial, and even when they themselves succeed in verbalizing the new rule, 3-year-olds continue to sort according to the original rule.

What the dimensional-change task shows is that 3-year-olds *are* capable of rule-based problem solving but with some definite limitations. Three-year-olds can handle two simple rules at a time—for example, if red, do this; if blue, do this. Two-year-olds, on the other hand, are able to learn and follow only one rule at a time. What the 3-year-old cannot yet do is to embed these simple rules within a more complex rule system, in which selection of a rule is contingent on a prior, higher-order, or inclusive rule. Successful performance on the dimensional-change tasks requires this sort of embedded rule structure. The child must be able to reason, if this is the color game (higher-order rule), then if red do this, and if blue do this; if this is the shape game (higher-order rule), then if car do this, and if flower do this.

Success on the dimensional-change task also requires that the child have sufficient short-term memory capacity to keep in mind several rules at the same time. The child must be capable of inhibiting the original response once a new response is called for. Finally, the child must have sufficient metacognitive ability to reflect on the rules that he or she has learned and to note the relations among them. The term *executive function* refers to these general problem-solving capabilities. Memory, inhibition, and self-awareness play a role in virtually every form of reasoning and problem solving. Recent research has shown that developmental improvements in executive function contribute to developmental advances on a wide range of cognitive tasks (Hughes, 2002; Keenan, 2000).

Developments in Rule-Based Reasoning Many situations require more complex problem-solving skills than simply learning to follow one rule or another. An example is a balance-scale problem originally devised by Inhelder and Piaget (1958) to study formal operational reasoning in older children. The child is shown a simple balance scale on which varying weights can be placed at varying distances from the fulcrum. The task is to predict whether the scale will balance or whether one side or the other will go down. Successfully performing the task requires that the child realize that both weight and distance are important and know how to combine the two factors in cases of conflict. The original Piagetian research revealed that children of different ages responded quite differently to the task, which Piaget analyzed in terms of the logical structures of concrete and formal operations.

These children are adding weights to a balance scale to test a prediction about what will happen and why. According to R. Siegler's research, what rules could a child use in reasoning about this kind of problem? What would determine which rule a child used? How is preschoolers' rule-based reasoning limited? (Janine Wiedel Photo Library/Alamy Images)

Siegler (1976, 1978) used the same balance-scale task using a different methodology and form of analysis. He began by carefully considering all the various ways in which children might attempt to solve the balance-scale problem. Such *task analysis* is a common information processing method (Kail & Bisanz, 1982). Based on this task analysis, Siegler identified four rules that children might use in solving balance problems:

Rule 1. The child judges that the side with more weights will go down or that, if the number of weights on each side is equal, the scale will balance.

Rule 2. The child uses Rule 1 but also takes distance into account.

Rule 3. The child uses Rule 2, always considering both weight and distance, and is correct whenever one or both are equal. If the two factors are in conflict, however (i.e., more weight on one side, greater distance on the other), the child becomes confused and does not know how to resolve the conflict.

Rule 4. The child overcomes the limitation of Rule 3, mastering the weight-times-distance rule: Downward force equals amount of weight multiplied by distance from the fulcrum. The Rule 4 child can therefore solve any version of the task.

A task analysis identifies possible ways of responding, but it does not tell us whether children actually use these approaches. Siegler's next step, therefore, was to test the psychological reality of the proposed rules. He devised six types of balance-scale problems, carefully constructed to yield different patterns of response across the different rules. Both the problem types and the predicted responses are shown in Table 8.3.

Siegler presented five versions of each problem type to children ranging in age from 5 to 17. Fully 90 percent of the children followed one of the four rules consistently. (We should note, however, that subsequent studies have sometimes found evidence for more than four rules—Boom, Hoijink, & Kunnen, 2001; Tudge, 1992). As expected, the complexity of the preferred rule increased with age; most 5-year-olds used Rule 1, whereas by age 17, Rules 3 and 4 were most common. Finally, interestingly, accurate performance on the problems involving conflict actually declined with age.

Siegler and others have applied his *rule-assessment method* to a number of tasks other than the balance-scale task (Klahr & Robinson, 1981; Ravn & Gelman, 1984; Siegler, 1981). In conservation tasks, for example, Siegler and Piaget agree that children solve the problem through mental action that logically combines information from both relevant dimensions (e.g., height and width in the case of conservation of quantity). There are two differences between Siegler's and Piaget's accounts, however—differences that in general

Questions for Thought and Discussion

What hierarchy of rules might you derive from a task analysis of a problem that you might encounter in your work?

TABLE 8.3 Types of Problems and Predicted Responses on the Siegler Balance-Scale Task

	RULE			
PROBLEM TYPE	**I**	**II**	**III**	**IV**
Balance	100	100	100	100
Weight	100	100	100	100
Distance	0 (Should say "Balance")	100	100	100
Conflict–weight	100	100	33 (Chance responding)	100
Conflict–distance	0 (Should say "Right down")	0 (Should say "Right down")	33 (Chance responding)	100
Conflict–balance	0 (Should say "Right down")	0 (Should say "Right down")	33 (Chance responding)	100

SOURCE: From R.S. Siegler. (1978). The origins of scientific reasoning. In R.S. Siegler (Ed.), *Children's Thinking: What Develops?* Mahwah, NJ: Erlbaum, p. 115. Copyright © 1978 by Lawrence Erlbaum Associates. Reprinted by permission.

divide the information processing and Piagetian approaches. The first difference concerns specificity and testability. Rules are more precisely defined than are Piagetian operations, and the rule-assessment methodology provides a more rigorous test of a proposed explanation than is typically the case in Piagetian research. The second difference is theoretical. Piaget's operations are general structures that are assumed to determine performance on a wide range of tasks, with the expected result that children will be consistent in their level of performance. Rules may be more domain specific, however, and there is no assumption that performance will necessarily be consistent from one task to another. Siegler finds that individual children may use rules of different levels on different tasks.

Reasoning by Analogy

Analogical reasoning
A form of problem solving in which the solution is achieved through recognition of the similarity between the new problem and some already understood problem.

In **analogical reasoning**, you solve a new problem by recognizing a similarity between the new problem and one you already understand. Some forms of analogic reasoning, including many verbal analogies, are complex and late to develop, which is why analogies are a common item on standardized tests. Some forms, however, are evident very early in development.

In one study, for example, 10- to 13-month-old infants were presented with the task shown in Figure 8.4 (Chen et al., 1997). Infants saw an attractive toy, such as the toy car pictured on the right side of the figure, but were not able to grasp and play with the toy immediately. A barrier intervened between infant and toy, and the toy was in any case too far away to reach. To solve the problem, therefore, the infant needed to push aside the barrier, grasp the string connected to the toy (while ignoring the other, nonhelpful string), and pull the toy within range. The infants were first given a chance to solve the problem on their own, and few could do so. When a parent then modeled the solution, however, many more infants succeeded.

The test for analogical problem solving followed. The infants received additional problems that retained the same general solution structure as the original problem but varied a number of specific perceptual features. For example (as the figure shows), a particular problem might have a different goal object, a different-colored barrier, or a different string arrangement. The question was whether infants could recognize the relation between the original problem and the new one and transfer the original solution appropriately. Not all

FIGURE 8.4 Analogic problem-solving task for infants.

In this experiment, researchers used goal objects, barriers, and alternative solutions to test the ability of infants to problem solve using analogic thinking. What learning did infants have to transfer to solve each successive challenge?

SOURCE: From Z. Chen, R.P. Sanchez, & T. Campbell. (1997). From beyond to within their grasp: The rudiments of analogical problem solving in 10- and 13-Month-Olds. *Developmental Psychology, 33*, 792. Copyright © 1997 by the American Psychogical Association. Reprinted by permission.

could, especially the younger ones. By the third problem, however, the average success rate had risen to better than 60 percent, much higher than in the initial trial. Although their process was nonverbal, the infants seemed to be engaging in reasoning: "This thing that's in my way is like the one I pushed aside before, and this string is like the one I pulled before, and so if I want to get this new toy. . . ."

As children develop, the relations they can recognize across problems gradually depend less on perceptual similarity. In addition, problem solving becomes embedded in language. Consider the following example of analogical problem solving in preschoolers (Brown, Kane, & Echols, 1986). Children first heard a story in which a genie needed to transport some jewels over a wall and into a bottle. The genie solved her problem by rolling up a piece of posterboard so that it formed a tube, placing one end of the tube in the mouth of the bottle, and rolling the jewels through the tube and into the bottle. The children were then asked to demonstrate a solution to the following problem: The Easter Bunny needs to transport eggs across a river and into a basket on the other side. Despite the presence of a piece of posterboard, few 3-year-olds spontaneously recognized the analogy to the genie task, although with help (for example, questioning about the central elements in each story) some eventually succeeded. Five-year-olds were much more likely to recognize the relevance of the original story and to discover immediately an analogical solution to the new task.

The basic capacity to reason by analogy appears to be present from early in life. What develops in analogic reasoning is the domain-specific knowledge about the particular items and relations that enter into particular analogies (Goswami, 1992, 1996). The point here is a simple one: If the child does not yet know what A or B is, then he or she cannot use the relation between A and B to reason analogically about C and D.

Contributions of Memory to Problem Solving

To solve any kind of problem effectively, a child or an adult must be able to keep all the relevant aspects of the problem in mind simultaneously and be able to retrieve relevant, previously learned information from long-term memory. Thus memory and problem solving are highly connected. One information processing theory that highlights the contributions of memory to problem solving is that of Robbie Case (1985, 1992; Case & Okamoto, 1996). Like Piaget, Case divides cognitive development into distinct stages—stages in many respects similar to Piaget's. However, Case's theory places greater emphasis on memory. In his view, the total problem-solving resources available to the child are divided into two components—operating space and short-term storage space.

Operating space refers to the resources necessary to carry out whatever cognitive operations are being employed for the problem at hand. In the case of the Siegler balance-scale task, for example, a child who used Rule 2 would first count the number of weights on each side of the fulcrum. Assuming that the weights were equal, the child would then count the number of pegs from the fulcrum to determine distance. Finally, the child would use the information about weight or distance to predict which side of the scale would go down. Each operation would require a certain amount of operating space. Here *space* is used metaphorically, not for some actual physical area in the brain but for how much available mental energy is needed for the activity.

Performing operations is one part of problem solving; remembering the results of those operations is another part. **Short-term storage space** refers to the resources the child needs to store results from previous operations while carrying out new ones. The Rule 2 child, for example, would need to remember both the overall goal of the task and the results of each preceding operation to execute the sequence just described. Without such memory, there could be little hope of a successful solution.

Many problems have solutions that depend on combining results from several cognitive operations. Such combining is possible only if short-term storage space is sufficient to hold all the relevant results. In Case's theory, limitations in short-term storage space contribute to young children's difficulties in problem solving. Because they can keep track of only a few things at a time, young children can do only a few things at a time. Advances in problem solving occur as short-term storage space expands, and the child can begin to combine operations that previously could only be performed separately. Why does short-term storage capacity increase? There are two possible explanations. One possibility is that total problem-solving resources expand with age. As total resources grow, so does the space available for short-term storage. In this view, older children simply have more resources available to them. Thus, it is not surprising that they can remember more and do more.

Plausible though this model may seem, Case's research leads him to prefer a second possibility. This possibility is that the growth in storage capacity results from a decrease in the space needed to perform operations. Cognitive resources must always be divided between operations and storage; if fewer resources are needed for one component, then

Operating space
In Case's theory, the resources necessary to carry out cognitive operations.

Short-term storage space
In Case's theory, the resources necessary to store results from previous cognitive operations while carrying out new ones.

What memory and strategy skills are needed for a child to win a family game of cards? What specific role does memory play in this success? According to Case's theory, what has changed to enable the child to succeed at the memory game? (Corbis RF/Corbis)

more are available for the other. In this second view, developmental changes in storage result from increases in the efficiency with which operations are performed. As children develop, they become more skilled at executing cognitive operations. Hence, they have more space left over for storage, and they can do more and more.

Case identifies two processes that contribute to increases in operational efficiency. One is practice, in which cognitive activities become more skilled and efficient through repetition. Thus, what once took effort and attention may eventually become automatic and routine. The other is biological maturation. Children develop cognitively at about the same pace, suggesting a biological contribution to development. Furthermore, Case notes that major changes in brain development occur at about the same time as the stage-to-stage transitions identified in his theory. Finally, research indicates that speed of information processing increases at a regular rate from early childhood to adulthood (Kail, 1991, 2000; Kail & Miller, 2006; Miller & Vernon, 1997). This increase in speed is so consistent across tasks and across samples that it appears to be maturational in origin. Thus, memory improves as children develop, and improvements in memory contribute to improvements in reasoning and problem solving.

Mechanisms of Cognitive Change

The information processing model identifies four main processes by which cognitive change occurs: encoding, automatization, strategy construction, and strategy selection. Siegler (1991) defines **encoding** as "identifying the most important features of objects and events and using the features to form internal representations" (p. 10). Encoding thus involves active *attention*. Information processing is always active rather than passive because the child attends only to some features of the environment and uses only some features to arrive at judgments. Encoding involves more than selective attention, however. The child forms some sort of mental representation of what he or she has attended to, and this representation guides subsequent problem solving.

The concept of encoding can be applied to the balance-scale task as an example. Recall that children who use Rule 1 base their judgments solely on the number of weights. Siegler (1976) tested such children's encoding of the relevant information. First, he allowed the children to observe an arrangement of the scale for 10 seconds. Then he covered the scale, brought another scale forward, and asked the children to reproduce the arrangement that they had just seen. Both 5-year-old and 8-year-old Rule 1 users were tested.

Siegler found that the 5-year-olds could reproduce the weights but not the distances, evidence that they had encoded only weight. The 5-year-olds also failed to benefit from training trials that showed them the results of various configurations of weight and distance. The children could not benefit from training because they did not encode the critical information. In contrast, the 8-year-olds were able to encode both weight and distance, even though they did not yet use distance information in making their judgments. Because of their sensitivity to both variables, the 8-year-olds were able to benefit from the training that had been ineffective with the 5-year-olds.

A second mechanism of cognitive change is **automatization.** At first, because it is new, a skill requires considerable attention and effort, and few resources, or "space," may be left for other kinds of cognitive processing. With practice, however, execution of the skill becomes more automatic, cognitive resources are freed, and more advanced forms of problem solving become possible. Automatization is a primary mechanism by which the cognitive system overcomes inherent limitations on the amount of information that can be processed.

A third mechanism of cognitive change is **strategy construction.** Like automatization, strategies serve to overcome processing limitations by increasing the efficiency with which information is handled. The child who realizes the organization inherent in a set of items, for example, may need to remember only the general categories and not every individual item. Similarly, a child who has developed the min strategy for adding numbers will need to count just twice rather than eight times when adding 2 plus 8.

Encoding
Attending to and forming internal representations of certain features of the environment; a mechanism of change in information processing theories.

Automatization
An increase in the efficiency with which cognitive operations are executed as a result of practice; a mechanism of change in information processing theories.

Questions for Thought and Discussion
How does the concept of automatization relate to Case's theory of conitive development?

Strategy construction
The creation of strategies for processing and remembering information; a mechanism of change in information processing theories.

Strategy selection
Progressively greater use of more effective strategies in place of less effective ones; a mechanism of change in information processing theories.

Strategy selection is a fourth mechanism closely related to strategy construction. Children often try out a variety of strategies in the process of developing competence in memory, arithmetic, and other kinds of problem solving as well (Ellis, 1997; Rosengren & Braswell, 2001). A main task for development is selecting the strategy or combination of strategies that provide the optimal solution. Over time, more effective strategies are increasingly used, while less effective strategies gradually are discarded (Siegler & Svetina, 2006).

In strategy selection, a sort of survival of the fittest takes place: The strategies that work are those that are maintained. Siegler (1996) argues that cognitive development during childhood in many respects is analogous to biological evolution in the history of a species. In both evolution and development, change builds on initial diversity and variation. In evolution, the diversity is in the distribution of genes in a species; in development, diversity lies in the variation in problem-solving approaches (multiple strategies, different encodings, etc.) in the initial response to a task. In both evolution and development, initial variation is followed by selection based on differential success: reproductive success in the case of evolution, problem-solving success in the case of development. And in both evolution and development, successful variants are preserved and passed on, producing adaptive change over time.

Information Processing and Academic Learning

In formal schooling, children are asked explicitly to learn and remember new information in many specific knowledge domains. As a result, researchers have applied principles of information processing to better understand and improve students' performance in school. How do strategy use, knowledge base, and metacognitive awareness apply to specific learning in academic settings? Following are three examples: strategy construction and selection in arithmetic; development of a conceptual knowledge base in physics; and metacognitive awareness in reading comprehension.

Strategy Construction and Selection in Arithmetic How do you come up with answers to simple addition problems, such as 4 + 2 and 3 + 5? Probably you simply know, having memorized many basic arithmetical facts. But what about young children who are just beginning to learn about mathematics? How do they come up with their answers?

Many research programs have examined the strategies children use to solve arithmetical problems (Ashcraft, 1990; Bisanz & LeFevre, 1990; Bjorklund & Rosenblum, 2001, 2002; Ginsburg, Klein, & Starkey, 1998; Siegler & Jenkins, 1989; Siegler & Shipley, 1995; Siegler & Shrager, 1984). Table 8.4 shows strategies that young children might use to solve the 3 + 5 problem. The strategies vary in both sophistication and likelihood of success.

TABLE 8.4 Children's Strategies for Solving Simple Addition Problems	
STRATEGY	**TYPICAL USE OF STRATEGY TO SOLVE 3 + 5**
Sum	Put up 3 fingers, put up 5 fingers, count fingers by saying "1, 2, 3, 4, 5, 6, 7, 8."
Finger recognition	Put up 3 fingers, put up 5 fingers, say "8" without counting.
Short-cut sum	Say "1, 2, 3, 4, 5, 6, 7, 8," perhaps simultaneously putting up one finger on each count.
Count-from-first-addend	Say "3, 4, 5, 6, 7, 8" or "4, 5, 6, 7, 8," perhaps simultaneously putting up one finger on each count.
Min (count-from-larger-addend)	Say "5, 6, 7, 8," or "6, 7, 8," perhaps simultaneously putting up one finger on each count beyond 5.
Retrieval	Say an answer and explain it by saying "I just knew it."
Guessing	Say an answer and explain it by saying "I guessed."
Decomposition	Say "35 is like 44, so it's 8."

SOURCE: Adapted from R.S. Siegler and E. Jenkins. (1989). *How Children Discover New Strategies.* Mahwah, NJ: Erlbaum, p. 59. Copyright © 1989 by Lawrence Erlbaum Associates. Adapted by permission.

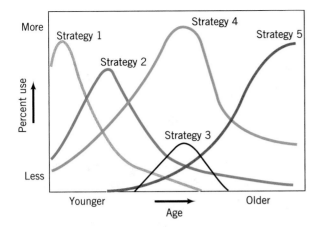

FIGURE 8.5 Siegler's overlapping waves model.
This model suggests that children use multiple strategies in problem solving and continue or discontinue using a particular strategy gradually over time. How would this graph look if children's strategy use followed a stage theory of development such as Piaget's?

Source: From R.S. Siegler. (1996). *Emerging Minds: The Process of Change in Children's Thinking.* New York: Oxford University Press, p. 89. Copyright © 1996 by Oxford University Press. Reprinted by permission.

One way to determine which strategy a child is using is simply to watch children as they work on the problems. Strategies such as putting up fingers or counting out loud are overt and thus directly observable. Another approach is to ask children how they arrive at their answers. A third approach makes use of a central information processing method: the measurement of response time as a guide to processes of solution. A child using the count-from-first-addend strategy, for example, should take longer to solve $3 + 7$ than to solve $3 + 5$; a child using the min strategy, however, should be equally quick on both problems. Response times across a range of problems can show which strategies are being used.

While a child might employ a range of strategies to solve a problem, their selection usually is not random but is adaptive to the problem at hand. A child may use the retrieval strategy for simple or familiar problems, for example, but fall back on a counting strategy when faced with a more complex task. In general, children seem to strive for a balance of speed and accuracy, selecting the fastest strategy that is likely to yield a correct response. With development, children progress from less efficient to more efficient strategies, culminating in the ability to retrieve answers from memory rather than continually having to calculate them anew. With development, speed and accuracy increase as well. These increases come in part from the emergence of more efficient strategies and in part from increased skill in executing any particular strategy. Strategy selection in subtraction, division, reading, and memory tasks, as well as in addition, follow the same pattern (Siegler, 1996, 1988).

Thus, children often have multiple ways of solving problems, and the transitions across development are often gradual rather than abrupt. This point is illustrated in Figure 8.5, showing Siegler's "overlapping waves" model (1996, 2000). This model contrasts with stage theories, in which children at a given stage have only one way of solving a problem and lower-level approaches are abruptly replaced by higher ones.

This research has clear implications for teaching arithmetic. One is that teachers should be sensitive to the beliefs and strategies that children bring to the classroom setting. Also, not all first graders will have the same strategies, and instruction, as far as possible, should be adjusted to the individual child's level of development. Lower-level strategies, such as counting on one's fingers, should not be discouraged necessarily, as children may need experience trying out other strategies to determine for themselves which are most effective. Educators must be sensitive to the natural sequence of development and children's need to build advanced knowledge on the basis of lower-level understanding.

Development of a Conceptual Knowledge Base in Physics The more you know, and the better integrated and organized your knowledge is within your domain of expertise, the better able you are to encode and retrieve accurate information from memory. Such a knowledge base also enables you to zero in quickly on the conceptually relevant aspects of newly encountered problems.

In a study of physics experts and novices, researchers presented physics problems and asked subjects to sort the problems into categories (Chi et al., 1981). Physics experts categorized the problems according to the underlying physical principles, such as conservation of energy

In this peer learning activity, the children are testing each other on solving simple problems in mathematics. What strategy is this girl using to solve the problem 6-5? According to R. Siegler's model, how will their problem-solving strategies change over time? (David Young-Wolff/PhotoEdit)

or rotational kinematics. Novices, in contrast, categorized on the basis of superficial surface features of the problems, such as whether they contained a ramp or a pulley. Because they immediately identify the type of problem at a conceptual level, physics experts are already well on the way to the solution, because each physical principle has unique equations and problem-solving strategies. Novice problem classifications do not facilitate problem solving, however, because they do not specify the principles and equations needed to solve the problem.

In addition, novices systematically misconstrue physics principles to fit their naive focus on material substance (Slotta et al., 1995). For example, novices tend to construe heat as a substance that can be added and subtracted, leading them to reason erroneously that adding two cups of 100 degree water yields one cup of 200 degree water! Experts, in contrast, identify heat as a form of energy embodied in the motion of molecules that can be transferred from substance to substance but cannot be added or subtracted (Smith, Carey, & Wiser, 1983). These results demonstrate that expert and novice knowledge is structured quite differently, and these differences systematically affect students' conceptual understanding of a domain, which in turn affects their ability to apply their knowledge successfully in problem solving.

The goal for educators, then, is to recognize the naïve understanding that students bring to conceptually complex knowledge domains such as physics and to use pedagogical practices that challenge rather than entrench those understandings (Slotta et al., 1995). Analyzing the structure of students' initial knowledge representation and strategy identification allows teachers to help students move toward conceptual understanding. This has also been shown for the acquisition of mathematics concepts (Vamvakoussi & Vosniadou, 2004); biology (Carey, 1985); astronomy (Vosniadou et al., 2004); and even marketing (Sujan et al., 1988).

Metacognitive Awareness in Comprehension Children's explicit understanding of how memory works encourages them to use memory strategies and to learn which strategies lead to the most effective recall in various situations. However, metacognitive skills of which we are not consciously aware also play an important role in mastering new material. One example of this kind of implicit metacognitive awareness is the ability to monitor one's current level of comprehension—to a conversation, a text, or a lecture. Such self-monitoring skills are essential in students' choice of what material to study and how much time to allocate to studying.

In a study of first- through seventh-grade children, for example, Dufresne and Kobasigawa (1989) presented students with two booklets of word pairs to study for a later recall test. One booklet presented "easy pairs" in which the terms were related to one another, whereas the other booklet presented more difficult, arbitrary pairs. Both first and third graders allocated equal study time to the two booklets. Fifth and seventh

---

Questions for Thought and Discussion

How would you analyze the knowledge in a lesson or skill that you might wish to teach to a child? What strategies could you teach to help the child acquire that knowledge or skill?

graders, however, spent more time studying the more difficult material. Thus, older children produced significantly better recall of the difficult items. Older children also differed in their explicit metacognitive skills, engaging in more self-testing strategies than younger children.

The metacognitive ability to monitor comprehension level also leads students to ask questions or review difficult material that they do not completely understand. Surprisingly, even college students often do not realize that they have failed to comprehend fully what another person has said (Siegler & Alibali, 2005). Studies of reading comprehension have demonstrated that one characteristic of good readers is that they consistently monitor their own comprehension. As a result, good readers are more likely than poor ones to slow down or return to difficult passages (Garner & Reis, 1981).

Thus, awareness of the limitations of your memory leads you to select and use mnemonic strategies more effectively. In the same way, your monitoring of your understanding of new material enables you to select and use study strategies more effectively. Research demonstrates that using appropriate study techniques is associated with better learning (Paris & Oka, 1986; Pressley et al., 1988). Successful interventions to improve students' classroom performance have focused on increasing students' metacognitive awareness (Lin, 2001).

Learning Objective 8.4: *Analyze the abilities and skills children use to solve problems, and give examples of how research on problem solving can be applied.*

1. What are children's problem-solving skills?
2. How does children's use of rule-based reasoning develop?
3. How does children's ability to reason by analogy develop?
4. How would you compare the theories of R. Case and R. Siegler concerning children's strategy use?
5. What are the four mechanisms of cognitive change?
6. What are some examples of applying research on strategy construction, strategy selection, knowledge bases, and metacognition to teaching and learning in school settings?

Questions for Thought and Discussion
What does information processing tell us about the structures and processes by which children become better rememberers and problem solvers?

Test Your Mastery...

The Core Knowledge Approach to Cognition

Much research in the information processing tradition has focused on knowledge acquisition within specific domains, such as chess or physics. The processes of information processing, however, can apply equally well to the acquisition of any kind of knowledge—that is, they are *domain-general*. Improvements in strategy selection or attentional control, for example, are equally relevant whether one happens to be learning about people or mathematics. In contrast to this view, core knowledge theorists have argued that in some ways understanding our environment is so essential to our survival that we are born with specialized, hard-wired **core knowledge**. Each core knowledge system applies only to a single topic, such as understanding human behavior or understanding the behavior of inanimate objects—that is, it is *domain-specific*. Core knowledge systems do not resemble adult understanding but instead consist of elementary principles that enable children to learn new information about each domain rapidly and easily (e.g., Gelman & Williams, 1998; Spelke & Van de Walle, 1993).

How might humans have come to possess built-in knowledge? Core knowledge theorists point out that core knowledge domains include aspects of the environment that not only are essential for modern humans, but were also needed by our evolutionary ancestors (Bjorklund & Blasi, 2005; Buss, 2005). For example, possessing a way to keep track of numerosity might be useful to any species that needs to know how much food is distributed across different parts of its territory. Similarly, any species that eats or might be eaten by other animals must be able to distinguish animate from inanimate objects and prey from

Learning Objective 8.5
Explain how aspects of information processing may begin with core knowledge.

Core knowledge
Domain-specific knowledge of the physical and social environment that appears to be inborn and has adaptive value in the evolution of a species.

predator. Because environmental challenges like these affect survival rates, natural selection may have favored individuals who could learn and adapt to them quickly, thus shaping core knowledge systems over evolutionary time (Bloom, 2004).

The origin of core knowledge in evolutionary history predicts that core knowledge should have three characteristics:

- First, all humans should possess core knowledge, which therefore should be universal cross-culturally.
- Second, core knowledge should be evident in other related species.
- Finally, because it is built in, core knowledge should be evident very early in development.

These predictions have led core knowledge theorists to investigate how human infants, young children, and nonhuman animals understand fundamental aspects of their environment (e.g., Feigenson, Dehaene, & Spelke, 2004).

Knowledge of the Physical World

Understanding the behavior of physical objects is central to our survival in a world in which we are continually surrounded by many such objects. As you read in Chapter 7, infants can mentally represent objects as continuing to exist when out of view, and they also know something about the typical behavior of physical objects. Core knowledge researchers point out that this physical knowledge emerges so early that it is unlikely to have been learned through infants' limited experience with the environment. Instead, some basic knowledge of the principles that govern the physical environment must be built in from the very beginning (e.g., Spelke, 2000). This basic knowledge includes understanding properties of solidity and principles of continuity and causality. In addition, infants have basic knowledge about their social worlds, including individuals' psychological states and behavioral intentions.

Understanding Solidity and Continuity Recall R. Baillargeon's rotating screen studies. These studies suggest that babies must know that objects are solid. If they did not know this, they would not be surprised to see the screen pass through objects in its path. Elizabeth Spelke and her colleagues inspected this idea further. They first showed 4- and 6-month-oldbabies a scene in which a hand dropped a ball behind a screen and onto the display floor. When the screen was raised, infants saw the ball sitting on the floor as expected. They were allowed to look at this outcome as long as they wanted. At first, babies were quite interested in the event, but after repeated trials, their looking time declined, indicating that they were bored with or habituated to the display. At this point, the researchers introduced a shelf into the display that rested about 12 inches above the floor. The hand again dropped the ball from the top of the display behind the screen. When the screen was raised, the ball could appear in either of two different positions. On "possible trials," the ball was resting on the shelf, exactly where adults predict it should be. On "impossible trials," the ball was sitting in its previous, familiar location on the floor of the display. To get there, however, the ball would have had to pass through the top shelf! Otherwise, it would have had to disappear above the top shelf and magically reappear below it. The researchers reasoned that if babies understood that the ball existed continuously (the *continuity principle*)behind the screen, and also maintained its solid form (the *solidity principle*), then babies should look longer at the impossible outcome, even though the ball appeared in the same location as it had during habituation. Infants at both ages did look longer at the impossible event, suggesting they knew that the object was demonstrating unusual behavior.

Laurie Santos and Marc Hauser (2002) have shown that rhesus monkeys also pass Spelke's solidity and continuity tests. The monkeys watched as an experimenter dropped an apple behind a screen toward one of two shelves. Just like 4-month-old human infants, the monkeys looked longer when the apple made an impossible reappearance on the bottom shelf!

Links to Related Material

In Chapter 7, you read about the infant's growing capacity to understand causality and to mentally represent objects that are out of sight. Here, you learn how these capacities are viewed by the core knowledge approach to cognitive development.

Using a different method, Karen Wynn (1992) has demonstrated that babies not only represent objects as continuing to exist even when out of view, but they can also perform simple mental operations on those representations. Wynn showed one group of babies a single Mickey Mouse doll on a stage. A screen then rotated up to hide the doll, and a hand carrying a second Mickey entered the display and carried the doll behind the screen. The hand emerged empty. Adults seeing this event quickly infer that the second Mickey must now be sitting behind the screen along with the first. Do babies, too, make this inference? To find out, Wynn then removed the screen. On possible trials, babies saw two Mickeys, just as expected. On impossible trials, however, only one of the dolls was revealed behind the screen, while the other appeared to have vanished. Five-month-old babies looked longer at this impossible outcome, suggesting that they were able to keep track of both Mickeys even after they were out of sight. A second group of babies saw a "subtraction event," in which a hand removed one of two Mickeys from behind the screen. In this case, babies looked longer at the impossible two-doll outcome. Rhesus macaque monkeys also successfully keep track of the number of objects (eggplants rather than Mickey Mouse dolls) present in this kind of addition/subtraction study (Hauser & Carey, 2003).

Understanding Physical Causality Representing objects and their properties is one important aspect of understanding the physical world. Understanding of *causality*—how objects interact with one another—is another. You will recall from Chapter 7 how Piaget concluded that infants' knowledge of cause and effect is based largely on their ability to act effectively to produce desired outcomes—for example, to push aside an obstacle to attain a goal. Researchers working with the core knowledge perspective have demonstrated that even infants with very little experience acting on their environment have some understanding of causality.

The most common strategy for studying causality has been to habituate infants to an event with a particular causal structure. For example, infants might repeatedly see a red ball that strikes a green ball and launches it into motion, much like the collision of two billiard balls on a pool table. Once babies are bored with this event, it is reversed, so that now the green ball launches the red ball into motion. Babies as young as 6 or 7 months of age recover interest in this reversed event, in which the green ball becomes the "launcher" and the red ball the "launchee."

How do we know that babies were responding to the change in the causal structure of the event and not just to the change in direction? In control conditions, other babies saw similar events, but ones that are not causal. For example, the two balls moved in the same way but never came into contact, or the second ball moved only after a long delay. When these babies viewed the reversal, they recovered interest, but not as much as babies who saw a reversal in both direction and causal relations (Cohen & Amsel, 1998; Leslie & Keeble, 1987). In addition to causality, these studies illustrate another physical principle that infants recognize: *contact*. Inanimate objects interact only through direct contact.

Thus, babies know a few principles of object behavior—that objects are solid, are continuous through time and space, and interact with one another only on contact (Spelke & Van de Walle, 1993). Other aspects of object behavior, such as the effects of gravity and inertia, may be learned gradually over the course of many months of experience (Baillargeon, 2004). For example, in Spelke's shelf studies, it is not until 9 months of age that babies respond to an impossible event in which the shelf is removed and the ball, defying gravity, floats in mid-air!

Figure 8.6 shows another method for studying infants' understanding of gravity and support. The contrast is between a possible event (enough contact between box and platform to support the box) and an impossible event (insufficient contact; yet the box remains on platform). By 6.5 months of age, infants look longer at the impossible event, suggesting that they appreciate the cause and effect relationship between contact and support (Baillargeon, et al., 1995). Younger infants do not respond the same way, however.

Infants of 3 or 4 months, for example, are not fazed by the impossible event of Figure 8.6 (Baillargeon et al., 1995). Thus, core knowledge is not complete knowledge.

Possible Event   Impossible Event

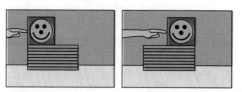
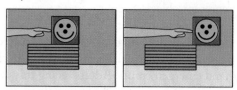

FIGURE 8.6 Infants' understanding of gravity and support.

By 6.5 months of age, infants pay attention to the "impossible" gravity-defying event in Baillargeon's study of infants' understanding of gravity and support. What other knowledge of the phsycial world do infants have? What other research supports the core knowledge view of cognitive development?

Source: How do infants learn about the physical world? In *Current Directions in Psychological Science, Vol. 3* (1994), p. 134. Fig. 1. Reprinted with permission of Cambridge University Press.

Infants still must learn a great deal about the physical world. The simple principles that infants have available to them enable them to learn more about objects more easily and quickly. According to core knowledge theorists, this knowledge has adaptive value for members of a species that pick up, eat, lose, find, and avoid running into thousands of objects every day.

Understanding the Social World Inanimate objects are not the only, or even the most important, entities with which humans interact. At birth, infants depend entirely on other humans to ensure their survival and well-being. As a species, humans have evolved to be the most socially sophisticated on earth, although we share many of our social skills with other primate species (Tomasello & Call, 1997). Social interaction is thus an ideal domain in which researchers might expect to find evidence of core knowledge.

A prime example, as you saw in Chapter 5, is the fact that infants appear to enter the world well-prepared to respond to the human face. Hours-old infants can imitate simple facial gestures such as tongue protrusion or mouth-opening performed by another person, despite the fact that they have no experience viewing other people's faces and have never seen their own faces (Meltzoff & Moore, 1977)! And, although they will imitate a human face, young infants will not imitate an inanimate box with a protruding "tongue" (Legerstee, 1991). From shortly after birth, infants also respond differently to human beings than to other stimuli. For example, infants vocalize more in the presence of a human face than in the presence of an inanimate object, even when the inanimate object is a moving, sounding puppet (Ellsworth, Muir, & Hains, 1993).

Understanding Human Behavior Understanding people's behavior involves knowing how people are different from other objects. Adults have a sophisticated understanding of mental states such as desires, thoughts, and beliefs. Young children have difficulty understanding mental capacities, which are not visible and must therefore be inferred. Human behavior, on the other hand, is visible, and it is applied to the environment in meaningful ways. Our behavior is intended to bring about desired goals—we reach for a cup in order to drink from it; we turn away from a wall to avoid running into it. Do infants understand that human behavior is meaningfully related to the environment in a way that the behavior of inanimate objects is not?

In one experiment by Amanda Woodward (1998), 6-month-old infants were habituated to an event in which a hand entered a stage and reached for one of two objects. On every trial, the hand reached in exactly the same manner and always to the same object—say, the ball. Adults interpret this event as *goal-directed*. That is, the purpose of the reach was to obtain the ball. Adults disregard as irrelevant other aspects of the event, such as whether the reach was right- versus left-handed or slow versus fast. Do babies, too, understand the significance of the goal of human reaches? To find out, Woodward tested babies with two new events in which the locations of the two objects were reversed. In the "old goal" event, the hand executed a novel reach, but the reach was directed to the same old goal. In the "new goal" event, the hand executed precisely the same reach as it had during habituation, but the reach was now directed to a new goal.

Links to Related Material
In Chapter 5, you read about the infant's preparedness for social interaction. Here, you learn how this preparedness relates to the core knowledge approach to cognitive development.

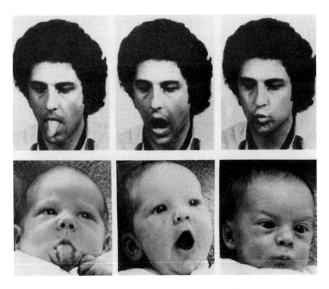

This photograph shows an adult model and corresponding infant responses in Meltzoff and Moore's study of neonatal imitation of other humans' facial expressions. How is this an example of core knowledge? From an evolutionary perspective, how might this inborn tendency to imitate human behavior have adaptive value?

Source: From A.N. Meltzoff and M.K. Moore. (1977). Imitation of facial and manual gestures by human neonates. *Science, 298,* 75. Copyright 1977 by the American Association for the Advancement of Science. Reprinted by permission.

Babies dishabituated when the hand reached for a new goal object, but not when the hand executed a new reach. This means that the babies understood that the goal of the reach is more significant than the manner in which the reach is executed. Babies do not, however, interpret the behavior of inanimate objects as similarly goal-directed. When they viewed the same set of events executed by an inanimate rod rather than a human hand, babies looked equally at both test events.

Understanding Psychological States A human (but not, for instance, a rock) can *see* a cup on the table, *attend* to the water inside it, *intend* to drink the water, and thus reach for the cup. Do babies appreciate such psychological states? Consider the following event. A mother and baby are playing together on the floor. At one point the mother turns her head and gazes toward the door of the room. The infant notices the mother's movement, stares for a moment at her face, and then turns and also gazes toward the door. This episode illustrates the phenomenon known as **joint attention:** the ability to follow the gaze of another and thus share the other's attentional focus. This skill, which emerges during the second half of the first year (Butterworth & Grover, 1988; Scaife & Bruner, 1975), seems to imply some appreciation of both perception and attention: Mommy sees something interesting; if I look where she's looking, I'll have the same experience. As predicted by the core knowledge approach, chimpanzees and even domestic dogs follow the gaze of other individuals (Call, Brauer, Kaminski, & Tomasello, 2003; Povinelli & Eddy, 1996).

Furthermore, suppose that what mother and baby see in the door is a stranger—some adult whom the baby has never encountered before. Uncertain how to respond, the baby turns back and looks at the mother's face. If the mother smiles and greets the stranger, the baby will probably respond positively as well; if the mother reacts with fear or distress, the baby's reaction will likely be similarly negative. The baby is engaging in **social referencing:** looking to another for cues about how to interpret and respond to an uncertain situation. Like joint attention, social referencing seems to imply some understanding that mother is experiencing a state of mind—in this case, an emotion that is relevant to the child's own emotional reaction. Like joint attention, social referencing is not present early in infancy but emerges around the end of the first year. And like joint attention, social referencing is specific to the human objects in the baby's environment. Infants do not follow the gaze of a favorite doll, and they do not turn to a teddy bear for guidance when trying to make sense of something new.

During the second year of life, infants begin to make inferences about people's *intentions* to perform particular actions as well their *desires* to obtain particular objects. For example, Malinda Carpenter, Nameera Akhtar, and Michael Tomasello (1998) demonstrated various actions, such as hitting a button to make a set of lights go on, to 16-month-old infants. The adult model concluded some actions with the comment, "There!" indicating that her behavior had been intentional. After other actions, the model exclaimed,

Joint attention
Use of directional gaze as a cue to identify and share the attentional focus of another.

Social referencing
Use of information gained from other people to interpret ambiguous situations and to regulate one's own behavior.

"Whoops!" indicating her behavior had been accidental. When infants were given the opportunity to imitate the model, they imitated the intentional actions much more often than the accidental ones. That is, they appeared to understand that some actions are deliberate and therefore worth imitating, while others are accidental and should not be imitated.

In a study by Andrew Meltzoff (1995), 18-month-old infants viewed an adult model who tried, but continually failed, to achieve an intended goal, such as putting a string of beads in a cup or pulling the rubber ends off of a small barbell. Infants were then given the opportunity to play with the objects. Would babies choose to imitate what they saw the adult model do, or would they imitate the adult's *intended*, but never actually witnessed, goal?

Infants were able to infer what the actor had intended to do. They imitated the intended action, despite the fact that they had never seen that action modeled! Infants did not do this when they saw an inanimate mechanical device execute the action, however. Babies appear to understand that human, but not machine, behavior is intentional (Meltzoff, 1995).

Infants this same age are able to infer people's *desires*. In the "broccoli study," 14- and 18-month-old infants viewed an adult sitting at a table with a plate of crackers, which most babies love, on one side and a plate of broccoli, which most babies despise, on the other. The adult looked at the crackers and presented a disgusted facial expression. When she looked at the broccoli, in contrast, she smiled in joy. The babies then got the chance to offer the adult one of the two plates of food. Fourteen-month-olds offered the adult the food they themselves liked—the crackers. They were unable to understand that another person's likes and desires might be different from their own. Older babies, in contrast, offered the adult the broccoli, correctly inferring that if she had expressed positive emotion toward it she would also want to eat it.

In all these examples, infants who are not yet 2 years old are demonstrating impressive skill in interpreting people's behaviors. All demonstrate that infants are sensitive to social information that is readily perceptible, such as gaze direction, facial expression, or tone of voice. However, infants are also using these perceptible signals to infer that people experience psychological states, such as attention, intention, or desire, that are not themselves visible.

Evaluating the Core Knowledge Approach

Critics of the core knowledge approach have argued that the methods for studying cognitive skills in babies are not adequate (e.g., Haith and Benson, 1998) or can have misleading results (Cohen & Marks, 2002). Studies showing that young babies understand basic physical or numerical principles can be difficult to replicate (Wakeley et al., 2000). Others have expressed skepticism about what it means to say that knowledge is built into human brains (Elman et al., 1996). The brain is highly plastic or flexible at birth, as discussed in Chapter 6. Therefore, it is unlikely that specific neurons are designated through our genetic code to represent knowledge per se. Furthermore, some studies raise questions about what it means to say that babies "know" about objects. For example, presented with Spelke's solidity task in which a ball drops behind a screen onto one of two shelves, 2-year-olds cannot predict that the ball should appear on the first shelf in its path. They are just as likely to say that the ball should appear on the bottom shelf, in violation of the solidity and continuity principles they supposedly understood at 4 months of age (Hood, Carey, & Prasada, 2000).

Many questions remain. For example, how does developmental change in core knowledge happen? How does learning affect core knowledge systems? How do new systems of knowledge emerge? What are the relations between information processing skills and core knowledge systems? Only recently have core knowledge researchers begun to address these questions (Spelke, 2000). Despite these criticisms, the wealth of research emerging from the core knowledge approach has revealed striking early competence in infants and young children that emerges seemingly before they have had any substantial experience with their environment. Collectively, these findings have led parents, psychologists, pediatricians, and companies that produce toys for babies to take seriously the idea that young children are able to think, reason, and learn about a lot of things much earlier than anyone previously thought.

Questions for Thought and Discussion

Do you think it would be possible to integrate the various approaches to cognitive development—Piaget's stages, Vygotsky's and other sociocultural approaches, information processing theory, and theory of mind—into a unified theory? Why, or why not?

Learning Objective 8.5: *Explain how aspects of information processing may begin with core knowledge.*

1. In what sense is core knowledge a biological approach to understanding cognitive development?
2. What specific knowledge of their physical environment do infants possess, and how do we know?
3. What understandings do infants have about human behavior and psychological states?
4. What roles do joint attention and social referencing play in developing core knowledge in infancy?
5. In what ways might core knowledge contribute to the development of information processing skills?

✔ *Test Your Mastery...*

Theory of Mind

Although the social-cognitive accomplishments of infancy are impressive, they differ significantly from adults' mature understanding of other people. Adults understand that human behavior is guided not only by feelings and desires, but also by *beliefs*—mental representations of the world around us. Beliefs can be accurate or inaccurate reflections of reality. For example, you might believe that your notebook is on the kitchen table because you remember putting it there, but that belief might be false if your sister moved it or if you forgot that you actually left it in the car. Psychologists use the term **theory of mind** to refer to children's understanding of the mental world. Do children realize that the mental world is distinct from the physical world? Do they realize that despite this distinction, the mental and the nonmental are connected—that our experiences lead us to have particular beliefs and that these beliefs then direct our behavior?

Theory-of-mind researchers have been particularly interested in children's understanding that people can have beliefs that do not correspond to reality. Understanding **false beliefs** provides clear evidence that the child appreciates the distinction between the mental and the nonmental. Figure 8.7 depicts a *false-belief task*. To any adult, the answer to the question of where Sally will search for her marble is obvious—in the basket, where she last saw it. She has no way of knowing that the marble has been moved during her absence. Note, however, that to arrive at this answer we must set aside our own knowledge of the true state of affairs to realize that Sally could believe something that differs from this true state—that she could hold a false belief. We can do this only if we realize that beliefs are mental representations that need not correspond to reality.

Three-year-old children typically have great difficulty understanding false beliefs. Most 3-year-olds fail tasks such as the one in Figure 8.7 and also have difficulty recapturing their own false beliefs. In another common false-belief task, children are shown a container that turns out to have unexpected contents—for example, a crayon box that actually holds candles. When asked what they initially believed was in the box, most 3-year-olds reply "candles," answering in terms of their current knowledge rather than their original, false belief. Four-year-olds are much more likely to understand that they can hold a belief that is false and that a representation can change even when the reality does not. They are also more likely to realize that others could hold false beliefs in the crayon-box or hidden-marble tasks (Astington & Gopnik, 1988).

Some have argued that infants' and young children's understanding of others as social beings and then later as mental beings is supported by core knowledge systems (e.g., Baron-Cohen, 1995; Leslie, Friedman, & German, 2004). Social understanding has adaptive value, and capacity for theory of mind can be inferred from evolution (Povinelli & Giambrone, 2001). Core knowledge theorists believe that as humans evolved to become a highly social species, we also evolved a unique, specialized knowledge system that supports social interaction (Baron-Cohen, 1995). Individuals with

Learning Objective 8.6
Describe how children develop a theory of mind.

Questions for Thought and Discussion
What if someone lacked the knowledge incorporated in a theory of mind? How would interactions with other people be affected?

Theory of mind
Thoughts and beliefs concerning the mental world.

False belief
The realization that people may hold beliefs that are not true, as a sign that a child possesses a theory of mind.

BOX 8.3   Brains in a Box: Do New Age Toys Deliver on the Promise?

It has become dangerously fashionable to label general—even trivial—pedagogical advice that is not grounded in scientific fact as "brain-based learning." For instance, findings about rapid synaptic proliferation in young children's brains have nurtured hopes that cognitive capabilities can be increased by teaching infants vocabulary and basic facts with audiovisual material. But proponents of these early education programs have conveniently overlooked the lack of direct empirical evidence linking neurological and learning processes (Stern, 2005, p. 745).

The brain-based learning movement that has swept education has become a societal preoccupation as well-intentioned parents scurry to find the best way to give their children a head start in learning. Fueled by findings of infant capabilities in perception, quantity, and language and by a research focus on the brain, parents and educators are looking for ways to enhance children's competencies before it is too late—before the mythical learning window closes at age 3. Toy companies were perfectly poised to quell parental fears—to offer what one toy chain boasted as "baby brain boosters" based on the exaggerated and sometimes unfounded science. And so it began . . .

In the past, toy aisles were filled with costumes, blocks, toys, and play dough. Today, these same aisles chime and blink with electronic learning pads, video games, DVD players, and so called educational toys. In 2004, the National Retail Federation boasted sales for these toys reaching in the hundreds of billions of dollars. And many of these dollars were spent on toys designed to increase infant and preschool intelligence despite the lack of evidence

suggesting that filling children's minds with discombobulated facts translated into meaningful learning. In fact, some of these toys even claimed to raise newborn *intelligence*, a promise that in scientific terms was untenable at best. Nonetheless, desire for these products was palpable. In 2002, Genius Products Inc., producers of the Baby Genius products, announced an 81 percent increase in gross revenues. That same year, Disney saw Baby Einstein yield $17 million in sales, up from $13 million the year before. Just as the car industry was using sex to sell cars, the toy industry started using brain development to sell toys.

In the last 30 years, researchers in child development have accumulated a great deal of information on how children learn. The science strongly suggests that this learning does not happen by assuming that children are empty vessels and that our job is to fill children's heads with facts. In this post-Skinnerian, -Piagetian era, infants and toddlers are seen as *active* explorers of their environments—capable discoverers who engage in meaningful learning. Infants also enter the world with some core knowledge. Their world is not one of William James's "blooming, buzzing, confusion," but rather one filled with discrete objects that move along trajectories, of language almost tailor-made to suit infants' capabilities, and of faces and social interaction. With these beginning points, infants are poised to delve into their surroundings and to construct (with the help of their mentors) a view of the physical and cultural world that resembles that of the adult.

Ah, but here is the rub—if infants can see objects and if they are sensitive to gravity at 8 months, should we not produce

better understanding of others' thoughts and motivations would have had an adaptive advantage over those who could not. Infants' sensitivity to human faces, human action, and psychological states is one source of evidence for these claims.

Another source of evidence that theory of mind might be built in comes from the study of individuals who do not understand human behavior or thought at all. *Autism* is a developmental disorder that may be characterized by mental retardation, language deficits, repetitive motor sequences, and most prominently by a profound lack of social engagement. Autistic children have been tested on simple false-belief tasks like the one in Figure 8.7 (Baron-Cohen, Leslie, & Frith, 1986, 2000). Although they have little difficulty with tasks that do not require an understanding of mental states, autistic children fail dramatically at solving simple false-belief problems. Baron-Cohen and colleagues suggest that the reason they fail and appear to lack interest in other people is that the core knowledge system for people is either missing or has failed to develop properly. Baron-Cohen (1995) has called this condition "mindblindness."

Impacts of Cognitive Skills on Theory of Mind

Like a child's own metacognitive awareness, understanding the mental activities of other people can be viewed as a specific body of knowledge that children must acquire through experience. Children who participate in activities that support learning about theory of mind tend to pass false-belief tasks earlier than children who engage in fewer such activities. Learning in social contexts, representational skills, and metacognitive skills are cognitive influences that affect children's acquisition of a theory of mind.

toys that encourage the learning of physics? If infants can distinguish different amounts of "stuff" and know that 3 is different from 2, should we not build toys that teach mathematics? If infants are sensitive to sounds in all of the world's languages, should we not offer toys that expose children to language so that they can become bi- or trilingual at the mere press of a button? Are we not building better brains and advancing children's natural propensities when we build on core knowledge and morph it into pedagogical learning? NO!

Importantly, science considers babies and toddlers to be ready learners who understand concepts *in context*. They learn that floors will support crawling by crawling and later walking. They learn that blocks will be supported in a structure by placing the block atop the pile and watching it balance or fall. They learn language not by passively overhearing isolated words or watching a video, but by having "conversations" with interactive partners. They learn quantity by asking for more juice or by setting a table for three versus four. Learning is not memorization. However, the toys (and some modern curricula in our schools) are selling the decontextualized learning of facts as the keys to later academic success. Parents have come to believe that young children need to watch educational videos, attend tutoring classes, drill with facts, and use expensive educational software to promote their well-being and intellectual growth.

How can we remedy the situation? When we remember that the world is a virtual classroom and that guided play is the best teacher, we can buy toys that encourage children to be the masters of their own play. We can buy toys that are 90 percent child and 10 percent toy as opposed to the other way around. We would avoid toys that direct children to look for one right, "fill-in-the-blank" answer. Why would we do these things? Because

PLAY = LEARNING, and research from early advances in reading and mathematics strongly suggests that this is so (Hirsh-Pasek & Golinkoff, 2003; Singer, Golinkoff, & Hirsh-Pasek, 2006).

Children who learn through play do better academically and socially. As members of the "Google" generation, 21st-century children will have facts at their fingertips. They don't need to be fed information through toys. They need to *play* and to become problem solvers and creative thinkers. Countless science lessons await children who play in the backyard exploring anthills and blades of grass. Lessons in mathematics abound when children divide birthday cake and separate the trail mix into sets of nuts and fruits. Cardboard boxes from local supermarkets offer foundations for makeshift taxicabs and storylines. Finger painting with pudding on freezer paper provides lessons in texture. Building blocks and construction toys build knowledge in physics. And costume drawers, puppets, red rubber balls, books, crayons, paints, rhythm instruments, and dolls all allow children to invent and discover.

It is time to bridge the gap between what we can learn from the science of child development and brain development and the kinds of toys we are buying for young children. To *truly* prepare children for their future in our global society, we must not be data blind and ignore the ways that children learn best. We must invent toys that can be assembled in more than one way and that serve as props for children's creativity. Learning occurs best in meaningful contexts, and not when children are served "Fact Food" in isolated clumps. Good toys are accoutrements that make everyday interactions more fun and expand the boundaries of children's ordinary experiences. Good toys naturally build social skills, academic skills, and bigger brains.

Learning in Social Contexts As Vygotsky would have predicted, language and play provide children with important sources of information about theory of mind. For example, children who receive training in mental state language (e.g., Mary *thought* that Fred went home) perform better on false-belief tasks than children who lack such training (Hale & Tager-Flusberg, 2003). Similarly, children from traditional Peruvian cultures who speak Quechua, a language that lacks mental state terms, struggle with false-belief tasks until the age of 7 or 8 (Vinden, 1996). Similarly, deaf children who do not learn sign language until they begin attending school acquire theory of mind understanding later than deaf children who have learned sign language from birth (Peterson, Wellman, & Liu, 2005). Pretend play provides another source of information about beliefs and mental states. When children engage in pretend play, they deliberately create situations that they know are not real. Moreover, successful play requires that all the children involved share the same mental representation of the play situation. Children who engage more often in pretend play demonstrate more sophisticated theory of mind skills (Astington & Jenkins, 1995).

Representational Skills Theory of mind also requires substantial representational skills. Young children find it quite difficult to keep two things in mind simultaneously. As you read in Chapter 7, they cannot simultaneously keep track of the height and width of a glass of liquid, for example, and thus fail to conserve. The inability to distinguish a false belief from reality may be related to the inability to distinguish appearance from reality. The **appearance–reality distinction** is the basis for separating the way things are from the way they appear. For example, if you show a child a picture of a red car, cover the picture with a transparent blue filter to make it look blue, and then ask what color the car "really and

Appearance–reality distinction
The realization that objects may not appear as they really are, as a sign that a child possesses a theory of mind.

FIGURE 8.7 Example of a false-belief task.

To answer correctly, the child must realize that beliefs are mental representations that may differ from reality. The ability to understand false beliefs is an indication that even young children have a theory of mind. The early appearance of this ability makes it a candidate for core knowledge.

Source: From U. Frith. (1989). *Autism: Explaining the Enigma.* Oxford: Basic Blackwell, p. 160. Copyright 1989 by Basil Blackwell. Reprinted with permission.

Links to Related Material

In Chapter 7, you read how young children have difficulty keeping two things in mind simultaneously, such as the height and width of a glass of liquid. Here, you read how this difficulty may relate to the appearance–reality distinction and the child's growing theory of mind.

truly is," a 3-year-old is likely to reply "blue." A 6-year-old will almost certainly (and perhaps scornfully) say "red." Suppose you next present a stone disguised as an egg and ask what this strange object "looks like." The 3-year-old, knowing that the apparent egg is really and truly a stone, answers "stone." The 6-year-old, on the other hand, again showing a capacity to distinguish appearance from reality, replies, "egg."

Problems in distinguishing appearance and reality are not limited to the visual realm. Children also come to realize that sounds or smells or touches may sometimes mislead, giving a false impression of their underlying source (Flavell, Flavell, & Green, 1983; Flavell, Green, & Flavell, 1989). And children must come to understand that people, as well as objects, can present misleading appearances—they may look nice, for example, when they are actually mean (Flavell et al., 1992). The ability to make such distinctions is not complete by age 6, however. We remain susceptible to being fooled by misleading appearances. But the preschool child makes major strides in mastering this important kind of knowledge (Flavell, 1986).

Both false-belief and appearance–reality tasks are based on the realization that mental representations can be different from physical reality. But such tasks also are based on the understanding that mental and physical realities are also linked. That is, what we believe follows from what we experience. The characters in Figure 8.7, for example, hold different beliefs about where the marble is because they have had different experiences.

It is not until about age 4 that children are able to appreciate this connection between experience and belief.

Metacognitive Skills Younger children do not have a good grasp of the relation between the physical and mental worlds, partly because younger children's metacognitive awareness of their own thought processes is limited. Young children's understanding of mental activities in others is similarly incomplete. Three-year-olds understand, for example, that a person who has looked into a box knows its contents, but a person who is merely in the same room as the box does not. However, 3-year-olds probably cannot tell you how they learned what is in the box—whether they learned through sight or touch or being told (O'Neill & Chong, 2001). Asked how to determine the color of an unseen object, 3-year-olds may try to determine this by touch rather than by looking (O'Neill, Astington, & Flavell, 1992). Four- and 5-year-olds may report that they have always known a fact that they just learned (Taylor, Esbensen, & Bennett, 1994). These results suggest that the development of metacognitive skills plays an important role in children's development of theory of mind.

Two general conclusions emerge from the studies of children's understanding of the origins of belief (Miller, 2000). First, the preschool period is a time of important accomplishments. By age 5 most children have a basic understanding of how experience leads to belief. The second conclusion is that children are not born with this knowledge but must acquire it. In contrast to core knowledge approaches, understanding the development of theory of mind depends on the significance of learning and the development of expertise.

Evaluating Theory of Mind Acquisition of a theory of mind is an extended developmental process. In addition, general information processing limitations may mask rather than promote children's true, underlying understanding of people's mental states (Leslie et al., 2004; Onishi & Baillargeon, 2005). The effects of inhibition, verbal competence, and learning on children's acquisition of theory of mind must be taken into account (Carlson & Moses, 2001; Ruffman et al., 2002). For example, children who have older brothers and sisters succeed on false-belief tasks sooner than do only children (Ruffman et al., 1998). Presumably, this result stems from the experiences (and opportunities for deception!) that older siblings provide. Infants may come into the world innately predisposed to study and interpret people and their behavior differently from inanimate objects (Gopnick & Meltzoff, 1997), but to develop a full theory of mind they also need information processing skills and learning from experience.

Learning Objective 8.6: *Describe how children develop a theory of mind.*

1. How do false-belief tasks help us study children's understanding of the mental world?
2. What can we learn about theory of mind from children with "mindblindness"?
3. What cognitive developments and information processing skills affect children's acquisition of a theory of mind?
4. What do studies of appearance–reality distinctions and experience–belief connections tell us about children's theory of mind?

✔ *Test Your Mastery...*

BOX 8.4   Contextual Model of Information Processing

- Infant is born with innate predispositions to gather certain kinds of information from the environment.
- Parents, teachers, and peers expose child to culturally appropriate knowledge. This differential exposure influences which domains the child will gain expertise in.
- Cultures and societies provide different opportunities to learn different kinds of knowledge.

Learning Objective 8.1
Define the information processing
approach and describe three methods of
studying information processing.

1. What are the goals of the information processing approach to cognition?

The goal of the *information processing approach* is to specify the steps by which the mind transforms sensory inputs into cognitive or behavioral outputs.

2. How does the information processing approach reflect a computer metaphor?

Psychologists have observed that *computers* can systematically transform a variety of inputs into a variety of outputs. To do so, computers require precise programs that specify each step of the transformation. Information processing theorists saw in the digital computer a useful metaphor for the human mind.

3. What are the strengths and limitations of connectionism in the information processing approach?

The *connectionist approach* has provided insight into a host of aspects of cognitive development, including infant perception, object permanence, Piagetian concrete operational concepts, category learning, and language. However, the use of connectionism as a tool for understanding cognition has also been criticized. Similarities between such networks and human brains often are exaggerated, and connectionist systems always require hundreds or even thousands of trials in order to learn simple tasks. These models never experience the "aha moments" of insight that humans often report, in which an answer simply becomes clear.

4. What can we learn from microgenetic studies of cognition?

There are five issues related to cognitive change for which *microgenetic techniques* can provide valuable data: first, the path of cognitive change: the sequences and levels through which children move in acquiring new knowledge; second, the rate of change: how quickly or slowly different forms of knowledge are mastered; third, the breadth of change: when a new competency is acquired and how narrowly or broadly it is applied; fourth, variability in the pattern of change: children often do not all follow the same route in mastering a new concept; and fifth, the sources of change: the experiences and processes through which new knowledge is constructed.

Learning Objective 8.2
Explain the information processing model of memory, and trace developmental changes in the kinds of memory.

1. What is the memory store model in the information processing approach?	In the *memory store model* the information first enters the sensory register, where a literal image of a stimulus can be held, but only for a matter of milliseconds. The information then moves to short-term or working, memory, the center for active and conscious processing. Although information typically remains in short-term memory for only a few seconds, various strategies may prolong it. Finally, the information may be transferred to long-term memory, where it can exist indefinitely. Getting the information to long-term memory is the goal when new information is to be learned.
2. What kinds of memory are present in infancy, and how are they different?	*Event memory* is when children develop scripts for sequences of familiar actions or routine events in their daily world. A script is a representation of the typical sequence of events in a familiar context, such as "birthday party" or "going to the store." *Constructive memory* refers to the ways that individuals interpret the information they take in from the world in terms of their preexisting knowledge, which affects what they remember. *Autobiographical memory* refers to specific, personal, and long-lasting memory about the self. Infants are also capable of recognition memory, which is the realization that some perceptually present stimulus or event has been encountered before, and recall memory, which refers to the retrieval of some past stimulus or event when the stimulus or event is not perceptually present.
3. How do researchers study recognition and recall memory in infants and young children?	Researchers study *recognition memory* in infancy through the habituation–dishabituation procedure. Even newborn infants show habituation across a range of modalities, including visual, auditory, and tactile. *Recall memory* is difficult to study in infancy because infants cannot produce verbal reports or drawings to show what they recall. However, studies of deferred imitation provide compelling evidence of recall memory in infancy.
4. How does memory change as children develop?	*Older children* remember better than younger children. On average, the older the child, the better the performance on memory measures. Research verifies that recall memory improves with age and that older children typically report more of their experiences than do younger children.

Learning Objective 8.3
Describe three cognitive tools that contribute to the development of memory during childhood.

1. What are mnemonic strategies, and how do they contribute to memory development in children?	A *mnemonic strategy* is any technique that people use to help them remember something. Individuals use three well-studied strategies: rehearsal, organization, and elaboration. Rehearsal is the saying over and over technique; organization is grouping into conceptual categories; and elaboration is linking items with a general image or story.
2. What does research on novices and experts tell us about the role of knowledge in cognitive development?	Where expertise is high, so is memory, and variations in expertise contribute to variations in memory. Variations in expertise contribute to developmental changes in memory across the span of childhood. Older children possess more expertise for most topics than do younger children, and this greater expertise is one reason they remember more. *Experts* have a greater quantity of knowledge and are able to represent more than just individual bits of information in memory. They are also capable of representing relationships among individual items. Expertise is also influential in reasoning and problem solving. Expertise affects the speed of processing. When knowledge about some domain is great, information relevant to that domain can be taken in and processed more rapidly, thus freeing cognitive resources for other activities.
3. What is metacognition, and how does this ability contribute to memory development?	*Metacognition* is knowledge about thinking. Children's thinking about memory (metamemory) changes as they develop. Even young children realize that there is such a thing as memory. By age 5 or 6, most children realize that familiar items are more easily remembered than unfamiliar ones. Research suggests that the knowledge behavior relationship is difficult to demonstrate empirically. However, training programs in memory strategies have been found to improve performance.

Learning Objective 8.4

Analyze the abilities and skills children use to solve problems, and give examples of how research on problem solving can be applied.

1. What are children's problem-solving skills?	Children utilize two kinds of *problem-solving skills*: (1) they form rules for combining information and making judgments and (2) they reason by analogy. Developmental changes in basic cognitive abilities affecting memory and knowledge also contribute to problem-solving ability.
2. How does children's use of rule-based reasoning develop?	Preschoolers are capable of *rule-based problem solving* but with some definite limitations. At first, children can follow only one rule at a time; eventually, however, higher-order rule following capabilities emerge. Finally, enough metacognitive ability develops, which allows the child to reflect on the rules he or she has learned and to note the relation among them. The term *executive function* refers to these problem-solving capabilities.
3. How does children's reason by analogy develop?	Some forms of analogical reasoning, including verbal analogies, are complex and late to develop. Some forms, however, are evident early in development. *Infants* are able to problem-solve in situations where the problem solving is modeled by a parent. As children develop, they can recognize relationships across problems and gradually depend less on perceptual similarity. Domain-specific knowledge about particular items and their relationships eventually develops.
4. How would you compare the theories of R. Case and R. Siegler concerning children's strategy?	In Case's theory, the total problem-solving resources available to the child are divided into the components of operating space and short-term storage space. Operating space refers to the available mental energy needed for an activity. Short-term storage space refers to the resources the child needs to store results from previous operations while carrying out new ones. Limitations in short-term storage space contribute to young children's difficulty to problem-solve. According to *Case*, developmental changes in storage result from the increase in the efficiency with which operations are performed. In contrast, in *Siegler's* theory children's strategy use increases as they acquire more information processing skills, which leads to cognitive change.

5. What are the four mechanisms of cognitive change?

Siegler identifies encoding, automatization, strategy construction, and strategy selection as the four mechanisms of cognitive change. *Encoding* is the identification and use of the most important features of objects and events to form internal representations. Young children are sometimes incapable of encoding critical information. *Automatization* is the process by which practice makes the skill automatic. Cognitive resources are freed, and more advanced forms of problem solving become possible. *Strategy construction* refers to the idea that children realize the organization inherent in a set of items, thus, increasing the efficiency with which information is handled. In *strategy selection*, the child chooses the strategy that supplies the optimal solution. In both theories, practice and biological maturation contribute to increases in operational efficiency.

6. What are some examples of applying research on strategy construction, strategy selection, knowledge bases, and metacognition to teaching and learning in school settings?

Research in children's strategy construction and selection informs *techniques for teaching* children how to solve basic arithmetic problems. Although a child might employ a range of strategies to solve a problem, their selection is usually not random but is adaptive to the problem at hand. Because not all children will have the same strategies, teachers need to be sensitive to the beliefs and strategies children bring to the classroom. Research with experts and novices finds that the experts' ability to identify a problem at the conceptual level allows them to solve the problem more quickly than the novices. The goal for educators is to recognize the naïve understanding of novices and how this influences their ability to apply their knowledge successfully in problem solving. Metacognitive awareness studies help us to understand the limitations of a child's memory. Successful interventions to improve students' classroom performance have focused on increasing students' metacognitive awareness and the use of mnemonic strategies.

Learning Objective 8.5

Explain how aspects of information processing
may begin with core knowledge.

1. In what sense is core knowledge a biological approach to understanding cognitive development?	*Core knowledge* theorists argue that in some ways understanding our environment is so essential to our survival that we are born with specialized hard-wired (biological) knowledge. Core knowledge is domain-specific and enables children to learn new information about each domain rapidly and easily.
2. What specific knowledge of their physical environment do infants possess, and how do we know?	Some *basic knowledge* of the principles that govern the physical environment must be built in from the very beginning. This basic knowledge includes understanding properties of solidity and principles of continuity and causality. In addition, infants have basic knowledge of their social worlds, including individuals' psychological states and behavior intentions. Researchers have provided evidence of this core knowledge in various studies.
3. What understandings do infants have about human behavior and psychological states?	Infants are capable of understanding *goal-directed behavior* or that a particular behavior has a specific purpose. They also engage in a process called *joint attention*, which is the ability to follow the gaze of another and thus share the other's attentional focus, and social referencing, or looking to another for cues about how to interpret and respond to an uncertain situation. Like joint attention, *social referencing* emerges around the end of the first year.

4. What roles do joint attention and social referencing play in developing core knowledge in infancy?	During the second year of life, infants begin to make *inferences about people's intentions* to perform particular actions as well as their desires to obtain particular objects. Researchers have confirmed that infants are able to infer an adult's intended action, despite the fact that they had never seen the actions modeled. Babies appear to understand that human behavior is intentional.
5. In what ways might core knowledge contribute to the development of information processing skills?	*Core knowledge* provides the infant with a basic knowledge of how to interpret people's behaviors. Research demonstrates that infants are sensitive to social information that is readily perceptible such as gaze direction, facial expression, or tone of voice. However, infants are also using these perceptible signals to infer that people experience psychological states, such as attention, intention, or desire, which are not themselves visible.

Learning Objective 8.6

Describe how children develop a theory of mind.

1. How do false-belief tasks help us study children's understanding of the mental world?	Understanding *false beliefs* provides clear evidence that the child appreciates the distinction between mental and nonmental. In addition, the ability to understand false beliefs is an indication that even young children have a theory of mind. Engaging children in false-belief tasks allows researchers to identify the developmental sequence that occurs in a child's ability to understand that they can hold a belief that is false and that a representation can change when reality does not.

2. What can we learn about theory of mind from children with "mindblindness"?	Researchers suggest that children who are *autistic* (mindblind) lack or have an undeveloped core knowledge system for people. That is why they tend to fail at solving false-belief problems.
3. What cognitive-development and information processing skills affect children's acquisition of a theory of mind?	Learning in *social contexts*, *representational skills*, and *metacognitive skills* are cognitive influences that affect children's acquisition of theory of mind.
4. What do studies of appearance–reality distinctions and experience–belief connections tell us about children's theory of mind?	The *appearance–reality distinction* is the basis for separating the way things are from the way they appear. Appearance–reality tasks are based on the understanding that mental and physical realities are linked. That is, what we believe follows what we experience. It is not until about age 4 that children are able to appreciate this connection between experience and belief.

Intelligence *and* Schooling

Masai children in Tanzania
(Tom Stoddart/Getty Images)

"We pick out the brightest children, those with the most potential, and then send them off with the goats," explains Johnson Kinyago, a Masai herder in Kenya. "It takes brains to identify each animal, find water, and ward off cattle rustlers. School is for those who are less quick."

It is not difficult to understand why schools based on the model so prevalent in industrialized societies might seem irrelevant to the Masai, one of the few migratory groups remaining in East Africa. Traditionally, these herders have followed their cattle from place to place, setting up temporary camps, and the schooling they have valued has been the kind needed to pursue their nomadic lifestyle. Today, however, changes have begun to appear in this traditional way of life. The Masai do not have enough land to support their population, and years of drought have depleted the cattle herds, leaving many people dependent on food aid. In the view of some Masai, formal schooling has become necessary.

For the Masai, changes in the environment are making it necessary to change the content of schooling. It is likely that along with this change will come some change in the idea of what constitutes intelligence. The best reader, for example, will not necessarily be the best herder. In industrialized cultures, the definition of intelligence is strongly linked to formal schooling. As you will see, the well-known IQ test was formulated to predict success in school. But intelligence, even in industrialized cultures, can be defined in various ways.

This chapter explores the concepts associated with intelligence and the functions and roles of the formal education process. However intelligence is defined, one critical question remains: how do we measure it? It is one thing to recognize intelligent behavior when we see it, but this is not an acceptable solution in schools or in the workplace. Thus, a significant emphasis in the psychology of intelligence is on assessment. In addition, from a contextual perspective, intelligence is meaningful in relation to culturally defined contexts such as, in the case of modern Western societies, schooling. Thus, in the latter half of this chapter, we will focus in particular on schooling as a context for child development. ■

Intelligence: IQ Testing and the Psychometric Approach

Learning Objective 9.1
Explain how intelligence traditionally is defined and measured.

Psychometrics
Conceptualization of intelligence that seeks to identify the trait or set of traits that characterize some people to a greater extent than others so that differences among individuals can be described.

General intelligence
According to Spearman, the one common factor (g) that underlies all intelligent behavior.

Specific intelligence
According to Spearman, the kinds of intelligence(s) that are needed to be successful on one particular task or in a certain situation.

Crytallized intelligence
According to Cattell, the abilities we acquire from experience, including general information and social norms.

Traditional definitions of intelligence are based on **psychometrics**, the idea that levels of intelligence can be identified by traits or sets of traits present in some people to a greater extent than in others. The psychometric approach has spawned the development of standardized tests of intelligence used in today's schools. The goal of testing is to identify and assess these traits so that differences among individuals can be described as measures of intelligence.

The psychometric approach is based in large part on the work of Charles Spearman (1927), a British psychologist and statistician. Spearman proposed that, although people can exhibit different types of intelligent behavior such as mathematical reasoning or verbal comprehension, there is one common factor that underlies all intelligent behavior. He called this common factor, "**g**," to indicate that it was **general intelligence**, required for successful performance in any domain. If a test of intelligence were measuring general intelligence, then any imperfect correlations among test items would reflect the **specific intelligence**, or "**s**," required for a particular item.

Spearman favored "g" as the central, most useful, and most significant type of intelligence. He believed that "g" represented the ability to engage in abstract reasoning, form relationships, and apply general principles. Specific intelligences or abilities, on the other hand, were only useful on certain tasks or situations. In addition, Spearman found that general intelligence was the best predictor of performance outside the testing situation.

Raymond Cattell (1971, 1987), a student of Spearman's, acknowledged the importance of both general and specific abilities but defined intelligence as either *crystallized* or *fluid*. **Crystallized intelligence** represents the abilities we acquire from experience, including, for example, general information and social norms. This intelligence is a function of the experience one has had within a particular culture. **Fluid intelligence**, on the other hand, represents more basic skills, including processing speed, working memory capacity, and the ability to detect relationships among various items. According to Cattell, fluid intelligence is more innate, or biologically influenced, whereas crystallized reflects cultural experience.

Measuring Intelligence

How is intelligence measured and used as a concept? Alfred Binet and Theodore Simon designed the first intelligence test in Paris in 1905. Binet and Simon had been hired by the Paris school authorities to develop a test that could be given to children who were having difficulty in school. The goal was to distinguish between children who were capable, perhaps with extra help, of succeeding in school and children who simply were not intelligent enough to cope with the regular curriculum. Once the latter group had been identified, these students could be placed in special classes from which they might benefit. This sort of tracking based on test performance has become controversial in recent years (Dornbusch, Glasgow, & Lin, 1996), but originally it had a humanitarian purpose (Slavin, 1990; Stipek, 2002).

Stanford-Binet The Stanford-Binet Intelligence Scale (Roid, 2003) is the direct descendant of the original Binet-Simon test. Although it can be used with adults, it is primarily a test of childhood intelligence, applicable to every age group except infancy. It is a global measure of intelligence, designed to yield a single **intelligence quotient (IQ)**, a score that summarizes the child's ability. And it stresses the kinds of verbal and academic skills that are important in school. Specifically, the current version of the Stanford-Binet assesses quantitative reasoning, fluid reasoning, visual-spatial processing, knowledge, and working memory.

The Stanford-Binet forumla for scoring on this test is $IQ =$ (mental age divided by chronological age) multiplied by100. This measure describes a child's intellectual ability relative to his or her age. For example, if a 4-year-old child is capable of doing the work that other 4-year-olds can do, the child would have an IQ of (4 divided by 4) $\times$ 100 = 100. An above-average child who is age 4 but can do the work of a 6-year-old would have an IQ of (6 divided by 4) $\times$ 100 = 150. A below-average child who is 4 but can do only the work of a 3-year-old would have an IQ of (3 divided by 4) $\times$ 100 = 75.

In this way, the IQ score used in the Stanford Binet test is a relative score. An IQ score of 100 is considered average, while the scores below and above 100 represent performance that is below and above average, respectively. The greater the discrepancy from the average, the higher or lower the IQs will be. This is not a weakness of this particular test. All intelligence tests are measures of relative performance, although they may use different items and different conceptualizations of what constitutes intelligence, because there is no absolute standard by which to assess intelligence.

IQ scores are assumed to be normally distributed in the general population. Thus, the scoring is set to yield an average, or normal, score of 100 with a standard deviation of 15. Approximately 96 percent of the population will score within two standard deviations of the average, or between the scores of 70 and 130. This means approximately 2 percent of the population scores below 70. People whose scores fall in this range and who have difficulty meeting age-appropriate expectations in everyday functioning are considered mentally retarded. The 2 percent of the population whose scores fall above 130 are considered intellectually gifted.

The Wechsler Scales A number of alternatives to the Stanford-Binet have been designed. The most commonly used is the series of tests designed by David Wechsler. These include the WIPSI (Wechsler Preschool and Primary Scale of Intelligence, intended for children from 4 to 6.5); the WISC-III and WISC-IV (Wechsler Intelligence Scale for Children,

Fluid intelligence
According to Cattell, an intelligence that is assumed to reflect a more innate, or biologically influenced, intelligence such as processing speed.

Questions for Thought and Discussion
Is there one basic type of intelligence that cuts across all tasks, or are there different kinds of intelligence? How much of your intelligence is due to experience and how much to inheritance?

Intelligence quotient (IQ)
Numerical representation of intelligence using the formula IQ = (mental age divided by chronological age) multiplied by 100; this measure describes a child's intellectual ability relative to his or her age.

intended for children ages 6 to 16); and the WAIS (Wechsler Adult Intelligence Scale, intended for those over 16).

Wechsler's changes in WISC-III included dividing the test into a *Verbal* section and a *Performance* section. Wechsler added the performance section to assess individuals whose verbal skills were impaired without an overall deficit in intelligence (such as students with reading disabilities). Items on the performance subscales relied heavily on visual-spatial skills and nonverbal logic. For example, on a block design task, children were shown a design and asked to reproduce it using bi-colored blocks. Further significant changes were made in WISC-IV to give greater emphasis to cognitive processes rather than products, such as problem-solving ability. The Verbal IQ and Performance IQ have been eliminated. Instead, the test is divided into ten subscales yielding information in four composite domains: verbal, perceptual, working memory, and processing speed.

Other Tests of Childhood Intelligence   The Kaufman Assessment Battery for Children, or KABC-II (Kaufman & Kaufman, 2004) marks an explicit effort to include cultural diversity and cultural fairness in the construction and administration of a test. The KABC-II thus attempts to answer one long-standing criticism of traditional IQ tests—that such measures may discriminate against children from poor or minority families. The KABC-II examines cognitive broad abilities, including visual processing, fluid reasoning, short-term memory, and long-term storage and retrieval.

The best-known measure of infant development is the Bayley Scales of Infant Development II (Bayley, 1993). Not surprisingly, measures of infant intelligence tend to stress sensorimotor skills, as opposed to the academic and verbal emphasis found in tests for older children. The Bayley test, for example, is divided into a motor scale (with items assessing control of the body, muscular coordination, manipulatory skill, and so on) and a mental scale (including items assessing sensory-perceptual acuity, vocalization, and memory) (see Table 9.1). Although scores on the Bayley Scales cannot be used to predict later IQ, they can be useful for charting infants' developmental progress, as well as for detecting neurological problems and developmental delays.

Evaluating Intelligence Tests

Two criteria are applied to determine whether a test that claims to measure intelligence really does so: reliability and validity. Any test of a stable attribute must demonstrate *reliability*; that is, it must be repeatable. If you tested a child's IQ on Monday and again on Thursday, the score should be very similar. If the child's IQ changed, for example, from a score of 120 to a score of 100, you would question the reliability of the test.

TABLE 9.1   Examples of Items from the Bayley Scales of Infant Development II

Age Placement (in months)	Ability Measured	Procedure	Credit
1	Habituates to rattle	Shake rattle at regular intervals behind child's head	If child shows an initial alerting response that decreases over trials
6	Smiles at mirror image	Place mirror in front of child	If child smiles at image in mirror
12	Pushes car	Push toy car while child watches, then tell child, "Push the car, push the car like I did"	If child intentionally pushes car so that all four wheels stay on table
17–19	Uses two different words appropriately	Record the child's spontaneous word usage throughout the exam	If child uses two (nonimitative) words appropriately
23–25	Points to five pictures	Show pictures of 10 common objects (e.g., dog book, car), say "Show me the"	If child either correctly points to or names at least five pictures

Source: From *Bayley Scales of Infant Development*, 2nd ed. Copyright (©) 1993 by The Psychological Corporation. Reprinted by permission. All rights reserved.

However, children's IQ scores change during early development. Tests differ in the skills they assess in very young children, and children develop at different rates, so IQ scores can vary dramatically in the first years of life. However, after approximately age 4 there is a fairly strong relationship between early IQ and later IQ, and the strength of this relationship increases by middle childhood (Sternberg, Grigorenko, & Bundy, 2001). By age 8 to 9, IQ is considered to be relatively stable and therefore should be reliable.

The issue of *validity* is addressed in the question, Does the test measure what it is supposed to measure? Do intelligence test scores really reflect differences in intelligence? Or might they reflect differences in something else, such as the way the test was administered, the child's state of mind, or socioeconomic differences? If IQ scores differ dramatically among different tests, then the validity of the tests must be challenged. If a test is valid, it is really measuring what it says it measures, and this also makes it reliable. On the other hand, a reliable test is not necessarily valid. That is, repeated administrations of it could yield the same inaccurate, or invalid, measure each time. How do we determine whether an IQ score is valid?

The most common approach is to determine *criterion validity*. This is done by first specifying some external measure, or criterion, of the attribute being assessed, and then seeing if scores on the test relate to performance on this external criterion. For tests of childhood IQ, the most common external criterion has been performance in school or on standardized tests of academic ability. Tests such as the Stanford-Binet, for example, correlate to academic performance (Brody, 1997; Neisser et al., 1996; Sternberg et al., 2001). Thus, on average, the higher the child's IQ, the better the child does in school.

This ability to predict important aspects of school success constitutes the argument for IQ tests as valid measures of intelligence. As you may know, however, there are exceptions to the correlation between IQ and performance in school. There are children with high IQs who do poorly in school, as well as children with average or below-average IQs who do well academically. Thus, knowing a child's IQ does not predict that child's school performance (or anything else) with certainty.

Nevertheless, IQ tests do measure something of what we mean by intelligence in our culture, because the tests were devised to predict school performance. Performance in school and in the occupational contexts to which school success often leads is important in our culture (Sternberg, 2004). IQ tests may not tap cognitive skills that are important in other cultures, however, such as the ability to navigate in a society in which sailing is important, or the ability to succeed in a small business at an age when most American and Canadian children have barely started school. In the same way, IQ tests may not tap skills that are important for some subgroups within a culture, such as the ability to do chores on the family farm or to cope with the challenges of inner-city life.

Learning Objective 9.1: *Explain how intelligence traditionally is defined and measured.*

1. Describe the psychometric approach to intelligence testing.
2. What is the Stanford-Binet, and how does it define and measure IQ?
3. Identify three IQ or developmental tests in addition to the Stanford-Binet that are commonly used with children.
4. In what ways can IQ tests be considered valid or not?

Individual and Group Differences in IQ

Jo has been blessed with two highly intelligent and well-educated parents who have offered a rich and stimulating environment ever since Jo's conception. Jo has been read to, sung to, talked to, played with, encouraged to paint, draw, run, jump, and explore all the exciting things the world has to offer. Chris has a loving but comparatively intellectually struggling mother who is working three menial jobs just to keep a roof over their heads. Chris is rarely read to and has little in the environment that is intellectually stimulating. Chris spends most days either working at a newspaper stand or caring for younger siblings as opposed to going to school regularly. Jo and Chris are both given IQ tests. What would you predict for their performance?

Questions for Thought and Discussion
What do you think would be gained and what would be lost if IQ tests were no longer used?

✔ *Test Your Mastery...*

Learning Objective 9.2
Identify factors that influence individual and group differences in IQ.

Your answer to that question will reveal much about your views on individual differences. Perhaps you predict that Jo will have an exceptionally high score, regardless of how we define intelligence. Because Jo has intelligent parents, a biological explanation seems logical. However, it is equally plausible that Jo would have a high score based on the rich home environment. You might equally logically predict that Chris would have a low score for genetic reasons or for environmental reasons. Is intelligence determined by relatively immutable biological factors, or is it a function of the experiences you have had? What causes individual and group differences in intelligence?

Genetic versus Environmental Influences on Individual IQ Scores

To what extent is an individual's intelligence related to his or her biological parents' intelligence? To what extent is an individual's intelligence related to the environment in which the individual was raised? As you saw in Chapter 3, three kinds of studies are used to answer these questions: family studies, adoption studies, and twin studies. Family or kinship studies capitalize on our knowledge of the degree of genetic relation among different sorts of relatives. Parent and child, for example, have 50 percent of their genes in common. Two siblings also share an average of 50 percent of their genes. In general, if we know the kinship relationship between two people, we know their degree of genetic similarity and can then see how similarity in IQ relates to similarity in genes. Recall from Chapter 3 that studies have found moderately strong correlations in IQ scores between parents and children (.50), and siblings (.55). As the degree of genetic relatedness decreases, so do correlations in IQ, with first cousins showing a correlation of only .26. Note, however, that these patterns might also be accounted for by environmental factors. Siblings, after all, usually share similar experiences, and parents typically are an important part of their children's environments.

You may also recall that studies of adopted children offer a way to disentangle the genetic and environmental explanations for parent-child similarity. Two sets of correlations are relevant. One is the correlation between the adopted child's IQ and the biological parents' IQs. In this case, the usual genetic basis for a correlation remains, but the environmental basis is ruled out. The other correlation of interest is that between the adopted child's IQ and the adoptive parents' IQs. In this case, the environmental basis remains, but the genetic contribution is ruled out.

Two main findings emerge from adoption studies (Plomin, Fulker, & Corley, 1997; Petrill et al., 2004). One concerns the pattern of correlations. Typically, the adopted child's IQ correlates more strongly with the IQs of the biological parents than with the IQs of the adoptive parents. This finding provides evidence for the importance of genetic factors. The biological parents make relatively little contribution to an adopted child's postnatal environment, but they do provide the child's genes. Studies of siblings find stronger correlations for biological siblings than for children adopted into the same home.

The second finding concerns average IQ. In most studies the mean IQ for samples of adopted children falls in the range of 105 to 110 (Capron & Duyme, 1989; van IJzendoorn, Juffer, & Poelhius, 2005). Adopted children thus tend to have above-average IQs. Why should this be? The most plausible explanation is an environmental one. Parents who adopt children are not a random subset of the population of parents, nor are adoptive homes a random subset of the population of homes. Adoptive parents tend to be highly motivated parents, and adoptive homes tend to be privileged in various ways (such as having a large number of books available and access to good-quality schools for the children). These factors apparently boost the IQs of children who grow up in such settings. Thus, adoption studies provide evidence for both genetic and environmental effects.

Links to Related Material

In Chapter 3, you read how family or kinship studies have been used to examine the role of nature versus nurture in human development. Here, you learn more about how kinship studies help us understand genetic versus environmental influences on IQ scores.

Adopted children and their adoptive parents tend to have above-average IQs. Why? How do adoption studies highlight the interactions of genes and environment in explaining intelligence? (Syracuse Newspapers/ Peter Chen/The Image Works)

TABLE 9.2 Correlations in IQ of Related and Unrelated Children Reared Together or Apart

RELATIONSHIP AND REARING CONDITION	AVERAGE CORRELATION	NUMBER OF PAIRS
Identical twins reared together	.86	4,672
Fraternal twins reared together	.60	5,533
Siblings reared together	.47	26,473
Unrelated children reared together	.32	714
Identical twins reared apart	.72	65

SOURCE: Adapted from T. J. Bouchard, Jr. and M. McGue. (1981). Familial studies of intelligence: A review. *Science*, p. 1056. Copyright 1981 by the American Association for the Advancement of Science. Adapted by permission.

The logic of the twin-study approach was explained in Chapter 3. If identical twins are separated early in life and reared in unrelated environments, then there is no environmental basis, other than prenatal experiences, for their developing similarly. The twins still share 100 percent of their genes, however, so any correlation in IQ would provide powerful evidence for the importance of genes. Table 9.2 summarizes results from studies of twins reared apart. The values in the table indicate that separated twins correlate quite substantially in IQ. The reported correlations are higher for identical twins reared apart than they are for fraternal twins reared in the same home (Bishop et al., 2003; Petrill, 2003; Segal, 1999)!

The Concept of Heritability

Family studies, adoption studies, and twin studies all point to the same conclusion: Both genes and the environment contribute to IQ. Researchers who attempt to determine the relative importance of genes and environment work with a set of statistical procedures for calculating the heritability of IQ. **Heritability** refers to the proportion of variance in a trait that can be attributed to genetic variance in the sample being studied. It is, in other words, an estimate of the extent to which differences among people come from differences in their genes as opposed to differences in their environments. The heritability statistic ranges from 0 (all of the differences are environmental in origin) to 1 (all of the differences are genetic in origin).

The most widely accepted contemporary estimates of the heritability of IQ place the value at about .4 to .7, with figures toward the lower end of the range more typical in childhood and higher values more typical for adult samples (Grigorenko, 2000; Hay, 1999; Plomin et al., 1997). By these estimates, then, approximately half to 2/3 of the variation in people's IQs results from differences in their genes. The heritability statistic has some limitations, however. It can be calculated in different ways, and the value obtained may vary depending on the method used and on the particular data that the researcher decides to emphasize. Also, whatever the heritability may be, the value is specific to the sample studied and cannot be generalized to other samples.

The sample-specific nature of heritability has two further important implications. First, a particular heritability value—based as it is on the current range of genes and environments—tells us nothing for certain about what might happen in the future. In particular, heritability does not tell us about the possible effects of improvements in the environment. Indeed, performance on IQ tests has improved steadily ever since the tests were first introduced, with an average gain of about 3 points per decade in industrialized societies, which is one reason that the tests must be periodically revised. This phenomenon is known as the **Flynn Effect**, after the researcher who has most fully documented the changes in performance (Flynn, 1999; Wicherts et al., 2004). Thus, however high heritability may be, improvements in the environment can still lead to gains in children's intelligence.

Second, heritability tells us nothing for certain about comparisons between samples that were not included in the heritability estimate. Whatever the heritability may be within one group, differences between groups could result solely from differences in their genes, solely from differences in their environments, or from some combination of genes and environment. Are there systematic group differences in intelligence?

Heritability
Proportion of variance in a trait that can be attributed to genetic variance in the sample being studied.

Flynn Effect
Observation that performance on IQ tests improves steadily over time, resulting in a need for revision and renorming.

Factors that Influence Performance on IQ Tests

Two provocative but agreed-upon facts fuel the debate over genetic and environmental contributions to intelligence:

- Racial and ethnic groups differ in their average scores on intelligence tests.
- Groups and individuals who score higher achieve higher levels of education and income.

It does not seem to matter where one travels in the world: ethnic groups differ in IQ scores. European New Zealanders score higher than Maori New Zealanders, Israeli Jews score higher than Israeli Arabs (Zeidner, 1990), and European Americans score higher than African Americans (Herrnstein & Murray, 1994). These IQ discrepancies between majority and minority populations rose to the center of international debate following the publication of Richard Herrnstein and Charles Murray's *The Bell Curve* (1994). This influential work acknowledged that group data cannot be applied to any one individual and further conceded that many Americans of African descent do outscore those of European descent. Nevertheless, the authors concluded that these significant group differences—often 15 or more points on an IQ test, the equivalent of approximately 1 or more standard deviations (Loehlin, 2000)—are, in part, hereditary at the population level (Herrnstein & Murray, 1994).

These children on average do not score as high on intelligence tests as do children in more affluent schools. How can group disparities in intelligence test scores be explained, and why is it important to do so? (Michael Newman/PhotoEdit)

The implications of this conclusion, whether or not it is scientifically justified, are not to be underestimated. If the racial disparity between European American and African American children is genetic, is it reasonable to expect similar disparities in educational and occupational outcomes for European American and African American students? If genetic factors are determining the difference in IQ scores, should the government be asked to fund or support programs such as Head Start and the affirmative action practices that grew out of the Civil Rights Act of 1964? The question clearly has major implications for public policy.

How can the origins of these group differences be explained? Potentially, there are three primary sources:

1. *Genetics:* The genetic explanation argues that group differences, and more specifically, the lower scores of African Americans, are a function of genetic endowment.

2. *Cultural bias in the test:* This argument explains the group differences as a result of differential experience with both the test items and the testing environment.

3. *Influence of the home environment:* This argument explains the group differences as a result of differential experiences and expectations in the way children are raised from infancy on and the socioeconomic conditions in which they live.

Genetics Heritability for European American samples is high, as you saw earlier. Comparable studies with African American samples have also yielded substantial heritabilities (Scarr, 1981). It appears that genes, therefore, are an important source of individual differences within groups. Proponents of *The Bell Curve* acknowledge that heritability is always sample-specific and that heritability within one group cannot be applied directly to a comparison between groups. However, they also argue that if genes are so important to differences within ethnic groups, it is plausible that they also contribute to differences between ethnic groups. In support of this position, they claim that environmental factors known to be important for intelligence do not vary appreciably between European Americans and African Americans. They also maintain that intervention programs to increase the intelligence of African American children have largely failed. Environmental differences, therefore, are not the cause.

Critics of this view point out that a number of additional issues must be addressed. First, race is largely a social construction rather than a biological one. This is demonstrated by the seemingly arbitrary ways in which racial labels are applied. For example, some cultures assign race by skin color, others by eye shape, and so on. In addition, scientists have been unable to locate "race" in the human genome (Sternberg, Grigorenko, & Kidd, 2005), but chromosomes related to "intelligence" have been identified (*American Journal of Human Genetics*, 2005). If intelligence varies by race, shouldn't race be a genetic factor?

Second, many African Americans in the United States in fact have European American ancestry in varying degrees, and the reverse. If genes contribute to group differences in IQ, then IQ scores among African Americans should be positively correlated with degree of European American ancestry. Studies provide no support for this prediction, however (Scarr et al., 1977).

Third, studies of transracial adoption show that African American children adopted into European American homes tend to score as well on IQ tests as European American children. Although the interpretation of this research is a point of debate (Levin, 1994; Sternberg, 2004; van IJzendoorn et al., 2005; Waldman, Weinberg, & Scarr, 1994), it appears that being reared in what Scarr and Weinberg call the "culture of the test" (that is, homes and schools that promote the kinds of knowledge emphasized on IQ tests) diminishes the racial differences in IQ. This finding undermines the genetic explanation for racial differences in IQ and also relates to the two other possible explanations for these differences. The first of these explanations is that IQ tests are biased in favor of the majority culture, and the second is that cultural expectations and interactions differ between racially defined groups. Both of these explanations point to the test-focused environment of the dominant group that facilitates performance.

Cultural Bias in the Tests   Traditional measures of IQ, such as the Wechsler and the Stanford-Binet, are believed to reflect a general ability that is not specifically taught. However, many question whether these tests are fair for all children. They argue that the communication style and certain types of knowledge required for successful performance on the test are culturally bound and that lack of exposure to these required skills undermines performance (Ceci, 1996; Sternberg, 2004; Sternberg et al., 2005). A primary issue is the administration of the tests. Intelligence tests are characterized by a series of factual questions (e.g., what is a knife?). This type of knowledge-seeking question is typical of European American parents and is observed in parent-child interactions from a very early age. However, children in African American families are rarely asked these kinds of questions; rather, adults and children engage in verbally rich exchanges of experiences and storytelling (Greenfield, Quiroz & Raeff, 2000). As a result, African American children may be unfamiliar with and uncomfortable in the traditional testing setting. In addition, it has frequently been argued that many test items are conceptualized unfairly in favor of the majority culture's perspective, particularly vocabulary items.

The cultural bias argument, although receiving mixed evidence when analyzing score differences, nonetheless is supported. First, when children's intelligence is assessed in infancy with habituation/recovery to visual stimuli, a task correlated with later intelligence scores, there are no racial or ethnic differences. Second, even items believed to assess more general and inborn abilities rather than those one might acquire through learning, such as the Block Design test from the WISC, are related to children's experience with games of this sort, including video games that require rapid mental rotation and manipulation of visual images (Sternberg, 2004; Subrahmanyam & Greenfield, 1996).

Third is the relatively recent concern of stereotype threat and its effect on the testing situation. As defined by Steele & Aronson (1995), **stereotype threat** occurs when a member of a group is asked to perform a task for which the prevailing view is that this group is deficient. In relation to intelligence, the testing situation can trigger awareness of the stereotype that your group is incompetent. This stereotype and its related anxiety then interfere with performance.

Stereotype threat
Anxiety about one's test performance based on membership in a group that is stereotyped for poor performance.

The stereotype threat effect has been well demonstrated with students of varying ages from young children (McKown & Weinstein, 2003) to adults (Steele & Aronson, 1995). The standard procedure in this work is to administer a test of verbal ability in a context in which students are reminded of their race, and tell the students that the test either does or does not provide an accurate assessment of their intelligence. When minority students

BOX 9.1   Reducing Stereotype Threat in Minority Populations

Stereotype threat is the extra pressure that people feel in situations in which their performance may confirm a negative stereotype about their group (Steele & Aronson, 1995). Importantly, students can suffer stereotype threat even if they do not believe the stereotype, but it is more damaging to performance when the stereotype is endorsed (Schmader, Johns, & Barquissau, 2004). Researchers have demonstrated stereotype threat under controlled laboratory conditions as well as in real-world classrooms (Good, Aronson, & Inzlicht, 2003). For instance, females tend to perform worse on assessments of mathematical ability when researchers invoke the stereotype that females are less capable in math (Cadinu, Maass, Rosabianca, & Kiesner, 2005). Invoking the stereotype may involve something as simple as solving math problems with male pictures in the examples versus pictures of females. In many classrooms the assertion that math is a male area is more blatant. Parents may also teach the stereotype with the feedback and expectations they provide during academic interactions such as homework (Bhanot & Jovanovic, 2005).

Stereotype threat is not limited to mathematics and females. For example, in a classic early study, Steele and Aronson (1995) found that African American students performed significantly worse than European Americans on a standardized test when the test was presented as diagnostic of their intellectual abilities. When the task was presented as a problem-solving task, the performance of the two groups was about equal. Simply asking students to indicate their race on a test form is sufficient to induce stereotype threat and impair the performance of African American students (Steele & Aronson, 1998). Even European American males, who normally do not suffer from stereotype threat, show impaired performance on difficult mathematics assessments when reminded of the stereotype that European Americans are inferior to Asian Americans in mathematics (Aronson et al., 1999).

Theorists believe that stereotype threat undermines academic performance primarily in two ways. First, in the short run, it raises anxiety and impairs test performance. For example, under conditions of stereotype threat, African American college students report feeling more anxious. Higher levels of anxiety have been confirmed through blood pressure measures (Blascovich et al., 2001).

The second way stereotype threat hurts academic performance is via the means students use to cope with the threat it poses to their self-esteem. To protect themselves, students may "disidentify," or disengage, from the threatened domain. Studies show that students tend to base their self-esteem on domains in which they can excel and devalue domains in which success is less likely (Marsh, Trautwein, Luedtke, Koeller, & Baumert, 2005). Disengagement can be short-lived, as when a student discounts the importance of a poor exam score. It can also contribute to a general disidentification with academics over time. For example, females asked to complete a difficult math task under stereotype threat conditions reported more negative thoughts specifically related to the

Q**uestions for Thought and Discussion**
Have you experienced stereotype threat? How have your experiences with group stereotypes affected your academic learning and performance?

were told that the test reflected their intelligence, their performance on the test decreased significantly compared to the minority students who were told that the test was not reflective of their intelligence.

Influence of the Environment   The third issue regarding race and IQ is whether differential environments characterize different ethnic groups and, if so, how do they affect IQ scores. One difference between the environments of many African American and European American children is the socioeconomic status (SES) of the family. In the United States, African American children are disproportionately more likely to be living in poverty. The consequences of living in poverty—poor nutrition, poor medical care, lack of educational resources—have a well-documented effect on intelligence test scores (Supplee, Shaw, Hailstones, & Hartman, 2004). Unfortunately, SES is not the simple explanation it promised to be, however. When children are matched for SES, the racial gap in intelligence test scores does not close (Neisser et al., 1996). Programs designed to overcome many effects associated with poverty (e.g., Head Start) are not associated with long-term gains in IQ scores, although they are associated with gains in school performance (Reynolds, 2003).

John Ogbu has offered one explanation for the persistent discrepancy in scores (1978, 1994). He argues that minority children do not believe that their effort and commitment will actually be rewarded, and might even be punished. Some African American students evidence this by rejecting doing schoolwork as "acting white." In addition, the argument has been made (Boykin, 1986, 1994) that the American school system, by its competitive and constrictive nature, is fundamentally at odds with an African American culture that emphasizes cooperation, community, and individuality of expression.

test and math than those who completed the task under no-threat conditions (Cadinu et al., 2005). Other research has indicated that stereotype threat actually interferes with the working memory capacity available to individuals in the stereotype conditions (Schmader & Johns, 2003).

Negative stereotypes (i.e., girls are bad at math) can create situational pressure that causes a decrease in performance. How do we help students demonstrate their actual ability and knowledge? Researchers have explored several means of alleviating stereotype threat. One approach is to redefine the testing situation to make it less threatening (Steele & Aronson, 1995). Although this manipulation has proved effective in laboratory settings, it would be difficult to readily apply it in real-world situations. For instance, it is not realistic to tell students that a test is not important, especially since very important implications are now associated with standardized test performance and NCLB (No Child Left Behind) legislation.

In real-world settings, directly countering the stereotype appears to help. For instance, when women are told that females perform just as well as males on specific kinds of math problems, their performance rises (Johns, Schmader, & Martens, 2005). This result suggests that teaching students about stereotype threat might offer a practical way to reduce its negative effects. Drawing students' attention to the accomplishments of members of their group also appears to inoculate vulnerable students against the threat (McIntyre, Paulson, & Lord, 2003). For example, women who are exposed to more positive role models, such as biographies of successful women, are less affected by stereotype threat.

The aim of one large-scale intervention was to directly tackle African American students' fears that others hold negative views about their intellectual abilities by increasing interactions among African American and European American students. The program, developed by Claude Steele and colleagues (Steele, Spencer, Hummel, et al., in press), created a racially integrated "living and learning" community in a 250-student wing of a large dormitory. The program included weekly study groups, rap sessions that focused on the personal side of college life, and frequent mastery workshops.

Participation in the weekly discussions of the personal side of college life proved especially effective in reducing students' stereotype threat and improving grades. Why? Many of the students had only limited contact with members of groups other than their own prior to college. By providing students the opportunity to get to know members of other groups on a more personal level, the program helped students realize that they shared many of the same concerns about college life (e.g., the fear of not measuring up). The discussions also created a climate of trust that allowed students to reevaluate their thinking about the ways others treated or reacted to them. They came to appreciate that behavior that seems driven by stereotypes often is not. They also learned that although many people do hold stereotypes, the stereotypes often reflect inexperience or ignorance and not the worst kind of prejudice.

We know from decades of research that cultural stereotypes are very difficult to change, even among young children. We also know that children gain knowledge of stereotypes at a very young age (Steele, 2003). However, the results of this intervention suggest that it is possible to create contexts—in classrooms and even entire schools—in which negative stereotypes do not apply.

Other research provides evidence about the contribution of the home environment to children's intelligence. Such studies have shown that IQ is not perfectly stable as children develop and that a particular child's IQ may go up or down by several points across childhood. Could those changes in IQ be linked to characteristics of the children's home environments?

One study (Sameroff et al., 1993) followed a sample of children and their parents from the time the children were 4 until they reached the age of 14. Included at both ages was an assessment of 10 risk factors in the child's family life (see Table 9.3). At both ages the children's IQs were negatively related to the number of risk factors; that is, the more risk factors present, the lower, on average, the IQs. No single category of risk emerged as critical; rather, what seemed important was the accumulation of different forms of risk. Furthermore, risk at age 4 proved predictive of IQ at age 13. Children with difficult early environments were most likely to experience continued problems in intellectual adaptation. The negative impact of early risk, it is important to note, is not limited to IQ scores but also extends to measures of language development and school performance (Burchinal et al., 2000; Caughy, 1996).

Undoubtedly, the most popular contemporary approach to measuring the home environment is an instrument called the HOME (Home Observation for Measurement of the Environment). There are infant versions of the HOME (Caldwell & Bradley, 1984), as well as versions for preschool, middle childhood, and adolescence (Bradley, 1994). The HOME assesses specific aspects of the child's environment, including quality of parent-child interaction and resources provided by the family for cognitive stimulation. In the infant version, for example, domains include the parents' verbal and emotional responsiveness

TABLE 9.3 Risk Factors in a Study of Family Environment and IQ	
RISK FACTOR	**DESCRIPTION**
Occupation	Head of household was unemployed or held unskilled occupation.
Mother's education	Mother did not complete high school.
Family size	Family has four or more children.
Father absence	Father was not present in the home.
Stressful life events	Family experienced 20 or more stressful events during the child's first 4 years.
Parenting perspectives	Parents held rigid or absolutist conceptions of children and childrearing.
Maternal anxiety	Mother was unusually high in anxiety.
Maternal mental health	Mother had relatively poor mental health.
Mother-child interaction	Mother showed little positive affect toward the child.

SOURCE: Adapted from A.J. Sameroff, R. Seifer, A. Baldwin, and C. Baldwin. (1993). Stability of intelligence from preschool to adolescence: The influence of social and family risk Factors, *Child Development, 64*, p. 85. Copyright 1993 by the Society for Research in Child Development. Adapted by permission.

to the child, avoidance of restriction and punishment, organization of space and time, provision of appropriate play materials, interactive involvement with the child, and provision of opportunities for variety in daily stimulation.

Measures on the HOME relate to contemporaneous measures of the child's intelligence at all ages. That is, scores on the infant version of the HOME correlate with infant intelligence (Barnard, Bee, & Hammond, 1984), scores on the preschool version correlate with preschool intelligence (Espy, Molfese, & DiLalla, 2001; Siegel, 1984), and scores on the middle childhood version correlate with childhood intelligence (Luster & Denbow, 1992). Other studies have demonstrated relationships between HOME scores in infancy and both IQ and school performance during the grade-school years (Bradley & Caldwell, 1984b; Olson, Bates, & Kaskie, 1992). Thus, the quality of the child's early environment is related to various aspects of the child's later intelligence.

Learning Objective 9.2: *Identify factors that influence individual and group differences in IQ.*

1. What is the evidence for genetic influences on IQ differences?
2. What is the evidence that home environment influences IQ?
3. How does cultural bias in testing work to influence IQ scores?
4. What is stereotype threat and how might it influence IQ scores?

Test Your Mastery...

Alternative Conceptions of Intelligence

Learning Objective 9.3
Identify alternative conceptions of intelligence.

The traditional, psychometric definition of intelligence and its uses in predicting school performance has been challenged, leading to the development of alternative conceptualizations of intelligence. Three influential alternatives are the evolutionary model, Sternberg's triarchic theory and dynamic testing, and Gardner's theory of multiple intelligences. These alternatives do not focus primarily on abilities associated with success in school. School and the disciplines taught in school are recent developments in human history. Reading and writing trace back fewer than 10,000 years. To this day, in some societies the majority of citizens cannot read, and formal education is unknown. Consequently, many theorists have sought other ways to define intelligence.

Evolutionary Approaches

According to the evolutionary model, intelligence is the ability to adapt to the environment, and is a product of natural selection occurring over tens of thousands of years. Many of the

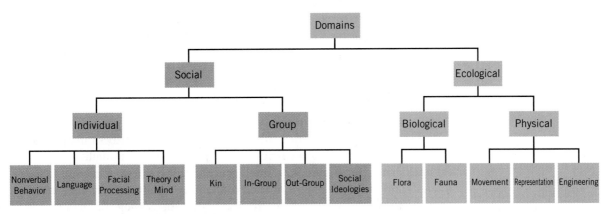

FIGURE 9.1   Domains in human evolutionary psychology.

These domains of species-typical experience have been proposed as biologically primary abilities for all humans. These abilities relate to solving problems of survival and reproduction and are part of human psychology. What other adaptive cognitive systems might you add to this model, and why?

SOURCE: From D. C. Geary. (1998). *Male, Female: The Evolution of Human Sex Differences.* Washington, DC: American Psychological Association, p. 180. Copyright 1998 by the American Psychological Association.

basic survival problems that our minds are designed to solve are not the ones common to modern life—such as learning to read, solving algebra equations, and operating complex machines—but rather are the problems our hunter-gatherer ancestors faced generation after generation. Those problems would have included finding food (along with knowing which foods to eat and which to avoid) and coping with the complexities of social life, such as attracting and choosing mates, recognizing kin, and "mind-reading" (inferring other's motives, intentions, desires, states of mind, and knowledge) (Tooby & Cosmides, 1995). Evolutionary psychologists believe that humans evolved a neuropsychological system specially adapted to solving these "ancient" problems. Moreover, this system is organized into specialized modules or cognitive systems dedicated to solving certain kinds of problems—specifically, problems related to human survival and reproduction. These specific cognitive systems emerge with species-typical experience over the course of development. One model of domains of human "species-typical" experience is shown in Figure 9.1 (Geary, 1998).

The social and ecological domains in Geary's model reflect the types of information that humans must process to survive and reproduce in their natural habitat. Thus, there are modules for language and for processing faces, modules for processing information about kin and strangers, modules for plants and for moving through the physical world, and so on. Geary proposes that many domains can be added, such as one for processing numerical information. Some evolutionary psychologists believe the number of modules dedicated to solving specific types of adaptive problems is quite large (Cosmides & Tooby, 2001).

Geary refers to the abilities shown in Figure 9.1 as **biologically primary abilities** that have been shaped by natural selection and evolved to deal with problems faced by our ancestors (Geary, 1995b; 2005). These abilities (e.g., language, face recognition) are universal, are found in all cultures, and are acquired easily by all normally developing children in all but the most deprived environments. Children are highly motivated to master these abilities and actively pursue opportunities to do so through play, social interaction, and exploration of objects and the environment (Geary, 2002).

Skills such as reading and higher mathematics are **biologically secondary abilities**—highly specialized neurocognitive systems that build on the primary abilities. Reading, for example, builds on the cognitive and brain systems involved in language acquisition and production. Biologically secondary abilities are products of culture, not biological evolution. Their acquisition depends on growing up in a culture that deliberately teaches the skills. For instance, children in nonliterate societies do not spontaneously learn to read. Although children readily (and happily) acquire biologically primary abilities without formal instruction, acquisition of biologically secondary abilities is much more variable.

Biologically primary abilities
Abilities that have been shaped by natural selection and evolved to deal with problems faced by our ancestors, and are therefore universal.

Biologically secondary abilities
Highly specialized neurocognitive systems that build on the primary abilities.

Such learning also often depends on tedious practice and external inducements (Geary, 2002). From the perspective of evolutionary theory, then, there are two distinct kinds of "intelligence," one natural and the other learned.

Sternberg's Triarchic Theory of Intelligence

Triarchic theory of intelligence
According to Sternberg, intelligence is composed of three overlapping aspects: (1) analytical intelligence, (2) creative intelligence and (3) practical intelligence.

Another alternative to the psychometric definition of intelligence is Robert Sternberg's **triarchic theory of intelligence**. Sternberg (1985, 2002) describes three overlapping components of intelligence: (1) analytical intelligence, (2) creative intelligence, and (3) practical intelligence (see Figure 9.2). Intelligence in this framework requires balancing one's interests and the requirements of one's community or culture to achieve success.

Analytical intelligence includes the information-processing abilities emphasized in the psychometric approach: such as the ability to acquire and apply problem-solving strategies, comparing and contrasting, and regulating one's performance. Although these skills are required for nonschool tasks (such as flying an airplane), they are easily seen in traditional school settings (such as learning how to convert fractions to decimals).

Creative intelligence requires thinking outside of the box to come up with creative solutions to problems. A hallmark of creative intelligence is the ability to apply information processing skills rapidly and efficiently, allowing more cognitive processing to be used for generating novel solutions. Tasks emphasizing creative intelligence ask us to imagine and invent.

Practical Intelligence requires applying intelligent behavior to everyday life, adapting our behavior, shaping our experiences, and selecting our environments. For example, if you know that you want to work with infants, but find that this requires certification in CPR, then you need to take a CPR class and become certified. If adaptation is not possible, for whatever reason, then people can *shape* the environment, changing it to suit one's own strengths. For example, a successful manager delegates tasks for which he or she has no interest or aptitude. If adapting to or shaping the environment is not possible, people can respond through practical intelligence by *selecting* an environment that more closely matches their strengths and needs. Sternberg's triarchic theory of intelligence defines intelligence in terms of the full range of complex human behavior and is not merely theoretical. The model can explain and predict success in a variety of cultures (Sternberg et al., 2000) and can be used to assess more accurately school children whose intellectual strengths are easily underestimated (Okagaki & Sternberg, 1993).

FIGURE 9.2 Sternberg's Triarchic Theory of Intelligence.

ANALYTICAL INTELLIGENCE (COMPONENTIAL)	Abstract thinking and logical reasoning Verbal and mathematical skills Knowledge acquisition skills Metacognitive skills
CREATIVE INTELLIGENCE (EXPERIENTIAL)	Creativity and divergent thinking Ability to deal with novelty Ability to invent solutions to problems Automaticity of skill performance
PRACTICAL INTELLIGENCE (CONTEXTUAL)	Ability to adapt to situations Ability to select options Ability to shape environments Application of knowledge to the real world

SOURCE: Based on information in Robert Sternberg. (1988). *The Triarchic Mind: A New Theory of Intelligence.* New York: Viking Press.

Sternberg's triarchic theory lends itself to improving the material on which children are tested (Sternberg & Grigorenko, 2002). *Dynamic testing* is a technique, based on Sternberg's model, for the fair testing of mental abilities by focusing on the acquisition of new abilities. Dynamic testing differs from static testing in that children are given feedback to improve their performance (Sternberg, 2004). Thus dynamic testing allows inferences about the skills a child currently possesses but also allows the examiner to predict the child's learning potential (Sternberg & Grigorenko, 2002).

In a powerful example of the difference that dynamic testing can make, Sternberg (2004) and his colleagues tested a group of Tanzanian children on several tasks measuring the skills that traditional intelligence tests assess (such as classification and verbal problem solving). All the children were given pretests, and then half were given less than an hour of instruction. Then the children were all tested again. Those who received the instruction showed significant improvement over the control group. Other research replicated these findings (Grigorenko, Meier, Lipka, et al., 2004). Thus, static assessments measure only what children have learned prior to dynamic testing. Dynamic testing revealed significant learning potential that otherwise was not visible (Sternberg, 2004). Underestimation of their abilities by traditional testing methods can leave children vulnerable to reduced academic involvement and encouragement.

Gardner's Theory of Multiple Intelligences

While Sternberg's theory proposes three kinds of intelligence, cognitive psychologist Howard Gardner believes that intelligence is even more diversified and multifaceted (1983, 1993, 1999). Gardner's thesis is that humans possess at least eight distinct *intelligences,* collectively defined as the "ability to solve problems or fashion products that are of consequence in a particular cultural setting or community"(Gardner, 1993, p. 15). Gardner's **multiple intelligences** are identified in Table 9.4.

According to Gardner, the existence of a distinct intelligence can be demonstrated through a number of kinds of evidence, or *signs*. Signs may include experimental evidence, factor analysis, information processing demonstrations, specifiable core operations, observable developmental change, an evolutionary history, deviations from normal development, and studies of giftedness. Taken together, evidence from these signs support the existence of multiple intelligences.

Questions for Thought and Discussion
How well does Gardner's theory of multiple intelligences apply to you and people you know?

Multiple intelligences
According to Gardner, there are eight unique, distinctive intelligences that explain problem solving, creation of new products, and discovery of new knowledge in eight distinct areas of culturally valued activities.

TABLE 9.4 Gardner's Multiple Intelligences		
TYPE OF INTELLIGENCE	**DESCRIPTION**	**RELATED VOCATIONS**
Linguistic	Sensitivity to spoken and written language; ability to use language to achieve goals	Writer, lawyer, poet
Logical-Mathematical	Ability to analyze problems logically, carry out mathematical operations, investigate issues scientifically	Mathematician, scientist
Musical	Appreciation of musical patterns; skill in the composition and performance of music	Musician, composer
Bodily kinesthetic	Ability to use one's body or part of the body (e.g., hands, feet) to solve problems or fashion products	Dancer, athlete, craftsperson
Spatial	Ability to perceive spatial relationships and manipulate patterns of space	Navigator, pilot, architect
Naturalist	Ability to recognize and classify flora and fauna	Biologist, naturalist
Interpersonal	Ability to understand the desires and intentions of other people and work effectively with others	Clinician, salesperson, politician
Intrapersonal	Capacity to understand oneself and to use this understanding to direct one's life effectively	Relevant to almost any occupation or profession

SOURCE: Adapted from H. Gardner. (1999). *Intelligence Reframed.* New York: Basic Books.

Giftedness and Creativity

Definitions of intelligence affect what we mean by *giftedness*. By one definition, gifted children are simply those who score at the top of the IQ range—IQs of 130 or 140 or above. This is the most common definition in American school systems. However, the standard IQ approach does not capture everything that the concept of giftedness embodies. Child psychologist Ellen Winner (1996, 2000) proposes that high-IQ children represent only one form of giftedness—they are gifted in the kinds of abilities (verbal skills, mathematical understanding, logical reasoning) that are stressed on IQ tests and in school. Even within the domain of IQ-type skills, however, such children might be gifted in math, for example, but only average on other dimensions. Winner argues that "global giftedness" is the exception rather than the rule; more typical is exceptional performance in just one domain of development. Furthermore, these domains include art and music, not just the verbal and mathematical abilities valued in school.

Exceptional performance in some domain is the starting point for any conception of **giftedness**. According to Winner, gifted children display three other characteristics. One is *precocity*—gifted children display exceptional abilities very early in development. Another is *marching to one's own drummer*. Gifted children learn in qualitatively different ways from other children, and much of what they learn they discover for themselves. Finally, gifted children possess *a rage to master*—they are strongly motivated, perhaps even driven, to conquer their domain of interest.

Where does giftedness come from? Winner's answer takes both nature *and* nurture in account, as do most psychologists and educators who have considered the question (Feldman, 1986; Gottfried et al., 1994). She dismisses as a "myth" the idea that parents or other environmental forces can turn any child into a gifted child. There must be a biological starting point, and only some children are born with the capacity to achieve exceptional levels in math or music or art. Biology alone is not sufficient, however; there must also be a supportive environment. Although gifted children in part create their own environment, to achieve their full potential they must receive help from parents, teachers, or other supportive adults.

Gifted children often are creative, but creativity is itself a subject of research. **Creativity** involves the ability to generate novel outcomes that are valued in some context. But what can children do that merits the label *creative* or that might be predictive of adult creativity? One approach emphasizes the distinction between convergent thinking and divergent thinking (Guilford, 1985; Wallach & Kogan, 1966). **Convergent thinking** is oriented towards right answers—the form of thinking we engage in when faced with a task (such as a mathematical problem or a logical deduction) for which there is a single, definite solution. Convergent thinking is what IQ tests measure. In contrast, **divergent thinking** involves the ability to generate multiple, original, possible solutions for tasks that do not have a single right answer. For example, thinking of unusual uses for a newspaper or coat hanger would be examples of divergent thinking, as would be generating different interpretations of an ambiguous drawing or visual abstraction.

Giftedness
Exceptional performance in some domain, characterized by precocity, qualitatively different learning, and strong motivation for mastery.

Creativity
The ability to generate novel outcomes that are valued in some context.

Convergent thinking
Right-answer–oriented thinking about problems for which there is a single, definite solution.

Divergent thinking
The ability to generate multiple, original, possible solutions for tasks that do not have a single right answer.

This drawing was made by a young girl identified as gifted in art (Winner, 1996). She drew the monkeys at age 5. This child produced 4,000 paintings in a span of three years. What three characteristics other than exceptional ability may identify her as gifted? (From "Gifted Children" by E. Winner, 1996, New York: Basic Books, pp. 84-85. Copyright © 1996 by Basic Books. Reprinted by permission.)

Tasks like these identify individual differences in the capacity for divergent thinking, differences that are evident from early childhood (Wallach & Kogan, 1966). Furthermore, differences in divergent thinking are only weakly related to IQ. Thus, tests of divergent thinking meet one of the criteria for a measure of creativity: They appear to tap something other than traditional IQ. At the same time, creativity requires more than a capacity for divergent thinking. Because of gaps between generating creative ideas and actually producing a creative product, measures of divergent thinking are not good predictors of real-world creative performance.

Contemporary theories of creativity stress the coming together or confluence of multiple contributions that must work together to make creativity possible (Sternberg and Lubart, 1991, 1995, 1996). Creativity requires a willingness to invest or commit a number of resources to the task at hand. The necessary cognitive resources include an aptitude for divergent thinking, knowledge in the specific problem domain, and an ability to evaluate the adequacy of the ideas that one generates. Cognitive factors must be combined with the right personality attributes—in particular, an ability to tolerate ambiguity and a willingness to take risks. There must be strong motivation to persist in the face of obstacles. And, as with giftedness, there must be a supportive environmental context. Cognitive abilities always develop and are expressed within an environmental context, and some children experience more supportive contexts than do others.

Learning Objective 9.3: *Identify alternative conceptions to intelligence.*

1. Describe the evolutionary approach to intelligence.
2. Define Sternberg's triarchic theory of intelligence.
3. What are the multiple intelligences identified in Gardner's model?
4. What relation does creativity have to traditional conceptions of intelligence?
5. What is giftedness?

Questions for Thought and Discussion
To what extent and in what ways are you creative? How might adults in your life have better nurtured your creativity?

✔ *Test Your Mastery...*

Schooling: Variations and Effects

Learning Objective 9.4
Evaluate different aspects of the schooling experience and how they affect cognitive development.

Children spend a large part of their developmental years in the formal educational settings provided by schools. They are exposed to formal instruction in the core academic subjects (e.g., math and reading), to the arts, and to technology, and they receive informal exposure to ideas and values from adults, peers, and society through the process of socialization. The average American child spends approximately 15,000 hours in school between the ages of 5 and 18. Most people think of school primarily as a setting designed to develop the cognitive abilities and knowledge bases of young children. Actually, school serves a variety of functions. It provides opportunities to learn information, to acquire and develop new skills, to participate in social activities and interactions, to participate in sports and games, to explore vocational choices, to examine and consider health options such as different food choices, and to develop friendships. Therefore, school is a place that potentially influences cognitive, socioemotional, and physical development.

The effects of schooling are difficult to assess, and they depend in many ways on how success is defined. In general terms, multiple indicators can be used to evaluate schooling. In terms of years of education completed, there are significant differences in earning power, life expectancy, and overall reported quality of life; individuals with more education have the advantage in each case (Wonacott, 2003). High school dropouts are at greater risk for a variety of problems, including increased time spent in the welfare system (Dillon, Liem, & Gore, 2003; National Center for Education Statistics, 2001).

Culture and the Cognitive Effects of Schooling

A difficulty in determining the effects of schooling in Western culture is its pervasiveness: Virtually every child goes to school. When we broaden our scope to encompass other cultures, this uniformity no longer holds. Of course, if we simply compare cultures with and without schooling, it will be difficult to interpret our results, because the cultures may differ in a number of ways apart from the presence or absence of school. Most informative, therefore, are cases in which only some children within a culture go to school or in which schooling has been recently introduced, allowing us to make a before-and-after comparison. Psychologists have been able to find and to study a number of such cases (Barber, 2005; Ceci, 1996; Cole, 1999). Several conclusions emerge.

A first conclusion is that some aspects of children's cognitive development seem to be less strongly and consistently affected by schooling than others. Many of the kinds of knowledge studied by Piaget, for example, are relatively unaffected. Schooling may influence the development of Piagetian concepts, especially the rate at which knowledge is acquired. However, most studies report (a) no clear qualitative differences between schooled and unschooled children in their mastery of concepts such as conservation, and (b) no lasting advantage for children who have been to school. In contrast, certain formal educational experiences, such as the methods and reasoning problems pursued in science and math, appear to facilitate the development of formal operations (Adey & Shayer, 1990; Huitt & Hummel, 2003). In general, college students outperform adults with no advanced educational experience, who then outperform adolescents (Huitt & Hummel, 2003; Mwamwenda, 1999).

Other aspects of cognitive development appear to be affected more by schooling. Schooling can affect memory. Schooled children not only perform better on a variety of memory tasks but also are more likely to use mnemonic strategies to help themselves remember. Schooling affects how children classify objects. Children who have been to school are more likely to group objects in terms of general categories (all of the foods together) rather than functional or thematic relations (ice cream and spoon together). Similarly, schooling affects how children think about words and use language, with schooled children more likely to think in terms of general categories and abstract relations. Finally, schooling improves children's metacognition—their ability to reflect and think about their cognitive processes (de Jager, Margo, & Reezigt, 2005) and to use scientific thinking skills (Yang, 2004).

Why does schooling produce these effects? Barbara Rogoff (1981) discusses four factors that may play roles.

1. Schooling directly teaches many of the specific skills on which schooled children excel. Classification, for example, is a common activity in school, and committing material to memory is even more common.

2. Schooling exerts its effects through emphasis on the search for general rules—for universal systems of knowledge (such as mathematics) within which specific instances can be understood.

3. There are differences between teaching in school and teaching outside school. Teaching in school often involves the verbal transmission of information that is far removed from its everyday context, a style of instruction that may promote verbally based, abstract modes of thought.

4. The primary goal of most forms of schooling is the development of literacy. Literacy, like verbally based teaching, promotes abstract, reflective styles of thinking. And reading, of course, can be the door to a vast world of experiences and knowledge that could never be acquired firsthand. In general, the more a people read, the more they know about a great many things, and reading exposure is strongly linked to cognitive development and subsequent attainment (Cunningham & Stanovich, 2003; Stanovich, Cunningham, & West, 1998).

The amount of schooling also appears to be important in the development of certain kinds of intelligence. It has long been known that a positive relation exists between number of years of education completed and IQ. In general, the more years of schooling people complete, the higher (on the average) are their IQs (Barber, 2005; Jencks, 1972). The usual

Links to Related Material
In Chapter 7, you read about Piaget's theory of cognitive development. Here, you learn more about how formal schooling may influence performance on Piagetian tasks.

Questions for Thought
and Discussion
Why does IQ predict success in school? Why does schooling then increase IQ?

explanation has been that more intelligent people stay in school longer. But it can also be argued that the cause and effect may also flow in the opposite direction—that is, that schooling may actually increase IQ (Barber, 2005; Ceci & Williams, 1997). Here are three examples. First, the IQ of children who drop out of school declines relative to that of children who stay in school, even when the two groups are initially equal in IQ. Second, children's IQs have been shown to decline slightly across the months of summer vacation and then to rise again during the school year. Third, children whose birthdays make them just barely old enough to qualify for school entry obtain higher IQ scores by age 8 than children whose birthdays make them fall just short. The point is that the two groups are virtually the same age, but one group has had a year more of schooling (Christian, Bachnan, & Morrison 2001).

Social Organization of Classroom Instruction

Among the impacts of schooling are the effects of the complex social structure of the classroom. Much research in this area has examined teacher-student interaction and how it is associated with academic achievement. The perceptions that students and teachers have of each other play a significant role. Elementary students, in general, have positive attitudes toward educators. They describe good teachers as interesting, fair, considerate, and caring, and as taking the time to get to know their students (Corbett & Wilson, 2002; Davis, 2003; Dodd, 1997). Not all children like school, but most come to school in the first years with positive attitudes toward learning.

Teacher Expectations   Attitudes are important because they affect teachers' motivation to engage with their students, which in turn, translates into student motivation and performance. One of the greatest challenges a teacher faces is to treat everyone equally and fairly. Unfortunately, teachers do not typically interact with everyone in the same way. Not surprisingly, children who are well behaved get more praise and encouragement from teachers, whereas more difficult students typically experience more criticism (Henricsson & Rydell, 2004). Teachers often have more positive expectations for students they perceive to be higher SES and higher ability, requiring them to work harder, criticizing them less often while praising them more, and giving them the benefit of the doubt on close calls in grading (Brophy, 1998).

Many children who do not perform well in school consistently have negative interactions with their teachers. These children are more likely to be in trouble for classroom behavior and for not completing their assignments (Stipek, 2002). Although consequences are needed in these cases, the educational environment can become a very unpleasant place for these children. Teachers also tend to have different achievement expectations for boys and girls (Jones & Myhill, 2004). Teachers' attitudes toward students can also affect how students interact with one another (Chang, 2003). For example, if a teacher is more tolerant of aggressive behavior in the classroom, students will have more positive attitudes toward aggressive students. Teachers are also less confident about their ability to teach students from certain groups, such as students learning English as a second language (Karabenick & Noda, 2004).

Even first graders can apparently tell what a teacher expects of them (Kuklinski & Weinstein, 2001; Weinstein, Gregory, & Strambler, 2004). What effect does differential treatment from the teacher have on a student's school performance, attitudes toward school, and behavior in school? Not surprisingly, researchers have found that the teachers' treatment of their students is associated with significant differences in outcomes. As early as first grade, teachers' beliefs about a student's ability to learn predicts the student's end-of-year achievement, even after controlling for differences in beginning-of-year performance (Weinstein, 2002). Students who perceive their teachers as supportive and caring are more motivated to engage in academic work than students who see their teachers as unsupportive and uncaring (McCombs, 2001; Newman, 2002).

Sometimes teachers communicate their beliefs in very subtle ways. For example, when a teacher asks a student a question, he or she can communicate a variety of expectations

BOX 9.2 Culture, Schooling, and the Mind

A central issue in the study of intelligence is whether all people the world over possess the same basic intellectual capacities or whether these capacities are profoundly shaped by cultural practices and institutions. The first systematic examination of this issue was an ambitious research project undertaken by A. R. Luria among the Uzbeki in Central Asia in the early 1930s (Luria, 1976, 1979).

At the time, many of the rural regions in Russia were undergoing a rapid social transformation. Although some of these regions could boast an ancient high culture, most of the citizenry had long been dependent on wealthy landowners and powerful feudal lords. Few were able to read. Much changed following the Russian Revolution. Women were emancipated, schools were established, and a collectivist agricultural economy was introduced. Luria and a team of assistants took advantage of the changes taking place to compare the thinking and reasoning of nonliterate groups living in villages and groups who had begun to participate in the new social structure through schooling and the collectivist economy.

Luria assessed a wide variety of cognitive skills, including perception, classification, and reasoning. In many respects, Luria followed procedures that cross-cultural researchers would advocate today. He conducted the experimental sessions in the local language in comfortable and familiar circumstances (e.g., around the evening campfire). And he avoided standard psychometric tests and tried to place the tasks in a familiar context using common materials.

Luria found striking differences between answers provided by the Uzbeki peasants' who lacked any formal schooling and those offered by men and women with some schooling and experience in the new economy. As the following exchange shows, those without schooling tended to respond (or not) on the basis of personal experience:

In the Far North, where there is snow, all bears are white. Novaya Zemlya is in the Far North and there is always snow there. What colors are the bears there?

There are different sorts of bears.
[The syllogism is repeated]

I don't know. I've seen a black bear, I've never seen any others . . .

Each locality has its own animals: If it's white, they will be white. If it's yellow they will be yellow.

But what kinds of bears are there in Navaya Zemlya?

We always speak only of what we see; we don't talk about what we haven't seen.

But what do my words imply?

Well, it's like this: our tsar isn't like yours, and yours isn't like ours. Your words can only be answered by someone who was there, and if a person wasn't there he can't say anything on the basis of your words.

But on the basis of my words—in the North, where there is always snow, the bears are white, can you gather what kind of bears there are in Navaya Zemlya?

If a man was sixty or eighty and had seen a white bear and had told about it, he could be believed, but I've never seen one and hence I can't say. That's my last word. Those who can tell, and those who didn't see can't say anything! (Luria, 1976, pp. 108–109)

Although the illiterate peasants performed somewhat better when the syllogisms related more directly to their everyday experiences, all of the villagers with some schooling and experience in the evolving economy were able to solve both familiar and unfamiliar logic problems by reasoning from the premises. On the basis of these and other data, Luria concluded that schooling and modernization led to qualitative shifts in reasoning.

After two expeditions, Luria returned to Moscow and made some of his findings public. The political climate at the time was not at all friendly toward Luria's conclusions. Although he clearly emphasized the benefits of collectivization, many people believed his results could be viewed as an insult to the Uzbeki people. Consequently, Luria's landmark study was not published until the 1970s (Cole, 1976).

Today, a growing number of researchers are traveling to distant cultures to test the universality of Western psychological theories. Like Luria, many of these researchers have found children and adults, especially those without schooling, to be quite perplexed by traditional psychological tasks. However, these researchers have also documented how well the same people could reason and solve problems in their daily lives. Recognizing the discrepancy in performance across contexts, many contemporary theorists have been unwilling to accept Luria's claim that schooling and modernization produce fundamental changes in modes of thinking (Cole, 1996; Rogoff, 2003). The issue of exactly which factors underlie cultural differences in performance on cognitive assessments continues to be debated. Nonetheless, the Central Asian study is highly regarded both for its unique historical value and for Luria's brilliant use of the clinical interview method (Cole, 1976).

concerning the student's ability and motivation. "John, what is the sum of 2 plus 13?" After asking the question, the teacher has several decisions to make. One of the most important is how long to wait for an answer. Waiting too long has the potential to embarrass John, to let the momentum of the lesson falter, and to encourage other students to divert their attention. Waiting too short a time can communicate to John that the teacher does not expect him to be able to answer the question. The recommended wait time for most questions is about six seconds. Teachers wait longer for students whom they perceive to possess more ability (Brophy, 1998).

How the teacher provides feedback also can communicate expectations to John. If a student perceives a negative view from the teacher, he or she may adopt that view and start to live up to it. This is called the educational **self-fulfilling prophecy** (Weinstein et al., 2004). In some cases, such as when the student adopts the teacher's positive views, the self-fulfilling prophecy can work to the student's advantage. The effect of the self-fulfulling prophecy is even stronger when a teacher emphasizes competition and public comparisons of children (Weinstein, 2002). Unfortunately, the potential negative effects of the self-fulfilling prophecy appear to be even stronger for students from at-risk groups such as minorities (McKown & Weinstein, 2002).

A challenge for educators, therefore, is to monitor their expectations and the subsequent treatment of their students. It is important to have positive, yet realistic, expectations for students of all kinds. Researchers have found that teachers can modify and increase their expectations for students with lower abilities (Sarason, 2004; Weinstein, Madison, & Kuklinski, 1995). Awareness of the problem is one of the first steps toward modifying these expectations.

Sometimes the communication of expectations is subtle; at other times teachers or students can state beliefs more bluntly. For example, a four-year-old comes home crying from her first day in preschool. She informs her mother that when she attempted to play at the science table, the boys pushed her away, saying, "Girls are not allowed at the science table. They do not do science." A quick phone call to the teacher resolved the situation, but the attitudes and the willingness to bluntly express and enforce them were already in place in these young students. Teachers and caregivers must recognize that it is not only their attitudes that matter, they must also set a good example in their actions toward others.

Class and School Size   Schools also are complex social systems. In the United States, students in small classes of about 13 to 17 score higher in reading and math than classes of about 22 to 25 and larger (Finn, Gerber, & Boyd-Zaharias, 2005). Students who attend small classes for at least three years increase their chances of graduating from high school. The beneficial effects are even more pronounced for students from at-risk groups, such as students from lower socioeconomic status families. Having a teacher's aide is not associated with the same benefits as a smaller class size. With fewer students, teachers are able to spend more time providing individual attention and getting to know students without sacrificing control of the classroom. Unfortunately, tight budgets in many states have been a factor in increasing class sizes across the country.

As children move from elementary to secondary school, they also tend to move from class to class more often, to interact with a greater number of teachers, and to have access to more activities outside the classroom. The relevant social context becomes the school as a whole. Researchers have found a significant relationship between student body size and a number of educational and social outcomes. Students from smaller schools consistently report more social support and caring from school personnel and are less likely to drop out than students from larger schools (Lee & Burkam, 2003). However, schools with 500 to 700 or fewer students have fewer people to ensure that school social activities, sports events, and organizations will function successfully. Young people are more likely to enter a greater number and variety of activities in these schools. In larger schools, the competition for slots in activity programs may be intense and lead to lower levels of overall participation. In some cases, larger schools may have the advantage of more resources overall, but this may be offset by greater competition for these resources.

School Transitions   One of the most stressful times for school children is the transition into a new school level. They must make many changes, including adjusting to new adult authority figures, physical environments, schedules, peers, and academic expectations. How well will the student respond to these changes? Their reactions are partially responsible for their success in school and may set the stage for peer and teacher interactions for years to come. What student and school factors contribute to successful transitions?

Self-fulfilling prophecy
In cases where a person adopts the views of another and either lives up to or lives down to those expectations.

Questions for Thought and Discussion
How did teachers' and parents' expectations of you affect your academic achievement?

This child is attending the first day of kindergarten. How might the child's prior experiences contribute to school readiness? Research shows that the stress of school transitions such as this one can have a major impact on children's achievement levels. How can effects of school transitions be mitigated through "stage-environment fit"? (Amy Etra/PhotoEdit)

Links to Related Material
In Chapter 11, you will read more about how children's early social and emotional development, including the quality of their relationship to their parents, influences their adjustment to school.

Questions for Thought
and Discussion
Which school transition had the greatest impact on you, how were you affected, and why?

Entry into kindergarten is a major developmental milestone. Children enter kindergarten with a variety of different experiences, expectations, abilities, and amounts of knowledge. Children with more experience in alternative care settings, either preschool or day care, tend to score higher on school readiness tests and to perform better in kindergarten and in subsequent academic grades (Broberg, Wessels, Lamb, & Hwang, 1997; Magnuson & Waldfogel, 2005a; Temple, Reynolds, & Miedel, 2000). These children also tend to report more positive attitudes toward school. Children with better communication and prosocial skills tend to make friends more easily in the school setting, form better relationships with teachers, and perform at higher levels than children with argumentative and aggressive styles (Fantuzzo & McWayne, 2002). Children who enter school with higher levels of reading readiness skills, such as phonological awareness and vocabulary, are also more likely to demonstrate higher levels of academic performance (Muter, Hulme, Snowling, & Stevenson, 2004; Share & Leikin, 2004; Whitehurst & Lonigan, 1998).

The majority of elementary schools use a format in which students spend most of the day with one primary teacher. This teacher often has a close, caring relationship with many of the children. In elementary school, the classroom is the main context for the child. The second major school transition for most students is the move from this intimate, self-contained classroom to an environment where they switch classrooms and teachers several times per day. Now there is less opportunity to form a close relationship with a supportive adult. The student also is in a more complex environment where the school is the primary social context, not the classroom. This change in school format typically occurs in early adolescence.

With each school transition, academic performance, self-esteem, motivation, and perception of academic competence tend to decline (Akos, 2002; Otis; Grouzet, & Pelletier, 2005). The decline is partially due to higher academic standards, but a number of school-related changes are also relevant. For example, upon the transition to middle school, there is often less individual attention and more whole-class instruction and more emphasis on teacher control and discipline (Gentry, Gable, & Rizza, 2002; Seidman, Aber, & French, 2004). Students rate their middle school and junior-high experiences less favorably than their elementary school experience (Akos, 2002; Akos & Galassi, 2004). They report that their middle school teachers are less friendly, care less about them, and stress competition more than mastery of skills compared to their elementary teachers.

The timing and number of school transitions appear to be particularly important for school success. In general, the earlier and more often transitions occur, the more difficult it is for the student to adjust successfully (Akos & Galassi, 2004; Eccles & Roeser, 1999). The number of transitions is influenced by whether a school utilizes a two-tier system of grades (typically an 8-4 arrangement with kindergarten through eighth grade in one school) or a 6-3-3 or 5-3-4 arrangement. The 8-4 arrangement has the benefit of requiring only one change of schools rather than two in the 6-3-3 or 5-3-4 arrangement. The 8-4 arrangement also places the major transition after many adolescents are well into puberty.

Every school system necessarily makes decisions that group students by age. These decisions include the age at which formal schooling should begin (typically 5 years of age in the United States) and the points at which movement will occur from one level or grade to the next (typically 1-year increments). In most communities, children do not remain in the same school throughout their educational careers, and thus decisions must also be made about how many transitions will be made from one school to another and when the transitions will occur. Most American students experience at least two transitions: from elementary school to either middle school (grades 6, 7, and 8) or junior high (grades 7 and 8 or 7, 8, and 9), and from middle school or junior high to high school.

It appears that all school transitions result in a temporary negative influence on students' competence. However, the earlier the school change occurs in adolescence, the more difficult it is for students. The inherent challenges posed by school transitions are magnified by the developmental changes that occur during early adolescence (Akos, 2002; Brough & Irvin, 2001; Trzesniewski, Donnellan, & Robins, 2003). Early adolescence is a time of heightened self-consciousness, a heightened desire and capacity for decision making and autonomy, an increased concern about close peer relations, and an increased need for supportive adults outside the home. It is, in short, a time when young people need what the new structure of schooling tends to discourage—a lack of fit. **Stage–environment fit** proceeds most smoothly when the environmental opportunities and challenges during a particular time period match the capacities and needs of the developing child. Psychologist Jacquelynne Eccles maintains that the typical middle school or junior high provides a poor fit for young adolescents, because early adolescence is a period of heightened risk for decline in self-esteem, lowered academic motivation, poorer academic performance, and increases in truancy and delinquency (Otis et al., 2005; Walls & Little, 2005).

School Effectiveness

As might be expected, school effectiveness is difficult to define and study (Friend & Pope, 2005; Wenglinsky, 2002). Some schools consistently produce more successful outcomes than others—their students score higher on achievement tests and are more likely to complete their schooling. Interestingly, the amount of money spent per student, assuming the school has reasonable resources, is not a major factor in determining school effectiveness (Hanushek, 1997; Skandera & Sousa, 2002). As you read, however, variations in school success (such as performance on standardized tests, attendance rates, and graduation rates) are associated with the financial or physical resources available to the school, with the overall size of the school, and with the size of classes within the school. Within certain broad limits, school and class size do not seem to be major contributors to school success, especially in relation to their high cost. Nevertheless, recent research indicates that small class size can be beneficial, especially in the early grades and especially for low-income students (Finn et al., 2005; Nye, Hedges, & Konstantopoulos, 2001).

What factors *do* influence school success? In general, effective schools are comfortable places to learn where education is actively pursued. These schools provide high, but reasonable, goals for their students and teachers while providing the expectations and support needed to obtain these goals (Corbett & Wilson, 2002; Rivkin, Hanushek, & Kain, 2005; Wenglinsky, 2002). Effective schools typically focus on tasks, practice firm but fair discipline, and provide a warm, friendly place to learn. These schools spend less time dealing with discipline problems and getting-started activities, such as collecting lunch money, and more time on educationally relevant exercises. Students in effective schools are helped to feel they are part of the school through opportunities to participate in school-related activities, as well as chances to have a voice in decisions concerning the school (Harlan & Rowland, 2002).

It is helpful if teaching is flexible and personalized and if students know their teachers. Interestingly, there is no universally accepted teaching program or technique. No researcher or educator has succeeded in identifying a teaching method or philosophy that has been proven to work equally well for all students. Many educational practices are highly effective for students with certain learning styles or abilities but are not as effective for others. It is important for the school and teacher to find an appropriate match between the students they have and the teaching methods they use. Students also tend to achieve better when they and their teacher share similar backgrounds (Goldwater & Nutt, 1999; Warikoo, 2004). The teaching program selected should be one that is evidence based, however, and has been tested and been shown to have a record of success. Using programs that we know work is one of the requirements of the No Child Left Behind Act (2003).

Schooling as a Mesosystem

The formal educational environment of schools is influenced by the people around it, such as peers, parents, and the general culture. Recall Bronfenbrenner's ecological systems theory (Bronfenbrenner, 1979). Schools fall within the environmental layer labeled the *microsystem,* as do families and peers. The *mesosystem* refers to interrelations among the child's microsystems, and schooling is a prime example because it depends very much on the relations that the child experiences between family and school, as well as between school and peers.

Peers are important at the time of the first school transition: the entry into school at age 5 or 6. Children who have several good friends when they start kindergarten are happier in school than are children who lack such friendships. They develop more positive

Stage–environment fit
Development proceeds most smoothly when the environmental opportunities and challenges during a particular time period match the capacities and needs of the developing child.

attitudes toward school; and they show greater gains in performance across the school year. Conversely, being rejected by peers is associated with unfavorable attitudes, poorer social development, and less adequate school performance (Gest, Domitrovich, & Welsh, 2005; Spinard et al., 2004).

Peer relations remain important as children progress through school. Association with academically oriented peers promotes academic motivation and achievement. Conversely, association with antisocial peers is linked to poor grades and dropping out of school (Fuligni et al., 2001; Wentzel & Watkins, 2002). Throughout grade school and high school, children who lack friends are less well adjusted in the classroom, show higher rates of absenteeism, are more at risk for being retained at a grade, and also are two to eight times more likely to drop out of school than children in general.

The family is also important to success in school. The importance of the family extends beyond stimulation of intellectual development. From the start of school, children's adjustment to school and their academic performance are linked to the quality of family relations and family support (Bradley et al., 2001; Cowan & Cowan, 2002; Hoglund & Leadbeater, 2004). Important aspects of family life include the number of parents or other adults in the home, the stability of the family structure, the quality of relations with the parents, and the degree of parental support for academic achievement. These factors, in turn, affect a variety of outcomes in the school setting, ranging from adjustment to kindergarten to coping with the transition to middle school or junior high, to the probability of dropping out of high school. Parents also affect their children's school success by influencing the peers with whom they associate, which contributes to academic attitudes and performance (Dishion, Bullock, & Granic, 2002).

Effective schools also tend to have supportive communities and parents (Englund, Luckner, Whaley, & Egeland, 2004). Parents can take an active role in their children's schooling in a number of ways, including parent-teacher conferences, monitoring of and help with homework, and guidance regarding the selection of curricular and career-track options (De Civita, Pagani, Vitaro, & Tremblay, 2004; Englund et al., 2004; Epstein, Sanders, & Simon, 2002). The dimension of parental involvement is itself an example of a contextual effect.

On average, low-income parents are less likely to be involved in their children's schooling than are middle-income parents. In many instances this lack of involvement is less a matter of interest and concern than of possibility. For parents coping with the challenges of poverty, dangerous neighborhoods, and uncertain employment, finding time and energy for their child's schooling may be a daunting task (Elias, Parker, & Rosenblatt, 2005; Lee & Burkham, 2002). In addition, many parents may lack the skills and experiences needed to help their child with their schoolwork.

It is important for teachers and schools to find ways to involve parents in the education of their children, besides merely sending home progress notes and holding parent-teacher conferences (Pedzek, Berry, & Renno, 2002; Sheldon & Epstein, 2005). Some communities have reading programs designed to increase the literacy of parents and their children. For example, programs that send home high-quality children's books with suggested extension activities for the adult and child have been shown to promote children's learning and family involvement (Dever, 2001; Rasinski & Stevenson, 2005). These programs appear to work well with all types of families, even those that do not usually participate in school-based events (e.g., low SES families, or those families in which the parents have limited English-language proficiency).

In addition to peers and parents, the child's general culture is an influential context for schooling. Because of the diversity of American society, different children often bring different experiences, beliefs, and values to the school setting. The potential importance of this dimension is expressed in the **cultural compatibility hypothesis:** Classroom instruction will be most effective when it matches patterns of learning that are familiar in the child's culture (Slaughter-DeFoe et al., 1990; Tharp, 1989).

A good example of this principle is found in a study of *wait-time*—the length of time one participant in a dialogue waits before responding to the other (Walsh & Sattes,

Cultural compatibility hypothesis
Classroom instruction will be most effective when it matches patterns of learning that are familiar in the child's culture.

2005; White & Tharp, 1988). Navajo children tend to pause when giving answers, creating the impression (at least for Anglo teachers) that they have finished responding. The result is that Navajo children are often interrupted before they have completed their answers. In this case, the teacher's wait-time is too short. In contrast, native Hawaiian children prefer a short wait-time because in their culture prompt response and overlapping speech patterns are signs of interest and involvement. Teachers, however, often interpret the Hawaiian child's quick responses as rude interruptions, and their attempts to curtail such behavior may lead to general uncertainty and inhibition. Thus, in both cases, though in different ways, the teacher's unfamiliarity with the child's cultural background can create problems for the child in school.

Ability Grouping

One of the greatest challenges facing public schools is to provide an equal opportunity for children to reach their potential even though the children come to school with different experiences and academic strengths. Different children may require different educational experiences to reach their potential. A high degree of student heterogeneity characterizes many schools in the United States, and educators and policy makers have a number of solutions for the issues raised by student homogeneity. One controversial issue is how to group students in the classroom. Much of this debate has centered on ability grouping.

Tracking   Ability grouping is designed to decrease the heterogeneity that teachers must work with in the classroom. In **tracking** or **between-class grouping**, students are assigned to particular classrooms based on some measure of ability, such as reading. In contrast, in **within-class grouping**, students already in a particular classroom are divided into groups for certain subjects. For example, the students in Mr. Smith's class might be divided into three reading groups based on academic ability. In the early school years, grouping is most likely to be at the within-class level—for example, the "red robins" and the "bluebirds" reading groups. By middle school and high school, grouping is more often at the between-class level—for example, separate curricula for college-bound and vocational-track students.

Is ability grouping a desirable educational practice? There is no simple answer to this question. The basic rationale behind the procedure—that instruction should be matched to the developmental level and interests of the individual student—is one with which no educator would disagree, and achieving such a fit is generally easier in a small and similar-ability group than in a larger, more diverse class. Supporters of ability grouping argue that by creating homogeneous groups of students, the teacher of a group can devise and deliver a curriculum that more closely meets the needs of all the students in the group. In theory, the more alike the students are in terms of knowledge, ability, and skill, the more easily a teacher can reach most of the students using a smaller number of examples. Some forms of ability grouping have been shown to work well for some students. In particular, placement in challenging educational tracks with peers of similar ability is generally beneficial for students of relatively high academic ability (Fuligni, Eccles, & Barber, 1995; Pallas et al., 1994).

Critics of ability grouping, especially between-class ability grouping, argue that students who are tracked receive a poorer educational environment, can be stigmatized, and demonstrate lower levels of academic performance (Saleh, Lazonder, & De Jong, 2005; Slavin, 1990; Stipek, 2002). Students in the low class may be labeled with demeaning names such as "the dummy group" or "the slow ones." Unfortunately, low-track classrooms often have less experienced teachers, fewer resources, and lower expectations (Achinstein, Ogawa, & Speiglman, 2004). Yes, a child's beliefs and the beliefs of others about one's abilities are powerful contributors to how one actually performs. Researchers have also found that low-ability students are more motivated to learn and achieve more in heterogeneous groupings (Saleh et al., 2005). Social injustice is also a concern. Assignment to a particular group may not accurately reflect a child's true ability or potential. Even when the placement is appropriate, children in

Tracking (between-class ability grouping)
Students are assigned to particular classrooms based on some measure of ability, often intelligence or some other measure of potential.

Within-class ability grouping
Students already in a particular classroom are divided into ability-based groups for instruction.

Questions for Thought and Discussion
What have been your experiences with between-class and within-class ability groupings? What were some benefits and drawbacks of these approaches?

It is not uncommon for a first-grade teacher to have some students who are still struggling to learn the letters of the alphabet and others who read fluently and independently. How does a teacher help each child achieve his or her potential when the classroom encompasses a wide range of motivation, ability, and knowledge? As a teacher, how would you work with students who have yet to demonstrate proficiency in basic skills while at the same time not holding back the educational development of the other children in the class? (Ellen B. Senisi)

lower-level tracks may not receive content that is sufficiently challenging to elicit their full potential, and the instruction they receive may not be of the same quality as that given their higher-track peers (Achinstein et al., 2004; Dornbusch et al., 1996). And low-income and minority children tend to be disproportionately represented in lower-level tracks (Ansalone, 2005; Dornbusch & Kaufman, 2001). Some have argued that, because of these factors, ability grouping is another institutional mechanism for oppressing these groups (Tieso, 2003).

Single-Gender Classrooms   Another issue in the grouping of students is whether to place boys and girls in different classrooms for certain academic subjects such as math and science. In elementary school, females tend to receive higher grades and demonstrate higher achievement than boys in all subjects, including math and science, which have historically been considered "masculine." However, females generally score lower than boys on standardized measures of math and science, beginning during high school and then in college (Nosek, Banaji, & Greenwald, 2002; Ryan & Ryan, 2005).

The attitude of females toward some subjects, especially math, is a cause of concern. During the middle school years, girls' attitudes toward math change (Herbert & Stipek, 2005; Watt, 2004). In general, girls in elementary school describe themselves as confident in their ability to do math. However, as they go through middle school, their confidence in their ability and their perception of math as a subject appropriate for girls declines. These findings are used as a partial explanation for why females are underrepresented in fields associated with math and science such as engineering and technology (Ryan & Ryan, 2005).

One concern is that females are exposed to treatment in co-ed classrooms that leads them to underperform in these academic subjects and choose not to pursue higher-level math and science classes and careers. Boys receive more total attention, both positive and negative, than girls according to some studies (Wittner & Honig, 1988; Dobbs, Arnold, & Doctoroff, 2004). This pattern extends throughout formal schooling and begins at a very young age (Sadker & Sadker, 1985). More specifically, boys are called on more often, and are asked more challenging and more critical thinking questions, as opposed to the more factual questions that are

Links to Related Material

In Chapter 13, you will learn more about gender differences and academic performance.

posed to girls (Altermatt, Jovanovic, & Perry, 1998; Klein, 1985). Students can be affected by these kinds of teacher and peer expectations. Some researchers have indicated that teachers can be trained through professional development activities to treat males and females more equitably in the classroom (Jones, Evans, Byrd, & Campbell, 2000).

Given that males and females appear to be treated differently in the co-ed classroom, it is reasonable to ask if there is evidence that single-sex classrooms are associated with greater achievement. Although there is much talk in the public sector regarding the effectiveness of single-sex or single-gender classes, the research examining their effectiveness has yielded a mixed bag of findings. Some studies find that girls make more progress in math and science in single-sex classrooms (Salomone, 2003; Shapka & Keating, 2003; Van de gaer, Pustjens, Van Damme, & De Munter, 2004), whereas other studies (Jackson & Smith, 2000) have found no differences in achievement or a combination of positive and negative outcomes for both males and females (Datnow, Hubbard, & Woody, 2001; Jackson, 2002).

Schools are not the only factors that influence the academic achievement of boys and girls. Parental and societal attitudes about gender roles play a significant role. Parental attitudes concerning school and educational expectations are transmitted to their children beginning at an early age. For example, parents' behavior is a strong predictor of both male and female participation in math, science, and computer activities (Simpkins, Davis-Kean, & Eccles, 2005). Despite the unpopularity of this view, gender differences also exist that may influence school performance. For example, boys are, on average, more aggressive and more physically active than girls (Campbell & Eaton, 1999). These characteristics may influence not only the child's behavior in the classroom but also the manner in which the teacher and other school personnel react to the child.

Mainstreaming and Inclusion: Teaching Students with Special Needs

An issue closely related to ability grouping is how the educational system is going to provide services for students with special needs. In the United States, public law (P.L.) 94-142, the 1975 Education for all Handicapped Children Act, required that all children with disabilities, whatever the nature or severity of their disability, be provided a free and appropriate education within the least restrictive environment possible (similar legislation exists in Canada). Later laws, such as the 1990 Individuals with Disabilities Education Act (IDEA), have clarified, strengthened, and expanded the 1975 legislation (Santrock, 2004). Prior to the implementation of these laws, many children with disabilities were segregated from their more typically developing peers in special classes or schools.

Now, instead of being segregated from their peers, many children with disabilities are placed in regular classrooms on at least a partial basis. The process of **mainstreaming** or **inclusion**, where students with learning disabilities are placed in regular classrooms for part of the school day, is designed to better prepare students for participation in society. Full inclusion or the placement of disabled students into the regular classroom full time has also become common.

Mainstreaming (inclusion)
Practice of planning special needs students in regular classrooms for part of the school day.

How effective are mainstreaming and full inclusion practices? In general, when disabled students are mainstreamed, they demonstrate higher academic performance, better attitudes toward school, better social skills, increased interaction with peers, and better preparation for post-school experiences than their nonmainstreamed peers (Power-deFur & Orelove, 2003). However, the effectiveness of mainstreaming depends on the severity of the disability, the support services available to the student and classroom teacher, and the attitudes of the teachers themselves (Heiman, 2002; Marshall, Stojanovik, & Ralph, 2002). Unfortunately, children with disabilities often are rejected by regular-classroom peers, and some children, as a result of their disability, have difficulty with social awareness and responsiveness (Sridhar & Vaughn, 2002). The achievement levels of nondisabled classmates are not negatively affected by the inclusion of children with disabilities, as long as appropriate support services are provided (Kochar & West, 2003).

Children with mild to moderate learning difficulties tend to perform best when they are provided the extra support and instruction they need (Weiner & Tardif, 2004). This typically can be accomplished in the full inclusion classroom if they receive consistent support from a special education teacher who consults with the classroom teacher and spends time in the classroom each day. Another approach is to use a pull-out program where the student receives instruction from a special education teacher in a resource area for part of the day and is mainstreamed for the remainder of the day.

In the regular classroom setting, teachers must make a concerted effort to promote peer acceptance of disabled students. Many educators use cooperative learning and peer-tutoring activities to accomplish this acceptance. These experiences are associated with improved peer acceptance and achievement gains for all children involved and have been used successfully in the teaching of math and reading (Fuchs & Fuchs, 2005; Mathes, Torgesen, & Allor, 2001). Just being exposed to children who possess different abilities or cultural backgrounds is not sufficient to alter attitudes and prejudice. It is necessary to engage in meaningful and cooperative interactions.

Motivation to Learn

Motivation
Mental processes that energize, direct, and sustain behavior.

Every day, teachers look into a sea of faces and meet expressions that range from bright-eyed and ready to learn to acute disinterest to total disengagement. There are the students that teachers know possess ability but who do just enough to get by. There are the students who give all they have and still cannot keep up. There are also students who just give up because they believe they will never be able to do it. How do we explain what does and does not motivate students to learn in the classroom? **Motivation** involves the processes that energize, direct, and sustain behavior. Many theoretical explanations have been offered for why we behave in certain ways. Learning or behavioral theory explains motivation as a result of external rewards and punishments. We are motivated to obtain reinforcement and to avoid punishment. Humanistic theory emphasizes people's freedom to choose their own destiny. Abraham Maslow, a humanist, argued in his hierarchy of needs theory that certain basic needs must be met before higher needs will be motivating. Therefore, a child who feels threatened or bullied in the school environment or who is hungry will not be motivated to learn because safety and food are more basic needs than cognitive pursuits. According to cognitive explanations of motivation, a person's thoughts guide their motivation. The emphasis is on perception, beliefs, and attributions of success and failure made by the individual student. Most research in motivation to achieve uses cognitive explanations.

Motivation to Achieve   A goal of schooling is to produce students who will be self-regulated, life-long learners. Students must persist in the face of difficulties, handle frustrations, and constructively cope with failure. For example, when Max has difficulty writing his name in cursive, he becomes frustrated and feels temporarily discouraged. But he then tries harder the next time. In contrast, when Brad has difficulty writing his name, he becomes discouraged and refuses to try again. How do we explain why one student maintains or even increases his or her level of motivation, whereas another student experiences a decrease in motivation?

Attributions
The perceived causes of outcomes.

Cognitive theories focus on the **attributions** made by students—the perceived causes of outcomes. What do we see as the cause of our failures and successes?

1. Is the cause external or internal to the person?
2. Is the cause stable or unstable?
3. Is the cause controllable by the person?

BOX 9.3   Conversations with a Special Educator

Kay Davis is an Instructional Programs coordinator in the Clark County School District in Las Vegas, Nevada. She grew up in Little Rock, Arkansas, and at age 40 is divorced with no children. Working with special educators of children with special needs is her life.

I came to this work through my own experiences as a student. In high school I worked as a peer tutor in the special education program and have worked in the field of special education ever since. My teachers encouraged me to pursue a career as a teacher. I began teaching out of field with a bachelor's degree in social science. But I wanted to be certified in special education, so I got a master's degree in special education.

Along the way I discovered that there are many opportunities for advancement in this field. My special education supervisor was working on a doctorate in administration and encouraged me to apply to programs. Upon deciding to qualify as a special education administrator as well as a special education teacher, I went to Virginia Tech, which had a doctoral program in special education administration and supervision.

Clark County is the fifth largest school district in the country. I am assigned to the Northwest Region, which has 61 schools. My job is to help teachers and administrators in preschool through high school solve problems and raise student achievement. This entails observing in classrooms, meeting with principals, and attending IEP meetings.

An IEP (Individualized Education Plan) describes the goals a team has set for a student with disabilities for the school year, as well as any special supports that are needed to help achieve those goals. I help develop the IEPs and train staff members in implementing them. Students who qualify for special education services in the public schools may include children with learning disabilities, Attention-Deficit Hyperactivity Disorder, emotional disorders, mental retardation, autism, hearing impairment, visual impairment, speech or language impairment, or developmental delay.

In my administrative role, I have to know what is happening in our schools so I can help staff plug in to and use resources to solve problems and keep student learning on track. I work in the context of a student support services team. The team is comprised of administrators supervising school psychologists, speech-language pathologists, and nurses. Six team members are specialist teachers, three are behavioral specialists, one is an early childhood specialist, one specializes in assistive technology, and one is a transition specialist. Our team is rounded out by two social workers and is led by a director. I am one of three coordinators. We provide technical assistance to our schools.

I'm established enough in my career where training others has become an important part of my job. Also, a major professional goal for me has been to present at national conferences, which I did recently at a meeting of the Council for Exceptional Children. My presentation was on administrator collaboration, explaining how school principals and special education administrators can work together for the benefit of all kids.

I'm also proud of an award I received from the Friends of FEAT (Families for Effective Autism Treatment). This parent advocacy organization had worked hard to develop a positive relationship with the school district and went to great lengths to surprise me with the award. I was very proud to have my efforts on behalf of kids with autism recognized in such a public way.

Being a special education administrator can be very stressful, partly because the rules for qualifying children for special services are very strict at the same time as they have gray areas. Sometimes I feel like the person who has to say no, although teams actually make the decisions. I have testified in hearings, and from this I have learned to make decisions based on collected data, knowledge of child development, and research-based practices. I don't always have to say no, of course, but when I do, it's easier for school staff and parents if I can explain clearly with empirical, practical, and scientific reasons.

So my job has challenges as well as rewards. And every day is different because every problem is different. Many times the solution to one problem can be used in other settings, and sometimes solutions open up a whole area of training or programming to focus on as a team. I view each challenge as a new learning opportunity.

The student who attributes failure to a lack of effort is making an attribution that is internal, unstable, and controllable. In contrast, the student who attributes failure to a lack of ability in some skill is making an internal, stable, and uncontrollable attribution. The attributions that a student makes can affect future motivation. For example, students who credit their success to internal, controllable factors, such as effort, are more likely to have higher self-esteem and increased motivation than those who use external factors such as luck (Horner & Gaither, 2004).

Researchers have identified interesting differences in the attributions of children who persist in the face of failure until they succeed and those who give up (Kaplan, Middleton,

Helpless orientation
Tendency to attribute failures to personal inadequacies, often a lack of ability.

Mastery orientation
Tendency to focus on the task rather than on ability and to believe that ability can be changed and improved.

Performance orientation
Tendency to focus on the outcome of the activity rather than on the process of improving skill or learning.

Questions for Thought and Discussion
What attributions do you tend to use for your academic successes and failures? What does this tendency tell you about your motivation?

Self-efficacy
According to Bandura, an individual's beliefs about his or her performance capabilities in a particular domain.

Link to Related Materials
In Chapter 12 you will learn more about how children's beliefs about their abilities, and particularly their beliefs about the role of effort in success, can affect their motivation and persistence in the face of failures.

Intrinsic motivation
Internal motivation to do something for its own sake.

Extrinsic motivation
External motivation; doing something to obtain some external reward.

Urdan, & Midgley, 2002; Pintrich, 1999; Wolters, 2004). Children with a **helpless orientation** tend to attribute their failures to personal inadequacies, often a lack of ability. Therefore, they often have low expectations for success, and they tend to give up quickly and avoid challenges. In contrast, children who persist in the face of failure tend to possess a **mastery orientation**. These children focus on the task rather than on their ability. They believe that ability can be changed and improved. Mastery-oriented students tend to thrive on challenges and to believe that increased effort will lead to success. Students who possess a **performance orientation** tend to focus on the outcome of the activity rather than on the process of improving skill or learning. They are focused on winning, and happiness is thought to result from winning and pleasing others. In contrast, mastery-oriented students tend to emphasize self-improvement.

Students are also influenced by the types of goals they set or choose to pursue, the types of tasks they are assigned, and the grading procedures that are used (Kaplan et al., 2002; Linnenbrink, 2005). Some teachers and parents set up goals for students to encourage the learning of certain skills. Others use goals that encourage competition or the obtaining of rewards. Learners adopt mastery goals as they seek to learn new things to improve their skills and abilities. Learners select performance goals as they attempt to prove that they can do something rather than to improve at the task.

The use of goal types tends to change over time (Middleton, Kaplan, & Midgely, 2004). Elementary programs generally emphasize learning goals. Many of the changes associated with the transition to middle school are likely to increase students' motivation to achieve performance goals rather than mastery goals (Wigfield & Eccles, 2002). For example, the shift to a greater focus on grades and competition nudges students toward focusing on obtaining awards, grades, and other outcomes. Students who continue to focus on learning goals tend to perform better in school than those who switch to performance goals (Stipek & Gralinski, 1996). In contrast, students who are concerned with getting good grades and pleasing others have less tendency to develop an adaptive pattern of self-regulated learning and performance (Pintrich, 1999).

Self-efficacy, a concept proposed by Albert Bandura, is an individual's beliefs about his or her performance capabilities in a particular domain. It is the belief that "I can," whereas helplessness is the belief, "I cannot." Self-efficacy includes a person's judgments about his or her ability to accomplish certain goals or tasks through action and confidence in his or her cognitive skills in academic situations. Bandura proposed that self-efficacy is a critical factor in whether or not students achieve (1997, 2001). Students with high levels of self-efficacy are more likely to commit cognitively to learning the material than those who are lower in self-efficacy (Stipek, 2002). They also are more likely to try to achieve, to set more challenging goals, and to succeed than students who do not believe in their own abilities.

Self-efficacy is positively correlated with self-regulated learning. Students who believe that they can learn and are confident in their abilities are more likely to use self-regulatory strategies and to be motivated to try (Margolis & McCabe, 2003; Pintrich, 1999). Self-efficacy tends to improve when students have opportunities to set goals that are specific, short-term, and challenging (Margolis & McCabe, 2003; Zimmerman & Schunk, 2001). These goals are seen as a commitment to self-improvement and give the student a chance to receive more immediate and relevant feedback.

Intrinsic and Extrinsic Motivation   Some tasks are interesting in and of themselves. For example, some children read because they like to read. **Intrinsic motivation** involves the internal motivation to do something for its own sake. In contrast, some children read because they want the reward that the teacher, parent, or school is offering for reading. This is **extrinsic motivation**—doing something in order to obtain some external reward.

In elementary education, many behaviors start off by being extrinsically motivating. It is difficult to learn to read, to master multiplication, and to complete the assignments that teachers assign. It is more fun to play. Educators hope that children will find these behaviors intrinsically motivating in the process of learning and mastering skills. Intrinsic motivation is associated with better school outcomes, such as persistence and performance, than extrinsic motivation (Hardré & Reeve, 2003; Otis, Grouzet, & Pelletier, 2005). However, students tend to be less intrinsically motivated and more extrinsically motivated as they progress through the school years, especially after a school transition (Lepper, Corpus, & Iyengar, 2005; Yeung & McInerney, 2005).

What happens when you provide extrinsic motivators for tasks that children find intrinsically motivating? Should you reward a child for doing something he or she likes to do? What is the harm of a gold star or an ice-cream cone? One concern is that the child may learn to do the activity for the external reward instead of the intrinsic value. Research shows that rewards that are tied to competence tend to promote motivation and interest. However, rewards that are not based on competence may eventually decrease motivation when the rewards are removed (Schunk, 2000). For example, providing rewards for simply spending time on a task does not give the student feedback about competence. It is unlikely to increase motivation. However, if the student is rewarded for accomplishing a task, he or she is more likely to feel competent, which is associated with increased motivation. The use of performance goals may be associated with an increase in achievement in older students, especially high school students, but is not recommended for elementary and middle school students (Midgley, Kaplan, & Middleton, 2001).

Other Factors Associated with Motivation   A student's beliefs about the importance of the task, interest in the task, and perceptions of the utility of the task to his or her future goals are all important factors in motivation (Pintrich, 1999). Where do these beliefs come from? Who and what influences whether a student sets learning or performance goals, has a certain learning orientation, acquires a good sense of self efficacy, and is intrinsically or extrinsically motivated?

The most important factor is the environment fostered by the school. Changes in motivation also are associated with the kinds of feedback that students receive from teachers and other adults. As students mature, the aspects of performance that teachers praise and the amount of criticism they use change. In the early grades, teachers are likely to praise effort and use little criticism, which helps younger students set learning rather than performance goals (Rosenholtz & Simpson, 1984). As students progress through the grades, teachers are more likely to reserve praise and reward achievement rather than effort. The focus on creating quality products and competition among students increases, which leads to a shift from learning goals to performance goals. Thus, it may take constant effort on the part of everyone involved in a child's education to encourage learning goals and a mastery orientation.

Parents also serve an important role in the motivation of students (Gonzalez-DeHass, Willeams, & Holbein, 2005). Parents can encourage performance in school and the setting of learning goals. Parents also can criticize and communicate expectations that are too low or too high. The encouragement of ability and effort is associated with the development of intrinsic motivation, whereas the rewarding of good grades and the punishment of bad grades are associated with the development of extrinsic motivation (James, 2005; Miserandino, 1996).

Parenting styles may also affect motivation (Casanova, Garcia-Linares, de la Torre, & Carpio, 2005; Leung & Kwan, 1998). Authoritative parents tend to have the highest achieving students. They tend to be more curious, prefer more challenging tasks, and are more interested in learning. At the some time, authoritarian parents tend to rely more on extrinsic factors, to nag more about homework and grades, and to closely supervise their children. These students tend to be less self-regulatory and to have lower levels of achievement. Permissive parents often are uninvolved with their children's schoolwork, and their children tend to demonstrate lower levels of self-regulatory behavior and school performance. The effects of parenting styles may be even greater for children at risk of school failure because of an economically disadvantaged family background (Casanova et al., 2005).

Questions for Thought and Discussion
How will your knowledge of parental impacts of parenting on children's academic achievement affect your behavior toward your children in the context of schooling?

✔ *Test Your Mastery...*

1. Identify the cognitive effects of schooling that have been found by researchers.
2. How do teacher expectations, class and school size, school transitions, and school effectiveness affect cognitive outcomes for children?
3. Define and describe the evidence for and against the effectiveness of tracking, mainstreaming, and single gender classrooms.
4. How do motivation to achieve, self-efficacy, and intrinsic versus extrinsic motivation affect schooling outcomes for children?

Culture, Diversity, and Schooling

Learning Objective 9.5
Identify the ways in which children's cultural and socioeconomic backgrounds might affect the schooling experience.

Today's schools are a reflection of today's diverse society, and there are several reasons why culture and diversity must be taken into consideration. These include the effects of a student's culture on his or her learning, the effects of the teacher's culture in the teaching process, and the effects of the dominant culture on school-related decisions, such as the content of curriculum. Many teachers do not have an adequate understanding of the cultural issues that are relevant to educating their students (Achinstein & Athanases, 2005; Pang, 2001), but teachers increasingly are asked to become skilled at instructing a wide range of students (Friend & Pope, 2005).

The mix of students from so many different backgrounds can add richness of experience to the classroom, which makes it more fun and meaningful for the educator and students. However, because of children's different experiences, opportunities, and expectations, they come to school differentially prepared to learn and with different preferred ways of learning. When children enter the school environment, they may be encountering a place that does not match the values and behavioral patterns with which they are familiar. For example, schools tend to encourage individual achievement and work. In contrast, many children are from cultural backgrounds that emphasize group cooperation rather than individual competition. When working with children and adults from cultural backgrounds that emphasize group cooperation, it may be helpful to: (1) provide critical feedback in private, (2) place more emphasis on cooperation than on competition, and (3) pay attention to group memberships (Jung & Stinnett, 2005; Lockwood, Marshall, & Sadler, 2005; Triandis, Brislin, & Hui, 1988).

Ethnicity

In the United States, approximately 42 percent of school children are from racial or ethnic minority groups, up dramatically from 22 percent in 1972 (National Center for Educational Statistics, 2005). In New York City, the largest school district in the United States, 84 percent of the students are minorities (New York: The State of Learning, 1999). *Ethnicity* refers to a person's cultural heritage or background.

A number of educational and social outcomes are associated with ethnicity, and many of them are tied to differences in socioeconomic status and group differences in attitudes toward education (Read & Zalk, 2001; Yeakey & Henderson, 2002; Zhang & Katsiyannis, 2002). For example, almost one-third of African American and Latino students attend schools in which 90 percent or more of the students are from these groups. Nationally, minority students are overrepresented in remedial and special education programs. Asian American students are much more likely to take higher level math and science courses in high school, and Asian American and European American students are much more likely to be enrolled in college preparatory programs.

Findings such as these have raised serious concerns that children from certain minority groups continue to experience educational segregation (Buck, 2002). This concern extends to the quality of schools and the overall educational opportunities available to the children who attend them. Some research has suggested, for example, that ethnic minority students are not challenged as much by educators, are presented with lower educational expectations, and are exposed to negative ethnic minority stereotypes (*stereotype threat*) in the school environment (Neal, McCray, & Webb-Johnson, 2003). For example, schools serving relatively high proportions of low-income children and children of color were rated by teachers to have more negative social climates (Stipek, 2004; Tennant, 2004). Teachers in these schools emphasized basic skills more and engaged in more didactic teaching and less constructivist teaching practices. Members of stigmatized groups also appear to be more affected by teacher underestimates of their ability than other children (McKown & Weinstein, 2002). A related concern is that, in contrast to the growing percentage of minority students in schools in the United States, approximately 90 percent of the teachers are European American (Banks et al., 1995; Orfield, 2001). Another issue associated with increased ethnic diversity is bilingual education. As many as 10 million children in the United States are from homes in which the primary language is not English. The education of students for whom English is not a first language is discussed further in Chapter 10.

Links to Related Material
Here, you learn how teacher expectations and school environments may influence the academic performance of low-income and minority children. In Chapter 10, you will read more about another dimension that affects the school experiences of ethnically diverse children: bilingual education.

Socioeconomic Status

One common denominator for many differences observed in the educational performance of various ethnic groups is socioeconomic status. In general, individuals from lower SES backgrounds have less educational achievement, fewer economic resources, and a lower relative standing in the community. For example, as mentioned previously, children from lower SES backgrounds are more likely to drop out of school than students from middle- and high-income families (National Center for Education Statistics, 2001). Children from lower social class families are much more likely to demonstrate lower levels of school achievement, have poorer attitudes toward school, and fail to graduate than children from middle- and high-income families (Arnold & Doctoroff, 2003; Elias, Parker, & Rosenblatt, 2005; Lee & Burkam, 2002).

The effects of SES are not direct but are exerted through other factors. For example, because poorer and less educated parents are more likely to live in poorer neighborhoods, their children are more likely to attend poorer quality schools. Children from these homes are also more likely to have lower quality health care (Arnold & Doctoroff, 2003). Given the social and personal stress that accompanies poverty, it is not surprising that children whose families are poor are less likely to be ready for kindergarten, more likely to fall behind in grade school, and more likely to drop out of high school (Duncan, Brooks-Gunn, & Klebanov, 1994; Elias et al., 2005; Schweinhart, 1994; Zill, Collins, West, & Hausken, 1995). Lower income parents also may be required to spend more time in the workforce to support their families and maintain their employment. The resulting lack of time can limit parents' ability to provide for the educational needs of their children.

Adults in lower SES homes often see education as a means of raising the quality of life for their children, but they also tend to be less educated themselves. In many cases they may have difficulty helping children with educational assignments (Drummond & Stipek, 2004). For example, children from lower SES homes are less likely to be read to during the preschool years (Coley, 2002; Payne, Whitehurst, & Angell, 1994; Purcell-Gates, 1996). Parents also may have had negative experiences in school that they pass on to their children in the form of lower educational aspirations or expectations (De Civita, Pagani, Vitaro, & Tremblay, 2004).

These results are averages, and therefore they do not necessarily apply to each individual family and child. Many children from lower SES homes receive a significant amount of help from their families and other adults. A key factor determining whether a child succeeds in a school in which the majority of children are low-income is expressed in the concept of *social capital*. **Social capital** refers to the community and family resources available to the child (Coleman, 1988; Furstenberg & Hughes, 1995). Children must have parents or other adults willing and able to invest time and effort in them, and the community must have resources and a commitment to a strong network of support for the child.

Links to Related Material
In Chapter 16, you will learn more about how the child's socioeconomic environment affects development.

Social capital
The community and family resources available for the child to draw upon.

An Ounce of Prevention: Compensatory Education

One of the best predictors of school performance is the level of skill, ability, and knowledge that a child possesses at school entry. Children who enter school better prepared to benefit from the formal educational opportunities provided (e.g., have higher levels of school readiness skills such as letter knowledge) tend to demonstrate higher subsequent performance in school. Children who enter ahead tend to maintain their relative standing compared to children who are less well prepared. This gap in knowledge tends to grow larger as they progress through the school years, a phenomenon called the Matthew Effect (Stanovich, 1986). Most explanations for the difference in achievement focus on the typically more disadvantaged home experiences of the lower SES child (Arnold & Doctoroff, 2003; Sirkin, 2005), with as many as two-thirds of children in poor urban areas entering school without the skills needed to learn (Coley, 2002; D'Angiulli, Siegel, & Hertzman, 2004; Zigler, 1988).

What can schools do to help prepare at-risk children for school and to facilitate their educational performance once they arrive? This question has been at the root of a major shift in philosophy in the U.S. educational and daycare systems. For many years the focus was to wait for children to fail and then to try to provide remediation services. Today, the emphasis is on trying to prevent failure in the first place through what is known as *compensatory education*. **Compensatory education** programs are designed to compensate, or make up for, the low-income child's frequent disadvantage in preparation for school.

Compensatory education
Programs, such as Head Start, designed to compensate, or make up for, a disadvantage in preparation for school that children from low-income families are expected to have.

The Abecedarian Project   The Abecedarian Project is one of the most successful of the many intervention efforts that were launched in the 1960s and 1970s (Gottlieb & Blair, 2004; Ramey et al., 2000; Ramey, Ramey, & Lanzi, 2001). Like many such projects, its focus was on low-income African American children and their families. Unlike many projects, however, it did not limit its intervention to the preschool years; rather, children were enrolled as infants, with an average age of 4 months at the start of the project. Half the infants were randomly assigned to the treatment group, and half were assigned to an untreated control group. The infants in the treatment group attended a specially constructed childcare center for 8 hours a day, 50 weeks a year. The center was very high quality, with a low teacher-to-child ratio and a curriculum designed to promote cognitive development. Children remained in the center until age 5, with appropriate changes in the curriculum as they grew older. The children also were given nutritional supplements and health benefits, and their mothers received instruction in principles of child development. Finally, for half the sample aspects of the intervention remained in effect through the first three years of elementary school.

The Abecedarian Project had an immediate effect, with some differences in development emerging between the treatment and control group participants as early as six months. The differences increased throughout the duration of the program. By preschool, the average IQ difference between treatment and control was 17 points. Although the superiority of the treatment participants decreased across the school years, it did not disappear. The treatment participants consistently outperformed their counterparts on various measures of academic achievement. In the most recent follow-up, some effects of the intervention were still evident on cognitive and academic measures at age 21 (Campbell et al., 2001).

In addition to demonstrating the possibility for long-term success, the Abecedarian Project provides evidence for the effectiveness of early, intense, and extended intervention. The greatest gains by far were shown by the children for whom intervention began early and extended late.

Head Start   The best-known compensatory education program is Head Start, a federally funded program first provided in 1965 as an eight-week summer program. It was designed

What is the rationale for offering compensatory education programs such as Head Start? What factors contribute to the success of such programs? What is the role of society's investment in social capital for children's futures? (Paul Conklin/PhotoEdit)

to help break the cycle of poverty by providing children of low-income families with a comprehensive program to meet their emotional, social, health, nutritional, and psychological needs. Head Start now serves children from birth to age 5 years and their families. Head Start has served more than 22 million children since it started, including approximately 900,000 in 2004 (Head Start Bureau, 2005). However, because of inadequate funding, Head Start serves only about one-half of eligible 3- and 4-year-old children, and Early Head Start serves only a fraction of the eligible toddlers and infants (Children's Defense Fund, 2003).

Do Head Start and other high-quality compensatory programs work? This is not an easy question to answer, but, in general, the answer is yes (Anderson et al., 2003; Love, Constantore, et al., 2004; Reynolds, 2003). Children who participate in Head Start demonstrate higher levels of school readiness (Ripple et al., 1999). This is especially true when compensatory programs continue after children start school (Children's Defense Fund, 2005; Ripple et al., 1999). The cognitive benefits of Head Start programs begin to fade when children enter school. For example, the intelligence test score gains demonstrated by Head Start participants relative to non-Head Start participants disappear after school entry. Head Start participants do not perform as well on standardized tests as do middle-class children. However, Head Start children are less likely to be placed in special education classes, to repeat a grade, and to drop out of high school than low-income children who did not attend a compensatory program (Magnuson & Waldfogel, 2005b; Neisser et al., 1996). Other social benefits for the participants of high-quality compensatory education programs include a lower teenage pregnancy rate and a decreased risk for juvenile delinquency (Anderson et al., 2003; Reynolds, 2003). The results of Head Start and other compensatory programs also apply to parents. The parents of children who participated in the Head Start and Early Head Start programs are more likely to read to their children and to use less physical punishment (Head Start Bureau, 2005; Manguson & Waldfogel, 2005b).

The six principles listed in Table 9.5 capture much of what is known about the contributors to successful intervention (Ramey and Ramey, 1998). The Abecedarian Project and Head Start illustrate many of the principles, including the principle of developmental timing (starting programs in infancy rather than waiting for the preschool years), and the principle of program intensity (the year-long, 5-day-a-week immersion in the program). On the positive side, it is clear that intervention programs *can* produce genuine and lasting benefits for children and their families, and that psychologists and educators have learned much about the factors that determine success. On the negative side, it is clear that

Questions for Thought and Discussion
If you were developing an intervention program for an at-risk population, what would your program emphasize, and how would you measure its effectiveness?

TABLE 9.5 Principles of Successful Intervention	
PRINCIPLE	**DESCRIPTION**
Developmental Timing	Programs that begin early and extend later in development are more successful.
Program Intensity	Programs that are more intensive (e.g., in terms of number of hours and range of activities) are more effective.
Direct Provision of Learning Experiences	Programs that provide direct learning experiences to children are more effective.
Program Breadth and Flexibility	Programs that provide more comprehensive services and use multiple pathways are more effective.
Individual Differences	Some children show greater benefits from participation than others.
Environmental Maintenance of Development	Maintenance of positive effects over time depends on adequate environmental supports.

SOURCE: Adapted from C.T. Ramey and S.L. Ramey. (1998). Early intervention and early experience. *American Psychologist, 53,* pp. 109–120. Copyright 1998 by the American Psychological Association. Adapted by permission.

success does not come easily; rather, a continued societal commitment is required to ensure that the necessary resources are devoted to the task.

Culture, Classrooms, and Academic Performance

The educational attainment of students is affected by family, school, and cultural factors. Cultural variations in the schooling that children receive can be a source of cognitive and achievement differences at the national level. This point is relevant to the discrepancy in mathematics achievement between Chinese and Japanese children and American children (Chen & Stevenson, 1995; Stevenson, Chen, & Lee, 1993; Stevenson et al., 1990). American children, on average, do not perform well in mathematics. This conclusion has emerged from several surveys of cross-national differences in mathematics ability in recent years. The contrast with children from Asian countries is especially marked. For example, in studies of mathematics achievement in 20 countries, American eighth and twelfth graders scored below the international average on virtually every measure taken (Garden, 1987; U.S. Department of Education, 2001). Children from China and Japan, in contrast, were consistently near the top of the range.

Why do American children do so poorly in mathematics? It is tempting to indict the school system. Some differences between Asians and Americans, however, are evident by age 5, before most children have even started school (Stevenson, Lee, & Stigler, 1986). Furthermore, Asian American students in the United States often outperform European American students, even though both groups are moving through the same school systems (Sue & Ozaki, 1990). These findings suggest that schools are not the sole explanation; the family environment also contributes.

The most ambitious attempt to identify family bases for academic achievement is a program of research by Stevenson and associates (Chen & Stevenson, 1995; Stevenson, Chen, & Lee, 1993; Stevenson et al., 1990). The child partici-

Cross-cultural studies confirm discrepancies in achievement between American and Asian students. How can these discrepancies be explained? How do those explanations point to the power of cultural differences to define group differences in academic achievement? (BrandXPictures/Getty)

"Big deal, an A in math. That would be a D in any other country."

pants for the initial phase of the project were first and fifth graders from the United States, China, and Japan. The children took a variety of achievement tests, and the results fit those of previous research—poorer performance in mathematics by American children than by children from China or Japan. Many of the first graders were retested in fifth and eleventh grade, and the original results were confirmed. If anything, the cross-national gap in achievement had widened.

The children's mothers also participated in the study, and it was their beliefs and practices that constituted the main focus of the research. The maternal interviews included a variety of questions designed to reveal differences among families and cultures that might lead to differences in academic performance. Mothers were asked, for example, to judge how well their children were doing in school and to indicate how satisfied they were with this progress. They were asked to give their beliefs about the bases for school success—in particular, to judge the relative contributions of ability and effort to doing well in school. And they were asked about various experiences at home that might contribute to school success, such as parental help with homework or the provision of a quiet place to study.

The Stevenson group's assessments made clear that mothers in all three cultures are interested in and supportive of their children's academic development. At the same time, the maternal interviews revealed cross-cultural differences in beliefs and practices that might well contribute to the superior performance of Asian children. Asian mothers, for example, were more likely than American mothers to regard effort as more important than ability for success in school. The emphasis on effort in the Chinese and Japanese families appears to fit with general and long-standing cultural beliefs about the malleability of human nature and the possibility of improving oneself through hard work (Kim, Yank, Atkinson, Wolfe, & Hong, 2001). Thus, Asian parents are more likely to believe that all children have the potential to succeed and that they can master any academic challenge if they work hard enough. Possibly as a result, Asian parents are much more likely to help their children with homework and to emphasize the importance of education as part of a student's obligation to family and community (Wang, 2004).

In line with these beliefs, Asian mothers were more likely than American mothers to provide help for their children's academic endeavors. In China, for example, 96 percent of the children received help with homework (the figure in the United States was 67 percent), and fully 95 percent of Chinese fifth graders and 98 percent of

Japanese fifth graders had their own desk at home at which to work (the figure for American children was 63 percent). Similar results emerged from a measure of time spent on academically related activities (e.g., reading, completing workbooks) outside school. Asian children spent more time in such endeavors than did American children.

Given the relatively poor performance of their children, American mothers might have been expected to be least satisfied with their children's academic achievement. However, just the reverse was true. American mothers were more satisfied with both their children's performance and their children's schools than were Chinese, Japanese, or Taiwanese mothers (Pezdek, Berry, & Renno, 2002). American mothers also gave higher (and therefore less realistic) evaluations of their children's cognitive and academic abilities than did mothers in the other two cultures. This pattern suggests a basis for the failure of many American mothers to nurture optimal academic performance in their children. These mothers may believe that their children are doing better than they really are, and thus may be satisfied with levels of performance that are not that high. Furthermore, these mothers may believe that academic success is primarily a function of immutable ability rather than changeable effort and thus may see little point in encouraging their children to try harder.

These conclusions have at least two qualifications (Hatano, 1990). First, the research does not claim that the childrearing practices of Asian cultures are producing generally superior children. American children do just as well as Chinese and Japanese children on measures of general intelligence, and differences in other domains of academic achievement are less marked and less consistent than those found for mathematics. In addition, Asian students also have less leisure time than U.S. students (Guan, 2003) and spend less time than American children in outside-of-school activities, such as music, art, and sports activities, which are not usually sponsored by public schools in Asian countries (Sit, Linder, Koenraad, & Sherrill, 2002). Second, the research does not claim that the differences in mathematics result solely from differences among families. Schools are also important, and schools contribute to the superior performance of Asian children in mathematics (Whitman, 2003).

For example, children in China and Japan spend more time in school than do children in the United States, with both longer school days and longer school years (Dandy & Nettlebeck, 2002; World Education Services, 2005). In addition, there is a focus on math and science in many Asian countries (United Nations Development Programme, 2002), and classrooms in China and Japan typically devote more instructional time to mathematics than do classrooms in the United States. Teachers and children in China and Japan spend a higher proportion of the allotted time actually teaching and doing mathematics as opposed to peripheral activities (e.g., handing out papers). Children from China and Japan do more math homework than do American children, and mathematics textbooks and curricula are more challenging in these countries than they are in the United States (Guan, 2003). In light of these and other differences, it is perhaps not surprising that the achievement gap persists.

✔ *Test Your Mastery...*

Learning Objective 9.5: *Identify the ways in which children's cultural and socioeconomic backgrounds might affect the schooling experience.*

1. Describe the ways in which students' ethnic or socioeconomic background might be related to the quality of their schooling experience.
2. What evidence have researchers found regarding the effectiveness of compensatory preschool programs, such as the Abecedarian Project or Head Start?
3. Why do children from Asian countries such as China, Japan, and Taiwan, outperform U.S. children on tests of math achievement?

BOX 9.4   Contextual Model of Intelligence and Schooling

Infant is born with individual genetic potential for different kinds of mental abilities.

Family, Neighborhood, and School Settings

- Good prenatal care and adequate nutrition, health care, and exercise provide an optimal environment for the achievement of individual potential.
- Family education and financial resources provide access to a wide variety of mentally stimulating activities.
- Family SES affects choice of neighborhood and access to well-equipped schools that encourage child to achieve full potential.
- Peer groups influence the value a child places on different types of activities.

Culture and Society

- Cultural and societal value placed on different kinds of activities (e.g., business versus art) can affect young person's vocational and career choices.

Learning Objective 9.1

Explain how intelligence is defined and measured.

1. Describe the psychometric approach to intelligence testing.	The *psychometric approach*, proposed by Spearman, suggests that one common factor underlies all intelligent behavior. He called this factor "g" to indicate general intelligence. Specific intelligences or abilities, on the other hand, are only useful on certain tasks or situations. Spearman found that general intelligence was the best predictor of performance outside the testing situation. Cattell acknowledged the importance of both general and specific abilities but defined intelligence as either crystallized or fluid. Crystallized intelligence represents the abilities we acquire from experience. Fluid intelligence represents more basic skills, including processing speed, working memory capacity, and the ability to detect a relationship among various items.
2. What is the Stanford-Binet, and how does it define and measure IQ?	The *Stanford-Binet* intelligence scale is primarily a test of childhood intelligence applicable to every age group except infancy. It is a global measure of intelligence designed to yield a single intelligence quotient (IQ), a score that summarizes the child's ability. It stresses the kinds of verbal and academic skills that are important in school—quantitative reasoning, fluid reasoning, visual-spatial processing, knowledge, and working memory.
3. Identify three IQ or developmental tests in addition to the Stanford-Binet that are commonly used with children.	The most commonly used alternative to the Stanford-Binet is a series of tests designed by David Wechsler. These include the *Wechsler Preschool and Primary Scale of Intelligence*, intended for children from 4 to 6.5, the WISC III and WISC IV (ages 6–16) and the WAIS, intended for those over 16. The *Kaufman Assessment Battery for Children* (K–ABC II) marks an explicit effort to include cultural diversity and cultural fairness in the construction and administration of a test. The best-known measure of infant development is the Bayley Scales of Infant Development II.
4. In what ways can IQ tests be considered valid?	Two criteria are applied to determine whether a test that claims to measure intelligence really does so. Any test of a stable attribute must demonstrate *reliability*; that is, it must be repeatable. The issue of *validity* is addressed in the question, "Does the test measure what it is supposed to measure?" If IQ scores differ dramatically among different tests, then the validity of the test must be challenged.

Learning Objective 9.2
Identify factors that influence individual and group differences in IQ.

1. What is the evidence for genetic influences on IQ differences?	Genes are an important source of individual differences in IQ. *Proponents* of the Bell Curve argue that environmental factors known to be important for intelligence do not vary appreciably between European Americans and African Americans. They also maintain that intervention programs to increase the intelligence of African American children have largely failed. Environmental differences, therefore, are not the cause. *Critics* of this viewpoint suggest that a number of additional issues must be considered. For one thing, race is largely a social construction. Furthermore, many African Americans and European Americans have mixed ancestry in varying degrees, and African American children who are adopted into European American homes tend to have higher IQs.
2. What is the evidence that home environment influences IQ?	One difference between the environment of African American and European American children is the *socioeconomic status* (SES) of the family. In the United States, African American children are disproportionately more likely to be living in poverty, producing a well-documented effect on intelligence scores. Researchers suggest that children with difficult early environments are most likely to score lower on IQs tests and have problems in intellectual adaptation. The quality of the child's early environment relates to various aspects of a child's later intelligence.
3. How does cultural bias in testing work to influence IQ scores?	A primary issue is the *administration* of the tests. Tests contain factual questions, a type of knowledge typically observed in European American parent-child interactions from an early age. African American children are rarely asked these kinds of questions, however; adults and children engage in a more egalitarian exchange of story-telling. As a result, African American children may be uncomfortable in the traditional testing setting. In addition, it has been argued that many test items are conceptualized unfairly in favor of the majority culture's perspective, especially the vocabulary items.
4. What is stereotype threat, and how does it influence IQ scores?	*Stereotype threat* occurs when a member of a group is asked to perform a task for which the prevailing view is that this group is different. This stereotype and its related anxiety then interfere with performance. The stereotype threat effect has been well documented with students of varying ages from young children to adults. When minority students were told that a test of verbal ability provided an accurate assessment of their intelligence, their performance on the test decreased significantly compared to the minority students who were told that the test did not reflect their intelligence.

1. Describe the evolutionary approach to intelligence.	According to the *evolutionary model*, intelligence is the ability to adapt to the environment. Many of the basic survival problems that our minds are designed to solve are the problems our hunter-gatherer ancestors faced generation after generation. Evolutionary psychologists believe that humans evolved a neuropsychological system especially adapted to solving these ancient problems. This system is organized into specialized cognitive systems dedicated to solving problems related to human survival and reproduction.
2. Define Sternberg's triarchic theory of intelligence.	Sternberg describes three overlapping components of intelligence: (1) *analytical*, (2) *creative*, and (3) *practical*. Intelligence in this framework requires balancing one's interests and the requirements of one's community or culture to achieve success. Analytical intelligence (componential) includes abstract thinking and logical reasoning, verbal and mathematical skills, knowledge acquisition skills, and metacognitive skills. Creative intelligence (experiential) includes creativity and divergent thinking, ability to deal with novelty, ability to invent solutions to problems, and automaticity of skill performance. Practical intelligence (contextual) includes the ability to adapt to situations, select options, shape environments, and application of knowledge to the real world.
3. What are the multiple intelligences identified in Gardner's model?	Gardner posits *eight distinctive intelligences*, collectively defined as the ability to solve problems or fashion products that are important in a particular cultural setting or community. The eight intelligences are (1) linguistic—ability to use language to achieve goals; (2) logical-mathematical—ability to analyze problems logically; (3) musical—appreciation and skill in the composition and performance of music; (4) bodily-kinesthetic—ability to use one's body to solve problems or fashion products; (5) spatial—ability to perceive spatial relationships; (6) naturalist—ability to recognize and classify flora and fauna; (7) interpersonal—ability to understand the desires and intentions of other people and work effectively with others; and (8) intrapersonal—capacity to understand oneself and use this understanding to direct one's life effectively.

4. What relation does creativity have to traditional conceptions of intelligence?	*Creativity* involves the ability to generate novel outcomes that are valued in some context. Contemporary theories of creativity stress the confluence of multiple contributions that must work together to make creativity possible. The necessary cognitive resources include an aptitude for divergent thinking, knowledge in the specific problem domain, and an ability to evaluate the adequacy of the ideas one generates. Cognitive factors must be combined with the ability to tolerate ambiguity and a willingness to take risks. Cognitive abilities always develop and are expressed within an environmental context, and some children experience more supportive contexts than do others.
5. What is giftedness?	By one definition, *gifted children* are simply those who score at the top of the IQ range. However, high-IQ children may represent only one form of giftedness. They are gifted in the kinds of abilities that are stressed on IQ tests and in school. Researchers suggest that "global giftedness" is the exception rather than the rule. More typical is exceptional performance in just one domain of development.

Learning Objective 9.4
Evaluate different aspects of the schooling experience and how these affect cognitive development.

1. Identify cognitive effects of schooling that have been found by researchers.	Some aspects of children's cognitive development are less strongly and consistently affected by schooling than others. The kinds of knowledge Piaget studied, for example, are relatively unaffected. Most studies report no clear qualitative differences between schooled children and unschooled children. In mastering concepts such as conservation, however, formal experiences and methods of reasoning used in science and math education facilitate the development of formal operations. Otherwise, *schooling* can affect memory, the development and use of mnemonic strategies, and classification of objects. Schooling also affects how children think about words and use language, as schooled children are more likely to think in terms of general categories and abstract relations. The development of literacy combined with verbal teaching promotes abstract, reflective styles of thinking, and reading exposure is strongly linked to cognitive development. Amount of schooling also appears to be important in the development of specific kinds of intelligence.

2. How do teacher expectations, class and school size, school transition, and school effectiveness affect cognitive outcomes for children?

One of the greatest challenges *teachers* face is treating everyone equally and fairly. Children who are well-behaved get more praise and encouragement from teachers, whereas more difficult students typically experience more criticism. Teachers often have more positive expectations for students they perceive to be higher SES and higher ability. Teachers also tend to have different achievement expectations for boys and girls. Students who perceive their teachers as supportive and caring are more motivated to engage in academic work than students who see their teachers as unsupportive and uncaring.

In the United States students in *small classes* of about 13 to 17 score higher in reading and math than those in classes of 22 to 25 or larger. The beneficial effects are even more pronounced for students from at-risk groups. Researchers have found that student body size affects a number of educational outcomes. Dropout rates are lower in smaller schools. Larger schools may have an advantage of more resources and activities overall, but this may be offset by the greater competition for these resources.

School transitions are a stressful time for children. Adjustments to new adult authority figures, physical environments, schedules, peers, and academic expectations add to the stress. Children who enter school with some preschool or day care experience tend to score higher on school readiness tests and have higher levels of reading readiness and academic performance. With each school transition, academic performance, self-esteem, motivation, and perception of academic competence tend to decline.

School effectiveness is difficult to define and study. In general, effective schools are comfortable places to learn where education is actively pursued. Students in effective schools are helped to feel they are part of the school through opportunities to participate in school-related activities, as well as chances to have a voice in decisions concerning the school. It is important for the school and teacher to find an appropriate match between the students they have and the teaching methods they use.

3. Define and describe the evidence for and against the effectiveness of tracking, single-gender classrooms, and mainstreaming.

Ability grouping, or tracking, is designed to decrease the heterogeneity that teachers must work with in the classroom. Students are assigned to particular classrooms based on some measure of ability, usually intelligence. In early school years, grouping is most likely to be at the within-class level (e.g., reading groups). By middle school and high school, grouping is more often at the between-class level (college bound versus vocational). Supporters of ability grouping argue that the practice permits teachers to devise and deliver a curriculum that more closely meets the needs of all the students in the group. Some forms of ability grouping have been shown to work well for some students. Critics argue that students who are tracked receive a poorer educational environment, can be stigmatized, and demonstrate lower levels of academic performance.

Another issue in the grouping of students is whether to place *boys and girls* in different classrooms for certain academic subjects, such as math and science. Girls' confidence in their ability to do math and their perception of math as an appropriate subject for girls decline in middle school. Females tend to underperform in these academic subjects and choose not to pursue higher-level math and science classes and careers. Research on the effectiveness of single-sex classes is mixed.

In *mainstreaming*, or inclusion, students with learning disabilities are placed in regular classrooms for all or part of the school day. In general, when students with special needs are mainstreamed, they demonstrate higher academic performance, better attitudes toward school, better social skills, increased interaction with peers, and better preparation for post-school experiences. However, the effectiveness of mainstreaming depends on the severity of the disability, the support services available to the student and classroom teacher, and the attitude of the teacher.

4. How do motivation to achieve, self-efficacy, and intrinsic versus extrinsic motivation affect schooling outcomes for children?

The *attributions* that a student makes can affect his or her future motivation to achieve. For example, students who credit their success to internal, controllable factors, such as effort, are more likely to have higher self-esteem and increased motivation than those who use external factors such as luck. Similarly, students who continue to focus on learning goals tend to perform better in school than those who switch to performance goals. In contrast, students who are concerned with performance—getting good grades and pleasing others—are less likely to develop an adaptive pattern of self-regulated learning and performance.

Self-efficacy (Bandura) is an individual's beliefs about his or her performance capabilities in a particular domain. Self-efficacy includes judgments about one's ability to accomplish certain goals or tasks through actions and confidence in one's cognitive skills in academic siutations. Students with high levels of self-efficacy are more likely to commit cognitively to learning the material. They are also more likely to try to achieve, set more challenging goals, and to succeed.

Intrinsic motivation involves the internal motivation to do something for its own sake. Extrinsic motivation involves doing something in order to obtain some external reward. Intrinsic motivation is associated with better school outcomes, such as persistence and performance. Students tend to be less intrinsically motivated as they progress through the school years, especially after a school transition.

Learning Objective 9.5

Identify the ways in which children's cultural and socioeconomic backgrounds might affect the schooling experience.

1. Describe the ways in which a student's ethnic or socioeconomic background might be related to the quality of his or her schooling experience.

Children's school environment may not match the values and behavioral patterns with which children are familiar. Educational outcomes associated with *ethnicity* are tied to differences in socioeconomic status and group differences in attitudes toward education. Nationally, minority students are overrepresented in remedial and special education programs, Asian American students are more likely to take higher level math and science courses in high school, and Asian American and European American students are more likely to be enrolled in college preparatory programs. Thus, some minority children continue to experience educational segregation. Also, individuals from lower *SES* backgrounds have less educational achievement, fewer economic resources, and a lower standing in the community. Children from lower social class families are more likely to demonstrate lower levels of school achievement, have poorer attitudes toward school, and fail to graduate than children from middle- and high-income families.

2. What evidence have researchers found regarding the effectiveness of compensatory preschool programs, such as the Abecedarian Project or Head Start?

Compensatory education programs are designed to compensate for a disadvantage in preparation for school that children from low-income families are expected to have. The Abecedarian Project is a successful intervention effort that was launched in the 1960s. Children were enrolled as infants and remained in the center until age 5. This experience had an immediate effect on IQ, and by preschool the average IQ difference between treatment and control was 17 points. The greatest gains were shown by children for whom intervention began early and extended late. The best known compensatory education program is the federally funded Head Start program. Head Start now serves children from birth to age 5 and their families and has served more than 22 million children since 1965. Children who participate in Head Start demonstrate higher levels of school readiness. While the cognitive benefits of Head Start programs begin to fade when children enter school, they are less likely to be placed in special education classes, to repeat a grade, and to drop out of high school than low-income children who did not attend a compensatory program.

3. Why do children from Asian countries such as China, Japan and Taiwan, outperform U.S. children on tests of math achievement?

Research findings suggest that schools are not the sole explanation; the family environment also contributes. Maternal interviews in the Stevenson study revealed cross-cultural differences in beliefs and practices that contribute to the superior performance of Asian students. Asian parents are more likely to believe that all children have the *potential to succeed* and that they can master any academic challenge if they work hard enough. As a result, Asian parents are more likely to help children with homework and to emphasize the importance of education as part of a student's obligation to family and community. American mothers were more satisfied with their children's performance and schooling than Asian mothers were and also gave higher evaluations of their children's cognitive and academic abilities. This pattern suggests why many American mothers fail to nurture optimal academic performance in their children.

Language *and* Communication

(Ellen B. Senisi/The Image Works)

"Padma's 12-month-old daughter, Manat, sat in the tub, playing happily. She cooed and laughed as her mother bathed her. Even though she could not "talk" yet, she communicated with her through sounds, gestures, and body language. Then Padma heard the word "baby." She turned around to see who was talking but there was no one else there. She realized it must have come from her daughter. Padma called her husband, Rajeem, and they listened to their daughter say "baby" over and over. It was an exciting day.

As a parent there are many first moments that stand out, but few rival the first words that your child speaks. There are also the challenges that accompany what seems like 100 questions in an hour coming from your 4-year-old. You will wonder how many times a single person can ask, "Why?" Then there is the seemingly sudden change to monosyllabic answers when you ask, "How was your day?" and you receive the standard middle-school answer of "Fine" or "All right."

In addition to its immediate glories and subsequent challenges, language is a mirror for parents, teachers, and childcare providers into the world of the child's thoughts, feelings, and desires. In this chapter we will explore the development of language from the child's first nonverbal attempts at communication to the beginnings of sentences and the learning of literacy. How do children master the particular language to which they are exposed? What contexts can aid or hinder children as they learn to communicate with the world around them? ■

Components of Language

Learning Objective 10.1

Define language and major components of language, including phonology, semantics, grammar, and pragmatics.

Language is a complex and dynamic system of conventional symbols that is used for thought and communication. A *symbol* is something that represents something else. For example, icons of a stylized man and woman are widely recognized symbols for public restrooms. Words also are symbols—they are sounds that represent specific meanings within a language. *Das brot, le pain,* and *bread* are symbols representing different types of flour-based baked goods in different countries. Thus symbols can be sounds such as those you hear when a word is spoken, or see when the word is written, or understand from gestures such as those used in American Sign Language (ASL).

All human languages are generative; that is, there is no limit to the number of meaningful sentences that can be created using a finite set of symbols and rules. Human languages also follow organizational rules of sound (*phonology*), form (*morphology*), order (*syntax*), meaning (*semantics*), structure (*grammar*), and function (*pragmatics*). The communication of messages can be understood broadly as a combination of form, content, and context. That is, particular symbols (sounds, words, letters, gestures, images) are presented in a particular way that will communicate a particular meaning to listeners or observers, who will use the message in a particular way in a particular social context. A simple social exchange—such as a prospective buyer asking a seller, "How much are the tickets?"—is actually a complex interplay of symbols with form, content, and context.

Sounds and Words

Without attached meaning, speech is only meaningless strings of sounds. A **phoneme** is the smallest unit of sound that can signal a difference in meaning. The sounds represented by *d* and *m* are phonemes, for example, signaling a difference in meaning between the sound sequences *dad* and *mad*. **Phonology** is the study of how sounds are made and combined to produce speech. Without thinking you can listen to someone speak a language or dialect you know and comprehend the complicated sequence of sounds the speaker is producing. If you do not know a language or a particular variant of a language, however, you cannot decipher a string of speech sounds, no matter how often or how carefully they are repeated.

In addition to discriminating and comprehending the individual sounds in language, a child must learn that these sounds combine to produce words with meaning. **Semantics** is the system of rules that determines how underlying concepts are expressed in words or word combinations. For example, *girl* means both female and young. In some contexts it can have a derogatory meaning, referring to a young girl's subordinate status. How does the meaning of *girl* change if you add sounds to it that represent other units of meaning, such as *y* or *ish*? What does it mean to say "my girl"? Children demonstrate an enormous capacity to soak up vocabulary and rapidly develop a large body of words, or *lexicon*.

Sentences and Communication

As children develop their lexicons, they begin to combine and modify words to communicate different meanings. And as they practice communicating, they learn **grammar**, the rules that determine the structure of language. Grammar includes *morphology* and *syntax*. *Morphology* is the structure of words and how change in parts of words alters their meaning. Parts of words function as grammatical markers that indicate tense, case, person, active and passive voice, or number. For example, English morphology includes the word structures that differentiate past from present (*waited* from *waits*) and singular from plural (*dog* from *dogs*). A *morpheme* is the smallest grammatical unit that possesses meaning.

Syntax specifies the rules that determine the structure of sentences, especially the order of words. For example, word order in English, Chinese, French, Russian, and other languages is SVO (subject-verb-object, as in "Jan ran home"), whereas Turkish, Japanese, Korean, Persian, and other languages are SOV (subject-object-verb, as in "Jan home ran"). To use language effectively, children need to learn morphology and syntax as well as words and their meanings.

In addition, the use of language to convey and receive meaning is more than just producing the correct sounds in an acceptable sequence. Children must learn to take turns in conversation, to stay on the current topic, and to understand how gestures and context can influence the meaning of what is being said. These rules for using language within the communicative context are called **pragmatics**. Children grow in their ability to carry on an interesting and informative conversation as they acquire a richer vocabulary and understand how to participate effectively in the communication process.

Phoneme
The smallest linguistic unit of sound that can signal a difference in meaning.

Phonology
Study of speech sounds that examines the rules governing the structure and sequence of speech sounds.

Semantics
System of rules that determines how underlying concepts are expressed in words or word combinations.

Grammar
System of rules that determines the structure of language including morphology and syntax.

Syntax
Aspect of grammar that specifies the rules that determine word order in sentences.

Pragmatics
Sets of rules related to language use within the communicative or social context.

This interaction, though nonverbal, is a form of symbolic communication. It also is linguistic, as it is rule-driven. Gestures can have the characteristics of type, form, sequence, meaning, structure or grammar, and function in the context of interaction. Do children learn systems such as ASL in the same way as they learn verbal language? (© Ellen B. Senisi)

Test Your Mastery...

Learning Objective 10.1: *Define language and major components of language, including phonology, semantics, grammar, and pragmatics.*

1. How is language defined as a means of symbolic communication?
2. What components of language do children learn?
3. What roles do phonology and semantics play in symbolic communication?
4. What roles do grammar and pragmatics play in symbolic communication?

Theories of Language Development

"Mine," 2-year-old Willa says, grabbing a toy. "I gots it." How ever did this young child learn to use a possessive pronoun and a complete sentence using first-person singular in reference to herself as the subject, a verb (however incorrect) meaning possession, and an object consisting of an indefinite third-person pronoun that she knows substitutes for the name of the toy? The question of how children learn language is one of the most challenging and fascinating topics in the study of development. There have been four major theoretical approaches to language development: the learning approach, the so-called nativist approach, the cognitive developmental approach, and the sociocultural approach. Today, most researchers acknowledge that all four of these approaches contribute to our understanding of language development in children.

Learning Approach

Learning Objective 10.2

Compare and contrast four major theories of language development.

The dominant theoretical approach to language development prior to the 1960s was the **learning approach**, which contends simply that language learning is based on experience. According to behavioral psychologist B. F. Skinner (1957), children learn language just as they learn any other skill or behavior, through operant conditioning. Skinner maintained that there is nothing unique or special about language. Children utter sounds at random, and caregivers reinforce the sounds that most resemble adult speech sounds through their attention, smiles, and verbal comments. Children then are more likely to repeat these sounds. Sounds that are not part of the child's native language are not reinforced, and the child gradually stops making them. Social-learning theory predicts that

Learning approach

Explanation of language learning, which contends that language learning is based on experience and emphasizes Skinner's operant conditioning principles.

children will imitate the sounds they hear older children and adults make. The sounds they produce are then selectively reinforced as words. This happens, for example, when a child says, "Hi" in response to a caregiver's greeting, and the caregiver responds with verbal praise and smiles.

The learning approach explains language development only in the context of operant conditioning, however. It cannot explain how children can produce novel combinations of words to form new sentences. That is, there are just too many word combinations for children to acquire them all exclusively through imitation and reinforcement. Children also produce word usages that are not reinforced. A preschool-age child may insist that "tooken" is a real word, for example, as in "She tooken the clothes to her room." According to learning theory, the use of "tooken" would be extinguished and replaced with "taken" through imitation and reinforcement. However, as many caregivers will attest, children produce and persist in novel and imaginative ways of saying things that they have never heard. Although reinforcement, observation, and imitation contribute to language development, they cannot fully explain it. Instead of learning specific sentences, young children appear to adopt a series of language rules that they learn to apply.

Nativist Approach

The first important challenge to Skinner's learning theory explanation of language development came from Noam Chomsky, a linguist at the Massachusetts Institute of Technology (MIT), around 1960. While Skinner's approach emphasized the role of the environment in language learning, the **nativist approach** proposed by Chomsky emphasized the interaction of inborn processes and biological mechanisms with environmental influences. Chomsky's followers believe that language acquisition must have a strong biological basis, because young children acquire language easily and rapidly (Chomsky, 1959, 1972; Lenneberg, 1967; Pinker, 1994). Chomsky (1957, 1972) proposed that the human brain has an innate capacity for acquiring language. Evidence for the inborn tendency to acquire language is found in the universality of human language abilities; in the regularity of the production of sounds, even among deaf children; and in the invariant sequences of language development, regardless of the specific language (Bloom, 1998; Volterra et al., 2005).

Chomsky's original model described language in terms of two types of processes. A language's *surface structure* consists of the rules governing the way that words and phrases can be arranged, which can vary considerably from one language to another. The *deep structure* of language, in contrast, refers to the inborn rules humans possess that underlie all language systems and guide the transformation of ideas into sentences. Specific vocabulary is part of the surface structure, for example, while the concepts that all languages express are part of the deep structure.

Chomsky argued that languages share a "universal grammar" represented in the deep structure. Language acquisition, therefore, requires a speech-analyzing mechanism, which Chomsky called the **language acquisition device (LAD)**. The LAD preprograms children's brains to analyze the language they hear and to figure out its rules. This process follows a developmental sequence, but according to Chomsky at least some of the basics of language are preprogrammed into the human organism. For example, nouns, verbs, and adjectives are universal in all languages; thus, the mental processes for discovering the rules that govern nouns, verbs, and adjectives are products of human evolution.

In any language, infinite word combinations are governed by a finite number of rules, and children learn these rules without merely imitating examples of them and without being told explicitly what they are. Children require only exposure to speech to develop a grammar and trigger explosive language development. Once children grasp the structural rules, or grammar, of the language, they can understand and produce an infinite array of sentences. In addition, according to the model, neural mechanisms for analyzing and processing speech

Questions for Thought and Discussion
What are some other examples of errors that reveal children's applications of language rules?

Nativist approach
Explanation of language development, proposed by Chomsky, that emphasizes innate mechanisms separate from cognitive processes.

Language acquisition device (LAD)
Chomsky's proposed brain mechanism for analyzing speech input; the mechanism that allows young children to acquire quickly the language to which they are exposed.

have evolved specifically for language acquisition and are concerned with the abstract structure of speech, not with its meaning or content. This means that language acquisition should place few demands on the child's cognitive abilities, making highly sophisticated language learning possible in young children.

Although the nativist approach had a major impact on how language development is viewed, researchers have had limited success in specifying the universal grammar that Chomsky believed underlies human languages. The innateness of grammatical knowledge has also been questioned. Challengers have asked why it takes children so long to apply grammatical rules successfully after they begin to use their innate ability to analyze language. The continuous and gradual improvement of language use may indicate that more learning and discovery are involved in language acquisition than nativist theory assumes.

Cognitive-Developmental Approach

Questions for Thought
and Discussion
If language has a strong biological basis, how did there come to be so many different languages? Do you think there will be more or fewer languages in the future? Why?

The *cognitive-developmental approach* to language focuses on the cognitive contributions to language acquisition. In nativist theory, language acquisition is somewhat separate from cognitive abilities because it is a product of innate mechanisms. In contrast, cognitive theorists assume that language is a by-product of cognitive development and that even very young children have a great deal of knowledge about the world that they use to help them learn language. For example, even before having words for objects or their qualities, children may classify them cognitively as "hard" or "soft" or "things that do (or do not) break when dropped or thrown." Thus, researchers suggest that children do not simply acquire a set of abstract linguistic rules. Rather, they acquire language forms that they can "map onto" cognitive concepts they already possess. Cognitive theories emphasize the learner's active role in the process rather than the hardware of the learning system.

The cognitive approach emphasizes the link between language learning and the child's developing understanding of concepts and relationships. As children mature cognitively, they are able to advance in language development as well. Evidence for this view comes from the progressive, stage-like, development of speech, shown in Table 10.1.

Researchers have debated whether language precedes thought or whether thought precedes language. Piaget (1976) argued that children must understand concepts before they can use words to describe the concepts. Therefore, children learn words in order to describe classes or categories they have already created. For example, children can learn the word "ball" because they already understand the characteristics that distinguish balls from other round things, such as apples. Also, children may need a concept of object permanence before they can begin using disappearance words, such as "all-gone" (Gopnik & Meltzoff, 1987).

Other theorists, however, have suggested that language can precede thought. Children can create cognitive categories in order to understand things that are labeled by words (Clark, 1983). For example, when children hear the word *ball* they may try to understand it by searching for characteristics that will enable them to classify balls separately from other round things in their environment that are not called *ball*.

Today, most theorists favor an interactionist view, in which language and thought are mutually reinforcing. In the early states of language development, concepts often precede words, whereas as the child matures language may increasingly influence thought. One major implication of the role of cognitive processes in language development is that caregivers need to recognize that the child's rate of language learning is tied closely to their cognitive development. This means that the child's ability to benefit from experience and feedback is limited as well as enabled by cognitive maturational factors, not just by their age. Therefore, it is important to take the child's cognitive level into account when making decisions about the learning environment that will most benefit the child.

Sociocultural Approach

Questions for Thought
and Discussion
What are some other examples of the two-way interaction between language and thought?

The *sociocultural approach* to language development, influenced by L. S. Vygotsky, stresses the cognitive abilities children bring to the task of language learning in conjunction with

TABLE 10.1 Stages in Learning to Speak and to Use Language—Birth to Age 4	
AGE	**SPEECH/LANGUAGE DEVELOPMENT**
0–3 Months	Sounds to communicate pleasure or pain Smiling and looking Crying and cooing Differentiation of cries to indicate source of discontent
4–6 Months	Vocal play using gurgling Speech-like babbling using sounds made with the lips (bilabials) Intentional use of gestures to communicate Use of sounds and gestures to prompt caretakers into action
7–12 Months	Increasing use of consonant-vowel combinations in babbling Use of speech sounds to attract and hold caretaker attention First words (e.g., "Ma Ma," "Bye Bye," "No") Repetition of sounds, syllables, and words (echolalia) First responding to verbal requests and questions
1–2 years	Increasing use of words and improvement in producing words clearly Asking of two-word questions First sentences (e.g., "Go night-night," "read story") Identification of objects and body parts when prompted Enjoyment of repetition of singing and rhyming games
2–3 years	Explosion in vocabulary Asking for the names for things Enjoyment of verbal concepts such as opposites Production of understandable two- to four-word sentences Use of exclamations ("Oh, no!" "Wow!")
3–4 Years	Speech normally fluent and clear Use of complete sentences of four or more words Narration of past events and experiences Observation of rules of conversation Enjoyment in telling invented stories First attempts to communicate grammatically

the cultural context, which affects early social interactions and therefore may differentially promote cognitive mastery. Vygotsky believed that thought becomes verbal and speech becomes rational at around age 2, when the sociocultural context becomes especially important. The history of the society in which a child is reared and the child's personal history are crucial determinants of the way the child will think. Language becomes a crucial tool for determining how the child will learn how to think, because modes of thought are transmitted to the child by means of words (Murray, 1993). The attitudes, beliefs, values, education, income, occupations, caregiving styles, and expectations of people interacting with the child will profoundly affect the child's learning.

The sociocultural approach emphasizes that the basis for language acquisition and use is social interaction (MacWhinney & Bates, 1993; Ninio & Snow, 1999). Sociocultural theorists maintain that the child's primary motivation for acquiring language is social interaction—to communicate ideas and to be understood. Thus the emphasis is on the *pragmatics* of language. Children are viewed as inherently social creatures, with language as their primary means of entering into and affecting their social world.

Language acquisition has preverbal origins. Social interaction begins at birth, and children therefore have many opportunities to learn about the nature of language well before their first words appear. Jerome Bruner (1983, 1999) has proposed that parents and other caregivers typically provide many structured opportunities for infants to learn language.

Language acquisition support system (LASS)
Bruner's proposed process by which parents assist children in learning language.

The LASS approach states that young children learn language through structured play experiences called formats. How do the hand gestures that go with a song such as "Itsy Bitsy Spider" aid this child's learning? (© Laura Dwight/Corbis Images)

Q**uestions for Thought and Discussion**
What formats or structured interactions did you enjoy as a child? What new formats might you present to a child in your care?

These opportunities make up what Bruner (in deliberate contrast to Chomsky's LAD) refers to as **LASS**, or the **language acquisition support system**.

The central component of LASS is the *format*, which consists of structured social interactions, or routines, that commonly take place between infants and their mothers. Familiar formats include looking at books together, playing naming games ("Where's your nose?" "Where's your mouth?"), action games (peekaboo and hide-and-seek), and singing songs with gestures ("The Itsy Bitsy Spider"). Such activities appear to be common across a range of cultures. Variations of the peekaboo game, for example, were found in all 17 cultural settings examined by Fernald and O'Neill (1993).

The format allows a child to learn specific language elements within a very restricted context—usually simply by memorizing words and their corresponding actions. Gradually, the parent may change the formats so that they include more elements or require a greater contribution from the child. In this way, additional language can be learned, and previously acquired responses can be applied in new ways. Within these formatted interactions, the parent also provides other sorts of scaffolding for language acquisition, such as simplifying speech, using repetition, and correcting the child's inaccurate or incomplete statements (Snow, Perlmann, & Nathan, 1987). Both children and adults bring a rich set of social-cognitive abilities to the interactions that underlie language learning (Snow, 1999; Tomasello, 2001).

As you can see, language acquisition cannot be explained by environmental input alone, which typically is inconsistent. For example, although parents reinforce their children for speaking in grammatically correct ways, they also sometimes smile at and praise their children for sentences that are ungrammatical (Brown, 1973). At the same time, children clearly do not learn in a social vacuum (Snow & Beals, 2001). Parents differ significantly in their language input styles. One result is that children raised in more economically disadvantaged homes are more likely to demonstrate vocabulary deficits compared to children from middle-income families (Farkas & Beron, 2004). This observation informs intervention programs that aim to aid literacy development. According to the intervention approach, language development in children depends on the quantity and quality of encouragement they receive, in and out of school. Opportunities to engage in active conversations, to answer questions, and to hear complex language being spoken are especially important for language development.

The sociocultural approach to language learning emphasizes the importance of the social context. Children interact verbally with adults and with each other, as well as with both print and images in a richly elaborated and socially rewarding context. Children learn language as needed to know and interact with their world. (Bananastock/Jupiter Images)

Learning Objective 10.2: *Compare and contrast four major theories of language development.*

1. What are the four major theories of language development?
2. In the behavioral view, through what processes do children learn language?
3. In the nativist view, how does biology take precedence over the environment in language learning?
4. How do the cognitive-developmental approach and the sociocultural approach differ in their explanations of language acquisition?

Preverbal Communication in Infancy

Children develop the ability to communicate meanings before they acquire any language. Children discriminate and attend to sounds and become aware of units of sound (*phonemes*). Phonemic awareness lets them distinguish like and unlike sounds, and they repeat sounds and syllables through verbal play. Children also utilize a variety of sounds and gestures to convey their wants, desires, moods, and feelings to their caregivers. Thus, communication is well established before the first word appears.

Learning Objective 10.3
Trace the developments in the first year of life that establish the preverbal basis for language learning.

Speech Perception

The ability to discriminate and attend to sounds is called *speech perception,* which enables listeners to divide speech, a continuous series of sound, into segments. As listeners divide the stream of sounds into syllables, words, and sentences, they also are attending to other characteristics of speech, such as rising and falling intonations, pauses between words and phrases, and the placement of stress. A foreign language may sound strange to you, for example, but you readily identify it as a language.

Infants perceive and distinguish *phonemes*—the smallest sound unit that signals a change in meaning. For example, 7-month-old infants can detect the difference between the consonant sounds in *pa* and *ma*. Young children also identify variants of sounds that combine to convey the same meaning. For example, the *a* in the word *car* sounds different when spoken by someone from Mississippi or from Brooklyn. But the variants fall within a class of sounds that convey the same meaning, with the result that an English-speaking listener would recognize both words as meaning "automobile."

When a sound variation changes from one phoneme category to another, a different meaning is produced (e.g., *car* to *core*). The sound difference between these two words may actually be smaller than between regional pronunciations of *car*. But *car* and *core* are perceived as different words with different meanings, because in English they represent different phonemes.

The English language uses about 45 phonemes: vowels such as *a, e,* and *u;* consonants such as *t, p,* and *k;* and blends of two consonants such as *th.* The number of phonemes varies across languages. According to Pinker (1994), the range extends from as few as 11 in Polynesian to as many as 141 in Khoisan (a "Bushman" language of southern Africa). You very likely would not recognize many of the phoneme distinctions in Khoisan, just as English has phonemic differences that speakers of Polynesian would not recognize as meaningful.

From an early age, infants show evidence of **categorical speech perception**—the ability to discriminate when two sounds represent two different phonemes as well as when they are in the same phonemic category. This ability to make "same-different" distinctions has been investigated in babies as young as 1 month old (Aslin, Jusczyk, & Pisoni, 1998; Jusczyk, 1997). The presence of categorical speech perception in infants so young suggests that this is an innate ability universal among children (Trehub, 1976).

Experience also plays an important role in early speech perception. Two-day-old infants already show a preference for hearing their own language (Moon, Cooer, & Fifer, 1993). And the more babies are exposed to a language, the sharper their phonemic discriminations become (Kuhl, 2001). Conversely, lack of exposure may dull or delay these

Categorical speech perception
The ability to detect differences in speech sounds that correspond to differences in meaning; the ability to discriminate phonemic boundaries.

abilities. For example, infants of Japanese-speaking parents usually are not exposed to the phonemic contrast between the sounds *r* and *l*, which are not differentiated in the Japanese language. Japanese speakers later attempting to learn English struggle to discriminate these sounds and also have difficulty pronouncing them (Miyawaki et al., 1975). Studies show that Japanese infants have no difficulty distinguishing *r* and *l*, however, suggesting that they gradually lose this ability through lack of exposure and use as they learn their native language (Eimas, 1975). Research identifies the timing of this loss as occurring between 7 and 11 months of age (Kuhl, 2001). This pattern has been demonstrated across a number of sound contrasts in a variety of languages. By the end of the first year, babies lose much of their ability to discriminate sound contrasts that are not present in the language to which they are exposed (Best, 1995; Werker & Tees, 1999).

Early Sounds and Gestures

Children develop language in stages tied to maturation. Before they develop language, infants use prelinguistic vocalizations that do not represent objects and events. Prelinguistic vocalizations include crying, cooing, and babbling, for example. During the first month, the primary sound that infants make is *crying*, which is produced by blowing air through the vocal tract and does not have distinct well-formed sounds. Crying serves as a means of communication to the parents or other caretakers. During the second month, infants begin *cooing*, using their tongues and extended vowel sounds to articulate. Coos appear to express feelings of pleasure or positive excitement. Infants tend not to coo when they are in discomfort.

Babbling
The first vocalizing that sounds like human speech.

Between 6 and 9 months of age infants begin **babbling**, the first vocalizing that sounds like human speech. All children appear to babble, even deaf children (Oller, 2000). In babbling, infants typically combine consonants and vowels, such as *ba* and *ga*, and repeat sound combinations such as the highly reinforcing "mama" and "dada." Despite similarities to real words, however, these first combinations are chance occurrences.

Although crying, cooing, and babbling are innate behaviors, they can be modified by experience (Volterra et al., 2004). Cooing increases when parents talk to the infant, smile at them, or coo in response to the child's prelinguistic sounds. Modeling and imitation may also play a role in babbling. At first, babbling is the same around the world. Soon, however, the language spoken by parents and other adults begins to have an influence. Adults often repeat the syllables uttered by their infants and combine syllables instead of using single syllable utterances. For example, adults often say "dadada" instead of "da." Repetition may aid the infant in discriminating these sounds from others and also may encourage the imitation of these sounds.

Echolalia
The automatic repetition of sounds, syllables, or words.

Around 10 to 12 months, infants tend to demonstrate **echolalia**, the automatic repetition of sounds, syllables, or words. These repetitions often sound like the child is carrying on a one-sided conversation. Then around 11 to 13 months many children speak their first word, an important milestone for parents. A range of approximately 8 to 18 months is considered normal (Bates, Thal, & Janowsky, 1992). Many children experience a gradual and continuous process of producing words as they build on their preverbal skills (Bates et al., 1987). For example, children appear to learn more quickly those words that involve sounds and syllables they are already using, suggesting that early speech builds on babbling skills (Schwartz et al., 1987).

Nonverbal aspects of communication, such as the use of gestures, are important preverbal skills (McNeill, 1992). All infants use gestures combined with other nonverbal responses to perform many of the functions of vocal language (Adamson, 1995). Before children can use words to ask for a toy, they indicate the object of their desire by reaching for it and looking back and forth between the object and a person. Infants first use gestures to communicate requests at about 8 to 10 months of age (Bruner, Roy, & Ratnre, 1982). Children also use gestures to symbolize objects or events (Acredelo et al., 1999), for example, holding out the arms to signify an airplane or raising the arms to indicate that an object is "big."

Research shows that when first words appear, children who do more gesturing also tend to use more words (Blake, 2000). In addition, teaching infants and toddlers a simple system of symbolic gestures (*signs*) has been shown to facilitate the mastery of spoken language (Goodwyn, Acredolo, & Brown, 2000). For example, repeatedly bringing the hand to the mouth may be a sign for "I want something to eat." It appears that infants seek to communicate through whatever means they have available, and initially they have more control over their hand movements than their speech production apparatus. The use of sign language does not slow or confuse the child's language development. Rather, gestures appear to be a natural early step on the road to effective communication.

Learning Objective 10.3: *Trace the developments in the first year of life that establish the preverbal basis for language learning.*

1. How does speech perception develop?
2. What preverbal speech sounds do infants use?
3. What is the role of nonverbal communication in language acquisition?

✔ *Test Your Mastery...*

Semantics: First Words and Vocabulary

The process of learning to speak involves learning not only the words to be used but also how to combine them to form coherent sentences that convey meaning. This semantic awareness is based on learning the system of rules governing the meaning or content of both individual words and word combinations.

Young children start off using a word to convey a range of possible meanings. One-year-old Kaylie called all nonbanana fruits "balls." Bananas were "bas" (as in the sheep sound). This became especially interesting when her grandfather became "ba-ba." He was now multiple bananas. In another case, a well-known investigator of children's language recounts how her 18-month-old daughter began to use the word *hi* to mean that some sort of cloth was covering her hands or feet (for example, her hands were inside a shirt or a blanket was laid across her feet). The child apparently had come to make this unlikely association as a result of her mother's showing her a finger puppet that nodded its head and said *hi*. Rather than interpreting the word as a greeting, the child had instead assumed it meant that the mother's fingers were covered by a cloth (Bowerman, 1976).

These anecdotes illustrate two points about semantic development. The first is that, although young children are amazingly adept at acquiring word meanings, the process of learning the meaning of words is not as simple a task as it might appear, especially around the age of 2. Not only do children hear adults speaking thousands of different words (one estimate is that 2-year-olds hear 20,000 to 40,000 words per day! [Chapman et al., 1992]), but they also must learn that words are of different types, such as those that stand for objects (*hat* and *Mommy*), actions (*eat* and *talk*), and states (*happy* and *red*).

Second, the more psychologists study word learning, the more they come to realize how closely this process is tied to children's concept development. Names of things (such as "cat") usually label an entire class of things (the family's pet kitten, a stuffed toy, Garfield), as do names of actions, states, and so on. Furthermore, the same thing can be called by many different names (for example, animal, horse, stallion, and Champ). This means that the kinds of words a child is capable of learning and using will change as they mature cognitively. How does the young child know what class of things to attach a new word to? And how does this learning develop? These questions are important in understanding language acquisition (Bloom, 1993).

Early Vocabulary Development

The acquisition of words and their meanings typically begins in the baby's second year. Infants' first words usually name things that are familiar or important to them, such as food, toys, and family members. These words also serve a variety of pragmatic functions,

Learning Objective 10.4
Describe the processes by which children first use words and develop vocabulary.

This child is using posturing and gesturing in nonverbal communication. She can achieve multiple purposes without the use of language by directing her parent's attention, for example, and by signifying her request to be given an object of desire. Research shows that children's use of gestures facilitates their acquisition of language. What are some examples of gestures used in association with speech to aid children's language learning? (© LWA-Dann Tardif/Corbis)

Children's first words often label common objects and parts of the body. Soon children begin to label everything in sight, with rapid accumulation of vocabulary. About how many words does a child learn in the first two years? (© Elizabeth Crews)

Q**uestions for Thought and Discussion**
What were your first words or those of a child you know?

Referential style
Style of early language learning in which children place more emphasis on language as a tool for labeling things; vocabularies tend to be richer in words that refer to objects.

including requesting things, asking questions, and complaining. Most children speak their first word at about 11–13 months, and then proceed to develop a vocabulary of about 8,000 to 14,000 words by the age of school entry. An average adult has a spoken vocabulary of about 40,000 to 60,000 words.

The acquisition of new words is initially slow in most children. They typically take 3 to 4 months to learn their first 10 to 30 words (de Villiers & de Villiers, 1999). By about 18 months, children may be able to produce about 50 words and to understand 100 or more (Benedict, 1979), and by age 2 they may understand as many as 900 words and speak 200 of them clearly. Semantic development proceeds faster for comprehension than for production; that is, children typically understand what words mean before they begin to say the words, and they comprehend more words than they speak (Rescorla, 1981). This pattern continues into adulthood.

After 18 months, often the number of new words learned grows rapidly (Reznick & Goldfield, 1992). The child may go from about 50 words to more than 300 in a few months. This rapid growth has been termed *the naming explosion*. Of the vast majority of the new words, in English speakers about 75 percent are nouns (Goldfield & Reznick, 1990). Children often maintain this rapid rate of vocabulary acquisition throughout the preschool period, when they can effortlessly acquire an average of nine new words per day (Rice, 1989). According to some estimates, the average 6-year-old learns as many as 22 new words per day. There normally are great individual differences in the size and range of vocabulary development. However, children who enter elementary school with a small vocabulary are at greater risk for reading failure than their schoolmates who possess larger vocabularies (Adams, 1990).

What sorts of words are present in children's early lexicons? Table 10.2 provides some typical examples. For most children, nouns (especially object words) predominate, and nouns remain more common than verbs and action words throughout language development. This is true for most languages, in which nouns are understood earlier, spoken earlier and more frequently, and even pronounced better (Camarata & Leonard, 1986; Gentner, 1982; Nelson, Hampson, & Shaw, 1993).

Individual and Cultural Differences

A major change in the study of language development in recent years has been the realization that there are important individual differences in how children go about the task of learning language (Goldfield & Snow, 2001; Pine, Lieven, & Rowland, 1997; Shore, 1995). One difference is in the size of children's early vocabularies. Another is in the rate at which children learn words. In one study (Fenson et al., 1994), the number of words that children produced at 16 months ranged from 0 to 347, an astonishing difference. At 25 months the range was from 7 to 668 words. Comparable differences were found for children's comprehension of words.

There also are differences in the types of words found in children's early lexicons (McCabe, 1989; Nelson, 1973). Some children, who display what is called a **referential style**,

TABLE 10.2 First Words in the Lexicons of Five Children	
CHILD	**WORDS**
Jane	Daddy, Mommy, Daniel, girl, ball, cracker, cookie, that, school, bye
Leslie	Daddy, ball, duck, doggie, kitty, donkey, bottle, apple, thank you, bowwow
Lisa	Daddy, Mommy, Daisy, puppy, ball, see, hi, yes, where
Paul	Daddy, Mommy, Papa, boat, truck, map, this, sit, umm
Mark	Ma, dog, milk, water, car, here, bye-bye, no

SOURCE: Adapted from K. Nelson. (1973). Structure and strategy in learning to talk. *Monographs of the Society for Research in Child Development, 38* (Serial No. 149). Copyright 1973 by the Society for Research in Child Development, Inc., University of Michigan, Center for Human Growth & Development.

follow the common nouns-first mode, described earlier. These children produce a large proportion of nouns, especially object names, and use language primarily to label things. Other children display an **expressive style**, which includes a larger mix of word types, more "stock phrases" (such as "What's that?" "Lemmee see"), and a greater emphasis on language as a pragmatic tool for expressing needs and for interacting socially. The two styles reflect different culturally defined ideas about the purpose of language, with referential children focusing on its informational function and expressive children more concerned with interpersonal uses. On average (and with many exceptions), referential children are more likely to be girls and firstborns, and to come from middle- or upper-class homes.

What could produce these two different patterns of early language acquisition? One influential model stresses the contexts within which language learning takes place and the interplay of biological and environmental factors (Nelson, 1985; Shore, 1995). This contextual explanation stresses the *transactional* nature of development. Certain characteristics that differentiate children with the two styles—such as gender and birth order—affect the type of language environment to which the children are exposed. For example, in some samples parents have been found to speak to their infant daughters more than to their infant sons, using more complex language and more supportive forms of speech (Gleason & Ely, 2002; Leaper, Anderson, & Sanders, 1998). This practice may reflect a greater expectation of verbal interaction from daughters. Similarly, parents tend to spend more time with firstborns than with later-born children, and speech to firstborns includes more learning devices and greater attention to the development of language abilities (Jones & Adamson, 1987). These different environments in turn may lead children to develop either a referential or an expressive pattern of vocabulary acquisition.

Children's First Words and Word Combinations

Psychologists have learned a great deal about children's semantic development by examining the kinds of errors they make. Word learning typically begins with a child's attaching a specific label to a specific object, such as learning that the pet terrier is a "doggie." Next, the child begins to extend that label to other examples of the same object, using "doggie" to label the dogs he or she sees in books or on TV. These extensions demonstrate that the child is forming an object category called *doggie* that is defined by certain features.

Expressive style
Style of early language learning in which children place more emphasis on language as a tool for talking about feelings and needs; vocabularies tend to be richer in social formulas and pronouns.

Unlike English-speaking children, these Korean children will learn action words—verbs—earlier and faster than they will learn object categories (nouns). This difference, noted for other language speakers as well, is cultural in origin. Korean parents use a higher proportion of verbs in their speech, and they tend to use verbs to give their young children clues to the meaning of words they do not yet know. (Purestock/photolibrary)

Overextensions
Early language error in which children use labels they already know for things whose names they do not yet know.

Most children, however, make errors when attempting to extend these early labels and may also use "doggie" to describe a cat, a fox, a rabbit, and so on. Such **overextensions** are common in the early stages of semantic development in many languages (Rescorla, 1980). Children's initial categories may be too broad, or children may not yet understand the specific features that define the concept. However, overextensions are more common in production than in comprehension. For example, a child who calls an apple a ball might, if shown an apple, a ball, and a pear, be able to *point* to the apple (Naigles & Gelman, 1995; Thomson & Chapman, 1977).

If overextensions do not always reflect a lack of understanding, then maybe they reflect a lack of vocabulary. If she does not know the word "apple," a child may use the name of a similar object, such as "ball," simply to achieve the communication function of talking about the object. Such errors may also result from momentary memory problems: a failure to retrieve the correct label under the time pressure of generating a word. Evidence suggests that all of these factors contribute to overextension errors (Behrend, 1988; Gershkoff-Stowe, 2001; Hoek, Ingram, & Gibson, 1986).

Underextensions
Early language error in which children fail to apply labels they know to things for which the labels are appropriate.

Another type of semantic error involves applying labels too narrowly rather than too broadly. A child who has learned to apply the label "bird" to robins and wrens, for example, may not apply it to seagulls or ostriches. Such **underextensions** are less common in production than are overextensions. Underextensions are frequent, however, in comprehension. For example, when shown a group of different animals, young children often do not point to the ostrich in response to the instruction "show me a bird," but instead select a nonmember of the category, such as a butterfly (Kay & Anglin, 1982).

Both overextensions and underextensions are indications that children, for a while, use words differently than do adults. *Coining* occurs when children create new words that are not part of the adult language. Children sometimes name an unfamiliar object by overextending the label of a similar object. For example, a child who sees a lawn rake for the first time may call it a fork, even though the child understands that the label is not correct. But another strategy that children use to deal with gaps in their vocabulary is simply to coin a new name for the object. The first-time viewer of a rake might instead call it a grass-comb. Here are more examples, taken from reports by Clark (1995) and Becker (1994): "fix-man" for mechanic, "many talls" for height, "nose-beard" for mustache. Word coining is common in young children, gradually decreasing as their lexicon grows (Windsor, 1993). Such inventiveness illustrates the tremendous creativity that children bring to the task of language learning.

Holophrase
A single word used to express a larger idea; common during second year of life.

Children's one-word utterances also have a special communicative function. You might expect that when children produce one-word utterances they are simply labeling objects in their environment—thus "ball" means "that's a ball," "Daddy" means "that's Daddy," and so forth. Although this is sometimes true, at other times young children use one word to express an entire sentence or idea. Thus, "ball" might mean "I want the ball," or "the ball hit me," or any of several other meanings. Such words are **holophrases**, meaning single-word sentences (Dore, 1985). Making sense of holophrases depends on the context and any other cues that point to the child's intended meaning.

Children begin to combine two or more words as they approach age 2. As with holophrases, they may sometimes use the same phrase to express different meanings, depending on its function. For example, "Daddy hat" may represent a name for an article of clothing, a demand for the father to take off his hat, or perhaps a simple description of the father's act of putting on his hat (Bloom, 1973). Again, contextual cues are important in interpreting what the child is trying to communicate.

Some functions of early word combinations are given in Table 10.3. Studies in various cultures reveal that the same dozen or so functions appear first in a variety of languages (Bowerman, 1975; Brown, 1973). Children everywhere need to be able to name, request, reject, and describe things, for example. This cross-language commonality also suggests that children's attempts to communicate during this period are influenced by their level of cognitive development. Because cognitive development is similar across different cultures, so too are aspects of early language.

TABLE 10.3 Some Functions of First Word Combinations

Function	Purpose	Examples
Nomination	Naming, labeling, or identifying	Bunny, cup, Leah
Negation	Rejecting or denying	No nap. Not wet.
Nonexistence	Describing something that is gone or finished	No milk. All-gone story.
Recurrence	Describing or demanding the repetition of something	More pat-a-cake. More juice.
Entity—attribute	Describing a characteristic of an object	Ball big. Bear little.
Possessor—possession	Naming two nouns, the first possessing the second	Mommy sock. Baby bottle.
Agent—action	Describing a person performing an action	Daddy jump.
Action—object	Describing an action being performed on an object	Hit ball. Bring book.
Agent—patient	Describing a person doing something to another person	Oscar Bert.
Action—patient Mommy.	Describing an action being performed on a person	Feed baby. Hug
Entity—location	Naming a noun and its place	Ball up. Baby chair.

Learning the Meaning of Words

Explanations have been proposed for *semantic development*—the processes by which children come to learn the meaning of words. In one process, children use grammatical cues to help them determine the meanings of certain words. That is, they use their knowledge of the meaning of utterances to help figure out grammatical structure. For example, knowing what "Give me that" means would help in determining what "Give me a hug" means. In this process, learning of grammar builds on prior knowledge of semantics.

The reverse is also possible. Once children have mastered some aspects of grammar, they can use this knowledge to make sense of new words. For example, imagine that a child who does not yet know the word *spatula* hears the sentence, "Give me the spatula." From its grammatical placement in the sentence, the child can infer that *spatula* is a noun and probably the name of an object. If the spatula is the only nearby object whose name she does not know, then the child is in position to pair the name and object correctly, thus learning a new word. If the child already knows the word *spatula* and hears the sentence, "Give me the gray spatula," then he or she can infer that *gray* must be an adjective. If a contrast is set up between adjectives (e.g., "Give me the gray spatula, not the white one"), then the child may learn a new color term.

There are many grammatical cues to word meaning in any language, based on syntax—the grammatical order of words in a sentence (Bloom, 1996, 2000). Table 10.4 summarizes some important examples of syntactic cues to word meaning in English, using a nonsense word for the new word that the child is attempting to decipher.

Experimental studies in which children have a chance to learn a new word based on the grammatical cues available in a sentence demonstrate that children can exploit a variety of grammatical cues—including all those listed in the table—to narrow down the possible meanings of new words (Bloom, 1996; Gleitman & Gillette, 1999; Hall, Lee, & Belanger, 2001). This process is called **syntactic bootstrapping**, because the child's prior knowledge of grammar underlies, or "bootstraps," the learning of semantics.

Most children have learned thousands of words by the time they start school, and most of these are words they learned on their own through exposure. Children's word learning can occur rapidly. Children as young as 3 can sometimes acquire the meaning of

Syntactic bootstrapping
Proposed mechanism of semantic development in which children use syntactic cues to infer the meanings of words.

TABLE 10.4 Syntactic Cues to Word Meaning

Syntactic Cues	Usual Type of Meaning	Examples
"This is a (the) *fep*."	Individual members of a (noun) category	cat, forest
"These are *fep*."	Multiple members of a category	cats, forests
"This is *fep*."	Specific individual	Fido, John
"This is some *fep*."	Nonindividuated stuff	water, sand
"John *feps*."	Action (verb) with one participant	sleeps, stands
"John *feps* Bill."	Action with two participants	pushes,
kisses		
"This thing is *feppy*."	Property (adjective)	big, good
"The dog is *fep* the table."	Spatial relationship	on, under

SOURCE: Adapted from P. Bloom. (2000). *How Children Learn the Meanings of Words* (p. 205). Cambridge, MA: MIT Press. Copyright 2000 by the MIT Press. Reprinted by permission.

a word after only one exposure to it, a process called *fast-mapping* (Carey, 1977; Heibeck & Markman, 1987). Preschoolers can use fast-mapping when watching TV programs or videos. They rapidly acquire new words used by the story characters (Rice & Woodsmall, 1988). In this way, for example, Natalie learned the meaning of words such as "backpack," "map," "Swiper," and "explorer" before the age of 3.

Learning the meaning of words is a difficult mental task. When a child sees a cat and hears Mommy say, "There's kitty," how does the child know that *kitty* refers to the cat rather than, say, its ears, its color, or its behavior? How does the child know that the reference is to the cat alone, not to the cat on the sofa or the cat with its toy? In any situation in which a child hears a new word, there are many logically possible meanings for that word. How does the child avoid the many false interpretations and find the one correct meaning?

Some psychologists suggest that when children hear a new word, they automatically make certain assumptions (usually accurate) regarding what it probably means. These assumptions act as *constraints*, ruling out many false possibilities and thus permitting

Through fast-mapping, children can sometimes acquire the meaning of a new word after only a brief exposure. What new words might these children acquire solely on the basis of this visit to the museum? (Thinkstock/Jupiter Images)

children to acquire the meanings of new words quickly (Markman, 1991; Waxman, 1990). What are some of these constraints that govern early word learning (Hollich, Hirsh-Pasek, & Golinkoff, 2000; Woodward & Markman, 1998)?

According to **lexical contrast theory** (Clark, 1987, 1993), when children hear an unfamiliar word, they automatically assume the new word has a meaning different from that of any word they already know. This assumption motivates them to learn exactly what the new word means. A second part of this theory holds that when a choice must be made, children always replace their current meanings with those they think are more conventional or correct. For example, a child who has been assuming that foxes are called "dogs" will replace the incorrect label upon learning that "fox" has its own separate meaning. This principle of lexical contrast helps the child better approximate adult understandings.

The **principle of mutual exclusivity** (Markman, 1989, 1991) states simply that children believe that objects can have only one name. When children hear a new word, they tend to assign it to an unknown object rather than an object for which they already have a label. This strategy limits the possible choices when a child is trying to attach meaning to a new word. Suppose, for example, that a toddler knows "kitty" but not "doggie." If an adult points toward a cat and a dog and says, "See the doggie," the child would assume that "doggie" cannot refer to the cat, because the child already knows a name for cats. The child then is more likely to attach the label to the correct referent.

Research supports the view that young children adhere to the principle of mutual exclusivity and that doing so helps them learn new words (Merriman, 1997; Woodward & Markman, 1998). The strategy also causes difficulty, temporarily, when children discover the hierarchical nature of word categories. A dog, for instance, can also be called doggie, puppy, hound, animal, mammal, a beagle, Frodo, and so forth. Two-year-olds sometimes balk at referring to their pet pooches by more than one name, which would be expected if children believe that objects have only one label (Gelman, Wilcox, & Clark, 1989; Mervis, 1987).

Although semantic constraints account well for some aspects of early word learning, not all psychologists are convinced that the idea is helpful (Bloom, 1998; Deak, 2000; Nelson, 1988; Tomasello & Merriman, 1995). Are children's word-learning biases really consistent and strong, for example? Are constraints present from the start of word learning, or do they emerge only later? Assuming they exist, are constraints innate or derived from experience? How much early word learning can constraints account for? Whatever position one takes on constraints, there is still the matter of how children use the speech around them to figure out exactly what words mean.

Roles of Parents and Children in Semantic Learning

Part of the answer to the puzzle of how children learn semantics lies in parents' roles in the process and the social-cognitive interaction between children and their parents. Parents are sensitive to their child's interest and attention, for example. Studies of parent-child interaction indicate that parents talk most about objects or events to which their children are already paying attention (Harris, Jones, & Grant, 1983) and that children are most successful at learning new words when parents have accurately judged their focus of attention (Tomasello & Farrar, 1986). In the "kitty" example, the mother would not have said "kitty" if the child's attention had been focused on the cat's ears, the nearby dog, or any of the other features of the situation. Because the parent labels what the child is attending to, the child is in a good position to link the label with its referent.

At the same time, children play an active role in this process. Even very young children are surprisingly good at discerning the *parent's* focus. By paying attention to what the parent attends to, the child learns to link what the parent says with the correct object or event (Baldwin, 1995; Baldwin & Moses, 2001). In addition, not all language learning is parent directed. Children initiate and direct many of the conversations from which they learn words and other aspects of language (Bloom et al., 1996).

Lexical contrast theory
Theory of semantic development holding that (1) children automatically assume that a new word has a meaning different from that of any other word they know and (2) children always choose word meanings that are generally accepted over more individualized meanings.

Principle of mutual exclusivity
Proposed principle of semantic development stating that children assume that an object can have only one name.

Thus, experience is necessary to complete the process of semantic development. Children can learn words only if their social environment provides them with sufficient information about what different words mean. Parents and other caregivers help their children in this task through *modeling*. Although children sometimes coin their own words, much of what they say reflects what they have heard, and children's early words tend to be those that are used most frequently by their parents. The more speech that parents address to young children, the faster children's early vocabularies grow (Hoff & Naigles, 2002; Snow, 1999). It is important, therefore, for children to have exposure to adult language and discourse. Good contexts for this exposure are mealtimes, drives in the car, shared errands, and playtimes.

Parents' modeling of words can occur either incidentally in the normal course of conversation or explicitly in an attempt to teach the child a new word. In what has been called the Original Word Game (Brown, 1958a), parents sometimes show a young child an object, tell the child its name, encourage the child to say the name, and then provide feedback as to the accuracy of the child's responses (Goddard, Durkin, & Rutter, 1985). Older children learn labels in a less structured fashion in everyday conversations between parent and child (Howe, 1981). Whether or not intended as teaching, such conversations can be a rich source of information about word meaning.

Learning Objective 10.4: *Describe the processes by which children first use words and develop vocabulary.*

1. How does children's cognitive development affect their semantic awareness?
2. What are the characteristics of children's first words, and at what rate do children acquire vocabulary?
3. What are some individual and cultural differences in children's language learning?
4. What can we learn about language learning from the semantic errors that children make?
5. By what processes do children learn the meanings of words?
6. What roles do parents and children themselves play in semantic development?

Grammar: Communicating in Sentences

After children acquire their first words, the next important linguistic milestone is putting two words together to convey one idea. Generally, this occurs between 18 and 24 months of age, or about 8 to 12 months after infants say their first word. There is a large age range, however, and most children who begin talking late catch up eventually. A child's first sentences usually employ speech that consists of a few essential words. For example, children may say "Me come" to indicate that you are to wait for them. Or children may hold out their hands and say, "Me ball," meaning, "Throw me the ball." What developmental steps are involved in the acquisition of grammar?

All languages are structured and follow certain rules called *grammar*. Many rules seem arbitrary, such as the English rule that adding *-ed* to a verb puts it in the past tense. But as nativist theorists suggest, some rules must have a biological basis because children naturally learn them very easily. Children learn grammar before they reach school age, when they are explicitly taught the structure of their language. Yet few adults can describe the rules of grammar in any detail and often make grammatical mistakes in their use of language!

The grammar of many languages involves three principal devices: word order, inflections, and intonation. Word order, or *syntax*, is significant in English, as in the sentence pairs "John hit the car" versus "The car hit John" or "I did pay" versus "Did I pay?" *Inflections* are endings added to words that modify their meanings. Common inflections include plural endings (videos), possessive endings (Jennifer's), and past-tense endings (worked). Some languages rely heavily on inflections to communicate meaning. In Turkish, for

✔ *Test Your Mastery...*

Learning Objective 10.5
Describe the processes by which children learn to communicate grammatically.

BOX 10.1 Conversations with a Speech-Language Pathologist

My name is Randi Chudnow Loeb. I'm 44 and I live with my husband and children in Sudbury, Massachusetts. I am a pediatric speech/language pathologist (SLP). In my current job I am a founder and co-director of Children's Speech and Language Services in Lexington, Massachusetts. In this private practice I evaluate and treat children ages 2 to18 who have a communication disorder of some kind. I see children individually, in dyads, and in small groups. My partner and I also supervise a staff of six speech-language pathologists. We do all of the intake work; that is, we talk to parents who are interested in having their children seen, read the relevant reports, talk to other professionals involved, and determine which clinician in our practice is best suited to work with the child.

I found this career path with the help of a career counselor. I had taken some time off after college to travel and think through my options. The career counselor gave me an aptitude test that pointed me in the direction of speech/language pathology. As part of the exploration process, I also interviewed several SLPs and spent the day with one. Once I decided to pursue a career in speech and language, I spent two and a half years getting a graduate degree in Communication Disorders at Emerson College, Boston. After that, I completed one clinical fellowship year in a hospital setting, to finish my training. My areas of expertise are autism spectrum disorders, nonverbal learning disability, and language-based learning disabilities.

Communications disorders include fluency disorders (affecting the flow and rhythm of speech), articulation disorders (inaccurate speech sound production due to faulty placement, timing, direction, pressure, speed, or integration of movements of the lips, tongue, velum, or pharynx), voice disorders (difficulty with vocal pitch, volume, or quality of speech), and language disorders. Language disorders may involve difficulty with social communication, word retrieval, understanding of language, language processing, language formulation and expression, and auditory processing. Speech and language disabilities have diverse causes, such as neurological problems, hearing loss, stroke, cerebral palsy, cognitive disability, or brain injury.

I get great satisfaction from my work, particularly when I feel like I am making a difference in the child's life and in the life of his or her family. It's very gratifying to watch a child master a skill and experience that light bulb switching on. These epiphanies are small moments that represent big triumphs. For example, once I went to our waiting room to get one of my kids for therapy. He said, whining, "Randi, I don't want to come with you. I don't want to work with you today." I must confess that I was a little bit hurt, even after 20 years of learning not to take these things personally. I asked him, "Why?" He paused and then responded, "Because the Penguin game is too hard." I was elated. This child with autism had reached a milestone. He had answered my Why-question with a relevant, logical reason. Together we celebrated—by *not* playing the Penguin game!

---

example, a verb can have up to 3,000 different inflections! *Intonation* can also alter meaning. A rising tone at the end of a sentence, for example, transforms a statement into a question. Children learn to recognize the changes in inflection that signals a parent's impatience with their rate of compliance to a request. Some other languages make greater use of intonation. In Chinese, for example, an end vowel spoken with a rising or falling tone can change the meaning of the word the vowel is in.

What would this cartoon caption say if it were grammatical? Researchers note that children's early sentences reflect the word order used in their language. That is, no child ever generates sentences by randomly combining words in all possible ways. Research shows that children are sensitive to word order even before they start producing sentences (© 1997 by NEA, Inc.)

Development of Grammar

As with semantic development, children's grammatical errors often reveal a great deal about their rule-learning processes. Errors are one of the best gauges of a child's current language level. Parents, childcare providers, educators, and others can use these errors to understand where children are developmentally in their language acquisition.

Most children begin to combine words into the first simple sentences at around 18 months. Precursors to sentence formation may be evident prior to this time, such as the meanings and pragmatic functions that children convey with their one-word holophrases. These one-word utterances, such as "Moon," meaning "I see the moon in the sky," may be combined with other one-word sentences, such as "Moon!" "See!" "Sky!" and then combined as "Moon see," "Sky moon," and the like. Many children begin to produce strings of single-word utterances, using one word to call attention to an object and then a second word to comment on the object, as in "Milk! Hot!" Multiple one-word utterances can be distinguished from the two-word sentences that will soon appear by the longer pause that occurs between the words (Branigan, 1979). The child seems to be on the brink of producing sentences.

By 18 to 24 months, infants string two words together into sentences, such as "Mommy sit" and "All-gone cookie." As children mature, their facility with the rule systems that govern language increases. They produce more sophisticated utterances, for example, using plural forms (cookies) and possessives (Mommy's). Researchers have discovered that children's first word combinations are not random but follow certain patterns. The first syntactic rules that many children develop seem to be built around individual base words that are combined with any number of other words. "All-gone," for example is a common base word with which the child can say, "All-gone doggie," "All-gone milk," and "All-gone Mommy" (Maratsos, 1983). Another child might develop rules around other words, for example, an object plus "on" as in "Hat on," "Shoe on," and so on, or "I" plus a verb or adjective, such as "I big," "I fall," "I make" (Bloom, Lightbrown, & Hood, 1975; Braine, 1976). Children show great variety of items and combinations in their initial sentences. As always, individual differences arise within the general patterns of development.

The next phase of grammatical development is **telegraphic speech**. As the child's sentences grow from two to three or four words and beyond, they become truncated, resembling telegram messages. Sentences focus on high-content words and omit unnecessary function words, such as *a*, *the*, and *of*, and also certain parts of words, such as endings and unstressed syllables. Thus, a child who hears "Ryan, we're going to the parade" may repeat "Ryan go 'rade." The telegraphic nature of children's speech diminishes over time, as children expand their utterances and add more and more elements of the adult language (Bowerman, 1982).

The rules children learn as they acquire grammar is evident in the mistakes they make. A good example is inflections. English uses inflectional rules to change a verb to the past tense (*-ed* is added, as in talk*ed* and play*ed*) and to change a noun from singular to plural (*-s* or *-es* is added, as in cup*s* and dish*es*). English also contains a large number of irregular forms, however, that are exceptions to these rules—the verb forms *go-went*, *eat-ate*, and *see-saw*, for example, and the noun forms *mouse-mice*, *foot-feet*, and *sheep-sheep*.

At first, children may produce a correct irregular form if it is part of a chunk of adult speech that they are copying. Thus, even 2-year-olds may be heard to say, "ate" or "feet." But as they begin to learn the inflectional rules of the language, children tend toward **overregularization**; that is, they sometimes apply the regular rules to nouns and verbs that have irregular forms. The child will be heard to say, "I knowed her" or "Look at the mans." Usage is inconsistent, so that a child may at one time say, "I ate" and at another time say, "I eated." Eventually, the correct and incorrect forms may merge, and the child may produce words such as "wented" and "mices." Thus, the application of rules, even when overextended, represents progress in language development. Children then need to learn the exceptions to the rules. Many of the exceptions will be learned by school age, but the process is not complete for quite some time.

Telegraphic speech
Speech from which unnecessary function words (e.g., *in, the, with*) are omitted; common during early language learning.

Overregularization
An early structural language error in which children apply inflectional rules to irregular forms (e.g., adding *-ed* to *say*).

Often when children overgeneralize a rule, the immediate temptation is to correct them. However, it is important to remember that this is a normal developmental phenomenon that occurs in only a minority of the cases in which children cope with irregular words. One extensive survey, based on more than 11,000 past tense utterances, reported overregularizations in only about 4 percent of the possible instances (Marcus et al., 1992). The recommendation is to model the correct use of the rule in conversation without overtly correcting the child. For example, if a child says, "I goed to the store," when telling you about his or her day, you could respond, "Yes, you went to the store today." This process gives the child more exposure to the correct application of the rule, encourages vocal expression, and does not focus on rule usage.

Interestingly, overregularizations are not limited to grammar. Similar phenomena are evident in phonological and semantic development. An example from semantics is the child who creates "yesternight" in analogy with "yesterday" (Maratsos, 1976). Nor are overregularizations limited to children who are learning English. Indeed, such errors may be more striking in more highly inflected languages that offer more opportunity for children to go astray (Slobin, 1985b).

Mechanisms of Grammar Acquisition

One process by which children acquire grammar is **semantic bootstrapping**—using word meanings to help learn about grammar (Bowerman, 1988; Pinker, 1987). This is theopposite of syntactic bootstrapping, discussed earlier: the idea that children use their knowledge of grammar to help learn about semantics. An example of semantic bootstrapping is using prior knowledge of noun and pronoun categories to determine the grammatical forms surrounding them in a sentence. In the sentence, "These pencils belong in this box," the child may know that *this* means one of something, while *these* means more than one. This knowledge may then help the child to form the plural and singular forms of the nouns in the sentence correctly (*pencils; box*). Children use semantic bootstrapping and syntactic bootstrapping reciprocally in language development.

Another process for the acquisition of grammar is children's use of innate cognitive strategies, which allow them to acquire grammatical rules rapidly. An example is children's development of rules for inflections of words, such as forming plurals. In an early study, Jean Berko (1958) asked children questions about imaginary entities, using nonsense names to rule out the possibility that children simply imitate what they hear adults say. In tests like the one shown in Figure 10.1, children were able to supply the correct inflectional ending, showing that they possessed a rule that they could apply to unfamiliar words.

After studying more than 40 languages, Slobin (1982, 1985a) identified more than 40 cognitive strategies he called *operating principles*, which describe how to learn the rules of any language. These operating principles comprise what Slobin refers to as the child's **language-making capacity (LMC).** Among the most important principles are (1) "Pay attention to the order of words," (2) "Avoid exceptions," and (3) "Pay attention to the ends of words." Another operating principle, important in many languages, is (4) "Pay attention to context." These strategies fit with what is known about children's language learning. For example, children focus increasingly on syntax (word order) in speech, and they use overregularization to avoid exceptions and apply inflectional rules across the board.

That children pay attention to word endings is shown in another interesting study (Daneman & Case, 1981). The study involved teaching children artificial language rules and examining which rules children acquired most easily. First, the children were taught the names of two new animals—"wugs" and "fips" (see Figure 10.2). Next, they learned two new verbs—"pum" (meaning to toss an animal vertically into the air) and "bem" (meaning to toss an animal horizontally across the table surface). Finally, the children were taught two variations of these verbs. If the animal's actions were observed by one other animal, the verbs describing them were "pumabo" or "bemabo"; if the animal's actions were observed by several other animals, the verbs became "akipum" or "akibem." The researchers

Semantic bootstrapping
Proposed mechanism of grammatical development in which children use semantic cues to infer aspects of grammar.

Questions for Thought
and Discussion
What is an example of language learning in which a child might use both semantic bootstrapping and syntactic bootstrapping at the same time?

Language-making capacity (LMC)
Slobin's proposed set of strategies or learning principles that underlie the acquisition of language.

FIGURE 10.1 Adding endings to "Wugs"

Data from this classic study showed that children's early use of inflectional endings involves the application of grammatical rules.

Source: From J. Berko. (1958). The child's learning of English morphology. *Word, 14*, 155. Reprinted by permission of Jean Berko Gleason.

This is a wug.

Now there is another one.

There are two of them.

There are two _____ .

hypothesized that if children use a strategy of paying attention to the ends of words, the verbs with a suffix (*-abo*) should be acquired more quickly than the verbs with a prefix (*aki-*). In support of Slobin's model, children learned the suffixed verbs more easily (Daneman & Case, 1981).

Another strategy children use to acquire grammar is to examine the various grammatical cues of their language, such as word order, endings, and intonation, and then choose the one they believe is most useful for learning the structure of the language. The cue they select varies from one language to another and also changes as children mature. This is called the *competition model*, because the child chooses among competing cues (Bates & MacWhinney, 1987; MacWhinney, 1987; MacWhinney & Chang, 1995).

Initially, children focus on the cue that is most *available*. In English and French, for example, children's first attempts to learn grammar involve word order. Because word order is

FIGURE 10.2 Artificial language concepts

These imaginary creatures were used in a study of children's strategies for learning grammatical rules for inflections—word prefixes and word endings.

Source: From M. Daneman and R. Case. (1981). Syntactic form, semantic complexity, and short-term memory: Influences on children's acquisition of new linguistic structures. *Developmental Psychology, 17*, 369. Copyright 1981 by the American Psychological Association. Reprinted by permission.

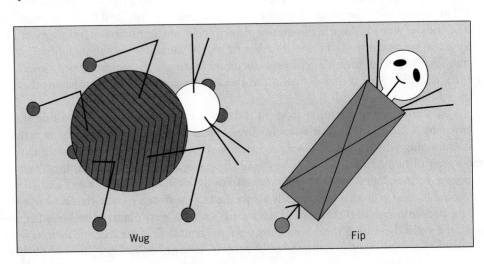

Wug   Fip

important in these languages, it is a cue that is frequently available to provide information useful for learning language rules. In contrast, in Turkish word order is less important, and children typically focus first on the inflections in the speech they hear. Later, children select the cues that are most *reliable*, meaning those that most consistently provide clues to grammatical structure. Later still, children note cues that are in *conflict* with one another and then choose the one that most often "wins out" and best reveals the language's structure. In this progression, children receive helpful input from adults in their speech environment, and that input helps the child make adaptive choices among the cues. The input is based on the pragmatics of language use. That is, children's mastery of language is motivated by the uses to which language can be put, and children use these pragmatic cues in learning language.

Recent work on the competition model using computer simulations suggests that learners cope with complexity and adjust their decisions through experience. Gradually, some connections strengthen among the shifting patterns of possible response. Some responses become more likely and others less so. This self-modifying system is an example of connectionism in the processing of information about language (see Chapter 8). An example in the domain of language is mastery of the English past tense. A computer programmed with the strategies identified in the competition model and given linguistic input shows patterns of acquisition of the past tense that are similar to those shown by children, even including a phase of overregularization errors prior to full mastery (MacWhinney & Leinbach, 1991). The computer and the child acquire not rules of grammar but patterns of response that fit the cues available to them (Klahr & MacWhinney, 1998; Marcus 2001; Pinker, 1999).

Links to Related Material
In Chapter 8, you read about connectionism as a model for cognitive development. Here, you learn how connectionist models may be useful in helping us understand language acquisition.

Environmental Contributions to Mastery of Grammar

What is the role of the environment, especially of the child's parents and other caregivers, in the mastery of grammar? How can caregivers ease the task of achieving that mastery? Research has demonstrated that both adults and children change aspects of their speech when talking to babies and toddlers (Newport, 1977; Snow & Ferguson, 1977). This is the *motherese* speaking style, which includes helpful linguistic adjustments. For example, some aspects of phonological development, such as the ability to discriminate phonemes, can be facilitated by motherese. Mothers tend to speak slowly and use short utterances, often

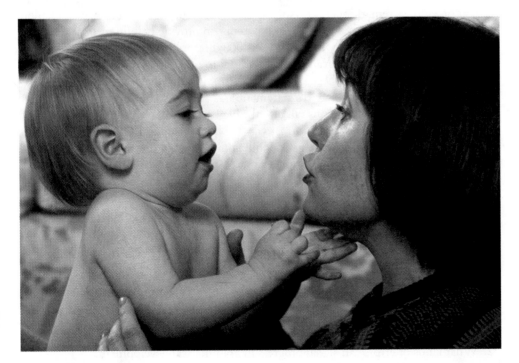

The form of speech known as motherese is one way that parents help their children master language. What are the characteristics of motherese? What other patterns characterize child-directed speech, and how do they help children in their language learning?
(© Jonathan Nourok/PhotoEdit)

three words or fewer. Usually, mothers pronounce words very clearly and with few grammatical errors. When talking about an object or situation, mothers label it frequently and use much repetition in their descriptions and comments. In addition, the focus of mothers' speech usually is on the here and now rather than on more distant or abstract events.

Fathers display many of the same speech adjustments, although they generally are less sensitive to the infant's level of linguistic development (McLaughlin et al., 1983; Ratner, 1988). Some researchers have suggested that the father's speech serves as a bridge between the fine-tuned adjustments of the mother and the complex and erratic speech of the outside world (Gleason & Weintraub, 1978; Mannle & Tomasello, 1987; Tomasello, Conti-Ramsden, & Ewert, 1990).

Adults, in general, modify their language in a similar way in a pattern of behavior called **child–directed speech.** The contributions of child-directed speech to a child's grammatical development are not clear, however (Furrow, Nelson, & Benedict, 1979; Hoff-Ginsberg, 1990; Hoff-Ginsberg & Shatz, 1982; Murray, Johnson, & Peters, 1990; Valian, 1999). While motherese has been shown to help in other areas of language development, its role in grammatical development remains to be established (Scarborough & Wyckoff, 1986; Schwartz & Camarata, 1985; Snow et al., 1987).

Other environmental contributions to learning aside from child-directed speech are modeling and feedback. As in semantic development, children imitate parental models of grammar. This imitation is not exact copying (Bloom et al., 1974; Ervin, 1964; Kuczaj, 1982; Tager-Flusberg & Calkins, 1990). Rather, the child adds something to the utterance that was just heard (*expanded imitation*); or copies it at some later time (*deferred imitation*); or copies a particular grammatical form using different words (*selective imitation*) (Snow, 1983; Whitehurst & Novak, 1973). Research suggests that these forms of imitation may be progressive in that a more advanced language structure first appears in a child's imitation of adult speech and then gradually finds its way into the child's spontaneous, original speech (Bloom, 1974; Snow & Goldfield, 1983).

Children also learn grammar through *feedback*—correction in response to utterances that are grammatically incorrect. Just as parental modeling provides evidence of correct language, feedback provides information about what is *not* correct in language. However, the role of feedback is a controversial topic in the study of language development (Bohannon et al., 1996; Morgan, Bonamo, & Travis, 1995; Valian, 1996). Parents rarely respond to their children's ungrammatical statements with simple disapproval, such as "No, you didn't say that right." Instead, parents usually give feedback about the accuracy of the content of a child's remark, such as "No, the block isn't red; it's blue" (Brown & Hanlon, 1970; Demetras, Post, & Snow, 1986). But parents do provide helpful feedback in other ways (Bohannon & Stanowicz, 1988; Moerk, 2000; Strapp, 1999).

Research has shown, for example, that adults frequently respond to children's ill-formed statements (such as, "Sheeps runned in barn, Mommy!") in one of three ways: *Expansions* involve repeating the child's statement and adding something to make it more complex ("Yes, the sheep and lambs ran into the big barn!"). *Recasts* involve restating what the child said in a different, more correct way ("Those sheep did run into that barn!"). *Clarification questions* signal that the listener did not understand the comment and that the child should attempt the communication again ("What happened? What did those sheep do?") (Demetras et al.,1986; Hirsh-Pasek et al., 1984; Penner, 1987).

Research suggests that these forms of feedback are helpful to children and that children appear to be receptive to such responses. For example, they are much more likely to imitate a correct grammatical form following a parental recast than following ordinary speech (Farrar, 1992). And there is evidence that providing children with such feedback can accelerate grammatical development (Farrar, 1990, 1992; Moerk, 1996).

Learning Objective 10.5: *Describe the processes by which children learn to communicate grammatically.*

1. What are children's first sentences like, and how do they change?
2. What kinds of errors can signal progress in grammatical development?

Questions for Thought and Discussion
Are you aware of having spoken motherese to a child? If you had not used child-directed speech, how would your communication to the child have been altered?

Child-directed speech
Simplified use of language forms and content for child listeners, also known as *motherese.*

✔ *Test Your Mastery...*

3. How do children acquire grammar through semantic bootstrapping?
4. How do we know that children use innate cognitive strategies to acquire grammar?
5. How do child-directed speech, imitation, and modeling help children learn language?
6. What kinds of feedback best help children acquire correct grammar?

Development of Pragmatics: Socially Appropriate Use of Language

A noticeable difference in the spoken language of a preschool-age child versus a school-aged child is seen in *pragmatics*—the practical knowledge of how to use language to communicate. The older children not only know more words, grammar, and syntax; they also become better conversationalists. They are more effective at using language to get people to do things they would like them to do. To accomplish this control, they must become more competent in pragmatics. When toddlers point to the refrigerator and say "Cup!" for example, they probably are not labeling the refrigerator but are asking the parent to get them a cup of juice. Pragmatics involves knowing how to begin and continue a conversation, how to ask for things, how to tell a story or joke, and how to adjust comments to a listener's perspective. Pragmatics also involves knowing how to conform to the cultural rules that govern how individuals are supposed to interact. Culture-based interaction rules cover subtle issues, for example, how far apart to stand from someone you are interacting with and whether to look into the person's eyes.

To be effective communicators, children first must learn to express their needs or desires in ways that others can understand. Babies cannot always convey their wants successfully and become frustrated by their parents' failure to understand exactly what they are requesting. This frustration is an important motivator for the child to acquire skills that will make communication more effective. At the same time, effective communication involves understanding what parents and others are saying in order to follow their directions, answer their questions, or comply with their requests. Communication, as always, is a two-way street.

The development of pragmatics is also associated with cognitive development. As children acquire perspective taking—the ability to perceive the world through the eyes of others—they advance in their abilities to make themselves understood to others. Preoperational preschool-age children assume that others will know what they want when they ask someone, "Give me that." As they mature cognitively, they understand the world from a less egocentric perspective and can state relevant details to communicate more effectively ("Please give me the cup on the table). Pragmatic skills develop rapidly between the ages of 3 and 5 as egocentric speech lessens (Beal & Flavell, 1983).

Learning Objective 10.6
Describe the means by which children learn the pragmatics of language use.

Speech Acts

Once children acquire language, they use speech to control others and to get their own way. The communication tools of the infant, however, are restricted to crying, facial expressions, and gestures (Reddy, 1999; Sachs, 2001). In one study, mothers played a turn-taking game (for example, taking turns squeezing a squeak toy) with their 1-year-old babies. After the game was well established, the mothers were instructed to stop taking turns, sit still, and remain silent. The babies reacted by behavior in ways clearly designed to communicate to the mother that it was her turn. They vocalized at her, pointed to the toy, and picked up the toy and gave it to her (Ross & Lollis, 1987).

With the acquisition of language, children add verbal responses to their repertoire of communication devices and achieve goals by directing words and phrases at other people. Such pragmatic uses of language are referred to as **speech acts** (Astington, 1988; Dore, 1976). Researchers have found that even the first words that infants utter serve pragmatic functions (Bretherton, 1988). "Mama," for example, is used both to call the mother and to

Speech acts
Speech used to perform pragmatic functions, such as requesting or complaining.

request things from her (as when the baby says "Mama" while pointing to a toy on a shelf). Later, "Mama" serves the more common purpose of naming the parent (Ninio & Snow, 1988). In the one-word period, babies begin to use relational words—those connecting several objects or events—in pragmatic ways toward multiple goals. For example, babies may use "More!" to request that an activity be continued, to describe a block being added to a pile, or to demand another cracker (McCune-Nicolich, 1981).

As their cognitive and linguistic abilities grow, children's speech acts increase in range and effectiveness. In one study, children's attempts to communicate using language doubled between 14 and 32 months of age, and the number of different types of speech acts more than tripled. In addition, the proportion of communications that could be comprehended—and therefore were more likely to be successful—rose from 47 to 94 percent (Snow et al., 1996). Children's comprehension of adults' speech acts is also important for adult and child to communicate effectively.

Discourse

Links to Related Material
In Chapter 7, you read about the cognitive-developmental phenomenon called egocentric speech. Here, you learn how children develop an understanding of socially appropriate discourse.

Speech during social interaction is called *discourse*, or social speech or conversation (Hicks, 1996; Rice, 1982). Unlike private speech, social speech is meant to be understood by a listener. As you read in Chapter 7, private speech—talking aloud with no intent to communicate—is normal and common during childhood, accounting for approximately 20 to 50 percent of what 1- to 4-year old children say (Berk, 1986).

When people have conversations, in addition to adhering to the grammatical rules of the language, they also must follow the social rules of discourse. The first of these is *turn taking*, with each participant alternating between the roles of speaker and listener. This basic rule of conversation may be learned during the preverbal period (Collis, 1985). Another conversational strategy, added around age 2, is *turnabout:* the speaker comments on what has been said while also adding a request to get the partner to respond again. The following exchange illustrates both the mother's and the child's use of turnabout:

Child: "I want to bring dolly."
Mother: "You want to bring dolly shopping? Won't she have to get dressed?"
Child: "Dolly has to put clothes on to go shopping. Help me find Dolly's dress."

Other rules of discourse are more complex, however, and are learned later. By 3 years of age, children begin to understand a range of requests for action not directly expressed as requests, such as "This room is a mess," which really means, "You need to clean up." The child learns *illocutionary intent*—what a person really means to say, even if the utterance is not completely consistent with it. When a parent says, "May I open it for you?" she or he is not really asking the child a question as much as offering help. And when a parent says, "I didn't mean to break it," he or she is doing more than describing intentions; the parent is actually apologizing to the child. Another example is the "answer obvious" rule. Statements phrased as questions are actually intended as directives, such as, "Could you hand me that pencil?" The answer is obvious in that the listener knows to hand the speaker the pencil rather than answer the question.

In these situations, how do listeners comprehend which function the speaker intends? Most often, people solve the problem by considering the context in which the remark is made (Shatz & McCloskey, 1984). Context cues would help identify a remark as a directive rather than a question, for example. The obviousness of the answer to a question is another kind of cue. These advanced discourse rules are more difficult to learn and require a higher level of cognitive development than that needed for simple turn taking. The answer-obvious rule is not apparent in children until about age 5 (Abbeduto, Davies, & Furman, 1988). And not until age 6 or 7 do children consistently use the discourse rules that one should (1) say something that relates to what the speaker has just said, (2) say something that is relevant to the topic under discussion, and (3) say something that has not already been said (Conti & Camras, 1984).

Social Referential Communication

An even more advanced conversational skill is to communicate information effectively about something that the other participant in the conversation does not know. An example is a child describing a video he or she saw to another child in such a way that the listener understands the content. This skill is called **social referential communication**—the communication that occurs when a speaker sends a message that a listener comprehends. The communication is *social* because it occurs between two people; it is *referential* because the message is in a symbolic form (the child uses language to convey the information rather than just show the video); and it is *communication* because it is understood by the listener (Whitehurst & Sonnenschein, 1985).

For children to engage in social referential communication effectively—as speakers or as listeners—they must learn a subset of important skills. In the role of speaker, the child must become aware of listener cues; that is, he or she must adjust messages to meet listeners' needs. If the listener is far away, for example, the message should be loud; if the listener is running out the door, the message should be brief; and if the listener is someone of high status (for example, a teacher), the message should be polite. Young children often fail to take into account listener cues and situational factors. A child may answer grandmother's questions on the phone by nodding the head and may even try to show her a picture from preschool. The child's ability to converse in challenging situations, such as on the phone or when he or she cannot see the listener's reactions, improves dramatically between the ages of 4 and 8.

Children sometimes adjust their speech in response to the listener's age. As mentioned previously, just as adults tend to use motherese when talking to young children, children as young as 4 also use simplified speech when speaking to toddlers or infants (Sachs & Devin, 1976; Shatz & Gelman, 1973). Adjusting to age of listener improves as children grow older. Fifth graders, for example, modify their speech more effectively when talking to younger children than do first graders (Sonnenschein, 1988). However, even older children tend to overestimate the comprehension abilities of young listeners (Miller, Hardin, & Montgomery, 2003; Montgomery, 1993).

Another useful listener cue involves *common ground*—information that is shared by both speaker and listener. If the listener knows when the speaker's birthday is, for example, then the message, "Come over on my birthday," will be sufficient. If the listener does not possess the information, however, the message will be inadequate. Kindergartners have some understanding of the common-ground principle, but this ability, too, improves with age (Ackerman & Silver, 1990; Ackerman, Szymanski, & Silver, 1990).

Perhaps the most important listener cues involve *feedback*. If the listener does not appear to understand what is being communicated, the speaker should change the message and try again. In simple situations with clear cues, even 2-year-olds show some ability to adjust their messages when a listener has misunderstood (Ferrier, Dunham, & Dunham, 2000; Shwe & Markman, 1997). In general, however, young children's sensitivity to listener feedback is limited, and they often persist with the same messages even when the listener is not understanding (Robinson, 1981).

Like speakers, listeners must be aware of context cues, including the information that has been given previously and the subject to which the information refers. In addition, when a message is uninformative or confusing, the listener must learn to recognize this fact and communicate the problem with a request for clarification. Children as young as 5 can sometimes detect a poorly constructed message or one that is missing critical information. At that age they often proceed regardless, however, whereas by age 7 the listener is more likely to seek clarification from the speaker (Ackerman, 1993).

Environmental factors play a role in the development of referential communication skills. One study found, for example, that children whose mothers provided specific feedback about the adequacy of messages developed communication skills most rapidly (Robinson, 1981). Caregivers also directly teach socially acceptable speech and social routines, such as saying, "please" and "thank you." Thus, as in the mastery of grammar, caregivers serve as

Social referential communication
Form of communication in which a speaker sends a message that a listener comprehends.

To become effective communicators, young children must acquire both speaker skills and listener skills. What rules of discourse are these children likely observing? How can we know whether their social referential communication is effective? What kinds of cues can they use to improve their comprehension? (Jennie Woodcock/Reflections/Corbis Images)

Links to Related Material
In Chapter 8, you read about children's developing theory of mind. Here, you learn more about how children's ability to understand another's state of mind influences how they use language with others.

✔ *Test Your Mastery...*

models for children as well as providing specific feedback. And as in other areas of language development, pragmatics skills also depend on the emergence of certain cognitive abilities. As children's egocentrism decreases, for example, they better appreciate how another person might receive messages. Moreover, as noted in Chapter 8, as children's theory-of-mind understanding improves, they come to realize that listeners with different cognitive capabilities (such as children versus adults) may interpret the same information differently (Chandler & Lalonde, 1996; Taylor, Cartwright, & Bowden, 1991).

Learning Objective 10.6: *Describe the means by which children learn the pragmatics of language use.*

1. What is involved in knowledge of pragmatics?
2. How do children use speech acts to communicate?
3. What strategies do children learn to apply in discourse?
4. What skills do children need for social referential communication?
5. What are some links between development in pragmatics and cognitive development?

Contexts That Influence Language Development

Children's language development is affected by a variety of contextual factors, including family characteristics, exposure to print and other media, the social and cultural setting that a child lives in, and exposure to multilingual experiences. Some environments place children at greater risk for lower levels or delays of language development, while others contribute to children's development of literacy.

Learning Objective 10.7
Discuss influences of family, technology, language, and culture on literacy and learning.

Learning Language in Diverse Family Contexts

A major aspect of the child's immediate environment is the child's parents and other primary caretakers. Adults differ in how well and how often they speak to children. As mentioned previously, however, complexity and variety in language experiences contribute to children's language development. The more words children hear spoken and explained, for example, the more words they integrate into their vocabulary (Weizman & Snow, 2001). Language experiences are dynamic rather than one way. That is, characteristics of children affect how adults communicate with them. For example, children who are more sociable are spoken to more often than shy children (Patterson & Fisher, 2000).

One factor that predicts the quality of a child's language environment is socioeconomic status, or SES. In general, children from low-income families experience significantly less oral and print language stimulation in their homes (Payne, Whitehurst, & Angell, 1994; Whitehurst & Lonigan, 1998) and in their neighborhoods (Purcell-Gates, 1996). For this reason primarily, children from lower SES families tend to have smaller vocabularies and enter school with lower levels of prereading skills and language development (Hecht et al., 2000). There also are significant differences in the quantity and quality of mother-child conversations across SES levels. Mothers from higher SES backgrounds typically provide much richer language experiences (Hoff, 2003). They ask more questions, produce longer utterances, use richer vocabulary, and actively encourage the development of language skills.

An example of the importance of family context is the at-risk status of children of single-parent teens, who also tend to come from lower SES homes. Children of teenage mothers on average score lower on measures of cognitive competence, especially language-based assessments (Luster et al., 2000). In particular, teen mothers tend to provide a less stimulating cognitive, educational, and verbal environment for the child (Culp et al., 1988; Moore et al., 1997). These risk factors seem to reflect the degree of interaction, feedback, and exposure to complex language that a child receives. Professionals interacting with families in helping contexts are alert to these risk factors and can design interventions to help children acquire the language and literacy skills they need in life. These skills developed in early childhood are excellent predictors of subsequent success in learning to read (Adams, 1990; Whitehurst & Lonigan, 1998). Unfortunately, children who start off poorly in reading tend to remain poor readers throughout their schooling and beyond (National Reading Panel, 2000; Torgesen & Burgess, 1998).

Questions for Thought and Discussion
How often did family members interact with you as a child? Were you included in conversations with adults? How do you think your family context affected your language development?

Early Experiences with Books and Oral Language

Children enter school differentially prepared to benefit from formal reading instruction and other demands school life places on them. In children without disabilities, these individual differences originate largely in early experiences in the home (Burgess, Hecht, & Lonigan, 2002). Adults in the home play an important role in oral language development. Caregivers serve as models, provide feedback, and expose children to opportunities to acquire new vocabulary. They also expose children to books and other printed matter.

In the United States, over the last 20 years many campaigns have been launched to get more people to read to their children. Reading with children is one of the most advocated early educational experiences, and research clearly shows a positive relationship between the amount of preschool reading exposure children receive and their subsequent school performance (Adams, 1990). On average, the more often a child is read to and the earlier the age of consistent shared reading experiences, the more easily a child learns to read.

Shared reading interaction provides an opportunity for exposure to more sophisticated language as well as to the formal rules associated with print. Thus, the quality of interaction with a child that occurs during shared reading is far more important than the act of reading with the child alone. In **dialogic reading**, for example, the adult asks challenging, open-ended questions about the content of a picture book rather than questions requiring a simple yes or no answer (Arnold et al., 1994; Lonigan et al., 1999). The adult follows up the child's answer with more questions, repeats and expands on the child's comments, provides praise, and encourages the child to relate the story content to his or her experiences. As a result, the child becomes the storyteller, and the adult becomes an active listener. In the process the child progressively uses more sophisticated language to communicate to the adult.

Questions for Thought and Discussion
How did you learn to read? What factors influenced your developing of prereading skills?

Dialogic reading
Technique of shared reading whereby the adult asks challenging, open-ended questions rather than questions that require a simple yes or no answer; the adult encourages the child to relate the story content to his or her experiences.

Dialogic reading practices are associated with better vocabulary and expressive language development in children, especially those from at-risk backgrounds (Whitehurst et al., 1988; Whitehurst & Lonigan, 2001). Few adults know to use this approach when reading with their child, but training programs have been very effective in teaching parents and day care providers to use dialogic reading (Huebner & Meltzoff, 2005). Adults' consistent use of this technique increased fourfold after training, and the language development of the 2- to 3-year-olds in the study increased significantly, as measured by the number of words they used and the length of utterances. The training method that appears to work best for adults with a high school education is in-person instruction supported by video demonstration (Huebner & Meltzoff, 2005). Figure 10.3 illustrates dialogic reading practices.

As you know, children who are read to more often have better prereading skills and are more prepared to benefit from formal literacy instruction provided by schools. **Emergent literacy** refers to a set of prereading skills on which the ability to read is based. These skills include important general linguistic skills, such as vocabulary acquisition, as well as alphabet knowledge and concepts about print (e.g., knowing that print is read from left to right) (Whitehurst & Lonigan, 1998).

An important emergent literacy skill is **phonological awareness**—the awareness of and ability to manipulate the sound structure of oral language (National Reading Panel, 2000; Rayner et al., 2001). Examples of phonological awareness are the ability to match sounds with symbols, to hear syllables within words, and to recognize words that rhyme. A child with phonological awareness would be able to follow the instruction, "Say bat. Now say bat without saying the /b/ sound."

Phonological awareness is considered necessary for normal reading development and is thought to be a major source of difficulty for children with reading problems (National Reading Panel, 2000; Wagner, Torgesen, & Rashotte, 1997). Children who are exposed to

Emergent literacy
Set of prereading skills that often precede actual reading, including concepts about print, phonological awareness, and alphabet knowledge.

Phonological awareness
Awareness of and ability to manipulate the sound structure of oral language.

FIGURE 10.3   Dialogic reading: an example

Father (reading from *Blueberries for Sal* by Robert McCloskey): "'Little Sal ate all of the berries she could reach from where she was sitting, then she started out to find her mother.' How many berries do you think she could reach, Aiden?"

Aiden: "Seven twenty."

Father: "That's a lot! How far can you reach from where you are sitting?"

Aiden: Reaches out with both arms to the front and sides and pretends to pick and eat blueberries.

Father: "What are you doing?"

Aiden: "I'm eating blueberries! Big ones."

Father: "Are they as good as the ones you have for breakfast sometimes?"

Aiden: Nods.

Father: "Look at this picture, Aiden. Did Little Sal save any berries in her pail?"

Aiden: "Kuplink, kuplank, kuplunk! (looks) No berries."

Father: "Good for you! You remembered the sound the berries make when Little Sal and her mother drop the berries in their pails. Now let's see how Little Sal can find her mother. 'She heard a noise from around a rock and thought, That is my mother walking along!' What happened?"

Aiden: "That's not her mother. That's the mother crow and the baby crows. Caw! Caw!"

Father: "Caw! Caw! (turning page) Ooops! Whose mother did Little Sal find?"

Aiden: "That's Little Bear's mother. Little Sal got mixed up. She's going with the wrong mother! Little Bear is lost too. Little Bear is going with Little Sal's mother! But don't worry, Daddy. It's okay."

more shared reading interactions with rhyming and alphabet books may acquire phonological awareness more rapidly than other children (Murry, Stahl & Ivey, 1996). Just as dialogic reading encourages vocabulary and expressive language skills, books that stress letter names and sounds encourage alphabet knowledge and the development of phonological awareness.

Children can begin building concepts about print at an early age. Very young children will play with books, turn the pages, and invent stories to go with the pictures. Eight-month-old Avery enjoyed handling a soft cloth book that featured textured farm animals with movable parts. Eighteen-month-old Josh knew immediately that a blank book he was given needed "writing" in it. Reading foundations are not built automatically, however. Children require active participation with adults in print-focused interactions that are age-appropriate in cognitive, emotional, social, and physical ways (Adams, 1990). Children benefit from a variety of verbal exchanges, such as story-telling, as well as interactions with print, such as pointing out letters or words on street signs or in stores.

There are several other effective approaches to reading, but books are only one medium for encouraging language development. There is a growing consensus that oral language such as story-telling, recitation, and song plays a central role in the development of reading (Dickinson, & Tabors, 2002). The No Child Left Behind Act (NCLBA, 2001) mandated that all children read at grade level by the end of third grade. NCLBA also mandated the use of programs whose effectiveness in the classroom has been documented. Those programs focus reading instruction on the four language categories: vocabulary, phonics (based on phonological awareness), phonemic awareness, and comprehension. NCLBA also emphasizes the interconnectedness of literacy and oral language development.

Early Experiences with Television and Computers

Nonprint and interactive media, such as television, computer programs, and video games, also influence children's language development. Exposure to television is almost universal in the United States and other industrialized countries. The amount of time spent viewing television varies dramatically, but in 2000 the average North American 2- to 6-year-old watched 1.5 to 2 hours per day. This increased to about 3.5 hours per day for middle school-aged children and decreased slightly in adolescence. Children from lower SES homes tend to spend more time watching television. The figures are higher today.

- Approximate number of studies examining TV's effects on children: 4,000.
- Number of minutes per week that the average child watches television: 1,680.
- The average child watches 3 hours of TV a day. The average youth watches 1,500 hours of TV a year.
- Percentage of day care centers that use TV during a typical day: 70.
- Percentage of 4- to 6-year-olds who, when asked to choose between watching TV and spending time with their fathers, preferred television: 54.
- Young children don't know the difference between programs and commercials.
- Number of 30-second TV commercials seen in a year by an average child: 20,000.
- Top-ranked advertisers on children's TV programs: food products and fast-food restaurants.
- Children who watch violence on TV are more likely to display aggressive behavior.
- Number of murders seen on TV by the time an average child finishes elementary school: 8,000 A.C. Nielsen Co. ttp://www.csun.edu/~vceed002/health/docs/tv& health.html; American Academy of Pediatrics ttp://www.aap.org/family/smarttv .htm; accessed October 21, 2005.

According to the latest longitudinal analysis of national data (Zimmerman & Christakis, 2005), children before age 3 watched TV an average of 2.2 hours per day. At 3 to 5 years, the daily average was 3.3 hours. When the children were tested at ages 6 and 7, it was

BOX 10.2 Teaching Children to Read

Reading, or getting meaning from print (Rayner et al., 2001), is arguably one of the most important skills that children acquire during the school years. In 1993, the U.S. Department of Education released the National Adult Literacy Survey. Approximately 23 percent of American adults read at Level 1, which is considered functionally illiterate, and approximately 27 percent read at Level 2, which is considered quite limited in reading skills. The report argued that many adults had difficulty with common tasks because their literacy level was insufficient. More recently, the National Reading Panel (2000) also indicated that, although most children in the United States learn to read, a significant number do not read well enough to function well in today's society, with its increasing literacy demands.

What is reading or literacy? Reading is a developmental skill. Young children typically develop a number of prereading skills that are associated with reading development. Emergent literacy, or the developmental precursors of reading skills in young children, includes alphabet knowledge, concepts about print (e.g., the directionality of print), vocabulary, and phonological awareness. Phonological awareness is the sensitivity to the sound structure of language that lets you manipulate spoken words into their constituent parts. Children who enter school with more developed emergent literacy skills, especially phonological awareness, typically learn to read more easily (Frost et al., 2005). As children learn to read, they acquire the alphabetic principle—that is, the understanding that there are systematic and predictable relationships between written letters and spoken sounds. As young children learn to read, the emphasis is usually on decoding, or reading individual words by using phonics or by sounding them out. As children develop a certain level of fluency with reading words, usually in second to third grade, the emphasis in reading shifts to reading comprehension. In general, the more fluently a child reads, the more easily the child will be able to comprehend what he or she reads (Eldredge, 2005). For example, children who spend all their cognitive energy recognizing and deciphering each word will have few cognitive resources left over for understanding what they are reading.

How should we teach reading? Historically, methods of teaching reading have been the subject of much controversy. One of the most heated debates has concerned the extent to which the rules of written language should be explicitly taught and emphasized. The **phonics (or code-oriented)** approach teaches children to analyze words into their constituent sounds. Phonics instruction teaches children the relationships between the letters of written language and the individual sounds, or phonemes, of spoken language. The goal of phonics instruction is to teach developing readers how to use the alphabetic principle. Specifically, it teaches children to use these relationships to read and write words. The **whole-language approach** assumes that reading instruction should focus on the level of the whole word, not the letters or other parts. Whole language emphasizes both reading for meaning and the use of sight words and context.

Which approach is best? Research clearly indicates that systematic and explicit phonics instruction is more effective than nonsystematic or no phonics instruction and that systematic and explicit phonics instruction improves word decoding, spelling, and reading comprehension (Blachman et al., 2004; National Center for Educational Statistics, 2003). Systematic phonics instruction provides practice with letter–sound relationships in a predetermined sequence. However, children benefit from the whole-language concept of immersion in real-world print. The use of shared reading activities and real print in the home and classroom is associated with gains in reading (Aram & Biron, 2004; Rasinski & Stevenson, 2005).

The No Child Left Behind Act requires that the effectiveness of educational programs used in the classroom must be demonstrated through rigorous scientific research. There are no easy, ready-made solutions for making every child a good reader. However, there now exists an extensive knowledge base showing us the skills that children must learn in order to read well. The National Reading Panel (2000) was asked to review the research in reading instruction and to identify methods that consistently lead to success in reading. They identified what were seen as the five essential components of reading instruction: (1) phonemic awareness skills, (2) phonics skills, (3) reading fluency, (4) vocabulary development, and (5) comprehension strategies. The important role of fluency and vocabulary in reading comprehension is a new target of emphasis in the teaching of reading. Individuals with poor vocabularies have difficulty understanding written text (Malatesha, 2005). Unfortunately, one of the best ways to develop a good vocabulary is to read a lot (Cunningham & Stanovich, 2003).

Many children—approximately 10 to 15 percent of school-age children—have difficulty learning to read, even though they possess normal levels of intelligence, do not have general learning difficulties, do not have sensory impairments, and have not experienced socioeconomic disadvantage (Vellutino, Fletcher, Snowling, & Scanlon, 2004). Although many people think that reading disability or dyslexia is caused by a visual problem, most reading disabilities are caused by a deficit in phonological awareness (Pogorzelski & Wheldall, 2005). For many children, this deficit is evident at school entry (Anthony et al., 2002). These children often have difficulty analyzing sounds in speech, and therefore, they often have difficulty detecting and using letter–sound correspondence information. This in turn impairs their ability to decode printed words automatically. Recent research has emphasized the importance of helping children develop their phonological awareness skills and of using explicit phonics programs (Blachman et al., 2005). A number of computer programs, teacher strategies, and peer-assisted learning techniques have been developed to help children with reading disabilities to become effective readers (Calhoon, 2005; Fasting, & Halaas Lyster, 2005; Hatcher, Hulme, & Snowling, 2005). Unfortunately, research also indicates that reading disability is a life-long disability, not a developmental delay that can be overcome with temporary interventions (Shaywitz & Shaywitz, 2005).

found that each hour of television viewing before age 3 was associated with lower scores on achievement, memory, intelligence, and reading tests. Thus, it is clear that television viewing has adverse effects on children's cognitive development before age 3 years.

These findings support earlier studies showing that children who spend more time viewing television spend less time reading and interacting with others and score lower on tests of academic skills assessments (Huston et al., 1999; Wright et al., 2001). This is especially true for children who watch more than two hours a day, especially prime time shows and cartoons. These studies focus on time spent, however, rather than on the type of programming. Children who watch high-quality educational programs, such as Sesame Street or Barney, especially children from lower SES backgrounds, tend to enter school more ready to read, have higher grades, read more books, and place more value on achievement (Anderson et al., 2001; Rice et al., 1990). Children from lower SES homes who view these programs also tend to acquire more vocabulary and alphabet knowledge. These positive outcomes associated with television viewing tend to be greater when viewing is limited to educational programs, when a caregiver views the program with the child, when the caregiver and child discuss the content, and when the content is linked to everyday learning experiences.

Although the viewing of high-quality children's programming may have some beneficial effects on certain preliteracy skills, such as number or letter recognition, or may serve to promote certain prosocial behaviors, such as sharing and manners, the American Academy of Pediatrics (AAP) has emphasized that many negative effects can result from TV viewing. In particular, research has shown that increased TV viewing is associated with a range of potential health problems, including aggression, lowered academic performance, distortions in body concept and self-image, increases in obesity, and attentional difficulties (American Academy of Pediatrics [AAP], 2001; Christakis et al., 2004). Some AAP guidelines for television viewing among children appear in Figure 10.4.

The effects of other media, such as computer and video games, have received less research attention than books and television. Most video games emphasize speed and action in violent plots, but a number of educational programs and games are also available. The effects of video game playing on development are not well studied. In general, the same recommendations that apply to television viewing should broadly apply to video game playing and computer time.

Phonics (or Code-Oriented)
An approach to teaching reading that teaches children to analyze words into their constituents.

Whole-Language Approach
Assumes that reading instruction should focus on the whole word. Emphasizes both reading for meaning and the use of sight words and context.

Links to Related Material
In Chapter 16, you will learn more about how television viewing affects children and families today.

FIGURE 10.4 TV viewing and child development

How much TV should children watch each day? Currently, the AAP recommends that television viewing be discouraged among children younger than 2 years and limited to no more than one to two hours of quality programming per day for children age 2 and older (AAP, 2001). In addition, the Academy recommends that parents:

- Remove television sets from children's bedrooms.

- Monitor the shows that children and adolescents are watching, to make sure that they are educational, informational, and nonviolent.

- View television programs with children and discuss their content.

- Use controversial programming as a place to begin family discussions regarding values, violence, sexuality, and substance use.

- With young children, instead of TV viewing, encourage interactive activities that promote optimal development, such as talking, playing, singing, and reading together.

- With older children, encourage alternative entertainment, including reading, sports, hobbies, and creative play.

SOURCE: Drawn from American Academy of Pediatrics, *Pediatrics*, 107, No. 2, February 2001, 423–426.

A difficult decision for many parents is how to regulate television and computer or video game time. Parents worry that these activities replace time that otherwise would be spent reading or engaging in educational and social activities. The assumption that children would spend more time in educational activities if they did not engage in media activities is referred to as the *displacement hypothesis*. It is not supported empirically, however. Limiting access to media is not enough. Rather, parents need to help fill children's time with other activities they deem more acceptable.

Language Development in Multilingual Settings

In many parts of the world children grow up learning two languages and sometimes more than two. In the United States, approximately 6 million children live in households in which a language other than English is spoken (U.S Census Bureau, 2003). There are many advantages to knowing multiple languages as an adult. For example, it opens many career opportunities in our increasingly diverse world where it is common to encounter people who are not native speakers of English. Research has shown that learning a second language enhances cognitive development (Bialystok, 1991). Bilingualism and multilingualism have been shown to foster classification skills, concept formation, analogical reasoning, visual-spatial skills, cognitive flexibility, and creativity. In addition, in a study comparing monolinguals and bilinguals (4 to 6 years of age), it was found that bilinguals were ahead of their monolingual peers in semantic development (Baker, 1993).

Children become bilingual in two ways. They can learn both languages simultaneously in early childhood, or they can master the first language and then acquire the second. Children of bilingual parents who are taught both languages in early childhood demonstrate no special problems with language development. In contrast, children who begin to acquire a second language at age 6 or 7 after speaking the first, usually take three to five years to develop second-language competence similar to that of children reared with the language (Hakuta, 1999).

In the United States, children who enter school with limited English proficiency present a challenge for educators. The best way to educate so-called Limited English-Proficient (LEP) children remains a matter of much debate. This debate has been fueled both by incorrect widespread beliefs concerning the wisdom of bilingual education and by ethnic prejudices. One claim of the older research literature was that bilingualism resulted in cognitive deficits. The foundations for this claim were that bilingual children show slower growth of language skills and the idea that hearing and learning two languages confuses children. It has now become clear, however, that bilingual children are more advanced in some areas of cognition and language development than monolingual children (Bialystok, 2001).

The benefits of bilingualism provide strong justification for bilingual education programs in schools. Children who become fluent in two languages do better than other children on tests of the kinds of intelligence that involve the use of creativity (Kessler & Quinn, 1987), problem solving (Bain, 1975; Kessler & Quinn, 1987), perspective taking, analytical reasoning, and metacognitive strategies (Bialystok & Herman, 1999).

Approaches to the challenge of educating limited English proficient children include the bilingual/multicultural model and the majority-only model (Brisk, 1998; Hakuta, 1999). Programs that follow a *bilingual model* use both the minority and the majority languages for instruction. This model has many variants depending on the specific emphases and time frame (structured immersion, transitional bilingual education, two-way bilingual education, and so on). All the variants, however, use two languages. Nevertheless, in the United States these programs are not truly bilingual, because the two languages are not given equal emphasis or time,

Questions for Thought and Discussion

What do you think is the best way to educate immigrant children in the United States today, and why?

The American Academy of Pediatrics recommends that television viewing be discouraged before the age of 2. For children over 2, viewing should be limited to only one to two hours per day of high-quality educational programming. (David J. Sams/Texas Imprint Photography)

Researchers recommend that children not be exposed to computers until around the age of 3. Research suggests that school-age children, such as these first graders, benefit from group investigation using educational software. Why is information literacy on the computer regarded as essential for children today? (Ellen B. Senisi)

as is the practice in other countries (Bialystok, 2001). The other model, in contrast, uses only the dominant or majority language as the language of instruction and content. In *English-only* programs, use of the minority language is minimized and may even be explicitly discouraged. In both models, the principal goal typically is to prepare students as quickly as possible for instruction in English.

Second-language and bilingual programs often reflect political rather than educational factors, with policy makers using scientific data to support their decisions. One main issue is how to best prepare children for what they must learn in the school curriculum to be successful (for example, math and science). A second issue is whether children who are learning two languages are delayed in learning the majority language. A third issue is the value of instructing minority children in their native tongue, which tells children that their cultural heritage is valued. Advocates of the bilingual model hope that it will help reduce the academic difficulties, school failures, and higher dropout rates of some minority groups. Deciding these issues requires an understanding of how the bilingual language learning process works.

One theory—the *single-system hypothesis*—is that bilingual children initially approach the task of learning two languages as if they were learning only one. That is, they do not separate the two forms of speech input but develop a single-language system that includes elements of each. Only as they mature cognitively do the children learn to differentiate the two tongues, gradually treating them as independent languages (Volterra & Taeschner, 1978). This theory grew from the observation that younger bilingual children practice *code-mixing,* or combining forms from the two languages within the same utterance (Redlinger & Park, 1980). Mixing occurs at all levels of speech, including articulation, vocabulary, inflections, and syntax. The assumption was that mixing reflects confusion and impedes learning. A related finding is that children in bilingual homes acquire both languages more slowly than do peers who are learning only one language. This lag gradually disappears, however, and the children's proficiency in both languages eventually reaches that of monolingual children in their language (Oller & Pearson, 2002).

BOX 10.3 Bilingual Education

President George W. Bush signed into law the *No Child Left Behind Act* (NCLB) on January 8, 2002. An amendment to the *Elementary and Secondary Education Act*, NCLB is built on four pillars: stronger accountability for results, more autonomy for states and communities, support for proven programs and teaching methods, and more choices for parents. Part of NCLB's amendment to the Elementary and Secondary Education Act was to consolidate the *Bilingual Education Program* and the *Emergency Immigrant Education Program* into the new *Title III State Formula Grant Program*. The purpose of Title III is to "ensure that limited English proficient students, including immigrant children and youth, develop English proficiency and meet the same academic content and academic achievement standards that other children are expected to meet" (U.S. Department of Education [USDOE], 2005, p. 2).

For more than three decades, English-language learners (ELLs) have been receiving special instruction in U.S. schools due to the 1974 ruling of *Lau vs. Nichols*. In this case, the U.S. Supreme Court found that when ELLs were placed in a classroom where they were unable to participate meaningfully because of their limited English proficiency, it "constituted discrimination on the basis of national origin in violation of Title VI of the Civil Rights Act" (Serpa, 2004, p. 3). Now, when there are 20 or more students of the same language group enrolled in a school, they are provided education in their native language, and when the number of ELLs sharing a language is less than 20, they are placed in English-as-a-second-language classes or receive tutoring.

With NCLB, the federal government is now holding schools and local educational agencies accountable for not only providing programs for ELLs, but also for increasing their English proficiency to the extent that they achieve academic success by meeting national standards (USDOE,

2005). Before NCLB, in June 1997, the international, professional organization, Teachers of English to Speakers of Other Languages (TESOL), developed a set of standards for the effective instruction of English as a second language in the United States. TESOL's standards supplement content area standards and reflect developmental stages of English-language proficiency in grade-level clusters, from pre-Kindergarten through grade 12 (Center for Applied Linguistics, 2002). In response to NCLB and Title III in particular, states have begun to create their own sets of standards for ELLs by building upon TESOL's standards and those standards created by other states and agencies.

Although the standards are becoming more aligned, the methods of instruction for ELLs vary between states, school districts, and even schools within the same city. A wide variety of programs targeting ELLs fall under the general heading of "bilingual education," which has been called "a simple label for a complex phenomenon" because many of these programs do not aim for a balanced use of two languages (Cazden & Snow, 1990, cited in Ovando, Combs, & Collier, 2006, p. 9).

The most popular forms of bilingual education are dual-language, bilingual transition, and immersion programs. Dual-language programs come the closest to providing genuine bilingual education. With dual-language instruction, students learn to speak, read, and write in two languages. Dual-language programs have proven to be the most effective instructional method for ELLs, according to standardized test scores (Merrow Report, 1998). Bilingual transition programs teach literacy and academic content in the students' native language while helping them to learn spoken English. "With the goal of English proficiency, the language in which academic subjects are taught gradually shifts from the students' first language to English" (Center for Research on Education,

More recent research strongly challenges the single-system hypothesis (Bialystok, 2001; Genesee, Nicoladis, & Paradis, 1995). Studies of infant speech perception, for example, indicate clearly that babies can differentiate sounds and phonemes found in different languages (Eilers & Oller, 1988; Moon et al., 1993). By 4 months of age, infants growing up in bilingual homes can differentiate sounds from the two languages, even when the languages are rhythmically similar (Bosch & Sebastian-Galles, 2001). Hence, perceptual confusion does not appear to be a problem.

In addition, children's code-mixing, such as substitution of a word in one language for the same word in the second language, may simply reflect the overextension principle. The child substitutes an unknown word from the first or second language simply because it is easier to do so (Vihman, 1985). Furthermore, parents frequently model language-mixing. Studies of bilingual children's home environments indicate that their parents often speak to them using parts of both languages simultaneously

Diversity & Excellence, 2001). Finally, immersion programs take many different forms, the most common being English-only immersion in which ELL students are placed in classrooms where English is the sole language of instruction, with the belief that they will develop English-language proficiency quickly. Support for students in English-only classrooms can be provided through modified curricula, materials, assessments, and bilingual teachers' aids, but these students are often left to sink or swim.

U.S. English and English First are two national groups that are instrumental in the *English Only Movement* (Crawford, 1997). With financial and ideological support mostly from private citizens, these groups work to promote legislation that would prohibit ELLs from being instructed in their native language. It is the English Only Movement that advocates immersing ELLs in English-language classrooms through the sink-or-swim method of instruction. A program that provides no specific support for ELLs within the context of immersion is problematic not only because students may suffer emotional trauma, but also because they will not have access to learning important academic concepts, causing them to fall behind their peers in all academic areas (Crawford, 1997).

Although immersion programs can be effective for learners whose language is valued and supported both at home and in the broader society, using both languages in the classroom is more effective for language minority students, whose language has less social status (Tucker, 1980, cited in Auerbach, 1993). Thus, language acquisition is not free from relations of power and their affective consequences (Auerbach, 1993).

The work of Jim Cummins (1979) shows that ELLs cannot adequately comprehend academic concepts before five or more years in an English-language setting. Cummins was the first to exemplify the distinction between conversational fluency and academic proficiency in a second language and the time it takes immigrant children to acquire each. *Basic interpersonal communicative skills* take about two years to develop, whereas *cognitive academic language proficiency* is not achieved until about five or more years in an English-language setting (Cummins, 1979). The age or grade level of an ELL is not of great importance in this respect because all ELLs who actually become proficient in a second language have to go through the same process of acquiring conversational fluency and later, grade-appropriate academic proficiency in that language (Cummins, 2003).

Virginia Collier (1995), a scholar of language acquisition, proposes that linguistic processes include both subconscious and conscious aspects of language development. She explains that the development of oral language can occur subconsciously because it is an innate ability of all humans. Meanwhile, the development of the written system of language must occur consciously, with the formal teaching of language in school (Collier, 1995). Collier claims that a person's academic success in a second language is dependent on their having a highly developed first-language system, both oral and written (1995). Stephen Krashen supports this assertion by stating that since "literacy transfers across languages, building literacy in the primary language is a short-cut to English literacy" (1999, p. 1). Krashen explains, "If we learn to read by understanding the messages on the page, it is easier to learn to read if we understand the language. And once we can read, we can read: The ability transfers to other languages" (1999, p. 1).

Thus, if it is feasible, it is more beneficial for schools to provide instruction in students' native languages so that they can progress cognitively and academically (Collier, 1995; Krashen, 1999). At the same time, they will receive English instruction that is meaningful and relevant to the curriculum. This way, once the students become proficient in English, they will not be cognitively and academically behind their native English-speaking peers. The problem lies in the fact that while first language instruction may be available for ELLs who speak Spanish as a first language, there are far fewer bilingual teachers who speak the wide variety of other languages spoken by children in U.S. schools.

and that parents generally respond positively to the child's code-mixing (Goodz, 1989; Lanza, 1997). Thus, mixing parts of two languages is not a sign of confusion or delay. Research that compares different approaches to educating bilingual children generally favors a bilingual model, in which both languages are used in the early grades and children can gradually develop competence in the majority language (Genesee, 1994; Greene, 1998).

Language Development Across Cultures

Language development proceeds in the same way across cultures. Children become more complex in their use of language as they mature cognitively and learn the pragmatics of their particular language. There appear to be general stages and rules of language development that apply across all languages and cultures, such as overgeneralization. Children develop language according to an invariant sequence of steps or stages that are closely tied to maturation. Children all over the world coo, babble, and show echolalia. Then simple words replace early nonspeech forms of communication. In addition, children demonstrate categorical perception of speech sounds and exhibit patterns such as the overgeneralization grammatical rules.

Children everywhere learn language through similar strategies and processes, and all languages are equally complex in their capacities for communicating meaning. Nevertheless, there are differences across cultures, showing the effects of immediate environments and broader cultural influences that surround the child. Recall, for example, that by the end of their first year, babies lose their ability to discriminate sound contrasts that are not present in the language to which they are exposed (Best, 1995).

Recall, too, that there are cultural preferences for language styles (Tardif, Gelman, & Xu, 1999). On the one hand, children with referential styles have vocabularies consisting mainly of nouns, especially words for objects, and they use language mainly to label things. Children with expressive styles, on the other hand, produce more action verbs, social formulas, and pronouns. They place greater emphasis on language as a pragmatic tool for expressing needs and for social interaction. The nouns-first referential pattern is more prevalent among children learning English than, for example, children learning Korean or Mandarin Chinese, who, are slower on average in acquiring object names (Choi, 1997, 2000; Kim, McGregor, & Thompson, 2000; Tardif, Gelman, & Xu, 1999). Korean and Mandarin Chinese children are faster to acquire verbs. These differences relate to differences in the speech input that parents provide, which, in turn, reflect cultural adaptations and values (Goldfield, 2000).

✔ *Test Your Mastery...*

Learning Objective 10.7: *Discuss influences of family, technology, language, and culture on literacy and learning.*

1. How do parents and family characteristics influence language learning?
2. How do exposure to books and oral language promote literacy?
3. What are some best practices for providing children with prereading skills?
4. What effects do television and computers have on language development?
5. What does research show about best practices in teaching bilingual learners?

BOX 10.4   Contextual Model of Language Development

Infant is born with innate capacity to learn human language and to engage in communicative actions with caretakers.

Family, Neighborhood, and School Settings

- Family's educational background affects the language they use when speaking to the child.
- Family's educational and financial resources affect number and variety of books, time spent reading to the child each day, and other literacy activities available in the home.
- Child observes and models parental vocabulary and grammar, as well as reading and other literacy habits.
- Work and family responsibilities and stress affect parents' availability to interact verbally with the child.
- Family SES affects neighborhood choice, which affects community and school resources available to the child to promote literacy activities.
- Language spoken at home by family determines the language(s) the child will learn. This language may or may not reinforce the language spoken at school.
- School policies on bilingual education affect children's opportunities for multilingual learning.

Culture and Society

- Pervasiveness of different media technology impact time that children could otherwise spend reading.
- Dominant language of culture will determine language needed for achievement in society.
- Societal attitudes toward minority languages and cultures affect child's ability to maintain a first language that is different from the language of the larger culture.

Summary for Chapter 10

Learning Objective 10.1

Define language and major components of language, including phonology, semantics, grammar, and pragmatics.

1. How is language defined as a means of symbolic communication?

Language is a complex and dynamic system of conventional symbols that is used for thought and communication. A symbol is something that represents something else. Words are also symbols, sounds that represent specific meanings within a language. All human languages are generative; there is no limit to the number of meaningful sentences that can be created using a finite set of symbols and rules.

2. What components of language do children learn?

A *phoneme* is the smallest unit of sound that can signal a difference in meaning. In addition to discriminating and comprehending the individual sounds of language, a child must learn that these sounds combine to produce words with meaning.

3. What roles do phonolgy and semantics play in symbolic communication?

Phonology is the study of how sounds are made and combined to produce speech. *Semantics* are expressed in words or word combinations. Children demonstrate an enormous capacity to soak up vocabulary and rapidly develop a large body of words, or lexicon. As children develop their lexicons, they begin to combine and modify words to create different meanings.

4. What roles do grammar and pragmatics play in symbolic communication?	*Grammar*, the rules that determine the structure of language, includes morphology and syntax. Morphology is the structure of words and how changes in parts of words alter their meaning. Syntax specifies the rules that determine the structure of sentences, especially the order of words. To use language effectively, children need to learn morphology and syntax as well as words and their meanings. In addition, children must learn to take turns in conversation, to stay on the current topic, and to understand how gestures and context can influence the meaning of what is being said. These rules for using language within the communicative context are called *pragmatics*.

Learning Objective 10.2

Compare and contrast four major theories of language development.

1. What are the four major theories of language development?	The dominant theoretical approach prior to the 1960s was the *learning approach* (Skinner), which contends that language learning is based on experience. The *nativist approach* proposed by Chomsky emphasized the interaction of inborn processes and biological mechanisms with environmental influences. The *cognitive-developmental approach* to language focuses on the cognitive contributions to language acquisition. The *sociocultural approach*, influenced by Vygotsky, stresses the cognitive abilities children bring to the task of language learning in conjunction with the cultural context, which affects early social interactions and therefore may differentially promote cognitive mastery.

2. In the behavioral view, through what processes do children learn language?

According to Skinner, children learn language just as they learn any other skill or behavior, through *operant conditioning*. Skinner maintained that there is nothing unique or special about language. Children utter sounds at random and are more likely to repeat the sounds that caregivers reinforce.

3. In the nativist view, how does biology take precedence over the environment in language learning?

Chomsky and his followers believe that language acquisition must have a strong *biological* - basis because young children acquire language early and rapidly. Evidence for the inborn tendency to acquire language is found in the universality of human language abilities; in the regularity of the production of sounds, even among deaf children; and in the invariant sequences of language development, regardless of the specific language.

3. How do the cognitive-developmental approach and the sociocultural approach differ in their expectations of language acquisition?

Cognitive theories emphasize the active role of the learner in the process of language acquisition. This approach emphasizes the link between language learning and the child's developing understanding of concepts and relationships. As children mature cognitively, they are able to advance in language development as well. Evidence for this view comes from the progressive, stage-like, development of speech. The *sociocultural approach* emphasizes that the basis for language acquisition and use is social interaction. In this view, the child's primary motivation for acquiring language is social interaction—to communicate ideas and to be understood.

Learning Objective 10.3

Trace the developments in the first year of life that establish the preverbal basis for language learning.

1. How does speech perception develop?	The ability to discriminate and attend to sounds is called *speech perception*, which enables listeners to divide speech, a continuous series of sound, into segments. As listeners divide the stream of sounds into syllables, words, and sentences, they also are attending to other characteristics of speech, such as rising and falling intonations, pauses between words and phrases, and the placement of stress. Infants perceive and distinguish phonemes—the smallest sound unit that signals a change in meaning. From an early age, infants show evidence of categorical speech perception—the ability to discriminate when two sounds represent two different phonemes as well as when they are in the same phonemic category. This ability to make "same-different" distinctions has been investigated in babies as young as 1 month old. Experience also plays an important role in early speech perception. Two-day-old infants already show a preference for hearing their own language. And the more babies are exposed to a language, the sharper their phonemic discriminations become. Conversely, lack of exposure may dull or delay these abilities.
2. What preverbal speech sounds do infants make?	Children develop language in stages tied to maturation. Before they develop language, infants use *prelinguistic vocalizations* that do not represent objects and events. Prelinguistic vocalizations include crying, cooing, and babbling, for example. During the first month, the primary sound that infants make is crying, which is produced by blowing air through the vocal tract and does not have distinct well-formed sounds. During the second month, infants begin cooing, using their tongues and extended vowel sounds to articulate. Coos appear to express feelings of pleasure or positive excitement. Infants tend not to coo when they are in discomfort. Between 6 and 9 months of age, infants begin babbling, the first vocalizing that sounds like human speech. All children appear to *babble*, even deaf children . Around 10 to 12 months, infants tend to demonstrate *echolalia*, the automatic repetition of sounds, syllables, or words. These repetitions often sound like the child is carrying on a one-sided conversation. Then around 11 to 13 months many children speak their first word, an important milestone for parents. A range of anywhere from approximately 8 to 18 months is considered normal for the utterance of the first word.
3. What is the role of nonverbal communication in language acquisition?	Nonverbal aspects of communication, such as the use of *gestures*, are important preverbal skills. All infants use gestures combined with other nonverbal responses to perform many of the functions of vocal language. Infants first use gestures to communicate requests at about 8 to10 months of age. Children also use gestures to symbolize objects or events.

Learning Objective 10.4

Describe the processes by which children first use words and develop vocabulary.

1. How does children's cognitive development affect their semantic awareness?

Researchers have debated whether language precedes thought or whether thought precedes language. Piaget argued that children must understand concepts before they can use words to describe the concepts. Therefore, children learn words in order to describe classes or categories they have already created. Other theorists, however, have suggested that language can precede thought. Children can create cognitive categories in order to understand things that are labeled by words. Today, most theorists favor an *interactionist view*, in which language and thought are mutually reinforcing. In the early stages of language development, concepts often precede words, whereas as the child matures language may increasingly influence thought. One major implication of the role of cognitive processes in language development is that caregivers need to recognize that the child's rate of language learning is tied closely to his or her cognitive development.

2. What are the characteristics of children's first words, and at what rate do children acquire vocabulary?

For most children, *nouns* (especially object words) predominate and remain more common than verbs and action words throughout language development. This is true for most languages, in which nouns are understood earlier, spoken earlier and more frequently, and even pronounced better. After 18 months, rapid growth often takes place in the number of new words learned. This rapid growth has been termed the *naming explosion*. Children often maintain this rapid rate of vocabulary acquisition throughout the preschool period, when they can effortlessly acquire an average of nine new words per day. According to some estimates, the average 6-year-old learns as many as 22 new words per day; however, there are generally great individual differences in the size and range of vocabulary development.

3. What are some individual and cultural differences in children's language learning?

One difference is in the *size* of children's early vocabularies. Another is in the *rate* at which children learn words. There is wide variability in the number of words in children's vocabularies, with word production ranging from several to hundreds. Comparable differences are found for children's comprehension of words. There also are differences in the types of words found in children's early lexicons. Some children display a *referential* style, producing a large proportion of nouns. Other children display an *expressive* style, which includes a larger mix of word types, more "stock phrases," and a greater emphasis on language as a pragmatic tool for expressing needs and for interacting socially. The two styles reflect different culturally defined ideas about the purpose of language, with referential children focusing on its informational function and expressive children more concerned with interpersonal uses.

4. What can we learn about language learning from the semantic errors that children make?

Psychologists have learned a great deal about children's semantic development by examining the kinds of errors they make. In early word learning, children attach a specific label to a specific object. Next the child begins to extend that label to other examples of the same object. These extensions demonstrate that the child is forming an object category that is defined by certain features. Most children, however, make errors when attempting to extend these early labels and may also use a specific label to describe something else. For example, they may call a cat or rabbit a "doggie." These *overextensions* are common in the early stages of semantic development. Overextensions may reflect either a lack of understanding or a lack of vocabulary. Young children may also apply labels too narrowly (*underextensions*), but are less common in production than overextensions. *Word coining* occurs when children create new words that are not a part of adult language and illustrate children's inventiveness and creativity. *Holophrases*, or single-word sentences have a special communicative function, which allow a young child to communicate effectively despite a limited vocabulary.

5. By what processes do children learn the meanings of words?

Explanations have been proposed for semantic development—the processes by which children come to learn the meaning of words. In one process, children use *grammatical cues* to help them determine the meanings of certain words. The reverse is also possible. Once children have mastered some aspects of grammar, they can use this knowledge to make sense of new words. There are many grammatical cues to word meaning in any language, based on syntax—the grammatical order of words in a sentence.

Experimental studies in which children have a chance to learn a new word based on the grammatical cues available in a sentence demonstrate that children can exploit a variety of grammatical cues to narrow down the possible meanings of new words. This process is called syntactic bootstrapping, because the child's prior knowledge of grammar underlies, or "bootstraps," the learning of semantics. Most children have learned thousands of words by the time they start school, and most of these words are those they learned on their own through exposure. Children's word learning can occur rapidly, sometimes after only a brief exposure, through a process called *fast-mapping*.

Children use assumptions, or constraints, to govern early word learning. Lexical contrast theory suggests that when children hear an unfamiliar word, they automatically assume the new word has a different meaning from any word they already know. This assumption motivates them to learn exactly what the new word means. In addition, children always replace their current meanings with those they think are more conventional or correct. The principle of mutual exclusivity states that children believe that objects can have only one name. This strategy limits the possible choices when a child is trying to attach meaning to a new word. Although semantic constraints account well for some aspects of early word learning, not all psychologists are convinced that the idea is helpful.

6. What roles do parents and children themselves play in semantic development?

Children can learn words only if their *social environment* provides them with sufficient information about what different words mean. Parents and other caregivers help their children in this task through modeling. Parents' modeling of words can occur either incidentally in the normal course of conversation, or explicitly in an attempt to teach the child a new word.

Learning Objective 10.5

Describe the processes by which children learn to communicate grammatically.

1. What are children's first sentences like, and how do they change?	Most children begin to *combine words* into the first simple sentences at around 18 months. Many children begin to produce strings of single-word utterances, using one word to call attention to an object and then a second word to comment on the object. Multiple one-word utterances can be distinguished from the two-word sentences that will soon appear by the longer pause that occurs between words. Children show great variety of items and combinations in their initial sentences. The next phase of grammatical development is *telegraphic speech*. As the child's sentences grow, they become truncated, resembling telegram messages. Sentences focus on high-content words and omit unnecessary function words.
2. What kinds of errors can signal progress in grammatical development?	As children learn the inflectional rules of language, they tend toward *overregularization*, or applying the regular rules to nouns and verbs that have irregular forms, for example, "I knowed her." Usage is inconsistent, but eventually the correct and incorrect forms may merge. Thus, the application of rules, even when overextended, represents progress in language development. Children then need to learn the exceptions to the rules.
3. How do children acquire grammar through semantic bootstrapping?	*Semantic bootstrapping* is using word meanings to help learn about grammar. An example of semantic bootstrapping is using prior knowledge of noun and pronoun categories to determine the grammatical forms surrounding them in a sentence. In the sentence, "These pencils belong in this box," the child may know that *this* means one of something, while *these* means more than one. This knowledge may then help the child to form the plural and singular forms of the nouns in the sentence correctly.

4. How do we know that children use innate cognitive strategies to acquire grammar?	Researchers have found that children's use of *innate cognitive strategies* allow them to acquire grammatical rules rapidly. An example is children's development of rules for inflections of words, such as forming plurals.
5. How do child-directed speech and imitation help children learn language?	In *child-directed speech*, adults modify their language when speaking to young children. Mothers tend to speak slowly and use short utterances. In addition the focus of mothers' speech is usually on the here and now rather than on more distant or abstract events. Imitation is not exact copying of parental models of grammar. Rather, the child adds something to the utterance that was just heard, or copies it at some later time, or copies a particular grammatical form using different words.
6. What kinds of feedback best help children acquire correct grammar?	Feedback provides information about what is not correct in language. Adults frequently respond to children's ill-formed statement in one of three ways. *Expansions* involve repeating the child's statement and adding something to make it more complex. *Recasts* involve restating what the child said in a different, more correct way. *Clarification* questions signal that the listener did not understand the comment and that the child should attempt the communication again. Research suggests that these forms of feedback are helpful to children, and children appear to be receptive to such responses.

Learning Objective 10.6

Describe the means by which children
learn the pragmatics of language use.

1. What is involved in knowledge of pragmatics?	*Pragmatics* is the practical knowledge of how to use language to communicate. Pragmatics involves knowing how to begin and continue a conversation, how to ask for things, how to tell a story or joke, and how to adjust comments to the listener's perspective. Pragmatics also involves knowing how to conform to the cultural rules that govern how individuals are supposed to interact. The development of pragmatics is also associated with cognitive development. As children acquire perspective taking, they advance in their abilities to make themselves understood to others. As children mature cognitively, they understand the world from a less egocentric perspective and can state relevant details to communicate more effectively.
2. How do children use speech acts to communicate?	With the acquisition of language, children add verbal responses to their repertoire of communication devices and achieve goals by directing words and phrases to other people. Such pragmatic uses of language are referred to as *speech acts*. Researchers have found that even the first words that infants utter serve pragmatic functions. In the one-word period, babies begin to use relational words, those connecting several objects or events, in pragmatic ways toward multiple goals. As their cognitive and linguistic abilities grow, children's speech acts increase in range and effectiveness. Children's comprehension of adults' speech acts is also important for adult and child to communicate effectively.
3. What strategies do children learn to apply in discourse?	Speech during social interaction is called *discourse*. When people have conversations, in addition to adhering to the grammatical rules of the language, they also must follow the social rules of discourse. The first of these is turn taking, with each participant alternating between the roles of speaker and listener. Another conversational strategy is turnabout, in which the speaker comments on what has been said while also adding a request to get the partner to respond again. By age 3 children understand a range of requests for action not directly expressed as requests. The child learns illocutionary intent, or what a person really means to say, even if the utterance is not completely consistent with it. Another example is the answer obvious rules. Statements phrased as questions are actually intended as directives. For example, the answer to "Could you hand me that pencil?" is obvious in that the listener knows to hand the speaker the pencil rather than answer the question.

4. What skills do children need for social referential communication?	*Social referential communication* involves a speaker sending a message that a listener comprehends. The communication is social because it occurs between two people; it is referential because the message is in a symbolic form; and it is communication because it is understood by the listener. To be effective, children must learn a subset of important skills. In the role of speaker, the child must become aware of listener cues, adjusting his or her messages to meet the listener's needs. Young children often fail to take into account listener cues and situational factors. Children also sometimes adjust their speech in response to the listener's age. Another useful listener cue involves common ground—information that is shared by both speaker and listener. Feedback is perhaps the most important listener cue. If the listener does not appear to understand what is being communicated, the speaker should change the message and try again. Listeners must also be aware of context cues, including information that has been given previously and the subject to which the information refers.
5. What are some links between development in pragmatics and cognitive development?	As in other areas of language development, *pragmatics skills* also depend on the emergence of certain cognitive abilities. As children's egocentric world decreases, for example, they better appreciate how another person might receive messages. As previously noted, as children's theory-of-mind understanding improves, they come to realize that listeners with different cognitive capabilities may interpret some information differently.

Learning Objective 10.7

Discuss the influences of family, technology,
language, and culture on literacy and learning.

1. How do parents and family characteristics influence language learning?	A major aspect of the child's immediate environment is the child's parents and other primary caretakers. Adults differ in how well and how often they speak to children. As mentioned previously, however, complexity and variety in language experiences contribute to children's language development. One factor that predicts the quality of a child's language environment is *socioeconomic status*, or SES. In general, children from low-income families experience significantly less oral and print language stimulation in their homes and neighborhoods. For this reason primarily, children from lower SES families tend to have smaller vocabularies and enter school with lower levels of prereading skills and language development. There also are significant differences in the quantity and quality of mother-child conversations across SES levels. An example of the importance of family context is the at-risk status of children of single-parent teens, who also tend to come from lower SES homes. Children of teenage mothers on average score lower on measures of cognitive competence, especially language-based assessments. Unfortunately, children who start off poorly in reading tend to remain poor readers throughout their schooling and beyond.

2. How do exposure to books and oral language promote literacy?

Reading with children is one of the most advocated early educational experiences, and research clearly shows a positive relationship between the amount of preschool reading exposure a child receives and the child's subsequent school performance. *Shared reading interaction* provides an opportunity for exposure to more sophisticated language as well as the formal rules associated with print. In *dialogic reading*, the adult asks challenging, open-ended questions about the content of a picture book and follows up the child's answer with more questions and provides praise. As a result, the child becomes the storyteller, and the adult becomes the active listener. Dialogic reading practices are associated with better vocabulary and expressive language development in children, especially those from at-risk backgrounds. In addition, children who are read to more often have better prereading skills and are more prepared to benefit from formal literacy instruction provided by school.

3. What are some best practices for providing children with prereading skills?

Children who are read to more often have better prereading skills and are more prepared to benefit from formal literacy instruction provided by schools. *Emergent literacy* refers to a set of prereading skills on which the ability to read is based. An important emergent literacy skill is phonological awareness—the awareness of and ability to manipulate the sound structure of oral language. Phonological awareness is considered necessary for normal reading development and is thought to be a major source of difficulty for children with reading problems. Children who are exposed to more shared reading interactions with rhyming and alphabet books may acquire phonological awareness more rapidly than other children. Just as dialogic reading encourages vocabulary and expressive language skills, books that stress letter names and sounds encourage alphabet knowledge and the development of phonological awareness. There are several other effective approaches to reading, but books are only one medium for encouraging language development. There is a growing consensus that oral language such as story-telling, recitation, and song plays a central role in the development of reading.

4. What effects do television and computers have on language development?

Research suggests that children who spend more time *viewing television* spend less time reading and interacting with others and score lower on tests of academic skills assessments. This is especially true for children who watch more than two hours a day, especially prime time shows and cartoons. These studies focus on time spent, however, rather than on the type of programming. Children who watch high-quality educational programs, such as Sesame Street or Barney, especially children from lower SES backgrounds, tend to enter school ready to read, have higher grades, read more books, and place more value on achievement. These positive outcomes associated with television viewing tend to be greater when viewing is limited to educational programs, when a caregiver views the program with the child, when the caregiver and child discuss the content, and when the content is linked to everyday learning experiences. However, research has shown that increased TV viewing is associated with a range of potential health problems, including aggression, lowered academic performance, distortions in body concept and self-image, increases in obesity, and attentional difficulties.

The effects of other media, such as computer and video games, have received less research attention than books and television. The effects of game playing on language development are not well studied. In general, the same recommendations that apply to television viewing should broadly apply to game playing and computer time.

Second-language and bilingual programs often reflect political rather than educational factors, with policy makers using scientific data to support their decisions. One main issue is how to best prepare children for what they must learn in the school curriculum to be successful (for example, math and science). A second issue is whether children who are learning two languages are delayed in learning the majority language. A third issue is the value of instructing minority children in their native tongue, which tells children that their cultural heritage is valued. Advocates of the bilingual model hope that it will help reduce the academic difficulties, school failures, and higher dropout rates of some minority groups. Deciding these issues requires an understanding of how the bilingual language learning process works.

One theory—the *single-system hypothesis*—is that bilingual children initially approach the task of learning two languages as if they were learning only one. That is, they do not separate the two forms of speech input but develop a single language system that includes elements of each. Only as they mature cognitively do the children learn to differentiate the two tongues, gradually treating them as independent languages. More recent research strongly challenges the single-system hypothesis. Studies of infant speech perception, for example, indicate clearly that babies can differentiate sounds and phonemes found in different languages. By 4 months of age, infants growing up in bilingual homes can differentiate sounds from the two languages, even when the languages are rhythmically similar. Hence, perceptual confusion does not appear to be a problem. Research that compares different approaches to educating bilingual children generally favors a *bilingual model* in which both languages are used in the early grades and children can gradually develop competence in the majority language.

Social *and* Emotional Worlds *of* Infants *and* Young Children

TEMPERAMENT
Learning Objective 11.1
DEFINE TEMPERAMENT AND DESCRIBE ITS ROLE IN CHILD DEVELOPMENT.
How Is Infant Temperament Measured?
Dimensions of Temperament
Understanding Different Temperament Profiles
Goodness of Fit: Parenting and Temperament
Stability of Temperament and Later Personality

EMOTIONS AND EARLY COMMUNICATION
Learning Objective 11.2
TRACE THE DEVELOPMENT OF EMOTIONS.
Understanding Emotions
Development of Emotional Expression
Emotions and Responding to Others
• Stranger Anxiety • Social Referencing
Emotions and Parent-Infant Interactions
• Parent-Infant Interaction Cycles • Parent-Infant Interaction Patterns • Problems in Parent-Infant Interaction
Emotions in Cross-Cultural Perspective
• Socialization of Emotions • Emotional Display Rules

ATTACHMENT TO OTHERS
Learning Objective 11.3
EXPLAIN THE ROLE OF ATTACHMENT IN CHILD DEVELOPMENT.
Why Do Infants Become Attached?
• Drive Reduction Theories • Other Psychoanalytic Perspectives • Ethological Approaches • Bowlby's Ethological Theory of Attachment
Individual Differences in Attachment
APPLICATIONS Promoting Healthy Parent-Infant Relationships
Causes and Consequences of Individual Differences in Attachment
• Temperament and Attachment • Consequences of Attachment • Attachment Across Generations
Culture and Attachment

ATTACHMENT RELATIONSHIPS IN A CHANGING WORLD
Learning Objective 11.4
DISCUSS SOCIETAL CHANGES THAT HAVE THE POTENTIAL TO AFFECT THE INFANT'S ATTACHMENT RELATION-SHIPS AND LATER DEVELOPMENT.
Nonparental Care and Attachment
The Changing Role of Fathers
Attachment and the Family Courts
RESEARCH & SOCIETY In the Child's Best Interest?
CONVERSATIONS with a CASA Volunteer Supervisor

SOCIAL AND EMOTIONAL DEVELOPMENT IN CONTEXTS OF RISK
Learning Objective 11.5
DISCUSS MAJOR HIGH-RISK CONTEXTS AND THEIR IMPACTS ON CHILDREN'S DEVELOPMENT.
Trauma
• Abuse and Neglect
Childhood Hospitalization
Severe Emotional Deprivation
Risk and Resilience

"When Eileen first held her newborn daughter, Avery, she felt almost overwhelmed with love for her. She thought of all the good things she wanted for her—health, well-being, a supportive family, and a satisfying work-life. She also thought of the challenges that lay ahead of her as a parent. Would she be able to provide her daughter with all that she needed to ensure a smooth and positive developmental path? When considering questions such as these, it is important for Eileen and other parents to keep in mind that they are not alone in their challenging new roles. Infants are born into social, cultural, and historical contexts consisting of extended family, neighborhoods, schools, communities, and the larger society. In addition, infants bring with them their own behaviors, which ultimately influence the lives they will lead.

This chapter uses an ecological model to examine biological and contextual influences on the social and emotional lives of infants. In what ways is early social and emotional development biologically based, and in what ways is it influenced by circumstances? To what extent are children born with a set of personality characteristics, emotions, or social tendencies? And to what extent is their development influenced by elements of the environment, such as family, neighborhood, and the larger culture? ■

Temperament

Temperament
The stable behavioral and emotional reactions that appear early and are influenced in part by genetic constitution.

Many parents who have had more than one child will find themselves making comments like Karen's, speaking of her two daughters, Jennifer and Brittany: "Jennifer was just always a bit more cautious and reserved. Although she was the younger one, it was Brittany who would rush headlong down the large slide at the Funland, and Jennifer who would stand back, uncertain that she wanted to try it. On the other hand, it was Jennifer who would spend her spare time reading while Brittany preferred ninja turtles. They're that way, even now. Brittany wanted to go to college several hundred miles from home, whereas Jennifer chose a school just an hour away." Karen's experience is common. Many parents can describe clear differences in the way that their children approach the world, and they believe that these differences are apparent from birth.

Most researchers who study child development agree that parents are picking up on a very real phenomenon called temperament. **Temperament** can be defined as "the stable behavioral and emotional reactions that appear early and are influenced in part by genetic constitution" (Kagan, 1994, p. 40). Many believe that these early tendencies to respond in predictable ways to environmental events provide the basis of adult personality (Caspi & Silva, 1995). Although researchers differ somewhat in their understanding of all the various aspects of temperament, they generally agree that qualities such as activity level, irritability,

How do you think your parents would have answered these questions about you?

Scale: 1 =Almost Never 6 =Almost Always

☐ The infant plays continuously for more than 10 minutes at a time with a favorite toy (rattle, mobile, etc.).

☐ The infant moves around much (kicks, grabs, squirms) during diapering and dressing.

☐ The infant greets a new toy (rattle, mobile) with a loud voice and much expression of feeling (whether positive or negative).

☐ The infant reacts (stares or startles) to sudden changes in lighting (flash bulbs, turning on lights).

☐ The infant gets sleepy at about the same time each evening (within 1/2 hour).

FIGURE 11.1 Sample questions from an Infancy Temperament Questionnaire

Source: James R. Cameron and David C. Rice, the Camereon-Rice Infant Temperament Questionnaire, derived with permission from the Revised Infant Temperament Questionnaire by W. B. Carey and S. C. McDevitt, 1978. See http://www.preventiveoz.org.

and sociability represent core dimensions of temperament (Goldsmith et al., 1987). For example, an infant may be more or less active, more or less responsive, more or less predictable in response, more or less persistent or distractible, more or less positive in mood, more or less receptive to novelty or adaptable to change, and so on.

Questions for Thought and Discussion
How might you describe temperamental differences between yourself and a sibling or between yourself and a parent? What are the nine dimensions of temperament described by child development researchers?

How Is Infant Temperament Measured?

Several different methods exist for measuring infant temperament. Parents may complete questionnaires regarding their infants' daily behavior. Two commonly used questionnaires are the Early Infancy Temperament Questionnaire (Medoff-Cooper, Carey, & McDevitt, 1993) and the Infant Temperament Questionnaire (Carey & McDevitt, 1978) (see Figure 11.1). Such questionnaires, like all self-report measures as you saw in Chapter 2, have the advantage of being easy to administer. However, parents' observations may be very subjective. Although parents may know their child's behavior better than anyone else does, their observations may reflect expectations based on gender or culture or may be influenced by personal circumstances such as stress level or marital satisfaction (Wolk, Zeanah, Garcia Coll, & Carr, 1992).

Links to Related Material
In Chapter 2, you read about some of the advantages and disadvantages of self-report methods, such as questionnaires. Here you learn more about how this method has been used to study infant temperament.

Other studies have found a good match between parents' perceptions and professionals' observations (Worobey & Blajda, 1989). Nevertheless, it is generally considered best to supplement parental ratings with other measures. Two common additional methods are behavioral ratings by others who know the infant well—such as doctors, nurses, or care providers—and direct observation by researchers (Bates, 1987). Observational ratings can be done either in a laboratory or in more natural settings (Bates & Bayles, 1984; Goldsmith & Rothbart, 1991). In some cases, physiological measures are also useful in describing temperament. For example, infants who tend to withdraw from novelty also exhibit higher heart rates in those situations (Kagan & Snidman, 1991). In general, it is best to use a combination of methods when trying to determine an infant's temperament.

Dimensions of Temperament

In their classic study of infant temperament, Thomas, Chess, and Birch (1970; Chess & Thomas, 1986; Thomas & Chess, 1977) followed 141 children from infancy to adulthood. This project, known as the **New York Longitudinal Study (NYLS)**, was begun in an effort to identify constitutional or inborn influences on children's behavior. Prior to this work, most researchers believed that individual differences in infants' behavior were due

New York Longitudinal Study (NYLS)
A well-known longitudinal study conducted by Thomas and Chess that examines infant temperament and its implications for later psychological adjustment.

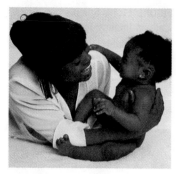

Of the three main patterns or profiles of temperament, researchers might describe this baby as an "easy child" rather than a "difficult" or "slow-to-warm-up" child. This mother seems to enjoy "goodness of fit" with her baby's temperament, but this is not always the case. Parents often have to learn to adjust their expectations and responses to better fit the temperament with which their infant was born. How might this picture be different if the mother were adapting her interaction to better suit her "slow-to-warm-up" child? (© Camille Tokerud/Photo Researchers)

Question for Thought and Discussion

How would you characterize your temperament? Has it remained stable since you were a child? Which aspects, if any, have changed?

to differences in parenting. Through the NYLS, however, researchers were able to identify nine dimensions of behavior that appear to have a biological basis.

1. *Activity level* refers to how physically active the infant is, and what the daily proportion is of active to inactive periods. For example, some infants may move around so much while they sleep that they must be re-covered several times a night, while other infants may move very little during sleep.

2. *Rhythmicity* is defined as predictability or regularity in the infant's patterns of sleep, feeding, and elimination. For example, some infants may eat exactly 4 ounces of formula every three hours, whereas other infants may vary from day to day in the amounts and times they eat.

3. *Approach–withdrawal* can be understood as the way in which an infant initially responds to a new stimulus, such as a new food, toy, or person. For example, some infants may smile and reach enthusiastically for a new toy, while others may either ignore it or push it away.

4. *Adaptability* refers to the ease with which an infant modifies his or her responses to change or novelty. For example, some infants may initially resist putting on a new snowsuit but then quickly adapt, so that after a few tries the change in clothing comes easily. Other infants may continue to resist the new snowsuit for weeks.

5. *Threshold of responsiveness* is defined as the intensity level of a stimulus that's needed before the infant responds. For example, an infant with a high threshold of responsiveness might be able to sleep through a lot of very loud noise, whereas an infant with a low threshold of responsiveness might startle at the sound of a door closing softly.

6. *Intensity of reaction* can be understood as the energy level of a response. For example, some infants will cry loudly as soon as they are hungry, while others may fuss only mildly.

7. *Quality of mood* refers to the amount of pleasant, friendly, joyful behavior that the infant exhibits, as compared to the amount of unpleasant, unfriendly, or crying behavior. For example, an infant who wakes up smiling and cooing is exhibiting positive mood, whereas an infant who wakes up fussing and frowning is exhibiting negative mood.

8. *Distractibility* is defined as the ease with which environmental stimuli can alter a child's behavior. For example, some infants will persist in fussing over a coveted cookie despite coaxing with any number of toys, while other infants will quickly forget the cookie and be easily distracted by the offered toy.

9. *Attention span and persistence* can be understood as the length of time an activity is pursued by an infant and the continuation of that activity in the face of obstacles. For example, some infants may play with the same toy for lengthy periods of time, and return to it following an interruption, whereas other infants may play with a toy for only a few minutes and then seem to forget about it.

Understanding Different Temperament Profiles

In addition to identifying these nine dimensions of temperament, Thomas, Chess, and Birch also noticed that certain characteristics of infant temperament seem to occur together in constellations or patterns. These patterns fall into three distinct types, plus a fourth mixed group that is not easily classifiable.

1. *The easy child* (40 percent of the NYLS sample) displays regularity in daily sleep, feeding, and elimination, responds well to new situations, adapts quickly to change, and is frequently cheerful.

2. *The difficult child* (10 percent of the NYLS sample) is irregular in daily sleep, feeding, and elimination patterns, is slow to accept change, and has intense, negative reactions.

3. *The slow-to-warm-up child* (15 percent of the NYLS sample) withdraws initially from new toys, food, or people, and is hesitant to accept change.

4. The remaining 35 percent of children in the NYLS sample displayed differing mixtures of the nine temperament dimensions and did not fit easily into any of the first three groups.

Goodness of Fit: Parenting and Temperament

Researchers generally believe that dimensions and patterns of temperament have a constitutional or biological basis. That is, infants come into the world with tendencies to react to their environments in certain ways (Goldsmith et al., 1987). However, temperament is not the same as personality. Nor does temperament directly determine personality. Instead, as you would expect using an interactional perspective on development, personality is shaped by the specific ways in which parents and other adults respond to the qualities of temperament that the infant displays. These responses shape the child's own growing sense of self.

The infant's constitutional way of behaving may match what parents expect from their child, or it may not match (Chess & Thomas, 1986). For example, Rosa was an outgoing person who expected that a happy infant should be physically active and should enjoy being swung vigorously in her mother's arms (an activity that many infants do enjoy). At 12 months, however, Natalie found such activities frightening rather than fun. Rosa also expected that her child would show affection with exuberant kisses and smiles, but Natalie was reserved and mild in her responses. Rosa worried that her baby didn't love her, and their relationship was becoming increasingly dominated by feelings of anxiety and frustration. It was a relief for Rosa to learn that there was nothing wrong with either Natalie or herself. She had a lovely, completely normal baby with a slow-to-warm-up temperament. By adjusting her expectations for and responses to Natalie's constitutional reactions, the two were able to develop a warm and accepting relationship.

Some parents are like Rosa and find themselves puzzled by a slow-to-warm-up or "shy" baby. Others, however, are like Emily and David, whose 20-month-old son, Zachary, was constantly in motion and had frequent, intensely negative reactions to minor daily events. Bedtime was a constant struggle, and Zachary often would not be asleep until after midnight. Mealtimes felt like a continual battle, with Emily practically begging him to "take just one more bite for Mommy." She worried that Zachary's behavior was somehow her fault, that she had done something to "cause" it, and tension grew between herself and David. Like Rosa, Emily and David felt relieved to learn that Zachary's temperament was something he had been born with. The challenge became that of finding ways to help Zachary cope with changes in his daily routine, even while they as parents became more patient with some of his unpredictability.

Such stories are common in clinical practice and represent instances where there is a poor fit between the child's temperament and the parents' expectations. When a good fit exists, family relationships become more harmonious and children develop a more positive sense of self as well as more flexible ways of coping with whatever temperamental tendencies they were born with. Improving the **goodness of fit** becomes a way of helping each child and each family realize their full potential as individuals and as relational partners.

Stability of Temperament and Later Personality

Researchers have found that toward the end of the first year, temperamental characteristics such as activity level and response to novelty are somewhat predictive of later behavior (Kagan & Snidman, 1991). However, it is much more difficult to predict later behavior based on temperamental differences in newborns (Gunnar et al., 1995). This lack of perfect prediction reminds us that development is not determined by any one single factor. Instead, children grow up in a social context that interacts with and shapes their inborn tendencies. Not only parents, but also peers, teachers, and other adults with whom the

Links to Related Material
In Chapter 3, you read how kinship studies have helped us understand the heritability of dimensions of temperament. Here you learn more about the manifestation of temperament in infant behavior, and the ways in which parents' own behaviors influence temperament.

Goodness of fit
The extent to which a baby's temperament fits with the behavioral expectations of parents and other adults in the environment.

In addition to the response of parents and other adults, other aspects of the environment may determine goodness of fit with a child's temperament. DeVries (1989) studied Masai infants in Africa and found that temperamentally difficult infants seemed to do better over time than temperamentally easy infants. The researchers speculate that in a region where food was scarce and maternal health was not optimal, fussier infants were more likely to get their needs met. Whether or not a particular temperament is adaptive clearly depends on goodness of fit with the total environment into which the infant is born. (Marilyn Parver/Danita Delimont)

child interacts will respond to the child's behavior in a negative or positive fashion, thus providing the child with important feedback. This feedback in turn will serve to shape the child's sense of self and expectations for the future.

For example, a classroom setting with lots of quiet individual seat-time may be well suited to a child with a low activity level and a long attention span. Other children, however, may find they are targets of frequent adult criticism in such a setting. They may do better in learning environments that allow for more physical activity and briefer engagements with learning tasks. The infant's personality ultimately depends on the ways in which a variety of others respond to his or her temperament throughout childhood. Temperament thus interacts with social context throughout a child's life.

✔ *Test Your Mastery...*

Learning Objective 11.1: *Define temperament and describe its role in child development.*

1. What is temperament?
2. How is infant temperament measured?
3. What are the nine dimensions of temperament?
4. What are the three major temperament profiles?
5. What is goodness of fit, and how does it affect the child's development?
6. Is temperament stable across time?

Emotions and Early Communication

Learning Objective 11.2
Trace the development of emotions.

The development of emotions is another area in which you can see the interaction between biology and social context. Researchers have noticed that people around the world associate particular facial expressions with specific emotions (Ekman & Friesen, 1972). Certain emotions, such as happiness, surprise, fear, anger, sadness, disgust, and interest, appear to be universally recognizable. For example, to people around the world bright eyes and a smile indicate happiness, whereas a squared mouth and downward pointing brows mean anger. Some researchers say that these universally recognizable facial expressions represent basic emotions that are present in infants (Izard, 1991).

Understanding Emotions

When 2-year-old Neema arrived at his new preschool center with his mother, his first response was to cuddle closer, burying his face in his mother's arms. When the director of the center approached him, he smiled shyly but still clung to his mother, wary of this new place and this new person. Over the next hour, the preschool director and his new teachers observed many emotional reactions in Neema: interest in the activities going on around him, excitement as he joined the other children in a brief jumping game, tears when his mother said goodbye to him, renewed interest as he rejoined the other children for some filling and spilling play in the water center, surprise and anger when another child grabbed the bucket he was holding, and happiness when it was returned to him.

Neema's emotions seemed clearly understandable to his caregivers in this situation. This section considers emotions more carefully from a theoretical perspective: What exactly are emotions? What characterizes emotional experiences and their occurrence?

An **emotion** can be understood as reactions, including feelings, thoughts, and behaviors, that arise in response to personally significant events or situations. The situations that elicit these responses can be any person, thought, or event that has significance for an individual. Emotions may involve physiological arousal (such as a rapidly beating heart), thoughts about the situation (such as Neema thinking about being in an unfamiliar setting with exciting new play opportunities as well as potentially scary new demands), and behavioral expressions (such as Neema demonstrating wariness by cuddling closer to Mom and expressing sadness through tears at her departure).

Many researchers today emphasize that emotions prepare a person to act in situations that have high personal relevance (Saarni, Mumme, & Campos, 1998). For Neema, for example, a new preschool setting has high personal relevance. His responses (wariness, interest, sadness, excitement, anger, happiness) helped him adapt to the situation and manage his experience there. Variously, for example, these responses motivated him to stay close to his mother, accept her departure, explore and participate in new activities with new people, and maintain possession of desired toys.

This definition of emotion represents a *functionalist approach* because it emphasizes a person's goals or intentions within a particular context and in relation to others (Barrett & Campos, 1987). This approach stresses the close link between emotions and actions and the fact that emotions serve a social function. Thus, emotions are transactional in nature—that is, they occur in social contexts and reflect ongoing interactions between people (Saarni, Mumme, & Campos, 1998).

Development of Emotional Expression

Because infants cannot tell us what they are feeling, much of our understanding of early emotional development has come about through studying infants' facial expressions (Malatesta, Izard, & Camras, 1991). Even newborns possess all the facial muscle movements necessary to produce virtually any adult emotional expression. Researchers have developed detailed coding procedures for assessing babies' facial expressions, involving separate ratings for the brow, eye, and mouth areas (Izard, 1989).

From birth, babies can indicate *distress* by crying and *interest* by staring attentively. As you saw in Chapter 5, one stimulus that babies reliably enjoy looking at is the human face, illustrating how evolution encourages parent-infant interaction right from the

Emotion
Reactions, including feelings, thoughts, and behaviors, that arise in response to personally significant events or situations.

Although researchers disagree about the extent to which emotions are differentiated at birth (Sroufe, 1979), most believe that the basic emotions can be detected in infants' facial expressions very early in life. How would you identify the emotions expressed by these infants? Do you think these emotions would be universally recognized? Babies' facial expressions of the basic emotions appear at different points in development (Camras, Malatesta, & Izard, 1991; Ekman, 1993), and there is some disagreement about exactly what the basic emotions are (Izard, 1993; Sroufe, 1996). (Image 100/photolibrary)

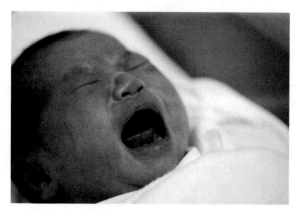  

These children are showing emotional states that researchers can infer from measurements of their facial features. How would you re-sequence the images to show the development of emotions over time? What does the chronology of emotional development tell us about the basic functions of emotions in supporting individual survival? What might account for the fact that complex emotional responses become more self-conscious as children grow older? (*Left*, Tongro Image Stock/Age Fotostock America, Inc.; *middle*, thislife pictures/Alamy; *right*, Photodisc/photolibrary)

Links to Related Material

In Chapter 5, you read how new-borns enjoy looking at the human face. Here, you learn more about how this inborn tendency sets the stage for social interaction.

Social smile
The broad grin that infants show in response to a human voice or face, typically beginning by 10 to 12 weeks of age.

Self-conscious emotions
The complex emotional responses (such as pride, guilt, and embarrassment) that typically arise in situations that involve injury or enhancement of one's sense of self.

beginning. Another inborn facial expression is *disgust*, which is elicited by unpleasant tastes or odors, usually signaling to the caregiver that feeding is not going the way it should (Rosenstein & Oster, 1988; Steiner, 1979).

In the first weeks of life, infants smile (demonstrating *pleasure* or *happiness*) when full, during REM sleep, and in response to a caregiver's gentle touching and vocalizing. By 10 to 12 weeks of age, the infant responds to a human voice or face with a broad grin called the **social smile** (Haviland & Lelwica, 1987).

Sadness and *anger*—demonstrated experimentally by removing a teething toy or by re-straining the baby's arm—are first evident in facial expressions at 3 or 4 months (Lewis, Alessandri, & Sullivan, 1990; Stenberg, Campos, & Emde, 1983). Facial expressions indi-cating *fear* do not appear until about 7 months. More complex emotional responses, such as those for *pride, guilt, shame,* and *embarrassment*, are not apparent until the child is 18 to 24 months of age (Tangney & Fischer, 1995). These more complex emotional responses are known as the **self-conscious emotions** because they typically arise in situations that in-volve injury or enhancement of one's sense of self. Their relatively late emergence most likely reflects advancements during the second year of life in the infant's emerging sense of self.

Emotions and Responding to Others

In addition to expressing emotions of their own, babies must learn to recognize and respond to the emotions of others. An infant's ability to recognize facial expressions of emotion seems to develop in stages (Baldwin & Moses, 1996; Nelson, 1987; Walker-Andrews, 1997). Babies younger than 6 weeks are not very good at scanning faces for detail. As a result, they do not recognize different emotional expressions (Field & Walden, 1982). Soon after, however, infants begin to show evidence of being able to discriminate among facial expressions. For example, babies who have been habituated to a photo of a smiling face show renewed attention when the photo is changed to a frowning face (Barrera & Maurer, 1981). Babies over six weeks of age discriminate even better when they view talking faces, although in these circumstances the voice may also provide important cues (Caron, Caron, & MacLean, 1988).

But do babies in this second stage have any real understanding of the emotions that are being expressed? Probably not. It is more likely that they simply can tell that the faces look different, without appreciating that a sad look represents unhappiness or a smiling face joy. After infants reach 5 to 6 months of age, however, they appear to develop a clearer understanding of the meanings of emotional expressions. This is shown, for example, by the fact that at this age babies begin to display the same emotion as is displayed on the face they are viewing (smiling at a happy face) and prefer some emotional expressions to others (Balaban, 1995; Haviland & Lelwica, 1987; Izard et al., 1995; Ludemann, 1991).

Near the end of the first year, infants begin to use information about other people's emotional expressions to regulate their own behavior (Feinman et al., 1992; Klinnert et al., 1983). Babies are especially likely to look to their mothers or fathers for this type of guidance when they are uncertain what to do next, such as when they encounter an unfamiliar object or person. They then use the parent's expression as a guide to how to react in the situation. Parents may sometimes aid this learning process by unconsciously exaggerating their expressions of emotions.

Stranger Anxiety Responding to others often involves responding to strangers. For example, Karen and Phil had moved to California before Jennifer was born. When Jennifer was 9 months old, they had an opportunity to visit Karen's in-laws on the East Coast. Phil's parents were very eager to finally see their first grandchild. With an enthusiastic greeting, Grandpa swooped Jennifer out of her mother's arms, and was taken aback when she burst into loud tears and reached for her mother. Karen explained apologetically that Jennifer had been very fearful of strangers lately.

Many infants respond to strangers the way that Jennifer did—with fear. Appropriately named **stranger anxiety**, this phenomenon begins at about 6 or 7 months of age and can continue into the second year. Not all infants show stranger anxiety to the same degree, however. Many different factors seem to influence the extent to which infants of this age show fear toward strangers. For example, Karen was a full-time mother, and Jennifer had little experience with strangers. There is some evidence that infants who are frequently exposed to strangers exhibit less stranger anxiety (Gullone & King, 1997). In addition, babies who are temperamentally shy may react more strongly. The circumstances of the meeting may also influence the baby's reaction. Infants may react more strongly in an unfamiliar setting or with strangers who approach them too quickly or otherwise behave in an unexpected manner (Thompson & Limber, 1991).

Social Referencing At 8 or 9 months of age, infants begin to seek emotional information from trusted adults when they are faced with uncertainty (Walden & Ogan, 1988). For example, one morning when LaShawn stopped to chat with a neighbor, the neighbor's Labrador retriever came bounding out, excitedly wagging its tail and sniffing the humans it encountered. Keshia, LaShawn's 10-month-old daughter, was sitting in her stroller. Keshia looked at her mother uncertainly as the dog approached. LaShawn smiled encouragingly. Keshia then also smiled and relaxed while the dog sniffed her legs. If LaShawn had responded to the dog's approach with a look of fear or concern, it is likely that Keshia would also have become distressed. Incidents such as this illustrate the phenomenon of *social referencing* (Feinman et al., 1992; Klinnert et al., 1983). With social referencing, the infant relies on trusted adults to provide them with the emotional information they need to interpret and respond appropriately to an ambiguous situation.

Stranger anxiety
A general fear of unfamiliar people that appears in many infants at around 7 months of age.

Social referencing
The infant's tendency to look to the parents for guidance when uncertain how to respond to an unfamiliar object or person.

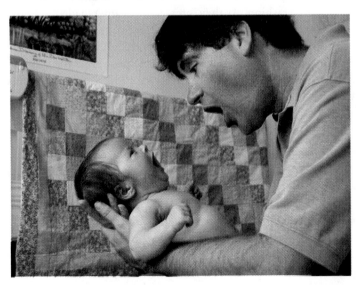

This picture highlights the development of emotions as essentially a result of social transactions. It also suggests the importance of learning how to interpret others' emotions, which may be a key to others' intentions. This baby is imitating, or mirroring, another's expression of emotion as seen in the other's facial expression. Do you think the baby may be having the same feelings? Do you think he or she knows the meaning of the emotion being expressed?
(Geri Engberg/The Image Works)

Links to Related Material
In Chapter 5, you read about how the visual-cliff procedure is used to study perception in infants. Here, you learn more about how social information from the parents can influence an infant's behavior in this procedure.

In a study that clearly illustrates this process, 1-year-old infants and their parents were studied as they interacted on the visual-cliff apparatus described in Chapter 5. The baby was placed on the shallow side, and the parent and an attractive toy were positioned at the other end, which was designed to simulate a drop of 30 cm. It thus deliberately presented the infant with an ambiguous situation—a drop that may or may not be safe. This ambiguous situation produced uncertainty in the infants, who generally responded with caution and with frequent looks to their parents, as if attempting to gain information about how to respond. The parents were instructed to respond to the infant's uncertainty by producing specific facial expressions, including fear, happiness, anger, interest, and sadness.

The question of interest to the researchers was whether the parents' emotional expression would influence the infant's behavior on the visual cliff. The results indicate that it did. When parents expressed joy or interest, most babies crossed over to the other side to reach them. When parents expressed fear or anger, however, very few babies ventured onto the side that represented an ambiguous depth (Sorce et al., 1985). Similar results have been found when parents were instructed to express different emotions toward an unfamiliar person or a new toy. Babies' willingness to approach and interact with the person or toy depended on the nature of the parents' reaction—both the facial expression and the tone of voice (Baldwin & Moses, 1994; Boccia & Campos, 1989; Mumme, Fernald, & Herrera, 1996). Thus, babies as young as 1 year appear able to use another person's emotional reactions as a gauge for understanding and adjusting to their environment.

Parents can use the infant's social referencing skills to their advantage. There is a window of time during an experience when parents can alter their responses to influence or change the baby's response. For example, by communicating a positive reaction to a surprising encounter, perhaps by smiling or speaking in a pleasant voice, parents can reduce the infant's uncertainty and possible distress (Hornik & Gunnar, 1988; Klinnert et al., 1984).

Emotions and Parent-Infant Interactions

During the first 3 or 4 months of life, much of the infant's contact with parents and other caregivers involves *face-to-face interactions*, such as those that occur during feeding, diapering, and, in some cultures, play. Western psychologists attach considerable significance to these early interactions, believing that they are fundamental to the development of an effective communication system between mother and baby and ultimately to the development of a close relationship (Brazelton & Yogman, 1986; Isabella, 1993, 1994).

Researchers investigate these early dyadic interactions in laboratory settings. The baby and parent sit facing each other, and the parent typically is instructed to play with the infant in her normal fashion. As they interact, one camera videotapes the parent's face and another videotapes the baby's. By replaying the two tapes side by side—often comparing only one frame at a time—investigators can examine the interactions in great detail. This technique, known as **microanalysis**, has helped reveal the subtle ways in which infants and parents influence one another (Kaye, 1982; Lamb, Thompson, & Frodi, 1982). Study of these early interactions has revealed two principal features—cycles and patterns—that characterize both newborn behavior in general and parent-infant dyadic exchanges in particular.

Microanalysis
A research technique for studying parent-infant interactions, in which the parent and baby are simultaneously videotaped with different cameras and then the tapes are examined side by side.

Parent-Infant Interaction Cycles   Newborns appear to cycle from states of attention and interest to states of inattention and avoidance. During the attention phase, they make eye contact with the caregiver and often display positive affect, such as by smiling and vocalizing, whereas during the inattention phase they avoid eye contact and are more likely to show distress. Some psychologists believe that periods of attention can become too arousing and stressful for infants and that infants keep this stimulation under control by turning away and perhaps by self-comforting, for instance, by putting the thumb in the mouth (Field, 1987; Gianino & Tronick, 1988). These early face-to-face interactions are important because they provide the baby with opportunities to regulate his or her own emotions through behaviors that increase positive feelings and decrease negative feelings (Fox, 1994; Thompson, Flood, & Lundquist, 1995).

Parent-Infant Interaction Patterns   Early, repeated interactions produce patterns of behavior between the caregiver and the infant. As parents come to recognize the baby's cycles of attention and inattention, they adjust their own behavior to better fit them. Microanalytic studies of parent-infant interaction during the first 4 months have shown that parents gradually learn to concentrate their emotional displays (talking, tickling, and smiling) during those times when the baby is attending to them. When the baby looks away, the parent's responses decline. Soon the infant and parent develop an **interactional synchrony** in behavior, so that they are both "on" or both "off" at about the same time (Kaye, 1982). In this way, parents maximize opportunities to "teach" the baby, and the baby can regulate the amount of interaction that takes place.

Once a synchronous pattern has developed between the parent and baby, a second pattern begins to emerge. The parent waits for the baby to respond and then responds back. Sometimes these responses are imitative (the mother produces the same sound that the baby has just made), sometimes they are repetitive (the father wiggles the baby's toes after each response), and sometimes they take other forms. But all of them serve to "answer" the infant's responses. This *turn-taking* pattern between caregivers and babies may represent the first conversational "dialogues," which later become more obvious as speech and language develop (Beebe et al., 1988; Masataka, 1993; Mayer & Tronick, 1985). Babies appear to enjoy turn-taking episodes, often displaying a good deal of smiling and positive vocalizations.

Problems in Parent-Infant Interaction   An issue with face-to-face interactions is what happens when they are disrupted. A revealing experimental technique involves having the mother present the baby with no expression at all. The results of this *still-face* procedure have been fairly consistent across a number of studies (Cohn & Tronick, 1983; Ellsworth, Muir, & Hains, 1993; Segal et al., 1995; Toda & Fogel, 1993). Generally, babies at first attempt to engage the mother's attention, sometimes by pointing, vocalizing, or looking at her inquisitively. When the mother fails to respond, the infants usually begin to show signs of distress and protest. They reduce their overall level of positive affect and often gaze in a different direction. These findings are consistent with the belief that the infant and mother develop an interaction pattern within the first few months that becomes comfortable for both of them. When one member of the pair (in this case, the mother) violates that pattern, however, the system is disrupted, and the other member (here, the baby) has difficulty coping with the new interactional style.

The importance of a smooth-running pattern of infant-caregiver interactions can also be seen in studies with mothers who are clinically depressed. These mothers have been found to be much less positive or responsive to their babies, and they do not synchronize well with the infants' behaviors. The babies, in turn, are less active and attentive and spend much of their time crying or displaying other forms of distress (Cohn et al., 1990; Field et al., 1990; Murray et al., 1996). Importantly, however, such infants do not display this sort of behavior with their nursery teachers (Pelaez-Nogueras et al., 1994), suggesting that it is the absence of a synchronous relationship with the caregiver that causes the infants to respond in this way.

Some studies suggest that the absence of a synchronous relationship may be a factor in child abuse. Disruption in mother-infant interaction caused by premature birth, for example, may relate to the fact that preterm infants are at greater risk for abuse than full-term babies. Studies have shown that preterm babies spend more time asleep, are less alert when awake, are more quickly overaroused by social stimulation, and spend more time averting their gaze from the caregiver. In turn, their mothers spend less time in face-to-face interaction with them, smile at and touch them less, and are less skilled at reading their emotional signals (Kropp & Haynes, 1987; Lester, Hoffman, & Brazelton, 1985; Malatesta et al., 1986). Prematurity does not prevent the development of a secure attach-

Interactional synchrony
The smooth coordination of behaviors between parent and baby.

Links to Related Material
In Chapter 5, you read about infants' arousal states. Here, you learn more about how parents use these states to time their interactions with infants during periods of alertnesss.

Question for Thought and Discussion
Based on your observations or experience, in what ways is the process of parent-child interaction both bidirectional and transactional?

ment relationship (van IJzendoorn et al., 1992), but it does disrupt normal face-to-face emotional interaction. This disruption interferes with the establishment of a synchronous relationship between mother and baby, which possibly increases the likelihood of abuse.

Another factor in mother-infant relationships is *affect mirroring,* or the degree to which mothers respond emotionally to emotional input from their infants (Legerstee & Varghese, 2001). Infant behavior patterns correspond to the level of maternal affect mirroring. That is, infants of mothers high in this measure display more positive affect, greater attention toward their mothers, and stronger preference for responsive input (smiles and the like) than do infants of mothers low in affect mirroring.

Emotions in Cross-Cultural Perspective

The emergence of emotions in infancy is guided primarily by biological processes and is universal across cultures (Izard, 1995). Even in early infancy, however, emotional development is influenced not only by the child's inborn tendencies and parents' responses to those tendencies, but also by broader cultural attitudes and practices. Culture shapes the way emotions are expressed, managed, and interpreted in a society.

Patterns of social interaction are not universal. For example, face-to-face interactions are based on the view that infants are autonomous conversational partners—with little to say, perhaps—from shortly after birth. Not all cultures attribute this characteristic to young infants, however. Cultural variations in early parent-infant interaction suggest that there are multiple pathways to the formation of emotional bonds between infants and others.

For example, the Kaluli people of the tropical rainforest of Papua New Guinea see their babies as helpless creatures who have "no understanding." Consequently, Kaluli do not engage in conversational dialogues with them. Mothers are highly attentive to their infants' cries and physical needs, however. Infants nurse on demand, although mothers often combine nursing with other activities and largely direct their attention elsewhere. Kaluli mothers greet their infants by name and use expressive vocalizations, but they avoid looking into the babies' eyes while doing so. The Kaluli believe it is impolite to look into a person's eyes when speaking to him or her, and they also associate the act with witchcraft. Although Kaluli mothers are almost always holding or carrying their infants, they tend to face them outward so that the infants can see and be seen by others (Ochs & Schieffelin, 1984). The practice of facing infants outward is common to many cultures, including some African American communities (Heath, 1983; Martini & Kirkpatrick, 1981; Sostek et al., 1981). The practice serves to encourage triadic (three-person) or multiparty interactions and reflects a more general cultural orientation toward embeddedness in a complex social world.

Socialization of Emotions   Early in life, infants display emotional expressions that parents recognize as sadness, interest, disgust, pleasure, surprise, anger, and fear. Although our biology provides a basis for these reactions, emotional behavior in all societies is governed by an elaborate set of rules that tell us how and when emotions should be expressed, as well as how emotions are managed, labeled, and interpreted (Lewis & Michaelson, 1983; Lewis & Saarni, 1985). In North America, small children are taught to hide their disappointment at receiving socks from Aunt Ellen for their birthday, for example, and not to whine when Mom refuses them candy before dinner.

This **socialization**—the process through which society molds a child's beliefs, expectations, and behavior—begins in the early months of life. Studies have shown that when playing with their infants, American mothers are more likely to model positive than negative emotions (Malatesta, 1985; Keller & Schoelmerich, 1987). The babies, in turn, tend to match these expressions (Haviland & Lelwica, 1987). This process may be one reason that over the course of the first year infants' positive emotional signals typically increase, while their negative responses decrease (Malatesta et al., 1989). In contrast, Gusii mothers in Kenya prefer to dampen intense emotional displays in their infants, whether positive or negative (Dixon, Tronick, Keeler, & Brazelton, 1981). Among the Utku of northern

Links to Related Material
In Chapter 7, you read about Vygotsky's concept of scaffolding, and how caretakers structure the child's participation in ongoing activities. Here, you learn more about how culture influences the types of social and emotional behaviors that parents encourage in their children.

Socialization
The process through which society molds a child's beliefs, expectations, and behavior.

In middle-class European American households, simple face-to-face interaction between the mother and baby peaks at about 3 to 4 months. After that, mothers increasingly direct their infant's attention outward toward objects and events in the world (Adamson & Bakeman, 1991; Lamb, Morrison, & Malkin, 1987). Japanese mothers, in contrast, continue to solicit their infants' attention and use objects to direct the babies' attention inward toward themselves for many months to come (Bornstein, Tal, & Tamis-LaMonda, 1991; Bornstein et al., 1990). (Ryuichi Sato/Taxi Japan/ Getty Images)

Canada, displays of anger in either gender are strongly discouraged once the child is weaned (Briggs, 1970).

In Japan, the expression of negative emotion is strongly discouraged. Japanese parents commonly model restraint of emotion and actively avoid confrontations and contests of will in which negative emotions are likely to be expressed. When Japanese parents oppose their children, they tend to express opposition indirectly via silence or withdrawal of attention (Azuma, 1996; Lebra, 1994; Miyake et al., 1986). In addition, researchers have found that mothers reinforce the smiles of their infant sons at a higher rate, while displaying a wider range of emotional expressions to their daughters. Researchers speculate that such experiences could provide the foundations for gender differences in boys' and girls' emotional expressiveness, with boys more restricted to the display of positive feelings and girls more comfortable with a broad range of emotions (Haviland & Malatesta, 1981; Malatesta & Haviland, 1985).

In cultures where infants are in nearly constant physical contact with caregivers, researchers have found that babies of both genders are less likely to express distress (Keller, Voelker, & Yovsi, 2005). For example, among the Inuit of Arctic Quebec, infants are almost always found in a pouch inside their mother's parka. Under these circumstances, small postural changes or movements are sufficient to elicit a response from caregivers. Indeed, observers often remark how little infants cry in communities where they are constantly held. Martha Crago, who studies language acquisition among the Inuit, noted:

> Infants wiggle and their mothers know they have awakened. They squirm and their mothers sense their hunger or discomfort. In some homes, I found the babies hardly needed to cry to have their needs known and responded to. I remember being with one family and finding that a whole day had gone by and I had never heard the one-month-old peep. Her mother would be carrying her in [her parka] and for no reason that was perceptible to me the infant would be taken out and fed. (Crago, 1988, p. 204).

Emotional Display Rules   Older infants and preschoolers generally learn to identify and label their emotions through everyday experiences. For example, parents might point out how a child is feeling ("You seem to be angry with Mommy" or "That baby must be feeling upset about dropping her ice cream cone") (Denham, Zoller, & Couchoud, 1994; Smiley & Huttenlocher, 1989). This information contributes to children's socialization into the rules for displaying emotions.

Question for Thought and Discussion

What emotional display rules were part of your socialization as a child in your family? How do you think your experiences with display rules affected your social and emotional development?

At first babies' affective expressions closely mirror their emotions, but over time children learn to control their emotional displays. What they express may not reflect what they are feeling (Saarni, 1989, 1990, 1999). Children may attempt to conceal emotions as they come to understand their culture's **emotional display rules**—cultural expectations regarding the appropriate expression of emotions (Davis, 1995; Malatesta & Haviland, 1982; Underwood, Coie, & Herbsman, 1992). Children begin to understand these implicit rules as early as age 2 (Lewis & Michaelson, 1985). For example, boys growing up in contemporary U.S. society may learn that displaying fear or pain is seen as less appropriate for boys than for girls, and so they may try to inhibit expressions of such emotions. Once again, we see that biology interacts with social context, and development is shaped by many forces in the child's life.

Learning Objective 11.2: *Trace the development of emotions.*

1. What are emotions?
2. How do emotions develop?
3. How do social referencing and stranger anxiety help infants regulate their own behavior?
4. What effect do face-to-face interactions have on infants' emotional development?
5. How does culture serve to shape face-to-face interactions and the expression of emotions?

Attachment to Others

At 13 months, Keshia enjoyed going on neighborhood picnics with her parents, LaShawn and Michael. There were always other families there to visit with, as well as interesting things to do and see. One day, LaShawn and Michael were sitting at a picnic table in the shade talking with some of the other parents. Keshia was a few feet away in a mixed-age group of small children. A new walker, she was excited to be able to join this group of "big kids" on her own two feet, and she was eager to join their game of tag. Although she did not really understand the rules, she played enthusiastically for several minutes. Suddenly, however, she became confused and wasn't quite sure which clump of grown-ups around her contained her parents. She stopped in mid-track and looked around fearfully, her face beginning to scrunch with tears. Just as she let out her first loud wail, she heard one of the other parents say, "There's Mommy and Daddy right over there." Sobbing, Keshia ran as fast as she could to her parents. LaShawn picked her up and held her on her lap. Almost instantly, Keshia's distress was gone. After only a minute, she was happy and smiling, ready to get down and begin exploring again.

Keshia's behavior is an example of **attachment**, which can be defined as the enduring emotional bond that exists between a child and those people who are significant in his or her life. Clearly evident by 12 months of age, attachment both furnishes the child with the sense of security necessary for exploring the environment and provides a safe haven and source of comfort during times of distress. Although specific attachment behaviors change as we grow older, attachment as an emotional experience remains with us throughout our lives.

John Bowlby (1969), a British psychiatrist, identified four stages in the formation of attachment relationships during the first years of life:

1. *Preattachment:* Orientation without discrimination (birth to 8–12 weeks). At birth, infants are predisposed to respond to the people around them in specific ways. They turn their heads and attempt to look at the source of voices they hear. They grasp and reach, smile and babble at the faces they see around them. Often, they cease crying when they hear or see someone approaching. These are social capabilities that infants are born with, and in the first few weeks of life they display these behaviors toward everyone. They do not seem to discriminate among the various people whom they see.

Emotional display rules
The expectations and attitudes a society holds toward the expression of certain emotions.

Test Your Mastery...

Learning Objective 11.3
Explain the role of attachment in child development.

Attachment
The enduring emotional bond that arises between infants and their parents or other primary caregivers.

2. *Beginnings of attachment:* *Discriminating responsiveness* (3 to 6–8 months). After a few months, infants remain friendly and responsive toward the people they see around them, but their responses become more intense toward the few people who are most involved in caring for them. At this age, babies will usually accept being held by a stranger, but will also clearly recognize their parents and other primary caretakers, and will show some preference for them. For example, when Keiko and Taki brought 5-month-old Masami to a convention with them, Masami was happy to be held by the various adults she met. However, by the end of the day Masami was tired and reached out her arms for her parents, clearly expressing her preference.

3. *Clear-cut attachment:* *Maintaining proximity* (6–8 months to about 3 years). During this phase, children make active efforts to maintain physical proximity with the parent or primary caretaker. They may follow a departing mother, cry when she leaves, greet her enthusiastically when she returns, and use her as a secure base from which to explore. Infants will show these clear-cut attachment behaviors only to selected people with whom they have had a substantial amount of contact. In addition, at this age the formerly friendly behavior toward strangers often subsides. Strangers are treated with caution and may even cause crying or fear.

4. *Formation of a goal-corrected partnership* (3–4 years and on). As children enter the preschool years, they become increasingly aware that their parents are separate individuals with goals of their own. As children gain greater insight into their parents' behaviors and motivations, they become better able to modulate their own reactions and responses. They become capable of complex relationships. This final phase marks the beginning of lifelong, mature attachment relationships.

This infant has developed an emotional tie to her parents, called attachment, which is the source of her sense of security and comfort in the world. Child psychologists have found that attachment has lifelong implications. Why is attachment so important? How does attachment develop? (Thinkstock/Alamy)

Links to Related Material
In Chapter 6, you read about motor develoment in the first two years of life. How do you think the infant's increasing motor skills might affect the infant's ability to display attachment behaviors toward the parent?

Why Do Infants Become Attached?

Beginning at about 6 or 7 months of age, most infants around the world begin to show clear attachment behaviors—such as following, clinging, and reaching—toward their parents or other primary caretakers (van IJzendoorn & Sagi, 1999). The apparent universality of this response has led many researchers to try to understand the process that leads infants to become attached to the people who care for them.

Drive Reduction Theories   For many years, drive reduction theories were used to explain why infants become attached to their primary caretakers. These theories have their roots in both Freud and behaviorism.

According to Freud, humans are motivated by biological drives, such as hunger or thirst. When these basic drives are satisfied, we feel pleasure. Freud believed that a primary focus of pleasure seeking in infancy is the mouth (Freud, 1933/1964). From this perspective, infants become attached to the people who feed them and provide them with this early source of pleasure.

Behaviorists proposed a similar theory in which infants' attachment behaviors represent learned responses. According to the behaviorists, the baby comes to associate the parents' presence with the relief they feel when their hunger is satisfied. From this point of view, attachment is a learned response rather than instinctual. Through repeated association with the pleasure of being fed, infants learn to prefer contact with those who feed them (Sears, Maccoby, & Levin, 1957). Although the Freudian and behavior perspectives differ in some of the concepts and terms they use, their similarity is apparent. Both emphasize hunger as a primary drive, and believe that attachment arises secondarily from early feeding experiences (Beller, 1957).

Other Psychoanalytic Perspectives   Freud believed that the infant's early attachment relationships are central to the formation of the child's personality. Because it is typically the mother who feeds the infant, he called this relationship the child's first love and the prototype for all later love relationships (Freud, 1940/1964). Other psychoanalytic theorists besides Freud have also contributed to our understanding of how infants form attachment relationships. Like Freud, these theorists believe that the infant's early relationship with the mother is paramount for later personality development. Unlike Freud, they place less emphasis on the infant's biological drives and feeding behavior.

One such theorist is Erik Erikson (1963). Erikson believed that there are eight stages of the life cycle. Each cycle represents a central psychosocial conflict that must be resolved for healthy development to occur. In infancy, the central conflict is one of trust versus mistrust. Will someone come to me when I cry? Can I depend on others to respond and to care for me? According to Erikson, infants become attached to the people who meet their needs and whom they come to trust.

Ethological Approaches   Both drive reduction and psychoanalytic theories speculated that attachment arises from the satisfaction of the infant's basic needs. That is, although these theories are different in their particulars, they all claim that attachment is a secondary phenomenon that arises from the infant's more basic biological needs. A radically different perspective is offered by ethological approaches. As you may recall from Chapter 1, *ethology* as a science examines the adaptation of animals to their natural habitat. Specifically, it is concerned with the biological basis of and evolutionary context for animal behavior. Early ethologists sought to understand human attachment by examining its analogues in animals. For example, Konrad Lorenz (1957) observed newborn goslings, which have an innate tendency to follow their mother. Lorenz discovered that if he was the first moving creature that baby geese saw after they hatched, then they would follow him as if he were their mother. He called this phenomenon *imprinting*, which can be defined as an experience that takes place during a critical period (just after birth), and results in attachment to the first moving object that is seen. It seemed evident then that animals are born with a set of built-in behaviors that promote survival by ensuring that the baby maintains physical proximity to the mother. Given the evolutionary basis for much of human behavior, it seemed reasonable to wonder whether innate mechanisms are at work in human attachment as well.

This possibility was supported by a series of classic experiments performed by Harry Harlow (Harlow, 1959; Harlow & Harlow, 1969). In these experiments, baby rhesus monkeys were placed in cages with two types of surrogate mothers. One "mother" was made of wire and provided food, while the other was a soft, terry-cloth "monkey" that did not provide food. In all the experiments, the baby monkeys showed a marked preference for the terrycloth "mother." Even though they received their food from the wire "mother," they spent most of their time clinging to and seeking comfort from the soft, terry cloth "mother."

Harlow's work cast serious doubt on theories claiming that infants become attached through the experience of feeding. Instead, findings from the field of ethology suggest that attachment is not a secondary phenomenon that arises when the infant's other, presumably more basic needs are met. Rather, the desire for physical contact with a comforting adult is itself a basic need that infants are born with.

Bowlby's Ethological Theory of Attachment   In 1950 the World Health Organization commissioned John Bowlby to study the effects of maternal deprivation on small children. Bowlby studied the behavior of children in residential nurseries, orphanages, and hospital wards, and what he found became the basis of contemporary attachment theory. He found that when small children are separated from their parents for a period of several weeks or more, they appear to go through what Bowlby described as stages in their emotional response to the prolonged separation. At first, they protest the separation through crying and active seeking of the lost parent. When the parent does not return, small children seem to withdraw into sadness, depression, and despair. Finally, they appear to recover, but when reunited with their parents they seem emotionally detached (Bowlby, 1952/1995). Bowlby

Harlow's experiments found that contact comfort, rather than feeding, was the most important determinant of a rhesus monkey's attachment to its caregiver. Did these experiments refute the theory that attachment arises from the satisfaction of basic needs? How are ethological theories different from drive reduction theories and other psychoanalytic theories? (Courtesy Harlow Primate Laboratory, University of Wisconsin)

believed that this detachment may represent a psychological defense against the deep pain, anxiety, and anger that the child experienced during the lengthy separation.

Bowlby (1969, 1973, 1980) believed that attachment is based primarily on the infant's need for security and safety and that it has its roots in our evolutionary past, when it was so important to avoid predators and other dangers during the helplessness of infancy. Attachment behaviors such as crying for, reaching toward, and following a primary caretaker have clear survival value. Bowlby believed that the need to form attachment relationships is an evolutionary adaptation of humans, and thus is both innate and universal. A psychiatrist by training, Bowlby also believed that the child's early attachment to his or her parents provides an important foundation for later social and emotional functioning (Bowlby, 1988).

Individual Differences in Attachment

Children around the world form attachment relationships with their parents or other primary caretakers, but not all attachment relationships are equal in quality. Most infants appear able to use their parents as a secure base from which to explore the world and as a safe haven to return to in times of distress, but some infants seem to do better at this than others. Mary Ainsworth, a research associate of Bowlby's, studied these individual differences in attachment behavior using a laboratory procedure called the **Strange Situation** (Ainsworth, Blehar, Waters, & Wall, 1978). The Strange Situation procedure is used to assess quality of attachment in infants between the ages of 12 and 24 months. It consists of seven three-minute episodes involving separation from and reunion with the parent (see Table 11.1). Most research using the Strange Situation has focused on the mother-infant relationship.

1. *Episode 1:* Mother and baby are brought into a room containing two chairs and some toys. The mother sits in the chair and puts the baby on the floor next to her. She is instructed to respond to the infant as she normally would, but not to initiate interaction. Of interest in this episode is the extent to which the infant is able to use the mother as a secure base from which to explore the toys.

2. *Episode 2:* A stranger (usually a female adult who works with the researcher but is unknown to the infant) enters the room. She sits in the other chair. She is quiet for a minute, talks to the mother for a minute, and then finally tries to engage the infant in play. Of interest in this episode is how the baby responds to the stranger: with undiscriminating friendliness? overwhelming fear? Or does the baby use the mother as a secure base and demonstrate a mixture of wariness and interest?

Q**uestion for Thought and Discussion**

What characteristics of infants and their behavior do you think may be the result of adaptations that contribute to the survival of our species?

Strange Situation

A standardized laboratory procedure devised by Mary Ainsworth for assessing the quality of the parent-infant attachment relationship.

TABLE 11.1 Strange Situation Procedure			
EPISODE PERSONS PRESENT		**DURATION**	**ACTION**
Mother, baby, observer		30 sec.	Mother, baby introduced to room
1	Mother, baby	3 min.	Mother sits, baby explores
2	Stranger, mother, baby	3 min.	Stranger enters, converses with mother, attempts to engage baby in play
3	Stranger, baby	3 min.[a]	First separation
4	Mother, baby	3 min.[b]	First reunion
5	Baby alone	3 min.[a]	Second separation
6	Stranger, baby	3 min.[a]	Stranger enters, attempts to comfort baby
7	Mother, baby	3 min.[b]	Second reunion

[a]Episode is curtailed if the baby is unduly distressed.
[b]Episode is prolonged up to 5 minutes if more time is required for baby to re-engage in play.

3. *Episode 3:* The mother leaves the room and the baby is alone with the stranger. Most infants exhibit some concern during this episode for the mother's whereabouts. Some cry, others watch the door for their mother's return. The brief separation in a strange place with a strange adult places a moderate amount of stress on most infants. This stress activates the child's need for comfort from an attachment figure.

4. *Episode 4:* The mother returns and the stranger leaves. Of interest in this episode is how the child responds to the mother's return. If the baby is distressed, does he or she seek contact with the mother? Does that contact serve to comfort the baby? If the baby is not distressed, does he or she greet the mother enthusiastically, happy for her return?

5. *Episode 5:* The mother leaves again and the baby is alone. Most infants become distressed during this episode. If the baby cries continuously for more than about 15 to 20 seconds, then the episode is cut short. The purpose of this episode is to place some additional stress on the child so that his or her need for contact with the mother becomes paramount.

6. *Episode 6:* The stranger returns. Of interest in this episode is how the infant responds to the stranger's presence when he or she is distressed. Typically, we would expect that, although an infant may accept contact from the stranger, this contact will not be truly effective in restoring the child's sense of security.

7. *Episode 7:* The mother returns and the stranger leaves. As in Episode 4, of interest here is how the child responds to the mother's return. If the baby is distressed, does he or she seek contact with the mother? Does that contact serve to comfort him or her? If the baby is not distressed, does he or she greet the mother enthusiastically, happy for her return?

Based on her observations of infants both at home and in the Strange Situation, Ainsworth (1967) identified three major patterns in the quality of attachment relationships that infants have with their parents or other primary caretakers: secure attachment (Group B), avoidant attachment (Group A), and ambivalent or resistant attachment (Group C).

1. A *securely attached* (Group B) infant is able to use the mother as a secure base from which to explore unfamiliar areas, objects, or people. If distressed by the separations, the securely attached infant seeks contact with the mother and is comforted by that contact. If not distressed, the securely attached infant greets the mother happily when she returns. In the United States, researchers have generally found that 60 to 70 percent of infants in low-risk, middle-class families are securely attached to their parents.

2. Infants who have an *avoidant attachment* (Group A) relationship show little distress during the separations, and when distressed they are easily comforted by the stranger. When the mother returns, they turn away from her and avoid contact with her rather than either greeting her happily or seeking comfort.

3. Infants who have an *ambivalent or resistant attachment* (Group C) relationship are extremely distressed by the separations, but seem unable to gain comfort from the mother when she returns. They continue to cry and will also express anger toward the mother.

In addition to these three patterns identified by Ainsworth, researchers have since recognized a fourth type, which they call *disorganized* (Group D) (Main & Solomon, 1986). Infants with disorganized attachment relationships exhibit a diverse array of

Links to Related Material
In Chapter 7, you read how Piaget emphasized the importance of active exploration during the sensorimotor period. To what extent do you think that a secure attachment relationship might promote active exploration in an infant?

Episode 3 is about to begin in this photo from a Strange Situation experiment in a research laboratory. What will happen next? What ideas are being tested? How will individual infants vary in their responses to this situation? How would you expect their responses to differ in the situation presented in Episode 6? (Courtesy of Jennie Noll)

BOX 11.1 Promoting Healthy Parent-Infant Relationships

Infant crying is one of the baby's earliest and most obvious attachment behaviors. Unlike smiling, which is rewarding to a parent, crying is typically experienced as disagreeable, thus motivating parents and other caretakers to find a way to end it. As such, it is one of the young infant's most powerful tools for communicating wants, preferences, and needs.

The history of expert advice to parents regarding responding to infant crying is mixed. Between 1920 and 1940, infant care pamphlets from the U.S. Children's Bureau urged mothers not to pick up their babies between feedings. Such behavior would only teach the baby "that crying will get him what he wants, sufficient to make a spoiled, fussy baby, and a household tyrant whose continual demands make a slave of the mother" (1924, p. 44). Although later advice encouraged mothers to follow their natural instincts, the concern that infants may be spoiled by attention to their cries persists for some parents.

In 1972, Mary Ainsworth and her colleagues (Ainsworth, Bell, & Stayton, 1972) demonstrated that infants whose mothers responded to their cries promptly and consistently throughout the first year of life cried less often at age 12 months than infants whose mothers did not respond to their cries. Instead of "spoiling" the infant, prompt responsiveness tended to make the infant more likely to learn and use other, more sophisticated types of social signals to communicate needs and wants. "Infants whose mothers have given them relatively much tender and affectionate holding in the earliest months of life are content with surprisingly little physical contact by the end of the first year; although they enjoy being held, when put down they are happy to move off into independent exploratory play" (Ainsworth et al., 1972, p. 1187).

In her later work, Ainsworth provided evidence that infants who had experienced prompt responsiveness to their cries throughout the first year of life were more likely to be classified as securely attached in the Strange Situation (Ainsworth, Blehar, Waters, & Wall, 1978). In addition, Ainsworth and her colleagues described a cluster of six maternal home behaviors that predicted secure attachment at one year. Key among these was the 9-point scale they identified as: "Sensitivity-insensitivity to the baby's signals and communications. . . . The optimally sensitive mother is able to see things from her baby's point of view. She is alert to perceive her baby's signals, interprets them accurately, and responds appropriately and promptly, unless no response is the most appropriate under the circumstances. She tends to give the baby what he seems to want, and when she does not she is tactful in acknowledging his communication" (p. 142).

At about the same time that Ainsworth was completing her groundbreaking work on maternal behavior and infant attachment,

Selma Fraiberg, a child psychiatrist, was doing her own pioneering work in the field of infant mental health (Fraiberg, Adelson, & Shapiro, 1987). In her work with high-risk families, Fraiberg observed that in some families, the baby is "burdened by the oppressive past of his parents from the moment he enters the world. The parent, it seems, is condemned to repeat the tragedy of his own childhood with his own baby in terrible and exacting detail" (p. 101). What Fraiberg found in her work with these families was that mothers at risk for abusing their infants could be helped through an ongoing, supportive relationship with an empathic professional who visited the mother and baby in their home at regular intervals over a period of several months. Through these relationships, mothers received compassion and support to remember the terror and pain of their own childhoods. In the process, their relationships with their own infant improved, and they were able to become protective and sensitive caretakers. Fraiberg states, "The key to our ghost story appears to lie in the fate of affects in childhood. Our hypothesis is that access to childhood pain becomes a powerful deterrent against repetition in parenting, while repression and isolation of painful affect provide the psychological requirements for identification with the betrayers and the aggressors. . . . In each case, when our therapy has brought the parent to remember and re-experience his childhood anxiety and suffering, the ghosts [in the nursery] depart and the afflicted parents become the protectors of their children against the repetition of their own conflicted past" (p. 135).

Today, the field of infant mental health is a thriving, international discipline (Osofsky & Fitzgerald, 2000) that has as one of its key tenets: intervention must directly support positive parent-infant relationships. Typically, such interventions involve videotaping parent-infant interactions and then viewing them together while offering support and providing specific feedback. Home visiting itself has become a crucial component of many intervention programs (Gomby, Culross, & Behrman, 1999). In particular, researchers found that mothers who participated in high-quality home visiting interventions availed themselves of more community resources, were more accepting and respectful of their infants, and had safer homes, more appropriate developmental expectations, and better understanding of noncorporal punishment (Culp et al., 2004). Through high-quality intervention programs, professionals are able to provide parents with a variety of educational and support services that empower them to better meet their infant's needs. When parents themselves are empowered, infants have a better foundation on which their own social, emotional, and cognitive development can flourish.

fearful, odd, or inconsistent behaviors during the Strange Situation. Disorganized attachment is often associated with maltreatment or other clinical concerns (Lyons-Ruth & Jacobvitz, 1999). The avoidant, ambivalent or resistant, and disorganized attachment relationships are all considered types of *insecure attachment*.

Causes and Consequences of Individual Differences in Attachment

Sensitive caretaking
Care that is sensitive to an infant's needs, promptly responsive, and effective at meeting those needs.

What causes these different types of attachment relationships? Ainsworth studied the early relationships that infants have with their parents (Ainsworth et al., 1978). She found that infants who are securely attached at one year have experienced **sensitive caretaking** throughout their first year of life—that is, care that is sensitive to their needs, promptly responsive, and effective at meeting those needs. Avoidant infants have experienced parenting that is often rejecting or overly intrusive. And the quality of care that ambivalent or resistant infants have received is inconsistent—that is, the parents respond to the infant with affection or indifference, depending on their mood. Disorganized infants have often experienced abuse or parental psychopathology. Researchers continue to find evidence that sensitive caretaking during the early years is key to the development of a secure attachment relationship (Belsky, 1999).

Temperament and Attachment Some researchers have wondered whether attachment relationships are affected by the infant's temperament, which, as you have seen, can influence parent-child interactions. For example, babies who tend to be more irritable may cause higher levels of stress in their parents. Also, parents whose economic, social, or psychological resources are strained may respond to an irritable infant with less sensitivity. Over time, this pattern may lead to the development of an insecure attachment relationship (van den Boom, 1994; Vaughn & Bost, 1999).

Consequences of Attachment Another question in attachment research is, why does it matter? One answer is that children who are securely attached as infants and preschoolers are more likely to develop *social competence*. They display a variety of socially competent behaviors throughout childhood. For example, they are more confident, show more empathy toward others, become popular with their peers, and are more cooperative with adults. Children with histories of insecure attachment histories are less likely to develop high levels of social competence (Cassidy et al., 1996; Fagot, 1997; Kerns, 1994; Thompson, 1999; Weinfield, Sroufe, Egeland, & Carlson, 1999). Interestingly, at least one study has found that mothers of insecurely attached children tended to be less skilled at recognizing their child's level of competence and responding appropriately (Meins, 1997).

In addition, securely attached babies are less likely to develop emotional or behavior problems than are insecurely attached infants (Erickson, Sroufe, & Egeland, 1985; Lewis et al., 1984). Securely attached children tend to be better at regulating their emotions (Conteras et al., 2000) and are more skilled as preschoolers in understanding emotions (Laible & Thompson, 1998). Secure attachment also benefits children in self-knowledge. By age 2 securely attached children have greater self-knowledge (self-recognition, knowledge of one's gender and name) than insecurely attached children. Securely attached children also show more knowledge of their mothers (Pipp, Easterbrooks, & Harmon, 1992).

Quality of attachment affects other social behaviors as well. Insecurely attached children are more likely to be biased in interpreting the behavior of other people (Cassidy et al., 1996). At age 5, insecurely attached children are more likely to interpret another's behavior as indicating hostility. An insecurely attached child might interpret being bumped by another child as ill will, for example, while a securely attached child might interpret this merely as an accident.

Attachment Across Generations Why do some mothers respond more sensitively to their babies than others? One answer seems to involve the mother's recollections of her own childhood experiences. As young children, individuals develop what are called **internal working models** of close relationships. These internal working models are mental schemas that children form as a result of repeated experiences with their parents and other caretakers. Through these repeated experiences, children develop expectations regarding relationships, especially whether others will be available and responsive to their needs, and whether they believe they are worthy of others' care and

Question for Thought and Discussion
Caretaker sensitivity and responsiveness are so important that interventions have been designed for parents of infants with attachment problems. Do you think society should mandate such interventions to improve parenting?

Internal working model
A person's internalized mental representations of significant relationships, usually formed as a result of repeated interactions over time with parents or other primary caretakers.

attention. These internalized expectations guide future relationship choices with friends, romantic partners, and one's children. They also affect behaviors and beliefs about oneself and others (Roisman et al., 2001; Thompson, 1999).

The concept of internal working models has proven key to understanding how attachment styles may be transmitted across generations. In particular, it is assumed that parents' styles of relating to their small children will be guided by their own internal working models of close relationships, based on their own experiences in childhood. To study whether parents' own internal working models influence the way they interact with their children, and their child's own subsequent attachment, researchers have used a semistructured interview called the **Adult Attachment Interview**. In this interview, individuals are asked to describe their relationships with their parents and to recall other significant attachment-related events in their past and present lives. Data from this interview are then used to classify parents in terms of four attachment styles (George, Kaplan, & Main, 1985; Main & Goldwyn, 1998), each corresponding to a childhood attachment relationship type.

Autonomous parents present an objective and balanced picture of their childhood, noting both the positive and negative experiences. This adult attachment style reflects a secure attachment in the parent's own childhood and is also associated with the formation of secure attachment relationships with one's own children.

Dismissing parents claim to have difficulty recalling their childhoods and appear to assign little significance to them. This adult attachment style is associated with the avoidant insecure childhood attachment pattern.

Preoccupied parents tend to dwell on their early experiences, often describing them in a confused or highly emotional manner. It is associated with the ambivalent or resistant childhood attachment pattern.

Finally, *unresolved* parents appear to have experienced significant emotional losses from their own childhood that they have not yet resolved, such as the loss of a parent or abuse. It is thought to be an adult analogue of the disorganized childhood attachment pattern.

Several studies have shown that the classifications derived from the Adult Attachment Interview are reasonably good predictors of the patterns of attachment that mothers form with their own babies (Posada et al., 1995; van IJzendoorn, 1992, 1995). Mothers' interviews during pregnancy predict their later attachment to their infants (Steele, Steele, & Fonagy, 1996; Ward & Carlson, 1995), and mothers' interviews when their children are age 6 correlate positively with mothers' attachment style when their children were age 1 (Main et al., 1985).

Intergenerational transmission of attachment is not predetermined, however. Instead, many parents who struggled with insecure attachments in their own childhood are nonetheless able to provide their own children with sensitive and responsive caretaking. In cases such as these, the sensitive caretaking that the infant experiences prevails over the parent's insecure attachment history, thus enabling the infant to develop a secure attachment relationship (Tarabulsy et al., 2005).

Culture and Attachment

Much of the research on attachment has been conducted with families in the United States. As a result, researchers have wondered whether studies done in other countries will produce similar results. To what extent is attachment a universal phenomenon? Van IJzendoorn and Sagi (1999) have identified four questions that we must answer when considering this issue. First, do infants around the world show similar patterns of attachment to their parents or other primary caretakers? The answer to this first question is a resounding yes. In all societies studied to date, infants are found to form important attachment relationships to the people who care for them. Moreover, infants universally show the same patterns of attachment.

The second question relates to the distribution of attachment patterns. Among low-risk middle-class families in the United States, 60 to 70 percent of infants are securely attached, 10 to 15 percent show avoidant attachments, 15 to 20 percent are ambivalent, and

Adult Attachment Interview
An instrument used to assess an adult's mental representations of attachment relationships, particularly those with his or her parents during childhood.

Question for Thought and Discussion
What pattern of attachment did you experience as a child? How do you think your experience might affect your attachment style with a child you care for?

5 to 10 percent are disorganized. Is this distribution typical of societies around the world? Here, the answer is no, possibly reflecting different cultural norms, values, and childrearing styles.

For example, a large percentage of avoidant attachments were found among infants in northern Germany. Researchers related this finding to an emphasis on early independence training in this society (Grossmann, Grossmann, Spangler, Suess, & Unzner, 1985). In contrast, a large percentage of ambivalent attachments was found in Japan. This finding may reflect the fact that Japanese infants rarely experience separation from their mothers, making the Strange Situation exceptionally stressful for them (Takahashi, 1990).

A large percentage of ambivalent attachments also was found among infants living on kibbutzim in Israel that practice communal sleeping arrangements (Sagi, van IJzendoorn, Aviezer, Donnell, & Mayseless, 1994). In the United States, different distributions of attachment relationships have been found among different ethnic groups and social classes (van IJzendoorn & Kroonenberg, 1988). Thus, the distribution of different patterns of attachment relationship seems to reflect differences in childrearing beliefs and practices. In all societies, however, the secure attachment pattern appears to be most common (van IJzendoorn & Sagi, 1999).

The third question about culture and attachment refers to the role of parental sensitivity. Is it true around the world that sensitive parenting leads to secure attachments? The answer to this question is complicated. Although sensitivity appears important in all cultures, cultures differ in the ways that parents demonstrate sensitivity toward their infants. For example, middle-class Puerto Rican mothers living in Puerto Rico use more physical control when interacting with their infants than middle-class European American mothers in the United States. Among the European American mothers, physical control is associated with greater maternal intrusiveness and so with insecure attachments, but among the Puerto Rican mothers physical control is associated instead with security (Carlson & Harwood, 2003). Thus, cultural definitions of what constitutes "sensitive care" must be taken into account.

The fourth question asks if in all societies secure attachments lead to greater social and emotional competence. As with the previous question, the answer here appears to be a qualified yes. That is, in all societies studied thus far, children with secure attachment histories appear to do better than children with insecure histories. However, social competence is a culturally defined ideal. In the United States a competent adult is self-confident, for example, but in other cultures, such as in Puerto Rico, a competent adult is modest and respectful toward others. It is possible that securely attached children are more likely to become socially competent, however social competence is defined (Harwood, Miller, & Lucca Irizarry, 1995).

✔ **Test Your Mastery...**

Learning Objective 11.3: *Explain the role of attachment in child development.*

1. Why do infants become attached?
2. What individual differences in attachment have researchers identified?
3. What are the causes and consequences of individual differences in attachment?
4. What role does culture play in shaping attachment?

Attachment Relationships in a Changing World

Learning Objective 11.4
Discuss societal changes that have the potential to affect the infant's attachment relationships and later development.

Vintage television shows from the 1950s, such as *Ozzie and Harriett* or *Leave It to Beaver*, portrayed a family life in which the mother stayed home and the father worked all day. Fathers were breadwinners and disciplinarians, whereas women were homemakers and nurturers. In recent years, the growing number of women in the workforce has produced radical changes in this traditional picture of the American family. Not only are more mothers of young children working full time, but the role of fathers also has been shifting toward greater involvement in the nurturance and direct care of their young children.

These and other societal changes have combined with technological advances to produce social and legal complexities in parent-child relationships undreamed of in previous generations. How do these changes shape the lives of young children today?

Nonparental Care and Attachment

Recent findings from the U.S. Census Bureau indicate that 65 percent of all working mothers have children under the age of 6 years, and nearly 55 percent of mothers with infants under 1 year were working outside the home (Bachu & O'Connell, 2000; U.S. Census Bureau, 2002). Demographic trends such as these have led researchers to wonder if the daily separation associated with full-time day care affects the quality of attachment or later social and emotional development (Clarke-Stewart, Gruber, & Fitzgerald, 1994; Lamb, 1998; McCartney, 1990).

Early research on the topic of day care produced much controversy and many conflicting findings (Belsky, 1988; Belsky & Rovine, 1988; Clarke-Stewart, 1989; Lamb, Sternberg, & Prodromidis, 1992). To help resolve the debate, the U.S. federal government funded a large-scale longitudinal study to explore a variety of outcomes associated with the onset, duration, and quality of day care. The study enrolled over 1,000 children shortly after birth in 10 localities across the nation (Little Rock, Arkansas; Irvine, California; Lawrence, Kansas; Boston, Massachusetts; Philadelphia and Pittsburgh, Pennsylvania; Charlottesville, Virginia; Morganton, North Carolina; Seattle, Washington; and Madison, Wisconsin). The NICHD (National Institute of Child Health and Development) Early Child Care Research Network has issued regular reports of its findings since the study began in 1994. No evidence was found that placing a child in day care *in itself* affects the security of the child's attachment to the caregiver at 15 months of age (NICHD Early Child Care Research Network, 1997). Evidence does indicate, however, that a child whose mother is low in sensitivity is more likely to be classified as insecurely attached when (1) the day care center does not provide a high level of care, (2) the child spends a great deal of time in day care, or (3) the child has had many different childcare arrangements.

The NICHD research team has reported findings on the children from birth through first grade, with assessments at 6, 15, 24, 36, and 54 months (NICHD Early Child Care Research Network, 2003). Findings thus far indicate that, by the first grade, children's social competence is best predicted by the overall sensitivity of maternal care that children have received throughout the first five years of life. Otherwise, it was found that greater accumulated hours in nonmaternal care throughout the first five years of life predicted more problem behaviors in school, as identified by teachers. These findings highlight the importance of mothers' sensitive interactions in shaping social and self-regulatory skills in early childhood.

In addition, quality of child care during the early years is a stronger predictor of academic success than of social competence in the first grade. Compared with children in lower-quality care, those in higher-quality care, in care that improved in quality over time, and in center-based care had better language, cognitive, and preacademic skills at age 4.5. However, children who spent more hours in day care exhibited higher levels of self-assertion and aggression at age 4.5 and during kindergarten, regardless of program quality (NICHD 2003).

Results from the NICHD study and other investigations indicate that early out-of-home child care is associated with both risks and benefits, even when considering factors such as ethnicity, family income and education, and family structure. Ideally, governmental and business policy changes would permit parents to be supported while they stayed at home with their newborns. However, in the United States most infants and children will spend part of their early years in nonparental care (Carnegie Task Force, 1994; Clark et al., 1997).

Question for Thought and Discussion

What factors do you think are most important in ensuring positive outcomes for children who spend time in day care? Who do you think should pay for quality child care?

This father's involvement with his child's daily care reflects significant ongoing changes in attachment relationships in the United States. Those changes also include the likelihood that this child will develop an attachment to a caregiver at this day care center. According to longitudinal research, what risks may be associated with full-time out-of-home day care? (Janine Wiedel Photolibrary/Alamy)

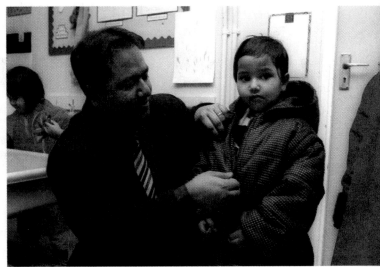

The Changing Role of Fathers

The growing number of women in the workforce has had an effect not only on the mother-infant relationship, but on the father-infant relationship as well. As women spend more hours in the workplace, fathers have generally spent more time in caretaking activities. For example, both Emily and David have continued to work full time since Zachary's birth. For three evenings a week, David serves as his primary caretaker. He feeds and bathes Zachary, changes his diapers, reads to him, plays with him, comforts him when he's distressed, and sings him to sleep at night.

Researchers have found that fathers can be just as nurturing and competent with childcare tasks as mothers (Parke & Tinsley, 1981; Russell, 1999). In addition, infants become attached to their fathers just as they do to their mothers. However, some differences have been found in the ways that mothers and fathers interact with their infants. In particular, mothers are more likely to spend time in caretaking tasks, such as changing, bathing, and feeding, whereas fathers spend more time in playful interactions (Lamb, 1987). Moreover, mothers and fathers tend to provide different kinds of play experiences for their infants. Fathers tend to engage in play that is physical and stimulating, such as bouncing and lifting the baby into the air, whereas mothers tend to engage in quieter, more structured play activities, such as clapping and singing games or peek-a-boo (Clarke-Stewart, 1980). Although fathers spend more time than they used to with their infants, most infants still spend more time each day with their mothers than with their fathers.

Attachment and the Family Courts

The significance of early attachment relationships has emerged as a critical battleground in the slow-moving court system, particularly in custody cases. In several high-profile custody cases in the 1990s, the attachment relationship formed with foster or adoptive parents was pitted against legal definitions of parenthood that have traditionally given priority to biological relatedness. One example is the case of Baby Jessica DeBoer, who was born in Iowa in 1991. Her birth mother, Cara Clausen, signed forms relinquishing her parental rights, and Baby Jessica was placed shortly after birth in the custody of Roberta and Jan DeBoer, who filed a petition to adopt her. A few weeks later, Cara Clausen filed a motion to revoke her release of custody on the grounds that she had not named the baby's true father in her original release of parental rights. She now named Daniel Schmidt as the baby's father, and the two were married about six months after Jessica's birth. Daniel Schmidt, who had not relinquished his parental rights to Jessica, filed an affidavit of paternity and a petition to intervene in the adoption proceeding.

About nine months later, a family court denied the DeBoers's petition to adopt, on the grounds that Daniel Schmidt had not abandoned his child and and should not have his parental rights terminated. The DeBoers then took this case to the Appellate Courts of Iowa, where the case took approximately one year to be heard. The case was later heard

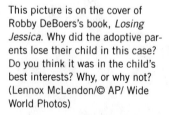

This picture is on the cover of Robby DeBoers's book, *Losing Jessica*. Why did the adoptive parents lose their child in this case? Do you think it was in the child's best interests? Why, or why not? (Lennox McLendon/© AP/ Wide World Photos)

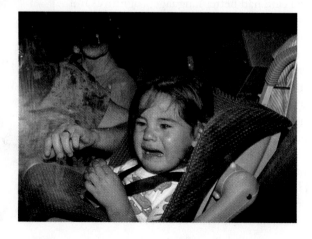

BOX 11.2   In the Child's Best Interest?

Societal changes, in combination with technological advances in the science of DNA testing, have yielded complex situations that pit our research-based understanding of attachment relationships against legal, biology-based definitions of parenthood espoused by the court. These cases have raised questions among psychologists regarding what constitutes the best interest of the child.

In one high-profile case, two mothers in Virginia named Paula Johnson and Whitney Rogers both had baby girls several hours apart in the same hospital in June 1995. Whitney and her boyfriend, Kevin Chittum, brought home a baby they named Rebecca, while Paula and her boyfriend, Carlton, brought home a baby they named Callie.

Three years later, Paula and Carlton had separated and were involved in child support disputes regarding Callie. The judge ordered paternity testing, which showed that neither Paula nor Carlton was Callie's biological parent. In the meantime, about 70 miles away, Kevin and Whitney had been raising the daughter they brought home and named Rebecca. Only a couple of weeks before Paula learned that Callie was not her biological child, Kevin and Whitney were killed on July 4, 1998, in a car accident. Rebecca was living with her grandparents when they were informed in a doctor's phone call that Rebecca probably was not their biological grandchild. Blood tests were performed, and later DNA testing confirmed that Rebecca was actually Paula and Carlton's biological child, while Callie was the biological child of Kevin and Whitney, now dead in one of the nation's worst 4th of July traffic accidents in 1998.

Callie and Rebecca had been "switched at birth." Some have estimated that every year two or three babies go home from hospitals with the wrong parents. However, only recently has technology advanced to the point where court-ordered DNA testing has become common in custody disputes. The increase in court-ordered DNA testing has also uncovered cases such as that of Callie and Rebecca. This "switched at birth" phenomenon poses complex social problems for all involved.

Paula Johnson had discovered that the child she had been raising was not her biological child, while the child she had given birth to was living with another family. Which child is "hers"? Should Paula sue for custody of Rebecca, her biological daughter? And what about Callie, the child she had been raising? Should Callie's biological grandparents sue for custody of her?

In Rebecca and Callie's case, both families sued for custody of both girls (the child they had been raising as well as the child they were biologically linked to). Paula Johnson also sued the hospital that had apparently committed the error. Ultimately, Johnson kept sole custody of Callie, and won joint custody of Rebecca with the grandparents who had been raising her.

by the Supreme Court of Iowa as well as courts in Michigan, where the DeBoers had moved. During all this time, Baby Jessica had remained with the DeBoers, as ordered by the courts. When Jessica was two years old, the courts finally determined that she should be moved from the DeBoers's home and placed in the custody of her biological parents, Cara and Daniel Schmidt. Many were deeply affected by filmed footage of 2-year-old Jessica being pried screaming from the arms of the only mother she had ever known, to go live with the strangers who were her biological parents.

Child development researchers and professionals who work in the family court system were motivated by the case of Baby Jessica and others like it to define more clearly what guidelines should be used when considering legal decisions designed to protect the child's best interest (Goldstein, Solnit, Goldstein, & Freud, 1996). Specific recommendations state that child placement decisions should (1) safeguard the child's need for emotional continuity in relationships, (2) reflect the child's own sense of time, (3) take into account the law's incapacity to make long-range predictions and to manage family relationships, and (4) provide the least detrimental available alternative for safeguarding the child's growth and development.

Cases like that of Baby Jessica violate these recommendations, first by allowing two years to pass before enforcing a decision. If Jessica had been returned to her biological parents at the age of six months, the consequences would have been less devastating for all concerned. By allowing two years to pass, Jessica had grown into a toddler with a deep emotional bond with the only parents she had ever known. In addition, researchers urge those who work in the family court system to recognize that long-range predictions about family relationships are impossible, and so trying to choose the "best family" for a child is not a workable solution. Instead, the courts need to consider factors such as the child's need for emotional continuity and the child's decidedly different sense of time in order to choose the least detrimental alternative when considering custody cases.

Questions for Thought and Discussion
How do court cases bring to the forefront the issue of how we define parenthood? Should court decisions be based primarily on biological relatedness?

BOX 11.3 CONVERSATIONS with a CASA Volunteer Supervisor

Padma Knight, 31, lives in the Washington, D.C. metropolitan area. She is a case supervisor with the Court Appointed Special Advocate (CASA) program of Montgomery County, Maryland, which is part of a national network of child advocacy organizations. The goal of CASA is to assist abused and neglected children in court proceedings to find safe, permanent homes as quickly as possible. This is accomplished through the recruitment, training, ongoing support, and supervision of volunteers from the community who are appointed by juvenile court judges to work one-on-one with children in the family juvenile court system. Padma supervises approximately 30 volunteers, conducts monthly meetings with them, and works to train and select new volunteers.

After earning her bachelor's of science degree in psychology from Mary Washington College in Virginia, Padma provided direct services at a group home for abused and neglected children in San Diego, California. For the past four years she has worked for CASA of Montgomery County.

CASA began in 1977 when a juvenile court judge felt that he did not know enough about some of his cases to make the best decisions. He thought that each child should have an individual outside of the court system to look over the situation and provide a detailed report to the judge to help him or her make a determination about what is best for the child. Since then, CASA has grown to over 950 programs nationwide and over 70,000 volunteers.

The entire system is overwhelmed. Social workers have upwards of 30 cases each, children's attorneys have up to 80 or 100 cases, and so they just don't have the time to do the intensive work. That is where the CASA program becomes useful to the system. Today, a judge hearing a case may appoint a CASA. Social workers, attorneys, and the child may also request a CASA but they are appointed at the judge's discretion. Usually we handle some of the most complicated, really contentious cases, where the sides are not coming to a decision.

CASA volunteers see children weekly, have time to interview everybody in the case, collect all of the information that others often don't have, and carefully consider what is in the child's best interest in an objective way. CASAs take into consideration the opinions of the mother, father, foster parents, counselors, and other adults in the child's life, as well as the child's opinion, if the child is able to voice one. However, CASAs make their own determination of what is in the child's best interest through their careful observation of the child and family during weekly meetings. They then advocate for the child's best interest during the court proceedings.

For example, one CASA became increasingly concerned about the number of people residing in the home with the child and the child's mother. In her report to the court, the CASA documented all the people thought to be living in the home and stated her concerns about the number of people, as well as the criminal history of some of the residents. At the hearing, the judge ordered that a list of the people in the home be provided to the social worker immediately. It was subsequently discovered that there was an ongoing investigation of one of the men living in the home and the child had to be removed for safety reasons.

The whole point is to advocate for best interest. We gather all of the information objectively and make a determination of what is in the child's best interest. We compare the information that we collect with that of the child's attorney and social worker, but we must keep in mind the agenda of these others. For example, guidelines in Maryland provide that if the child's attorney believes that the child has "considered judgment" or the ability to talk and reason, then the attorney must advocate for what the child wants, regardless of the ramifications of that decision. Although they take

Padma Knight. (Courtesy of Padma Knight)

✔ *Test Your Mastery...*

Learning Objective 11.4: *Discuss societal changes that have the potential to affect the infant's attachment relationships and later development.*

1. What effects does nonparental care have on attachment and later socioemotional development?
2. What does research tell us about the role of fathers in early development?
3. What guidelines, based on child development research, should be brought to bear in court-related child placement decisions?

into consideration the child's opinion, CASAs look at the entire situation. They talk to foster parents and therapists, and investigate how the parents are doing with whatever they need to do in order to earn back custody. The CASA might not agree with any other person involved with the case but, in the end, all parties give their opinions and observations to the judge, who makes a final decision. For example, a CASA had been working with a teenage boy who had been living in the same group home for about two years. As the CASA gathered information and met with the group home staff and the boy's father, he learned that the distant location of the group home was preventing the father from participating in his son's treatment and visiting on a regular basis. The CASA advocated for the boy to be moved to a group home that would better meet his special needs and that would be closer to his father's home. As a result, the boy was moved to a group home that was only a few miles from his father and was better equipped to handle the boy's mental health issues.

In an especially rewarding case, a CASA was assigned to a 12-year-old boy, and at her first hearing only three months later, the CASA made strong recommendations about the child's placement. The child had been eligible for adoption for the last couple of years but had been placed in a group home. The CASA strongly advocated that the boy be placed immediately in a foster home or a preadoptive home. This conflicted with the social worker's recommendation that the boy remain in this group home. Based solely on the CASA's report and verbal recommendations, the judge ruled that the boy be moved to a new home within the week. The young boy started having visits with a prospective adoptive family, and his new foster family also offered to adopt him. Now this boy has two chances to have a permanent home.

My job is to assist these volunteers in their advocacy roles. Part of my role as a case supervisor is keeping the CASAs focused. They are trained to be impartial and objective, but over time may need help refocusing their objectivity. Sometimes we need to ask them "for what are we really advocating?" The whole goal is to advocate for permanency for these children, that they are placed in the most permanent situation, be that with their parents, or a relative, or through adoption. Furthermore, we need to see that that they are receiving all of the services that they need, such as counseling and medical care.

An individual who is seeking to become a CASA volunteer must undergo two interviews and pass a careful background check. Understanding the motivations of the volunteers is very important to the success of the program. Volunteers must have a serious commitment to helping these children. My psychology background helps me in making these assessments.

To become a CASA case supervisor, individuals must have direct service experience. After college I worked in a residential group home for children, helping residents with their homework and social skills, and leading groups. After that I provided in-home support services to families. Once parent(s) had done everything they needed to do to get their children back, I met with them on a weekly basis to work on parenting skills. The aim was to ensure that the placement would be successful so that the kids would not have to be removed again. We would discuss how to handle problems and conflicts, as well as parenting goals and how to accomplish them.

In Montgomery County, all CASA case supervisors have direct service experience. My co-workers have worked in the foster care, adoption, and probation systems, and have worked with the children, the parents, and the child welfare system. I had worked with CASA volunteers in both of my other jobs so I was familiar with the program.

I find working for CASA to be very rewarding. Compared to my jobs in direct service, I find that my efforts at CASA have a broader impact. As a case supervisor I feel that I am able to influence change in many areas of a case, instead of one specific area. I am also able to see the case come to a conclusion, which, when it works out, can be extremely gratifying.

In considering this as a career, a person first and foremost has to have a desire to help, to be involved in an extremely complicated and sometimes extremely frustrating system. The emotional rewards are great when you see that a child is better off and you have made a difference. But those rewards do not come every day. Sometimes there is a lot of time between them, and often there are many disappointments and frustrations. To consider a career in this field, an individual must be prepared for that and be willing to stick with it despite the difficulties. But if you have the dedication, this field can be exceptionally rewarding. I don't know many things more satisfying then making a positive difference in someone's life, especially a child's.

For more information on CASA check out their Web site: http://www.nationalcasa.org/

Social and Emotional Development in Contexts of Risk

As you have seen, early social development is influenced by a child's temperament and emotions, as well as by significant attachment relationships and larger cultural norms. In addition, early social development is influenced by external factors that may impinge upon what would otherwise be a normal developmental path, placing particular kinds of stress on the developing child. These special circumstances, often considered high-risk

Learning Objective 11.5
Discuss major high-risk contexts and their impacts on children's development.

contexts for development, help to explain further how early experience lays the groundwork for later social, emotional, and cognitive development. These special circumstances include, for example, war and dislocation, abuse and neglect, serious illness, and severe emotional deprivation.

Trauma

Posttraumatic stress disorder (PTSD) is a disorder in which a particularly stressful event results in later emotional symptoms, including reexperiencing of the event, decreased responsiveness to the outside world, tendency to startle easily, and nightmares. Like adults, children are susceptible to developing PTSD following traumatic events such as earthquakes (Pynoos et al., 1993), school shootings (Pynoos, Frederick, & Nader, 1987), and catastrophic floods (Green et al., 1994).

Rates of PTSD are significant, often initially affecting at least a third of exposed children. One recent study found that these events are not strongly associated with the onset of psychiatric disorders in children (Sandberg et al., 2001). Nevertheless, evidence suggests that the effects may linger into adulthood. Clinicians have noted an association between recalled childhood trauma and adult depression (Hill, 2003).

A major area of research interest has been the effect of war on children. Here again, significant stress reactions are not rare. For example, one study found that 70 percent of Kuwaiti children reported moderate to severe posttraumatic stress following the first Gulf War (Nader et al., 1993), and PTSD was noted in a quarter of Bosnian adolescents and Kurdish children displaced from their homelands during times of conflict (Ahmad, 1992; Weine et al., 1995). The effect of witnessing violence in war may be additive. That is, the more frequently children witness violence, the more likely they are to suffer ill effects (Allwood, Bell-Dolan, & Husain, 2002). In January 2005 the dean of the Psychological Research Center at Baghdad University reported that 28 percent of Iraqi children were suffering from PTSD as a consequence of the war there, and the number was rising (http://www.msnbc.msn.com/id/6836120/).

Abuse and Neglect Although the family typically is a source of security and protection for the young child, sometimes it can be just the opposite. Child abuse is a tragic reality of some households, and it is a problem that may be growing (Emery & Laumann-Billings, 1998). Abuse and neglect have major developmental consequences for growing children. By 1 year of age, maltreated infants tend to lag in both social and cognitive development, and these problems continue into childhood and adolescence (Trickett & McBride-Chang, 1995). A great deal of recent research has focused on the attachment process in infants who have been abused or are at risk for abuse (Cicchetti & Carlson, 1989; Rogosch et al., 1995).

Sensitive and responsive caregiving growing out of mutual infant-caregiver regulation is thought to provide the basis for secure attachment. But, as noted, many abusive mothers fail to develop a smooth and effective communication system with their infants. Although babies will become attached even to mothers whose caregiving is of poor quality, the attachment relationship suffers. Perhaps for this reason, insecure attachment, particularly the disorganized patterns, occur more frequently among maltreated infants (Carlson et al., 1989; Rogosch et al., 1995).

Some parents maltreat their infants in ways that involve physical punishment and active hostility. Many maltreated infants exhibit signs of disorganized attachment in Ainsworth's Strange Situation, such as freezing, assuming unusual postures or expressions, and making interrupted or mistimed movements (Main & Solomon, 1986, 1990). These children are especially at risk for developing a variety of behavior problems (Lyons-Ruth, Alpern, & Repacholi, 1993).

This child in Fallujah, Iraq, may be among those suffering from posttraumatic stress disorder. Researchers have attempted to identify which specific factors associated with traumatic experiences make stress reactions more likely. In the case of war, evidence suggests that relocation and the disruption of school life or peer relationships caused by relocation may be especially important—more so than other potential factors, such as parenting and overall family functioning (Thabet & Vostanis, 1999). According to research, what will determine individual differences in the resilience of these children to their experiences of war? (Cpl. Mike Escobar/Second Marine Division)

The conclusions that can be drawn from research on abused children support a transactional model of attachment (Crittenden & Ainsworth, 1989). Evolution has provided that babies will become attached even to caregivers who provide minimal or deviant care, but the interactions between these mothers and babies clearly affect the quality of the relationship that develops. This in turn affects the child's later social, emotional, and cognitive development (van IJzendoorn et al., 1992).

Childhood Hospitalization

Hospitalization is another experience that you might expect to be stressful for children. Hospital stays of more than seven days have become less frequent overall in the past 20 years. Still, this trend is not universal, evidenced by a rise in the incidence of childhood cancers. Also, though extended hospitalizations for injuries have decreased, those for mental disorders have increased (Chabra & Chavez, 2000). Early research (Rutter, 1976) found that a hospital stay in itself does not necessarily cause problems over time. For example, 10-year-olds who had been hospitalized for seven or fewer days before age 5 were no more likely than other children to suffer from maladjustment or other behavioral difficulties. However, repeated hospitalization was associated with a variety of behavior problems years later. In addition, recent research has found evidence for adverse effects of repeated hospitalizations on the families of children suffering from asthma, including greater financial strain and higher levels of conflict (Chen et al., 2003). Parents' attitudes about a child's hospitalization can be an important determinant of the quality of the child's experience (Whelan & Kirkby, 2000). Parent stress can match and even exceed that of children, making it an important factor in the impact of hospitalization.

The condition for which the child is receiving treatment also influences the effects of hospitalization. Specific characteristics of a child's illness are likely to influence the emotional impact of the illness and the hospitalizations associated with it. Mrazek (1991) identified several such illness-specific risk factors, such as time of onset, degree of deformity or disability it produces, and prognosis for the future.

Severe Emotional Deprivation

In Romania in 1989, the repressive regime of Nicolae Ceausescu was overthrown. At that time, over 150,000 children were found languishing in Romania's orphanages, malnourished and neglected, many of them dying of infectious diseases. Most of these children had experienced severe emotional and physical deprivation. When others around the world saw televised documentaries of the appalling conditions of Romania's orphans, many were eager to adopt them. This provided researchers with a unique opportunity to view the developmental course of babies and young children who had been institutionalized and living in conditions of severe emotional and physical deprivation.

Does severe emotional and physical deprivation have long-lasting effects on the developmental course of children, even when those children are later adopted into loving homes? What percentage of profoundly deprived children is able to recover following adoption and go on to achieve normal psychological functioning? Are certain types of behavior problems more strongly associated with early deprivation than others? Is there a developmental window during which certain events, such as the formation of an attachment relationship, must occur in order to ensure normal development?

In 2001, British psychologist Michael Rutter reported on 156 Romanian orphans who had been adopted before age 42 months by parents in England and compared them to 50 children from nondepriving circumstances who had been adopted within the United Kingdom before the age of 6 months (Rutter, Kreppner & O'Connor, 2001). Upon entry into their new country, the Romanian orphans were seriously underweight and malnourished, in poor physical health, and showed significant developmental delays. Later, at ages 4 and 6 years, all the children were examined again for a variety of behavioral problems,

Links to Related Material

In Chapter 3, you read about adoption as a pathway to parenthood. Here, you learn more about the implications of age at adoption for long-term outcomes. In Chapter 16, you will read more about the foster care system and families created through adoption.

Resilience
The capacity to resume a normal developmental path despite adversities.

including attachment disorders, ADHD, emotional difficulties, autism, cognitive impairment, peer difficulties, and conduct problems.

Rutter found that the Romanian children who had experienced severe emotional and physical deprivation prior to their adoption were more likely than the nondeprived British adoptees to exhibit behavior problems in four of seven domains: attachment problems, ADHD, autistic-like problems, and cognitive impairment. In addition, these behavior problems were much more likely to occur among children who had left Romania after their second birthday. The Romanian children who had been adopted before 6 months of age showed growth and developmental progress that closely resembled that of the children who were adopted within the UK. After 6 months of age, the risk of developing behavior problems increased in a linear fashion, with the largest degree of risk found for children who were severely deprived and adopted after the age of 2. But even then 20 to 25 percent of those children showed no behavior problems at the age of 6 years. Although it is sometimes assumed that prolonged early deprivation leads inevitably to lasting psychological damage, the results of this study suggest otherwise. Researchers found **resilience**—the ability to resume a normal developmental path despite adversities—as well as long-term vulnerability among these severely deprived children.

Similar findings were reported in a Canadian study (Fisher, Ames, Chisholm, & Savoie, 1997), which compared three groups of children: Canadian-born children who had not been adopted; Romanian-born children who had spent at least 8 months in a Romanian orphanage; and Romanian-born children adopted before the age of 4 months. Researchers in this study found no significant differences between the Canadian children and the early adopted Romanian children, but did find that the later-adopted Romanian children were more likely to exhibit a variety of behavior problems.

Risk and Resilience

Studies suggest that both *risk* and *resilience* exist among children who experience severe early emotional and physical deprivation. In particular, the longer the period of time that a child experiences these severely depriving conditions, the more likely it is that the experience will result in long-term social and emotional damage. However, even among children who experienced the severely depriving conditions described by Rutter up to the age of 3.5 years, a sizable minority (20 to 25 percent) appeared able to rebound and resume a normal developmental course after adoption into a loving family.

Risk and resilience emerge as important themes in the work of other child development researchers. Werner (1990; Werner & Smith, 2001) followed into middle adulthood nearly 700 children born in 1955 on the Hawaiian island of Kauai. Half of these children lived in chronic poverty, half in relative affluence. Roughly a third of the children in this cohort had developed learning or behavioral problems by young adulthood. This was particularly true among children who had been exposed to multiple risk factors, such as perinatal illness, parental psychopathology, family instability, and chronic poverty. However, a group of 72 children (about 10 percent of the entire cohort) who had experienced multiple risk factors at early ages nonetheless grew into caring and competent adults. Protective factors for these and other vulnerable children within the cohort were identified and include the mother's caregiving competence, as well as the child's social maturity, autonomy, sense of self-efficacy, scholastic competence, and emotional support from extended family and friends. Many researchers believe that these factors represent sources of resilience that enable children reared under adverse conditions to make a successful life adaptation in adulthood, despite the odds.

Learning Objective 11.5: *Discuss major high-risk contexts and their impacts on children's development.*

1. What are some specific conditions that might present high-risk challenges to children's development?
2. Are all children equally affected by growing up in high-risk environments?

 *Test Your Mastery...*

BOX 11.4   Contextual Model of Emotional and Social Development

Infant is born with biologically based temperamental characteristics.

Family, Community, and School Settings

- Parents bring own temperament, personality, attachment history, marital satisfaction, and personality to bear on relationship with infant.
- Parents and other important caretakers, such as day care providers and preschool teachers, work together to make sure they agree on what constitutes an optimal environment for infants and young children.
- Parents' social support networks, work environment, and educational and economic resources influence the parents' own well-being, which in turn affects emotional availability to the infant and young child.

Culture and Society

- Parents are influenced by larger cultural beliefs and practices regarding childrearing.

Summary for Chapter 11

Learning Objective 11.1
Define temperament and describe its role in child development.

1. What is temperament?	*Temperament* is defined as the stable behavioral and emotional reactions that appear early and are influenced in part by genetic constitution. Generally, qualities such as activity level, irritability, and sociability represent core dimensions of temperament.
2. How is infant temperament measured?	*Self-report* questionnaires such as the Early Infant Temperament Questionnaire and the Infant Temperament Questionnaire are used. Two common additional methods are *behavioral ratings* by doctors, nurses, or care providers, and *physiological measures* such as monitoring heart rate.
3. What are the nine dimensions of temperament?	(1) *Activity level*, referring to level of physical activity; (2) *rhythmicity*, or regularity of sleep patterns; (3) *approach-withdrawal*, the child's initial response to new stimulus; (4) *adaptability*, or response to new experience; (5) *threshold of responsiveness*, the intensity level of stimulus required for response; (6) *intensity of reaction*, or the energy level of the infant's response; (7) *quality of mood*, pleasant vs. unpleasant; (8) *distractibility*, how easily the child is distracted, and (9) *attention span and persistence*, length of time an activity is pursued in the face of obstacles.
4. What are the three major temperament profiles?	Certain characteristics of infant temperament seem to occur together in constellations or patterns. The *easy* child displays regularity in daily sleep, feeding, and elimination, responds well to new situations, adapts quickly to change, and is frequently cheerful. The *difficult* child is irregular in daily sleep, feeding and elimination patterns, slow to accept change, and has intense, negative reactions. The *slow-to-warm-up* child initially withdraws from new toys, food, or people and is hesitant to accept change.
5. What is goodness of fit, and how does it affect the child's development?	*Goodness of fit* refers to the connection between the child's temperament and the parents' expectations. When a good fit exists, family relationships become more harmonious and children develop a more positive sense of self as well as more flexible ways of coping with whatever temperamental tendencies they were born with.

6. Is temperament stable across time?	*Temperamental characteristics* such as activity level and response to novelty are somewhat predictive of later behavior. However, the social context the child grows up in and the variety of responses from others throughout childhood will also influence one's temperament.

Learning Objective 11.2
Trace the development of emotions.

1. What are emotions?	*Emotions* can be understood as reactions, including feelings, thoughts, and behaviors, that arise in response to personally significant events or situations. The situations that elicit these responses can be any person, thought, or event that has significance for an individual. Emotions may involve physiologic arousal, thoughts about the situation, and behavioral expressions.
2. How do emotions develop?	Much of our understanding of *emotional development* has come about through studying infants' facial expressions. Babies indicate distress by crying, interest by staring attentively, and disgust when an unpleasant taste or odor is encountered. A smile demonstrates pleasure or happiness when full, during REM sleep, and in response to a caregiver's gentle touching and vocalizing. By 10–12 weeks of age, the infant responds to the human voice or face with a broad grin called the social smile. Sadness and anger are demonstrated by 3 or 4 months, and facial expressions of fear appear around 7 months of age. More complex emotional responses such as pride, guilt, shame and embarrassment are not apparent until the child is between 18 and 24 months of age. Babies must also learn to recognize and respond to others' emotions, Babies who are 6 weeks of age are able to begin to recognize different facial expressions. After 5 to 6 months of age, infants appear to develop a clearer understanding of emotional expressions. Near the end of the first year, infants begin to use information about other people's emotional expressions to regulate their own behavior.
3. How do social referencing and stranger anxiety help infants to regulate their own behavior?	*Stranger anxiety* begins at about 6 months of age and can continue into the second year, and is the expression of fear when around someone unfamiliar. Not all infants show stranger anxiety to the same degree. There is some evidence that infants who are exposed frequently to strangers exhibit less stranger anxiety. Babies are likely to look to their mothers or fathers for guidance when they encounter an unfamiliar object or person. At about 8 months of age, infants begin to seek emotional information from trusted adults when they are faced with uncertainty. With *social referencing*, the infant relies on trusted adults to provide them with the emotional information they need to interpret and respond appropriately to an ambiguous situation.

4. What effect do face-to-face interactions have on infants' emotional development?	*Face-to-face interactions* occur during feeding, diapering, and, in some cultures, play. Many Western psychologists believe that these interactions are fundamental to the development of an effective communication system between mother and baby and ultimately to the development of a close relationship.
5. How does culture serve to shape face-to-face interactions and the expression of emotions?	The emergence of emotions in infancy is guided primarily by biological processes and is universal across cultures. However, *culture* shapes the way emotions are expressed, managed, and interpreted in a society. For example, not all cultures believe that infants are autonomous conversation partners; therefore, they may not engage their infant during face-to-face interactions. Similarly, in some cultures mothers hold infants facing outward, so that they can see and be seen by others. This practice serves to encourage three-person interactions and reflects a more general cultural orientation toward embeddedness in a complex social world. On the other hand, Japanese mothers solicit their infants' attention and use objects to direct their babies' attention inward toward themselves for many months.

Learning Objective 11.3
Explain the role of attachment in child development.

1. Why do infants become attached?	Beginning at about 6 or 7 months of age, most infants around the world begin to show clear attachment behaviors, such as following, clinging, and reaching toward their parents or other primary caretakers. *Freud* believed that infants become attached to the people who feed them and provide them with this early source of pleasure. *Behaviorists* propose that infants' attachment behaviors represent learned responses. Babies associate the parents' presence with the relief they feel when their hunger is satisfied. In this view, the attachment is a learned response rather than instinctual. According to *Erikson*, infants become attached to the people who meet their needs and whom they come to trust. Findings from the field of *ethology* suggest that the desire for physical contact with a comforting adult is a basic need that infants are born with. *Bowlby* believed that the need to form attachment relationships is an evolutionary adaptation of humans, and thus is both innate and universal.

<table>
<tr><td>

2. What individual differences in attachment have researchers identified?

</td><td>

Based on her observation of infants both at home and in the Strange Situation, Ainsworth identified three major patterns in the quality of attachment relationships that infants have with their parents or primary caretakers. A *securely attached* infant is able to use the mother as a secure base from which to explore unfamiliar areas, objects, or people. If distressed by the separations, the infant seeks contact with the mother and is comforted by that contact. If not distressed, the infant greets the mother happily when she returns. Infants who have an *avoidant attachment* show little distress during the separations, and when distressed they are easily comforted by the stranger. When the mother returns, they turn away from her and avoid contact with her rather than greeting her happily or seeking comfort. Infants who have an *ambivalent or resistant attachment* relationship are extremely distressed by the separations, but seem unable to gain comfort from the mother when she returns. They continue to cry and will also express anger towards the mother.

</td></tr>
<tr><td>

3. What are the causes and consequences of individual differences in attachment?

</td><td>

Infants who are securely attached have experienced sensitive caretaking throughout their first year of life. Avoidant infants have experienced parenting that is often rejecting or overly intrusive, and resistant infants have experienced parenting that is inconsistent. Disorganized infants have often experienced abuse or parental psychopathology. In addition, a lack of goodness of fit between parenting style and an infant's temperament may also lead to the development of an insecure attachment relationship. Children who are *securely attached* as infants and preschoolers are more likely to develop social competence. In other words, they are more confident, show more empathy toward others, become popular with their peers, and are more cooperative with adults. Similarly, securely attached babies are less likely to develop emotional or behavior problems than are insecurely attached infants. Insecurely attached children are more likely to be biased in interpreting the behavior of other people.

</td></tr>
<tr><td>

4. What role does culture play in shaping attachment?

</td><td>

Researchers have identified four questions that must be answered in considering the role that *culture* plays in shaping attachment. First, do infants around the world show similar patterns of attachment to their parents or primary caregivers? This answer is a resounding yes. Second, what is the distribution of attachment patterns? Among low-risk middle-class families in the United States, 60 to 70 percent of infants are securely attached, 10 to 15 percent show avoidant attachments, 15 to 20 percent are ambivalent, and 5 to 10 percent are disorganized. This distribution is not typical of societies around the world. For example, a large percentage of avoidant attachments were found in northern Germany, perhaps because of an emphasis on early independence. Also, a large percentage of ambivalent attachments also was found among infants living on kibbutzim in Israel that practice communal sleeping arrangements. Third, what role does parental sensitivity play in shaping attachment? Although sensitivity appears important in all cultures, cultures differ in the ways that parents demonstrate sensitivity toward their infants. For example, middle-class Puerto Rican mothers living in Puerto Rico use more physical control when interacting with their infants than middle-class European American mothers in the United States. Among the European American mothers, physical control is associated with greater maternal intrusiveness and so with insecure attachments, but among Puerto Rican mothers, physical control is associated instead with security. Fourth, in all societies do secure attachments lead to greater social and emotional competence? In all societies studied thus far, children with secure attachment histories appear to do better than children with insecure histories. However, social competence is a socially defined ideal.

</td></tr>
</table>

Learning Objective 11.4
Discuss societal changes that have the potential to affect the infant's attachment relationship and later development.

1. What effect does nonparental care have on attachment and later socioemotional development?

The National Institute of Child Health and Development *Early Child Care Research Network* has issued regular reports of its findings since the study began in 1994. Findings thus far indicate that, by the first grade, children's social competence is best predicted by the overall sensitivity of maternal care that the children have received throughout the first five years of life. Otherwise, it was found that greater accumulated hours in nonmaternal care throughout the first five years of life predicted more problem behaviors in school, as identified by teachers. These findings highlight the importance of mothers' sensitive interactions in shaping social and self-regulatory skills in early childhood. In addition, the quality of child care during the early years is a stronger predictor of academic success than of social competence in the first grade.

2. What does research tell us about the role of fathers in early development?

Researchers have found that *fathers* can be just as nurturing and competent with childcare tasks as mothers. Infants become attached to fathers just as they do to their mothers. There are some differences, however, in the ways that mothers and fathers interact with their infants. Mothers are more likely to spend time in caretaking tasks, such as changing, bathing, and feeding, whereas fathers spend more time in playful interactions. Fathers also tend to engage in play that is physical and stimulating, such as bouncing and lifting the baby into the air, whereas mothers tend to engage in quieter, more structured play activities, such as clapping and singing games or peek-a-boo.

3. What guidelines, based on child development research, should be brought to bear in court-related child placement decisions?

Child development researchers and professionals who work in the family court system recommend that *child placement decisions should* (1) safeguard the child's need for emotional continuity in relationships; (2) reflect the child's own sense of time; (3) take into account the law's incapacity to make long-range predictions and to manage family relationships; and (4) provide the least detrimental available alternative for safeguarding the child's growth and development.

Learning Objective 11.5
Discuss major high-risk contexts and their impacts on child development.

1. What are some specific conditions that might present high-risk challenges to children's development?

These *special circumstances* include war and dislocation, abuse and neglect, serious illness, and severe emotional deprivation. Children are susceptible to developing posttraumatic stress disorder (PTSD) following traumatic events such as war, earthquakes, school shootings, and catastrophic floods. Evidence suggests that the effects of childhood trauma may linger into adulthood. Children who are abused or neglected are at risk for developing a variety of behavior problems and tend to lag in social and cognitive development. Similarly, repeated hospitalizations are associated with various behavior problems of children and adverse affects on their families. Children who are severely deprived both emotionally and physically are more likely to exhibit attachment problems, ADHD, autistic-like problems, and cognitive impairment.

2. Are all children equally affected by growing up in high-risk environments?

Studies suggest that *both risk and resilience* exist among children who experience severe emotional and physical deprivation. The longer the period of time that a child experiences those severely depriving conditions, the more likely it is that the experience will result in long-term social and emotional damage. However, researchers have found that some children appear to be able to rebound and resume a normal developmental course after adoption into a loving family. Protective factors for these vulnerable children include the mother's caregiving competence, as well as the child's social maturity, autonomy, sense of self-efficacy, scholastic competence, and emotional support from extended family and friends. Many researchers believe that these factors represent sources of resilience that enable children reared under adverse conditions to make a successful life adaptation into adulthood, despite the odds.

Self *and* Identity

(LWA/Dann Tardiff/Blend Images/Jupiter Images)

IDENTITY AND SOCIETY

Learning Objective 12.5

EXPLAIN HOW INDIVIDUALS CONSTRUCT THEIR PERSONAL AND ETHNIC OR CULTURAL IDENTITIES.

Erikson and Marcia on Identity Crisis

Social and Cultural Influences on Identity

Ethnic Identity

APPLICATIONS Possible Selves and Academic Achievement

Identity Construction as an Ongoing Process

66 "Anyone can cook aloo gobi," wails Jess. "But who can bend a ball like Beckham?" Jess (Jesminder Bjamra), a passionate soccer player, comes from a traditional Indian family. Her parents are Sikhs who fled from Uganda to England. Beckham is David Beckham, one of England's premier professional soccer players, Jess's idol.

The passage is from the 2002 film *Bend It Like Beckham.* The main characters in the movie are two athletically gifted 18-year-old girls, Jess and Jules, who dream about playing professional soccer in America. At the moment, however, their best option is playing on a community women's team where the girls have a chance to be noticed by American scouts.

There is a catch, though. Jess's family is impatient with her obsession with the sport. Her father disapproves of her running "half-naked" in front of men. In the meantime, her mother insists that Jess learn the wifely art of cooking perfect chapatis, while harboring hopes that her daughter will study law and marry a nice boy. To play, Jess must erect a wall of lies between her and her family. But not to play would be to deny the very core of her being.

Bend It Like Beckham is a story of the clash of aspirations between immigrant parents and assimilated children. At its heart is another theme common to moviegoers—the story of a young person who follows a dream despite seemingly insurmountable odds. Every generation has several such films—*Saturday Night Fever, Flashdance, Rocky, Rudy, Working Girl, Billy Elliot, Legally Blonde*—in which the protagonist struggles against barriers of social class or culture, gender, family expectations, or all in combination for self-fulfillment. These films may hold special appeal to Western audiences, who by and large endorse the maxim "To thine own self be true." What, though, is the self? We address that question in this chapter. ■

Existential self

One of two parts of the self proposed by William James, the "I" self is the subjective experiencer of the world.

Categorical self

One of two parts of the self proposed by William James, the "Me" self is an objective entity seen and evaluated in the world.

Self-system

Harter's conceptualization of the self that includes three distinct, interrelated units: self-knowledge, self-evaluation, and self-regulation.

Self-knowledge, or self-awareness

The part of the self-system concerned with children's knowledge about themselves.

Over the years, psychologists have conceptualized the self using several schemes. One early and influential view, first proposed by William James (1890, 1892), divides the self into two major components: subjective "I" and objective "me." The "I," or **existential self**, is the subjective experiencer of the world, whereas the "Me," or **categorical self**, is an objective entity seen and evaluated in the world. The *I* includes a sense of personal identity, a sense of being able to do things (personal agency), and an awareness of one's continuing existence across time; the *Me* includes traits such as physical appearance, personality traits, and cognitive abilities (Harter, 2003).

According to a more recent view, the "self" is a broad concept that can be divided into three distinct but interrelated units: self-knowledge, self-evaluation, and self-regulation (Harter, 1999, 2003). Together these form the **self-system**.

- **Self-knowledge**, also referred to as *self-awareness,* is concerned with the questions, What do children know about themselves as distinct, enduring individuals? When do they acquire this knowledge? How does this knowledge relate to understanding other aspects of their social and physical environments?

- **Self-regulation** is concerned with the questions, How and when do children acquire self-control? What variables influence this process?

- **Self-evaluation** concerns the questions, Does the child have high or low self-esteem? What factors influence children's opinions of themselves? How do these opinions affect their behavior? When you describe yourself, you include your perceptions of your unique traits and attributes and how you evaluate and feel about these. Your self knowledge and self-esteem and other self-evaluations are pulled together to form an identity, a process that takes a long time to complete and is influenced by many factors.

The self-system is involved in the ongoing development of a personal identity. **Identity** is concerned with the questions, Who am I? Where am I headed in my life? What variables influence the process of identity development?

Theories of the Self

Psychoanalytic Approaches to the Self

The self-system and identity encompass a broad range of topics and issues. Perhaps for that reason, no theoretical perspective has explained them completely. The *psychoanalytic perspective*, as proposed by Freud, stresses the biological urges of the id, which pushes children through universal stages of psychosexual development, shown in Table 1.1 in Chapter 1. Psychoanalytic theory focuses on early childhood experiences and conflict resolution. Erik Erikson, a neo-Freudian, proposed that the personality evolves through systematic stages based on the way an individual meets a basic challenge or resolves a crisis. Erikson's theory of psychosocial development emphasized the influence of social factors such as peers, teachers, and parents (Erikson, 1950, 1968). He also emphasized development across the lifespan, while Freud focused on early childhood. Erikson proposed eight stages of psychosocial development, also shown in Table 1.1.

Cognitive-Developmental Approaches to the Self

Those working from the cognitive-developmental framework tend to use the information processing theory to focus on how children's cognitive abilities to process information limit and shape the development of the self, while other theorists have proposed normative models of self-development based largely on Piaget's theory (Selman, 1980). Children's information processing abilities—how they encode, interpret, and remember information—contribute to the creation of self-relevant cognitive structures that in turn influence how further information is processed. Specifically, researchers believe that over time each child develops a **self-schema**, an internal notion of "who I am," composed of various features and characteristics. As a child encounters new information, the self-schema works to filter, interpret, and organize that information. Whenever we encounter new events or information, we attempt to understand them in terms of these cognitive structures. For example, children whose self-esteem is high are apparently more attuned to information that is consistent with a positive view of themselves. They may be likely to notice compliments, which, in turn, should further enhance their self-image (Christiansen, Wood, & Barrett, 2003). Children low in self-esteem, in contrast, are more aware of information that confirms their negative feelings and thus likely serves to decrease self-esteem even more.

Environmental/Learning Approaches to the Self

Social-learning theorists have proposed a number of psychological processes that are relevant to the self. Social-learning approaches emphasize that people change if their environment changes. Therefore, people are influenced by their interactions with others in specific social situations. For example, an assertive girl will become passive if her assertive behavior is no longer reinforced. A boy may be very outgoing with his female friends but be very shy around other girls. The development of the self is proposed to be a very

Self-regulation
The part of the self-system concerned with self-control.

Self-evaluation
The part of the self-system concerned with children's opinions of themselves and their abilities.

Identity
A well-organized conception of the self made up of values, beliefs, and goals to which the individual is committed.

Learning Objectives 12.1
Compare and contrast five theoretical perspectives on the development of self concepts.

Self-schema
An internal notion of "who I am," composed of the various features and characteristics about the self.

Links to Related Material
In Chapters 7 and 8, you read how children develop schemas or mental models about the world, and how these schemas influence information processing. Here, you learn more about how schemas influence the information that children process about themselves.

Self-efficacy
Bandura's term for people's ability to succeed at various tasks, as judged by the people themselves.

Questions for Thought
and Discussion
How have your beliefs about self-efficacy directly affected decisions you made recently? Do you think that following your self-efficacy judgments is always wise?

In sizing up her chances of success in this situation, this child is making judgments based on her sense of self-efficacy. How will her decisions affect her present and potentially her future behavior? (Erik Isakson/Rubberball/Jupiter Images)

Questions for Thought
and Discussion
From an evolutionary perspective, what would be the selective value of self-awareness for primates such as humans?

individual process that depends on each person's subjective social experiences and social environments.

Albert Bandura proposed a model of self-evaluation built around the concept of **self-efficacy**, a person's ability, as judged by that person, to carry out various behaviors and acts (Bandura, 1997, 2001). Bandura observed that just as infants and young children do not understand the operations of the physical and social world very well, they do not know much about their own skills and abilities. In everyday situations parents must frequently warn children, for example, that they are swimming out too far or that a particular library book will be too difficult for them to understand. Such verbal instructions from parents, along with many trial-and-error experiences, help young children gradually learn the limits of their talents and capabilities—that is, accurately judge their self-efficacy (Plumert, 1995).

As children grow, two other mechanisms promote the development of self-efficacy judgments. One is modeling, which children come to use as a way of estimating the likelihood of success at a task. For example, a child might reason, "If that little girl [who is my size and age] can jump over that fence, I can probably do it, too." Another way children learn to estimate their potential for success is through awareness of internal bodily reactions. For example, feelings of emotional arousal (e.g., tension, a nervous stomach, or a fast heart rate) frequently become associated with failures. Self-efficacy judgments are important because they are believed to affect children's behavior significantly. Bandura contends, for example, that greater feelings of self-efficacy produce increased effort and persistence on a task and thus, ultimately, a higher level of performance. This concept is especially relevant in the area of children's academic achievement and how it relates to their self-evaluations.

Evolutionary and Biological Approaches to the Self

Two approaches to the self fall under the framework of evolutionary and biological approaches—Bowlby's attachment theory and evolutionary psychology. Historically, Bowlby's theory has proved the more influential. In his landmark writings on attachment, John Bowlby discussed his belief that the sense of self begins to develop within the context of infant-caregiver interactions and is promoted by responsive caregiving. Babies whose caregivers are sensitive and responsive should construct an internal model of the self as lovable and worthy of attention. Babies whose caregivers are neglectful and insensitive should form models of the self as unworthy (Nair & Murray, 2005).

In recent years, evolutionary psychologists have taken up the issue of the self. Great strides in the study of animal self-awareness were made in 1970 with the publication of a paper on primate mirror self-recognition by Gordon Gallup, Jr. Gallup described an experimental procedure that provided compelling evidence that chimpanzees are able to recognize their images in mirrors. Since Gallup's pioneering study, scientists have tested many other species for mirror self-recognition. Among primates, only hominids (orangutan, bonobo, chimpanzee) show clear evidence of self-recognition (de Veer, Gallop, Theall, & van den Bos, 2003). Studies suggest that bottle-nosed dolphins may also have the capacity for self-recognition (Herman, 2002).

Sociocultural Approaches to the Self

The sociocultural approach focuses on the socialization of the self and self-understanding through participation in cultural practices, customs, and institutions. Socialization practices reflect each culture's model of the self. These models, in turn, derive from societal ideals and values and vary from culture to culture. Cultural models of the self vary across a number of dimensions (Cross & Gore, 2003; Mascolo & Li, 2004). Of these models, the most extensively documented is the relationship of the self to others. For example, cultural communities with roots in Western European traditions tend to draw a clear distinction between the self and others. In this view, the self is independent, self-contained, and autonomous. In many other cultures, the boundary between the self and others is less clearly drawn. In this model, which is common in many East Asian, Central and South American, and Native American groups, the self and others are seen as interdependent or interconnected.

Although the self–other dimension has been most widely studied cross-culturally, conceptions of the self vary in other ways as well. Cultures differ in the age at which they assign "selfhood" or person-status to an individual. In some cultures, children are not considered "persons" until they have lived for several months or even a year or more. Cultures also vary in their definitions of the ideal self. In European American communities, for example, the ideal person is independent and achievement oriented. In these communities, individuals strive to distinguish themselves from the crowd. Personal economic and psychological needs take precedence over those of the group. In contrast, in many East Asian societies, the ideal person is closely connected with others and does not stand out. In these communities, individuals strive to conform, maintain harmonious interpersonal relations, and bring favor to the family (Mascolo & Li, 2004).

Although every culture provides a broad outline of the ideal self, cultures also provide some options. The range of possible selves varies widely across cultures. In diverse, heterogeneous cultures, there is a veritable supermarket of identities from which to choose. In other societies, there are relatively few options (for example, some cultures may limit a woman's options to those of wife and mother) (Cross & Gore, 2003). The sociocultural approaches emphasize the importance of caregiver practices and adult responses to behaviors as well as broader cultural themes. For example, from the first days of an infant's life, caregivers adopt practices that are largely compatible with their own cultural views of the self.

Questions for Thought and Discussion
How did social and cultural contexts shape your self-concept?

Learning Objective 12.1: *Compare and contrast five theoretical perspectives on the development of the self-system.*

1. According to contemporary views, what are the three components of the self-system?
2. How do cognitive-developmental approaches differ from psychoanalytic approaches to the development of self?
3. How do environmental/learning approaches contribute to our understanding of the development of self?
4. What are examples of biological and evolutionary approaches to questions about the self?
5. What important information do sociocultural approaches provide in understanding the self?

Test Your Mastery...

Self-Knowledge

What do children know about the self, and when do they know it? It is not uncommon to hear a toddler proudly announce that he is a big boy or that his name is Jeremy. But he may, as yet, have very little understanding of his physical characteristics (heavy or slight), his personality (shy or bold), or his living conditions (middle-class or poor). Children's self-knowledge develops steadily across the childhood years and is interwoven with the development of other cognitive and socialization processes.

When does a baby first understand that he or she exists separately from the surrounding world? Some researchers believe that babies have an inborn awareness of their existence, or at least that this awareness develops within the first weeks of life (Butterworth, 1995; Gibson, 1993). Others argue that none of what babies do requires us to assume they have self-awareness prior to their first birthday (Kagan, 1991). Most now agree that a sense of self begins to develop in the first two to three months of life as infants discover that they can cause things to happen in the world around them (Rachat, 2003).

Learning Objective 12.2
Trace the development of self-knowledge from infancy, identifying the processes by which changes in the self-system occur.

BOX 12.1 Culture and the Self

Some psychologists have observed that different cultures tend to hold different conceptions of the relationship between self and other (Markus and Kitayama, 1991). In the United States, the emphasis is typically on attending to oneself, appreciating the ways in which one is unique from others, and asserting oneself. In many other cultures, the emphasis is generally on being attentive to and fitting in with others and on interpersonal harmony. These basic ideas about the self in relation to others can affect the way people think, react, and even feel, in various situations.

How does a young child develop a particular self-orientation? Children develop their sense of self in relation to others within their cultural context. For example, ideas about the "self" are instantiated through parenting practices, especially the style of mother-child interactions (Keller et al., 2004). In one cross-cultural study, researchers studied 116 families in Costa Rica, Cameroon, and Greece to see how a "proximal style" of parenting (high degree of body contact and physical stimulation, e.g., holding, caressing) or a "distal style" of parenting (high degree of face-to-face contact and use of objects as cognitive stimulation) relates to the development of self-concept. How did these styles of parenting relate to how quickly babies developed a sense of themselves as separate, autonomous beings? How quickly did babies develop a sense of self-regulation through compliance with mothers' requests (e.g., to bring her a familiar object)?

Keller and her colleagues found, as expected, that the Greek toddlers, whose mothers most often employed the distal style of parenting, exhibited the most instances of self-recognition at 18 to 20 months of age. Cameroon (Nso) toddlers, whose mothers had mostly used a proximal style of parenting, demonstrated the most instances of self-regulation. Interestingly, the Costa Rican toddlers, whose mothers had generally employed a combination of proximal and distal styles, were at a midpoint between the Greek and Nso toddlers in measures of their self-recognition and self-regulation. This study provides evidence for the idea that parents' interaction styles with their young children tend to influence children's later ideas about themselves in relation to others.

In another study (Wang, 2004), researchers interviewed 3- to 9-year-old middle-class children in the United States and China, noting differences in the children's conceptions of themselves in the context of their personal memories. In China, children recounted prior events with an emphasis on their role in relation to others and the social interactions that occurred, with relatively little mention of personal opinions and emotions. In the United States, in contrast, children retold events in which they had played a central role. American children tended to express more emotions and personal opinions. This pattern held for both the children's early and recent memories. These cultural differences in self-conception became more pronounced among the older children.

In an earlier study, Wang and colleagues (2000) examined conversations about past events between mothers and their 3-year-old daughters in China and the United States. They found that, in China, mothers tended to play a more directive role in helping their daughters to retell past events, determining the structure and even the content of the story. In contrast, the U.S. mothers asked their daughters more open-ended questions, allowing them far more choice in how the story was retold. The U.S. mothers also tended to offer more praise of their daughters' personal achievements during the event that they were discussing. In general, the interactions between the Chinese mothers and daughters tended to be more hierarchical, while those between U.S. mothers and daughters were more egalitarian. These studies highlight the influence of culture on children's concepts of self and relationships.

What differences might you predict in cultural influences on the development of self-concept between these preschoolers in China and American children in a similar setting in the United States? (Ellen B. Senisi/The Image Works)

Discovery of the Self in Infancy

Perceptual processes are thought to play an important role in infants' first coming to recognize their separateness (Rochat, 2003). For example, as you read in Chapters 5 and 11, within only weeks after birth, infants can imitate certain adult facial expressions. This finding means that newborns can connect sensory (visual) input with the corresponding motor responses—a capability that lays the groundwork for their realizing that they can interact with and affect the world around them (Bremner, 2002).

By 3 months of age, infants seem to perceive that they control their own body movements. One study had babies seated in an apparatus in which they could see live images of their legs transmitted on two TV monitors in front of them. Different images—sometimes reversed or upside down—were presented on each TV, and it was clear from the babies' looking responses that they could easily detect when the timing or direction of the leg movements they viewed did not correspond to what they were actually doing (Rochat & Morgan, 1995). Similar research has reported the same findings with infants' arm movements (Schmuckler, 1995).

Studies of perception also have shown that in the months that follow, the self becomes more clearly defined. For example, when 6-month-olds are taught to look for an object located in one position relative to themselves—say, to the left—and then are rotated to the opposite orientation—so that the object is to their right—they continue to search for the object by looking left. The addition of visual cues or landmarks to encourage more appropriate searching has little effect on babies of this age. This approach results in unsuccessful searching, however, and gradually gives way to more effective, environmentally guided, perceptual strategies as the baby approaches 1 year. But in using themselves as anchor points when searching, young infants demonstrate at least a crude awareness of their own separate existence (Morin, 2004; Rochat, 2003).

Along with infants' knowledge that they exist apart from the things around them comes an understanding of **personal agency**—that is, an understanding that they can be the agents or causes of events that occur in their worlds. Now babies move toys and put things in their mouths and bang blocks, all suggesting an awareness both that they are separate from these things and that they can do something with them (Tomasello & Haberl, 2003; van Leeuwen, Kaufmann, & Walther, 2000). Personal agency also appears to develop through babies' early interactions with caregivers (Barnard & Sumner, 2002; Crockenburg & Leerkes, 2004; Kotchick, Dorsey, & Heller, 2005). Theorists concur that when parents are more sensitive and responsive to their infants' signals, babies more quickly develop an understanding of the impact they can have on their environments (such as, "I can make Mommy come by crying"). The importance of caregiver interactions is a theme in the factors that influence self and identity development.

Babies first acquire an understanding of the self as separate from the mother. In one study, babies aged 6 months and older watched an adult model eat a Cheerio. They were then given one and instructed to feed it either to themselves or to their mothers. Significantly more babies at each age were able to follow the first instruction than were able to follow the second (Pipp, Fischer, & Jennings, 1987). These results show that infants learn to direct actions and speech toward themselves before they direct those same responses toward their mothers or others (Rochat, 2003; Rochat & Striano, 2002). Thus, self-knowledge of personal agency ("I can do it to me") precedes mother-knowledge ("I can do it to her"). This difference reverses by age 2, when toddlers are better able to direct actions toward their mothers and others than toward themselves. Older infants become more self-conscious and more focused on interpersonal relations and play (Pipp-Siegel & Foltz, 1997).

Self-Recognition

As babies approach age 2, they display an increasing awareness of the self. Perhaps the form of self-knowledge that has attracted the most research is infants' ability to recognize what they look like. A number of researchers have investigated the development of **visual self-recognition** by examining babies' reactions to mirror reflections. The major issue in this research concerns whether babies actually recognize the reflected images as themselves.

During their first year, babies will smile and vocalize at their mirror reflections (Neilsen & Dissanayake, 2004). They will also spend time in self-exploration, observing their own movements, and they seem to enjoy the experience of watching themselves move. There is also some evidence that babies distinguish between their own images and

Links to Related Material
In Chapters 5 and 11, you read about infants' early capacities to imitate adult facial expressions. Here, you learn more about how this and other early perceptual capacities may be linked to the infant's developing sense of agency.

Personal agency
The understanding that one can be the cause of events.

Visual self-recognition
The ability to recognize oneself; often studied in babies by having them look into mirrors.

Does this baby recognize the face in the mirror? How do researchers use visual self-recognition in their research on the development of infants' sense of self and other? How will this child respond in similar experiments at the age of 2? (© Joseph Pobereskin/Stone/Getty)

that of another child. When infants as young as 3 months of age are shown still images of themselves and another baby, they exhibit a clear preference for looking at the other child, indicating not only that they can discriminate between the two images but that their own is familiar to them (Bornstein & Arterberry, 2003; Rochat & Striano, 2002).

By about 5 months of age, this procedure reveals another interesting finding. When the image a baby normally sees in a mirror is altered (such as by placing colored marks on the cheeks of both babies), the looking preference changes, and infants spend more time looking at their own images (Neilsen, Dissanayake, & Kashima, 2003). Whether babies this young realize that what they are seeing is themselves, however, is not known.

One sure way to know if a toddler recognizes herself in a mirror is if she labels the image ("It's me!" or "Amy!"). Pronouns such as *me* and *mine,* as well as the child's name, enter the child's vocabulary during the second year of life (Lewis & Ramsey, 2004). By the second birthday, most children can apply these labels to their reflections in mirrors. But do children recognize mirror images as themselves before they can apply the appropriate labels? To answer this question, psychologists use the "mark test" described earlier. A colored mark is surreptitiously placed on the infant's face in a location where she could not normally see it, such as on her forehead (Vyt, 2001). The baby is then placed before a mirror, and the investigators note whether she attempts to touch the mark. If she does, they conclude that she understands that the marked face in the mirror is her own. Using this measure, researchers have not found self-recognition in infants under 15 months of age. Self-recognition does not occur reliably until about 24 months (Courage, Edison, & Howe, 2004).

Visual self-recognition has also been investigated with a variety of other techniques, including comparing infants' reactions to videotapes or photographs of themselves with their reactions to tapes or photos of similar peers (Courage et al., 2004; Neilson et al., 2003) and having infants point to pictures of themselves in a group after hearing their names (Courage et al., 2004; Damon & Hart, 1982). Evidence from these measures places self-recognition several months later than do the mirror-technique findings (Rochat, 2003).

Self-Recognition over Time Daniel Povinelli and colleagues (Barth, Povinelli, & Cant, 2004) have explored how self-recognition endures over time, with some surprising results. In one study (Povinelli, 1995), 2- to 4-year-old children were asked to play a game in which the experimenter repeatedly praised each child and patted him or her on the head. This provided an opportunity to place a large colorful sticker on the child's head. Just minutes later, the child was invited to watch a videotape of the game, which clearly showed the experimenter placing the sticker on the child's head, and the child then playing for a few minutes adorned with the sticker.

None of the 2-year-olds searched for the stickers on their own bodies, and only 25 percent of the 3-year-olds did so—even though they typically could label their video image with a confident "That's me!" An important distinction characterized the 4-year-olds, who not only searched for the stickers but did so immediately on seeing the videotape showing the sticker placement. Povinelli concluded that a young child does not connect his or her current physical self with the selves that existed at various points in the past. This idea was supported by the results of another study, in which the children were shown live video feedback instead of the delayed feedback described earlier. In this case, the 2- and 3-year-olds began to reach for the stickers when they saw the stickers being placed on their heads. Evidently, the children did not respond in the same way to the delayed feedback because, although they recognized the delayed images as sharing physical characteristics with their present selves, the images did not move as the children were moving (Povinelli, 1995).

These experimental procedures require children to use mirror or video information to reach for a spot of rouge or some other mark on themselves, but children's responses may demonstrate more than the dawning of self-recognition. Mark-directed behavior also is thought to reflect the broad shift in cognitive development that occurs as a child approaches the age of 2 (Courage & Howe, 2002).

Individual Differences in Self-Recognition Regardless of the method used, self-recognition appears at different ages for different infants. What could be the source of these differences? One hypothesis is that self-recognition relates to temperament (Lewis & Wolan Sullivan, 2005). Specifically, babies who react strongly in stress situations (and so are usually classified as difficult) are thought to develop a sense of self earlier than do other babies in order to deal better with the intensity of the stimulation they experience. Consistent with this idea, infants who react most strongly to vaccinations at 6 months of age also are most likely to show mirror self-recognition at 18 months of age (Lewis & Ramsay, 1997).

Another source of individual differences in self-recognition is attachment (Harel, Eshel, Ganor, & Scher, 2002; Siegel & Hartzell, 2003). Children who are securely attached have a better understanding of both personal agency and physical characteristics than do children in other attachment classifications (Meins, Fernyhough, & Wainwright, 2003; Symons, 2004; Thompson, Easterbrooks, & Padilla-Walker, 2003). Thus, a secure attachment relationship appears to promote the development of the self.

Why might this be? As we indicated earlier, some psychologists believe that mother-child interaction provides an infant the opportunity to first develop a concept of a separate self. Secure attachment to the caregiver promotes exploration and cognitive development in the baby—all factors that may contribute to the development of self-recognition. What about the relationship between attachment and self-recognition in cases where children have been abused and neglected? Maltreated infants tend to be less securely attached and displayed less evidence of self-recognition (Jung, Meen & Cicchetti, 2004; Macfie, Cicchetti, & Toth, 2001; Weinfield, Whaley, & Egeland, 2004). Moreover, the maltreated infants responded more negatively to their mirror reflections, and their language was less likely to involve descriptions of themselves or of their internal states and feelings (Eigsti & Cicchetti, 2004). Behaviors such as these may indicate the beginnings of a low sense of self-worth.

Awareness of Self and Others When do infants know that the leg they see moving is theirs while also knowing that the hand touching their leg is not? The consequence of infants' increasing awareness of their own identities may be a greater awareness of the separateness and distinctiveness of others. That is, as we become more self-aware, we should simultaneously become more other-aware. There is some evidence that infants draw distinctions between themselves and others at a very young age. For example, infants 4 months of age responded differently to a live video of an adult mimicking their behavior than to a live video of themselves. Infants' behaviors toward the mimicker were more social, with more smiling and longer gazes. In addition, when the video images of both infant and adult were frozen for 1 minute, infants made more attempts to reengage the adult image, suggesting recognition that another person is a potential social partner. This difference was present in both 4- and 9-month-old children, with a large increase in reengagement behaviors across the two ages (Rochat & Striano, 2002).

Further evidence for children's developing appreciation of the existence and individuality of others can be found in an early type of play termed *synchronic imitation*. In synchronic imitation, preverbal children play with similar toys in a similar fashion (Neilsen & Dissanayake, 2004). For example, one toddler might bang a spoon, followed by another toddler banging a spoon, a pattern that the toddlers repeat to their great glee. To synchronize play with that of a peer, a child must have some understanding of the other child's intentions and behavior. This type of play would thus seem to require some degree of self- and other-awareness. Consistent with this view, 18-month-olds who give evidence of mirror self-recognition display more synchronic imitation with same-age peers (and also with adults) than do infants who do not recognize themselves in the mirror (Nadal, 2004).

Self-recognition has also been linked to the emergence of the self-conscious emotions of embarrassment, pride, shame, empathy, and guilt (Lewis & Wolan Sullivan, 2005). To experience this class of emotions, children need to be able to evaluate the self relative to

Links to Related Material
Here, you learn about the child's developing sense of self and other. In Chapter 15, you will read more about children's early peer interactions.

some social standard, and they need to have developed self-awareness. A number of studies have linked these affective experiences with the development of prosocial behavior and a moral sense (Kochanska et al., 2002; Leary & Tangney, 2003).

Developmental Changes in Self-Descriptions

Psychologists have typically assessed older children's self-knowledge by examining their descriptions of themselves. This method has taken various forms, ranging from very unstructured interviews, which might include general questions (such as "Who are you?") to very structured questionnaires, which require answers to written items (such as "How old are you?" and "What is your favorite outdoor game?"). Regardless of the method used, researchers have found a predictable pattern of development (Bornholt, 2005).

By the age of 2, many children display knowledge of some of their most basic characteristics. For example, they know whether they are girls or boys, and they are aware that they are children rather than adults (Campbell, Shirley, & Caygill, 2002; Harter, 1988). These category labels are undoubtedly learned through modeling and other learning processes, as children repeatedly hear themselves referred to with phrases such as "my little boy" or as they receive approval when they correctly state their age or other personal characteristic. In the preschool years, as shown in Table 12.1, self-descriptions are very concrete and usually involve physical features, possessions, and preferences (Sakuma, Endo, & Muto, 2000). Thus a 4-year-old might say that she lives in a big house, has a dog, and likes ice cream. This information, however, is not always completely accurate, and children's descriptions are often unrealistically positive. During this period there is a focus on objective, here-and-now attributes—a finding that corresponds well with Piaget's description of preoperational children's view of the world.

But is it incorrect to assume, as some psychologists have, that 4-year-olds can comprehend specific personal characteristics but not more general traits, such as being messy or having a big appetite? The self-description a young child offers seems to depend heavily on how the information is sought. Children give more general responses when questions are structured to encourage generality ("Tell me how you are at school with your friends") than when questions seek more specific information ("Tell me what you did at school with friends today") (Harter, 1999, 2003). When seeking information from children, it is important to remember that children's responses often reflect as much about how the question is asked as the question itself.

In middle childhood, self-descriptions change in several ways, reflecting the shift to concrete operational abilities (Harter, 2003). Rather than limiting their statements to the here and now and the physical, 6- to 10-year-olds begin to talk about less tangible characteristics, such as emotions ("Sometimes I feel sad"). They also can combine separate

TABLE 12.1 Children's Self-Descriptions during Three Age Periods			
AGE PERIOD	**PIAGETIAN STAGE**	**FOCUS OF SELF-DESCRIPTIONS**	**EXAMPLES**
Early Childhood	Preoperational	Physical characteristics, possessions, preferences	"I have freckles." "My cat is white." "I like pizza."
Middle Childhood	Concrete operations	Behavioral traits and abilities, emotions, category membership	"I'm a good singer." "I'm a happy kid." "I'm a cheerleader."
Adolescence	Formal operations	Attitudes, personality attributes (sometimes opposing or associated with different roles), beliefs	"I'm patriotic." "I can be persuasive." "I'm not a quitter." "I support gun control."

attributes (good at climbing, jumping, and running) into an overall category ("I'm a good athlete"). The accuracy of children's information improves during this period, although they generally continue to stress their positive, rather than negative, characteristics (Butler, 2005; Ruble & Dweck, 1995).

In later childhood, descriptions may be based on social comparisons with others, as children evaluate their skills or talents relative to those of friends or classmates ("I'm the best skater on the street") (Boulton, 2005; Spinath & Spinath, 2005). Children also can include opposing attributes ("I'm good at spelling, but bad at math") in their descriptions. The earlier tendency to stress positive attributes now sometimes gives way to more intense negative self-evaluations and more general feelings of low self-worth (Harter, 2003).

As children enter adolescence, their self-descriptions continue to change (Harter, 2003; Harter, Whitesell, & Junkin, 1998). The formal operational child thinks and self-describes in more abstract and hypothetical terms. Rather than focusing on physical characteristics and possessions (as in early childhood) or on behavioral traits and abilities (as in middle and later childhood), the adolescent is concerned with attitudes ("I hate chemistry"), personality attributes ("I'm curious"), and beliefs involving hypothetical situations ("If I meet someone who has a different idea about something, I try to be tolerant of it") (Elliot & Dweck, 2005; Watt, 2004).

By middle adolescence, the self typically differentiates into more roles. For example, adolescents give different responses when asked to describe themselves in the classroom, at home, and with friends. Sometimes these differences involve opposing or conflicting attributes, such as being shy in the classroom but outgoing with friends. For the first time, conflicts in self-descriptions can produce feelings of confusion and distress (Harter, 2003; Harter & Whitsell, 2002).

Later in adolescence, opposing characteristics are often combined into single personality styles ("cheerful" and "sad" are combined into "moody"), and this more complex view of the self comes to be viewed as legitimate and normal (Harter, 2002, 2003). Adolescents now can display **false self-behavior**, meaning that, when necessary, they can purposely behave ("act") in ways that do not reflect their true selves. The limits of self-development are not yet known, but the self apparently continues to differentiate throughout adolescence and adulthood (Harter, 1999; Schunk & Miller, 2002).

As we have seen, the child's perception of the self becomes more sophisticated and refined with age. Cognitive development is one critical factor in the revisions of self descriptions as children mature. The self is a product of these cognitive changes and the feedback the child receives from others. As children mature, they also become better at interpreting information they receive from others and incorporating it into their conceptualization of the self. As children internalize the expectations of those around them, they develop an *ideal self* that they use to evaluate their *real self*.

Learning Objective 12.2: *Trace the development of self-knowledge from infancy, identifying the processes by which changes in the self-system occur.*

1. How can you tell when an infant discovers the self as a separate entity with personal agency?
2. How does self-recognition change over time in relation to recognition of others?
3. How do children's self-descriptions change from early childhood to adolescence?
4. How do individual and cultural differences shape the development of self-concept?

Self-Control

Some parents report that they sometimes can "see" their children's minds working as they try to decide whether to pursue a course of action. For example, is taking the cookie, toy, or next step worth whatever trouble might ensue? Young children seem to try to stop themselves, but once the thought has occurred to them the behavior follows. How does

False self-behavior
Behaving in a way that is knowingly different from how one's true self would behave.

Questions for Thought and Discussion
Are you aware of displaying false self-behavior? In what contexts? What are the main contrasts between your ideal and real self?

Test Your Mastery...

Learning Objective 12.3
Analyze the mechanisms and processes by which children develop self-control.

the self come to regulate, or control, children's behavior? *Self-control* refers to the many processes by which humans control or regulate their behaviors, states, and inner feelings and is an important element in the construction of the self (Rueda, Posner, & Rothbart, 2005). In addition, self-control is the foundation of how humans are able to function in societies and to use socialization (Baumeister & Vohs, 2004).

Self-regulation is a crucial aspect of human development. If children did not learn to control their behavior—to avoid the things they must avoid, to wait for the things they cannot have right away, to alter strategies that are not working—they constantly would be at the mercy of the moment-to-moment pushes and pulls of their environments. They would simply be "weathervanes," as Bandura puts it (1986, p. 335). The development of self-control is one of the child's most impressive accomplishments. Self-control indicates at the very least that the child knows what demands are made by the surrounding world, realizes what behaviors relate to those demands, and understands how to adjust behaviors to meet the demands (Muller & Hrabok, 2005). How does such self-control develop, and what are its effects? Higher self-control is associated with better adjustment, higher self-esteem, better relationships and interpersonal skills, and better school performance (Tangney, Baumeister, & Boone, 2004).

Erik Erikson (1950) identified the period from about 18 months to 3 years as the second stage of personality development—autonomy versus shame and doubt. This stage is characterized by a shift from the external control of behavior to self-control. According to Erikson, young children begin to use their own judgments more and to substitute these judgments for those of their caregivers. Toddlers learn to adjust to the limits set by adults. The "terrible twos," for example, often are seen as a time where the child is constantly pushing limits, rules, and boundaries set by adults. Toddlers begin to test the idea that they are individuals with some degree of control over their world. Caregivers who meet these attempts at control as a normal part of child development can help the child gain self-control. By providing contexts in which children can assert their self-will, parents can help to avoid unnecessary conflict as the child develops self-control.

During early infancy, self-regulation mostly involves involuntary biological processes (Rothbart & Posner, 1985; Stifter & Braungart, 1995). For instance, babies reflexively squint in response to a bright light. Even young infants control sensory input by turning away or falling asleep when stimulation from caregivers or surroundings becomes overwhelming. Such responses serve important regulatory functions, but there is no evidence that the infants who engage in them are cognitively aware of what is happening.

By the beginning of the second year, babies have developed many voluntary behaviors and can act on their environments in purposeful ways. Children act to accomplish things or to produce outcomes, such as when a baby grabs for a toy he or she would like to play with or pushes over a tower of blocks to watch it crash to the floor. But at this point, the child's ability to monitor behaviors and to adjust them as necessary is still limited (Huichang, Junli, & Hongxue, 2005).

During the third year, most children consistently begin to regulate their activities to produce outcomes. They pay attention to simple standards set by others or by themselves and monitor their activities in relation to those standards. For instance, a child making a birthday cake out of sand may try several combinations of mud, water, sticks, and grass to get it just right. As children come to recognize standards, they also begin to react affectively when they meet or fail to meet them. Thus, we begin to see the expression of the self-conscious emotions of pride, shame, guilt, and embarrassment (Lewis, 2000; Liew, Eisenberg, & Reiser, 2004).

The changes in self-regulation observed during the early years reflect two important developments. First, regulation shifts from external to internal control. Initially, caregivers largely regulate children's behavior either directly or indirectly by supporting or scaffolding children's own efforts at self-regulation. Gradually, however, regulation shifts to the child. Second, self-control grows more elaborate and sophisticated as children exercise their developing powers of discretion.

Questions for Thought
and Discussion

How would we be "weathervanes" in the absense of self-control? How do other species exhibit self-control in their behavior?

Is this 3-year-old likely to comply with her father's request to pick up this mess? Why, or why not? What factors will determine the child's committed and situational compliance in the development of self-regulation? (SW Products/Photodisc/ Getty Images)

Compliance

One of the earliest indices of self-control is **compliance**—children's ability to obey requests or adopt the standards of behavior given by authority figures. Children begin to understand caregiver wishes and expectations around the end of the first year (Suzuki, 2005). However, during the months that follow, children are more likely to refuse, ignore, or subvert parents' behavioral requests than comply with them (Huichang, Junli, & Hongxue, 2005).

The kinds of situations in which parents expect compliance vary widely. For instance, sometimes caregivers direct children to stop or refrain from doing something—for example, playing with the electric socket, interrupting when mom is on the phone, going in the street. To comply with these requests, children must be able to inhibit a behavior. In other situations, parents want their children to perform desired behavior such as brushing teeth, saying "thank you," and helping with chores (Lagattuta, 2005).

To study the development of compliance, researchers look at children's behavior in both kinds of situations (termed "Don't" and "Do" situations). For example, Grazyna Kochanska and colleagues (Kochanska, Coy, & Murray, 2001) followed a group of children longitudinally from shortly after their first birthdays until age 4. As you can see in Figure 12.1, compliance in the "Don't" situations increased dramatically during the second year of life. By the time they were 4, children complied with parental prohibitions nearly 80 percent of the time. In contrast, compliance in the "Do" situation was far more difficult to achieve.

The quality of children's compliance differed between the two contexts. In the "Don't" situation, children usually complied wholeheartedly, which Kochanska termed **committed compliance**. Committed compliance describes children's behavior when they embrace the caregiver's agenda, adopt it as their own, and follow caregiver directives in a self-regulated ways (for example, saying, "No, no! Don't touch!"). Compliance in the "Do" situation, on the other hand, was less likely and usually given grudgingly. In this type of compliance, termed **situational compliance**, children essentially cooperate with parental directives but with little enthusiasm. Situational compliance requires sustained caregiver support, such as reminding the child to continue or framing the activity as some kind of game (for example, toy cleanup). Situational compliance is often fleeting and disappears if caregivers become distracted, leave the room, or otherwise withdraw control.

Compliance
The child's ability to go along with requests or adopt the standards of behavior espoused by caregivers.

Committed compliance
Compliant behavior that results from a child's internalizing the instruction of an adult; results in positive emotion.

Situational compliance
Obedience that results from a child's awareness of an adult's will in a particular situation and does not reflect enduring behavioral change.

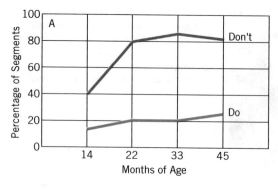

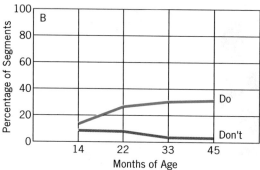

FIGURE 12.1

Longitudinal study of children's compliance

These graphs compare 2 children's committed and situational compliance at ages 14, 22, 33, and 45 months in both the "Do" and the "Don't" contexts. Which of these contexts is easier for children to learn compliance, and which is more challenging for them? Why did researchers distinguish between committed compliance and situational compliance? How did children's compliance change over time?

SOURCE: From The development of self-regulation in the first four years of life. G. Kochanska, K.C. Coy, and K.T. Murray. (2001). *Child Development, 72,* 1101. Copyright by the Society for Research in Child Development. Reprinted by permission.

Links to Related Material
Here, you learn about the development of compliance in childhood. In Chapter 16, you will read more about how different parenting styles lead to different types of compliance in children.

As you can see in Figure 12.1, it is clear that "Do" requests are more challenging for young children than "Don't" demands. Why this is so is open to interpretation. One possibility is that the ability to inhibit a behavior matures before the ability to sustain a prolonged flow of behavior (Rothbart & Rueda, 2005). Another possibility is that parents impose "Don't" commands earlier and expect children to comply with them at a younger age than "Do" commands. It is noteworthy that many "Don't" commands involve safety issues (e.g., "*Don't* jump on the bed;" "*Don't* poke the dog;" "*Don't* touch the stove"). Young children also must develop adequate cognitive abilities (such as memory and planning) to comply with requests and to regulate the negative emotions that may result from thwarting their desires (Liew, Eisenberg, & Reiser, 2004; Rueda, Posner, & Rothbart, 2005).

There are also striking individual differences in the ease with which parents and children achieve compliance. Some children are eager to comply with caregivers, whereas others readily comply with one parent but not the other. For other children, achieving compliance is a struggle regardless of who else is involved in the interaction. What factors might underlie these individual differences?

One contributing factor may be children's temperament. As you have read, children vary in their fearfulness and ability to regulate their behavior (inhibitory control). Researchers have found that children who are more cautious or able to inhibit a dominant response tend to be more compliant (Kochanska, Friesenborg, Lange, & Martel 2004; Murray & Kochonska, 2002; Rothbart & Hwang, 2005). Another factor is the quality of the relationship between parent and child. Parental warmth and postive expressivity are associated with higher levels of self-control in young children and teens (Eisenberg, Zhou, Spinrad, et al., 2005; Huichang, Junli, & Hongxue, 2005). As you will see in Chapter 16, authoritative parenting practices are associated with higher levels and earlier attainment of self-control, whereas authoritatian parenting practices are associated with lower levels of self-control (Zhou, Eisenberg, Wang, & Reiser, 2004).

Children are most likely to comply in dyads marked by a happy mood in which partners are mutually responsive to one another's needs and desires (Kochanska, 2002). Mothers in dyads with a mutually responsive orientation have a history of being responsive to their children's signals of need, signs of distress, bids for attention, and social overtures

(Kochanska, 1997; Kochanska, Aksan, & Knaack, 2004). During the second year, children whose mothers were responsive to their needs as infants tend to adopt a similar attitude—or what Kochanska terms a *responsive stance*—toward maternal wishes. Children with a responsive stance happily embrace the mother's agenda and eagerly comply with her requests. Kochanska believes that a responsive stance is an intermediate step between simple cooperation and genuine internalization of parental values and standards.

Studies of Japanese mother-child relations provide additional support for Kochanska's model. As you have seen, the mother-child relationship in Japan is unusually close, and mothers are highly responsive (even indulgent in the view of many Westerners) to infants' needs. Japanese parents try to avoid direct confrontations and contests of will with their children, rarely scold them directly, and often back down when children resist their requests (Bornstein & Cote, 2004; Cote & Bornstein, 2000). Although giving children such a free reign might seem destined to create demanding tyrants, Japanese children actually make fewer demands on parents, give fewer commands, and are less likely to assert that they will not obey (Caudill & Schooler, 1973). The "terrible twos," a phenomenon American parents are led to believe is unavoidable and normative, is unheard of in Japan.

To understand why Japanese children tend to be more compliant than their American counterparts and at a younger age, we can return to Kochanska's model. The goal of Japanese parenting techniques is to encourage children to *want* to adhere to parental and societal values and standards (Bornstein & Cote, 2004; Fogel, Stevenson, & Messinger, 1992; Rothbaum et al., 2000). In other words, by creating a warm, close, and responsive parent-child relationship, Japanese parents are fostering a receptive stance in their children.

American parents, in contrast, try to *convince* children to go along with parental requests (Fogel et al., 1992). To convince them, American parents often are forced to resort to power assertion or appeals to the parents' authority. Power assertion encompasses a range of behaviors, including taking toys from children, spanking, and verbal threats. Although power assertion is often effective in the short run (e.g., a child who is slapped upon touching an attractive toy will likely stop immediately), it is less likely to promote the internalization of values and standards than other parenting techniques.

Undoubtedly, many reasons explain why Japanese and American parents adopt such different approaches to the socialization of self-control. Nonetheless, a number of theorists contend that the American approach is a natural outgrowth of a cultural emphasis on autonomy and independence (Bornstein & Cote, 2004; Fogel et al., 1992; Rogoff, 2003; Rothbaum et al., 2000). American parents begin to encourage children to assert their own wishes and desires from a very early age. As a result, toddlers and preschoolers often have their own opinions about a variety of issues, including the reasonableness of parental requests and directives! The Japanese approach, in contrast, may reflect a greater cultural emphasis on interdependence and interpersonal harmony.

Delay of Gratification

As children grow older and spend more time outside the immediate supervision of adults, they learn to inhibit completely forbidden behaviors and to delay gratification through behaviors that might be more appropriate at a later time. And children inhibit behaviors and delay gratification even when no one is watching them. How does this kind of self-control develop?

A common method for studying resistance to temptation uses the **forbidden-toy technique**, which is similar to the "Don't" situation already described. Typically, an experimenter puts a child in a room where there is an attractive toy and tells the child not to touch or play with the toy. Outside the room, observers monitor the child's behavior through a two-way mirror. The investigators usually are interested in how long the child waits before breaking the rule or how much time the child spends playing with the forbidden toy.

Researchers have experimented to learn whether the self-instructional statements children make during their waiting time affects their ability to resist temptation. In one study,

Forbidden-toy technique
An experimental procedure for studying children's resistance to temptation in which the child is left alone with an attractive toy and instructed not to play with it.

3- to 7-year-old children were placed in a room with several attractive toys on a table behind them. They were instructed not to turn around and look at the toys while the experimenter was out of the room. One group of children also was told that, to help keep them from looking, they should repeat out loud a relevant statement, such as "I must not turn around." Children in a second group were told to use an irrelevant self-instruction, such as "Hickory, dickory, dock." Those in a third group were given no self-instructional advice and waited silently. For younger children, producing a verbal self-instruction led to greater resistance to temptation than remaining silent. But the semantic content of the instruction did not matter—the relevant and irrelevant instructions worked equally well. For older children, the content of the self-instruction did make a difference, with the relevant statement proving most effective (Hartig & Kanfer, 1973).

Several other factors have been shown to influence children's behavior in forbidden-toy settings (Putnam, Spiritz, & Stifter, 2002). For example, on one hand, seeing an adult model break the rule and play with the toy makes children more likely to do so (Grusec et al., 1979). On the other hand, providing children with a good rationale for following the prohibition ("Don't touch the toy; it's fragile and might break") increases the likelihood that they will resist (Parke, 1977), as does teaching children to develop their own plans or strategies for dealing with the temptation (Patterson, 1982; Yang & Yu, 2002).

In contrast to behaviors that are explicitly forbidden, some behaviors merely need to be delayed until a more appropriate time or place or until a more desired goal can be achieved. This situation is analogous to many choices children (and adults) encounter every day. Should I use this week's allowance to buy a small toy, or should I combine it with next week's and buy a larger toy? Should I eat this snack now, or should I save my appetite for a better meal later? A popular approach to studying children's self-control in these kinds of situations has been the **delay-of-gratification technique**. Typically, the child is presented with two choices: a small reward that is available immediately or a larger reward that can only be obtained later. This experimental task is more complex than those tasks involving resistance to temptation; thus, more factors have been shown to influence children's ability to delay gratification (Mischel, 2003; Mischel & Ayduk, 2002; Putnam, Spritz, & Stifter, 2002).

Children who, while waiting for a better reward, were directed to make a relevant statement ("I am waiting for the marshmallow"), an irrelevant statement ("One, two, three"), or no statement differed in their ability to delay their gratification. Either of the self-statements increased waiting time for younger children, but only the relevant verbalizations were of assistance to the older children (Karniol & Miller, 1981). Thus, children were more successful when they used strategies to help them wait.

Another method that helps children delay gratification is to reduce or alter the attention they pay to the tempting object (the smaller but immediately available reward) (Peake, Hebl, & Mischel, 2002; Qiaoyan & Fengqiang, 2005). When the object is out of sight, for example, children will wait much longer. The same is true when they spend the waiting time playing with a toy or engaging in some other distracting activity. Even when they are thinking about the tempting object, children will wait longer if they are instructed to think about its objective properties (say, the shape or color of a candy bar) rather than about its appealing properties (the candy bar's smell or taste).

As children grow older, their understanding of these distraction and delay strategies increases (Lizhu et al., 2005; Mischel & Ayduk, 2004; Yang & Yu, 2002). For example, when presented with various waiting techniques and asked to select the ones that would work best, preschoolers display little knowledge of what strategies would be more effective. Third graders, however, show an impressive understanding. By sixth grade, the majority of children seem to know that redirecting one's attention from the reward and other forms of distraction are useful methods for delaying gratification (Mischel & Ayduk, 2004; Yates, Yates, & Beasley, 1987).

Children's use of distraction strategies may be related to their ability to delay gratification. Toddlers who were able to use self-distraction to cope with a period of separation from their mothers were found at age 5 to be able to delay gratification for longer periods

Delay-of-gratification technique
An experimental procedure for studying children's ability to postpone a smaller, immediate reward in order to obtain a larger, delayed one.

How will their ages affect the ability of these children to resist temptation? The ability to delay gratification appears to be a personality trait that remains stable over time. What strategies help children develop self-control in the delay-of-gratification technique and the forbidden-toy technique? (© Jeneart LTD/The Image Bank/Getty Images)

compared to children who did not show that early coping ability (Sethi et al., 2000). Researchers also explored how delay of gratification relates to children's reactions to their mother's behavior in a play setting. The key predictor of preschool delay of gratification was toddlers' response to their mothers. The greatest success in delay of gratification at age 5 was observed in the children who as toddlers had distanced themselves from controlling mothers or had engaged with noncontrolling mothers. Not surprisingly, the ability to delay gratification has been linked to children's social competence. Children who respond impulsively often experience problems in their social interactions with other children, in part because they fail to acquire all the necessary information about a situation before making a decision (Eisenberg, Pidada, & Liew, 2001; Frankel & Feinberg, 2002; Hughes et al., 2000). Children who have been rejected or excluded often demonstrate an imparied ability to self-regulate (Baumeister et al., 2005; Twenge, Catanese, & Baumeister, 2003).

Finally, children's ability to cope with temptation in experimental situations appears to reflect a surprisingly stable personality characteristic. In one study, adolescents who had participated as preschoolers in delay-of-gratification research were studied again 10 years later. Parents were asked to complete several questionnaires concerned with aspects of their children's present skills in three areas: cognitive skills, social competence, and ability to cope with stress. The results indicated that children who had been better at delaying gratification in their early years were much more likely to be rated by parents as stronger in each of these three areas. For example, children who had waited the longest during the experimental procedures were later reported to be the most academically successful, the best at getting along with peers, the best at coping with problems, and the most confident and self-reliant (Mischel, Shoda, & Peake, 1988; Shoda, Mischel, & Peake, 1990). Thus, a child's early ability to delay gratification may be one long-term predictor of that child's eventual success and happiness (Bembenntly & Karabenick, 2004; Spinrad, Stifter, Donelson-McCall, & Turner, 2004; Wulfert et al., 2002).

> **Questions for Thought and Discussion**
> *Why do you think the ability to delay gratification is so important in child development?*

Internalization and Development of Conscience

When the teacher is not in the room, what keeps the children from going wild? What keeps Sam from grabbing the toy he wants from his friend? What determines whether or not the teenager abstains from sexual behavior? As you have seen, children generally become more effective in regulating their behaviors with age and experience. However, although it is important to follow the rules when authority figures are present, it is possibly more important to learn to behave and control one's emotions when they are not. How do we gain the ability to control ourselves using broader societal standards? **Internalization** is the process by which individuals, especially children, accept a society's standards of behavior as their own. Children learn about the acceptable behaviors, beliefs, and attitudes through the process of socialization. Among the most powerful agents of socialization are the family and schools (Wills & Resko, 2004).

As children develop a sense of self and gain the ability to regulate their behaviors and emotions, they also develop a **conscience**—internal standards of conduct they use to control their behavior, which typically produce discomfort when violated. Because conscience includes emotional discomfort from doing something wrong, it requires that the individual internalize a set of moral standards—internal rules and values that do not need external monitoring (Akson & Kochanska, 2005; Kochanska, 2004). Conscience also requires the control of behavior based on the belief that certain behaviors are right whereas others are wrong. A child may not take the cookie while his mother is watching, for example, but will wait until she is not looking to select the one of his choice. Another child may refrain, however, believing that taking the cookie without asking is the wrong thing to do.

Children's development of committed compliance is associated with the internalization of parental and societal values and rules (Kochanska, 2002). In contrast, situational compliance depends on caregiver control. Committed compliance and situational compliance begin to develop in early infancy and increase with age (Forman, Akson, & Kochanska, 2004). Committed compliance is also associated with authoritative parenting

Internalization
The process by which individuals, especially children, accept a society's standards of behavior as their own.

Conscience
Internal standards of conduct that are used to control one's behavior and typically produce discomfort when they are violated.

What is the association between religiosity and the development of internalization (conscience) and committed compliance in children? What other social and cultural factors foster children's development of self-regulation? (© Syracuse Newspapers/Albert Fanning/The Image Works)

behaviors (Kochanska & Akson, 2004; Kochanska et al., 2005). Caregivers who foster a warm, responsive interaction pattern are more likely to encourage the development of internalization and committed compliance in their children as well as development of morals and a value system (Royal & Baker, 2005). The use of threats and force, on the other hand, is negatively associated with the development of internalization and committed compliance in children.

The transmission of religiosity, through parents and other agents such a church system, is also a factor in the development of conscience. Religiosity, defined as the degree of involvement in religious organizations and observances, is associated with higher self-esteem, lower risk of substance use, and lower risk of dangerous sexual behaviors (Carothers et al., 2005; King & Furrow, 2004; Wills et al., 2003). However, although religious involvement is associated with fewer sexual encounters, adolescents who are religiously involved and sexually active are less likely to use medically approved methods of contraception (McKay, 2003). This pattern is most likely related to the finding that parental public religiosity is associated with decreased frequency of parent-child conversations about sex and birth control (Regnerus, 2005).

Children and teens are exposed to new roles, attitudes, and values outside the home that may conflict with those of their parents. How parents respond to the conflict can be important (Padilla-Walker & Thompson, 2005). The extent of parental control of exposure to new ideas is associated with the self-reported importance of values to parents. Parents use more controlling strategies to defend values that are the most important to them. In some situations, the controlling behaviors also may create conflict in the child-parent relationship.

✔ Test Your Mastery...

Learning Objective 12.3: *Analyze the mechanisms and processes by which children develop self-control.*

1. What are two general trends in the development of self-regulation?
2. How do children learn different types of compliance?
3. What can we learn about self-control from experiments using the forbidden-toy and delay-of-gratification techniques?
4. By what process do children develop a conscience?
5. What role do parenting styles play in children's development of self-control?

Self-Evaluation and Self-Esteem

Learning Objective 12.4
Describe the development of self-esteem and ways to measure it.

As children grow, they not only come to understand more about themselves but also begin to evaluate this information. Participation in school and in athletic teams and clubs encourages children to compare themselves with other children and also with their images of who they would like to be. Such self-evaluations usually bring both good news and bad, as children come to recognize their strengths and weaknesses and their positive and negative attributes. Self-evaluation, like self-knowledge, develops as children grow and is influenced by both cognitive and socialization variables (Burton & Mitchell, 2003).

Understanding and Measuring of Self-Esteem

The evaluative opinions children develop about themselves have been referred to as their **self-esteem**, or **self-worth** (Harter & Whitsell, 2003). Self-esteem is assumed to include not only children's cognitive judgments of their abilities but also their affective reactions (pride, shame, and so on) to these self-evaluations. In other words, it is not just how a child does on a task that matters, but also how they feel about it.

This concept is not new. Two traditional views of self-esteem have long been part of the developmental literature. According to the idea of the **looking-glass self** (Cooley, 1902), the psychological portraits we paint of ourselves are based on how we think others see us. That is, we view other people's reactions to us as "reflections" of who we are. The **competence view of the self** (James, 1892) holds that our level of self-esteem results from a combination of what we would like to achieve and how confident we feel about achieving it—an idea very similar to the more recent concept of self-efficacy (Cervone, Mor, & Orom, 2004; Madduz & Gosselin, 2003).

Methods of Measurement   The most common method of assessing children's self-esteem has been through questionnaires. Typically, such instruments present children with a list of questions designed to tap their opinions of themselves in a variety of situations or contexts (such as, "Are you usually willing to help when a friend needs a favor?" and "Do you think you are artistic?"). The responses to these questions can be combined and analyzed to produce an overall score that represents the child's level of self-esteem (Ghaderi, 2005; Zhen & Yousui, 2004).

Attempts to capture self-esteem in a single score, however, have met with the same problems as attempts to describe children's intelligence with a single IQ score. Intuitively, it seems unlikely that children would evaluate themselves similarly in all areas—academics, appearance, athletics, and so on. And research has demonstrated that evaluations across different areas are usually not consistent (Marsh & Ayotte, 2003; Marsh, Ellis, & Craven, 2003).

So how should we conceptualize self-esteem? Even for infants self-esteem appears to be multifaceted and depends on the evaluative information available to children as well as their ability to use that information. By age 7 to 8, children in Western cultures usually have formed at least four broad areas of self-esteem: academic competence, social competence, physical/athletic competence, and physical appearance (Harter, 2003; Marsh & Ayotte, 2003). These categories become increasingly more refined and distinct with age. As children mature, they also gain the ability to combine their separate self-evaluations into a general psychological image of themselves—an overall sense of self-esteem (Harter, 2003). Thus, self-esteem assumes a hierarchical structure, with each separate self-evaluation contributing unequally to self-esteem. Some children attach more importance to certain self-judgments and weight these more heavily. Unfortunately, during childhood and adolescence, perceived physical attractiveness correlates more highly with overall or global self-worth than any other self-esteem factor (Harter, 2003; Hong, Xiting, & Cheng, 2004; Hymel et al., 1999). Because self-esteem is multifaceted, it is important to measure multiple domains of experience to obtain accurate assessments of self-worth in both children and adults.

Harter's *Self-Perception Profile for Children*   An alternative to the single-score method of measurement is to divide children's lives conceptually into a number of domains (social skills, physical skills, and so on) and then assess children's self-evaluations separately in

Self-esteem, or self-worth
A person's evaluation of the self and the affective reactions to that evaluation.

Looking-glass self
The conception of the self based on how one thinks others see him or her.

Competence view of the self
Self-evaluation that includes both what one would like to achieve and one's confidence in being able to achieve it.

Links to Related Material
In Chapter 11, you read about how quality of attachment may influence later social and emotional development, including self-esteem. Here, you learn more about the development and measurement of self-esteem during childhood.

each. The results are then reported as a profile across the various domains. For example, Susan Harter has developed a set of popular instruments for measuring self-esteem at various stages of development. Each instrument assesses self-evaluations in specific domains as well as overall self-worth. The *Self-Perception Profile for Children* (Harter, 1985b; Van den Bergh & De Rycke, 2003), designed for children ages 8 and older, assesses children's opinions of their overall worth as well as their self-evaluations in five separate domains: scholastic competence, athletic competence, social acceptance, behavioral conduct, and physical appearance. Three additional domains—close friendship, romantic appeal, and job competence—are included on the adolescent version of the scale (Harter, 1988b; Shirk, Burwell, & Harter, 2003; Winstok & Enosh, 2004). There are also versions for use with college students and adults, which include an even greater number of domains (Harter, 1999; McAuley et al., 2005).

Each item on the questionnaire presents two related statements, one describing a competent child and the other a less competent child. A child completing the instrument selects the statement that best describes him or her and then marks the box indicating whether the statement is "really true for me" or "sort of true for me" (see Figure 12.2).

Children respond to six items in each of the six areas, and their scores are used to construct a profile of their self-esteem. Results allow the researcher to note both global self-worth and differences from one domain to the next. It should be noted that the tester cannot simply sum an individual's scores across the separate domains to obtain a score of

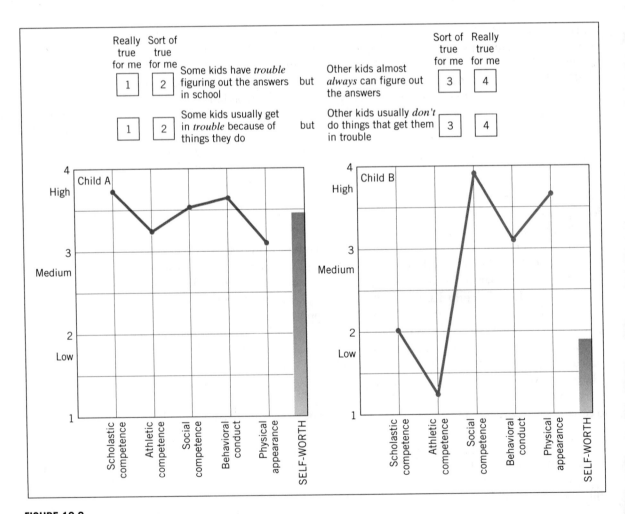

FIGURE 12.2

Two sample items from the *Self-Perception Profile.*

These graphs chart the self-perceptions of two children on the six areas of Harter's instruments for measuring self-esteem. How would you describe the differences between these two children in their self-evaluations? Used by permission.

FIGURE 12.3

A sample item from the *Self-Perception Profile* for younger children.

In Harter's *Pictorial Scale of Perceived Competence*, younger children choose a picture in a pair that they feel best represents them a little or a lot. This pair, for example, shows a girl who is good at puzzles and a girl who is not good at puzzles. Used by permission.

global self-worth. The "global" score reflects responses to its own separate scale. In addition, the global score is imperfectly predicted by responses to the other scales.

To assess the looking-glass self, Harter constructed additional items that asked children to rate how they believed other people felt about them. Consistent with that model, youngsters who felt others had high regard for them also rated themselves high on the self-worth items. To examine the competence view of the self, she asked children to rate how important each of the areas was to them. In support of this model, children who rated themselves as very competent in areas they felt were important also had high self-worth scores (Alves-Martins et al., 2002; Harter, 1986). Harter concluded from her research that older children's feelings of self-esteem are based on both how they believe others evaluate them and how they evaluate themselves (Harter, 2003; Harter & Whitsell, 2003; Lyon, Rainey, & Bullock, 2002).

Preschoolers differ from older children in their levels of self-understanding, their self-descriptions, and their general cognitive development. Measuring their self-concepts thus presents a unique challenge. For younger children between the ages of 4 and 7, Harter modified the *Self-Perception Profile* to create the *Pictorial Scale of Perceived Competence and Social Acceptance* (Harter, 2003; Harter & Pike, 1984). As shown in Figure 12.3, its items consist of pictures—for example, a girl who is good at puzzles (left) and a girl who is not good at puzzles (right). The child points to the circle indicating whether a picture is a little like her (small circle) or a lot like her (large circle). Because children below age 8 may not be able to form an overall judgment of their self-worth, only four individual content areas are assessed.

Harter's pictorial scale has been used widely to assess children's self-evaluations in early childhood education and intervention programs. Recent research has raised questions about the validity and applicability of the assessment tool, but testing of a revised version of the scale for adolescents in a Norwegian study confirmed its general validity and improved reliability (Wichstrom, 1995). Studies in 1999 and 2000 found that the *Self-Perception Profile for Children* had cross-cultural validity and could be used reliably, for example, with Arab children in the United Arab Emirates and Dutch-speaking Belgian children (Eapen & Naqvi, 2000; Van Den Bergh & Marcoen, 1999). Other researchers have argued that the instrument is not developmentally appropriate for preschool-age children and may not be well suited for use with some minority populations, such as children in urban Head Start programs (Billows, 2002; Fantuzzo et al., 1996).

Marsh's *Self-Description Questionnaire*   Another principal measure of the self is the *Self-Description Questionnaire* (SDQ), developed by Herbert Marsh and colleagues (Marsh, Barnes, & Cairns, 1984; Marsh, Ellis, et al., 2005). This measure is based on the belief that individuals develop a multidimensional and hierarchical self-concept. Different versions have been devised for preadolescents, adolescents, and young adults (Byrne, 1996; Guerin,

Early adolescence is a time of increased self-consciousness and often lower self-esteem. What factors are believed to be responsible for this change? How does the tendency to focus on personal appearance affect adolescents' self-esteem? Are there gender differences in self-esteem as well? (Michael Newman/PhotoEdit)

Self-consciousness
A concern about the opinions others hold about one.

L**inks to Related Material**
In Chapter 7, you read about Piaget's formal operational stage of cognitive development. Here, you learn how this stage may affect self-consciousness and self-esteem in early adolescence.

Marsh, & Famose, 2004; Marsh, Parada, & Ayotte, 2004), and for preschool-age children (Marsh, Ellis, & Craven, 2002).

The new version of the SDQ for 4- to 5-year-olds uses an interview procedure in which the child is first asked a "yes" or "no" question, such as the following:

Can you run fast?

Do you like the way you look?

Do you have lots of friends?

Do your parents smile at you a lot?

Are you good at counting?

After answering "yes" or "no," the child is asked to clarify whether he or she means "yes/no always" or "yes/no sometimes." Using this procedure, preschoolers are able to distinguish among different aspects of self-concept (physical ability, appearance, relationships with peers, relationships with parents, verbal skills, and math skills).

The Developmental Progression of Self-Esteem

The developmental course of self-esteem is relatively consistent. Self-esteem changes as children mature cognitively and as they experience the world around them. Although very young children may not have a well-developed sense of overall self-worth, the self-esteem scores of preschool and kindergarten children are generally high. Self-esteem drops slightly during the first years of elementary school. During middle and later childhood, self-esteem scores are generally stable, with perhaps a small trend toward improvement (Rhodes et al., 2004). But the transition to adolescence often poses problems. Many investigators have found that at about age 11 or 12, self-esteem scores dip, only to increase again over the subsequent years (Birndorf, Ryan, Aninger, & Aten, 2005; Harter & Whitsell, 2002). Several explanations have been offered for the drop in self-esteem in early adolescence. These include the stress of school transitions and increased self-consciousness.

One factor that may play a role in the temporary deterioration of self-esteem is the child's level of **self-consciousness**, or concern about the opinions of others (Baumeister & Twenge, 2003). Cognitive-developmental theorists suggest that this tendency increases with the emergence of formal operational abilities. At this stage, children become so much better at taking the perspective of others that they develop a preoccupation with how other people regard their appearance, behavior, and so forth (Bell & Bromnick, 2003). The increased self-consciousness leads to more critical self-evaluations, which in turn leads to lower self-esteem (Ogai, 2004; Vartanian, 2000).

The dip in self-worth among early adolescents may also be partially caused by the biological changes associated with puberty. Some researchers have suggested that pubertal changes produce physical and psychological stress in children that leads to depression and other negative emotional states (Michael & Eccles, 2003). Other evidence has shown that the relationship between puberty and depression is connected with the young person's body image, self-esteem, and experience of stressful life events (Benjet & Hernandez-Guzman, 2002; Marcotte et al., 2002). Thus, the physical changes associated with puberty likely represent one element of a complex array of factors that dampen self-esteem in early adolescence.

An environmental variable that contributes to a drop in self-esteem involves whether children remain in their own school or move to a new one following sixth grade. Several studies report that moving to a new school usually produces a noticeable decline in self-esteem scores, especially if the new school is large and ethnically diverse (Akos & Galassi, 2004; Cantin & Boivin, 2004). Children who remain in the same school show no such change. This phenomenon appears to affect a wide range of young people, including African Americans and Latinos. The drop in self-esteem associated with the transition to junior high school is present regardless of ethnicity or gender (Akos & Galassi, 2004; Seidman et al., 1994).

Gender Differences in Self-Esteem

Girls and boys exhibit some general differences in self-esteem measures. In self-evaluative judgments across different domains, boys show much less variability than girls from one domain to the next (Birndorf et al., 2005; Harter, 2003; Watt, 2004). Although girls typically evaluate their conduct in a more positive light than do boys, they provide much more negative assessments of their physical appearance and athletic competence. These gender differences are consistent cross-culturally and across development, holding from elementary school through college. Females' perceptions of their athletic abilities are thought to arise from the traditionally greater emphasis on males' athletic prowess and participation, whereas their low ratings of their physical appearance are believed to stem from the greater cultural emphasis on female appearance and the more limited yet unrealistic expectations of what constitutes female beauty.

Changes in self-esteem also differ for boys and girls. Self-ratings of perceived physical appearance again are a source of male-female contrast. Beginning in the fourth grade, girls' perceptions of their physical attractiveness decline markedly. By the last half of high school, girls have dramatically lower self-ratings than do boys, whose scores decline only a little with age. This trend may be particularly troubling given that perceived physical appearance has been shown to be an effective predictor of global self-worth (Harter, 1999; Hong et al., 2004). Females' self-perceptions of physical appearance vary among different groups, however. Research with adults has found that African American women typically rate their appearance more favorably than do Caucasian women. School is another important area and a potential source of gender differences in self-esteem.

Academic Self-Concept

The factors affecting self-esteem have been investigated in the classroom, especially children's perceptions of their **academic competence**, or **academic self-concept**. Prior to entering school, children have no basis for an academic self-concept (Marsh, Ellis, & Craven, 2002). Some researchers have examined the reactions of infants and preschoolers to other sorts of achievement tasks, however, and have found that a developmental progression does exist (Kelly, Brownell & Campbell, 2000; Stipek, Recchia, & McClintic, 1992; Turner & Johnson, 2003). Infants, for example, have little understanding of success and failure and so do not behave in ways that give any evidence of self-evaluation. However, even before the age of 2, children begin to show that they anticipate how adults will react to their achievements, such as when they look up for approval after making a stack of blocks. They also express delight at their successes and display negative reactions to their failures. By age 3, most children prefer to engage in activities at which they win rather than lose.

Children's academic self-concept generally is highest in kindergarten and steadily declines through at least fourth grade (Nurmi & Aunola, 2005). One cause of this decline may be as simple as the fact that older children realize that bragging is not socially appropriate and so increasingly avoid giving glowing descriptions of their abilities (Ruble & Frey, 1987). Another factor may be the role of socialization. For example, gender differences develop where males typically have higher self-concepts for math than girls and girls have higher self-concepts for English (Herbert & Stipek, 2005; Watt, 2004).

Dweck's Motivational Model of Achievement   Children's academic self-concept, derives mainly from their academic performance (Marsh, Trautwein, Ludtke, Koeller, & Baumert, 2005). Those who do well in school are likely to develop high opinions of their competence, whereas poor performers are likely to develop low opinions. How well a child performs in school depends partly on his or her academic abilities and partly on the amount of effort and motivation the child puts forth.

Based on over 20 years of research, Carol Dweck and her colleagues have developed a theoretical model that attempts to explain the complex role that motivation plays in children's academic success (Dweck, 1999, 2002; Ellis & Dweck, 2005). The model focuses

Links to Related Material
Here, you learn about gender differences in self-esteem. In Chapter 13, you will read more about the impact of gender on child development.

Questions for Thought and Discussion
What are some examples of effects of your gender roles and experiences on your self-esteem?

Academic competence, or academic self-concept
The part of self-esteem involving children' perceptions of their academic abilities.

Links to Related Material
In Chapter 9, you read about the influence of teacher's expectations on children's academic performance. Here, you learn more about the role of achievement motivation in children's school performance.

on two patterns of *achievement motivation* that have been observed in both younger and older children and that are reflected in their affect, cognitions, and behavior.

Children in achievement situations generally react to failure experiences in one of two ways (Dweck, 2002; Grant & Dweck, 2003). Some children display a *mastery-oriented* pattern. Despite having just failed at a task or problem, these children retain a positive mood and express high expectations for success on future attempts. As a result, they tend to persist at the task, and they seek out similar challenging problems. This motivational pattern usually leads to improved academic performance over time.

Other children, however, display a *helpless* pattern. When they encounter failure, their affect conveys sadness or disappointment, and they express doubt that they can ever succeed at the task. These children show little persistence in the activity and tend to avoid similar challenges in the future. Academic performance in these children often remains considerably below what it could be. What could produce these very different responses to failure?

Dweck's model proposes that at the heart of the problem are children's feelings of self-worth. Children who develop the helpless pattern typically believe that their self-worth depends on the approval and positive judgments of others. As a way of validating their self-worth, they seek out situations in which success involves receiving such approval. If the situation instead produces failure, these children view the absence of approval as a blow to their "goodness" as a person (self-worth), which then leads to the helpless pattern of negative affect, low expectations for future success, low persistence, and avoidance of similar situations.

In contrast, children who develop the mastery-oriented pattern do not believe that their self-worth depends on the opinions of others. They tend to seek out situations in which, whether successful or not, they will learn from their experiences. When these children fail, therefore, they view it simply as an opportunity to improve their ability on the task and so display the opposite pattern of affect, expectations, and persistence.

The Development of Motivation: Work with Preschool Children   Dweck and colleagues have examined the achievement motivation of preschool-age children and have found that even at these young ages, children display patterns of persistence or helplessness. In these studies, 4- and 5-year-olds were asked to solve several puzzles, but only one could actually be solved. The others had been modified—for example, in a jigsaw puzzle, pieces might have been removed and pieces from a different puzzle added. After spending time with the puzzles, children were given the opportunity to indicate which one they would like to play with again. More than a third of the children said they would like to work on the single solved puzzle again, despite having just completed it.

Interestingly, when asked to explain their choice, these "nonpersisters" did not say that the solved puzzle was challenging or that repeating it would provide them with good practice. Instead, these young children said things like "Because it was the easiest" or "Because I already know how to do it." These children also displayed negative affect toward the task and expressed lower expectations for success on another task. Children who chose to persist on one of the unsolved puzzles showed the more positive pattern of reactions (Grant & Dweck, 2003; Smiley & Dweck, 1994).

Children's Implicit Theories of Intelligence   In older children, the model becomes more complex. Beyond 10 years of age or so, children's cognitive abilities permit them to develop certain self-conceptions (Dweck, 2002; Dweck & Leggett, 1988; Elliot & Dweck, 2005). One of these is a "theory of intelligence." Some children come to believe in an **entity model**, in which the amount of a person's intelligence is fixed and unchangeable. Others subscribe to an **incremental model**, in which a person's intelligence can grow with experience and learning. A second self-conception involves children's "attributions for success or failure." Some children believe that success or failure results primarily from the amount of ability a person has, while other children believe it depends on the amount of effort a person applies to a task.

Entity model
The belief that a person's intelligence is fixed and unchangeable.

Incremental model
The belief that a person's intelligence can grow through experience and learning.

Children who develop the helpless pattern, as you might expect, generally believe that the amount of their intelligence is fixed (entity model) and that their lack of success derives from a lack of ability. These two beliefs combine to give the child little reason for optimism in the face of failure—after all, ability is unchangeable and the child simply has too little of it. Predictably, then, these children feel helpless and hopeless and are likely to give up or avoid challenging tasks.

A very different outlook, however, results from the two opposite beliefs, which are generally held by mastery-oriented children. If intelligence can grow (incremental model) and success depends largely on one's effort, then failure experiences need not lead to feelings of despair or pessimism. These children believe they can do better next time simply by trying harder. Similarly, Mueller and Dweck (1998) found that children who are praised for their effort are more likely to persist and succeed following failure than children who are praised for their ability.

Research has also supported this portion of the model. For example, one study found that fifth-grade children who displayed elements of the helpless pattern (nonpersistence and low expectations for future success) following failure on a task were more likely to hold the entity view of intelligence, whereas children displaying the mastery-oriented pattern tended to believe in the incremental view (Cain & Dweck, 1995). Similar results have been demonstrated in older children and adults (Oikawa, 2005; Riemann, 2003; Spinath, Spinath, & Riemann, 2003).

Girls—especially bright girls—are especially vulnerable to the helpless pattern. Girls are also more likely to hold an entity theory of intelligence (Ziegler & Stoeger, 2004). Compared with boys, girls more often pick tasks at which they can perform well and show impairment when tasks grow difficult. When the going gets tough, girls are also more likely to blame their abilities (Dweck, 2004).

What motivation pattern has this child most likely developed? What model of achievement probably is part of his academic self-concept? According to Dweck's research, what effect could the teacher's praise have on the child's future academic performance? (© LWA-Dann Tardif/Corbis)

Effects of Praise and Criticism   Many caregivers, parents, and teachers assume that praise is good and criticism is detrimental. Another important component of Dweck's model of achievement motivation concerns caregivers' responses to children's performance. How are failures and successes handled? What aspects of the child's performance are the targets of praise or criticism? The answers to these questions are of substantial consequence. Dweck (1999, 2004) asserts that the feedback children receive from adults is the source of patterns of motivation and have more impact than the child's temperament.

Dweck's team hypothesized that criticism could have a negative impact on children. Specifically, the researchers targeted criticism that judged the children themselves ("I am disappointed in you") and that judged their stable traits rather than their situation-specific effort ("You can try harder next time"). In contrast, criticism that focused on the children's effort or strategies was thought to promote the desirable mastery-oriented motivational pattern. The researchers hypothesized that praise directed toward the child's efforts or problem-solving processes would be beneficial, just as with criticism. Praise could end up having a negative impact, however, when focused on children's enduring traits.

To test these hypotheses, kindergartners participated in a role-playing exercise in which they imagined they had done some well-intentioned act for their teacher that ended up being a disappointment. For example, in one scenario, the children imagined creating a picture of a family and then realizing that a child in the painting had no feet:

> You spend a lot of time painting a picture of a family to give to your teacher. You pick out colors you think are nice and carefully draw each person. As you are about to give it to your teacher you say to yourself, "Uh oh, one of the kids has no feet." But you worked really hard on the picture and want to give it to her. You say, "Teacher, here's a picture for you." (Heyman, Cain, & Dweck, 1992, p. 404)

Interestingly, noting a flaw in the picture did not concern kindergartners. Reactions changed, however, when the scenario included criticism from the teacher ("What, no feet? I don't call this drawing the right way. I'm disappointed"). In this scenario, about a third of the young children responded by lowering their own evaluation of the painting. What they had thought was fine was now judged to be inadequate. Children with this downward reaction also reported more negative emotion and were less willing to persist on the task—evidence of a helpless reaction (Dweck, 1999, 2002). "Helpless" children also imagined that their painting's shortcoming would elicit negative reactions from their parents and teachers ("You are very bad" or "That's bad work"). Finally, this negativity extended to children's self-evaluations. Nearly two-thirds of the helpless children said that their performance indicated they were not being good kids—a sentiment shared by fewer than 10 percent of the mastery-oriented children. Thus, it appears that a strong relationship exists between the child's motivation pattern and his or her reactions to criticism.

Dweck and colleagues have also demonstrated the effects of differing kinds of criticism and praise using hypothetical scenarios (Dweck, 2002; Kamins & Dweck, 1999). Feedback was provided in response to children's errors. Some children received criticism that offered information about their strategy use—for example, "Maybe you should think of another way to do it." Other criticism focused on the child's behavior ("That's not what I call doing it the right way") or on the child as a whole ("I'm disappointed in you"). Children who received strategy-specific feedback fared the best, giving their work the highest self-rating, reporting the most positive overall feelings, and providing the best solutions for future improvement.

Analogous results were found for children's responses to praise. Receiving person-oriented praise was actually associated with increased vulnerability to failure, whereas praise directed at effort or strategy use produced the most mastery-oriented responses. In explaining these findings, Dweck proposes that believing that one is good when one does something correctly leaves one open to the alternative conclusion that one is bad when failure results. Thus, despite the common intuition that praise is bound to be beneficial for children, research suggests that certain forms of praise can have later negative consequences. Praise works especially well when it is perceived as sincere and when it encourages performance attributions to controllable causes, promotes autonomy, and conveys reasonable and attainable expectations and standards (Henderlong & Lepper, 2002).

Dweck also suggests that performance-based praise may underlie girls' greater vulnerability to helplessness (She & Fisher, 2002). Girls are usually the stars of elementary school. According to Dweck, young girls—especially bright ones—are likely fed a steady diet of praise during the early years of school. They are, after all, generally better behaved than boys and comply more readily with adult requests (Herbert & Stipek, 2005). Moreover, very capable girls are unlikely to struggle very much with the academic demands of the first years of school. The lesson girls may learn is that they can measure their traits from the outcomes and praise they receive.

Because the requirements of the classroom are less compatible with the needs of the average boy, boys are more likely to experience both failure and criticism. These early difficulties may, however, prove advantageous over time, because they teach boys that persistence can lead to success. In sum, teacher and caregiver feedback can affect children's self-evaluations and overall estimations of their self-worth. These can lead to changes in self-esteem over time. It is important for adults to recognize that their criticism and praise, though well intentioned, can have serious and sometimes unexpected outcomes.

Role of Social Comparisons   You have seen that academic self-image is affected by children's academic performance and by the types of attributions they make regarding failure. But the general decline in self-esteem during the elementary years may also involve social comparisons. Children, like adults, contrast their abilities with those of others and draw conclusions about themselves from those assessments—a process called **social comparison**. This process begins as early as kindergarten, but its function changes with age (Dweck, 2004; Stipek & Tannatt, 1984; Wheeler & Suls, 2005).

Kindergartners use what their classmates are doing or saying primarily as a way of making friends or learning how things are done. For example, a child may comment to a classmate that they are coloring on the same page of their books. Social comparisons, at

Questions for Thought and Discussion
Why is praise directed toward effort, skills, and knowledge better than praise directed at personal qualities? What might be some ways to foster a mastery orientation to achievement without abandoning person-oriented praise?

Social comparison
Comparing one's abilities to those of others.

this point, do not appear to have much impact on the child's self-image (Elliot & Dweck, 2005; Wheeler & Suls, 2005). As children proceed through the early grades, however, their social comparisons increasingly involve academic performance, and they begin to use the comparisons to evaluate their own competence relative to others (Rankin, Lane, Gibbons, & Gerrard, 2004).

By second grade, children's spontaneous self-evaluative remarks become positively correlated with the number of social comparisons they make. That is, children with lower opinions of their competence make fewer social comparisons (Ruble & Frey, 1991). Why? One interpretation of this finding is that in continually comparing their performance with that of peers, many children unhappily discover that their work is not as good as they had believed. A child who once found great pleasure in drawing may discover that his artwork is not as attractive as that of his classmates. As a result, he may lower his opinion of his drawings but also begin to avoid comparing his work with that of other children. If this interpretation is correct, we would expect academically successful children to seek out more information about their performance than children who are lower achievers. And research has found just that: High-achieving students show more interest in comparing their performance with that of classmates and also in discovering the correct answers to problems (Ruble & Flett, 1988). At the same time, the presence of high-ability peers can reduce academic self-concept (Wheeler & Suls, 2005).

This developmental change in the use of social comparisons is not inevitable, however, and can be influenced by the atmosphere of the educational environment. For example, in Israel the communal kibbutz environment places more emphasis on cooperative than on competitive learning and fosters concern with mastering skills rather than with surpassing others. As a result, even older children in the kibbutz environment have been found to use social comparison primarily as a means of acquiring new abilities and much less for self-evaluation (Butler & Ruzany, 1993). Social comparisons are more likely to be interpreted in a positive way when the individuals perceive the social environment as cooperative rather than competitive (Buunk, Zurriaga, Piero, Nauta, & Gasalvez, 2005).

The relation between social comparison and academic self-concept, then, is bidirectional. Social comparisons can affect children's self-image by giving them information about how they are performing relative to other children. But children's self-image may affect their willingness to engage in social comparisons, depending on how pleasant or unpleasant they expect the resulting information to be (Marsh et al., 2005; Wheeler & Suls, 2005).

Role of Parenting Styles   Children's academic self-concept is also affected by the attitudes, expectations, and behaviors of their parents. Studies have shown that parents' perceptions of their children's academic abilities are one of the best predictors of the children's self-perceptions of ability (Eccles et al., 2000; Herbert, Stipek, & Stipek, 2005; Midgett et al., 2002).

Parental expectations produce their effects on children's self-perceptions through parents' interactions with children on academic tasks. Parents who display an authoritative style (discussed in Chapter 16), which combines warmth and limit-setting, tend to use more scaffolding techniques when working with their children (Marchant, Paulson, & Rothisberg, 2001), and these children tend to be more cognitively competent (Fang, Xiong, & Guo, 2003; Joussemet et al., 2005; Kim & Chung, 2003). The fathers of children with high academic self-concept are warmer and more supportive in their interactions than the fathers of children with lower academic self concept.

Parents also communicate levels of social support. The child's perception of parental involvement and any educational barriers they might put into place is also important (Wettersten et al., 2005). This finding is consistent with other research in which college students recalled that continuing support from their fathers was instrumental in their success in school (Kim & Chung, 2003).

It is also important for parents and other caregivers to regard the child's interests and efforts with appreciation rather than merely praising them. For example, when a child

Links to Related Material
Here, you learn about the role that parenting plays in the development of children's positive academic self-concept. In Chapter 16, you will learn more about different parenting styles and their effects on child development.

shows interest in bugs, you can treat the interest seriously and help the child learn more about bugs. Praise in isolation may distract the child from his or her interest. It is also important for children to gain experience from tasks and activities that offer a real challenge instead of those that are merely frivolous (Walker & Satterwhite, 2002). Fun is important, but it is also important for a child to develop a sense of accomplishment from their actions and abilities (Shirk, Burwell, & Harter, 2003).

Effects of Academic Self-Concept   Academic self-concept strongly influences academic achievement (Marsh et al., 2005; Wang & Xu, 2005). Studies examining feelings of competence and perceived self-efficacy report that children who view themselves as academically skilled are more motivated to succeed, more persistent in their work, and more willing to seek out challenging tasks or problems (Harter, 2003; Mau, 2003; Zang & Zang, 2003). A high academic self-concept, even when it overestimates the child's abilities, also correlates positively with (and probably contributes to) a high level of self-esteem (Burnett, 2004).

Children with low opinions of their academic abilities, in contrast, are less motivated to work. Even among children whose academic skills are high, those who hold an incorrectly low opinion of their competence approach new tasks with less effort and optimism than do their classmates (Phillips, 1987; Spinath & Spinath, 2005). Thus, for some children, academic success may hinge as much on academic self-concept as on academic ability. Subjective perception of ability (rather than actual ability) determines whether children will attempt or avoid challenges.

Cultural Perspectives on Understanding the Self

Because self-esteem is associated with self-perception and is influenced by social comparisons and societal expectations, it follows that children from different cultures experience differences in their self-evaluations. Some researchers have found that members of many Asian countries report lower levels of self-esteem than do members of Western cultures (Spencer-Rodgers, Peng, Wang, & Hou, 2004). In one recent study, however, mentioned earlier in this chapter, Chinese girls perceived themselves more positively than did American girls (Aimin & Guiying, 2004). One reason for differences in self-esteem may be differential perceptions of parental satisfaction, which could influence a young person's own sense of satisfaction with self (Oishi & Sullivan, 2005).

The need for individuation is thought to be very important in Western countries. For Asians standing out for its own sake appears to be less desirable than for individuals from Western cultures (Tafaradi, Marshall, & Katsura, 2004). In addition, Americans tend to view themselves as above average on positive characteristics but below average on negative characteristics, the better-than-average effect, more often than members of cultures that stress modesty and adherence to group norms (Silvera & Seger, 2004). Members of Western cultures are more likely to make self-enhancing statements, whereas those from more collectivistic cultures are more even-handed in their self evaluations (Ross, Heine, Wilson, & Sugimori, 2005).

Q**uestions for Thought and Discussion**
How was your academic self-concept influenced by a teacher or school guidance counselor?

✔ ***Test Your Mastery...***

Learning Objective 12.4: *Describe the development of self-esteem, ways to measure it, and the contexts that shape the way children evaluate themselves.*

1. What is self-esteem, and how is it measured?
2. How does self-esteem change across childhood and adolescence and differ for boys and girls?
3. What factors are believed to contribute to the formation of academic self-concept?
4. What roles do children's theories of intelligence and attributions play in achievement motivation?
5. What roles do criticism, praise, and social comparison play in the development of academic self-concept?
6. What is the impact of academic self-concept on children's development and future prospects?

BOX 12.2   Conversations with a School Guidance Counselor

Alfonso G. Smith, age 33, grew up in Fayetteville, North Carolina, where he lives with his wife Arnicia and son Solomon. Alfonso is a guidance counselor in the Fayetteville public school system. He credits his success in a job he loves to his blessings in life.

I have been blessed with being given a lot. I have grown up in a loving home with two parents who nurtured me and supported me in all that I did. I have family and friends, who have helped me tremendously during times that I have had various needs. I believe in the truth of the saying, "To whom much is given, much is required." Now I have been put into a position in which I can work to help others, and it is something that I love to do.

I have always enjoyed helping others. As a teen, I had a gift for working with children, as I served as a summer camp counselor at Camp Geronimo in Fort Bragg, North Carolina. I have always valued people more than money, so when I finally decided on a career path, education was at the forefront. I believe that I am fulfilling part of my purpose through my efforts in the public school system.

After obtaining a BS degree in Human Development at the University of North Carolina at Greensboro, Alfonso worked for two years with American Express. He found that work with large companies tends to be very money-focused. His people-centered approach thus tended to conflict with the needs of the company. He went back to school to earn his graduate degree, an MS, from North Carolina A&T State University. Alfonso then worked as an elementary school guidance counselor, in which he was the only counselor in schools totaling 300 to 350 students! He is currently in a high school in which he is one of seven counselors, and he loves it.

I still have a caseload of well over 300 students (counselors' caseloads are determined by the students' last names, and I have A–Cas), but I truly benefit from being part of a guidance team. We are able to draw on our different strengths and experiences to serve the needs of a very diverse school population.

As a high school guidance counselor (and varsity basketball coach), I do a lot of counseling with students, ranging from social issues to academic issues. I find myself giving the students lots of encouragement, because of the many challenges that our youth face today. I try my best to serve purposely as a positive influence in the lives of the students I work with directly, as well as others I come into contact with. I help students to move successfully from their freshman year of high school through their senior year to graduation. I also prepare students for postsecondary education and/or career paths. In high school (compared to elementary school), I enjoy the fact that we are able to see evidence of "the fruits of our labors" at the end of each year, because of graduation.

As you work, day in and day out, in a helping profession, it is easy to feel a bit taken for granted. It is a great feeling when you see that young man or young woman you have been working with (and struggling with, correcting, rebuking, encouraging, etc.) successfully reach a monumental goal. It is very rewarding, even more so when students come back to say, "Hey, you made a difference in my life, and I thank you." I have received cards in which students say, "Thank you for believing in me, when my family didn't believe in me, and when I did not even believe in myself." Those acknowledgments have great value to me.

I sincerely believe that I am fulfilling my purpose, and this is very important. Because the reality is that we do get some "thank you's" and appreciation shown our way, but it would be a mistake to work just to get the kudos. It is important that your entire sense of self-worth does not revolve around working in other people's lives. I have become a better counselor for others as I have learned more about my own strengths and weaknesses.

Identity and Society

Who am I? What am I going to do with my life? These and many other questions surface in earnest during adolescence. We have examined how perceptions of the self and our self-evaluations change as we mature. During adolescence, the various self-perceptions are pulled together to form an identity—an overall sense of who we are, where we are going, and how we fit into society.

Contemporary views of identity development indicate that it is a lengthy process, continuing through adulthood, and is very complex. Identity development begins with attachment and the development of a sense of self and then is processed throughout the lifespan. Adolescence is the first time when cognitive, physical, and social development are at a point that the individual can examine and synthesize childhood identities to construct a pathway toward adult maturity. In contrast, younger children model themselves after other people. We continue to construct our identity as we mature into adulthood. Adults add new areas of self-evaluation, such as parenting and marriage, and these influence our perception of who we are.

Learning Objective 12.4
Explain how individuals construct their personal and ethnic or cultural identities.

Erikson and Marcia on Identity Crisis

Erik Erikson (Erikson, 1950, 1968) proposed the most comprehensive and influential theory of identity development. Identity versus confusion is the fifth developmental stage of Erikson's theory, which typically is experienced during the adolescent years. During this stage, adolescents examine who they are, what they are all about, and where they are going in life. During this time, they are faced with new roles, such as vocational and romantic roles, and new experiences. **Identity crisis** is a temporary period of distress during which adolescents experiment with alternatives before settling on values and goals.

As adolescents explore and search for an identity they often experiment with different values. James Marcia has said that Erikson's theory contains four statuses of identity, or ways of resolving the identity crisis (Marcia, 1994, 2002; Peterson, Marcia, & Capendale, 2004). Individuals can be classified into one of the four identity statuses depending on the extent of the crisis and commitment to a meaningful alternative.

The following statuses describe Marcia's ways of resolving the identity crisis.

- **Identity diffusion** is the term for the state adolescents are in when they have not yet experienced a crisis or made any commitments.
- In **identity moratorium**, adolescents are in the middle of a crisis, but their commitments are only vaguely defined or are missing altogether.
- In **identity foreclosure**, the adolescent has made a commitment without experiencing a crisis. In this situation the adolescent has often accepted commitments that have been imposed by families with an authoritarian parenting style. The adolescent has not had sufficient opportunities to explore alternatives independently.
- In **identity achievement**, the adolescent has experienced a crisis and has then made a commitment.

Although Marcia's ideas have been very influential in conceptualizing identity development, the currently favored term to use in place of crisis is *exploration*. Contemporary theorists have reduced the focus on this period as a time of psychosocial crisis and have placed more emphasis on the finding that identity development is not traumatic or disturbing for most adolescents. Thus, identity development is more accurately characterized as exploration and trying out life's possibilities, followed by commitment to a self structure (Arnett, 2000).

Identity crisis
Period of identity development during which the adolescent is selecting from among meaningful alternatives.

Identity diffusion
Term for state adolescents are in when they have not yet experienced a crisis or made any commitments.

Identity moratorium
Term for state when adolescents are in the middle of a crisis, but their commitments are only vaguely defined or missing altogether.

Identity foreclosure
Term for state when the adolescent has made a commitment without experiencing a crisis; typically, the adolescent has been handed down commitments.

Identity achievement
Term for state when the adolescent has experienced a crisis and has then made a commitment.

Achieving a clear identity in adolescence may involve more of an exploration of life's possibilities than a psychosocial crisis. According to Marcia's theory, what stages of identity formation might these youths experience? How will their relationships at home, with friends, and at school affect their identity? (Adrian Sherratt/Alamy)

Social and Cultural Influences on Identity

Identity development depends to a large degree on the development of cognitive resources. Another major influence is the social environment of the individual, especially family, friends, school, and the larger social climate of the times. According to Marcia (2003), young adolescents must be confident that they have parental support. Parents who use democratic processes, typical of the authoritative parenting style, encourage the adolescent to participate in family decision making, which fosters identity achievement (Berzonsky, 2004; Reis & Youniss, 2004). Identity foreclosure is associated with autocratic behavior, such as refusing to permit adolescents to express themselves, and with the authoritarian parenting style. Families that promote individuality, self-assertion, connectedness, sensitivity, and openness to the views of others are fostering identity development. Encouraging adolescents to develop their own point of view while providing a secure base from which to explore their ever widening world also enhances identity formation (Zimmerman & Becker-Stoll, 2002).

Another source of ideas, values, and experiences are the adolescent's peers. Adolescents spend much more time with their friends than younger children do. Close friends provide emotional support and model different roles for the adolescent. These relationships help the adolescent explore options, again in the context of a caring and secure environment (Meeus, Oosterwegel, & Vollebergh, 2002). Peers can serve as a sounding board for ideas and provide feedback on the adolescent's thoughts, worries, and emotions.

Children also spend a significant amount of time in schools and are greatly influenced by their experiences there. They are exposed to different viewpoints, ideas, and values that can provide an opportunity for higher-level thinking; opportunities to assume responsible roles through extracurricular activities; and vocational opportunities and information (through teachers and counselors). Adolescents benefit from the chance to discuss ideas with older peers and adults and from the presence of role models (Chen et al., 2003; Flouri & Buchanan, 2002). For example, encouraging low-SES and ethnic minority students to stay in school and go to college may be easier when these students see examples of individuals that have successfully made this transition (Stanton-Salazar & Spina, 2003; Zirkel, 2002).

Cognitive developments that relate to social and cultural contexts for the development of self include skills involved in "reading" people. As children mature, they become more sophisticated in their understanding of other people. They become better at making inferences about the personality traits, viewpoints, and behaviors of others. *Social perception*—the processes by which people come to understand each other—becomes better organized and more differentiated. In particular, children become more adept at **person perception**—the mental processes we use to form judgments and draw conclusions about the characteristics and motives of others.

Person perception
Mental processes we use to form judgments and draw conclusions about the characteristics and motives of others.

Young children tend to focus their descriptions of others, like their self-descriptions, on concrete, easily seen activities and behaviors and shared emotions. As children discover consistencies in the behaviors of other people around them, they become more likely to use personality traits in their descriptions (Droege & Stipek, 1993; Stipek, 1990). As abstract thinking develops, children's descriptions of others they know begin to integrate the person's personality and dispositions, typical behaviors, and physical characteristics.

Children also become more sophisticated in their use of attributions. Not until middle school do they indicate that there are limits to the degree to which effort can improve performance in academic and social environments. For example, they may come to an understanding that sometimes no matter how hard another person tries, they will not succeed at a particular task. As children's descriptions of others become more complex, the question that arises is whether they think of themselves as more complex than others. Although a common belief, there is little evidence that people think more complexly about the self than others (Locke, 2002).

As children develop more advanced perceptions of others, they also begin to gain an understanding of how other people feel and think (Doubleday & Droege, 1993; McHugh, Barnes-Holmes, & Barnes-Holmes, 2004). Recall that *perspective taking*—the capacity to imagine and understand what another person may be thinking and feeling—plays a significant role in the ability to communicate with others and is important in social problem solving (Batson et al., 2003; Eisenberg et al., 2005). It is important for children to begin to understand that emotions, their own and those of others, can influence decision making (Prencipe & Zelazo, 2005; Suzuki &, Koyasu, & An, 2004). Interestingly, when individuals are socially excluded they tend to perform more poorly on cognitive tasks (Baumeister, Twenge, & Nuss, 2002). Perspective taking is also associated with the ability to make higher-level moral judgments (Selman, 1994).

As with other aspects of the self and identity development, parental interaction styles and other caregiver behaviors have been shown to predict perspective taking. For example, people who feel secure in their relationships may be predisposed to perceive others as loving and responsive, while people who feel insecure or rejected in their relationships may perceive others as cold and rejecting (Baumeister et al., 2005; Twenge, Catanese, & Baumeister, 2003).

Ethnic Identity

Ethnic identity

Sense of lasting ehtnic group membership and the attitudes and feelings associated with that membership; is central to the process of identity development.

In addition to the influences of cognitive development, caregivers, and exposure to experiences in school, identity is influenced by the broader cultural context in which it occurs. For adolescents who are members of ethnic or cultural minorities, **ethnic identity**—a sense of lasting ethnic group membership and the attitudes and feelings associated with that membership—is central to the process of identity development. As adolescents develop cognitively, they may become more sensitive to feedback from the broader social environment and may also become aware of the potential for prejudice and discrimination. A positive sense of ethnic identity may provide the resources adolescents need to cope with stresses related to encounters with prejudice and discrimination (Davalos, Chavez, & Guardiola, 2005; Wong, Eccles & Sameroff, 2003). Adolescents are aided in the development of a strong, positive, ethnic identity when they are encouraged to learn and understand the history, traditions, and values of their group, and when they have opportunities to interact frequently with peers who share similar experiences (Phinney, Romero, & Nava, 2001). Tatum (1997) outlines five stages of racial identity development among African American youth:

- Pre-encounter: the child absorbs the beliefs and values of the dominant culture.
- Encounter: an event forces a young person to acknowledge the impact of racism.
- Immersion: the young person spends time exploring and learning about his or her racial identity.
- Internalization: the young person gains a sense of security about his or her racial or cultural identity.
- Commitment: this personal sense of security is translated into actions to benefit the community.

For example, Michael grew up in a largely white, middle-class suburb in the Midwest. At school and at home, he was exposed to ideals of racial egalitarianism. In elementary school and around his neighborhood, he played with boys who were African American as well as European American. As he and his friends approached puberty, girls became a source of interest. It was at this time that one of his European American friends hurled a racial insult at him, the first time that this had happened to him. This event marked his transition into the "encounter" stage identified by Tatum. Michael, hurt by his friend's betrayal, began to spend more time with other African American youth at his middle school, where he felt accepted and understood as he coped with the myriad changes associated with puberty. He was happy when several of his African American

Questions for Thought and Discussion
How might you describe your most hoped-for and most feared possible self? Where are you in your development of self-identity?

BOX 12.3 Possible Selves and Academic Achievement

I want to be smart and hope to get a scholarship to college and to graduate from college and own a business. . . . I want to be out on my own too. I want to have an apartment. [Eventually] I want to build me a house and have children. (Kerpelman, Shoffner, & Ross-Griffin, 2002, p. 294)

This comment was offered by one adolescent in response to the question, "Who do you expect to become during the next 5 years?" Self-concept grows more differentiated during adolescence in relation to time. In contrast to younger children, adolescents are able to think flexibly about the self in terms of the past, present, and future. Future-oriented components of the self are referred to as **possible selves**. Possible selves represent a person's goals and embody dreams, hopes, and fears (Markus & Nurius, 1986). Possible selves include hoped-for selves and feared selves. Hoped-for selves represent "what we would like to become." These selves are domain-specific (e.g., career, family) and include abstract goals as well as the scripts, plans, and strategies for achieving the goals. Feared selves are the possible selves that an individual does *not* want to become. Together, hoped-for and feared selves motivate behavior as people are energized to pursue images they hope for and strive to avoid images they fear (Oyserman & Markus, 1990).

A growing number of researchers are beginning to examine adolescent educational aspirations and achievement in light of the theory of possible selves (e.g., Kerpelman et al., 2002; Packard & Nguyen, 2003; Yowell, 2000, 2002). The reasoning behind this approach is quite straightforward. Adolescents who view their future selves as academically successful should be motivated to engage in behaviors that lead to success in school and avoid behaviors (e.g., truancy, substance use) that interfere with academic achievement. Conversely, adolescents who do not include an academically successful self among their possible selves should be less motivated to engage in behavior associated with school success.

Indeed, studies have documented a link between possible selves and academic behaviors and achievement (Oyserman, Gant, & Ager, 1995; Oyserman & Markus, 1990; Oyserman & Saltz, 1993).

Given the established link between school-focused possible selves and academic performance, might it be possible to improve a student's engagement in school and, ultimately, academic performance by targeting his or her academic self-concept? Daphna Oyserman and colleagues (Oyserman, Terry, & Bybee, 2002) developed an after-school intervention to do just that. The nine-week intervention, *Schools-to-Jobs,* involved a sequence of activities focused on helping adolescents (1) create and detail academically successful possible selves; (2) connect possible selves for the coming year to specific strategies to attain these selves; (3) connect their short-term possible selves and strategies to adult possible selves; and (4) develop skills to effectively work with others to attain these possible selves.

The researchers implemented the intervention with three cohorts of low-income urban African American middle-school students. Evaluation of the intervention showed that, compared with a control group that received no intervention, students in the *Schools-to-Jobs* program reported better school attendance and more bonding to school (e.g., "I feel I really belong at school"). They also expressed more concern about doing well in school, more "balanced" possible selves, and more realistic strategies for achieving their possible selves.

The findings to date suggest that the *Schools-to-Jobs* program can positively impact student attitudes toward school. Additional research is needed to document more specific behavioral changes and to see whether the effects of the intervention last over time. Meanwhile, this study offers a promising means to foster educational achievement—especially among youth lacking role models and mentors who embody and reinforce the long-term importance of school success.

friends from high school also chose to attend the nearby state university, where he selected biology as a major. While at college, he moved into Tatum's stage of immersion when he became interested in electives offered in African American history, literature, and art. He began spending time at the African American cultural center, talking to other students about their rich history, tradition, and experiences as a people. He finally decided to join an African American fraternity. After graduation from college, he moved on to graduate studies in radiology, where his peer group expanded again to include European Americans who were comfortable with his and their own racial backgrounds. His transition into the stage of internalization occurred at this time, as his studies consumed him and his peers in their shared goal of becoming radiologists. Finally, after he had passed his board exams and had settled into his new job with his wife and growing family, he began to spend time volunteering with African American youth organizations and after-school programs, where he sought to be an active role model. His transition into Tatum's final stage of commitment had begun.

Possible selves
Future-oriented components of the self that represent a person's goals and embody dreams, hopes, and fears.

Links to Related Material
Here, you learn about the development of a positive sense of ethnic identity among minority youth. In Chapter 16, you will read more about the role that ethnic background can play in child development

These youths identify themselves as African Americans, and they clearly value their shared ethnic identity. According to Tatum's theory, how did their ethnic identity likely develop? What is important about our ethnic, racial, cultural, and group identities in our ongoing construction of identity? (Steve Skjold/Alamy)

Identity Construction as an Ongoing Process

Identity construction is complex and continues throughout the lifespan (Kroger, 2002, 2003; Marcia, 2002). Our perceptions of the roles we play and their importance in determining who we are change as we mature (Dweck, Higgins, & Grant-Pillow, 2003). People become parents, for example, and undertake careers. Erikson proposed that identity issues pop up later in life for individuals, even those who formed a positive sense of self identity during adolescence (Hoare, 2002).

As individuals move through adolescence into young adulthood, an increasing number will reach identity achievement, but this tends to occur at different rates for different domains of identity (Kroger, 1996; Schwartz, Cote, & Arnett, 2005; Waterman, 1999). The process of identity formation may be even more complex for members of ethnic minorities (Harter, 2002). Marcia (1996, 2002) proposed that identity formation is actually a series of commitments. As we explore new roles and opportunities and acquire new knowledge and responsibilities, it is likely that our identity will change.

✔ *Test Your Mastery...*

Learning Objective 12.5: *Explain how individuals construct their personal and ethnic or cultural identities.*

1. What four identity statuses did Marcia propose for resolving an identity crisis or exploration?
2. What cognitive abilities and social relationships facilitate identity formation?
3. Through what process do adolescents develop their ethnic, racial, or cultural identity?
4. When does identity development begin and end?

BOX 12.4   Contextual Model of the Self and Identity

Infant is born with genetic potential for a range of skills, abilities, and personal characteristics.

Family, Neighborhood, and School Settings

- Parents encourage child's exploration and development of a positive sense of self through warm interactions and opportunities to try a range of activities.
- Schools and teachers provide opportunities and feedback.
- Peers reinforce specific behaviors and activities in the child, and provide positive or negative feedback.

Culture and Society

- Cultures provide differential support for specific types of activities.
- Cultural stereotypes regarding gender, class, and ethnicity may influence opportunities available to child.

Learning Objective 12.1

Compare and contrast five theoretical perspectives on the development of the self-system.

1. According to contemporary views, what are the three components of the self-system?

The contemporary view is that "self" is a broad concept that can be divided into three distinct but interrelated units: *self-knowledge, self-evaluation*, and *self-regulation*. Together these form the self-system. Self-knowledge, or self-awareness, asks, what do children know about themselves as distinct, enduring individuals? When do they acquire this knowledge, and how does it relate to their social and physical environments? Self-regulation asks, how and when do children acquire self-control? What variables influence this process? Self-evaluation asks, does the child have high or low self-esteem? What factors influence children's opinions of themselves, and how do these opinions affect their behavior? A person uses self-knowledge, self-esteem, and other self-evaluations to form an identity. Identity asks, who am I? Where am I headed in my life?

2. How do cognitive-developmental approaches differ from psychoanalytic approaches to the development of self?

The *psychoanalytic* perspective, as proposed by Freud, stresses the biological urges of the id, which pushes children through universal stages of psychosexual development. Psychoanalytic theory focuses on early childhood experiences and conflict resolution. Erik Erikson, a neo-Freudian, proposed that the personality evolves through systematic stages based on the way an individual meets a basic challenge or resolves a crisis. Erikson's theory of psychosocial development emphasized the influence of social factors such as peers, teachers, and parents. He also emphasized development across the lifespan, while Freud focused on early childhood.

Those working from the *cognitive-developmental* perspective tend to use information-processing theory to focus on how children's cognitive abilities to process information limit and shape the development of the self. Children's information processing abilities—how they encode, interpret, and remember information—contribute to the creation of self-relevant cognitive structures that in turn influence how further information is processed. Over time each child develops a self-schema, an internal notion of "who I am."

3. How do environmental/learning approaches contribute to our understanding of the development of self?

Social-learning approaches emphasize that people change if their environment changes. People are influenced by their interactions with others in specific social situations. The development of the self is an individual process that depends on each person's subjective social experiences and social environments. Albert Bandura proposed a model of self-evaluation built around the concept of self-efficacy—a person's ability, as judged by that person, to carry out various behaviors and acts. As children mature, two other mechanisms promote the development of self-efficacy judgments: modeling, which children use to estimate the likelihood of success at a task; and awareness of internal bodily reactions associated with successes and failures. Self-efficacy judgments are believed to affect children's behavior significantly.

4. What are examples of biological and evolutionary approaches to questions about the self?

Bowlby's *attachment theory* and *evolutionary psychology* are two approaches in the evolutionary and biological framework. In his influential writings on attachment, John Bowlby discussed his belief that the sense of self begins to develop within the context of infant-caregiver interactions and is promoted by responsive caregiving. Evolutionary psychologists consider the adaptive value of the self-system for a species. Early studies of animal self-awareness began with primate self-recognition. For example, Gordon Gallup, Jr. showed that chimpanzees are able to recognize their images in mirrors.

5. What important information do sociocultural approaches provide in understanding the self?

Sociocultural approaches focus on the socialization of the self and self-understanding through participation in cultural practices, customs, and institutions. Socialization practices reflect each culture's model of the self. For example, cultural communities with roots in western European traditions tend to draw a clear distinction between the self and others. In this view, the self is independent, self-contained, and autonomous. In many other cultures, however, the boundary between the self and others is less clearly drawn. Cultures also differ in the age at which they assign "selfhood" or person-status to an individual, as well as in their definitions of the ideal self. In European American communities, for example, the ideal person is independent and achievement oriented. In contrast, in many East Asian societies, the ideal person is closely connected with others and does not stand out. In many cultures, individuals ideally strive to conform, maintain harmonious interpersonal relations, and bring favor to the family.

Learning Objective 12.2

Trace the development of self-knowledge from infancy, identifying the processes by which changes in the self-system occur.

1. How can you tell when an infant discovers the self as a separate entity with personal agency?

Perceptual processes are thought to play an important role in infants' first coming to recognize their separateness. By 3 months of age, infants seem to perceive that they control their own body movements. Along with infants' knowledge that they exist apart from the things around them comes an understanding of personal agency, that is, an understanding that they can be the agents or causes of events that occur in their worlds. Babies manipulate objects, suggesting an awareness both that they are separate from things and that they can do something with them. *Personal agency* also appears to develop through babies' early interactions with caregivers Theorists concur that when parents are more sensitive and responsive to their infants' signals, babies more quickly develop an understanding of their impact on their environments and the self as separate from the mother.

2. How does self-recognition change over time in relation to recognition of others?

Evidence suggests that infants draw distinctions between themselves and others at a very young age. Their developing appreciation of the existence and individuality of others can be found in an early type of preverbal play, *synchronic imitation*, in which children play with similar toys in a similar fashion. To synchronize play with that of a peer, a child must have some understanding of the other child's intentions and behavior, requiring some degree of self- and other-awareness. Consistent with this view, 18-month-olds who give evidence of mirror self-recognition display more synchronic imitation with same-age peers (and also with adults) than do infants who do not recognize themselves in the mirror. *Self-recognition* has also been linked to the emergence of the self-conscious emotions of embarrassment, pride, shame, empathy, and guilt. To experience this class of emotions, children need to be able to evaluate the self relative to some social standard, and they need to have developed self-awareness.

3. How do children's self-descriptions change from early childhood to adolescence?

By the age of 2, many children display knowledge of some of their most basic characteristics. For example, they know whether they are girls or boys and that they are children rather than adults. In the preschool years, *self-descriptions* are very concrete and usually involve physical features, possessions, and preferences. This information, however, is not always completely accurate, and children's descriptions are often unrealistically positive. During this period, there is a focus on objective, here-and-now attributes. In middle childhood, self-descriptions of 6- to 10-year-olds reflect the shift to concrete operational abilities. They begin to talk about less tangible characteristics, such as emotions, and can combine separate attributes into an overall category. The accuracy of children's information improves during this period, although they generally continue to stress their positive characteristics. In later childhood, descriptions may be based on social comparisons with others, as children evaluate their skills or talents relative to those of friends or classmates. Children also can describe opposing attributes of the self. As children enter adolescence, the formal operational child thinks and self-describes in more abstract and hypothetical, and sometimes negative, terms. Adolescents are concerned with attitudes, personality attributes, and beliefs involving hypothetical situations. By middle adolescence, the self is differentiated in terms of social roles, and in later adolescence, opposing characteristics are often integrated into single personality styles.

4. How do individual and cultural differences shape the development of self-concept?	Children develop a sense of self in relation to others within their *cultural context*. Researchers have found evidence for the idea that parents' interaction styles with their young children tend to influence children's later ideas about themselves in relation to others. Children's conceptions of themselves also differ in the context of their personal memories. In China, children recounted prior events with an emphasis on their role in relation to others and the social interactions that occurred. In the United States, in contrast, children retold events in which they had played a central role and tended to express more emotions and personal opinions. These cultural differences in self-conception became more pronounced among older children.

Learning Objective 12.3

Analyze the mechanisms and processes
by which children develop self-control.

1. What are two general trends in the development of self-regulation?	The changes in *self-regulation* observed during the early years reflect two important developments. First, regulation shifts from external to internal control. Initially, caregivers largely regulate children's behavior either directly or indirectly by supporting or scaffolding children's own efforts at self-regulation. Gradually, however, regulation shifts to the child. Second, self-control grows more elaborate and sophisticated as children exercise their developing powers of discretion.
2. How do children learn different types of compliance?	Children begin to understand caregiver wishes and expectations around the end of the first year. However, young children are more likely to refuse, ignore, or subvert parents' behavioral requests than comply with them. Researchers have found that the quality of children's *compliance* differs between the two contexts of "Do" and "Don't." In the "Don't" situation, children usually comply wholeheartedly, or display committed compliance. Committed compliance describes children's behavior when they embrace the caregiver's agenda, adopt it as their own, and follow caregiver directives in self-regulated ways. Compliance in the "Do" situation, on the other hand, is less likely and is usually given grudgingly. In this type of compliance, termed situational compliance, children essentially cooperate with parental directives but with little enthusiasm.

3. What can we learn about self-control from experiments using the forbidden-toy and delay-of-gratification techniques?

As children grow older, their ability to exercise *self-control* through distraction and delay strategies increases. Preschoolers display little knowledge of what strategies would be effective, but by sixth grade, most children seem to know that redirecting one's attention from the reward and other forms of distraction are useful methods for delaying gratification. Even toddlers use distraction strategies to delay gratification, however. Toddlers who used self-distraction to cope with a period of separation from their mothers were found at age 5 to be able to delay gratification for longer periods compared to children who did not show that early coping ability. A key predictor of preschool delay of gratification is toddlers' response to their mothers: The greatest success in delay of gratification at age 5 was observed in the children who as toddlers had distanced themselves from controlling mothers or had engaged with noncontrolling mothers. Thus, the development of self-control is linked to children's social competence. Children who respond impulsively often experience problems in their social interactions with other children, in part because they fail to acquire all the necessary information about a situation before making a decision. Children who have been rejected or excluded often are less able to self-regulate. Ability to cope with temptation appears to be a stable personality characteristic, and a child's early ability to delay gratification may predict the child's eventual success and happiness.

4. By what process do children develop a conscience?

As children develop a sense of self and gain the ability to *regulate* their behaviors and emotions, they also develop a conscience, or internal standards of conduct they use to control their behavior, which typically produce discomfort when violated. Children's development of committed compliance is associated with the *internalization* of parental and societal values and rules. In contrast, situational compliance depends on caregiver control. Caregivers who foster a warm, responsive interaction pattern are more likely to encourage the development of internalization and *committed compliance* in their children as well as development of morals and a value system The transmission of religiosity, through parents and other agents such as a church system, is also a factor in the development of conscience.

5. What role do parenting styles play in children's development of self-control.	Parental warmth and positive expressivity are associated with higher levels of self-control in young children and teens. *Authoritative* parenting practices are associated with higher levels and earlier attainment of self-control, whereas *authoritarian* and *indulgent* parenting practices are associated with lower levels of self-control.

Learning Objective 12.4

Describe the development of self-esteem, ways to measure it, and the contexts that shape the way children evaluate themselves.

1. What is self-esteem, and how is it measured?	The evaluative opinions children develop about themselves is referred to as their self-esteem, or self-worth. Children's *self-esteem* is assumed to include both cognitive judgments and affective reactions to those judgments. The most common *method* of assessing children's self-esteem is through questionnaires. Instruments such as Harter's *Self-Perception Profile for Children* and Marsh's *Self-Description Questionnaire* present children with a list of questions designed to tap their opinions of themselves in a variety of situations or contexts. The responses to these questions can be combined and analyzed to produce an overall score that represents the child's level of self-esteem. Researchers have found that by age 7 to 8, children in Western cultures usually have formed at least four broad areas of self-esteem: academic competence, social competence, physical/athletic competence, and physical appearance. These categories become increasingly more refined and distinct with age. As children mature, they also gain the ability to combine their separate self-evaluations into a general psychological image of themselves—an overall sense of self-esteem.

2. How does self-esteem change across childhood and adolescence and differ for boys and girls?	The *developmental course of self-esteem* is relatively consistent. Self-esteem changes as children mature cognitively and as they experience the world around them. Self-esteem drops slightly during the first years of elementary school. During middle and later childhood, self-esteem scores are generally stable, with a small trend toward improvement. But the transition to adolescence often poses problems. Many investigators have found that at about age 11 or 12, self-esteem scores dip, only to recover over the subsequent years. This drop in self-esteem in early adolescence may be due to the stress of school transitions, increased self-consciousness about the opinions of others, and the biological changes associated with puberty. An environmental

variable that contributes to a drop in self-esteem involves whether children remain in their own school or move to a new one following sixth grade. Several studies report that moving to a new school usually produces a noticeable decline in self-esteem, especially if the new school is large and ethnically diverse. Girls and boys exhibit some general differences in self-esteem measures, with boys showing much less variability than girls from one domain to the next. Girls typically evaluate their conduct more positively than do boys, but provide more negative assessments of their physical appearance and athletic competence. These gender differences are consistent cross-culturally and across development, holding from elementary school through college. Beginning in the fourth grade, girls' perceptions of their physical attractiveness decline markedly. By the last half of high school, girls have dramatically lower self-ratings than do boys, whose scores decline only a little with age. This trend may be troubling, because perceived physical appearance has been shown to be an effective predictor of global self-worth.

3. What factors are believed to contribute to the formation of academic self-concept?

Children's perceptions of their *academic competence*, or academic self-concept, represent one factor that affects self-esteem. Infants have little understanding of success and failure and so do not behave in ways that suggest self-evaluation. Before the age of 2, however, children begin to show that they anticipate how adults will react to their achievements, such as when they look up for approval after finishing a task. Children's academic self-concept generally is highest in kindergarten and steadily declines through at least fourth grade. Older children learn that bragging is not socially appropriate and so increasingly avoid giving glowing descriptions of their abilities. In addition, gender socialization factors develop where males typically have higher self-concepts for math than girls and girls have higher self-concepts for English.

4. What roles do children's theories of intelligence and attributions play in achievement motivation?

Some children come to believe in an *entity model* of intelligence, in which intelligence is fixed and unchangeable. Others develop an *incremental model*, in which a person's intelligence can grow with experience and learning. These models relate to children's "attributions for success or failure." Some believe that success or failure depends on how much ability one has, while others believe it depends on how much effort one applies to a task. Children who attribute their lack of success to a lack of ability tend to learn helplessness and fail to persist. Children who focus on effort and skills-building, on the other hand, have reason for optimism in the face of failure. They become mastery-oriented, believing they can do better in the future by trying harder.

5. What roles do criticism, praise, and social comparison play in the development of academic self-concept?

The feedback children receive from adults is the source of patterns of motivation and has more impact than the child's temperament. Experiments show that a strong relationship exists between the child's motivation pattern and his or her reactions to both criticism and praise from parents and teachers. Receiving *person-oriented praise*, for example, is associated with increased vulnerability to failure, whereas praise directed at *effort or strategy* use produces the most mastery-oriented responses. Equating correctness with goodness leaves one open to the self-judgment that one is bad when failure results. Thus, certain forms of praise are not always beneficial for children. Praise works when it is perceived as sincere, encourages performance attributions to controllable causes, promotes autonomy, and conveys reasonable and attainable expectations and standards. People contrast their abilities with those of others and draw conclusions about themselves from those assessments, a process called social comparison. This process begins as early as kindergarten, but its function changes with age. Kindergartners use what their classmates are doing or saying primarily as a way of making friends or learning how things are done. As children proceed through the early grades, however, their social comparisons increasingly involve academic performance, and they begin to use the comparisons to evaluate their own competence relative to that of others. By second grade, children with lower opinions of their competence make fewer social comparisons, because by continually comparing their performance with that of peers, many children unhappily discover that their work is not as good as they had believed. High-achieving students show more interest in comparing their performance and also in discovering the correct answers to problems. At the same time, the presence of high-ability peers can reduce academic self-concept. Social comparison is strongly influenced by the atmosphere of the educational environment, with more positive results in educational environments that are more cooperative than competitive. Thus, the relationship between social comparison and academic self-concept is bidirectional. Social comparisons can affect children's self-image, which in turn affects their willingness to engage in social comparisons.

6. What is the impact of academic self-concept on children's development and future prospects?

Academic self-concept strongly influences academic achievement. Children who view themselves as academically skilled are more motivated to succeed, more persistent in their work, and more willing to seek out challenging tasks or problems. A high academic self-concept, even when it overestimates the child's abilities, also correlates positively with (and probably contributes to) a high level of self-esteem. Children with low opinions of their academic abilities, on the other hand, are less motivated to work. Even among children whose academic skills were high, those who held an incorrectly low opinion of their competence approached new tasks with less effort and optimism than did their classmates. Subjective perception of ability (rather than actual ability) determines whether children will attempt or avoid challenges.

Learning Objective 12.5

Explain how individuals construct their personal and ethnic or cultural identities.

1. What four identity statuses did Marcia propose for resolving an identity crisis or exploration?

Identity diffusion is the term for the state adolescents are in when they have not yet experienced a crisis or made any commitments. In *identity moratorium*, adolescents are in the middle of a crisis, but their commitments are only vaguely defined or are missing altogether. In *identity foreclosure*, the adolescent has made a commitment without experiencing a crisis. In this situation the adolescent has often accepted commitments that have been imposed by families with an authoritarian parenting style. The adolescent has not had sufficient opportunities to explore alternatives independently. Finally, in *identity achievement*, the adolescent has experienced a crisis and has then made a commitment.

2. What cognitive abilities and social relationships facilitate identity formation?

As children mature, they become more sophisticated in their understanding of other people. They become better at making inferences about the personality traits, viewpoints, and behaviors of others. *Social perception*, or the processes by which people come to understand each other, becomes better organized and more differentiated. In particular, children become more adept at person perception—the mental processes we use to form judgments and draw conclusions about the characteristics and motives of others. Children also become more sophisticated in their use of descriptions and attributions and in perspective taking—the capacity to imagine and understand what another person may be thinking and feeling. Perspective taking plays a significant role in the ability to communicate with others, is important in social problem solving, and is associated with the ability to make higher-level moral judgments. Parental interaction styles and other caregiver behaviors have been shown to predict perspective taking.

3. Through what process do adolescents develop their ethnic, racial, or cultural identity?

Ethnic identity—a sense of lasting group membership based on race, ethnicity, or cultural heritage, and the attitudes and feelings associated with that membership—is central to the process of identity development. As adolescents develop cognitively, they may become more sensitive to minority status and feedback from the broader social environment and may also become aware of the potential for prejudice and discrimination. A strong, positive sense of ethnic identity may provide the resources adolescents need to cope with stresses related to encounters with prejudice and discrimination. Adolescents are aided in this when they are encouraged to learn and understand the history, traditions, and values of their group, and when they have opportunities to interact frequently with peers who share similar experiences. Five stages of racial identity development have been identified among African American youth: In the pre-encounter the child absorbs the beliefs and values of the dominant culture. In the encounter stage, an event forces the young person to acknowledge the impact of racism. In the immersion stage, the person spends time exploring and learning about his or her racial identity. In the internalization stage, the person gains a sense of security about his or her racial or cultural identity; and in the commitment stage, this personal sense of security is translated into actions to benefit the community.

4. When does identity development begin and end?

Identity construction is complex, begins in infancy, and continues throughout the lifespan. Our perceptions of the roles we play and their importance in determining who we are change as we mature. *Identity achievement* occurs at different rates for different domains of identity, but as we explore new roles and opportunities and acquire new knowledge and responsibilities, it is likely that our identity will change.

Sex Differences *and* Gender Role Development

CHAPTER 13

SEX DIFFERENCES: PERCEIVED AND REAL

Learning Objective 13.1

DESCRIBE PHYSICAL, COGNITIVE, AND SOCIAL/PERSONALITY SEX DIFFERENCES THAT RESEARCHERS HAVE FOUND.

Physical Differences
- Vulnerability • Activity Level • Motor Development

Cognitive Differences
- Language and Verbal Abilities • Quantitative Abilities • Spatial Abilities

APPLICATIONS Should Schools Teach Visual-Spatial Skills?

Social and Personality Differences
- Emotional Development • Self-Control • Aggression • Prosocial Behavior
- Activities and Interests • Friends and Companions

INFLUENCES ON SEX DIFFERENCES AND GENDER ROLE DEVELOPMENT

Learning Objective 13.2

COMPARE AND CONTRAST BIOLOGICAL AND SOCIAL INFLUENCES ON SEX DIFFERENCES AND GENDER ROLE DEVELOPMENT.

Biological Influences
- Genes and Hormones • Hormonal Regulation and Abnormalities

RESEARCH & SOCIETY When Genotype and Phenotype Don't Match
- Brain Lateralization

Social Influences
- Society and the Media • Teachers • Parents • Siblings • Peers

THE CHILD'S ACTIVE PARTICIPATION IN GENDER ROLE DEVELOPMENT

Learning Objective 13.3

EXPLAIN AND ILLUSTRATE HOW CHILDREN PARTICIPATE ACTIVELY IN THEIR GENDER ROLE DEVELOPMENT.

Self-Selecting Processes
Role of Cognition in Gender Identity
- Kohlberg's Cognitive-Developmental Approach • Schema Theory

GENDER ROLE DEVELOPMENT

Learning Objective 13.4

TRACE THE DEVELOPMENT OF GENDER ROLE KNOWLEDGE AND BEHAVIOR.

Development of Gender Knowledge
Flexibility of Gender Stereotypes

CONVERSATIONS with Men in Nontraditional Roles
Influences of Gender Knowledge on Behavior
- Toy Preferences • Motivation • Memory • Social Judgments

DEVELOPMENT OF SEXUAL RELATIONSHIPS AND BEHAVIOR:
Learning Objective 13.5
DISCUSS THE DEVELOPMENT OF SEXUAL RELATIONSHIPS AND BEHAVIOR.
Emergence of Romantic and Sexual Interest
Origins of Sexual Orientation
• Biological Influences • Social Influences
Gender Identity and Transsexualism

When Kaylie was born, her parents Jennifer and Steven were determined to rear her free of gender stereotypes. When she was an infant, they purchased green and yellow sleepers for her, and dressed her in outfits with some traditional "boy" themes such as soccer balls and tools, as well as some traditional "girl" themes such as butterflies and flowers. When she was a toddler, they got a wide variety of toys for her to play with, ranging from blocks, legos, and toy cars to baby dolls and toy dishes. For her first Halloweens, she was dressed in gender-neutral costumes, a tiger one year and a lion the next. By the time she was 3, Kaylie had a strong preference for pink and lavender outfits with flowers and hearts on them. She was indifferent to the blocks and roadset her parents had purchased for her, preferring to dress up in princess clothes and pretend to feed her baby dolls. She chose toys and other products that featured Dora the Explorer, Barbie, and the Disney Princesses while actively avoiding products that featured Spiderman, Thomas the Train, or Bob the Builder. When shopping with her mother, she would sometimes ask, "Is this for boys or girls?" and then would want to purchase an item only if assured it was for girls. She was eager to enroll in dance classes and informed her parents that she wanted to be either a fairy princess or a ballerina for Halloween this year. Jennifer and Steven were amazed. Was it true after all that biology hardwired boys and girls for different interests, or were the environmental pressures toward gendered behavior stronger than their own efforts to counteract it?

This chapter considers sex differences and gender role development, including where they come from and how they develop. Psychologists do not all agree on the use of the terms *gender* and *sex* (Deaux, 1993; Ruble & Martin, 1998). Some use these terms interchangeably, others distinguish between them, and still others suggest that differentiating between these two terms perpetuates a false notion that we can separate out the effects of nature and nurture (Halpern, 2000). In this textbook the term *sex* refers to differences between males and females, regardless of the origin of those differences. The term *gender* refers to sociocultural expectations that people have about what those differences mean. When referring to a *sex difference*, we are saying simply that males and females differ as groups in relation to a particular trait or characteristic. Thus, identifying a sex difference is not the same as claiming either a biological or an environmental origin of that difference.

The term **gender stereotype** refers to widely held beliefs in a culture regarding how males and females should behave. In most cultures, for example, gender stereotypes associated with maleness include traits such as competitiveness, dominance, and aggressiveness, whereas gender stereotypes associated with femaleness include characteristics such as nurturance, dependence, and sensitivity (Best, 2001; Williams & Best, 1990). These widely held beliefs are enacted in everyday life in the **gender roles** that males and females adopt (Deaux, 1993; Gentile, 1993). **Gender identity** refers to one's perception of oneself as male or female. **Gender typing,** on the other hand, is the process by which children develop the beliefs, behaviors, attitudes, and roles that their society deems appropriate for their gender. Gender typing, apparent in 3-year-old Kaylie's feminine preferences, is assumed to involve a combination of biological, social, and cognitive influences (Huston, 1985; Powlishta et al., 2001). ∎

Sex Differences: Perceived and Real

Learning Objective 13.1
Describe physical, cognitive, and social/personality sex differences that researchers have found.

This section discusses sex differences that are commonly observed during childhood or adolescence. At issue, however, is how to interpret research on sex differences. In cases where studies have yielded conflicting results, how do we know which results to believe?

To help make sense of discrepant results, researchers use *meta-analysis.* In meta-analysis, researchers apply statistical rules to a group of studies that all examine the same thing. Because meta-analysis is based on large amounts of data collected by numerous researchers under widely varying conditions, researchers are better able to draw firm conclusions about the behavior or attribute under study. Meta-analyses are not available for every behavior and attribute related to sex differences, but you should pay special attention to differences that are supported by meta-analysis.

Also keep in mind that sex differences represent only the average difference across all males and females. For example, we often hear (and indeed we shall see) that boys typically outperform girls on mental rotation tasks. But what does this mean? Consider Figure 13.1, which shows two possible models that people may have in mind when they hear that a sex difference exists. In (*a*), males and females differ so markedly that there is no overlap in their scores. To use our example, according to this model all men are better at mental rotation tasks than all women. When the topic of sex differences is raised, the picture represented by graph (*a*) often comes to mind. However, this pattern virtually *never* arises in real life, and indeed it is not the case when it comes to mental rotation tasks.

In (*b*), to continue our example, males on average outperform females with regard to visual-spatial skills, but there is considerable overlap between males and females. What this means is that many women are in reality better than many men at this skill. The variability on this skill among men and women is greater than the group differences between them. The general pattern depicted in (*b*) is the most common pattern for understanding virtually all sex differences that are reported.

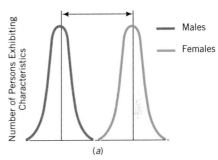

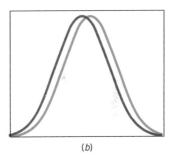

FIGURE 13.1   Two Possible Patterns for Sex Differences

Pattern (*a*) shows completely separate sex differences, while pattern (*b*) shows overlapping sex differences. Which pattern is more prevalent, and what is the meaning of that finding?

Gender stereotypes
Widely held beliefs in a culture regarding how males and females should behave.

Gender role
A pattern or set of behaviors considered appropriate for males or females within a particular culture.

Gender identity
One's perception of oneself as male or female.

Gender typing
The process by which children develop the behaviors and attitudes considered appropriate for their gender.

How did these children become so "gendered" at such a young age? To what extent are their "masculine" and "feminine" preferences hardwired, and to what extent are they learned? How do sex differences and gender roles develop? (© Lawrence Migdale/Photo Researchers)

Differences among males and among females are greater than differences between males and females. All sex differences are the product of both biological and environmental processes acting in concert.

Physical Differences

Physical differences include differences in physical maturity and vulnerability, in activity level, and in motor development. At birth, girls generally are healthier and more developmentally advanced than boys, despite being somewhat smaller and lighter. Although girls are less muscular, they are better coordinated neurologically and physically (Garai & Scheinfeld, 1968; Lundqvist & Sabel, 2000; Reinisch & Sanders, 1992; Tanner, 1990). On average, girls also reach developmental milestones earlier than boys. For instance, on average girls lose their first tooth at a younger age and begin (and end) puberty sooner.

Vulnerability Males are physically more vulnerable than females from conception on. They are more likely to be miscarried, to suffer from physical and mental illnesses and various kinds of hereditary abnormalities, and to die in infancy (Hartung & Widiger, 1998; Jacklin, 1989). Males are also more likely to suffer physical injuries. This probably reflects a constellation of factors, including boys' higher activity level and greater risk-taking tendencies (Byrnes, Miller, & Schafer, 1999; Laing & Logan, 1999).

Activity Level On average, boys have higher activity levels than girls. This sex difference first emerges during the prenatal period, when male fetuses are on average more active in the womb (Almli, Ball, & Wheeler, 2001; DiPietro et al., 1996). Meta-analytic studies show that this difference is maintained through infancy and childhood (Campbell & Eaton, 1999; Eaton & Enns, 1986). Interestingly, sex differences in activity level are small when children are playing alone. Boys' activity levels increase substantially when they are in the company of other boys—as any casual observer of a preschool classroom, birthday party, or school lunch line can attest (Maccoby, 1998).

Motor Development During infancy, sex differences in motor development are minimal. Sex differences in large and fine motor development are evident in early childhood, however. Boys have the edge in skills that require strength. By age 5, boys can jump farther, run faster, and throw farther than girls. Beginning in the preschool years, boys are also able to throw more accurately than girls. This sex difference increases during adolescence, in part because of physical changes and in part because of practice.

Girls, in turn, have an advantage in gross motor skills, such as hopping and skipping, that require a combination of balance and precise movement. Girls also have better fine motor skills and so initially have an easier time tying shoes and performing tasks required in school, such as writing, cutting paper, and the like.

Cognitive Differences

According to popular stereotypes, girls are better at verbal tasks, whereas boys are better at mathematics. In fact, studies using meta-analysis reveal that the differences between males and females in these two cognitive domains are quite small (Hyde, Fennema, & Lamon, 1990; Hyde & Linn, 1988). Furthermore, the differences that do exist are often restricted to specific age groups, to specific kinds of tasks, or to very high-achieving groups. Nevertheless, some differences are observed.

Language and Verbal Abilities There is little doubt that girls outperform boys in some kinds of verbal skills (Feingold, 1992, 1993). As infants, girls produce more sounds at an earlier age than do boys (Harris, 1977); they use words sooner; and the size of their early vocabularies is larger (Bauer, Goldfield, & Reznick, 2002; Galsworthy et al., 2000; Huttenlocher et al., 1991). On a variety of measures of grammar and language complexity (sentence length, use of pronouns, use of conjunctions, and so on), girls begin to show marked superiority at about 2 years of age, and the differences continue through adolescence (Koenigsknecht & Friedman, 1976; Schacter et al., 1978).

Throughout the school years, girls achieve higher scores in reading and writing (Campbell, Hombo, & Mazzeo, 2000; Halpern, 2000). Early differences in learning to read may originate in sex differences in the ability to detect the sounds of language (phonology), as girls outperform boys across a range of phonological tasks (Majeres, 1999). Recent reports of performance on standardized exams of reading and writing show that girls continue to outperform boys at the end of high school (National Center for Education Statistics, 2003; (http://nces.ed.gov/nationsreportcard/reading/results2003/scalegender-all.asp; Willingham et al., 1997).

One source of the gender gap in reading and writing is that males are more likely than females to have serious problems with speech and written language. Compared with girls, boys are more likely to suffer from language difficulties, such as stuttering. They are also more likely to have dyslexia and other types of learning disorders that make learning to read and write difficult (Miles, Haslum, & Wheeler, 1998; Nass, 1993).

There is considerable evidence that sex differences in verbal and language abilities are biologically based. Of particular importance is brain **lateralization**—the specialization of functions in the right and left hemispheres. Scientists believe that prenatal exposure to high levels of testosterone—which occurs normally during the development of male fetuses—slows the development of the left hemisphere and enhances the development of the right hemisphere (Rosen, Galaburda, & Sherman, 1990). This process may produce two results significant for sex differences in cognitive abilities.

Lateralization
The specialization of functions in the right and left hemispheres of the brain.

One is that the right hemisphere is relatively more established in newborn boys. You may recall from Chapter 6 that the right hemisphere is specialized for quantitative and spatial abilities. This may help account for the male advantage in spatial tasks. Second, the brains of females are less lateralized. That is, female superiority on verbal and language tasks may derive from the fact that they use both hemispheres to process language, whereas males' language processing tends to be localized in the left hemisphere.

Although language skills appear to have biological underpinnings, environment plays a significant role as well. Girls usually experience a richer language environment than boys. A meta-analysis of mother-child talk showed that mothers vocalize more to daughters, imitate their vocalizations more, and generally maintain a higher level of mother-infant vocal exchange (Leaper, Anderson, & Sanders, 1998). Parents also believe that daughters have greater reading ability than sons, even when actual ability differences do not support this belief (Eccles, Arbreton, et al., 1993; Wigfield et al., 2002).

L inks to Related Material
In Chapter 6, you read about lateralization of the hemispheres of the brain. In this chapter, you learn more about how lateralization relates to gender differences in certain cognitive abilities.

Quantitative Abilities During elementary school girls and boys are equally interested in mathematics (Andre et al., 1999; Eccles, Jacobs, et al., 1993; Folling-Albers & Hartinger, 1998; Wigfield et al., 1997). Even at this young age, however, girls and boys appear to excel at different kinds of mathematics. Throughout elementary and junior high school, girls are better at computational problems, whereas boys do better on average with mathematical reasoning (Hyde et al., 1990; Seong, Bauer, & Sullivan, 1998).

By adolescence, boys express greater interest in mathematics than do girls (Gardner, 1998; Wigfield et al., 2002). They also begin to perform significantly better than girls on standardized exams, but not in math courses. On average, boys achieve higher scores on SAT mathematics exams than girls, whereas girls tend to receive higher grades in mathematics courses (Benbow, 1992; Snyder & Hoffman, 2000). The sex difference in performance on standardized exams is especially marked among students of very high ability (Benbow, 1992; Bielinkski & Davison, 1998; Willingham & Cole, 1997).

Recent studies in the United States shed some light on male-female differences. These studies looked at how girls and boys solve mathematical problems—not just whether they solve them correctly. Compared with boys, first-grade girls are more likely to use strategies such as counting on one's fingers, which are almost certain to produce correct solutions. Boys, in contrast, tend to use strategies such as retrieval, which places them at greater risk for making mistakes (Carr & Davis, 2001; Carr & Jessup, 1997; Carr, Jessup, & Fuller, 1999).

Some researchers believe that these early differences in the types of strategies preferred by girls and boys contribute to differences in mathematical achievement that persist over time. By third grade, despite their earlier retrieval-based mistakes, boys are better able to rapidly and automatically retrieve correct answers to arithmetic problems. This ability may lay the foundation for later-developing mathematical competencies. How quickly students retrieve mathematical facts is predictive of their performance on both computational and mathematical reasoning tasks (Geary et al., 2000; Royer et al., 1999). Speedy retrieval may especially advantage males on timed tests, such as college entrance exams.

There is also a sex difference in the kinds of strategies used to solve mathematical reasoning problems. Starting in first grade, girls are more likely to use concrete strategies, such as counting, whereas boys use more abstract approaches (Fennema et al., 1998). By third grade, girls prefer the conventional strategies taught in school, whereas boys on average are more likely to use estimation or some kind of unconventional strategy (Hopkins, McGillicuddy-De Lisi, & De Lisi, 1997).

Differences in strategy preferences can also help explain why girls tend to perform better in mathematics courses, yet obtain lower scores than boys on standardized exams. Although the orthodox approaches used by girls tend to produce correct solutions on conventional problems, they are less likely to yield good results on unconventional ones (see Table 13.1 for an illustration). Consequently, girls may perform well on school exams designed to test whether they can correctly apply a taught strategy, but they are less able to solve trickier problems that require a novel approach. Conversely, although mathematics teachers may not always appreciate the creative solutions offered by male students, those approaches may confer an advantage on males outside of the classroom (Gallagher & De Lisi, 1994; Gallagher et al., 2000).

TABLE 13.1 Two Types of SAT Math Problems

Problem 1 is easily solved using a formula, but Problem 2 is more easily solved using non-conventional procedures, such as visualization, estimation, ruling out, and the like. In the United States, females tend to have better success with the first type of problem.

Problem 1.

P	Q	R
4/n	5/n	1/4

If $PQ = QR$ on the number line above, what is the length of PR?

(A) 1/12
(B) 1/9
(C) 1/8
(D) 1/6
(E) 3/16

Answer: (A) 1/12

Problem 2.

A blend of coffee is made by mixing Colombian coffee at $8 a pound with espresso coffee at $3 a pound. If the blend is worth $5 a pound, how many pounds of the Colombian coffee are needed to make 50 pounds of the blend?

(A) 20
(B) 25
(C) 30
(D) 35
(E) 40

Answer: (A) 20

SOURCE: Adapted by permission from A. M. Gallagher and R. De Lisi. (1994). Gender differences in Scholastic Aptitude Test mathematics problem solving among high-ability students. *Journal of Educational Psychology, 86*, 204–211.

Why boys and girls approach mathematical problems differently is not well understood. Some studies have suggested that girls have less confidence in their mathematical abilities than do boys (Pajares & Miller, 1994; Stipek & Gralinski, 1991; Wigfield et al., 1997). However, more recent work suggests that the gender gap in beliefs involving mathematical competence is decreasing (Jacobs et al., 2002; Marsh & Yeung, 1998). Another possibility is that girls are more concerned with following rules and meeting teacher expectations (Dweck, 1999). Finally, it is possible that the stereotype threat phenomenon discussed in Chapter 9— contributes to the gender gap in girls' performance or standardized mathematics tests (Good, Aronson, & Inzlicht, 2003).

Spatial Abilities As already noted, males repeatedly outperform females in tasks involving spatial abilities (Feingold, 1993; Halpern, 2000). Some sex differences in spatial abilities are observed as early as the preschool years. On average, boys outperform girls on the Maze Subtest of the Weschler Preschool and Primary Scale of Intelligence (Fairweather & Butterworth, 1977; Wechsler, 1967). Four-year-old boys also outperform girls on spatial transformation tasks like that shown in Figure 13.2 and show superior performance on three-dimensional spatial tasks such as copying Lego models (Levine et al., 1999; McGuiness & Morley, 1991).

There is some evidence that sex differences in spatial abilities increase in adolescence and adulthood, although the extent of the difference varies with the task (Voyer, Voyer, & Bryden, 1995). One type of task on which adolescent and adult males and females differ markedly involves mental rotation (Linn & Petersen, 1986; Masters & Sanders, 1993). An example of a mental-rotation task appears in Figure 13.3. Another task at which females generally have more difficulty is the water-level task, shown in Figure 13.4 (Vasta & Liben, 1996).

What might account for sex differences in spatial abilities? One explanation, as noted, emphasizes the biological explanation of brain lateralization. The right hemisphere is specialized for quantitative and spatial tasks, and the development of the right hemisphere is

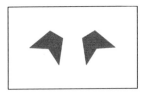
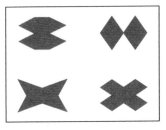

FIGURE 13.2 Spatial Transformation Task

In this task, children select which of the four cards shows what the two pieces in the top card would look like if placed together.

Source: S. C. Levine, J. Huttenlocher, A. Taylor, and A. Langrock. (1999). Early sex differences in spatial skill. *Developmental Psychology, 35*, 940–949.

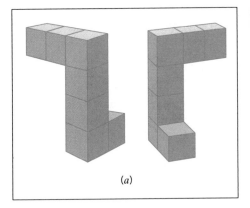
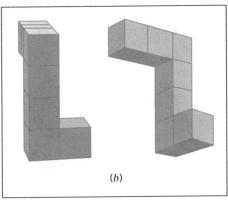

(a)   *(b)*

FIGURE 13.3 Mental-Rotation Task

Which set of of objects is the same, (a) or (b)?
Answer: (a) The objects in (b) are different.

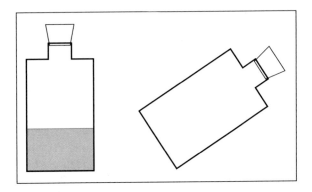

FIGURE 13.4
Water-Level Task

Draw a line to predict how the water will look when the bottle is tilted.

BOX 13.1   Should Schools Teach Visual-Spatial Skills?

One of the most robust and reliable findings in research on sex differences is a male advantage on tasks that involve spatial reasoning, such as mental rotation and spatial visualization. At the same time, there is ample evidence that certain experiences promote the development of spatial skills (Baenninger & Newcombe, 1989, 1995). Cross-cultural research shows superior spatial abilities among children and adults in cultures that depend heavily on hunting and other activities that require extensive travel (Dasen, 1975). Moreover, when females travel and hunt as frequently as males, they exhibit comparable spatial skills (Berry, 1966).

Everyday, practical experience performing tasks that entail spatial demands also enhances spatial competence in modern societies. For instance, Ross Vasta and colleagues (Vasta et al., 1997) found that individuals in occupations that provide extensive experience with liquids in containers—namely, bartenders and servers—perform better than adults of equal age, gender, and education on the water-level task depicted in Figure 13.4. Experience playing computer and video games has also been linked to spatial competence. Under naturalistic conditions, it is difficult to know whether time spent playing these games promotes the development of spatial skills or whether children (and adults) with better spatial skills enjoy playing those games more and so devote more time to them.

A recent study that tracked children's cognitive development over the course of the first two years of elementary school supports the idea that some kinds of activities promote the development of spatial abilities (Huttenlocher, Levine, & Vevea, 1998). Children in this study were tested four times—October and April during kindergarten and October and April during first grade. Children's spatial skills increased over the two-year period, but most children showed greater growth during the months they were in school (October through April) than when they were mostly at home. These findings suggest that typical school activities, such as puzzle play and basic pregeometry instruction, facilitate children's development of spatial competence. Interestingly, children who entered kindergarten with very strong spatial abilities did not improve differentially during the school year. This suggests that the home environments of these spatially gifted children may have included more opportunities to practice spatial skills than the home environments of the other children.

Training studies provide further evidence for the effect of experience on spatial abilities. In one study, female college students were taught how to solve the water-level problem (Vasta, Knott, & Gaze, 1996). This task has proved notoriously difficult for college-age women. Estimates suggest that up to 50 percent of them do not recognize that the water level will remain horizontal when the container is tilted (Halpern, 2000). Simply by receiving practice on a series of problems of increasing complexity (without feedback), females were able to solve problems as accurately as males.

The fact that spatial skills can be taught has led some theorists to argue that spatial thinking should be included in the school curriculum. Schools offer remedial programs for reading—an area in which boys are at increased risk for educational failure. Significant numbers of girls—and more than a few boys—exhibit serious deficiencies in spatial competence. Yet schools generally make little effort to address these limitations (Halpern, 2000).

Questions for Thought and Discussion
What are some examples of activities that might make males better than females on spatial tasks? Are there activities common among females that promote spatial skills just as well?

promoted by male hormones. Another explanation emphasizes experiential factors. From early childhood, boys are more likely to participate in activities that promote spatial skills. They spend more time building with blocks, constructing models, and playing computer and video games and sports (Baenninger & Newcombe, 1989, 1995; Serbin et al., 1990; Subrahmanyam & Greenfield, 1994; Subrahmanyam et al., 2001).

Nora Newcombe, an expert on the development of spatial cognition, has argued that scientists should direct their attention to the fact that spatial skills are trainable (Newcombe, Mathason, & Terlecki, 2002). It is widely accepted that spatial skills are important in daily life (e.g., hooking up the computer, packing the trunk of the car, orienteering), as well as in various professions, such as science, engineering, and medicine (Gardner, 1993; Shea, Lubinski, & Benbow, 2001).

Social and Personality Differences

Questions for Thought and Discussion
How might society benefit if more people developed better spatial skills? Do you think spatial reasoning should be taught in school?

We turn next to social and personality differences between boys and girls, including differences in temperament, emotional development, self-control, aggression, prosocial behavior, activities and interests, and friends and companions. As you saw in Chapter 11, infants are born with a basic temperament, on which personality is based. Some babies are easygoing, whereas others are often fussy and irritable. It is clear that temperament varies from infant to infant. But are some dimensions of infant temperament more typical of girls and others more typical of boys?

From the first days of life, girls seem better equipped for social interaction than boys. As infants, girls maintain greater eye contact with caregivers (Connellan et al., 2000; Hittleman & Dickes, 1979). By 3 months of age, they engage in more face-to-face communication (Lavelli & Fogel, 2002). Girls also smile more during social interactions (Cossette et al., 1996). These differences persist into adulthood. Adult women maintain eye contact and smile more during social exchanges than do adult males (Hall, 1984; LaFrance, Hecht, & Paluck, 2003).

Despite these differences, there is no evidence to suggest that females are inherently more sociable than males (Maccoby, 1998; Mathiesen & Tambs, 1999; McCrae et al., 2002). What appears to be a female propensity for social interaction during the first months of infancy is most likely related to male infants' greater fussiness and irritability and their less developed ability to regulate their emotional states (Calkins et al., 2002; Weinberg et al., 1999).

Emotional Development As they grow older, both boys and girls become better able to manage their emotions. This improvement is due to both biological maturation and the development of emotion regulation strategies (Compas et al., 2001). Sex differences in the strategies used to regulate emotional states have been observed among children as young as age 2. In one study, for example, toddlers were promised an attractive toy but were made to wait before being allowed to play with it. The girls coped with the stress of the situation by seeking comfort from their mothers, whereas the boys were more likely to distract themselves by playing with the other objects in the room (Raver, 1996).

This gender difference in coping style grows larger over the course of childhood (Broderick, 1998; Copeland & Hess, 1995). By adolescence, these behavioral styles are incorporated into *gender scripts*, or widely accepted expectations for behavior. Adolescents expect females to turn to other people when upset and males to find something else to do (Broderick & Korteland, 2002). A recent meta-analysis of the adult coping literature confirms the same pattern in adulthood. Females are more likely to seek social support and talk about upsetting events. Males, in contrast, are more likely to employ distraction or to engage in some kind of physical activity (Tamres, Janicki, & Helgeson, 2002).

One possible reason girls talk about their feelings with other people more than boys is that they are socialized to do so (Fivush & Buckner, 2000). Studies of parent-child reminiscing in Western cultures find that mothers and fathers talk more about the emotional aspects of events with daughters than with sons (Eisenberg, 1999; Fivush, 1998; Flannagan & Perese, 1998). Most intriguing is that parents seem to highlight sadness when talking with daughters (Chance & Fiese, 1999; Fivush & Buckner, 2000; Kuebli & Fivush, 1992). This focus on sadness does not appear to be elicited by the girls themselves, as young girls and boys mention sadness equally often. Later in childhood, however, females are likely to report feeling sad than are males (Hughes & Dunn, 2002).

There are gender differences in the expression of other negative emotions as well. Parent-child conversations about anger are more common with sons than daughters (Brody, 1999; Fivush, 1991). Boys are also more likely to express anger, both in face-to-face interactions and when describing past events (Hubbard, 2001; Peterson & Biggs, 2001). In addition, boys are more likely to deny feeling afraid. Boys are also less likely to follow cultural display rules regarding the expression of disappointment. For instance, upon receiving a disappointing gift, girls are better able to mask their disappointment and look pleased. Boys not only are more likely to show disappointment in this situation but also are less capable of hiding it, even when given incentives to do so (Cole, 1986; Davis, 1995; McDowell, O'Neil, & Parke, 2000).

Self-Control As you saw in Chapter 12, the emergence of self-control is one of the hallmark achievements of the preschool period. Children with self-control are able to inhibit impulsive and aggressive behavior, delay immediate gratification, and comply with caregiver requests and prohibitions.

Links to Related Material
In Chapter 12, you read about the development of self-control in children. Here, you learn more about gender differences in self-control.

There is some evidence that girls develop self-regulatory capabilities more rapidly than boys. During early childhood, boys have considerably more difficulty than girls with tasks that demand impulse control—for example, whispering on command, walking slowly on a line, and playing games such as Simon Says (Kochanska et al., 1996). Girls also have been found to comply more readily and at a younger age than boys with parental requests to perform unpleasant tasks, such as picking up toys, and prohibitions against touching fragile or dangerous objects (Kochanska & Askan, 1995; Kochanska, Coy, & Murray, 2001; Kuczynski & Kochanska, 1990).

Children with limited self-control are at risk for problem behaviors, such as angry outbursts and other kinds of disruptive actions. Prior to age 4 or 5, girls and boys engage in disruptive and impulsive behavior equally often (Achenbach, Edelbrock, & Howell, 1987). After this age, however, striking sex differences are found. Whereas most girls show a steady decline in problem behaviors, boys show a lesser decline and, in some cases, even an increase (Prior et al., 1993).

Aggression Perhaps the clearest and largest sex difference in behavior is that males generally display more physical aggression than do females—especially aggression involving violence. For example, FBI arrest statistics indicate that in the United States, males commit about 89 percent of the murders and 79 percent of the aggravated assaults (FBI Uniform Crime Reports, 2003, Table 33: Ten-Year Arrest Trends by Sex, 1994–2003, p. 275). Most other countries report similar statistics (Kenrick & Trost, 1993). However, between 1994 and 2003 in the United States, arrests of females for aggravated assault rose by 14 percent to 21 percent of the total arrests for that crime, a significant increase. A recent study of over 4,500 preschoolers in eight countries found that boys were universally reported to be more physically aggressive than girls the same age (LaFreniere et al., 2002), engaging more frequently in acts such as kicking, pinching, and hitting. Boys are also more likely to defy authority and to damage property.

When other forms of aggression are considered, however, the situation becomes more complex (Eagly & Steffen, 1986; Hyde, 1984, 1986). Although boys are more likely to display physical aggression, girls are more likely to engage in what is called *relational aggression*. In relational aggression, girls attempt to harm other children, particularly other girls, through the social relationships that girls are taught to value. This is done through activities such as gossip and exclusion (Crick et al., 2001; Offord, Lipman, & Duku, 2001; Underwood, 2003). Gender differences in the types of aggression that children use have been found to occur as young as preschool (Ostrov & Keating, 2004) and to persist through high school (Cillessen & Mayeux, 2004; Rose, Swenson, & Waller, 2004).

Prosocial Behavior Girls are generally rated as more generous, helpful, and cooperative than boys by their teachers and peers (Shigetomi, Hartmann, & Gelfand, 1981; Zarbatany et al., 1985). Some evidence suggests that girls have better emotional perspective-taking abilities and experience more empathy (Dodge & Feldman, 1990; Zahn-Waxler et al., 1992; Zahn-Waxler, Robinson, & Emde, 1992). But when researchers have examined children's actual behavior, they have found few sex differences (Eagly & Crowley, 1986; Eisenberg, Martin, & Fabes, 1996); thus, if a difference exists in prosocial behavior, it is very small.

Activities and Interests Gender differences in activity preferences emerge between the first and second birthdays. Boys show more interest in blocks, transportation toys (such as trucks and airplanes), and objects that can be manipulated. They also engage in more large-motor activities, including rough-and-tumble play (DiPietro, 1981; O'Brien & Huston, 1985; Roopnarine, 1984).

Girls prefer doll play, dress-up, artwork, and domestic play, such as cooking. They also prefer more sedentary activities, such as reading and drawing, over more vigorous ones. This sex difference in participation in

Sex differences in social behavior can be clearly demonstrated. Studies in diverse countries show, for example, that boys are more physically aggressive and competitive than girls. Does this mean that girls are not aggressive or competitive or that they express aggression and competition differently? (Eastcutt/Mamatiuk/The Image Works)

vigorous physical activity is maintained throughout childhood and adolescence (Bradley et al., 2000). However, whereas boys tend to stick to a rather narrowly defined group of toys and games, girls display a wider range of interests over time and are more likely than boys to engage in activities preferred by the opposite sex (Bussey & Bandura, 1992; Eisenberg, Tryon, & Cameron, 1984; Fagot & Leinbach, 1993).

Because sex differences in play preferences emerge so early, it is tempting to believe that somehow boys are born to prefer mechanical toys and girls to prefer dolls. As we shall see, however, parents encourage sex-typed play from the first months of life. This is especially true for boys, who experience considerable pressure from both parents and peers to play with toys deemed appropriate for their sex.

In addition to differing in play preferences, boys and girls exhibit sex-stereotyped television preferences (Huston & Wright, 1998). Boys prefer noneducational cartoons, action programs, and sports. Girls lose interest in noneducational cartoons before boys and prefer shows with relationship themes (Wright et al., 2001).

Beginning during the preschool years, boys use computers more than girls do (Funk, Germann, & Buchman, 1997; Greenfield, 1994; Huston et al., 1999; Rideout et al., 1999). One national survey of children age 2 to 18 found the gender difference to lie in computer use in school. While more boys than girls reported using (or were reported by parents to have used) computers in school the day before, there were no differences in the percentage using computers outside of school (Roberts et al., 1999). These findings are consistent with the results of other studies indicating that boys tend to monopolize computers in the classroom, particularly in periods of uncontrolled access (Cassell & Jenkins, 1998; Kinnear, 1995; Schofield, 1995).

Boys spend far more time playing computer and video games than do girls (Harrell et al., 1997; Roberts et al., 1999; Wright et al., 2001). This gender gap persists despite the increasing availability of electronic games for girls (Rideout et al., 2003; Subrahmanyam & Greenfield, 1998). An analysis of popular games revealed that nearly 80 percent had aggressive or violent themes (Dietz, 1998; Rideout, Vandewater, & Wartella, 2003). These themes appeal primarily to boys, who often prefer violent games, including those that depict realistic human violence (Funk et al., 1997; Gailey, 1996).

By adolescence, males express greater interest in mathematics and science than do females (Gardner, 1998; Wigfield et al., 2002). A cross-national study (based on data collected in 1990–1991) confirmed the same pattern of interests in the United States, Japan, and Taiwan. Interestingly, the sex difference was smaller in the United States than in the two Asian communities. The researchers attributed the cultural difference to the more egalitarian gender roles found in the United States (Evans, Schweingruber, & Stevenson, 2002). In addition, recent studies reveal that the gender difference in interest in mathematics and science is decreasing in the United States. One survey of a national sample found that although 59 percent of male adolescents reported preferring mathematics and science over English and social studies, 53 percent of females did as well (Gallup Poll, 1997). Although many females are as interested in science as males, their specific interests within the domain of science differ. Male students tend to be more interested in the physical sciences. Female students, in contrast, tend to express more interest in the biological sciences (Adamson et al., 1998; Burkam, Lee, & Smerdon, 1997; Jones, Howe, & Rua, 2000).

Friends and Companions Children's social relationships show striking sex differences. Beginning in early childhood, boys play in larger groups, whereas girls generally limit their group size to two or three. Boys report having a greater number of friends. Girls have fewer but more intimate friendships.

Computer games for young girls significantly lack themes of violence, but with this exception, boys and girls use computers similarly. During adolescence, no sex differences have been found in the use of the computer for chatting, visiting Web sites, using e-mail, doing schoolwork, or using the computer in a job (Gallup Poll, 1997; Roberts et al., 1999). In addition, adolescent males and females are equally confident about their computer abilities and equally skilled (Gallup Poll, 1997; North & Noyes, 2002). (Kim Karpeles/Alamy)

Links to Related Material
In Chapters 14 and 15, you will learn more about the development of aggression, prosocial behavior, and children's friendships.

Test Your Mastery...

Boys' and girls' groups also are characterized by different interactional processes. Interactions among girls tend to involve more self-disclosure and intimacy (Brown, Way, & Duff, 1999; Lansford & Parker, 1999). Social interaction among boys often involves issues of dominance and leadership, whereas girls' interactions stress turn taking and equal participation by group members (Benenson, 1993; Benenson, Apostoleris, & Parnass, 1997; Maccoby, 1990, 1995). When school-aged children were placed in mixed-gender pairs to solve simple arithmetic problems, it was found that boys used more controlling acts and more negative interruptions whereas girls used more affiliating acts; interestingly, when placed in same-gender pairs, all children used more collaborative types of communication (Leman, Ahmed, & Ozarow, 2005). When attempting to resolve a conflict or to influence others to do something, boys take a more heavy-handed approach, often using threats or physical force. Girls are more likely to use verbal persuasion or to abandon the conflict altogether (Leaper, Tenenbaum, & Shaffer, 1999; Miller, Danaher, & Forbes, 1986; Pettit et al., 1990; Sheldon, 1990, 1992).

Learning Objective 13.1: *Describe physical, cognitive, and social/personality sex differences that researchers have found.*

1. What physical sex differences have researchers found?
2. What cognitive sex differences have researchers found?
3. What social and personality sex differences have researchers found?

Influences on Sex Differences and Gender Role Development

Learning Objective 13.2
Compare and contrast biological and social influences on sex differences and gender role development.

Research has clearly shown the existence of a number of sex differences. Understanding the origins of those differences has proved a greater challenge. In the following sections, we discuss how biological factors and socialization contribute to the development of sex differences and gender roles. We turn first to biological factors. These include the genetic, structural, and physiological processes that distinguish males and females.

Biological Influences

Sex differentiation
The biological process through which physical differences between sexes emerge.

Like most other species, humans exhibit *sexual dimorphism*—that is, the male and female are biologically different for the purpose of reproduction. The process through which these biological differences emerge is called **sex differentiation**. Many of the biological influences on gender role development appear to result from nature's preparing the individual in this way to participate in the reproduction process.

Links to Related Material.
In Chapter 3, you read about the role that the sex chromosomes play in determining gender. Here, you learn more about prenatal gender differentiation and the influence on development of prenatal exposure to sex hormones.

Genes and Hormones As you read in Chapter 3, the sex chromosomes—the X and the Y chromosomes—determine whether individuals develop as boys or girls. The X chromosome is similar in size to the autosomes and carries a good deal of genetic material, whereas the Y chromosome is much smaller and has many fewer genes. When the pair of sex chromosomes inherited from the parents consists of two X chromosomes (XX), the person is female; when it is made up of one of each type (XY), the person is male.

The sex chromosomes have no influence at all on the fertilized zygote for about 6 weeks. At that time, if the embryo is genetically male (XY), the Y chromosome causes a portion of the embryo to become the male gonadal structure—the testes. Once this is accomplished, the Y chromosome does not appear to play any further role in the process of sex differentiation. If the embryo is genetically female (XX), the sex chromosomes produce no change at 6 weeks. At 10 to 12 weeks, however, one X chromosome causes a portion of the embryo to become female gonads—the ovaries. From this point on, sex differentiation is guided primarily by the hormones produced by the testes and the ovaries. In addition to genes on the sex chromosomes, other genes can affect males and females differently. Usually, this occurs when the expression of a trait requires the presence of certain levels of sex hormones. Such traits are called **sex-limited traits.** The gene for baldness, for example, may be carried by either men or women, but the characteristic appears primarily in men because high levels of male hormones are needed for it to be expressed.

Sex-limited traits
Genes that affect males and females differently but that are not carried on the sex chromosomes.

A major step in sex differentiation begins when the newly formed embryonic gonads begin to secrete hormones of different types. The internal sex organs of the fetus become either male or female in the third month of gestation. When a Y chromosome causes testes to develop in the embryo, these glands secrete hormones called *androgens*, which cause the male internal reproductive organs to grow (they also secrete a chemical that causes the female organs to shrink). At 5 months, if androgens are present, the external sex organs also develop as male, producing a penis and scrotal sac. If androgens are not present at 3 months, the internal sex organs, and later the external sex organs, develop as female. The hormones produced mainly by the ovaries, estrogen and progesterone, do not play their principal role in sex differentiation until puberty.

Somewhere between 3 and 8 months after conception, sex hormones are believed to affect the development and organization of the fetal brain. The two major types of organizing effects involve hormonal regulation (how often the body releases various hormones) and brain lateralization.

Hormonal Regulation and Abnormalities In adult humans, the pituitary gland controls the production of hormones by the gonads. One effect of these hormones is to activate certain social behaviors, including aggression, maternal behaviors, and sexual activity. Some theorists believe that sex differences in these and other social behaviors may be largely controlled by such hormones (Hines & Green, 1991). In support of this idea, researchers have given pregnant hamsters or monkeys extra doses of testosterone (a type of androgen), for example, and found that the female offspring tended to be more aggressive, dominant, and adventurous—characteristics more common in males of the species (Hines, 1982).

Are naturally occurring variations in testosterone during the prenatal period related to the gender role behavior of human offspring? Researchers measured testosterone levels in maternal blood samples obtained during routine prenatal care (Hines et al., 2002). When their children were 3 years of age, the parents completed a questionnaire about their children's involvement with sex-typed toys, games, and activities. Among girls, higher levels of testosterone during the prenatal period were linked with lower levels of sex typing; that is, they played with toys typed for both boys and girls. Among boys, however, there was no relationship between prenatal testosterone levels and gender role behavior.

Another way to study the effects of hormones on development is to study cases of hormonal abnormality, such as **congenital adrenal hyperplasia (CAH).** CAH occurs when too much androgen is produced during pregnancy. This overproduction usually is the result of an inherited enzyme deficiency that causes the adrenal glands to produce androgens, regardless of the presence or absence of testes (Breedlove & Hampson, 2002). This problem typically begins after the internal sex organs have been formed but before the external sex organs appear. The effects on males of the extra dose of androgens are fairly mild. These boys are somewhat more inclined toward intense physical activity than are normal boys, but they do not appear to be more aggressive or antisocial (Berenbaum & Hines, 1992; Berenbaum & Snyder, 1995; Hines & Kaufman, 1994).

If, however, the fetus is genetically female (XX), she will have ovaries and normal internal sex organs, but the excessive androgen will cause the external organs to develop in a masculine direction. Often the clitoris will be very large, resembling a penis, and sometimes a scrotal sac will develop (although it will be empty, because there are no testes).

In a number of reported cases, such females have been mistaken at birth for males and raised as boys (Money & Annecillo, 1987). In most cases, however, the problem is discovered at birth and corrected by surgically changing the external sex organs and by administering drugs to reduce the high levels of androgens. Although these procedures return the girls to biological normality, the early androgen exposure appears to have some long-term effects. CAH females often have better spatial abilities (but poorer verbal skills) than normal females (Kelso et al., 2000). Many of these girls also become "tomboys," preferring rough outdoor play and traditional male-stereotyped toys, while having little interest in dolls, jewelry, or activities typical of young females (Leveroni & Berenbaum, 1998).

Congenital adrenal hyperplasia (CAH)
A recessive genetic disorder in which the adrenal glands produce unusually high levels of male hormones known as androgens.

BOX 13.2 When Genotype and Phenotype Don't Match

Both biology and society have provided researchers with test cases that demonstrate the critical role that prenatal hormones play in the development of gender-typed behavior. In one landmark case in the 1960s, one of a pair of identical 8-month-old twin boys suffered severe injury to his penis following an accident during circumcision. Learning that it would not be possible to reconstruct the penis, the anguished parents sought advice from Dr. John Money, a leading sex researcher at Johns Hopkins University.

Dr. Money believed that it would be better for the boy to live as a female than as a physically deformed male. He recommended that the child be raised as a girl. This would involve surgical construction of female genitalia and hormone treatments. In the hope of giving their baby the best chance for a normal life, the parents agreed and proceeded to raise their son—renamed Brenda—as a girl, assured by the doctors that she would remain unaware of her original biology.

The details of this extraordinary case were first made public in 1972 (Money & Ehrhardt, 1972). In the report, the authors mentioned Brenda's tomboyishness but focused primarily on the ways in which her behavior and interests conformed to female stereotypes, especially in contrast to those of her identical twin brother. In this and subsequent updates on the twins' development, the intervention was portrayed as an unqualified success (Money, 1975).

The case received a great deal of attention in both the scientific literature and the popular press. *Time Magazine* opined, "This dramatic case provides strong support . . . that conventional patterns of masculine and feminine behavior can be altered. It also casts doubt on the theory that major sexual differences, psychological as well as anatomical, are immutably set by the genes at conception" (*Time*, 1973, cited in Colapinto, 2000, p. 69).

In reality, the case turned out to offer strong support for the biological determinants of psychological gender. From early on, Brenda displayed more interest in toys and activities commonly preferred by boys despite the parents' best efforts to encourage stereotypically female interests and behavior. Everyone, including her twin brother, Brian, noticed Brenda's masculinity.

Brenda's boyish looks and mannerisms elicited daily teasing and ridicule from peers as early as kindergarten. During early adolescence, Brenda made a brief but concerted effort to look and act more feminine, but the result was an appearance so unusual that even strangers would stop and stare. Moreover, Brenda did not *feel* like a girl—she felt like a freak.

Finally, Brenda rebelled. She abandoned her efforts to dress and behave like a girl, resisted the annual visits to the research

David Reimer's difficult childhood as Brenda was captured in this book by John Colapinto, *As Nature Made Him: The Boy Who Was Raised as a Girl.* ("As Nature Made Him: The Boy Who Was Raised as a Girl," by John Colapinto. Courtesy of Harper-Collins Publishers)

hospital where she was treated, and refused to undergo the vaginal surgery needed to complete her transformation. When Brenda was 14, the physicians assigned to her case declared the sex reassignment a total failure and advised Brenda's parents to tell her the truth. Brenda decided immediately to take steps to return to her original gender as a male and took the name David. He eventually married and became father to three stepchildren.

In 2004, at the age of 38, depressed over the loss of his job, recently separated from his wife, and grieving his twin brother who had died two years previously, David took his own life. As is often the case, David's suicide appears to have had multiple causes. It is difficult to say how much of a role his nightmare childhood finally played in his decision to end his life.

It was many years before the rest of the world learned the truth about the twins. Milton Diamond, a biologist who specialized in the effects of prenatal sex hormones on development and who had for years expressed skepticism about the case, and Keith Sigmundson, a psychiatrist who had been involved in the twins' treatment, convinced David to go public with his story (Diamond & Sigmundson, 1997). In 2000, a book was published about his life, *As Nature Made Him: The Boy Who Was Raised as a Girl*, by John Colapinto.

In retrospect, one of the most remarkable aspects of this case is that so many people readily accepted the premise that it would be easy to change a boy into a girl. One explanation is that the prevailing view in the United States in the 1960s and early 1970s was that sexual orientation and sex-typed behavior, like many other behaviors, were primarily the products of socialization and different types of behavioral reinforcement. Today, the view is nearly the opposite, and many scholars warn that experiential factors, rather than biological ones, are being overlooked (Lewontin, 2000; Oyama, 2000).

Androgen insensitivity
A genetic defect in males that prevents the body cells from responding to androgens, the masculinizing hormones.

Another type of hormonal disorder is known as **androgen insensitivity,** a genetic defect in males that prevents the body cells from responding to androgens, the masculinizing hormones. The testes will produce hormones, but neither internal nor external male sex organs will develop. The substance that usually shrinks the potential female internal sex organs will be effective, however, leaving the fetus with neither a uterus nor an internal male system. The external organs will develop as female. Studies have shown that androgen-insensitive individuals are generally feminine in appearance, preferences, and abilities (Breedlove & Hampson, 2002).

Taken together, evidence from animals and humans suggests that fetal sex hormones play an important part in producing differences between males and females. But hormonal processes are complex, and scientists still do not understand exactly how they interact with socialization processes.

Brain Lateralization As you will recall from Chapter 6, the human brain is divided into left and right hemispheres that perform different functions. The left half both controls and receives information from the right side of the body, including the right ear, hand, and foot and the right visual field of each eye. The right hemisphere controls and receives information from the left side. The left hemisphere is primarily responsible for language and speech processes, whereas the right side appears to be more involved with quantitative and spatial abilities (Springer & Deutsch, 1998).

Because the division of these functions corresponds to the cognitive sex differences discussed in this chapter, some psychologists believe that differences in brain lateralization may be important for understanding certain differences in male and female behavior. For example, as noted earlier, some data suggest that males are more lateralized—that is, their left and right hemispheres function more independently—than are females (Bryden, 1982; McGlone, 1980).

Studies of language and verbal abilities provide some support for the idea that brain lateralization plays a role in gender differences. For example, sex differences in hemisphere specialization have been found in both 3- and 6-month-old infants. When they responded to recordings of a voice speaking, female infants showed stronger brain-wave reactions to right-ear (left-hemisphere) presentations, whereas male infants showed stronger reactions to left-ear (right-hemisphere) presentations (Shucard & Shucard, 1990; Shucard et al., 1981). At 2 and 3 years of age, both sexes begin to process verbal stimuli (such as spoken words) through the right ear and nonverbal stimuli (such as music) through the left ear (Harper & Kraft, 1986; Kamptner, Kraft, & Harper, 1984). But at this point, males begin to show evidence of greater lateralization than females—for example, performing much better in response to verbal stimuli presented in the right ear than the left ear but showing the opposite tendency for nonverbal stimuli (Kraft, 1984).

Other research has reported that verbal abilities in males whose left hemispheres have been damaged (such as through strokes or tumors) are much more impaired than are those in females with a similar degree of damage in that area (McGlone, 1980; Sasanuma, 1980). More recently, studies using functional magnetic resonance imaging have shown that when males perform tasks involving sounds, activation is more localized to a specific region of the left hemisphere, whereas females show more activation in both hemispheres (Shaywitz et al., 1995). These results suggest that language functioning in females is more equally spread between the two hemispheres.

The role of brain lateralization in spatial abilities has also been examined in a study of children's haptic (touch) performance. Children in the study first felt a pair of hidden shapes, one with each hand, for 10 seconds. They were then asked to pick out the two shapes from a visual display. For boys, left-hand (right-hemisphere) performance was better than right-hand performance. For girls, left- and right-hand performances were equal (Witelson, 1976). The evidence from research on brain lateralization suggests that some sex differences may literally exist in our brains.

Social Influences

Clearly, biological factors make important contributions to gender role development. They do not, however, operate in isolation. Rather, biological processes interact with environmental forces in shaping gender development. Environmental influences on the development of gender are usually viewed in terms of socialization. The socialization of gender occurs on mul-

Questions for Thought and Discussion

How are sexual identity and sex-typed behavior a product of biology? To what extent are they a product of environment? How would you describe the relationship between these factors?

What are these girls learning about being female in their society? What parts do role models and the differential treatment of males and females in their society play in these girls' gender scripts and behavior? (John Birdsall/The Image Work)

Questions for Thought
and Discussion
In what settings and social roles do children learn the behaviors and attributes regarded as appropriate for their gender? How important is it that males and females have equal access to various social roles?

tiple levels, and includes schools, parents, peers, and the larger society. The following sections highlight two means of socialization—modeling and differential treatment of boys and girls.

Society and the Media In all cultures, children are socialized to gender roles, although the specifics of these roles may differ across time and place. One way children learn about gender roles is through modeling, by observing those around them. Modeling is a powerful means of transmitting values, attitudes, beliefs, and behavioral practices from generation to generation (Bandura, 1986). Gender knowledge is no exception.

In many societies, mass media have greatly expanded the variety of models available to children. Television, especially, communicates a great deal about social practices and behavior. Analyses of the contents of both network programs and commercials—in the United States and around the world—indicate that TV has generally portrayed characters in traditional gender roles (Allan & Coltrane, 1996; Craig, 1992; Furnam, Abramsky, & Gunter, 1997; Gilly, 1988; Signorelli, 2001; Signorelli & Bacue, 1999). This is especially the case for children's noneducational cartoons (Leaper et al., 2002; Thompson & Zerbinos, 1995, 1997). Thus, it should not be surprising that children who are the heaviest TV viewers also hold the most stereotyped perceptions of male and female sex roles (Luecke-Aleksa et al., 1995; McGhee & Frueh, 1980; Signorella, Bigler, & Liben, 1993).

A second way in which children learn about gender roles in society is through observing and experiencing the differential treatment of males and females. Differential treatment can take various forms (Bussey & Bandura, 1999; Leaper, 2002). In some cultures, access to formal education and different types of vocational apprenticeships differs for males and females. Societies also have division of labor by sex, although the specific tasks assigned to each gender and the extent to which tasks are shared across genders vary widely across cultures.

Differential treatment is also evident in the social opportunities and experiences available to males and females. For instance, worldwide, boys are generally granted greater autonomy than girls. They have greater freedom of movement and can be found farther from home without adult supervision (Whiting & Edwards, 1988). As a consequence, males have greater opportunities to explore the environment, pursue risky adventures, and work out interpersonal conflicts without adult intervention.

An additional type of differential treatment concerns the expectations societies have for boys' and girls' behaviors. Different expectations translate into different socialization pressures. In Japan, for example, the expectations for self-control are greater for girls than for boys. Consequently, girls exhibit greater self-regulatory capabilities at a younger age than do boys (Olson & Kashiwagi, 2000).

Questions for Thought
and Discussion
Have you observed or experienced gender bias from teachers? Why do you think this occurs? How important do you think it is to counter this tendency, and why?

Teachers Do boys and girls experience differential treatment in the school? Some evidence indicates that teachers treat boys and girls differently. For example, studies show that teachers give more attention to boys than to girls, although much of that contact is negative. For instance, boys receive more disapproval and scolding for misbehavior than girls (Huston, 1983; Pollack, 1998). Also, some studies have found that teachers call on boys more often and allow them more time to speak (AAUW, 1992; Duffy, Warren, & Walsh, 2001; Sadker & Sadker, 1994). However, other studies do not find a difference in the amount of attention teachers direct to male and females students (Kleinfeld, 1996). Interestingly, girls see themselves as participating in class as much as boys. Moreover, when asked whom teachers call on most often and pay the most attention to, the majority of both middle and high school males and females report a **gender bias**—in this case favoring girls over boys (AAUW/Greenberg-Lake, 1990; Harris, 1997).

If boys do receive more attention from teachers than girls, it may be in part because they tend to actively demand attention. A majority of over 1,000 sixth- through twelfth-grade teachers responding to a survey reported that boys demanded more attention in the classroom than girls (Harris, 1997). A recent observational study of middle school science classrooms found that half of the teachers called on boys more often than girls, but that in these classrooms the boys volunteered to answer questions more often than the girls (Altermatt, Jovanovic, & Perry, 1998).

Some studies suggest that teachers attribute greater ability in math and science to males (Li, 1999), although other studies do not find a gender difference in teachers' beliefs about ability (Helwig, Anderson, & Tindal, 2001). Teachers' beliefs that girls and boys are different in abilities or interests are reflected in the number and kinds of questions they ask of each gender, as well as the amount of encouragement they provide (She, 2000).

Evidence that girls and boys have different experiences in school has fostered concern that schools shortchange students of both genders. Some advocates argue that schools undermine girls' self-confidence and career aspirations and discourage interest in traditionally male domains such as math and science (AAUW, 1992; Oakes, 1990). Partly in response to these assertions, schools and other organizations have done much to transform the educational experiences of many girls. With the exception of physics, female high school students now enroll in as many mathematics and science courses as males (Sanders, Koch, & Urso, 1997), and they achieve scores within 5 to 10 points of males on standardized tests of mathematics and science (National Center for Education Statistics, 1997). In 2002 average scores on science achievement tests for 13-year-olds were the same for boys and girls (National Center for Education Statistics, 2003).

Concern is now growing that schools are failing to meet the needs of boys (AAUW, 2001; Gally, 2002; Lesko, 2000; Noble & Bradford, 2000; Skelton, 2001). Boys do appear to be falling behind girls in educational achievement. The gender gap in reading and writing has actually widened, with males scoring on average about 15 points lower than girls on standardized tests (National Center for Education Statistics, 1997; 2003).

Parents Children's learning about gender roles through modeling and differential treatment is also influenced by parents. Because parents are important figures in children's lives, they are especially significant models for what it means to be male or female (Bussey & Bandura, 1999). It can be difficult to isolate the effects of modeling by parents from other models, however, such as television characters, classmates, and other adults.

One way to study parental influences is to examine gender role development in families in which parents' roles deviate from cultural norms. That is, parents model behavior different from what children typically observe in other settings. Researchers have examined the gender role development of children in single-parent households; in alternative households, such as are found in communes; and in households headed by same-sex parents. These studies find few differences in gender role development among children from different types of families (Anderson, Amlie, & Ytteroy, 2002; Golombok et al., 2003; Serbin, Powlishta, & Gulko, 1993; Stevens et al., 2002; Stevenson & Black, 1988; Weisner & Wilson-Mitchell, 1990). And when differences are found, they tend to be small and specific to children of a particular age, gender, or socioeconomic status.

The fact that researchers have had so little luck linking variations in gender role development to differences in parents' roles does not mean that no link exists. Rather,

Gender bias
Preferring or responding to children of one gender more positively or more often than the other.

Questions for Thought and Discussion
What models do the media offer for what it means to be male and female? How important were these models in shaping your gender role development? How did you decide which messages to pay attention to and which to ignore?

simply knowing whether a parent is, for example, married or employed reveals little about what children actually observe in the home. Studies that have examined parents' attitudes and behavior show that in homes where parents perform nontraditional jobs and chores, children hold less stereotyped ideas about the proper roles of men and women (Deutsch, Servis, & Payne, 2001; Hoffman & Youngblade, 1999; Serbin et al., 1993; Weisner, Garnier, & Loucky, 1994). Interestingly, however, even in homes where parents enthusiastically endorse egalitarian ideals, girls, and especially boys, often maintain strong preferences for sex-typed peers, toys, and clothing (Weisner & Wilson-Mitchell, 1990).

Differential treatment of boys and girls by their parents includes instruction, opportunities, and attitudes. For instance, parents are sometimes quite explicit in teaching sons or daughters skills traditionally associated with one or the other gender—as when fathers recruit sons, but not daughters, to help with home repairs. Differential treatment can be largely unconscious. You have seen, for example, that parents talk about emotions differently with sons and daughters. A consequence of this differential treatment is that boys and girls learn different ways of expressing and coping with emotions.

Studies show that parents also offer sons and daughters different opportunities, for example, for kinds of play (Lytton & Romney, 1991). During infancy, parents are more likely to physically stimulate boys than girls (Frisch, 1977; MacDonald & Parke, 1986), and this emphasis on physical play with boys is maintained during early childhood. Both mothers and fathers tend to engage in more physical play with sons and pretend play with daughters; however, rough physical play is especially likely among fathers and sons (Jacklin, DiPietro, & Maccoby, 1984; Lindsey & Mize, 2001; Lindsey, Mize, & Pettit, 1997).

In wealthy cultures that place a premium on play, differential treatment is also apparent in parents' selection of toys (Lytton & Romney, 1991). Parents tend to give boys more sports equipment, vehicles, and tools, and girls more dolls and toy kitchen sets (Fisher-Thompson, 1993; Rheingold & Cook, 1975; Robinson & Morris, 1986). In many families, infants are given sex-typed toys within the first few months of life—long before they can express any kind of toy preferences (Pomerleau et al., 1990). Children begin to demonstrate preferences for same-sex toys between their first and second birthdays. Parents encourage gender-appropriate play during this period by more often offering gender-appropriate or neutral toys than those traditionally viewed as appropriate for the other sex (Eisenberg et al., 1985; Wood, Desmarais, & Gugula, 2002). Parents are likely to express approval (smile, act excited, comment approvingly) for gender-appropriate play and activities and to respond negatively to behaviors considered characteristic of the other sex (Fagot & Hagan, 1991; Fagot & Leinbach, 1987; Leaper et al., 1995). Parents' gender typing of play tends to be stronger with sons than daughters, and this is especially true of fathers. Fathers appear to be more concerned that their male child be masculine and that their female child be feminine, whereas mothers tend to treat their sons and daughters alike (Bronstein, 1994; Fisher-Thompson, 1993; Jacklin et al., 1984; Lindsey et al., 1997; Siegal, 1987; Turner & Gervai, 1995).

Sex typing of play is important because different kinds of play provide opportunities to acquire and practice different skills. Female-stereotyped play, such as pretense involving domestic themes, encourages nurturance, communication skills, and emotional and social understanding. Pretense also depends more heavily on language than the kinds of activities parents more often enjoy with sons—such as physical play and construction activities. In turn, these male-stereotyped activities foster a different set of knowledge and abilities, including visual-spatial skills and physical strength, endurance, and coordination.

As children move into the elementary school years, parents begin to provide them with other kinds of experiences, such as dance classes, music lessons, and sports activities. One ongoing study of a group of approximately 600 children has found that parents provide different experiences for sons and daughters (Eccles et al., 2000). As shown in Table 13.2, these experiences tend to reflect gender stereotypes and to parallel gender differences in interests and achievement that emerge in later childhood and adolescence.

Alexia Fotopoulos spent her early years traveling with her mother Danielle and the other members of the Carolina Courage, a professional women's soccer team. What adult expectations regarding women and sports is Alexia likely to be exposed to? (© Chris Kelly/www.digitalsportsarchive.com)

TABLE 13.2 Parents' Provision of Experiences for Daughters and Sons (Grades 2, 3, and 5)

ACTIVITY	GIRLS	BOYS
Have child read to you	3.10	2.90
Play sports with child	2.63	3.36
Do active, outdoor activities with child	3.20	3.56
Take child to paid sporting event	1.71	1.91
Encourage child to do math- or science-related activities at home	4.01	4.35
Encourage child to work on or play with a computer outside of school	3.70	4.04
Encourage child to read	6.04	5.69
Encourage child to play competitive sports	3.58	4.43
Encourage child to play noncompetitive sports	4.54	4.94
Encourage child to take dance lessons	3.56	2.15
Encourage child to take dancing for fun	3.85	2.53
Encourage child to watch sports on TV	2.61	3.07
Encourage child to take music lessons	4.26	3.52
Encourage child to play a musical instrument	4.32	3.67
Enourage child to build, make, or fix things	3.83	4.67
Encourage child to learn cooking and other homemaking	4.01	3.59

Ratings were made on 7-point scales: 1 = *never/strongly discourage*; 7 = *almost every day/strongly encourage*. All differences between girls' and boys' mean ratings are statistically significant. What patterns do you find in these data?

SOURCE: Adapted by permission from J.S. Eccles, C. Freedman-Doan, P. Frome, J. Jacobs, & K.S. Yoon. (2000). Gender role socialization in the family: A longitudinal approach. In T. Eckes & H. M. Trautner (Eds.), *The Developmental Social Psychology of Gender*. Mahway, NJ: Erlbaum.

Parents often hold different expectations for sons and daughters. Even before newborns leave the hospital, parents use very different terms to describe their little boys (e.g., "firmer," "better coordinated," "stronger") (Rubin, Provenzano, & Luria, 1974). As infants become mobile, mothers tend to perceive their infant sons to have better crawling abilities—and daughters to have worse crawling skills—than they really do (Mondschein, Adolph, & Tamis-LeMonda, 2000). During middle childhood, parents rate sons as more capable in sports than daughters (Eccles et al., 2000), and when boys and girls achieve success in sports, parents attribute the success to different factors. Boys' sports achievements are attributed to "natural talent," whereas girls' achievements are attributed to "hard work" (Eccles, Jacobs, et al., 1993).

Parents hold different expectations for boys and girls in the academic realm as well. As noted earlier, parents believe daughters' reading ability to be greater than sons' (Eccles, Arbreton, et al., 1993; Wigfield et al., 2002). They also believe that mathematics is more natural for boys than for girls, and they tend to underestimate girls' mathematics abilities and overestimate boys' (Eccles et al., 2000). Similar findings have emerged in science (Tenenbaum & Leaper, 2003). As in mathematics, there is no gender difference in science aptitude or achievement during elementary school. Nonetheless, parents generally endorse the cultural stereotype that boys are better in science than girls.

Parents' gender-stereotyped expectations contribute to children's gender role development in two ways. First, the expectations lead parents to provide boys and girls with different opportunities to develop specific skills and competencies. Second, parents' views of their children's abilities influence children's own developing sense of competence and interests (Eccles et al., 2000; Tiedemann, 2000; Wigfield et al., 2002). Children whose parents rate their ability as low in a domain tend to rate their own ability lower than it really is.

Siblings Most studies of gender role socialization have focused on parents, peers, or non-family influences, such as schools and the media. Recently, researchers have begun to explore the impact that siblings have on gender role development, especially the potential impact of an opposite-sex sibling on one's interests, activities, and behavior.

Rust and colleagues (Rust et al., 2000) examined this question in a massive study of British children. Participants included over 2,000 3-year-olds with older siblings under the age of 12 and a comparable number of children without siblings (singletons). Parents completed a questionnaire that included items about children's toys, activities, and interpersonal characteristics. According to parents, preschoolers with same-sex older siblings engaged in more sex-typed play and exhibited more sex-typed interpersonal behavior than children with an older sibling of the opposite sex. The ratings for children without siblings fell between the two sibling groups.

Interestingly, having an older brother had a bigger effect on the younger siblings than having an older sister. Compared with singletons and children with older sisters, younger boys *and* girls with older brothers exhibited more masculinized toy and activity preferences and interpersonal characteristics, and less feminized ones. Although boys with older sisters exhibited more feminine interests and behaviors, the presence of an older sister did not decrease their masculine traits.

Why might having an older brother matter more? One possibility is that the activities of older brothers are more highly regarded. As you have seen, it is more acceptable for girls to behave like boys than for boys to behave like girls. And girls are more likely to imitate male models than boys are to imitate females.

Another possibility is that older brothers exert greater pressure on younger siblings to engage in the kinds of activities they prefer. Studies of preschool peer groups show that boys—at least among European American samples—use more forceful control tactics than girls, and consequently have more influence over girls than girls have over boys. Younger brothers may be less influenced by their older sisters both because sanctions against cross-sex play are stronger for boys and because the older sisters are less successful (or perhaps less interested) in inducing their little brothers to play with them or to play what the girls want to play.

Studies also suggest that older siblings continue to influence the gender role development and behavior of their younger brothers and sisters, sometimes even more than parents. One study (McHale et al., 2001) even found that the gender role orientations of older siblings (ages 10 to 12 years) were strong predictors of second-borns' gender role attitudes, sex-typed personality characteristics, and masculine leisure activities.

Sibling influence can extend to one's relations with peers, especially among females. Compared with girls with older sisters, girls with older brothers reported more controlling behavior with their friends. These findings suggest that girls learn male-typical control strategies in their interactions with their older brothers, which they then utilize in their friendships (Updegraff, McHale, & Crouter, 2000).

The extent to which siblings contribute to one another's gender role development varies depending on the quality of their relationship, the amount of time they spend together, exposure to other socialization influences, and so forth. Moreover, some children may be more open to the influence of an opposite-sex sibling. For example, one study found that having a brother and the associated opportunities to engage in male-stereotyped play enhanced girls' spatial abilities, but only for girls believed to have an inherited predisposition to acquire spatial skills fairly easily. Girls for whom spatial tasks were expected to be challenging did not benefit from having a brother and, in fact, developed better spatial skills when there were no boys in the house (Casey, Nuttall, & Pezaris, 1999).

Peers The peer group is another powerful socialization force in children's lives. Studies consistently show that peers reinforce one another for engaging in gender-typed play and punish those who deviate from established norms. Although boys and girls are both criticized by peers for cross-sex play, the consequences are especially severe for boys (Carter & McCloskey, 1984; Fagot, 1977; Lamb & Roopnarine, 1979; Zucker et al., 1995).

TABLE 13.3 Under What Circumstances Is It Permissible to Have Contact with the Other Gender in Middle Childhood?

Rule: The contact is accidental.

Example: You're not looking where you are going and you bump into someone.

Rule: The contact is incidental.

Example: You go to get some lemonade and wait while two children of the other gender get some. (There should be no conversation.)

Rule: The contact is in the guise of some clear and necessary purpose.

Example: You may say, "Pass the lemonade," to persons of the other gender at the next table. No interest in them is expressed.

Rule: An adult compels you to have contact.

Example: "Go get that map from X and Y and bring it to me."

Rule: You are accompanied by some of your own gender.

Two girls may talk to two boys though physical closeness with your own partner must be maintained and physical intimacy with the others is disallowed.

Rule: The interaction or contact is accompanied by disavowal.

You say someone is ugly or hurl some other insult or (more commonly for boys) push or throw something at them as you pass by.

SOURCE: Reprinted by permission from L.A. Sroufe, C. Bennett, M. Englund, J. Urban, & S. Shulman. (1993). The significance of gender boundaries in preadolescence: Conntemporary correlates and antecedents of boundary relations and maintenance. *Child Development, 64*, 455–466.

Children actively maintain strictures against cross-sex interaction throughout middle childhood. One revealing study of preadolescents at a summer camp described a set of "rules" that dictate children's interactions with members of the opposite sex (see Table 13.3). These guidelines have come to be known as "the cootie rules," because children observing them often behave as though they have been contaminated by just being near a member of the opposite sex (Sroufe et al., 1993). Basically, the rules state that one cannot freely choose to interact with a peer of the opposite sex, but they acknowledge that contact is sometimes inevitable or unavoidable. Under those circumstances, it is acceptable. Interestingly, children who adhere most closely to the rules and maintain them most actively are liked the most by peers and judged to be most socially competent by adults.

It is not surprising that children spend much of their time in the company of same-sex peers. In some societies, **gender segregation** is imposed by adults, who manage children's lives in ways that separate boys and girls. For instance, in some societies, boys are assigned chores (such as herding) that take them away from home, whereas girls are given domestic duties that keep them near adult women and other girls (Whiting & Edwards, 1988). In other societies, children attend single-sex schools or are kept largely separate in

Gender segregation
The physical separation of children into same-sex groups.

Children develop their gender identies in the context of same-sex peer groups, which have a powerful influence on social and emotional development. In contrast, gender role development during adolescence takes place in mixed-sex peer groups. How is gender segregation supported by strong social norms in the culture of childhood? (Ellen B. Senisi/The Image Works)

other ways. As you have seen, however, gender segregation also prevails in societies where children are free to associate—indeed, are *encouraged* to associate—with opposite-sex peers. Gender segregation emerges at around age 3 and is routinely observed in mixed-sex settings, such as day care and preschool. Although children regularly play with the opposite sex in homes and in neighborhoods, they have a powerful tendency to seek out companions of the same sex and to avoid children of the opposite sex (Hartup, 1983; Leaper, 1994; Maccoby & Jacklin, 1974).

The causes of gender segregation are not well understood (Fagot, Rodgers, & Leinbach, 2000; Maccoby, 2000; Powlishta et al., 2001). One explanation is that children are naturally attracted to children with play styles that are compatible with their own, and boys and girls exhibit different play styles beginning at an early age (Moller & Serbin, 1996). However, children tend to react positively to same-sex peers before they have had time to learn about their play styles (Martin, 1989; Serbin & Sprafkin, 1986). Children also exhibit a preference for same-sex adults (Serbin & Sprafkin, 1986). Children's preference for same-sex companions extends to "own-sex" favoritism, which colors their perception of a wide variety of sex-typed traits (Powlishta, 1995).

Whatever the causes of gender segregation, same-sex groupings are important for children's gender role development. As we will discuss further in Chapter 15, boy and girl groups differ in size, nature of activities, and norms for social interaction. According to Eleanor Maccoby (1998), a prominent gender theorist, the dynamics of interaction in boys and girls groups are so different that the groups constitute separate "cultures of childhood." These "peer cultures," in turn, foster the development of distinct sets of socioemotional skills and propensities.

Learning Objective 13.2: *Compare and contrast biological and social influences on sex differences and gender role development.*

1. How does biology influence sex differences and gender role development?
2. What are the various social influences that have been found on sex differences and gender role development?

The Child's Active Participation in Gender Role Development

So far, our discussion of socialization portrays children as responding passively to pressures from outside. However, young children play an active role in their own gender socialization, both through selecting which models they will attend to and what beliefs they construct about gender. Children actively participate in their gender role socialization through self-selecting processes such as their selection of models. Although children of both genders can learn male and female gender stereotypes by viewing models, children tend to focus on models of their own gender. Children are better able to recall and imitate the behavior of same-sex models (Bussey & Bandura, 1984, 1992; Perry & Bussey, 1979). In addition, children are sensitive to the gender appropriateness of the model's activity. If a male child, for example, believes that a behavior is "female," he is unlikely to imitate it even if it is modeled by a male (Masters, 1979; Raskin & Israel, 1981).

Self-Selecting Processes

The tendency to attend more to self-select same-sex models is especially strong for boys, who often resist imitating behaviors modeled by females. In contrast, although girls prefer to imitate adult women, they will also imitate adult men (Bussey & Perry, 1982; Slaby & Frey, 1975). Generally, both boys and girls are more likely to imitate models perceived to be powerful. The greater likelihood of cross-sex imitation by girls may reflect their perception that culture invests males with higher status and greater rewards (Williams, 1987).

Questions for Thought and Discussion

What support is there for single-sex schools? Would single-sex schooling be more effective at certain ages? What criteria would you use to determine whether single-sex education "works" and benefits both sexes?

✔ *Test Your Mastery...*

Learning Objective 13.3

Explain and illustrate how children participate actively in their gender role development.

Another way that children participate in their gender socialization is through gradually internalizing external sanctions (such as negative reactions from parents and peers) as self-sanctions. As children acquire knowledge about the likely consequences of gender-linked conduct, they come to regulate their actions accordingly (Bussey & Bandura, 1999). Children's regulation of their own sex-typed play was graphically illustrated in a study that examined preschoolers' reactions to opportunities to play with a variety of gender-typed toys or toys linked to the other gender (Bussey & Bandura, 1992). When only other-sex toys were available, some boys attempted to have the stereotypically feminine toys removed. When that failed, the boys did all they could to avoid playing with the toys. One boy was reported to fling the baby doll across the room and turn his back on it. Others transformed the toys into more masculine props, such as using the egg beater in the kitchen set as a drill or gun. Children's self-ratings correspond to these behavioral observations. At age 4, both boys and girls rated themselves more positively when they played with own-sex toys and negatively when they played with toys usually associated with the other sex.

Other studies show that young children adapt their toy preferences to win approval from peers (Serbin et al., 1979). In one study (Banerjee & Lintern, 2000), boys and girls between the ages of 4 and 9 described their activity and toy preferences twice—once when alone and once when facing a group of same-sex peers. Older children did not change their self-descriptions in front of peers, but younger boys presented themselves as more sex-typed in front of peers than they did when alone.

Role of Cognition in Gender Identity

As you can see, the process of "self-socialization" requires a good deal of knowledge about gender and related attributes. What do children know about gender and when? Children participate actively in their gender role socialization through the knowledge and beliefs they construct about gender roles. This knowledge guides the gender-typed behaviors we commonly observe (Liben & Bigler, 2002; Martin, Ruble, & Szkrybalo, 2002), contributing to the development of cognitive models of change. Two approaches to understanding the role of cognition are Kohlberg's cognitive-developmental theory and schema theory.

Kohlberg's Cognitive-Developmental Approach The earliest cognitive model of gender role development was proposed by Lawrence Kohlberg (1966). Kohlberg believed that children construct their gender identity, or perception of themselves as male or female, from what they see and hear around them. Once established, this gender identity serves to organize and regulate children's gender learning and behavior.

A key component of Kohlberg's model is the development of **gender constancy**—the belief that one's own gender is fixed and irreversible (Kohlberg & Ullian, 1974; Slaby & Frey, 1975). Children who have achieved gender constancy understand that their sex is a permanent attribute tied to biological properties and that changes in superficial characteristics such as hair length, clothing, or activities will not turn them into a member of the opposite sex.

Kohlberg proposed that gender constancy develops in three stages—gender identity ("I am a boy/girl"), **gender stability** ("I will grow up to be a man/woman"), and **gender consistency** ("I cannot change my sex"). Furthermore, according to Kohlberg's theory, children reliably behave in gender-typed ways only after they have developed gender constancy late in the preschool years (Bhana, 1984; De Lisi & Gallagher, 1991; Munroe, Shimmin, & Munroe, 1984).

Studies of the development of gender constancy in societies as diverse as Egypt, Kenya, and Nepal, as well as North America, have confirmed that children the world over progress through Kohlberg's stages in the proposed order (Gibbons, 2000). The idea that gender constancy precedes children's adherence to gender norms, however, is not supported by empirical research. Children show gender-typed toy preferences, emulate same-sex models, and reward peers for gender-appropriate behavior years before they understand that gender is a permanent, unchanging attribute. Moreover, some studies have failed to

Gender constancy
The belief that one's own gender is fixed and irreversible.

Gender stability
The awareness that all boys grow up to be men and all girls become women.

Gender consistency
The recognition that an individual's gender remains the same despite changes in dress, hairstyle, activities, or personality.

demonstrate a link between levels of gender constancy and gender-appropriate preferences and behaviors, or have found just the opposite of what Kohlberg originally proposed (Ruble & Martin, 1998).

Schema Theory Another cognitive model for understanding children's construction of gender is *schema theory*—based on the idea that individuals have mental models for how things should be. Proponents of this approach explain developmental changes in children's gender role behavior in terms of mental models that children use to organize their experiences concerning gender. Children form **gender schemas**—cognitive representations of the characteristics associated with being either male or female (Bem, 1981; Liben & Signorella, 1987; Martin & Halverson, 1987). According to this theory, children categorize gender-relevant stimuli (people, toys, activities) as "for girls" or "for boys." These categorizations are an expression of our inborn tendency to organize and classify information from the environment, applied to the many gender-distinguishing cues (such as clothing, names, and occupations) in that environment.

The child then adopts one of the schemas—girl or boy—which affects the child in two ways. First, it prompts the child to pay greater attention to information relevant to his or her own gender. A girl may notice television ads for a new Disney Princess doll, for example, whereas a boy may be more attuned to commercials announcing the release of a new action hero movie. Second, it influences the child's self-regulated behavior. For instance, a girl may decide to play with Barbie dolls and a boy to take karate lessons (Bem, 1993; Martin, 1993; Powlishta, 1995).

Gender schema theory has much in common with Kohlberg's theory. In both approaches, for example, children are motivated to behave in ways that are consistent with what they know or believe about gender. An important difference between the two theories, however, is the level of knowledge or understanding required for the child to begin to act in accordance with gender norms. Kohlberg believed that children do not behave in sex-typed ways until they achieve gender constancy, a milestone not attained until late in the preschool years. According to gender schema theory, children begin to organize their experiences and behave in ways compatible with gender norms as soon as they can identify themselves as male or female—an achievement typically reached between the ages of 2 and 3.

Research supports the idea that young children use gender to categorize their world and that knowledge of gender categories influences children's processing of information. The link between gender role knowledge and gender-typed behavior is less straightforward. For example, children often show gender-typed toy preferences even before they can label themselves as girls or boys and before they can identify specific toys as more appropriate or typical for one gender or the other. These children may understand more about gender roles than they are given credit for (Levy, 1999; Liben & Bigler, 2002; Martin et al., 2002).

Some children show impressive knowledge of gender role stereotypes but nonetheless choose to behave in non–gender-typed ways (Martin, 1993; Martin et al., 2002). It is also the case that some children develop *idiosyncratic gender schemas*, or gender schemas that include dimensions more typically associated with the opposite sex. For instance, a "tomboy" may have a schema that is different from the schemas of more feminine girls (Liben & Bigler, 2002). In our chapter opening example, Kaylie appears to be developing a gender-typed schema of what being a "girl" means. Another 3-year-old girl, growing up with older sisters who are on the local girls' soccer team, a mother who is a carpenter, and an uncle who owns a florist shop down the street, may develop a gender schema that is less typically "feminine."

Learning Objective 13.3: *Explain and illustrate how children participate actively in their gender role development.*

1. What self-selecting processes do children demonstrate with regard to models and sanctions?
2. What role does cognition play in children's gender role development?

Gender schemas
Cognitive representations of the characteristics associated with being either male or female.

Questions for Thought and Discussion
What are some examples of things in your everyday life that you pay attention to or ignore probably because they relate to your gender schema?

✔ **Test Your Mastery...**

Gender Role Development

We have discussed several sources that influence children's gender roles. How does children's understanding of gender roles and gender stereotypes, as well as their gender-based behaviors and gender identity, develop over time? As you have read, by 3 years of age, almost all children display gender identity. Gender stability follows at about 4 years of age and gender consistency at about 5. Males and females progress through these stages at approximately the same rate (Bem, 1989; Fagot, 1985; Martin & Little, 1990). This progression has been demonstrated in a variety of cultures, although children in many non-Western cultures appear to proceed through the stages at later ages (Munroe, Shimmin, & Munroe, 1984). The development of gender knowledge is part of this process.

Learning Objective 13.4
Trace the development of gender role knowledge and behavior.

Development of Gender Knowledge

Research shows that children develop some knowledge about gender categories during the first 2 years of life. By just 2 months of age, infants can discriminate male and female voices (Jusczyk, Pisoni, & Mullennix, 1992). By the end of the first year, children are able to categorize people by gender on the basis of features such as voice pitch and hair length (Leinbach & Fagot, 1993; Patterson & Werker, 2002; Poulin-Dubois et al., 1994; Walker-Andrews et al., 1991).

Once the categories of male and female are established, children begin to associate other attributes with gender. By about 2, children can reliably sort pictures of males and females and their accessories (clothes, tools, and appliances) into separate piles and accurately point to pictures of things for males and things for females (Fagot, Leinbach, & Hagan, 1986; O'Brien & Huston, 1985). There is some evidence that toddlers also have some awareness of the typical activities of men and women at around age 2 (Poulin-Dubois et al., 2002). Within about 1 year, they are able to verbally label toys as for boys or for girls (Weinraub et al., 1984).

Over the course of early childhood, children begin to incorporate more abstract concepts into their gender stereotypes. For example, perhaps as early as age 2 and certainly by age 4, children come to associate hardness and items such as bears and eagles with boys and softness, flowers, butterflies, and the color pink with girls (Eichstedt et al., 2002; Leinbach, Hort, & Fagot, 1997). During middle childhood, children gradually add information about occupations, behavioral traits, and personality differences to their stereotypes (Best & Williams, 1993; Liben & Bigler, 2002; Serbin et al., 1993; Signorella et al., 1993).

Children's *gender stereotypes*—defined at the beginning of this chapter as beliefs regarding how males and females should behave—mirror those of the adults in their cultural communities (Williams & Best, 1990). Cross-cultural studies show that male stereotypes are generally learned earlier than female stereotypes, although there are exceptions. Female stereotypes are learned earlier in Germany and in Latin/Catholic cultures (Brazil, Chile, Portugal, Venezuela), where the adult-defined female stereotype is more positive than the male (Best, 2001).

Flexibility of Gender Stereotypes

Children's gender stereotypes change over the course of childhood, becoming more flexible. During the preschool years, most children view gender roles in inflexible, absolute terms (consistent with Piaget's preoperational stage of cognitive development) and consider cross-sex behaviors to be serious violations of social standards.

By middle childhood, children begin to realize that gender roles are socially determined rules and conventions that can be viewed flexibly and broken without major consequences (Serbin et al., 1993; Stoddart & Turiel, 1985; Trautner, 1992). This flexibility reflects several developmental achievements, including more advanced classification skills

BOX 13.2 Conversations with Men in Nontraditional Roles

Lavorick Robinson *is a 29-year-old preschool teacher from Odessa, Texas. He lives with his wife, Isabel, and their three children—Ashley age 4, Erik age 3, and Jalen age 5 months—in Lubbock, Texas. He has a B.A. in Human Development & Family Studies from Texas Tech University.*

" I always knew I wanted to work with kids. During the summer, I'd get jobs working with the Boys and Girls Club. After I finished school, I tried working with various age groups as a substitute teacher. I found I really liked working with the younger kids. They're a lot of fun."

In the fall of 2003, Lavorick answered an ad for an assistant teacher at Early Odyssey Developmental School, an NAEYC-accredited preschool program in Lubbock. He got the job and became lead teacher for the 3-year-old room in January 2005.

Lavorick says of his job, "There are days when I go home tired but rarely do I go home in a bad mood. I think I enjoy the kids as much as they enjoy me. Every day is fun. It's very fulfilling watching them grow and feeling like you're a part of that growth."

Lavorick believes that he can be particularly helpful to the children

Lavorick Robinson with two children from his preschool classroom. (Courtesy of Lavorick Robinson)

who don't have fathers living in their homes. "Some kids don't have a male figure in their lives. I can fill that void for them, and for the kids that do have a dad at home, I can be an extension of that role for them at school."

He feels that overall people in his life have been supportive of his choice to become a preschool teacher. He states, "I think a lot of men would find it fulfilling to work with kids, but for macho reasons are afraid to—what will their friends think and all that. I think young men shouldn't feel afraid of going into this field if they want to."

Stanley Bermudez *is a 40-year-old artist and stay-at-home dad. He lives with his wife and their two daughters—Lucia age 4, and Aida age 2—in Lubbock, Texas. Stanley is from Venezuela. He moved to Texas when he was 18 to study art at Sam Houston State University. Later, he went on to complete his Master's in Fine Arts at Radford University in Virginia.*

In 2001, his wife Maria was offered a full-time position as assistant professor in Marriage and Family Therapy at Texas Tech University. He states, "We both agreed it was important for one of us to be home with the kids, and we both agreed that it made sense under the circumstances for it to be me."

Stanley finds his role satisfying. "The kids are close to me. I love my Dad but I'm not as close to him as I am to my Mom. I like that my own daughters will come and talk to me about whatever is on their minds, just as they do with Maria."

As a dad, Stanley feels his parenting style differs somewhat from that of his wife's. "I wrestle and rough house with the kids more than Maria would. I also expose them to art a lot—we go to museums and art openings. Otherwise, I think what I do with them is pretty much the same as what Maria would do."

He describes his own family as very supportive of his decision to stay at home with the kids, but thinks that Maria's family

(Bigler & Liben, 1992; Trautner, 1992), a growing awareness of the cultural relativity of gender norms (Carter & Patterson, 1982; Damon, 1977; Levy, Taylor, & Gelman, 1995; Stoddart & Turiel, 1985), and an increasingly sophisticated understanding of biology. For instance, one study presented children with a story of a baby who had been raised on an island with only members of the opposite sex. When asked which gender characteristics the baby would eventually display, children younger than age 9 or 10 predicted that the baby's biological sex would determine its later characteristics. Children above that age, in contrast, believed that the baby would be more influenced by the social environment and so would adopt the characteristics of the opposite sex (Taylor, 1996).

The transition to junior high school appears to increase adolescents' flexibility toward the roles of males and females. This may occur because the fairly dramatic change in setting and routine forces young adolescents to rethink many of their previous ideas (Katz & Ksansnak, 1994). Nevertheless, in junior high and high school, reorganized gender stereotypes become increasingly rigid again (Alfieri, Ruble, & Higgins, 1996).

may be more ambivalent. "They ask me a lot, 'Have you gotten a job yet?' It's hard for them to understand—this is my job right now. I went to school to study art, and I have a chance to work on my art while I'm at home with the kids, plus I try to teach one art course each semester at the university. But what I'm doing is very important for the kids. I like that I can be with them. It is my job right now."

Stanley feels that his experience as a stay-at-home dad has strengthened his and Maria's marriage. "I'm involved with the kids day in and day out, and it has helped build respect between us. I have a better appreciation for Maria as a mother, and I think we are both more aware and accepting of each other's differences as parents."

When asked what he would like to share with others about his experience, Stanley stated, "Any man who becomes a father should try being a stay-at-home dad at least once, at least for a few months, just to see what it is like to be at home with the kids. Some men are laid off and end up being stay-at-home dads, but not out of choice. For me it was a choice. My advice to other dads is to try it and see what it takes. I think it can make you better appreciate what most women do, and also help you become closer to your kids."

Zach Laymon *is a 29-year-old massage therapist. He recently moved with his new wife Micah, to Hawaii, from Lubbock, Texas. Zach started out as a phlebotomist, then became a lab assistant, and finally managed the referral testing department within a lab at a hospital in Lubbock. However, he did not find his work at the hospital fulfilling. "People were never quick to thank you but always quick to jump on you. A friend was in massage school and I volunteered to be one of her practice massages. It was my first professional experience with massage and I thought it was amazing."*

Zach began attending the Healing Arts Institute in Lubbock while continuing to work full-time at the hospital. In 2001, he left the hospital to start his own business as a massage therapist. He observes, "I feel appreciated through the repeat

"Siblings," by Stanley Bermudez (Painting by S. Bermudez)

business of my clients. I have a feeling of financial success. I have built a practice from nothing and now I earn a good living with it. I feel like I'm hands-on helping people. In the hospital, drawing blood, people were tense when they came to me. Now, it's nice to feel that I'm really making a difference in people's lives. A person might come into my office bent over with pain, hardly able to walk, and after several months of treatment the pain is gone. It's very moving and inspirational."

When asked about other people's reactions to his profession, Zach states, "This is the buckle of the Bible belt here. I've really had to prove myself. Friends and family have been supportive, but the general public is a little wary. Most males don't succeed as legitimate, licensed massage therapists, but I have. It's a source of satisfaction to me. I achieved this, and I did it all on my own. Now I have confidence that, if my girlfriend and I get married and move to a different part of the country, I can open another business and succeed again."

Influences of Gender Knowledge on Behavior

Gender knowledge, present very early in childhood, profoundly influences children's behavior. Gender labeling is the basis for their toy and activity preferences. It influences their motivation, accuracy, and expectancies for success. It even influences their memory and social judgments. What are some examples of these influences?

Toy Preferences As you have read, sex differences in children's play emerge between the first and second birthdays, before children of both sexes can reliably identify toys as being more appropriate or typical for girls or boys (Campbell, Shirley, & Caygill, 2002; Serbin et al., 2001). Consequently, gender knowledge probably is not critical for the emergence of sex-typed play. It does become critical, however, as children grow older.

One way to study the effects of gender knowledge on play is to present children with toys described as being "for boys" (for example, "I think boys like the toys in this box better than girls do") or "for girls" or "for both boys and girls." Studies using this procedure show that by the preschool years, children spend more time exploring own-sex toys and rate own-sex toys as more attractive, even if the opposite sex or neutral toys are actually more appealing—that is, *if* children remember the labels, and not all children do (Bradbard et al., 1986; Frey & Ruble, 1992; Martin, Eisenbud, & Rose, 1995).

Motivation Gender labeling also influences children's motivation, accuracy, and expectancies for success. In one study (Montemayor, 1974), 6- to 8-year-old children were shown a novel game (Mr. Munchie) that involved throwing marbles into a clown's body. Some children were told that the game was a toy for boys, "like basketball" others were told it was a girls' game, "like jacks"; and yet others were given no information about the game. Children performed better, reported liking the game more, and gave the game higher ratings when told the game was for their own sex versus the other sex.

Gender labels have an impact on children's motivation and performance on a variety of tasks, including academic ones (Gold & Berger, 1978; Stein, Pohly, & Mueller, 1971). These studies confirm that children, especially boys, are vulnerable to stereotypes at a young age. This vulnerability may make children less inclined to try activities they deem appropriate for the opposite sex. Once children decide that an activity is more appropriate for the other sex (for example, that "reading is for girls"), their performance on the activity may decline. In this way, the gender label serves to maintain both the stereotype and the sex difference (Carter & Levy, 1988; Levy & Carter, 1989).

Memory Gender stereotypes influence what children remember. Children remember more about same-sex peers and activities than other-sex peers and activities (Ruble & Stangor, 1986; Signorella et al., 1993; Stangor & McMillan, 1992). Gender information also influences children's memory for scripted sequences of behaviors. Boys, but not girls, show better memory for own-gender than other-gender scripts (Bauer, 1993; Boston & Levy, 1991; Levy & Fivush, 1993).

Children's recall is better when information is consistent with the gender schemas they have formed. For example, in several studies, children were shown a series of pictures or photographs, each depicting either a male or female performing a gender-stereotyped activity. The children later were shown two pictures and asked which one they had seen earlier. Children had more accurate memory for gender-consistent pictures (such as a woman ironing clothes) than for gender-inconsistent pictures (such as a man ironing clothes) (Bigler & Liben, 1990; Boston & Levy, 1991; Liben & Signorella, 1993). Children sometimes even misremember information so as to make it consistent with their stereotypes (Martin & Halverson, 1983; Signorella & Liben, 1984). These kinds of memory distortions appear to peak at about 5 to 6 years and then decline with age (Stangor & Ruble, 1987; Welch-Ross & Schmidt, 1996).

Social Judgments Children—like adults—use gender knowledge to make inferences and judgments about other people. As in gender-related recall, young children are better able to make stereotypic inferences when given own-sex cues than when given other-sex cues. For example, a girl told about a child who likes to play with kitchen sets would likely infer that the same child would also like to play with dolls. She would be less likely, however, to draw appropriate inferences if told about a boy who likes to play with trucks.

By around age 8, children are able to use other-gender cues to draw inferences about the opposite sex. Developmental differences also emerge when children are presented conflicting information about another person, such as a boy who enjoys playing with dolls. Young children tend to reason simply on the basis of the child's gender and infer that because the unfamiliar child is a boy, he probably will like to play with trucks. Older children rely more on individuating information (for example, the unfamiliar child's individual interests, traits, or appearance) and infer that this particular boy may not behave in sex-stereotyped ways (Berndt & Heller, 1986; Biernat, 1991; Martin, 1989).

A recent study of Chinese and Israeli school-age children shows that the extent to which children draw inferences that run counter to gender stereotypes also depends on cultural attitudes toward behavior that deviates from the norm (Lobel et al., 2001). Chinese society places a high value on conformity to group norms and expectations, and children's individual deviations from those norms may be deemphasized. Chinese children, especially boys, are less likely to rely on individuating information than their Western counterparts. Hence, they are more likely to infer that a boy described as engaging in a stereotypically feminine activity would nonetheless have masculine toy and occupation preferences.

The range of possible inferences increases as children gain additional stereotypic information about the sexes. For example, when told of a boy who admired another child's bicycle, school-age boys and girls were likely to suggest that the boy was the kind of person who likes to steal things. In contrast, when the character was a girl, children were more likely to claim that by admiring the other child's bicycle, she was simply trying to be friendly (Heyman, 2001).

Learning Objective 13.4: *Trace the development of gender role knowledge and behavior.*

1. What is the developmental progression of gender knowledge?
2. What is the developmental course for children's flexibility regarding gender stereotypes?
3. How does gender knowledge influence behavior?

✔ *Test Your Mastery...*

Development of Sexual Relationships and Behavior

Throughout childhood, the dominant theme in children's relations with the opposite sex is segregation. Some researchers believe that gender segregation during early and middle childhood contributes to the development of sexual orientation (Bem, 1996, 2000). For most children as they move into adolescence, hetereosexual attraction becomes increasingly powerful, opposing the forces of cross-sex avoidance.

There is marked individual variation in sexuality and **sexual orientation**—heterosexual or homosexual attraction and preference. Nonetheless, most adolescents develop a sexual attraction to those of the opposite sex, and the peer culture of adolescence is dominated by a heterosexual orientation. How do romantic and sexual interest develop, and how do adolescents manage the transition to adult sexual relationships?

Learning Objective 13.5
Discuss the development of sexual relationships and behavior.

Sexual orientation
A person's sexual preference. Heterosexuals are attracted to members of the opposite sex, and homosexuals are attracted to members of the same sex.

These young people are exploring their friendships in low-risk contexts, in ways that will contribute to the development of their sexual orientation, romantic interests, and sexual relationships. What biological factors may be involved in sexual orientation? (Myrleen Ferguson Cate/PhotoEdit)

Children are aware of each other as potential romantic and sexual partners from early on. Romantic themes involving dating, courtship, and marriage dominate much of girls' play. In the meantime, boys engage in "locker room" talk about girls (Maccoby, 1998). "Kiss-and-chase" games that are the mainstay of elementary school playgrounds in industrialized societies are observed in cultures around the world as well (Sutton-Smith & Roberts, 1973). During middle childhood when children are at the peak of opposite gender avoidance, children tease each other for "liking" or "loving" a child of the opposite sex (Maccoby, 1998; Thorne, 1993).

Emergence of Romantic and Sexual Interest

How do children move from these kinds of immature relationships to the sexually mature relationships of adulthood? Until recently, sexual maturation was highly regulated by cultural practices and prescribed social expectations, such as initiation rites and rules governing contact between the sexes before marriage. In some cultures, this remains true even today. But in many communities, young people must negotiate their entry into dating and sexuality with little direct support or guidance from parents or other adults. In these communities, the peer group serves as an important context for the development of heterosexual relationships.

This transition occurs through a series of stages (Brown, 1999; Dunphy, 1963; O'Sullivan, Graber, & Brooks-Gunn, 2001). Boys and girls typically report experiencing their first romantic interests, or "crushes," between the ages of 7 and 10. Most often, these crushes are directed at unavailable objects, such as teachers and celebrities.

Between the ages of 10 and 14 years, young people spend increasing amounts of time in mixed-sex groups just "hanging out" and going places together. Initially, there is little intimacy in these encounters, but gradually, activities such as dances and parties that require more intimacy become more frequent. Games with some sexual content (e.g., Spin the Bottle, Man Hunt, and Seven Minutes of Heaven) and kissing and touching breasts or genitals over clothes become more common (O'Sullivan et al., 2001). Nonetheless, having numerous peers around remains important to ensure that behavior remains within culturally acceptable bounds.

By middle adolescence (15 to 16 years), approximately half of U.S. adolescents are involved in a romantic relationship (Feiring, 1996). Nonetheless, couples continue to spend much of their time in mixed-sex groups that include peers involved in romantic relationships and other adolescents who are just friends. During later adolescence, romantic relationships involve greater levels of emotional and sexual intimacy. The relationships are also longer in duration and involve more solitary activities than those observed in younger adolescents (O'Sullivan et al., 2001).

Research generally reports significant correspondence between stages of dating (e.g., casual, steady, engaged) and sexual activity (e.g., kissing, petting, intercourse) (Jessor & Jessor, 1977; McCabe & Collins, 1984; Miller et al., 1986). National surveys show that by twelfth grade, approximately 60 percent of youth in the United States have had sexual intercourse (Centers For Disease Cantrol, 2002).

Large numbers of adolescents do not conform to the normative model just described, and there are many sources of difference. There may be cultural differences, for example, in the order in which sexual behaviors emerge (Smith & Udry, 1985). Individuals raised in conservative religious communities may delay sexual intercourse into adulthood. Gay, lesbian, and bisexual young people typically do not have their first same-sex sexual experience within a romantic relationship, in part because of the difficulty of dating someone of the same sex within the heterosexual-dominated adolescent peer culture (Diamond, Savin-Williams, & Dube, 1999; Herdt & Boxer, 1993). And some adolescents may skip stages altogether or recycle through the various stages several times (Brown, 1999).

Origins of Sexual Orientation

Most adolescents develop a heterosexual orientation, but homosexuality has been found in all cultures that have been studied (Crompton, 2003). Calculating the actual number of gay people in a society has proven very difficult. Estimates of homosexuality depend in large part on how it is defined. For example, asking people if they have ever had any kind of same-sex experience yields quite different results than asking people if they have had a same-sex partner in the past five years. Also, many more people report being attracted to someone of the same sex than report having a sexual experience with someone of the same sex. And more report having a same-sex sexual experience than self-identify as gay or lesbian. The more homosexuality is stigmatized in a society, the more likely it is to be underreported.

These and other factors make it difficult to obtain accurate information regarding the actual number of gay people living in different societies. Surveys in North America and Europe estimate that the percentage of men and women who identify themselves as gay is between 2 and 5 percent of the population (Diamond, 1993). When the criteria include same-sex experiences (without self-identification as gay), then estimates rise to between 8 and 10 percent (B. Erens et al., 2003). In addition, an unknown but significant number of individuals identify themselves as bisexual.

How does an erotic attraction to one or the other sex or both sexes develop? Most research on the development of sexual orientation has focused on how some individuals develop an attraction to members of their own sex. This research bias reflects cultural norms for heterosexuality. After all, most children in modern societies are right-handed, but that has not led researchers to study only how left-handedness develops. Nonetheless, researchers have focused on the development of a nonheterosexual orientation as a puzzle to be understood. To explain it, researchers have looked to both biological and social influences.

Biological Influences Research on twins and families suggests that sexual orientation may be in part hereditary. Although rates vary widely from study to study, the chances that both members of a pair of twins will have a homosexual orientation are significantly greater for identical (monozygotic) twins than for fraternal (dizygotic) twins (Hershberger, 2001; Zucker, 2001). Studies also find gay men and lesbian women to have more gay and lesbian siblings than heterosexuals. Gay males are more likely to have gay male siblings, and lesbians are—to a lesser degree—more likely to have lesbian siblings (Bailey & Bell, 1993; Bailey & Benishay, 1993; Bailey, Pillard, et al., 1993; Pillard, 1990).

How might genes influence the development of sexual orientation? Genes influence the production or effects of prenatal hormones. As you have read, hormones produced by the newly formed testes masculinize the fetus, which includes both the development of the reproductive organs and the organization of the fetal brain. Some researchers believe that sexual orientation is established during this process (Meyer-Bahlberg, 1993; Reinisch, Ziemba-Davis, & Sanders, 1991).

As you have seen, hormone levels are influenced by both genetic and environmental factors. Whether a person is chromosomally male (XY) or female (XX), hormonal imbalances—such as those caused by CAH and androgen insensitivity—can affect the individual's gender-related behavior, personality traits, and sexual preferences (Berenbaum & Snyder, 1995; Dittmann et al., 1990; Zucker et al., 1996). Moreover, girls exposed prenatally to unusually high levels of masculinizing androgens, typically through the use of prescription steroids, are more likely to develop a lesbian or bisexual orientation than girls whose mothers did not take the drugs (Meyer-Bahlberg et al., 1995). It is not known, however, if the same processes occur in gays and lesbians who are not affected by these disorders or drugs.

Further evidence to support the role of hormones in sexual orientation is the existence of a birth order difference between gay and heterosexual men (Hershberger, 2001). Specifically, homosexual boys tend to be later in birth order than heterosexual boys. Moreover, the later birth order of gay men depends on the number of older brothers and not on the number of older sisters (Blanchard & Bogaert, 1996; Blanchard & Zucker, 1994; Blanchard et al., 2002). The birth order effect is believed to be due to a maternal immune reaction that lessens the effects of male androgens on male fetuses during the prenatal period (Blanchard & Klassen, 1997).

Social Influences An alternative explanation of sexual orientation involves socialization. There is little empirical evidence, however, for explanations based on socialization as a cause of sexual orientation. For example, having a nonheterosexual parent does not predispose a child to become gay or lesbian (Bailey & Dawood, 1998; Golombok & Tasker 1996; Gottman, 1990; Patterson, 1992; Tasker & Golombok, 1997). In one study of the sons of gay fathers, researchers found that the sons' identification as either gay or heterosexual was unrelated to the amount of time they had lived with their fathers, the extent to which they accepted their fathers' homosexuality, or the quality of their relationships with their fathers (Bailey, Nothnagel, & Wolfe, 1995). In general, the proportion of children reared by gay, lesbian, or bisexual parents who adopt a nonheterosexual identity is comparable to that of children raised by heterosexual parents. Thus, childrearing alone does not determine sexual orientation.

Gender Identity and Transsexualism

Transsexualism
The condition in which a person assumes the identity and permanently acts the part of the gender opposite to his or her biological sex.

Finally, a word should be said about **transsexualism**, or the condition in which a person assumes the identity and permanently acts the part of the gender opposite to his or her biological sex. Often, people assume that homosexuality and transsexualism are the same thing, but they are not. As described above, gender identity refers to one's perception of oneself as male or female, whereas sexual orientation refers to the gender of the person(s) to whom one is sexually attracted. People with same-sex orientations typically are comfortable with themselves as males or females. Transsexuals, however, describe a sense of extreme discomfort with the gender they were assigned at birth, usually on the basis of external genitalia. They report feeling that they are actually the opposite gender trapped inside a man or woman's body. Such individuals may undergo hormonal treatment under the supervision of medical personnel and therapists. This hormonal treatment is often a first step toward permanent sex reassignment. After a trial period of living as a member of the opposite sex, permanent sex reassignment may be accomplished through surgery. Transsexuals are likely to report a greater sense of personal fulfillment following reassignment to the sex they feel they actually belong to (Israel & Tarver, 1997). Following sex reassignment, transsexuals can be straight or gay in their sexual orientation.

Test Your Mastery...

Learning Objective 13.5: *Discuss the development of sexual relationships and behavior.*

1. How do romantic and sexual interest emerge?
2. What do we know about the origins of sexual orientation?
3. What is transsexualism?

BOX 13.4 Contextual Model of Gender Development

Infant is born typically with clear anatomic gender, male or female, with exposure to sex hormones having occurred prenatally.

Family and School Settings

- Parents' own gender expectations and attitudes influence toys and books they buy and activities they encourage for the child.
- Parents provide gender role models in their occupations, relationship with one another, and choice of activities around the home.
- Schools and teachers encourage traditional or nontraditional gendered behavior in the curriculum and materials they provide, as well as in the activities and behavior they encourage in both boys and girls.
- Peers provide important feedback regarding acceptable and unacceptable gendered behavior.

Culture and Society

- Different cultures provide different models for men and women engaged in a variety of activities.
- Media, both print and electronic, provide models for gendered or nongendered behavior.

Learning Objective 13.1
Describe physical, cognitive, and social/personality sex differences that researchers have found.

1. What physical sex differences have researchers found?

Differences are seen in *physical maturity, vulnerability, activity level, and motor development.* At birth, girls are generally healthier and more developmentally advanced than boys despite being smaller and lighter. Girls are less muscular but are better coordinated neurologically and physically. On average, girls reach developmental milestones earlier than boys. Males are physically more vulnerable than females from conception on. They are more likely to be miscarried, to suffer from physical and mental illness and injuries, and to die in infancy. On average, boys have higher activity levels than girls even in the womb. Sex differences in infancy are minimal in motor development. However, they are evident in early childhood. Boys can jump farther, run faster, and throw farther than girls by age 5. Girls have the advantage in gross motor skills such as hopping and skipping, and also in fine motor skills like tying shoes, writing, and cutting paper.

2. What cognitive sex differences have researchers found?

Research has shown that sex differences in *verbal and language abilities* are biologically based. Of particular importance is *brain lateralization*, the specialization of functions in the right and left hemispheres. Prenatal exposure to high levels of testosterone by male fetuses slows the development of the left hemisphere and enhances the development of the right hemisphere for male fetuses. This process may produce two results significant for sex differences in cognitive abilities. One is that the *right hemisphere* is relatively more established in newborn boys. The right hemisphere is specialized for quantitative and spatial abilities, while the left hemisphere is specialized to process language. This may explain why boys outperform girls in some tests of spatial abilities. It may also account for the fact that baby girls produce more sounds at an earlier age, use words sooner, and have larger vocabularies than boys.

3. What social and personality sex differences have researchers found?

There are sex differences in *temperament, emotional development, self-control, aggression, prosocial behavior, activities and interests, and friends and companions.* Baby girls tend to maintain eye contact and smile at caregivers more than baby boys. This difference persists into adulthood. Sex differences in the strategies used to regulate emotional states have been observed among children as young as 2. In a stressful situation, girls tend to seek out comfort from their mothers, while boys are more likely to distract themselves by playing with a toy. In adolescence, girls are expected to turn to other people when they are upset, and boys are expected to find something else to do. Boys are more likely to express anger, both in face-to-face interactions and when describing past events. Boys are also more likely to deny feeling afraid. In the area of self-control, girls tend to develop self-regulatory capabilities more rapidly than boys. The clearest and largest sex difference in behavior is that males generally display more physical aggression than do females. Girls are generally rated as more generous, helpful, and cooperative (prosocial behavior) than boys. Gender differences in activity preferences emerge between the first and second birthdays. Boys prefer more vigorous physical activities, and other activities appear to follow gender-stereotyped play, with girls preferring doll play, dress-up, and domestic play and boys preferring blocks, trucks, and airplanes. However, parents encourage sex-typed play from the first months of life. This is especially true for boys, who experience considerable pressure from both parents to play with toys deemed appropriate for their sex. Children's social relationships show striking sex differences. Boys play in larger groups, whereas girls limit their group size to two or three. Girls have fewer, but more intimate, friendships. Social interaction among boys often involves issues of dominance and leadership, while girls' interactions stress turn taking and equal participation by group members.

Learning Objective 13.2

Compare and contrast biological and social influences on sex differences and gender role development.

1. How does biology influence sex differences and gender role development?

A major step in *sex differentiation* begins when the newly formed embryonic gonads begin to secrete *hormones* of different types. Somewhere between 3 and 8 months after conception, sex hormones are believed to affect the development and organization of the fetal brain. These hormones activate certain social behaviors, including aggression, maternal behaviors, and - sexual activity. Similarly, psychologists believe that differences in brain lateralization may be important for understanding certain differences in male and female behavior. Researchers believe that naturally occurring variations in testosterone during the prenatal period may be related to the gender behavior of human offspring. In addition, fetuses who are exposed to incorrect amounts of testosterone are prone to disorders in the development of sex organs.

2. What are the various social influences that have been found on sex differences and gender role development?

The socialization of gender occurs on multiple levels and includes schools, parents, peers, and the larger society. Two means of socialization are *modeling* and *differential treatment* of boys and girls. One way children learn about gender roles is through modeling, by observing those around them. Modeling is a powerful means of transmitting values, attitudes, beliefs, and behavioral practices from generation to generation. In particular, television communicates a great deal about social practices and behavior. TV generally portrays characters in traditional gender roles. The second way in which children learn about gender roles in society is through observing and experiencing differential treatment of males and females. Differential treatment is evident in access to formal education, division of labor by sex, the availability of social opportunities, and the treatment boys and girls experience in school. Parents provide an especially significant model for what it means to be male or female, often holding different expectations for sons and daughters. Finally, siblings and peer groups exert great influence on a child's gender role socialization.

Explain and illustrate how children
participate actively in their gender role
development.

1. What self-
selecting
processes do
children
demonstrate with
regard to models
and sanctions?

Children participate actively in their gender role socialization through their *selection of models* and have the tendency to attend more to same-sex models. This is especially true for boys, who often resist imitating behaviors modeled by females. Although girls prefer to imitate adult women, they will also imitate adult men. Both girls and boys are more likely to imitate models perceived to be powerful. Cross-sex imitation by girls may reflect their perception that culture invests males with higher status and greater rewards. In addition, children participate in their gender socialization through gradually internalizing external sanctions as self-sanctions. In other words, as children acquire knowledge about the likely consequences of gender-linked conduct, they come to regulate their actions accordingly.

2. What role
does cognition
play in children's
gender role
development?

Kohlberg believed that children *construct gender identity* from what they see and hear around them. This gender identity serves to organize and regulate children's gender learning and behavior. Children come to believe that one's own gender is fixed and irreversible (gender constancy). This belief develops in three stages: gender identity, gender stability, and gender consistency. Gender constancy is developed by the late preschool years. Similarly, schema theories propose that children construct gender based on mental models for how things should be. Children form gender schemas, which are cognitive representations of the characteristics associated with being either male or female. Thus, children categorize gender-relevant stimuli as "for girls" or "for boys." In both approaches, children are motivated to behave in ways that are consistent with what they know or believe about gender.

Learning Objective 13.4

Trace the development of gender role
knowledge and behavior.

1. What is the developmental progression of gender knowledge?	Children develop some knowledge about *gender categories* during the first two years of life. At 2 months of age, infants can discriminate male and female voices At age 1, children are able to categorize people by gender on the basis of features such as voice pitch and hair length. By age 2, children can reliably sort pictures of males and females into separate piles and accurately point to pictures of things for males and females. Over the course of early childhood, children begin to incorporate more abstract concepts in their gender stereotypes.
2. What is the developmental course for children's flexibility regarding gender stereotypes?	Gender stereotypes become more *flexible* over the course of childhood. During the preschool years, most children view gender roles as inflexible and absolute. Cross-sex behaviors are seen as serious violations of social standards. By middle childhood, children begin to realize that gender roles are socially determined and can be broken without any major consequences. The transition to junior high school appears to increase adolescents' flexibility toward the roles of males and females.
3. How does gender knowledge influence behavior?	Gender knowledge, present very early in childhood, profoundly influences children's behavior. *Gender labeling* is the basis for their toy and activity preferences, influencing their motivation, accuracy, and expectancies for success. Sex differences in children's play emerge between the first and second birthdays. By the preschool years, children spend more time exploring own-sex toys and rate own-sex toys as more attractive. Children are more motivated by own-sex games and activities and are more likely to remember more about same-sex peers and to use gender knowledge to make inferences about judgments of other people.

Learning Objective 13.5
Discuss the development of sexual relationships and behavior.

1. How do romantic and sexual interests emerge?	Boys and girls typically report experiencing their first romantic interests or "crushes" between the ages of 7 and 10. Most often, these crushes are directed at unavailable objects such as teachers or celebrities. Between the ages of 10 and 14 years, young people spend increasing amounts of time in mixed sex groups. By *middle adolescence* (15 to 16 years), approximately half of U.S. adolescents are involved in a romantic relationship. During *later adolescence*, romantic relationships involve greater levels of emotional and sexual intimacy. National surveys show that by the twelfth grade, approximately 60 percent of youth in the United States have had sexual intercourse. However, there are individual and cultural differences, and not all adolescents conform to this normative model.
2. What do we know about the origins of sexual orientation?	Research on twins and families suggests that *sexual orientation* may be in part hereditary. The chances that both members of a pair of twins will have a homosexual orientation are significantly greater for identical twins. And gay men and lesbian women have more gay and lesbian siblings than heterosexuals. Some researchers believe that sexual orientation is established during prenatal development when the fetus is exposed to sex hormones. Similarly, some research suggests a birth order effect on sexuality. It is believed that there may be a maternal immune reaction that lessens the effects of male androgens on the male fetus during the prenatal period. Therefore, there is some evidence that a later birth order may produce a difference between a gay and heterosexual man. An alternative explanation of sexual orientation involves socialization, although there is little empirical evidence. In general, the proportion of children reared by gay, lesbian, or bisexual parents who adopt a nonheterosexual identity is comparable to that of children raised by heterosexual parents. However, researchers agree that sexual orientation is the product of the interaction between biological and environmental influences.

3. What is transsexualism?

Transsexualism is a condition in which a person assumes the identity and permanently acts the part of the gender opposite to his or her biological sex. Homosexuality and transsexualism are not the same thing. People with same-sex orientations are typically comfortable with themselves as males or females. In contrast, transsexuals describe a sense of extreme discomfort with the gender they were assigned at birth, usually on the basis of external genitalia. They report feeling trapped inside a man's or woman's body. Transsexuals are likely to report a greater sense of personal fulfillment following sex reassignment. Following sex reassignment, transsexuals can be straight or gay in their sexual orientation.

Moral Development

B ut our fish said, "No! No!

Make that cat go away!

Tell that Cat in the Hat

You do NOT want to play.

He should not be here.

He should not be about.

He should not be here

When your mother is out!"

Many readers will recognize this excerpt from the well-loved children's book, *The Cat in the Hat*. It is a cold and rainy day; mother is out, and Sally and her brother are bored. A mischievous cat appears on the doorstep with promises of "good games" and amusing "tricks" that will undoubtedly annoy mother. Despite the warnings of the fish (the parental voice), the children let the cat into the house and all kinds of chaos ensues. The children grow concerned, but the cat shows up with an amazing machine that restores order and all is well, except, perhaps, the children's state of mind. They wonder—should we tell mother, or not? (And, the author asks, would you?)

Generations of children have felt the rush of adrenaline as the cat breaks rule after rule in this story and its sequel, *The Cat in the Hat Comes Back*. The stories appeal strongly to children who are old enough to know about family and societal rules and to spend increasing amounts of time unsupervised and outside of direct adult control. They delight in imagining what they might do—if they could be certain they would not be caught. Would

they eat cake in the bathtub? Fly kites in the house? Juggle mother's china? Try on father's shoes?

The violations depicted by Dr. Seuss are relatively minor—and that is part of their appeal to young listeners. By the time children are old enough to appreciate Dr. Seuss, they can already distinguish between the fanciful infractions of the Cat in the Hat and more serious transgressions, and most children would not find serious transgressions so amusing. Why this is so, and how children come to understand various kinds of rules and to follow them even when parents or other authority figures are not around, is the focus of this chapter.

Morality involves issues of right and wrong, good and evil. If any society is going to survive, it must have rules that make clear to its citizens what is permitted and what is prohibited. Children's moral development involves the ways they come to understand and follow (or not follow) the rules of their social world. Until fairly recently, the study of moral development was left primarily to philosophers and religious scholars. Today, developmental psychologists also have a great deal of interest in this topic.

Theories of Moral Development

Learning Objective 14.1
Compare and contrast four theoretical approaches to the study of moral development.

Two theoretical issues have dominated the study of moral development. One is whether children's moral beliefs and behaviors reside in the child and simply emerge over time or whether they reside in the culture and are transmitted to the child. The second issue involves the generality of moral rules. If they emerge from the child, they must have a large biological component, making them universal for all members of our species. On the other hand, if they develop within the social group, they are more arbitrary and thus can vary from one culture to the next. These two questions lie at the heart of much of the research on this topic.

Piaget's Model of Moral Development

Piaget's model of moral development grew out of his early work with children in Geneva, Switzerland, during the 1920s and 1930s. To investigate how children's conceptions of morality develop, Piaget observed children playing common street games, such as marbles. He closely examined how youngsters created and enforced the rules of their games, and he questioned them about circumstances under which the rules could be modified or even ignored.

In addition, Piaget presented children with **moral dilemmas** to solve. These took the form of short stories in which the child had to determine which of two characters was "naughtier." For example, in one story a little boy named Augustine accidentally makes a large ink stain on the tablecloth while trying to be helpful and fill his father's ink pot, whereas a little boy named Julian makes a small ink spot on the tablecloth while engaging in the forbidden act of playing with his father's pen. Piaget asked the children, "Who is naughtier, Augustine or Julian? And why?"

From this research, Piaget developed a four-stage model of moral development that focused on the way children follow rules (Piaget, 1932). In the first stage (2 to 4 years), children have no real conception of morality. Much of their behavior involves play and imaginative games that have no formal rules, although at times they may invent certain restrictions as part of the play (e.g., all green blocks must be put in the same pail). The idea of following someone else's rules does not appear consistently until the second stage (5 to 7 years). When rule following emerges, children approach the concept in an absolute manner. Social rules are viewed as externally dictated (*heteronomous*), commands are presented by people in authority (usually parents), and rules cannot be changed. Children in this second stage, called the stage of **moral realism,** do not think to question the purpose or correctness of a rule, even though they may not like to follow it. Thus, Piaget observed that younger children playing marble games were usually very inflexible about changing any rules, even if it would have made the game more convenient or more fun.

Piaget noted two interesting characteristics that grow out of this absolutist orientation. Most children in the second stage evaluate moral situations only in terms of their physical and objective consequences. These children saw acts causing more damage as more morally wrong than acts causing less damage, regardless of the actor's motives or intentions. Hence, from the perspective of moral realism, the helpful Augustine was usually seen as naughtier than the disobedient Julian because Augustine made the larger ink stain.

Another characteristic of this stage is a belief in *immanent justice*. Because these children believe so firmly in the authority of a rule, they feel that punishment must always occur when the rule is broken. Thus, if a child steals a cookie when no one is looking and then loses his baseball the following day, he may assume that he has been punished for the theft.

In Piaget's third stage (8 to 11 years), the child gradually realizes that rules are agreements created by people to help or protect one another. Obeying these rules is no longer viewed simply as following someone else's orders but as an autonomous or personal decision to cooperate with others. Piaget observed, for example, that third-stage children could adapt marble-game rules if necessary to fit the circumstances of the moment (too many players, too few marbles, and so on).

Furthermore, at this stage children's more advanced cognitive abilities allow new factors to enter into their moral evaluations. What a person was trying or meaning to do—that is, the person's motives or intentions—may become as important as the outcome of the behavior. Accordingly, with increasing age, children were more likely to judge Julian's forbidden behavior naughtier, even though it caused less damage. Because the morality of following a rule is now evaluated in relation to other factors in the situation, Piaget referred to this third stage as **moral relativism**.

In the final stage, which Piaget discussed only briefly, children become more *autonomous* in their moral reasoning, capable of viewing rules critically and developing new rules when the circumstances require it. They also begin to extend their moral reasoning beyond the personal level to larger societal and political concerns and to abstract principles of justice.

Piaget emphasized children's interactions with peers. During their early years, children learn that parents usually dictate and enforce the rules of behavior. In their desire to

Piaget studied common children's games as a way of examining children's conceptions of rules and responses to rule infractions. Do moral precepts arise from human nature or are they entirely learned? (Michael Newman/PhotoEdit)

Moral dilemmas
Stories used by Piaget and others to assess children's levels of moral reasoning.

Moral realism
Piaget's second stage of moral development, in which children's reasoning is based on objective and physical aspects of a situation and is often inflexible.

Moral relativism
Piaget's third stage of moral development, in which children view rules as agreements that can be altered and consider people's motives or intentions when evaluating their moral conduct.

please their parents, children adopt the belief that they live in a world where rules must be followed. But the one-way nature of this rule system keeps children from expressing their own points of view or appreciating that there can be different opinions on moral questions. Piaget believed that through their interactions with peers, children learn that there can be several perspectives on an issue and that rules are the result of negotiating, accommodating, and respecting the points of view of other people.

Research has generally supported Piaget's account of children's moral development. Numerous studies show that with age, children increasingly consider motives and intentions when evaluating the morality of actions (Berg & Mussen, 1975; Lickona, 1976). In addition, various cognitive measures, including perspective-taking and mental state understanding, have been associated with children's level of moral judgment (Dunn & Herrera, 1997; Kurdek, 1980). And as Piaget observed, children's peer relations provide many opportunities to tackle moral issues, such as kindness and unkindness, exclusion from play, failure to share, and so forth. Research also confirms Piaget's claim that children advance their moral reasoning through discussions with peers (Kruger, 1992; Walker, Hennig, & Krettenauer, 2000). Consistent with his prediction, children with punitive parents who reinforce strict adherence to rules tend to display less mature moral reasoning and behavior (Hoffman, 1983, 2000; Walker & Taylor, 1991).

Other aspects of Piaget's theory are not as well supported. Parents play a more important and unique role in the development of children's morality than Piaget envisioned. Piaget also appears to have underestimated the moral reasoning abilities of young children. For example, when Piaget's dilemmas are presented in ways that make intentions more important—by clearly stating the intention at the end of the story or by adding pictures like that shown in Figure 14.1—even young children can take motives into account (Chandler, Greenspan, & Barenboim, 1973; Helwig, Zelazo, & Wilson, 2001; Jones & Thomson, 2001).

Other research shows that even young children consider a variety of factors in addition to motives and damage when assessing a character's morality. For example, young children believe that taking a toy from a friend is more wrong than taking a toy from a nonfriend (Slomkowski & Killen, 1992). Most important, children in many societies judge the breaking of moral rules (e.g., right and wrong) more harshly than the violation of social conventions (e.g., polite and impolite).

Questions for Thought
and Discussion
What advice might a Piagetian give to those wishing to reduce aggressive behavior and promote prosocial behavior?

FIGURE 14.1

Illustration for Considering Motives in Moral Judgments

This illustration is intended to convey motive, action, and outcome in a story. When pictures such as these accompany stories involving moral dilemmas, even 4- to 6-year-olds sometimes use actor's motives as a basis for evaluating their behavior. On what basis might a child in Piaget's heteronomous stage conclude that the action shown in the picture was wrong?

SOURCE: From S. A. Nelson. (1980). Factors influencing young children's use of motives and outcomes as moral criteria. *Child Development, 51,* 823–829. Copyright © 1980 by the Society for Research in Child Development. Reprinted by permission.

Kohlberg's Stages of Moral Development

A second influential theory of moral development was proposed by Lawrence Kohlberg, who drew much of his inspiration and methodology from Piaget's earlier work (Colby & Kohlberg, 1987; Kohlberg, 1969, 1981). Like Piaget, Kohlberg rejected the idea that moral development is a simple transmission of moral rules from parents and other adults to children.

Kohlberg's method, like Piaget's, involved presenting children and adults with moral dilemmas to assess their level of moral reasoning. But Kohlberg's stories did not require a simple choice as to who was naughtier. Instead, they presented the child with a dilemma in which a story character must choose between obeying a law (or rule), for example, or breaking the law for the benefit of an individual person. For example, Kohlberg presented the following story about Judy, a 12-year-old girl.

Judy's mother promised her that she could go to a special rock concert coming to their town if she saved up her baby-sitting and lunch money to buy a ticket to the concert. Judy managed to save the fifteen dollars the ticket cost plus another five dollars. But then her mother changed her mind and told Judy that she had to spend her money on new clothes for school. Judy was disappointed and decided to go to the concert anyway. She bought a ticket and told her mother that she had only been able to save five dollars. That Saturday she went to the performance and told her mother that she was spending the day with a friend. A week passed without her mother finding out. Judy then told her older sister, Louise, that she had gone to the performance and had lied to her mother about it. Louise wonders whether to tell their mother what Judy did. Should Louise, the older sister, tell their mother that Judy lied about the money or should she keep quiet? Why?

SOURCE: L. Kohlberg, (1984). *Essays on Moral Development: The Psychology of Moral Development* (Vol. II). San Francisco: Harper and Row.

In this dilemma, and for others like it, the child is asked to indicate what the character should do and why. In Kohlberg's model, the second question (Why?) is more important because it presumably reveals the child's level of moral reasoning. The actual content of a person's answer (e.g., Yes, Louise should tell their parents about Judy's lies versus No, she should not tell) is less important than the reasoning behind the answer.

In Heinz's dilemma, presented next, perhaps Kohlberg's most famous example, children were asked to explain their moral reasoning in a life or death situation:

In Europe, a woman was near death from cancer. One drug might save her, a form of radium that a druggist in the same town had recently discovered. The druggist was charging $2000, ten times what the drug cost him to make. The sick woman's husband, Heinz, went to everyone he knew to borrow the money, but he could get together only about half of what it cost. He told the druggist that his wife was dying and asked him to sell it cheaper or let him pay later. But the druggist said no. The husband got desperate and broke into the man's store to steal the drug for his wife. Should the husband have done that? Why or why not? (adapted from Snarey, 1985)

From his research, Kohlberg concluded that moral reasoning develops in three predictable levels—termed **preconventional, conventional,** and **postconventional**— containing six stages in all. The model is described in Table 14.1. In his later writings, Kohlberg suggested that the sixth and last stage is more theoretical than real. Few individuals ever attain this level, and none of the individuals that Kohlberg studied ever displayed it (Kohlberg, Levine, & Hewer, 1983).

Movement from stage to stage in Kohlberg's model closely follows the Piagetian process of accommodation. Movement occurs when children can no longer handle new information within their current view of the world—or, in Piagetian terms, can no longer assimilate new information within the existing structure of schemes. Kohlberg's model places

Questions for Thought
and Discussion
How might children's answers to these questions reflect Kohlberg's stages of moral development?

Preconventional level
Kohlberg's first two stages of moral development. Moral reasoning is based on the assumption that individuals must serve their own needs.

Conventional level
Kohlberg's third and fourth stages of moral development. Moral reasoning is based on the view that a social system must be based on laws and regulations.

Postconventional level
Kohlberg's final stages of moral development. Moral reasoning is based on the assumption that the value, dignity, and rights of each individual person must be maintained.

particular importance on *role-taking* opportunities, which occur when children participate in decision-making situations with others and exchange differing points of view on moral questions. Contradictory viewpoints produce cognitive conflict, or dissonance, which the child eventually resolves by reorganizing his or her thinking into a more advanced stage of

---

TABLE 14.1 Kohlberg's Stage Model of Moral Reasoning

Level I Preconventional Morality

Moral decisions are made on the basis of reward and punishment and the satisfaction of one's own needs.

Stage 1: Avoidance of Punishment

In this stage, emphasis is placed on avoiding punishment. The needs of others are not considered. For example, if you find a walletful of money, you might return it to its rightful owner because you're afraid of getting caught and being punished.

—Louise should tell on Judy because she will get blamed if Judy gets caught and she knew about it.
—Louise should not tell because she will get in trouble with her sister if she does.

Stage 2: Satisfaction of One's Own Needs

In this stage, right actions are those that satisfy one's own needs. The needs of others are considered for what they can bring you in return. For example, if you find a wallet, you might keep it because it satisfies your immediate interest, or you might return it because then the owner may owe you something.

—Louise should tell on Judy because she will win favor with her parents for informing them.
—Louise should not tell on Judy because Judy might tell on her one day.

Level II Conventional Morality

Moral decisions are made on the basis of conforming to others' expectations, including the general social order.

Stage 3: Good Girl/Bad Girl

In this stage, the emphasis is on living up to the expectations of others, or of gaining approval from others by being nice or good. If you find a wallet, you should keep it because you reason that is what the other person would do, or return it because then others will view you as a nice or good person.

—Louise should not tell because others will view her as a rat who betrays her sister.
—Louise should tell about Judy's dangerous lying because her family would see her as a bad sister if she did not.

Stage 4: Law and Order

In this stage, a person is oriented toward satisfying the expectation of authorities and toward maintaining the social order by doing one's duty. If you find a wallet, you should return it because "If everyone were to keep things that belong to others, there would be social anarchy."

—Louise should not tell because her little sister told her the truth in confidence, and if everyone went around betraying confidences, then no one would be able to trust anyone else.
—Louise should tell, because she has a duty to protect her sister and the well-being of her family.

Level III Postconventional Morality

Correct behavior is defined in terms of individual rights and the consensus of society.

Stage 5: Social Contract

In this stage, emphasis is on the contractual commitment that individuals have with society. The laws of society are made to uphold the common good. When two of these laws come into conflict (e.g., the right to life versus the right to profit), then a person and society must weigh their relative value. If you find a wallet, you should return it because honesty and integrity are personal values that are also to the benefit of society as a whole.

—Louise should tell on Judy because her little sister places herself at risk by lying, and we should value the safety of family members even if it means betraying a confidence.
—Louise should not tell on Judy because Judy spoke to her in confidence, and the social harm of lightly betraying a confidence is greater than the harm it does to their parents to not know the truth about where Judy went that night.

Stage 6: Universal Ethical

Correct behavior is defined as a decision of conscience in accord with self-chosen ethical principles that are logical, universal, and consistent. When laws violate principles, one must act in accordance with principles of justice.

—Louise should tell her parents what Judy did because her sister's safety is a moral imperative that goes beyond the issue of betraying a confidence.

reasoning. This process occurs gradually, so although any individual's reasoning can be generally classified into one of the levels, he or she may approach certain moral issues at a higher or lower stage.

Several other characteristics of Kohlberg's stage model are similar to Piaget's theory. For instance, each stage forms a *structured whole*, with children in that stage generally responding consistently to different dilemmas and situations. Also, the stages follow an *invariant sequence*, so all children experience them in the same order and with no regression to earlier stages. Finally, the progression of stages is regarded as *universal* for all people and all cultures.

Like Piaget's model of moral development, Kohlberg's theory is supported by a good deal of empirical research. Kohlberg's methods have been replicated and show that individuals progress through the preconventional, conventional, and postconventional sequence proposed by Kohlberg in the predicted order (Armon & Dawson, 1997; Rest et al., 1999; Walker, 1989). One study followed a group of boys from age 10 through adulthood (Colby et al., 1983). As shown in Figure 14.2, at age 10, the boys primarily used preconventional reasoning—emphasizing obeying authority or acting in one's own self-interest. From the ages of 14 to 24, Stage 3 reasoning predominated. During these years, the boys were concerned with conforming to expectations to win others' approval. Even by age 36, only a small number were reasoning at the postconventional (Stage 5) level.

Research has not supported the cross-cultural validity of Kohlberg's model, however. Is the model universal, applying equally well to people of all cultures? Studies in preliterate societies show that individuals rarely progress to the fifth stage. In societies where the majority of people receive formal schooling, the percentage of individuals displaying Stage 5 reasoning increases but remains in the minority (Snarey, 1985). Thus, apparently the majority of the world's population rarely reasons at the postconventional level. This raises questions. Perhaps Kohlberg is presenting a model of how Western societies think people *should* reason. If this is the case, then this theory of moral development reflects Western ideals that are not applicable to all people everywhere.

A related concern is that Kohlberg's moral dilemmas do not adequately address moral issues and concepts found in other cultures (Snarey & Keljo, 1991). In some Chinese cultures, for example, the conflict between what is right for the individual and what is right for society is not ideally resolved by choosing one over the other (as is required in Kohlberg's hypothetical dilemmas). Instead, the most appropriate solution is thought to be reconciliation between the two interests by arriving at a compromise solution (Dien, 1982). According to Hindu beliefs in India, the very fact that Louise finds herself in a

Both Piaget and Kohlberg believed that children's moral reasoning is strongly influenced by their interactions with peers. The interaction in this photo, for example, may cause one of the girls discover or doubt some point of view on a moral question or may lead her to resolve her thinking into a more advanced stage of moral reasoning. (Charles D. Winters/Photo Researchers)

Questions for Thought and Discussion

Which of Kohlberg's levels and stages does your moral reasoning reflect? What is an example of a dilemma or conflict that you think may have contributed to your moral development?

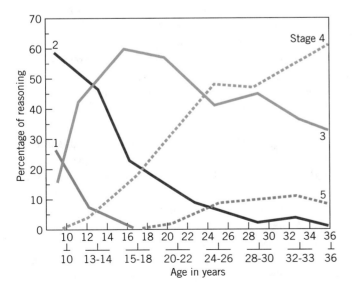

FIGURE 14.2

A Longitudinal Study of Moral Development

This graph shows the mean percentage of moral reasoning by age group for each of Kohlberg's first five stages of moral development. By what age did preconventional moral reasoning most sharply decline? Notice the relationship of those curves to the ones for conventional moral reasoning. How would you account for the fact that less than 10 percent of the children attained postconventional moral reasoning as adults?
SOURCE: From A. Colby, L. Kohlberg, J.C. Gibbs, and M. Lieberman. (1983). A longitudinal study of moral judgment. *Monographs of the Society for Research in Child Development, 48*, 1–2. Reprinted by permission.

dilemma is an indication of her prior sins or negligence, which she will not escape by committing further negligent actions, such as ignoring her sister's lies (Shweder & Much, 1987). Thus, Kohlberg's model is not applicable in all cultural groups.

Applicability should be universal not only across cultures but between sexes. Recall that Kohlberg studied boys' moral reasoning and focused on justice reasoning as the best indicator of moral development. In one early study, Kohlberg reported that females' moral reasoning generally was not as advanced as that of males (Kohlberg & Kramer, 1969). Not surprisingly, this news was not well received, particularly by women. In response, psychologist Carol Gilligan asserted that women's moral reasoning is not inferior to that of males but is different. Specifically, Gilligan claimed that females are socialized to an "ethic of care" that is devalued in Kohlberg's system. She argued that females evaluate Kohlberg's dilemmas in terms of issues of responsibility, care, and sacrifice—whether someone has an *obligation* to do something based on the value of a personal relationship rather than on whether someone has the right to do something based on laws or rules (Gilligan, 1982).

Contrary to both Kohlberg's and Gilligan's ideas, research has provided little evidence that males and females differ in their moral reasoning. When levels of formal education are equal, males and females at any age score similarly on Kohlberg's tasks (Dawson, 2002; Jadack et al., 1995; Walker, 1991, 1995). Moreover, themes of both justice and care appear in the responses of both sexes. Consistent with Gilligan's views, however, females in their moral judgments tend to focus more on issues of caring about the well-being of other peoples (Garrod, Beal, & Shin, 1990; Gilligan & Attanucci, 1988; Smetana, Killen, & Turiel, 1991). This is particularly true when individuals reflect on moral issues in their own lives (Jaffee & Hyde, 2000; Wark & Krebs, 1996) and may also reflect gender socialization as much as moral development.

Turiel's Moral Domains

Elliot Turiel's model has much in common with those of Piaget and Kohlberg, including the methods used to assess children's reasoning. Like Piaget and Kohlberg, Turiel and colleagues interview children about hypothetical situations. Some stories involve themes similar to those in the stories of Piaget and Kohlberg (e.g., lying, stealing, breaking a promise). Others involve other rule violations, such as undressing on the playground, not saying grace before snack, a boy's wanting to become a nurse and care for infants when he grows up, and the like (Turiel, Killen, & Helwig, 1987). The stories are designed to depict rule violations in three distinct *domains*.

The **moral domain** is concerned with people's rights and welfare. Issues concerning fairness and justice, such as lying, stealing, and killing, fall into this category. The *social domain* involves **social conventions,** the rules that guide social relations among people. Being polite, wearing appropriate clothing, and addressing people using the proper titles (Mrs. Jones, Dr. Brown, etc.) are behaviors that characterize this domain. There are also *matters of personal choice*, in which individual preferences take priority. These preferences do not violate the rights of others or harm others, and they are not socially regulated (or only weakly so). In many American families, these personal choice matters include one's hairstyle, choice of clothing, and preferred leisure activities or use of time.

A central premise of Turiel's model is that children can distinguish among these domains from a very early age. Of particular interest is the distinction between moral rules and social conventions. According to Piaget and Kohlberg, rules and conventions initially fall within a single domain for children and do not divide into separate cognitive categories until later on. Turiel's research indicates, however, that in many societies children understand by age 3 that moral violations (e.g., hitting another child) are more wrong than violations of social conventions (e.g., eating ice cream with fingers). And children as young as 4 assert that a moral transgression would be wrong even if an adult did not see it and there was no rule to prohibit it (Smetana & Braeges, 1990).

How do children come to make these distinctions among moral domains? According to Turiel, children understand the moral domain through their social interactions—especially

Questions for Thought and Discussion
How might Kohlberg's model aid those who want to reduce childhood aggression and increase prosocial behavior?

Moral domain
In Turiel's model, the cognitive domain in which individuals make decisions about right and wrong.

Social conventions
Rules used by a society to govern everyday behavior and maintain order. In Turiel's model, the chief characteristic of the social domain versus the domain of personal choice.

with peers—as they both become victims of immoral acts and witness the consequences of such acts for others. Children's understanding of conventions in the social domain is assumed to result from their experiences in a variety of social settings, with the conventions differing from one setting to another. The domain model predicts that children in all cultures will distinguish between the moral and social domains at an early age but that particular social conventions will vary cross-culturally (Turiel, 2002; Turiel & Wainryb, 1994; Wainryb, 1993).

Turiel's model, too, is supported by evidence. Studies show that moral reasoning involves different independent cognitive domains and that children distinguish between them from an early age. For example, preschool children in the United States generally believe that breaking a moral rule (such as stealing) is always wrong, whereas breaking a social convention (such as eating with your hands) is conditional. It depends on the setting and situation. They also believe that it is wrong to do something immoral whether or not an explicit rule about it exists; ignoring a social convention, however, is acceptable if there is no specific rule prohibiting it.

Similarly, in situations involving harm and justice (moral rules), children judge that peers, parents, and other adults all have the authority to intervene to protect another person. And they believe it is illegitimate for a teacher or other authority figure to compel a child to violate moral rules. At the same time, children believe that teachers and other authority figures have the right to make their own rules in their own arenas of influence. So teachers can make rules in the classroom but not in children's homes. Finally, when asked which is more wrong, a minor moral misdeed (stealing an eraser) or a major social-conventional transgression (wearing pajamas to school), most children choose the former (Catron & Masters, 1993; Laupta & Turiel, 1993; Smetana & Braeges, 1990; Smetana, Schlagman, & Adams, 1993; Tisak & Turiel, 1988).

Children in Western societies appear to reason in ways consistent with Turiel's model. But do children in all cultures of the world draw similar distinctions among moral rules, social conventions, and matters of personal choice? Research shows significant cultural variability in how children classify various kinds of rule violations. To illustrate, consider some of the transgressions rated as most and least serious by Hindu Brahman 8- to 10-year-olds (see Table 14.2).

To understand how a child would come to judge a widow's eating fish as seriously morally wrong, it is necessary to place judgments of morality in a broader context of beliefs, including religious beliefs. Hindu beliefs specify that eating fish will stimulate the sexual appetite and lead the widow to behave immorally instead of fulfilling her obligation to seek salvation so she can be reunited with the soul of her husband (Shweder et al., 1987). Instances such as these have led some critics to question the universality of Turiel's moral, social, and personal domains.

Questions for Thought and Discussion
What are examples of issues that some Americans regard as matters of personal choice but that others classify as rule violations in the moral domain?

Questions for Thought and Discussion
How might you use Turiel's model to teach children moral reasoning skills?

TABLE 14.2 Transgressions Rated Most and Least Serious by Hindu Brahman 8- to 10-Year-Olds

Serious Transgressions

The day after his father's death, the eldest son had a haircut and ate chicken.

A family member eats beef regularly.

A widow in a community eats fish two or three times a week.

Less Serious Transgressions

A person meets a foreigner who is wearing a watch. He asks how much it costs and whether the foreigner will give it to him.

In school, a girl drew a picture. One of her classmates came, took it, and tore it up.

Not a Transgression

A boy played hooky from school. The teacher told the boy's father and the father warned the boy not to do it again. But the boy did it again, and the father beat him with a cane (the father's actions).

SOURCE: Based on information from R.A. Shweder, M. Mahapatra, and J.G. Miller. (1987). Culture and moral development. In J. Kagan and S. Lamb (Eds.), *The Development of Morality in Young Children* (pp. 40–41). Chicago: University of Chicago Press.

What rules of morality dictate when we must help others? What is the source of these rules? What rules guide your helping behavior as a member of your society, and how did you come to understand those rules? (Jeff Isaac Greenberg/Photo Researchers)

Cultural construction approach
Explanations of children's moral behavior as cultural constructions based on experience as a member of a society.

Questions for Thought and Discussion
How might you use the cultural construction approach in teaching moral reasoning skills to children?

✔ *Test Your Mastery...*

Learning Objective 14.2
Identify factors in children's lives that significantly influence their moral development.

Cultural Construction Approach

The **cultural construction approach** to moral development focuses on how larger cultural beliefs and values influence children's understanding of moral and social rules (Buzzelli, 1995; Edwards, 1987; Miller, Bersoff, & Harwood, 1990; Shweder, Mahapatra, & Miller, 1987; Tappan, 1997). Researchers taking this perspective emphasize that children actively construct their understanding of morality. This construction is a social process in which other people assist children's moral development by structuring and interpreting situations through the lens of a particular moral system.

For example, in one study 7-, 11-, and 18-year-olds in India and the United States were given a series of vignettes in which one person refused to help another person (Miller, Bersoff, & Harwood, 1990). The severity of the need involved varied from severe (a person trained in CPR refuses to give someone mouth-to-mouth resuscitation) to moderate (a person with aspirin refuses to share it with someone who has a severe headache) and minor (a person refuses to give someone a ride to an art store for a special sale). The results of the study indicated that in severe or life-threatening situations, the majority of respondents at all ages in both the United States and India felt that a person has a moral obligation to help another if he or she was able to do so. However, at moderate levels of need, the perception of moral obligation dropped off dramatically in the United States, but not among respondents in India. In other words, children and young adults in India appeared to construe moral obligations more broadly than in the United States, perceiving duty to others more morally binding across a broader range of situations.

Much cultural research on moral development focuses on children's involvement in moral situations that naturally arise during everyday life. For example, how do caregivers foster children's moral development in the context of sibling interactions (Dunn, 1987; Edwards, 1987; Whiting & Edwards, 1988)? How does participation in cultural institutions (such as schools, churches, and community service organizations) contribute to children's moral development (Eccles & Barber, 1999; Lewis, 1995; Youniss, McLellan, & Mazer, 2001)?

Learning Objective 14.1: *Compare and contrast four theoretical approaches to the study of moral development.*

1. What is Piaget's model of moral development?
2. How do Kohlberg's stages of moral development differ from Piaget's model?
3. Is there evidence that males and females have different kinds or levels of moral reasoning?
4. To what extent do Turiel's domains of morality have cross-cultural validity?
5. How does the cultural construction approach to moral development differ from other approaches?

Influences on Moral Development

In addition to social and cultural values and institutions, other influences on moral development include individual life experiences, peer interactions, parental discipline, personality factors such as temperament, and emotions or moral affect. These influences affect both moral reasoning and moral behavior, which often are not the same thing. People capable of high levels of moral reasoning may also be capable of highly immoral behavior. At the same time, people may behave morally without being able to explain their reasoning. Studies based on Kohlberg's method have found only a modest relation between a child's level of moral reasoning and the child's moral behavior (Blasi, 1980, 1983; Kohlberg, 1987; Kohlberg & Candee, 1984; Rholes & Lane, 1985; Straughan, 1986).

BOX 14.1   When Are We Obligated to Help Others? Cultural Differences in Children's Perceptions

How might a child answer this question: If a stranger is on the roadside next to a broken down car, do you have an obligation to help? Will that child's answer change if he sees it is his best friend in need of help? What if it was a person he did not like? What if external circumstances made it difficult to help? According to research by Joan Miller and her colleagues, the answers to these questions are culturally variable.

Miller's research focuses on the role of culture in moral development, specifically expanding *the morality of caring*. The morality of caring was introduced as an alternative model of morality by Gilligan (Gilligan & Wiggins, 1988). The model broadened the scope of traditional morality research by adding interpersonal relationships to the limited issues of justice and individual rights that traditional theorists such as Kohlberg (1971) defined as morality. Miller's work fits within this newer framework of the morality of caring (Miller, 1997). Gilligan theorized that the morality of caring was gender related and, although there was never confirming evidence of such a distinction, it did leave a path open for looking at "subgroup diversity," such as culture, within the field of morality. Miller has expanded on the model by investigating differences in Hindu Indian and European American cultures (Bersoff & Miller 1993; Miller, 1995; Miller, Bersoff & Harwood 1990; Miller & Luthar 1989).

Miller et al. (1990) compared the moral judgments of Indian and American second graders, sixth graders, and college students. Participants were given vignettes in which an agent declined to help another person for a selfish reason. The relationship between the people in the vignette varied across conditions—they were strangers, friends, or part of a parent-young child relationship. The level of help needed also varied from life-threatening to moderate and minor need. Both Indians and Americans see helping as desirable. However, Indians judge that there is a moral responsibility to help, whereas Americans tend to consider it as a matter of personal choice.

This observation was most salient in a non–life-threatening condition. Both Indians and Americans judge that whether or not to help the agent in life-threatening situations is a moral issue. However, Americans are more likely to judge helping as a moral issue if the person is a close friend or relative. This emerges as a linear pattern in the American responses, where a moral judgment is assigned to issues in a declining order of need and role of the agent involved, with parent-child major-need most often assessed to be a moral decision. Indians judge more situations across the board as moral decisions, regardless of level of need or role of the agent; whether the person in need of help is a stranger or a close relative and whether the need is great or minor, the choice is a moral one that is seen as legitimately subject to social sanction and as governed by an objective obligation.

American and Indian second graders tend to be more similar in their moral judgments than their older counterparts are to each other. Whereas Indian children reflect their older counterparts, American children tend to judge situations as moral more often than do American adults. As children grow, they develop a morality that increasingly reflects their culture, rather than a specific gender or a universal morality. Miller hypothesizes that the similarity in children's moral judgments may stem from the universal need for nurturing as infants, which leads children to more often assess helping as a moral issue. However, as children are exposed to their own cultural practices and beliefs, their reasoning about why an issue is moral becomes increasingly based on those cultural practices and not on the experience of infant dependency (Miller, 1984; Miller et al., 1990).

Although Americans categorize a broader range of helping instances as personal choice and Indians categorize them more frequently as moral imperatives, Indians are much more forgiving of breaches in these moral decisions and are less likely to hold agents accountable when they do not live up to a responsibility (Miller & Luthar, 1989).

An important distinction according to Miller (1997) is that Hindu Indians don't need to like someone in order to help them—the decision is one of interpersonal responsibility. Americans see personal liking, common interests, and tastes as an integral part of the decision of whether or not to help in a given situation. Miller and Bersoff (1998) found liking and level of need were key factors for Americans in deciding when to help family and friends. However, liking played no role in the decision for Indian respondents.

Miller's research shows how cultural practices influence moral development in many ways. When are we obligated to help others is just one of the questions that illustrates how culture affects the ways we see and interact with the world. If a particular culture prizes individual autonomy, then when to help someone will be seen as a personal choice rather than a moral decision. If, however, the cultural values reflect the person as "an inherent part of a social body" (Miller, 1997), then whether or not to help a person is more likely a moral imperative.

In keeping with Bronfenbrenner's ecological model, researchers also are concerned with how aspects of parents' lives, such as their employment, directly and indirectly affect children's involvement in prosocial and antisocial activities (Elder & Conger, 2000; Fletcher, Elder, & Mekos, 2000). Researchers agree that social and family factors play a role in moral development, although they disagree as to the nature and importance of that role.

Peer Influences on Moral Reasoning

Both Piaget and Kohlberg emphasized that children's interactions with peers are an important impetus for moral growth. One indirect test of the role of peers in children's moral development is whether children with greater peer experience have more advanced moral reasoning. This appears to be the case, as correlational studies show a positive relationship between aspects of a child's peer interactions (such as popularity) and the child's level of moral maturity (Dunn, Cutting, & Demetriou, 2000; Enright & Satterfield, 1980; Schonert-Reichl, 1999). The influence between peer relations and moral development goes both ways, however: Children who reason competently about moral issues are likely to be attractive companions and friends.

Other researchers have followed in Piaget's footsteps and observed children's social interactions around moral events. These studies have been conducted in homes and schools and on playgrounds with children age 2 through early adolescence (Much & Shweder, 1978; Nucci & Nucci, 1982a, 1982b; Nucci & Turiel, 1978; Turiel, 2002). These studies consistently show that situations involving issues of fairness and harm arise frequently in children's interactions with peers. Moreover, children respond to moral transgressions from a very early age, usually by talking about the injury or loss experienced by the victim and asking the perpetrator to consider how it would feel to be the victim of the transgression.

Other researchers have used experiments to study the impact of peer interaction on moral reasoning (Berkowitz, Gibbs, & Broughton, 1980; Kruger 1992; Kruger & Tomasello, 1986; Walker et al., 2000). These studies involve older elementary school children and adolescents who are asked to respond individually to moral dilemmas. Respondents then are paired with peer partners and asked to discuss the dilemmas and reach a consensus in moral judgment. Following the discussion, each child is interviewed again, sometimes months or even years later. Results show that discussing moral issues with peers can foster advances in children's moral reasoning. Interactions among peers with different perspectives on the dilemmas are most beneficial (Berkowitz et al., 1980). Peer interactions that promote moral growth differ in important ways from parent-child interactions associated with higher levels of moral reasoning (Walker et al., 2000).

Parent Influences on Moral Reasoning

Dialogues with parents also can foster moral growth (Holstein, 1972; Parikh, 1980). In one investigation, for example, Lawrence Walker and John Taylor recruited children ranging in age from 6 to 16 and their parents to participate in two laboratory sessions two years apart. First, both parents and children responded individually to a set of Kohlberg's moral dilemmas and to a real-life dilemma they had recently experienced in their own lives. They were asked to discuss a dilemma on which they had shown disagreement during the individual interviews. They also discussed a real-life dilemma that had been volunteered by the child. The same procedure was repeated two years later.

The study showed that parents lowered their level of moral reasoning during the family conversations, whereas children raised theirs. These findings are consistent with Vygotsky's notion of a zone of proximal development. By aiming their reasoning at—but not beyond—the upper bounds of the child's capabilities, parents provided a scaffold for the child's acquisition of a more advanced moral understanding.

Walker and Taylor also found that when discussing hypothetical dilemmas, parents tended to challenge children's reasoning and adopted a didactic style. During discussions of the child's real-life dilemma, in contrast, parents tended to be more supportive and to focus on drawing out the child's opinion and coming to understand it. Interestingly, the quality of the interactions about the real-life dilemmas—but not the hypothetical ones—predicted children's moral reasoning two years later (Walker & Taylor, 1991). Another way parents influence children's moral understanding is through discipline for misconduct. When parents punish children, they generally hope that children will not only avoid engaging in the inappropriate behaviors again but also will gradually assume responsibility for enforcing the rules. The development of self-regulation often involves learning to control the desire to engage in forbidden behavior. Children seem to accomplish this self-regulation by *internalizing* the rules and prohibitions presented by their parents (Buzzelli, 1995; Hoffman, 1994; Tappan, 1997).

The effectiveness of discipline in promoting internalization of the parents' values and morals depends on the style of punishment and the child's temperament. (Grusec & Goodnow, 1994). Three general classes of parental discipline have been identified (Hoffman, 1970, 1984). The *power assertion* style involves the use of commands, threats, and physical force. The *love withdrawal* style uses verbal disapproval, ridicule, or withholding affection from the child. The *induction* style involves reasoning with the child to explain why certain behaviors are prohibited and often engenders guilt in the child by pointing out how the misbehavior may have caused harm or distress to someone else. Evidence from several studies suggests that American children who have been disciplined through an induction approach display the most advanced levels of moral reasoning; love-withdrawal techniques result in somewhat lower levels; and power assertion produces the least mature forms of reasoning (Boyes & Allen, 1993; Hart, 1988b; Weiss et al., 1992).

Will this parent's discipline strategy promote moral development? Which discipline style has proven most effective in fostering moral reasoning and behavior? What aspects of a child's temperament contribute to effective parent-child interactions on issues of moral development? (Christina Kennedy/PhotoEdit)

Psychological Factors that Influence Moral Behavior

Another factor that affects how well discipline promotes internalization involves the child's temperament. *Fearfulness*, for example, is an inborn trait that influences whether children will internalize their parents' rules (Kochanska, 1993, 1995, 1997). For fearful children, prone to timidity and anxiety, gentle discipline and the avoidance of power assertion tactics work best to promote the child's development of conscience (internalization). For fearless children, a cooperative and responsive approach works best, because it capitalizes on the child's positive motivation to accept the parents' values. The goodness-of-fit concept discussed in Chapter 11 thus applies here as well. The type of discipline that is most effective with a particular child is the one that best "fits" with the child's personality and temperament (Kochanska & Thompson, 1997).

Links to Related Material
In Chapter 11, you read about the concept of goodness of fit. Here, you learn more about how goodness of fit relates to parental discipline strategies and children's development of conscience.

Does morality represent a consistent personality trait that each of us carries with us? Hartshorne and May (1932) explored this problem by exposing over 10,000 children (ages 8 to 16) to situations that provided opportunities for dishonesty. The settings included homes, schools, and churches, and the behaviors of interest were various forms of lying, cheating, and stealing. Each situation was designed so that dishonest behavior would "pay off" for the child, but the apparent risk of being detected varied. In reality, the researchers were always aware of whether the child was being honest. The children were also interviewed about their attitudes regarding dishonesty.

The results showed little consistency across situations. The fact that a child stole in one context was not useful in predicting whether the child would cheat in another. And there was very little correspondence between children's verbal pronouncements of moral values and their actual behavior. Hartshorne and May thus concluded that children's moral behavior does not reflect a personality trait but is situation-specific, depending primarily on the circumstances at hand. A reanalysis of the data from this classic study indicated that some degree of consistency did exist for similar situations (Burton, 1963, 1984). Nevertheless, it remained clear that the children were usually willing to adjust their moral conduct to fit the demands of the moment. Those demands often include peer pressure and obedience to authority, which are known to encourage both prosocial and antisocial behavior.

Learning Objective 14.2: *Identify factors in children's lives that significantly influence their moral development.*

1. According to research, how do peer interactions influence moral development?
2. How do parenting styles and child-parent interactions influence moral development?
3. What psychological factors influence individuals' moral development?
4. To what extent is moral behavior a product of personality factors versus situational factors?

✔ *Test Your Mastery...*

Learning Objective 14.3
Define the dimensions of prosocial behavior and identify sources of variation in prosocial behavior.

Prosocial behavior
The aspect of moral conduct that includes socially desirable behaviors, such as sharing, helping, and cooperating; often used interchangeably with altruism by modern researchers.

Empathy
The ability to vicariously experience another's emotional state or condition.

Sympathy
Feeling of concern for another in reaction to the other's situation or emotional state, not necessarily involving an experience of the other's emotional state.

Prosocial Behavior

Moral behavior is defined by how people act as opposed to how they think. **Prosocial behavior** includes acts that society considers desirable and attempts to encourage in children. Three forms of prosocial behavior have been studied extensively: *helping* (which includes comforting and caregiving), *sharing*, and *conflict resolution* (Eisenberg & Fabes, 1998). It is widely believed that the roots of prosocial behavior lie in the capacity to feel empathy and sympathy.

Empathy and Sympathy

Moral action requires more than moral thoughts; it also requires what have come to be known as moral affect, or moral emotions, including empathy and sympathy. **Empathy** is the ability to experience another's emotional state or condition vicariously—essentially, to feel what the other is feeling. **Sympathy,** in contrast, is concern for another in response to his or her situation or emotional state without necessarily sharing the same emotions (Eisenberg, 1986). Recall that evolutionary theorists believe that the capacity to feel these emotions is present in both humans and some nonhuman primate species (Flack & de Waal, 2000).

Martin Hoffman (2000) proposes a five-stage model of the development of empathy. Stage one is a precursor of empathy, apparent during the first months of life, when infants cry reflexively upon hearing the cries of other infants. Interestingly, infants do not cry when they hear their own tape-recorded crying, nor do they react as strongly to other equally noxious nonsocial stimuli (Martin & Clark, 1982; Sagi & Hoffman, 1976).

In the second stage, infants respond to another's distress as though they themselves were in distress. During this developmental interval, infants feel empathy in response to distress but lack clear boundaries between the self and others. Consequently, infants respond to others' distress by comforting themselves (e.g., sucking their thumbs) or seeking comfort from caregivers.

During the third stage, as children develop a sense of themselves as distinct individuals, their reactions to others' distress change. When confronted with someone who is distressed, they realize the distress is the other's, not their own. However, because young children have difficulty distinguishing between their own and others' thoughts and feelings, the help they offer tends to reflect what they would like and not necessarily what is most helpful to the other person. For example, one 14-month-old responded to a crying friend with a sad look, then gently took the friend's hand and brought him to his own mother, although the friend's mother was nearby (Hoffman, 1978, 2000). During this stage, children begin to feel sympathy for others.

During the fourth stage, children develop greater empathy, feeling what others are actually feeling, because they now understand how other people have inner states different from their own. Children can offer more appropriate help and comfort, although they may not always do so. A child may understand why a sibling is distressed and how best to comfort her, for example, but may choose to do the opposite (Dunn, 1988)!

During the final stage, which emerges in middle childhood, children are able to consider the broader features of other people's lives. Thus, they are able to empathize with those they imagine to have generally sad or unpleasant lives because of illness, poverty, and the like. By around age 7 or 8, children can comprehend social categories that define groups and so come to understand the plight of entire classes of people, such as the homeless, social outcasts, and victims of war.

Helping and Sharing

Research findings on the development of early helping behavior are largely consistent with Hoffman's five-stage theory of the development of empathy. One series of longitudinal studies, conducted by Carolyn Zahn-Waxler and colleagues, tracked changes in children's reactions

This child is showing empathy toward another child in a particular social context. How does empathy develop, and what are some other basic prosocial behaviors?
(© P. Davidson/The Image Works)

BOX 14.2   CONVERSATIONS with a Marriage and Family Therapist

Sandra Rigazio-DiGilio
(Courtesy of Sandra Rigazio-DiGilio)

Sandra Rigazio-DiGilio is a licensed marriage and family therapist and a licensed psychologist, as well as a professor in the School of Family Studies at the University of Connecticut— Storrs. She grew up in Springfield, Massachusetts, and at age 51 now lives in Connecticut with her husband, Dr. Anthony J. Rigazio-DiGilio, her daughter Elizabeth (15), and her son Nicholas (13). Sandra's clinical practice involves working with families who are living through the dying process of one of their children. We asked her to talk about her practice and the career path that led her to this important work.

The grieving process spans a phase of life that includes caring for the child through many iterations of illness, accepting the dying process, the death itself, bereavement, and reorganization. During this journey, children and families often wish to retell portions of their lives, and to think through how they understand their changing circumstances. I use both narrative therapy and videography to assist children and families to tell their stories, review their histories, and express their hopes for the future—not just for themselves, but also for wider audiences.

The concrete gift of videos is enormously powerful for both givers and the receivers, offering opportunities for individuals, families, and communities to focus on events that seem untenable, and to find ways to define, experience, and interpret these events. Additionally, videos allow people's stories to live on, even for those not yet born, reinforcing the continuity of family history. The making and sharing of tapes reinforces social ties that add meaning and value to life.

What I have found is that children who are living through the dying process seem to find an intuition that healthy individuals only capture later in life. They have an incredible capacity to connect with others, be humorous, and be wise. Their spirituality connects them to a plane beyond life as we know it and draws others significant to them into this plane. The understandings and connectedness that emerge when hearing their stories about life, dying, death, and life beyond are heartfelt. Significant others stretch to listen to the worldviews held in the minds of these children and to express themselves during these intimate encounters.

My Italian heritage taught me that the dying process is an immensely important part of living life. The ways in which we work through it profoundly color our perceptions of our families and ourselves for generations to come. As a child, I found that adults beyond my family who were usually capable of comforting me through my personal dilemmas were made uneasy by the stories of death and dying that I was experiencing. This uneasiness—which I saw throughout my pre-professional life—was my main impetus for choosing this clinical subspecialty.

Dr. Rigazio-DiGilio's undergraduate degree is in human development and family relations. Her graduate degrees are in rehabilitation counseling, marriage and family therapy, and counseling psychology. In her clinical practice, she works within a wide community context, emphasizing the resources and relationships that can be brought to bear to support families through the dying process. These resources include hospitals, schools, community services, churches, and extended family networks. Some families share the videos to affect the community and wider social contexts, even public policy. Videos may relate to causes for particular illnesses, such as support for individuals with AIDS; education for dying with dignity; goals of spirituality; or support for others working though similar illnesses, such as self-help groups and family support networks. "Thus," Sandra says, "the spirit of the children's stories is used to create a better place after their passing."

I have been working with children and families in this capacity for well over 25 years and still feel an absolute privilege to be invited into such a significant life transition. I also see the many ways these events can affect individuals across different ages and over the life span. Particularly noteworthy are my experiences with adolescents working through the dying process of one of their siblings. It is often the case that their own uncertainties and fears remove them from the process in ways they later—as adults—negatively evaluate. For these individuals, the tapes provide a reminder of the resources and capabilities they did have.

For example, I recently received a letter from a young man whose sister died when he was 15. Twenty years before, he had not kept a promise to take his sister hiking while she was still capable of walking. During the process of therapy, he decided to make a videotape of a walk in the woods, which they later watched together from her bedside. His sister later titled the tape, "My Walk with My Brother—and I Did Not Even Lose My Breath." In his letter to me, he wrote, "I knew I was too young to understand or accept what was happening to my sister. I was angry. I have felt that perhaps I did not do enough to make her feel I loved her. However, when I watched my son laugh at my video of the woods, I knew I must have had an impact on my sister. A memory from so long ago leaves me with a precious thought of how hard I tried to be there, using the resources I had. Obviously, I did a good job."

While the topic of death and dying is scary, especially in untimely death, the work families can do with therapists as a guide can be enormously rewarding. The children's stories live on. The tapes, and how they were made, shared, and discussed, become their living legacy—cherished gifts that can be shared for future generations to come.

to others' distress during the second and third years of life (Zahn-Waxler & Radke-Yarrow, 1982; Zahn-Waxler et al., 1992; Zahn-Waxler et al., 2001).

In each study mothers reported their children's reactions when confronted with the distress of another in the context of everyday activities. In some studies, these reports were supplemented by home and laboratory visits during which mothers and experimenters staged events designed to elicit concern. For example, the mother might pretend to cry, cough, or choke, or feign an injury to her knee. Coders recorded the children's reactions to the incidents. Typical behaviors included giving hugs or kisses or words of comfort (e.g., "You be okay"), putting on a bandage, asking if the mother was all right, and showing concern or distress in facial expressions.

As Hoffman's theory predicts, when confronted with someone distressed, the younger toddlers primarily became distressed themselves. But many of the older toddlers actually attempted to help the victim, although the help was not always appropriate, as when one youngster tried to feed his cereal to his "ailing" father (Zahn-Waxler, Radke-Yarrow, et al., 1992). As the children grew older, both the frequency and sophistication of the helping increased. With age, children were increasingly likely to express their concern verbally, fetch a bandage or a blanket, or ask another adult to intervene.

Similar age-related increases in helping have been reported in studies of siblings and peers. Young children show an increased tendency to comfort a sibling in distress between the ages of 15 and 36 months—but only if the child was not the cause of the sibling's distress (Dunn, 1988). Observations in preschools reveal that young children also will comfort peers in distress, especially if the pair have an ongoing friendly relationship (Farver & Branstetter, 1994).

Other signs of early prosocial behavior come from observations of children as they follow parents and older siblings about during their daily activities (Rogoff, 1990, 2003). Toddlers are often eager to help others perform household chores (Rheingold, 1982). There are cultural variations in how often young children have the opportunity to help, however, and how others respond to their offers of help. In communities where children are integrated into the lives of adults, toddlers' imitation of adult activities is expected and encouraged, and even small children are assigned simple chores (Rogoff, 2003). In many cultures participation in chores is associated with prosocial behavior (Elder & Conger, 2000; Whiting & Whiting, 1975).

Helping behavior increases with age. Compared with younger children, older children and adolescents are more likely to help even at some cost to themselves, perhaps because older children are better able to recognize possible physical, psychological, or moral gains from assisting others (Eisenberg & Fabes, 1998).

Individuals of any age do not always offer help, even when they can. Obstacles to helping at all ages include not knowing how to help, lack of confidence in one's ability to help, and fear that helping will make the situation worse or otherwise will be unappreciated. In addition, children and adolescents sometimes fail to help because they feel that someone else is responsible or that it is not appropriate for them to help (Eisenberg & Fabes, 1998). Studies show that children are more likely to help when they have been shown how to assist and when they have been assigned responsibility to help (Peterson, 1983a, 1983b; Staub, 1971).

A related prosocial behavior is sharing. As you know, young children do not always readily share. Still, like helping, sharing emerges remarkably early. Babies as young as 1 year will often hand a toy or food to their parent or to another child. Sharing can serve a variety of interpersonal functions. For young children who have as yet only limited verbal capabilities, sharing is one way to initiate or maintain social interactions with adults or peers (Eckerman, Davis, & Didow, 1989; Hay et al., 1995). It also may be a means by which children resolve conflicts among themselves (Butovskaya et al., 2000; Caplan et al., 1991). Children are especially likely to share when they are involved in a give-and-take relationship with the other person and have experienced some "receiving" as well as "giving" (Hay & Murray, 1982; Levitt et al., 1985). Also, as with helping, older children are more likely to share than are younger ones (e.g., Benenson et al., 2003; Eisenberg & Fabes, 1998).

Conflict Resolution

A third type of prosocial behavior is conflict resolution. Although estimates vary, conflict among peers and siblings occurs fairly regularly during childhood and adolescence (Buhrmester & Furman, 1990; DeHart, 1999; Hartup et al., 1988; Hay, 1984; Laursen & Collins, 1994). Because many conflicts escape the notice of adults, some mechanism must exist that keeps children's conflicts from escalating out of control.

Children resolve conflict in three ways. *Negotiation* includes compromise and intervention by a third party, such as another peer or a teacher. *Disengagement* includes withdrawal (walking away from the dispute) and shifting the focus or topic. *Coercion* occurs when one party is forced to give in to the demands of another, sometimes in response to threats or other aggressive ploys (Jensen-Campbell, Graziano, & Hair, 1996; Vuchinich, 1990).

A meta-analysis of studies of peer conflict among North Americans asked the question, how does the use of these conflict resolution strategies change with age (Laursen, Finkelstein, & Betts, 2001)? Children tend to resolve disputes through coercion and refraining from disengagement. Adolescents, in contrast, tend to favor negotiation, and they employ disengagement and coercion equally often. Young adults strongly favor negotiation and use coercion infrequently. The data also showed that children tend to display more effective conflict resolution skills in hypothetical dilemmas than in actual disputes, where even adolescents tend to rely on coercive techniques. Methods of conflict resolution also vary depending on the relationship (e.g., friends, acquaintances), where negotiation tends to increase with closer ties. Also, negotiation increases as children's verbal abilities, understanding of mental and emotional states, and self-regulatory capacities advance.

How do children "make peace" with one another following conflict (Verbeek, Hartup, & Collins, 2000)? **Peacemaking** refers to a friendly postconflict reunion between former opponents. Postconflict peacemaking behaviors vary considerably, both among nonhuman primates and human children. Peacemaking can follow the conflict immediately or after a delay or cooling-off period. In some species, peacemaking involves conspicuous behaviors that are rarely observed in other social contexts, whereas in other species the behaviors are more implicit (de Waal, 1993). Among chimpanzees, after a conflict one protagonist will reach out to the other, inviting proximity and physical contact. The chimps will hug, groom intensively, kiss, or have sex. Sometimes a mediator will bring the two together and then withdraw, leaving the protagonists calmed and close to each other. Major reconciliations are accompanied by loud vocalizations by other members of the group (de Waal, 2000). Studies show that children use both verbal and nonverbal behaviors to reconcile with peers, including sharing of toys or food, invitations to play, apologies, and touching or hugs.

Peacemaking
A friendly postconflict reunion between former opponents often characterized by invitations to play, hugs, apologies, object sharing, and silliness.

Individual Differences Individual differences in prosocial behavior also exist. Some children seem inordinately caring and compassionate, whereas others appear to care little about the welfare of other beings. There is some evidence that genetic factors contribute to these differences. Studies involving adult twins have found greater similarity in self-reported empathy and altruism among pairs of identical twins than among fraternal twin pairs (Davis, Luce, & Kraus, 1994; Rushton et al., 1986). Similar findings were reported in a recent study of toddler twins (Zahn-Waxler et al., 2001). Identical twins received more similar scores on measures of empathic concern and prosocial behavior than did fraternal twins.

Researchers doubt there is a gene for kindness, however. Individual differences in prosocial responding likely relate to differences in temperament. Studies have linked children's tendencies to feel negative emotions such as anxiety, sadness, and guilt, as well as their responses to these emotions, with their tendency to feel empathy and sympathy. Children who experience negative emotions but are not overcome by them are especially likely to feel sympathy for the plight of others. In contrast, children who are overcome by high levels of negative emotions tend to focus on themselves (Eisenberg et al., 1998; Eisenberg et al., 2000). Of course, feeling bad is not always sufficient to prompt action. Inhibited or cautious children may not always be able to bring themselves to help someone even if they want to (Barrett & Yarrow, 1977; Denham & Couchoud, 1991).

Peacemaking rituals are part of the culture of these children. What Kalmyk peacemaking rituals are you aware of from your own and others' culture histories? What other cultural factors shape patterns of prosocial behavior in a society? (Marina Butovskaya and Olga Vorotnikova)

Gender Differences A widely held gender stereotype is that females are more kind, generous, and caring than males (Eagly, Wood, & Diekman, 2000; Shigetomi, Hartmann, & Gelfand, 1981). However, empirical evidence suggests only a modest sex difference favoring girls (Eagly & Crowley, 1986; Eisenberg & Fabes, 1998). Even across different cultures, girls and boys do not differ significantly in peacemaking, although they sometimes differ in the methods they use to make peace. For example, one approach used often by boys but rarely by girls is acting silly to make others laugh.

As infants and toddlers, girls tend to display more personal distress, empathy, and other expressions of concern than boys, though the difference is not great (Zahn-Waxler et al., 2001). Sex differences in empathy grow larger with age and are greatest when measured by self-report. Girls are also more likely to be kind and considerate but are not more inclined to share, comfort, or help (Eisenberg & Fabes, 1998).

Social and Cultural Differences The first national survey of altruism and empathy ever conducted in the United States, the National Opinion Research Center at the University of Chicago (2002), asked people questions about 15 different acts of altruism, such as talking with someone who is depressed, helping with housework, giving up a seat to a stranger, giving money to a charity, volunteering, helping someone find a job, or helping in another way, such as lending money. The study found, based on self-reports, that more frequent religious observances (such as church attendance) were associated with more frequent charitable behavior. Thus, religious observance is a social factor in prosocial behavior.

Cultural factors in prosocial behavior include differences in peacemaking techniques (Butovskaya et al., 2000). One cross-cultural study observed postconflict reunions among middle-income children in day care centers and schools in four diverse cultural communities: preschool-age children in large cities in the United States and Sweden and 6- and 7-year-old elementary school children in two Russian communities. One community was composed of ethnic Russians living in a large city. The other was composed of Kalmyk children. Traditionally nomadic herdsman, Kalmyks in Russia now live in villages and towns near the Caspian Sea.

In each of the four communities, children in conflict were more likely to seek each other out for peaceful interaction than children who had not engaged in conflict, and the interaction usually was initiated within 2 minutes of the conflict. Older children were more inclined to make peace than younger children. In Sweden, for example, postconflict peacemaking occurred 60 percent of the time among 5- and 6-year-olds, 42 percent of the time among 4-year-olds, and only 17 percent of the time among 3-year-olds.

When compared with their Russian counterparts, the Kalmyk children showed a greater peacemaking tendency, reflecting stronger cultural and religious emphasis on peaceful coexistence. Kalmyk and Russian children also used ritualized peacemaking rhymes, called *mirilka*. During the peacemaking rituals, children held hands and recited *mirilka*, such as "Make peace, make peace, don't fight, if you fight, I'll bite, and we can't bite since we're friends" (Butovskaya et al., 2000, p. 249). Sometimes, Kalmyk peers brought the opponents together and encouraged them to recite the rhymes publicly to signify the end of conflict.

✔ *Test Your Mastery...*

Learning Objective 14.3: *Define the dimensions of prosocial behavior and identify sources of variation in prosocial behavior.*

1. What is prosocial behavior, and how is it manifested?
2. What are Hoffman's five stages in the development of empathy?
3. What methods of conflict resolution and peacemaking can be observed in children?
4. What are some individual and gender differences in prosocial behavior?
5. What social and cultural factors shape differences in prosocial behavior?

Determinants of Prosocial Behavior

Theorists seek to explain the origins, causes, or determinants of behavior. Explanations for prosocial behavior can be found in evolutionary or biological factors, cognitive and emotional factors in human psychology, and sociocultural factors relating to socialization in the family, community, and way of life. Evolutionary explanations begin with the idea that altruistic behaviors are those that benefit someone else but offer no obvious benefit—and perhaps even some cost—to the individual performing them. Giving money to a charity, sharing a candy bar, and risking one's life to save someone else's are examples. Yet, altruism is a universal trait among humans and some other species, so there must be a biological or evolutionary basis for this behavior. How can behavior that does not increase a person's own chances of survival and reproduction be passed on in the species? It would seem, instead, that people who act selfishly and think first about themselves would be more likely to survive to pass along their genes. This dilemma, called the *paradox of altruism* has been debated since the time of Charles Darwin (Campbell & Christopher, 1996; Krebs, 1987; MacDonald, 1988a; Post et al., 2002).

Kin Selection and Reciprocal Altruism

Sociobiologists have attempted to resolve the paradox of altruism problem by showing how self-sacrifice can contribute to a gene pool through kin selection (Dawkins, 1976; Maynard Smith, 1976). **Kin selection** proposes that humans (and some other animals) behave in ways that increase the chances for the survival and reproduction of their genes rather than of themselves. A person can pass on genes either by reproducing or by increasing the reproductive chances of someone who has the same or similar genes, that is, a relative. The more genes a second individual shares with the first, the more adaptive it becomes to try to save that individual's life (and reproductive capability). A mother, therefore, would be more likely to risk her life for her child than for her husband, because her child shares many of her genes. Similarly, any family member, or kin, would be favored over any unrelated individual.

But people perform acts of altruism directed toward nonfamily members—even strangers—every day. How does evolutionary theory explain such behavior? Here, a process called **reciprocal altruism** comes into play. According to this idea, people are genetically programmed to be helpful because (1) it increases the likelihood that they will someday in turn receive aid from the person they helped or from some other altruistic member of their group, or (2) by helping someone else in their social group, they help ensure that genes similar to their own will be passed on in the species (Trivers, 1971, 1983).

Moral Affect and Moral Reasoning

Although the capacity for prosocial behavior is grounded to some extent in biology, cognitive and emotional factors also play a role. Researchers have measured children's emotional arousal and facial expressions as they viewed videotapes designed to induce feelings of sympathy for a story character. Children whose responses were strongest were shown to be most likely to share or to display other prosocial behaviors when given the opportunity (Eisenberg & Fabes, 1998; Fabes et al., 1994; Miller et al., 1996). This finding relates to individual differences in prosocial behavior.

Cognitive-developmental studies predict a positive relationship between a child's moral reasoning and his or her altruistic behavior, which research generally supports (Eisenberg, 1986, 1987; Eisenberg et al., 1995; Krebs & Van Hesteren, 1994). These studies evaluate children's levels of moral reasoning through the use of *prosocial dilemmas*. These stories differ from those of Piaget and Kohlberg in that they place less emphasis on breaking rules or laws. Instead, the story character usually must decide whether to help someone, often at some personal expense. For example, one story requires a little girl to choose between helping a hurt child and being on time for a birthday party (Eisenberg, 1982). Findings show a connection between how children think about moral issues and how they act.

Learning Objective 14.4
Explain the biological, cognitive, and sociocultural determinants of prosocial behavior.

Questions for Thought
and Discussion
Do you believe that altruism ever occurs in the absence of internal or external rewards? If so, what is an example?

Kin selection
A proposed mechanism by which an individual's altruistic behavior toward kin increases the likelihood of the survival of genes similar to those of the individual.

Reciprocal altruism
A proposed mechanism by which an individual's altruistic behavior toward members of the social group may promote the survival of the individual's genes through reciprocation by others or may ensure the survival of similar genes.

Links to Related Material

In Chapter 8, you read about false-belief tasks and children's developing theory of mind. Here, you learn that performance on false-belief tasks relates to conflict resolution skills in elementary school.

The ability to understand a situation from someone else's point of view is central to this process. In several studies, children who were better at telling a story from another person's point of view were more prosocial with peers (Eisenberg, 1986, 1987; Eisenberg et al., 1995). Understanding (but not necessarily experiencing) the mental state or feelings and emotions of another person is also correlated with prosocial behavior (Garner, Jones, & Miner, 1994; Moore & Eisenberg, 1984). And children who do well as preschoolers on various types of "mind-reading" tasks (for example, the false-belief tasks described in Chapter 8) are better able to resolve conflicts with friends during elementary school (Dunn, 1999).

Because it is internalized, altruistic behavior is largely self-reinforcing, affecting moral affect even in the absence of external rewards or approval. Children witnessing the joy experienced by someone they helped, for example, or sharing that person's relief from distress are reinforcing their helping behavior. There can be no doubt that much of children's prosocial behavior occurs because it rewards the giver as well as the receiver.

Social Participation and Socialization

Over the course of childhood and adolescence, prosocial behaviors increase in frequency. Developmental changes in children's affective and cognitive capabilities contribute to this increase, but increases in prosocial responding also coincide with changes in children's social experiences. Among these are changes in the settings children inhabit, the roles they play, the kinds of activities they engage in, and the expectations of others. Thus, children's opportunities for prosocial behavior change, beginning with the family context. For example, children who routinely perform chores and contribute to family well-being and the functioning of the household often develop a stronger prosocial orientation than their peers who do not participate in family life in this way (Grusec, Goodnow, & Cohen, 1996).

One source of supporting evidence is the Six Cultures Study introduced in Chapter 1 (Whiting & Whiting, 1975). In this study, researchers observed children between the ages of 3 and 11 in six different countries. They found that children in Kenya, Mexico, and the Philippines displayed more nurturant behavior (e.g., offering help and support) than children in Okinawa, India, or the United States. The factor most strongly associated with nurturing behavior was the assignment of chores to children, especially the care of infants. Moreover, the degree to which children within each culture participated in the infant care and household work was predictive of their level of nurturance.

Is there any evidence that opportunities for activities such as these promote prosocial commitment in children? What other parent behaviors promote prosocial behavior?
(Jim West/Alamy)

A study of Iowa farm youth followed more than 400 seventh graders over a period of six years during a time when many Iowa farmers were struggling economically (Elder & Conger, 2000). As is true in many farm families, the farm youth in this study made a significant economic contribution to the household through their labor on the farm and the money they earned by raising livestock or in part-time jobs. Even as seventh graders, the adolescents took their responsibilities quite seriously. Most rated their chores as very important, a higher rating than that provided by agemates from nonfarm families. When interviewed as twelfth graders about what made their work important, many of the respondents focused on the importance of being counted on and the experience of being interconnected with others. As one boy noted, "If I help the family, it saves the family money as a whole. So we can take the money we save . . . and apply it to maybe . . . a new truck" (Elder & Conger, 2000, p. 90). For many adolescents, voluntary community service may serve a similar function, providing opportunities to practice helping others and perhaps increasing feelings of prosocial commitment (Johnson et al., 1998; Yates & Youniss, 1996).

Prosocial commitment is fostered through parental communication of values, modeling, and reinforcement. Recall that parents may foster a prosocial orientation through the values they communicate to children (Grusec & Goodnow, 1994). Children whose parents employ inductive techniques and talk with them about the impact of their actions on others display more mature moral reasoning than children of parents who use other disciplinary techniques (Hoffman, 1975; Krevans & Gibbs, 1996). People who have shown unusually high levels of altruism tend to report that they learned values of caring, generosity, and respect for all human life from their parents and other influential adults (Oliner & Oliner, 1988).

Children learn not only from what parents say but also from what they do. Laboratory studies have shown that children share more or are more helpful after observing a model performing similar behaviors (e.g., Eron & Huesmann, 1986; Lipscomb, McAllister, & Bregman, 1985; Radke-Yarrow & Zahn-Waxler, 1986). Children are especially likely to imitate adults with whom they have a positive relationship.

Some psychologists have attempted to use modeling in applied settings to increase prosocial behavior. Children's educational television, for example, often includes moral themes and prosocial messages (Jordan, Schmitt, & Woodard, 2001). A recent meta-analysis of 34 studies (with a total sample of over 5,000 children) found that viewing prosocial TV programming has modest positive effects on prosocial behavior. These effects increased with the use of supplemental materials, such as guided lessons, games, and discussion designed to enhance program content (Mares & Woodard, 2005).

Children also display more altruism when their altruistic behavior is reinforced. Laboratory studies routinely demonstrate the positive effects of reward and praise on children's prosocial behaviors (Eisenberg & Murphy, 1995; Gelfand & Hartmann, 1982). Praise is especially effective in promoting altruism if it emphasizes that the child is a generous or helpful person ("You were a very nice girl for sharing your candy") (Mills & Grusec, 1989). Applied psychologists have used reward programs as a way of increasing prosocial behaviors in the classroom and other natural settings (CPPRG, 1999; Walker, Colvin, & Ramsey, 1995).

Studies in natural settings and situations show that preschool children often respond positively to altruistic behavior, such as by smiling, thanking the child, or doing something nice in return (Eisenberg et al., 1981). Older siblings who are cooperative and helpful also tend to promote prosocial interactions among younger family members (Dunn & Munn, 1986). And mothers, like peers, often respond to altruistic behavior with some form of praise or verbal approval (Eisenberg et al., 1992; Mills & Grusec, 1988). Parental reinforcement also is key to adolescent involvement in community activities, particularly when the parents themselves do not participate (Fletcher, Elder, & Mekos, 2000).

Test Your Mastery...

Learning Objective 14.4: *Explain the biological, cognitive, and sociocultural determinants of prosocial behavior.*

1. What is a possible evolutionary basis for altruistic behavior?
2. What cognitive abilities and emotional responses help make altruism self-reinforcing?
3. What socialization methods help shape prosocial behavior?
4. What are some examples of socially mediated opportunities for prosocial behavior?

Learning Objective 14.5

Distinguish kinds of aggression and the factors that contribute to aggressive behavior in children.

Aggression

Behavior that is intended to cause harm to persons or property and that is not socially justifiable.

Instrumental aggression

Aggression whose purpose is to obtain something desired.

Hostile aggression

Aggression whose purpose is to cause pain or injury.

Physical aggression

Aggression expressed through hitting, kicking and biting

Verbal aggression

Aggression expressed in name calling, teasing, and threats.

Relational aggression

Aggression designed to damage or disrupt social relationships.

Aggression

The same kinds of determinants (biological, evolutionary, cognitive-developmental, psychological, and sociocultural) are at work in antisocial behavior. At the opposite end of the spectrum from prosocial behavior is the antisocial behavior of **aggression**. Whether it takes the form of hitting, verbal ridicule, or malicious gossip, aggression is a common and important aspect of child development that has been studied extensively (Coie & Dodge, 1998; Loeber & Farrington, 1998).

Different kinds of aggressive behavior in children can be distinguished. **Instrumental aggression** is aggressive behavior aimed at obtaining something desirable, for example, when one preschooler shoves another to try to grab a toy. **Hostile aggression**, in contrast, is aggression aimed specifically at inflicting pain or harm (Berkowitz, 1993). Studies focus on aggressive behavior that is intended to cause harm to persons or property and that is not socially justifiable. Thus, aggression is based on a social judgment that takes into account both the individual's motives and the context in which the behavior occurs (Coie & Dodge, 1998; Parke & Slaby, 1983). Researchers have identified three general types of hostile aggression.

- **Physical aggression**—hitting, kicking, and biting
- **Verbal aggression**—name calling, teasing, and threats
- **Relational aggression**—spreading damaging rumors, social exclusion (Crick, 1995; Crick & Grotpeter, 1995)

Age and Gender Differences in Aggression

Types of aggression occur in different proportions among children of different ages and sexes. By the end of their second year, children begin to use physical aggression, such as hitting and pushing, to resolve conflicts (Tremblay et al., 1999). Physical and instrumental aggression decline over the preschool years, while verbal and relational aggression increase. Decline in physical aggression coincides with improved ability to resolve conflicts verbally and to control emotions and actions.

Most children continue to show a decline in overt **physical aggression** during elementary school and through adolescence. Some children manifest serious problems with aggression at this age, however, and other forms of antisocial behavior (Cairns et al., 1989; Loeber & Hay, 1993). And for some adolescents there is a marked increase in serious acts of physical violence (Coie & Dodge, 1998; Haapasalo & Tremblay, 1994). The peak age of onset for violent crime is 16, when about 5 percent of male adolescents report their first act of serious violence. When considering youths between the ages of 12 and 20 who report having committed at least one serious violent act at any age, prevalence for males ranges from about 8 to 20 percent, and for females, it ranges from 1 to 18 percent (*Youth Violence: A Report of the Surgeon General*, 2001, http://www.surgeongeneral.gov/library/youthviolence/default.htm).

As you can see in Figure 14.3, there is a large difference in the number of males and females who engage in physically violent behavior during adolescence and early adulthood.

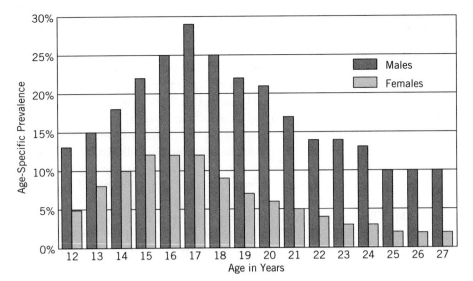

FIGURE 14.3
Violence by Age and Sex
This graph compares the prevalence of self-reported violence for males and females of different ages. How do these data support the idea that aggression has biological determinants?

SOURCE: From J.D. Coie and K.A. Dodge. (1998). Aggression and antisocial behavior. In W. Damon (Series Ed.) & N. Eisenberg (Vol. Ed.), *Handbook of Child Psychology: Volume 3. Social, Emotional, and Personality Development* (5th ed.). New York: Wiley. Reprinted by permission.

This sex difference in rates of physical aggression begins long before adolescence and is observed in all cultures of the world. Boys begin to display more physical and verbal aggression as preschoolers and continue to do so throughout the elementary-school years (Loeber & Hay, 1997).

Beginning with the preschool years and extending into adolescence, girls display more relational aggression than boys (Crick, Bigbee, & Howes, 1996; Crick, Casas, & Mosher, 1997; Crick et al., 1999). In the later elementary grades, aggression by boys toward other boys becomes increasingly physical, but aggression by boys toward girls drops markedly. Aggression by girls remains primarily relational and is directed predominantly toward other girls (Cairns et al., 1989; Galen & Underwood, 1997; Underwood, 2003).

Biological Determinants of Aggression

From an evolutionary standpoint, one major function of aggression is to increase the likelihood of survival of an individual's or group's genes. Aggression may help an individual or group to obtain food, protect the young, or preserve valuable hunting territory. In such cases, evolutionary processes favor the stronger, smarter, or more skillful members of the species.

Aggression in many species can lead to physical combat. Some conflicts do not progress to this point, however, but are resolved when one animal displays threatening gestures (such as certain facial expressions and body postures) and the other animal backs down, perhaps making submissive gestures. Such behaviors also have adaptive value for individuals and groups—the attacker may gain possession of desired property, and those who retreat may avoid injury or death.

Primates live in social groups with a **dominance hierarchy,** in which members of the group are ranked or fit somewhere on a dominance ladder. Individuals control those lower in the hierarchy (often simply by threats) but submit to those higher on the ladder. Although dominance hierarchies are established and maintained through aggression, such a structure ultimately reduces the overall physical conflict that might otherwise occur in the group (Pellegrini & Bartini, 2001; Strayer & Noel, 1986). The structure and function of dominance hierarchies in children's social interactions work in a similar fashion.

Hormones, genes, and temperament influence an individual's level of aggression, which is stable over many years (Farrington, 1994; Loeber & Stouthamer-Loeber, 1998). Longitudinal research indicates that frequent peer aggression at age 8 is a good predictor of aggression and other antisocial behaviors at age 30 (Eron et al., 1987). This degree of stability lends itself well to a genetic or biological explanation of the behavior. Numerous studies have

Dominance hierarchy
A structured social group in which members higher on the dominance ladder control those who are lower, initially through aggression and conflict, but eventually simply through threats.

Questions for Thought and Discussion
Do you think that humans are aggressive by nature, making warfare inevitable? If not, why is there persistent conflict?

shown a link between levels of the male hormone, testosterone, and *adult* aggressiveness (Archer, 1991). Evidence for a link between hormone levels and aggression among adolescent males, however, is mixed. Some studies have found that boys rated as more aggressive by their peers or parents have higher-than-average levels of testosterone (Olweus et al., 1988; Sussman et al., 1987), whereas other studies have found no evidence that increases in testosterone are related to increases in aggression (Halpern et al., 1994). There is some evidence that testosterone levels are more closely linked to social dominance than aggression per se and that hormone levels can change in response to particular kinds of competitive experiences (Coie & Dodge, 1998). If hormone levels do contribute to individual differences in aggression, the process is likely to be indirect and to vary with age (Archer, 1994).

Numerous studies of adult twins have reported more similar levels of aggression among identical (monozygotic) twins than among fraternal (dizygotic) twins or other siblings (DiLalla, 2002). Recent twin studies involving children have also demonstrated significant genetic effects on aggression (Deater-Deckard & Plomin, 1999; Taylor, Iacono, & McGue, 2001; Vierikko et al., 2003). Genes have a stronger influence on aggression than on other forms of antisocial behavior, such as delinquency. In addition, they play a stronger role during childhood and adulthood than during adolescence, when environmental factors matter more (Miles & Carey, 1997).

One manifestation of genetic effects is temperament. Recall from Chapter 11 that some babies are born with "difficult" response styles. They fuss, cry, and are more demanding than other infants of the same age. This personality dimension is quite stable across childhood, prompting researchers to investigate whether it bears some relation to the development of aggressive behavior. One team of researchers tested this hypothesis by asking a group of mothers to rate their 6-month-old infants on a temperament questionnaire that allowed the researchers to identify difficult babies. Over the next five years, the same mothers periodically evaluated their children's aggressive behavior. As predicted, the early temperament ratings were quite good predictors of which children would later display greater amounts of aggression (Bates et al., 1991). Other longitudinal studies have reported similar results extending into adolescence (Caspi et al., 1995; Olson et al., 2000).

As children move into the preschool years, other temperament dimensions, such as impulsivity and poor self-regulation, become predictive of later aggressiveness. Children who are highly impulsive during early childhood are more likely to engage in fighting and delinquency during early adolescence, aggression and criminal activity during late adolescence, and violence in adulthood (Caspi et al., 1995; Tremblay et al., 1994).

Why might temperament predict later antisocial behavior? One possibility is that a difficult early temperament reflects a stable underlying problem that manifests itself in different ways at different ages. Another possibility is that difficult babies are not really difficult but are just seen that way by parents. Parents may either directly or indirectly communicate to such children that they are difficult, which may motivate the children to behave in ways that match parental expectations. Still another possibility is that children with difficult temperaments elicit or evoke harsh and punitive parenting, which makes them more antisocial (Ge et al., 1996; O'Connor et al., 1998; Rubin et al., 2003).

Cognitive and Affective Influences on Aggression

Aggression is a subject with which most youngsters are familiar. From an early age, children can identify aggressive behavior and realize that it is considered undesirable. Even first graders show strong agreement on peer nominations of aggression (Younger & Piccinin, 1989; Younger, Schwartzman, & Ledingham, 1985). By the age of 5, children can comprehend more complex forms of aggressive behavior, such as **displaced aggression,** in which a child who has been the object of aggression reacts by striking out at something else (Miller & DeMarie-Dreblow, 1990; Weiss & Miller, 1983).

Aggressive children (especially boys) show certain cognitive differences from their classmates. For example, their levels of moral reasoning and empathy (Cohen & Strayer, 1996) tend to be lower, and they are less likely to take into account a person's motives when

Links to Related Material
In Chapter 11, you read about dimensions of temperament. Here, you learn more about how early temperament may relate to the development of aggressive behavior.

Displaced aggression
Retaliatory aggression directed at a person or an object other than the one against whom retaliation is desired.

These children, known to peers as a bully, have misread a social situation. They have interpreted a classmate's behavior as an act of hostile aggression and are exacting revenge. How does this fit with research on the relationship between cognitive development and social behavior? (*Left*, © Richard Hutchings/PhotoEdit; *right*, © Jonathan Nourok/PhotoEdit)

making a moral judgment (Sanvitale, Saltzstein, & Fish, 1989). In addition, aggressive children often display a "self-protective" interpretation of their social world; that is, they tend to minimize the negative feelings that other children have toward them (Zabriski & Coie, 1996). Consistent with this idea is the finding that children who have positively biased self-perceptions (believing themselves to be more socially accepted than their peers report them to be) are more likely to show high levels of both physical and relational aggression than are children without such a bias (David & Kistner, 2000).

Aggressive children also have been found to differ in two other aspects of social cognition—the process by which they come to understand the social world in which they live (Dodge & Crick, 1990). Using an information processing model, Kenneth Dodge and his associates found that aggressive children have difficulty reading social cues in the environment (Crick & Dodge, 1994; Dodge & Crick, 1990; Quiggle et al., 1992). Their studies typically involve videotaped episodes in which one child is harmed or provoked by a peer whose intentions are unclear. In these situations, aggressive children are much more likely to attribute hostile or malicious motives to the provoker. And when cues are provided to suggest that the provoker's intentions are not hostile, aggressive children have more difficulty understanding and using these cues (Dodge & Crick, 1990; Dodge & Somberg, 1987). Thus, these children may be aggressive because they do not view the world in the same way that most children do (Waas, 1988; Waldman, 1996). Children whose aggression stems from these sorts of attributional problems are most likely to display hostile aggression (Crick & Dodge, 1996).

Second, Dodge believes that aggressive children also frequently have another difficulty processing social information—deciding how to respond to a provocation from another child (Dodge & Crick, 1990). In such situations, these children are most likely to select an aggressive response as the best way to respond, apparently because they believe that this approach will produce the most positive outcomes. Aggressive children with this type of processing difficulty are most likely to display instrumental aggression to obtain something they want (Crick & Dodge, 1996).

Sociocultural and Family Determinants of Aggression

In addition to biological and cognitive factors, social, cultural, and situational factors are also important determinants of aggressive behavior. Aggression is culturally channeled, socially sanctioned, and shaped through learning principles (Bandura, 1986, 1989, 1994). That is, children learn when, where, with whom, and how to be aggressive through their social experiences. For example, gender differences in physical aggression may result because boys—by their own report—expect less disapproval for this sort of behavior than girls do and are less bothered by the disapproval when it occurs (Boldizar, Perry, & Perry, 1989; Perry, Perry, & Weiss, 1989). Environmental influences such as family processes, peer relations, and media such as television strongly influence aggression.

Family Processes Children's aggression often stems from their interactions with parents and siblings. Parents of aggressive children deal with misbehavior more through power-assertion methods of discipline, using physical punishment, than through verbal

Coercive family process
The method by which some families control one another through aggression and other coercive means.

explanation or reasoning (Chamberlain & Patterson, 1995; Rubin, Stewart, & Chen, 1995; Schwartz et al., 1997). Thus, parents may be modeling aggressive behavior to their children, who go on to imitate what they see. Also, these parents may be interacting with their children in ways that promote, even perpetuate, aggression. Evidence suggests that these processes often continue from one generation to the next, such that as adults aggressive children are more likely to have aggressive children themselves (Serbin et al., 2002).

Studies have found that families of aggressive children commonly display a troublesome pattern of interactions, referred to as the **coercive family process** (Patterson, 1982; Patterson, Reid, & Dishion, 1992; Snyder & Patterson, 1995). In these households, negative interaction patterns between parents and children are unwittingly reinforced and can become firmly entrenched, resulting in a child who is "out of control." How do such patterns become established? An example is Laura and her 9-year-old daughter, Jennifer. At times, Laura ignores Jennifer's messy bedroom, but at other times, stressful circumstances in Laura's own life leads her to explode with threats. Jennifer must clean her room immediately, "or else." Jennifer is used to her mother's inconsistency in such matters. She begins to whine, scream, argue, and otherwise behave unpleasantly while avoiding the task of cleaning her bedroom. Angered by her daughter's refusal to obey, Jennifer escalates her threats and criticisms but does not act on them. Eventually, exhausted by the conflict, Laura gives in and stalks away angrily. Jennifer, in turn, ends her unpleasant behavior—at least temporarily. Experiencing relief at the abrupt ending of Jennifer's tantrum, the mother is reinforced in her behavior of "giving in." Jennifer, in turn, is reinforced in her belief that it is worthwhile to throw tantrums rather than comply with undesirable parental requests.

The long-term consequences of this pattern is that the child is more likely to ignore parental commands in the future. To get the child to comply, the parent must escalate threats, which leads to other coercive tactics (e.g., slapping, hitting). The child, in turn, must escalate tantrums or other bad behavior. The result is an out-of-control child, and often an out-of-control parent as well.

Family members achieve their goals through coercive behaviors rather than through cooperative, prosocial means. The connection between this sort of parenting and later aggression in young girls is not known (Keenan & Shaw, 1997; McFayden-Ketchum et al., 1996), but for young boys the outcomes are clear. Boys who learn this style of interaction at home—and who fail to learn more positive interpersonal skills—also display aggression in other settings and often go on to delinquency and other serious forms of antisocial behavior (Conger et al., 1994; DeBaryshe, Patterson, & Capaldi, 1993; Patterson, 1995; Vuchinich, Bank, & Patterson, 1992).

Peer Relations Aggression is a social problem primarily because it causes harm to others. In addition, by failing to acquire appropriate social skills, aggressive children run the risk of being rejected by their peer group and becoming outcasts (Asher & Coie, 1990; Lochman & Wayland, 1994). Overtly aggressive children often have poor interpersonal skills, and unpopular, rejected children often are aggressive. These behaviors probably are mutually reinforcing. But does this mean that highly aggressive children never have friends? Or that they are never members of stable social groups?

These questions were addressed in a large-scale study of the social patterns of overtly aggressive children (Cairns et al., 1988). To begin, the researchers identified a group of boys and girls in the fourth and seventh grades as very aggressive, based on reports from their teachers, principals, and counselors. Next, for comparison, the researchers selected a group of nonaggressive children who were similar in age, gender, race, and other related characteristics. The social patterns of the two groups were measured through interviews with classmates, ratings by teachers, and self-ratings.

The data from these measures were analyzed to answer several questions. First, did the children group themselves into social clusters, in which certain children spent a great deal of time together? If so, which children were members of these groups? Were any of the clusters made up predominantly of aggressive children? Finally, how often were aggressive children nominated as "best friends" by their classmates?

The results proved somewhat surprising. In the identified social clusters, aggressive individuals were just as likely to be members as those who were nonaggressive. Children high in aggression often tended to hang around together, forming their own clusters. And aggressive children had just as many peer nominations as best friend as did nonaggressive children. The best-friend relationships, however, involved aggressive children nominating one another and nonaggressive children nominating one another.

These findings, once again, demonstrate how studies of children in their natural environments often turn up unexpected results. The widely held belief that aggressive behavior automatically sentences a child to a life of social isolation is clearly overstated. Many aggressive children have networks of friends who are similar to themselves. Although these clusters may encourage and thus perpetuate antisocial behavior, they also appear to provide friendships and social support. Thus, although many aggressive children may fail to develop good interpersonal skills and may be rejected by their peers, some are socially competent enough to make and maintain friends.

Television and Real-Life Violence   The prevalence of violence on television is well documented. Surveys of TV programming from the early 1970s to the early 1990s revealed that over 70 percent of children's prime time programs and over 90 percent of Saturday morning dramatic programming depicted violent acts. The average number of violent acts per hour was 5.3 during prime time and 23 on Saturday mornings (Huston & Wright, 1998).

The amount of aggression and violence shown on TV is particularly striking in light of the amount of TV children watch—about 24 hours per week for the typical school-age child (Comstock & Scharrer, 2001). The number of violent acts viewed during these hours adds up—by age 21, the average child has witnessed about 8,000 television murders (Huston & Wright, 1998).

Beginning with Albert Bandura in the 1960s, researchers have repeatedly demonstrated that children can learn new forms of aggression, and can be stimulated to perform them, by viewing a violent film model (Bandura, 1973, 1983, 1994). But does the average child really become more aggressive simply as a result of watching a typical diet of current network programming? The answer, based on dozens of studies and reports, appears to be yes (Bushman & Huesmann, 2001; Comstock & Scharrer, 1999). Moreover, the effects of violence can take several forms.

The most obvious effect is that children imitate the violent acts they see. They are especially likely to do so when the violence is performed by the "good guys" and also when the aggression successfully achieves its purpose. A somewhat less obvious effect is that TV violence increases the likelihood of all other forms of aggression in children, even those that do not resemble the behavior of the television models. And the effects are long term. Similarly, researchers have reported that for both boys and girls viewing TV violence from ages 6 to 10 was associated with elevated aggressive behavior 15 years later in young adulthood (Huesmann et al., 2003). This relationship held up regardless of factors such as socioeconomic status and intellectual ability. The relationship between violence and aggression appears to be circular: Television violence stimulates aggression, and more aggressive children also tend to watch more violent television (Huesmann, Lagerspetz, & Eron, 1984). Violence on TV can also make children more tolerant of aggression and less bothered by it (Parke & Slaby, 1983).

Not all the violence children witness is vicarious. Many children also experience repeated violence firsthand in their everyday lives. Sometimes it occurs in the home among family members, perhaps in the form of spouse or child abuse. And increasingly, children around the world are exposed to political, religious, ethnic, or community violence (Cairns, 1987, 1996; Garbarino et al., 1992; Garbarino & Kostelny, 1996; Kostelny & Garbarino, 1994; Leavitt & Fox, 1993; Straker, 1992). Children exposed to both vicarious and real-life violence tend to display increased use of aggressive words, aggressive play, and a general preoc-

Links to Related Material
In Chapter 10, you read about the effects of TV viewing on children's cognitive development. Here, you learn more about the specific effects of viewing violence on TV.

Questions for Thought and Discussion
What aspects of American society do you think might increase violence and aggression among children? What aspects might decrease it?

Violence on television, like personally experienced violence in real life, has been shown to be a common cause of children's aggression.
(© Etta Hulme/Reprinted by permission of NEA, Inc.)

cupation with aggressive themes. Children who have a secure relationship with one or both parents generally fare the best in these environments, whereas any conflict or animosity within the family increases the likelihood that the children will be affected by the violence.

Learning Objective 14.5: *Distinguish kinds of aggression and the factors that contribute to aggressive behavior in children.*

1. What kinds of aggressive behavior do children exhibit?
2. How does antisocial behavior vary by age and sex?
3. What evolutionary, biological, and genetic factors may cause aggressive behavior?
4. What are some social-cognitive and affective characteristics of violent children?
5. What coercive family process contributes to children's antisocial behavior?
6. How do experiences of violence, both real and on TV, affect children's social behavior?

![✔] **Test Your Mastery...**

Controlling Childhood Aggression

Learning Objective 14.6
Discuss methods of reducing juvenile violence and aggression.

Parents, teachers, and public officials often look to child development research for help in solving real-life problems. This has been the case with efforts to reduce juvenile violence and aggression, a task in which legal and judicial methods generally fail. Despite enormous attention to the issue, the contributions of research to violence prevention have seemed disappointing (Pettit & Dodge, 2003). Childhood aggression is a complex problem that must be treated in the broader context of troubled children's lives. And we must recognize that our powers of intervention are limited, particularly among older youth.

Recent years have seen progress in understanding the development of antisocial behavior. We have learned that antisocial youth may follow one of a number of routes, or "developmental trajectories" (Lacourse et al., 2002). Consequently, "one-size-fits-all" interventions are unlikely to work equally well with all children. We also have learned that preventing the development of antisocial behavior in the first place is generally more effective than treating youth after they have begun to engage in problem behavior (Fields & McNamara, 2003). And we have learned much about which kinds of interventions do work—and which do not. It was once believed that aggression is a means of venting steam and can thus be prevented by having the aggressive child channel energy into other behaviors or experience aggression vicariously. Hitting a punching bag or watching a wrestling match, then, could take the place of engaging in aggressive behaviors. Psychoanalytic theory refers to these substitute behaviors as forms of **catharsis.** The cathartic process has been used to defend the existence of violent TV programs and aggression-related toys (Feshbach & Singer, 1971). Research

Catharsis
The psychoanalytic belief that the likelihood of aggression can be reduced by viewing aggression or by engaging in high-energy behavior.

evidence, however, does not support this theory. As you have seen, viewing violence on TV increases rather than decreases the probability of aggression. And studies with both children and adults indicate that engaging in high-activity behaviors does not make aggression any less likely (Bushman, 2002; Geen, 1983). Not surprisingly, methods aimed at curbing aggression through catharsis have generally proved ineffective (Parke & Slaby, 1983).

Parent and Child Training

It is well established that parents' childrearing methods are related to their children's aggression (Coie & Dodge, 1998; Stormshak et al., 2000). One of the most straightforward and successful approaches to handling this source of aggression has been the use of parent training techniques (Forehand & Kotchick, 2002; Kazdin, 2002; Reid, 1993). Drawing on principles of behavior modification, child development professionals have trained parents in more effective ways of interacting with their children. Parents learn to reduce the use of negative remarks, such as threats and commands, and replace them with positive statements and verbal approval of children's prosocial behaviors. They are also trained in applying nonphysical punishment in a consistent and reasonable manner when discipline is required. The results of this form of intervention have often been dramatic in changing both the parents' and the children's behavior.

Children can be trained as well, especially to change their cognitive strategies for dealing with social informaiton. This approach has been used with children ranging in age from preschoolers to adolescents. One **cognitive training** approach involves preventing aggression through training children in problem-solving techniques. Children learn to deal with problem situations more effectively by first generating and examining various strategies for confronting the problem and then following a systematic plan for dealing with it. With younger children, problem-solving training often is begun in a laboratory setting. The children first hear stories in which a character faces potential conflict and then are trained to analyze the problem and develop constructive solutions. Gradually, the children are encouraged to apply these new skills in real-life situations (Lochman et al., 1984; Shure, 1989). Similar programs have been used with aggressive adolescents (Goldstein & Glick, 1994; Guerra & Slaby, 1990).

One limitation of this approach is that for many aggressive children, the difficulty lies not in their ability to generate multiple and appropriate solutions to interpersonal conflicts but in their ability to execute the behaviors. Often, heightened emotion interferes with children's ability to inhibit aggressive actions. Laboratory studies with adults have shown that if this emotional response can be replaced with empathy, aggression can be prevented or decreased (Baron, 1983). Programs for increasing children's empathy—by teaching them to take the perspective of the other child and to experience that child's emotional reactions—have found some success in reducing conflict and aggression (Feshbach & Feshbach, 1982; Frey, Hirschstein, & Guzzo, 2000; Gibbs, 2003).

Another approach is to focus on the assumptions or attributions children make about others' behavior (Graham & Hoehn, 1995; Graham, Hudley, & Williams, 1992; Graham & Juvonen, 1998b). The premise of this approach is that aggressive children are likely to interpret ambiguous, provocative actions by their peers (such as bumping into them in the school hallway) as intentional and hostile. This attribution produces anger, which then gives rise to aggressive, retaliatory behavior.

Researchers developed a cognitive intervention program designed to interrupt this sequence leading up to the aggression (Hudley & Graham, 1993). The study involved urban African American children in grades 4 to 6 who had been selected on the basis of teacher and peer ratings of their aggression. Most of the children had been rated high on aggression, but some had been rated low (so that not all children selected to participate in the study were stigmatized as problem students). Each research participant was assigned to one of three groups: an experimental group that received attribution training, an attention control group that received training only in academic skills, and a third control group that received no training.

Cognitive training
Interventions designed to change the way people think about themselves, others, situations, and options.

School-based programs offer universal interventions to teach conflict resolution and other prosocial attitudes and behaviors. What needs to happen for such programs to be successful? (Ellen B. Senisi/The Image Works)

The attribution training involved teaching the children to recognize cues to another person's intentions (such as facial expressions), to encourage nonhostile attributions when the peer's actions were ambiguous (for example, "he probably did it by accident"), and to generate nonaggressive responses to the peer's behavior. The training continued for six weeks and included a variety of methods, such as storytelling, role playing, videos, and group brainstorming.

Before and after the training, all research participants were given a series of assessments designed to determine how likely they were to (a) attribute hostile intentions in an ambiguous situation, (b) become angry in response to such attributions, and (c) respond with aggressive behavior. The data for those children initially rated high on aggression are shown in Figure 14.4. Obviously, the attributional training worked very well. On each of the three measures, children in the experimental group scored the lowest on aggression in

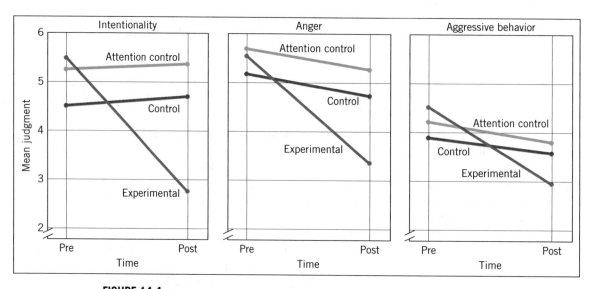

FIGURE 14.4

Results of a Cognitive Intervention Study

In this intervention study with African-American children, the experimental group received attributional training and decreased in aggression the most on the three measures of interest.

SOURCE: Adapted from C. Hudley & S. Graham. (1993). An attributional intervention to reduce peer-directed aggression among African-American Boys. *Child Development, 64,* 124–138. Copyright (c) 1993 by the Society for Research in Child Development. Reprinted by permission.

the posttest that followed the training and showed by far the greatest change. These data suggest not only that attributions play a role in producing aggression toward peers in everyday classroom situations but also that cognitive interventions designed to change these attributions can reduce such aggression.

The researchers caution, however, that other factors in the situation should not be overlooked. One is that not all aggression is directed toward peers and that this approach may not reduce problems involving vandalism, defiance of authority, theft, gang-related activities, and so forth. Perhaps a more important point is that given the difficult conditions under which many lower-SES urban children live, attributing hostile intentions to peer provocations may often be accurate and retaliating with aggression may seem a useful survival response in such a setting.

School-Based Programs

An alternative approach to controlling aggression is to shift the focus away from the individual child and toward the school—one of the primary socialization contexts of children's lives. Several intervention programs share a common goal of reducing aggressive behavior and increasing prosocial behavior by altering the social environment of the school (Battistich et al., 2000; Flannery et al., 2003; Grossman et al., 1997; Nucci, 2001). Although the specifics of the programs differ, all aim to create caring school communities. These so-called **universal interventions** involve all children in a classroom or school and not just children deemed to have problem behaviors. Key to the success of the programs is helping teachers foster a prosocial orientation among students toward classmates and their community. Universal interventions, which may include special curricula devoted to improving children's social problem-solving skills, have been shown to have positive effects, although the impact on children with serious problems with aggression is modest (Greenberg, Domitrovich, & Bumbarger, 2001).

Two examples cited by the American Psychological Association as widely tested and successful early interventions in school settings are the PeaceBuilders Program and RCCP (Resolving Conflict Creatively Program)(American Psychological Association, 2003). The PeaceBuilders Program is used by 200,000 students in New York City schools and in 12 other school systems across the country. It focuses on teacher-led activities for learning choice making, conflict resolution using constructive strategies, and acceptance of individual and cultural differences. The RCCP program focuses on providing opportunities for children to improve their social competence and on creating positive school climate.

Universal interventions
School-based programs for improving children's social competence and reducing aggression.

Learning Objective 14.6: *Discuss methods of reducing juvenile violence and aggression.*

1. Why is catharsis unreliable and often ineffective as a means of treating childhood aggression?
2. What kinds of interventions have been shown to reduce childhood aggression?
3. What training has proven helpful to parents of aggressive children?
4. What three kinds of cognitive training have been used with aggressive children?
5. What makes universal school-based interventions such as Fast Track effective?

✔ *Test Your Mastery...*

BOX 14.3   Intervening in the Lives of Aggressive Children

Although numerous interventions aimed at aggressive children have proved promising in the short term, the challenge is to maintain the reduction in aggression and other antisocial behaviors over time. Increasingly, researchers believe that effective treatment of antisocial and aggressive children requires a multifaceted approach that addresses parenting skills, teacher-parent communication, the social behaviors and reasoning skills of at-risk children, and the behaviors of peers.

One intensive, comprehensive program is the Fast Track intervention. Fast Track targets children who display problem behaviors at the beginning of elementary school. The intervention is designed to address the multiple problems that characterize these "early-starting" aggressive children: They tend to come from poor families and neighborhoods, experience ineffective parenting, have poor relations with peers, do poorly in school, and attend schools that cannot control disruptive and violent behavior. The program seeks to improve these various areas of children's lives.

Fast Track begins in first grade and continues through tenth grade. It includes both a universal curriculum for all children and a specialized program that targets high-risk children and their families. The universal curriculum fosters emotion regulation and prosocial skills in the regular education classroom. The specialized program includes weekly enrichment sessions during school hours. High-risk children and their parents participate in these sessions, which are designed to further advance children's social skills and peer relations and to improve parenting skills, parent-child relations, and the parent-school partnership. The children also receive academic tutoring. In addition, the program includes home visits designed to develop trusting relationships with the parents and children and to promote general problem-solving skills for the entire family (CPPRG, 1992, 1999).

According to the *Fast Track Project* Web site (http://www.fast-trackproject.org/), the six components of the elementary school phase of the Fast Track intervention (grades 1–5) include:

- Teacher-led classroom curricula (called PATHS) as a universal intervention directed toward the development of emotional concepts, social understanding, and self-control (including weekly teacher consultation about classroom management); and the following five programs administered to the high-risk intervention subjects.

- Parent training groups designed to promote the development of positive family-school relationships and to teach parents behavior management skills, particularly in the use of praise, time-out, and self-restraint.

- Home visits for the purpose of fostering parents' problem-solving skills, self-efficacy, and life management.

- Child social skill training groups (called Friendship Groups).

- Child tutoring in reading.

- Child friendship enhancement in the classroom (called Peer Pairing).

As you can see, this is a multifaceted intervention that addresses diverse factors affecting children's social behavior: children's cognitive, affective, and interactional awareness and skills; literacy development; teacher training and support; and parent training and support. Does Fast Track work? A longitudinal study designed to assess the effectiveness of this comprehensive program was initiated in 1990. Nearly 900 first-graders with behavior problems were randomly assigned to intervention (Fast Track) or control classrooms. The results of ongoing evaluations are promising. By fourth grade, 48 percent of children in the control group had been placed in special education, compared with 36 percent of children in the intervention group. The intervention also lowered arrest rates. By eighth grade, 42 percent of the control group had been arrested, contrasting with 38 percent of Fast Track children. And among children in ninth grade, the intervention reduced serious conduct disorders by more than a third, from 21 percent to 13 percent (Conduct Problems Prevention Research Group, 2002; Crawford, 2002).

Fast Track is an expensive program. Is the reduction in rates of serious antisocial behavior obtained so far worth the cost? Kenneth Dodge, one of the program directors, thinks so. He observes, "If each career criminal costs society $1.3 million and the Fast Track program costs $40,000 per child, the program will prove to be a wise economic investment if just 3 percent of children are saved from careers of violent crime" (Crawford, 2002, p. 38). Because of its success, today the Fast Track program has been adopted in several school systems in the United States, as well as in Great Britain, Australia, and Canada.

BOX 14.4   Contextual Model of Moral Development

Child is born with human biological propensities for aggression and prosocial behavior. In addition, individual differences in temperament influence the child's behavioral profile.

Family, Neighborhood, and School Settings

- Parents, siblings, peers, and teachers provide models for prosocial behavior, conflict resolution skills, and aggression.
- Parents and other caretakers provide discipline and guidance that influence the development of conscience.
- Parents' own temperament influences how they respond to the child's temperament, impacting on their ability to modify or shape specific aspects of the child's temperament.

Community Influences

- Parents' socioeconomic status influences where they can afford to live. Children who grow up in more crime-ridden neighborhoods are more likely to be exposed to a larger number of peer models for violence and aggression.
- Parents' own experience of stress in their workplace may influence time and patience that they have to provide guidance and consistent discipline.

Cultural Influences

- Violent and aggressive or prosocial behaviors are modeled for children in the media.
- Children learn conflict resolution tactics that are valued in the larger culture.

Learning Objective 14.1

Compare and contrast four theoretical approaches to the study of moral development.

1. What is Piaget's model of moral development?

Piaget presented children with moral dilemmas to solve in which the child had to determine which of two characters was "naughtier." He developed a *four-stage model* of moral development based on the way children follow rules. In the first stage (2 to 4 years), children have no real conception of morality and no formal rules. The idea of following someone else's rules appears consistently in the second stage (5 to 7 years). Social rules are viewed as absolute, externally dictated (*heteronomous*) by authority figures (usually parents), and unchangeable. Children in this stage of moral realism do not question the purpose or correctness of a rule and tend to evaluate moral situations only in terms of their physical consequences. Another characteristic of this second stage is a belief in imminent justice—that punishment must always follow rule breaking. In Piaget's third stage (8 to 11 years), the child gradually realizes that rules are agreements created by people to help or protect one another. Children's more advanced cognitive abilities allow new factors to enter into their moral evaluations. Thus, a person's motives or intentions become as important as the outcome of the behavior. Piaget referred to this third stage as moral relativism. In the final stage, children become more autonomous in their moral reasoning, capable of viewing rules critically and developing new rules when circumstances require. They also begin to extend their moral reasoning beyond the personal level to larger societal and political concerns and to abstract principles of justice.

2. How do Kohlberg's stages of moral development differ from Piaget's model?

Kohlberg, like Piaget, presented moral dilemmas to assess individuals' level of moral reasoning. Kohlberg's dilemmas had story characters who had to choose between obeying a rule or breaking a rule for an individual's benefit. Kohlberg concluded that moral reasoning develops in *three predictable levels*: preconventional, conventional, and postconventional, containing six stages in all. In preconventional morality, moral decisions are made on the basis of reward and punishment and the satisfaction of one's own needs. In conventional morality, moral decisions are made on the basis of conforming to others' expectations, including the general social order. In postconventional morality correct behavior is defined in terms of individual rights and the consensus of society. Movement from stage to stage in Kohlberg's model closely follows the Piagetian process of accommodation. Kohlberg's stages, like Piaget's, formed structured wholes, followed an invariant sequence, and were regarded as universal.

3. Is there evidence that males and females have different kinds or levels of moral reasoning?	Research has provided *little evidence* that males and females differ in their moral reasoning. When levels of formal education are equal, male and females at any age score similarly on Kohlberg's tasks. Females in their moral judgments tend to focus more on issues of caring about the well-being of other people. This tendency may reflect gender socialization as much as moral development.
4. To what extent do Turiel's domains of morality have cross-cultural validity?	Children in Western societies appear to reason in ways consistent with Turiel's model. Research shows significant *cultural variability* in how children classify various kinds of rule violations. Judgments of morality must be placed in a broader context of beliefs, including religious beliefs. Critics have questioned the universality of Turiel's moral, social, and personal domains.
5. How does the cultural construction approach to moral development differ from other approaches?	The *cultural construction approach* to moral development focuses on how larger cultural beliefs and values influence children's understanding of moral and social rules. Researchers taking this perspective emphasize that children actively construct their understanding of morality through social interaction and experience. This construction is a social process in which other people assist children's moral development by structuring and interpreting situations through the lens of a particular moral system.

Learning Objective 14.2
Identify factors in children's lives that significantly influence their moral development.

1. According to research, how do peer interactions influence moral development?	Children with greater peer experience have more advanced moral reasoning. Correlational studies show a positive relationship between a child's peer acceptance, for example, and the child's level of moral maturity. The influence between *peer relations and moral development* goes both ways; that is, children who reason competently about moral issues are more likely to attract companions and friends. Studies show that issues of fairness and harm arise frequently in children's interactions with peers. Children respond to moral transgressions from an early age, talk about a victim's injury or loss, and express empathy. Experiments on the impact of peer interaction on moral reasoning show that discussing moral issues with peers fosters advances in children's moral reasoning.
2. How do parenting styles and child-parent interactions influence moral development?	Parents influence children's moral understanding, for example, through discipline for misconduct. The effectiveness of discipline in promoting internalization of the parents' values and morals depends on the style of punishment and the child's temperament. The *power assertion* style uses commands, threats, and physical force. The *love withdrawal* style uses verbal disapproval, ridicule, or withholding of affection from the child. The *induction style* involves reasoning with the child to explain why certain behaviors are prohibited and often engenders guilt in the child by pointing out how the misbehavior may have caused harm or distress to someone else. Studies suggest that American children disciplined through an induction approach display the most advanced levels of moral reasoning and the power assertion style the least.
3. What psychological factors influence individuals' moral development?	*Fearfulness* is an inborn trait that influences whether children will internalize their parents' rules. For fearful children, prone to timidity and anxiety, gentle discipline and the avoidance of power assertion tactics work best to promote the child's development of conscience (internalization). For fearless children, a cooperative and responsive approach works best, because it capitalizes on the child's positive motivation to accept the parents' values.

4. To what extent is moral behavior a product of personality factors versus situational factors?

According to researchers, children's moral behavior does not reflect a personality trait but is *situation-specific*, depending primarily on the circumstances at hand. Children are usually willing to adjust their moral conduct to fit the demands of the moment. Those demands often include peer pressure and obedience to authority, which are known to encourage both prosocial and antisocial behavior.

Learning Objective 14.3
Define the dimensions of prosocial behavior and identify sources of variation in prosocial behavior.

1. What is prosocial behavior and how is it manifested?

Prosocial behavior includes acts that society considers desirable and attempts to encourage in children. Three forms of prosocial behavior have been studied extensively: helping (which includes comforting and caregiving), sharing, and conflict resolution. It is widely believed that the roots of prosocial behavior lie in the capacity to feel empathy and sympathy.

2. What are Hoffman's five stages in the development of empathy?

Stage one is a precursor of empathy, apparent during the first months of life, when infants cry reflexively upon hearing the cries of other infants. In the *second stage*, infants respond to another's distress as though they themselves were in distress. During this developmental interval, infants feel empathy in response to distress but lack clear boundaries between the self and others. Consequently, infants respond to others' distress by comforting themselves (e.g., sucking their thumbs) or seeking comfort from caregivers. During the *third stage*, as children develop a sense of themselves as distinct individuals, they realize that the distress is someone else's, not their own. They begin to feel sympathy for others. During the *fourth stage*, children develop greater empathy, feeling what others are actually feeling, because they now understand how other people have inner states different from their own. During the *final stage*, which emerges in middle childhood, children are able to consider the broader features of other people's lives.

3. What methods of conflict resolution and peacemaking can be observed in children?	Children resolve conflict in three ways. *Negotiation* includes compromise and intervention by a third party, such as another peer or a teacher. *Disengagement* includes withdrawal and shifting the focus or topic. *Coercion* occurs when one party is forced to give in to the demands of another, sometimes in response to threats or other aggressive ploys. Children tend to resolve disputes through coercion and to refrain from disengagement. Adolescents, in contrast, tend to favor negotiation, and they employ disengagement and coercion equally often. Young adults strongly favor negotiation and use coercion infrequently. Peacemaking refers to a friendly postconflict reunion between former opponents. Peacemaking can follow the conflict immediately or after a delay or cooling-off period. Studies show that children use both verbal and nonverbal behaviors to reconcile with peers, including sharing of toys or food, invitations to play, apologies, and touching or hugs.
4. What are some gender and individual differences in prosocial behavior?	A widely held gender stereotype is that females are more kind, generous, and caring than males. However, empirical evidence suggests only a modest sex difference favoring girls. Even across different cultures, girls and boys do not differ significantly in peacemaking, although they sometimes differ in the methods they use to make peace.

As infants and toddlers, girls tend to display more personal distress, empathy, and other expressions of concern than boys. *Sex differences in empathy* grow larger with age and are greatest when measured by self-report. Girls are also more likely to be kind and considerate but are not more inclined to share, comfort, or help. As individuals, some children seem inordinately caring and compassionate, whereas others appear to care little about the welfare of other beings. Genetic factors contribute to these differences insofar as individual differences in prosocial responding relate to differences in *temperament*. Studies have linked children's tendencies to feel and respond to negative emotions, such as anxiety, sadness, and guilt, with their tendency to feel empathy and sympathy. In contrast, children who are overcome by high levels of negative emotions tend to focus on themselves, while inhibited or cautious children may not be able to bring themselves to help someone even if they want to. |
| **5. What social and cultural factors shape differences in prosocial behavior?** | Studies have found that more frequent religious observances (such as church attendance) were associated with more frequent charitable behavior. Thus, religious observance is a social factor in prosocial behavior. *Cultural factors* in prosocial behavior include differences in peacemaking techniques. One cross-cultural study observed postconflict reunions among middle-income children in day care centers and schools in four diverse cultural communities. In each of the four communities, children in conflict were more likely to seek each other out for peaceful interaction than children who had not engaged in conflict. |

Learning Objective 14.4

Explain the biological, cognitive, and sociocultural determinants of prosocial behavior.

1. What is a possible evolutionary basis for altruistic behavior?	*Sociobiologists* have attempted to resolve the paradox of altruism by showing how self-sacrifice can contribute to a gene pool through kin selection. Kin selection proposes that humans behave in ways that increase the chances for the survival and reproduction of their genes rather than of themselves. A person can pass on genes either by reproducing or by increasing the reproductive chances of someone who has the same or similar genes, that is, a relative. Also, according to *reciprocal altruism*, people are genetically programmed to be helpful because it increases the likelihood that they will someday in turn receive aid, and by helping someone else in their social group, they help ensure that genes similar to their own will be passed on in the species.
2. What cognitive abilities and emotional responses help make altruism self-reinforcing?	The ability to understand a situation from someone else's *point of view* is central to altruism. In several studies, children who were better at telling a story from another person's point of view were more prosocial with peers. Understanding (but not necessarily experiencing) the mental state or feelings and emotions of another person is also correlated with prosocial behavior. Children who do well as preschoolers on various types of "mind-reading" tasks are better able to resolve conflicts with friends during elementary school. Because it is internalized, altruistic behavior is largely self-reinforcing, affecting moral affect even in the absence of external rewards or approval.
3. What socialization methods help shape prosocial behavior?	Children whose parents employ *inductive techniques* and talk with them about the impact of their actions on others display more mature moral reasoning than children of parents who use other disciplinary techniques. People who have shown unusually high levels of altruism tend to report that they learned values of caring, generosity, and respect for all human life from their parents and other influential adults. Prosocial commitment is fostered through parental communication of values, modeling, and reinforcement.

4. What are some examples of socially mediated opportunities for prosocial behavior?

Children's opportunities for prosocial behavior begin with the family context. For example, children who routinely perform chores and con*tribute to family well-being* and the functioning of the household often develop a stronger prosocial orientation than their peers who do not participate in family life in this way. Laboratory studies have shown that children share more or are more helpful after *observing a model* performing similar behaviors. Children are especially likely to imitate adults with whom they have a positive relationship. Children also display more altruism when their altruistic behavior is *reinforced*. Praise is especially effective in promoting altruism if it emphasizes that the child is a generous or helpful person. Studies in natural settings and situations show that preschool children often respond positively to altruistic behavior, such as by smiling, thanking the child, or doing something nice in return.

Learning Objective 14.5

Distinguish kinds of aggression and the factors that contribute to aggressive behavior in children.

1. What kinds of aggressive behavior do children exhibit?

Instrumental aggression is behavior aimed at obtaining something desirable, for example, when one preschooler shoves another to try to grab a toy. *Hostile aggression*, in contrast, is aimed specifically at inflicting pain or harm. Researchers have identified three general types of hostile aggression. Physical aggression is hitting, kicking, and biting; verbal aggression is name calling, teasing, and threats; and relational aggression is spreading damaging rumors and social exclusion.

2. How does antisocial behavior vary by age and sex?

Types of aggression occur in different proportions among children of different ages and sexes. By the end of their second year, children begin to use physical aggression, such as hitting and pushing, to resolve conflicts. *Physical and instrumental aggression* decline over the preschool years, while *verbal and relational aggression* increase. Decline in physical aggression coincides with improved ability to resolve conflicts verbally and to control emotions and actions. Most children continue to show a decline in overt physical aggression during elementary school and through adolescence. Some children manifest serious problems with aggression, however, and some adolescents show marked increase in serious acts of violence. Among youths between the ages of 12 and 20 who report having committed a serious violent act at any age, prevalence for males ranges from about 8 to 20 percent, and for females, from 1 to 18 percent. Boys display more physical and verbal aggression as preschoolers and continue to do so throughout the elementary school years. Beginning in the preschool years, girls display more relational aggression than boys, and this aggression is directed mainly toward other girls. In the later elementary grades, boys' aggression toward other boys becomes more physical, but boys' aggression toward girls drops.

3. What evolutionary, biological, and genetic factors may cause aggressive behavior?

From an *evolutionary standpoint*, one major function of aggression is to increase the likelihood of survival of an individual's or group's genes. Aggression may help an individual or group to obtain food, protect the young, or preserve hunting territory. In such cases, evolutionary processes favor the stronger, smarter, or more skillful members of the species. *Hormones, genes,* and *temperament* influence an individual's level of aggression, which is stable over many years. Longitudinal research indicates that frequent peer aggression at age 8 is a good predictor of aggression and other antisocial behaviors at age 30. This degree of stability lends itself well to a genetic or biological explanation of the behavior. One manifestation of genetic effects is temperament. As children move into the preschool years, temperament dimensions, such as impulsivity and poor self-regulation, become predictive of later aggressiveness. Children who are highly impulsive during early childhood are more likely to engage in fighting and delinquency during early adolescence, aggression and criminal activity during late adolescence, and violence in adulthood.

4. What are some social-cognitive and affective characteristics of violent children?

Aggressive children (especially boys) tend to have lower levels of moral reasoning and empathy, and they are less likely to take into account another's motives when making a moral judgment. In addition, aggressive children often display a "self-protective" interpretation of their social world; that is, they tend to minimize the negative feelings that other children have toward them. Children with falsely positive self-perceptions (thinking better of themselves than others do) are more likely to show high levels of both physical and relational aggression than are children without such a bias. Aggressive children also have been found to have difficulty reading social cues in the environment and processing social information. Aggressive children with these types of processing difficulties are more likely to display instrumental aggression to obtain something they want.

5. What coercive family process contributes to children's antisocial behavior?

Studies have found that families of aggressive children commonly display a troublesome pattern of interactions, referred to as the *coercive family process*. In these households, negative interaction patterns between parents and children are unwittingly reinforced and can become firmly entrenched, resulting in a child who is "out of control." The long-term consequences of this pattern is that the child is more likely to ignore parental commands in the future. Family members achieve their goals through coercive behaviors rather than through cooperative, prosocial means. Boys who learn this style of interaction at home, and who fail to learn more positive interpersonal skills, also display aggression in other settings and often go on to delinquency and other serious forms of antisocial behavior.

6. How do experiences of violence, both real and on TV, affect children's social behavior?

Beginning with Albert Bandura in the 1960s, researchers have repeatedly demonstrated that children can learn to perform new forms of aggression by viewing a violent film model. Children *imitate* the violent acts they see, especially when the violence is performed by the "good guys" and achieves its purpose. TV violence increases the likelihood of all forms of aggression in children, and the effects are long term. Violence on TV can also make children more tolerant of aggression and less bothered by it. Not all the violence children witness is vicarious. Many children also experience violence in their everyday lives, as in the form of spouse or child abuse. And increasingly, children around the world are exposed to political, religious, ethnic, or community violence. Children exposed to both vicarious and real-life violence tend to display increased use of aggressive words, aggressive play, and a general preoccupation with aggressive themes.

Learning Objective 14.6
Discuss methods of reducing juvenile violence and aggression.

1. Why is catharsis unreliable and often ineffective as a means of treating childhood aggression?

It was once believed that aggression can be prevented by channeling aggressive energy into other behaviors or experiencing aggression vicariously. Hitting a punching bag or watching a wrestling match, then, could take the place of engaging in aggressive behaviors. Psychoanalytic theory refers to these substitute behaviors as forms of *catharsis*. Research does not support this theory, however. Viewing violence increases rather than decreases the probability of aggression. Engaging in high-activity behaviors does not make aggression less likely. Methods aimed at curbing aggression through catharsis have generally proved *ineffective*.

2. What kinds of interventions have been shown to reduce childhood aggression?

Cognitive intervention programs can interrupt the sequence leading to aggression. Attribution training, for example, involves teaching children to recognize cues to another person's intentions (such as facial expressions), to encourage nonhostile attributions when the peer's actions are ambiguous (for example, "he probably did it by accident"), and to generate nonaggressive responses to the peer's behavior. Children who received attribution training scored the lowest on aggression.

3. **What training has proven helpful to parents of aggressive children?**

It is well established that parents' childrearing methods are related to their children's aggression. A successful approach to handling this source of aggression is *parent training techniques*. Drawing on principles of behavior modification, child development professionals have trained parents in more effective ways of interacting with their children. Parents learn to reduce the use of negative remarks, such as threats and commands, and replace them with positive statements and verbal approval of children's prosocial behaviors. They also learn to apply nonphysical punishment when discipline is required.

4. **What three kinds of cognitive training have been used with aggressive children?**

One cognitive training approach involves training children in *problem-solving techniques*. Children learn to generate and examine various strategies for confronting a problem and then follow a systematic plan for dealing with it. Programs for increasing children's *empathy* have found some success in reducing conflict and aggression. A third approach is to focus on the assumptions or *attributions* children make about others' behavior. The premise of this approach is that aggressive children are likely to interpret ambiguous, provocative actions by their peers (such as bumping into them in the school hallway) as intentional and hostile. This attribution produces anger, which then gives rise to aggressive, retaliatory behavior.

Relationships with Peers

(Tom Prettyman/PhotoEdit)

CHAPTER

TRACE THE DEVELOPMENT OF PEER SOCIABILITY AND FRIENDSHIP IN CHILDREN.

- Determinants of Friendship • Behavior with Friends • Intimacy • Effects of Friendship

DISCUSS PEER SOCIOMETRIC STATUS AND ITS CONSEQUENCES FOR CHILDREN'S DEVELOPMENT.

- Peer Status and Problem-Solving Skills
- Stability of Peer Status

RESEARCH & SOCIETY Bullying and Victimization in School

APPLICATIONS Enhancing Peer Competence among Shy Children

ANALYZE THE SOCIAL CONTEXTS OF PEER RELATIONSHIPS IN CHILDHOOD AND ADOLESCENCE.

- Conformity to Peers
- Siblings and Peers • Parents and Peers

CONVERSATIONS with a Community Mental Health Practitioner

hen 3-year-old Kaylie started preschool, her mother, Jennifer, was surprised at the peer dynamics she found occurring among Kaylie's agemates. Bailey was a "Queen Bee" with a loyal following of two little girls, who together asserted their dominance through informing other girls in the class: "I'm not going to invite you to my birthday party." Another group of girls, with whom Kaylie became friends, comprised the majority. Within that group, Kaylie particularly enjoyed playing with three other girls, but even among them, friendships were asserted and disputed and reasserted on almost a regular basis. One little girl seemed on the outside of many of the peer interactions, watching and hovering and trying to be recognized, but rarely included in play. Among the boys, one seemed particularly prone to problem solving through hitting and name-calling. Kaylie described him as "mean," and it was clear to Jennifer that the teachers spent a large proportion of their time dealing with his misbehavior, as well as teaching the other children appropriate ways to respond to his provocations. Jennifer was happy that Kaylie seemed in the majority with a group of friendly girls, but she wondered, Were the children playing social roles at age 3 that would continue into grade school? How did such roles arise, and what did they mean in the long run for the children who played them?

For most children, interacting with peers is a major activity of daily life. Peer relations are therefore a major context for and influence on child development. This chapter examines the development of peer sociability and friendship and the research that addresses some of the questions asked by Kaylie's mother about individual differences in peer acceptance. This chapter also explores the development of peer groups and connections between peer and family relationships. ■

Peer Sociability

Learning Objective 15.1
Trace the development of peer sociability and friendship in children.

Questions for Thought and Discussion
Is experience with peers necessary for development? Could a child reared solely in the company of adults develop normally? Why, or why not?

Unlike older children, infants cannot spontaneously seek out their peers for companionship or pleasure. If infants find themselves together, it is because adults have placed them together. Adults often do place babies together, however, and the likelihood of such contact is increasing as more and more mothers enter the labor force (NICHD Early Child Care Research Network, 1997). Three or four infants may be cared for in the home of one mother, or half a dozen or so may occupy the infant room of a day care center.

Interest in other children emerges quite early. Infants as young as 6 months look at, vocalize to, smile at, and touch other infants (Hay, 1985; Hay, Nash, & Pedersen, 1983). Such behaviors are limited in both frequency and complexity. These behaviors also have been characterized as *object-centered*, because infants' early interactions often center on some toy of mutual interest. Indeed, toys remain an important context for interaction throughout infancy (at least in cultures that emphasize early object play).

Relations with peers change in various ways as babies develop (Brownell & Brown, 1992; Eckerman & Peterman, 2001). LaShawn loves to watch Kiaree's early interactions with her same-age cousin. These interactions began before the age of 1 year with simple and discrete behaviors, such as a touch or a smile. At about 1 year, Kiaree and her cousin begin to coordinate these behaviors into more complex combinations, such as a touch in conjunction with a smile, perhaps followed by a vocalization. Moreover, one-way social acts become increasingly reciprocal between the two of them as their interactions evolve into more truly social interchanges. The children also become more and more likely to imitate one another's behavior and to take pleasure in that activity (Howes, 1992). Their

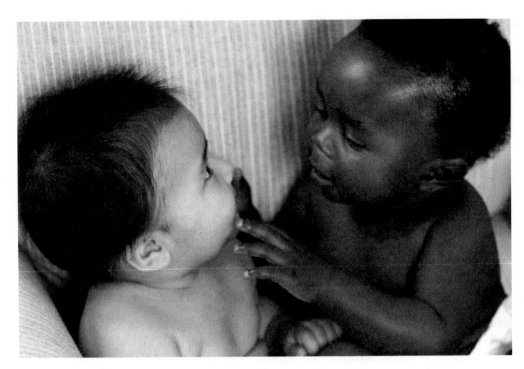

Children show interest in one another from an early age. How will the interest that these infants show in one another change and develop as they grow older? (Brand X/Jupiter Images)

positive emotional responses to one another become more marked as they begin to derive obvious enjoyment from each other's company, often greeting one another with delighted coos and hugs. Unfortunately, negative responses also become more evident, especially in disputes over toys. Nevertheless, most of their social interchanges remain positive, and LaShawn notices that the cognitive level of their play is generally higher when they are playing together than when they are playing alone (Rubenstein & Howes, 1976).

As Kiaree enters the preschool years, her social world becomes larger, with a greater number and variety of playmates (Howes, 1983, 1987). LaShawn notices that her social world also becomes more differentiated—that is, Kiaree is able to direct different behaviors to different people and to form somewhat different relations with different peers (Ross & Lollis, 1989). Her social interactions become more complex as symbolic forms of play (for example, the ability to have conversations and to engage in pretend play) begin to predominate over physical forms of play. Kiaree also becomes better able to use words effectively to win time for herself with a desired toy, saying "You play with it and then it will be my turn," rather than simply grabbing or pushing. At the same time, she becomes more skilled at adjusting her communications to the different needs of different listeners (Garvey, 1986; Shatz & Gelman, 1973), as her first truly collaborative problem solving emerges (Brownell & Carriger, 1990; Holmes-Lonergan, 2003).

Types of Play

Much of the research concerned with peer relations during the preschool years has focused on children's play. One common approach to categorizing play is shown in Table 15.1. As you can see, the categories vary in the cognitive complexity of the play, ranging from the simple motor exercise of functional play to the give-and-take intricacies of games with rules. As would be expected, children of different ages are likely to engage in different types of play. Functional play emerges early and predominates during the infant and toddler years, whereas games with rules are infrequent among children younger than grade-school age (Rubin, Fein, & Vandenberg, 1983).

The category of *pretend play* or *sociodramatic play* has been of special interest to investigators of preschool development. As you saw in Chapter 7, studies have demonstrated that both the frequency and complexity of pretend play increase across the preschool years (Garvey, 1990). For example, 2-year-old Zachary picks up a toy truck and pushes it along

TABLE 15.1 Types of Play Classified According to Cognitive Level

Type	Description	Examples
Functional	Simple, repetitive muscular movements performed with or without objects	Shaking a rattle; jumping up and down
Constructive	Manipulation of objects with intention of creating something	Building a tower of blocks; cutting and pasting pictures
Pretend	Use of an object or person to symbolize something that it is not	Pretending that a log is a boat; playing "house" with friends.
Games With Rules	Playing games in accordance with prearranged rules and limits	Playing hopscotch; playing checkers

SOURCE: Based on information from S. Smilansky. (1968). *The Effects of Sociodramatic Play on Disadvantaged Preschool Children.* New York: Wiley.

Links to Related Material
In Chapter 7, you read about some of the cognitive developments that underlie changes in pretend play across the preschool years. Here, you learn more about the development of different types of pretend play.

Parallel play
When two or more young children play next to each other, using the same sorts of materials and perhaps even talking now and then, yet without any genuine interaction.

the couch, making "vroom" sounds. By 3, he is able to extend his pretend play regarding vehicles beyond toys that look like trucks to any object, such as a wooden block. By 4, he is using multiple cars and trucks, including passengers and objects they might be transporting, in rapidly shifting sequences: "Vroom. The car comes down the road and the people get in. Vroom. Here comes the dumptruck full of cement." By 5, he is beginning to build elaborate roadways with friends, complete with towns and storylines.

Another popular approach to categorizing play is shown in Table 15.2. Here, the focus is on the social organization rather than the cognitive level of the child's play. The usual assumption has been that the various types of play develop in the order shown in the table. Thus, 1-year-olds are most likely to be found in solitary or onlooker behavior, while 4- and 5-year-olds are more likely to be found in associative and cooperative play. In **parallel play,** two or more children play next to each other, using the same sorts of materials and perhaps even talking, yet without any genuine interaction. For example, at 2, Natalie and Kiaree enjoy sitting in the sandbox together, shoveling, digging, filling, and spilling, each child busy with her own sand toys, and generally interacting only when one girl wants a toy that the other one has. Anyone who has watched groups of 2-year-olds playing can verify that such "semisocial" play is common in the early ages.

The categories listed in Table 15.2 were developed more than 70 years ago (Parten, 1932). Although recent research verifies that children today show the same general patterns of play, research also suggests some qualifications and complexities in the developmental picture (Howes & Tonyan, 1999; Rubin, Bukowski, & Parker, 1998). For one thing, not all children progress in the order shown in the table. A child might move directly from solitary behavior to cooperative play, for example, without an intervening phase of parallel

TABLE 15.2 Types of Play Classified According to Social Level

Type	Description
Onlooker	Watching others play without participating oneself
Solitary	Playing alone and independently, with no attempt to get close to other children
Parallel	Playing alongside other children and with similar materials but with no real interaction or cooperation
Associative	Playing with other children in some common activity but without division of labor or subordination to some overall group goal
Cooperative	Playing in a group that is organized for the purpose of carrying out some activity or attaining some goal, with coordination of individual members' behavior in pursuit of the common goal

SOURCE: Based on information from M. B. Parten. (1932). Social participation among preschool children. *Journal of Abnormal and Social Psychology, 27,* 243–269.

Parallel play is a familiar sight among young children. These three children play with sand toys in physical proximity to one another, but do not elaborate play themes together. In what ways do you think the sand play of older preschoolers might differ from that of 2-year-olds? (Kwame Zikomo/SUPERSTOCK)

play (Smith, 1978). Nor do the early categories of play necessarily disappear as children grow older. Solitary and parallel play are still common among 3- and 4-year-olds, for example (Tieszen, 1979).

What does change with age is the cognitive maturity of the play. The nonsocial play of 1- and 2-year olds consists mainly of various kinds of functional play (see Table 15.1). Older children are more likely to embed even their nonsocial play in a constructive or dramatic context (Rubin, Watson, & Jambor, 1978). Because of this interplay of cognitive and social factors, modern scales to assess play typically include both cognitive and social dimensions (Howes, Unger, & Seidner, 1989; Rubin, 1989).

As children develop, their play continues to evolve through the hierarchies shown in Tables 15.1 and 15.2. By age 8 or 9, children have become enthusiastic participants in games with rules, as any visit to a school playground or toy store will readily verify (Eifermann, 1971). By middle childhood, children's play is also more likely to fall within the most advanced of the categories in Table 15.2—cooperative play.

These changes in both the cognitive level and the social organization of play in turn relate to more general factors in the child's development. Increased experience with peers clearly plays a role, as children spend more and more time with a wider variety of children. The effects of experience are evident even before this time. From infancy on, children with more extensive peer experience are more positive and skilled in peer play (Howes & James, 2002; NICHD Early Child Care Research Network, 2001). Advances in cognitive level also contribute. In particular, gains in perspective-taking skills during middle childhood may underlie both the newfound facility at games with rules and the general ability to interact cooperatively.

Questions for Thought
· and Discussion
What are some examples of your play as a child that reflect the social and cognitive levels of play?

Friendship

According to the dictionary, the word *peer* means "equal." Clearly, however, some peers (to borrow from George Orwell's *Animal Farm*) are more equal than others. The closest and most significant peer relationship is friendship. What do children mean by the word *friend?* How do friendships form and influence children's behavior and development?

Consider the following answers in response to the question, "What is a friend?"

"A friend is a person you like. You play around with them."

"Friends don't snatch or act snobby, and they don't argue or disagree. If you're nice to them, they'll be nice to you."

These children coordinate their activities to achieve a common goal. What social level of play is illustrated here? (© Laura Dwight Photography)

Friendship
An enduring relationship between two individuals, characterized by loyalty, intimacy, and mutual affection.

Q**uestions for Thought and Discussion**
How do you define friendship? What factors have determined who your friends are? How are you and your friends similar?

L**inks to Related Material**
In Chapter 13, you read about the preference for same-sex friendships that is often evident in childhood. Here, you learn more about factors that influence the development of friendships.

"A person who helps you do things. When you need something, they get it. You do the same for them."

"Someone you can share things with and who shares things with you. Not material things; feelings. When you feel sad, she feels sad. They understand you."

"A stable, affective, dyadic relationship marked by preference, reciprocity, and shared positive affect."

It does not take much psychological insight to guess that these answers were given by respondents of different ages—or to figure out which is the definition offered by professional researchers. The first four answers (drawn from studies by Rubin, 1980, and Youniss and Volpe, 1978) came from children ranging in age from 6 to 13. The last (from Howes, 1987, p. 253) is typical of how psychologists define **friendship.** When psychologists say that friendship is "a stable, affective, dyadic relationship marked by preference, reciprocity, and shared positive affect," they mean that friendship is an emotional tie between two people that endures over time, and is marked by a desire to spend time with one another, give and take, and shared positive emotions.

Despite their diversity, the different definitions share some common elements. All agree that there is something special about a friend that does not apply to peers in general. All state or imply that friendship is not just any sort of relationship, but a relationship of affection—friends like each other. And all acknowledge that friendship is a two-way, reciprocal process. One child may like another child, but liking alone does not make one a friend. For friendship to exist, the affection must be returned.

As the examples indicate, the presence of these common elements does not rule out the possibility that children's reasoning about friendship might change with age. At a general level, a description of the changes that occur should sound familiar, because such changes parallel more general advances in the way children think about the world (Hartup & Abecassis, 2002; Rawlins, 1992). Young children's thinking about friendship tends to focus on concrete, external attributes—a friend is someone who is fun to play with and who shares things. Older children are more capable of penetrating beneath the surface to take into account more abstract aspects of friendship, such as caring for another person. For young children, friendship is often a momentary state dependent on specific acts just performed or about to be performed. Older children are more likely to see friendship as an enduring relationship that persists across time and even in the face of occasional conflicts. Finally, although even young children realize the importance of mutual liking between friends, qualities such as loyalty and intimacy do not become central in children's thinking about friendship until late childhood or adolescence.

Determinants of Friendship   Friends are not selected randomly. As children develop, they are exposed to many different people, but only a few of these potential friends ever become actual friends. On what basis are these selections made? Studies of friendship formation show a rare unanimity in that one general factor is central to most friendship choices (Aboud & Mendelson, 1996; Hartup & Stevens, 1997). This factor is similarity. Children tend to pick friends who are similar to themselves. Similarity is not the only criterion used. Children may sometimes seek out friends who are more popular than they are (Hirsch & Renders, 1986) or who have a higher socioeconomic status (Epstein, 1983). Nevertheless, similarity seems to be a major contributor to most friendship selections.

Various kinds of similarity are important. One is similarity in age. Friendships are most common among children who are close in age. Mixed-age friendships are found, of course, especially when children move outside the same-age groupings imposed by school (Epstein, 1989). Even when not constrained by adults, however, most children tend to pick friends who are about the same age (Berndt, 1988).

Similarity in gender is also important. As you saw in Chapter 13, a preference for same-sex friends emerges in the preschool years and becomes quite strong by middle childhood. Throughout much of childhood, gender is a better predictor of friendship choices than age (Epstein, 1986; Maccoby, 2000b). By adolescence, cross-sex romantic relationships have

The most important peer relationship is that of friendship. What aspects of friendship are evident between the children in this photo? (©André Gallant)

begun to emerge (Shulman & Collins, 1997). Even here, however, same-sex friendships continue to predominate (Hartup, 1993).

Although the variables of age and gender are important, they do not completely explain friendship selection. What seems important in addition to general similarity with a peer is specific similarity in behaviors and interests—what psychologists call *behavioral homophyly*. In short, one reason that children become friends is that they like to do the same sorts of things. For example, on her first day of middle school, Min was glad that several of her elementary school friends would be there with her, but nonetheless she was nervous about finding new friends in the socially larger and more complex environment. When she went to choir, her first elective, she discovered that one of the other sopranos enjoyed singing the same kind of music that she did. They began talking about the voice and piano lessons they had both taken when they were younger, and soon found that they also both enjoyed dance lessons after school. By the end of the semester, the two girls had become close friends and had arranged their schedules so that they could take dance classes together as well. This pattern is evident as early as the preschool period (Rubin et al., 1994), and it eventually extends to various settings in which children find themselves. Among older children, friends tend to be similar in their orientation toward school. They show correlations, for example, in educational aspirations and achievement test scores (Ide et al., 1981). They also tend to be similar in what Thomas Berndt (1988) labels their "orientation toward children's culture," or what they like to do outside of school (music, sports, games, and so on). They tend to be similar in general behavior patterns and personality—for example, in the tendency to be shy or aggressive (Kupersmidt, DeRosier, & Patterson, 1995; Poulin et al., 1997). An important dimension of similarity for many adolescents is ethnic and racial identity, or the degree to which the adolescent identifies with the culture and values of a specific ethnic or racial group (Hamm, 2000).

Although the relationship between similarity and friendship is well established, the causal basis for it is less clear. Do children become friends because they have similar interests and preferences, or do children develop similar interests and preferences because they are friends? Answering this question requires longitudinal study, in which patterns of similarity can be traced over time. Such studies suggest that in this case cause and effect flow in both directions (Epstein, 1989; Hartup, 1996). Children who later become friends are more similar initially than are children who do not become friends, indicating that similarity is indeed a determinant of friendship selection. But children who are friends become more similar over time, indicating that friendship also promotes further similarity.

Through what processes are friendships initially formed? A study by John Gottman (1983) provides an exceptionally detailed account. The participants in Gottman's research were children between the ages of 3 and 9, none of whom knew one another at the start of the study. Pairs of same-age children were randomly formed, and each pair then met in the home of one of the children for three play sessions across a period of four weeks. The questions were whether the children would become friends and, if so, what processes led to friendship formation.

Gottman found that some of the children did indeed become friends, whereas others did not. What aspects of the interaction proved important in differentiating the two groups? Children who became friends were more successful at establishing a *common-ground activity*—that is, agreeing on what to do—than were children who did not become friends. Eventual friends showed greater *communication clarity* and were more successful at *exchanging information* than were nonfriends. Eventual friends were more skillful at *resolving conflict*—an important skill, for conflict is frequent in young children's interactions. And eventual friends were more likely to engage in *self-disclosure,* or sharing of personal information about oneself.

Elements of Successful Friendship Formation

- Finding common-ground activities
- Communicating clearly
- Exchanging information
- Resolving conflict
- Self-disclosure

Other studies of friendship formation support Gottman's conclusion that processes such as exchange of information and resolution of conflict play central roles (Grusec & Lytton, 1988). Friendship formation processes do not disappear once a friendship has been formed. The same kinds of skills that help build a friendship are also central to the ways friends continue to interact.

Links to Related Material
In Chapter 14, you read about the development of prosocial behavior. Here, you learn how prosocial behavior relates to the development of children's friendships.

Behavior with Friends   That behavior is different with friends than with nonfriends seems almost part of the definition of friendship. But exactly how does behavior differ as a function of friendship? Children spend more time with friends than with nonfriends, and they typically derive more pleasure from interacting with friends (Newcomb & Bagwell, 1995). Friends are fun to be with. In addition, prosocial behavior characterizes friendship relationships. As you read in Chapter 14, *prosocial behavior* refers to forms of conduct that society considers desirable and ecourages in children's development. Examples of prosocial behavior include helping someone in need, comforting someone in distress, and sharing with others. It seems reasonable to expect that such clearly positive behaviors will be more likely with friends than with peers in general.

For the most part, this commonsense prediction is borne out by research. Children share more with friends than with classmates who are merely acquaintances (Jones, 1985). Cooperation in carrying out some common task is greater among friends than nonfriends, as is equity in dividing any rewards that are obtained (Berndt, 1981). Even as early as the preschool years, children may cooperate and share more with friends than with nonfriends (Matsumoto et al., 1986), and they are more likely to offer help to a friend in distress than to a mere acquaintance (Costin & Jones, 1992). Preschoolers also provide positive reinforcement more often to friends than to peers in general (Masters & Furman, 1981).

Despite this evidence, not all studies find that prosocial behaviors are more likely with friends. In one series of studies, elementary school children actually shared less with friends than with acquaintances (Berndt, 1986). According to Berndt, the critical element may be the presence of perceived competition with the friend. Research indicates that children believe friends should be equal (Tesser, 1984). Sharing too freely threatens this principle, because it may result in the friend "winning the contest" by ending up with the greater amount. The resulting inequality then is a threat to the friendship. Allowing a nonfriend to "win" is less threatening, however, so children are more willing to share with nonfriends. By adolescence, this threat diminishes, and sharing is more likely with friends than with nonfriends, even under competitive conditions.

Conflict is a less positive side of peer interaction. Psychologists define conflict broadly as occurring "when one person does something to which a second person objects" (Hay, 1984, p. 2). The core notion is opposition between individuals, conveyed by words such as *refusing, denying, objecting,* and *disagreeing* (Hartup, 1992a).

Thus defined, conflict clearly is a frequent component of peer interaction (Shantz & Hartup, 1995). It also occurs frequently in interactions between friends (Shantz, 1987). Some conflict arises simply because friends spend so much time together. But the likelihood of conflict also reflects the freedom and security that friends feel with one another, and thus their ability to criticize and disagree without threatening the relationship (Hartup et al., 1993).

The important difference between friends and nonfriends is not the probability of conflict but the ways conflict is handled (Laursen, Finkelstin, & Betts, 2001). Although exceptions certainly occur, conflicts tend to be less heated among friends than among nonfriends. Friends use "softer" modes of managing conflict. That is, they are more likely to attempt to reason with the other person and less likely to get into extended chains of disagreement (Hartup 1992a). They are also more likely to resolve the conflict in an equitable, mutually satisfactory way. And they are more likely to forgive and forget and to continue playing together following the conflict. Thus, the ability to resolve conflicts satisfactorily plays a role both in forming and in maintaining a friendship. The ability to overcome conflict and remain close can be seen as one definition of *friendship*.

Intimacy   The idea that intimacy is central to friendship is expressed in the definition of a friend as someone with whom to share one's innermost thoughts and feelings. It is usually not until late childhood or adolescence that the emphasis on intimacy emerges in children's talk about friendship.

Do friends interact in more intimate ways than do nonfriends? Children's own statements about friendship provide one source of evidence. If a girl says she shares things with her best friend that she can share with no one else, there seems little reason to doubt the accuracy of her statement. In one series of studies, statements of this sort were absent among kindergartners, but were offered by approximately 40 percent of the sixth-grade participants (Berndt, 1986a).

Children who are friends or are in the process of becoming friends are more likely than nonfriends to talk about feelings and to engage in self-disclosure (Gottman, 1983). Because this difference emerges as early as the preschool years, these data suggest that intimacy may be a characteristic of friendship long before children begin to talk about intimacy as being important. Nevertheless, the frequency of such intimate disclosures increases as children grow older (Berndt & Perry, 1990; Buhrmester & Prager, 1995). The importance of intimacy as a determinant of the quality of friendship is greater for adolescents than for younger children (Buhrmester, 1990; Hartup, 1993). In addition to age differences, there are gender differences in this aspect of friendship: Girls' friendships are characterized by a higher degree of emotional intimacy than are those of boys (Buhrmester, 1996; Jenkins, Goodness, & Buhrmester, 2002). This difference begins to emerge by middle childhood and increases into adolescence.

Effects of Friendship   Friendship can have a number of positive effects on the ways children interact—for example, increasing the likelihood of prosocial behavior and successful conflict resolution. There are long-term impacts of childhood friendship as well. Do children with many friends develop differently than children with few or no friends? Do children with high-quality friendships differ in their development from children whose friendships are less satisfactory? Research on the long-term consequences of friendship confirms positive answers to these questions. One long-term benefit of friendship, already discussed in Chapter 9, is that children with satisfactory friendships adjust more successfully to school than do children who lack such support. Another long-term effect of friendship is on the child's self-esteem. As noted in Chapter 12, children vary in how positively

Links to Related Material
In Chapter 12, you read about relationships that researchers have found among friendship, school adjustment, and self-esteem. Here, you learn more about the positive effects of friendship in children's lives.

Social support
Resources (both tangible and intangible) provided by other people in times of uncertainty or stress.

they feel about different aspects of their lives (academic abilities, physical prowess, and so on). The successes or failures that a child experiences in a particular domain affect these feelings of self-worth. For example, as you would expect, children who do well in school tend to feel better about their academic competence than children who do less well.

Children's success in forming friendships and being accepted in peer groups also affects self-esteem. In most (but not all) studies, children with relatively satisfactory friendships have more positive scores on the Self-Perception Profile (described in Chapter 12) than do children who lack such friendships (Berndt, 2002; Berndt & Keefe, 1995; Keefe & Berndt, 1996). As you might expect, the greatest differences tend to be on the social acceptance subscale, but the effects are not limited to perceptions of peer relations. Global self-worth—the most general index of self-evaluation—also tends to be higher in children who have satisfactory friendships. Friendship also provides **social support,** defined as the resources other people provide in times of uncertainty or stress. We all need such support on occasion, even if the help is simply in the form of someone "being there" during a difficult time. Research with adults has shown that success in obtaining support is an important determinant of people's ability to cope with stress (Cohen & Wills, 1985).

Four kinds of social support in the lives of children (Bryant, 1985; Reid et al., 1989) are:

- *Emotional support*—behaviors of others that offer needed comfort or reassurance and in general enhance the self-esteem of the recipient. Providing reassurance after a potentially embarrassing failure is a form of emotional support, as is lending a sympathetic ear when a friend has frustrations to vent.

- *Instrumental support*—provision of tangible resources to help solve practical tasks—for example, helping a friend to repair a bicycle's flat tire, sell lemonade, build a treehouse, or perform a chore like cleaning the garage.

- *Informational support*—provision of information or advice about how to cope with problems—for example, advising a friend as to which language arts teacher has the reputation for being "most fun," what activities are needed to obtain a particular scouting badge, or what birthday gift a mutual friend might find particularly desirable.

- *Companionship support*—sharing of activities and experiences, such as going to the movies together, hanging out at the mall, sleeping over at one another's house, or playing games together.

Just as they can take many forms, supports can come from many sources. In one study, friends were judged second only to parents as sources of emotional support, and friends headed the list when children were in need of companionship (Reid et al., 1989). Furthermore, the value of friends as sources of support increases as children grow older (Berndt, 1989b; Denton & Zarbatany, 1996). Older children, as we have seen, emphasize such qualities as intimacy and trust in their thinking about friendship and in their behavior with friends. It is not surprising, then, that development brings an increased tendency to turn to friends in times of need.

 **Test Your Mastery...**

Learning Objective 15.1: *Trace the development of peer sociability and friendship in children.*

1. How does early sociability emerge in infants and young children?
2. What types of play do researchers use to study the development of children's play?
3. How do the social and cognitive levels of play compare?
4. How does children's understanding of friendship develop?

Peer Acceptance

Learning Objective 15.2
Discuss peer sociometric status and its consequences for children's development.

For some children, life in the peer group is much more enjoyable and fulfilling than it is for others. Children form opinions—sometimes positive, sometimes negative—about many of their peers, and children are themselves the subject of evaluation by others in the peer group. What factors determine whether a child is generally liked or disliked by other children?

To determine how children are doing in their peer group, the most common approach has been to ask the children. The assumption is that a child's peers should be the best judges of that child's standing among peers. Peer-based evaluations of social standing are referred to as **sociometric techniques** (Asher & Hymel, 1981; Cillessen & Bukowski, 2000).

Researchers have used a variety of sociometric approaches. In the *nomination technique,* the child is asked to name some specific number of well-liked peers—for example, "Tell me the names of three kids in the class you especially like." The technique can also be directed to negative relations—"Tell me the names of three kids in the class you don't like very much." In the *rating-scale technique,* the child is asked to rate classmates along the dimension of interest. The child might be asked, for example, to rate each classmate on a 5-point scale ranging from "really like to play with" to "really don't like to play with." In the *paired-comparison technique,* the child is presented with the names of two classmates at a time and asked to pick the one whom he or she likes better. Because all pairs are eventually presented, the technique yields an overall measure of liking for each target child.

Sociometric scores have been shown to correlate with teacher ratings of popularity and peer competence—that is, the children who are identified by their peers as well liked also tend to be the ones whom teachers identify as popular (Green et al., 1980). Sociometric scores also correlate with direct observations of children's social interactions (Bukowski & Hoza, 1989). Sociometric assessments by children even as young as preschool age show correlations with external measures (Denham & McKinley, 1993; Wu et al., 2001).

Peer Status

Children who are *popular* are well-liked by their peers. In sociometric studies, such children receive high ratings and are the objects of many positive choices and few, if any, negative choices. **Popular-prosocial children** are high in social competence and generally also do well academically. They are well-liked by other children for their abilities to solve conflicts peacefully and to interact with their peers in cooperative yet assertive ways. Popular children tend to be friendly, socially visible, outgoing in their behavior, and reinforcing in their interactions with others (Newcomb, Bukowski, & Pattee, 1993). Three sets of skills seem to be especially important (Asher, Renshaw, & Hymel, 1982). Popular-prosocial children are skilled at *initiating interaction* with other children. They enter ongoing groups smoothly and set about making friends in a carefully paced but confident manner, not forcing themselves on other children but also not giving up at the slightest rebuff. Popular children are also skilled at *maintaining interaction.* They reinforce other children, show sensitivity to the needs and wishes of others, and communicate effectively in the role of both speaker and listener. Third, popular children are skilled at *resolving conflict.* The popular child knows how to defuse touchy situations in ways agreeable to all parties, using reasoning rather than force and drawing on general principles of fairness and general rules for how people should interact. As you can see, the kinds of social skills that help make a child popular are the same sorts of skills that are important for forming and maintaining friendships. Popular-prosocial children are children who have the qualities desirable in a friend.

Children who are sociometrically *average* do not receive scores or numbers of nominations that are extreme in either direction, positive or negative. **Rejected children** receive few positive nominations from their peers but many negative ones. The rejected child seems to be actively disliked. There are two types of rejected children. The first and most common group is **rejected-aggressive children.** Peers report, and behavioral observations confirm, that many rejected children score high in aggression. Aggression leads to being rejected by the peer group, but being rejected also increases later aggression (Dodge et al., 2003). Rejected-aggressive children often show antisocial behavior that is inappropriate to the situation at hand and disruptive of ongoing group activities. In boys, this aggression is likely to take the form of overt physical and verbal aggression, whereas in girls aggression is more likely to be relational.

A second, smaller group are **rejected-withdrawn children.** These children often find social interactions to be very anxiety-provoking. Their attempts to enter new groups or to

Children display individual differences in peer status from an early age. What qualities are these children displaying with their peers? What do you think their sociometric status is likely to be? Why? (Ellen B. Senisi/ The Image Works)

make new friends tend to be clumsy and often end in rebuff. Over time, they develop a perception of themselves as unlikable and expect that others will scorn or attack them. Partly as a consequence of the negative response from peers that they experience, as well as the resulting loneliness and poor self-regard, these children are at risk for continued anxiety and depression (Rubin, Burgess, & Coplan, 2002). Finally, the submissive interaction style of rejected-withdrawn children places them at greater risk for abuse by bullies (Boivin & Hymel, 1997; Hart, Yang, Nelson, et al., 2000; Ladd & Burgess, 1999).

Neglected child
A child who receives few nominations of any sort, positive or negative, in sociometric assessments by peers. Such children seem to be ignored by the peer group.

The **neglected child** receives few nominations of any sort, positive or negative, from peers; thus, the neglected child seems to be less disliked than ignored. These children are often perceived by their peers as shy. This perception is not surprising, as neglected children are less talkative and less socially active than others (Evans, 2001; Younger, Schneider, Wadeson, Guirguis, & Bergeron, 2000). For some children, this apparent shyness may reflect a lack of interest in ongoing social interactions. For others, it may reflect social anxiety (Coplan, Prakash, O'Neil, & Armer, 2004). However, the social skills of peer-neglected children do not differ from those of average children in terms of cooperativeness, behavioral conduct, and relations with adults (Hymel, Woody, & Bowker, 1993). Often, neglected status is temporary; when assessed at a different time, these children may be average in their sociometric status.

Controversial child
A child who receives both many positive and many negative nominations in sociometric assessments by peers.

Finally, the **controversial child,** as the name suggests, receives a mixed evaluation from the peer group, earning both positive and negative nominations. As befits their in-between sociometric status, controversial children typically show a mixture of positive and negative social behaviors (Newcomb, Bukowski, & Pattee, 1993). Like rejected children, controversial children tend to rank high on measures of aggression. But, like popular children, they also tend to score high on measures of sociability. Like the status of neglected children, controversial status is often temporary.

Social problem-solving skills
Cognitive skills needed to resolve social dilemmas.

Peer Status and Problem-Solving Skills   Some investigators have examined the relationship between **social problem-solving skills,** or the skills needed to resolve social dilemmas, and peer acceptance (Rubin & Krasnor, 1986; Rubin & Rose-Krasnor, 1992). An example of an approach to assessing social problem-solving skills is shown in Table 15.3.

TABLE 15.3 Examples of Items Used to Assess Children's Social Problem-Solving Skills

STIMULUS	NARRATION	QUESTIONS
Picture of one girl swinging and another girl standing nearby	This girl's name is Laurie, and this is Kathy. Laurie is five years old. Kathy is seven years old. Kathy is older than Laurie. Kathy has been on the swing for a long, long time. Laurie would really like to play on the swing.	What do you think Laurie could say or do so that she could play on the swing? If that didn't work, what else could Laurie do or say so that she could play on the swing? What do you think you would do or say if you wanted to play on the swing?
Picture of a boy riding a tricycle and a girl standing nearby	This boy's name is Bert and this girl's name is Erika. They are both five years old. Bert, the boy, has been on the tricycle for a long, long time. Erika, the girl, would like to ride the tricycle.	What do you think Erika could say or do so that she could ride the tricycle? If that didn't work, what else could Erika do or say so that she could have the tricycle? What do you think you would do or say if you wanted to ride on the tricycle?
Picture of a school setting with two girls sitting near each other	This girl's name is Kim and this is Jenny. Kim and Jenny are both five years old. They are both the same age. Kim and Jenny are in the same class at school, but this is Jenny's first day at the school. Jenny is a new girl in the class. Kim would like to get to know Jenny better.	What do you think Kim could say or do to get to know Jenny? If that didn't work, what else could Kim do or say to get to know Jenny? What do you think you would do or say to get to know Jenny?

SOURCE: Excerpted from K. H. Rubin. (1988). *The Social Problem-Solving Test—Revised* (pp. 3, 4). Waterloo, Ontario: University of Waterloo Press. Copyright © 1988 by K. H. Rubin. Reprinted by permission.

Studies suggest that problem-solving and other cognitive skills contribute to variations in peer acceptance. Both rejected and neglected children show deficits in the kind of social problem-solving skills illustrated in Table 15.3 (Rubin & Krasnor, 1986; Rubin & Rose-Krasnor, 1992). The kinds of solutions such dilemmas call for are precisely the behaviors that rejected and neglected children fail to show. In addition, unpopular children often score lower in perspective-taking skills than their more popular peers (Jennings, 1975), and rejected children have difficulty judging the intentions behind the behavior of others, a deficiency that may contribute to their high levels of aggression (Dodge, 1986).

Stability of Peer Status An important question in the study of peer relations concerns the stability of sociometric status over time. Do popular children remain popular and unpopular children unpopular as they grow up? Or do children simply outgrow their problems as they develop? Longitudinal studies indicate that children with problems do not automatically outgrow them (Cillessen, Bukowski, & Haselager, 2000; McDougall et al., 2001). At the same time, early peer status does not perfectly predict later development. For many children, however, early rejected status, either aggressive or withdrawn, predicts continuing rejection. The category of rejection is especially stable over time, and rejected children are at greatest risk for a number of problems later in life, including juvenile delinquency, dropping out of school, and mental illness (Laird et al., 2001; Parker et al., 1995).

Problems in peer relations are not just a source of anxiety and unhappiness in childhood. Such problems place children at greater than average risk for a variety of negative outcomes later in life. Can children who are having difficulty in the peer group be helped by intervention programs designed to improve their success?

A variety of intervention approaches have been tried (Ladd, Buhs, & Troop, 2002; Ramsey, 1991; Schneider, Rubin, & Ledingham, 1985). Some are grounded in social-learning theory. Modeling, for example, has been used in an attempt to increase social skills and social acceptance (Schunk, 1987). Shaping of desirable social behaviors through reinforcement has also been explored (O'Connor, 1972). Other approaches have their origins in cognitive-developmental theory. Included in this category are attempts to improve peer relations through teaching perspective-taking skills (Chandler, 1973) and through training in social problem-solving abilities (Pepler, King, & Byrd, 1991; Urbain & Kendell, 1980). Still other programs are more eclectic, encompassing a number of different training techniques in an effort to promote the needed social skills (Mize & Ladd, 1990).

One approach, **peer-mediated intervention** (Odom & Strain, 1984), focuses not only on the target child but also on the group of peers with whom the child interacts. The

Questions for Thought and Discussion
Were you ever a bully or a victim of bullying as a child? What was your sociometric status in your peer group? How did your peers react to your bullying or victimization?

Peer-mediated intervention
Form of intervention for children with sociometric problems in which responses of the peer group are utilized to elicit more effective social behaviors from the target children.

BOX 15.1 Bullying and Victimization in School

According to surveys, 40 to 80 percent of students experience unpleasantness at the hands of peers, including humiliation, taunting, threats, and social ostracism at school (Bosworth, Espelage, & Simon, 1999; Hoover, Oliver, & Hazler, 1992; Juvonen & Graham, 2001). For most students, these negative experiences are relatively infrequent and have no serious impact on long-term adjustment. For others, however, victimization is frequent and longstanding. One recent study estimates that approximately 10 percent of students are picked on and harassed by peers at least two to three times per month. A sizable number are bullied several times per week, and many of these victims are tormented by peers for years (Sohlberg & Olweus, 2003). Not surprisingly, these children are at heightened risk for a variety of problems, including loneliness, depression, anxiety, low self-esteem, peer rejection, academic difficulties, or even, in certain circumstances, outbursts of school violence such as occurred at Columbine or Virginia Tech (Ladd & Ladd, 2001).

In recent years, investigators have devoted considerable effort to understanding the phenomena of peer bullying and victimization. One thing we have learned is that bullying is largely a group phenomenon. Studies show that peers are present during the vast majority of bullying episodes (Atlas & Pepler, 1998; Hawkins, Pepler, & Craig, 2001; Olweus, 2001). Despite their presence, students seldom intervene and put a halt to attacks on peers:

The leaders . . . made it a point to give [Mick] a new derogatory nickname each day—"Brillo" and "Helmet" were two—making fun of his hair, of course. They all thought it was hilarious. Sometimes they'd start to chant—"Don't let Mick eat"—and it was like a rallying cry. They would blow snot on his sandwich or simply steal his food. One day they stole a bee from the biology lab and put it in his tuna sandwich. I didn't join in the teasing, but looking back on it, I can't believe I just sat there and let it happen around me. (Kindlon & Thompson, 1999, p. 7)

Why do students so often stand by and watch as others are teased, assaulted, and humiliated by peers? Research suggests that most children do not support the practice of bullying, find it uncomfortable to watch, and admire peers who try to stop it (Charach, Pepler, & Ziegler, 1995; Rigby & Slee, 1993). Nonetheless, while a significant minority of youth report that they know they should try to halt bullying, peers intervene only 10 to 20 percent of the time (Atlas & Pepler, 1998; Hawkins et al., 2001; Salmivalli, 2001).

One reason children choose not to intervene is that they believe that victims bring harassment on themselves. Children may elicit attacks by showing off, tattling, spreading rumors, or otherwise behaving obnoxiously (Graham & Juvonen, 1998a; Olweus, 2001). In such cases, children (and often adults) may feel that the victim "deserves" the rough treatment. Of course, even children who behave badly have the right to a safe school environment.

It is noteworthy, too, that provocative victims (or "bully/victims") constitute only a minority of children who are picked on by peers. Research consistently shows that most victims (80 percent) do not actively provoke others but rather are perceived as weak and vulnerable (Olweus, 2001). Even these victims may be seen as bringing on attacks, however, by appearing weak and by failing to defend themselves (Graham & Juvonen, 1998a). Boys in particular are unlikely to come to the aid of peers who express fear (Terwogt, 2002).

Students also fail to stop bullying because they fear the group will turn on them if they do. As one fifth-grade boy observed, "It's a real risk if you want to try to stick up for someone because you could get rejected from the group or whatever. Some people do, and nothing happens because they are so high up that other people listen to them. But most people would just

---

attempt is to utilize responses from these other children (for example, offers to play, praise for desirable behavior) to promote more effective social behaviors in the target child. Intervention efforts have beneficial effects (Asher, Parker, & Walker, 1996; Erwin, 1993; Schneider & Byrne, 1985), though they are limited in some ways. Not all children benefit from intervention, and we have little information about the long-term impacts of such programs. Nevertheless, rejected children, who may be most at risk for later problems, can be helped through intervention to improve their social status (Asher, 1985).

One technique that has proved especially effective with rejected children is training in academic skills (Coie & Krehbiel, 1984). Apparently, improvement in the rejected child's academic performance has a beneficial impact on the child's self-concept and general classroom behavior, and these changes in turn affect how the peer group evaluates the child.

Peer Relations in Cultural Perspective

Most of what we know about the bases for children's sociometric standing comes from research in a narrow range of cultural settings, such as school settings in North America. Recent years

Questions for Thought and Discussion

Were you or a member of your family shy or withdrawn as a child? How did this characteristic affect development? What kinds of responses were most helpful?

find themselves in the same boat. And, we've all been there before, so we know what that's like" (Adler & Adler, 1998, pp. 67–68).

As understanding of bullying has grown, it has become increasingly clear that we cannot expect students to work out peer problems on their own. Researchers have developed a number of school-based programs to reduce school bullying. One successful program is a large-scale intervention implemented by Dan Olweus and colleagues in Norwegian schools.

The *Olweus Bullying Prevention Program* has four major goals (Olweus, 1997).

- The first is to increase awareness of the bullying problem.
- Second, the program aims to actively involve teachers and parents. Implicit in this goal is the recognition that adults have some responsibility to control what goes on among students at school.
- A third goal is to develop clear rules against bullying. These rules include explicit statements that bullying is not allowed, that students are to help those who are bullied, and that students should attempt to include in their activities peers who are easily left out.
- A final goal is to provide support and protection of victims.

These four goals are translated into specific actions. Teachers and parents are provided information on what is generally known about the causes and consequences of bullying and victimization, as well as information specific to their school setting, gleaned from student responses to (anonymous) questionnaires about bullying at their school. The questionnaire information helps school staff to increase supervision for times and locations that bullying has occurred most often (for example, lunch and break times).

Steps also are implemented in the classroom. Each classroom establishes and enforces clear rules against bullying, and teachers regularly hold meetings with students to discuss bullying. When students violate class rules and bully others,

teachers intervene swiftly and seriously. They sit down and discuss the incident with bullies and victims and their parents.

Finally, teachers work directly with victims and their parents. Teachers help victims learn how to assert themselves in the classroom and how to respond effectively to taunts and threats. They also help victims' parents find ways to improve their children's relations with peers by establishing new peer contacts or acquiring the social skills required to maintain existing friendships. Teachers also support victims by enlisting the help of neutral or well-adjusted peers to alleviate the victims' predicaments in various ways.

Olweus has reported between 50 and 70 percent declines in bullying in Norwegian schools that have implemented the intervention, while control schools show increases in bullying (Olweus, 1997, 2001). The first systematic evaluation of the Olweus Bullying Prevention Program in the United States (Limber, 2004) was conducted in the mid-1990s, involving 18 middle schools in South Carolina. After one year of implementation, researchers observed:

- Large, significant decreases in boys' and girls' reports of bullying others.
- Large, significant decreases in boys' reports of being bullied and in boys' reports of social isolation.

An evaluation of the Olweus program in 12 elementary schools in the Philadelphia area (Black, 2003) revealed that among those schools that had implemented the program with at least moderate fidelity:

- There were significant reductions in self-reported bullying and victimization.
- There were significant decreases in adults' observations of bullying (in the cafeteria and on the playground).

SOURCE: http://www.clemson.edu/olweus/evidence.html

have seen the extension of sociometric research to settings outside of the United States and Canada. The picture that emerges from these studies is in some respects similar to what is found with North American samples and in some respects different. In North American samples, one of the strongest and most consistent predictors of peer rejection is aggression. This finding extends across a range of cultures. Similar aggression–rejection links have now been demonstrated in China (Chen, Rubin, & Li, 1995), Italy (Attili, Vermigli, & Schneider, 1997), the Netherlands (Cillessen et al., 1992), and Costa Rica (Kupersmidt & Trejos, 1987). These findings confirm that hitting other children is not an effective way to win friends or earn group approval, whatever the specific cultural setting in which the child is developing.

Other findings from North American samples are not generalizable to other cultures. Recall that American children who are shy and reserved in their interactions with peers are at risk of being neglected by the peer group. In China, however, there is no association between a reserved pattern of behavior and neglect. On the contrary, Chinese children who are quiet and nonassertive tend to be above average in popularity. They also are rated by their teachers as especially competent, and they hold a disproportionate number of leadership positions within the school (Chen, 2002; Chen, Rubin, & Sun, 1992).

BOX 15.2   Enhancing Peer Competence among Shy Children

Shy/withdrawn children interact infrequently with their peers, tend to withdraw from social encounters, are likely to be timid and reserved, and talk less than their nonshy peers (Evans, 2001, Younger, Schneider, Wadeson, Guirguis, & Bergeron, 2000). Shy children display such inhibition in unfamiliar social situations, in the presence of peers, and in the classroom. Interestingly, in the more familiar atmosphere of their home, they are often less inhibited with parents and family (Evans, 2001).

One of the most noticeable characteristics of shy/withdrawn children is their tendency to talk considerably less than others. Mary Ann Evans (2001) of the University of Guelph reports that children who are very shy talk infrequently in class, take longer to make their first remarks in class, and their statements are usually significantly shorter than those of their classmates. Such shy children frequently prefer not to answer questions in class and, when called on by the teacher, often fail to respond. According to Evans, such lack of verbal participation in class may actually lead to the teacher's perception that the shy child has poorer academic competence. Shy children's "communication reticence" is evident not only to their teachers, but also to their peers. Alastair Younger of the University of Ottawa asked 227 children from grades 1, 3, 5, and 7 how they could tell that a peer was shy. The overwhelming majority of children from all grade levels responded that shy children "do not talk much" (Younger, Schneider, & Pelley, 1993; Younger et al., 2000).

Shy/withdrawn children are aware of their shyness and view themselves negatively in some areas. Shelley Hymel of the University of British Columbia, Erik Woody of the University of Waterloo, and Anne Bowker of Carleton University (Hymel, Woody, & Bowker, 1993) report that shy/withdrawn, elementary school-aged children view themselves more negatively in social and athletic areas and, to some extent, in terms of physical appearance. Not surprisingly, shy/withdrawn children report being

Applications

lonely. According to Shelley Hymel and colleagues, however, shy children are not completely lacking in positive social skills. Although poorer in social skills such as leadership and sense of humor than their more outgoing peers, they are equal in other skills such as cooperativeness, behavioral conduct, and relations with adults. Nevertheless, shy/withdrawn children tend to perceive themselves as less socially competent than others. As Hymel points out, such negative self-perceptions can lead to a vicious cycle whereby negative self-perceptions can lead a child to develop negative expectations of social interactions, and thus to behave in ways that may actually evoke negative experiences from their peers.

Shy/withdrawn children tend to undervalue their social skills and view themselves as disliked by the peer group. But are they really viewed negatively by the peer group? As discussed in this chapter, some researchers have argued that shy/withdrawn children are not disliked by their peers, but rather occupy the sociometric status of "Neglected"—neither liked nor disliked. Others have argued that such children tend to be among those in the "Rejected" category, although perhaps for different reasons than for aggressive children. Which of these is true?

Alastair Younger has suggested that children's view of their shy/withdrawn peers may depend on age. Younger has reported that in early elementary school grades, children do not pay much attention to the behavior of shy/withdrawn peers (Younger, Gentile, & Burgess, 1993). Although many peers are aware of the presence of shy classmates, even in the first grade (Younger, Schneider, & Pelly, 1993), the behavior of shy children is not viewed negatively (Younger, Gentile, & Burgess, 1993). With increasing age, however, children not only pay more attention to the behavior of shy peers, but also view it more negatively. Thus, the same behaviors that led to being "Neglected" at an earlier age may lead some (although by no means all) shy children to be "Rejected" in later elementary

How might cultural values affect the meaning that children and adults give to the reserved, cooperative behavior shown by the children in this classroom? (Ellen B. Senisi/The Image Works)

school. As Lynne Alden (2001) of the University of British Columbia suggests, shyness can interfere with the development of children's peer relationships, and negative experiences with peers can serve to exacerbate the shy child's already-existing self-doubt and social anxiety. Indeed, Michel Boivin of Laval University and Shelley Hymel of the University of British Columbia (Boivin & Hymel, 1997) have observed that some shy/withdrawn children may come to be victimized by peers, and be made fun of and called names.

Researchers Ken Rubin, Kim Burgess, and Rob Coplan (2003) suggest that, partly as a consequence of this negative peer response, and the loneliness and poor self-regard that ensues, some shy children may be more likely to experience anxiety and depression at later ages. Indeed, Kim Burgess and Alastair Younger (2006), in research conducted at the University of Ottawa, found that preadolescent children in grades 6 and 7 who were highly withdrawn tended, in fact, to report more depression and anxiety, and, in some cases, reported experiencing more somatic symptoms such as headaches, stomach aches, fatigue, and nausea, than did their nonwithdrawn peers. Thus, shyness/withdrawal, particularly when accompanied by peer rejection, may have the potential to lead to unhappiness and emotional distress as children develop.

Shy/withdrawn children can be helped in various ways. In the classroom setting, teachers can take a number of steps to gently encourage the participation of shy children. Interviews with several teachers conducted by Mary Ann Evans (2001) suggest the value of maintaining a quiet, orderly class. Teachers also report that it is helpful to spend time alone with the shy child after school, engaging him or her in discussion about family and interests, leading to the development of trust and a relationship. Teachers can also gently reinforce children's participation in class discussion, without drawing notice to them, through patient attention and encouragement.

From the peer side of things, children who are shy and withdrawn can often benefit from social skills training interventions.

Such interventions can be most successful when conducted in a group of children with similar problems. Helen Bienert and Barry Schneider (1995) of the University of Ottawa report that modeling social skills such as how to approach others, how to initiate activities, and how to begin and respond to conversation, followed by practice in the group, can be an effective intervention (see also Sweeney & Rapee, 2001). Interventions that include pairing the shy/withdrawn child with a non-shy peer, perhaps a peer who is a couple of years younger than the shy child, have also been found to be helpful (Furman, Rahe & Hartup, 1979; Zimbardo, 1981).

Parents can also help. As Evans (2001) noted, many shy/withdrawn children are less inhibited at home (see also Zimbardo, 1981). It can be beneficial to encourage the shy child to invite a friend over to spend time in this less threatening setting (Zimbardo, 1981). Although parents of shy children may often want to shield their child from stressful situations, Kim Burgess and Ken Rubin point out that such overcontrol and overprotection may actually serve to maintain or exacerbate the child's anxiety (Burgess, Rubin, Cheah, & Nelson, 2001). Lynne Alden (2001) suggests that gently encouraging a shy child to "engage" life can help the child learn to cope with social anxiety. In their book, *The Shy Child,* Philip Zimbardo and Shirley Radl (1999) offer valuable examples of such encouragement that can help children build confidence in social interactions, including practicing making eye contact, developing a sense of humor, developing listening skills, and so on. It is also valuable to help shy children to focus on their areas of competence and interest, be they academic, hobbies, or other activities, to help them view themselves as persons with strengths in various areas, rather than just perceived weaknesses in the areas of social interaction (Zimbardo & Radl, 1999).

These are some ways in which shy children can be helped and encouraged. Other suggestions for shy children, as well as for their parents and teachers can be found at the very helpful web site—www.shykids.com.

Why might a similar behavior pattern lead to such different outcomes in different cultures? The most likely answer concerns cultural values and expectations. In China, a cautious, self-restrained style of interpersonal interaction is regarded as a sign of competence and maturity (Ho, 1986). Adults therefore encourage this behavior pattern in children, and children come to value it and reward it in their peers. In any culture there are expectations about appropriate forms of behavior—expectations held by children as well as adults. Children whose behavior is in accord with cultural values and expectations are the ones who are most likely to find acceptance in the peer group.

Learning Objective 15.2: *Discuss peer sociometric status and its consequences for children's development.*

1. What are the categories of peer sociometric status identified by researchers?
2. What long-term effects does peer rejection have on development?
3. What are social problem-solving skills, and how do these relate to peer status?
4. What cultural differences have been found in peer acceptance?

✔ *Test Your*
M a s t e r y . . .

Learning Objective 15.3
Analyze the social contexts of peer relationships in childhood and adolescence.

Group
A collection of individuals who interact regularly in a consistent, structured fashion and who share values and a sense of belonging to the group.

Cliques
A kind of group typical in adolescence, consisting usually of 5 to 10 members whose shared interests and behavior patterns set them apart from their peers.

Crowds
Large, loosely organized groups that serve to structure social identity in high school.

The Social Contexts of Peer Relationships

Peer relations are a major part of most children's lives. However, relationships with peers go beyond the joys and challenges of finding friends and companions to spend time with. They also provide contexts that influence children's behavior and development. In this section, we will examine some of the ways in which peer groups serve as a social context for development, as well as some of the interconnections between the contexts of peer and family relationships.

A striking developmental change in peer relations is the increased importance of groups as a context for peer interaction. For psychologists, the term **group** describes something more than just a collection of two or more individuals. Hartup (1983) suggests the following criteria for determining that a group exists: "social interaction occurs regularly, values are shared over and above those maintained in society at large, individual members have a sense of belonging, and a structure exists to support the attitudes that members should have toward one another" (p. 144).

Preschool children occasionally interact in ways that seem to fit this definition. The same four boys or girls, for example, may play together in similar ways every day, demonstrating clear leader-and-follower roles in their play as well as a clear sense of "we" versus "they" in their relations with those outside their group. During the grade school years, membership in groups assumes greater significance in the lives of most children. Some groups are formal with a significant adult input, such as Girl Scouts, Boy Scouts, 4-H, and Little League. Other groups are more informal, child-created, and child-directed, reflecting mutual interests of the group members.

In the early teen years, the more loosely structured groups of middle childhood coalesce into *cliques*. **Cliques** are small groups of five to seven friends who interact frequently and whose shared interests and behavior patterns set them apart from both their peers and the adult world. Typically, clique members are similar in family background, values, and attitudes. In early adolescence, cliques are usually same-sex, but by the mid-teens mixed-sex cliques are more common. Cliques offer members a place to find emotional support and companionship, as well as a place to begin to explore one's social (and sexual) identity during the teen years.

During high school, groups of cliques often come together to form *crowds*. **Crowds** are large, loosely organized groups that serve to structure social identity in high school (Stone & Brown, 1999). Most adults will remember a variety of high school crowds by their general label and reputation: the "jocks," who typically are popular and involved in athletics; the "geeks" or "nerds," who often are considered technologically sophisticated but

What different crowds do you think the boy and girl in this photo belong to? How do these groups serve to structure social life and identity in high school? (Corbis/photolibrary)

socially awkward; the "goths," who distinguish themselves with their dark clothing, chains, and body piercings; the "headbangers" or, in previous generations, "druggies," who use drugs and are known for skipping school and getting into fights; and others.

Crowds such as these provide adolescents with a forum for exploring social identity. After high school, the power of crowds declines in the lives of individuals. However, even in adulthood, people seek like-minded groups of others with whom they socialize and often identify with in terms of personal interests and lifestyle choices.

Conformity to Peers   To many adults, the importance of peer-group membership for the grade-schooler or adolescent raises the disturbing possibility that peers may come to outweigh parents as a source of behaviors and values—that is, that the desire to conform or "fit in" with a peer group will lead young people to engage in behaviors that parents have taught them is objectionable. What do we know about the influence of peers and in particular about the relative influence of peers and parents?

Peers can be an important source of values, but the degree of importance depends on a number of factors (Berndt, 1989a; Urberg, 1999). Peer influence varies with age, reaching a peak by some measures in early adolescence and declining thereafter (Berndt, 1979; Constanzo, 1970). Peer influence also varies from child to child. Some children are much more susceptible to peer pressures to conform than others (Berndt, 1996; Hartup, 1999). And peer influence, as well as the relative importance of peers and parents, varies from one area of life to another. In areas such as clothing, music, and choice of friends, for example, peers often are more important than parents, especially by adolescence, when membership in a specific peer group is often expressed through conformity in these matters. In areas such as academic planning and occupational aspirations, however, parents usually have the dominant voice (Berndt, Miller, & Park, 1989; Sebald, 1989; Steinberg, 2001).

Peers also can be a negative influence in problem areas such as smoking (Urberg, Degirmencioglu, & Pilgrim, 1997); drinking (Cleveland & Wiebe, 2003); drug use (Dinges & Oetting, 1993; Mounts & Steinberg, 1995); bullying (Espelage, Holt, & Henkel, 2003); delinquency (Jessor & Jessor, 1977); and gang violence (Lahey et al., 1999). Nevertheless, peer group membership is enjoyable for children, often nurtures positive behaviors and values, and promotes a number of social skills that remain valuable throughout life. Furthermore, surveys reveal that the common perception of a clash in values between peers and parents is overstated. On most questions, peers and parents are more similar than different in their views (Brown, 1990; Newman, 1982). In part, this similarity results from the fact that parents help determine the peers with whom the child associates (Collins et al., 2000).

Family-Peer Connections

For most children, the family and the peer group are the two most important microsystems within which development occurs. How do these two major social worlds relate? How do children's relations with their siblings compare with their peer relations, and how do parents contribute to children's peer relations? On the one hand, both sibships and friendships are intimate, long-lasting relationships that are the context for frequent and varied interactions—usually positive in tone but including moments of conflict and rivalry as well. Both relationships involve partners who are close in age, and hence interactions are likely to be more egalitarian and symmetrical than are interactions with adults, such as parents or teachers.

On the other hand, siblings (unless they are twins) are not identical in age, and the younger–older contrast introduces a basic asymmetry that is not necessarily found with friends. Furthermore, siblings, unlike friends, are not together by choice and do not have the option of terminating the relationship if negative aspects begin to outweigh positive ones. As one researcher put it, "Siblings do not choose each other, very often do not trust or even like each other, and may be competing strongly for parental affection and interest; the sources of conflict and hostility in this relationship are likely to be very different from those leading to tension in a friendship" (Dunn, 1992, p. 7).

Questions for Thought and Discussion
What labels and reputations identified crowds in your high school? How did membership in a crowd affect your development during adolescence?

Questions for Thought
and Discussion
*How would you compare and
contrast your sibships with your
friendships while growing up?*

Siblings and Peers This analysis suggests that we should expect both similarities and differences between sibling and peer relations. Siblings can perform the same roles and fulfill the same needs as are important among friends—as playmates or social companions, for instance, as sources of affection, or as confidants for intimate interchanges (Buhrmester, 1992). Less positively, siblings, like friends, may also sometimes be targets of hostility and conflict. Especially among younger children, conflicts among siblings are a depressingly familiar experience for many parents (Dunn, 1993). Some conflict is inevitable in any long-term, intimate relationship, and siblings, like friends, are no exception to this rule.

Along with these general similarities in sibling and peer relations come differences. Some differences follow from the differences in age between siblings and the contrasting roles played by the younger and older child. Sibling interchanges, especially early in development, tend to be less symmetrical and egalitarian than those among friends, both because of the younger-older contrast and because of the forced, rather than chosen, nature of the sibling relationship. This factor also contributes to differences in the domain of conflict. Although conflicts occur in both relationships, they tend to be more frequent between siblings than between friends (Buhrmester, 1992), and they also take somewhat different forms in the two contexts. Children are less likely to reason with siblings than with friends, less likely to attempt to take the sibling's point of view, and more likely to judge perceived transgressions negatively when the perpetrator is a sibling (Slomkowski & Dunn, 1993). Again, the involuntary nature of the sibling relationship may account for the siblings–friends differences.

Do particular children tend to show the same sorts of behaviors with peers as with siblings? Does the overall quality of a child's peer relations mirror the quality of relations with siblings? The answers turn out to be "sometimes but not always" (Dunn & McGuire, 1992). Research makes clear that there is no simple, direct carryover of relations forged with siblings to relations with peers. Some examinations of the issue report little, if any, association between how children behave with siblings and how they behave with peers (Abramovitch et al., 1986; Volling, Youngblade, & Belsky, 1997). Such findings demonstrate once again the importance of context for children's behavior: What we see in one social context does not necessarily hold true when we move to a different context.

In other studies, sibling–peer connections emerge, but they are seldom strong. Links tend to be greater with friendship (another intense, dyadic relationship) than with peer relations in general (Stocker & Dunn, 1990). Some studies have shown positive correlations between cooperation with siblings and cooperation with friends (Stocker & Mantz-Simmons, 1993); between aggression with siblings and aggression toward peers (Vandell et al., 1990); and between the overall quality of sibling relations and the quality of peer relations (Seginer, 1998). Other studies have shown negative correlations. For example, children with relatively hostile sibling relations sometimes form especially close friendships (Stocker & Dunn, 1990). Similarly, children who are unpopular with peers may rank high on affection and companionship with their siblings (East & Rook, 1992). What seems to be happening in these cases is a kind of compensation: When one component of children's social world is unsatisfactory, they may try especially hard to obtain pleasure and support from other components.

Parents and Peers How do relations with parents and peers contribute to children's success in school? This question relates to an aspect of the mesosystem (Bronfenbrenner, 1979)—the relationship between two microsystems: life with parents and life in the peer group. First, what do parents do that helps or hinders their children's success with peers? Many studies show that parents do a variety of things that can be important (Kerns, Contreras, & Neal-Barnett, 2000; Parke & Ladd, 1992; Parke et al., 2002).

Parents' contribution to peer relations can begin very early in life, before most children even begin to interact with peers. As you read in Chapter 11, infants differ in the security of the attachments they form with parents, and these differences, in turn, relate to the sensitivity and responsiveness of caregiving practices. Also, secure attachment in infancy is associated with a number of positive outcomes in later childhood, including positive peer

Links to Related Material
*In Chapter 11, you read about
the relation of quality of
attachment to later peer
relations. Here, you learn more
about the impact of early
attachment relationships on the
quality of children's friendships.*

relations. Children who were securely attached as infants tend to do well on measures of social competence and popularity later in childhood (Bohlin, Hagekull, & Rydell, 2000; Fagot, 1997; Kerns, Klepac, & Cole, 1996). Security of attachment is also related to quality of friendships. Children with a history of secure attachment tend to form more harmonious and well-balanced friendships than do children with a history of less satisfactory attachments (Kerns, 1996; Youngblade & Belsky, 1992). Infant attachment is a stronger predictor of friendship quality than of general peer status (Schneider, Atkinson, & Tardif, 2001).

Most research on attachment security as a predictor of later developmental outcomes has concentrated on mothers. We know less, therefore, about the possible importance of early relations with fathers. The studies that do exist, however, suggest that a secure attachment with the father also relates positively to later success with peers (Schneider et al., 2001).

Parents also contribute to the development of the forms of play that occupy such a central position in children's early interactions with their peers. Before they embark on pretend or dramatic play with peers, many children have spent dozens of hours engaged in such play with their parents at home. Observational studies verify that joint pretend play is a frequent activity in many households and that parents (mothers, in particular, in these studies) often assume a directive role in such play (Tamis-LeMonda, Uzgiris, & Bornstein, 2002). Research suggests, moreover, that children can acquire social skills in play with parents that carry over to later interactions with peers. It has been shown, for example, that parents' expression of positive emotions during play is linked to children's subsequent expression of positive emotions with peers, which is related to acceptance by the peer group (Isley et al., 1999). Similarly, mothers' use of reasoning that asks the child to take the perspective of the other is related to the children's subsequent success in resolving conflicts with friends (Herrera & Dunn, 1997).

Parents may also take a direct role in promoting and managing their children's encounters with peers. Gary Ladd (1992) identified four ways that parents may influence the frequency and nature of peer interactions:

1. As *designers* of the child's environment, parents make choices that affect the availability of peers and the settings (such as a safe versus a hazardous neighborhood) within which peer interactions take place.

2. As *mediators,* parents arrange peer contacts for their children and regulate their choice of play partners.

3. As *supervisors,* parents monitor their children's peer interactions and offer guidance and support.

4. As *consultants,* parents provide more general advice and emotional support with respect to peer relations, especially in response to questions and concerns from the child.

Research indicates that parents vary in the frequency and skill with which they perform these four roles and that these variations in parental behavior relate to variations in children's peer relations (Ladd & Pettit, 2002). It has been found, for example, that peer acceptance in preschool relates to the extent to which parents initiate and direct play opportunities for their children (Ladd & Hart, 1992). Play among children, especially toddlers or preschoolers, proceeds more smoothly and happily when a parent is present to facilitate (Bhavnagri & Parke, 1991). In addition, play opportunities are more frequent and friendship networks are larger when children grow up in safe neighborhoods with closely spaced houses that are conducive to peer interaction (Medrich et al., 1982). Parents' initiation of peer contacts for their children has also been shown to relate positively to peer acceptance in Russia and China (Hart et al., 1998). Parental monitoring of interaction with peers has been found to be beneficial in Denmark (Arnett & Balle-Jensen, 1993); Australia (Feldman et al., 1991); and China (Chen et al., 1998).

What childrearing strategies nurture or fail to nurture the social skills necessary for success with peers? One consistent correlate of sociometric status and social skills is

How do parents indirectly and directly influence their children's peer relations? What could these parents do to facilitate their children's positive relationships with peers? (Peter Hvizdak/The Image Works)

parental warmth (MacDonald, 1992). Children who come from homes characterized by high levels of warmth, nurturance, and emotional expressiveness tend to do well in the peer group. Conversely, children whose home lives are less harmonious are at risk for peer problems as well, especially in cases of physical abuse or neglect. Children who have been abused show special difficulty in responding appropriately when peers exhibit signs of distress (Klimes-Dougan & Kistner, 1990). Children who have been maltreated also show heightened levels of aggressiveness and social withdrawal (Mueller & Silverman, 1989). Abused children tend to fare poorly on sociometric measures, and their unskilled behavior with peers often perpetuates their difficulties (Bolger & Patterson, 2001; Cicchetti et al., 1992).

The parent's methods of controlling and disciplining the child also can be important (Dekovic & Janssens, 1992; Dishion, 1990; Hart et al., 1992). Parents of popular children tend to be intermediate in the degree of control they exert, neither rigidly directing the child's every action nor allowing too much leeway because of lack of time or interest. When discipline becomes necessary, parents of popular children tend to prefer verbal rather than physical methods, reasoning with the child and negotiating rather than imposing solutions. In contrast, techniques of power assertion (threats and physical punishment) tend to characterize the home lives of children with peer problems (Ladd & Pettit, 2002).

Parents contribute to the child's success with peers and also to failure. Many children reared in difficult circumstances nonetheless show good adjustment later in life. In one study, researchers explored whether peers might buffer children from the effects of exposure to marital conflict and physical aggression in the family environment (Criss et al., 2002). The researchers found that children exposed to higher levels of family adversity in early childhood exhibited more problem behaviors in grade 2. However, children reared in adverse circumstances who had positive peer relations displayed far fewer behavior problems than other children raised in comparable family situations. The results of this study suggest that positive peer relations can serve as a protective factor against family adversity.

Peer Relations as a Source of Resilience

It is well established that children exposed to adverse family environments during early childhood are at elevated risk for the development of behavior problems. Of course, exposure to difficult family experiences does not foreordain adjustment problems. Many children reared in difficult circumstances nonetheless show good adjustment later in life.

Questions for Thought and Discussion

How did parenting styles and childrearing strategies in your family affect your peer relations during childhood and adolescence?

Psychologists refer to children who adapt positively in the face of significant adversity as **resilient children** (Luthar, Cicchetti, & Becker, 2000; Masten et al., 1999).

Studies of resilient children have revealed that a variety of factors contribute to children's ability to overcome negative experiences. These include personal characteristics of the child (e.g., socially responsive temperament, high self-esteem), aspects of the family (e.g., the availability of alternative caregivers), and characteristics of the child's wider social network (e.g., supportive neighbors or social agencies) (Cochran & Niego, 2002; Werner & Smith, 1982). In one study, researchers explored whether peers might buffer children from the effects of exposure to a family environment characterized by high levels of marital conflict and physical aggression (Criss et al., 2002).

The investigation was part of a larger, longitudinal study of children's socialization known as the Child Development Project (Pettit et al., 2001). More than 550 children and their families in Tennessee and Indiana were recruited for the study when they registered for kindergarten. The families were primarily of middle-class and European American backgrounds. During the summer before children entered kindergarten, the parents were interviewed and completed questionnaires about a variety of issues. Based on the parents' responses, each family was rated on three dimensions of family adversity—ecological disadvantage, violent marital conflict, and harsh discipline.

Data on children's peer relations were collected during kindergarten and first grade. To assess children's peer relations, the researchers used two of the sociometric techniques described earlier. During individual interviews, children were shown a class roster and asked to nominate up to three peers they liked and three peers they disliked. They were also asked to rate how much they liked each peer. The measures provided an index of how much each child was generally liked by peers as well as his or her number of friends.

Children's adjustment was based on teacher ratings. During the spring of grade 2, teachers completed the Child Behavior Checklist, a widely used checklist of behavior problems that includes such items as "gets in many fights" and "disobedient at school."

As expected, the researchers found that children exposed to higher levels of family adversity in early childhood exhibited greater numbers of problem behaviors in grade 2. However, children reared in adverse circumstances but who had positive peer relations displayed far fewer behavior problems than other children raised in comparable family situations. Moreover, the positive impact of peers was found for all three kinds of family adversity.

The results of this study suggest that positive peer relations can serve as a protective factor against family adversity. The findings also raise a number of intriguing questions. One question is how peer relations might moderate the effects of negative family environments. Theorists have proposed a number of explanations. One possibility is that positive peer relationships provide a "remedial" context in which children can practice certain skills not picked up at home (Price, 1996). For instance, a child whose parents are too overstressed to help the child learn how to manage his or her emotions may learn how to do so in the context of peer interaction.

Another possibility is that relationships with peers may foster the child's engagement in school and foster positive relations with teachers. A positive orientation toward school may in turn decrease the child's tendency toward social deviance. A third possibility is that peers may serve as a form of "behavioral intervention." The negative reactions of peers, and possibly the peers' parents, to inappropriate behavior (e.g., aggression) may teach the at-risk child that behaviors that are normative in his or her own home are unacceptable outside of it.

Finally, children's relationships with peers may also indirectly modify parents' behaviors. By interacting with the parents of their children's friends, mothers may learn more effective means of discipline and of resolving marital conflicts (Fletcher et al., 1995). Establishing a network of relations with other parents may also reduce family stress by providing social support. Thus, peer relations may lead to improvements in the behavior of children at risk via their positive influence on parenting.

Resilient children
Children who adapt positively in the face of significant adversity.

BOX 15.3 Conversations with a Community Mental Health Practitioner

Beth Muller with family friend (Courtesy of Beth Muller)

Beth Muller, 49, is an instructor in the Department of Psychiatry, University of Connecticut School of Medicine. She grew up in the Northeast, and lives in West Hartford with her husband and daughter. She works with high-risk children in Connecticut, many of whom are referred by the juvenile justice system.

Since I got my nursing degree in 1980, I have played many roles in many different contexts, but all within the framework of nursing. For seven years, I taught nursing students at Yale University at the master's level, training them to be therapists in child and adolescent psychiatry. In my current position, I'm helping to create programs to serve the mental health needs for poor and indigent children in Connecticut, with a special emphasis on kids in the juvenile justice system. I also do direct service, including psychiatric evaluations and providing psychiatric medication. Our mission is to provide psychiatric care for populations with limited access. For example, I go into the inner city and I see kids who are in the juvenile justice system who cannot return to the community safely without mental health support. There is a huge lack of child psychiatrists in the state of Connecticut, so my current licensing allows me to have an independent practice to do psychiatric evaluation and medication for children and adolescents.

I am an Advanced Practice Registered Nurse (APRN), a nurse with special training beyond the master's degree that allows me to do specialized work. I also train medical residents here at UConn, and soon we will be adding nursing and social work students for a multidisciplinary program that is being developed here.

I also am working on a Ph.D. in child development, with an emphasis on children's cultural contexts. I use my cultural knowledge everyday in my work with these kids. I'm in the clinics dealing with people from a variety of cultural backgrounds, particularly from Puerto Rico, Central America, and the African American community. My awareness of the importance of cultural values has enabled me to develop treatment plans that are congruent with the family's values and cultural backgrounds. For example, different cultural groups view the activity level of children differently. How a parent experiences what is normal versus pathological can be very different from that of the dominant culture, and it is important that we understand that, and develop a treatment plan that is sensitive to cultural differences. I also enjoy teaching students about the importance of cultural frameworks, both in evaluating mental illness and in providing competent care.

In my work, I play many roles. I teach, provide consultation on kids with severe mental health needs, prescribe medication, do research, and coordinate care as we track kids through the state. I case manage kids and oversee their care, making sure they get the services they need and the right level of care. We also partner with many state agencies to develop these treatment and intervention programs for high-need children and families. For example, I work closely with probation and parole officers. We're creating services that were never there before. The bad news is that we can't keep up. One of our tasks is to train medical residents for public and community psychiatry, with an ultimate goal of filling the exponentially growing need we have for new providers.

I chose this profession for myself because I wanted my work to be meaningful, to have the opportunity to have my work make a difference every day. I work to make it possible for high-need kids to be safely maintained in their communities. So, kids who are not normally getting good care are now getting top-notch care. For example, I was treating a 12-year-old who had been arrested for drug dealing and for carrying a 2 x 4 board as a weapon. While he was being interviewed he kept saying, "I would never use drugs." During the interview, we discovered that his father was unknown, his mother was incarcerated, and his drug dealing was supporting a family of eight—five younger siblings, a grandmother, and a great-aunt. What else could he have done? He had no access to a regular-paying job that would support a family. He was carrying the 2 x 4 to fight off gangs who were trying to interfere with his business. He never started a fight. It really shook me to the core. This kid was incredibly bright. We have to think about context before we make judgments or place labels about what is pathological and what is not. Incidents like this really shape your vision.

We are in desperate need of people who have the desire and the will to take on these challenges in the mental health field. The need is huge. The reward is that, even though I am exhausted at times, at the end of the day I feel as though I have done something that gives back to our community and our children.

Learning Objective 15.3: *Analyze the social contexts of peer relationships in childhood and adolescence.*

1. How do peer groups develop in childhood and adolescence?
2. What is the function of high school "crowds" in adolescent social and emotional development?
3. What is the relationship between peer groups and conformity in childhood and adolescence?
4. What connections have researchers found between peer and sibling relationships?
5. In what ways do parents influence the development of children's peer relationships?

✔ *Test Your Mastery...*

BOX 15.4 **Contextual Model of Peer Relationships**

Child is born with dimensions of temperament that predispose him or her toward greater or lesser sociability.

Family, Neighborhood, and School Settings

- Parents lay the foundation for secure attachment relationships through their responsiveness to the child's needs.
- Parents and other caregivers model and reinforce good social problem-solving skills, as well as warm, positive relationships.
- Children have the opportunity to practice their developing social skills in peer group settings within the extended family, the neighborhood, and school settings.
- Children participate in the social networks that are created and structured by their parents.
- Children increasingly create their own social networks as they grow old enough to choose preferred activities and companions.
- Children experience themselves socially in relation to a peer group, and adopt a sense of self that is consistent with the feedback they get from others.

Cultural and Societal Settings

- Expectations regarding appropriate social behavior, and sanctions for violating these norms, are communicated by adults and media within the larger culture.

Learning Objective 15.1
Trace the development of peer
sociability and friendship in children.

---

1. How does early sociability emerge in infants and young children?

Infants as young as *6 months* look at, vocalize to, smile at, and touch other infants. These behaviors have been characterized as object-centered, because infants' early interactions often center on some toy of mutual interest. At about *one year*, infants begin to coordinate these behaviors into more complex combinations, such as a touch in conjunction with a smile, perhaps followed by a vocalization. Moreover, one-way social acts become increasingly reciprocal between young children as interactions evolve into more truly social interchanges. As children enter the *preschool years*, their social world becomes larger. They are able to direct different behaviors to different people and to form somewhat different relationships. The complexity of their social interactions increases as symbolic forms of play begin to predominate over physical forms of play.

---

2. What types of play do researchers use to study the development of children's play?

Functional play, such as shaking a rattle or jumping up and down, emerges early and predominates during the infant and toddler years. Games with rules are infrequent among children younger than grade-school age. *Constructive* play is the manipulation of objects with the intention of creating something, like a block tower, or cutting and pasting pictures. Pretend play or *sociodramatic* play has been of special interest to investigators of preschool development. Studies have demonstrated that both the frequency and the complexity of pretend play increase across the preschool years.

---

3. How do the social and cognitive levels of play compare?

The nonsocial play of 1- and 2-year-olds consists mainly of various kinds of functional play. *Older children* are more likely to embed even their nonsocial play in a constructive or dramatic context. Because of this interplay of cognitive and social factors, modern scales to assess play typically include both cognitive and social dimensions. By age 8 or 9, children have become enthusiastic participants in games with rules. By middle childhood, children's play is also more likely to consist of cooperative play. These changes in both the cognitive level and the social organization of play relate to more general factors in the child's development.

4. How does children's understanding of friendship develop?	Young children's thinking about friendship tends to focus on concrete, external attributes. A friend is someone who is fun to play with and who shares things. *Older children* are more capable of taking into account more abstract aspects of friendship, such as caring for another person. For young children, friendship is often a momentary state dependent on specific acts just performed or about to be performed. Older children are more likely to see friendship as an enduring relationship that persists across time and even in the face of occasional conflicts. Although even young children realize the importance of mutual liking between friends, qualities such as loyalty and intimacy do not become central in children's thinking about friendship until late childhood or adolescence.

Learning Objective 15.2
Discuss peer sociometric status and its consequences for children's development.

1. What are the categories of peer sociometric status identified by researchers?	*Popular-prosocial* children are high in social competence and generally do well academically. They are well-liked by other children for their abilities to solve conflicts peacefully and to interact with their peers in cooperative yet assertive ways. Popular-prosocial children are skilled at initiating and maintaining interaction. They reinforce other children, show sensitivity to the needs and wishes of others, and communicate effectively. Rejected children, on the other hand, are actively disliked. For *rejected-aggressive* children, their aggression leads to being rejected by the peer group, which contributes to later aggression. Rejected-aggressive children often show antisocial behavior. *Rejected-withdrawn* children, on the other hand, often find social interactions to be anxiety-provoking. Their attempts to enter new groups or to make new friends tend to be clumsy and often end in rebuff. These children may be at risk for anxiety and depression, and their submissive interaction style places them at greater risk for abuse by bullies. The neglected child is viewed by peers neither positively nor negatively and tends to be ignored. *Neglected* children often are perceived by their peers as shy, for they are less talkative and less socially active. Finally, the *controversial* child receives a mixed evaluation from the peer group, viewed as both positive and negative by peers. Like rejected children, controversial children tend to be aggressive, but, like popular children, they also tend to be sociable. Sociometric statuses may be temporary.

2. What long-term effects does peer rejection have on development?	*Early rejected status*, either aggressive or withdrawn, predicts continuing rejection. The category of rejection is especially stable over time, and rejected children are at greatest risk for a number of problems later in life, including juvenile delinquency, dropping out of school, and mental illness. Problems in peer relations are not just a source of anxiety and unhappiness in childhood. Such problems place children at greater than average risk for a variety of negative outcomes later in life.

3. What are social problem-solving skills, and how do these relate to peer status?

Interventions have been used to help children having trouble with peer relationships. Modeling, for example, can increase social skills and social acceptance. Shaping of desirable social behaviors through reinforcement also can work. Children can be taught perspective-taking skills and receive training in social problem-solving abilities. Peer-mediated intervention uses responses from a group to promote effective social behaviors in the target child. A technique that is effective with rejected children is training in academic skills. Apparently, improvement in the rejected child's academic performance has a beneficial impact on the child's self-concept and general classroom behavior, and these changes in turn affect how the peer group evaluates the child.

4. What cultural differences have been found in peer acceptance?

In North American samples, a strong predictor of peer rejection is aggression, and this finding extends across a range of cultures. Similar *aggression–rejection* links have now been demonstrated in China, the Netherlands, and Costa Rica. These findings confirm that hitting other children is not an effective way to win friends or earn group approval, whatever the specific cultural setting in which the child is developing. Other findings from North American samples are not generalizable to other cultures. In China, for example, children who are *shy and reserved* in their interactions with peers are not at risk of being neglected by the peer group as would be the case in the United States. Chinese children who are quiet and nonassertive tend to be above average in popularity, are rated by their teachers as especially competent, and hold more leadership positions in the school.

Learning Objective 15.3

Analyze the social contexts of peer relationships in childhood and adolescence.

1. How do peer groups develop in childhood and adolescence?

A striking developmental change is the *increased importance of groups* as a context for peer interaction. Preschool children occasionally interact in small groups or play together in similar ways every day. They demonstrate leader-and-follower roles in their play and a sense of "we" versus "they" in their relations with children outside the group. During the grade school years, membership in groups assumes greater significance. Some groups are formal with significant adult input, whereas other groups are more informal, child-created, and child-directed. In the early teen years, the more loosely structured groups of middle childhood coalesce into cliques— small groups of five to seven friends who interact frequently and share certain interests and behavior patterns. In early adolescence, cliques are usually same-sex, but by the mid-teens mixed-sex cliques are more common. During high school, groups of cliques often come together to form crowds—large, loosely organized groups that serve to structure social identity in high school.

2. What is the function of high school "crowds" in adolescent social and emotional development?

Crowds provide adolescents with a forum for exploring social identity. After high school, the power of crowds declines in the lives of individuals. However, even in adulthood, people seek like-minded groups of others with whom they socialize and often identify with in terms of personal interests and lifestyle choices.

3. What is the relationship between peer groups and conformity in childhood and adolescence?

Peers can be an important source of values, but peer influence varies with age, reaching a peak in early adolescence and then declining. Some children are much more susceptible to peer pressures to conform than others. In areas such as clothing, music, and choice of friends, peers often are more important than parents, especially by adolescence, when membership in a specific peer group is often expressed through conformity in these areas. In academic planning and occupational aspirations, however, *parents* usually have the dominant voice. Peers also can be a negative influence in problem areas such as smoking, drinking, drug use, bullying, delinquency, and gang violence.

4. What connections have researchers found between peer and sibling relationships?

Siblings can perform the *same roles* and fulfill the same needs as are important among friends: for example, as playmates or social companions, as sources of affection, or as confidants for intimate interchanges. Less positively, siblings, like friends, may also sometimes be targets of hostility and conflict. *Some differences* between sibling and peer relations stem from differences in age and the contrasting roles played by the younger and older sibling. Sibling interchanges tend to be less symmetrical and egalitarian than interchanges among friends. Although conflicts occur in both relationships, they tend to be more frequent between siblings than between friends. Children are less likely to reason with siblings than with friends, less likely to attempt to take the sibling's point of view, and more likely to judge perceived transgressions negatively when the perpetrator is a sibling.

5. In what ways do parents influence the development of children's peer relationships?

Parents' contribution to peer relations can begin before most children even begin to interact with peers. *Secure attachment* with parents in infancy is associated with positive outcomes in later childhood, including positive peer relations. Children who were securely attached as infants tend to do well on measures of social competence and popularity later in childhood. Security of attachment is also related to quality of friendships. Children with a history of secure attachment tend to form more harmonious and well-balanced friendships than do children with a history of less satisfactory attachments. Secure attachment with the father, as well as the mother, positively relates to later success with peers. Parents also contribute to the development of the forms of play that children use in their early peer interactions. Social skills in play with parents carries over to later interactions with peers. Parents also typically take a direct role in promoting and managing their children's encounters with peers.

Families *and* Society

(Ariel Skelley/Corbis)

Jennifer was a single mom with a well-paying job. She was able to provide Kaylie with a roomy house in a safe neighborhood, dance lessons, and an excellent private school and health care. When Jennifer unexpectedly lost her job, they moved in with relatives in another part of the country. This change, necessitated by Jennifer's economic circumstances, brought with it numerous changes in the context of Kaylie's life. One positive change was that Kaylie and Jennifer now had the direct support of extended family. Kaylie had regular contact with grandparents, aunts, uncles, and cousins, and Jennifer had day-to-day support with child care. Other changes were less positive. Jennifer and Kaylie had given up the spaciousness and privacy of their own house and now shared a small bedroom in someone else's house. They had also lost their excellent private health care, and they now struggled with every health-related decision. The neighborhood they moved to was nearer a downtown area and less safe than the one they had moved from. There was less choice with regard to Kaylie's school, and the public schools in their new town were plagued with problems. There was no more money for extras like dance lessons, and Jennifer did not have long-standing relationships with Kaylie's new teachers, a definite change in the quality of Kaylie's mesosystem. These multiple changes made Jennifer more aware of the various ways in which the opportunities that she as a parent provided had served to shape Kaylie's life on many levels.

As is evident with the case of Jennifer and Kaylie, families shape the context of their children's lives in multiple ways. Parents not only provide their children with caregiving, socialization, and guidance. They also influence their children's lives indirectly through such things as cultural background, attitudes and values, and socioeconomic opportunities and constraints. In this chapter, we will examine some of the ways in which families influence child development. Children encounter many people who influence them as they develop. For most, however, the family is one of the earliest and most important sources of direct influence. In this section, we look at the role of socialization within the family. ■

Learning Objective 16.1
Analyze the influence of parenting practices and children's contributions to childhood socialization.

Parental warmth
A dimension of parenting that reflects the amount of support, affection, and encouragement the parent provides to the child.

Parental control
A dimension of parenting that reflects the degree to which the child is monitored, disciplined, and regulated.

Parenting style
The overall pattern of childrearing provided by a parent, typically defined by the combination of warmth and control that the parent demonstrates.

Parenting Styles

Parents differ in how they choose to socialize their children. The goal in most studies of childrearing is twofold: to identify the important differences among parents and to determine what effects, if any, these variations have on children's development. What are the significant dimensions along which parenting might vary? The most influential conceptualization of parenting style was developed by Diana Baumrind (1971, 1989, 1991). In her research, Baumrind observed preschool-age children in their homes and at school. She also collected information from parents about their typical behaviors and their child's. Through her work and that of others, two major dimensions have consistently emerged as important in understanding individual differences in parenting styles (Maccoby & Martin, 1983). One is **parental warmth** (sometimes labeled *acceptance/responsiveness*)—the amount of support, affection, and encouragement the parent provides, as opposed to hostility, shame, or rejection. The second dimension is **parental control** (sometimes labeled *demandingness*)—the degree to which the child is monitored, disciplined, and regulated, as opposed to being left largely unsupervised.

Baumrind's model combines the dimensions of warmth and control to yield four **parenting styles**, or overall patterns of childrearing, summarized in Table 16.1. As you

TABLE 16.1 Parenting Styles

Parental Warmth		Parental Control	
		High	**Low**
	High	Authoritative	Permissive
	Low	Authoritarian	Uninvolved

CHARACTERISTICS OF DIFFERENT PARENTING STYLES

Authoritative parenting

Is accepting of child; displays frequent expressions of affection

Sets high standards for behavior

Maintains consistent discipline and limit setting

Employs reason rather than force

Listens to child's point of view

Authoritarian parenting

Shows little warmth; may be actively rejecting

Sets high standards for behavior

Expects strict obedience

Uses harsh, punitive discipline

Does not listen to child's point of view

Permissive parenting

Is highly accepting; displays frequent expressions of affection

Is undemanding with regard to child's behavior

Has lax rules, is inconsistent about discipline

Employs reason rather than force

Encourages child to express his or her point of view

Uninvolved parenting

Is emotionally detached; withdrawn

Is undemanding with regard to child's behavior

can see, the **authoritative parenting** style is characterized as high on both warmth and control. Authoritative parents tend to be caring and sensitive toward their children, while at the same time setting clear limits and maintaining a predictable environment. They also often provide rationales for why they expect certain behavior from the child.

In contrast, the **authoritarian parenting** style couples high control with low warmth. Authoritarian parents are very demanding. They exercise strong control over their children's behavior, and they tend to enforce their demands with threats and harsh punishment. They display little warmth or affection toward the child. The **permissive parenting** style represents a third possible combination of the two dimensions. Permissive parents are high in warmth but low in control. These parents are loving and emotionally sensitive but set few limits on behavior and provide little in the way of structure or predictability. Finally, the **uninvolved parenting** style (also termed *disengaged* or *neglectful* parenting style) is the label for parents who are low on both dimensions. These parents set few limits on their children, but they also provide little in the way of attention, interest, or emotional support.

The Baumrind approach has proved successful in identifying individual differences among parents across a range of different populations and child ages. As noted, however, the measurement of parental characteristics is usually just the first step in studies of parenting. A further step is to determine how the variations in parenting affect children's development. Baumrind reported, and later studies have largely confirmed, that the authoritative style is associated with the most positive child outcomes (Baumrind, 1971;

Authoritative parenting
In Baumrind's model, a style of parenting characterized by firm control in the context of a warm and supportive relationship.

Authoritative parenting
In Baumrind's model, a style of parenting characterized by firm control in the context of a cold and demanding relationship.

Permissive parenting
In Baumrind's model, a style of parenting characterized by low levels of control in the context of a warm and supportive relationship.

Uninvolved parenting
In Baumrind's model, a style of parenting characterized by low levels of both control and warmth; also termed disengaged or neglectful parenting.

Questions for Thought and Discussion
Which of Baumrind's parenting styles best describes yours or your parents?

The authoritative style of childrearing is characterized by firm control in the context of a warm and supportive relationship. Why do you think the authoritative childrearing style is effective? (© Tony Freedman/PhotoEdit)

Parke & Buriel, 1998; Steinberg, 2001). Children of authoritative parents tend to be curious, self-confident, and well behaved. They perform well in school, are popular with peers, and are responsive to parental messages. Their self-esteem is high, and their probability of engaging in deviant activities (such as drug use in adolescence) is low.

The other parenting styles are linked to more negative outcomes in different ways. Children of authoritarian parents tend to be anxious, easily upset, and low in self-confidence. They often react with anger and aggression when frustrated, a tendency that negatively affects their relations with peers. They are at risk for both conduct problems and internalizing problems such as depression and anxiety. The children of permissive parents, on the other hand, tend to be impulsive, immature, and disobedient. They are overly dependent on adults, do not persist well in the face of difficulty, and often do not do well in school.

Finally, the uninvolved style seems to be associated with the most negative outcomes, given that uninvolved parents are low in both warmth and control. Children of uninvolved parents often form insecure attachments in infancy. They show low social competence as they develop and are at heightened risk for substance abuse, delinquency, and other mental health problems in adolescence. At the extreme, the uninvolved style becomes *neglect*, a form of child abuse associated with a range of negative outcomes.

These characterizations are "ideal types" that do not apply to every child. That is, not all instances of authoritative rearing lead to positive outcomes, and children whose parents exhibit one of the other styles are certainly not doomed to failure. Many such children turn out fine. Also, the effects of the different styles may vary across different social and cultural groups.

Contextual Influences on Parenting Styles

Much of the research on Baumrind's parenting styles has been done with European American, predominantly middle-class, families. Extension of the model to other populations reveals both similarities and differences. For example, the authoritative style has been shown to be beneficial across a range of different populations. These include subgroups within the United States, such as African American, Latino, and Asian American samples (Brody & Flor, 1998; Glasgow et al., 1997; Steinberg et al., 1991). They also include samples from other countries, such as China and India (Chen, Liu, & Li, 2000; Pinto, Folkers, & Sines, 1991). However, the benefits of authoritative rearing—and the superiority of this style to other methods of childrearing—do not extend to all populations.

Authoritarian parenting is more common in many groups other than the European American samples that have been the focus of research. This is true for African American and Asian American families in the United States, as well as for samples of Chinese parents and children (Greenberger & Chen, 1996; Parke & Buriel, 1998). Two factors appear to account for this finding: (1) cultural beliefs and values, and (2) socioeconomic realities.

In China, for example, family unity, respect for elders, and obedience to authority are the central goals of socialization, and parental concern for children is expressed more through close supervision and frequent teaching than through displays of overt physical affection (Chao, 2001; Chao & Tseng, 2002). Many African American families in the United States share a similar emphasis on communal values, respect for parents and other adults, and close control of children's activities.

Authoritarian parenting styles also vary regionally in the United States and tend to be more common in southern and midwestern states and in rural communities. Many parents believe that spanking, which most psychologists oppose, is the most effective way to teach children right from wrong. Physical punishment is common among many cultural minorities, including many African American and some immigrant groups. Yet, the use of physical punishment among these groups is not associated with the negative effects found in European American communities.

For example, for families living in dangerous neighborhoods and under conditions of poverty, reasoning with the child and encouraging independence can increase risk. Firm

Questions for Thought and Discussion
What are your views concerning the use of physical punishment in the socialization of children?

and immediate control may be a higher priority for parents in such circumstances—and may be adaptive for the overall well-being of the child (Furstenberg, 1993). Thus, in some contexts the authoritarian style might actually be beneficial for children's development. Authoritarian rearing appears to have beneficial—or at least not clearly detrimental—effects for many African American children in the United States (Lamborn, Dornbusch, & Steinberg, 1996), as well as for Chinese families in China and Chinese American families in the United States (Chao & Tseng, 2002). Some studies suggest the same outcomes for the children of families living in poverty (Baldwin, Baldwin, & Cole, 1990).

Thus, the meaning of a particular parental style cannot be defined solely in terms of objective attributes, such as amount of physical discipline or expressions of overt affection. The meaning lies, rather, in how the child interprets the parents' practices, which in turn depends on the overall cultural context in which they occur. One Asian American student makes this point well in talking about the firm and at times even punitive control that characterizes his culture's parenting: "That's how we know our parents love us" (Bronfenbrenner, 1993, p. 39). Another cross-cultural perspective on parenting styles—parental acceptance-rejection theory (PARTheory)—is presented in the Research & Society feature.

Questions for Thought and Discussion

Based on your own observations and experiences, what would you predict as answers to the five core questions that PARTheory addresses?

Parenting Roles: Mothers and Fathers

Much of the research on parenting has focused on mothers. There are theoretical reasons for this emphasis, in that many of the theories that have guided socialization research have stressed the importance of the mother's role. There are also pragmatic reasons—mothers typically have more responsibility for early child care within the family than fathers. In addition, mothers often have more flexible work hours than fathers do, making them more available for participation in research.

Recent years have seen an increased interest in the role of fathers in children's development (Lamb, 1997; Parke, 1996, 2002). How do mothers and fathers typically compare in their caregiving activities? There are wide variations across families, and no single pattern is going to characterize all fathers. In recent years, fathers have assumed an increased role in children's care, in part because of social changes that have allowed more mothers to enter the workforce (Pleck, 1997; Yeung et al., 2001). In general, however, fathers—despite the increased involvement—devote less time to child care than do mothers. Furthermore, the time they spend tends to be distributed differently. Although research suggests that most fathers are as skilled and sensitive in performing basic caregiving

BOX 16.1   Cross-Cultural Perspectives on Parental Acceptance and Rejection

Parental acceptance-rejection theory (PARTheory) is an evidence-based theory of socialization and lifespan development that seeks to predict and explain major causes, consequences, and correlates of parental acceptance and rejection within the United States and worldwide (Rohner, 1986; Rohner & Khaleque, 2005; Rohner, Khaleque, & Cournoyer, 2005; Veneziano & Muller, 2005). In PARTheory, parental acceptance-rejection together are said to form a bipolar dimension of *parental warmth*, with parental acceptance at the positive end of the continuum and parental rejection at the negative end. Thus, the warmth dimension relates to the quality of the affectional bond between parents and their children, and to the physical, verbal, and symbolic behaviors parents use to express these feelings. The positive end, or acceptance, is marked by love, affection, care, comfort, nurturance, support, or concern that parents can feel and express toward their children. The negative end, or rejection, is marked by the absence or significant withdrawal of these feelings and behaviors, and by the presence of a variety of physically and psychologically hurtful behaviors and affects.

Parents anywhere can express rejection in three major ways. They can be cold and unaffectionate, indifferent and neglecting, or hostile and aggressive. In addition, children can experience parental rejection subjectively in the form of undifferentiated rejection. Undifferentiated rejection refers to children's belief that their parents do not really love them or care about them, even though there might not be clear behavioral indicators that the parents are cold and unaffectionate, hostile and aggressive, or indifferent and neglecting toward them. One of the major predictions of PARTheory is that parental rejection has the same negative effects on the psychological adjustment and behavioral functioning of children (and adults) universally.

Much of parental acceptance–rejection is symbolic. Therefore, to understand why rejection has consistent negative effects on children, one must understand its symbolic nature. In the context of ethnic and cross-cultural studies one must strive to understand people's culture-based interpretations of parents' love-related behaviors to fully comprehend the acceptance–rejection process. That is, even though parents everywhere may express acceptance or rejection, the way they do it is highly variable and saturated with cultural and sometimes idiosyncratic meaning. For example, parents anywhere might praise or compliment their children, but the way in which they do it in one sociocultural setting might have no meaning (or a totally different meaning) in another setting. This point is illustrated in the following incident:

> A few years ago I interviewed a high-caste Hindu woman about family matters in India. Another woman seated nearby distracted my attention. The second woman quietly and carefully peeled an orange and then removed the seeds from each segment. Her 9-year-old daughter became increasingly animated as her mother progressed. Later, my Bengali interpreter asked me if I had noticed what the woman was doing. I answered that I had, but that I had not paid much attention to it. "Should I have?" "Well," she answered, "you want to know about parental love and affection in West Bengal, so you should know. . . ." She went on to explain that when a Bengali mother wants to praise her child—to show approval and affection for her child—she might give the child a peeled and seeded orange. Bengali children understand completely that their mothers have done something special for them, even though mothers may not use words of praise—for to do so would be unseemly, much like praising themselves. (Rohner, 1994, p. 113)

Research & Society

PARTheory has the following distinctive characteristics: (1) It is a continually evolving theoretical perspective—developed over a period of about 45 years. (2) It draws extensively from worldwide, cross-cultural evidence as well as from every major ethnic group in the United States. (3) It draws from literary and historical insights as far back as two thousand years. (4) It draws from more than two thousand empirical studies on issues of parental acceptance–rejection published since the turn of the twentieth century. (5) It emphasizes a universal or global perspective on parenting. (6) And it emphasizes a multimethod approach to the study of parental acceptance–rejection.

The theory attempts to answer the following five classes of questions concerning parental acceptance and rejection:

1. What happens to children who perceive themselves to be loved (accepted) or unloved (rejected) by their parents?

2. To what extent do the effects of childhood rejection extend into adulthood?

activities (e.g., feeding, diapering, putting to bed) (Parke, 2002), most fathers do not perform such activities very often. Instead, fathers' interactions with their children tend to center around physical stimulation and play, especially with boys. This emphasis emerges early in infancy and continues through childhood (Russell & Russell, 1987).

This pattern is not universal, however. Father as play partner is a common role across many cultures, but there are exceptions. In Sweden, for example, there are no

3. Why do some children and adults cope more effectively than others with the experiences of childhood rejection?

4. Why are some parents warm, loving, and accepting, and others cold, aggressive, neglecting, and rejecting?

5. How is the total fabric of a society, as well as the behavior and beliefs of people within the society, affected by the fact that most parents in that society tend to either accept or reject their children?

PARTheory is divided into three distinguishable subtheories:

1. *Personality Subtheory* attempts to predict and explain major personality or psychological consequences of perceived parental acceptance and rejection in childhood and adulthood. The subtheory assumes that the emotional need for positive response from parents and other attachment figures is a powerful motivator for children. When this need is not adequately met by parents and other attachment figures, children are predisposed emotionally and behaviorally to respond in specific ways. In particular, the subtheory postulates that rejected children tend to feel anxious and insecure. Moreover, they are likely to be hostile, aggressive, passive aggressive, or to have problems with the management of hostility and aggression; to be dependent or defensively independent, depending on the form, frequency, and intensity of rejection; to have impaired self-esteem; to have impaired self-adequacy; to be emotionally unresponsive; to be emotionally unstable and to have a negative worldview. More than 50 studies within the United States and cross-culturally have tested these assumptions (Khaleque & Rohner, 2002). All of them came to the same conclusion—the experience of parental acceptance or rejection appears to be universally associated with the form of psychological maladjustment, regardless of variations in culture, ethnicity, gender, and geographical boundaries.

2. *Coping Subtheory* deals with the fact that some children cope emotionally with the experiences of rejection more effectively than other children. As noted earlier, studies in the United States and across the world confirm the assumption that the vast majority of children—regardless of geographic location, race, and ethnicity, and other defining conditions—tend to be negatively affected by parental rejection (Rohner, 2005). A small fraction of rejected children, however, are "affective copers." They are children who experience significant parental rejection but who nonetheless continue to be reasonably well adjusted psychologically. It is not that these children are untouched by the pain of rejection, because they *are* touched. However, their overall psychological adjustment more closely resembles the type of adjustment of accepted children than that of the vast majority of rejected children. Given this fact, what gives some children the resilience to withstand the pain of rejection more effectively than most children? At this time, PARTheorists do not have clear and comprehensive answers to this question.

3. *Sociocultural Systems Subtheory* attempts to predict and explain major causes and sociocultural correlates of parental acceptance and rejection worldwide. First, this subtheory attempts to predict and explain why some parents are warm and loving, whereas others are cold, neglecting/rejecting, or hostile/aggressive. Second, the subtheory attempts to predict and explain how the total fabric of a society—as well as the behavior and beliefs of individuals within that society—is affected by the fact that most parents in that society tend to either accept or reject their children. The subtheory predicts, for example, that children are more likely to develop beliefs about the supernatural world (God and spiritual beings) as malevolent (i.e., hostile, treacherous, destructive, or negative in some other way) in societies where they tend to be rejected. On the other hand, the supernatural world is expected to be perceived as benevolent (i.e., warm, generous, protective, or positive in some other way) in societies where most children are raised with love and acceptance. Cross-cultural evidence confirms these predictions (Rohner, 1975, 1986). Sociocultural systems subtheory also predicts—and cross-cultural evidence confirms—that parental acceptance and rejection tend to be associated worldwide with many other sociocultural correlates, such as household structure, artistic preferences, and occupational choices of individuals (Rohner, 1986, 2005; Rohner, Khaleque, & Cournoyer, 2005).

mother-father differences in the tendency to engage children in play (Lamb et al., 1982), and the same is true for Israeli kibbutz families (Sagi et al., 1985). In both instances, the society's egalitarian political views may account for the similarity in parental roles (though with definite limitations—mothers still perform most of the basic caregiving activities).

What fathers do with their children is one of the questions of interest in research on the father's role. The other question is what effects these paternal behaviors have. What do we know about fathers' contribution to children's development? In Chapter 13 you read that fathers, on average, seem to hold stronger views about gender-appropriate behavior than mothers and are more likely to treat boys and girls in ways that might promote sex

Links to Related Material
In Chapters 11 and 13, you read about young children's attachment to their fathers and fathers' attitudes about gender. Here, you learn more about the role of fathers in children's lives.

This photo suggests that fathers can provide the same quality of nurturance and limit setting that mothers do. Why do you think mothers' and fathers' parenting styles are similar? What social and cultural factors might encourage or limit the involvement of fathers in their children's lives? (Comstock Images/Age Fotostock America, Inc.)

Questions for Thought and Discussion

Do you think that children raised by their fathers develop differently from those raised by their mothers?

Links to Related Material

In Chapter 11, you read about infant temperament. Here, you learn more about how different dimensions of child temperament affect the parenting that they receive.

differences in development. In Chapter 11 you read that fathers as well as mothers can serve as attachment objects for infants. Almost all babies with a father in the home become attached to their fathers, and the probability of a secure attachment is as great with the father as with the mother (Van IJzendoorn & De Wolff, 1997). Furthermore, secure attachment to the father is equally predictive of later positive outcomes.

How do children's relationships with the father compare generally to their relationships with the mother? Evidence comes from 116 studies that examine parent-child relationships as a function of both sex of parent and sex of child (Russell & Saebel, 1997). In total, the studies span a range of ages and a variety of measures of parent-child relations. Differences occur on some measures for some samples; that is, some children have closer or more satisfactory or more intense relations with one parent than with the other (Collins & Russell, 1991; Russell, Mize, & Bissaker, 2002). In the majority of cases, however, relations with the two parents—for both sons and daughters—are more alike than different.

Research on mother-father similarity in parenting style shows similar effects on children. In general, the attributes that characterize successful parenting for fathers turn out to be the same as those that are important for mothers—namely, a warm relationship with the child, firm but not punitive control, and frequent use of verbal reasoning. Thus, just as for mothers, the authoritative style of parenting appears most adaptive for fathers' socialization of their children (Marsiglio et al., 2000).

The Child's Contribution

Parenting style may lead to particular outcomes in children, but the reverse is also possible: Characteristics of the child can influence parenting style. Following a classic paper by Richard Bell (1968), researchers have increasingly studied how characteristics of the child can influence parents' behavior. As you saw in Chapter 11, infants enter the world with individual temperaments, including variations in irritability, emotionality, and sociability that affect the ways parents interact with them (Putnam, Sanson, & Rothbart, 2002). Infants with difficult temperaments, for example, receive more total caregiving time in the early months of life than do infants in general, presumably because their characteristics force attention in a way that those of easier-to-handle babies do not (Crockenberg, 1986). By the second half of the first year, however, mothers of difficult infants tend to soothe their infants less and become less involved, presumably because they have too often been frustrated and unrewarded in their efforts (van den Boom & Hoeksma, 1994). Other aspects of temperament that affect parent behavior are activity level and inhibition or timidity.

Some parents adapt more successfully than others to the child's characteristics, described in Chapter 11 as the idea of goodness of fit. Development proceeds most successfully when parents are able to match their caregiving practices to the nature and needs of the child. Early difficult temperament often leads to continued difficult temperament and various behavioral problems in later childhood (Gallagher, 2002). However, parental response to the difficult temperament is a determining factor in later outcomes. Some parents are successful at gradually moderating their child's problematic attributes, whereas others respond to the child in ways that perpetuate or even aggravate the difficulties. Thus the developmental process is transactional. Characteristics of the child elicit particular behaviors from the parent. Parental behaviors in turn alter characteristics of the child. The child then brings different characteristics to future socialization encounters with the parent, and so on throughout development.

Effects of children's characteristics on parental behavior thus are not limited to the early years or to inborn temperamental qualities. Child effects are a pervasive finding across a range of ages and socialization contexts. For example, children who are compliant are likely to receive milder and more verbal forms of discipline than children whose compliance is more forced or situational (Kochanska, 1997). Children who resist maternal requests elicit stronger demands and more restrictions from the mother than children who are easier to control (Kuczynski & Kochanska, 1995). Adolescents who engage in antisocial behavior receive harsher forms of parental discipline than adolescents who are better behaved (Neiderheiser et al., 1999).

Nevertheless, parent and child do not play equal roles or have equal impact in most socialization exchanges (Maccoby, 2002), and parent-child correlations are also the result of many factors other than adaptation to children's temperament and behavior.

Learning Objective 16.1: *Analyze the influence of parenting practices and children's contributions to childhood socialization.*

1. What major parenting styles affect child development?
2. How do cultural and socioeconomic factors influence parenting styles?
3. To what extent do mothers and fathers play different roles in parenting?
4. What is the child's contribution to the socialization process?

✔ *Test Your Mastery...*

The Family as a Social System

Determining what mothers or fathers do is important, but a sole focus on one or even both parents provides an incomplete picture of life in the family, for several reasons. Many families contain more members than one child and his or her parents. Families include siblings and sometimes grandparents and other family members as well. Even when not living in the same household, most children have at least semiregular contact with extended family members. Researchers often study families, both within and outside the household unit, from a **family systems** perspective. In this perspective, the family is viewed as a complex set of interacting relationships, all of which are influenced by larger social and cultural factors, as well as by the individual characteristics and behaviors of each family member.

For example, when Luis's company opened a new site in Florida, he began to travel extensively for work. Rosa found the long weeks at home alone with 1-year-old Natalie wearing. She began to feel fatigued and irritable. When Luis was home on weekends, he also was tired, preoccupied with home maintenance needs, and not as helpful with the baby as he had been in the past. They began having minor arguments, and Rosa felt that she had less energy for playtime with Natalie. Rosa's mother decided to come from Puerto Rico and stay for a while to help out while Luis was away. Rosa's sister and brother-in-law also stopped by more often to help and to visit. This social support eased some of the stress that Rosa was feeling until Luis eventually was able to resume his normal family life at home.

This story illustrates several factors that often influence family life. First, parents interact not only with their child but with one another as well. The quality of the marital relationship can affect parental mood and responsiveness toward the infant (Belsky, 1981). From this perspective, the family is a system, and interactions between any two members can indirectly affect relationships with other members.

Second, parents' employment status and satisfaction with their jobs can affect their mood and responsiveness. Mothers who feel forced to work but wish they could stay at home, or mothers who would prefer to work but feel obliged to stay at home often are more irritable or less responsive to their infants than mothers whose employment status is congruent with their preferred lifestyle (Greenberger & Goldberg, 1989). Similarly, when fathers lose their jobs and find themselves at home full-time when they would prefer not to be, marital conflicts can arise and tempers can grow short toward the children (Conger, Patterson, & Ge, 1995). In addition to emotional satisfaction, the degree of financial stability provided by a parent's job also has a tremendous influence on the child's life. Greater financial resources can ensure better neighborhoods, better schools, more spacious homes and yards, and greater access to material comforts and a variety of extracurricular activities and educational opportunities.

Third, children's lives are influenced not only by the parents' marital satisfaction and job status, but also by the presence or absence of social support. Parents who have access to both friends and extended family who can provide them with emotional and physical

Learning objective 16.2
Identify the ways that families function as a social system.

Family systems
A theoretical perspective that views the family as a complex set of interacting relationships, all of which are influenced by larger social and cultural factors, as well as by the individual characteristics and behaviors of each family member.

support are able to be warmer and more responsive to their children (Crockenberg, 1981; Parke & Buriel, 1998). Social support also can provide parents with a buffer during times of personal and family stress.

Siblings

Links to Related Material
In Chapter 15, you read about sibling relations in relation to peer relationships. Here, you learn more about the possible effects of sibling relationships on other aspects of development.

In 2003, 66 percent of all U.S. families with children had more than one child (Fields, 2003). It has been estimated that in the United States and Europe approximately 80 percent of children have siblings or half-siblings over the course of their lifetime. Most spend more time with their siblings than with their parents, and for many, relationships with siblings will be the longest lasting relationships they ever have (Dunn, 2002). Chapter 15 explored sibling relations in relation to peer relationships. What do we know about sibling relations and their possible effects on other aspects of development?

One thing we know is that sibling relations come in many forms. In terms of birth order, any child is either the older or the younger member of a sibling dyad. Siblings can be the same gender or different genders. They can be close in age or widely separated. And they can number from two to a dozen or more. The modal number of children for U.S. families is two, and only 6 percent of families have four or more children (Fields & Casper, 2001). Growing up with lots of siblings is a less common experience than was once the case. There also are variations in the *quality* of the sibling relationship—variations that are largely independent of characteristics such as age spacing or gender composition. Some siblings have closer and more positive relations than others, and for many this closeness remains true throughout development. Judy Dunn, a leading researcher of sibling relations, summarizes the differences in quality as follows:

> Some siblings show affection, interest, cooperation, and support in the great majority of their interactions. When interviewed they describe their affection and positive feelings vividly. Other siblings show hostility, irritation, and aggressive behavior, and describe their dislike very clearly. Other children are ambivalent about their relations with their siblings, and show both hostility and positive interest in one another. (Dunn, 2002, p. 224)

What causes such striking variations? As is true for many aspects of development, temperament plays a role. Siblings typically get along best when they have similar temperaments—for example, both active and outgoing (Brody, 1996). Because temperament is only moderately heritable, many siblings will not have similar temperaments. Furthermore, a difficult temperament for either member of a sibling pair is predictive of eventual difficulties in their relationship (Brody, Stoneman, & McCoy, 1994).

Parents can also be important in sibling relations. The same qualities that make up successful parenting in general—warmth, reasoning, firm but nonpunitive control—also enhance the probability of positive relations among siblings (Brody, 1998; Furman & Lanthier, 2002). The parents' own relationship also contributes. Positive relations among siblings are most likely when the parents' relationship is positive (MacKinnon, 1989).

One strong predictor of difficulty in the sibling relationship is differential treatment by parents—that is, one sibling receiving more attention and affection and less discipline than the other sibling (Dunn, 2002; Furman & Lanthier, 2002). The child's *interpretation* of the treatment is also important (Kowal & Kramer, 1997; Kowal et al., 2002). When children perceive that they are being treated unequally and regard the differential treatment as unfair, difficulties in the sibling relationship are most likely.

Both conflict and cooperation are frequent components of sibling interactions. What do you remember about the sibling interactions in your home while you were growing up? (*Top,* © Carolyn A. McKeone/Photo Researchers; *bottom,* ©Jeff Greenberg/Photo Researchers)

Sibling Relationships over Time   For the firstborn child in a family, sibling relations begin with the birth of a second child. It is not a happy time for most firstborns. The arrival of a second child is associated with a decline in both the amount and the positiveness of mother-child interaction for the firstborn (Baydar, Greek, & Brooks-Gunn, 1997). It is also associated with an increase in behavior problems for the older child. The arrival of a sibling often inaugurates what has long been regarded as a worrisome aspect of sibling relations: **sibling rivalry**, or negative, competitive feelings between two or more siblings.

Initially, a new sibling has little to offer to an older child in the family. By about a year of age, however, the younger sibling begins to present possibilities as a play partner. By the time a baby brother or sister reaches age 2 or 3, most siblings are spending much time together. These interactions tend to be marked by strong expressions of emotion on both sides of the sibling pair, with the balance of positive and negative emotions varying markedly across dyads. In one case, a sibling pair produced 56 conflicts in an hour (Dunn, 1993)!

As they develop, interactions between siblings change in various ways (Brody, 1996). Interactions become less physical and more verbal and become more wide-ranging in topics and concerns. In addition to serving as play partners, siblings begin to perform various other roles for each other. They can be sources of support in times of stress, as well as sources of advice or information when some problem arises. They provide help with schoolwork, for example, and consult each other on family issues and other personal matters (Tucker, McHale, & Crouter, 2001). Typically, information and support flow from older to younger sibling, but this is not always the case, especially as children grow older.

As children develop, changes take place in the balance or symmetry of their interactions and relationship. Initially, older siblings take the lead in most dealings with their younger siblings, initiating both positive and negative actions more often and generally directing the course of the interaction. Younger siblings, in turn, are more likely to give in to and imitate their older partner (Teti, 1992). Such asymmetry lessens with age, and by adolescence the relations between siblings typically are more egalitarian. The younger sibling is sometimes the dominant member and can be the one who provides nurturance or help (Buhrmester & Furman, 1990).

Another change that is evident by adolescence is a decline in the relative importance of siblings as sources of intimacy or help. As you read in Chapter 15, by adolescence friends come to play these roles more often. Children thus have less motivation to turn to their siblings when they are in need of emotional or instrumental support (Buhrmester & Furman, 1990).

Effects of Siblings   Siblings spend thousands of hours together as they grow up, they imitate each other frequently from early in life (Abramovitch, Corter, & Pepler, 1980), and they eventually exchange information and opinions (often conflicting ones!) on dozens of different issues. Few aspects of development are not potentially affected by growing up with siblings.

Growing up with siblings—perhaps especially older siblings—has cognitive benefits, as noted in Chapter 8. Benefits include accelerated development of theory-of-mind skills (Ruffman et al., 1998). Sibling interactions are a common context for frequent teasing, tricks, and sharing of emotions. It is no surprise, therefore, that such interactions can help children learn about other minds and how they can differ from their own.

Siblings can also be effective teachers of one another. Research suggests that siblings are more likely to teach and more skillful in teaching a younger child than are peers, even older ones (Azmitia & Hesser, 1993). Many parents capitalize on this fact by entrusting an older child to convey a household chore or a social expectation to a younger brother or sister, such as how to dress, how to behave at church, or what to say when Grandma gives you a gift.

Siblings also affect aspects of each other's social development, especially in gender role development. Siblings, especially older ones, are both models of gender role behavior and potential agents of reinforcement or punishment for behaviors they see in their siblings. As you saw in Chapter 13, same-sex older siblings promote gender-typical behavior, and opposite-sex siblings make counter-stereotypical behavior more likely (McHale et al., 2001; Rust et al., 2000). The social skills and expectations that children first acquire in interactions with siblings affect—for better or for worse—how they behave and how successful they are when they enter the larger world of peers.

Cultural differences may be significant in sibling socialization. In Western societies, older siblings occasionally take care of younger ones, but the caregiving role is not a generally expected, culturally mandated part of being an older sibling. However, older siblings serve as

Sibling rivalry
Feelings of competition, resentment, and jealousy that can arise between siblings.

Questions for Thought
 and Discussion
Was sibling rivalry a factor in your family system? What impact do you think birth order had on your development?

Links to Related Material
In Chapter 8, you read about the development of theory of mind. Here, you learn more about how sibling interactions can improve a child's theory-of-mind skills.

principal caregivers for younger children in a large number of the world's cultures (Zukow-Goldring, 2002). Millions of children around the world receive much of their socialization in their early years not from adults but from older siblings. Older siblings are socialized by the adults of the community to assume the role of caregiver—a prime example of the guided participation model of cultural transmission stressed in the sociocultural approach to development.

Grandparents

In 2002, 5.6 million or 8 percent of all U.S. children were living in a home with one or more grandparents—in some instances with one or more parents as well. In almost half the cases, the grandparent was the child's primary caretaker (Fields, 2003). Millions of other children visit and receive visits from grandparents, and surveys indicate that such contacts are moderately frequent in a majority of cases (Smith & Drew, 2002). Surveys also suggest that grandparents value their role. Being a grandparent is ranked as the third most important role in life, following the roles of spouse and parent (Kivett, 1985).

Grandparents can be a source of emotional or financial support for the parents. Grandparents can be mentors, playmates, babysitters, or substitute parents for grandchildren. In one survey, most grandchildren reported having engaged in the following activities (among others) with their grandparents: having treats, playing games, going on trips, taking part in family events, joining in religious activities, talking about school, and learning about family history (Eisenberg, 1988).

In many cultural groups, the extended family represents a common, desirable, and beneficial living arrangement. What positive effects do you think an extended family living arrangement might provide for child development? (© Michael Newman/PhotoEdit)

The extent to which grandparents are involved in their grandchildren's lives depends partly on family structure. In families with two parents, grandparents tend to stay more in the background and have less direct involvement with the grandchildren. When one parent is absent, however, the role of grandparents often increases, and children similarly report an increased closeness to them. Among the 4 percent of U.S. children with no parents, about half live with their grandparents, and in these cases grandparents play a maximal role in the child's life (America's Children: Key National Indicators of Well Being, 2005, http://www.childstats.gov).

Another factor is gender. On average, grandmothers are more involved in and derive more satisfaction from the grandparent role than grandfathers (Creasey & Koblewski, 1991; Somary & Stricker, 1998). Research on grandparenting as a function of gender of child or age of child has yet to yield consistent results (Smith & Drew, 2002). However, such research does reveal changes with age in how children perceive their grandparents, from a view of the grandparent as a dispenser of gifts or treats in early childhood to an emphasis on companionship and support by late childhood and adolescence.

The presence of a grandmother can be very important in the case of teenage motherhood. Co-residence of daughter and mother becomes more likely when a new baby arrives, especially among African Americans, and a grandmother in the home can be a source of both expertise and welcome hands-on help (Stevens, 1984). Having a grandmother present is not always a benefit, however. In some cases the presence of her own mother can interfere with the new mother's comfort level and effectiveness in her parenting role, with detrimental effects on both her parenting skills and the child's development (Moore & Brooks-Gunn, 2002).

Families in Cultural Perspective

The presence of grandparents in the home is much more typical in some cultures than in European American families. In China, for example, three-generation households are common (Shu, 1999), and the same is true for African American families in the United States. In many cultures—including African Americans—the modal family pattern is not the nuclear family but the **extended family.** An extended family unit consists not only of children and parents but also other adult relatives. For African Americans, the extended

Extended family
A family unit that consists not only of parents and children but also of at least one and sometimes several other adult relatives.

Social networks provide young parents with emotional, instrumental, informational, companionship, and material support. In what ways might this new mothers' support group provide members with each kind of support? Why are parents' social networks important to a child's development? (Eric Risberg/ © AP/Wide World Photos)

family is a legacy of family patterns in parts of Africa where newly married couples join one of the parents' households rather than starting a household of their own.

As with any long-established cultural tradition, the extended family is associated with beneficial effects in cultures in which it is the norm. This is true for African Americans in the United States. The extended family structure provides social and financial support to members of the younger generation, facilitates the transmission of cultural history and values, and reduces the probability of negative developmental outcomes (Taylor, Casten, & Flickinger, 1993; Wilson, 1995). In Sudan the nuclear family is a relatively recent development, and children who live in nuclear families have more problems in development than those growing up in the more traditional extended family (El Hassan Al Awad & Sonuga-Barke, 1992). Similar findings have been reported for children in Korea (Hwang & St. James-Roberts, 1998).

Social Support and the Family System

Families do not exist in a vacuum. Typically, they have grandparents, aunts and uncles, friends, neighbors, childcare providers, coworkers, and other adults who offer emotional support, information, and concrete help with childrearing tasks. The saying "It takes a whole village to rear a child," derives from a Swahili proverb, "One hand cannot bring up (or nurse) a child," meaning that child rearing is a community effort (Scheven, 1981). A person's **social network** is comprised of individuals who "make a difference" in that person's life (Cochran & Niego, 2002). Researchers who study the impact of social networks have differentiated among different kinds of social support that individuals within a social network may offer a person.

Social network
The network of individuals and other social contacts that a person relies on for social support.

- *Emotional support* refers to expressions of empathy and encouragement that inspire confidence and help a person through a time of discouragement or worry.
- *Instrumental support* consists of concrete help, typically with household chores or child care. When Luis was away on business, Rosa was grateful to have her sister come by and help with Natalie while she ran errands and did chores.
- *Informational support* refers to advice or information. After Michelle brought her preterm twin boys home from the hospital, she sought out other mothers of twins for tips on coping with two babies at once. She also talked to child professionals knowledgeable about preterm birth, so that she would know what to look for in her own sons' development.
- *Companion support* consists of opportunities to engage in enjoyable activities with other adults, such as going to the movies or a ballgame.

Finally, *material support* refers to people who can provide financial assistance or other material support during difficult times. For example, when Jennifer, a single mother, lost her job, she and her daughter lived with relatives for a period of time. The provision of a home to live in is an example of material support. Also, when Jennifer was pregnant with Kaylie, she had received a diaper-changing table, crib, infant carrier, and clothes from other mothers with children who had outgrown them—another example of material support. Studies of parents' social networks show that emotional support, childrearing advice, and assistance with child care are particularly helpful to young parents, especially when they are single, divorced, or separated (Cochran & Niego, 2002; Weinraub et al., 2002). In particular, women who report having access to childcare support from social network members have more positive interactions with their children, are emotionally warmer with them, and more sensitive to their needs.

Researchers have identified four ways that social support is beneficial to families (Crockenberg, 1988). First, support can reduce the amount of stress in a parent's life. Babysitting, childrearing advice, and material support provide relief from daily burdens that might otherwise accumulate to overwhelming proportions. A parent overwhelmed with stress is less likely to be an effective parent.

Another way that social support helps is to buffer the parent from the adverse affects of stressful events. A difficult, frustrating day can be put into perspective through the companionship and emotional support offered by a friend or family member. Again, the reduction of stress in a parent's life improves the ability to parent competently.

Social support also aids in the construction of effective coping strategies. For example, after moving to the United Sates from India, Padma was frustrated by the increased disrespectfulness of her 7-year-old daughter, Parminder. As she got to know her new co-workers better, she became aware that their children behaved in ways similar to what she observed in Parminder. Padma spent time discussing with them the parenting strategies they used to elicit greater cooperation and respect from their children. She tried these strategies herself and found that they helped to reduce her sense of frustration and to improve Parminder's behavior. Finally, parents who themselves experience emotional support and nurturance from others are more likely to feel cared about, which often results in an increased capacity to nurture others, including one's children. Researchers have found, however, that a parent's access to rich and rewarding social networks can be limited by socioeconomic factors such as family income, parents' own educational experiences, and occupational level.

Parents' access to positive social networks has been linked to many positive developmental outcomes in children, including happiness with the family, stronger peer-related social skills, and the development of positive peer friendships (Cochran & Niego, 2002). In addition, children benefit both emotionally and cognitively through regular contact with responsive and dependable adult network members. Adult network members may provide children with outings, for example, such as trips to the park or zoo, and opportunities to engage in everyday activities such as gardening or cooking—all in the context of a warm and caring relationship.

Test Your Mastery...

Learning Objective 16.2: *Identify the ways that families function as a social system.*

1. How do sibling relationships influence child development?
2. How do grandparents influence child development?
3. How does culture affect family relationships and their relative importance for child development?
4. What are the kinds and functions of social support?
5. In what ways does social support affect a family's functioning?

Learning Objective 16.3
Describe and evaluate the influence of different social contexts on families and children.

Families in Social Context

Children's lives are embedded in families, schools, neighborhoods, and communities. Thus, they are influenced by specific aspects of the larger social, historical, economic, technological, and cultural environment. Consider, for example, the impacts of family multimedia use on children's development, also discussed in Chapters 7, 10, and 14.

Different types of media are omnipresent in American family life today (Dorr, Rabin, & Irlen, 2002; Roberts, Foehr, Rideout, & Brodie, 1999). In 1999, among U.S. households, virtually all had a television (99 percent), a VCR (97 percent), a radio (97 percent), and a CD player (90 percent). Over two-thirds of families had cable or satellite service (74 percent), a video game player (70 percent), or a computer (69 percent), and nearly half of families had premium cable (44 percent) or access to the Internet (45 percent).

Families and the Media

As the presence of different types of media in the home has risen, so have concerns regarding their effects on children's development. A national survey (Roberts et al., 1999) found that on average, children age 2 to 18 years spent about 5.5 hours per day in personal, non-school uses of media and technology at home, including television, VCR and DVD players, video games, computer games or other online usage, and musical CDs. Differences were found according to age (children age 14 to 18 were more likely than younger children to use media alone or in their bedrooms); gender (boys were more likely to use video game players); social class (higher-income homes were more likely to have Internet access, as well as more books and other print media, whereas lower-income homes were more likely to have televisions and video game players in children's bedrooms); and ethnicity (European American children averaged 6 hours per day total media exposure, whereas Latino children averaged about 7 hours, and African American children almost 8 hours).

The ecology of home media use among America's children has raised concerns for many parents, educators, and child development professionals. These concerns have focused on too little time spent reading; too much time spent watching TV, videos, and DVDs; objectionable content of both visual and audio media; and time spent with all media in the absence of parental supervision and interaction (Dorr et al., 2002).

What can families do to alleviate the negative impact of multimedia in their children's lives? Adults can actively mediate children's viewing by providing explanation, evaluation, and feedback. In those conditions, children's understanding of program content, learning from educational programs, and prosocial attitudes and behaviors increase. In addition, the more parents talk to their children about the content of what they are viewing, the

Links to Related Material
In Chapters 7, 10, and 14, you read about the influence of television viewing on children's cognitive and linguistic development, as well as on the development of aggressive behavior. Here, you learn more about the presence of media in American homes today and what parents can do to monitor its impact.

Parental restriction of media viewing, as well as supervision and interaction regarding programming content, helps children make good choices and better understand what they view on TV. (Index Stock/Alamy)

more children's opinions of the programming change to match those of their parents (Dorr et al., 2002). Following are other ways that parents can reduce the negative impact of multimedia use on children's lives.

- Restrict usage according to time of day, number of hours per day, and specific content.
- Model balanced interactions with media by reducing overall hours of parents' viewing and computer use and increasing the time spent reading.
- Organize the household to deemphasize viewing practices (e.g., place the television in a back room; remove televisions and video game players from bedrooms) and emphasize reading (e.g., place books and other printed media in the family room and children's bedrooms).
- Provide parental guidance, communication, and models for positive family interaction, such that children will be less likely to be swayed by whatever they observe in the media.

Families, Schools, and Communities

Most children grow up in communities where their lives are affected not only by parents and teachers, but also by many adults in the larger community—extended family, clergy, teachers, coaches, mentors, and so on. The partnerships and connections that exist among these people influence a child's success in school as well as the quality of children's and families' lives outside of school (Epstein & Sanders, 2002).

Researchers who examine such partnerships have developed models for understanding relations among families, schools, and the larger community. Through much of the 20th century, theories emphasized the separateness of teachers' and parents' roles in schooling. Parents were to provide basic life skills and social competencies in the early years, then hand their well-socialized children to the schools for academic training. Today, society's expectations have changed, and more people recognize a need for partnerships between families and schools, with the family preparing and supporting the child academically outside of school even as schools serve a significant socializing influence in children's lives. These changed expectations are consistent with a theoretical model that views the multiple developmental contexts of childhood as interdependent, embedded, or overlapping (Bronfenbrenner, 1986; Epstein & Sanders, 2002).

Research indicates that when parents are involved in their children's formal education and school life, academic performance improves and the children have more positive school attitudes and higher career aspirations. This is true regardless of the parents' educational background or socioeconomic status (Gutman & McLoyd, 2000; Sanders & Herting, 2000). In addition, parent-child discussions about schoolwork, school programs, and plans for the future have a strong effect on student achievement. Conversely, when schools invite parental involvement in clear ways, more parents become involved. How can families, schools, and communities act in partnership to further children's academic success and overall well-being? Several types of partnership have been identified (Epstein & Sanders, 2002):

- Parents can support children's education through early literacy learning, involvement and support with homework, and discussion of future college and career plans.
- Schools can invite and encourage parents' active participation by welcoming, informing, and guiding them in specific school activities.
- Parents, schools, and communities can work together to provide information about children's health, safety, supervision, nutrition, discipline, and home conditions that support learning and development. In turn, parents can provide schools with important information regarding their goals, family life, and the children's needs and abilities.
- Families and schools can work together to improve communication to better accomplish these goals.

- Parents can support the school through volunteer activities and can support their children's learning through home activities that are coordinated with the school curriculum. For example, schools can inform parents that their children will be learning about whales and other sea mammals during a specific two-week period at school. Schools and parents can then work together to provide complementary home learning activities—for example, organizing a trip to a local aquarium or identifying books, movies, and documentaries that are available at the library.

- Schools can strengthen parents' participation in school decisions by encouraging strong parent associations, as well as parent and community representation on school governing boards and committees.

- Schools and parent groups can make connections with local agencies, businesses, churches, cultural associations, and other community groups. Through these connections, families can be kept informed of health services, cultural events, after-school programs and activities, and community service opportunities.

Socioeconomic Influences

As you have read in previous chapters, *socioeconomic status (SES)* is understood to be a combination of parental education, occupation, and income. Usually, these influences are interrelated, with lower levels of education often constraining both income and occupational mobility, and higher levels of education typically correlating with higher income and occupational status.

Researchers have found that SES strongly influences parenting. Several studies have found that higher-SES mothers address more speech to their children and use more complex vocabulary and syntax when speaking to their children. In addition to differences in verbal interaction, lower-SES mothers tend to be more controlling and restrictive of their children's behavior and are more likely to have an authoritarian parenting style (Hoff, Laursen, & Tardif, 2002). Across many different cultural groups, lower-SES parents have been found to place greater emphasis on obedience and conformity to authority, whereas higher-SES parents tend to place greater emphasis on personal initiative and autonomy (Harwood et al., 1996; Kohn, 1977).

What causes these differences? When the individual components of SES (education, occupation, and income) are examined separately, researchers have found that level of education is associated most reliably with differences in parenting practices and styles. However, low income and poverty present unique challenges to parenting, and so provide a defining context for children's development, particularly in relation to the physical settings of childhood.

In the United States, property taxes that families pay typically are returned to the neighborhood in the form of material resources—money for school personnel, equipment, and activities; money for parks and recreation facilities; money for the policing necessary to keep a neighborhood safe from violence and toxins. Because poorer families living in

Children living in poor neighborhoods are more likely to attend inadequately financed schools and to live in areas with inadequately maintained or nonexistent parks and recreation facilities, and higher exposure to neighborhood violence and environmental toxins. In what other ways is socioeconomic status likely to affect children's lives? (David Grossman/The Image Works)

inexpensive homes pay less money in local taxes, the neighborhoods that they live in typically receive less in material goods from the local government. Neighborhoods thus show distinctive characteristics according to the average socioeconomic status of the families that live there. Moreover, children living in high-poverty neighborhoods are more likely to grow up in physical settings that include inadequately financed schools, inadequately maintained or nonexistent parks and recreation facilities, and higher exposure to neighborhood violence and environmental toxins. Below a certain threshold, then, low income has a profound influence on many children's lives. Unfortunately, minority children are disproportionately likely to be living in high-poverty neighborhoods.

Families Living in the Context of Poverty

In the United States, poverty is defined by comparing a household's total income with a predefined threshold level of income that varies with family size and inflation. In 2005, the poverty threshold levels for two-, three-, and four-person families, respectively, were $12,830, $16,090, and $19,350 (Federal Register, 2005). Typically, official U.S. poverty thresholds are lower than the amounts of money Americans say are necessary to "get along in their community," "live decently," or avoid hardship (Magnuson & Duncan, 2002). In 2003, 17 percent of U.S. children lived in families with incomes below the poverty threshold. As can be seen in Table 16.2, some groups of children are more likely to live in poverty than other groups.

Compared to nonpoor children, poor children are at greater risk of academic failure, poor physical health, and behavior problems. Researchers have found that providing learning experiences in early childhood has a strong effect on children's later school achievement and cognitive functioning. Early learning experiences include providing children with learning-oriented toys or a library card and educational experiences such as music classes or trips to museums and zoos, as well as reading to them. Unfortunately, children from poor families are less likely to receive these early learning experiences (Bradley & Caldwell, 1984; Magnuson & Duncan, 2003). Lack of available money plays a large role in this: poor parents have less money to spend on resources such as books, educational toys, dance classes, or family museum memberships. In addition, lack of reliable transportation may inhibit certain types of outings, such as trips to the library. Financial resources thus play a major role in parents' abilities to provide their children with an optimal home learning environment.

TABLE 16.2 Percentage of Children Under Age 18 Living Below the Poverty Threshold	
All Children	**18%**
Children Aged 0–5	20%
Children Aged 6–17	16%
Children in Female-Headed Households	42%
Children in Married-Couple Households	9%
African American Children	**34%**
Female-Headed Households	50%
Married-Couple Households	11%
Hispanic Children	**30%**
Female-Headed Households	51%
Married-Couple Households	21%
Asian American Children	**12%**
Female-Headed Households	37%
Married-Couple Households	9%
European American Children	**14%**
Female-Headed Households	37%
Married-Couple Households	8%

SOURCES: *America's Children: Key National Indicators of Well-Being, 2005*; U.S. Census Bureau, 2004; http://www.childtrendsdatabank.org/indicators/4poverty.cfm.

The stress associated with struggling to make ends meet in poor families affects not only the home learning environment. Parental psychological distress, combined with lessened access to certain types of social support, can also create a home environment characterized by more frequent negative parent-child interactions and harsher discipline (Magnuson & Duncan, 2003). In addition, poor families are more likely to live in neighborhoods characterized by the following conditions.

- Environmental toxins in soil and paint
- Community violence
- Ineffective schools
- Concentrated poverty, in which 40 percent or more of families in the neighborhood live below the official poverty threshold
- Less effective neighborhood and institutional control of problem behaviors, including delinquency, gang-related violence, and drug trafficking
- Negative peer influences

Families in low-income neighborhoods often are more protective and controlling with their children in an effort to protect them from unsafe elements in the environment. At the same time, they may feel frustrated in their efficacy as parents to provide adequate protection. Such efforts may lead to greater restriction of children's activities, increased social isolation, and greater risk of parental depression and negative parent-child interactions (Magnuson & Duncan, 2003). Finally, as you read in Chapter 6, poor children are significantly more likely than nonpoor children to lack health insurance, a fact that has important ramifications for their overall health and development.

Ethnicity and Race   Often, the terms *ethnicity, minority,* and *race* are used interchangeably. Generally, "ethnicity" refers to the geographic location and cultural identity of one's ancestral heritage—for example, Irish, Italian, Russian, Armenian, Korean, Mexican, and so on. For families that have immigrated in the past few generations, this cultural heritage may be kept alive through family memories and the continued celebration of certain festivals or the enjoyment of specific foods. For families that migrated to the United States generations ago, active participation in or memory of a specific ethnic heritage may have faded, but Americans who trace their family roots back discover that their ancestors came to the United States from a specific place or places in the world, and thus they, too, have an "ethnic heritage."

Ethnic background can have an impact on child development, depending on how recently the family arrived in the new country, whether or not the family lives in an ethnic enclave, and whether or not a family's ethnic background has "minority" status within the larger society (Rumbaut & Portes, 2001).

For example, Eileen and Kevin's grandparents had immigrated from Ireland early in the 20th century. They settled in a Boston neighborhood heavily populated by their Irish countrymen. A hundred years later, Eileen and Kevin enjoyed wearing green on St. Patrick's Day, had traveled to Ireland on vacation, and enjoyed insider jokes and stories related to being Irish in Boston. However, they were not involved in any Irish American cultural groups or political causes. They attended a university in Boston, but after college they moved to a suburban area where being Irish was in the background of their lives. Aside from continuing to celebrate St. Patrick's Day and planning to take their daughter, Avery, to Ireland someday, they maintained little connection to their Irish heritage.

Rosa and Luis had been born and grew up in a Puerto Rican neighborhood in urban Connecticut. For both of them, English was their native language, although they understood and spoke Spanish. They also both attended a local community college, where Rosa received training as an LPN. Luis worked with a federal disaster relief agency that kept him on the road often for work.

Despite their native command of the English language, and despite the fact that they had finished high school and gone on to receive relevant college training, both Rosa and Luis felt they were "outsiders" in the suburban neighborhood they had moved to. Their

Links to Related Material
In Chapter 6, you read that poor children are less likely than nonpoor children to have access to good health care. Here, you learn more about the impact of poverty on children's lives.

outward appearance led some to classify them racially as "black," a label they did not identify with. They also became aware that "assimilating" into mainstream American culture was not as easy for them as it was for some of their childhood friends who were much lighter-skinned—primarily because of the different racial categories that were applied to them and the different perceptions that many people had based on this classification. Rosa found herself increasingly drawn to Puerto Rican and Latino groups that were active in political issues in her region. Her own identity as a Puerto Rican became more salient to her, and she began to immerse herself in the literature, history, and politics of Puerto Rico, particularly in relation to the larger United States. When their daughter Natalie was born, Rosa and Luis chose to move from the integrated suburban neighborhood where they had been living to a Puerto Rican neighborhood, so that Natalie would grow up with the opportunity to form strong connections with her Puerto Rican heritage and identity.

Jennifer had grown up in a small town in West Texas. Her ancestors had immigrated to the United States from Germany in the mid-19th century. In the 150 years since then, they had intermarried with people from Sweden, Ireland, and England. In addition, her great-grandmother had been a member of the Cherokee Nation. As an adolescent, she was not sure what countries her ancestors had come from, but was certain it was "lots of different ones." She was not aware that she had a Native American ancestor. When asked in a high school class what her ethnic background was, she answered, "white."

As you can see from the stories of these families, ethnic identity is something that all Americans begin with, but for some it seems to fade in importance, whereas for others it remains in the foreground. For some young people in the United States, ethnic identity is amorphous with little meaning attached to it, to the point where ethnic background becomes confused with racial labels, as was the case for Jennifer. For others, it becomes a prominent dimension of their sense of self. Researchers have distinguished between two types of ethnic identities that young people may maintain (Rumbaut & Portes, 2001). In *symbolic identity*, a young person may celebrate specific aspects of an ethnic heritage, such as holidays, foods, or music. However, these connections usually remain within the family of origin and typically are not central to a young person's public identity. Such a situation is evident in the story of Avery's family. By the time she was in the third grade, she knew that her family came from Ireland and hoped to visit there one day. However, aside from wearing green on St. Patrick's Day and having a fondness for the Irish soda bread that her mother still purchased occasionally on trips into the city, this identity had little public meaning for Avery.

For some children, however, ethnic backgrounds remain alive and important. This is particularly likely to happen when members of the dominant culture perceive a child's group as a "minority" group, particularly one that U.S. society defines as "nonwhite." In these cases, children are more likely to develop what is called a *resistant identity* (Rumbaut & Portes, 2001; Steinberg, 2001) in which young people will, with pride, consciously claim an ethnic heritage and frequently immerse themselves in the language, history, politics, and culture of that heritage (Tatum, 2003).

Such a situation is evident for Natalie. By the time she was in high school, she was deeply involved with Puerto Rican and Latino cultural and political groups. Although English was her native language, her parents had placed her in a bilingual Spanish-English elementary school so that she would maintain her Spanish while learning about Latino history and culture in a more formal setting. In high school, she spent time volunteering at a Head Start that served Puerto Ricans, and her goal after college was to work at the local Hispanic health agency. For Natalie, being Puerto Rican became a central aspect of her sense of identity. In addition, although several of her cousins were viewed by mainstream U.S. society as "white," she knew that her physical appearance set her apart visibly. She was aware that this made her and others like her more subject to prejudice and discrimination.

In contrast to ethnic heritage, "race" is a set of social categories that people are assigned to on the basis of perceived physical or genetic differences (rather than cultural, geographic, linguistic, or religious differences). Categories of "race" have shifted over time (Jacobson, 1998). For example, in the 18th century, the Irish were considered a separate "race" in the United States. One hundred years later, Italians and Jews were so categorized. Following World War II, increased awareness of the dangers inherent in such classifications among people led to the creation of the three-race system ("Caucasians," "Blacks," and "Asians") common to many today (Gould, 1996; Jacobson, 1998). Increasingly, however, the inadequacies of such a racial classification system are being recognized. Although apparently based on biological differences, in reality many people in the world do not fit easily into this set of classifications. For example, people from India are variously classified as "Asian" or "Caucasian," as are Native American and Polynesian groups. Similarly, many groups within the Americas (often known by the umbrella term "Hispanics" or "Latinos") represent a racially mixed background including Europeans, Africans, and Native American populations. As we saw in the story of Rosa and Luis, many Latinos who migrate to the United Sates find themselves forced into black-white racial classifications that seem arbitrary at best (particularly evident when two siblings from the same family are given different racial classifications based on differing skin color or hair type!). Among African Americans, the arbitrariness of racial designations is underlined by the commonness of white ancestors in a cultural context in which a white woman can bear a black child, but a black woman cannot bear a child classified as white (Rumbaut & Portes, 2001).

Unfortunately, despite the arbitrariness of racial classifications, they continue to exert a profound effect on economic and social life in America. In the United States, children who are identified as black or Hispanic are more likely to live in poverty and to grow up in neighborhoods with substandard schools and high violence. They are less likely to attend a four-year college and more likely to end up in prison or unemployed. The inequitable distribution of opportunities and resources within the United States, and the impact that this has on the development of children, remains a subject of debate and controversy among researchers interested in the intersection of public policy and child development (Danziger, Sandefur, & Weinberg, 1994; Wilson, 1996).

Families classified as "nonwhite" ethnic minorities often provide specific ethnic and racial socialization for their children. This may include messages emphasizing racial pride, heritage and traditions, acceptance of racial background, and positive self-image, as well as socialization for recognizing and handling situations of prejudice, discrimination, and blocked opportunities. There is some evidence that providing children with a sense of ethnic pride, combined with a recognition of racial barriers and prospects for upward mobility, contribute to positive outcomes for children in many ethnic minority families (Garcia Coll & Pachter, 2002).

Families and Immigration

In the 1990s, roughly 40 percent of the United States' total population growth was due to net immigration (that is, the number of incoming minus the number of outgoing migrations). This relative growth rate through immigration is equaled in U.S. history only by the decade 1901–1910. In 2003, the U.S. foreign-born population was 33.5 million, comprising the largest immigrant population in modern history (Larsen, 2004).

In addition to a dramatic increase in the volume of immigration, the demographic profile of U.S. immigrants has also changed dramatically in the past few decades. In 1940, only 13 percent of immigrants were from Asia and Latin America while 86 percent came from Europe and Canada. By 1990, this pattern had reversed, with 84 percent coming from Asia and Latin America, and less than 13 percent from Europe and Canada (U.S. Census Bureau, 1992; Rumbaut, 1994). In 2003, 53 percent of all foreign-born persons living in the United States were from Latin America, an additional 25 percent were from Asia, and fewer than 14 percent had their origins in Europe (Larsen, 2004). Consistent with these statistics, only 62 percent of children born in the United States in 1995 were white non-Latinos whose parents had also been born in the United States (Hernandez, 1997). It is estimated that by 2020, 53% of U.S. children will be classified as white, non-Hispanic (Child Trends Databank, 2006; http://www.childtrendsdatabank.org/indicators/60 Race and Ethnic Composition. cfm).

Acculturation is the process through which different cultural groups change and adapt to one another. Typically, people think of the immigrant group as changing in a unilinear fashion in the direction of the host culture, leading to assimilation. However, acculturation is a multidirectional and multidimensional process. Cultural contact affects and changes the host group as well as the immigrant group. For example, many forms of food,

Questions for Thought and Discussion
How did your cultural, ethnic, racial, and/or minority-group classification or identification affect your development during childhood and adolescence?

Acculturation
The process through which different cultural groups change and adapt to one another.

BOX 16.2 Building Tolerance in a Diverse Society

As a society becomes more diverse, the likelihood of between-group conflicts also increases, thus producing a need for interventions aimed at reducing intergroup conflict. A classic example of efforts to promote tolerance is known as the Robber's Cave experiment (Sherif, Harvey, White, Hood, & Sherif, 1961). In this experiment, Muzafer Sherif and his colleagues brought together 22 unacquainted fifth-grade boys into two summer camps. The boys engaged in the usual camp activities such as crafts and hiking, but there was a twist. The researchers planned some unexpected challenges for them, such as preparing their own meal when no one else had done so. As a result, "leaders" and "followers" developed in the two camps. The groups also adopted names for themselves ("Rattlers" and "Eagles") as an expression of their solidarity. Although the two camps were initially unaware of each other, after a few days the researchers had the groups "accidentally" meet and engaged them in various planned sports competitions, which eventually gave way to a solid group identity for each camp—and also resulted in an "us" versus "them" mentality. The rivalry between the two camps even escalated to the point of violence. Sherif and his colleagues, however, were able to help the Rattlers and Eagles resolve their intergroup conflict and even develop cross-group friendships through a series of engineered "crises" in which they were required to problem-solve and collaborate as one team instead of two. What Sherif in this experiment achieved suggests that promoting cooperation for a common goal is an effective way to decrease conflict among groups that are at odds.

Due to the increased immigration of people from non-European countries since the 1960s, when Sherif and his colleagues conducted their study, the United States has become far more diverse. Can the principles of their Robber's Cave experiment still be applied with children in a modern context? The answer seems to be yes. About 10 years ago, Dr. Linda Hansell of the University of Pennsylvania founded PARTNERS, a model program in Philadelphia schools. As Dr. Hansell noted in her online article describing the program, "[I]n the field of multicultural education, the focus seems to be on exposing students to different cultures through literature and cultural fairs, rather than through planned interactions between diverse groups of students" (Hansell, 2000).

In the 1950s, a well-known psychologist, Gordon Allport, said that in order for prejudice to be reduced, people must be encouraged to do things together often, in service of a common goal, over an extended period of time. In addition, their efforts must be supported by some larger organization. Another researcher, Thomas Pettigrew, emphasized friendship and emotional experiences as critical to this transformation. The main goal of the PARTNERS program is to promote deep-rooted friendships and mutual appreciation among students from diverse racial, ethnic, and socioeconomic backgrounds, in the spirit of Allport's ideas regarding meaningful contact. About 1,800 students from grades 1 through 8 (about 50 percent of color, mostly African American, working-class urban, and the other 50 percent white, middle-class suburban) take part each year in the special social and "creative, curriculum-centered projects" sponsored by PARTNERS.

In these projects, students are paired with a "partner" for the entire academic year. Alternating schools, they visit each other's school every month, where they engage in many different

art, music, and festivals currently enjoyed in the United States are a result of cultural interchange with groups that have migrated from other countries. In addition, changes that follow migration can occur along multiple dimensions, such as language, childrearing practices, and ethnic pride (Garcia Coll & Pachter, 2002). Also, many individuals from immigrant backgrounds develop bicultural patterns of beliefs and behaviors, rather than simply abandoning their culture of origin for the host culture. In the phenomenon known as *globalization*, people maintain cultural identification and contact with others like themselves wherever they happen to be in the world, creating enduring global networks based on a variety of factors, including national origin.

Children who grow up in immigrant families typically face the task of integrating the culture of origin that exists in their home with the host culture they find at school. This integration occurs on multiple levels, including language, values, and expectations for behavior. Studies have explicitly examined intergenerational differences among children and their immigrant parents. For example, in a study of 200 Puerto Rican parents and their married children living in New York City, researchers found that the traditional Puerto Rican value placed on the primacy of family diminished intergenerationally according to educational upward mobility (Procidano and Rogler, 1989; Rogler and Santana Cooney, 1984). However, intergenerational interactions and supportive patterns between parents and children remained strong and stable.

Similarly, in a study of intergenerational Mexican American families in Los Angeles (Rueschenberg & Buriel, 1989), researchers found that acculturation was linked to

In the last 20 years, the vast majority of immigrant families have come to the United States from countries in Latin America and Asia. How have current immigration patterns changed what is taught in schools, as well as what experiences are available to people in the larger society? (© Lawrence Migdale/Photo Researchers)

activities and intercultural lessons together (e.g., reading books from a different culture), which have been designed jointly by teachers from both schools. Between visits, the pairs of children write each other "pen pal"-style letters to get to know each other better. Similar to the principles of Robber's Cave, they also take part in outdoor "team-building days" at a local camp, participating in activities that are designed to require them to cooperate, communicate, and solve problems as a team.

Self-reflection is an important component of building tolerance, so that individuals can monitor their feelings and reactions to the new information they are receiving. PARTNERS asks children to engage regularly in periods of personal reflection, as well as dialogue. They discuss their reactions to the program with the class and in personal journals. Older students (middle school level) are encouraged to think about their experiences in the context of the larger social problems that they are becoming aware of—racism, economic inequality, and violence.

Parental involvement has been a key component of the program. Many parents volunteer each year, accompanying their children on visits, helping with activities and field trips, and serving on an advisory board. Teachers take part in workshops every month, where they intermingle with teachers from the partner school, and discuss issues related to the program and diversity in general. In addition to involving adults in a meaningful way, PARTNERS helps build children's ties to the relevant communities. They take tours of each other's school and make maps of each other's neighborhoods. Along the way, they take note of local cultural, recreational, and other resources that each place offers. By developing a personal connection to the other community, the students seem better equipped to relinquish fears and biases they may have had about it. Furthermore,

the children's assignment to create an "ideal community" from the strengths of each place helps the students to work as a team with a common, positive social vision.

Another important, timely effort has involved bringing together Jewish-Israeli and Palestinian youth for dialogue. Ifat Maoz (Maoz, 2000) discusses a series of workshops that were conducted, based also on the principles of Allport's intergroup contact theory. This is a potentially much harder situation due to the actual conflict Israelis and Palestinians are continually engaged in over territory and resources. The workshops, conducted in 1998, involved 67 Palestinian and 64 Jewish-Israeli high school students. Questionnaires about attitudes and stereotypes were given before and after. The encounters involved mixed groups of about five to seven students from each school. Two facilitators, one Israeli and one Palestinian, led meetings for the two days. A series of dialogues was designed to take students from building ties to discussing the national conflicts. First, students played games to get acquainted, then lighter discussions of culture and school were introduced, and finally students' perceptions of the Jewish-Palestinian conflict and intergroup issues were discussed. Narration of personal stories was included, aimed at helping the students see the human side of their experiences and to feel empathy. Participants indicated that there was some change for the better in their attitudes about each other's group, and some continued to pursue connections with the other group after the close of the workshop, even up to a year later. Although more research is needed to determine whether the workshop was indeed the cause of the changes in perception, the promise of this and even more long-term encounters of "transformative dialogue" is exciting and hope inspiring.

---

variables external to the family system (such as achievement orientation), but was not related to internal family system variables (such as cohesiveness and authority of parents). This finding suggests that the basic internal organization of the family, including the role of parental authority, remained relatively unchanged during the acculturation process. Two additional studies (Delgado-Gaitin, 1993; Phinney, Ong, and Madden, 2000) have found that immigrant Mexican American parents and their children in Southern California held comparable values regarding *familism* (devotion to family well-being) and *respeto* (respect).

Findings such as these highlight the complexity of the process of intergenerational change, yet suggest that children may retain many of their immigrant parents' central values. There is increasing evidence that the transmission of culture across generations is individual and dynamic (Fisher, Jackson, & Villarruel, 1998). That is, the content and significance of culture change across time depend on a variety of social network, individual, and family demographic variables (Portes & Rumbaut, 1990).

Learning Objective 16.3: *Identify and evaluate the influence of different social contexts on families and children.*

1. What role do the mass media play in children's lives in the United States?
2. How do relations among the family, schools, and the larger community affect children's development?
3. In what ways does socioeconomic status influence child development?

✔ *Test Your Mastery...*

4. What are the impacts of poverty as a context for child development?
5. How do ethnicity and race provide socializing contexts for child development?
6. How does immigration in the United States function as a socializing context for child development?

Families in a Changing Society

Learning Objective 16.4
Discuss how social change influences family life in the United States today.

A family is people and a family is love
That's a family
They come in all different sizes
And different kinds
But mine's just right for me.
There's a girl I know who lives with her mom
Her dad lives far away
Although she sees her parents just
One at a time
They both love her every day.

Lyrics from Barney song, "My Family's Just Right for Me." Coypright © 1993, Capital Records.

In 1970, 40 percent of all U.S. households were married couples with children. By 2004, this number had dropped to 23 percent. In 2003, just 68 percent of children under the age of 18 lived with two married parents, down from 87 percent in 1970. Twenty-six percent lived in homes headed by single women, while 6 percent lived just with their fathers (Fields, 2003). In addition, an increasing number of children live in alternative family structures, such as those created by remarriage following divorce, adoption, same-sex parents, and mothers who choose single parenthood.

Divorce and Blended Families

Divorce is an increasing reality in the lives of many children. Between 1960 and 1980 the divorce rate in the United States more than doubled, and at present almost half of new U.S. marriages end in divorce (Hetherington & Stanley-Hagan, 2002). Currently, about two-thirds of U.S. children live in a two-parent home, and in some ethnic groups the percentage is considerably lower (U.S. Bureau of the Census, 2001). The shift from two-parent to one-parent families reflects the fact that a larger proportion of unmarried women are having children, as well as rising divorce rates among couples with children (Fields, 2003).

Because much of what we will say about the effects of divorce will be negative, we should begin with two qualifications. First, the findings are on-the-average outcomes that do not apply to every child. Not all children are negatively affected by divorce, and the effects that do occur vary in severity across different children. Second, evaluations of the negative consequences of divorce must be placed in the context of the alternative, which in many cases is for parents to stay together in an unhappy marriage in which conflict in the home is a daily occurrence. Experts disagree about the extent to which an unhappy marriage should be preserved for the sake of the children (Hetherington & Kelly, 2002; Wallerstein, Lewis, & Blakeslee, 2000). Most, however, believe that in some instances divorce may be the better of two unfortunate alternatives.

Effects of Divorce Children whose parents have divorced do not fare well when compared with children from intact families. Negative outcomes for children of divorce have been demonstrated across virtually every aspect of development that has been examined (Amato, 2001; Clarke-Stewart et al., 2000; Hetherington & Stanley-Hagan, 2002).

Effects are generally most evident in the time period immediately following the divorce (Hetherington, 1989). Typically, the first year or so following a divorce is a time of heightened anxiety, depression, and parent–child conflict. Often, both child and parent are struggling to adjust to new and stressful circumstances, and the negative reactions of each can affect the other in a cyclical, escalating fashion.

Although the obvious immediate effects of divorce generally dissipate with time, the consequences do not necessarily disappear. Children whose parents have divorced remain at risk for a variety of problems, including antisocial behavior, lower self-esteem, difficulties in school, and poor relations with both siblings and peers (Hetherington, Bridges, & Isabella, 1998). Effects may persist into adolescence, as shown by a heightened probability of precocious sexual activity, substance abuse, and school dropout (Hetherington & Clingempeel, 1992). They may also persist into adulthood: Children of divorce are more likely to have their own marriages end in divorce (Amato, 1996).

Effects of divorce vary to some extent as a function of both the age and the gender of the child. Preschool-age and early-school-age children are in some ways especially vulnerable, because they lack the cognitive resources to understand the reasons for the divorce and may assume that they themselves were somehow to blame (Zill, Morrison, & Coiro, 1993). On the other hand, each segment of the developmental span presents its own vulnerabilities and possibilities for damage; adolescence, for example, can be an especially challenging time to cope with the dissolution of a marriage. Boys are typically more affected by divorce than girls, at least in terms of overt effects (for example, increased aggression, defiant behavior). Girls, however, may be more vulnerable to internalizing effects, such as sadness and self-blame (Hetherington & Stanley-Hagan, 2002). Nevertheless, in most ways the negative consequences of divorce appear greater for boys than for girls.

Determinants of Effects   Documenting effects is just one of the goals in research on divorce. A further important goal is to determine why the effects occur—and why outcomes are more positive for some children than for others.

Some of the effects associated with divorce result from conditions present prior to the divorce. It perhaps goes without saying that families in which the parents are on the verge of divorce do not present the most harmonious home atmosphere. Studies indicate that the problems shown by children of divorce were often evident prior to the parents' separation (Hetherington & Stanley-Hagan, 2002).

Changes in the child's experiences following the divorce are also important. One of the parents, with whom the child has lived his or her entire life (typically the father), is no longer in the home, and thus a source of affection and support is no longer so readily available. In many cases the family's economic situation worsens appreciably, and the financial circumstances put additional stress on a mother who is now trying to cope with the role of single parent. Often the mother's parenting practices become harsher and less consistent, with predictable negative effects on the children's behavior (Hetherington & Kelly, 2002). More positively, when mothers are able to maintain an authoritative style of parenting, their children are more likely to adapt successfully following divorce (Wolchik et al., 2000).

The behavior of the noncustodial parent (in more than 80 percent of cases this is the father) is also important. Sheer amount of time with the father does not appear to be critical, but the quality of the time is. Children generally adjust most successfully when the relationship with the father is warm and supportive (Amato & Gilbreth, 1999; Whiteside & Becker, 2000).

Although mother-only custody remains the usual outcome for divorces in the United States, *joint custody*—that is, equally shared rights and responsibilities for the two parents—is becoming increasingly common. As with any post divorce arrangement, the success of joint custody depends on how committed and effective each parent is in the parenting role, as well as how successfully the parents are able to work together. In general, however, joint custody appears to increase the chances of successful adjustment following divorce (Bauserman, 2002).

Remarriage   Approximately 75 percent of divorced parents eventually remarry (although, sadly, an even higher proportion of these marriages, compared to first marriages, will end in divorce) (Hetherington & Stanley-Hagan, 2002). The addition of a stepparent to the child's life brings both challenges and opportunities. When both parents bring children to

Blended family
A new family unit, resulting from remarriage, which consists of parents and children from previously separate families.

the new marriage, then there are stepsiblings as well and more new challenges. The conjunction of two families to form a new one is referred to as a **blended family.**

Initially, adjustment to the new family situation following remarriage is often shaky—for both child and stepparent. This is especially true during early adolescence (a shaky time in general for parenting!) and for girls' adjustment to a stepfather (Hetherington, 1993). Boys are more likely to adjust favorably to a stepfather, presumably because they perceive less threat to their relationship with the mother than do girls.

Because mothers usually obtain custody of the child following divorce, less is known about the effects of a new stepmother in the home. Studies indicate, however, that this situation can also be a difficult one—perhaps even more than the more typical new-stepfather case (Mekos, Hetherington, & Reiss, 1996). As with stepfathers, however, initial difficulties are often (though unfortunately not always) smoothed out with time. Important in both cases is the relationship between the newly married parents, as well as the support (or at least not active hostility) of the noncustodial biological parent.

Despite the difficulties just noted, stepparents can be a wonderful addition to the lives of children who have experienced a divorce. Especially when stepparents are involved with the children and skillful in their parenting efforts, positive effects on family life and children's development are evident (Hetherington & Stanley-Hagan, 2002). Unfortunately, stepparents, on average, are less involved and less skillful than parents in general; thus, not all children reap these potential benefits.

Single-Parent Families

The proportion of U.S. children under 18 living in single-parent families has increased dramatically in recent decades, from fewer than 10 percent in 1960 to over one-quarter in 2003. Not only have single-parent families become more common over the past few decades, but so have the conditions leading to their formation. In 1970, divorce and separation accounted for 86 percent of children in single-parent homes. By 1997, this number had declined to 58 percent. Concomitantly, children living in single-parent families headed by a never-married mother increased from 6 percent in 1970 to 37 percent in 1997 (Weinraub, Horvath, & Gringlas, 2002).

In general, researchers have found that children growing up in single-parent families have poorer outcomes than children growing up in two-parent families. Children reared in single-parent homes are more likely to drop out of high school, have a baby before the age of 20 years, and be out of work as young adults than those from a similar background who grew up in two-parent homes. In addition, they are at greater risk for psychological problems and for poor school performance (Murray & Golombok, 2005).

Why do so many children from single-parent families show poor outcomes? Some researchers have wondered whether it is because of father absence per se or other factors, such as economic stress, social isolation, or parental conflict surrounding divorce. To answer this question, researchers have examined single-parent families that have been formed through different circumstances—for example, those resulting from divorce and separation, those formed by professional women who have never married but choose to have a child on their own, and those formed through teen motherhood.

In one such study (Carlson & Corcoran, 2001), data from the National Longitudinal Survey of Youth were used to examine the effect of various family structures on behavioral and cognitive outcomes for children age 7 to 10. This large-scale study found that financial resources, mother's mental health, and overall quality of the home environment are particularly important for children's behavior. Family income and mother's own intellectual aptitude predicted children's school performance.

Single-Parent Families Formed Through Divorce Studies that have looked specifically at single-parent families formed through divorce and separation have found that divorce brings a unique set of challenges. For example, following Karen and Philip's divorce, Karen grieved over the loss of her marriage and wrestled with feelings of failure as a spouse. Although her relationship with Philip had become conflictual and acrimonious, she nonetheless missed his daily presence. After Philip moved out, Karen needed to find new household routines that felt comfortable for herself and her two school-age daughters, Jennifer and Brittany. Jennifer and Brittany also missed their father's presence, and felt angry and resentful about his absence.

In addition, Karen's financial situation changed considerably following the divorce. She had previously worked part-time in a job with flexible hours that allowed her to be home when school let out, shepherd Jennifer and Brittany to various extracurricular activities, and make a family dinner each evening. Following the divorce, Karen had to begin working full-time, which necessitated changes in their household routine. Jennifer and Brittany spent afternoons at the home of a family friend until Karen picked them up at 5:30. Dinner was often a haphazard affair as Karen adjusted to the new demands in her life. Karate lessons became too expensive and were sacrificed. Daily trips to the pool for swim practice became difficult to manage. Karen wondered whether they would be able to keep the house they had lived in for many years, or whether they would need to sell it and move to a smaller house in a less desirable neighborhood. Jennifer and Brittany cried and grew sullen at the prospect of entering a new school district and leaving their friends.

The life changes that typically follow divorce, including increased loneliness, task overload, and financial stress, pose significant challenges for competent parenting (Weinraub et al., 2002). Quality of parenting often diminishes in the first months and years after a divorce, with newly single parents more irritable and unresponsive in their interactions with their children and less effective in their supervision and discipline. Although most families are able to find a new homeostasis within two years, after which family functioning usually improves (Hetherington & Stanley-Hagan, 2002), poorer outcomes among children of divorce nonetheless appear related to stresses associated with family dissolution and reorganization, increased financial insecurity, diminished quality of parenting, as well as preexisting and continuing conflict between custodial parents.

Single Parents Who Have Never Married   As mentioned, the proportion of single-parent families formed by parents who have never been married has increased dramatically in recent decades. How do these families differ from single-parent families formed through divorce? What are the unique contexts they offer for child development? Two subgroups of never-married parents are adolescent single parents and older professional women.

Adolescent parents (usually mothers) are the most disadvantaged of single parents. Of all adolescent mothers, 79 percent are not married. African American teen mothers are less likely to be married than other teen mothers and following the birth of the baby are more likely than European Americans to live with their family of origin in an extended family situation.

Adolescent parents are more likely than other parents to come from poor families of low educational backgrounds living in impoverished neighborhoods. Typically, they have attended poor-quality schools and have suffered from school failure. They are more likely to drop out of school than other teens, and their life circumstances often limit their ability to become self-sufficient. Attaining a higher level of education and controlling future births are important factors in improving the life course of a teen mother (Weinraub et al., 2002).

The relatively disadvantaged life circumstances of many teen mothers combine with their young age to create a context that affects the development of their children in unique ways. The adolescent who becomes a parent, like all parents, must develop an identity as a mother and negotiate new family dynamics that arise following a baby's birth. In addition, adolescent parents are at the same time confronted with their own developmental needs related to being an adolescent: finding an identity of their own and negotiating autonomy from the family of origin. Combining these two major life transitions (becoming a parent and being an adolescent) into the same time period can place

In the 1990s, the birth of a child to sitcom character Murphy Brown, a single professional woman, stirred a national controversy regarding the importance of fathers in children's lives. Murphy Brown's choice to have a child on her own became a rallying point for proponents on both sides of the political spectrum. If aired today, do you think this sitcom situation would cause the same furor that it did 15 years ago? (CBS/Landov LLC)

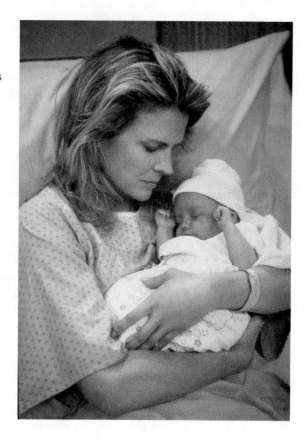

considerable stress on the teen mother (Moore & Brooks-Gunn, 2002). In addition, the financial and educational limitations typically experienced by adolescent mothers contribute to making teen parenthood an exceptionally difficult life circumstance to traverse successfully. The high rates of problem behavior among children of teen parents attest to this difficulty.

The fastest growing group of single parents in the United States today is that of the older, professional woman who has never married but who chooses to have a child on her own. Called *single mothers by choice* (SMC), these women first came to national attention in the 1990s, when the television sitcom character, Murphy Brown, chose to bring a child into the world knowing that she would not have the help or support of a partner. Typically, single mothers by choice are in their upper 30s and early 40s, European American, and of upper-middle-class socioeconomic status. Like Murphy Brown, they are usually financially secure, well educated, and employed in well-paying professional jobs (Weinraub et al., 2002). Although some of these mothers choose single parenthood through adoption, the majority elect to have children through anonymous donor insemination (ADI).

Research on outcomes for children reared by women who are single mothers by choice is limited, reflecting the relative recency of the growth of this phenomenon in our society. A national support and informational group for these women, called SMC, was founded in 1981 by Jane Mattes with just 8 members and currently has over 2,000 members. However, research thus far indicates that children reared by single mothers by choice may not face the same developmental risks as children in single-parent homes created through divorce or teen parenthood. In a recently initiated longitudinal study of SMC families created through ADI, researchers actually found fewer emotional and behavioral difficulties among these children than among a comparison group of married ADI families (Murray & Golombok, 2005). However, the children reported on in this study are only two years old. Follow-up on their development over the years will help us better understand the effects of growing up in this unique context.

Adoptive and Foster Families

In 2000, adopted children made up 2.5 percent of the U.S. child population. The vast majority of these (87 percent) represented domestic adoptions, or adoptions within the United States, whereas the remaining 13 percent were international adoptions. Among internationally adopted children, nearly half (48 percent) were from Asian countries, with another 33 percent from Latin America, and 16 percent from Europe. Families within the United States with adopted children differ from other families in significant ways. They are more likely to be European American (76 percent), are older, and are better off economically on average than other U.S. families. In addition, 17 percent of adopted children were of a different race than their parents (U.S. Census Bureau, 2003, http://www.census.gov/prod/2003pubs/censr-6.pdf).

Adoptions occur for many reasons, under many circumstances, and at many points in adopted children's lives—all of which complicate the task of determining what effects, if any, adoption has on children's development. However, as you saw in Chapter 11, children who are adopted before the age of 6 months, even from severely depriving circumstances, are no more likely than nonadopted children to experience behavioral, emotional, or academic problems (Rutter, Kreppner & O'Connor, 2001). After the age of 6 months, the risk of developmental problems among adopted children increases in a linear way. That is, the older the child is at the age of adoption, the greater the risk is that the child will have behavior problems. The greatest risk is found among children who were severely deprived and adopted after the age of 2. However, even among later adopted children, 20 to 25 percent showed no behavior problems at the age of 6 years.

The majority of adopted children, particularly those adopted as infants, clearly develop in ways that are indistinguishable from those of children being reared by their biological parents. However, certain groups of adopted children appear to be at greater risk for the later development of problems. In particular, children who at the time of adoption are older have had more adverse experiences, such as health problems, multiple changes in caregiving environment, or a history of neglect or abuse; in addition, boys show higher risk for adjustment and behavioral problems than girls (Brodzinsky & Pinderhughes, 2002).

Although nearly half of international adoptees are infants, in 1998 only 2 percent of children adopted domestically through the U.S. foster care system were infants. Yet,

Links to Related Material
In Chapter 11, you read about the impact of early deprivation on children's development. Here, you learn more about how early deprivation may affect children who are in foster care.

BOX 16.3   Conversations with a Child Protective Services Administrator

Diane Kindler, age 58, grew up in central Massachusetts and today is single with an 18-year-old son, David. She is deputy division director at Casey Family Services, Maine Division. Diane recalls that during college she had experiences working with children, which she enjoyed. She was considering both journalism and social work when an entry-level opportunity in social work opened up in Boston, where she was living at the time. Before that she worked for a large insurance company to pay the bills until she could get a job she wanted. She earned a B.A. in sociology and an MSW (Master's degree in social work), working first in Massachusetts in public welfare and then in child protective services in Maine.

After graduate school in North Carolina, I returned to Maine as a child protective supervisor. I then worked for a private children's mental health agency in a variety of administrative roles. I was in private practice as a social worker for 12 years with a focus on working with children and families, especially those affected by divorce, existing in the child welfare system, or involved in adoption. In 1999 I came to Casey Family Services as a team leader to start a new post-adoption program. Three years ago I became the division deputy.

I am responsible for the day-to-day operations of our division. Casey Family Services is the direct service branch of the Annie E. Casey Foundation. In the Maine Division we provide an array of child welfare services, including family preservation, foster care, reunification services, and post-adoption services. I supervise the six team leaders, who, in turn, supervise all our social workers and family support specialists. I provide clinical direction for our division and am available to help staff with crises and problems as they arise. I work most closely with the division director and the team leaders, but I also have contact with many other staff and with clients. I facilitate a parents' support group that meets biweekly.

At Casey we have the unique opportunity to combine direct service with participation in other activities, such as research. One of our goals is to develop new methods of child welfare practice that work, are cost effective, and can be replicated in the larger child welfare system. In my first years at Casey I developed and ran a post-adoption services program that was part of a larger research project. This project led to the development of a new model of providing post-adoption services to families who adopt children from the child welfare system.

My work is never, ever, boring. I think that most of the time what we do matters. It is a privilege to have worked with so many fine parents—birth, foster, and adoptive. Tremendous progress has been made in finding permanent homes and families for children in the child welfare system rather than letting them drift in and out of foster care and institutions. I am very proud to see that some children I have worked with have been adopted by families who love them unconditionally. I have also seen individuals become better parents and able to care for their children. Years later I have had some clients tell me specifically how something I did helped them.

Child welfare is always affected by the political climate, and there can be a tendency toward action based on the most recent tragedy rather than on a real attempt to put into place what we know people need in order to take care of their children. Our society likes quick fixes. Social workers and the like are low on the professional totem pole in a society that tends to measure people by how much money they have.

To do this work well you have to be able to see how more alike we are than different. That is, the best social workers I have known are people who understand that they are not very different from their clients. In fact, given a few different experiences, rolls of the dice, and misfortunes, *they* would be the clients. You should not do this work if for any reason you cannot maintain a respectful attitude toward your clients. Also, you have to enjoy the work and find satisfaction in the contributions you are making to people's lives, as it is too hard and too poorly paid to do if you don't.

Questions for Thought
and Discussion

How did family structure affect your development during childhood and adolescence? What forces of social and cultural change might affect your childrearing decisions and behaviors as a parent today?

infants less than 12 months of age are the largest group of children to enter and remain in the child welfare system. Of the almost 600,000 children in foster care nationwide, a fifth are infants. In addition, since many infants in foster care experienced prenatal exposure to drugs or were low birthweight, they are more likely than other children to have serious medical problems, disabilities, and developmental delays (Dicker & Gordon, 2004).

The U.S. foster care system itself has been described as "in crisis." Although the number of children needing foster care has risen, the number of foster families available has dropped. In addition, the U.S. foster care system also confronts serious issues related to the inability of the system to return children to their homes or place them with adoptive families quickly (Haugaard & Hazan, 2002). This inability often results in multiple moves from home to home, a situation that can cause serious problems in the child's ability to form positive attachment relationships, thus impacting emotional and mental health.

Families Headed by Gay and Lesbian Parents

Families with same-sex parents can be formed in a number of ways. Most commonly, the children of gay or lesbian parents are the result of a previous heterosexual relationship of a parent who has now committed to a gay or lesbian sexual orientation. However, lesbian and gay couples may also choose to add children to their families through adoption or donor insemination. Becoming parents through adoption carries its own special risks, given the context of anti-gay sentiment found in some child protective service (CPS) systems, agencies, and host countries.

Because of the fear of discrimination that prevents many lesbian or gay individuals from revealing their sexual orientation, the actual number of gay and lesbian families with children is not known. The 2000 U.S. Census counted nearly 600,000 same-sex partner households. Of these, 34 percent of female and 22 percent of male couples had children under the age of 18 living with them. However, many people may not wish to reveal their sexual orientation. In addition, many lesbians and gay men are not in partnerships when they choose to become parents and so are counted as single parents when they adopt or, in the case of a woman, bear a child through anonymous donor insemination. Thus, estimates of the number of children being raised in families with gay and lesbian parents range from 1 to 5 million (Patterson, 2002). This means, of course that at least a million and possibly many more children are growing up in households with a gay or lesbian parent or parents. Some estimates place the number as high as 10 to 14 million (Patterson, 1995).

Research on the possible effects of such a family structure is a fairly recent endeavor. Such research faces a number of methodological challenges, and all who evaluate the research agree that more study is needed (Golombok, 2000; Patterson, 2002; Patterson & Chan, 1999). Thus far, however, the findings seem clear: There is no evidence that growing up with lesbian or gay parents has negative effects on children's development—or indeed any consistent effects of any sort that differentiate such children from those in other family arrangements. This conclusion holds across a range of outcomes, including self-esteem, intelligence, family relations, and peer relations. It holds as well for the most frequently examined outcomes: gender role development and sexual identity. As you saw in Chapter 13, children of lesbian or gay parents are not in general either more or less strongly sex-typed than children of heterosexual parents. As adolescents and young adults, they appear no more likely to adopt a same-sex sexual orientation than young adults in general.

Links to Related Material
In Chapter 13, you read about the development of sexual orientation. Here, you learn more about the development of children growing up in families headed by gay and lesbian parents.

There is no evidence thus far that growing up with gay or lesbian parents has a negative effect on children's development. (Maya Barnes/The Image Works)

Although many children in gay and lesbian households are the result of prior heterosexual marriages, lesbian and gay couples are also more likely to bear children through unconventional means. For example, Mark and John are a gay male couple. Their good friends and next-door neighbors, Vicky and Irene, are a lesbian couple. Both couples have been together for many years, and both would like to have a child. They finally decide that Vicky will bear a child via donor insemination using Mark's sperm. Their resulting son, Jason, lives with Vicky and Irene but sees Mark and John on a daily basis. He is a happy, well-adjusted child who has two fathers and two mothers, all of whom are actively involved in his life.

As a society, we have come a long way since the days when television shows such as *Ozzie and Harriet, Father Knows Best*, and *Leave It to Beaver* presented us with the image of a "normal" family consisting of a wage-earner dad, stay-at-home mom, and two or more children. Although factors such as poverty, lack of social support, and family conflict have a negative impact on child development, the evidence so far suggests that family structure per se does not. When financial and social resources are adequate, family conflict is low, and parenting styles are authoritative, then most children seem to have the context they need to thrive developmentally.

✔ *Test Your Mastery...*

Learning Objective 16.4: *Discuss how social change influences family life in the United States today.*

- How do divorce and remarriage affect child development?
- What are three types of single-parent families, and how do these family settings affect child development?
- In what different ways are families formed through adoption?
- How do gay and lesbian family structures work as a context for child development?

BOX 16.4   Contextual Model of Family and Society

Child is born or adopted into a given family with a specific genetic inheritance and prenatal history.

Family, Neighborhood, and School Settings

- Family's socioeconomic status (SES) is influenced by education, occupation, and income. A family's SES influences such factors as the safety and resources of the neighborhood they live in, the quality of the schools the children go to, and the recreational opportunities available in the community.
- Parents' workplace stress, finances, health, and social support affect the time and resources they have to meet the everyday demands of parenting, thus affecting the quality of parent-child interactions.
- Presence of siblings and extended family also influences the context of child development.

Culture and Society

- Family has an ethnic background that may or may not involve recent immigration and that may or may not be reflected in the dominant culture.
- Larger cultural values influence childrearing beliefs and practices, including attitudes toward family structure and composition, moral development, interpersonal relationships, and gender roles.

Summary for Chapter 16

Learning Objective 16.1
Analyze the influence of parenting practices and children's contributions to childhood socialization.

1. What major parenting styles affect child development?

Based on measures of warmth and control, researchers have identified four parenting styles, or overall patterns of childrearing. The *authoritative* parenting style is high on both warmth and control. Authoritative parents tend to be caring and sensitive toward their children, while at the same time setting clear limits and maintaining a predictable environment. They also often provide rationales for why they expect certain behavior from the child. In contrast, the authoritarian parenting style combines high control with low warmth. *Authoritarian* parents are demanding, exercise strong control over their children's behavior, and tend to enforce demands with threats and harsh punishment. They display little warmth or affection toward the child. *Permissive* parents are high in warmth but low in control. These parents are loving and emotionally sensitive but set few limits on behavior and provide little in the way of structure or predictability. The *uninvolved* parenting style (also termed *disengaged* or *neglectful* parenting style) describes parents who are low in both warmth and control. They set few limits on their children but also provide little attention, interest, or emotional support.

2. How do cultural and socioeconomic factors influence parenting styles?

Much of the research on parenting styles has involved European American middle-class families. However, the *authoritative* style has been shown to be beneficial for child development across a range of different populations, including African American, Latino, and Asian American samples, as well as samples from China and India. However, the benefits of authoritative parenting styles do not extend to all populations. *Authoritarian parenting* is more common in African American and Asian American families, as well as in Chinese families. Factors that account for this finding are cultural beliefs and values, and socioeconomic realities. In China, for example, family unity, respect for elders, and obedience to authority are central goals of socialization, and parental concern for children is expressed more through close supervision and frequent teaching than through displays of overt physical affection. Many African American families share a similar emphasis on communal values, respect for parents and other adults, and close control of children's activities. Authoritarian parenting styles also vary regionally in the United States and tend to be more common in southern and midwestern states and in rural communities. Physical punishment is common among many cultural minorities, including African Americans and some immigrant groups. Yet, the use of physical punishment among these groups is not associated with the negative effects found in European American communities. Economic and personal necessities also influence parenting styles. For families living in dangerous neighborhoods and under conditions of poverty, reasoning with the child and encouraging independence can increase risk. Firm and immediate control may be a higher priority for parents in such circumstances and may be adaptive for the overall well-being of the child.

3. To what extent do mothers and fathers play different roles in parenting?

In recent years, *fathers* have assumed an increased role in children's care, in part because of social changes that have allowed more mothers to enter the workforce. Despite increased involvement, fathers generally devote less time to child care than do mothers. Fathers' interactions with their children tend to center around physical stimulation and play, especially with boys. This emphasis emerges early in infancy and continues through childhood. Fathers, on average, seem to hold stronger views about gender-appropriate behavior than mothers and are more likely to treat boys and girls in ways that might promote sex differences in development. Almost all babies with a father in the home become attached to their fathers, and the probability of a secure attachment is as great with the father as with the mother.

4. What is the child's contribution to the socialization process?

Infants enter the world with individual *temperaments*, including variations in irritability, emotionality, and sociability, which affect the ways that parents interact with them. Infants with difficult temperaments, for example, receive more total caregiving time in the early months than do easier-to-handle babies. By the second half of the first year, however, mothers of difficult infants tend to soothe their infants less and become less involved, as they too often have been frustrated and unrewarded in their efforts. Other aspects of temperament that affect parent behavior are activity level and inhibition or timidity. Some parents adapt more successfully than others to the child's characteristics (goodness of fit). Development proceeds most successfully when parents are able to match their caregiving practices to the nature and needs of the child. Thus the developmental process is transactional. Characteristics of the child elicit particular behaviors from the parent. Parental behaviors in turn alter characteristics of the child. The child then brings different characteristics to future socialization encounters with the parent, and so on throughout development.

Learning Objective 16.2
Analyze the ways that families function as a social system.

1. How do sibling relationships influence child development?

Siblings spend thousands of hours together as they grow up, imitate each other frequently, and eventually exchange information and opinions on many issues. Most aspects of development are potentially affected by growing up with siblings. Growing up with siblings has *cognitive* benefits, such as accelerated development of theory-of-mind skills, partly because sibling interactions often involve teasing, tricks, and sharing of emotions. Siblings can also be effective teachers of one another, even more so than peers. Siblings also affect each other's *social* development, especially gender-role development. Older siblings are models of gender role behavior and agents of reinforcement or punishment for behaviors they see in their siblings. Same-sex older siblings promote gender-typical behavior, and opposite-sex siblings make counter-stereotypical behavior more likely. The social skills and expectations that children first acquire in interactions with siblings affect how they behave and how successful they are when they enter the larger world of peers.

2. How do grandparents influence child development?

Grandparents can be a source of emotional or financial support for the parents and can be mentors, playmates, babysitters, or substitute parents for grandchildren. On average, grandmothers are more involved in and derive more satisfaction from the grandparent role than grandfathers. The presence of a grandmother can be very important in the case of teenage motherhood. Co-residence of daughter and mother becomes more likely when a new baby arrives, especially among African Americans, and a grandmother in the home can be a source of both expertise and welcome hands-on help. Having a grandmother present is not always a benefit, however. In some cases the presence of her own mother can interfere with the new mother's comfort level and effectiveness in her parenting role, with detrimental effects on both her parenting skills and the child's development.

3. How does culture affect family relationships and their relative importance for child development?

In some cultures the presence of grandparents in the home is typical. In China, for example, three-generation households are common, and the same is true for African American families in the United States. In many cultures, the modal family pattern is not the nuclear family but the extended family. An *extended family unit* consists not only of children and parents but also other adult relatives. For African Americans, the extended family is a legacy of family patterns in parts of Africa where newly married couples join one of the parents' households rather than starting a household of their own. As with any long-established cultural tradition, the extended family is associated with beneficial effects in cultures in which it is the norm. The extended family structure provides social and financial support to members of the younger generation, facilitates the transmission of cultural history and values, and reduces negative developmental outcomes.

4. What are the kinds and functions of social support?

A person's social network is comprised of individuals who "make a difference" in that person's life. Researchers who study the impact of social networks have differentiated kinds of social support that individuals within a social network may offer a person. *Emotional* support refers to expressions of empathy and encouragement that inspire confidence and help a person through a time of discouragement or worry. *Instrumental* support consists of concrete help, typically with household chores or child care. *Informational* support refers to advice or information. *Companion* support consists of opportunities to engage in enjoyable activities with other adults. *Material* support refers to people who can provide financial assistance or other material support during difficult times.

5. In what ways does social support affect a family's functioning?

Social support can reduce the amount of *stress* in a parent's life and buffer the parent from the adverse effects of stressful events. A difficult, frustrating day can be put into perspective through the companionship and emotional support offered by a friend or family member. Parents who experience emotional support and nurturance from others often have greater capacity to nurture others, including their children. Parents' access to *positive social networks* has been linked to many positive developmental outcomes in children, including happiness with the family, stronger peer-related social skills, and the development of positive peer friendships. In addition, children benefit both emotionally and cognitively through regular contact with responsive and dependable adult network members.

Learning Objective 16.3

Identify and evaluate the influence of different social contexts on families and children.

1. What role do the mass media play in children's lives in the United States?

As the presence of different types of *media* in the home has risen, so have concerns regarding their effects on children's development. On average, children age 2 to 18 years spend about 5.5 hours per day in personal, nonschool uses of media and technology at home, including television, VCR and DVD players, video games, computer games or other online usage, and music CDs. The ecology of home media use among America's children has raised concerns for many parents, educators, and child development professionals. These concerns have focused on too little time spent reading, too much time spent watching media, objectionable media content, and time spent with media in the absence of parental supervision and interaction.

2. How do relations among the family, schools, and the larger community affect children's development?

Research indicates that when *parents* are involved in their children's formal education and school life, academic performance improves and the children have more positive school attitudes and higher career aspirations. This is true regardless of the parents' educational background or socioeconomic status. In addition, parent-child discussions about schoolwork, school programs, and plans for the future have a strong effect on student achievement. When *schools* invite parental involvement in clear ways, more parents become involved. Parents can support children's education through early literacy learning, involvement and support with homework, and discussion of future college and career plans. Parents, schools, and *communities* can work together to provide information about children's health, safety, supervision, nutrition, discipline, and home conditions that support learning and development. Parents can support the school through volunteer activities and home activities coordinated with the school curriculum. Schools can encourage strong parent associations and parent representation on school governing boards. Schools and parent groups can make connections with local agencies, businesses, churches, and other groups to serve the needs of families and the community.

3. In what ways does socioeconomic status influence child development?

Researchers have found that *SES* strongly influences parenting. Higher-SES mothers address more speech to their children and use more complex vocabulary and syntax when speaking to their children. In addition to differences in verbal interaction, lower-SES mothers tend to be more controlling and restrictive of their children's behavior and are more likely to have an authoritarian parenting style. Across many different cultural groups, lower-SES parents have been found to place greater emphasis on obedience and conformity to authority, whereas higher-SES parents tend to place greater emphasis on personal initiative and autonomy. When the individual components of SES (education, occupation, and income) are examined separately, researchers have found that level of education is associated most reliably with differences in parenting practices and styles.

4. What are the impacts of poverty as a context for child development?

Poor children are at *greater risk* of academic failure, poor physical health, and behavior problems. Children from poor families are less likely to receive early learning experiences that affect children's later school achievement and cognitive functioning. Poor parents have less money to spend on books, educational toys, dance classes, or family museum memberships. In addition, lack of reliable transportation may inhibit educational outings, such as trips to the library. Finances also may limit parents' abilities to provide an optimal home learning environment. Significant stress is associated with struggling to make ends meet in poor families. Psychological distress, combined with lack of social support, can create a home environment with frequent negative parent-child interactions and harsher discipline. Families in low-income neighborhoods often are more protective and controlling in an effort to protect children from unsafe elements in the environment. Such efforts may lead to greater restriction of children's activities, increased social isolation, and greater risk of parental depression. Finally, poor children are significantly more likely than nonpoor children to lack health insurance, which affects their overall health and development.

5. How do ethnicity and race provide socializing contexts for child development?

The effects of *ethnic background* on child development depend on how recently the family arrived, whether or not the family lives in an ethnic enclave, and whether or not a family's ethnic background has "minority" status within the larger society. For some, ethnic identity fades in importance, while for others it remains strong and becomes an important part of their sense of self. In symbolic identity, a young person may celebrate specific aspects of an ethnic heritage, such as holidays, foods, or music. However, these connections typically are not central to a young person's public identity. In resistant identity, young people who are members of "minority" groups consciously claim an ethnic heritage and immerse themselves with pride in the language, history, politics, and culture of that heritage. Ethnic background may become confused with racial labels. "Race" is a set of social categories to which people are assigned on the basis of perceived physical or genetic differences. Racial categories have shifted over time, oversimplifying human diversity and generally failing as a classification system. Despite the arbitrariness of racial classifications, they continue to exert a profound effect on economic and social life in America. In the United States, children who are identified as black or Hispanic are more likely to live in poverty and to grow up in neighborhoods with substandard schools and high violence. They are less likely to attend a four-year college and more likely to end up in prison or unemployed. The inequitable distribution of opportunities and resources within the United States, and the impact that this has on the development of children, remains a subject of debate and controversy among those interested in impacts of public policy on child development. Families classified as "nonwhite" ethnic minorities often provide specific ethnic and racial socialization for their children, including messages emphasizing racial pride; heritage and traditions; positive self-image; and ways of recognizing and handling situations of prejudice, discrimination, and blocked opportunities. There is some evidence that providing children with a sense of ethnic pride combined with recognition of racial barriers and prospects for upward mobility contribute to positive outcomes for children in many ethnic minority families.

6. How does immigration in the United States function as a socializing context for child development?

In 2003, 53 percent of all foreign-born persons living in the United States were from Latin America, an additional 25 percent were from Asia, and fewer than 14 percent had their origins in Europe. Acculturation is the process through which different cultural groups change and adapt to one another. Typically, people think of the immigrant group as changing in a unilinear fashion in the direction of the host culture, leading to assimilation. However, acculturation is a multidirectional and multidimensional process. Cultural contact affects and changes the host group as well as the immigrant group. Children who grow up in immigrant families typically face the task of integrating the culture of origin that exists in their home with the host culture they find at school. This integration occurs on multiple levels, including language, values, and expectations for behavior.

Learning Objective 16.4

Discuss how social change influences family life in the United States today.

1. How do divorce and remarriage affect child development?

Children whose parents have divorced do not fare as well as children from intact families. Negative outcomes for *children of divorce* arise in every aspect of development. Typically, the first year or so following a divorce is a time of heightened anxiety, depression, and parent-child conflict. Children whose parents have divorced remain at risk for antisocial behavior, lower self-esteem, difficulties in school, and poor relations with both siblings and peers. Preschool-age and early-school-age children are in some ways especially vulnerable because they lack the cognitive resources to understand the reasons for the divorce and may assume that they were somehow to blame. Adolescence also can be an especially challenging time to cope with the dissolution of a marriage. Boys typically are more overtly affected by divorce than girls. Girls, however, may be more vulnerable to internalizing effects, such as sadness and self-blame. The negative effects of divorce appear greater for boys than for girls. The addition of a stepparent to the child's life brings both challenges and opportunities. When both parents bring children to the new marriage, then there are stepsiblings in the blended family. Adjustment to the new family situation following remarriage is often shaky for both child and stepparent. This is especially true during early adolescence and for girls' adjustment to a stepfather. Boys are more likely to adjust favorably to a stepfather. The situation of a new stepmother in the home also can be difficult. However, stepparents with good parenting skills can be a wonderful addition to the lives of children of divorce.

2. What are three types of single-parent families, and how do these family settings affect child development?

One type of single-parent family is formed through *divorce*. The life changes that typically follow divorce, including increased loneliness, task overload, and financial stress, pose significant challenges for competent parenting. Quality of parenting often diminishes in the first months and years after a divorce, with newly single parents more irritable and unresponsive in their interactions with their children and less effective in their supervision and discipline. Poorer outcomes relate to stresses associated with family dissolution and reorganization, increased financial insecurity, diminished quality of parenting, and preexisting or continuing conflict between custodial parents. Another type of single-parent family involves single parents who have never married. The proportion of these single-parent families has increased dramatically in recent decades.

Two subgroups of never-married parents are adolescent single parents and older professional women. *Adolescent parents* (usually mothers) are the most disadvantaged of single parents. Of all adolescent mothers, 79 percent are not married. African American teen mothers are less likely to be married than other teen mothers and following the birth of the baby are more likely to live with their family of origin in an extended family situation. Adolescent parents are more likely to come from poor families of low educational backgrounds living in impoverished neighborhoods. Adolescents who become parents must develop an identity as parents at the same time as they must meet their own developmental needs as adolescents. In addition to this stress on the teen mother, financial and educational limitations contribute to making teen parenthood an exceptionally difficult life circumstance. The high rates of problem behavior among children of teen parents attest to this difficulty.

The fastest growing group of single parents in the United States today is that of the older, professional woman who has never married but who chooses to have a child on her own. Typically, *single mothers by choice* are in their upper 30s and early 40s, European American, and of upper-middle-class socioeconomic status. Research thus far indicates that children reared by single mothers by choice may not face the same developmental risks as children in single-parent homes created through divorce or teen parenthood.

3. In what different ways are families formed through adoption?

In 2000, adopted children accounted for 2.5 percent of the U.S. child population. The vast majority of these (87 percent) represented *domestic adoptions*, or adoptions within the United States, whereas the remaining 13 percent were *international adoptions*. Adoptions occur for many reasons, under many circumstances, and at many points in adopted children's lives. Although nearly half of international adoptees are infants, in 1998 only 2 percent of children adopted domestically through the U.S. foster care system were infants.

4. How does gay and lesbian family structure work as a context for child development?

Research on the possible effects of *gay and lesbian family structure* provides no evidence that growing up with lesbian or gay parents has negative effects on children's development, or any consistent effects that differentiate such children from those in other family arrangements. This conclusion holds across a range of outcomes, including self-esteem, intelligence, family relations, and peer relations. It holds as well for the most frequently examined outcomes: gender role development and sexual identity. Children of lesbian or gay parents are not more or less strongly sex-typed than children of heterosexual parents. As adolescents and young adults they appear no more likely to adopt a same-sex sexual orientation than young adults in general. Although factors such as poverty, lack of social support, and family conflict have a negative impact on child development, the evidence so far suggests that family structure per se does not.

Glossary

A-not-B error Infants' tendency to search in the original location in which an object was found rather than in its most recent hiding place. A characteristic of stage 4 of object permanence.

Academic competence, or academic self-concept The part of self-esteem involving children's perceptions of their academic abilities.

Accommodation In Piaget's theory of cognitive development, adaptation through changing existing cognitive structures to fit with new experiences; that is, changing our cognitive structures—what we understand—to fit in with environmental realities.

Acculturation The process through which different cultural groups change and adapt to one another.

Adult Attachment Interview An instrument used to assess an adult's mental representations of attachment relationships, particularly those with his or her parents during childhood.

Age of viability The age (presently around 23 or 24 weeks) at which the infant has a chance to survive if born prematurely.

Aggression Behavior that is intended to cause harm to persons or property and that is not socially justifiable.

Alleles Genes for the same trait located in the same place on a pair of chromosomes.

Amniocentesis A procedure for collecting cells that lie in the amniotic fluid surrounding the fetus. A needle is passed through the mother's abdominal wall into the amniotic sac to gather discarded fetal cells. These cells can be examined for chromosomal and genetic defects.

Amniotic sac A fluid-containing watertight membrane that surrounds and protects the embryo and fetus.

Analogical reasoning A form of problem solving in which the solution is achieved through recognition of the similarity between the new problem and some already understood problem.

Androgen insensitivity A genetic defect in males that prevents the body cells from responding to androgens, the masculinizing hormones.

Anorexia nervosa A severe eating disorder, usually involving excessive weight loss through self-starvation, most often found in teenage girls.

Anoxia A deficit of oxygen to the cells, which can produce brain or other tissue damage.

Apgar exam An exam administered immediately after birth that assesses the newborn's vital functions, such as heart rate and respiration.

Appearance-Reality Distinction The realization that objects may not appear as they really are, as a sign that a child possesses a theory of mind.

Artificial neural networks Multiple interconnected processing units arranged in layers in a computer, just as the brain consists of multiple interconnected neurons.

Assimilation In Piaget's theory of cognitive development, adaptation through interpreting new experiences in terms of existing cognitive structures; that is, the fitting in or interpretation of new experiences in terms of what we already understand.

Assisted discovery An educational approach based on Vygotsky's idea that children learn through interactions between teachers and students as well as between students.

Assisted reproductive technologies (ART) Techniques, such as *in vitro* fertilization or donor insemination, intended to help couples or individuals achieve a pregnancy through means other than sexual intercourse.

Attachment The enduring emotional bond that arises between infants and their parents or other primary caregivers.

Attention The selection of particular sensory input for perceptual and cognitive processing and the exclusion of competing input.

Attention-Deficit Hyperactivity Disorder (ADHD) A developmental disorder characterized by difficulty in sustaining attention, hyperactivity, and impulsive and uncontrolled behavior.

Attributions The perceived causes of outcomes.

Authoritarian parenting In Baumrind's model, a style of parenting characterized by firm control in the context of a cold and demanding relationship.

Authoritative parenting In Baumrind's model, a style of parenting characterized by firm control in the context of a warm and supportive relationship.

Autobiographical memory Specific, personal, long-lasting memory regarding the self.

Automatization An increase in the efficiency with which cognitive operations are executed as a result of practice. A mechanism of change in information processing theories.

Autosomes The 22 pairs of human chromosomes, other than the sex chromosomes.

Average age The average age for attaining a motor milestone is the age at which 50% of babies in a population have mastered that skill.

Axon A long fiber extending from the cell body in a neuron; conducts activity from the cell.

Babbling The first vocalizing that sounds like human speech.

Behavior genetics The field of study that explores the role of genes in producing individual differences in behavior and development.

Behavioral and social-learning approaches Perspectives on development that give greatest importance to environmental influences and learning experiences as sources of development.

Biologically primary abilities Abilities that have been shaped by natural selection and evolved to deal with problems faced by our ancestors, and are therefore universal.

Biologically secondary abilities Highly specialized neurocognitive systems that build on the primary abilities.

Blended family A new family unit, resulting from remarriage, which consists of parents and children from previously separate families.

Body Mass Index (BMI) A person's weight divided by height.

Brain stem The lower part of the brain, closest to the spinal cord; includes the cerebellum, which is important for maintaining balance and coordination.

Brazelton Neonatal Behavioral Assessment Scale The most comprehensive of newborn assessment instruments; assesses attention and social responsiveness, muscle tone and physical movement, control of alertness, and physiological response to stress.

Bulimia Nervosa A disorder of food binging and sometimes purging by self-induced vomiting, typically observed in teenage girls.

Case study A research method that involves only a single individual, often with a focus on a clinical issue.

Catch-up growth Accelerated growth that follows a period of delayed or stunting growth resulting from disease or malnutrition. The pace of growth during childhood and adolescence is influenced by both nature and nurture factors.

Categorical self One of two parts of the self proposed by William James, the "Me" self is an objective entity seen and evaluated in the world.

Categorical speech perception The ability to detect differences in speech sounds that correspond to differences in meaning; the ability to discriminate phonemic boundaries.

Catharsis The psychoanalytic belief that the likelihood of aggression can be reduced by viewing aggression or by engaging in high-energy behavior.

Centration Piaget's term for the young child's tendency to focus on only one aspect of a problem at a time, a perceptually biased form of responding that often results in incorrect judgments.

Cephalocaudal Literally, head to tail. This principle of development refers to the tendency of body parts to mature in a head-to-foot progression.

Cerebral cortex The thin sheet of gray matter that covers the brain.

Cerebrum The highest brain center; includes both hemispheres of the brain and the interconnections between them.

Certified Nurse-Midwife A health care provider who has been trained in both nursing and midwifery, and who provides a full range of gynecological and obstetric primary care services to women.

Cesarean section Surgical delivery of the fetus directly from the uterus; performed when normal delivery is prohibited.

Child-directed speech Simplified use of language forms and content for child listeners, also known as motherese.

Chorionic villus sampling (CVS) A procedure for gathering fetal cells earlier in pregnancy than is possible through amniocentesis. A tube is passed through the vagina and cervix so that fetal cells can be gathered at the site of the developing placenta.

Chromosomes Chemical strands in the cell nucleus that contain the genes. The nucleus of each human cell has 46 chromosomes, with the exception of the gametes, which have 23.

Chronological age Age as measured in years.

Chronosystem Bronfenbrenner's term for historical contexts and the passage of time as a context for studying human development.

Class inclusion The knowledge that a subclass cannot be larger than the superordinate class that includes it. In Piaget's theory of cognitive development, a concrete operational achievement.

Classical conditioning A pattern of learned response involving reflexes, in which a neutral stimulus acquires the power to elicit the same response as an unconditioned stimulus through association or pairing. The neutral stimulus becomes conditioned. Through this process an organism learns to respond to conditioned stimuli in the same way that it responds to unconditioned stimuli.

Cliques A kind of group typical in adolescence, consisting usually of 5 to 10 members whose shared interests and behavior patterns set them apart from their peers.

Coercive family process Gerald Patterson's term for the method by which some families control one another through aggression and other coercive means.

Cognition Higher-order mental processes, such as reasoning and problem solving, through which humans attempt to understand the world.

Cognitive development Changes in the ways that children think about and make sense of the world and solve problems.

Cognitive training Interventions designed to change the way people think about themselves, others, situations, and options.

Cohort effect A problem sometimes found in cross-sectional research in which people of a given age are affected by factors unique to their generation.

Collective monologue Piaget's term for young children's tendency to use egocentric speech with each other during play, resulting in noncommunication.

Committed compliance Compliant behavior that results from a child's internalizing the instruction of an adult; results in positive emotion.

Compensatory education Programs, such as Head Start, designed to compensate, or make up for, a disadvantage in preparation for school that children from low-income families are expected to have.

Competence view of the self Self-evaluation that includes both what one would like to achieve and one's confidence in being able to achieve it.

Compliance The child's ability to go along with requests or adopt the standards of behavior espoused by caregivers.

Computer simulation Programming a computer to perform a cognitive task in the same way in which humans are thought to perform it. An information processing method for testing theories of underlying process.

Conception The combining of the genetic material from a male gamete (sperm) and a female gamete (ovum); fertilization.

Congenital adrenal hyperplasia (CAH) A recessive genetic disorder in which the adrenal glands produce unusually high levels of male hormones known as androgens.

Congenitally organized behaviors Early behaviors of newborns that do not require specific external stimulation and that show more adaptability than simple reflexes.

Connectionism Information processing approach using computer simulations that approximate the structure of neural connections within the human brain, enabling programs to solve cognitive tasks and modify their solutions in response to experience.

Conscience Internal standards of conduct that are used to control one's behavior and typically produce discomfort when they are violated.

Conservation The knowledge that the quantitative properties of an object or collection of objects are not changed by a change in appearance. In Piaget's theory of cognitive development, a concrete operational achievement.

Constructive memory The ways that individuals interpret the information they take in in terms of their preexisting knowledge, which affects what they remember.

Constructivism The idea that children actively construct their knowledge of the world.

Continuity versus discontinuity A scientific controversy about the process of development as constant and connected (continuous) or uneven and disconnected (discontinuous).

Controversial child A child who receives both many positive and many negative nominations in sociometric assessments by peers.

Conventional level Kohlberg's third and fourth stages of moral development. Moral reasoning is based on the view that a social system must be based on laws and regulations.

Convergent thinking Right-answer-oriented thinking about problems for which there is a single, definite solution.

Core knowledge Domain-specific knowledge of the physical and social environment that appears to be inborn and has adaptive value in the evolution of a species.

Correlation The relation between two variables, described in terms of direction and strength.

Cosleeping A practice in which babies and young children sleep in the same bed or room with one or both parents.

Creativity The ability to generate novel outcomes that are valued in some context.

Cross-cultural studies Research designed to determine the influence of culture on some aspect of development and in which culture typically serves as an independent variable.

Crossing over The exchange of genetic material between pairs of chromosomes during meiosis.

Cross-sectional design A research method in which people of different ages are studied simultaneously to examine the effects of age on some aspect of behavior.

Cross-sequential design A research method combining longitudinal and cross-sectional designs.

Crowds Large, loosely organized groups that serve to structure social identity in high school.

Crystallized intelligence According to Cattell, the abilities we acquire from experience, including general information and social norms.

Cultural compatibility hypothesis Classroom instruction will be most effective when it matches patterns of learning that are familiar in the child's culture.

Cultural construction approach Explanations of children's moral behavior as cultural constructions based on experience as a member of a society.

Cultural/historical development Development that occurs over decades and centuries and leaves a legacy of tools and artifacts, value systems, institutions, and practices.

Cultural psychology Study of a single culture from the perspective of members of that culture, the goal being to identify the values and practices important to the culture.

Culture The accumulated knowledge of a people encoded in their language and embodied in the physical artifacts, beliefs, values, customs, institutions, and activities passed down from one generation to the next.

Decentering Piaget's term for the gradual decline in egocentrism that occurs across development.

Decentration The ability to keep in mind multiple aspects of a situation simultaneously.

Defensive reflex A natural reaction to novel stimuli that tends to protect the organism from further stimulation and that may include orientation of the stimulus receptors away from the stimulus source and a variety of physiological changes.

Deferred imitation Imitation of a model observed some time in the past.

Delay-of-gratification technique An experimental procedure for studying children's ability to postpone a smaller, immediate reward in order to obtain a larger, delayed one.

Dendrite One of a net of short fibers extending out from the cell body in a neuron; receives activity from nearby cells and conducts that activity to the cell body.

Dependent variable The variable that is predicted to be affected by an experimental manipulation. In psychology, usually some aspect of behavior.

Descriptive research Research based solely on observations, with no attempt to determine systematic relations among the variables.

Developmental niche Three interconnected dimensions of culture that shape children's lives, thus affecting physical, cognitive, linguistic, social, and emotional development in childhood.

Developmental psychology The branch of psychology devoted to the study of changes in behavior and abilities over the course of development.

Dialogic reading Technique of shared reading whereby the adult asks challenging, open-ended questions rather than questions that require a simple yes or no answer; adult encourages the child to relate the story content to his or her experiences.

Discovery learning An educational approach based on Piaget's idea that children learn by acting on the world individually, not by passively taking in information.

Displaced aggression Retaliatory aggression directed at a person or an object other than the one against whom retaliation is desired.

Divergent thinking The ability to generate multiple, original, possible solutions for tasks that do not have a single right answer.

DNA (deoxyribonucleic acid) A stair-like, double-helix molecule that carries genetic information on chromosomes.

Dominance hierarchy A structured social group in which members higher on the dominance ladder control those who are lower, initially through aggression and conflict, but eventually simply through threats.

Dominant gene A relatively powerful allele whose characteristics are expressed in the phenotype regardless of the allele with which it is paired.

Doula A woman who has been trained to provide a woman with continuous one-on-one support during childbirth, primarily in the form of nonmedical physical and emotional care.

Dual representation The realization that an object can be represented in two ways simultaneously.

Dynamic systems approach Thelen's model of the development of motor skills, in which infants who are motivated to accomplish a task create a new motor behavior from their available physical abilities.

Echolalia The automatic repetition of sounds, syllables, or words.

Ecological systems model Brofenbrenner's model of development, which focuses on individuals and their relationships and interactions within their environmental contexts.

Egocentric speech In Piaget's theory, the tendency for preoperational children to assume that listeners know everything that they know, revealing difficulty with perspective taking.

Egocentrism In Piaget's theory of cognitive development, a self-centered view of the world in which preoperational children have only a limited ability to represent the psychological experiences of others.

Electroencephalograph (EEG) An instrument that measures brain activity by sensing minute electrical changes at the top of the skull.

Embryo The developing organism from the third week, when implantation is complete, through the eighth week after conception.

Emergent literacy Set of prereading skills that often precede actual reading including concepts about print, phonological awareness, and alphabet knowledge.

Emotion Reactions, including feelings, thoughts, and behaviors, that arise in response to personally significant events or situations.

Emotional display rules The expectations and attitudes a society holds toward the expression of certain emotions.

Empathy The ability to vicariously experience another's emotional state or condition.

Encoding Attending to and forming internal representations of certain features of the environment; a mechanism of change in information processing theories.

Entity model The belief that a person's intelligence is fixed and unchangeable.

Equilibration In Piaget's theory, the process of self-regulation in which individuals naturally seek to maintain or restore balance within their cognitive system.

Ethnic identity Sense of lasting ethnic group membership and the attitudes and feelings associated with that membership is central to the process of identity development.

Ethnographic methods Methods of study employed in cultural psychology, in which the researcher lives as a member of a culture and gathers information about the culture through various techniques (e.g., observations, interviews) over an extended period of time.

Ethology The study of animal behavior in its natural environment from an evolutionary perspective.

Event memory Recall of things that have happened in experience.

Evolutionary and biological approaches Viewing development principally as a product of evolutionary adaptation and biological processes.

Evolutionary developmental psychology A theoretical approach that emphasizes the evolutionary origins of human thought patterns, emotions, and cognitive abilities.

Existential self One of two parts of the self proposed by William James; the "I" self is the subjective experiencer of the world.

Exosystem Social systems that can affect children but in which they do not participate directly; the third layer of context in the ecological systems model.

Experience-dependent processes The creation of new synaptic connections through exposure to experiences specific to the individual.

Experience-expectant processes The preservation of important synaptic connections early in development through exposure to experiences in the expectable environment.

Expertise Organized factual knowledge regarding some content domain.

Expressive style Style of early language learning in which children place more emphasis on language as a tool for talking about feelings and needs; vocabularies tend to be richer in social formulas and pronouns.

Extended family A family unit that consists not only of parents and children but also of at least one and sometimes several other adult relatives.

Extrinsic motivation External motivation; doing something to obtain some external reward.

False belief The realization that people may hold beliefs that are not true, as a sign that a child possesses a theory of mind.

False self behavior Behaving in a way that is knowingly different from how one's true self would behave.

Family systems A theoretical perspective that views the family as a complex set of interacting relationships, all of which are influenced by larger social and cultural factors, as well as by the individual characteristics and behaviors of each family member.

Fetal alcohol syndrome (FAS) A set of features in the infant and child caused by the mother's use of alcohol during pregnancy; typically includes facial malformations and other physical and mental disabilities.

Fetal distress A condition of abnormal stress in the fetus, reflected during the birth process in an abnormal fetal heart rate.

Fetus The developing organism from the 9th week to the 38th week after conception.

Fluid intelligence According to Cattell, an intelligence that is assumed to reflect a more innate or biologically influenced, intelligence such as processing speed.

Flynn Effect Observation that performance on IQ tests improves steadily over time, resulting in a need for revision and renorming.

Forbidden-toy technique An experimental procedure for studying children's resistance to temptation in which the child is left alone with an attractive toy and instructed not to play with it.

Fraternal (dizygotic) twins Twins who develop from separately fertilized ova and who thus are no more genetically similar than are other siblings.

Friendship An enduring relationship between two individuals, characterized by loyalty, intimacy, and mutual affection.

Functional imaging techniques Methods (such as PET, fMRI, and ERP) of measuring brain activity associated with behavior.

Gender bias Preferring or responding to children of one gender more positively or more often than the other.

Gender consistency The recognition that an individual's gender remains the same despite changes in dress, hairstyle, activities, or personality.

Gender constancy The belief that one's own gender is fixed and irreversible.

Gender identity One's perception of oneself as male or female.

Gender role A pattern or set of behaviors considered appropriate for males or females within a particular culture.

Gender schemas Cognitive representations of the characteristics associated with being either male or female.

Gender segregation The physical separation of children into same-sex groups.

Gender stability The awareness that all boys grow up to be men and all girls become women.

Gender stereotypes Widely held beliefs in a culture regarding how males and females should behave.

Gender typing The process by which children develop the behaviors and attitudes considered appropriate for their gender.

Gene A segment of DNA on the chromosome that codes for the production of proteins. The basic unit of inheritance.

Gene–environment correlation Situation in which genes and environment affect development similarly because the genes the child receives from the parents are compatible with the environment the parents provide (passive); because the child evokes environmental effects consistent with genetic predispositions (evocative); or because children seek out experiences and shape their environments that suit them (active).

General intelligence (g) According to Spearman, the one common factor that underlies all intelligent behavior.

Genetic counseling The practice of advising prospective parents about genetic diseases and the likelihood that they might pass on defective genetic traits to their offspring.

Genotype The arrangement of genes underlying a trait.

Gestation The length of time from conception to birth, typically calculated from the date of a woman's last menstrual period.

Giftedness Exceptional performance in some domain, characterized by precocity, qualitatively different learning, and strong motivation for mastery.

Glial cells Cells of the brain that support and nourish neurons (the other kind of brain cell) and form the myelin sheath around axons.

Goodness of fit The extent to which a baby's temperament fits with the behavioral expectations of parents and other adults in the environment.

Grammar System of rules that determines the structure of language, including morphology and syntax.

Group A collection of individuals who interact regularly in a consistent, structured fashion and who share values and a sense of belonging to the group.

Guided participation The process by which young children become competent by participating in everyday, purposeful activities under the guidance of more experienced partners.

Habituation A type of learning in which a behavioral response decreases or disappears as a result of repeated exposure to a stimulus.

Habituation–dishabituation A method commonly used by researchers to study infants' early perceptual abilities that relies on babies' natural responses to changes in stimulation.

Haptic perception The perceptual experience that results from active exploration of objects by touch.

Health A state of complete physical, mental, and social well-being and not merely the absence of disease or infirmity.

Helpless orientation Tendency to attribute failures to personal inadequacies, often a lack of ability.

Hemispheric specialization The tendency of the right and left sides of the brain to specialize with regard to different functions skills.

Heritability Proportion of variance in a trait that can be attributed to genetic variance in the sample being studied.

Higher mental functions Complex mental processes that are intentional, self-regulated, and mediated by language and other sign systems.

Holophrase A single word used to express a larger idea; common during second year of life.

Hostile aggression Aggression whose purpose is to cause pain or injury.

Hypothesis A predicted relation between a phenomenon and a factor assumed to affect it that is not yet supported by a great deal of evidence. Hypotheses are tested in experimental investigations.

Hypothetical-deductive reasoning A form of problem solving characterized by the ability to generate and test hypotheses and draw logical conclusions from the results of the tests. In Piaget's theory, a formal operational achievement.

Identical (monozygotic twins) Twins who develop from a single fertilized ovum and thus inherit identical genetic material.

Identification The Freudian process through which the child adopts the characteristics of the same-sex parent during the phallic stage.

Identity A well-organized conception of the self made up of values, beliefs, and goals to which the individual is committed; in Erikson's theory, the component of personality that develops across the eight stages of life and that motivates progress through the stages.

Identity achievement Term for state when the adolescent has experienced a crisis and has then made a commitment.

Identity crisis Period of identity development during which the adolescent is selecting from among meaningful alternatives.

Identity diffusion Term for state adolescents are in when they have not yet experienced a crisis or made any commitments.

Identity foreclosure Term for state when the adolescent has made a commitment without experiencing a crisis; typically, the adolescent has been handed down commitments.

Identity moratorium Term for state when adolescents are in the middle of a crisis, but their commitments are only vaguely defined or missing altogether.

Incremental model The belief that a person's intelligence can grow through experience and learning.

Independent variable The variable in an experiment that is systematically manipulated.

Infant mortality rate The number of deaths in the first year of life per 1,000 live births.

Infantile amnesia The inability to remember experiences from the first two or three years of life.

Infertility Difficulty in achieving a pregnancy, defined in medicine as failure to conceive after a year of sexual intercourse without the use of contraceptives.

Information processing model A way of viewing cognition, memory, and intelligence as neurophysiological processes or by analogy with the structures and functions of the computer.

Instrumental aggression Aggression whose purpose is to obtain something desired.

Intelligence quotient (IQ) Numerical representation of intelligence using the formula IQ = (mental age divided by chronological age) multiplied by 100; this measure describes a child's intellectual ability relative to his or her age.

Intentional behavior In Piaget's theory, behavior in which the goal exists prior to the action selected to achieve it; made possible by the ability to separate means and end.

Interactional synchrony The smooth coordination of behaviors between parent and baby.

Internal working model A person's internalized mental representations of significant relationships, usually formed as a result of repeated interactions over time with parents or other primary caretakers.

Internalization 1. In Vygotsky's theory, a term for the child's incorporation of culturally meaningful information, primarily through language and interactions with others in culturally meaningful settings. 2. In theories of moral development, the process by which individuals, especially children, accept a society's standards of behavior as their own.

Intersubjectivity A commitment to find common ground on which to build shared understanding.

Interview methods Collecting information through verbal reports gathered via interviews or questionnaires.

Intrinsic motivation Internal motivation to do something for its own sake.

Invariants Aspects of the world that remain the same even though other aspects have changed. In Piaget's theory, different forms of invariants are understood at different stages of development.

***In vitro* fertilization** An assisted reproductive technology in which a mature ovum is removed and fertilized by sperm in a laboratory dish.

Joint attention Use of directional gaze as a cue to identify and share the attentional focus of another.

Kin selection A proposed mechanism by which an individual's altruistic behavior toward kin increases the likelihood of the survival of genes similar to those of the individual.

Language acquisition device (LAD) Chomsky's proposed brain mechanism for analyzing speech input; the mechanism that allows young children to acquire quickly the language to which they are exposed.

Language acquisition support system (LASS) Bruner's proposed process by which parents assist children in learning language.

Language-making capacity (LMC) Slobin's proposed set of strategies or learning principles that underlie the acquisition of language.

Lateralization The specialization of functions in the right and left hemispheres of the brain.

Learning approach Explanation of language learning, which contends that language learning is based on experience and emphasizes Skinner's operant conditioning principles.

Lexical contrast theory Theory of semantic development holding that (1) children automatically assume that a new word has a meaning different from that of any other word they know and (2) children always choose word meanings that are generally accepted over more individualized meanings.

Locomotion The movement of a person through space, such as walking and crawling.

Longitudinal design A research method in which the same individuals are studied repeatedly over time.

Looking-glass self The conception of the self based on how one thinks others see him or her.

Macrosystem The culture and subcultures in which the child lives, the fourth layer of context in the ecological systems model.

Mainstreaming (inclusion) Practice of placing special needs students in regular classrooms for part of the school day.

Malnutrition A deficit of one or more essential nutrients needed by the body.

Mastery orientation Tendency to focus on the task rather than on ability and to believe that ability can be changed and improved.

Maturation The process of attaining physical maturity.

Meiosis The process by which germ cells produce four gametes (sperm or ova), each with half the number of chromosomes of the parent cell.

Memory In information processing theory, the process by which information is taken in, stored, and retrieved.

Menarche Onset of menstruation among girls.

Mental representation The use of symbols to picture and act on the world internally.

Mesosystem The interrelationships among the child's microsystems, the second layer of context in the ecological systems model.

Meta-analysis A method of reviewing the research literature on a given topic that uses statistical procedures to establish the existence and the size of effects.

Metamemory Knowledge about memory.

Microanalysis A research technique for studying parent-infant interactions, in which the parent and baby are simultaneously videotaped with different cameras and then the tapes are examined side by side.

Microgenetic development Moment-to-moment learning of individuals as they work on specific problems.

Microgenetic method A research method in which a small number of individuals are observed repeatedly in order to study an expected change in a developmental process.

Microsystem The environmental system closest to the child, such as the family or school, the first layer of context in the ecological systems model.

Midbrain A part of the brain that lies above the brain stem; serves as a relay station and as a control area for breathing and swallowing and houses part of the auditory and visual systems.

Mitosis The process by which body cells reproduce, resulting in two identical cells.

Mnemonic strategies Techniques (such as rehearsal or organization) that people use in an attempt to remember something.

Modeling Changes in behavior as a result of observing the behavior of a model, usually through imitation.

Moral dilemmas Stories used by Piaget and others to assess children's levels of moral reasoning.

Moral domain In Turiel's model, the cognitive domain in which individuals make decisions about right and wrong.

Moral realism Piaget's second stage of moral development, in which children's reasoning is based on objective and physical aspects of a situation and is often inflexible.

Moral relativism Piaget's third stage of moral development, in which children view rules as agreements that can be altered and consider people's motives or intentions when evaluating their moral conduct.

Motivation Mental processes that energize, direct, and sustain behavior.

Multiple intelligences According to Gardner, eight unique, distinctive intelligences that explain problem solving, creation of new products, and discovery of new knowledge in eight distinct areas of culturally valued activities.

Mutations Sudden and permanent changes in genetic material.

Myelin A sheath of fatty material that surrounds and insulates the axon, resulting in speedier transmission of neural activity.

Nativist approach Explanation of language development, proposed by Chomsky, that emphasizes innate mechanisms separate from cognitive processes.

Naturalistic observation Systematic observation of behavior in natural settings.

Nature versus nurture A scientific controversy about the main causes of developmental change as biological and genetic (nature) or environmental and experiential (nurture).

Negative correlation A correlation in which two variables change in opposite directions.

Neglected child A child who receives few nominations of any sort, positive or negative, in sociometric assessments by peers. Such children seem to be ignored by the peer group.

Neuron A nerve cell, consisting of a cell body, axon, and dendrites. Neurons transmit activity from one part of the nervous system to another.

Neurotransmitter A chemical that transmits electrical activity from one neuron across the synapse to another neuron.

New York Longitudinal Study (NYLS) A well-known longitudinal study conducted by Thomas and Chess that examines infant temperament and its implications for later psychological adjustment.

Nonshared environment A concept used in behavior genetics to refer to aspects of the environment that children experience differently, leading to individual differences.

Normative versus idiographic development A research choice between identifying commonalities in typical human development (normative) or the causes of individual differences (idiographic).

Obesity A condition of excess fat storage; often defined as body mass index above the 95th percentile.

Object permanence The knowledge that objects have a permanent existence that is independent of our perceptual contact with them. In Piaget's theory, a major achievement of the sensorimotor period.

Objectivity A characteristic of scientific research; it requires that the procedures and subject matter of investigations should be formulated so that they could, in principle, be agreed on by everyone.

Observational learning A pattern of learning based on vicarious reinforcement in which an observer's behavior changes as a result of observing and imitating a model.

Ontogenetic development Development across years of an individual's life, such as childhood.

Operant conditioning A pattern of learned response involving voluntary behavior, in which the consequences of the behavior (reinforcement or punishment) strongly influence whether the organism will repeat the behavior.

Operating space In Case's theory, the resources necessary to carry out cognitive operations.

Operations Piaget's term for the various forms of mental action through which older children solve problems and reason logically.

Orienting reflex A natural reaction to novel stimuli that enhances stimulus processing and includes orientation of the eyes and ears to optimize stimulus reception, inhibition of ongoing activity, and a variety of physiological changes.

Overextensions Early language error in which children use labels they already know for things whose names they do not yet know.

Overregularization An early structural language error in which children apply inflectional rules to irregular forms (e.g., adding -ed to say).

Parallel play When two or more young children play next to each other, using the same sorts of materials and perhaps even talking now and then, yet without any genuine interaction.

Parental control A dimension of parenting that reflects the degree to which the child is monitored, disciplined, and regulated.

Parental warmth A dimension of parenting that reflects the amount of support, affection, and encouragement the parent provides to the child.

Parenting style The overall pattern of childrearing provided by a parent, typically defined by the combination of warmth and control that the parent demonstrates.

Peacemaking A friendly postconflict reunion between former opponents often characterized by invitations to play, hugs, apologies, object sharing, and silliness.

Peer collaboration In Vygotsky's view, the cooperative learning that takes place when peers of roughly equal cognitive ability work together to solve a problem.

Peer learning In Piaget's view, the teaching and learning that takes place between peers with lesser and greater knowledge or experience (novice and expert).

Peer-mediated intervention Form of intervention for children with sociometric problems in which responses of the peer group are utilized to elicit more effective social behaviors from the target children.

Perception The interpretation of sensory stimulation based on experience.

Performance orientation Tendency to focus on the outcome of the activity rather than the process of improving skill or learning.

Permissive parenting In Baumrind's model, a style of parenting characterized by low levels of control in the context of a warm and supportive relationship.

Person perception Mental processes we use to form judgments and draw conclusions about the characteristics and motives of others.

Personal agency The understanding that one can be the cause of events.

Phenotype The characteristic of a trait that is expressed or observable. The phenotype results from an interaction of genotype and environment.

Phoneme The smallest linguistic unit of sound that can signal a difference in meaning.

Phonics (or codes oriental) An approach to learning to read that teaches children to analyze words into their constituent sounds.

Phonological awareness Awareness of and ability to manipulate the sound structure of oral language.

Phonology Study of speech sounds that examines the rules governing the structure and sequence of speech sounds.

Phylogenetic development Development of the species.

Physical aggression Aggression expressed through hitting, kicking, biting, and other physical means.

Pincer grasp Grasping an object between the thumb or forefinger.

Placenta An organ that forms where the embryo attaches to the uterus. This organ exchanges nutrients, oxygen, and wastes between the embryo or fetus and the mother through a very thin membrane that does not allow the passage of blood.

Plasticity The capacity of the brain to be affected by experience as it develops.

Polygenic inheritance The case in which a trait is determined by a number of genes.

Popular-prosocial children These children are high in social competence and generally also do well academically. They are well-liked by other children for their abilities to solve conflicts peacefully and to interact with their peers in cooperative yet assertive ways.

Positive correlation A correlation in which two variables change in the same direction.

Possible selves Future-oriented components of the self that represent a person's goals and embody dreams, hopes, and fears.

Postconventional level Kohlberg's final stages of moral development. Moral reasoning is based on the assumption that the value, dignity, and rights of each individual person must be maintained.

Postural development The increasing ability of the baby to control parts of his or her body, especially the head and trunk.

Pragmatics Sets of rules related to language use within the communicative or social context.

Preconventional level Kohlberg's first two stages of moral development. Moral reasoning is based on the assumption that individuals must serve their own needs.

Preference method A research method for the study of visual ability in infancy. Two visual stimuli are presented simultaneously, and the amount of time the infant looks at each is measured.

Prehension The ability to grasp and manipulate objects with the hands.

Prereaching Early direction of arm movements toward an object.

Pretend play Symbolic play other than object play, solitary or with others, with or without props, involving pretense or make-believe.

Preterm Describes babies born before 38 weeks gestation.

Primary sexual characteristics Pubertal changes to the reproductive organs.

Principle of mutual exclusivity Proposed principle of semantic development stating that children assume that an object can have only one name.

Private speech In Vygotsky's theory, children's self-talk, speech that they produce and direct toward themselves during problem solving.

Production deficiency The failure to generate memory strategies spontaneously, even though the child is capable of executing and benefiting from a strategy.

Prosocial behavior The aspect of moral conduct that includes socially desirable behaviors, such as sharing, helping, and cooperating; often used interchangeably with altruism by modern researchers.

Protein (PEM) Type of malnutrition that results from a diet that is chronically insufficient in protein and energy.

Proximodistal Literally, near to far. This principle of development refers to the tendency of body parts to develop in a trunk-to-extremities direction.

Psychometrics Conceptualization of intelligence that seeks to identify the trait or set of traits that characterize some people to a greater extent than others so that differences among individuals can be described.

Psychosexual development Freud's theory that people progress through stages of personality development based on the strength and location of sexual pleasure (libido) in the body (oral, anal, phallic, latent, genital).

Psychosocial development Erikson's theory that people progress through stages of personality development based on their resolution of conflicts between potentially positive or negative outcomes of behavioral changes.

Puberty The period in which chemical and physical changes in the body occur that enable sexual reproduction.

Punishment Any consequence that decreases the occurrence of a behavior. Punishment may be positive (something unpleasant happens) or negative (something pleasant is removed).

Qualitative identity The knowledge that the qualitative nature of something is not changed by a change in its appearance. In Piaget's theory, a preoperational achievement.

Quasi-experiment Comparison of groups differing on some important characteristic.

Rapid eye movement (REM) sleep A stage of light sleep, characterized by rapid moving of the eyes behind the closed eyelids, in which dreaming occurs.

Reaction range The term for the range of ability or skill that genes set. The value achieved within this range is determined by the environment.

Recall memory The retrieval of some past stimulus or event that is not perceptually present.

Recessive gene A relatively weak allele whose characteristics are expressed in the phenotype only when it is paired with another recessive gene.

Reciprocal altruism A proposed mechanism by which an individual's altruistic behavior toward members of the social group may promote the survival of the individual's genes through reciprocation by others or may ensure the survival of similar genes.

Recognition memory The realization that some perceptually present stimulus or event has been encountered before.

Referential style Style of early language learning in which children place more emphasis on language as a tool for labeling things; vocabularies tend to be richer in words that refer to objects.

Reinforcement Any consequence that increases the occurrence of a behavior. Reinforcement may be positive (something pleasant happens) or negative (something unpleasant stops happening).

Rejected children Children who receive few positive and many negative nominations in sociometric assessments by peers. Such children seem to be disliked by the peer group.

Rejected-aggressive children These children score high in aggression. They often show antisocial behavior that is inappropriate to the situation at hand and disruptive of ongoing group activities.

Rejected-withdrawn children These children often find social interactions to be very anxiety-provoking. Their attempts to enter new groups or to make new friends tend to be clumsy and often end in rebuff. They are at risk for abuse by bullies.

Relational aggression Aggression designed to damage or disrupt social relationships.

Repression Freud's term for the process through which desires or motivations are driven into the unconscious, associated with the phallic stage of psychosexual development.

Resilience The capacity to resume a normal developmental path despite adversities.

Resilient children children who adapt positively in the face of significant adversity.

Reversibility Piaget's term for the power of operations to correct for potential disturbances and thus arrive at correct solutions to problems.

Rule-based strategies Set procedures for acting on the environment and solving problems.

Scaffolding A method of teaching in which the adult adjusts the level of help provided in relation to the child's level of performance, the goal being to encourage independent performance.

Scatter plot A graphic illustration of a correlation between two variables.

Scientific method The system of rules used by scientists to conduct and evaluate their research.

Script A representation of the typical sequence of actions and events in some familiar context.

Secondary sexual characteristics Other pubertal bodily changes, such as breast development in girls, voice change in boys, and the development of pubic hair in both sexes.

Secular trend Changes over time in physical growth, such as adult height and age of menarche.

Selective attention Concentration on a stimulus or event with attendant disregard for other stimuli or events.

Self-conscious emotions The complex emotional responses (such as pride, guilt, and embarrassment) that typically arise in situations that involve injury or enhancement of one's sense of self.

Self-consciousness A concern about the opinions others hold about one.

Self-efficacy According to Bandura, an individual's beliefs about his or her performance capabilities in a particular domain.

Self-esteem, or self-worth A person's evaluation of the self and the affective reactions to that evaluation.

Self-evaluation The part of the self-system concerned with children's opinions of themselves and their abilities.

Self-fulfilling prophecy In cases where a person adopts the views of another and either lives up to or down to those expectations.

Self-knowledge, or self-awareness The part of the self-system concerned with children's knowledge about themselves.

Self-regulation The part of the self-system concerned with self-control.

Self-schema An internal notion of "who I am," composed of the various features and characteristics about the self.

Self-system Harter's conceptualization of the self that includes three distinct, interrelated units: self-knowledge, self-evaluation, and self-regulation.

Semantic bootstrapping Proposed mechanism of grammatical development in which children use semantic cues to infer aspects of grammar.

Semantics System of rules that determines how underlying concepts are expressed in words or word combinations.

Sensation The experience resulting from the stimulation of a sense organ.

Sensitive caretaking Care that is sensitive to an infant's needs, promptly responsive, and effective at meeting those needs.

Sensitive period A period of development during which certain behaviors are more easily or quickly learned.

Sensorimotor schemes Skilled and generalizable action patterns by which infants act on and understand the world. In Piaget's theory, the cognitive structures of infancy.

Seriation The ability to order stimuli along some quantitative dimension, such as length. In Piaget's theory, a concrete operational achievement.

Sex chromosomes The pair of human chromosomes that determines one's sex. Females have two X chromosomes; males have an X and a Y.

Sex differentiation The biological process through which physical differences between sexes emerge.

Sex-limited traits Genes that affect males and females differently but that are not carried on the sex chromosomes.

Sexual orientation A person's sexual preference. Heterosexuals are attracted to members of the opposite sex, and homosexuals are attracted to members of the same sex.

Short-term storage space In Case's theory, the resources necessary to store results from previous cognitive operations while carrying out new ones.

Sibling rivalry Feelings of competition, resentment, and jealousy that can arise between siblings.

Situational compliance Obedience that results from a child's awareness of an adult's will in a particular situation and does not reflect enduring behavioral change.

Size constancy The experience that the physical size of an object remains the same even though the size of its projected image on the eye varies.

Skeletal maturity (bone age) The degree of maturation of an individual as indicated by the extent of hardening of the bones.

Small for gestational age (SGA) Describes babies born at a weight in the bottom 10% of babies of a particular gestational age.

Social capital The community and family resources available for the child to draw upon.

Social comparison Comparing one's abilities to those of others.

Social conventions Rules used by a society to govern everyday behavior and maintain order. In Turiel's model, the chief characteristic of the social domain versus the domain of personal choice.

Social-learning theory Any theory that adds observational learning to classical and operant learning as a process through which children's behavior changes.

Social network The network of individuals and other social contacts that a person relies on for social support.

Social problem-solving skills Cognitive skills needed to resolve social dilemmas.

Social referencing Use of information gained from other people to interpret ambiguous situations and to regulate one's own behavior; among infants, the tendency to look to the parents for guidance when uncertain how to respond to an unfamiliar object or person.

Social referential communication Form of communication in which a speaker sends a message that a listener comprehends.

Social smile The broad grin that infants show in response to a human voice or face, typically beginning by 10 to 12 weeks of age.

Social support Resources (both tangible and intangible) provided by other people in times of uncertainty or stress.

Socialization The process through which society molds a child's beliefs, expectations, and behavior.

Sociocognitive conflict Piaget's term for cognitive conflict that arises during social interaction, when one's way of thinking is challenged.

Sociocultural approach Theoretical perspective expressed by Vygotsky, emphasizing children's learning through interaction with others and problem solving within the context of society and culture.

Sociodramatic play In sociocultural approaches to development, pretend play in which participants enact social roles and themes.

Sociogenesis The process of acquiring knowledge or skills through social interactions.

Sociometric techniques Procedures for assessing children's social status based on evaluations by the peer group; may involve ratings of degree of liking, nominations of liked or disliked peers, or forced-choice judgments between pairs of peers.

Solitary pretense Form of symbolic play in which children pretend by themselves.

Specific intelligence (s) According to Spearman, the kinds of intelligence that are needed to be successful on one particular task or in a certain situation.

Speech acts Speech used to perform pragmatic functions, such as requesting or complaining.

Stage–environment fit Development proceeds most smoothly when the environmental opportunities and challenges during a particular time period match the capacities and needs of the developing child.

Stage theory Any theory in which qualitative change is said to occur across an invariant sequence of stages, leading to concurrences of behavior.

Stages of cognitive development Piaget's four stages or periods of development, based on the means by which children know the world, from sensorimotor and preoperational intelligence to operational intelligence and formal operations.

States of arousal The states of alertness that infants display, from deep sleep to alert activity and crying.

Stereotype threat Anxiety about one's test performance based on membership in a group that is stereotyped for poor performance.

Strange Situation A standardized laboratory procedure devised by Mary Ainsworth for assessing the quality of the parent-infant attachment relationship.

Stranger anxiety A general fear of unfamiliar people that appears in many infants at around 8 months of age.

Strategy construction The creation of strategies for processing and remembering information; a mechanism of change in information processing theories.

Strategy selection Progressively greater use of more effective strategies in place of less effective ones; a mechanism of change in information processing theories.

Structured observation Observation of behavior in settings that are controlled by the investigator.

Sudden Infant Death Syndrome (SIDS) The sudden and unexpected death of an apparently healthy infant under the age of 1.

Symbolic function The ability to use one thing (such as a mental image or word) as a symbol to represent something else.

Symbolic play Form of play in which the child uses one thing in deliberate pretense to stand for something else.

Sympathy Feeling of concern for another in reaction to the other's situation or emotional state, not necessarily involving an experience of the other's emotional state.

Synapses The small spaces between neurons, across which neural activity is communicated from one cell to another.

Syntactic bootstrapping Proposed mechanism of semantic development in which children use syntactic cues to infer the meanings of words.

Syntax Aspect of grammar that specifies the rules that determine word order in sentences.

Telegraphic speech Speech from which unnecessary function words (e.g., in, the, with) are omitted; common during early language learning.

Temperament The stable behavioral and emotional reactions that appear early and are influenced in part by genetic constitution.

Teratogen An agent that can cause abnormal development in the fetus.

Theory A broad set of statements describing the relation between a phenomenon and the factors assumed to affect it.

Theory of mind Thoughts and beliefs concerning the mental world.

Tracking (between-class ability grouping) Students are assigned to particular classrooms based on some measure of ability, often intelligence or some other measure of potential.

Transitivity The ability to combine relations logically to deduce necessary conclusions—for example, if AB and BC, then AC. In Piaget's theory, a concrete operational achievement.

Transsexualism The condition in which a person assumes the identity and permanently acts the part of the gender opposite to his or her biological sex.

Triarchic theory of intelligence According to Sternberg, intelligence is composed of three

overlapping aspects: (1) analytical intelligence, (2) creative intelligence, and (3) practical intelligence.

Ulnar grasp An early grasp using the whole palm.

Ultrasound imaging A noninvasive procedure for detecting physical defects in the fetus. A device that produces sound waves is moved over the pregnant woman's abdomen, and reflections of these waves form an image of the fetus.

Umbilical cord A soft cable of tissue and blood vessels that connects the fetus to the placenta.

Underextensions Early language error in which children fail to apply labels they know to things for which the labels are appropriate; also termed disengaged or neglectful parenting.

Uninvolved parenting In Baumrind's model, a style of parenting characterized by low levels of both control and warmth.

Universal interventions School-based programs for improving children's social competence and reducing aggression.

Universals of development Aspects of development or behavior that are common to children everywhere.

Utilization deficiency The failure of a recently developed mnemonic strategy to facilitate recall.

Variable Any factor that can take on different values along a dimension.

Verbal aggression Aggression expressed in name calling, teasing, and threats.

Vestibular sensitivity The perceptual experience that results from motion of the body and the pull of gravity.

Visual acuity The clarity with which visual images can be perceived.

Visual cliff A research method for the study of depth perception in infancy. The infant is placed on a glass-covered table near an apparent drop-off, and perception of depth is inferred if the infant avoids the drop.

Visual self-recognition The ability to recognize oneself; often studied in babies by having them look into mirrors.

Whole-language approach Assumes that reading instruction should focus on the leved of the whole word, not the letters or other parts.

Within-class ability grouping Students already in a particular classroom are divided into groups for instruction in certain subjects, such as reading or math.

X-linked disorders Disorders that travel on the X chromosome, leaving males more vulnerable to their expression.

Zone of proximal development The distance between what a child can accomplish independently and what the child can accomplish with the help of an adult or more capable peer.

Zygote A fertilized ovum.

References

Abbeduto, L., Davies, B., & Furman, L. (1988). The development of speech act comprehension in mentally retarded individuals and nonretarded children. *Child Development, 59*, 1460–1472.

Abel, E. L. (1980). Fetal alcohol syndrome: Behavioral teratology. *Psychological Bulletin, 87*, 29–50.

Abel, E. L. (1981). Behavioral teratology of alcohol. *Psychological Bulletin, 90*, 564–581.

Aboud, F. E., & Mendelson, M. J. (1996). Determinants of friendship selection and quality: Links to childmother attachment. In W. M. Bukowski, A. F. Newcomb, & W. W. Hartup (Eds.), *The company they keep: Friendship in childhood and adolescence*. New York: Cambridge University Press.

Abramovitch, R., Corter, C., & Pepler, D. J. (1980). Observation of mixed-sex sibling dyads. *Child Development, 51*, 217–229.

Abramovitch, R., Corter, C., Pepler, D. J., & Stanhope, L. (1986). Sibling and peer interaction: A final follow-up and a comparison. *Child Development, 57*, 217–229.

Abramovitch, R., Freedman, J. L., Thoden, K., & Nikolich, C. (1991). Children's capacity to consent to participation in psychological research: Empirical findings. *Child Development, 62*, 1100–1109.

Achenbach, T. M., Edelbrock, C., & Howell, C. T. (1987). Empirically based assessment of the behavioral/emotional problems of 2-and 3-year-old children. *Journal of Abnormal Child Psychology, 15*, 629–650.

Achinstein, B., & Athanases, S.Z. (2005). Focusing new teachers on diversity and equity: Toward a knowledge base for mentors. *Teaching & Teacher Education: An International Journal of Research & Studies, 21*, 843–862.

Achinstein, B., Ogawa, R. T., & Speiglman, A. (2004). Are we creating separate and unequal tracks of teachers? The effects of state policy, local conditions, and teacher characteristics on new teacher socialization. *American Educational Research Journal, 41*, 557–603.

Ackerman, B. P. (1993). Children's understanding of the speaker's meaning in referential communication. *Journal of Experimental Child Psychology, 55*, 56–86.

Ackerman, B. P., & Silver, S. (1990). Children's understanding of private keys in referential communication. *Journal of Experimental Child Psychology, 50*, 217–242.

Ackerman, B. P., Szymanski, J., & Silver, D. (1990). Children's use of common ground in interpreting ambiguous referential utterances. *Developmental Psychology, 26*, 234–245.

Acredelo, L. P., Goodwyn, S. W., Horobin, K. D., & Emmons, Y. D. (1999). The signs and sounds of early language development. In L. Balter & C. S. Tamis-LeMonda (Eds.), *Child psychology: A handbook of contemporary issues*. Philadelphia: Psychology Press.

Adair, L. (1999). Filipino children exhibit catch-up growth from age 2 to 12 years. *Journal of Nutrition, 129*, 1140–1148.

Adams, M. J. (1990). *Beginning to read: Thinking and learning about print*. Cambridge: Massachusetts Inst. of Tech.

Adams, R. J. (1989). Newborns' discrimination among mid- and long-wavelength stimuli. *Journal of Experimental Child Psychology, 47*, 130–141.

Adams, R. J. (1995). Further exploration of human neonatal chromatic-achromatic discrimination. *Journal of Experimental Child Psychology, 60*, 344–360.

Adams, R. J., & Courage, M. L. (1998). Human newborn color vision: Measurement with chromatic stimuli varying in excitation purity. *Journal of Experimental Child Psychology, 67*, 22–34.

Adamson, L. B. (1995). Communication development during infancy. Madison, WI: Brown & Benchmark.

Adamson, L. B., & Bakeman, R. (1991). The development of shared attention during infancy. In R. Vasta (Ed.), *Annals of child development* (Vol. 8). London: Kingsley.

Adamson, L. B., Foster, M. A., Roark, M. L., & Reed, D. B. (1998). Doing a science project: Gender differences during childhood. *Journal of Research in Science Teaching, 35*, 845–857.

Adey, P., & Shayer, M. (1990). Accelerating the development of formal thinking in middle and high school students. *Journal of Research in Science Teaching, 27*, 267–285.

Adler, P. A., & Adler, P. (1998). Peer power: Preadolescent culture and identity. New Brunswick, NJ: Rutgers University Press.

Adolph, K. E. (2000). Specificity of learning: Why infants fall over a veritable cliff. *Psychological Science, 11*, 290–295.

Ahmad, A. (1992). Symptoms of post-traumatic stress disorder among displaced Kurdish children in Iraq: Victims of man-made disaster after the Gulf war. *Nordic Journal of Psychiatry, 46*, 314–319.

Aimin, W., & Guiying, R. (2004). A comparative study of self-concept in Chinese and American children. *Chinese Mental Health Journal, 18*(5), 294–299.

Ainsworth, M. D. S. (1967). Infancy in Uganda: Infant care and the growth of love. Baltimore: Johns Hopkins University Press.

Ainsworth, M. D. S., Bell, S. M., & Stayton, D. J. (1972). Individual differences in the development of some attachment behaviors. *Merrill-Palmer Quarterly, 18*, 123–143.

Ainsworth, M. D. S., Blehar, M. C., Waters, E., & Wall, S. (1978). *Patterns of attachment: A psychological study of the Strange Situation*. Hillsdale, NJ: Erlbaum.

Akos, P. (2002). Student perceptions of the transition from elementary to middle school. *Professional School Counseling, 5*, 339–345.

Akos, P., and Galassi, J. P. (2004). Middle and high school transitions as viewed by students, parents, and teachers. *Professional School Counseling, 7*(4), 212–221.

Akson, N., & G. (2005). Conscience in childhood: Old questions, new answers. *Developmental Psychology, 41*, 506–516.

Alan Guttmacher Institute. (2004). U.S. teenage pregnancy statistics: overall trends, trends by race and ethnicity and state-by-state information. New York: Alan Guttmacher Institute. Retrieved March 17, 2006 from http://www.guttmacher.org/pubs/state_pregnancy_trends.pdf

Alden, L. (2001). Interpersonal perspectives on social phobia. In W. Ray Crozier & Lynne E. Alden (Eds.), *International Handbook of Social Anxiety* (pp. 381–404). New York: Wiley.

Alexander, D. (1998). *Prevention of mental retardation: Four decades of research. Mental Retardation and Development Disabilities Research Reviews, 4*, 50–58.

Alfieri, T., Ruble, D. N., & Higgins, E. T. (1996). Gender stereotypes during adolescence: Developmental changes and the transition to junior high school. *Developmental Psychology, 32*, 1129–1137.

Allan, K., & Coltrane, S. (1996). Gender display in television commercials: A comparative study of television commercials in the 1950s and 1980s. *Sex Roles, 35*, 185–203.

Allison, K. R., Dwyer, J. J. M., Goldenberg, E., Fein, A., Yoshida, K. K., Boutilier, M. (2005). Male adolescents` reasons for participating in physical activity, barriers to participation, and suggestions for increasing participation. *Adolescence, 40*(157), 155–170.

Allwood, M. A., Bell-Dolan, D., & Husain, S. A. (2002). Children's trauma and adjustment reactions to violent and nonviolent war experiences. *Journal of the American Academy of Child and Adolescent Psychiatry, 41*, 450–457.

Almli, C. R., Ball, R. H., & Wheeler, M. E. (2001). Human fetal and neonatal movement patterns: Gender differences and fetal-to-neonatal continuity. *Developmental Psychobiology, 38*, 252–273.

Als, H., Duffy, F. H., & McAnulty, G. B. (1988). Behavioral differences between preterm and full-term newborns as measured with the APIB System Scores: I. *Infant Behavior and Development, 11*, 305–318.

Altermatt, E. R., Jovanovic, J., & Perry, M. (1998). Bias or responsivity? Sex and achievement-level effects on teachers' classroom questioning practices. *Journal of Educational Psychology, 90*, 516–527.

Alves Martins, M., Peixoto, F., Gouveia Pereira, M., Amaral, V., & Pedro, I. (2002). Self-esteem and academic achievement among adolescents. *Educational Psychology, 22*, 51–62.

Amato, P. R. (1996). Explaining the intergenerational transmission of divorce. *Journal of Marriage and the Family, 58*, 628–640.

Amato, P. R. (2001). Children of divorce in the 1990s: An update of the Amato and Keith (1991) meta-analysis. *Journal of Family Psychology, 15*, 355–370.

Amato, P. R., & Gilbreth, J. G. (1999). Nonresident fathers and children's well-being: A meta-analysis. *Journal of Marriage and the Family, 61*, 557–573.

America's Children: Key National Indicators of Well Being. (2005). http://www.childstats.gov

American Academy of Pediatrics. (2000a). Changing concepts of sudden infant death syndrome: Implications for infant sleeping environment and sleep position. *Pediatrics, 105*, 650–656.

American Academy of Pediatrics. (2000b). Diagnosis and evaluation of the child with attention-deficit/hyperactivity disorder. *Pediatrics, 105*, 1158–1170.

American Academy of Pediatrics. (2001), Policy statement: Children, adolescents, and television. *Pediatrics, 107*, 423–426.

American Academy of Pediatrics (2005). *Breast-feeding and the Use of Human Milk Pediatrics, 115*(2), 496–506.

American Association on Mental Retardation. (2002). *Mental retardation: Definitions, classifications, and system of supports,* 10th Edition, Washington, DC.

American Association of University Women. (1992). *How schools shortchange girls: A study of major findings on girls and education.* Washington, DC: AAUW Educational Foundation, Wellesley College Center for Research on Women.

American Association of University Women. (2001). *Beyond the gender wars: A conversation about girls, boys, and education.* Washington, DC: AAUW.

American Association of University Women/ Greenberg-Lake. (1990). *Expectations and aspirations: Gender roles and self-esteem.* (Data Report and Banners). Washington, DC: Greenberg-Lake.

American Cancer Society. *Cancer Information Database.* (2004). American Cancer Society. Atlanta, GA.

American College of Obstetricians and Gynecologists. (2000). *The menopause years.* Washington, DC: American College of Obstetricians and Gynecologists.

American Journal of Human Genetics. (2005). *American Journal of Human Genetics,* 77: 318–326.

American Psychiatric Association Work Group on Eating Disorders. (2000). *Practice guideline for the treatment of patients with eating disorders,* Second Edition. Retrieved March 17, 2006 from http://www.psych.org/psych_pract/treatg/pg/eating_revisebook_index.cfm

American Psychological Association. (2002). Ethical principles of psychologists and code of conduct. *American Psychologist, 57,* 1060–1073.

American Psychological Association. (2003). Two successful violence prevention programs highlight the importance of early intervention. APA Press Releases (http://www.apa.org/releases/violence_prevent.html).

Anderson, G. M., & Allison, D. J. (1990). Intrauterine growth retardation and the routine use of ultrasound. In R. B. Goldbloom & R. S. Lawrence (Eds.), *Preventing disease: Beyond the rhetoric.* New York: Springer-Verlag.

Anderson, N., Amlie, C., & Ytteroy, E. A. (2002). Outcome for children with lesbian or gay parents: A review of studies from 1978 to 2000. *Scandinavian Journal of Psychology, 43,* 335–351.

Anderson, D. R., Huston, A. C., Schmitt, K. L.; & Linebarger, D. L. (2001). Early childhood television viewing and adolescent behavior: The recontact study. *Monographs of the Society for Research in Child Development, 66,* vii–147.

Anderson, D. R., Lorch, E. P., Field, D. E., Collins, P. A., & Nathan, J. G. (1986). Television viewing at home: Age trends in visual attention and time with TV. *Child Development, 57,* 1024–1033.

Anderson, J. R., Reder, L. M., & Simon, H. A. (1996). Situated learning and education. *Educational Researcher, 25,* 511.

Anderson, L. M., Shinn, C., Fullilove, M. T., Scrimshaw, S. C., Fielding, J. E., Normand, J., & Carande-Kulis, V. G. (2003). The effectiveness of early childhood development programs: A systematic review. *American Journal of Preventive Medicine, 24,* 32–46.

Andre, T., Whigham, M., Hendrickson, A., & Chambers, S. (1999). Competency beliefs, positive affect, and gender stereotypes of elementary students and their parents about science versus other school subjects. *Journal of Research in Science Teaching, 36,* 719–747.

Ansalone, G. (2005). Getting our schools on track: Is detracking really the answer? *Radical Pedagogy, 6,* http://radicalpedagogy.icaap.org/content/issue6_2/ansalone.html.

Ansell, N. & Young L. (2004). Enabling households to support successful migration of AIDS orphans in southern Africa. *AIDS Care, 16* (1): 310.

Anthony, J. L, Lonigan, C. J., Burgess, S. R., Driscoll, B., Phillips, B. M., and Bloomfield, B. G. (2002). Structure of preschool phonological sensitivity: Overlapping sensitivity to rhyme, words, syllables, and phonemes. *Journal of Experimental Child Psychology, 82,* Special Issue: Reflections, 65–92.

Antonini, A., & Stryker, M. P. (1993). Rapid remodeling of axonal arbors in the visual cortex. *Science, 260,* 1819–1821.

Apgar, V. (1953). A proposal for a new method of evaluation of the newborn infant. *Current Researches in Anesthesia and Analgesia, 32,* 260–267.

Appel, L. F., Cooper, R. G., McCarrell, N., Sims-Knight, J., Yussen, S. R., & Flavell, J. H. (1972). The development of the distinction between perceiving and memorizing. *Child Development, 43,* 1365–1381.

Aram, D., & Biron, S. (2004). Joint storybook reading and joint writing interventions among low ses preschoolers: Differential contributions to early literacy. *Early Childhood Research Quarterly, 19,* 588–610.

Archer, J. (1991). The influence of testosterone on human aggression. *British Journal of Psychology, 82,* 128.

Archer, J. (1992). *Ethology and human development.* London: Harvester Wheatshead and Barnes & Noble.

Archer, J. (1994). Testosterone and aggression: A theoretical review. *Journal of Offender Rehabilitation,* 21, 339.

Armon, C., & Dawson, R. L. (1997). Developmental trajectories in moral reasoning across the lifespan. *Journal of Moral Education, 26,* 433–453.

Arnett, J. J. (2000). Emerging adulthood: A theory of development from the late teens through the twenties. *American Psychologist, 55,* 469–480.

Arnett, J., & Balle-Jensen, L. (1993). Cultural bases of risk behavior: Danish adolescents. *Child Development, 64,* 1842–1855.

Arnold, D. H., & Doctoroff, G. L. (2003). The early education of socioeconomically disadvantaged children. *Annual Review of Psychology, 54,* 517–545.

Arnold, D. H., Lonigan, C. J., & Whitehurst, G. J. (1994). Accelerating language development through picture book reading: Replication and extension to a videotape training format. *Journal of Educational Psychology,* 86, 235–243.

Aronson, J., Lustina, M., Good, C., Keough, K., Brown, J. L., & Steele, C. M. (1999). When white men can't do math: Necessary and sufficient factors in stereotype threat. *Journal of Experimental Social Psychology,* 35, 11–23.

Arthur, M. W., & Blitz, C. C. (2000). Bridging the gap between science and practice in drug abuse prevention through needs assessment and strategic community planning. *Journal of Community Psychology,* 28(3): 24–155.

Asbury, K., Dunn, J. F., Pike, A., & Plomin, R. (2003). Nonshared environmental influences on individual differences in early behavioral development: A monozygotic twin differences study. *Child Development,* 74(3), 933–943.

Ashcraft, M. H. (1990). Strategic processing in children's mental arithmetic: A review and proposal. In D. F. Bjorklund (Ed.), *Children's strategies: Contemporary views of cognitive development.* Hillsdale, NJ: Erlbaum.

Asher, S. R. (1985). An evolving paradigm in social skill training research with children. In B. H. Schneider, K. H. Rubin, & J. E. Ledingham (Eds.), *Children's peer relations: Issues in assessment and intervention.* New York: Springer-Verlag.

Asher, S. R., & Coie, J. D. (Eds.). (1990). *Peer rejection in childhood.* New York: Cambridge University Press.

Asher, S. R., & Hymel, S. (1981). Children's social competence in peer relations: Sociometric and behavioral assessment. In J. D. Wine & M. D. Smye (Eds.), *Social competence.* New York: Guilford.

Asher, S. R., Parker, J. G., & Walker, D. L. (1996). Distinguishing friendship from acceptance: Implications for intervention and assessment. In W. M. Bukowski, A. F. Newcomb, & W. W. Hartup (Eds.), *The company they keep: Friendship in childhood and adolescence.* New York: Cambridge University Press.

Asher, S. R., Renshaw, P. D., & Hymel, S. (1982). Peer relations and the development of social skills. In S. G. Moore (Ed.), *The young child: Reviews of research* (Vol. 3). Washington, DC: National Association for the Education of Young Children.

Aslin, R. N., Jusczyk, P. W., & Pisoni, D. B. (1998). Speech and auditory processing during infancy: Constraints on and precursors to language. In W. Damon (Series Ed.) & D. Kuhn & R. S. Siegler (Vol. Eds.), *Handbook of child psychology: Vol. 2. Cognition, perception, and language* (5th ed.). New York: Wiley.

Aslin, R. N., Pisoni, D. B., & Jusczyk, P. W. (1983). Auditory development and speech perception in infancy. In P. H. Mussen (Series Ed.) & M. M. Haith & J. J. Campos (Vol. Eds.), *Handbook of child psychology: Vol. 2. Infancy and developmental psychology* (4th ed.). New York: Wiley.

Astington, J. W. (1988). Children's production of commissive speech acts. *Journal of Child Language, 15,* 411–423.

Astington, J. W. & Gopnick, A. (1988). Knowing you've changed your mind: Children's understanding of representational change. In J.W. Astington, P.L. Harris & D.R. Olson (Orgs.), *Developing theories of mind,* 193–225. Cambridge: Cambridge University Press.

Astington, J. W., & Jenkins, J. M. (1995). Theory of mind and social understanding. *Cognition and Emotion, 9,* 151–165.

Atkinson, M. A. (1980). Some practical uses of a natural lifetime, *Human Studies, 3,* 33–46.

Atkinson, R. C., & Shiffrin, R. M. (1971). The control of short-term memory. *Scientific American,* 225, 82.

Atlas, R. S., & Pepler, D. J. (1998). Observations of bullying in the classroom. *Journal of Educational Research, 92,* 86–99.

Attili, G., Vermigli, P., & Schneider, B. H. (1997). Peer acceptance and friendship patterns within a cross-cultural perspective. *International Journal of Behavioral Development, 21,* 277–288.

Auerbach, E. R. (1993). Reexamining English only in the ESL classroom. *TESOL Quarterly,* 27(1), Retrieved September 29, 2005, from NCBE's TESOL Web site: http://www.ncela.gwu.edu/pubs/tesol/tesolquarterly/reexamin.htm

Azmitia, M. (1996). Peer interactive minds: Developmental, theoretical, and methodological issues. In P. B. Baltes & V. M. Staudinger (Eds.), *Interactive minds: Life-span perspectives on the social foundations of cognition*. New York: Cambridge University Press.

Azmitia, M., & Hesser, J. (1993). Why siblings are important agents of cognitive development: A comparison of siblings and peers. *Child Development, 64*, 430–444.

Azuma, H. (1996). Cross-national research on child development: The Hess-Azuma collaboration in retrospect. In D. Schwalb & B. Schwalb (Eds.), *Japanese childrearing: Two generations of scholarship*. New York: Guilford.

Baenninger, M., & Newcombe, N. (1989). The role of experience in spatial test performance: A meta-analysis. *Sex Roles, 20*, 327–344.

Baenninger, M., & Newcombe, N. (1995). Environmental input to the development of sex-related differences in spatial and mathematical ability. *Learning and Individual Differences, 7*, 363–382.

Bahrick, L. E. (1983). Infants' perception of substance and temporal synchrony in multimodal events. *Infant Behavior and Development, 6*, 429–451.

Bahrick, L. E. (1992). Infants' perceptual differentiation of amodal and modality-specific audio-visual relations. *Journal of Experimental Child Psychology, 53*, 180–199.

Bahrick, L. E., & Lickliter, R. (2000). Intersensory redundancy guides attentional selectivity and perceptual learning in infancy. *Developmental Psychology, 36*, 190–201.

Bahrick, L. E., Netto, D., & Hernandez-Reif, M. (1998). Intermodal perception of adult and child faces and voices by infants. *Child Development, 69*, 1263–1275.

Bahrick, L. E., & Pickens, J. N. (1994). Amodal relations: The basis for intermodal perception and learning in infancy. In D. J. Lewkowicz & R. Lickliter (Eds.), *The development of intersensory perception: Comparative perspectives*. Hillsdale, NJ: Erlbaum.

Bailey, J. M., & Bell, A. P. (1993). Familiality of female and male homosexuality. *Behavior Genetics, 23*, 313–322.

Bailey, J. M., & Benishay, D. (1993). Familial aggregation of female sexual orientation. *American Journal of Psychiatry, 150*, 272–277.

Bailey, J. M., & Dawood, K. (1998). Behavioral genetics, sexual orientation, and the family. In C. P. Patterson & A. R. D'Augelli (Eds.), *Lesbian, gay, and bisexual identities in families: Psychological perspectives*. New York: Oxford University Press.

Bailey, S. M., & Garn, S. M. (1986). The genetics of maturation. In F. Falkner & J. M. Tanner (Eds.), *Human growth: A comprehensive treatise*. New York: Plenum.

Bailey, J. M., Nothnagel, J., & Wolfe, M. (1995). Retrospectively-measured individual differences in childhood sex-typed behavior among gay men: Correspondences between self and maternal reports. *Archives of Sexual Behavior, 24*, 613–622.

Bailey, J. M., Pillard, R. C., Neale, M. C., & Agyei, Y. (1993). Heritable factors influence sexual orientation in women. *Archives of General Psychiatry, 50*, 217–223.

Baillargeon, R. (1987a). Object permanence in 3 1/2- and 4 1/2-old-infants. *Developmental Psychology, 23*, 655–664.

Baillargeon, R. (1987b). Young infants' reasoning about the physical and spatial properties of a hidden object. *Cognitive Development, 2*, 179–200.

Baillargeon, R. (2004). Infants' physical world. *Current Directions in Psychological Science, 13*(3), 89–94.

Baillargeon, R., Kotovsky, L., & Needham, A. (1995). The acquisition of physical knowledge in infancy. In D. Sperber, D. Primack, & A. J. Primack (Eds.), *Causal cognition: A multidisciplinary debate*. New York: Clarendon Press.

Bain, B. (1975). Toward an integration of Piaget and Vygotsky: Bilingual consideration. *Linguistics, 160*, 520.

Bakeman, R., Adamson, L. B., Konner, M., & Barr, R. G. (1990). !Kung infancy: The social context of object exploration. *Child Development, 61*, 794–809.

Baker, C. (1993). *Foundations of bilingual education and bilingualism*. Multilingual Matters Ltd.

Baker-Ward, L., Ornstein, P. A., & Holden, D. J. (1984). The expression of memorization in early childhood. *Journal of Experimental Child Psychology, 37*, 555–575.

Balaban, M. T. (1995). Affective influences on startle in five-month-old infants: Reactions to facial expressions of emotion. *Child Development, 66*, 28–36.

Baldwin, D. A. (1995). Understanding the link between joint attention and language. In C. Moore & P. J. Dunham (Eds.), *Joint attention: Its origins and role in development*. Hillsdale, NJ: Erlbaum.

Baldwin, A., Baldwin, C., & Cole, R. E. (1990). Stress-resistant families and stress-resistant children. In J. E. Rolf, A. S. Masten, D. Cicchetti, K. N. Wechterlein, & S. Weintraub (Eds.), *Risk and protective factors in the development of psychopathology*. New York: Cambridge University Press.

Baldwin, D. A., & Moses, L. J. (1994). Early understanding of referential intent and attentional focus: Evidence from language and emotion. In C. Lewis & P. Mitchell (Eds.), *Children's early understanding of mind*. Hillsdale, NJ: Erlbaum.

Baldwin, D. A., & Moses, L. J. (1996). The ontogeny of social information gathering. *Child Development, 67*, 1915–1939.

Baldwin, D. A., & Moses, L. J. (2001). Links between social understanding and early word learning: Challenges to current accounts. *Social Development, 10*, 309–329.

Bandura, A. (1965). Influence of models' reinforcement contingencies on the acquisition of imitative responses. *Journal of Personality and Social Psychology, 1*, 589–595.

Bandura, A. (1973). *Aggression: A social learning analysis*. Englewood Cliffs, NJ: Prentice Hall.

Bandura, A. (1983). Psychological mechanisms of aggression. In R. G. Geen & E. I. Donnerstein (Eds.), *Aggression: Theoretical and empirical reviews* (Vol. 1). New York: Academic Press.

Bandura, A. (1986). *Social foundations of thought and action: A social cognitive theory*. Englewood Cliffs, NJ: Prentice Hall.

Bandura, A. (1989). Regulation of cognitive processes through perceived self-efficacy. *Developmental Psychology, 25*, 729–735.

Bandura, A. (1992). Social cognitive theory. In R. Vasta (Ed.), *Six theories of child development: Revised formulations and current issues*. London: Kingsley.

Bandura, A. (1994). Social cognitive theory of mass communication. In J. Bryant & D. Zillman (Eds.), *Media effects: Advances in theory and research*. Hillsdale, NJ: Erlbaum.

Bandura, A (1997). *Self-efficacy: The exercise of control*. New York: Freeman.

Bandura, A. (2001). Social cognitive theory: An agentic perspective. *Annual Review of Psychology, 52*, 126.

Banerjee, R., & Lintern, V. (2000). Boys will be boys: The effect of social evaluation concerns on gender-typing. *Social Development, 9*, 397–408.

Banks, M. S., & Ginsburg, A. P. (1985). Infant visual preferences: A review and new theoretical treatment. In H. W. Reese (Ed.), *Advances in child development and behavior* (Vol. 19). Orlando, FL: Academic Press.

Banks et al. (2005). Teaching diverse learners. In Linda Darling-Hammund & John Bransford (Eds.)., *Preparing teachers for a changing world: What teachers should learn and be able to do*.

Barber, N. (2005). Educational and ecological correlates of IQ: A cross-national investigation. *Intelligence, 33*, 273–284.

Bard, C., Hay, L., & Fleury, M. (1990). Timing and accuracy of visually directed movements in children: Control of direction and amplitude components. *Journal of Experimental Child Psychology, 50*, 102–118.

Barinaga, M. (1993). Death gives birth to the nervous system. But how? *Science, 259*, 762–763.

Barkley, R. A. (1998). *Attention-deficit hyperactivity disorder: A handbook for diagnosis and treatment* (2nd ed.). New York: Guilford.

Barkow, J. H., Cosmides, L., & Tooby, J. (Eds.). (1992). *The adapted mind: Evolutionary psychology and the generation of culture*. New York: Oxford University Press.

Barnard, K. E., Bee, H. L., & Hammond, M. A. (1984). Home environment and cognitive development in a healthy, low-risk sample: The Seattle study. In A. W. Gottfried (Ed.), *Home environment and early cognitive development*. New York: Academic Press.

Barnard, K. E., & Sumner, G. A. (2002). Promoting awareness of the infant's behavioural patterns: Elements of anticipatory guidance for parents. In J. Gomes-Pedro, J.K. Nugent, G.J. Young, & T.B. Brazelton (Eds.), *The infant and family in the twenty-first century*. New York: Brunner-Routledge.

Barnett, C. R., Leiderman, P. H., Grobstein, R., & Klaus, M. H. (1970). Neonatal separation:The maternal side of interactional deprivation. *Pediatrics, 45*, 197–205.

Baron, R. A. (1983). The control of human aggression: A strategy based on incompatible responses. In R. G. Geen & E. I. Donnerstein (Eds.), *Aggression: Theoretical and empirical reviews* (Vol. 2). New York: Academic Press.

Baron-Cohen, S. (1995). *Mindblindness: An essay on autism and theory of mind*. Cambridge, MA: MIT Press.

Baron-Cohen, S. (2000). The cognitive neuroscience of autism: Evolutionary approaches. In M. Gassaniga (Ed.), *The new cognitive neurosciences* (2nd ed.). Cambridge, MA: MIT Press.

Baron-Cohen, S., Leslie, A. M., & Frith, U. (1986). Mechanical, behavioural and intentional understanding of picture stories in autistic children. *British Journal of Developmental Psychology, 4*, 113–125.

Barrera, M., & Maurer, D. (1981a). The perception of facial expressions by the three-month-old. *Child Development, 52*, 203–206.

Barrera, M., & Maurer, D. (1981b). Recognition of mother's photographed face by the three-month-old infant. *Child Development, 52*, 714–716.

Barrett, K. C., & Campos, J. J. (1987). Perspectives on emotional development: II. A functionalist approach to emotions. In J. Osofsky (Ed.),

Handbook of infant development, 2nd ed., (pp. 555–578). New York: Wiley.

Barrett, D. E., & Yarrow, M. R. (1977). Prosocial behavior, social inferential ability, and assertiveness in children. *Child Development, 48,* 475–481.

Barth, J., Povinelli, D. J., & Cant, J. G. H. (2004). Bodily origins of self. In D. Beike, J. L. Lampinen, & D. A. Behrend (Eds.), *The self and memory* (pp. 11–43). New York: Psychology Press.

Bartrip, J., Morton, J., & de Schonen, S. (2001). Response to mother's face in 3-week to 5-month-old infants. *British Journal of Developmental Psychology, 19,* 219–232.

Bates, J. E. (1987). Temperament in infancy. In J. D. Osofsky (Ed.), *Handbook of infant development* (2nd ed.). New York: Wiley.

Bates, J. E., & Bayles, K. (1984). Objective and subjective components in mothers' perceptions of their children from age 6 months to 3 years. *Merrill-Palmer Quarterly, 30,* 111–130.

Bates, J. E., Bayles, K., Bennett, D. S., Ridge, B., & Brown, M. M. (1991). Origins of externalizing behavior problems at eight years of age. In D. Pepler & K. H. Rubin (Eds.), *Development and treatment of childhood aggression.* Hillsdale, NJ: Erlbaum.

Bates, E., & MacWhinney, B. (1987). Competition, variation, language learning. In B. MacWhinney (Ed.), *Mechanisms of language acquisition.* Hillsdale, NJ: Erlbaum.

Bates, E., & Roe, K. (2001). Language development in children with unilateral brain injury. In C. A. Nelson & M. Luciana (Eds.), *Handbook of developmental cognitive neuroscience* (pp. 281–307). Cambridge, MA: MIT Press.

Bates, E., Thal, D., Janowsky, J. S. (1992). Early language development and its neural correlates. In Segalowitz, Sidney J. Rapin I. (Eds.), *Handbook of neuropsychology.* Vol. 7. New York, Elsevier Science, pp. 691–10.

Batson, Lishner, D. A., et al. (2003). As you would have them do unto you: Does imagining yourself in the other's place stimulate moral action? *Personality & Social Psychology Bulletin, 29,* 1190–1201.

Battistich, V., Schaps, E., Watson, M., Solomon, D., & Lewis, C. (2000). Effects of the Child Development Project on students' drug use and other problem behaviors. *Journal of Primary Prevention, 21,* 75–99.

Bauer, D. J., Goldfield, B. A., & Reznick, J. S. (2002). Alternative approaches to analyzing individual differences in the rate of early vocabulary development. *Applied Psycholinguistics, 23,* 313–326.

Bauer, P. J. (1993). Memory for gender-consistent and gender-inconsistent event sequences by twenty-five-month-old children. *Child Development, 64,* 285–297.

Bauer, P. J. (2002). Early memory development. In U. Goswami (Ed.), *Blackwell handbook of childhood cognitive development.* Malden, MA: Blackwell Publishers.

Bauer, P. J., & Fivush, R. (1992). Constructing event representations: Building on a foundation of variation and enabling relations. *Cognitive Development, 2,* 381–401.

Bauer, D. J., Goldfield, B. A., & Reznick, J. S. (2002). Alternative approaches to analyzing individual differences in the rate of early vocabulary development. *Applied Psycholinguistics, 23,* 313–326.

Bauer, P. J., Hertsgaard, L. A., & Dow, G. A. (1994). After 8 months have passed: Long-term recall of events by 1- to 2-year-old children. *Memory, 2,* 353–382.

Bauer, P. J., & Mandler, J. M. (1992). Putting the horse before the cart: The use of temporal order in recall of events by one-year-old children. *Developmental Psychology, 28,* 441–452.

Bauer, P. J., & Travis, L. L. (1993). The fabric of an event: Different sources of temporal invariance differentially affect 24-month-olds' recall. *Cognitive Development, 8,* 319–341.

Bauer, P. J., Wenner, J. A., Dropik, P. L., & Wewerka, S. S. (2000). Parameters of remembering and forgetting in the transition from infancy to early childhood. *Monographs of the Society for Research in Child Development, 65*(4, Serial No. 263).

Bauerfeld, S. L., & Lachenmeyer, J. R. (1992). Prenatal nutritional status and intellectual development: Critical review and evaluation. In B. B. Lahey & A. E. Kazdin (Eds.), *Advances in clinical child psychology* (Vol. 14). New York: Plenum.

Baumeister, R. F., DeWall, C. N., Ciarocco, N. J., & Twenge, J. M. (2005). Social exclusion impairs self-regulation. *Journal of Personality & Social Psychology, 88,* 589–604.

Baumeister, R. F. & Vohs, K. D. (2004). *Handbook of self regulation: Research, theory, and applications.* New York: Guilford.

Baumeister, R.F., & Twenge, J.M. (2003). The social self. In T. Milon, & M.J. Lerner (Eds.), *Handbook of personality: Personality & social psychology,* Vol. 5. Hoboken, NJ: John Wiley & Sons.

Baumeister, R. F., Twenge, J. M., & Nuss, C. K. (2002). Effects of social exclusion on cognitive processes: Anticipated aloneness reduces intelligent thought. *Journal of Personality and Social Psychology, 83,* 817–827.

Baumrind, D. (1971). Current patterns of parental authority. *Developmental Psychology Monograph, 4,* 1103.

Baumrind, D. (1989). Rearing competent children. In W. Damon (Ed.), *Child development today and tomorrow.* San Francisco: Jossey-Bass.

Baumrind, D. (1991). The influence of parenting style on adolescent competence and substance abuse. *Journal of Early Adolescence, 11,* 56–95.

Bauserman, M. (2002). Child adjustment in joint-custody versus sole-custody arrangements: A meta-analytic review. *Journal of Family Psychology, 16,* 91–102.

Baydar, N., Greek, A., & Brooks-Gunn, J. (1997). A longitudinal study of the effects of the birth of a sibling during the first 6 years of life. *Journal of Marriage and the Family, 59,* 939–956.

Bayley, N. (1956). Individual patterns of development. *Child Development, 27,* 45–74.

Bayley, N. (1993). *Bayley Scales of Infant Development: Birth to two years* (2nd ed.). New York: Psychological Corporation.

Baylies, C. (2002). The impact of AIDS on rural households in Africa: A shock like any other? *Development and Change, 33* (4), 611, September.

Beal, C. R., & Flavell, J. H. (1983). Young speakers' evaluations of their listener's comprehension in a referential communication task. *Child Development, 54,* 148–153.

Bearison, D. (1982). New directions in studies of social interactions and cognitive growth. In F. C. Serafica (Ed.), *Social-cognitive development in context.* New York: Guilford.

Bearison, D., & Dorval, B. (2002). *Collaborative cognition: Children negotiating ways of knowing.* Westport, CT: Ablex.

Beauchamp, D. K., Cowart, B. J., Mennella, J. A., & Marsh, R. R. (1994). Infant salt taste: Developmental, methodological, and contextual factors. *Developmental Psychobiology, 27,* 353–365.

Becker, J. (1994). "Sneak-shoes," "sworders," and "nose-beards": A case study of lexical innovation. *First Language, 14,* 195–211.

Beckwith, L., & Parmelee, A. (1986). EEG patterns of preterm infants, home environment, and later IQ. *Child Development, 57,* 777–789.

Beebe, B., Alson, D., Jaffe, J., Feldstein, S., & Crown, C. (1988). Vocal congruence in mother-infant play. *Journal of Psycholinguistic Research, 17,* 245–259.

Bedard, J., & Chi, M. T. H. (1992). Expertise. *Current Directions in Psychological Science, 1,* 135–139.

Behrend, D. A. (1988). Overextensions in early language comprehension: Evidence from a signal detection approach. *Journal of Child Language, 15,* 63–75.

Behrend, D. A., Rosengren, K. A., & Perlmutter, M. (1989). A new look at children's private speech: The effects of age, task difficulty, and parental presence. *International Journal of Behavioral Development, 12,* 305–320.

Behrman, R. E., Kliegman, R. M., & Jenson, H. B. (Eds.). (2000). *Nelson textbook of pediatrics* (16th ed.). Philadelphia: W. B. Saunders.

Beier, E. G. (1991). Freud: Three contributions. In G. A. Kimble, M. Wertheimer, & C. L. White (Eds.), *Portraits of pioneers in psychology.* Hillsdale, NJ: Erlbaum.

Beilin, H. (1992a). Piaget's enduring contribution to developmental psychology. *Developmental Psychology, 28,* 191–204.

Beilin, H. (1992b). Piaget's new theory. In H. Beilin & P. B. Pufall (Eds.), *Piaget's theory: Prospects and possibilities.* Hillsdale, NJ: Erlbaum.

Bell, R. Q. (1968). A reinterpretation of the direction of effects of socialization. *Psychological Review, 75,* 81–95.

Bell, J. H., & Bromnick, R. D. (2003). The social reality of the imaginary audience: A grounded theory approach. *Adolescence, 38,* 205–220.

Beller, E. K. (1957). Dependency and autonomous achievement striving related to orality and anality in early childhood. *Child Development, 28,* 287–315.

Bellinger, D. C., & Adams, H. F. (2001). Environmental pollutant exposures and children's cognitive abilities. In R. J. Sternberg & E. L. Grigorenko (Eds.), *Environmental effects on cognitive abilities.* Mahwah, NJ: Erlbaum.

Bellinger, D. C., Leviton, A., Needleman, H. L., Waternaux, C., & Rabinowitz, M. (1986). Low-level lead exposure and infant development in the first year. *Neurobehavioral Toxicology and Teratology, 8,* 151–161.

Belsky, J. (1981). Early human experience: A family perspective. *Developmental Psychology, 17,* 323.

Belsky, J. (1988). The "effects" of infant day care reconsidered. *Early Childhood Research Quarterly, 3,* 235–272.

Belsky, J. (1999). Interactional and contextual determinants of attachment security. In J. Cassidy & P. R. Shaver (Eds.), *Handbook of attachment: Theory, research, and clinical applications.* New York: Guilford.

Belsky, J. Goode, M. K., & Most, R. K. (1980). Maternal stimulation and infant exploratory competence: Cross-sectional, correlational, and experimental analyses. *Child Development, 51,* 1168–1178.

Belsky, J., & Rovine, M. (1988). Nonmaternal care in the first year of life and infantparent attachment security. *Child Development, 59,* 157–167.

Bem, S. L. (1981). Gender schema theory: A cognitive account of sex typing. *Psychological Review, 88,* 354–364.

Bem, S. L. (1989). Genital knowledge and gender constancy in preschool children. *Child Development, 60,* 649–662.

Bem, S. L. (1993). *The lenses of gender: Transforming the debate on sexual inequality.* New Haven, CT: Yale University Press.

Bem, D. J. (1996). Exotic becomes erotic: A developmental theory of sexual orientation. *Psychological Review, 103,* 320–335.

Bem, D. J. (2000). Exotic becomes erotic: Interpreting the biological correlates of sexual orientation. *Archives of Sexual Behavior, 29,* 531–548.

Bembenntly, H., & Karabenick, S. A. (2004). Inherent association between academic delay of gratification, future time perspective, and self-regulated learning. *Educational Psychology Review, 16,* 35–57.

Benasich, A. A., & Brooks-Gunn, J. (1996). Maternal attitudes and knowledge of child-rearing: Associations with family and child outcomes. *Child Development, 67,* 1186–1205.

Benbow, C. P. (1992). Academic achievement in mathematics and science of students between ages 13 and 23: Are there differences among students in the top one percent of mathematical ability? *Journal of Educational Psychology, 84,* 51–61.

Benenson, J. F. (1993). Greater preference among females than males for dyadic interaction in early childhood. *Child Development, 64,* 544–555.

Benenson, J. F., Apostoleris, N. H., & Parnass, J. (1997). Age and sex differences in dyadic and group interaction in early childhood. *Developmental Psychology, 33,* 538–543.

Benenson, J. F., Markovits, H., Roy, R., & Denko, P. (2003). Behavioural rules underlying learning to share: Effects of development and context. *International Journal of Behavioral Development, 27,* 116–121.

Benjet, C., & Hernandez-Guzman, L. (2002). A short-term longitudinal study of pubertal change, gender, and psychological well-being of Mexican early adolescents. *Journal of Youth and Adolescence, 31* (6), 429–442.

Benson, J. B. (1990). The significance and development of crawling in human infancy. In J. E. Clark & J. H. Humphrey (Eds.), *Advances in motor development research* (Vol. 3). New York: AMS Press.

Benson, J. B., & Uzgiris, I. C. (1985). Effects of self-initiated locomotion on infant search activity. *Developmental Psychology, 21,* 923–931.

Berenbaum, S. A., & Hines, M. (1992). Early androgens are related to childhood sex-typed toy preferences. *Psychological Science, 3,* 203–206.

Berenbaum, S. A., & Snyder, E. (1995). Early hormonal influences on childhood sex-typed activity and playmate preferences: Implications for the development of sexual orientation. *Developmental Psychology, 31,* 31–42.

Berg, W. K., & Berg, K. M. (1987). Psychophysiological development in infancy. In J. Osofsky (Ed.), *Handbook of infant development* (2nd ed.). New York: Wiley.

Berg, N. E., & Mussen, P. (1975). The origins and development of concepts of justice. *Journal of Social Issues, 31,* 183–201.

Berger, P. L. & Luckmann, T. (1966). *The social construction of reality: A treatise its the sociology of knowledge.* Garden City, NY: Anchor Books.

Berk, L. E. (1986). Development of private speech among preschool children. *Early Child Development & Care, 24,* 113–136.

Berk, L. E. (1994). Why children talk to themselves. *Scientific American, 271,* 78–83.

Berk, L. E., & Garvin, R. A. (1984). Development of private speech among low-income Appalachian children. *Developmental Psychology, 20,* 271–286.

Berk, L. E., & Landau, S. (1993). Private speech of learning disabled and normally achieving children in classroom academic and laboratory contexts. *Child Development, 64,* 556–571.

Berko, J. (1958). The child's learning of English morphology. *Word, 14,* 150–177.

Berkowitz, L. (1993). *Aggression: Its causes, consequences, and control.* New York: Academic Press.

Berkowitz, M. W., Gibbs, J. C., & Broughton, J. M. (1980). The relation of moral judgment stage disparity to developmental effects of peer dialogues. *Merrill-Palmer Quarterly, 26,* 341–357.

Berndt, T. J. (1979). Developmental changes in conformity to peers and parents. *Developmental Psychology, 15,* 608–616.

Berndt, T. J. (1981). Age changes and changes over time in prosocial intentions and behavior between friends. *Developmental Psychology, 17,* 408–416.

Berndt, T. J. (1986). Sharing between friends: Contexts and consequences. In E. C. Mueller & C. R. Cooper (Eds.), *Process and outcome in peer relationships.* New York: Academic Press.

Berndt, T. J. (1988). The nature and significance of children's friendships. In R. Vasta (Ed.), *Annals of child development* (Vol. 5). Greenwich, CT: JAI Press.

Berndt, T. J. (1989a). Friendships in childhood and adolescence. In W. Damon (Ed.), *Child development today and tomorrow.* San Francisco: Jossey-Bass.

Berndt, T. J. (1989b). Obtaining support from friends during childhood and adolescence. In D. Belle (Ed.), *Children's social networks and social supports.* New York: Wiley.

Berndt, T. J. (1996). Transitions in friendship and friends' influence. In J. A. Graber, J. Brooks-Gunn, & A. C. Petersen (Eds.), *Transitions through adolescence: Interpersonal domains and context.* Mahwah, NJ: Erlbaum.

Berndt, T. J. (2002). Friendship quality and social development. *Current Directions in Psychological Science, 11,* 710.

Berndt, T. J., & Heller, K. A. (1986). Gender stereotypes and social inferences: A developmental study. *Journal of Personality and Social Psychology, 50,* 889–898.

Berndt, T. J., & Keefe, K. (1995). Friends' influence on adolescents' adjustment to school. *Child Development, 66,* 1312–1329.

Berndt, T. J., Miller, K. E., & Park, K. (1989). Adolescents' perceptions of friends' and parents' influence on aspects of their school adjustment. *Journal of Early Adolescence, 9,* 419–435.

Berndt, T. J., & Perry, T. B. (1990). Distinctive features and effects of adolescent friendships. In R. Montemayor, G. R. Adams, & T. P. Gullotta (Eds.), *From childhood to adolescence: A transitional period?* London: Sage.

Bernier, J. G., & Siegel, D. H. (1994). Attention-deficit hyperactivity disorder: A family ecological systems perspective. *Families in Society, 75,* 142–150.

Berry, J. W. (1966). Temme and Eskimo perceptual skills. *International Journal of Psychology, 1,* 207–229.

Berry, J. B. (Ed.). (1997). *Handbook of cross-cultural psychology.* Boston: Allyn and Bacon.

Berry, J. W. (1997). Immigration, acculturation, and adaptation. *International Journal of Applied Psychology, 46,* 534.

Bersoff, D. M., & Miller, J. G. (1993). Culture, context, and the development of moral accountability judgments. *Developmental Psychology, 29*(4), 664–676.

Bertenthal, B. I. (1996). Origins and early development of perception, action, and representation. *Annual Review of Psychology, 47,* 431–459.

Bertenthal, B. I., Campos, J. J., & Haith, M. M. (1980). Development of visual organization: The perception of subjective contours. *Child Development, 51,* 1072–1080.

Bertenthal, B. I., Campos, J. J., & Kermoian, R. (1994). An epigenetic perspective on the development of self-produced locomotion and its consequences. *Current Directions in Psychological Science, 3,* 140–145.

Berzonsky, M. D. (2004). Identity style, parental authority, and identity commitment. *Journal of Youth and Adolescence, 6,* 1.

Best, C. T. (1995). Learning to perceive the sound pattern of English. In C. K. Rovee-Collier & L. P. Lipsitt (Eds.), *Advances in infancy research* (Vol. 9). Norwood, NJ: Ablex.

Best, D. L. (2001). Cross-cultural gender roles. In J. Worell (Ed.), *Encyclopedia of women and gender* (Vol. 1). San Diego, CA: Academic Press.

Best, D. L., & Williams, J. E. (1993). A cross-cultural viewpoint. In A. E. Beall & R. J. Sternberg (Eds.), *The psychology of gender.* New York: Guilford.

Bever, T. G. (Ed.). (1982). *Regressions in mental development: Basic phenomena and theories.* Hillsdale, NJ: Erlbaum.

Bhana, K. (1984). The development of gender understanding in children. *South African Journal of Psychology, 14,* 10–13.

Bhanot, R., & Jovanovic, J. (2005). Do parents' academic gender stereotypes influence whether they intrude on their children's homework? *Sex Roles, 52,* 597–607.

Bhavnagri, N., & Parke, R. D. (1991). Parents as direct facilitators of children's peer relationships: Effects of age of child and sex of parent. *Journal of Social and Personal Relationships, 8,* 423–440.

Bialystok, E. (1991). Metalinguistic dimensions of bilingual language proficiency. In E. Bialystok (Ed.), *Language processing in bilingual children* (pp. 113–140). New York: Cambridge University Press.

Bialystok, E. (2001). *Bilingualism in development: Language, literacy, and cognition.* New York: Cambridge University Press.

Bialystok, E., & Herman, J. (1999). Does bilingualism matter for early literacy? *Bilingualism: Language & Cognition, 2,* 35–44.

Bielinski, J. C., & Davison, M. L. (1998). Gender differences by item difficulty interactions in multiple-choice mathematics items. *American Educational Research Journal, 35,* 455–476.

Biernat, M. (1991). A multicomponent, developmental analysis of sex typing. *Sex Roles, 24,* 567–586.

Bienert, H., & Schneider, B. (1995). Deficit-specific social skills training with peer-nominated aggressive-disruptive and sensitive-isolated preadolescents. *Journal of Clinical Child Psychology, 24,* 287–299.

Bigler, R. S., & Liben, L. S. (1990). The role of attitudes and interventions in gender-schematic processing. *Child Development, 61,* 1440–1452.

Bigler, R. S., & Liben, L. S. (1992). Cognitive mechanisms in children's gender stereotyping: Theoretical and educational implications of a cognitive-based intervention. *Child Development, 64,* 1351–1363.

Billows, W. D. (2002). Cross-validation of the self-esteem impact indicator measure for individuals with serious and persistent mental illness. *Dissertation Abstracts International: Section B: The Science and Engineering, 62,* 47–73.

Birndorf, S., Ryan, S., Auinger, P., & Aten, H. (2005). High self-esteem among adolescents: Longitudinal trends, sex differences, and protective factors. *Journal of Adolescent Health, 37,* 194–201.

Birnholz, J. C., & Benacerraf, B. R. (1983). The development of human fetal hearing. *Science, 222,* 516–518.

Bisanz, J., & Lefevre, J. (1990). Strategic and non-strategic processing in the development of mathematical cognition. In D. F. Bjorklund (Ed.), *Children's strategies: Contemporary views of cognitive development.* Hillsdale, NJ: Erlbaum.

Bishop, A. P., Mehra, B., Bazzell, I. & Smith, C. (2003). Participatory action research and digital libraries: Reframing evaluation. In Ann Peterson Bishop, Nancy A. Van House, and Barbara P. Buttenfield (Eds.), *Digital library use: Social practice in design and evaluation* (pp. 161–189). Cambridge, MA: MIT Press.

Bjorklund, D. F. (1987). How age changes in knowledge base contribute to the development of children's memory: An interpretive review. *Developmental Review, 7,* 93–130.

Bjorklund, D. F. (Ed.). (1990). *Children's strategies: Contemporary views of cognitive development.* Hillsdale, NJ: Erlbaum.

Bjorklund, D. F. (1997). The role of immaturity in human development. *Psychological Bulletin, 122,* 153–169.

Bjorklund, D. F. (2000). *Children's thinking* (3rd ed.). Belmont, CA: Wadsworth.

Bjorklund, D. F., & Coyle, T. R. (1995). Utilization deficiencies in the development of memory strategies. In F. E. Weinert & W. Schneider (Eds.), *Memory performance and competencies: Issues in growth and development.* Mahwah, NJ: Erlbaum.

Bjorklund, D. F., & Blasi, C. H. (2005). Evolutionary developmental psycholoy, in D. M. Buss (Ed.), *The handbook of evolutionary psychology* (pp. 828–850). Hoboken, NJ: Wiley.

Bjorklund, D. F., Muir-Broaddus, J. E., & Schneider, W. (1990). The role of knowledge in the development of strategies. In D. F. Bjorklund (Ed.), *Children's strategies: Contemporary views of cognitive development.* Hillsdale, NJ: Erlbaum.

Bjorklund, D. F., & Pellegrini, A. D. (2000). Child development and evolutionary psychology. *Child Development, 71,* 1687–1708.

Bjorklund, D. F., & Pellegrini, A. D. (2002a). Evolutionary perspectives on social development. In P. K. Smith & C. H. Hart (Eds.), *Blackwell handbook of childhood social development.* Malden, MA: Blackwell Publishers.

Bjorklund, D. F., & Pellegrini, A. D. (2002b). *The origins of human nature: Evolutionary developmental psychology.* Washington, DC: American Psychological Association.

Bjorklund, D. F., & Rosenblum, K. E. (2001). Children's use of multiple and variable addition strategies in a game context. *Developmental Science, 4,* 184–194.

Bjorklund, D. F., & Rosenblum, K. E. (2002). Context effects in children's selection and use of simple arithmetic strategies. *Journal of Cognition and Development, 3,* 225–242.

Bjorklund, D. F., & Schneider, W. (1996) The interaction of knowledge, aptitude, and strategies in children's memory performance. In H. W. Reese (Ed.), *Advances in child development and behavior* (Vol. 26). San Diego, CA: Academic Press.

Blachman, B. A., Schatschneider, C., & Fletcher, J. M. (2004). Effects of intensive reading remediation for second and third graders and a 1-year follow-up. *Journal of Educational Psychology, 96,* 444–461.

Black, S. (2003). *An ongoing evaluation of the bullying prevention program in Philadelphia schools: Student survey and student observation data.* Paper presented at Centers for Disease Control's Safety in Numbers Conference, Atlanta, GA.

Blake, J. (2000). *Routes to child language.* New York: Cambridge University Press.

Blake, R., Turner L. M., Smoski, M. J., Pozdol, S. L, Stine, W. L. (2003). Visual recognition of biological motion is impaired in children with autism. *Psycholological Science, 14,* 15–17.

Blanchard, R., & Bogaert, A. F. (1996). Homosexuality in men and number of older brothers. *American Journal of Psychiatry, 153,* 27–31.

Blanchard, R., & Klassen, P. (1997). H-Y antigen and homosexuality in men. *Journal of Theoretical Biology, 185,* 373–378.

Blanchard, R., & Zucker, K. J. (1994). Reanalysis of Bell, Weinberg, and Hammersmith's data on birth order, sibling sex ratio, and parental age in homosexual men. *American Journal of Psychiatry, 151,* 1375–1376.

Blanchard, R., Zucker, K. J., Cavacas, A., Allin, S., Bradley, S. J., & Schachter, D. C. (2002). Fraternal birth order and birth weight in probably prehomosexual feminine boys. *Hormones and Behavior, 41,* 321–327.

Blascovich, J., Spencer, S. J., Quinn, D. M., & Steele, C. M. (2001). African Americans and high blood pressure: The role of stereotype threat. *Psychological Science, 12,* 225–229.

Blasi, A. (1980). Bridging moral cognition and moral action: A critical review of the literature. *Psychological Bulletin, 88,* 145.

Blasi, A. (1983). Moral cognition and moral action: A theoretical perspective. *Developmental Review, 3,* 178–210.

Blass, E. M., & Smith, B. A. (1992). Differential effects of sucrose, fructose, glucose, and lactose. *Developmental Psychology, 28,* 804–810.

Bloom, L. (1973). *One word at a time.* The Hague, Netherlands: Mouton.

Bloom, L. (1993, Winter). Word learning. *SRCD Newsletter,* 113.

Bloom, L. (1998). Language acquisition in developmental contexts. In W. Damon (Series Ed.) & D. Kuhn & R. S. Siegler (Vol. Eds.), *Handbook of child psychology:* Vol. 2. *Cognition, perception, and language* (5th ed.). New York: Wiley.

Bloom, L., Hood, L., & Lightbrown, N. P. (1974). Imitation in language development: If, when, and why. *Cognitive Psychology, 6,* 380–420.

Bloom, L., Lightbrown, P., & Hood, L. (1975). Structure and variation in child language. *Monographs of the Society for Research in Child Development, 40*(2, Serial No. 160).

Bloom, L., Margulis, C., Tinker, E., & Fujita, N. (1996). Early conversations and word learning: Contributions from child and adult. *Child Development, 67,* 3154–3175.

Bloom, P. (1996). Controversies in language acquisition: Word learning and the part of speech. In R. Gelman & T. Au (Eds.), *Perceptual and cognitive development.* San Diego, CA: Academic Press.

Bloom, P. (2000). *How children learn the meanings of words.* Cambridge, MA: MIT Press.

Bloom, P., & Markson, L. (1998). Intention and analogy in children's naming of pictorial representations. *Psychological Science, 9,* 200–204.

Boccia, M., & Campos, J. J. (1989). Maternal emotional signals, social referencing, and infants' reactions to strangers. In N. Eisenberg (Ed.), *New directions for child development*: No. 44. *Empathy and related emotional responses.* San Francisco: Jossey-Bass.

Bogartz, R., Shinskey, J. L., & Schilling, T. H. (2000). Object permanence in five-and-a-half-month-old infants? *Infancy, 1,* 403–428.

Bohannon, J. N. I, Padgett, R. J., Nelson, K. E., & Mark, M. (1996). Useful evidence on negative evidence. *Developmental Psychology, 32,* 551–555.

Bohannon, J. N., III, & Stanowicz, L. (1988). The issue of negative evidence: Adult responses to children's language errors. *Developmental Psychology, 24,* 684–689.

Bohlin, G., Hagekull, B., & Rydell, A. (2000). Attachment and social functioning: A longitudinal study from infancy to middle childhood. *Social Development, 9,* 24–39.

Boivin, M. & Hymel, S. (1997). Peer experiences and social self-perceptions: A sequential model. *Developmental Psychology, 33,* 135–145.

Boldizar, J. P., Perry, D. G., & Perry, L. C. (1989). Outcome values and aggression. *Child Development, 60,* 571–579.

Bolger, K. E., & Patterson, C. J. (2001). Developmental pathways from child maltreatment to peer rejection. *Child Development, 72,* 549–568.

Boom, I., Hoijink, H., & Kunnen, S. (2001). Rules in the balance: Classes, strategies, or rules for the balance scale task? *Cognitive Development, 16,* 717–735.

Borke, H. (1975). Piaget's mountains revisited: Changes in the egocentric landscape. *Developmental Psychology, 11,* 240–243.

Bornholt, L. (2005). *Ask-kids Inventory for Children, Manual.* Australian Council for Educational Research (ACER).

Bornstein, M. H., & Arterberry, M. E. (1999). Perceptual development. In M. H. Bornstein & M. E. Lamb (Eds.), *Developmental psychology: An advanced textbook* (4th ed.). Mahwah, NJ: Erlbaum.

Bornstein, M. H., & Arterberry, M. E. (2003). Recognition, discrimination and categorization of smiling by 5-month-old infants. *Developmental Science, 6* (5), 585–599.

Bornstein M. H., & Cote L. R. (2004). Mothers' parenting cognitions in cultures of origin, acculturating cultures, and cultures of destination. *Child Development, 75*(1), 221–235.

Bornstein, M. H., DiPietro, J. A., Hahn, C., Painter, K., Haynes, O. M., & Costigan, K. A. (2002). Prenatal cardiac function and postnatal cognitive development: An exploratory study. *Infancy, 3,* 475–494.

Bornstein, M. H., Haynes, O. M., Pascual, L., Painter, K. M., & Galperin, C. (1999). Play in two societies: Pervasiveness of process, specificity of structure. *Child Development, 70,* 317–331.

Bornstein, M. H., & Sigman, M. D. (1986). Continuity in mental development from infancy. Child Development, 57, 251–274.

Bornstein, M. H., Tal, J., & Tamis-LaMonda, C. S. (1991). Parenting in cross-cultural perspective: The United States, France, and Japan. In M. H. Bornstein (Ed.), *Cultural approaches to parenting.* Hillsdale, NJ: Erlbaum.

Bornstein, M. H., & Tamis-LaMonda, C. S. (1990). Activities and interactions of mothers and their firstborn infants in the first six months of life: Covariation, stability, continuity, correspondence, and prediction. *Child Development, 61,* 1206–1217.

Bornstein, M. H., Toda, H., Azuma, C. S., Tamis-LeMonda, C. S., & Ogino, M. (1990). Mother and infant activity and interaction in Japan and in the United States: II. A comparative microanalysis of naturalistic exchanges focused on the organization of infant attention. *International Journal of Behavioral Development, 13,* 289–308.

Bosch, L., & Sebastian-Galles, N. (2001). Evidence of early language discrimination abilities in infants from bilingual environments. *Infancy, 2,* 29–50.

Boston, M. B., & Levy, G. D. (1991). Changes and differences in preschoolers' understanding of gender scripts. *Cognitive Psychology, 6,* 417–432.

Bosworth, K., Espelage, D. L., & Simon, T. R. (1999). Factors associated with bullying behavior in middle school students. *Journal of Early Adolescence, 19,* 341–362.

Bouchard, T. J., Jr. (1997). IQ similarity in twins reared apart: Findings and responses to critics. In R. J. Sternberg & E. L. Grigorenko (Eds.), *Intelligence, heredity, and environment.* New York: Cambridge University Press.

Bouchard, T. J., Jr. (2004) Genetic influence on human psychological traits. *Directions in Psychological Science, 13*(4), 148–151.

Bouchard, T. J. Jr., Lykken, D. T., McGue, M., Segal, N. L., & Tellegen, A. (1990). Sources of human psychological differences: The Minnesota Study of Twins Reared Apart. *Science, 250,* 223–228.

Bouchard, T. J., Jr., & McGue, M. (1981). Familial studies of intelligence: A review. *Science, 212,* 1055–1059.

Bouchard, T.J., & McGue, M. (2003). Genetic and environmental influences on human psychological differences. *Journal of Neurobiology, 54*(1), 445.

Boulton, M. J. (2005). Predicting changes in children's self-perceptions from playground social activities and interactions. *British Journal of Developmental Psychology, 23,* 209–226.

Bottoms, B. L., & Goodman, G. S. (Eds.). (1996). *International perspectives on child abuse and children's testimony: Psychological research and law.* Thousand Oaks, CA: Sage.

Bottoms, B. L., Goodman, G. S., Schwartz-Kenney, B. M., Sachsenmaier, T., & Thomas, S. (1990, March). *Keeping secrets: Implications for children's testimony.* Paper presented at the American Psychology and Law Society Meeting, Williamsburg, VA.

Bowerman, M. (1975). Cross-linguistic similarities at two stages of syntactic development. In E. H. Lenneberg & E. E. Lenneberg (Eds.), *Foundations of language: A multidisciplinary approach.* New York: Academic Press.

Bowerman, M. (1976). Semantic factors in the acquisition of rules for word use and sentence construction. In D. M. Morehead & A. E. Morehead (Eds.), *Normal and deficient child language.* Baltimore: University Park Press.

Bowerman, M. (1982). Reorganizational processes in lexical and syntactic development. In E. Wanner & L. R. Gleitman (Eds.), *Language acquisition: The state of the art.* New York: Cambridge University Press.

Bowerman M. (1988). Inducing the latent structure of language. In F. S. Kessel (Ed.), *The development of language and language researchers: Essays in honor of Roger Brown.* Hillsdale, NJ: Erlbaum.

Bowlby, J. (1952/1995). *Maternal care and mental health.* Northvale, NJ: Jason Aronson.

Bowlby, J. (1969). *Attachment and loss*: Vol. 1. *Attachment.* New York: Basic Books.

Bowlby, J. (1973). *Attachment and loss*: Vol. 2. *Separation.* New York: Basic Books.

Bowlby, J. (1980). *Attachment and loss*: Vol. 3. *Loss.* New York: Basic Books.

Bowlby, J. (1982). *Attachment and loss*: Vol. 1. *Attachment* (2nd ed.). New York: Basic Books. (Original work published 1969)

Bowlby, J. (1988). *A secure base: Parent-child attachment and healthy human development.* New York: Basic Books.

Boyes, M. C., & Allen, S. G. (1993). Styles of parentchild interaction and moral reasoning in adolescence. *Merrill-Palmer Quarterly, 39,* 551–570.

Boykin, A. (1986). The triple quandary and the schooling of Afro-American children. In U. Neisser (Ed.), *The school achievement of minority children: New perspectives* (pp. 57–92). Hillsdale, NJ: Erlbaum.

Boykin, A. W. (1994). Reformulating educational reform. Toward the proactive schooling of African American children. In R. J. Rossi (Ed.), *Educational reforms and students at risk.* New York: Teachers College Press.

Brackbill, Y., Adams, G., Crowell, D. H., & Gray, M. L. (1966). Arousal level in neonates and preschool children under continuous auditory stimulation. *Journal of Experimental Child Psychology, 4,* 178–188.

Bradbard, M. R., Martin, C. L., Endsley, R. C., & Halverson, C. F. (1986). Influence of sex stereotypes on children's exploration and memory: A competence versus performance distinction. *Developmental Psychology, 22,* 481–486.

Bradley, C. B., McMurray, R. G., Harrell, J. S., & Deng, S. (2000). Changes in common activities of 3rd though 10th graders: The CHIC study. *Medicine and Science in Sports and Exercise, 32,* 2071–2078.

Bradley, R. H. (1994). The HOME inventory: Review and reflections. In H. W. Reese (Ed.), *Advances in child development and behavior* (Vol. 25). San Diego, CA: Academic Press.

Bradley, R. H., & Caldwell, B. M. (1984b). The relation of infants' home environments to achievement test performance in first grade: A follow-up study. *Child Development, 55,* 803–809.

Bradley, R. H., Corwyn, R. F., Burchinal, M., McAdoo, H. P., & Coll, C. G. (2001). The home environments of children in the United States Part II: Relations with behavioral development through age 13. *Child Development, 72,* 1868–1886.

Bradley, R. H., Mundfrom, D. J., Whiteside, L., Casey, P. H., & Barrett, K. (1994). A factor analytic study of the Infant-Toddler and Early Childhood versions of the HOME inventory administered to White, Black, and Hispanic American parents of children born preterm. *Child Development, 65,* 880–888.

Braine, M. D. S. (1976). Children's first word combinations. *Monographs of the Society for Research in Child Development, 41*(1, Serial No. 164).

Braine, M. D. S., & Rumain, B. (1983). Logical reasoning. In P. H. Mussen (Series Ed.) & J. H. Flavell & E. M. Markman (Vol. Eds.), Handbook of child psychology: Vol. 3. *Cognitive development* (4th ed.). New York: Wiley.

Branigan, G. (1979). Some reasons why successive single word utterances are not. *Journal of Child Language, 6,* 411–421.

Brazelton, T. B., & Nugent, J. K. (1995). *Neonatal Behavioral Assessment Scale* (3rd ed.). London: Mac Keith Press.

Brazelton, T. B., & Yogman, M. W. (Eds.). (1986). *Affective development in infancy.* Norwood, NJ: Ablex.

Breedlove, S. M., & Hampson, E. (2002). Sexual differentiation of the brain and behavior. In J. B. Becker, S. M. Breedlove, D. Crews, & M. M. McCarthy (Eds.), *Behavioral endocrinology* (2nd ed). Cambridge, MA: MIT Press.

Bremner, J. G. (2002). The nature of imitation by infants. *Infant Behavior & Development, 25,* 65–67.

Bretherton, I. (1988). How to do things with one word: The ontogenesis of intentional message making in infancy. In M. D. Smith & J. L. Locke (Eds.), *The emergent lexicon.* San Diego, CA: Academic Press.

Bretherton, I. (1995). The origins of attachment theory: John Bowlby and Mary Ainsworth. In S. Goldberg, R. Muir, & J. Kerr (Eds.), *Attachment theory: Social, developmental, and clinical perspectives.* Hillsdale, NJ: Analytic Press.

Briggs, J. (1970). *Never in anger.* Cambridge, MA: Harvard University Press.

Brisk, M. (1998). *Bilingual education: From compensatory to quality schooling.* Mahwah, NJ: Erlbaum.

Broberg, A., Wessels, H., Lamb, M. E, Hwang, C. (1997). Effects of day care on the development of cognitive abilities in 8 year olds: A longitudinal study. *Developmental Psychology, 33*(1), 62–69.

Broderick, P. C. (1998). Early adolescent gender differences in the use of ruminative and distracting coping strategies. *Journal of Early Adolescence, 18,* 173–191.

Broderick, P. C., & Korteland, C. (2002). Coping style and depression in early adolescence: Relationships to gender, gender role, and implicit beliefs. *Sex Roles, 46,* 201–213.

Brody, G. H. (Ed.). (1996). *Sibling relationships: Their causes and consequences.* Norwood, NJ: Ablex.

Brody, G. H. (1998). Sibling relationship quality: Its causes and consequences. *Annual Review of Psychology, 49,* 124.

Brody, G.H., & Flor, D. L. (1998). Maternal resources, parenting practices, and child competence in rural single-parent African American families. *Child Development, 69,* 803–816.

Brody, G. H., Stoneman, Z., & McCoy, J. K. (1994). Forecasting sibling relationships in early adolescence from child temperament and family processes in middle childhood. *Child Development, 65,* 771–778.

Brody, L. R. (1999). *Gender, emotion, and the family.* Cambridge, MA: Harvard University Press.

Brody, N. (1997). Intelligence, schooling, and society. *American Psychologist, 52,* 1046–1050.

Brodzinsky, D. M., & Pinderhughes, E. (2002). Parenting and child development in adoptive families. In M. H. Bornstein (Ed.), *Handbook of parenting* (2nd ed., Vol. 1). Mahwah, NJ: Erlbaum.

Bronfenbrenner, U. (1979). *The ecology of human development: Experiments by nature and design.* Cambridge, MA: Harvard University Press.

Bronfenbrenner, U. (1986). Recent advances in research on human development. In R. K. Silbereisen, K. Eyferth, & G. Rudinger (Eds.), *Development as action in context: Problem behavior and normal youth development.* New York: Springer-Verlag.

Bronfenbrenner, U. (1992). Ecological systems theory. In R. Vasta (Ed.), *Six theories of child development: Revised formulations and current issues.* London: Kingsley.

Bronfenbrenner, U. (1993). The ecology of cognitive development: Research models and fugitive findings. In R. H. Wozniak & K. W. Fischer (Eds.), *Development in context*. Hillsdale, NJ: Erlbaum.

Bronfenbrenner, U., & Morris, P. A. (1998). The ecology of developmental processes. In W. Damon (Series Ed.) & R. M. Lerner (Vol. Ed.), *Handbook of child psychology*: Vol. 1. *Theoretical models of human development* (5th ed.). New York: Wiley.

Bronstein, P. (1994). Differences in mothers' and fathers' behaviors toward children: Cross-cultural comparison. *Developmental Psychology, 20,* 995–1003.

Brooke, J. (1991, June 15). Signs of life in Brazil's industrial valley of death. *New York Times International*, p. 2.

Brooks-Gunn, J. (1987). Pubertal processes and girls' psychological adaptation. In R. M. Lerner & T. L. Foch (Eds.), *Biological psychosocial interactions in early adolescence*. Hillsdale, NJ: Erlbaum.

Brooks-Gunn, J. (1991). Maturational timing variations in adolescent girls, consequences of. In R. M. Lerner, A. C. Petersen, & J. Brooks-Gunn (Eds.), *Encyclopedia of adolescence* (Vol. 2). New York: Garland.

Brooks-Gunn, J., & Reiter, E. O. (1990). The role of pubertal processes. In S. S. Feldman & G. R. Elliott (Eds.), *At the threshold: The developing adolescent*. Cambridge, MA: Harvard University Press.

Brophy, J. E. (1998). *Motivating students to learn*. Boston, MA: McGraw-Hill.

Brough, J.A., & Irvin, J.L. (2001). Parental involvement supports academic improvement among middle schoolers: What research says. *Middle School Journal, 32,* 56–61.

Brown, A. L., Kane, M. J., & Echols, K. (1986). Young children's mental models determine transfer across problems with a common goal structure. *Cognitive Development, 1,* 103–122.

Brown, B. (1999). Optimizing expression of the common human genome for child development. *Current Directions in Psychological Science, 8,* 37–41.

Brown, B. B. (1990). Peer groups and peer cultures. In S. S. Feldman & G. R. Elliott (Eds.), *At the threshold: The developing adolescent*. Cambridge, MA: Harvard University Press.

Brown, K. W., & Gottfried, A. W. (1986). Development of cross-modal transfer in early infancy. In L. P. Lipsitt & C. K. Rovee-Collier (Eds.), *Advances in infancy research* (Vol. 4). Norwood, NJ: Ablex.

Brown, L. M., Way, N., & Duff, J. L. (1999). The others in my I: Adolescent girls' friendships and peer relations. In N. G. Johnson, M. C. Roberts, & J. Worell (Eds.), *Beyond appearance: A new look at adolescent girls*. Washington, DC: American Psychological Association.

Brown, R. (1958a). How shall a thing be called? *Psychological Review, 65,* 14–21.

Brown, R. (1973). *A first language: The early stages*. Cambridge, MA: Harvard University Press.

Brown, R., & Hanlon, C. (1970). Derivational complexity and order of acquisition in child speech. In J. R. Hayes (Ed.), *Cognition and the development of language*. New York: Wiley.

Browne, C. A., & Woolley, J. D. (2001). Theory of mind in children's naming of drawings. *Journal of Cognition and Development, 2,* 389–411.

Brownell, C. A., & Brown, E. (1992). Peers and play in infants and toddlers. In V. B. Van Hasselt & M.

Hersen (Eds.), *Handbook of social development*. New York: Plenum.

Brownell, C. A., & Carriger, M. S. (1990). Changes in cooperation and self-other differentiation during the second year. *Child Development, 61,* 1164–1174.

Brownlow, S., Dixon, A. R., Egbert, C. A., & Radcliffe, R. D. (1997). Perception of movement and dancer characteristics from point-light displays of dance. *Psychological Record, 47(3),* 411–421.

Bruckner, H., & Bearman, P. (2005). After the promise: the STD consequences of adolescent virginity pledges. *Journal of Adolescent Health, 36,* 271–278.

Bruer, J. T. (1999). *The myth of the first three years: A new understanding of how learning occurs throughout life*. Riverside, NJ: Simon and Schuster.

Bruner, J. (1983). *Child's talk: Learning to use language*. New York: Norton.

Bruner, J. (1999). The intentionality of referring. In P. D. Zelazo, J. W. Astington, & D. R. Olson (Eds.), *Developing theories of intention*. Mahwah, NJ: Erlbaum.

Bruner, J., Roy, C., & Ratner, N. (1982). The beginnings of request. In K. E. Nelson (Ed.), *Children's language* (Vol. 3). Hillsdale, NJ: Erlbaum.

Bryan, J., Osendarp, S., Hughes, D., Calvaresi, E., Baghurst, K., &Van Klinken, J. W. (2004). Nutrients for cognitive development in school-aged children. *Nutrition Reviews, 62(8),* 295–306.

Bryant, B. K. (1985). The neighborhood walk: Sources of support in middle childhood. *Monographs of the Society for Research in Child Development, 50(3,* Serial No. 210).

Bryden, M. P. (1982). *Laterality: Functional asymmetry in the intact brain*. New York: Academic Press.

Buck, J. B. (2002). Re-segregating America's public schools. In C.C. Yeakey & R.D. Henderson (Eds.), *Surmounting the odds: Equalizing educational opportunity in the new millennium*. Greenwich, CT: IAP.

Buckingham, D., & Shultz, T. R. (2000). The developmental course of distance, time, and velocity concepts: A generative connectionist model. *Journal of Cognition and Development, 1,* 305–345.

Buhrmester, D. (1990). Intimacy of friendship, interpersonal competence, and adjustment during preadolescence and adolescence. *Child Development, 61,* 1101–1111.

Buhrmester, D. (1992). The developmental courses of sibling and peer relationships. In F. Boer & J. Dunn (Eds.), *Children's sibling relationships: Developmental and clinical issues*. Hillsdale, NJ: Erlbaum.

Buhrmester, D. (1996). Need fulfillment, interpersonal competence, and the developmental contexts of early adolescent friendship. In W. M. Bukowski, A. F. Newcomb & W. W. Hartup (Eds.), *The company they keep: Friendship in childhood and adolescence*. New York: Cambridge University Press.

Buhrmester, D., & Furman, W. (1990). Perceptions of sibling relationships during middle childhood and adolescence. *Child Development, 61,* 1387–1398.

Buhrmester, D., & Prager, K. (1995). Patterns and functions of self-disclosure during childhood and adolescence. In K. J. Rotenberg (Ed.), *Disclosure processes in children and adolescents*. New York: Cambridge University Press.

Bukowski, W. M., & Hoza, B. (1989). Popularity and friendship: Issues in theory, measurement,

and outcome. In T. J. Berndt & G. W. Ladd (Eds.), *Peer relationships in child development*. New York: Wiley.

Burchinal, M. R., Roberts, J. E., Hooper, S., & Zeisel, S. A. (2000). Cumulative risk and early cognitive development: A comparison of statistical risk models. *Developmental Psychology, 36,* 793–807.

Burgess, S. R., Hecht, S. A., & Lonigan, C. J. (2002). Relations of the preschool HLE and oral language, phonological sensitivity, and word decoding: A one-year longitudinal study. *Reading Research Quarterly, 37,* 408–427.

Burgess, K., Rubin, K., Cheah, C., & Nelson, L. (2001). Behavioral inhibition, social withdrawal, and parenting. In W. Ray Crozier & Lynne E. Alden (Eds.), *International Handbook of Social Anxiety* (pp. 137–158). New York: Wiley.

Burkam, D. T., Lee, V. E., & Smerdon, B. (1997). Gender and science learning early in high school: Subject matter and laboratory experiences. *American Educational Research Journal, 34,* 297–331.

Burnett, P. C. (2004). Enhancing students' self-perceptions: The impact of programs and teacher feedback. *Australian Journal of Guidance & Counselling, 14,* 34–47.

Burton, R. V. (1963). The generality of honesty reconsidered. *Psychological Review, 70,* 481–499.

Burton, R. V. (1984). A paradox in theories and research in moral development. In W. M. Kurtines & J. L. Gewirtz (Eds.), *Morality, moral behavior, and moral development*. New York: Wiley.

Burton, S., & Mitchell, P. (2003). Judging who knows best about yourself: Developmental change in citing the self across middle childhood. *Child Development, 74(2),* 426–443.

Bushman, B. J. (2002). Does venting anger feed or extinguish the flame? Catharsis, rumination, distraction, anger and aggressive responding. *Personality and Social Psychology Bulletin, 28,* 724–731.

Bushman, B. J., & Huesmann, L. R. (2001). Effects of televised violence on aggression. In D. G. Singer & J. L. Singer (Eds.), *Handbook of children and the media*. Thousand Oaks, CA: Sage.

Bushnell, I. W. R., Sai, F., & Mullin, J. T. (1989). Neonatal recognition of the mother's face. *British Journal of Developmental Psychology, 7,* 315.

Buss, D. M. (1999). *Evolutionary psychology: The new science of the mind. Boston*: Allyn and Bacon.

Buss, D. M. (Ed.), (2005). *The handbook of evolutionary psychology*. Hoboken, NJ: Wiley.

Bussey, K., & Bandura, A. (1984). Gender constancy, social power, and sex-linked modeling. *Journal of Personality and Social Psychology, 47,* 1292–1302.

Bussey, K., & Bandura, A. (1992). Self-regulatory mechanisms governing gender development. *Child Development, 63,* 1236–1250.

Bussey, K., & Bandura, A. (1999). Social-cognitive theory of gender development and differentiation. *Psychological Review, 106,* 676–713.

Bussey, K., & Perry, D. G. (1982). Same-sex imitation: The avoidance of cross-sex models or the acceptance of same-sex models? *Sex Roles, 8,* 773–784.

Butler, R. (2005). Competence assessment, competence, and motivation between early and middle childhood. In A.J. Elliot & C.S. Dweck (Eds.), *Handbook of competence and motivation*. New York: Guilford.

Butler, R., & Ruzany, N. (1993). Age and socialization effects on the development of social comparison motives and normative ability assessment in kibbutz and urban children. *Child Development, 64*, 532–543.

Butovskaya, M., Verbeek, P., Ljungberg, T., & Lunardini, A. (2000). A multicultural view of peace-making among young children. In F. Aureli & F. B. M. de Waal (Eds.), *Natural conflict resolution.* Berkeley: University of California Press.

Butterworth, G. (1995). The self as an object of consciousness in infancy. In P. Rochat (Ed.), *The self in infancy: Theory and research.* Amsterdam: Elsevier.

Butterworth, G., & Grover, L. (1988). The origins of referential communication in human infancy. In L. Weiskrantz (Ed.), *Thought without language* (pp. 5–24). Oxford: Clarendon.

Buunk, B. P., Zurriaga, R., Piero, J. M., Nauta, A., & Gasalvez, I. (2005). Social comparisons at work related to a cooperative social climate and to individual differences in social comparison orientation. *Applied Psychology: An International Review, 54*, 61–80.

Buzzelli, C. A. (1995). Teacher-child discourse in the early childhood classroom: A dialogic model of self-regulation and moral development. In S. Reifel (Ed.), *Advances in early education and day care* (Vol. 7). Greenwich, CT: JAI Press.

Byrne, B. M. (1996). *Measuring self-concept across the life span: Issues and instrumentation.* Washington, DC: American Psychological Association.

Byrnes, J. P. (1988). Formal operations: A systematic reformulation. *Developmental Review, 8*, 66–87.

Byrnes, J. P., Miller, D. C., & Schafer, W. D. (1999). Gender differences in risk taking: A meta-analysis. *Psychological Bulletin, 125*, 367–383.

Cadinu, M. R., Maass, A., Rosabianca, A., & Kiesner, J. (2005). Why do women underperform under stereotype threat? Evidence for the role of negative thinking. *Psychological Science, 16*, 572–578.

Cain, K. M., & Dweck, C. S. (1995). The relation between motivational patterns and achievement cognitions through the elementary years. *Merrill-Palmer Quarterly, 41*, 25–52.

Cairns, E. (1987). *Caught in crossfire: Children and the Northern Ireland conflict.* Belfast: Appletree Press.

Cairns, E. (1996). *Children and political violence.* Oxford: England: Blackwell.

Cairns, R. B., Cairns, B. D., Neckerman, H. J., Gest, S. D., & Gariepy, J. (1988). Social networks and aggressive behavior: Peer support or peer rejection? *Developmental Psychology, 24*, 815–823.

Cairns, R. B., Cairns, B. D., Neckerman, H. J., Ferguson, L. L., & Gariepy, J. (1989). Growth and aggression: I. Childhood to early adolescence. *Developmental Psychology, 25*, 320–330.

Caldera, Y. M., Huston, A. C., & O'Brien, M. (1989). Social interactions and play patterns of parents and toddlers with feminine, masculine, and neutral toys. *Child Development, 60*, 70–76.

Caldwell, B.M., & Bradley, R.H. (1984). *Home observation for measurement of the environment.* Little Rock: University of Arkansas.

Calhoon, M. B. (2005). Effects of a peer-mediated phonological skill and reading comprehension program on reading skill acquisition for middle school students with reading disabilities. *Journal of Learning Disabilities, 38*, 424–433.

Calkins, S. D., Dedmon, S. E., Gill, K. L., Lomax, L. E., & Johnson, L. M. (2002). Frustration in infancy: Implications for emotion regulation, physiological processes, and temperament. *Infancy, 3*, 175–197.

Call, J., Brauer, J., Kaminski, J., & Tomasello, M. (2003). Domestic dogs (*Canis familiaris*) are sensitive to the attentional state of humans.. *Journal of Comparative Psychology, 117*, 257–263.

Camarata, S., & Leonard, L. B. (1986). Young children pronounce object words more accurately than action words. *Journal of Child Language, 13*, 51–65.

Campbell, A., Shirley, L., & Caygill, L. (2002). Sex-typed preferences in three domains: Do two-year-olds need cognitive variables? *British Journal of Psychology, 93*, 203–217.

Campbell, D., & Eaton, W. O. (1999). Sex differences in the activity level of infants. *Infant and Child Development, 8*, 1–17.

Campbell, F. A., Pungello, E. P., & Miller-Johnson, S. (2001). The development of cognitive and academic abilities: Growth curves from an early childhood educational experiment. *Developmental Psychology, 37*, 231–242.

Campbell, J. R., Hombo, C. M., & Mazzeo, J. (2000). *NAEP 1999 trends in academic progress: Three decades of student performance.* Washington, DC: U.S. Department of Education.

Campbell, R. L., & Christopher, J. C. (1996). Moral development theory: A critique of its Kantian presuppositions. *Developmental Review, 16*, 147.

Campbell, S. B. (2000). Attention-deficit/hyperactivity disorder: A developmental view. In A. Sameroff, M. Lewis, & S. M. Miller (Eds.), *Handbook of developmental psychopathology* (2nd ed.). New York: Plenum.

Campos, J. J., Bertenthal, B. I., & Kermoian, R. (1992). Early experience and emotional development: The emergence of wariness of heights. *Psychological Science, 3*, 61–64.

Campos, J. J., Hiatt, S., Ramsay, D., Henderson, C., & Svejda, M. (1978). The emergence of fear on the visual cliff. In M. Lewis & L. Rosenblum (Eds.), *The origins of affect.* New York: Plenum.

Campos, R. G. (1989). Soothing pain-elicited distress in infants with swaddling and pacifiers. *Child Development, 60*, 781–792.

Camras, L. A., Malatesta, C. Z., & Izard, C. E. (1991). The development of facial expressions in infancy. In R. Felman & B. Rime (Eds.), *Fundamentals of nonverbal behavior.* Cambridge: Cambridge University Press.

Cantin, S., & Boivin, M. (2004). Change and stability in children's social network and self perceptions during transition from elementary to junior high school. *International Journal of Behavioral Development, 28*(6), 561–570.

Caplan, M., Vespo, J. E., Pedersen, J., & Hay, D. F. (1991). Conflict and its resolution in small groups of one- and two-year-olds. *Child Development, 62*, 1513–1524.

Capron, C., & Duyme, M. (1989). Assessment of effects of socio-economic status on IQ in a full cross-fostering study. *Nature, 340*, 552–554.

Cardon, L. R. (1994). Specific cognitive abilities. In J. C. DeFries, R. Plomin, & D. W. Fulker (Eds.), *Nature and nurture during middle childhood.* Oxford, England: Blackwell.

Carey, S. (1977). The child as word learner. In M. Halle, J. Bresnan, & G. A. Miller (Eds.), *Linguistic theory and psychological reality.* Cambridge, MA: MIT Press.

Carey, S. (1985). *Conceptual change in childhood.* Cambridge, MA: MIT Press.

Carey, W. B., & McDevitt, S. C. (1978). Revision of the Infant Temperament Questionnaire. *Pediatrics, 61*, 735–739.

Carlson, M. J., & Corcoran, M. E. (2001). Family structure and children's behavioral and cognitive outcomes. *Journal of Marriage & Family, 63*(3), 779–793.

Carlson, S. M., & Moses, L. J. (2001). Individual differences in inhibitory control and children's theory of mind. *Child Development, 72*, 1032–1053.

Carlson, V., Cicchetti, D., Barnett, D., & Braunwald, K. G. (1989). Finding order in disorganization: Lessons from research on maltreated infants' attachments to their caregivers. In D. Cicchetti & V. Carlson (Eds.), *Child maltreatment: Theory and research on the causes and consequences of child abuse and neglect.* New York: Cambridge University Press.

Carlson, V. J., and Harwood, R. L. (2003). Attachment, culture, and the caregiving system: The cultural patterning of everyday experiences among Anglo and Puerto Rican mother-infant pairs. *Infant Mental Health Journal, 24*(1), 53–73.

Carmichael, S. L., & Shaw, G. M. (2000). Maternal life event stress and congenital anomalies. *Epidemiology, 11*, 30–35.

Carnegie Task Force. (1994). *Starting points: Meeting the needs of our youngest children.* New York: Carnegie Corporation of New York.

Carothers, S. S., Borkowski, J. G., Lefever, J. B., & Whitman, T. (2005). Religiosity and the socioemotional adjustment of mothers and their children. *Journal of Family Psychology, 19*, 263–275.

Caron, A. J., Caron, R. F., & MacLean, D. J. (1988). Infant discrimination of naturalistic emotional expressions: The role of face and voice. *Child Development, 59*, 604–616.

Carp, E. Wayne. (1998). *Family matters: Secrecy and disclosure in the history of adoption.* Cambridge, MA: Harvard University Press.

Carpenter, M., Akhtar, N., & Tomasello, M. (1998). 14- through 18-month-old infants differentially imitate intentional and accidental actions. *Infant Behavior and Development 21*, 315–330.

Carr, M., & Davis, H. (2001). Gender differences in arithmetic strategy use: A function of skill and preference. *Contemporary Educational Psychology, 26*, 330–347.

Carr, M., & Jessup, D. L. (1997). Gender differences in first grade mathematics strategy use: Social and metacognitive influences. *Journal of Educational Psychology, 98*, 318–328.

Carr, M., Jessup, D. L., & Fuller, D. (1999). Gender differences in first-grade mathematics strategy use: Parent and teacher contributions. *Journal for Research in Mathematics Education, 30*, 20–46.

Carter, D. B., & Levy, G. D. (1988). Cognitive aspects of early sex-role development: The influence of gender schemas on preschoolers' memories and preferences for sex-typed toys and activities. *Child Development, 59*, 782–792.

Carter, D. B., & McCloskey, L. A. (1984). Peers and maintenance of sex-typed behavior: The development of children's conceptions of cross-gender behavior in their peers. *Social Cognition, 2*, 294–314.

Carter, D. B., & Patterson, C. J. (1982). Sex roles as social conventions: The development of children's conceptions of sex-role stereotypes. *Developmental Psychology, 18*, 812–824.

Carver, L. J., & Bauer, P. J. (2001). The dawning of a past: The emergence of long-term explicit memory in infancy. *Journal of Experimental Psychology: General, 130*, 726–745.

Casanova, P. F., Garcia-Linares, M. C., de la Torre, M. J., & Carpio, M. (2005). Influence of family and socio-demographic variables on students with low academic achievement. *Educational Psychology, 25*, 423–435.

Case, R. (1985). *Intellectual development.* New York. Academic Press.

Case, R. (1992). *The mind's staircase: Exploring the conceptual underpinnings of children's thought and knowledge.* Hillsdale, NJ: Erlbaum.

Case, R., & Okamoto, Y. (1996). The role of central conceptual structures in the development of children's thought. *Monographs of the Society for Research in Child Development,* 61 (12, Serial No. 246).

Casey, B. J., Davidson, M. & Rosen, B. (2002). The Basics of fMRI and its application to developmental science. *Developmental Science, 5,* 301–309.

Casey, B. J., & de Haan, M. (2002). Introduction: New methods in developmental science. *Developmental Science, 5,* 265–267.

Casey, M. B., Nuttall, R. L., & Pezaris, E. (1997). Mediators of gender differences in mathematics college entrance test scores: A comparison of spatial skills with internalized beliefs and anxieties. *Developmental Psychology, 33,* 669–680.

Casey, M. B., Nuttall, R. L., & Pezaris, E. (1999). Evidence in support of a model that predicts how biological and environmental factors interact to influence spatial skills. *Developmental Psychology, 35,* 1237–1247.

Caspi, A. (1998). Personality development across the life course. In W. Damon (Series Ed.) & N. Eisenberg (Vol. Ed.), *Handbook of child psychology,* Vol. 3: *Social, Emotional, and Personality Development* (pp. 311–388). New York: Wiley.

Caspi, A., Henry, B., McGee, R. O., Moffitt, T. E., & Silva, P. A. (1995). Temperamental origins of child and adolescent behavior problems: From age 3 to age 15. *Child Development, 66,* 55–68.

Caspi, A., & Silva, P.A. (1995). Temperamental qualities at age three predict personality traits in young adulthood: Longitudinal evidence from a birth cohort. *Child Development, 66,* 486–498.

Cassell, J., & Jenkins, H. (1998). Chess for girls? Feminism and computer games. In J. Cassell & H. Jenkins (Eds.), *From Barbie to Mortal Kombat: Gender and computer games.* Cambridge, MA: MIT Press.

Cassia, V. M., Simion, F., & Umilta, C. (2001). Face preference at birth: The role of an orienting mechanism. *Developmental Science, 4,* 101–108.

Cassidy, J., Kirsh, S. J., Scolton, K. L., & Parke, R. D. (1996). Attachment and representations of peer relationships. *Developmental Psychology, 32,* 892–904.

Catron, T. F., & Masters, J. C. (1993). Mothers' and children's conceptualizations of corporal punishment. *Child Development, 64,* 1815–1828.

Cattell, R. B. (1971). *Abilities: Their structure, growth, and action.* Boston: Houghton Mifflin.

Cattell, R. B. (1987). *Intelligence: Its structure, growth, and action.* New York: North-Holland.

Caudill, W., & Schooler, C. (1973). Child behavior and child rearing in Japan and the United States: An interim report. *Journal of Nervous and Mental Disease, 157,* 323–338.

Caughy, M. O. (1996). Health and environmental effects on the academic readiness of school-age children. *Developmental Psychology, 32,* 515–522.

Cavallotti, D., Casilla, G., Piantelli, G., Verrotti, C., Fieni, S. & Gramellini, D. (2004). Early complications of prenatal invasive diagnostics: Perspective analysis. *Acta Bio Medica Ateneo Parmense, 75*(1), 23–26.

Cavanaugh, J. C., & Perlmutter, M. (1982). Metamemory: A critical examination. *Child Development, 53,* 11–28.

CDC National Center for Health Statistics. Health, United States (2004). *With Chartbook on Trends in the Health of Americans.* Hyattsville, MD.

CDC National Center for Health Statistics. (2005). Prevalence of overweight among children and adolescents: United States, 1999–2002. Retrieved March 17, 2006 from http://www.cdc.gov/nchs/ products/pubs/pubd/hestats/overwght99.htm

CDC National Center for Infectious Diseases. (2005). Retrieved December 19, 2005 from http://www.cdc.gov/ncbddd/fas/fasask.htm#how

Ceci, S. J. (1996). *On intelligence: A bioecological treatise on intellectual development* (expanded ed.). Cambridge, MA: Harvard University Press.

Ceci, S. J., & Bruck, M. (1995). *Jeopardy in the courtroom: A scientific analysis of children's testimony.* Washington, DC: American Psychological Association.

Ceci, S. J., & Bruck, M. (1998). Children's testimony. In W. Damon (Series Ed.) & I. E. Sigel & K. A. Renninger (Vol. Eds.), *Handbook of child psychology*: Vol. 4. *Child psychology in practice* (5th ed.). New York: Wiley.

Ceci, S. J., & Williams, W. M. (1997). Schooling, intelligence, and income. *American Psychologist, 52,* 1051–1058.

Celi, A. C. (2005). Immigration, race/ethnicity, and social and economic factors as predictors of breastfeeding initiation. (eng; includes abstract). *Archives of Pediatrics & Adolescent Medicine 159*(3), 255–260.

Center for Applied Linguistics. (2002). ESL standards for Pre-K 12 students. Retrieved March 22, 2005, from Center for Applied Linguistics Web site: http://www.cal.org/eslstandards/

Centers for Disease Control. (2002). Trends in sexual risk behaviors among high school students-United States. *Morbidity and Mortality Report Weekly, 51,* 856–859.

Centers for Disease Control and Prevention. (2004). Gonorrhea. CDC Fact Sheet. Retrieved March 6, 2006, from http://www.cdc.gov/ std/Gonorrhea/ STDFact-Gonorrhea.htm#common.

Centers for Disease Control and Prevention. (2006). [Article Title]. MMWR 2002; 51:[897899]. Retrieved March 16, 2006 from http://www.cdc.gov/mmwr/PDF/wk/mm5140.pdf

Center for Research on Education, Diversity & Excellence. (2001). Practitioner brief #3. Retrieved October 11, 2005, from Center for Applied Linguistics Web site: http://www.cal.org/crede/ pubs/PracBrief3.pdf

Cervone, D., Mor, N., & Orom, H. (2004). Self-efficacy beliefs on the architecture of personality: On knowledge, appraisal, and self-regulation. In Roy F. Baumeister, & Kathleen D. Vohs (Eds.), *Handbook of self-regulation: Research, theory, and applications* (pp. 188–210). New York: Guilford Press.

Chabra, A., & Chavez, G. F. (2000). A comparison of long pediatric hospitalizations in 1985 and 1994. *Journal of Community Health*: 25(3), 199–10.

Chamberlain, J., McDonagh, R., Lalonde, A., & Arulkumaran, S. (2003). Averting maternal death and disability: The role of professional associations in reducing maternal mortality worldwide. *International Journal of Gynecology and Obstetrics, 83,* 94–102.

Chamberlain, P., & Patterson, G. R. (1995). Discipline and child compliance in parenting. In M. H. Bornstein (Ed.), *Handbook of parenting*: Vol. 4. *Applied and practical parenting.* Mahwah, NJ: Erlbaum.

Chance, C., & Fiese, B. H. (1999). Gender-stereotyped lessons about emotion in family narratives. *Narrative Inquiry, 9,* 243–255.

Chandler, M. J. (1973). Egocentrism and antisocial behavior: The assessment and training of social perspective-taking skills. *Developmental Psychology, 9,* 326–332.

Chandler, M. J., Greenspan, S., & Barenboim, C. (1973). Judgments of intentionality in response to videotaped and verbally presented moral dilemmas: The medium is the message. *Child Development, 44,* 315–320.

Chandler, M. J., & Lalonde, C. (1996). Shifting to an interpretive theory of mind: 5-to-7-year-olds' changing conceptions of mental life. In A. J. Sameroff & M. M. Haith (Eds.), *The five to seven year shift: The age of reason and responsibility.* Chicago: University of Chicago Press.

Chang, L. (2003). Variable effects of children's aggression, social withdrawal, and prosocial leadership as functions of teacher beliefs and behaviors. *Child Development, 74,* 535–548.

Chao, R. (2001). Extending the research on the consequences of parenting style for Chinese Americans and European Americans. *Child Development, 72,* 1832–1843.

Chao, R., & Tseng, V. (2002). Parenting of Asians. In M. H. Bornstein (Ed.), *Handbook of parenting* (2nd ed., Vol. 3). Mahwah, NJ: Erlbaum.

Chapman, M. (1988). *Constructive evolution: Origins and development of Piaget's thought.* Cambridge: Cambridge University Press.

Chapman, M. (1992). Equilibration and the dialectics of organization. In H. Beilin & P. B. Pufall (Eds.), *Piaget's theory: Prospects and possibilities.* Hillsdale, NJ: Erlbaum.

Chapman, R. S., Streim, N. W., Crais, E. R., Salmon, D., Strand, E. A., & Negri, N. A. (1992). Child talk: Assumptions of a developmental process model for early language learning. In R. A. Chapman (Ed.), *Processes in language acquisition and disorders.* St. Louis, MO: Mosby Year Book.

Charach, A., Pepler, D., & Ziegler, S. (1995). Bullying at school. *Education Canada, 37,* 12–18.

Chase, W. G., & H. A. Simon. (1973). The mind's eye in chess. In W. G. Chase (Ed.), Academic Press, *Visual Information Processing.* New York: Academic Press.

Chavajay, P., & Rogoff, B. (1999). Cultural variation in management of attention by children and their caregivers. *Developmental Psychology, 35,* 1079–1090.

Chen, C., Greenberger, E., Lester, J., Dong, Q., & Guo, M. (1998). A cross-cultural study of family and peer correlates of adolescent misconduct. *Developmental Psychology, 34,* 770–781.

Chen, C., & Stevenson, H. W. (1995). Motivation and mathematics achievement: A comparative study of Asian-American, Caucasian-American, and East Asian high school students. *Child Development, 66,* 1215–1234.

Chen, E., Bloomberg, G. R., Fisher, E. B. Jr., & Strunk, R. C. (2003). Predictors of repeat hospitalizations in children with asthma: The role of psychosocial and socioenvironmental factors. *Health Psychology, 22,* 12–18.

Chen, X. (2002). Peer relationships and networks and socio-emotional adjustment: A Chinese perspective. In B. Cairns & T. Farmer (Eds.), *Social networks from a developmental perspective.* New York: Cambridge University Press.

Chen, X. Liu, M., & Li, D. (2000). Parental control, warmth, and indulgence and their relations to adjustment in Chinese children: A longitudinal study. *Journal of Family Psychology, 14,* 401–419.

Chen, X., Rubin, K. H., & Li, Z. (1995). Social functioning and adjustment in Chinese children: A longitudinal study. *Developmental Psychology, 31,* 531–539.

Chen, X., Rubin, K. H., & Sun, Y. (1992). Social reputation and peer relationships in Chinese and Canadian children: A cross-cultural study. *Child Development, 63,* 1336–1343.

Chen, Z., Sanchez, R. P., & Campbell, T. (1997). From beyond to within their grasp: The rudiments of analogical problem solving in 10- and 13-month-olds. *Developmental Psychology, 33,* 790–801.

Chen, Z., & Siegler, R. S. (2000). Across the great divide; Bridging the gap between understanding of toddlers' and older children's thinking. *Monographs of the Society for Research in Child Development, 65,* (2), Serial No. 261.

Cherny, S. S., & Cardon, L. R. (1994). General cognitive ability. In J. C. DeFries, R. Plomin, & D. W. Fulker (Eds.), *Nature and nurture during middle childhood.* Oxford, England: Blackwell.

Cherny, S. S., Fulker, D. W., Corley, R. P., Plomin, R., & DeFries, J. C. (1994a). Continuity and change in infant shyness from 14 to 20 months. *Behavior Genetics, 24,* 365–379.

Chess, S., & Thomas, A. (1986). *Temperament in clinical practice.* New York: Guilford Press.

Chess, S., & Thomas, A. (1987). *Origins and evolution of behavior disorders: From infancy to early adult life.* Cambridge, MA: Harvard University Press.

Chi, M. T., Feltovich, P. J., & Glaser, R. (1981). Categorization and representation of physics problems by experts and novices. *Cognitive Science, 5,* 121–152.

Chi, M. T. H., Glaser, R., & Farr, M. J. (Eds.). (1988). *The nature of expertise.* Hillsdale, NJ: Erlbaum.

Chi, M. T. H., & Koeske, R. D. (1983). Network representation of a child's dinosaur knowledge. *Developmental Psychology, 19,* 29–39.

Children's Defense Fund. (2003). *Head Start reauthorization: Questions and answers.* Washington, DC.

Children's Defense Fund. (2005). *Head start basics 2005.* Washington, D.C.

Childs, C. P. & Greenfield, P. M. (1980). Informal modes of learning and teaching: The case of Zinacanteco weaving. In N. Warren (Ed.), *Studies in cross-cultural psychology,* Vol. 2, (pp. 269–316). New York: Academic Press.

Choi, S. (1997). Language-specific input and early semantic development: Evidence from children learning Korean. In D. I. Slobin (Ed.), *The crosslinguisitic study of language acquisition*: Vol. 5. *Expanding the contexts.* Mahwah, NJ: Erlbaum.

Choi, S. (2000). Caregiver input in English and Korean: Use of nouns and verbs in book-reading and toy-play contexts. *Journal of Child Language, 27,* 69–96.

Chomsky, N. (1959). A review of B. F. Skinner's Verbal Behavior. *Language, 35,* 26–58.

Chomsky, N. (1972). *Studies on semantics in generative grammar.* The Hague & Paris: Mouton.

Christakis, D. A., Zimmerman, F. J., DiGiuseppe, D. L., & McCarty, C. A. (2004). Early television exposure and subsequent attentional problems in children. *Pediatrics, 113,* 708–771.

Christian, K., Bachnan, H. J., & Morrison, F. J. (2001). Schooling and cognitive development. In R. J. Sternberg & E. L. Grigorenko (Eds.), *Environmental effects on cognitive abilities.* Mahwah, NJ: Erlbaum.

Christiansen, T. C., Wood, J. V., & Barrett, L. F. (2003). Remembering everyday experience through the prism of self-esteem. *Personality & Social Psychology Bulletin, 29,* 51–62.

Cicchetti, D., & Carlson, V. (Eds.), (1989). *Child maltreatment: Theory and research on the causes and consequences of child abuse and neglect.* New York: Cambridge University Press.

Cicchetti, D., Lynch, M., Shonk, S., & Manly, J. T. (1992). An organizational perspective on peer relations in maltreated children. In R. D. Parke & G. W. Ladd (Eds.), *Family-peer relationships: Modes of linkage.* Hillsdale, NJ: Erlbaum.

Cillessen, A. H. N., & Bukowski, W. M. (Eds.). (2000). Recent advances in the measurement of acceptance and rejection in the peer system. *New Directions for Child and Adolescent Development,* No. 88.

Cillessen, A. H. N., Bukowski, W. M., & Haselager, G. J. T. (2000). Stability of sociometric categories. In A. H. N. Cillessen & W. M. Burkowski (Eds.), *New Directions for Child and Adolescent Development,* No. 88. *Recent Advances in the measurement of acceptance and rejection in the peer system.* San Francisco: Jossey-Bass.

Cillessen, A. H. N., & Mayeux, L. (2004). From censure to reinforcement: Developmental changes in the association between aggression and social status. *Child Development, 75,* 147–163.

Cillessen, A. H. N., Van IJzendoorn, H. W., Van Lishout, C. F. M., & Hartup, W. W. (1992). Heterogeneity among peer-rejected boys: Subtypes and stabilities. *Child Development, 63,* 893–905.

Clark, E.V. (1983). Meaning and concepts. In P.Mussen (Ed.), *Handbook of child psychology* (Vol. 3). New York: Wiley.

Clark, E. V. (1987). The principle of contrast: A constraint on language acquisition. In B. MacWhinney (Ed.), *Mechanisms of language acquisition.* Hillsdale, NJ: Erlbaum.

Clark, E. V. (1993). *The lexicon in acquisition.* New York: Cambridge University Press.

Clark, E. V. (1995). Later lexical development and word learning. In P. Fletcher & B. MacWhinney (Eds.), *The handbook of child language.* Cambridge, MA: Blackwell.

Clark, R., Hyde, J. S., Essex, M. J., & Klein, M. H. (1997). Length of maternity leave and quality of motherinfant interactions. *Child Development, 68,* 364–383.

Clarke, A. M., & Clarke, A. D. B. (1976). *Early experience: Myth and evidence.* London: Open Books Publishing.

Clarke-Stewart, K. A. (1980). The father's contribution to children's cognitive and social development in early childhood. In F.A. Pedersen (Ed.), *The father-infant relationship: Observational studies in the family setting.* New York: Praeger.

Clarke-Stewart, K. A. (1989). Infant day care: Maligned or malignant? *American Psychologist, 44,* 266–273.

Clarke-Stewart, K. A., Gruber, C. P., & Fitzgerald, L. M. (1994). *Children at home and in day care.* Hillsdale, NJ: Erlbaum.

Clarke-Stewart, K. A., Vandell, D. L., McCartney, K., Owen, M. T., & Booth, C. (2000). Effects of parental separation and divorce on very young children. *Journal of Family Psychology, 14,* 304–326.

Cleveland, H. H., & Wiebe, R. P. (2003). The moderation of adolescent-to-peer similarity in tobacco and alcohol use by school levels of substance use. *Child Development, 74,* 279–291.

Clewell, W. H., Johnson, M. L., Meier, P. R., Newkirk, J. B., Zide, S. L., Hendee, R. W., et al. (1982). A surgical approach to the treatment of fetal hydrocephalus. *New England Journal of Medicine, 306,* 1320–1325.

Cochran, M., & Niego, S. (2002). Parenting and social networks. In M. H. Bornstein (Ed.), *Handbook of parenting* (2nd ed., Vol. 4). Mahwah, NJ: Erlbaum.

Cohen, D., & Strayer, J. (1996). Empathy in conduct-disordered and comparison youth. *Developmental Psychology, 32,* 988–998.

Cohen, G., Roux, J. C., Grailhe, R., Malcolm, G., Changeux, J. P., Lagercrantz, H. (2005). Perinatal exposure to nicotine causes deficits associated with a loss of nicotinic receptor function. *Proceedings of the National Academy of Sciences of the United States of America, 102*(10), 3817–3821.

Cohen, L. B. (1998). An information-processing approach to infant perception and cognition. In F. Simion & G. Butterworth (Eds.), *The development of sensory, motor and cognitive capacities in early infancy: From perception to cognition.* Hove, UK: Psychology Press.

Cohen, L. B., & Amsel, G. (1998). Precursors to infants' perception of the causality of a simple event. *Infant Behavior and Development, 21,* 713–731.

Cohen, L. B., & Marks, K. S. (2002). How infants process addition and subtraction events. *Developmental Science, 5,* 186–212.

Cohen, L. B., & Strauss, M. S. (1979). Concept acquisition in the human infant. *Child Development, 50,* 419–424.

Cohen, S., & Wills, T. A. (1985). Stress, social support, and the buffering hypothesis. *Psychological Bulletin, 98,* 310–357.

Cohn, J. F., Campbell, S. B., Matias, R., & Hopkins, J. (1990). Face-to-face interactions of postpartum depressed and nondepressed motherinfant pairs at 2 months. *Developmental Psychology, 26,* 15–23.

Cohn, J. F., & Tronick, E. Z. (1983). Three-month-old infants' reaction to simulated maternal depression. *Child Development, 54,* 185–193.

Coie, J. D., & Dodge, K. A. (1998). Aggression and antisocial behavior. In W. Damon (Series Ed.) & N. Eisenberg (Vol. Ed.), *Handbook of child psychology*: Vol. 3. *Social, emotional, and personality development* (5th ed.). New York: Wiley.

Coie, J. D., & Krehbiel, G. (1984). Effects of academic tutoring on the social status of low-achieving, socially rejected children. *Child Development, 55,* 1465–1478.

Colapinto, J. (2000). *As nature made him.* New York: HarperCollins.

Colby A., Kohlberg, L., Gibbs, J. C., & Lieberman, M. (1983). A longitudinal study of moral judgment. *Monographs of the Society for Research in Child Development, 48*(12, Serial No. 200).

Colby, A., & Kohlberg, L. (1987). *The measurement of moral judgment* (Vols. 12). New York: Cambridge University Press.

Cole, M. (1976). Foreword. In A. R. Luria. *Cognitive development: Its cultural and social foundations.* Cambridge, MA: Harvard University Press.

Cole, M. (1996). *Cultural psychology: A once and future discipline.* Cambridge, MA: Harvard University Press.

Cole, M. (1999). Culture in development. In M. H. Bornstein & M. E. Lamb (Eds.), *Developmental psychology: An advanced textbook* (4th ed.). Mahwah, NJ: Erlbaum.

Cole, P. M. (1986). Children's spontaneous control of facial expression. *Child Development, 57,* 1309–1321.

Cole, T. J. (2000). Secular trends in growth. (eng; includes abstract), *The Proceedings of the Nutrition Society 59*(2), 317–341.

Coleman, J.S. (1988). Social capital in the creation of human capital. *American Journal of Sociology, 94,* 95–120.

Coley, R. J. (2002). *An uneven start: Indicators of inequality in school readiness.* Policy Information Report. Policy Information Center, Educational Testing Service, Princeton, NJ.

Collier, V. P. (1995). Acquiring a second language for school. *Directions in Language & Education,* 1(4). Retrieved April 17, 2005, from National Clearinghouse for English Language Acquisition Web site: http://www.ncela.gwu.edu/pubs/directions/04.htm

Collins, W. A., Maccoby, E. E., Steinberg, L., Hetherington, E. M., & Bornstein, M. H. (2000). Contemporary research on parenting: The case for nature and nurture. *American Psychologist, 55,* 218–232.

Collins, W. A., & Russell, G. (1991). Mother-child and father-child relationships in middle childhood and adolescence: A developmental analysis. *Developmental Review, 11,* 99–136.

Collis, G. M. (1985). On the origins of turn-taking: Alternation and meaning. In M. D. Barrett (Ed.), *Children's single-word speech.* New York: Wiley.

Colombo, J. (2001). The development of visual attention in infancy. *Annual Review of Psychology, 52,* 337–367.

Committee for Ethical Conduct in Child Development Research. (1990, Winter). Report from the Committee for Ethical Conduct in Child Development Research. SRCD Newsletter, pp. 57.

Commons, M. L., Miller, P. M., & Kuhn, D. (1982). The relation between formal operational reasoning and academic course selection and performance among college freshmen and sophomores. *Journal of Applied Developmental Psychology, 3,* 110.

Compas, B. R., Conner-Smith, J. J., Saaltzman, H., Thomsen, A. H., & Wadsworth, M. E. (2001). Coping with stress during childhood and adolescence: Problems, progress, and potential in theory and development. *Psychological Bulletin, 127,* 87–127.

Comstock, G., & Scharrer, E. (1999). *Television: What's on, who's watching, and what it means.* San Diego, CA: Academic Press.

Comstock, G., & Scharrer, E. (2001). The use of television and other film-related media. In D. Singer & J. L. Singer (Eds.), *Handbook of children and the media.* Thousand Oaks, CA: Sage.

Condition of Education. National Center for Educational Statistics. NCES Number 2005094.

Condry, K. F., Smith, W. C., & Spelke, E. S. (2001). Development of perceptual organization. In F. Lacerda, C. von Hofsten, & M. Heimann (Eds.), *Emerging cognitive abilities in early infancy.* Mahwah, NJ: Erlbaum.

Conger, R. D., Ge, X., Elder, G. H., Lorenz, F. O., & Simons, R. L. (1994). Economic stress, coercive family process, and developmental problems of adolescents. *Child Development, 65,* 541–561.

Conger, R. D., Patterson, G. R., & Ge, X. (1995). It takes two to replicate: A mediational model for the impact of parents' stress on adolescent adjustment. *Child Development, 66,* 80–97.

Connellan, J., Baron-Cohen, S., Wheelwright, S., Batki, A., & Ahluwalia, J. (2000). Sex differences in human neonatal social perception. *Infant Behavior and Development, 23,* 113–118.

Constanzo, P. R. (1970). Conformity development as a function of self-blame. *Journal of Personality and Social Psychology, 14,* 366–374.

Conteras, J. M., Kerns, K. A., Weimer, B. L., Gentzler, A. L., & Tomich, P. L. (2000). Emotion regulation as a mediator of associations between mother-child attachment and peer relationships in middle childhood. *Journal of Family Psychology, 14,* 111–124.

Conti, D. J., & Camras, L. A. (1984). Children's understanding of conversational principles. *Journal of Experimental Child Psychology, 38,* 456–463.

Cooley, C. H. (1902). *Human nature and the social order.* New York: Charles Scribner's Sons.

Copeland, E. P., & Hess, R. S. (1995). Differences in young adolescents' coping strategies based on gender and ethnicity. *Journal of Early Adolescence, 15,* 203–219.

Coplan, R. Prakash, K., O'Neil, K., & Armer, M. (2004). Do you "want" to play? Distinguishing between conflicted shyness and social disinterest in early childhood. *Developmental Psychology, 40,* 244–258.

Corbett, D., & Wilson, B. (2002). What urban students say about good teaching. *Educational Leadership, 60*(1), 18–22.

Cornelius, M. D., & Day, N. L. (2000). The effects of tobacco use during and after pregnancy on exposed children. *Alcohol Research and Health, 24,* 242–249.

Cornelius, M. D., Ryan, C. M., Day, N. L., Goldschmidt, L., & Willford, J. A. (2001). Prenatal tobacco effects on neuropsychological outcomes among preadolescents. *Journal of Developmental and Behavioral Pediatrics, 22,* 217–225.

Cornelius, M. D., Taylor, P., Geva, D., & Day, N. (1995). Prenatal tobacco exposure and marijuana use among adolescents: Effects on offspring gestational age, growth, and morphology. *Pediatrics, 95,* 738–743.

Cosmides, L., & Tooby, J. (2001). Unraveling the enigma of human intelligence: Evolutionary psychology and the multimodular mind. In R. J. Sternberg & J. C. Kaufman (Eds.), *The evolution of intelligence.* Mahwah, NJ: Erlbaum.

Cossette, L., Pomerleau, A., Malcuit, F., & Kaczorowski, J. (1996). Emotional expressions of female and male infants in a social and nonsocial context. *Sex Roles, 35,* 693–710.

Costin, S. E., & Jones, D. C. (1992). Friendship as a facilitator of emotional responsiveness and prosocial interventions among young children. *Developmental Psychology, 28,* 941–947.

Cote, L. R., & Bornstein, M. H. (2000). Social and didactic parenting beliefs and behaviors among Japanese American and South American mothers of infants. *Infancy, 1,* 363–374.

Courage, M. L., Edison, S. C., & Howe, M. L. (2004). Variability in the early development of visual self-recognition. *Infant Behaviour & Development, 27,* 509–532.

Courage, M. L., & Howe, M. L. (2002). From infant to child: The dynamics of cognitive change in the second year of life. *Psychological Bulletin, 128,* 250–277.

Cowan, P. A. (1978). *Piaget with feeling.* New York: Holt, Rinehart & Winston.

Cowan, P. A., & Cowan, C. P. (2002). What an intervention design reveals about how parents affect their children's academic achievement and behavior problems. In J. G. Borkowski, S. L. Ramey, & M. Bristol-Power (Eds.), *Parenting and the child's world: Influences on academic, intellec-*

tual, and social-emotional development. Mahwah, NJ: Erlbaum.

Coyle, T. R. (2001). Factor analysis of variability measures in eight independent samples of children and adults. *Journal of Experimental Child Psychology, 78,* 330–358.

Coyle, T. R., & Bjorklund, D. F. (1997). Age differences in, and consequences of, multiple- and variable-strategy use on a multitrial sort-recall task. *Developmental Psychology, 33,* 372–380.

Cox, B. D., & Lightfoot, C. (Eds.). (1997). *Sociogenetic perspectives on internalization.* Mahwah, NJ: Erlbaum.

CPPRG. (1999). Initial impact of the Fast Track prevention trial for conduct problems: I. The high-risk sample. *Journal of Consulting and Clinical Psychology, 67,* 631–647.

CPPRG. (2002). Evaluation of the first 3 years of the Fast Track prevention trial with children at high risk for adolescent conduct problems. *Journal of Abnormal Child Psychology, 30,* 19–35.

Crago, M. B. (1988). Cultural context in the communicative interaction of young Inuit children. Unpublished doctoral dissertation. McGill University.

Craig, R. S. (1992). The effect of television's daily part in gender portrayals in television commercials: A continuing analysis. *Sex Roles, 26,* 197–211.

Crawford, J. (1997). The English only movement. In *James Crawford's Language Policy and Website Emporium.* Retrieved September 28, 2005, from http://ourworld.compuserve.com/homepages/JWCRAWFORD/engonly.htm

Crawford, N. (2002). Science-based program curbs violence in kids. *Monitor on Psychology, 33,* 38.

Creasey, G. L., & Koblewski, P. J. (1991). Adolescent grandchildren's relationships with maternal and paternal grandmothers and grandfathers. *Journal of Adolescence, 14,* 373–387.

Creasy, R., & Resnick, R. (1999). *Maternal-fetal medicine* (4th ed.), Philadephia, PA.: Saunders.

Crick, N. R. (1995). Relational aggression: The role of intent attributions, feelings of distress, and provocation type. *Development and Psychopathology, 7,* 313–322.

Crick, N. R., Bigbee, M. A., & Howes, C. (1996). Gender differences in children's normative beliefs about aggression: How do I hurt thee? Let me count the ways. *Child Development, 67,* 1003–1014.

Crick, N. R., Casas, J. F., & Mosher, M. (1997). Relational and overt aggression in preschool. *Developmental Psychology, 33,* 579–588.

Crick, N. R., & Dodge, K. A. (1994). A review and reformulation of social information-processing mechanisms in children's social adjustment. *Psychological Bulletin, 115,* 74–101.

Crick, N. R., & Dodge, K. A. (1996). Social information-processing mechanisms in reactive and proactive aggression. *Child Development, 67,* 993–1002.

Crick, N. R., & Grotpeter, J. K. (1995). Relational aggression, gender, and social-psychological adjustment. *Child Development, 66,* 710–722.

Crick, N. R., Nelson, D. A., Morales, J. R., Cullerton-Sen, C., Cases, J. F., & Hickman, S. E. (2001). Relational victimization in childhood and adolescence: I hurt you through the grapevine. In J. Juvonen & S. Graham (Eds.), *Peer harassment in school: The plight of the vulnerable and the victimized.* New York: Guilford.

Crick, N. R., Werner, N. E., Casas, J. F., O'Brien, K. M., Nelson, D. A., Grotpeter, J. K., et al. (1999).

Childhood aggression and gender: A new look at an old problem. In D. Bernstein (Ed.), *Nebraska symposium on motivation*: Vol. 45. *Gender and motivation*. Lincoln: University of Nebraska Press.

Criss, M. M., Pettit, G. S., Bates, J. E., Dodge, K. A., & Lapp, A. L. (2002). Family adversity, positive peer relationships, and children's externalizing behavior: A longitudinal perspective on risk and resilience. *Child Development, 73,* 1220–1237.

Crittenden, P. M., & Ainsworth, M. D. S. (1989). Child maltreatment and attachment theory. In D. Cicchetti & V. Carlson (Eds.), *Child maltreatment: Theory and research on the causes and consequences of child abuse and neglect*. New York: Cambridge University Press.

Crockenberg, S. (1981). Infant irritability, mother responsiveness, and social support influences on the security of infant-mother attachment. *Child Development, 52,* 857–865.

Crockenberg, S. B. (1986). Are temperamental differences in babies associated with predictable differences in care giving? In J. V. Lerner & R. M. Lerner (Eds.), *New directions for child development: No. 31. Temperament and social interaction during infancy and childhood*. San Francisco: Jossey-Bass.

Crockenberg, S. (1988). Social support and parenting. In W. Fitzgerald, B. Lester & M. Yogman (Eds.), *Research on support for parentings and infants in the postnatal period* (pp. 67–92). New York: Ablex.

Crockenburg, S. C., & Leerkes, E. M. (2004). Infant and maternal behaviours regulate infant reactivity to novelty at 6 months. *Developmental Psychology, 40,* 1123–1132.

Crockett, L. J., & Petersen, A. C. (1987). Pubertal status and psychosocial development: Findings from the early adolescence study. In R. M. Lerner & T. L. Foch (Eds.), *Biological psychosocial interactions in early adolescence*. Hillsdale, NJ: Erlbaum.

Crook, C. K. (1979). The organization and control of infant sucking. In H. W. Reese & L. P. Lipsitt (Eds.), *Advances in child development and behavior* (Vol. 14). New York: Academic Press.

Cross, S. E., & Gore, J. S. (2003). Cultural models of the self. In M. R. Leary & J. P. Tangney (Eds.), *Handbook of self and identity*. New York: Guilford.

Crouchman, M. (1985). What mothers know about their newborns' visual skills. *Developmental Medicine and Child Neurology, 27,* 455–460.

Crowley, K., Callanan, M. A., Jipson, J., Galco, J., Topping, K., & Shrager, J. (2001). Shared scientific thinking in everyday parent-child activity. *Science Education, 85,* 712–732.

Croyle, R. T. (2000). Genetic counseling. In A. Kazdin (Ed.), *Encyclopedia of psychology*. Washington, DC: APA.

Culhane, M., Fowler, M. G., Lee, S. S., McSherry, G., Brady, M., & O'Donnell, K. (1999). Lack of long-term effects of in utero exposure to zidovudine among uninfected children born to HIV-infected women. *Journal of the American Medical Association, 281,* 151–157.

Culp, A., Culp, R., Hechtner-Galvin, T., Howell, C., Saathoff-Wells, T., & Marr, P. (2004). First-time mothers in home visitation services utilizing child development specialists. *Infant Mental Health Journal, 25,* 115.

Cummins, J. (1979). Cognitive/academic language proficiency, linguistic interdependence, the optimum age question and some other matters. *Working Papers on Bilingualism, 19,* 121–129.

Cummins, J. (2003). Basic interpersonal communicative skills and cognitive academic language proficiency. In *Dr. Cummins' ESL and Second Language Learning Web*. Retrieved April 17, 2005, from the I teach I learn.com Web site: http://www.iteachilearn.com/cummins/bicscalp.html

Cunningham, A., & Stanovich, K. (2003). Reading can make you smarter: The more children read, the greater their vocabulary and the better their cognitive skills. *Principal—What Principals Need to Know about Reading, 83,* 2, November/December 2003, 34–39.

Curtin, S. C., & Park, M. M. (1999). Trends in the attendant, place, and timing of births and in the use of obstetric interventions: United States 19891997. *National Vital Statistics Report, 47* (27), 112.

Curtiss, S. (1977). Genie: *A psycholinguistic study of a modern day "wild child."* New York: Academic Press.

Damon, W. (1977). Measurement and social development. *Counseling Psychologist, 6,* 13–15.

Damon, W. (1984). Peer education: The untapped potential. *Journal of Applied Developmental Psychology, 5,* 331–343.

Damon, W., & Hart, D. (1982). The development of self-understanding from infancy through adolescence. *Child Development, 53,* 841–864.

D'Andrade, R.G. (1984). Cultural meaning systems. In R.A. Schweder & R.A. Levine (Eds.), *Culture theory: Essays on mind, self and emotion*. Cambridge: Cambridge University Press.

Daneman, M., & Case, R. (1981). Syntactic form, semantic complexity, and short-term memory: Influences on children's acquisition of new linguistic structures. *Developmental Psychology, 17,* 367–378.

Dannemiller, J. L., & Stephens, B. R. (1988). A critical test of infant pattern preference models. *Child Development, 59,* 210–216.

Danner, F. W., & Day, M. C. (1977). Eliciting formal operations. *Child Development, 48,* 1600–1606.

Danziger, S. H., Sandefur, G., & Weinberg, D. (1994). *Confronting poverty: Prescriptions for change*, Cambridge, MA: Harvard University Press.

Darwin, C. (1872). *The expression of emotions in man and animals*. London: Murray.

Dasen, P. R. (1975a). Concrete operational development in Canadian Eskimos. *International Journal of Psychology, 10,* 165–180.

Dasen, P. R. (1975b). Concrete operational development in three cultures. *Journal of Cross-Cultural Psychology, 6,* 156–172.

Datnow, A., Hubbard, L., & Woody, E. (2001). Is single gender schooling viable in the public sector? Lessons from California's pilot program. Final report. (ED471051).

Davalos, D. B., Chavez, E. L., & Guardiola, R. J. (2005). Effects of perceived parental school support and family communication on delinquent behaviors in Latinos and white Non-Latinos. *Cultural Diversity & Ethnic Minority Psychology, 11*(1), 57–68.

David, C. F., & Kistner, J. A. (2000). Do positive self-perceptions have a "dark side"? Examination of the link between perceptual bias and aggression. *Journal of Abnormal Child Psychology, 28,* 327–337.

Davies, W., Isles, A. R. & Wilkinson, L. S. (2001). Imprinted genes and mental dysfunction. *Annals of Medicine, 33,* 428–436.

Davis, H.A. (2003). Conceptualizing the role and influence of student-teacher relationships on children's social and cognitive development. *Educational Psychologist, 38,* 207–234.

Davis, T. L. (1995). Gender differences in masking negative emotions: Ability or motivation? *Developmental Psychology, 31,* 660–667.

Davis, J. V. (2003). Transpersonal psychology. In Taylor, B. and Kaplan, J. (Eds), *The Encyclopedia of Religion and Nature*. Bristol, England: Thoemmes Continuum.

Davis, M. H., Luce, C., & Kraus, S. J. (1994). The heritability of characteristics associated with dispositional empathy. *Journal of Personality, 62,* 369–391.

Davis-Floyd, R. E. (1992). *Birth as an American rite of passage*. Berkeley: University of California Press.

Davis-Floyd, R. (1994). The technocratic body: American childbirth as cultural expression. *Social Science and Medicine, 38*(8), 1125–1140.

Dawkins, R. (1976). *The selfish gene*. New York: Oxford University Press.

Dawson, T. L. (2002). New tools, new insights: Kohlberg's moral judgement stages revisited. *International Journal of Behavioral Development, 26,* 154–166.

Day, M. C. (1975). Developmental trends in visual scanning. In H. W. Reese (Ed.), *Advances in child development and behavior* (Vol. 10). New York: Academic Press.

Day, N. L., Richardson, G. A., Goldschmidt, L., & Cornelius, M. D. (2000). Effects of prenatal tobacco exposure on preschoolers' behavior. *Journal of Developmental and Behavioral Pediatrics, 21,* 180–188.

Day, R. H. (1987). Visual size constancy in infancy. In B. E. McKenzie & R. H. Day (Eds.), *Perceptual development in early infancy: Problems and issues*. Hillsdale, NJ: Erlbaum.

D'Angiulli, A., Siegel, L. S., & Hertzman, C. (2004). Schooling, socioeconomic context, and literacy development. *Educational Psychology, 24,* 867–883.

Dandy, J., & Nettelbeck, T. (2002). A cross-cultural study of parent's academic standards and educational aspirations for their children. *Educational Psychology, 22,* 621–627.

de Haan, M. (2001). The neuropsychology of face processing in infancy. In C. A. Nelson & M. Luciana (Eds.), *Handbook of developmental cognitive neuroscience*. Cambridge, MA: MIT Press.

de Haan, M., & Nelson, C. A. (1998). Discrimination and categorisation of facial expressions of emotions during infancy. In A. Slater (Ed.), *Perceptual development: Visual, auditory, and speech perception in infancy*. Hove, UK: Psychology Press.

de Haan, M., & Nelson, C. A. (1999). Brain activity differentiates face and object processing in 6-month-old infants. *Developmental Psychology, 35,* 1113–1121.

de Jager, B., Margo, J., & Reezigt, G. (2005). The development of metacognition in primary school learning environments. *School Effectiveness and Improvement, 16,* 179–196.

de Veer, M. W., Gallop, G. G., Theall, L. A., & van den Bos, R. (2003). An 8-year longitudinal study of mirror self-recognition in chimpanzees (Pan troglodytes). *Neuropsychologia, 41,* 229–234.

de Villiers, J. G., & de Villiers, P. A. (1999). Language development. In M. H. Bornstein & M. E. Lamb (Eds.), *Developmental psychology: An advanced textbook* (4th ed.). Mahwah, NJ: Erlbaum.

de Waal, F. B. M. (1993). Reconciliation among primates: A review of empirical evidence and unresolved issues. In W. A. Mason & S. Mendoza

(Eds.), *Primate social conflict*. Albany: State University of New York Press.

de Waal, F. B. M. (2000). Primates—a natural heritage of conflict resolution. *Science, 289,* 586–590.

Deater-Deckard, K., & Plomin, R. (1999). An adoption study of etiology of teacher and parent reports of externalizing behavior problems in middle childhood. *Child Development, 70,* 144–154.

Deak, G. O. (2000). Hunting the fox of word learning: Why "constraints" fail to capture it. *Developmental Review, 20,* 29–80.

Deaux, K. (1993). Sorry, wrong number—A reply to Gentile's call. Sex or gender? *Psychological Science, 4,* 125–126.

DeBaryshe, B. D., Patterson, G. R., & Capaldi, D. M. (1993). Performance model for academic achievement in early adolescent boys. *Developmental Psychology, 29,* 795–804.

DeCasper, A. J., & Fifer, W. P. (1980). Of human bonding: Newborns prefer their mothers' voices. *Science, 208,* 1174–1176.

DeCasper, A. J., & Prescott, P. A. (1984). Human newborns' perception of male voices: Preference, discrimination, and reinforcing value. *Developmental Psychobiology, 17,* 481–491.

DeCasper, A. J., & Spence, M. J. (1986). Newborns prefer a familiar story over an unfamiliar one. *Infant Behavior and Development, 9,* 133–150.

DeCasper, A. J., & Spence, M. J. (1991). Auditory mediated behavior during the perinatal period: A cognitive view. In M. J. S. Weiss & P. R. Zelazo (Eds.), *Newborn attention: Biological constraints and the influence of experience.* Norwood, NJ: Ablex.

De Civita, M., Pagini, L., Vitaro, F., & Tremblay, R.E. (2004). The role of maternal educational aspirations in mediating the risk of income source on academic failure in children from persistently poor families. *Children & Youth Services Review, 26,* 749–769.

DeFries, J. C., Plomin, R., & Fulker, D. W. (Eds.). (1994). *Nature and nurture during middle childhood.* Oxford, England: Blackwell.

Dehaene-Lambertz, G. (1999). Cerebral specialization in acoustical and linguistics processings in infants. *Brain and Language, 69,* 417–419.

De Haan, M., & Thomas, K. M. (2002). Applications of ERP and fMRI techniques to developmental science. *Developmental Science, 5*(3), 335–343.

DeHart, G. B. (1999). Conflict and averted conflict in preschoolers' interactions with siblings and friends. In W. A. Collins & B. Laursen (Eds.), *Minnesota symposia on child psychology*: Vol. 30. *Relationships as developmental contexts.* Mahwah, NJ: Erlbaum.

Dejin-Karlsson, E., Hanson, B. S., Estergen, P., Sjoeberg, N., & Marshal, K. (1998). Does passive smoking in early pregnancy increase the risk of small-for-gestational age infants? *American Journal of Public Health, 88,* 1523–1527.

De Jonge, A., & Lagro-Janssen, A. (2004). Birthing positions. A qualitative study into the views of women about various birthing positions. *Journal of Psychosomatic Obstetrics & Gynecology, 25,* 47–55.

Dekovic, M., & Janssens, J. M. A. M. (1992). Parents' childrearing style and child's sociometric status. *Developmental Psychology, 28,* 925–932.

Delgado-Gaitin, C. (1993). Parenting in two generations of Mexican American families. *International Journal of Behavioral Development, 16,* 409–427.

De Lisi, R., & Gallagher, A. M. (1991). Understanding of gender stability and constancy in Argentinean children. *Merrill-Palmer Quarterly, 37,* 483–502.

De Lisi, R., & Goldbeck, S. L. (1999). Implications of Piagetian theory for peer learning. In A. M. O'Donnell & A. King (Eds.), *Cognitive perspectives on peer learning.* Mahwah, NJ: Erlbaum.

De Lisi, R., & Staudt, J. (1980). Individual differences in college students' performance on formal operations tasks. *Journal of Applied Developmental Psychology, 1,* 201–208.

DeLoache, J. S. (2000). Dual representation and young children's use of scale models. *Child Development, 71,* 329–338.

DeLoache, J. S. (2002). The symbol-mindedness of young children. In W. W. Hartup & R. A. Weinberg (Eds.), *Minnesota symposia on child psychology*: Vol. 32. *Child psychology in retrospect and prospect.* Mahwah, NJ: Erlbaum.

DeLoache, J. S., Miller, K. F., & Pierretsoukas, S. L. (1998). Reasoning and problem solving. In W. Damon (Series Ed.) & D. Kuhn & R. S. Siegler (Vol. Eds.), *Handbook of child psychology*: Vol. 2. *Cognition, perception, and language* (5th ed.). New York: Wiley.

DeLoache, J. S., Miller, K. F., & Rosengren, K. (1997). The credible shrinking room: Very young children's performance in symbolic and non-symbolic tasks. *Psychological Science, 8,* 308–313.

DeLoache, J. S., & Smith, C. M. (1999). Early symbolic representation. In I. E. Sigel (Ed.), *Development of mental representation.* Mahwah, NJ: Erlbaum.

DeLoache, J. S., Uttal, D., & Pierroutsakos, S. L. (2000). What's up? The development of an orientation preference for picture books. *Journal of Cognition and Development, 1,* 81–95.

DeMarie, D., & Ferron, J. (2003). Capacity, strategies, and metamemory: Tests of a three-factor model of memory development. *Journal of Experimental Child Psychology, 84,* 167–193.

Demetras, M. J., Post, K. N., & Snow, C. E. (1986). Feedback to first language learners: The role of repetitions and clarification questions. *Journal of Child Language, 13,* 275–292.

Demos, V. (1986). Crying in early infancy: An illustration of the motivational function of affect. In T. B. Brazelton & M. Yogman (Eds.), *Affect and early infancy.* Norwood, NJ: Ablex.

DeNavas-Walt, C., Proctor, B.D., & Mills, R. J. (2004). Income, poverty, and health insurance coverage in the United States: 2003, *U.S. Census Bureau Current Population Reports,* August 2004.

Denham, S. A., & Couchoud, E. A. (1991). Social-emotional predictors of preschoolers' responses to adult negative emotion. *Journal of Child Psychology and Psychiatry and Allied Disciplines, 32,* 595–608.

Denham, S. A., & McKinley, M. (1993). Sociometric nominations of preschoolers: A psychometric analysis. *Early Education and Development, 4,* 109–122.

Denham, S. A., Zoller, D., & Couchoud, E. A. (1994). Socialization of preschoolers' emotion understanding. *Developmental Psychology, 30,* 928–936.

Denton, K., & Zarbatany, L. (1996). Age differences in support processes in conversations between friends. *Child Development, 67,* 1360–1373.

De Ribaupierre, A., Rieben, L., & Lautrey, J. (1991). Developmental change and individual differences: A longitudinal study using Piagetian tasks. *Genetic, Social, and General Psychology Monographs, 117,* 285–311.

Dettwyler, K. A., & Stuart-Macadam, P. (1995). *Breastfeeding: Biocultural perspectives.* New York: Aldine De Gruyter,

Deutsch, F. M., Servis, L. J., & Payne, J. D. (2001). Paternal participation in child care and its effects on children's self-esteem and attitudes toward gendered roles. *Journal of Family Issues, 22,* 1000–1024.

Dever, M.T. (2001). Family literacy bags: A vehicle for parent involvement and education. *Journal of Education & Family Review, 8,* 17–28.

Devlin, B, Daniels, M. & Roeder, K. (1997). The heritability of IQ. *Nature, 388,* 468–471.

DeVries, M. W. (1989). Difficult temperament: A universal and culturally embedded concept. In W.B. Carey & S. McDevitt (Eds.), *Clinical and educational applications of temperament research.* Berwyn, PA.: Swets North America.

DeVries, R. (1969). Constancy of generic identity in the years three to six. *Monographs of the Society for Research in Child Development, 34* (3, Serial No. 127).

DeVries, R., & Zan, B. (1994). *Moral classrooms, moral children: Creating a constructivist atmosphere in early education.* New York: Teachers College Press.

Diamond, L. M., Savin-Williams, R. C., & Dubé, E. M. (1999). Sex, dating, passionate friendships, and romance: Intimate peer relations among lesbian, gay, and bisexual adolescents. In W. Furman, B. B. Brown, & C. Feiring (Eds.), *The development of romantic relationships in adolescence.* Cambridge: Cambridge University Press.

Diamond, M. (1993). Homosexuality and bisexuality in different populations. *Archives of Sexual Behavior, 22,* 291–310.

Diamond, A., Prevor, M. B., Callender, G., & Druin, D. P. (1997). Prefrontal cortex cognitive deficits in children treated early and continuously for PKU. *Monographs of the Society for Research in Child Development, 62*(4, Serial No. 252).

Diamond, M., & Sigmundson, H. K. (1997). Sex reassignment at birth. Long-term review and clinical implications. *Archives of Pediatric Adolescent Medicine, 151,* 298–304.

Dick, D. M., Rose, R. J., Viken, R. J., & Kaprio, J. (2000). Pubertal timing and substance use: Associations between and within families across adolescence. *Developmental Psychology, 36,* 180–189.

Dickinson, D. K., & Tabors, P. O. (2002). Fostering language and literacy in classrooms and homes. Supportive language learning. *Young Children, 57,* 10–18.

Dien, D. S. F. (1982). A Chinese perspective on Kohlberg's theory of moral development. *Developmental Review, 2,* 331–341.

Dietrich, K. N. (1999). Environmental toxicants and child development. In H. Tager-Flusberg (Ed.), *Neurodevelopmental disorders.* Boston: MIT Press.

Dietz, T. L. (1998). An examination of violence and gender role portrayals in video games: Implications for gender socialization and aggressive behavior. *Sex Roles, 38,* 425–442.

Dillon, C. O., Liem, J. H., & Gore, S. (2003). Navigating disrupted transitions: Getting back on track after dropping out of high school. *American Journal of Orthopsychiatry, 73,* 429–440.

Dinges, M. M., & Oetting, E. R. (1993). Similarity in drug use patterns between adolescents and their friends. *Adolescence, 28,* 253–266.

DiLalla, L. F. (2002). Behavior genetics of aggression in children: Review and future directions. *Developmental Review, 22,* 593–622.

DiPietro, J. (1981). Rough and tumble play: A function of gender. *Developmental Psychology, 17,* 50–58.

DiPietro, J. A., Bornstein, M. H., Costigan, K. A., Pressman, E. K., Hahn, C., Painter, K., et al. (2002). What does fetal movement predict about behavior during the first two years of life? *Developmental Psychobiology, 40,* 358–371.

DiPietro, J. A., Hodgson, D. M., Costigan, K. A., Hilton, S. C., & Johnson, T. R. B. (1996). Fetal neurobehavioral development. *Child Development, 67,* 2553–2567.

DiPietro, J. A., Hodgson, D. M., Costigan, K. A., & Johnson, T. R. B. (1996). Fetal antecedent of infant temperament. *Child Development, 67,* 2568–2583.

DiPietro, J. A., Suess, P. E., Wheeler, J. S., Smouse, P. H., & Newlin, D. B. (1995). Reactivity and regulation in cocaine-exposed neonates. *Infant Behavior and Development, 18,* 407–414.

Dishion, T. J. (1990). The family ecology of boys' peer relations in middle childhood. *Child Development, 61,* 874–892.

Dishion, T. J., & Bullock, B. M. (2002). Parenting and adolescent problem behavior: An ecological analysis of the nurturance hypothesis. In J. G. Borkowski, S. L. Ramey, & M. Bristol-Power (Eds.), *Parenting and the child's world: Influences on academic, intellectual, and social-emotional development.* Mahwah, NJ: Erlbaum.

Dishion, T. J., Bullock, B. M., & Granic, I. (2002). Pragmatism in modeling peer influence: Dynamics, outcomes, and change processes. In D. Cicchetti & S. Hinshaw (Eds.), How prevention intervention studies in the field of developmental psychopathology can inform developmental theories and models [Special Issue]. *Development and Psychopathology,* 969–981.

Dittmann, R. W., Kappes, M. H., Kappes, M. E., Borger, D., Meyer-Bahlberg, H. F. L., Stegner, H., et al. (1990). Congenital adrenal hyperplasia: II. Gender-related behavior and attitudes in female patients and sisters. *Psychoneuroendocrinology, 15,* 410–420.

Dittrich, W. H., Troscianko, T., Lea, S., & Morgan, D. (1996). Perception of emotion from dynamic point-light displays represented in dance. *Perception, 25*(6), 727–738.

Dixon, S., Tronick, E., Keeler, C., & Brazelton, T. B. (1981). Mother-infant interaction among the Gusii of Kenya. In T.M. Field, A.M. Sostek, P. Vietze, & P.H. Leiderman (Eds.), *Culture and early interaction.* Hillsdale, NJ: Erlbaum.

Dobbs, J., Arnold, D.H., & Doctoroff, G.L. (2004). Attention in the preschool classroom: The relationships among child gender, child misbehavior, and types of teacher attention. *Early Child Development & Care, 174,* 281–295.

Dodd, A. W. (1997, May). Creating a climate for learning: Making the classroom more like an ideal home. *NASSP Bulletin.*

Dodge, K. A. (1986). A social information processing model of social competence in children. In M. Perlmutter (Ed.), *Minnesota symposia on child psychology:* Vol. 18. *Cognitive perspectives on children's social and behavioral development.* Hillsdale, NJ: Erlbaum.

Dodge, K. A., & Crick, N. R. (1990). Social-information processing bases of aggressive behavior in children. *Personality and Social Psychology Bulletin, 16,* 8–22.

Dodge, K. A., & Feldman, E. (1990). Issues in social cognition and sociometric status. In S. R. Asher & J. D. Coie (Eds.), *Peer rejection in childhood.* New York: Cambridge University Press.

Dodge, K. A., Lansford, J. E., Burks, V. S., Bates, J. E., Pettit, G. S., Fontaine, R., et al. (2003). Peer rejection and social information-processing factors in the development of aggressive behavior problems in children. *Child Development, 74,* 374–393.

Dodge, K. A., & Somberg, D. R. (1987). Hostile attributional biases among aggressive boys are exacerbated under conditions of threats to the self. *Child Development, 58,* 213–224.

Doise, W., & Mugny, G. (1984). *The social development of the intellect.* Oxford: Pergamon.

Donaldson, M. (1982). Conservation: What is the question? *British Journal of Psychology, 73,* 199–207.

Dore, J. (1976). Children's illocutionary acts. In R. Freedle (Ed.), *Comprehension and production.* Hillsdale, NJ: Erlbaum.

Dore, J. (1985). Holophrases revisited: Their "logical" development during dialog. In M. D. Barrett (Ed.), *Children's single-word speech.* New York: Wiley.

Dornbusch, S. M. (1994, February). *Off the track.* Presidential address presented at the meeting of the Meeting of the Society for Research in Adolescence, San Diego, CA.

Dornbusch, S. M., Glasgow, K. L., & Lin, I.-C. (1996). The social structure of schooling. *Annual Review of Psychology, 47,* 401–429.

Dorr, A., Rabin, B. E., & Irlen, S. (2002). Parenting in a multimedia society. In M.H. Bornstein (Ed.), *Handbook of parenting,* vol. 5: *Practical issues in parenting* (pp. 349–374), 2nd ed. Mahwah, NJ: Erlbaum.

Doubleday, C. N., & K. L. Droege. (1993). Cognitive developmental influences on children's understanding of television. In Gordon L Berry and Joy Keiko Asamen (Eds), *Children and Television* (pp. 23–37). Newbury Park, CA: Sage.

Dougherty, T., & Haith, M. M. (1993, March). *Processing speed in infants and children: A component of IQ?* Paper presented at the meeting of the Society for Research in Child Development, New Orleans.

Dowling, M., & Bendell, D. (1988). Characteristics of small-for-gestational-age infants. *Infant Behavior and Development, 11,* 77.

Droege, K. L., & Stipek, D. J. (1993). Children's use of dispositions to predict classmates behavior. *Developmental Psychology, 29,* 646–654.

Drummond, K. V,. & Stipek, D. (2004). Low-income parents' beliefs about their role in children's academic learning. *The Elementary School Journal, 104,* 197–213.

Duckworth, E. (1987). *The having of wonderful ideas and other essays on teaching and learning.* New York: Teachers College Press.

Duffy, F. H., Als, H., & McAnulty, G. B. (1990). Behavioral and electrophysiological evidence for gestational age effects in healthy preterm and full-term infants studied two weeks after expected due date. *Child Development, 61,* 1271–1286.

Duffy, J., Warren, K., & Walsh, M. (2001). Classroom interactions: Gender of teacher, gender of student, and classroom subject. *Sex Roles, 45,* 579–593.

Dufresne, A., & Kobasigawa, A. (1989). Children's spontaneous allocation of study time: Differential and sufficient aspects. *Journal of Experimental Child Psychology, 47,* 274–296.

Duncan, G. J., Brooks-Gunn, J., & Klebanov, P. K. (1994). Economic deprivation and early childhood development. *Child Development, 65,* 296–318.

Duncan, R. M., & Pratt, M. W. (1997). Microgenetic change in the quantity and quality of preschooler's private speech. *International Journal of Behavioral Development, 20,* 367–383.

Dunn, J. (1987). The beginnings of moral understanding: Development in the second year. In J. Kagan & S. Lamb (Eds.), *The emergence of morality in young children.* Chicago: University of Chicago Press.

Dunn, J. (1988). *The beginnings of social understanding.* Cambridge, MA: Harvard University Press.

Dunn, J. (1992). Sisters and brothers: Current issues in developmental research. In F. Boer & J. Dunn (Eds.), *Children's sibling relationships: Developmental and clinical issues.* Hillsdale, NJ: Erlbaum.

Dunn, J. (1993). *Young children's close relationships.* Newbury Park, CA: Sage.

Dunn, J. (1999). Siblings, friends, and the development of social understanding. In W. A. Collins & B. Laursen (Eds.), *Minnesota symposia on child psychology:* Vol. 30. *Relationships as developmental contexts.* Mahwah, NJ: Erlbaum.

Dunn, J. (2002). Sibling relationships. In P. K. Smith & C. H. Hart (Eds.), *Blackwell handbook of childhood social development.* Malden, MA: Blackwell Publishers.

Dunn, J., Cutting, A. L., & Demetriou, H. (2000). Moral sensibility, understanding others, and children's friendship interactions in the preschool period. *British Journal of Developmental Psychology, 18,* 159–177.

Dunn, J., & Herrera, C. (1997). Conflict resolution with friends, siblings, and mothers: A developmental perspective. *Aggressive Behavior, 23,* 343–357.

Dunn, J., & Kendrick, J. (1982). The speech of two- and three-year-olds to infant siblings: "Baby talk" and the context of communication. *Journal of Child Language, 9,* 579–595.

Dunn, J., & McGuire, S. (1992). Sibling and peer relationships in childhood. *Journal of Child Psychology and Psychiatry and Allied Disciplines, 33,* 67–105.

Dunn, J., & Munn, P. (1986). Siblings and the development of prosocial behaviors. *International Journal of Behavioral Development, 9,* 265–284.

Dunphy, D. C. (1963). The social structure of urban adolescent peer groups. *Sociometry, 26,* 230–246.

Dweck, C. S. (1999). *Self-theories: Their role in motivation, personality, and development.* Philadelphia: Psychology Press.

Dweck, C. (2002). Messages that motivate: How praise molds students' beliefs, motivation, and performance (in surprising ways). In Aronson, J. (Ed.), Improving academic achievement: *Impact of psychological factors on education* (pp. 37–60). San Diego, CA: Academic Press.

Dweck, C. S. (2004). The role of mental representation in social development. *Merrill-Palmer Quarterly, 50* (4), 428–444.

Dweck, C. S., Higgins, E. T., & Grant-Pillow, H. (2003). Self-systems give unique meaning to self variables. In M. R. Leary and J. P. Tangney (Eds.), *Handbook of Self and Identity* (pp. 239–252). New York: Guilford.

Dweck, C. S., & Leggett, E. L. (1988). A social-cognitive approach to motivation and personality. *Psychological Review, 95,* 256–273.

Eagly, A. H., & Crowley, M. (1986). Gender and helping behavior: A meta-analytic review of the social psychological literature. *Psychological Bulletin, 100*, 283–308.

Eagly, A. H., & Steffen, V. J. (1986). Gender and aggressive behavior: A meta-analytic review of the social psychological literature. *Psychological Bulletin, 100*, 309–330.

Eagly, A. H., Wood, W., & Diekman, A. B. (2000). Social role theory of sex differences and similarities: A current appraisal. In T. Eckes & H. M. Trautner (Eds.), *The developmental social psychology of gender*. Mahwah, NJ: Erlbaum.

Eapen, V., & Naqvi, A. (2000). Cross-cultural validation of Harter's self-perception profile for children in the United Arab Emirates. *Annals of Saudi Medicine, 20*(1), 811.

East, P. L., & Rook, K. S. (1992). Compensatory patterns of support among children's peer relationships: A test using school friends, nonschool friends, and siblings. *Developmental Psychology, 28*, 163–172.

Eaton, W. O., & Enns, L. R. (1986). Sex differences in human motor activity level. *Psychological Bulletin, 100*, 19–28.

Eccles, J. S., Arbreton, A., Buchanan, C., Jacobs, J., Flanagan, C., Harold, R., et al. (1993). School and family effects on the ontogeny of children's interests, self-perceptions, and activity choice. In J. Jacobs (Ed.), *Nebraska symposium on motivation*: Vol. 40. *Developmental perspectives on motivation*. Lincoln: University of Nebraska Press.

Eccles, J. S., & Barber, B. L. (1999). Student council, volunteering, basketball, or marching band: What kind of extracurricular involvement matters? *Journal of Adolescent Research, 14*, 10–43.

Eccles, J. S., Freedman-Doan, C., Frome, P., Jacobs, J., & Yoon, K. S. (2000). Gender-role socialization in the family: A longitudinal approach. In T. Eckes & H. M. Trautner (Eds.), *The developmental social psychology of gender*. Mahwah, NJ: Erlbaum.

Eccles, J. S., Jacobs, J. E., Harold, R. D., Yoon, K. S., Arbreton, A., & Freedman-Doan, C. (1993). Parents and gender-role socialization during the middle childhood and adolescent years. In S. Oskamp & M. Costanzo (Eds.), *Gender issues in contemporary society*. Thousand Oaks, CA: Sage.

Eccles, J. S., & Roeser, R. W. (1999). School and community influences on human development. In M. H. Bornstein & M. E. Lamb (Eds.), *Developmental psychology: An advanced textbook* (4th ed.). Mahwah, NJ: Erlbaum.

Eckerman, C. O., Davis, C. C., & Didow, S. (1989). Toddlers' emerging ways of achieving social coordinations with a peer. *Child Development, 60*, 440–453.

Eckerman, C. O., Hsu, H., Molitor, A., Leung, E. H. L., & Goldstein, R. F. (1999). Infant arousal in an en-face exchange with a new partner: Effects of prematurity and perinatal biological risk. *Developmental Psychology, 35*, 282–293.

Eckerman, C. O., & Peterman, K. (2001). Peers and infant social/communicative development. In G. Bremner & A. Fogel (Eds.), *Blackwell handbook of infant development*. Malden, MA: Blackwell Publishers.

Eckstein, S., & Shemesh, M. (1992). The rate of acquisition of formal operational schemata in adolescence: A secondary analysis. *Journal of Research in Science Teaching, 29*, 441–451.

Edelman, G. M. (1993). Neural Darwinism: Selection and reentrant signaling in higher brain function. *Neuron, 10*, 115–125.

Edwards, C. (1987). Culture and the construction of moral values: A comparative ethnography of the moral encounters in two cultural settings. In J. Kagan & S. Lamb (Eds.), *The emergence of morality in young children*. Chicago: University of Chicago Press.

Eibl-Eibesfeldt, I. (1989). *Human ethology*. Hawthorne, NY: Aldine de Gruyter.

Eichstedt, J. A., Serbin, L. A., Poulin-Dubois, D., & Sen, M. G. (2002). Of bears and men: Infants' knowledge of conventional and metaphorical gender stereotypes. *Infant Behavior and Development, 25*, 296–310.

Eifermann, R. R. (1971). Social play in childhood. In R. E. Herron & B. Sutton-Smith (Eds.), *Child's play*. New York: Wiley.

Eigsti, I., & Cicchetti, D. (2004). The impact of child maltreatment on expressive syntax at 60 months. *Developmental Science, 7*, 88–102.

Eilers, R. E., & Oller, D. K. (1988). Precursors to speech: What is innate and what is acquired? In R. Vasta (Ed.), *Annals of child development* (Vol. 5). Greenwich, CT: JAI Press.

Eimas, P. D. (1975). Auditory and phonetic coding of the cues for speech: Discrimination of the [r-l] distinction by young infants. *Perception and Psychophysics, 18*, 341–347.

Eisen, M. L., Quas, J. A., & Goodman, G. S. (Eds.). (2002). *Memory and suggestibility in the forensic interview*. Mahwah, NJ: Erlbaum.

Eisenberg, A. R. (1988). Grandchildren's perspectives on relationships with grandparents: The influence of gender across generations. *Sex Roles, 19*, 205–217.

Eisenberg, A. (1999). Emotion talk among Mexican American and Anglo American mothers and children from two social classes. *Merrill-Palmer Quarterly, 45*, 267–284.

Eisenberg, N. (1982). The development of reasoning regarding prosocial behavior. In N. Eisenberg (Ed.), *The development of prosocial behavior*. New York: Academic Press.

Eisenberg, N. (1986). *Altruistic emotion, cognition, and behavior*. Hillsdale, NJ: Erlbaum.

Eisenberg, N. (1987). The relation of altruism and other moral behaviors to moral cognition: Methodological and conceptual issues. In N. Eisenberg & J. Strayer (Eds.), *Empathy and its development*. New York: Cambridge University Press.

Eisenberg, N., Cameron, E., Tryon, K., & Dodez, R. (1981). Socialization of prosocial behavior in the preschool classroom. *Developmental Psychology, 17*, 773–782.

Eisenberg, N., Carlo, G., Murphy, B., & Van Court, P. (1995). Prosocial development in late adolescence: A longitudinal study. *Child Development, 66*, 1179–1197.

Eisenberg, N., Fabes, R. A., Carlo, G., & Troyer, D. (1992). The relations of maternal practices and characteristics to children's vicarious emotional responsiveness. *Child Development, 63*, 583–602.

Eisenberg, N., & Fabes, R. A. (1998). Prosocial development. In W. Damon (Series Ed.) & N. Eisenberg (Vol. Ed.), *Handbook of child psychology*: Vol. 3. *Social, emotional, and personality development* (5th ed.). New York: Wiley.

Eisenberg, N., Fabes, R. A., Shepard, S. A., Murphy, B. C., Jones, S., & Guthrie, I. K. (1998). Contemporaneous and longitudinal prediction of children's sympathy from dispositional regulation and emotionality. *Developmental Psychology, 34*, 910–924.

Eisenberg, N., Fabes, R. A., Guthrie, I. K., & Reiser, M. (2000). Dispositional emotionality and regulation: Their role in predicting quality of social

functioning. *Journal of Personality and Social Psychology, 78*, 136–157.

Eisenberg, N., Martin, C. L., & Fabes, R. A. (1996). Gender development and gender effects. In D. C. Berliner & R. C. Calfee (Eds.), *Handbook of educational psychology*. New York: Macmillan Library Reference.

Eisenberg, N., & Murphy, B. (1995). Parenting and children's moral development. In M. H. Bornstein (Ed.), *Handbook of parenting*: Vol. 4. *Applied and practical parenting*. Mahwah, NJ: Erlbaum.

Eisenberg, N., Pidada, S., & Liew, J. (2001). The relations of regulation and negative emotionality to Indonesian children's social functioning. *Child Development, 72*, 1747–1763.

Eisenberg, N., Tryon, K., & Cameron, E. (1984). The relation of preschoolers' peer interaction to their sex-typed toy choices. *Child Development, 55*, 1044–1050.

Eisenberg, N., Wolchik, S. A., Hernandez, R., & Pasternack, J. F. (1985). Parental socialization of young children's play: A short-term longitudinal study. *Child Development, 56*, 1506–1513.

Eisenberg, N., Zhou, Q., Spinrad, T. L., Valiente, C., Fabes, R. A. & Liew, J. (2005). Relations among positive parenting, children's effortful control, and externalizing problems: A three-wave longitudinal study. *Child Development, 76*(5), 1055–1071.

Ekman, P. (1993). Facial expression and emotion. *American Psychologist, 48*, 384–392.

Ekman, P., & Friesen, W. (1972). Constants across culture in the face and emotion. *Journal of Personality and Social Psychology, 17*, 124–129.

El Abd, S., Turk, J., & Hill, P. (1995). Annotation: Psychological characteristics of Turner syndrome. *Journal of Child Psychology and Psychiatry, 36*, 1109–1125.

Elbert, T., Pantev, C., Wienbruch, C., Rockstrub, B. & Taub, E. (1995). Increased cortical representation of the fingers of the left hand in string players. *Science, 270*(5234), 305–307.

Elder, G. H., & Caspi, A. (1988). Human development and social change: An emerging perspective on the life course. In N. Bolger, A. Caspi, G. Downey, & M. Moorehouse (Eds.), *Persons in context: Developmental processes*. New York: Cambridge University Press.

Elder, G. H., & Conger, R. D. (2000). *Children of the land*. Chicago: University of Chicago Press.

Eldredge, J. L. (2005). Foundations of fluency: An exploration. *Reading Psychology: An International Journal, 26*, 161–181.

El Hassan Al Awad, A. M., & Sonuga-Barke, E. J. S. (1992). Childhood problems in a Sudanese City: A comparison of extended and nuclear families. *Child Development, 63*, 906–914.

Elias, M. J., Parker, S., & Rosenblatt, J. L. (2005). Building educational opportunity. In Goldstein, S. & Brooks, R.B. (Eds), pp. 315–336. New York: Kluwer.

Ellis, S. (1997). Strategy choice in sociocultural context. *Developmental Review, 17*, 490–524.

Ellis, B. J., & Garber, J. (2000). Psychosocial antecedents of variations in girls' pubertal timing: Maternal depression, stepfather presence, and marital and family stress. *Child Development, 71*, 485–501.

Ellis, S., & Siegler, R. S. (1994). Development of problem solving. In R. J. Siegler (Ed.), *Handbook of perception and cognition*: Vol. 12. *Thinking and problem solving*. New York: Academic Press.

Elliott, A. J., & Dweck, C. S. (2005). *Handbook of competence and motivation.* New York: Guilford Press.

Ellsworth, C. P., Muir, D. W., & Hains, S. M. J. (1993). Social competence and person-object differentiation: An analysis of the still-face effect. *Developmental Psychology, 29,* 63–73.

Elman, J., Bates, E., Johnson, M., Karmiloff-Smith, A., Parisi, D., & Plunkett, K. (1996). *Rethinking innateness.* Cambridge, MA: MIT Press.

Elmer-DeWitt, P. (1994, January 17). The genetic revolution. *Time,* pp. 46–53.

Emde, R. N. (1992). Individual meaning and increasing complexity: Contributions of Sigmund Freud and Rene Spitz to developmental psychology. *American Psychologist, 28,* 347–359.

Emde, R. N., & Harmon, R. J. (Eds.). (1984). *Continuities and discontinuities in development.* New York: Plenum.

Emde, R. N., Plomin, R., Robinson, J., Corley, R., DeFries, J., Fulker, D. W., et al. (1992). Temperament, emotion, and cognition at fourteen months: The MacArthur Longitudinal Twin Study. *Child Development, 63,* 1437–1455.

Emery, R. E., & Laumann-Billings, L. (1998). An overview of the nature, causes, and consequences of abusive family relationships: Toward differentiating maltreatment and violence. *American Psychologist, 53,* 121–135.

Englund, M.M., Luckner, A.E., Whaley, G.J.L., & Egeland, B. (2004). Children's achievement in early elementary school: Longitudinal effects of parental involvement, expectations, and quality of assistance. *Journal of Educational Psychology, 96,* 723–730.

Ennis, R. H. (1976). An alternative to Piaget's conceptualization of logical competence. *Child Development, 47,* 903–919.

Ennouri, K., & Bloch, H. (1996). Visual control of hand approach movements in newborns. *British Journal of Developmental Psychology, 14,* 327–338.

Enright, R. D., & Satterfield, S. J. (1980). An ecological validation of social cognitive development. *Child Development, 51,* 156–161.

Epstein, J. L. (1983). Selections of friends in differently organized schools and classrooms. In J. L. Epstein & M. Karweit (Eds.), *Friends in school.* New York: Academic Press.

Epstein, J. L. (1986). Friendship selection: Developmental and environmental influences. In E. C. Mueller & C. R. Cooper (Eds.), *Process and outcome in peer relationships.* New York: Academic Press.

Epstein, J. L. (1989). The selection of friends: Changes across the grades and in different school environments. In T. J. Berndt & G. W. Ladd (Eds.), *Peer relationships in child development.* New York: Wiley.

Epstein, J. L. (2002). *School, family, and community partnerships: Your handbook for action* (2nd ed.). Thousand Oaks, CA: Corwin Press.

Epstein, J. L., & Sanders, M. G. (2002). Family, school, and community partnerships. In M.H. Bornstein (Ed.), *Handbook of parenting,* vol. 5: *Practical issues in parenting* (pp. 407–438), 2nd ed. Mahwah, NJ: Erlbaum.

Erikson, E. (1950). *Childhood and society.* New York: Norton.

Erikson, E. H. (1963). *Childhood and society.* New York: Norton.

Erickson, M. F., Sroufe, L. A., & Egeland, B. (1985). The relationship between quality of attachment and behavior problems in pre-school in a high-risk sample. In I. Bretherton & E. Waters (Eds.), *Growing points of attachment theory and research. Monographs of the Society for Research in Child Development, 50*(12, Serial No. 209).

Eron, L. D., & Huesmann, L. R. (1986). The role of television in the development of prosocial and antisocial behavior. In D. Olweus, J. Block, & M. Radke-Yarrow (Eds.), *Development of antisocial and prosocial behavior.* Orlando, FL: Academic Press.

Eron, L. D., Huesmann, L. R., Dubow, E., Romanoff, R., & Yarmel, R. W. (1987). Aggression and its correlates over 22 years. In D. H. Crowell, I. M. Evans, & C. R. O'Donnell (Eds.), *Childhood aggression and violence: Source of influence, prevention, and control.* New York: Plenum.

Ervin, S. M. (1964). Imitation and structural change in children's language. In E. H. Lenneberg (Ed.), *New directions in the study of language.* Cambridge, MA: MIT Press.

Erwin, P. (1993). *Friendship and peer relations in children.* Chichester, England: Wiley.

Espelage, D. L., Holt, M. K., & Henkel, R. R. (2003). Examination of peer-group contextual effects on aggression during early adolescence. *Child Development, 74,* 205–220.

Esposito N. (1999) Marginalised women's comparisons of their hospital and free-standing birth centre experience: A contract of inner city birthing centres. *Health Care for Women International, 20*(2): 11–126.

Espy, K. A., Molfese, V. J., & DiLalla, L. F. (2001). Effects of environmental measures on intelligence in young children: Growth curve modeling of longitudinal data. *Merrill-Palmer Quarterly, 47,* 42–73.

Ethics Committee of the American Society for Reproductive Medicine. (2001). Preconception gender selection for nonmedical reasons. *Fertil. Steril., 75,* 861–864.

Evans, D., & Miguel E. (2004). *Orphans and schooling in Africa: A longitudinal analysis.* Center for International and Development Economics Research, October (http://repositories.cdlib.org/iber/cider/C05-143/).

Evans, E. M., Schweingruber, H., & Stevenson, H. W. (2002). Gender differences in interest and knowledge acquisition: The United States, Taiwan, and Japan. *Sex Roles, 47,* 153–167.

Evans, M. A. (2001). Shyness in the classroom and at home. In W. Ray Crozier & Lynne E. Alden (Eds.), *International Handbook of Social Anxiety* (pp. 159–183). New York: Wiley.

Fabes, R. A., Eisenberg, N., Karbon, M., Troyer, D., & Switzer, G. (1994). The relations of children's emotion regulation to their vicarious emotional responses and comforting behavior. *Child Development, 65,* 1678–1693.

Fabricius, W. V., & Steffe, L. (1989, April). *Considering all possible combinations: The early beginnings of a formal operational skill.* Paper presented at the meeting of the Society for Research in Child Development, Kansas City, MO.

Fagan J. F., III. (1973). Infants' delayed recognition memory and forgetting. *Journal of Experimental Child Psychology, 16,* 424–450.

Fagan, J. F., III. (1976). Infants' recognition of invariant features of faces. *Child Development, 47,* 627–638.

Fagot, B. I. (1977). Consequences of moderate cross-gender behavior in preschool children. *Child Development, 48,* 902–907.

Fagot, B. I. (1985). Beyond the reinforcement principle: Another step toward understanding sex role development. *Developmental Psychology, 21,* 1097–1104.

Fagot, B. I. (1997), Attachment, parenting, and peer interactions of toddler children. *Developmental Psychology, 33,* 489–499.

Fagot, B. I., & Hagan, R. (1991). Observations of parent reactions to sex-stereotyped behaviors: Age and sex effects. *Child Development, 62,* 617–628.

Fagot, B. I., & Leinbach, M. D. (1987). Socialization of sex roles within the family. In D. B. Carter (Ed.), *Current conceptions of sex roles and sex typing: Theory and research.* New York: Praeger.

Fagot, B. I., & Leinbach, M. D. (1993). Gender-role development in young children: From discrimination to labeling. *Developmental Review, 13,* 205–224.

Fagot, B. I., Leinbach, M. D., & Hagan, R. (1986). Gender labeling and the adoption of sex-typed behaviors. *Developmental Psychology, 22,* 440–443.

Fagot, B. I., Rodgers, C. S., & Leinbach, M. D. (2000). Theories of gender socialization. In T. Eckes & H. M. Trautner (Eds.), *The developmental social psychology of gender.* Mahwah, NJ: Erlbaum.

Fairweather, H., & Butterworth, G. (1977). The WPPSI at four years: A sex difference in verbal-performance discrepancies. *British Journal of Educational Psychology, 7,* 85–90.

Fang, P., Xiong, D., & Guo, C. (2003). The effect of parenting styles on children's academic achievement. *Psychological Science (China), 26,* 78–81.

Fantuzzo, J. W., McDermott, P. A., Manz, P. H., Hampton, V. R., & Burdick, N. A. (1996). The pictorial scale of perceived competence and social acceptance: Does it work with low-income urban children? *Child Development, 67,* 1071–1084.

Fantuzzo, J., & McWayne, C. (2002). The relationship between peer-play interactions in the family context and dimensions of school readiness for low-income preschool children. *Journal of Educational Psychology, 94*(1), 79–87.

Fantz, R. L. (1961). The origin of form perception. *Scientific American, 204,* 66–72.

Fantz, R. L. (1963). Pattern vision in newborn infants. *Science, 140,* 296–297.

Faraone, S. V., & Biederman, J. (2000). Nature, nurture, and attention deficit hyperactivity disorder. *Developmental Review, 20,* 568–581.

Farkas, G., & Beron, K. (2004). The detailed age trajectory of oral vocabulary knowledge: Differences by class and race. *Social Science Research, 33,* 464–497.

Farrar, M. J. (1990). Discourse and the acquisition of grammatical morphemes. *Journal of Child Language, 17,* 607–624.

Farrar, M. J. (1992). Negative evidence and grammatical morpheme acquisition. *Developmental Psychology, 28,* 90–98.

Farrington, D. P. (1994). Childhood, adolescent, and adult features of violent males. In L. R. Huesmann (Ed.), *Aggressive behavior: Current perspectives.* New York: Plenum.

Farver, J. M. (1993). Cultural differences in scaffolding pretend play: A comparison of American and Mexican mother-child and sibling-child pairs. In K. MacDonald (Ed.), *Parent-child play: Descriptions and implications.* Albany: State University of New York Press.

Farver, J. M. (1999). Activity setting analysis: A model for examining the role of culture in development. In A. Göncü (Ed.), *Children's engagement in the world: Sociocultural perspectives.* Cambridge: Cambridge University Press.

Farver, J. M., & Branstetter, W. H. (1994). Preschoolers' prosocial responses to their peers' distress. *Developmental Psychology, 30,* 334–341.

Farver, J. M., & Howes., C. (1993). Cultural differences in American and Mexican mother-child pretend play. *Merrill-Palmer Quarterly, 39,* 344–358.

Farver, J. M., & Wimbarti, S. (1995). Indonesian children's play with their mothers and older siblings. *Child Development, 66,* 1493–1503.

Fasting, R. B., & Lyster, S. H. (2005). The effects of computer technology in assisting the development of literacy in young struggling readers and spellers. *European Journal of Special Needs Education, 20,* 21–40.

Federal Register. (2005). (Vol. 70, No. 33), pp. 8373–8375. *From the Federal Register Online via GPO Access [wais.access.gpo.gov]* http://aspe.hhs.gov/poverty/05fedreg.htm

Feigenson, L., Dehaene, S., & Spelke, E. S.(2004). Core systems of number. *Trends in Cognitive Sciences. 8,* 307–314.

Feingold, A. (1992). Sex differences in variability in intellectual abilities: A new look at an old controversy. *Review of Educational Research, 62,* 61–84.

Feingold, A. (1993). Cognitive gender differences: A developmental perspective. *Sex Roles, 29,* 91–112.

Feinman, S., Roberts, D., Hsieh, K., Sawyer, D., & Swanson, D. (1992). A critical review of social referencing in infancy. In S. Feinman (Ed.), *Social referencing and the social construction of reality in infancy.* New York: Plenum.

Feiring, C. (1996). Concepts of romance in 15-year-old adolescents. *Journal of Research on Adolescence, 6,* 181–200.

Feldman, D. H. (1986). *Nature's gambit: Child prodigies and the development of human potential.* New York: Basic Books.

Feldman, P. J., Dunkel-Schetter, C., Sandman, C. A., & Wadhwa, P. D. (2000). Maternal social support predicts birth weight and fetal growth in human pregnancy. *Psychosomatic Medicine, 62,* 715–725.

Feldman, R. (2006). From biological rhythms to social rhythms: Physiological precursors of mother–infant synchrony. *Developmental Psychology, 42*(1), 175–188.

Feldman, S., Rosenthal, D. A., Mont-Reynauld, R., & Leung, K. (1991). Ain't misbehavin': Adolescent values and family environments as correlates of misconduct in Australia, Hong Kong, and the United States. *Journal of Research on Adolescence, 1,* 109–134.

Fennema, E., Carpenter, T. P., Jacobs, V. R., Franke, M. L., & Levi, L. W. (1998). A longitudinal study of gender differences in young children's mathematical thinking. *Educational Researcher, 27,* 6–11.

Fenson, L., Dale, P. S., Reznick, J. S., Bates E., Thal, D. J., & Pethick, S. J. (1994). Variability in early communicative development. *Monographs of the Society for Research in Child Development, 59*(5, Serial No. 242).

Ferber R. (1995). Introduction: Pediatric sleep disorders medicine. In Ferber, R. Kryger, M. (Eds.), *Principles and practice of sleep medicine in the child,* p. 15. Philadelphia: WB Saunders.

Fernald, A., & O'Neill, D. K. (1993). Peekaboo across cultures: How mothers and infants play with voices, faces, and expectations. In K. MacDonald (Ed.), *Parent-child play.* Albany: State University of New York Press.

Ferrier, S., Dunham, P., & Dunham, F. (2000). The confused robot: Two-year-olds' responses to breakdowns in conversation. *Social Development, 9,* 337–347.

Feshbach, N. D., & Feshbach, S. (1982). Empathy training and the regulation of aggression: Potentialities and limitations. *Academic Psychology Bulletin, 4,* 399–413.

Feshbach, S., & Singer, R. D. (1971). *Television and aggression: An experimental field study.* San Francisco: Jossey-Bass.

Field, T. M. (1987). Affective and interactive disturbances in infants. In J. D. Osofsky (Ed.), *Handbook of infant development* (2nd ed.). New York: Wiley.

Field, T. M. (2001). *Touch.* Cambridge, MA: MIT Press.

Field, T. M., Healy, B., Goldstein, S., & Guthertz, M. (1990). Behavior-state matching and synchrony in mother-infant interactions of nondepressed versus depressed dyads. *Developmental Psychology, 26,* 7–14.

Field, T. M., & Walden, T. A. (1982). Production and perception of facial expressions in infancy and early childhood. In H. W. Reese & L. P. Lipsitt (Eds.), *Advances in child development and behavior* (Vol. 16). New York: Academic Press.

Fields, J. (2003). *America's families and living arrangements:* 2003. Current Population Reports, P20553. U.S. Census Bureau, Washington, DC.

Fields, J., & Casper, L. M. (2001). *America's families and living arrangements: March 2000.* Washington, DC: U.S. Census Bureau.

Fields, S. A., & McNamara, J. R. (2003). The prevention of child and adolescent violence. A review. *Aggression and Violent Behavior, 8,* 61–91.

Finn, J. D., Gerber, S. B., Achilles, C. M., & Boyd-Zaharias, J. (2001). The enduring effects of small classes. *Teachers College Record, 103,* 145–183.

Fischer, K. W., & Bidell, T. R. (1998). Dynamic development of psychological structures in action and thought. In W. Damon (Series Ed.) & R. M. Lerner (Vol. Ed.), *Handbook of child psychology:* Vol. 1. *Theoretical models of human development* (5th ed.). New York: Wiley.

Fisher, L., Ames, E., Chisholm, K., & Savoie, L. (1997). Problems reported by parents of Romanian orphans adopted to British Columbia. *International Journal of Behavioral Development, 20,* 67–82.

Fisher, C. B., Jackson, J. F., & Villarruel, F. A. (1998). The study of African American and Latin American children and youth. In W. Damon (Series Ed.), *Handbook of child psychology:* Vol. 1. *Theoretical models of human development* (5th ed.) (pp. 1145–1207). New York: Wiley.

Fisher, C. B., & Tryon, W. W. (Eds.). (1990). *Ethics in applied developmental psychology: Emerging issues in an emerging field.* Norwood, NJ: Ablex.

Fisher-Thompson, D. (1993). Adult toy purchases for children: Factors affecting sex-typed toy selection. *Journal of Applied Developmental Psychology, 14,* 385–406.

Fivush, R. (1998). Gendered narratives: Elaboration, structure, and emotion in parent-child reminiscing across the preschool years. In C. P. Thompson & D. J. Herrmann (Eds.), *Autobiographical memory: Theoretical and applied perspectives.* Mahwah, NJ: Erlbaum.

Fivush, R. (1991a). Gender and emotion in mother-child conversations about the past. *Journal of Narrative and Life History, 1,* 325–341.

Fivush, R. (1991b). The social construction of personal narratives. *Merrill-Palmer Quarterly, 37,* 59–81.

Fivush, R. (1998). Gendered narratives: Elaboration, structure, and emotion in parent-child reminiscing across the preschool years. In C. P. Thompson & D. J. Herrmann (Eds.), *Autobiographical memory:*

Theoretical and applied perspectives. Mahwah, NJ: Erlbaum.

Fivush, R., & Buckner, J. P. (2000). Gender, sadness, and depression: The development of emotional focus through gendered discourse. In A. H. Fischer (Ed.), *Gender and emotion: Social psychological perspectives.* New York: Cambridge University Press.

Fivush, R., Sales, J. M., Goldberg, A., Bahrick, L., & Parker, J. (2004). Weathering the storm: Children's long-term recall of Hurricane Andrew. *Memory, 12,* 104–118.

Flack, J. C., & de Waal, F. B. M. (2000). "Any animal whatever": Darwinian building blocks of morality in monkeys and apes. In L. D. Katz (Ed.), *Evolutionary origins of morality: Cross disciplinary perspectives.* Thorveton, UK: Imprint Academic.

Flannagan, D., & Perese, S. (1998). Emotional references in mother-daughter and mother-son dyads' conversations about school. *Sex Roles, 39,* 353–367.

Flannery, D. J. Vazsonyi, A. T., Liau, A. K., Guo, S., Powell, K. E., Atha, H., et al. (2003). Initial behavior outcomes for the PeaceBuilders universal school-based violence prevention program. *Developmental Psychology, 39,* 292–308.

Flavell, J. H. (1963). *The developmental psychology of Jean Piaget.* Princeton, NJ: Van Nostrand.

Flavell, J. H. (1970). Developmental studies of mediated memory. In H. W. Reese & L. P. Lipsitt (Eds.), *Advances in child development and behavior* (Vol. 5). New York: Academic Press.

Flavell, J. H. (1971). First discussant's comments. What is memory development the development of? *Human Development, 14,* 272–278.

Flavell, J. H. (1985). *Cognitive development* (2nd ed.). Englewood Cliffs, NJ: Prentice Hall.

Flavell, J. H. (1986). Development of children's knowledge about the appearance-reality distinction. *American Psychologist, 41,* 418–425.

Flavell, J. H., Beach, D. H., & Chinsky, J. M. (1966). Spontaneous verbal rehearsal in a memory task as a function of age. *Child Development, 37,* 283–299.

Flavell, J. H., Flavell, E. R., & Green, F. L. (1983). Development of the appearance-reality distinction. *Cognitive Psychology, 15,* 95–120.

Flavell, J. H., Friedrichs, A., & Hoyt, J. (1970). Developmental changes in memorization processes. *Cognitive Psychology, 1,* 324–340.

Flavell, J. H., Green, F. L., & Flavell, E. R. (1989). Young children's ability to differentiate appearance-reality and level 2 perspective taking in the tactile modality. *Child Development, 60,* 201–213.

Flavell, J. H., Lindberg, N. A., Green, F. L., & Flavell. E. R. (1992). The development of children's understanding of the appearance-reality distinction between how people look and what they are really like. *Merrill-Palmer Quarterly, 38,* 513–524.

Flavell, J. H., Miller, P. H., & Miller, S. A. (2002). *Cognitive development* (4th ed.). Upper Saddle River, NJ: Prentice Hall.

Flavell, J. H., Shipstead, S. G., & Croft, K. (1980). What young children think you see when their eyes are closed. *Cognition, 8,* 369–387.

Fletcher, A. C., Darling, N.E., Steinberg, L., & Dornbusch, S. (1995). The company they keep: Relation of adolescents' adjustment and behavior to their friends' perceptions of authoritative parenting in the social network. *Developmental Psychology, 31,* 300–310.

Fletcher, A. C., Elder, G. H., & Mekos, D. (2000). Parental influences on adolescent involvement in community activities. *Journal of Research on Adolescence, 10,* 29–48.

Flieller, A. (1999). Comparison of the development of formal thought in adolescent cohorts aged 10 to 15 years (1967–1999 and 1972–1993). *Developmental Psychology, 35*, 1048–1058.

Flynn, J. R. (1999). Searching for justice: The discovery of IQ gains over time. *American Psychologist, 54* (1), 5–20.

Flynn, E., O'malley, C., & Wood, D. (2004). A longitudinal, microgenetic study of the emergence of false belief understanding and inhibition skills. *Developmental Science, 7*(1), 103–115.

Fodor, J. (1986). The modularity of mind. In Pylyshyn, Z and Demopoulos, W. (Eds.), *Meaning and Cognitive Structure, 318*, 129–135.

Fogel, A., Stevenson, M. B., & Messinger, D. (1992). A comparison of the parent-child relationship in Japan and the United States. In J. L. Roopnarine & D. B. Carter (Eds.), *Annual advances in applied developmental psychology*: Vol. 5. *Parent-child socialization in diverse cultures.* Norwood, NJ: Ablex.

Folling-Albers, M., & Hartinger, A. (1998). Interest of boys and girls in elementary school. In L. Hoffman, A. Krap, K. A. Renninger, & J. Baumert (Eds.), *Interest and learning.* Kiel, Germany: Institute for Science Education.

Ford, C., & Beach, F. (1951). *Patterns of sexual behavior.* New York: Harper & Row.

Forehand, R., & Kotchick, B. A. (2002). Behavioral parent training: Current challenges and potential solutions. *Journal of Child and Family Studies, 11*, 377–384.

Forman, D. R., Aksan, N., & Kochanska, G. (2004). Toddlers' responsive imitation predicts preschool conscience. *Psychological Science, 15*, 699–704.

Forman, E. A., & Cazden, C. B. (1985). Exploring Vygotskian perspectives in education: The cognitive value of peer interaction. In J. V. Wertsch (Ed.), *Culture, communication, and cognition: Vygotskian perspectives.* Cambridge: Cambridge University Press.

Forman, E. A., & McPhail, J. (1993). Vygotskian perspective in children's collaborative problem solving activity. In E. A. Forman, N. Minick, & C. A. Stone (Eds.), *Contexts for learning: Sociocultural dynamics in children's development.* Oxford: Oxford University Press.

Foster, G. (2004). Safety nets for children affected by HIV/AIDS in southern Africa. In Robyn Pharoah, (Ed.), *Monographs for the African Humanity Security Initiative*, No. 109, December.

Fox, N. A. (Ed.) (1994). The development of emotion regulation: Biological and behavioral considerations. *Monographs of the Society for Research in Child Development, 59*(23, Serial No. 240).

Fraiberg, S. H., Adelson, E. & Shapiro, V. (1987). Ghosts in the Nursery: A Psychoanalytic approach to the problems of impaired Infant-mother relationships. In Fraiberg L (Ed.), *Selected Writings of Selma Fraiberg.* Columbus, Ohio: Ohio State University Press, pp. 100–136. An earlier version of this chapter appeared in the *Journal of the American Academy of Child Psychiatry, 14* (3), Summer 1975, pp. 387–422.

Francis, P. L., Self, P. A., & Horowitz, F. D. (1987). The behavioral assessment of the neonate: An overview. In J. D. Osofsky (Ed.), *Handbook of infant development* (2nd ed.). New York: Wiley.

Franco, P., Seret, N., Van Hees, J. N., Scaillet, S., Groswasser, J., & Kahn, A. (2005). Influence of swaddling on sleep and arousal characteristics of healthy infants. *Pediatrics, 115*(5), 1307–1311.

Frank, M., & Zigler, E. F. (1989). *The parental leave crisis: Toward a national policy.* New Haven, CT: Yale University Press.

Frankel, F., & Feinberg, D. (2002). Social problems associated with ADHD vs. ODD in children referred for friendship problems. *Child Psychiatry and Human Development, 33*, 125–146.

Frauenglass, M. H., & Diaz, R. M. (1985). Self-regulatory functions of children's speech: A critical analysis of recent challenges to Vygotsky's theory. *Developmental Psychology, 21*, 357–364.

Fredriks, A. M., van Buuren, S., Burgmeijer, R. J., Meulmeester J. F., Beuker. R. J., Brugman, E., Roede, M.J., Verloove-Vanhorick, S. P., & Wit, J. M. (2000). Continuing positive secular growth change in the Netherlands 1955–1997. *Pediatric Research, 47* (3), 316–323.

Freeburg, T. J., & Lippman, M. Z. (1986). Factors influencing discrimination of infant cries. *Journal of Child Language, 13*, 3–13.

Freedland, R. L., & Bertenthal, B. I. (1994). Developmental stages in interlimb coordination: Transition to hands-and-knees crawling. *Psychological Science, 5*, 26–32.

Freud, S. (1933/1964). *New introductory lectures.* Harmondsworth: Penguin.

Freud, S. (1940/1964). An outline of psychoanalysis. In J. Strachey (Ed. & Trans.), *The standard edition of the complete psychological works of Sigmund Freud* (Vol. 23). London: Hogarth.

Frey, K. S., Hirschstein, M. K., & Guzzo, B. A. (2000). Second Step: Preventing aggression by promoting social competence. *Journal of Emotional and Behavioral Disorders, 8*, 102–112.

Frey, K. S., & Ruble, D. N. (1992). Gender constancy and the "cost" of sex-typed behavior: A test of the conflict hypothesis. *Developmental Psychology, 28*, 714–721.

Fried, P. (1989). Postnatal consequences of maternal marijuana use in humans. *Annals of the New York Academy of Sciences, 562*, 123–132.

Fried, P. (2002a). Adolescents prenatally exposed to marijuana: Examination of facets of complex behaviours and comparisons with the influence of in utero cigarettes. *Journal of Clinical Pharmacology, 42*(11 Suppl.), 97S–102S.

Fried, P. (2002b). Pregnancy and effects on offspring from birth through adolescence. In F. Grotenhermen & E. Russo (Eds.), *Cannabis and cannabinoids: Pharmacology, toxicology, and therapeutic potential*, pp. 269–278. New York: Haworth Press.

Fried, P. A., O'Connell, C. M., & Watkinson, M. A. (1992). Sixty- and 72-month follow-up of children prenatally exposed to marijuana, cigarettes, and alcohol: Cognitive and language assessment. *Developmental and Behavioral Pediatrics, 13*, 383–391.

Friedman, J. M. (1981). Genetic disease in the offspring of older fathers. *Obstetrics and Gynecology, 57*, 745–749.

Friend, M., & Pope, K. L. (2005). Creating schools in which all students can succeed. *Kappa Delta Pi Record, 41*, 56–61.

Frisch, H. L. (1977). Sex stereotypes in adult-infant play. *Child Development, 48*, 1671–1675.

Frith, U. (1989). *Autism: Explaining the enigma.* Oxford, England: Basil Blackwell.

Frodi, A. M., Lamb, M. E., Leavitt, L. A., & Donovan, W. L. (1978). Fathers' and mothers' responses to infant smiles and cries. *Infant Behavior and Development, 1*, 187–198.

Frost, J., Madsbjerg, S., & Niedersoe, J. (2005). Semantic and phonological skills in predicting reading development: From 3-16 years of age. *Dyslexia: An International Journal of Research & Practice, 11*, 79–92.

Frye, D. (1999). Development of intention: The relation of executive function to theory of mind. In P. D. Zelazo, J. W. Astington, & D. R. Olson (Eds.), *Developing theories of intention.* Mahwah, NJ: Erlbaum.

Fuchs, D., & Fuchs, L. S. (2005). Peer-assisted learning strategies: Promoting word recognition, fluency, and reading comprehension in young children. *Journal of Special Education, 39*, 34–44.

Fuligni, A. J., Eccles, J. S., Barber, B. L., & Clements, P. (2001). Early adolescent peer orientation and adjustment during high school. *Developmental Psychology, 27*, 28–36.

Funk, J. B., Germann, J. N., & Buchman, D. D. (1997). Children and electronic games in the United States. *Trends in Communication 2*, 111–126.

Furman, W., Rahe, D., & Hartup, W. (1979). Rehabilitation of socially withdrawn preschool children through mixed-age and same-age socialization. *Child Development, 50*, 915–922.

Furman, W., & Lanthier, R. (2002). Parenting siblings. In M. H. Bornstein (Ed.), *Handbook of parenting* (2nd ed., Vol. 1). Mahwah, NJ: Erlbaum.

Furnam, A., Abramsky, S., & Gunter, B. (1997). A cross-cultural content analysis of children's television advertisements. *Sex Roles, 37*, 91–99.

Furrow, D., Nelson, K., & Benedict, H. (1979). Mothers' speech to children and syntactic development: Some simple relationships. *Journal of Child Language, 6*, 423–442.

Furstenberg, F. F. (1993). How families manage risk and opportunity in dangerous neighborhoods. In W. J. Wilson (Ed.), *Sociology and the public agenda.* Newbury Park, CA: Sage.

Furstenberg, F. F., & Hughes, M. E. (1995). Social capital and successful development among at-risk youth. *Journal of Marriage & Family, 57*, 580–592.

Gailey, C. W. (1996). Mediated messages: Gender, class, and cosmos in home video games. In P. M. Greenfield & R. R. Cocking (Eds.), *Interacting with video.* Norwood, NJ: Ablex.

Galen, B. R., & Underwood, M. K. (1997). A developmental investigation of social aggression among children. *Developmental Psychology, 33*, 589–600.

Gallagher, A. M., & De Lisi, R. (1994). Gender differences in Scholastic Aptitude Test-mathematics problem solving among high-ability students. *Journal of Educational Psychology, 86*, 204–211.

Gallagher, K. C. (2002). Does child temperament moderate the influence of parenting on adjustment? *Developmental Review, 22*, 623–643.

Gallagher, A. M., De Lisi, R., Holst, P. C., McGillicuddy-De Lisi, A. V., Morely, M., & Cahalan, C. (2000). Gender differences in advanced mathematical problem solving. *Journal of Experimental Child Psychology, 75*, 165–190.

Gallahue, D. L., & Ozmun, J. C. (1995). *Understanding motor development: Infants, children, adolescents, adults* (3rd ed.). Madison, WI: Brown & Benchmark.

Gallup Poll. (1997). *U.S. teens and technology.* Retrieved February 9, 2003 from www.nsf.gov/od/lpa/nstw/teenov.htm.

Gally, M. (2002, Jan. 23). Research: Boys to men. *Education Week.* Retrieved February 9, 2003 from www.edweek.org/ew/newstory.cfm?slug519boys.h21.

Galsworthy, M. J., Dionne, G., Dale, P. S., & Plomin, R. (2000). Sex differences in early verbal and non-verbal cognitive development. *Developmental Science, 3*, 206–215.

Garai, J. E., & Scheinfeld, A. (1968). Sex differences in mental and behavioral traits. *Genetic Psychology Monographs, 7*, 169–299.

Garbarino, J., Dubrow, N., Kostelny, K., & Pardo, C. (1992). *Children in danger: Coping with the consequences of community violence.* San Francisco: Jossey-Bass.

Garbarino, J., & Kostelny, K. (1996). The effects of political violence on Palestinian children's behavior problems: A risk accumulation model. *Child Development, 67*, 33–45.

Garcia Coll, C., & Pachter, L. M. (2002). Ethnic and minority parenting. In M.H. Bornstein (Ed.), *Handbook of parenting,* vol 4: *Social conditions and applied parenting* (pp. 1–20), 2nd ed. Mahwah, NJ: Erlbaum.

Garden, R. A. (1987). The second IEA mathematics study. *Comparative Education Review, 31*, 47–68.

Gardner, H. (1983). *Frames of mind: The theory of multiple intelligences.* New York: Basic Books.

Gardner, H. (1993a). *Frames of mind: The theory of multiple intelligences* (10th anniversary ed.). New York: Basic Books.

Gardner, H. (1993b). *Multiple intelligences.* New York: Basic Books.

Gardner, H. (1999). *Intelligence reframed: Multiple intelligence in the 21st century.* New York: Basic Books.

Gardner, P. L. (1998). The development of males' and females' interest in science and technology. In L. Hoffman, A. Krap, K. A. Renninger, & J. Baumert (Eds.), *Interest and learning.* Kiel, Germany: Institute for Science Education.

Garner, P. W., Jones, D. C., & Miner, J. L. (1994). Social competence among low-income preschoolers: Emotion socialization practices and social cognitive correlates. *Child Development, 65*, 622–637.

Garner, R., & Reis, R. (1981). Monitoring and resolving comprehension obstacles: An investigation of spontaneous text lookbacks among upper-grade good and poor comprehenders. *Reading Research Quarterly, 16*, 569–582.

Garrod, A., Beal, C., & Shin, P. (1990). The development of moral orientation in elementary school children. *Sex Roles, 22*, 13–26.

Garton, A. (1992). *Social interaction and the development of language and cognition.* Hillsdale, NJ: Erlbaum.

Garvey, C. (1986). Peer relations and the growth of communication. In E. C. Mueller & C. R. Cooper (Eds.), *Process and outcome in peer relationships.* New York: Academic Press.

Garvey, C. (1990). *Play.* Cambridge, MA: Harvard University Press.

Gaskins, S. (1999). Children's daily lives in a Mayan village: A case study of culturally constructed roles and activities. In A. Göncü (Ed.), *Children's engagement in the world: Sociocultural perspectives.* New York: Cambridge, University Press.

Gaub, M., & Carlson, C. L. (1997). Gender differences in ADHD: A meta-analysis and critical review. *Journal of the American Academy of Child and Adolescent Psychiatry, 36*, 1036–1045.

Gauvain, M. (1998). Cognitive development in social and cultural context. *Current Directions in Psychological Science, 7*, 188–192.

Ge, X., Conger, R. D., Cadoret, R. J., Neiderhiser, J. M., Yates, W., Troughton, E., & Stewart, M. A. (1996). The developmental interface between nature and nurture: A mutual influence model of child antisocial behavior and parents' behaviors. *Developmental Psychology, 32*, 574–589.

Ge, X., Conger, R. D., & Elder, G. H. Jr. (2001a). Pubertal transition, stressful life events, and the emergence of gender differences in adolescent de-

pressive symptoms. *Developmental Psychology, 37*, 404–417.

Geary, D. C. (1995b). Reflections of evolution and culture in children's cognition: Implications for mathematical development and instruction. *American Psychologist, 50*, 24–37.

Geary, D. C. (1998). *Male, female: The evolution of human sex differences.* Washington, DC: American Psychological Association.

Geary, D. C. (2002). Principles of evolutionary educational psychology. *Learning and Individual Differences, 12*, 317–345.

Geary, D. C., & Bjorklund, D. F. (2000). Evolutionary developmental psychology. *Child Development, 71*, 57–65.

Geary, D. C., Saults, S. J., Liu, F., & Hoard, M. K. (2000). Sex differences in spatial cognition, computational fluency, and arithmetical reasoning. *Journal of Experimental Child Psychology, 77*, 337–353.

Geen, R. G. (1983). Aggression and television violence. In R. G. Geen & E. I. Donnerstein (Eds.), *Aggression: Theoretical and empirical reviews* (Vol. 2). New York: Academic Press.

Gelfand, D. M., & Hartmann, D. P. (1982). Response consequences and attributions: Two contributors to prosocial behavior. In N. Eisenberg (Ed.), *The development of prosocial behavior.* New York: Academic Press.

Gelman, R. (1972). Logical capacity of very young children: Number invariance rules. *Child Development, 43*, 75–90.

Gelman, S. A., Wilcox, S. A., & Clark, E. V. (1989). Conceptual and lexical hierarchies in young children. *Cognitive Development, 4*, 309–326.

Gelman, R., & Williams, E. (1998). Enabling constraints for cognitive development and learning: Domain specificity and epigenesis. In D. Kuhn and R. Siegler (Eds.), *Cognition, perception and language.* Vol. 2. *Handbook of Child Psychology* (5th ed.) (pp. 575–630). New York: Wiley.

Genesee, F. (Ed.). (1994). *Educating second language children.* New York: Cambridge University Press.

Genesee, F., Nicoladis, E., & Paradis, J. (1995). Language differentiation in early bilingual development. *Journal of Child Language, 22*, 611–631.

Genome International Sequencing Consortium. (2001). Initial sequencing and analyses of the human genome. *Nature, 409*, 860–921.

Gentile, D. A. (1993). Just what are sex and gender, anyway? A call for a new terminological standard. *Psychological Science, 4*, 120–122.

Gentner, D. (1982). Why nouns are learned before verbs: Linguistic relativity versus natural partitioning. In S. A. Kuczaj (Ed.), *Language development* (Vol. 2). Hillsdale, NJ: Erlbaum.

Gentry, M., Gable, R. K., & Rizza, M. G. (2002). Students' perceptions of classroom activities: Are there grade-level and gender differences? *Journal of Educational Psychology, 94*(3), 539–544.

George, C., Kaplan, N., & Main, M. (1985). The Adult Attachment Interview. Unpublished manuscript, University of California, Department of Psychology, Berkeley.

Gershkoff-Stowe, L. (2001). The course of children's naming errors in early word learning. *Journal of Cognition and Development, 2*, 131–155.

Gest, S. D., Domitrovich, C. E., & Welsh, J. A. (2005). Peer academic reputation in elementary school: Associations with changes in self-concept and academic skills. *Journal of Educational Psychology, 97*, 337–346.

Ghaderi, A. (2005). Psychometric properties of the self-concept questionnaire. *European Journal of Psychological Assessment, 21*, 139–146.

Ghatala, E. S., Levin, J. R., Pressley, M., & Goodwin, D. (1986). A componential analysis of the effects of derived and supplied strategy utility information on children's strategy selections. *Journal of Experimental Child Psychology, 41*, 76–92.

Ghim, H. R. (1990). Evidence for perception organization in infants: Perception of subjective contours by young infants. *Infant Behavior and Development, 13*, 221–248.

Gianino, A., & Tronick, E. Z. (1988). The mutual regulation model: The infant's self and interactive regulation coping and defense. In T. Field, P. McCabe, & N. Schneiderman (Eds.), *Stress and coping.* Hillsdale, NJ: Erlbaum.

Gibbons, J. L. (2000). Gender development in cross-cultural perspective. In T. Eckes & H. M. Trautner (Eds.), *The developmental social psychology of gender.* Mahwah, NJ: Erlbaum.

Gibbs, J. C. (2003). *Moral development and reality: Beyond the theories of Kohlberg and Hoffman.* Thousand Oaks, CA: Sage.

Gibson, E. J. (1969). *Principles of perceptual learning and development.* New York: Appleton-Century-Crofts.

Gibson, E. J. (1988). Exploratory behavior in the development of perceiving, acting, and the acquiring of knowledge. *Annual Review of Psychology, 39*, 141.

Gibson, E. J. (1993). Ontogenesis of the perceived self. In U. Neisser (Ed.), *The perceived self: Ecological and interpersonal sources of self-knowledge.* Cambridge, MA: Cambridge University Press.

Gibson, E. J., & Pick, A. (2000). *Perceptual learning and development: An ecological view.* New York: Oxford University Press.

Gibson, E. J., & Walk, R. D. (1960). The "visual cliff." *Scientific American, 202*, 64–71.

Gibson, E. J., & Walker, A. (1984). Development of knowledge of visual-tactual affordances of substance. *Child Development, 55*, 453–460.

Gibson, J. J. (1966). *The senses considered as perceptual systems.* Boston: Houghton Mifflin.

Gilbert, W. M., Nesbitt, T. S., & Danielsen, B. (1999). Childbearing beyond age 40: Pregnancy outcomes in 24,032 cases. *Obstetrics and Gynecology, 93*, 9–14.

Gilligan, C. (1982). *In a different voice: Psychological theory and women's development.* Cambridge, MA: Harvard University Press.

Gilligan, C., & Attanucci, J. (1988). Two moral orientations: Gender differences and similarities. *Merrill-Palmer Quarterly, 34*, 223–237.

Gilligan, C., & Wiggins, G. (1988). The origins of morality in early childhood relationships. In C. Gilligan, J. Ward, & J. Taylor (Eds.), *Mapping the moral domain: A contribution of women's thinking to psychological theory and education* (pp. 111–138). Cambridge, MA: Harvard University Press.

Gilly, M. (1988). Gender roles in advertising: A comparison of television advertisements in Australia, Mexico, and the United States. *Journal of Marketing, 52*, 75–85.

Ginsburg, H. J., Klein, A., & Starkey, P. (1998). The develop-ment of children's mathematical thinking: Theory, research, and practice. In W. Damon (Series Ed.) & I. E. Sigel & K. A. Renninger (Vol. Eds.), *Handbook of child psychology*: Vol. 4. *Child psychology in practice* (5th ed.). New York: Wiley.

Ginsburg, H., & Opper, S. (1988). *Piaget's theory of intellectual development* (3rd ed.). Englewood Cliffs, NJ: Prentice Hall.

Giusti, R. M., Iwamoto, K., & Hatch, E. E. (1995). Diethylstilbestrol revisited: A review of the long-term health effects. *Annals of Internal Medicine, 122*, 778–788.

Glasgow, K. L., Dornbusch, S. M., Troyer, L., Steinberg, L., & Ritter, P. I. (1997). Parenting style, adolescents' attributions, and educational outcomes in nine heterogeneous high schools. *Child Development, 68*, 507–529.

Glassman, M. (1994). All things being equal: The two roads of Piaget and Vygotsky. *Developmental Review, 14*, 186–214.

Glassy, D. & Romano, J. (2003). Committee on Early Childhood, Adoption, and Dependent Care. Selecting appropriate toys for young children: The pediatrician's role. *Pediatrics, 111*, 911–913.

Gleason, J. B., & Ely, R. (2002). Gender differences in language development. In A. McGillicuddy-De Lisi & R. De Lisi (Eds.), *Advances in applied developmental psychology*: Vol. 21. *Biology, society, and behavior: The development of sex differences in cognition*. Westport, CT: Ablex.

Gleason, J. B., & Weintraub, S. (1978). Input and the acquisition of communicative competence. In K. E. Nelson (Ed.), *Children's language* (Vol. 1). New York: Gardner.

Gleitman, L. R., & Gillette, J. (1999). The role of syntax in verb learning. In W. C. Ritchie & T. K. Bhatia (Eds.), *Handbook of child language acquisition*. San Diego, CA: Academic Press.

Goddard, M., Durkin, K., & Rutter, D. R. (1985). The semantic focus of maternal speech: A comment on Ninio and Bruner (1978). *Journal of Child Language, 12*, 209–213.

Gold, D., & Berger, C. (1978). Problem-solving performance of young boys and girls as a function of task appropriateness and sex identity. *Sex Roles, 4*, 183–193.

Goldenberg, R. L. (1995). Small for gestational age infants. In B. P. Sachs, R. Beard, E. Papiernik, & C. Russell (Eds.), *Reproductive health care for women and babies*. New York: Oxford University Press.

Goldfield, B. A. (2000). Nouns before verbs in comprehension vs. production: The view from pragmatics. *Journal of Child Language, 27*, 501–520.

Goldfield, B. A., & Reznick, J. S. (1990). Early lexical acquisition: Rate, content, and the vocabulary spurt. *Journal of Child Language, 17*, 171–183.

Goldfield, B. A., & Snow, C. E. (2001). Individual differences: Implications for the study of language acquisition. In J. B. Gleason (Ed.), *The development of language* (5th ed.). Boston: Allyn and Bacon.

Goldman, A. S. (1980). Critical periods of prenatal toxic insults. In R. H. Schwartz & S. J. Yaffe (Eds.), *Drug and chemical risks to the fetus and newborn*. New York: Alan R. Liss.

Goldsmith, H. H., Buss, A. H., Plomin, R., Rothbart,M. K., Thomas, A., Chess, S., et al. (1987). Roundtable: What is temperament. Four approaches. *Child Development, 58*, 505–529.

Goldsmith, H. H., & Rothbart, M. K. (1991). Contemporary instruments for assessing early temperament by questionnaire and in the laboratory. In J. Strelau & A. Angleitner (Eds.), *Explorations in temperament: International perspectives on theory and measurement*. New York: Plenum.

Goldstein, A. P., & Glick, B. (1994). Aggression replacement training: Curriculum and evaluation. *Simulation and Gaming, 25*, 9–26.

Goldstein J, Solnit, A. J., Goldstein, S., Freud, A. (1996). *The Best Interests of the child: The least detrimental alternative*. New York: The Free Press.

Goldwater, O. D., & Nutt, R. L. (1999). Teachers' and students' work-culture variables associated with positive school outcome. *Adolescence, 34*, 653–664.

Golombok, S. (2000). *Parenting: What really matters?* London: Routledge.

Golombok, S., Cook, R., Bish, A., & Murray, C. (1995). Families created by the new reproductive technologies: Quality of parenting and social and emotional development of the children. *Child Development, 66*, 285–298.

Golombok, S. & MacCallum, F. (2003). Outcomes for parents and children following non-traditional conception: What do clinicians need to know? *Journal of Child Psychology & Psychiatry, 44*(3), 303–315.

Golombok, S., Perry, B., Burston, A., Murray, C., Mooney-Somers, J., Stevens, M., et al. (2003). Children with lesbian parents: A community study. *Developmental Psychology, 39*, 20–33.

Golombok, S., & Tasker, F. L. (1996). Do parents influence the sexual orientation of their children? Findings from a longitudinal study of lesbian families. *Developmental Psychology, 32*, 3–11.

Gomby, D. S., Culross, P. L., & Behrman, R. E. (1999). Home visiting: Recent program evaluations-Analysis and recommendations. *The Future of Children, 9*, 4–26.

Gonzolez-DeHass, A. R., Willems, P. P., & Holbein, M. F. (2005). Examining the relationship between parental involvement and student motivation. *Educational Psychology Review, 17*, 99–123.

Good, C., Aronson, J., & Inzlicht, M. (2003). Improving adolescents' standardized test performance: An intervention to reduce the effects of stereotype threat. *Journal of Applied Developmental Psychology, 24*, 645–662.

Goodman, R., & Stevenson, J. (1989). A twin study of hyperactivity: II. The aetiological role of genes, family relationships, and perinatal adversity. *Journal of Child Psychology and Psychiatry, 30*, 691–709.

Goodman, G. S., Hirschmann, J. E., Hepps, D., & Rudy, L. (1991). Children's memory for stressful events. *Merrill-Palmer Quarterly, 37*, 109–158.

Goodman, G. S., Pyle Taub, S., Jones, D. P. H., England, P., Port, L. K., Rudy, L., et al. (1992). Testifying in criminal court. *Monographs of the Society for Research in Child Development, 57*(5, Serial No. 229).

Goodnow, J. J. (1990). The socialization of cognition: What's involved? In J. W. Stigler, R. A. Shweder, & G. Herdt (Eds.), *Cultural psychology: Essays on comparative human development*. New York: Cambridge University Press.

Goodnow, J. J. (1996). Acceptable ignorance, negotiable disagreement: Alternative views of learning. In D. R. Olson & N. Torrance (Eds.), *The handbook of education and human development: New models of learning, teaching, and schooling*. Cambridge, MA: Blackwell.

Goodwyn, S. L., Acredolo, L. P., & Brown, C. A. (2000). Impact of symbolic gesturing on early language development. *Journal of Nonverbal Behavior, 24*, 81–103.

Goodz, N. S. (1989). Parental language mixing in bilingual families. *Journal of Infant Mental Health, 10*, 25–34.

Gopnik, A., & Meltzoff, A. N. (1987). Early semantic developments and their relationship to object permanence, means-ends understanding and categorization. In K. Nelson & A. VanKleek (Eds.), *Children's language* (Vol. 6). Hillsdale, NJ: Erlbaum.

Gopnik, A. & Meltzoff, A. (1997). Words, thoughts, and theories. Cambridge, MA: MIT Press.

Gorman, K. S., & Pollitt, E. (1992). Relationship between weight and body proportionality at birth, growth during the first year of life, and cognitive development at 36, 48, and 60 months. *Infant Behavior and Development, 15*, 279–296.

Goswami, U. (1992). *Analogical reasoning in children*. Hove, UK: Erlbaum.

Goswami, U. (1996). Analogical reasoning and cognitive development. In H. W. Reese (Ed.), *Advances in child development and behavior* (Vol. 26). New York: Academic Press.

Goswami, U. (2004). Neuroscience and education. *British Journal of Educational Psychology, 74*, 1–14.

Gotlieb, S. J., Baisini, F. J., & Bray, N. W. (1988). Visual recognition memory in IVGR and normal birthweight infants. *Infant Behavior and Development, 11*, 223–228.

Gottlieb, G., & Blair, C. (2004). How early experience matters in intellectual development in the case of poverty. *Prevention Science, 5*, 245–252.

Gottesman, I. I. (1974). Developmental genetics and ontogenetic psychology: Overdue détente and propositions from a matchmaker. In A. Pick (Ed.), *Minnesota symposia on child psychology* (Vol. 8). Minneapolis: University of Minnesota Press.

Gottfried, A. W., Gottfried, A. E., Bathurst, K., & Guerin, D. W. (1994). *Gifted IQ: Early developmental aspects*. New York: Plenum Press.

Gottman, J. M. (1983). How children become friends. *Monographs of the Society for Research in Child Development, 48*(3, Serial No. 201).

Gottman, J. S. (1990). Children of gay and lesbian parents. In F. W. Bozett & M. B. Sussman (Eds.), *Homosexuality and family relations*. New York: Harrington Park Press.

Goudena, P. P. (1987). The social nature of private speech of preschoolers during problem solving. *International Journal of Behavioral Development, 10*, 187–206.

Göncü, A., Mistry, J., & Mosier, C. (2000). Cultural variations in the play of toddlers. *International Journal of Behavioral Development, 24*, 321–329.

Graber, J. A., Brooks-Gunn, J., Paikoff, R. L., & Warren, M. P. (1994). Prediction of eating problems: An 8-year study of adolescent girls. *Developmental Psychology, 30*, 823–834.

Graber, J. A., Brooks-Gunn, J., & Petersen, A. C. (Eds.). (1996). *Transitions through adolescence: Interpersonal domains and context*. Mahwah, NJ: Erlbaum.

Graham, F. K., & Clifton, R. K. (1966). Heart-rate change as a component of the orienting response. *Psychological Bulletin, 65*, 305–320.

Graham, S., & Hoehn, S. (1995). Children's understanding of aggression and withdrawal as social stigmas: An attributional analysis. *Child Development, 66*, 1143–1161.

Graham, S., Hudley, C., & Williams, E. (1992). Attributional and emotional determinants of aggression among African-American and Latino young adolescents. *Developmental Psychology, 28*, 731–740.

Graham, S., & Juvonen, J. (1998b). A social cognitive perspective on peer aggression and victimization. In R. Vasta (Ed.), *Annals of child development* (Vol. 13). London: Kingsley.

Grant, H., & Dweck, C. S. (2003). Clarifying achievement goals and their impact. *Journal of Personality and Social Psychology, 85*, 541–553.

Grantham-McGregor, S., Ani, C., & Fernald, L. (2001). The role of nutrition in intellectual development. In R. J. Sternberg & E. L. Grigorenko (Eds.), *Environmental effects on cognitive abilities*. Mahwah, NJ: Erlbaum.

Green, B. L., Grace, M., Vary, J. G., Kramer, T., Gleser, G. C., & Leonard, A. (1994). Children of disaster in the second decade: A 17-year follow-up of Buffalo Creek survivors. *Journal of the American Academy of Child and Adolescent Psychiatry, 33,* 71–79.

Green, J. A., Jones, L. E., & Gustafson, G. E. (1987). Perception of cries by parents and nonparents: Relation to cry acoustics. *Developmental Psychology, 23,* 370–382.

Green, K. D., Forehand, R., Beck, S. J., & Vosk, B. (1980). An assessment of the relationship among measures of children's social competence and children's academic achievement. *Child Development, 51,* 1149–1156.

Greenberg, M. T., Domitrovich, C., & Bumbarger, B. (2001). The prevention of mental disorders in school-age children: Current state of the field. *Prevention and Treatment, 4,* Article 001a. Online article available at http://hournals.apa.org/prevention/volume4/pre004001a.html.

Greenberger, E., & Chen, C. (1996). Perceived family relationships and depressed mood in early and late adolescence: A comparison of European and Asian Americans. *Developmental Psychology, 32,* 707–716.

Greenberger, E., & Goldberg, W. A. (1989). Work, parenting, and the socialization of children. *Developmental Psychology, 25,* 22–35.

Greene, J. P. (1998). *A meta-analysis of the effectiveness of bilingual education.* Claremont, CA: Tomas Rivera Policy Institute.

Greenfield, P. M. (1966). On culture and conservation. In J. S. Bruner, R. R. Oliver, & P. M. Greenfield (Eds.), *Studies in cognitive growth.* New York: Wiley.

Greenfield, P. M. (1984). A theory of the teacher in the learning activities of everyday life. In B. Rogoff & J. Lave (Eds.), *Everyday cognition* (pp. 117–138). Cambridge, MA: Harvard University Press.

Greenfield, P.M. (1994). Video games as cultural artifacts. *Journal of Applied Developmental Psychology, 15,* 311.

Greenfield, P. M. (2004). *Weaving generations together: Evolving creativity in the Zinacantec Maya.* Santa Fe, NM: SAR Press.

Greenfield, P. M., & Lave, J. (1982). Cognitive aspects of informal education. In D. Wagner & H. Stevenson (Eds.), *Cultural perspectives on child development* (pp. 181–207). San Francisco: Freeman.

Greenfield, P. M., Maynard, A. E., & Childs, C. P. (2003). Historical change, cultural learning, and cognitive presentation in Zinacantec Maya children. *Cognitive Development, 18,* 455–491.

Greenfield P. M., Quiroz, B., & Raeff, C. (2000). Cross-cultural conflict and harmony in the social construction of the child. *New Directions for Child and Adolescent Development, 87,* 93–108.

Greenough, W. T., & Black, J. E. (1999). Experience, neural plasticity, and psychological development. In N. A. Fox, L. A. Leavitt, & J. G. Warhol (Eds.), *The role of early experience in infant development.* Pompton Plains, NJ: Johnson and Johnson Pediatric Institute.

Greenough, W. T., Black, J. E., & Wallace, C. S. (1987). Experience and brain development. *Child Development, 58,* 539–559.

Gressens, P. (2000). Mechanisms and disturbances of neuronal migration. *Pediatric Research, 48* (6), 725–730.

Grigorenko, E. L. (2000). Heritability and intelligence. In R. J. Sternberg (Ed.), *Handbook of intelligence.* New York: Cambridge University Press.

Grigorenko, E. L., Meier, E., Lipka, J., Mohatt, G., Yanez, E., & Sternberg, R. J. (2004). Academic and practical intelligence: A case study of the Yup'ik in Alaska. *Learning and Individual Differences, 14,* 183–207.

Grossman, D., Neckerman, H., Koepsell, T., Liu, P. Y., Asher, K. N., Belands, K., et al. (1997). Effectiveness of a violence prevention curriculum among children in elementary school: A randomized controlled trial. *Journal of the American Medical Association, 277,* 1605–1611.

Grossman, E. D., Donnelly, M., Price, P., Morgan, V., Pickens, D., Neighbor, G., & Blake, R. (2000). Brain areas involved in perception of biological motion. *Journal of Cognitive Neuroscience, 12*(5), 711–720.

Grossmann, K., Grossmann, K. E., Spangler, G., Suess, G., & Unzner, L. (1985). Maternal sensitivity and newborns' orientation responses as related to quality of attachment in northern Germany. In I. Bretherton & E. Waters (Eds.), *Growing points of attachment theory and research. Monographs of the Society for Research in Child Development, 50*(12, Serial No. 209).

Grotevant, D., Perry, Y. V., & McRoy, R. G. (2005). Openness in adoption: Outcomes for adolescents within their adoptive kinship networks. In D. M. Brodzinsky & J. Palacios (Eds.), *Psychological Issues in Adoption.* Westport, CT: Greenwood Publishing Group.

Grusec, J. E., & Goodnow, J. J. (1994). Impact of parental discipline methods on the child's internalization of values: A reconceptualization of current points of view. *Developmental Psychology, 30,* 419.

Grusec, J. E., Goodnow, J. J., & Cohen, L. (1996). Household work and the development of concern for others. *Developmental Psychology, 32,* 999–1007.

Grusec, J. E., Kuczynski, L., Rushton, J. P., & Simutis, Z. M. (1979). Learning resistance to temptation through observation. *Developmental Psychology, 15,* 233–240.

Grusec, J. E., & Lytton, H. (1988). *Social development: History, theory, and research.* New York: Springer-Verlag.

Guan, Y. (2003). Spare-time life of Chinese children. *Journal of Family & Economic Issues, 24,* 365–371.

Guerin, F., Marsh, H. W., & Famose, J. P. (2004). Generalizability of the PSDQ and its relationship to physical fitness: The European French connection. *Journal of Sport & Exercise Psychology, 26,* 19–38.

Guerra, N. G., & Slaby, R. G. (1990). Cognitive mediators of aggression in adolescent offenders: 2. Intervention. *Developmental Psychology, 26,* 269–277.

Guilford, J. P. (1985). The structure-of-intellect model. In B. B. Wolman (Ed.), *Handbook of intelligence.* New York: Wiley.

Guillemin, J. (1993). Cesarean birth: Social and political aspects. In B. K. Rothman (Ed.), *Encyclopedia of childbearing.* Phoenix, AZ: Oryx Press.

Gullone, E., & King, N. J. (1997). Three-year follow-up of normal fear in children and adolescents aged 7 to 18 years. *British Journal of Developmental Psychology, 15,* 97–111.

Gunnar, M. R., Malone, S., Vance, G., & Fisch, R. O. (1985). Coping with aversive stimulation in the neonatal period: Quiet sleep and plasma cortisol levels during recovery from circumcision. *Child Development, 56,* 824–834.

Gunnar, M. R., Proter, F. L., Wolf, C.M., Rigatuso, J., & Larson, M. C. (1995). Neonatal stress reactivity: Predictions of later emotional temperament. *Child Development, 66,* 113.

Gustafson, G. E., & Harris, K. L. (1990). Women's responses to young infants' cries. *Developmental Psychology, 26,* 144–152.

Gustafson, G. E., Wood, R. M., & Green, J. A. (2000). Can we hear the causes of infants' crying? In R. G. Barr, B. Hopkins, & J. A. Green (Eds.), *Crying as a sign, a symptom, and a signal: Clinical, emotional, and developmental aspects of infant and toddler crying.* New York: Cambridge University Press.

Gutman, L. M. & McLoyd, V. C. (2000). Parents' management of their children's education within the home, at school, and in the community: An examination of African-American families living in poverty. *The Urban Review, 32,* 1–24.

Haapasalo, J., & Tremblay, R. E. (1994). Physically aggressive boys from age 6 to 12: Family background, parenting behavior, and prediction of delinquency. *Journal of Consulting and Clinical Psychology, 62,* 1044–1052.

Hack, M., Weissman, B., & Borawski-Clark, E. (1996) Catch-up growth during childhood among very-low-birth-weight children. (eng; includes abstract). *Archives Of Pediatrics & Adolescent Medicine, 150* (11),1122–1131.

Hack, M., Klein, N. K., & Taylor, H. G. (1995). Long-term developmental outcomes of low birth weight infants. *The future of children* (Vol. 5, No. 1). Los Angeles: Packard Foundation.

Hadjistavropoulos, H. D., Craig, K. D., Grunau, R. V. E., & Johnston, C. C. (1994). Judging pain in newborns: Facial and cry determinants. *Journal of Pediatric Psychology, 19,* 485–491.

Hagen, J.W., & Hale, G. A. (1973). The development of attention in children. In A. D. Pick (Ed.), *Minnesota symposia on child psychology* (Vol. 7). Minneapolis: University of Minnesota Press.

Hagerman, R. J. (1996). Biomedical advances in developmental psychology: The case of Fragile X syndrome. *Developmental Psychology, 32,* 416–424.

Haight, W. L., Parke, R. D., & Black, J. E. (1997). Mothers' and fathers' beliefs about and spontaneous participation in their toddlers' pretend play. *Merrill-Palmer Quarterly, 43,* 271–290.

Haight, W. L., Wang, X., Fung, H., Williams, K., & Mintz, J. (1999). Universal, developmental, and variable aspects of young children's play: A cross-cultural comparison of pretending at home. *Child Development, 70,* 1477–1488.

Hainline, L. (1998). The development of basic visual abilities. In A. Slater (Ed.), *Perceptual development: Visual, auditory, and speech perception in infancy.* Hove, UK: Psychology Press.

Hainline, L., & Abramov, I. (1992). Assessing visual development: Is infant vision good enough? In C. Rovee-Collier & L. P. Lipsitt (Eds.), *Advances in infancy research* (Vol. 7). Norwood, NJ: Ablex.

Haith, M. M. (1966). The response of the human newborn to visual movement. *Journal of Experimental Child Psychology, 3,* 235–243.

Haith, M. M. (1980). *Rules that babies look by.* Hillsdale, NJ: Erlbaum.

Haith, M. M. (1986). Sensory and perceptual processes in early infancy. *Journal of Pediatrics, 109,* 158–171.

Haith, M. M. (1990). Progress in the understanding of sensory and perceptual processes in early infancy. *Merrill-Palmer Quarterly, 36,* 109.

Haith, M. M. (1991). Gratuity, perception-action integration and future orientation in infant vision. In F. Kessel, A. Sameroff, & M. Bornstein (Eds.),

The past as prologue in developmental psychology: Essays in honor of William Kessen. Hillsdale, NJ: Erlbaum.

Haith, M. M. (1994). Visual expectations as the first step toward the development of future-oriented processes. In M. M. Haith, J. B. Benson, R. J. Roberts Jr., & B. F. Pennington (Eds.), *The development of future-oriented processes.* Chicago: University of Chicago Press.

Haith, M. M. (1998). Who put the cog in infant cognition? *Infant Behavior and Development, 21,* 161–179.

Haith, M. M., & Benson, J. B. (1998). Infant cognition. In W. Damon (Series Ed.) & D. Kuhn & R. S. Siegler (Vol. Eds.), *Handbook of child psychology:* Vol. 2. *Cognition, perception, and language* (5th ed.). New York: Wiley.

Haith, M. M., Benson, J. B., Roberts, R. J. Jr., & Pennington, B. F. (Eds.). (1994). *The development of future-oriented processes.* Chicago: University of Chicago Press.

Haith, M. M., Wentworth, N., & Canfield, R. L. (1993). The formation of expectations in early infancy. In C. Rovee-Collier & L. P. Lipsitt (Eds.), *Advances in infancy research* (Vol. 8). Norwood, NJ: Ablex.

Hakuta, K. (1999). The debate on bilingual education. *Journal of Developmental and Behavioral Pediatrics, 20,* 36–37.

Hale, M., & Tager-Flusberg, H. (2003). The influence of language on theory of mind: A training study. *Developmental Science, 6,* 3–46.

Hall, J. A. (1984). *Nonverbal sex differences: Communication accuracy and expressive style.* Baltimore: Johns Hopkins University Press.

Hall, D. G., Lee, S. C., & Belanger, J. (2001). Young children's use of syntactic cues to learn proper names and count nouns. *Developmental Psychology, 37,* 298–307.

Halpern, C. T., Udry, J. R., Campbell, B., & Suchindraw, C. (1994). Relationships between aggression and pubertal increases in testosterone: A panel analysis of adolescent males. *Social Biology, 40,* 8–24.

Halpern, D. F. (2000). *Sex differences in cognitive abilities* (3rd ed.) Mahwah, NJ: Erlbaum.

Halpern, L. F., MacLean, W. E. Jr., & Baumeister, A. A. (1995). Infant sleepwake characteristics: Relation to neurological status and the prediction of developmental outcome. *Developmental Review, 15,* 255–291.

Hamilton, B. E., Martin, J. A.., & Sutton, P. D. (2004). Births: Preliminary data for 2003, *National Vital Statistics Reports, 53*(9). Centers for Disease Control and Prevention. Retrieved February 25, 2004, from http://www.cdc.gov/nchs/data/nvsr/nvsr53/nvsr53_09.pdf

Hamm, J. V. (2000). Do birds of a feather flock together? The variable bases for African American, Asian American, and European American adolescents' selection of similar friends. *Developmental Psychology, 36,* 209–219.

Hansell, L. (2000). Putting contact theory into practice: Using the PARTNERS program to develop intercultural Competence Electronic Magazine of Multicultural Education [online], 2(2), 35 paragraphs. Accessed June 20, 2007, from http://www.eastern.edu/publications/emme/200fall/hansell.html

Hanushek, E. (1997). Assessing the effects of school resources on student performance: An update. *Educational Evaluation and Policy Analysis, 19*(2), 141–164.

Hardré, P., & Reeve, J. (2003). A motivational model of rural students' intentions to persist in, versus drop out, of high school. *Journal of Educational Psychology, 95,* (2), 347–356.

Harel, J., Eshel, Y., Ganor, O., & Scher, A. (2002). Antecedents of mirror self-recognition of toddlers: Emotional availability, birth order, and gender. *Infant Mental Health Journal, 23* (3), 293–310.

Harkness, S., Raeff, C., & Super, C. M. (Eds.). (2000). New directions for child and adolescent development: No. 87. *Variability in the social construction of the child.* San Francisco: Jossey-Bass.

Harkness, S., & Super, C.M. (2002). Culture and parenting. In M.H. Bornstein (Ed.), *Handbook of parenting,* 2nd edition (pp. 253–280). Mahwah, NJ: Erlbaum.

Harlan, J. C., & Rowland, S. T. (2002). Behavior management strategies for teachers : Achieving instructional effectiveness, student success, and student motivation—every teacher and any student can! (2nd ed.). Springfield, IL: Charles C. Thomas.

Harlow, Harry F. (1959). Love in Infant Monkeys. *Scientific American* (June), pp. 2–8.

Harlow, H. F., & Harlow, M. K. (1969). Effects of various mother-infant relationships on rhesus monkey behaviors. In B. M. Foss (Ed.), *Determinants of infant behavior* (Vol.4). London: Methuen.

Harper, L. V., & Kraft, R. H. (1986). Lateralization of receptive language in preschoolers: Test-retest reliability in a dichotic listening task. *Developmental Psychology, 22,* 553–556.

Harrell, J. S., Gansky, S. A., Bradley, C. B., & McMurray, R. G. (1997). Leisure time activities of elementary school children. *Nursing Research, 46,* 246–253.

Harris, L. J. (1977). Sex differences in the growth and use of language. In E. Donelson & J. E. Gullahorn (Eds.), *Women: A psychological perspective.* New York: Wiley.

Harris, L. (1997). *The Metropolitan Life survey of the American teacher 1997: Examining gender issues in public schools.* New York: Louis Harris and Associates.

Harris, M., Jones, D., & Grant, J. (1983). The nonverbal context of mothers' speech to infants. *First Language, 4,* 21–30.

Harris, P. L. (1989). Object permanence in infancy. In A. Slater & G. Bremner (Eds.), *Infant development.* Hillsdale, NJ: Erlbaum.

Hart, D. (1988b). A longitudinal study of adolescents' socialization and identification as predictors of adult moral judgment development. *Merrill-Palmer Quarterly, 34,* 245–260.

Hart, C. H., DeWolf, D. M., Wozniak, P., & Burts, D. C. (1992). Maternal and paternal disciplinary styles: Relations with preschoolers' playground behavioral orientations and peer status. *Child Development, 63,* 879–892.

Hart, C. H., Yang, C., Nelson, D. A., Jin, S., Bazarskaya, N., Nelson, L., et al. (1998). Peer contact patterns, parenting practices, and preschoolers' social competence in China, Russia, and the United States. In P. T. Slee & K. Rigby (Eds.), *Children's peer relations.* London: Routledge.

Harter, S. (1985b). *The Self-Perception Profile for Children.* Denver, CO: University of Denver.

Harter, S. (1986). Processes underlying the construction, maintenance, and enhancement of the self-concept in children. In J. Suls & A. Greenwald (Eds.), *Psychological perspectives on the self* (Vol. 3). Hillsdale, NJ: Erlbaum.

Harter, S. (1988a). Developmental processes in the construction of the self. In T. D. Yawkey & J. E. Johnson (Eds.), *Integrative processes and socialization: Early to middle childhood.* Hillsdale, NJ: Erlbaum.

Harter, S. (1988b). The Self-Perception Profile for Adolescents. Unpublished manual, University of Denver, Denver, CO.

Harter, S. (1999). *The construction of the self: A developmental perspective.* New York : Guilford.

Harter, S. (2002). Authenticity. In C.R. Snyder, & S.J. Lopez (Eds.)., *Handbook of positive psychology.* New York: Oxford University Press.

Harter, S. (2003). The development of self-representations during childhood and adolescence. In M. R. Leary and J. P. Tangney (Eds.), *Handbook of Self and Identity,* (pp. 610–642). New York: Guilford.

Harter, S., & Pike, R. (1984). The Pictorial Scale of Perceived Competence and Social Acceptance for young children. *Child Development, 55,* 1969–1982.

Harter, S., & Whitesell, N. R. (2002). Beyond the debate: Why some adolescents report stable self-worth over time and situation, whereas others report changes in self-worth. *Journal of Personality, 71,* 1027–1058.

Harter, S., Whitesell, N. R., & Junkin, L. J. (1998). Similarities and differences in domain-specific and global self-evaluation of learning-disabled, behaviorally disordered, and normally achieving adolescents. *American Educational Research Journal, 35,* 653–680.

Hartig, M., & Kanfer, F. H. (1973). The role of verbal self-instructions in children's resistance to temptation. *Journal of Personality and Social Psychology, 25,* 259–267.

Hartshorn, H., and May, M. (1932). *Studies in the nature of character: Studies in the organization of character,* Vol. 3. New York: Macmillan.

Hartung, C. M., & Widiger, T. A. (1998). Gender differences in the diagnosis of mental disorders: Conclusions and controversies of the DSM-IV. *Psychological Bulletin, 123,* 260–278.

Hartup, W. W. (1983). Peer relations. In P. H. Mussen (Series Ed.) & E. M. Hetherington (Vol. Ed.), *Handbook of child psychology:* Vol. 4. *Socialization, personality, and social development* (4th ed.). New York: Wiley.

Hartup, W. W. (1992a). Conflict and friendship relations. In C. U. Shantz & W. W. Hartup (Eds.), *Conflict in child and adolescent development.* Cambridge: Cambridge University Press.

Hartup, W. W. (1993). Adolescents and their friends. In B. Laursen (Ed.), *New directions for child development:* No. 60. *Close friendships in adolescence.* San Francisco: Jossey-Bass.

Hartup, W. W. (1996). The company they keep: Friendships and their developmental significance. *Child Development, 67,* 1–13.

Hartup, W. W. (1999). Constraints on peer socialization: Let me count the ways. *Merrill-Palmer Quarterly, 45,* 172–183.

Hartup, W. W., & Abecassis, M. (2002). Friends and enemies. In P. K. Smith & C. H. Hart (Eds.), *Blackwell handbook of childhood social development.* Malden, MA: Blackwell Publishers.

Hartup, W. W., French, D. C., Laursen, B., Johnson, M. K., & Ogawa, J. R. (1993). Conflict and friendship relations in middle childhood: Behavior in a closed-field situation. *Child Development, 64,* 445–454.

Hartup, W. W., Laursen, B., Stewart, M. I., & Eastenson, A. (1988). Conflict and the friendship relations of young children. *Child Development, 59,* 1590–1600.

Hartup, W. W., & Stevens, N. (1997). Friendships and adaptation in the life course. *Psychological Bulletin, 121*, 355–370.

Harwood, R. L., Miller, J. G., & Irizarry, N. L. (1995). *Culture and attachment*. New York: Guilford.

Harwood, R. L., Schoelmerich, A., Ventura-Cook, E., Schulze, P. A., & Wilson, A. (1996). Culture and class influences on Anglo and Puerto Rican mothers' beliefs regarding long-term socialization goals and child behavior. *Child Development, 67*, 2446–2461.

Hasselhorn, M. (1992). Task dependency and the role of category typicality and metamemory in the development of an organizational strategy. *Child Development, 63*, 202–214.

Hatano, G. (1990). The nature of everyday intelligence. *British Journal of Developmental Psychology, 8*, 245–250.

Hatano, G., & Inagaki, K. (1998). Cultural contexts of schooling revisited: A review of the Learning Gap from a cultural psychology perspective. In S. G. Paris & H. M. Wellman (Eds.), *Global prospects for education: Development, culture, and schooling*. Washington, DC: American Psychological Association.

Hatcher, P. J., Hulme, C., & Snowling, M. J. (2004). Explicit phoneme training combined with phonic reading instruction helps young children at risk of reading failure. *Journal of Child Psychology & Psychiatry, 45*, 338–358.

Haugaard, J., & Hazan, C. (2002). Foster parenting. In M.H. Bornstein (Ed.), *Handbook of parenting*, Vol 1: *Children and parenting* (pp. 313–328), 2nd ed. Mahwah, NJ: Erlbaum.

Hauser, M. D., & Carey, S. (2003). Spontaneous representations of small numbers of objects by rhesus macaques: Examinations of content and format. *Cognitive Psychology, 47*, 367–401.

Hauspie, R. C., Vercauteren, M., & Susanne, C. (1997). Secular changes in growth and maturation: An update. *Acta Paediatr Suppl, 23*, 20–27.

Haviland, J. M., & Lelwica, M. (1987). The induced affect response: 10-week-old infants' response to three emotion expressions. *Developmental Psychology, 23*, 97–104.

Haviland, J., & Malatesta, C. (1981). A description of the development of nonverbal signals: Fallacies, facts, and fantasies. In C. Mayo & N. Henley (Eds.), *Gender and nonverbal behavior*. New York: Springer.

Hawkins, D. L., Pepler, D. J., & Craig, W. M. (2001). Naturalistic observations of peer interventions in bullying. *Social Development, 10*, 512–527.

Hay, D. F. (1984). Social conflict in early childhood. In G. J. Whitehurst (Ed.), *Annals of child development* (Vol. 1). Greenwich, CT: JAI Press.

Hay, D. F. (1985). Learning to form relationships in infancy: Parallel attainments with parents and peers. *Developmental Review, 5*, 122–161.

Hay, D. (1999). The developmental genetics of intelligence. In M. Anderson (Ed.), *The development of intelligence*. Hove, UK: Psychology Press.

Hay, D. F., Castle, J., Stimsom, C., & Davies, L. (1995). The social construction of character in toddlerhood. In M. Killen & D. Hart (Eds.), *Morality in everyday life*. New York: Cambridge University Press.

Hay, D. F., & Murray, P. (1982). Giving and requesting: Social facilitation of infants' offers to adults. *Infant Behavior and Development, 5*, 301–310.

Hay, D. F., Nash, A., & Pedersen, J. (1983). Interaction between six-month-old peers. *Child Development, 54*, 557–562.

Hayne, H., Boniface, J., & Barr R. (2000) The development of declarative memory in human infants: Age-related changes in deferred imitation. *Behavioral Neuroscience, 114*, 77–83.

Head Start. (2005). Program fact sheet. U.S. Department of Health and Human Services. Washington, DC. http://www2.acf.dhhs.gov/programs/hsb/research/2005.htm

Heath, S. B. (1983). *Ways with words: Language, life, and work in communities and classrooms*. New York: Cambridge University Press.

Hebb, D. O. (1949). *The organization of behavior*. New York: Wiley.

Hecht, S. A., Burgess, S. R., Torgesen, J. K., Wagner, R. K., & Rashotte, C. (2000). Explaining social class differences in growth of reading skills from beginning kindergarten through fourthgrade: The role of phonological awareness, rate of access, and print knowledge. *Reading & Writing: An Interdisciplinary Journal, 12*, 99–127.

Heibeck, T., & Markman, E. M. (1987). Word learning in children: An examination of fast mapping. *Child Development, 58*, 1021–1034.

Heiman, T. (2002). Inclusive schooling: Middle school teachers' perceptions. *School Psychology International, 23* (1), 174–186.

Heinze, S.D., & Sleigh, M.J. (2003). Epidural or no epidural anaesthesia: Relationships between beliefs about childbirth and pain control choices. *Journal of Reproductive & Infant Psychology, 21* (4), 323–333.

Helwig, C. C., Zelazo, P. D., & Wilson, M. (2001). Children's judgments of psychological harm in normal and noncanonical situations. *Child Development, 72*, 66–81.

Helwig, R., Anderson, L., & Tindal, G. (2001). Influence of elementary student gender on teachers' perceptions of mathematics achievement. *Journal of Educational Research, 95*, 93–102.

Henderlong, J., & Lepper, M.R. (2002). The effects of praise on children's intrinsic motivation: A review and synthesis. *Psychological Bulletin, 128*, 774–795.

Henricsson, L., & Rydell, A. M. (2004). Elementary school children with behavior problems: Teacher-child relations and self-perception. A prospective study. *Merrill-Palmer Quarterly, 50*, 193–203.

Herbert, J., & Stipek, D. (2005). The emergence of gender differences in children's perceptions of their academic competence. *Journal of Applied Developmental Psychology, 26*, 276–295.

Herdt, G., & Boxer, A. M. (1993). *Children of Horizons: How gay and lesbian teens are leading a new way out of the closet*. Boston: Beacon.

Herman, L. M. (2002). Exploring the cognitive world of the bottlenosed dolphin. In M. Bekoff, C. Allen, & G. M. Burghardt (Eds.), *The cognitive animal: Empirical and theoretical perspectives on animal cognition*. Cambridge, MA: MIT Press.

Hernandez, D. J. (1997). Child development and the social demography of childhood. *Child Development, 68*, 149–169.

Herrera, C., & Dunn, J. (1997). Early experiences with family conflict: Implications for arguments with a close friend. *Developmental Psychology, 33*, 869–881.

Herrnstein, R. J., & Murray, C. (1994). *The bell curve: Intelligence and class structure in American life*. New York: Free Press.

Hershberger, S. L. (2001). Biological factors in the development of sexual orientation. In A. R. D'Augelli & C. J. Patterson (Eds.), *Lesbian, gay, and bisexual identities and youth: Psychological perspectives*. New York: Oxford University Press.

Hetherington, E. M. (1993). An overview of the Virginia longitudinal study of divorce and remarriage with a focus on early adolescence. *Journal of Family Psychology, 7*, 1–18.

Hetherington, E. M. (1989). Coping with family transitions: Winners, losers, and survivors. *Child Development, 60*, 1–14.

Hetherington, E. M., Bridges, M., & Isabella, G. M. (1998). What matters? What does not? Five perspectives on the association between marital transitions and children's adjustment. *American Psychologist, 53*, 167–184.

Hetherington, E. M., & Clingempeel, W. G. (1992). Coping with marital transitions: A family systems perspective. *Monographs of the Society for Research in Child Development, 57*(Serial No. 227).

Hetherington, E. M., & Kelly, J. (2002). *For better or worse: Divorce reconsidered*. New York: Norton.

Hetherington, E. M., & Parke, R.D. (1979). *Child psychology: A contemporary viewpoint*. New York: McGraw-Hill.

Hetherington, E. M., & Stanley-Hagan, M. S. (2002). Parenting in divorced and remarried families. In M. Bornstein (Ed.), *Handbook of parenting*. (2nd ed., Vol. 3). Mahwah, NJ: Erlbaum.

Heyes, C., & Huber, L. (Eds.). (2000). *The evolution of cognition*. Cambridge, MA: MIT Press.

Heyman, G. (2001). Children's interpretation of ambiguous behavior: Evidence for a "boys are bad" bias. *Social Development, 10*, 230–247.

Heyman, G. D., Dweck, C. S., & Cain, K. M. (1992). Young children's vulnerability to self-blame and helplessness: Relationship to beliefs about goodness. *Child Development, 63*, 401–415.

Hewlett, B. S. (1992). The parent-infant relationship and social-emotional development among the Aka pygmies. In J. L. Roopnarine & D. B. Carter (Eds.). *Annual advances in applied development psychology: Vol. 5. Parent-child socialization in diverse cultures*. Norwood, NJ: Ablex.

Hicks, D. (1996). *Discourse, learning, and schooling*. New York: Cambridge University Press.

Hill, J. (2003). Early identification of individuals at risk for antisocial personality disorder. *British Journal of Psychiatry, 182*(Suppl. 144), s11–s14.

Hinds, P., & Kiesler, S. (2002). *Distributed work*. Cambridge, MA: MIT Press.

Hines, M. (1982). Prenatal gonad hormones and sex differences in human behavior. *Psychological Bulletin, 92*, 56–80.

Hines, M., Golombok, S., Rust, J., Johnston, K. J., Golding, G., & the Avon Longitudinal Study of Parents and Children Study Team. (2002). Testosterone during pregnancy and gender role behavior in children: A longitudinal, population study. *Child Development, 73*, 1678–1687.

Hines, M., & Green, R. (1991). Human hormonal and neural correlates of sex-typed behaviors. *Review of Psychiatry, 10*, 536–555.

Hines, M., & Kaufman, F. R. (1994). Androgen and the development of human sex-typical behavior: Rough-and-tumble and sex of preferred playmates in children with congenital adrenal hyperplasia (CAH). *Child Development, 65*, 1042–1053.

Hirsh-Pasek, K., & Golinkoff, R. M. (1996). *The origins of grammar: Evidence from early language comprehension*. Cambridge, MA: MIT Press.

Hirsh-Pasek, K., Treiman, R., & Schneiderman, M. (1984). Brown and Hanlon revisited: Mothers' sensitivity to ungrammatical forms. *Journal of Child Language, 11*, 81–88.

Hittelman, J. H., & Dickes, R. (1979). Sex differences in neonatal eye contact time. *Merrill-Palmer Quarterly, 25,* 171–184.

Hmelo-Silver, C. E., Pfeffer, M. G. (2004). Comparing expert and novice understanding of a complex system from the perspective of structures, behaviors and functions. *Cognitive Science, 28,* 127–138.

Ho, D. Y. F. (1986). Chinese patterns of socialization: A critical review. In M. H. Bond (Ed.), *The psychology of Chinese people.* New York: Oxford University Press.

Hoare, C. H. (2002). *Erikson on development in adulthood: New insights from the unpublished papers.* New York: Oxford University Press, pp. 2–84.

Hoek, D., Ingram, D., & Gibson, D. (1986). Some possible causes of children's early word overextensions. *Journal of Child Language, 13,* 477–494.

Hoff, E. (2003). The specificity of environmental influence: Socioeconomic status affects early vocabulary development via maternal speech. *Child Development, 74,* 1368–1378.

Hoff, E., Laursen, B., & Tardif, T. (2002). Socioeconomic status and parenting. In M.H. Bornstein (Ed.), *Handbook of parenting,* vol. 2: *Biology and ecology of parenting* (pp. 23–152), 2nd ed. Mahwah, NJ: Erlbaum.

Hoff, E., & Naigles, L. (2002). How children use speech to acquire a lexicon. *Child Development, 73,* 418–433.

Hoff-Ginsberg, E. (1990). Maternal speech and the child's development of syntax: A further look. *Journal of Child Language, 17,* 85–99.

Hoff-Ginsberg, E., & Shatz, M. (1982). Linguistic input and the child's acquisition of language. *Psychological Bulletin, 92,* 3–26.

Hoffman, L. W., & Youngblade, L. M. (1999). *Mothers at work: Effects on children's well being.* New York: Cambridge University Press.

Hoffman, M. L. (1970). Moral development. In P. H. Mussen (Ed.), *Carmichael's manual of child psychology* (3rd ed., Vol. 2). New York: Wiley.

Hoffman, M. L. (1975). Altruistic behavior and the parent-child relationship. *Journal of Personality and Social Psychology, 31,* 937–943.

Hoffman, M. L. (1978). Empathy, its development and prosocial implications. In C. B. Keasey (Ed.), *Nebraska symposium on motivation* (Vol. 25). Lincoln: University of Nebraska Press.

Hoffman, M. L. (1983). Affective and cognitive processes in moral internalization: An information processing approach. In E. R. Higgins, D. Ruble, & W. Hartup (Eds.), *Social cognition and social development: A socio-cultural perspective.* New York: Cambridge University Press.

Hoffman, M. L. (1984). Empathy, its limitations, and its role in a comprehensive moral theory. In J. L. Gewirtz & W. Kurtines (Eds.), *Morality, moral development, and moral behavior.* New York: Wiley.

Hoffman, M. L. (1994). Discipline and internalization. *Developmental Psychology, 30,* 26–28.

Hoffman, M. L. (2000). *Empathy and moral development.* New York: Wiley.

Hofsten, C. Von (1982). Eye-hand coordination in the newborn. *Developmental Psychology, 18,* 450–461.

Hofsten, C. von, & Siddiqui, A. (1993). Using the mother's actions as a reference for object exploration in 6- and 12-month-old infants. *British Journal of Developmental Psychology, 11,* 61–74.

Hogan, D., & Tudge, J. R. H. (1999). Implications of Vygotsky's theory for peer learning. In A. M.

O'Donnell & A. King (Eds.), *Cognitive perspectives on peer learning.* Mahwah, NJ: Erlbaum.

Hogberg, U., Wall, S., & Brostrom, G. (1986). The impact of early medical technology on maternal mortality in late 19th century Sweden. *International Journal of Gynecology and Obstetrics, 24,* 251–261.

Hogge, W. A. (1990). Teratology. In I. R. Merkatz & J. E. Thompson (Eds.), *New perspectives on prenatal care.* New York: Elsevier.

Hoglund, W. L., & Leadbeater, B. J. (2004). The effects of family, school, and classroom ecologies on changes in children's social competence and emotional and behavioral problems in first grade. *Developmental Psychology, 40,* 533–544.

Holden, C. (1986). High court says no to administration's Baby Doe rules. *Science, 232,* 1595–1596.

Hollich, G. J., Hirsh-Pasek, K., & Golinkoff, R. M. (2000). Breaking the language barrier: An emergentist coalition model of word learning. *Monographs of the Society for Research in Child Development, 65*(3, Serial No. 262).

Holmes, J. (1995). "Something there is that doesn't love a wall": John Bowlby, attachment theory, and psychoanalysis. In S. Goldberg, R. Muir, & J. Kerr (Eds.), *Attachment theory: Social, developmental, and clinical perspectives.* Hillsdale, NJ: Analytic Press.

Holmes-Lonergan, H. A. (2003). Preschool children's collaborative problem solving interactions: The role of gender, pair type, and task. *Sex Roles. 48,* 505–517.

Holstein, C. B. (1972). The relation of children's moral judgment level to that of their parents and to communication patterns in the family. In R. C. Smart & M. S. Smart (Eds.), *Readings in child development and relationships.* New York: Macmillan.

Hong, Y. (2001). Chinese students' teachers and students' inferences of effort and ability. In F. Salili, C. Chiu, & Y. Hong (Eds.), *Student motivation: The culture and context of learning.* New York: Plenum Publishers.

Hong, C., Xiting, H., & Cheng, G. (2004). A correlational study between physical self-satisfaction and self-worth of middle school students. *Psychological Science* (China), *27,* 817–820.

Hood, B., Carey, S., & Prasada, S. (2000). Predicting the outcomes of physical events: Two-year-olds fail to reveal knowledge of solidity and support. *Child Development, 71,* 1540–1554.

Hoover, J. H., Oliver, R., & Hazler, R. J. (1992). Bullying: Perceptions of adolescent victims in the midwestern USA. *School Psychology International, 12,* 5–16.

Hopkins, B. (1991). Facilitating early motor development: An intracultural study of West Indian mothers and their infants living in Britain. In J. K. Nugent, B. M. Lester, & T. B. Brazelton (Eds.), *The cultural context of infancy*: Vol. 2. *Multicultural and interdisciplinary approaches to parentinfant relations.* Norwood, NJ: Ablex.

Hopkins, K. B., McGillicuddy-De Lisi, A. V., & De Lisi, R. (1997). Student gender and teaching methods as sources of variability in children's computational arithmetic performance. *Journal of Genetic Psychology, 158,* 333–345.

Horner, S.L., & Gaither, S.M. (2004). Attribution retraining instruction with a second-grade class. *Early Childhood Education Journal, 31,* 165–170.

Hornik, R., & Gunnar, M. R. (1988). A descriptive analysis of infant social referencing. *Child Development, 59,* 626–634.

Horon, I. L. (2005). Underreporting of maternal deaths on death certificates and the magnitude of

the problem of maternal mortality. *American Journal of Public Health, 95,* 478–482.

Hoy, E. A., Bill, J. M., & Sykes, D. H. (1988). Very low birthweight: A long-term developmental impairment? *International Journal of Behavioral Development, 11,* 37–67.

Hoyert, Kung, & Smith. (2003). Deaths: Preliminary Data for 2003. *National Vital Statistics Reports,* 53(15).

Howard, B. J., & Wong, J. (2001). Sleep disorders. In *Review / American Academy of Pediatrics, 22*(10), 327–369.

Howe, C. (1981). *Acquiring language in a conversational context.* Orlando, FL: Academic Press.

Howe, M. L. (2000). *The fate of early memories.* Washington, DC: American Psychological Association.

Howes, C. (1983). Patterns of friendship. *Child Development, 54,* 1041–1053.

Howes, C. (1987). Social competence with peers in young children: Developmental sequences. *Developmental Review, 7,* 252–272.

Howes, C. (1992). *The collaborative construction of pretend.* New York: SUNY Press.

Howes, C., & James, J. (2002). Children's social development within the socialization context of childcare and early childhood education. In P. K. Smith & C. H. Hart (Eds.), *Blackwell handbook of childhood social development.* Malden, MA: Blackwell Publishers.

Howes, C., & Tonyan, H. (1999). Peer relations. In L. Balter & C. S. Tamis-Lemonda (Eds.), *Child psychology: A handbook of contemporary issues.* Philadelphia: Psychology Press.

Howes, C., Unger, O., & Seidner, L. B. (1989). Social pretend play in toddlers. Parallels with social play and with solitary pretend. *Child Development, 60,* 77–84.

Hsu, A. & Slonim, A. D. (2006). Preventing pediatric trauma: The role of the critical care professional. *Critical Connections, Society for Critical Care Medicine.* Retrieved March 17, 2006 from http://www.sccm.org/publications/critical_connections/ 2006_01Feb/ pedTrauma.pdf

Hubbard, J. A. (2001). Emotion expression processes in children's peer interaction: The role of peer rejection, aggression, and gender. *Child Development, 72,* 1426–1438.

Hudley, C., & Graham, S. (1993). An attributional intervention to reduce peer-directed aggression among African-American boys. *Child Development, 64,* 124–138.

Huebner, C. E., & Meltzoff, A. N. (2005). Intervention to change parent-child reading style: A comparison of instructional methods. *Journal of Applied Developmental Psychology, 26,* 296–313.

Huesmann, L. R., Lagerspetz, K., & Eron, L. D. (1984). Intervening variables in the television violence-aggression relation: Evidence from two countries. *Developmental Psychology, 20,* 746–775.

Huesmann, L. R., Moise-Titus, J., Podolski, C.-L., & Eron, L. D. (2003). Longitudinal relations between children's exposure to TV violence and their aggressive and violent behavior in young adulthood: 1977–1992. *Developmental Psychology, 39,* 201–221.

Hughes, C. (2002). Executive functions and development: Emerging themes. *Infant and Child Development, 11,* 201–209.

Hughes, C. & Dunn, J. (2002). "When I say a naughty word". A longitudinal study of young children's accounts of anger and sadness in themselves and close others. *British Journal of Developmental Psychology, 20,* 515–535.

Hughes, C., White, A., Sharpen, J., & Dunn, J. (2000). Antisocial, angry, and unsympathetic: "Hard-to-manage" preschoolers' peer problems and possible cognitive influences. *Journal of Child Psychology and Psychiatry and Allied Disciplines, 41,* 169–179.

Huichang, C., Junli, Y., & Hongxue, Z. (2005). A correlational research on delaying self-control of 2-year-olds and their family factors. *Psychological Science* (China), *28,* 285–289.

Huitt, W., & Hummel, J. (2003). Piaget's theory of cognitive development. Retrieved October 11, 2004, from http://chiron.valdosta.edu/whuitt/col/cogsys/piaget.html

Human Genome Project [special issue]. (2001, February 16). *Science, 291.*

Hunt, M. (1997). *How science takes stock: The study of meta-analysis.* New York: Russell Sage Foundation.

Hurley, J. C., & Underwood, M. K. (2002). Children's understanding of their research rights before and after debriefing: Informed assent, confidentiality, and stopping participation. *Child Development, 73,* 132–143.

Huston, A. C. (1983). Sex-typing. In P. H. Mussen (Series Ed.) & E. M. Hetherington (Vol. Ed.), *Handbook of child psychology:* Vol. 4. *Socialization, personality, and social development* (4th ed.). New York: Wiley.

Huston, A. C. (1985). The development of sex typing: Themes from recent research. *Developmental Review, 5,* 1–17.

Huston, A. C., & Wright, J. C. (1998). Mass media and children's development. In W. Damon (Series Ed.) & I. E. Sigel & K. A. Renninger (Vol. Eds.), *Handbook of child psychology:* Vol. 4. *Child psychology in practice* (5th ed.). New York: Wiley.

Huston, A. C., Wright, J. C., Marquis, J., & Green, S. B. (1999). How young children spend their time: Television and other activities. *Developmental Psychology, 35,* 912–925.

Hutchins, E. (1983). Understanding Micronesian navigation. In D. Gentner & A. Stevens (Eds.), *Mental models.* Hillsdale, NJ: Erlbaum.

Huttenlocher, P. R. (1990). Morphometric study of human cerebral cortex development. *Neuropsychologia, 28,* 517–527.

Huttenlocher, J., Haight, W., Bryk, A., Seltzer, M., & Lyons, T. (1991). Early vocabulary growth: Relation to language input and gender. *Developmental Psychology, 27,* 236–248.

Huttenlocher, J., Levine, S., & Vevea, J. (1998). Environmental input and cognitive growth: A study using time-period comparisons. *Child Development, 69,* 1012–1029.

Huttenlocher, J., Newcombe, N., & Vasilyeva, M. (1999). Spatial scaling in young children. *Psychological Science, 10,* 393–398.

Hutton, N. (1996). Health prospects for children born to HIV-infected women. In R. R. Faden & N. E. Kass (Eds.), *HIV, AIDS, and childbearing.* New York: Oxford University Press.

Hwang, H. J., & St. James-Roberts, I. (1998). Emotional and behavioral problems in primary school children from nuclear and extended families in Korea. *Journal of Child Psychology and Psychiatry, 39,* 973–979.

Hyde, J. S. (1984). How large are gender differences in aggression? A developmental meta-analysis. *Developmental Psychology, 20,* 722–736.

Hyde, J. S. (1986). Gender differences in aggression. In J. S. Hyde & M. C. Linn (Eds.), *The psychology of gender: Advances through meta-analysis.* Baltimore: Johns Hopkins University Press.

Hyde, J. S., Fennema, E., & Lamon, S. J. (1990). Gender differences in mathematics performance: A meta-analysis. *Psychological Bulletin, 107,* 139–153.

Hyde, J. S., & Linn, M. C. (1988). Gender differences in verbal ability: A meta-analysis. *Psychological Bulletin, 104,* 53–69.

Hymel, S., Tarulli, D., Hayden Thomson, L., & Terrell-Deutsch, B. (1999). Loneliness through the eyes of children. In K. J. Rotenberg & S. Hymel (Eds.), *Loneliness in childhood and adolescence* (pp. 80–106). New York: Cambridge University Press.

Hymel, S., Woody, E., & Bowker, A., (1993). Social withdrawal in childhood: Considering the child's perspective. In K. Rubin & J. Asendorpf (Eds.), *Social withdrawal, inhibition, and shyness in childhood.* (pp. 237–262). Hillsdale NJ: Lawrence Erlbaum Associates.

Ike, N. (2000). Current thinking on XYY syndrome. *Psychiatric Annals, 30,* 91–95.

Inhelder, B., & Piaget, J. (1958). *The growth of logical thinking from childhood to adolescence.* New York: Basic Books.

Isabella, R. A. (1993). Origins of attachment: Maternal interactive behavior across the first year. *Child Development, 64,* 605–621.

Isabella, R. A. (1994). The origins of infant–mother attachment: Maternal behavior and infant development. In R. Vasta (Ed.), *Annals of child development* (Vol. 10). London: Kingsley.

Isley, S. L., O'Neil, R., Clatfelter, D., & Parke, R. (1999). Parent and child expressed affect and children's social competence: Modeling direct and indirect pathways. *Developmental Psychology, 35,* 547–560.

Israel, G., & Tarver, D. (1997). *Transgender care: Recommended guidelines, practical information, and personal accounts.* Philadelphia, PA: Temple University Press.

Izard, C. (1989). *The maximally discriminative facial movement coding system (MAX)* (rev. ed.). Newark: University of Delaware, Information Technologies and University Media Services.

Izard, C. (1991). *The psychology of emotions.* New York: Plenum.

Izard, C. (1993). Organizational and motivational functions of discrete emotions. In M. Lewis & J. Haviland (Eds.), *Handbook of emotions.* New York: Guilford.

Izard, C. (1995). Innate and universal facial expressions: Evidence from developmental and cross-cultural research. *Psychological Bulletin, 115,* 288–299.

Izard, C. E., Fantauzzo, C. A., Castle, J. M., Haynes, O. M., Rayias, M. F., & Putnam, P. H. (1995). The ontogeny and significance of infants' facial expressions in the first 9 months of life. *Developmental Psychology, 31,* 997–1013.

Jacklin, C. N. (1989). Female and male: Issues of gender. *American Psychologist, 44,* 127–133.

Jacklin, C. N., DiPietro, J. A., & Maccoby, E. E. (1984). Sex-typing behavior and sex-typing pressure in child/parent interactions. *Archives of Sexual Behavior, 13,* 413–425.

Jackson, C. (2002). Can single-sex classes in co-educational schools enhance the learning experiences of girls and/or boys? An exploration of pupils' perceptions. *British Educational Research Journal, 28,* 37–48.

Jackson, C., & Smith, I. D. (2000). Poles apart? An exploration of single-sex and mixed-sex educational environments in Australia and England. *Educational Studies, 26,* 409–422.

Jacobs, J. E., Lanza, S., Osgood, D. W., Eccles, J. S., & Wigfield, A. (2002). Changes in children's self-competence and values: Gender and domain differences across grades one though twelve. *Child Development, 73,* 509–527.

Jacobson, M. F. (1998). *Whiteness of a different color: European immigrants and the alchemy of race, Matthew Frye Jacobson.* Cambridge, MA: Harvard University Press.

Jacobson, J. L., & Jacobson, S. W. (1988). New methodologies for assessing the effects of prenatal toxic exposure on cognitive functioning in humans. In M. Evans (Ed.), *Toxic contaminants and ecosystem health: A Great Lakes focus.* New York: Wiley.

Jacobson, J. L., Jacobson, S. W., Padgett, R. J., Brimitt, G. A., & Billings, R. L. (1992). Effects of prenatal PCB exposure on cognitive processing efficiency and sustained attention. *Developmental Psychology, 28,* 297–306.

Jacobvitz, D., & Sroufe, L. A. (1987). The early caregiver-child relationship and attention-deficit disorder with hyperactivity in kindergarten: A prospective study. *Child Development, 58,* 1496–1504.

Jadack, R. A., Hyde, J. S., Moore, C. F., & Keller, M. L. (1995). Moral reasoning about sexually transmitted diseases. *Child Development, 66,* 167–177.

Jaffee, S., & Hyde, J. S. (2000). Gender differences in moral orientation: A meta-analysis. *Psychological Bulletin, 126,* 703–726.

James, H.S. (2005). Why did you do that? An economic examination of the effect of extrinsic compensation on intrinsic motivation and performance. *Journal of Economic Psychology, 26,* 549–566.

James, W. (1890). *Principles of psychology.* New York: Holt.

James, W. (1892). *Psychology: The briefer course.* New York: Holt.

Jamison, W. (1977). Developmental inter-relationships among concrete operational tasks: An investigation of Piaget's stage concept. *Journal of Experimental Child Psychology, 24,* 235–253.

Jencks, C. (1972). *Inequality.* New York: Basic Books.

Jenkins, S. R., Goodness, K., & Buhrmester, D. (2002). Gender differences in early adolescent's relationship qualities, self-efficacy, and depression symptoms. *Journal of Early Adolescence, 22,* 277–309.

Jenni, O. G., & O'Connor, B. B. (2005). *Children's sleep: An interplay between culture and biology, pediatrics, 115*(1), 204–216.

Jennings, K. D. (1975). People versus object orientation, social behavior, and intellectual abilities in preschool children. *Developmental Psychology, 11,* 511–519.

Jensen-Campbell, L. A., Graziano, W. G., & Hair, E. C. (1996). Personality and relationships as moderators of interpersonal conflict in adolescence. *Merrill-Palmer Quarterly, 42,* 148–164.

Jessor, R., Colby, A., & Shweder, R. A. (Eds.). (1996). Ethnography and human development: Context and meaning in social inquiry. Chicago: University of Chicago Press.

Jessor, R., & Jessor, S. L. (1977). *Problem behavior and psychosocial development.* New York: Academic Press.

Johansson, G. (1973). Visual perception of biological motion and a model for its analysis. *Perception and Psychophysics, 14,* 201–211.

Johns, M., Schmader, T., & Martens, A. (2005). Knowing is half the battle: Teaching stereotype threat as a means of improving women's math performance. *Psychological Science, 16*(5), 175–179.

Johnson, M. H. (2001). Functional brain development during infancy. In G. Bremner & A. Fogel (Eds.), *Blackwell handbook of infant development*. Malden, MA: Blackwell Publishers.

Johnson, M. H. (2002). Imaging techniques and their application in developmental psychology [Special issue]. *Developmental Science, 5*(3).

Johnson, M. H., & de Haan, M. (2001). Developing cortical specialisation for visual-cognitive function: The case of face recognition. In J. L. McClelland & R. S. Siegler (Eds.), *Mechanisms of cognitive development: Behavioural and neural perspectives*. Mahwah, NJ: Erlbaum.

Johnson, M. K., Beebe, T., Mortimer, J. T., & Snyder, M. (1998). Volunteerism in adolescence: A process perspective. *Journal of Research on Adolescence, 8*, 309–332.

Johnson, M. H., Dziurawiec, S., Ellis, H., & Morton, J. (1991). Newborns' preferential tracking of facelike stimuli and its subsequent decline. *Cognition, 40*, 119.

Johnson, S. P. (1997). Young infants' perception of object unity: Implications for development of attentional and cognitive skills. *Current Directions in Psychological Science, 6*, 5–11.

Johnson, S. P., & Aslin, R. N. (1995). Perception of object unity in 2-month-old infants. *Developmental Psychology, 31*, 739–745.

Johnston, L. D., O'Malley, P. M., Bachman, J. G., & Schulenberg, J. E. (2005). Monitoring the future national survey results on drug use, 1975–2004. Volume I: *Secondary school students* (NIH Publication No. 05-5727). Bethesda, MD: National Institute on Drug Abuse, 680 pp.

Jones, D. C. (1985). Persuasive appeals and responses to appeals among friends and acquaintances. *Child Development, 56*, 757–763.

Jones, C., & Adamson, L. B. (1987). Language use in mother–child and mother-child-sibling interactions. *Child Development, 58*, 356–366.

Jones, K., Evans, C., Byrd, R., & Campbell, K. (2000). Gender equity training and teacher behavior. *Journal of Instructional Psychology, 27*, 173–177.

Jones, K. L., Smith, D. W., Ulleland, C. N., & Streissguth, A. P. (1973). Pattern of malformation in offspring of chronic alcoholic mothers. *Lancet, 1*, 1267–1271.

Jones, M. C. (1965). Psychological correlates of somatic development. *Child Development, 36*, 899–911.

Jones, M. G., Howe, A., & Rua, M. J. (2000). Gender differences in students' experiences, interests, and attitudes toward science and scientists. *Science Education, 84*, 180–192.

Jones, S., & Myhill, D. (2004). "Troublesome Boys" and "Compliant Girls": Gender identity and perceptions of achievement and underachievement. *British Journal of Sociology of Education, 25*, 547–561.

Jones, E. F., & Thomson, N. R. (2001). Action perception and outcome valence: Effects on children's inferences of intentionality and moral and liking judgments. *Journal of Genetic Psychology, 162*, 154–166.

Joos, S. K., Pollitt, E., Mueller, W. H., & Albright, D. L. (1983). The Bacon Chow study: Maternal nutritional supplementation and infant behavioral development. *Child Development, 54*, 669–676.

Jordan, H. E., & Kindred, J. E. (1948). *Textbook of embryology* (5th ed.). New York: Apple-Century-Crofts.

Jordan, A. B., Schmitt, K. L., & Woodard, E. H. (2001). Developmental implications of commercial broadcasters' educational offerings. *Journal of Applied Developmental Psychology, 22*, 87–101.

Joseph, J. (2000). Not in their genes: A critical view of the genetics of attention-deficit hyperactivity disorder. *Developmental Review, 20*, 539–567.

Journal of Clinical Psychiatry. (2002). *Journal of Clinical Psychiatry, 63* (Suppl. 12), 505.

Joussemet, M., Koestner, R., Lekes, N., & Landry, R. (2005). A longitudinal study of the relationship of maternal autonomy support to children's adjustment and achievement in school. *Journal of Personality, 73*, 1215–1235.

Jung, W.S., & Stinnett, T.A. (2005). Comparing judgements of social, behavioral, and school adjustment functioning for Korean, Korean-American, and Caucasian-American children. *School Psychology International, 26*, 317–329.

Jungmeen, K., & Cicchetti, D. (2004). A longitudinal study of child maltreatment, mother-child relationship quality and maladjustment: The role of self-esteem and social competence. *Journal of Abnormal Child Psychology, 32*, 341–354.

Jusczyk, P. W. (1997). *The discovery of spoken language*. Cambridge, MA: MIT Press.

Jusczyk, P. W., Pisoni, D. B., & Mullennix, J. (1992). Some consequences of stimulus variability on speech processing by 2-month-old infants. *Cognition, 43*, 253–291.

Juvonen, J., & Graham, S. (2001). Preface. In J. Juvonen & S. Graham (Eds.), *Peer harassment in school: The plight of the vulnerable and victimized*. New York: Guilford.

Kaback, M. (2000). Population-based genetic screening for reproductive counseling: The Tays-Sachs disease model. *European Journal of Pediatrics, 159* (Suppl. 3), S 192–195.

Kagan, J. (1991). The theoretical utility of constructs for self. *Developmental Review, 11*, 244–250.

Kagan, J. (1994). *Galen's prophecy*. New York: Basic Books.

Kagan, J., & Snidman, N. (1991). Temperamental factors in human development. *American Psychologist, 46*, 856–862.

Kail, R., & Bisanz, J. (1992). The information-processing perspective on cognitive development in childhood and adolescence. In R. J. Sternberg & C. A. Berg (Eds.), *Intellectual development*. New York: Cambridge University Press.

Kail, R. V. (1991). Developmental change in speed of processing during childhood and adolescence. *Psychological Bulletin, 109*, 490–501.

Kail, R. V., & Miller, C. A. (2006). Developmental change in processing speed: Domain specificity and stability during childhood and adolescence. *Journal of Cognition and Development. 7*, 119–137.

Kail, R. V. (2000). Speed of information processing: Developmental changes and links to intelligence. *Journal of School Psychology, 38*, 51–61.

Kail, R., & Bisanz, J. (1992). The information-processing perspective on cognitive development in childhood and adolescence. In R. J. Sternberg & C. A. Berg (Eds.), *Intellectual development*. New York: Cambridge University Press.

Kaitz, M., Meirov, H., Landman, I., & Eidelman, A. I. (1993). Infant recognition by tactile cues. *Infant Behavior and Development, 16*, 333–341.

Kamii, C., & DeVries, R. (1993). *Physical knowledge in preschool education: Implications of Piaget's theory* (rev. ed.). New York: Teachers College Press.

Kamins, M. L., & Dweck, C. S. (1999). Person versus process praise and criticism: Implications for contingent self-worth and coping. *Developmental Psychology, 35*, 835–847.

Kamptner, L., Kraft, R. H., & Harper, L. V. (1984). Lateral specialization and social-verbal development in preschool children. *Brain and Cognition, 3*, 42–50.

Kaplan, A., Middleton, M., Urdan, T., & Midgley, C. (2002). Achievement goals and goal structures. In C. Midgley (Ed.)., *Goals, goal structures, and patterns of adaptive learning*. Hillsdale, NJ: Erlbaum.

Karabenick, S. A., & Noda, P. A. C. (2004). Professional development implications of teachers` beliefs and attitudes toward English language learners. *Bilingual Research Journal, 28*(1), 55–75.

Karmel, B. Z., & Maisel, E. B. (1975). A neuronal activity model for infant visual attention. In L. B. Cohen & P. Salapatek (Eds.), *Infant perception: From sensation to cognition*: Vol. 1. *Basic visual processes*. New York: Academic Press.

Karniol, R., & Miller, D. T. (1981). The development of self-control in children. In S. S. Brehm, S. M. Kassin, & F. X. Gibbons (Eds.), *Developmental social psychology: Theory and research*. New York: Oxford University Press.

Karp, H. (2002). *The happiest baby on the block : The new way to calm crying and help your baby sleep longer*. New York: Bantam.

Katz, P. A., & Ksansnak, K. R. (1994). Developmental aspects of gender role flexibility and traditionality in middle childhood and adolescence. *Developmental Psychology, 30*, 272–282.

Kaufman, A. S., & Kaufman, N. L. (1983). *Kaufman Assessment Battery for children*. Circle Pines, MN: American Guidance Service.

Kavsek, M. J. (2002). The perception of static subjective contours in infancy. *Child Development, 73*, 331–344.

Kawabata, H., Gyoba, J., Inoue, H., & Ohtsubo, H. (1999). Visual completion of partly occluded grating in infants under one month of age. *Vision Research, 39*, 3586–3591.

Kawasaki, C., Nugent, J. K., Miyashita, H., Miyahara, H., & Brazelton, T. B. (1994). The cultural organization of infants' sleep. *Children's Environments, 11*, 135–141.

Kay, D. A., & Anglin, J. M. (1982). Overextension and underextension in the child's expressive and receptive speech. *Journal of Child Language, 9*, 83–98.

Kaye, K. (1982). *The mental and social life of babies*. Chicago: University of Chicago Press.

Kazal, L. A. (2002). Prevention of iron deficiency in infants and toddlers. *American Family Physician, 66*(7), 1217–1227.

Kazdin, A. E. (2002). Psychosocial treatments for conduct disorder in children and adolescents. In P. E. Nathan & J. M. Gorman (Eds.), *A guide to treatments that work* (2nd ed.). London: Oxford University Press.

Keating, D. P. (1988). Byrnes' reformulation of Piaget's formal operations: Is what's left what's right? *Developmental Review, 8*, 376–384.

Kee, D. W., & Guttentag, R. (1994). Resource requirements of knowledge access and recall benefits of associative strategies. *Journal of Experimental Child Psychology, 57*, 211–223.

Keefe, M. R. (1987). Comparison of neonatal nighttime sleepwake patterns in nursery versus rooming-in environments. *Nursing Research, 36*, 140–144.

Keefe, K., & Berndt, T. J. (1996). Relations of friendship quality to self-esteem in early adolescence. *Journal of Early Adolescence, 16*, 110–129.

Keenan, T. (2000). Mind, memory, and metacognition: The role of memory span in children's developing understanding of the mind. In J. W. Astington (Ed.), *Minds in the making: Essays in honor of David R. Olson*. Malden, MA: Blackwell Publishers.

Keenan, K., & Shaw, D. (1997). Developmental and social influences on young girls' early problem behavior. *Psychological Bulletin, 121*, 95–113.

Keil, F. C. (1998). Cognitive science and the origins of thought and knowledge. In W. Damon (Series Ed.) & R. M. Lerner (Vol. Ed.), *Handbook of child psychology*: Vol. 1. *Theoretical models of human development* (5th ed.). New York: Wiley.

Keller, H. & Scholmerich, A. (1987). Infant vocalizations and parental reactions during the first four months of life. *Developmental Psychology, 23*, 62–67.

Keller, H., Völker, S., & Yovsi, R. D. (2005). Conceptions of parenting in different cultural communities. The case of West African Nso and Northern German women. *Social Development, 14*(1), 158–180.

Keller, H., Yovsi, R., Borke, J., Kartner, J., Jensen, H., & Papaligoura, Z. (2004). Developmental consequences of early parenting experiences: Self-recognition and self-regulation in three cultural communities. *Child Development, 75*, 1745–1760.

Kellman, P. J. (1996). The origins of object perception. In R. Gelman & T. Au (Eds.), *Perceptual and cognitive development*. San Diego, CA: Academic Press.

Kellman, P. J., & Banks, M. (1998). Infant visual perception. In W. Damon (Series Ed.) & D. Kuhn & R. S. Siegler (Vol. Eds.), *Handbook of child psychology*: Vol. 2. *Cognition, perception, and language* (5th ed.). New York: Wiley.

Kelly, S.A., Brownell, C., & Campbell, S. B. (2000). Mastery motivation and self-evaluative affect in toddlers: Longitudinal relations with maternal behavior. *Child Development, 71*, 1061–1071.

Kelso, W. M., Nicholls, M. E. R., Warne, G. L., & Zacharin, M. (2000). Cerebral lateralization and cognitive functioning in patients with congenital adrenal hyperplasia. *Neuropsychology, 14*, 370–378.

Kenrick, D. T., & Trost, M. R. (1993). The evolutionary perspective. In A. E. Beall & R. J. Sternberg (Eds.), *The psychology of gender*. New York: Guilford.

Kerns, K. A. (1994). A longitudinal examination of links between mother-child attachment and children's friendships in early childhood. *Journal of Social and Personal Relationships, 11*, 379–381.

Kerns, K. A. (1996). Individual differences in friendship quality: Links to child-mother attachment. In W. M. Bukowski, A. F. Newcomb, & W. W. Hartup (Eds.), *The company they keep: Friendship in childhood and adolescence*. New York: Cambridge University Press.

Kerns, K. A., Contreras, J. M., & Neal-Barnett, A. M. (Eds.). (2000). *Family and peers: Linking two social worlds*. Westport, CT: Praeger.

Kerns, K. A., Klepac, L., & Cole, A. (1996). Peer relationships and preadolescents' perceptions of security in the child-mother relationship. *Developmental Psychology, 32*, 457–466.

Kerpelman, J. L., Shoffner, M. F., & Ross-Griffin, S. (2002). African American mothers' and daughters' beliefs about possible selves and their strategies for reaching the adolescents' future academic and career goals. *Journal of Youth and Adolescence, 31*, 289–302.

Kessen, W. (1979). The American child and other cultural inventions. *American Psychologist, 34*, 815–820.

Kessler, C., & Quinn, M.E. (1987). Language minority children's linguisitc and cognitive creativity. *Journal of Multilingual & Multicultural Development, 8*, 173–186.

Khaleque, A., & Rohner, R. P. (2002). Perceived parental acceptance-rejection and psychological adjustment: A meta-analysis of cross cultural and intracultural studies. *Journal of Marriage and the Family, 64*, 54–64.

Khoury, M. J.; McCabe, L. L., & McCabe, E. R. B. (2003). Population screening in the age of genomic medicine. *New England Journal of Medicine, 348*(1), 50–59.

Kim, H., & Chung, R. H. (2003). Reltionship of recalled parenting style to self-perception in Korean American college students. *Journal of Genetic Psychology, 164*, 481–492.

Kim, M., McGregor, K. K., & Thompson, C. K. (2000). Early lexical development in English- and Korean-speaking children: Language-general and language specific patterns. *Journal of Child Language, 27*, 225–254.

Kimm, S. Y., & Obarzanek, E. (2002) Childhood obesity: a new pandemic of the new millennium *Pediatrics, 110*, 1003–1007.

Kindlon, D., & Thompson, M. (1999). *Raising cain: Protecting the emotional life of boys*. New York: Ballantine.

King, P. E., & Furrow, J. L. (2004). Religion as a resource for positive youth development: Religion, social capital, and moral outcomes. *Developmental Psychology, 40*, 703–713.

Kinnear, A. (1995). Introduction of microcomputers: A case study of patterns of use and children's perceptions. *Journal of Educational Computing Research, 13*, 27–40.

Kisilevsky, B. S., & Muir, D. W. (1984). Neonatal habituation and dishabituation to tactile stimulation during sleep. *Developmental Psychology, 20*, 367–373.

Kivett, V. R. (1985). Grandfathers and grandchildren: Patterns of association, helping, and psychological closeness. *Family Relations, 34*, 565–571.

Klahr, D., & MacWhinney, B. (1998). Information processing. In W. Damon (Series Ed.) & D. Kuhn & R. S. Siegler (Vol. Eds.), *Handbook of child psychology*: Vol. 2. *Cognition, perception, and language* (5th ed.). New York: Wiley.

Klahr, D., & Robinson, M. (1981). Formal assessment of problem solving and planning processes in preschool children. *Cognitive Psychology, 13*, 113–148.

Kleeman, W. J., Schlaud, M., Fieguth, A., Hiller, A. S., Rothamel, T., & Troger, H. D. (1999). Body and head position, covering of the head by bedding, and risk of sudden infant death syndrome (SIDS). *International Journal of Legal Medicine, 112*, 22–26.

Klein, S.S. (Ed.) (1985). *Handbook for achieving sex equity through education*. Baltimore, MD: Johns Hopkins University Press.

Kleinfeld, J. S. (1996). The surprising ease of changing the belief that the schools shortchange girls. In R. J. Simon (Ed.), *From data to public policy: Affirmative action, sexual harassment, domestic violence and social welfare*. Lanham, MD: University Press of America.

Klimes-Dougan, B., & Kistner, J. (1990). Physically abused pre-schoolers' responses to peers' distress. *Developmental Psychology, 26*, 599–602.

Klinnert, M. D., Campos, J. J., Sorce, J. F., Emde, R. N., & Svejda, M. (1983). Emotions as behavior

regulators: Social referencing in infancy. In R. Plutchik & H. Kellerman (Eds.), *Emotions in early development*: Vol. 2. *The emotions*. New York: Academic Press.

Klinnert, M. D., Sorce, J. F., Emde, R. N., Stenberg, C., & Gaensbaurer, T. (1984). Continuities and change in early emotional life: Maternal perceptions of surprise, fear, and anger. In R. N. Emde & R. J. Harmon (Eds.), *Continuities and discontinuities in development*. New York: Plenum.

Knops, N. B. B., Kommer, C. A., Sneeuw, Brand, R., Hille E. T. M., Ouden, A. L.,Wit, J.-M., & S. Pauline Verloove-Vanhorick. (2005). Catch-up growth up to ten years of age in children born very preterm or with very low birth weight. *BMC Pediatrics, 5*, 26–35.

Kochanska, G. (1993). Toward a synthesis of parental socialization and child temperament in early development of conscience. *Child Development, 64*, 325–347.

Kochanska, G. (1995). Children's temperament, mothers' discipline, and security of attachment: Multiple pathways to emerging internalization. *Child Development, 66*, 597–615.

Kochanska, G. (1997). Multiple pathways to conscience for children with different temperaments: From toddlerhood to age 5. *Developmental Psychology, 33*, 228–240.

Kochanska, G. (2002). Committed compliance, moral self, and internalization: A mediational model. *Developmental Psychology, 38*, 339–351.

Kochanska, G. (2004). Conscience in childhood: Past, present, and future. *Merrill-Palmer Quarterly*.

Kochanska, G., & Aksan, N. (1995). Mother-child mutually positive affect, the quality of child compliance to requests and prohibitions, and maternal control as correlates of early internalization. *Child Development, 66*, 236–254.

Kochanska, G., & Aksan, N. (2004). Conscience in childhood: Past, present, and future. Invited article for the 50th anniversary issue of *Merrill Palmer Quarterly, 50*, 299–310.

Kochanska, G., Aksan, N., & Knaack, A. (2004). Maternal parenting and children's conscience: Early security as a moderator. *Child Development, 75*, 1229–1242.

Kochanska, G., Coy, K. C., & Murray, K. T. (2001). The development of self-regulation in the first four years of life. *Child Development, 72*, 1091–1111.

Kochanska, G., Forman, D. R., Aksan, N., & Dunbar, S. B. (2005). Pathways to conscience: Early mother-child mutually responsive orientation and children's moral emotion, conduct, and cognition. *Journal of Child Psychology and Psychiatry, 46*, 19–34.

Kochanska, G., Friesenborg, A.E., Lange, L.A., & Martel, M.M. (2004). Parents' personality and infants' temperament as contributors to their emerging relationship. *Journal of Personality & Social Psychology, 86*, 744–759.

Kochanska, G., Gross, J. N., Li, M-H., & Nichols, K. E. (2002). Guilt in young children: Development, determinants, and relations with a broader system of standards. *Child Development, 73*, 461–482.

Kochanska, G., Murray, K., Jacques, T. Y., Koenig, A. L., & Vandergeest, K.A. (1996). Inhibitory control in young children and its role in emerging internalization. *Child Development, 67*, 490–507.

Kochanska, G., & Thompson, R. A. (1997). The emergence and development of conscience in toddlerhood and early childhood. In J. E. Grusec & L. Kuczynski (Eds.), *Handbook of parenting and the transmission of values*. New York: Wiley.

Kochlar, C.A., & West, L.L. (1996). *Handbook for successful inclusion.* Gaithersburg, MD: Aspen Publishers.

Kodish, E. (2005). *Ethics and research with children: A case-based approach.* New York: Oxford University Press.

Koenigsknecht, R. A., & Friedman, P. (1976). Syntax development in boys and girls. *Child Development, 47,* 1109–1115.

Kohlberg, L. (1966). A cognitive-developmental analysis of children's sex role concepts and attitudes. In E. E. Maccoby (Ed.), *The development of sex differences.* Stanford, CA: Stanford University Press.

Kohlberg, L. (1969). Stage and sequence: The cognitive-developmental approach to socialization. In D. A. Goslin (Ed.), *Handbook of socialization theory and research.* Chicago: Rand McNally.

Kohlberg, L. (1971). From is to ought: How to commit the naturalistic fallacy and get away with it in the study of moral development. In T. Mischel (Ed.), *Cognitive development and epistemology* (pp. 151–236). New York: Academic.

Kohlberg, L. (1987). The development of moral judgment and moral action. In L. Kohlberg (Ed.), *Child psychology and childhood education: A cognitive-developmental view.* New York: Longman.

Kohlberg, L. (1981). *Essays on moral development:* Vol. 1. *The philosophy of moral development.* New York: Harper & Row.

Kohlberg, L. (1984). *The psychology of moral development: The nature and validity of moral stages.* San Francisco: Harper & Row.

Kohlberg, L., & Candee, D. (1984). The relationship of moral judgment to moral action. In W. M. Kurtines & J. L. Gewirtz (Eds.), *Morality, moral behavior, and moral development.* New York: Wiley.

Kohlberg, L., & Kramer, R. (1969). Continuities and discontinuities in childhood and adult moral development. *Human Development, 12,* 93–120.

Kohlberg, L., Levine, C., & Hewer, A. (1983). *Moral stages: A current formulation and a response to critics.* Basel, Switzerland: Karger.

Kohlberg, L., & Ullian, D. Z. (1974). Stages in the development of psychosexual concepts and attitudes. In R. C. Friedman, R. M. Richart, & L. VandeWiele (Eds.), *Sex differences in behavior.* New York: Wiley.

Kohlberg, L., Yaeger, J., & Hjertholm, E. (1968). Private speech: Four studies and a review of theories. *Child Development, 39,* 817–826.

Kohn, M.L. (1977). *Class and conformity: A study of values* (2nd ed). Chicago: University of Chicago.

Kolb, B. (1989). Brain development, plasticity, and behavior. *American Psychologist, 44,* 1203–1212.

Kolb, B. (1995). *Brain plasticity and behavior.* Mahwah, NJ: Erlbaum.

Kolb B., Wishaw, I. Q. (2003). *Fundamentals of human neuropsychology* (5th ed.). New York: Freeman.

Konner, M. J. (1976). Maternal care, infant behavior and development among the Kung. In R. B. Lee & I. DeVore (Eds.), *Kalahari hunter-gatherers.* Cambridge, MA: Harvard University Press.

Korner, A. F., & Thoman, E. (1970). Visual alertness in neonates as evoked by maternal care. *Journal of Experimental Child Psychology, 10,* 67–78.

Kosslyn, S. M., Pascual-Leone, A., Felician, O., Camposano, S., Keenan, J. P., Thompson, W. L., Ganis, G., Sukel, K. E., & Alpert, N. M. (1999). The role of area 17 in visual imagery: convergent evidence from PET and rTMS. *Science, 284,* 167–170.

Kostelny, K., & Garbarino, J. (1994). Coping with the consequences of living in danger: The case of Palestinian children and youth. *International Journal of Behavioral Development, 17,* 595–611.

Kotchick, B. A.; Dorsey, S., & Heller, L. (2005). Predictors of parenting among African American single mothers: Personal and contextual factors. *Journal of Marriage and Family, 67*(2), 448–460.

Kotulak, R. (1996). *Inside the brain. Revolutionary discoveries of how the mind works.* Kansas City: Andrews and MacMeel, Universal Press Syndicate Company.

Kowal, A., & Kramer, L. (1997). Children's understanding of parental differential treatment. *Child Development, 68,* 113–126.

Kowal, A., Kramer, L., Krull, J. L., & Crick, N. R. (2002). Children's perceptions of the fairness of parental preferential treatment and their socioemotional well-being. *Journal of Family Psychology, 16,* 297–306.

Kozlowski, L. T. & Cutting, J. E. (1977). Recognizing the gender of walkers from dynamic point-light displays. *Perception and Psychophysics, 21,* 575–580.

Kozlowski, L. T., & Cutting, J. E. (1978). Recognizing the gender of walkers from point-lights mounted on ankles: Some second thoughts. *Perception & Psychophysics, 23*(5), 459.

Kozulin, A. (1990). *Vygotsky's psychology.* Cambridge, MA: Harvard University Press.

Kraft, R. H. (1984). Lateral specialization and verbal/spatial ability in preschool children: Age, sex and familial handedness differences. *Neuropsychologia, 22,* 319–335.

Krashen, S. D. (1999). Bilingual education: Arguments for and (bogus) arguments against. In J.E. Alatis (Ed.), *Proceedings of Georgetown University Roundtable of Languages and Linguistics.* Washington, D.C.: Georgetown University Press. Retrieved October 11, 2005, from http://ourworld.compuserve.com/homepages/jwcrawford/Krashen3.htm

Krebs, D. (1987). The challenge of altruism in biology and psychology. In C. Crawford, M. Smith, & D. Krebs (Eds.), *Sociobiology and psychology: Ideas, issues, and applications.* Hillsdale, NJ: Erlbaum.

Krebs, D. L., & Van Hesteren, F. (1994). The development of altruism: Toward an integrative model. *Developmental Review, 14,* 103–158.

Kreitler, S., & Kreitler, H. (1989). Horizontal decalage: A problem and its solution. *Cognitive Development, 4,* 89–119.

Kreutzer, M. A., Leonard, C., & Flavell, J. H. (1975). An interview study of children's knowledge about memory. *Monographs of the Society for Research in Child Development, 40* (1, Serial No. 159).

Krevans, J., & Gibbs, J. C. (1996). Parents' use of inductive discipline: Relations to children's empathy and prosocial behavior. *Child Development, 67,* 3263–3277.

Kroger, J. (1996). *Identity in adolescence: The balance between self and other.* London: Routledge.

Kroger, J. (2002). Identity processes and contents through the years of late adulthood. *Identity, 2,* 81–99.

Kroger, J. (2003). What transits in an identity status transition? *Identity: An international Journal of Theory & Research, 3,* 197–220.

Kropp, J. P., & Haynes, O. M. (1987). Abusive and nonabusive mothers' ability to identify general and specific emotion signals of infants. *Child Development, 58,* 187–190.

Kruger, A. C. (1992). The effect of peer and adult-child transactive discussions on moral reasoning. *Merrill-Palmer Quarterly, 38,* 191–211.

Kruger, A. C., & Tomasello, M. (1986). Transactive discussions with peers and adults. *Developmental Psychology, 22,* 681–685.

Kuchuk, A., Vibbert, M., & Bornstein, M. H. (1986). The perception of smiling and its experiential correlates in three-month-old infants. *Child Development, 57,* 1054–1061.

Kuczaj, S. A. (1982). Language play and language acquisition. In H. W. Reese (Ed.), *Advances in child development and behavior* (Vol. 17). New York: Academic Press.

Kuczynski, L., & Kochanska, G. (1990). Development of children's noncompliance strategies from toddlerhood to age 5. *Developmental Psychology, 26,* 398–408.

Kuczynski, L., & Kochanska, G. (1995). Function and content of maternal demands: Developmental significance of early demands for competent action. *Child Development, 66,* 616–628.

Kuebli, J., & Fivush, R. (1992). Gender differences in parent-child conversations about past emotions. *Sex Roles, 27,* 683–698.

Kuhl, P. K. (2001). Speech, language, and developmental change. In F. Lacerda, C. von Hofsten, & M. Heimann (Eds.), *Emerging cognitive abilities in early infancy.* Mahwah, NJ: Erlbaum.

Kuhl, P. K., & Meltzoff, A. N. (1982). The bimodal perception of speech in infancy. *Science, 218,* 1138–1141.

Kuhl, P. K., & Meltzoff, A. N. (1988). Speech as an intermodal object of perception. In A. Yonas (Ed.), *Minnesota symposia on child psychology:* Vol. 20. *Perceptual development in infancy.* Hillsdale, NJ: Erlbaum.

Kuhn, D. (1995). Microgenetic study of change: What has it told us? *Psychological Science, 6,* 133–139.

Kuhn, D., Ho, V., & Adams, C. (1979). Formal reasoning among pre- and late-adolescents. *Child Development, 50,* 1128–1135.

Kuklinski, M. R., & Weinstein, R. S. (2001). Classroom and developmental differences in a path model of teacher expectancy effects. *Child Development, 72,* 1554–1578.

Kulin, H. E. (1991). Puberty, hypothalamic-pituitary changes of. In R. M. Lerner, A. C. Peterson, & J. Brooks-Gunn (Eds.), *Encyclopedia of adolescence* (Vol. 2). New York: Garland.

Kuller, J. A. (1996). Chorionic villus sampling. In J. A. Kuller, N. C. Cheschier, & R. C. Cefalo (Eds.), *Prenatal diagnosis and reproductive genetics.* St. Louis, MO: Mosby.

Kupersmidt, J. B., DeRosier, M. E., & Patterson, C. P. (1995). Similarity as the basis for children's friendships: The roles of sociometric status, aggressive and withdrawn behavior, academic achievement, and demographic characteristics. *Journal of Social and Personal Relationships, 12,* 439–452.

Kupersmidt, J. B., & Trejos, S. L. (1987, April). *Behavioral correlates of sociometric status among Costa Rican children.* Paper presented at the meeting of the Society for Research in Child Development, Baltimore.

Kurdek, L. A. (1980). Developmental relations among children's perspective taking, moral judgment, and parent-rated behaviors. *Merrill-Palmer Quarterly, 26,* 103–121.

Kurtz, B. E., & Borkowski, J. G. (1987). Development of strategic skills in impulsive and reflective children: A longitudinal study of metacognition.

Journal of Experimental Child Psychology, 43, 129–148.

Kwong, T. E., Varnhagen, C. K. (2005). Strategy development and learning to spell new words: Generalization of a process. *Developmental Psychology, 41*(1), 148–159.

Laboratory of Comparative Human Cognition. (1983). Culture and cognitive development. In P. H. Mussen (Series Ed.) & W. Kessen (Vol. Ed.), *Handbook of child psychology*: Vol. 1. *History, theory, and methods* (4th ed.). New York: Wiley.

Lacourse, E., Cote, S., Nagin, D. S., Vitaro, F., Brendgen, M., & Tremblay, R. E. (2002). A longitudinal-experimental approach to testing theories of antisocial behavior development. *Development and Psychopathology, 14,* 909–924.

Ladd, B. K., & Ladd, G. W. (2001). Variations in peer victimization: Relations to children's maladjustment. In J. Juvonen & S. Graham (Eds.), *Peer harassment in school: The plight of the vulnerable and victimized.* New York: Guilford.

Ladd, G. W. (1992). Themes and theories: Perspectives on processes in family-peer relationships. In R. D. Parke & G. W. Ladd (Eds.), *Family-peer relationships: Modes of linkage.* Hillsdale, NJ: Erlbaum.

Ladd, G. W., Buhs, E. S., & Troop, W. (2002). Children's interpersonal skills and relationships in school settings: Adaptive significance and implications for school-based prevention and intervention programs. In P. K. Smith & C. H. Hart (Eds.), *Blackwell handbook of childhood social development.* Malden, MA: Blackwell Publishers.

Ladd, G. W., & Hart, C. H. (1992). Creating informal play opportunities: Are parents' and preschoolers' initiations related to children's competence with peers? *Developmental Psychology, 28,* 1179–1187.

Ladd, G. W., & Pettit, G. (2002). Parents' and children's peer relationships. In M. H. Bornstein (Ed.), *Handbook of parenting* (2nd ed., Vol. 5). Mahwah, NJ: Erlbaum.

LaFrance, M., Hecht, M. A., & Paluck, E. L. (2003). The contingent smile: A meta-analysis of sex differences in smiling. *Psychological Bulletin, 129,* 305–334.

LaFreniere, P., Masataka, N., Butovskaya, M., Chen, Q., Dessen, M. A., Atwanger, K., et al. (2002). Cross-cultural analysis of social competence and behavior problems in preschoolers. *Early Education and Development, 13,* 201–219.

Lagattuta, K. H. (2005). When you shouldn't do what you want to do: Young children's understanding of desires, rules, and emotions. *Child Development, 76,* 713–733.

Lahey, B. B., Gordon, R. A., Loeber, R., Stouthamer-Loeber, M., & Farrington, D. P. (1999). *Journal of Abnormal Child Psychology, 27,* 247–260.

Laible, D. J., & Thompson, R. A. (1998). Attachment and emotional understanding in preschool children. *Developmental Psychology, 34,* 1038–1045.

Laing, G. J., & Logan, S. (1999). Patterns of unintentional injury in childhood and their relation to socio-economic factors. *Public Health, 113,* 291–294.

Laird, R. D., Jordan, K. Y., Dodge, K. A., Pettit, G. S., & Bates, J. E. (2001). Peer rejection in childhood, involvement with antisocial peers in early adolescence, and the development of externalizing behavior problems. *Development and Psychopathology, 13,* 337–354.

Lamaze, F. (1970). *Painless childbirth: Psychoprophylactic method.* Chicago: Henry Regnery.

Lamb, M. E. (1987). *The father's role: Cross-cultural perspectives.* Hillsdale, NJ: Erlbaum.

Lamb, M. E. (Ed.). (1997). *The role of the father in child development* (3rd ed.). New York: Wiley.

Lamb, M. E. (1998). Nonparental child care: Context, quality, correlates, and consequences. In W. Damon (Series Ed.) & I. E. Sigel & K. A. Renninger (Vol. Eds.), *Handbook of child psychology*: Vol. 4. *Child psychology in practice* (5th ed.). New York: Wiley.

Lamb, M. E., Morrison, D. C., & Malkin, C. M. (1987). The development of infant social expectations in face-to-face interaction: A longitudinal study. *Merrill-Palmer Quarterly, 33,* 241–254.

Lamb, M. E., & Roopnarine, J. L. (1979). Peer influences on sex-role development in preschoolers. *Child Development, 50,* 1219–1222.

Lamb, M. E., & Poole, D. A. (1998). *Investigative interviews of children: A guide for helping professionals.* Washington, DC: American Psychological Association.

Lamb, M. E., Sternberg, K., & Prodromidis, M. (1992). Nonmaternal care and the security of infant-mother attachment: A reanalysis of the data. *Infant Behavior and Development, 15,* 71–83.

Lamb, M. E., Thompson, R. A., & Frodi, A. M. (1982). Early social development. In R. Vasta (Ed.), *Strategies and techniques of child study.* New York: Academic Press.

Lamborn, S. D., Dornbusch, S. M., & Steinberg, L. (1996). Ethnicity and community context as moderators of the relation between family decision making and adolescent adjustment. *Child Development, 67,* 283–301.

Lancy, D. F. (1996). *Playing on the mother ground: Cultural routines for children's development.* New York: Guilford.

Langer, O. (1990). Critical issues in diabetes and pregnancy. In I. R. Merkatz & J. E. Thompson (Eds.), *New perspectives on prenatal care.* New York: Elsevier.

Langlois, J. H., Roggman, L. A., Casey, R. J., Ritter, J. M., Reiser-Danner, L. A., & Jenkins, V. Y. (1987). Infant preference for attractive faces: Rudiments of a stereotype? *Developmental Psychology, 23,* 363–369.

Lansford, J. E., & Parker, J. G. (1999). Children's interactions in triads: Behavioral profiles and effects of gender and patterns of friendships among members. *Developmental Psychology, 35,* 80–93.

Lanza, E. (1997). *Language mixing in infant bilingualism: A sociolinguistic perspective.* Oxford: Oxford University Press.

Larsen, L. J. (2004). The foreign-born population in the United States: 2003. *Current Population Reports,* P20551, U.S. Census Bureau, Washington, DC.

Larsson, G., Bohlin, A. B., & Tunell, R. (1985). Prospective study of children exposed to variable amounts of alcohol in utero. *Archives of Disease in Childhood, 60,* 316–321.

Laupta, M., & Turiel, E. (1993). Children's concepts of authority and social contexts. *Journal of Educational Psychology, 85,* 191–197.

Laursen, B., & Collins, W. A. (1994). Interpersonal conflict during adolescence. *Psychological Bulletin, 115,* 197–209.

Laursen, B., Finkelstein, B. D., & Betts, N. T. (2001). A developmental meta-analysis of peer conflict resolution. *Developmental Review, 21,* 423–449.

Lavelli, M., & Fogel, A. (2002). Developmental changes in mother-infant face-to-face communication: Birth to 3 months. *Developmental Psychology, 38,* 288–305.

Le, T. N., & Stockdale, G. D. (2005). Individualism, collectivism, and delinquency in Asian American adolescents. *Journal of Clinical Child & Adolescent Psychology, 34*(4), 681–691.

Leaper, C. (Ed.). (1994). New directions for child development: No. 65. *Childhood gender segregation: Causes and consequences.* San Francisco: Jossey-Bass.

Leaper, C. (2002). Parenting girls and boys. In M. H. Bornstein (Ed.), *Handbook of parenting* (2nd ed., Vol. 1). Mahwah, NJ: Erlbaum.

Leaper, C., Anderson, K. J., & Sanders, P. (1998). Moderators of gender effects on parents' talk to their children: A meta-analysis. *Developmental Psychology, 34,* 327.

Leaper, C., Breed, L., Hoffman, L., & Perlman, C. A. (2002). Variations in the gender-stereotyped content of children's television cartoons across genres. *Journal of Applied Social Psychology, 32,* 1653–1662.

Leaper, C., Leve, L., Strasser, T., & Schwartz, R. (1995). Mother-child communication sequences: Play activity, child gender, and marital status effects. *Merrill-Palmer Quarterly, 41,* 307–327.

Leaper, C., Tenenbaum, H. R., & Shaffer, T. G. (1999). Communication patterns of African American girls and boys from low-income, urban background. *Child Development, 70,* 1489–1503.

Leary, M. R., & Tangney, J. P. (2003). The self as an organizing construct in the behavioural and social sciences. In M.R. Leary and J.P. Tangney (Eds.), *Handbook of self and identity.* New York: Guilford Press.

Leavitt, L., & Fox, N. (Eds.). (1993). *Psychological effects of war and violence on children.* Hillsdale, NJ: Erlbaum.

Lebra, T. S. (1994). Mother and child in Japanese socialization: A Japan-U.S. comparison. In P. M. Greenfield & R. R. Cocking (Eds.), *Cross-cultural roots of minority child development.* Hillsdale, NJ: Erlbaum.

Lecanuet, J.-P. (1998). Fetal responses to auditory and speech stimuli. In A. Slater (Ed.), *Perceptual development: Visual, auditory, and speech perception in infancy.* Hove, UK: Psychology Press.

Lee, V.E., & Burkam, D. T. (2002). *Inequality at the starting gate: Social background differences in achievement as children begin school.* Washington, DC: Economic Policy Institute. (BBB25681).

Lee, V. E., & Burkam, D. T. (2003). Dropping out of high school: The role of school organization and structure. *American Educational Research Journal, 40*(2), 353–393.

Leger, D. W., Thompson, R. A., Merritt, J. A., & Benz, J. J. (1996). Adult perception of emotion intensity in human infant cries: Effects of infant age and cry acoustics. *Child Development, 67,* 3238–3249.

Legerstee, M. (1991). The role of person and object in eliciting early imitation. *Journal of Experimental Child Psychology, 51,* 423–433.

Legerstee, M., Anderson, D., & Schaffer, A. (1998). Five- and eight-month-old infants recognize their faces and voices as familiar and social stimuli. *Child Development, 69,* 37–50.

Legerstee, M., & Varghese, J. (2001). The role of maternal affect mirroring on social expectancies in three-month-old infants. *Child Development, 72,* 1301–1313.

Leiderman, P. H., & Seashore, M. J. (1975). Mother-infant separation: Some delayed consequences. In *Parent-infant interaction* (CIBA Foundation Symposium No. 33). New York: Elsevier.

Leinbach, M. D., & Fagot, B. I. (1993). Categorical habituation to male and female faces: Gender schematic processing in infancy. *Infant Behavior and Development, 16,* 317–332.

Leinbach, M. D., Hort, B. E., & Fagot, B. I. (1997). Bears are for boys: Metaphorical associations in young children's gender stereotypes. *Cognitive Development, 12,* 107–130.

Leman, P. J., Ahmed, S. & Ozarow, L. (2005). Gender, gender relations, and the social dynamics of children's conversations. *Developmental Psychology, 41*(1), 64–74.

Lempers, J. D., Flavell, E. R., & Flavell, J. H. (1977). The development in very young children of tacit knowledge concerning visual perception. *Genetic Psychology Monographs, 95,* 353.

Lenneberg, E. H. (1967). *Biological foundations of language.* New York: Wiley.

Lepper, M.R., Corpus, J.H., & Iyengar, S.S. (2005). Intrinsic and extrinsic motivational orientations in the classroom: Age differences and academic correlates. *Journal of Educational Psychology, 97,* 184–196.

Lesko, N. (Ed.). (2000). *Masculinities at school.* London: Sage.

Leslie, A. M., Friedman, O., & German, T. P. (2004). Core mechanisms in "theory of mind". *Trends in Cognitive Sciences, 8,* 529–533.

Leslie, A. M., & Keeble, S. (1987). Do six-month-olds perceive causality? *Cognition, 25,* 265–288.

Lester, B. M. (1984). A biosocial model of infant crying. In L. P. Lipsitt (Ed.), *Advances in infancy research* (Vol. 3). Norwood, NJ: Ablex.

Lester, B. M. (2000). Prenatal cocaine exposure and child outcome: A model for the study of the infant at risk. *Israel Journal of Psychiatry and Related Sciences, 37,* 223–235.

Lester, B. M., Boukydis, C. F. Z., & Twomey, J. E. (2000). Maternal substance abuse and child outcome. In C. H. Zeanah Jr. (Ed.), *Handbook of infant mental health* (2nd ed.). New York: Guilford.

Lester, B. M., Hoffman, J., & Brazelton, T. B. (1985). The rhythmic structure of mother-infant interaction in term and preterm infants. *Child Development, 56,* 15–27.

Lester, B. M., & Tronick, E. Z. (2001). Behavioral assessment scales: The NICU Network Neurobehavioral Scale, the Neonatal Behavioral Assessment Scale, and the Assessment of the Preterm Infant's Behavior. In L. T. Singer & P. S. Zeskind (Eds.), *Biobehavioral assessment of the infant.* New York: Guilford Press.

Leung, P.W., & Kwan, K.S. (1998). Parenting styles, motivational orientations, and self-perceived academic competence: A mediational model. *Merrill-Palmer Quarterly, 44,* 1–19.

Leveroni, C. L., & Berenbaum, S. A. (1998). Early androgen effects on interest in infants: Evidence from children with congenital adrenal hyperplasia. *Developmental Neuropsychology, 14,* 321–340.

Levin, I., & Druyan, S. (1993). When sociocognitive transaction among peers fails: The case of misconceptions in science. *Child Development, 63,* 1571–1591.

LeVine, R. A. (1984). Properties of culture: An ethnographic view. In R.A. Schweder & R.A. Levine (Eds.) *Culture theory: Essays on mind, self and emotion* (pp. 67–87). Cambridge: Cambridge University Press.

Levine, S. C., Huttenlocher, J., Taylor, A., & Langrock, A. (1999). Early sex differences in spatial skill. *Developmental Psychology, 35,* 940–949.

Levitt, M. J., Weber, R. A., Clark, M. C., & McDonnell, P. (1985). Reciprocity of exchange in toddler sharing behavior. *Developmental Psychology, 21,* 122–123.

Levy, G. (1999). Gender-typed and non-gender-typed category awareness in toddlers. *Sex Roles, 41,* 851–873.

Levy, G. D., & Carter, D. B. (1989). Gender schema, gender constancy, and gender-role knowledge: The roles of cognitive factors in preschoolers' gender-role stereotype attributions. *Developmental Psychology, 25,* 444–449.

Levy, G. D., & Fivush, R. (1993). Scripts and gender: A new approach for examining gender-role development. *Developmental Psychology, 13,* 126–146.

Levy, G. D., Taylor, M. G., & Gelman, S. A. (1995). Traditional and evaluative aspects of flexibility in gender roles, social conventions, moral rules, and physical laws. *Child Development, 66,* 515–531.

Lewis, M. (1995). Embarrassment: The emotion of self-exposure and evaluation. In J. Tangney & K. Fischer (Eds.), *Self-conscious emotions: The psychology of shame, guilt, embarrassment, and pride.* New York: Guilford.

Lewis, M. (2000). The emergence of human emotions. In M. Lewis & J. Haviland-Jones (Eds.), *Handbook of emotions* (2nd ed.). New York: Guilford.

Lewis, M., Alessandri, S. M., & Sullivan, M. W. (1990). Violation of expectancy, loss of control, and anger expression in young infants. *Developmental Psychology, 26,* 745–751.

Lewis, M., Feiring, C., McGuffog, C., & Jaskir, J. (1984). Predicting psychopathology in six-year-olds from early social relations. *Child Development, 55,* 123–136.

Lewis, M., & Michaelson, L. (1983). *Children's emotions and moods: Developmental theory and measurement.* New York: Plenum.

Lewis, M., & Michaelson, L. (1985). Faces as signs and symbols. In G. Zivin (Ed.), *Development of expressive behavior: Biological-environmental interaction.* New York: Academic Press.

Lewis, M., & Ramsey, D. S. (1997). Stress reactivity and self-recognition. *Child Development, 68,* 621–629.

Lewis, M., & Ramsey, D. (2004). Development of self-recognition, personal pronoun use, and pretend play during the 2nd year. *Child Development, 75,* 1821–1831.

Lewis, M., & Saarni, C. (1985). Culture and emotions. In M. Lewis & C. Saarni, *The socialization of emotions* (pp. 1–17). New York: Plenum.

Lewis, M., & Wolan Sullivan, M. (2005). The development of self-conscious emotions. In A.J. Elliot, & C.S. Dweck (Eds.)., *Handbook of competence and motivation.* New York: Guilford.

Lewkowicz, D. J. (2000). The development of temporal intersensory perception: An epigenetic systems/limitations view. *Psychological Bulletin, 126,* 281–308.

Lewkowicz, D. J., & Lickliter, R. (Eds.) (1994). *The development of intersensory perception: Comparative perspectives.* Hillsdale, NJ: Erlbaum.

Lewkowicz, D. J., & Turkewitz, G. (1981). Intersensory interaction in newborns: Modification of visual preferences following exposure to sound. *Child Development, 52,* 827–832.

Lewontin, R. (2000). *It ain't necessarily so: The dream of the human genome and other illusions.* New York: New York Review of Books.

Li, Q. (1999). Teachers' beliefs and gender differences in mathematics: A review. *Educational Research, 41,* 63–76.

Liben, L. S., & Bigler, R. (2002). The developmental course of gender differentiation: Conceptualizing, measuring, and evaluating constructs and pathways. *Monographs of the Society for Research in Child Development, 67*(2, Serial No. 269).

Liben, L. S., & Signorella, M. L. (Eds.). (1987). New directions for child development: No. 38. *Children's gender schemata.* San Francisco: Jossey-Bass.

Liben, L. S., & Signorella, M. L. (1993). Gender-schematic processing in children: The role of initial interpretations of stimuli. *Developmental Psychology, 29,* 141–149.

Lickliter, R., & Bahrick, L. E. (2000). The development of infant intersensory perception: Advantages of a comparative convergent-operations approach. *Psychological Bulletin, 126,* 260–280.

Lickona, T. (Ed.). (1976). *Moral development and behavior: Theory, research, and social issues.* New York: Holt, Rinehart and Winston.

Lieberman E, Ernst E. K., Rooks J. P., Stapleton S., & Flamm B. (2004). Results of the national study of vaginal birth after cesarean in birth centers. *Obstet. Gynecol., 104,* 93–342.

Liew, J., Eisenberg, N., & Reiser, M. (2004). Preschoolers' effortful control and negative emotionality, immediate reaction to disappointment, and quality of social functioning. *Journal of Experimental Child Psychology, 89,* 298–313.

Limber, S. P. (2004). Implementation of the Olweus Bullying Prevention Program: Lessons learned from the field. In D. Espelage & S. Swearer (Eds.), *Bullying in American schools: A social-ecological perspective on prevention and intervention* (pp. 351–363). Mahwah, NJ: Erlbaum.

Lin, X. (2001). Designing metacognitive activities. *Educational technology research and development, 49*(2), 23–40.

Lindberg, M. A. (1980). Is knowledge base development a necessary and sufficient condition for memory development? *Journal of Experimental Child Psychology, 30,* 401–410.

Lindsey, E. W., & Mize, J. (2001). Contextual differences in parent-child play: Implications for children's gender role development. *Sex Roles, 44,* 155–176.

Lindsey, E. W., Mize, J., & Pettit, G. S. (1997). Differential play patterns of mothers and fathers of sons and daughters: Implications for children's gender role development. *Sex Roles, 37,* 643–661.

Linn, M. C., & Petersen, A. C. (1986). A meta-analysis of gender differences in spatial ability: Implications for mathematics and science achievement. In J. S. Hyde & M. C. Linn (Eds.), *The psychology of gender: Advances through meta-analysis.* Baltimore: Johns Hopkins University Press.

Linnenbrink, E.A. (2005). The dilemma of performance-approach goals: The use of multiple goal contexts to promote students' motivation and learning. *Journal of Educational Psychology, 97,* 197–213.

Lipscomb, T. J., McAllister, H. A., & Bregman, N. J. (1985). A developmental inquiry into the effects of multiple models on children's generosity. *Merrill-Palmer Quarterly, 31,* 335–344.

Lipsitt, L. P., Engen, T., & Kaye, H. (1963). Developmental changes in the olfactory threshold of the neonate. *Child Development, 34,* 371–376.

Lizhu, Y., Jiangyang, W., Wen, L., Cuskelly, M., & Zhang, A. (2005). Strategies used by 3 to 5 years old children on a self-imposed delay of gratification task including a cross-cultural comparison between China and Austria. *Acta Psychologica Sinica, 37,* 224–232.

Lobel, M., Dunkel-Schetter, C., & Scrimshaw, S. C. M. (1992). Prenatal maternal stress and prematurity: A prospective study of socioeconomically disadvantaged women. *Health Psychology, 11*(1), 32–40.

Lobel, T. E., Gruber, R., Govrin, N., & Mashraki-Pedhatzur, S. (2001). Children's gender-related inferences and judgments: A cross-cultural study. *Developmental Psychology, 37*, 839–846.

Lochman, J. E., Burch, P. P., Curry, J. F., & Lampron, L. B. (1984). Treatment and generalization effects of cognitive-behavioral and goal-setting interventions with aggressive boys. *Journal of Consulting and Clinical Psychology, 52*, 915–916.

Lochman, J. E., & Wayland, K. (1994). Aggression, social acceptance and race as predictors of negative adolescent outcomes. *Journal of the American Academy of Child and Adolescent Psychiatry, 33*, 1026–1035.

Lockman, J. J. (1984). The development of detour ability during infancy. *Child Development, 55*, 482–491.

Lockman, J. J., & Adams, C. D. (2001). Going around transparent and grid-like barriers: Detour ability as a perception-action skill. *Developmental Science, 4*, 463–471.

Lockman, J. J., & McHale, J. P. (1989). Object manipulation in infancy: Developmental and contextual determinants. In J. J. Lockman & N. L. Hazen (Eds.), *Action in social context: Perspectives on early development.* New York: Plenum.

Locke, K. D. (2002). Are descriptions of the self more complex than descriptions of others? *Personality & Social Psychology Bulletin, 28*, 1094–1105.

Lockwood, P., Marshala, T. C., & Sadler, P. (2005). Promoting success or preventing failure: Cultural differences in motivation by positive and negative role models. *Personality & Social Psychology Bulletin, 31*, 379–392.

Loeber, R., & Hay, D. F. (1993). Developmental approaches to aggression and conduct problems. In M. Rutter & D. F. Hay (Eds.), *Development through life: A handbook for clinicians.* Oxford: Blackwell Publishers.

Loeber, R., & Hay, D. F. (1997). Key issues in the development of aggression and violence from childhood to early adulthood. *Annual Review of Psychology, 48*, 371–410.

Loeber, R., & Farrington, D. P. (Eds.). (1998). *Serious and violent juvenile offenders: Risk factors and successful interventions.* Thousand Oaks, CA: Sage.

Loeber, R., & Stouthamer-Loeber, M. (1998). Development of juvenile aggression and violence: Some common misconceptions and controversies. *American Psychologist, 53*, 242–259.

Loehlin, J. C. (1992). *Genes and environment in personality development.* Newbury Park, CA: Sage.

Loehlin, J. C. (2000). Group differences in intelligence. In R. J. Sternberg (Ed.), *Handbook of intelligence.* New York: Cambridge University Press.

Loehlin J. C., Horn J. M. & Willerman, L. (1997). *Heredity, environment, and IQ in the Texas Adoption Project.*

Loehlin, J. C., Neiderhiser, J. M., & Reiss, D. (2005). Genetic and environmental components of adolescent adjustment and parental behavior: A multivariate analysis. *Child Development, 76* (5), 1104–1115,

Lonigan, C. J., Bloomfield, B. G., Brenlee, G., & Anthony, J. T. (1999). Relations among emergent literacy skills, behavior problems, and social competence in preschool children from low- and middle-income backgrounds. *Topics in Early Childhood Special Education, 19*, 40–53.

Lorenz, K. Z. (1937). The companion in the bird's world. *Auk, 54*, 245–273.

Lorenz, K. (1957). Companionship in bird life. In C. Scholler (Ed.), *Instinctive behavior.* New York: International Universities Press.

Lorenz, K. Z. (1950). Innate behaviour patterns. *Symposia for the Study of Experimental Biology, 4*, 211–268.

Loudon, I. (1993). *Death in childbirth: An international study of maternal care and maternal mortality, 1800–1950.* New York: Oxford University Press.

Lourenco, O., & Machado, A. (1996). In defense of Piaget's theory: A reply to 10 common criticisms. *Psychological Review, 103*, 143–164.

Love, J. M., Constantine, J., Paulsell, D., Boller, K., Ross, C., Raikes, H., Brady-Smith, C., & Brooks-Gunn, J. (2004). The role of early head start programs in addressing the child care needs of low-income families and toddlers: Influences on child care use and quality. U.S. Department of Health and Human Services Head Start Bureau. Administration for children, youth, and families, Washington, D.C.

Lowrey, G. H. (1978). *Growth and development of children* (7th ed.). Chicago: Yearbook Medical Publishers.

Lozoff, B., Wolf, A. W., & Davis, N. S. (1984). Cosleeping in urban families with young children in the United States. *Pediatrics, 74*, 171–182.

Ludemann, P. M. (1991). Generalized discrimination of positive facial expressions by seven- and ten-month-old infants. *Child Development, 62*, 55–67.

Luecke-Aleksa, D., Anderson, D. R., Collins, P. A., & Schmitt, K. L. (1995). Gender constancy and television viewing. *Developmental Psychology, 31*, 773–780.

Lundqvist, C., & Sabel, K-G. (2000). Brief report: The Brazelton Neonatal Behavioral Assessment Scale detects differences among newborn infants of optimal health. *Journal of Pediatric Psychology, 25*, 577–582.

Luria, A. R. (1976). *Cognitive development: Its cultural and social foundations.* Cambridge, MA: Harvard University Press.

Luria, A. R. (1979). *The making of mind: A personal account of Soviet psychology.* Cambridge, MA: Harvard University Press.

Luster, T., Bates, L., Fitzgerald, H., Vandenbelt, M., & Key, J. P. (2000). Factors related to successful outcomes among preschool children born to low-income adolescent mothers. *Journal of Marriage & the Family, 62*, 133–146.

Luster, T., & Denbow, E. (1992). Home environment and maternal intelligence as predictors of verbal intelligence: A comparison of preschool and school-age children. *Merrill-Palmer Quarterly, 38*, 151–175.

Luthar, S. S., Cicchetti, D., & Becker, B. (2000). The construct of resilience: A critical evaluation and guidelines for future work. *Child Development, 71*, 543–562.

Lyon, D. W., Rainey , B. B., & Bullock, C. N. (2002). The effects of glasses on the self-concept of school-aged children. *Journal of Optometric Vision Development, 33*, 29–32.

Lyon, T. D., & Flavell, J. H. (1993). Young children's understanding of forgetting over time. *Child Development, 64*, 789–800.

Lyons-Ruth, K., Alpern, L., & Repacholi, B. (1993). Disorganized infant attachment classification and maternal psychosocial problems as predictors of hostile-aggressive behavior in the pre-school classroom. *Child Development, 64*, 572–585.

Lyons-Ruth, K., & Jacobvitz, D. (1999). Attachment disorganisation: Unresolved loss, relational violence, and lapses in behavioral and attentional strategies. In J. Cassidy & P.R. Shaver (Eds.), *Handbook of attachment: Theory, research and clinical applications* (pp. 520–554). New York: Guilford Press .

Lytton, H., & Romney, D. M. (1991). Parents' sex-related differential socialization of boys and girls: A meta-analysis. *Psychological Bulletin, 109*, 267–296.

Maccoby, E. E. (1990). Gender and relationships: A developmental account. *American Psychologist, 45*, 513–521.

Maccoby, E. E. (1995). The two sexes and their social systems. In P. Moen, G. H. Elder, Jr., & K. Luscher (Eds.), *Examining lives in context: Perspectives on the ecology of human development.* Washington, DC: American Psychological Association.

Maccoby, E. E. (1998). The two sexes: Growing up apart, coming together. Cambridge, MA: Harvard University Press.

Maccoby, E. E. (2000a). Parenting and its effects on children: On reading and misreading behavior genetics. *Annual Review of Psychology, 51*, 127.

Maccoby, E. E. (2000b). Perspectives on gender development. *International Journal of Behavioral Development, 24*, 398–406.

Maccoby, E. E. (2002). Parenting effects: Issues and controversies. In J. G. Borkowski, S. L. Ramey, & M. Bristol-Power (Eds.). *Parenting and the child's world: Influences on academic, intellectual, and social-emotional development.* Mahwah, NJ: Erlbaum.

Maccoby, E. E., & Jacklin, C. N. (1974). *The psychology of sex differences.* Stanford, CA: Stanford University Press.

Maccoby, E. E., & Martin, J. A. (1983). Socialization in the context of the family: Parent-child interaction. In P. H. Mussen (Series Ed.) & E. M. Hetherington (Vol. Ed.), *Handbook of child psychology*: Vol. 4. *Socialization, personality, and social development* (4th ed.). New York: Wiley.

MacDonald, K. B. (1988a). The interfaces between sociobiology and developmental psychology. In K. B. MacDonald (Ed.), *Sociobiological perspectives on human development.* New York: Springer-Verlag.

MacDonald, K. B. (1992). Warmth as a developmental construct: An evolutionary analysis. *Child Development, 63*, 753–773.

MacDonald, K., & Parke, R. D. (1986). Parent-child physical play: The effects of sex and age of children and parents. *Sex Roles, 15*, 367–378.

MacDorman M. F, Martin, J. A., Mathews, T. J., Hoyert, D. L., & Ventura, S. J. (2005). Explaining the 2001–2002 infant mortality increase: data from the linked birth/infant death data set. *Natl. Vital. Stat. Rep., 53*(12), 122.

MacFarlane, A. (1975). Olfaction in the development of social preferences in the human neonate. In *Parent-infant interaction* (CIBA Foundation Symposium No. 33). Amsterdam: Elsevier.

Mackay, Robert W. (1973). Conceptions of children and models of socialization. In Dreitzel, H.P. (Ed.), *Recent Sociology.* No. 5, New York: Macmillan, pp. 27–43, reprinted in Waksler, F.C. (Ed.), *Studying the social worlds of children.* Basingstoke, England: Falmer, 1991, pp. 23–37.

MacKinnon, C. E. (1989). An observational investigation of sibling interactions in married and divorced families. *Developmental Psychology, 25*, 36–44.

Mactie, J., Cicchetti, D., & Toth, S. L. (2001). The development of dissociation in maltreated preschool-aged children. *Development and Psychopathology, 13*, 233–254.

MacWhinney, B. (1987). The competition model. In B. MacWhinney (Ed.), *Mechanisms of language acquisition*. Hillsdale, NJ: Erlbaum.

MacWhinney, B., & Bates, E. (1993). *The crosslinguistic study of sentence processing*. Cambridge: Cambridge University Press.

MacWhinney, B., & Chang, F. (1995). Connectionism and language learning. In C. A. Nelson (Ed.), *Minnesota symposia on child psychology*: Vol. 28. *Basic and applied perspectives on learning, cognition, and development*. Mahwah, NJ: Erlbaum.

MacWhinney, B., & Leinbach, J. (1991). Implementations are not conceptualizations: Revising the verb learning model. *Cognition, 40*, 121–157.

Madansky, D., & Edelbrock, C. (1990). Cosleeping in a community sample of 2- and 3-year-old children. *Pediatrics, 86*(2), 197–203.

Madduz, J. E., & Gosselin, J. T. (2003). Self-efficacy. In M.R. Leary, & J.P. Tangney (Eds.), *Handbook of self and identity*. New York: Guilford Press.

Magnuson, K. A., & Duncan, G. J. (2002). Parents in poverty. In M.H. Bornstein (Ed.), *Handbook of parenting*, vol. 4: *Social conditions and applied parenting* (pp. 95–122), 2nd ed. Mahwah, NJ: Erlbaum.

Magnuson, K. A., & Waldfogel, J. (2005). Early childhood care and education: Effects on ethnic and racial gaps in school readiness. *The Future of Children, 15*(1), 169–196.

Magnusson, D., Bergman, L. R., Rudiger, G., & Torestad, B. (Eds.). (1994). *Problems and methods in longitudinal research: Stability and change*. New York: Cambridge University Press.

Main, M., & Goldwyn, R. (1998). Adult attachment rating and classification systems. In M. Main (Ed.), *Assessing attachment through discourse, drawings, and reunion situations*. New York: Cambridge University Press.

Main M., Kaplan, N., & Cassidy, J. (1985). Security in infancy, childhood and adulthood: A move to the level of representation. In I. Bretherton & E. Waters (Eds.), *Growing points of attachment theory and research. Monographs of the Society for Research in Child Development, 50*(12, Serial No. 209).

Main, M., & Solomon, J. (1986). Discovery of a disorganized/disoriented attachment pattern. In T. B. Brazelton & M. W. Yogman (Eds.), *Affective development in infancy*. Norwood, NJ: Ablex.

Main M., & Solomon, J. (1990). Procedures for identifying infants as disorganized/disoriented during the Ainsworth Strange Situation. In M. Greenberg, D. Cicchetti, & M. Cummings (Eds.), *Attachment during the preschool years*. Chicago: University of Chicago Press.

Majeres, R. L. (1999). Sex differences in phonological processes: Speeded matching and word reading. *Memory and Cognition, 27*, 246–253.

Makame, V., & Frantham-Mcgregor, S. (2002). Psychological well-being of orphans in Dar Es Salaam, Tanzania. *Acta Paediatrica, 91* (4), 459–465.

Malatesha, J. R. (2005). Vocabulary: A critical component of comprehension. *Reading & Writing Quarterly: Overcoming Learning Difficulties, 21*, 209–219.

Malatesta, C. Z. (1985). Developmental course of emotion expression in the human infant. In G. Zivin (Ed.), *Development of expressive behavior: Biological-environmental interaction*. New York: Academic Press.

Malatesta, C. Z., Culver, C., Tesman, J. R., & Shepard, B. (1989). The development of emotion expression during the first two years of life.

Monographs of the Society for Research in Child Development, 54(12, Serial No. 219).

Malatesta, C. Z., Grigoryev, P., Lamb, C., Albin, M., & Culver, C. (1986). Emotion socialization and expressive development in preterm and full term infants. *Child Development, 57*, 316–330.

Malatesta, C. Z., & Haviland, J. M. (1982). Learning display rules: The socialization of emotion expression in infancy. *Child Development, 53*, 991–1003.

Malatesta, C. Z., & Haviland, J. M. (1985). Signs, symbols, and socialization. In M. Lewis & C. Saarni (Eds.), *The socialization of emotion* (pp. 89–115). New York: Plenum Press.

Malatesta, C. Z., Izard, C. E., & Camras, L. (1991). Conceptualizing early infant affect: Emotions as fact, fiction, or artifact? In K. Strongman (Ed.), *International review of studies on emotion*. New York: Wiley.

Malina, R. M. (1990). Physical growth and performance during the transitional years (916). In R. Montemayor, G. R. Adams, & T. Gullotta (Eds.), *From childhood to adolescence*: Vol. 2. *Advances in adolescent development*. London: Sage.

Mandel, D., Kemler Nelson, D. G., & Jusczyk, P. W. (1996). Infants remember the order of words in a spoken sentence. *Cognitive Development, 11*, 181–196.

Mandoki, M. W., Summer, G. S., Hoffman, R. P., & Riconda, D. L. (1991). A review of Klinefelter's syndrome in children and adolescents. *Journal of the American Academy of Child and Adolescent Psychiatry, 30*, 167–172.

Mangelsdorf, S. C., Plunkett, J. W., Dedrick, C. F., Berlin, M., Meisels, S. J., McHale, J. L., et al. (1996). Attachment security in very low birth weight infants. *Developmental Psychology, 32*, 914–920.

Manke, B., Saudino, K. J., & Grant, J. D. (2001). Extreme analyses of observed temperament dimensions. In R. N. Emde & J. K. Hewitt (Eds.), *Infancy to early childhood*. New York: Oxford University Press.

Mannino, D. M., Moorman, J. E., Kingsley, B., Rose, D., & Repace, J. (2001). Health effects related to environmental tobacco smoke exposure in the United States. *Archives of Pediatric and Adolescent Medicine, 155*, 36–41.

Mannle, S., & Tomasello, M. (1987). Fathers, siblings, and the Bridge Hypothesis. In K. E. Nelson & A. VanKleeck (Eds.), *Children's language* (Vol. 6). Hillsdale, NJ: Erlbaum.

Mannuzza, S., & Klein, R. G. (2000). Long-term prognosis in attention-deficit/hyperactivity disorder. *Child and Adolescent Psychiatric Clinics of North America, 9*, 1711–1726.

Mao, A., Burnham, M. M., Goodlin-Jones, B. L., Gaylor, E. E., & Anders, T. F. (2004). A comparison of the sleepwake patterns of cosleeping and solitary-sleeping infants. *Child Psychiatry & Human Development, 35*(2), 95–105.

Maoz, I. (2000). An experiment in peace: Reconciliation-aimed workshops of Jewish-Israeli and Palestinian youth. *Journal of Peace Research, 37*, 721–736. Electronic version.

Maquet, P. (2001). The role of sleep in learning and memory. *Science, 294*(5544), 1048–1052.

Maratsos, M. (1976). *Language development: The acquisition of language structure*. Morristown, NJ: General Learning Press.

Maratsos, M. (1983). Some current issues in the study of the acquisition of grammar. In P.H. Mussen (Series Ed.) & J.H. Flavell & E.M. Markman (Vol. Eds.), *Handbook of child psychology: Vol.3. Cognitive development* (4th ed.). New York: Wiley.

March of Dimes (2005). Retrieved December 19, 2005, from http://www.marchofdimes.com/professionals/14332_1169.asp

Marchant, G. J., Paulson, S. E., & Rothlisberg, B. A. (2001). Relations of middle school students' perceptions of family and school contexts with academic achievement. *Psychology in the Schools, 38*, 505–519.

Marcia, J. E. (1994). The empirical study of ego identity. In H. A. Bosma, T. L.Graafsma, H. D. Grotevant, & D. J. Delevita (Eds.), *Identity and development: An interdisciplinary approach* (pp. 67–80). Thousand Oaks: Sage Publications.

Marcia, J. E. (2002). Identity and psychosocial development in adulthood. *Identity, 2*, 7–28.

Marcia, J. E. (2003). Treading fearlessly: A commentary on personal persistence, identity development, and suicide. *Monographs of the Society for Research in Child Development, 68*(2), 131–138.

Marcotte, D., Fortin, L., Potvin, P., & Papillon, M. (2002). Gender differences in depressive symptoms during adolescence: Role of gender-typed characteristics, self-esteem, body image, stressful life events, and pubertal status. *Journal of Emotional and Behavioral Disorders, 10*, 29–42.

Marcus, G. F. (2001). *The algebraic mind: Integrating connectionism and cognitive science*. Cambridge, MA: MIT Press.

Marcus, G. F., Pinker, S., Ullman, M., Hollander, M., Rosen, T. J., & Xu, F. (1992). Overregularization in language acquisition. *Monographs of the Society for Research in Child Development, 57*(4, Serial No. 228).

Mares, L., & Woodard, E. (2005). The positive effects of television on children's social interactions. In R. Carveth & J. Bryant (Eds.), *Meta-analyses of media effects*. Mahwah, NJ: Erlbaum.

Mareschal, D. French, R. M., & Quinn, P. C. (2000). A connectionist account of asymmetric category learning in early infancy. *Developmental Psychology, 36*, 635–645.

Mareschal, D., & Johnson, S. P. (2002). Learning to perceive object unity: A connectionist account. *Developmental Science, 5*, 151–185.

Margolis, H., & McCabe, P. (2003). Self-efficacy: A key to improving the motivation of struggling learners. *Preventing School Failure, 47*, 4,162–170.

Markman, E. M. (1989). *Categorization and naming in children: Problems of induction*. Cambridge, MA: MIT Press.

Markman, E. M. (1991). The whole object, taxonomic, and mutual exclusivity assumptions as initial constraints on word meanings. In S. A. Gelman & J. P. Byrnes (Eds.), *Perspectives on language and thought: Interrelations in development*. Cambridge: Cambridge University Press.

Markus, H. R. & Kitayama, S. (1991). Culture and self: Implications for cognition, emotion, and motivation. *Psychological Review, 98*(2), 224–253.

Marlier, L., Schaal, B., & Soussignan, R. (1998). Neonatal responsiveness to the odor of amniotic and lacteal fluids: A test of perinatal chemosensory continuity. *Child Development, 69*, 611–623.

Marsh, H. W., & Ayotte, V. (2003). Do multiple dimensions of self-concept become more differentiated with age? The differential distinctiveness hypothesis. *Journal of Educational Psychology, 95*, 687–706.

Marsh, H. W., Barnes, J., & Cairns, L. (1984). Self-Description Questionnaire: Age and sex effects in the structure and level of self-concept for preadolescent children. *Journal of Educational Psychology, 76*(5), 940–956.

Marsh, H. W, Ellis, L. A., & Craven, R. G. (2002). How do preschool children feel about themselves? Unraveling measurement and multidimensional self-concept structure. *Developmental Psychology, 38*, 376–393.

Marsh, H. W., Ellis, L. A., Parada, R. H., Richards, G., & Heubeck, B. G. (2005). A short version of the self description questionnaire III: Operationalizing criteria for short-form evaluation with new applications of confirmatory factor analyses. *Psychological Assessment, 17*, 81–102.

Marsh, H. W., Parada, R. H., & Ayotte, V. (2004). A multidimensional perspective of relations between self-concept (Self Description Questinnaire ll) and adolescent mental health (Youth Self Report). *Psychological Assessment, 16*, 27–41.

Marsh, H. W., Trautwein, U., LÜdtke, O., KÖller, O., & Baumert, J. (2005). Academic self-concept, interest, grades and standadized test scores: Reciprocal effects models of causal ordering. *Child Development, 76*, 397–416.

Marsh, H. W., & Yeung, A. S. (1998). Longitudinal structural equation models of academic self-concept and achievement: Gender differences in the development of math and English constructs. *American Educational Research Journal, 35*, 705–738.

Marshall, J., Ralph, S., & Palmer, S. (2002). I wasn`t trained to work with them: mainstream teachers` attitudes to children with speech and language difficulties. *International Journal of Inclusive Education, 6*(3):199–215.

Marsiglio, W., Amato, P., Day, R. D., & Lamb, M. E. (2000). Scholarship on fatherhood in the 1990s and beyond. *Journal of Marriage and the Family, 62*, 1173–1191.

Martin, C. L. (1989). Children's use of gender-related information in making social judgments. *Developmental Psychology, 25*, 80–88.

Martin, C. L. (1993). New directions for investigating children's gender knowledge. *Developmental Review, 13*, 184–204.

Martin, C. L., Eisenbud, L., & Rose, H. (1995). Children's gender-based reasoning about toys. *Child Development, 66*, 1453–1471.

Martin, C. L., & Halverson, C. E. (1983a). The effects of sex-typing schemas on young children's memory. *Child Development, 54*, 563–574.

Martin, C. L., & Halverson, C. F. (1983b). Gender constancy: A methodological and theoretical analysis. *Sex Roles, 9*, 775–790.

Martin, C. L., & Halverson, C. F. (1987). The roles of cognition in sex role acquisition. In D. B. Carter (Ed.), *Current conceptions of sex roles and sex typing: Theory and research.* New York: Praeger.

Martin, C. L., & Little, J. K. (1990). The relation of gender understanding to children's sex-typed preferences and gender stereotypes. *Child Development, 61*, 1427–1439.

Martin, C. L., Ruble, D. N., & Szkrybalo, J. (2002). Cognitive theories of early gender development. *Psychological Bulletin, 128*, 903–933.

Martin, G. B., & Clark, R. D. (1982). Distress crying in neonates: Species and peer specificity. *Developmental Psychology, 18*, 39.

Martin J. A., Kochanek, M. S., Strobino, D. M., Guyer, B., & MacDorman, M. F. (2005). Annual summary of vital statistics—2003. *Pediatrics, 115*, 619–634.

Martini, M., & Kirkpatrick, J. (1981). Early interactions in the Marquesas Isalnds. In T. M. Field, A. M. Sostek, P. Vietze, & P. H. Leiderman (Eds.), *Culture and early interactions.* Hillsdale, NJ: Erlbaum.

Martorano, S. C. (1977). A developmental analysis of performance on Piaget's formal operational tasks. *Developmental Psychology, 13*, 666–672.

Martorell, R. (1984). Genetics, environment, and growth: Issues in the assessment of nutritional status. In A. Velasquez & H. Bourges (Eds.), *Genetic factors in nutrition.* Orlando, FL: Academic Press.

Masataka, N. (1993). Effects of contingent and noncontingent maternal stimulation on the social behavior of three- to four-month-old Japanese infants. *Journal of Child Language, 20,* 303–312.

Masataka, N. (1999). Preference for infant-directed singing in 2-day-old infants of deaf parents. *Developmental Psychology, 35*, 1001–1005.

Mascolo M. E.,& Li, J. (2004). *Culture and developing selves: Beyond dichotomization.* San Francisco. CA: Jossey-Bass.

Masten, A. S., Hubbard, J. J., Gest, S. D., Tellegen, A., Garmezy, N., & Ramiriez, M. (1999). Competence in the context of adversity: Pathways to resilience and maladaptation from childhood to late adolescence. *Development and Psychopathology, 11*, 143–169.

Masters, J. C. (1979). Modeling and labeling as integrated determinants of children's sex-typed imitative behavior. *Child Development, 50*, 364–371.

Masters, J. C., & Furman, W. (1981). Popularity, individual friendship selection, and specific peer interaction among children. *Developmental Psychology, 17*, 344–350.

Masters, M. S., & Sanders, B. (1993). Is the gender difference in mental rotation disappearing? *Behavior Genetics, 23*, 337–341.

Mathes, P. G., Torgesen, J. K., & Allor, J. H. (2001). The effects of peer-assisted literacy strategies for first-grade readers with and without additional computer-assisted instruction in phonological awareness. *American Educational Research Journal, 38*, 371–410.

Mathiesen, K. S., & Tambs, K. (1999). The EAS Temperament Questionnaire-factor structure, age trends, reliability, and stability in a Norwegian sample. *Journal of Child Psychology and Psychiatry and Allied Disciplines, 40*, 431–439.

Matsumoto, D., Haan, N., Yabrove, G., Theodorou, P., & Carney, C. C. (1986). Pre-schoolers' moral actions and emotions in Prisoner's Dilemma. *Developmental Psychology, 22*, 663–670.

Mau, W. (2003). Factors that infleuence persistence in science and engineering career aspirations. *Career Development Quarterly, 51*, 234–243.

Maurer, D. (1985). Infants' perception of facedness. In T. M. Field & N. A. Fox (Eds.), *Social perception in infants.* Norwood, NJ: Ablex.

Maurer, D., & Lewis, T. L. (2001). Visual acuity and spatial contrast sensitivity: Normal development and underlying mechanisms. In C. A. Nelson & M. Luciana (Eds.), *Handbook of developmental cognitive neuroscience.* Cambridge, MA: MIT Press.

Maurer, D., & Maurer, C. (1988). *The world of the newborn.* New York: Basic Books.

Maurer, D., Stager, C. L., & Mondloch, C. J. (1999). Cross-modal transfer of shape is difficult to demonstrate in one-month-olds. *Child Development, 70*, 1047–1057.

Mavalankar, D. V. & Rosenfield, A. (2005). Maternal mortality in resource-poor settings: Policy barriers to care. *American Journal of Public Health, 95*, 200–203.

Mayer, N. K., & Tronick, E. Z. (1985). Mothers' turn-giving signals and infant turn-taking in mother-infant interaction. In T. M. Field & N. A. Fox (Eds.), *Social perception in infants.* Norwood, NJ: Ablex.

Mayes, L. C., & Fahy, T. (2001). Prenatal drug exposure and cognitive development. In R. J. Sternberg & E. L. Grigorenko (Eds.), *Environmental effects on cognitive abilities.* Mahwah, NJ: Erlbaum.

Maynard Smith, J. (1976). Group selection. *Quarterly Review of Biology, 51*, 277–283.

McArthur, L.Z., & Baron, R.M. (1983). Toward an ecological theory of social perception. *Psychological Review, 90.* 215–238.

McAuley, E., Elavsky, S., Motl, R. W., Konopack, J. F., Hu. L., & Marquez, D. X. (2005). Physical activity, self-efficacy, and self-esteem: Longitudinal relationships in older adults. *Journals of Gerontology-Series B: Psychological Sciences and Social Sciences, 60* B, 268–275.

McCabe, A. E. (1989). Differential language learning styles in young children: The importance of context. *Developmental Review, 9,* 120.

McCabe, M. P., & Collins, J. K. (1984). Measurement of depth of desired and experienced sexual involvement at different stages of dating. *Journal of Sex Research, 20*, 377–390.

McCartney, K. (Ed.). (1990). New directions for child development: No. 49. *Child care and maternal employment: A social ecology approach.* San Francisco: Jossey-Bass.

McCombs, B.L. (2001). What do we know about learners and learning? The learner-centered framework: Bringing the educational system into balance. *Educational Horizons, 79* (4), 182–193.

McCrae, R. R., Costa, P. T. Jr., Terracciano, A., Parker, W. D., Mills, C. J., De Fruyt, F., et al. (2002). Personality trait development from age 12 to age 18: Longitudinal, cross-sectional and cross-cultural analyses. *Journal of Personality and Social Psychology, 83*, 1456–1468.

McCune-Nicolich, L. (1981). The cognitive bases of relational words in the single word period. *Journal of Child Language, 8*, 15–34.

McDonough, L., & Mandler, J. M. (1994). Very long-term recall in infants: Infantile amnesia reconsidered. *Memory, 2*, 339–352.

McDougall, P., Hymel, S.,Vaillancourt, T., & Mercer, L. (2001). The consequences of childhood peer rejection. In M. Leary (Ed.), *Interpersonal rejection.* London: Oxford University Press.

McDowell, D. J., O'Neil, R., & Parke, R. D. (2000). Display rule application in a disappointing situation and children's emotional reactivity. *Merrill-Palmer Quarterly, 46*, 306–324.

McFayden-Ketchum, S. A., Bates, J. E., Dodge, K. A., & Pettit, G. S. (1996). Patterns of change in early childhood aggressive-disruptive behavior: Gender differences in predictions from early coercive and affectionate mother-child interactions. *Child Development, 67*, 2417–2433.

McGhee, P. E., & Frueh, T. (1980). Television *viewing* and the learning of sex-role stereotypes. *Sex Roles, 6*, 179–188.

McGlone, J. (1980). Sex differences in human brain asymmetry: Critical survey. *Behavioral and Brain Sciences, 3*, 215–227.

McGraw, M. B. (1940). Suspension grasp behavior of the human infant. *American Journal of the Disabled Child, 60*, 799–811.

McGuiness, D., & Morley, C. (1991). Sex differences in the development of visuo-spatial ability in pre-school children. *Journal of Mental Imagery, 15*, 143–150.

McHale, S. M., Updegraff, K. A., Helms-Erikson, H., & Crouter, A. C. (2001). Sibling influences on gender development in middle childhood and early adolescence: A longitudinal study. *Developmental Psychology, 37*, 115–125.

McHugh, L., Barnes-Holmes, Y., & Barnes-Holmes, D. (2004). Perspective-taking as relational responding: A developmental profile. *Psychological Record, 54,* 115–144.

McIntyre, R. B., Paulson, R. M., & Lord, C. G. (2003). Alleviating women's mathematics stereotype threat through salience of group achievements. *Journal of Experimental Social Psychology, 39,* 83–90.

McKay, A. (2003). Sex *Research Update. Canadian Journal of Human Sexuality, 12*(3–4), 183–188.

McKenna, J. (1996). Sudden Infant Death Syndrome in cross-cultural perspective: Is infant-parent cosleeping protective? *Annual Review of Anthropology, 25* (1), 201–216.

McKown, C., & Weinstein, R. S. (2002). Modeling the role of child ethnicity and gender in children's differential response to teacher expectations. *Journal of Applied Social Psychology, 32,* 159–184.

McKown, C., & Weinstein, R. (2003). The development and consequences of stereotype-consciousness in childhood. *Child Development, 74,* 498–515.

McKusick, V. A. (1998). *Mendelian inheritance in man* (12th ed.). Baltimore: Johns Hopkins University Press.

McLaughlin, B., White, D., McDevitt, T., & Raskin, R. (1983). Mothers' and fathers' speech to their young children: Similar or different? *Journal of Child Language, 10,* 245–252.

McNeill, D. (1992). *Hand and mind: What gestures reveal about thought.* Chicago: University of Chicago Press.

McPherson, S. L. & Thomas, J. R. (1989). Relation of knowledge and performance in boys' tennis: Age and expertise. *Journal of Experimental Child Psychology, 48,* 190–211

Medoff-Cooper, B., Carey, W. B., & McDevitt, S. C. (1993). The Early Infancy Temperament Questionnaire. *Journal of Developmental and Behavioral Pediatrics, 14,* 230–235.

Medoff-Cooper, B., & Ratcliffe, S. J. (2005). *Development of preterm infants. Advances in Nursing Science, 28*(4), 356–363.

Medrich, E. A., Roizen, J. A., Rubin, V., & Buckley, S. (1982). *The serious business of growing up: A study of children's lives outside school.* Berkeley: University of California Press.

Meeus, W., Oosterwegel, A., & Vollebergh, W. (2002). Parental and peer attachment and identity development in adolescence. *Journal of Adolescence, 25,* 93–106.

Meichenbaum, D. H., & Goodman, J. (1971). Training impulsive children to talk to themselves: A means to develop self-control. *Journal of Personality and Social Psychology, 34,* 942–950.

Meins, E. (1997). Security of attachment and maternal tutoring strategies: Interaction within the zone of proximal development. *British Journal of Developmental Psychology, 15,* 129–144.

Meins, E., Fernyhough, C., & Wainwright, R. (2003). Pathways to understanding construct validity and predictive validity of maternal mind-mindedness. *Child Development, 74,* 1194–1211.

Mekos, D., Hetherington, E. M., & Reiss, D. (1996). Sibling differences in problem behavior and parental treatment in nondivorced and remarried families. *Child Development, 67,* 2148–2165.

Meltzoff, A. N. (1988). Infant imitation after a 1-week delay: Long-term memory for novel and multiple stimuli. *Developmental Psychology, 24,* 470–476.

Meltzoff, A. N. (1995). Infants' understanding of people and things: From body imitation to folk psychology. In *The body and the self,* edited by Jose Bermudez, Anthony J. Marcel, and Naomi Eilan. Cambridge, MA: MIT Press.

Meltzoff, A. N., & Borton, R. W. (1979). Intermodal matching by human neonates. *Nature, 282,* 403–404.

Meltzoff, A. N., & Moore, M. K. (1977). Imitation of facial and manual gestures by human neonates. *Science, 198,* 75–78.

Meltzoff, A. N., & Moore, M. K. (1994). Imitation, memory, and the representation of persons. *Infant Behavior and Development, 17,* 83–99.

Meltzoff, A. N., & Moore, M. K. (1999a). A new foundation for cognitive development in infancy: The birth of the representational infant. In E. K. Scholnick, K. Nelson, S. A. Gelman, & P. H. Miller (Eds.), *Conceptual development: Piaget's legacy.* Mahwah, NJ: Erlbaum.

Meltzoff, A. N., & Moore, M. K. (1999b). Persons and representation: Why infant imitation is important for theories of human development. In J. Nadel & G. Butterworth (Eds.), *Imitation in infancy.* Cambridge: Cambridge University Press.

Menard, S. (1991). *Longitudinal research.* Newbury Park, CA: Sage.

Menig-Peterson, C. L. (1975). The modification of communicative behaviors in preschool-aged children as a function of the listener's perspective. *Child Development, 46,* 1015–1018.

Merriman, W. E. (1997). CALLED: A model of early word learning. In R. Vasta (Ed.), *Annals of child development* (Vol. 13). London: Kingsley.

Merrow Report (1998). *Lost in translation: Latinos, schools and society* [Videocassette]. Learning Matters, Inc. (Production Company). New York: PBS Home Video. http://www.pbs.org/merrow/tv/transcripts/lost_english.pdf

Mervis, C. B. (1987). Child-basic object categories and early lexical development. In U. Neisser (Ed.), *Concepts and conceptual development: Ecological and intellectual factors in categorization.* New York: Cambridge University Press.

Meyer-Bahlberg, H. F. L. (1993). Psychobiologic research on homosexuality. *Child and Adolescent Psychiatric Clinics of North America, 2,* 489–500.

Meyer-Bahlberg, H. F. L., Ehrhardt, A. A., Rosen, L. R., Gruen, R. S., Veridiano, N. P., Vann, F. H., et al. (1995). Prenatal estrogens and the development of homosexual orientation. *Developmental Psychology, 31,* 12–21.

Michael, A., & Eccles, J. S. (2003). When coming of age means coming undone: Links between puberty and psychosocial adjustment among European American and African American girls. In C. Hayward (Ed.), *Gender differences at puberty.* New York, Cambridge University Press.

Midgett, J., Ryan, B. A., Adams, G. R., & Corville-Smith (2002). Complicating achievement and self-esteem: Considering the joint effects of child characteristics and parent-child interactions. *Contemporary Educational Psychology, 27,* 132–143.

Middleton, M. J., Kaplan, A., & Midgley, C. (2004). The change in middle school students' achievement goals in mathematics over time. *School Psychology of Education, 7,* 289–311.

Midgley, C., Kaplan, A., & Middleton, M. (2001). Performance-approach goals: Good for what, for whom, under what circumstances, and at what cost? *Journal of Educational Psychology, 93,* 77–86.

Midwifery Task Force, Inc. (2005). *The Midwives Model of Care.* Retrieved March 10, 2006 from http://www.cfmidwifery.org/ mmoc/define.aspx.

Miles, D. R., & Carey, G. (1997). Genetic and environmental architecture of human aggression. *Journal of Personality and Social Psychology, 72,* 207–217.

Miles, T. R., Haslum, M. N., & Wheeler, T. J. (1998). *Gender ratio in dyslexia. Annals of Dyslexia, 48,* 27–55.

Miller, A. M. & Harwood, R. L. (2001). Long-term socialisation goals and the construction of infants' social networks among middle class Anglo and Puerto Rican mothers. *International Journal of Behavioral Development, 25*(5), 450–457.

Miller, A. M., & Harwood, R. L. (2002). The cultural organization of parenting: Change and stability of behavior patterns during feeding and social play across the first year of life. *Parenting: Science and Practice, 2,* 241–272.

Miller, J. G. (1997). Culture and self: Uncovering the cultural grounding of psychological theory, The self across psychology: Self-recognition, self-awareness, and the self concept. *Annals of the New York Academy of Sciences, 818,* 217–231. New York: New York Academy of Sciences.

Miller, J. G., & Bersoff, D. M. (1998). The role of liking in perceptions of the moral responsibility to help: A cultural perspective. *Journal of Experimental Social Psychology, 34*(5), 443–469.

Miller, J. G., Bersoff, D. M., & Harwood, R. L. (1990). Perceptions of social responsibilities in India and in the United States: Moral imperatives or personal decisions? *Journal of Personality and Social Psychology, 58*(1), 33–47.

Miller, J. G., & Luthar, S. (1989). Issues of interpersonal responsibility and accountability: A comparison of Indians' and Americans' moral judgments. *Social Cognition, 3,* 237–261.

Miller, K. F. (1984). Child as the measurer of all things: Measurement procedures and the development of quantitative concepts. In C. Sophian (Ed.), *Origins of cognitive skills.* Hillsdale, NJ: Erlbaum.

Miller, L. T. & Vernon, P.A. (1997). Developmental changes in speed of information processing in young children. *Developmental Psychology, 33* (3), 549–554.

Miller, P. A., Eisenberg, N., Fabes, R. A., & Shell, R. (1996). Relations of moral reasoning and vicarious emotion to young children's prosocial behavior toward peers and adults. *Developmental Psychology, 32,* 210–219.

Miller, P. H. (1990). The development of strategies of selective attention. In D. F. Bjorklund (Ed.), *Children's strategies: Contemporary views of cognitive development.* Hillsdale, NJ: Erlbaum.

Miller, P. H., & Coyle, T. R. (1999). Developmental change: Lesson from microgenesis. In E. K. Scholnick, K. Nelson, S.A. Gelman, & P.H. Miller (Eds.), *Conceptual development: Piaget's legacy.* Mahwah, NJ: Erlbaum.

Miller, P. H., & DeMarie-Dreblow, D. (1990). Social-cognitive correlates of children's understanding of displaced aggression. *Journal of Experimental Child Psychology, 49,* 488–504.

Miller, P. H. (2001). *Theories of developmental psychology* (4th ed.). New York: Worth.

Miller, P. H., & Seier, W. L. (1994). Strategy utlization deficiencies in children: When, where, and why. In H. W. Reese (Ed.), *Advances in child development and behavior,* Vol. 25 (pp. 107–156). New York: Academic Press.

Miller, P. J., Mintz, J., Hoogstra, L., Fung, H., & Potts, R. (1992). The narrated self: Young children's construction of self in relation to others in conversational stories of personal experience. *Merrill-Palmer Quarterly, 38,* 45–67.

Miller, P. M., Danaher, D. L., & Forbes, D. (1986). Sex-related strategies for coping with interpersonal conflict in children aged five to seven. *Developmental Psychology, 22*, 543–548.

Miller, S. A. (1976). Nonverbal assessment of Piagetian concepts. *Psychological Bulletin, 83*, 405–430.

Miller, S. A. (1982). Cognitive development: A Piagetian perspective. In R. Vasta (Ed.), *Strategies and techniques of child study*. New York: Academic Press.

Miller, S. A. (1986). Certainty and necessity in the understanding of Piagetian concepts. *Developmental Psychology, 22*, 318.

Miller, S. A. (1995). Parents' attributions for their children's behavior. *Child Development, 66*, 1557–1584.

Miller, S. A. (2000). Children's understanding of pre-existing differences in knowledge and belief. *Developmental Review, 20*, 227–282.

Miller, S. A., & Brownell, C. A. (1975). Peers, persuasion, and Piaget: Dyadic interaction between conservers and nonconservers. *Child Development, 46*, 992–997.

Miller, S. A., Hardin, C. A., & Montgomery, D. E. (2003). Young children's understanding of the conditions for knowledge acquisition. *Journal of Cognition and Development, 4*, 325–356.

Mills, R. S. L., & Grusec, J. E. (1988). Socialization from the perspective of the parent-child relationship. In S. Duck (Ed.), *Handbook of personal relationships*. Chichester, England: Wiley.

Mills, R. S. L., & Grusec, J. E. (1989). Cognitive, affective, and behavioral consequences of praising altruism. *Merrill-Palmer Quarterly, 35*, 299–326.

Minde, K. (1993). Prematurity and illness in infancy: Implications for development and intervention. In C. H. Zeanah Jr. (Ed.), *Handbook of infant mental development*. New York: Guilford.

Minde, K. (2000). Prematurity and serious medical conditions in infancy: Implications for development, behavior, and intervention. In C. H. Zeanah Jr. (Ed.), *Handbook of infant mental health* (2nd ed.). New York: Guilford.

Mischel, W. (2003). Challenging the Traditional Personality Psychology Paradigm. In Ed. Robert J. Sternberg's *Psychologists defying the crowd: Stories of those who battled the establishment and won*. (pp. 139–156) Washington, DC: American Psychological Association..

Mischel, W., & Ayduk, O. (2002). Willpower in a cognitive-affective processing system: The dynamics of delay of gratification. In R.F. Baumeister, & K.D. Vohs (Eds.), *Handbook of self-regulation: Research, theory, and applications*. New York: Guilford

Mischel, W., & Ayduk, O. (2004). Willpower in a cognitive-affective processing system: The dynamics of delay of gratification. In R. F. Baumeister & K. D. Vohs (Eds.), *Handbook of self-regulation: Research, theory, and applications* (pp. 991–929). New York: Guilford.

Mischel, W., Shoda, Y., & Peake, P. K. (1988). The nature of adolescent competencies predicted by preschool delay of gratification. *Journal of Personality and Social Psychology, 54*, 687–696.

Miserandino, M. (1996). Children who do well in school: Individual differences in perceived competence and autonomy in above average children. *Journal of Educational Psychology, 88*, 203–214.

Miyake, K., Campos, J., Bradshaw, D., & Kagan, J. (1986). Issues in socioemotional development. In H. Stevenson, H. Azuma, & K. Hakuta (Eds.),

Child development and education in Japan. New York: Freeman.

Miyawaki, K., Strange, W., Verbrugge, R., Liberman, A. M., Jenkins, J. J., & Fujimura, O. (1975). An effect of linguistic experience: The discrimination of the [r] and [l] by native speakers of Japanese and English. *Perception and Psychophysics, 18*, 331–340.

Mize, J., & Ladd, G. W. (1990). A cognitive-social learning approach to social skill training with low-status preschool children. *Developmental Psychology, 26*, 388–397.

Modgil, S., & Modgil, C. (1976). *Piagetian research: Compilation and commentary* (Vols. 18). Windsor, England: NFER.

Moerk, E. L. (1996). Input and learning processes in first language acquisition. In H. W. Reese (Ed.), *Advances in child development and behavior* (Vol. 26). San Diego, CA: Academic Press.

Moerk, E. L. (2000). *The guided acquisition of first language skills*. Stamford, CT: Ablex.

Molfese, D. L., & Molfese, V. J. (1979). Hemispheric and stimulus differences as reflected in the cortical responses of newborn infants to speech stimuli. *Developmental Psychology, 15*, 505–511.

Moller, L., & Serbin, L. A. (1996). Antecedents of toddler gender segregation: Cognitive consonance, gender-typed toy preferences and behavioral compatibility. *Sex Roles, 35*, 445–460.

Mondloch, C. J., Lewis, T. L., Budreau, D. R., Maurer, D., Dannemiller, J. L., Stephens, B. R., & Kleiner-Gathercoal, K. A. (1999). Face perception during early infancy. *Psychological Science, 10*, 419–422.

Mondschein, E. R., Adolph, K. E., & Tamis-LeMonda, C. S. (2000). Gender bias in mothers' expectations about infant crawling. *Journal of Experimental Child Psychology, 77*, 304–316.

Money, J. C. (1975). Ablatio penis: Normal male infant sex-reassigned as a girl. *Archives of Sexual Behavior, 4*, 65–71.

Money, J. C., & Annecillo, C. (1987). Crucial period effect in psychoendocrinology: Two syndromes, abuse dwarfism and female (CVAH) hermaphroditism. In M. H. Bornstein (Ed.), *Sensitive periods in development: Interdisciplinary perspectives*. Hillsdale, NJ: Erlbaum.

Money, J. C., & Ehrhardt, A. A. (1972). *Man and woman, boy and girl*. Baltimore: Johns Hopkins University Press.

Montemayor, R. (1974). Children's performance in a game and their attraction to it as a function of sex-typed labels. *Child Development, 45*, 152–156.

Montgomery, D. E. (1993). Young children's understanding of interpretive diversity between different-age listeners. *Developmental Psychology, 29*, 337–345.

Monzó, L. D., & Rueda, R. A. (2006). Sociocultural perspective on acculturation: Latino immigrant families negotiating discipline practices. *Education & Urban Society, 38* (2), 188–203.

Moon, C., Cooper, R. P., & Fifer, W. P. (1993). Two-day-olds prefer their native language. *Infant Behavior and Development, 16*, 495–500.

Moore, B. S., & Eisenberg, N. (1984). The development of altruism. In G. J. Whitehurst (Ed.), *Annals of child development* (Vol. 1). Greenwich, CT: JAI Press.

Moore, K. A., Morrison, D. R., & Greene, A. D. (1997). Effects on children born to adolescent mothers. In R.A. Maynard (Ed.), *Kids having kids: Economic costs and social consequences*

of teen pregnancy (pp. 145–180). Washington, DC: Urban Institute Press.

Moore, M. R., & Brooks-Gunn, J. (2002). Adolescent parenthood. In M. H. Bornstein (Ed.), *Handbook of parenting* (2nd ed., Vol. 3). Mahwah, NJ: Erlbaum.

Morbidity and Mortality Weekly Report. (2004). Retrieved March 17, 2006 from http://www.cdc.gov/mmwr/preview/mmwrhtml/mm5329a3.htm

Morell, V. (1993). The puzzle of the triple repeats. *Science, 260*, 1422–1423.

Morelli, G., Rogoff, B., Oppenheim, D., & Goldsmith, D. (1992). Cultural variations in infants' sleeping arrangements: Questions of independence. *Developmental Psychology, 28*, 604–613.

Morgan, J. L., Bonamo, K. M., & Travis, L. L. (1995). Negative evidence on negative evidence. *Developmental Psychology, 31*, 180–197.

Morgane, P. J., Austin-LaFrance, R., Bronzino, J., Tonkiss, J., Diaz-Cintra, S., Cintra, L., et al. (1993). Prenatal malnutrition and development of the brain. *Neuroscience and Biobehavioral Reviews, 17*, 911–28.

Morin, A. (2004). A neurocognitive and socioecological model of self-awareness. *Genetic, Social, & General Psychology Monographs, 130*, 197–202.

Moro, E. (1918). Das erste Trimenon. *Munch. med. Wschr., 65*, 1147–1150.

Morrongiello, B. A., Fenwick, K. D., Hiller, L., & Chance, G. (1994a). Sound localization in newborn human infants. *Developmental Psychobiology, 27*, 519–538.

Morrongiello, B. A., Humphrey, G. K., Timney, B., & Choi, J. (1994b). Tactual object exploration and recognition in blind and sighted children. *Perception, 23*, 833–848.

Morton D. H., Morton C. S., Strauss K. A., Robinson D.L., Puffenberger E. G., Hendrickson C., & Kelley R. I. (2003). Pediatric medicine and the genetic disorders of the Amish and Mennonite people of Pennsylvania. *American Journal of Medical Genetics, 121C*, 517,

Moshman, D. (1998). Cognitive development beyond childhood. In D. Kuhn & R. S. Siegler (Vol. Eds.) & W. Damon (Series Ed.), *Handbook of child psychology*: Vol. 2. *Cognition, perception, and language* (5th ed.). New York: Wiley.

Mounts, N. S., & Steinberg, L. (1995). An ecological analysis of peer influence on adolescent grade point average and drug use. Developmental Psychology, 31, 915–922.

Mrazek, D. A. (1991). Chronic pediatric illness and multiple hospitalizations. In M. Lewis (Ed.), *Child and adolescent psychiatry: A comprehensive textbook*. Baltimore: Williams & Wilkins.

Much, N., & Shweder, R. A. (1978). Speaking of rules: The analysis of culture in breach. In W. Damon (Ed.), *New directions for child development*: No. 2. *Moral development*. San Francisco: Jossey-Bass.

Mueller, C. (1996). Multidisciplinary research of multimodal stimulation of premature infants: An integrative review of the literature. *Maternal-Child Nursing Journal, 24*, 18–31.

Mueller, W. H. (1986). The genetics of size and shape in children and adults. In F. Falkner & J. M. Tanner (Eds.), *Human growth: A comprehensive treatise* (2nd ed., Vol. 3). New York: Plenum.

Mueller, E., & Silverman, N. (1989). Peer relations in maltreated children. In D. Cicchetti & V. Carlson (Eds.), *Child maltreatment: Theory and research on the causes and consequences of child abuse and neglect*. New York: Cambridge University Press.

Muir, D., & Clifton, R. K. (1985). Infants' orientation to the location of sound sources. In G. Gottlieb & N. A. Krasnegor (Eds.), *Measurement of audition and vision in the first year of postnatal life: A methodological overview*. Norwood, NJ: Ablex.

Muller, U., & Hrabok, M. (2005). Handbook of self-regulation: Research, theory, and application. *Canadian Psychology, 46*, 106–108.

Mumme, D. L., Fernald, A., & Herrera, C. (1996). Infants' responses to facial and vocal emotional signals in a social referencing paradigm. *Child Development, 67*, 3219–3237.

Munakata, Y. (1998). Infant perseveration and implications for object permanence theories: A PDP model of the AB task. *Developmental Science, 1*, 161–184.

Munakata, Y., McClelland, J. L., Johnson, M. H., & Siegler, R. S. (1997). Rethinking infant knowledge: Toward an adaptive process account of successes and failures in object permanence tasks. *Psychological Review, 104*, 686–713.

Munakata, Y. & McClelland, J. L. (2003). Connectionist models of development. *Developmental Science, 6*, 413–429.

Munroe, R. H., Shimmin, H. S., & Munroe, R. L. (1984). Gender understanding and sex role preference in four cultures. *Developmental Psychology, 20*, 673–682.

Murata, P. J., McGlynn, E. A., Siu, A. L., & Brook, R. H. (1992). *Prenatal care*. Santa Monica, CA: Rand.

Murphy, K., McKone, E., & Slee, J. (2003). Dissociations between implicit and explicit memory in children: The role of strategic processing and the knowledge base. *Journal of Experimental Child Psychology, 84*, 124–165.

Murray, F. B. (1982). Learning and development through social interaction and conflict: A challenge to social learning theory. In L. Liben (Ed.), *Piaget and the foundation of knowledge*. Hillsdale, NJ: Erlbaum.

Murray, L., Fiori-Cowley, A., Hooper, R., & Cooper, P. (1996). The impact of postnatal depression and associated adversity on early mother-infant interactions and later outcome. *Child Development, 67*, 2512–2526.

Murray, C., Golombok, S. (2005). Solo mothers and their donor insemination infants: follow-up at age 2 years. *Human Reproduction, 20*(6), 1655–1660,

Murray, A. D., Johnson, J., & Peters, J. (1990). Fine-tuning of utterance length to preverbal infants: Effects on later language development. *Journal of Child Language, 17*, 511–525.

Murray, B. A., Stahl, S. A., & Ivey, M. G. (1996). Developing phoneme awareness through alphabet books. *Reading and Writing, 8*, 307–322.

Murray, K. T., & Kochanska, G. (2002). Effortful control: Factor structure and relation to externalizing and internalizing behaviors. *Journal of Abnormal Child Psychology, 30*(5), 503–514.

Murray, Thomas, R. (1993). *Comparing Theories of Child Development*, Third Edition. Belmont, CA: Wadsworth Publishing Company.

Mussen (Series Ed.) & J. H. Flavell & E. M. Markman (Vol. Eds.), *Handbook of child psychology*: Vol. 3. *Cognitive development* (4th ed.). New York: Wiley.

Muter, V., Hulme, C., Snowling, M. J. & Stevenson, J. (2004) Phonemes, rimes, vocabulary and grammatical skills as foundations of early reading development: evidence from a longitudinal study. *Developmental Psychology, 40*, 665–681.

Mwamwenda, T. S. (1999). Undergraduate and graduate students' combinatorial reasoning and formal operations. *Journal of Genetic Psychology, 160* (4), 503–505.

Nadal, J. (2004). Do children with autism understand imitation as intentional interaction? *Journal of Cognitive & Behavioral Psychotherapies, 4*, 165–177.

Nader, K., Pynoos, R., Fairbanks, L., Al-Ajeel, M., & Al-Asfour, A. (1993). A preliminary study of PTSD and grief among the children of Kuwait following the Gulf crisis. *British Journal of Clinical Psychology, 32*, 407–416.

Naigles, L. G., & Gelman, S. A. (1995). Overextensions in comprehension and production revisited: Preferential-looking in a study of dog, cat, and cow. *Journal of Child Language, 22*, 19–46.

Nair, H., & Murray, A. D. (2005). Predictors of attachment security in preschool children from intact and divorced families. *Journal of Genetic Psychology, 166*, 245–263.

Nass, R. D. (1993). Sex differences in learning abilities and disabilities. *Annals of Dyslexia, 43*, 61–77.

Nastasi, B.K., Clements, D.H., & Battista, M.T. (1990). Social-cognitive interactions, motivation, and cognitive growth in logo programming and CAI problem-solving environments. *Journal of Educational Psychology, 82* (i), 150–158.

Nathanielsz, P. W. (1995). The role of basic science in preventing low birth weight. *The future of children* (Vol. 5, No. 1). Los Angeles: Packard Foundation.

National Center for Education Statistics. (1997). *Digest of education statistics 1997* (NCES 98015). Washington, DC: U.S. Department of Education.

National Center for Education Statistics (2001). *Internet access in U.S. public schools and classrooms: 1994-2000* (NCES 2001071). Washington, DC: Office of Educational Research and Improvement.

National Center for Education Statistics (2003). *Digest of Education Statistics, 2002* (NCES 2003060), Chapter 2.

National Center on Birth Defects and Developmental Disabilities (2005). Fetal alcohol syndrome. Retrieved March 10, from http://www.cdc.gov/ncbddd/fas/fasask.htm#how

National Center for Infectious Disease (2005). Cytomegalovirus (CMV) Infection Retrieved March 6, 2006, from http://www.cdc.gov/ncidod/diseases/cmv.htm.

National Center for Health Statistics, 2006. Preliminary Births for 2004. Retrieved March 16, 2006 from http://www.cdc.gov/nchs/ products/pubs/pubd/hestats/prelim_births/prelim_births04.htm

National Institute of Neurological Disorders & Stroke (2005). Retrieved March 16, 2006 from http://www.ninds.nih.gov/disorders/brain_basics/understanding_sleep.htm.

National Institutes of Health, National Institute of Mental Health, 1999. Retrieved March 17, 2006 from http://www.surgeongeneral.gov/library/mentalhealth/home.html

National Reading Panel (2000). Report of the National Reading Panel: Teaching children to read: An evidence-based assessment of the scientific research literature on reading instruction: Reports of the subgroups. Washington, DC: National Institute of Child Health and Development.

National Opinion Research Center. (2002). *Altruism in contemporary America: A report from the national altruism study*. Chicago: University of Chicago Press.

Neal, L., McCray, A .D., & Webb-Johnson, G. (2003). The effects of African American movement styles on teachers' perceptions and reactions. *Journal of Special Education, 377*, 49–57.

Needham, A. (2001). Object recognition and object segregation in 4.5-month-old infants. *Journal of Experimental Child Psychology, 78*, 324.

Needleman, H. L., Schell, A. S., Bellinger, D., Leviton, A., & Alldred, E. N. (1990). The long-term effects of exposure to low doses of lead in childhood: An 11-year follow-up report. *New England Journal of Medicine, 322*, 83.

Neiderhiser, J. M., Reiss, D., Hetherington, E. M., & Plomin, R. (1999). Relationships between parenting and adolescent adjustment over time: Genetic and environmental contributions. *Developmental Psychology, 35*, 680–692.

Neilsen, M., & Dissanayake, C. (2004). Pretend play, mirror self-recognition and imitation: A longitudinal investigation through second year. *Infant Behavior & Development, 27*, 342–365.

Neilsen, M., Dissanayake, C., & Kashima, Y. (2003). A longitudinal investigation of self-other discrimination and the emergence of mirror self-recognition. *Infant Behavior and Development, 26*, 213–226.

Neisser, U., Boodoo, G., Bouchard, T. J. Jr., Boykin, A. W., Brody, N., Ceci, S. J., et al. (1996). Intelligence: Knowns and unknowns. *American Psychologist, 51*, 77–101.

Nelson, C. A. (1987). The recognition of facial expressions in the first two years of life: Mechanisms of development. *Child Development, 58*, 889–909.

Nelson, C. A., & Luciano, M. (Eds.). (2001). *Handbook of developmental cognitive neuroscience*. Cambridge, MA: MIT Press.

Nelson, E. A. S., Schiefenhoevel, W., & Haimerl, F. (2000). Child care practices in nonindustrialized societies. *Pediatrics, 105*, e75.

Nelson, K. (1973). Structure and strategy in learning to talk. *Monographs of the Society for Research in Child Development, 38*(12, Serial No. 149).

Nelson, K. (1985). *Making sense: The acquisition of shared meaning*. Orlando, FL: Academic Press.

Nelson, K. (1988). Constraints on word learning? *Cognitive Development, 3*, 221–246.

Nelson, K. (1996). *Language in cognitive development: The emergence of the mediated mind*. New York: Cambridge University Press.

Nelson, K., Hampson, J., & Shaw, L. K. (1993). Nouns in early lexicons: Evidence, explanations, and implications. *Journal of Child Language, 20*, 61–84.

New, R.S., & Richman, A.L. (1996). Maternal beliefs and infant care practices in Italy and the United States. In S. Harkness & C.M. Super (Eds.), *Parents' Cultural Beliefs Systems* (pp. 385–404). New York: Guilford Press.

Newcomb, A. F., & Bagwell, C. L. (1995). Children's friendship relations: A meta-analytic review. *Psychological Bulletin, 117*, 306–347.

Newcomb, A. F., Bukowski, W. M., & Pattee, L. (1993). Children's peer relations: A meta-analytic review of popular, rejected, neglected, controversial, and average sociometric status. *Psychological Bulletin, 113*, 991–928.

Newcombe, N. S., Drummey, A. B., Fox, N. A., Lie, E., & Ottinger-Alberts, W. (2000). Remembering early childhood: How much, how, and why (or why not). *Current Directions in Psychological Science, 9*, 55–58.

Newcombe, N. S., Mathason, L., & Terlecki, M. (2002). Maximization of spatial competence: More important than finding the cause of sex differences. In A. V. McGillicuddy-De Lisi & R. De Lisi (Eds.), *Biology, society, and behavior: The* development of sex differences in cognition. Greenwich, CT: Ablex.

Newman, P. R. (1982). The peer group. In B. B. Wolman (Ed.), *Handbook of developmental psychology*. Engelwood Cliffs, NJ: Prentice Hall.

Newman, R. S. (2002). How self-regulated learners cope with academic difficulty: The role of adaptive help seeking. *Theory into Practice, 41*, 132–138.

Newport, E. L. (1977). Motherese: The speech of mothers to young children. In N. J. Castellan, D. B. Pisoni, & G. Potts (Eds.), *Cognitive theory* (Vol. 2). Hillsdale, NJ: Erlbaum.

Newport, E. L. (1991). Contrasting concepts of the critical period for language. In S. Carey & R. Gelman (Eds.), *The epigenesis of mind: Essays on biology and cognition*. Hillsdale, NJ: Erlbaum.

New York: The state of Learning. (1999). A report from the regents and State Department of education to the Governor and Legislature.

NICHD Early Child Care Research Network. (1997a). Child care in the first year of life. *Merrill-Palmer Quarterly, 43*, 340–360.

NICHD Early Child Care Research Network (1997b). The effects of infant child care on infant-mother attachment security: Results of the NICHD Study of Early Child Care. *Child Development, 68*, 860–879.

NICHD Early Child Care Research Network (1999). Child care and mother-child interaction in the first three years of life. *Developmental Psychology, 35*, 1399–1413.

NICHD Early Child Care Research Network. (2001). Child care and children's peer interaction at 24 and 36 months: The NICHD Study of Early Child Care. *Child Development, 72*, 1478–1500.

NICHD Early Child Care Research Network. (2002). Early child care and children's development prior to school entry: Results from the NICHD Study of Early Child Care. *American Educational Research Journal, 39*, 133–164.

NICHD Early Child Care Research Network (2003). Does amount of time spent in child care predict socio- emotional adjustment during the transition to kindergarten? *Child Development, 74*, 976–1005.

Ninio, A., & Snow, C. E. (1988). Language acquisition through language use: The functional sources of children's early utterances. In Y. Levy, I. M. Schlesinger, & M. D. S. Braine (Eds.), *Categories and processes in language acquisition*. Hillsdale, NJ: Erlbaum.

Ninio, A., & Snow, C. E. (1999). The development of pragmatics: Learning to use language appropriately. In W. C. Ritchie & T. K. Bhatia (Eds.), *Handbook of child language acquisition*. San Diego, CA: Academic Press.

NIH (2000). *NIH Consensus Statement: Phenylketonuria: Screening and management*. Washington, DC: National Institutes of Health.

No Child Left Behind Act of 2001. Retrieved from http://www.ed.gov/ policy/elsec/leg/esea02/107-110.pdf on 2-26-2006.

No Child Left Behind (2003). A parents' guide. Washington, DC: U.S. Department of Education.

Noble, C., & Bradford, W. (2000). *Getting it right for boys and girls*. London: Routledge.

Nord, M., Andrews, M., & Carlson, S. (2004). *Household Food Security in the United States*, 2004/ERR-11, USDA, Economic Research Service, Retrieved March 16, 2006 from http://www.ers.usda.gov/publications/fanrr42/fanrr42.pdf

North, A. S., & Noyes, J. M. (2002). Gender influences on children's computer attitudes and cognition. *Computers in Human Behavior, 18*, 135–150.

Nosek, B.A., Banaji, M.R., & Greenwald, A.G. (2002). Math = male, me = female, therefore math ? me. *Journal of Personality & Social Psychology, 83*, 44–59.

Nucci, L. P. (2001). *Education in the moral domain*. New York: Cambridge University Press.

Nucci, L. P., & Nucci, M. S. (1982a). Children's responses to moral and social conventional transgressions in free-play settings. *Child Development, 53*, 1337–1342.

Nucci, L. P., & Nucci, M. S. (1982b). Children's social interactions in the context of moral and conventional transgressions. *Child Development, 53*, 403–412.

Nurmi, J.E., & Aunola, K. (2005). Task-motivation during the first school years: A person-oriented approach to longitudinal data. *Learning & Instruction, 15*, 103–122.

Nuttall, R. L., & Pezaris, E. (2001). Spatial-mechanical reasoning skills versus mathematical self-confidence as mediators of gender differences on mathematics subtests using cross-national gender-based items. *Journal for Research in Mathematics Education, 32*, 28–57.

Nybo-Anderson, A. M., Wohlfahrt, J., Christens, P., Olsen, J., & Melbye, M. (2000). Maternal age and fetal loss: population based register linkage study. *BMJ, 24*, 320(7251), 170–812.

Nye, B., Hedges, L. V., & Konstantopoulos, S. (2001). Are effects of small classes cumulative? Evidence from a Tennessee experiment. *Journal of Educational Research, 94*, 336–345.

Nyiti, R. M. (1982). The validity of "cultural differences explanations" for cross-cultural variation in the rate of Piagetian cognitive development. In D. A. Wagner & H. W. Stevenson (Eds.), *Cultural perspectives on child development*. San Francisco: W. H. Freeman.

Oakes, J. (1990). Opportunities, achievement, and choice: Women and minority students in science and mathematics. In C. B. Cazden (Ed.), *Review of research in education* (Vol. 16). Washington, DC: American Educational Research Association.

O'Brien, M., & Huston, A. C. (1985). Development of sex-typed play behavior in toddlers. *Developmental Psychology*, 21, 866–871.

Ochs, E., & Schieffelin, B. B. (1984). Language acquisition and socialization: Three developmental stories. In R. Shweder & R. LeVine (Eds.), *Culture theory: Essays on mind, self and emotion* (pp. 276–320). New York: Cambridge University Press.

O'Connor, R. D. (1972). Relative efficacy of modeling, shaping, and the combined procedures for modification of social withdrawal. *Journal of Abnormal Psychology, 79*, 327–334.

O'Connor, T. G., Deater-Deckard, K., Fulker, D., Rutter, M., & Plomin, R. (1998). Genotype-environment correlations in late childhood and early adolescence: Antisocial behavioral problems and coercive parenting. *Developmental Psychology 34*, 970–981.

O'Connor, T. G., Heron, J., Golding, J., Beveridge, M., & Glover, V. (2002). Maternal antenatal anxiety and children's behavioural/ emotional problems at 4 years. *British Journal of Psychiatry, 180*, 502–508.

Ochs, E., & Schieffelin, B. B. (1984). Language acquisition and socialization: Three developmental stories and their implications. In R. Schweder & R. LeVine (Eds.), *Culture theory: Essays on mind, self, and emotion*. Cambridge: Cambridge University Press.

Odom, S. L., & Strain, P. S. (1984). Peer-mediated approaches to promoting children's social interaction: A review. *American Journal of Orthopsychiatry, 54*, 544–557.

Oehler, J. M., & Eckerman, C. D. (1988). Regulatory effects of human speech and touch in premature infants prior to term age. *Infant Behavior and Development, 11*, 249.

Offord, D. R., Lipman, E. L., & Duku, E. K. (2001). Epidemiology of problem behavior up to age 12 years. In R. Loeber & D. P. Farrington (Eds.), *Child delinquents: Development, intervention, and service needs*. Thousand Oaks, CA: Sage.

Ogai, Y. (2004). The relationship between two aspects of self-oriented perfectionism and self-evaluative depression: Using coping styles of uncontrollable events as mediators. *Japanese Journal of Psychology, 75*, 199–206.

Ogbu, J. (1978). *Minority education and caste: The American system in cross-cultural perspective*. New York, Academic Press.

Ogbu, J. U. (1994). Minority status, cultural frame of reference and literacy. In D. Keller-Cohen (Ed.), *Literacy: Interdisciplinary conversations* (pp. 43–62). Albany: State University of New York Press.

Ogle, A., & Mazzullo, L. (2002). *Before your pregnancy*. New York: Ballantine Books.

Ohring, R., Graber, J. A., & Brooks-Gunn, J. (2002). Girls' recurrent and concurrent body dissatisfaction: Correlates and consequences over 8 years. *International Journal of Eating Disorders, 31*, 404–415.

O'Neill, D. K. (1996). Two-year-olds' sensitivity to a parent's knowledge state when making requests. *Child Development, 67*, 659–677.

O'Neill, D. K., Astington, J. W., & Flavell, J. H. (1992). Young children's understanding of the role that sensory experiences play in knowledge acquisition. *Child Development, 63*, 474–490.

O'Neill, D. K., & Chong, S. C. F. (2001). Preschool children's difficulty understanding the types of information obtained through the five senses. *Child Development, 72*, 803–815.

O'Sullivan, L. F., Graber, J. A., & Brooks-Gunn, J. (2001). Adolescent gender development. In J. Worell (Ed.), *Encyclopedia of women and gender* (Vol. 1). San Diego, CA: Academic Press.

Oikawa, M. (2005). Participants' theories of intelligence and pursuit of nonconscious goals. *Japanese Journal of Educational Psychology, 53*, 14–25.

Oishi, S., & Sullivan, H. W. (2005). The mediating role of parental expectations in culture and well-being. *Journal of Personality, 73*, 1267–1294.

Okagaki, L., & Frensch, P. (1994). Effects of video game playing on measures of spatial performance: Gender effects in late adolescence. *Journal of Applied Developmental Psychology, 15*, 33–58.

Okagaki, L., & Frensch, P. A. (1996). Effects of video game playing on measures of spatial performance: Gender effects in late adolescence. In P.M. Greenfield, & R.R. Cocking (Eds.), *Interacting with video* (115–140). Westport, CT: Ablex Publishing.

Okami, P., Weisner, T. S., and Olmstead, R. (2002). Outcome correlates of parent-child bedsharing: An 18-year longitudinal study. *Journal of Developmental and Behavioral Pediatrics, 23* (4), 244–253.

Oliner, S. P., & Oliner, P. M. (1988). *The altruistic personality: Rescuers of Jews in Nazi Europe.* New York: Free Press.

Oller, D. K. (2000). *The emergence of the speech capacity.* Mahwah, NJ: Erlbaum.

Oller, D. K., & Pearson, B. Z. (2002). Assessing the effects of bilingualism. In D. K. Oller (Ed.), *Language and literacy in bilingual children.* Clevedon, UK: Multilingual Matters.

Olson, H. (1994). The effects of prenatal alcohol exposure on child development. *Infants and Young Children, 6,* 10–25.

Olson, S. L., Bates, J. E., Sandy, J. M., & Lanthier, R. (2000). Early developmental precursors of externalizing behavior in middle childhood and adolescence. *Journal of Abnormal Child Psychology, 28,* 119–133.

Olson, S. L., Bates, J. E., & Kaskie, B. (1992). Caregiver-infant interaction antecedents of children's school-age cognitive ability. *Merrill-Palmer Quarterly, 38,* 309–330.

Olson, S. L., & Kashiwagi, K. (2000). Teacher ratings of behavioral self-regulation in preschool children: A Japanese/U.S. comparison. *Journal of Applied Developmental Psychology, 21,* 609–617.

Olweus, D. (1997). Bully/victim problems in school: Facts and intervention. *European Journal of Psychology of Education, 12,* 495–510.

Olweus, D. (2001). Peer harassment: A critical analysis and some important issues. In J. Juvonen & S. Graham (Eds.), *Peer harassment in school: The plight of the vulnerable and victimized.* New York: Guilford.

Olweus, D., Mattison, A., Schalling, D., & Low, H. (1988). Circulating testosterone levels and aggression in adolescent males: A causal analysis. *Psychosomatic Medicine, 50,* 261–272.

Onishi, K. H. & Baillargeon, R. (2005). Do 15-month-old infants understand false beliefs? *Science, 308,* 255–258.

Oram, M. W., & Perrett, D. I. (1996). Integration of form and motion in the anterior superior temporal polysensory area (STPa) of the macaque monkey. *Journal of Neurophysiology, 76,* 109–129.

Orfield, G. (Ed.) (2001). *Diversity challenged: Evidence on the impact of affirmative action.* Harvard Civil Rights Project, Cambridge, MA.

Ornstein, P. A. Baker-Ward, L., Gordon, B. N., Pelphrey, K. A., Tyler, C. S., & Gramzow, E. (2006). The influence of prior knowledge and repeated questioning on children's long-term retention of the details of a pediatric examination. *Developmental Psychology. 42,* 332–344.

Ornstein, P. A., Naus, M. J., & Liberty, C. (1975). Rehearsal and organizational processes in children's memory. *Child Development, 56,* 818–830.

Osherson, D. N. (1990). *An invitation to cognitive science.* Cambridge, MA: MIT Press.

Osofsky, J. D., & Fitzgerald, H. E. (Eds.). (2000). *Handbook of infant mental health.* (Vols. 1–4). New York: Wiley.

Ostrov, J. M., & Keating, C. F. (2004). Gender differences in preschool aggression during free play and structured interactions: An observational study. *Social Development, 13,* 255–277.

Otis, N., Grouzet, F. M., & Pelletier, L. G. (2005). The latent motivational change in academic setting: A three-year longitudinal study. *Journal of Educational Psychology, 97,* 170–183.

Ottaviano, S., Giannotti, F., Cortesi, F., Bruni, O., & Ottaviano, C. (1996). Sleep characteristics in healthy children from birth to 6 years of age in the urban area of Rome. *Sleep, 19,* 13.

Ovando, C. J., Combs, M. C., & Collier, V. P. (2006). *Bilingual & ESL classrooms: Teaching in multicultural contexts.* New York: McGraw-Hill.

Owen, D. R. (1979). Psychological studies in XYY men. In H. L. Vallet & I. H. Porter (Eds.), *Genetic mechanisms of sexual development.* New York: Academic Press.

Oyama, S. (2000). *Evolution's eye: A systems view of the biology-culture divide.* Durham, NC: Duke University Press.

Oyserman, D., Gant, L., & Ager, J. (1995). A socially contextualized model of African American identity: Possible selves and school persistence. *Journal of Personality and Social Psychology, 69,* 1216–1232.

Oyserman, D., & Markus, H. (1990). Possible selves and delinquency. *Journal of Personality and Social Psychology, 59,* 112–125.

Oyserman, D., & Saltz, E. (1993). Competence, delinquency, and attempts to attain possible selves. *Journal of Personality and Social Psychology, 65,* 360–374.

Oyserman, D., Terry, K., & Bybee, D. (2002). A possible selves intervention to enhance school involvement. *Journal of Adolescence, 25,* 313–326.

Paarlberg, K. M., Vingerhoets, A., Passchier, J., & Dekker, G. A. (1995). Psychosocial factors and pregnancy outcome: A review with emphasis on methodological issues. *Journal of Psychosomatic Research, 39,* 563–595.

Pachter, L. M., & Harwood, R. L. (1996). Culture and child behavior and psychosocial development. *Developmental and Behavioral Pediatrics, 17*(3), 191–197.

Packard, B. W-L., & Nguyen, D. (2003). Science career-related possible selves of adolescent girls: A longitudinal study. *Journal of Career Development, 29,* 251–263.

Padilla-Walker, L. M., & Thompson, R. A. (2005). Combating conflicting messages of values: A closer look at parental strategies. *Social Development, 14* (2), 305–323.

Paikoff, R. L., & Brooks-Gunn, J. (1990). Physiological processes: What role do they play during the transition to adolescence? In R. Montemayor, G. R. Adams, & T. Gullotta (Eds.), *From childhood to adolescence*: Vol. 2. *Advances in adolescent development.* London: Sage.

Pajares, F., & Miller, M. D. (1994). Role of self-efficacy and self-concept beliefs in mathematical problem solving: A path analysis. *Journal of Educational Psychology, 86,* 193–203.

Pallas, A. M., Entwisle, D. R., Alexander, K. L., & Stluka, M. F. (1994). Ability-group effects: Instructional, social, or institutional? *Sociology of Education, 67,* 27–46.

Paneth, N. S. (1995). *The problem of low birth weight. The future of children* (Vol. 5. No. 1). Los Angeles: Packard Foundation.

Pang, V. O. (2001). *Multicultural education: A caring-centered, reflective approach.* New York: McGraw-Hill.

Panigrahy, A., Filiano, J. J., Sleeper, L. A., et al. (1997). Decreased kainite binding in the arcuate nucleus of the sudden infant death syndrome. *Journal of Neuropathological Experimental Neurology, 56,* 1253–1261.

Parikh, B. (1980). Development of moral judgment and its relation to family environment factors in Indian and American families. *Child Development, 51,* 1030–1039.

Paris, S. G., & Oka, E. R. (1986). Children's reading strategies, meta-cognition, and motivation. *Developmental Review, 6,* 25–56.

Parke, R. D. (1977). Some effects of punishment on children's behavior-revisited. In E. M. Hetherington & R. D. Parke (Eds.), *Contemporary readings in child psychology.* New York: McGraw-Hill.

Parke, R. D. (1996). *Fatherhood.* Cambridge, MA: Harvard University Press.

Parke, R. D. (2002). Fathers and families. In M. H. Bornstein (Ed.), *Handbook of parenting* (2nd ed., Vol. 3). Mahwah, NJ: Erlbaum.

Parke, R. D., & Buriel, R. (1998). Socialization in the family: Ethnic and ecological perspectives. In W. Damon (Series Ed.)& N. Eisenberg (Vol. Ed.), *Handbook of child psychology:* Vol. 3. *Social, emotional, and personality development* (5th ed.). New York: Wiley.

Parke, R. D., & Ladd, G. W. (Eds.). (1992). *Family-peer relationships: Modes of linkage.* Hillsdale, NJ: Erlbaum.

Parke, R. D., Simpkins, S. D., McDowell, D. J., Kim, M., Killian, C., Dennis, J., et al. (2002). Relative contributions of families and peers to children's social development. In P. K. Smith & C. H. Hart (Eds.), *Blackwell handbook of childhood social development.* Malden, MA: Blackwell Publishers.

Parke, R. D., & Slaby, R. G. (1983). The development of aggression. In P. H. Mussen (Series Ed.) & E. M. Hetherington (Vol. Ed.), *Handbook of child psychology:* Vol. 4. *Socialization, personality, and social development* (4th ed.). New York: Wiley.

Parke, R. D., & Tinsley, B. R. (1981). The father's role in infancy: Determinants of involvement in caregiving and play. In M.E. Lamb (Ed.), *The role of the father in child development* (2nd ed., pp. 429–457). New York: Wiley.

Parker, J. G., Rubin, K. H., Price, J. M., & DeRosier, M. E. (1995). Peer relationships, child development, and adjustment: A developmental psychopathology perspective. In D. Cicchetti & D. J. Cohen (Eds.), *Developmental psychopathology:* Vol. 2. *Risk, disorder, and adaptation.* New York: Wiley.

Parmelee, A. H., & Garbanati, J. (1987). Clinical neurobehavioral aspects of state organization in newborn infants. In A. Kobayashi (Ed.), *Neonatal brain and behavior.* Nagoya, Japan: University of Nagoya Press.

Parmelee, A. H., & Sigman, M. D. (1983). Perinatal brain development and behavior. In P. H. Mussen (Series Ed.) & M. M. Haith & J. J. Campos (Vol. Eds.), *Handbook of child psychology*: Vol. 2. *Infancy and developmental psychobiology* (4th ed.). New York: Wiley.

Parten, M. B. (1932). Social participation among preschool children. *Journal of Abnormal and Social Psychology, 27,* 243–269.

Pascalis, O., De Schonen, S., Morton, J., & Deruelle, C. (1995). Mother's face recognition by neonates: A replication and an extension. *Infant Behavior and Development, 18,* 79–85.

Pasch, L. A. (2001). Confronting fertility problems. In A Baum, T Revenson, & J Singer (Eds.). *The Handbook of Health Psychology.* Mahwah, NJ: Lawrence Erlbaum.

Passarotti, A. M., Paul, B. M., Bussiere, J. R., Buxton, R. B., Wong, E. C., & Stiles, J. (2003). The development of face and location processing: An FMRI study. *Developmental Science, 6,* 100–117.

Patterson, C. J. (1992). Children of lesbian and gay parents. *Child Development, 63,* 1025–1042.

Patterson, C. J. (1995). Lesbian and gay parenthood. In M. H. Bornstein (Ed.), *Handbook of parenting*: Vol. 3. *Status and social conditions of parenting.* Mahwah, NJ: Erlbaum.

Patterson, C. J. (2002). Lesbian and gay parenthood. In M. Bornstein (Ed.). *Handbook of parenting* (2nd ed., Vol. 3). Mahwah, NJ: Erlbaum.

Patterson, C. J., & Chan, R. W. (1999). Families headed by lesbian and gay parents. In M. E. Lamb (Ed.), *Parenting and child development in "nontraditional" families*. Mahwah, NJ: Erlbaum.

Patterson, G. R., Reid, J. B., & Dishion, T. J. (1992). *Antisocial boys*. Eugene, OR: Castalia.

Patterson, M. L., & Werker, J. F. (2002). Infants' ability to match dynamic phonetic and gender information in the face and voice. *Journal of Experimental Child Psychology, 81*, 93–115.

Patterson, G. R. (1982). *Coercive family process*. Eugene, OR: Castalia.

Patterson, G. R., & Fisher, P. A. (2002). Recent development in our understanding of parenting: Bidirectional effects, causal modeling, and the search for parsimony. In Marc H. Bornstein (Ed.), *Handbook of parenting*: Vol. 5: *Practical issues in parenting* (2nd ed.), pp. 59–88. Mahwah, NJ: Lawrence Erlbaum.

Payne, A. C., Whitehurst, G. J., & Angell, A. L. (1994). The role of the home literacy environment in the development of language ability in preschool children from low-income families. *Early Childhood Research Quarterly, 9*, 427–440.

Peake, P. K., Hebl, M., & Mischel, W. (2002). Strategic attention deployment for delay of gratification in working and waiting situations. *Developmental Psychology, 38*, 313–326.

Pecheux, M., Lepecq, J., & Salzarulo, P. (1988). Oral activity and exploration in 12-month-old infants. *British Journal of Developmental Psychology, 6*, 245–256.

Pederson, D. R., & Ter Vrugt, D. (1973). The influence of amplitude and frequency of vestibular stimulation on the activity of two-month-old infants. *Child Development, 44*, 122–128.

Peiper, A. (1963). *Cerebral function in infancy and adulthood*. New York: Consultants Bureau.

Pelaez-Nogueras, M., Field, T., Cigales, M., Gonzalez, A., & Clasky, S. (1994). Infants of depressed mothers show less "depressed" behavior with their nursery teachers. *Infant Mental Health Journal, 15*, 358–367.

Pelham, W. E., & Hinshaw, S. P. (1992). Behavior intervention for attention-deficit hyperactivity disorder. In S. M. Turner, K. S. Calhoun, & H. E. Adams (Eds.), *Handbook of clinical behavior therapy* (2nd ed.). New York: Wiley.

Pellegrini, A. D., & Bartini, M. (2001). Dominance in early adolescent boys: Affiliative and aggressive dimensions and possible functions. *Merrill-Palmer Quarterly, 47*, 142–163.

Penner, S. G. (1987). Parental responses to grammatical and ungrammatical child utterances. *Child Development, 58*, 376–384.

Pennington, B. F. (2001). Genetic methods. In C. A. Nelson & M. Lucian. (Eds.), *Handbook of developmental cognitive neuroscience*. Cambridge, MA: MIT Press.

Pepler, D. J., King, G., & Byrd, W. (1991). A social-cognitively based social skills training program for aggressive children. In D. J. Pepler & K. H. Rubin (Eds.), *The development and treatment of childhood aggression*. Hillsdale, NJ: Erlbaum.

Perry, D. G., & Bussey, K. (1979). The social learning theory of sex differences: Imitation is alive and well. *Journal of Personality and Social Psychology, 37*, 1699–1712.

Perry, D. G., Perry, L. C., & Weiss, R. J. (1989). Sex differences in the consequences that children anticipate for aggression. *Developmental Psychology, 25*, 312–319.

Peters, D. P. (1991). The influence of stress and arousal on the child witness. In J. Doris (Ed.), *The suggestibility of children's recollections*. Washington, DC: American Psychological Association.

Petersen, A. C. (1987). The nature of biological-psychosocial interactions: The sample case of early adolescence. In R. M. Lerner & T. L. Foch (Eds.), *Biological-psychosocial interactions in early adolescence*. Hillsdale, NJ: Erlbaum.

Petersen, A. C. (1988). Adolescent development. *Annual Review of Psychology, 39*, 583–607.

Peterson, C., & Wellman, H. M. & Liu, D. (2005). Steps in theory-of-mind development for children with deafness or autism. *Child Development, 76*, 502–517.

Peterson, L. (1983a). Influence of age, task competence, and responsibility focus on children's altruism. *Developmental Psychology, 19*, 141–148.

Peterson, L. (1983b). Role of donor competence, donor age, and peer presence on helping in an emergency. *Developmental Psychology, 19*, 873–880.

Peterson, C., & Biggs, M. (2001). "I was really, really, really mad!" Children's use of evaluative devices in narratives about emotional events. *Sex Roles, 45*, 801–825 .

Peterson, D. M., Marcia, J. E., & Carpendale, J. I. M. (2004). Identity: Does thinking make it so? In C. Lightfoot, C. Lalonde, & M. Chandler (Eds.), *Changing conceptions of psychological life*. Mahwah, NJ: Erlbaum.

Petrill, S.A., Plomin, R., DeFries, J.C., & Hewitt, J.K. (2003). Nature, nurture, and adolescent development. In S.A. Petrill, R. Plomin, J.C. DeFries, & J.K. Hewitt (Eds.), *Nature, nurture, and the transition to early adolescence* (pp. 3-12). New York: Oxford University Press.

Petrill, S. A., Lipton, P. A., Hewitt, J. K., Plomin, R., Cherny, S. S., Corley, R., & DeFries, J. C. (2004). Genetic and environmental contributions to general cognitive ability through the first 16 years of life. *Developmental Psychology, 40*, 805–812.

Pettit, G. S., Bakshi, A., Dodge, K. A., & Coie, J. D. (1990). The emergence of social dominance in young boys' play groups: Developmental differences and behavior correlates. *Developmental Psychology, 26*, 1017–1025.

Pettit, G. S., & Dodge, K. A. (2003). Violent children: Bridging development, intervention, and public policy. *Developmental Psychology, 39*, 187–188.

Pettit, G. S., Laird, R. D., Dodge, K.A., Bates, J. E., & Criss, M. M. (2001). Antecedents and behavior-problem outcomes of parental monitoring and psychological control in early adolescence. *Child Development, 72*, 583–598.

Pezdek, K., Berry, T., & Renno, P.A. (2002). Children's mathematics achievement: The role of parents' perceptions and their involvement in homework. *Journal of Educational Psychology, 94*, 771–777.

Phillips, D. A. (1987). Socialization of perceived academic competence among highly competent children. *Child Development, 58*, 1308–1320.

Phillips, R. B., Sharma, R., Premachandra, B. R., Vaughn, A., J., & Reyes-Lee, M. (1996). Intrauterine exposure to cocaine: Effect on neurobehavior of neonates. *Infant Behavior and Development, 19*, 71–81.

Phinney, J. S., Ong, A., & Madden, T. (2000). Cultural values and intergenerational value discrepancies in immigrant and non-immigrant families. *Child Development, 71*, 528–539.

Phinney, J. S., Romero, I., & Nava, M. (2001). The role of language, parents, and peers in ethnic

identity among adolescents in immigrant families. *Journal of Youth & Adolescence, 30*, 135–153.

Piaget, J. (1926). *The language and thought of the child*. New York: Harcourt Brace.

Piaget, J. (1932). *The moral judgment of the child*. London: Routledge and Kegan Paul.

Piaget, J. (1951). *Play, dreams, and imitation in childhood*. New York: Norton.

Piaget, J. (1952). *The origins of intelligence in children*. New York: International Universities Press.

Piaget, J. (1954). *The construction of reality in the child*. New York: Basic Books.

Piaget, J. (1957). Logique et equilibre dans les comportements du sujet. In L. Apostel, B. Mandelbrot, & J. Piaget (Eds.), *Etudes d'epistemologie genetique* (Vol. 2). Paris: Presses Universitaires de France.

Piaget, J. (1965). *Developments in pedagogy*. Reprinted in H. E. Gruber & J. J. Vonèche (Eds.), *The essential Piaget: An interpretive reference and guide* (pp. 696–719). New York: Basic Books, 1977.

Piaget, J. (1968). *On the development of memory and identity*. Barre, MA: Clark University Press and Barre Publishers.

Piaget, J. (1969). *The child's conception of time*. London: Routledge & Kegan Paul.

Piaget, J. (1970). *The child's conception of movement and speed*. London: Routledge & Kegan Paul.

Piaget, J. (1971). *Science of education and the psychology of the child*. New York: Viking.

Piaget, J. (1972). Intellectual evolution from adolescence to adulthood. *Human Development, 15*, 112.

Piaget, J. (1976). *To understand is to invent: The future of education*. New York: Penguin.

Piaget, J. (1977). *The development of thought: Equilibration of cognitive structures*. New York: Wiley.

Piaget, J. (1983). Piaget's theory. In P. H. Mussen (Series Ed.) & W. Kessen (Vol. Ed.), *Handbook of child psychology*: Vol. 1. *History, theory, and methods* (4th ed.). New York: Wiley.

Piaget, J., & Inhelder, B. (1956). *The child's conception of space*. London: Routledge & Kegan Paul.

Piaget, J., & Inhelder, B. (1974). *The child's construction of quantities*. London: Routledge & Kegan Paul.

Piaget, J., Inhelder, B., & Szeminska, A. (1960). *The child's conception of geometry*. New York: Basic Books.

Piaget, J., & Szeminska, A. (1952). *The child's conception of number*. New York: Basic Books.

Pick, H. L. Jr. (1992). Eleanor J. Gibson: Learning to perceive and perceiving to learn. *Developmental Psychology, 28*, 787–794.

Pillard, R. C. (1990). The Kinsey scale: Is it familial? In D. P. McWhirter, S. A. Sanders, & J. M. Reinsch (Eds.), *Homosexuality/heterosexuality: Concepts of sexual orientation*. The Kinsey Institute series, Vol. 2. New York: Oxford University Press.

Pine, J. M., Lieven, E. V. M., & Rowland, C. F. (1997). Stylistic variation at the "single-word stage": Relations between maternal speech characteristics and children's vocabulary composition and usage. *Child Development, 68*, 807–819.

Pinker, S. (1987). The bootstrapping problem in language acquisition. In B. MacWhinney (Ed.), *Mechanisms of language acquisition*. Hillsdale, NJ: Erlbaum.

Pinker, S. (1994). *The language instinct: How the mind creates language*. New York: William Morrow.

Pinker, S. (1999). *Words and rules*. New York: HarperCollins.

Pinquart, M., & Silbereisen, R. K. (2004). Human development in times of social change: Theoretical considerations and research needs. *International Journal of Behavioral Development, 28*(4), 289–298.

Pinto, A., Folkers, E., & Sines, J. O. (1991). Dimensions of behavior and home environment in school-age children: India and the United States. *Journal of Cross-Cultural Psychology, 22,* 491–508.

Pintrich, P.R. (1999). The role of motivation in promoting and sustaining self-regulated learning. International *Journal of Educational Research, 31,* 459–470.

Pinyerd, B. (1994). Temperament and mother-infant interaction. *Neonatal Network, 13*(4), 16.

Pipp, S., Easterbrooks, M. A., & Harmon, R. J. (1992). The relation between attachment and knowledge of self and mother in one- to three-year-old infants. *Child Development, 63,* 738–750.

Pipp, S., Fischer, K. W., & Jennings, S. (1987). Acquisition of self- and mother knowledge in infancy. *Developmental Psychology, 23,* 86–96.

Pipp-Siegel, S., & Foltz, C. (1997). Toddlers' acquisition of self/other knowledge: Ecological and interpersonal aspects of self and other. *Child Development, 68,* 69–79.

Pleck, J. H. (1997). Paternal involvement: Levels, sources, and consequences. In M. E. Lamb (Ed.), *The role of fathers in child development* (3rd ed.). New York: Wiley.

Plomin, R. (2000a). Behavioral genetics. In M. Bennett (Ed.), *Developmental psychology: Achievements and prospects.* Philadelphia: Psychology Press.

Plomin, R. (2000b). Behavioral genetics in the 21st century. *International Journal of Behavioral Development, 24,* 30–34.

Plomin, R., DeFries, J. C., McClearn, G. E., & Rutter, M. (1997). *Behavioral genetics* (3rd ed.). New York: W. H. Freeman.

Plomin, R., Fulker, D. W., Corley, R., & DeFries, J. C. (1997b). Nature, nurture, and cognitive development from 1 to 16 years: A parentoff-spring adoption study. *Psychological Science, 8,* 442–447.

Plomin, R., & McGuffin, P. (2003). Psychopathology in the postgenomic era. *Annual Review of Psychology, 54,* 205–228.

Plomin, R., & Rutter, M. (1998). Child development, molecular genetics, and what to do with genes once they are found. *Child Development, 69,* 1223–1242.

Plumert, J. M. (1995). Relations between children's overestimation of their physical abilities and accident proneness. *Developmental Psychology, 31,* 866–876.

Plunkett, K., Karmiloff-Smith, A., Bates, E., Elman J. L. & Johnson M. (1997). Connectionism and developmental psychology. *Journal of Child Psychology and Psychiatry, 38,* 53–80.

Pogorzelski, S., & Wheldall, K. (2005). The importance of phonological processing for older low-progress readers. *Educational Psychology in Practice, 2,* 122.

Pollack, W. (1998). *Real boys: Rescuing our sons from the myths of boyhood.* New York: Random House.

Pomerleau, A., Bolduc, D., Malcuit, G., & Cossette, L. (1990). Pink or blue: Environmental gender stereotypes in the first two years of life. *Sex Roles, 22,* 359–367.

Pomerleau, A., Malcuit, G., & Sabatier, C. (1991). Child-rearing practices and parental beliefs in three cultural groups of Montral: Quebècois, Vietnamese, Haitian. In M. H. Bornstein (Ed.), *Cultural approaches to parenting.* Hillsdale, NJ: Erlbaum.

Poole, D. A., & Lindsay, D. S. (2002). Children's suggestibility in the forensic context. In M. L. Eisen, J. A. Quas, & G. S. Goodman (Eds.), *Memory and suggestibility in the forensic context.* Mahwah, NJ: Erlbaum.

Porter, R. H., Balogh, R. D., & Makin, J. W. (1988). Olfactory influences on mother-infant interaction. In C. Rovee-Collier & L. P. Lipsitt (Eds.), *Advances in infancy research* (Vol. 5). Norwood, NJ: Ablex.

Portes, A., & Rumbaut, R. G. (1990). *Immigrant America: A portrait.* Berkeley: University of California Press.

Posada, G., Waters, E., Crowell, J. A., & Lay, K. (1995). Is it easier to use a secure mother as a secure base? Attachment Q-sort correlates of the Adult Attachment Interview. In E. Waters, B. E. Vaughn, G. Posada, & K. Kondo-Ikemura (Eds.), Caregiving, cultural, and cognitive perspectives on secure-base behavior and working models. *Monographs of the Society for Research in Child Development, 60*(23, Serial No. 244).

Post, S. G., Underwood, L. G., Schoss, J. P., & Hurlbut, W. B. (Eds.). (2002). *Altruism and altruistic love: Science, philosophy, and religion in dialogue.* London: Oxford University Press.

Poulin, F., Cillessen, A. H. N., Hubbard, J. A., Coie, J. D., Dodge, K. A., & Schwartz, D. (1997). Children's friends and behavioral similarity in two social contexts. *Social Development, 6,* 224–236.

Poulin-Dubois, D., Serbin, L. A., Eichstedt, J. A., Sen, M. G., & Beissel, C. F. (2002). Men don't put on make-up: Toddlers' knowledge of the gender stereotyping of household activities. *Social Development, 11,* 166–181.

Poulin-Dubois, D., Serbin, L. A., Ken-Yon, B., & Derbyshire, A. (1994). Infants' intermodal knowledge about gender. *Developmental Psychology, 30,* 436–442.

Povinelli, D. J. (1995). The unduplicated self. In P. Rochat (Ed.), *The self in infancy. Theory and research.* Amsterdam: Elsevier.

Povinelli, D. J., & Eddy, T. J. (1996). What young chimpanzees know about seeing. *Monographs of the Society for Research in Child Development, 61.* No. 247, Chicago: University of Chicago Press.

Povinelli, D. J. & Giambrone, S. (2001). Reasoning about beliefs: A human specialization? *Child Development, 72,* 691–695.

Power, T. G. (2000). *Play and exploration in children and animals.* Mahwah, NJ: Erlbaum.

Power-deFur, L.A., & Orelove, F.P. (1997). *Inclusive education: Practical implementation of the least restrictive environment.* Gaithersburg, MD: Aspen Publishers.

Powlishta, K. K. (1995). Intergroup processes in childhood: Social categorization and sex role development. *Developmental Psychology, 31,* 781–788.

Powlishta, K. K., Sen, M. G., Serbin, L. A., Poulin-DuBois, D., & Eichstedt, J. A. (2001). From infancy through middle childhood: The role of social and cognitive factors in becoming gendered. In R. K. Unger (Ed.), *Handbook of the psychology of women and gender.* New York: Wiley.

Prader, A., Tanner, J. M., & Von Harnack, G. A. (1963). Catch up growth following illness or starvation. *Journal of Pediatrics, 62,* 646–659.

Prencipe, A., & Zelazo, P. D. (2005). Development of affective decision-making for self and other: Evidence for the integration of first- and third-person perspectives. *Psychological Science, 16,* 501–505.

Pressley, M. (1992). How not to study strategy discovery. *American Psychologist, 47,* 12401–241.

Pressley, M., Borkowski, J. G., & O'Sullivan, J. (1985). Children's metamemory and the teaching of memory strategies. In D. L. Forrest-Pressley, G. E. MacKinnon, & T. G. Waller (Eds.), *Metacognition, cognition, and human performance: Vol. 1. Theoretical perspectives.* New York: Academic Press.

Pressley, M., Forrest-Pressley, D., & Elliot-Faust, D. J. (1988). What is strategy instructional enrichment and how to study it: Illustrations from research on children's prose memory and comprehension. In F. E. Weinert & M. Perlmutter (Eds.), *Memory development: Universal changes and individual differences.* Hillsdale, NJ: Erlbaum.

Price, J. M. (1996). Friendship of maltreated children and adolescents: Contexts for expressing and modifying relationship history. In W. M. Bukowski, A. F. Newcomb, & W. H. Hartup (Eds.), *The company they keep.* New York: Cambridge University Press.

Price-Williams, D., Gordon, W., & Ramirez, M. (1969). Skill and conservation: A study of pottery-making children. *Developmental Psychology, 1,* 769.

Prior, M., Smart, M. A., Sanson, A., & Oberklaid, F. (1993). Sex differences in psychological adjustment from infancy to 8 years. *Journal of the Academy of Child and Adolescent Psychiatry, 32,* 291–304.

Proceeding of the National Academy of Sciences. (2002). *Proceedings of the National Academy of Sciences, 99* (1), 309–314.

Procidano, M., & Rogler, L. H. (1989). Homogamous assortative mating among Puerto Rican families: Intergenerational processes and the migration experience. *Behavior Genetics, 19,* 343–354.

Purcell-Gates, V. (1996). Stories, coupons, and the TV Guide: Relationships between home literacy experiences and emergent literacy knowledge. *Reading Research Quarterly, 31,* 406–428.

Putnam, S. P., Sanson, A. V., & Rothbart, M. K. (2002). Child temperament and parenting. In M. H. Bornstein (Ed.), *Handbook of parenting* (2nd ed., Vol. 1). Mahwah, NJ: Erlbaum.

Putnam, S. P., Spiritz, B. L., & Stifter, C. A. (2002). Mother-child coregulation during delay of gratification at 30 months. *Infancy, 3,* 209–225.

Pynoos, R., Frederick, C., & Nader, K. (1987). Life threat and post-traumatic stress in school-age children. *Archives of General Psychiatry, 44,* 1057–1063.

Pynoos, R., Goenjian, A., Tashjian, M., Krakashian, M., Manjikian, A., Manoukian, G., et al. (1993). Post-traumatic stress reactions in children after the 1988 Armenian earthquake. *British Journal of Psychiatry, 163,* 239–247.

Qiaoyan, X., & Fengqiang, G. (2005). Mischel's researches on the delay of gratification. *Psychological Science* (China), 28, 238–240.

Quas, J. A., Goodman, G. S., Bidrose, S., Pipe, M., Craw, S., & Ablin, D. S. (1999). Emotion and memory: Children's long-term remembering, forgetting, and suggestibility. *Journal of Experimental Child Psychology, 72,* 235–270.

Quiggle, N. L., Garber, J., Panak, W. F., & Dodge, K. A. (1992). Social information processing in aggressive and depressed children. *Child Development, 63,* 1305–1320.

Radke-Yarrow, M., & Zahn-Waxler, C. (1986). The role of familial factors in the development of prosocial behavior: Research findings and questions. In D. Olweus, J. Block, & M. Radke-Yarrow (Eds.), *Development of antisocial and prosocial behavior.* Orlando, FL: Academic Press.

Rakic, P. (1988). Specifications of cerebral cortical areas. *Science, 241,* 170–176.

Ramey, C. T., Campbell, F. A., Burchinal, M., Skinner, M. L., Gardner, D. M., & Ramey, S. L. (2000). Persistent effects of early childhood education on high-risk children and their mothers. *Applied Developmental Psychology, 4,* 214.

Ramey, C. T., & Ramey, S. L. (1998). Early intervention and early experience, *American Psychologist, 53,* 109–120.

Ramey, C. T.; Ramey, S. L.; Lanzi, R. G. (2001). Intelligence and experience. In R.J. Sternberg & E. L. Grigorenko, (Eds.), *Environmental effects on cognitive abilities* (pp. 83–115).

Ramsey, P. G. (1991). *Making friends in school: Promoting peer relationships in early childhood.* New York: Teachers College Press.

Rankin, J. L., Lane, D. J., Gibbons, F. X., & Gerrard, M. (2004). Adolescent self-consciousness: Longitudinal age changes and gender differences in two cohorts. *Journal of Research on Adolescence, 14,* 121.

Rasinski, T., & Stevenson, B. (2005). The effects of fast start reading: A fluency-based home improvement reading program, on the reading achievement of beginning readers. *Reading Psychology, an International Quarterly, 26,* 109–125.

Raskin, P. A., & Israel, A. C. (1981). Sex-role imitation in children: Effects of sex of child, sex of model, and sex-role appropriateness of modeled behavior. *Sex Roles, 7,* 1067–1077.

Ratner, N. B. (1988). Patterns of parental vocabulary selection in speech to very young children. *Journal of Child Language, 15,* 481–492.

Raver, C. C. (1996). Relations between social contingency in mother-child interaction and 2-year-olds' social competence. *Developmental Psychology, 32,* 850–859.

Ravn, K. E., & Gelman, S. A. (1984). Rule usage in children's understanding of "big" and "little." *Child Development, 55,* 2141–2150.

Rawlins, W. K. (1992). *Friendship matters: Communication, dialectics, and the life course.* New York: Aldine de Gruyter.

Rayner, K., Foorman, B. R., Perfetti, C. A., Pesetsky, D., & Seidenberg, M. S. (2001). How psychological science informs the teaching of reading. *Psychological Science in the Public Interest, 2,* 31–74.

Read, P. T., & Zalk, S. R. (2001). Academic environments: Gender and ethnicity in U.S. higher education. In J. Worrell (Ed.), *Encyclopedia of women and gender.* San Diego,: Academic Press.

Recht, D. R., & Leslie, L. (1980). Effect of prior knowledge on good and poor readers' memory of text. *Journal of Educational Psychology, 80,* 16–20.

Reddy, V. (1999). Prelinguistic communication. In M. Barrett (Ed.), *The development of language.* Hove, UK: Psychology Press.

Redlinger, W. E., & Park, T. (1980). Language mixing in young bilinguals. *Journal of Child Language, 7,* 337–352.

Regnerus, M. D. (2005). Talking about sex: Religion and patterns of parent-child communication about sex and contraception. *Sociological Quarterly, 46*(1), 79–105.

Reid, J. B. (1993). Prevention of conduct disorder before and after school entry: Relating interventions to developmental findings. *Development and Psychopathology, 5,* 243–262.

Reid, M., Landesman, S., Treder, R., & Jaccard, J. (1989). "My Family and Friends": Six- to twelve-year-old children's perceptions of social support. *Child Development, 60,* 896–910.

Reinisch, J. M., Ziemba-Davis, M., & Sanders, S. A. (1991). Hormonal contributions to sexual dimorphic behavioral development in humans. *Psychoneuroendocrinology, 16,* 213–278.

Reinisch, J. M., & Sanders, S. A. (1992). Prenatal hormonal contributions to sex differences in human cognitive and personality development. In A. A. Gerall & H. Moltz (Eds.), *Sexual differentiation. Handbook of behavioral neurobiology* (Vol. 11). New York: Plenum Press.

Reinisch, J. M., Ziemba-Davis, M., & Sanders, S. A. (1991). Hormonal contributions to sexual dimorphic behavioral development in humans. *Psychoneuroendocrinology, 16,* 213–278.

Reis, O., & Youniss, J. (2004). Patterns in identity change and development in relationships with mothers and friends. *Journal of Adolescent Research, 19,* 31–44.

Reisman, J. E. (1987). Touch, motion and perception. In P. Salapatek & L. Cohen (Eds.), *Handbook of infant perception*: Vol. 1. *From sensation to perception.* New York: Academic Press.

Reiss, D., Neiderhiser, J. M., Hetherington, E. M., & Plomin, R. (2000). *The relationship code: Deciphering genetic and social patterns in adolescent development.* Cambridge, MA: Harvard University Press.

Rescorla, L. A. (1980). Overextension in early language development. *Journal of Child Language, 7,* 321–335.

Rescorla, L. A. (1981). Category development in early language. *Journal of Child Language, 8,* 225–238.

Rest, J., Narvaez, D., Bebeau, M. J., & Thoma, S. J. (1999). *Postconventional moral thinking: A neo-Kohlbergian approach.* Mahwah, NJ: Erlbaum.

Reynolds, A. J. (2003). The added value of continuing early intervention into the primary grades. In Reynolds, A.J. & Wang, M.C. (Eds.) *Early childhood programs for a new century,* pp 163–196. Washington DC: Child Welfare League of America.

Reznick, J. S., & Goldfield, B. A. (1992). Rapid change in lexical development in comprehension and production. *Developmental Psychology, 28,* 406–413.

Rheingold, H. L., & Cook, K. V. (1975). The contents of boys' and girls' rooms as an index of parents' behavior. *Child Development, 46,* 459–463.

Rheingold, H. L., Hay, D. F., & West, M. J. (1976). Sharing in the second year of life. *Child Development, 47,* 1148–1156.

Rheingold, H. L. (1982). Little children's participation in the work of adults, a nascent prosocial behavior. *Child Development, 53,* 114–125.

Rhodes, J., Roffman, J., Reddy, R., Fredriksen, K., & Way, N. (2004). Changes in self-esteem during the middle school years: A latent growth curve study of individual and contextual influences. *Journal of School Psychology, 42,* 243–261.

Rholes, W. S., & Lane, J. W. (1985). Consistency between cognitions and behavior: Cause and consequence of cognitive moral development. In J. B. Pryor & J. D. Day (Eds.), *The development of social cognition.* New York: Springer-Verlag.

Riccio, C. A., Hynd, G. W., Cohen, M. J., & Gonzalez, J. J. (1993). Neurological basis of attention deficit hyperactivity disorder. *Exceptional Children, 60,* 118–124.

Rice, M. L. (1982). Child language: What children know and how. In T.M. Field, A. Huston, H.C. Quay, L. Troll, & G.E. Finley (Eds.), *Review of human development research.* New York: Wiley.

Rice, M. L. (1989). Children's language acquisition. *American Psychologist, 44,* 149–156.

Rice, M. L., Huston, A. C., & Truglio, R. (1990). Words from "Sesame Street": Learning vocabulary white viewing. *Developmental Psychology, 26,* 421–428.

Rice, M. L., & Woodsmall, L. (1988). Lessons from television: Children's word learning when viewing. *Child Development, 59,* 420–429.

Richter, L. (2004).The impact of HIV/AIDS on the development of children. In Robyn Pharaoh, ed., *Monographs for the African Humanity Security Initiative,* No. 109, December.

Rideout, V. J., Foehr, U. G., Roberts, D. F., & Brodie, M. (1999). *Kids and media at the new millennium.* Executive summary. Menlo Park, CA: Kaiser Family Foundation.

Rideout, V. J., Vandewater, E. A., & Wartella, E. A. (2003). *Zero to six: Electronic media in the lives of infants, toddlers, and preschoolers.* A Kaiser Family Foundation Report. Menlo Park, CA: Kaiser Family Foundation.

Riemann, G. (2003). A joint project against the backdrop of a research tradition: An introduction to 'doing biographical research' [36 paragraphs]. Forum Qualitative Sozialforschung/Forum: Qualitative Social Research [On-line Journal], 4(3). Available at: http://www.qualitative-research.net/fqs-texte/3-03/3-03hrsg-e.htm

Rieser, J., Yonas, A., & Wikner, K. (1976). Radial localization of odors by human newborns. *Child Development, 47,* 856–859.

Rigby, K., & Slee, P. (1993). Children's attitudes toward victims. In D. Tattum (Ed.), *Understanding and managing bullying.* Oxford: Heinemann School Management.

Ripple, C. H., Gilliam, W. S., & Chanana, N. (1999). Will fifty cooks spoil the broth? The debate over entrusting Head Start to the states. *American Psychologist, 54,* 327–343.

Rivkees, S. A. (2003). Developing circadian rhythmicity in infants. *Pediatrics, 112*(2), 373–382.

Rivkin, S. G., Hanushek, E. A., & Kain, J. F. (2005). Teachers, schools, and academic achievement. *Econometrica, 73*(2), 417–458.

Rivera, S. M., Wakeley, A., & Langer, J. (1999). The drawbridge phenomenon: Representational reasoning or perceptual preference? *Developmental Psychology, 35,* 427–435.

Robbins, W. J., Brady, S., Hogan, A. G., Jackson, C. M., & Greene, C. W. (1928). *Growth.* New Haven, CT: Yale University Press.

Roberts, D. F., Foehr, U. G., Rideout, V. J., & Brodie, M. (1999). *Kids and media at the new millenium: A comprehensive national analysis of children's media use.* Menlo Park, CA: Kaiser Family Foundation.

Robinson, E. J. (1981). The child's understanding of inadequate messages and communication failure: A problem of ignorance or egocentrism? In W. P. Dickson (Ed.), *Children's oral communication skills.* New York: Academic Press.

Robinson, C. C., & Morris, J. T. (1986). The gender-stereotyped nature of Christmas toys received by 36-, 48-, and 60-month old children: A comparison between nonrequested vs. requested toys. *Sex Roles, 15,* 21–32.

Rochat, P. (1989). Object manipulation and exploration in 2- to 5-month-old infants. *Developmental Psychology, 25*, 871–884.

Rochat, P., & Morgan, R. (1995). Spatial determinants in the perception of self-produced leg movements by 3- to 5-month-old infants. *Developmental Psychology, 31*, 626–636.

Rochat, P., & Striano, T. (2002). Who's in the mirror? Self-other discrimination in specular images by four- and nine-month-old infants. *Child Development, 73*, 35–46.

Rochat, P. (2003). Five levels of self-awareness as they unfold early in life. *Consciousness and cognition: An International Journal, 12*, 717–731.

Rochat, P., & Striano, T. (2002). Who's in the mirror? Self-other discrimination in specular images by four- and nine-month-old infants. *Child Development, 73*, 35–46.

Roder, B, Rosler, F., & Hennighausen, E. (1997). Different cortical activation patterns in blind and sighted humans during encoding and transformation of haptic images. *Psychophysiology, 34*, 292–307.

Roder et al. (2000). Event-related potentials during auditory language processing in congenitally blind and sighted people. (eng; includes abstract) By Röder, B., Rösler, F., Neville, H. J. *Neuropsychologia, 38* (11), pp. 1482–1502;

Roffwarg et al., (1966). Ontogenetic development of the human sleep-dream cycle. *Science, 152*, 604–619.

Rogers, T. T., & McClelland, J. L. (2005). A parallel distributed processing approach to semantic cognition: Applications to conceptual development. In L. Gershkoff-Stowe & D. Rakison (Eds.). *Building object categories in developmental time* (pp. 335–387). Mahwah, NJ: Erlbaum.

Rogler, L. H., & Santana Cooney, R. (1984). *Puerto Rican families in New York City: Intergenerational processes.* Maplewood, NJ: Waterfront.

Rogoff, B. (1990). *Apprenticeship in thinking.* New York: Oxford University Press.

Rogoff, B. (1998). Cognition as a collaborative process. In W. Damon (Series Ed.) & D. Kuhn & R. S. Siegler (Vol. Eds.), *Handbook of child psychology: Vol. 2. Cognition, perception, and language* (5th ed.). New York: Wiley.

Rogoff, B. (2003). *The cultural nature of human development.* New York: Oxford University Press.

Rogoff, B., & Chavajay, P. (1995). What's become of research on the cultural basis of cognitive development? *American Psychologist, 50*, 859–887.

Rogoff, B., Mistry, J., Göncü, A., & Mosier, C. (1993). Guided participation in cultural activity by toddlers and caregivers. *Monographs of the Society for Research in Child Development, 58* (8, Serial No. 236).

Rogosch, F. A., Cicchetti, D., Shields, A., & Toth, S. L. (1995). Parenting dysfunction in child maltreatment. In M. H. Bornstein (Ed.), *Handbook of parenting: Vol. 4. Applied and practical parenting.* Mahwah, NJ: Erlbaum.

Rohner, R. P. (1975). *They love me, they love me not: A worldwide study of the effects of parental acceptance and rejection.* New Haven, CT: HRAF Press. [Reprinted by Rohner Research Publications]

Rohner, R. P. (1986). *The warmth dimension: Foundations of parental acceptance-rejection theory.* Newbury Park, CA: Sage Publications, Inc.[Reprinted by Rohner Research Publications]

Rohner, R. P. (1994). Patterns of parenting: The warmth dimension in cross-cultural perspective. In W. J. Lonner and R. S. Malpass (Eds.), *Readings in psychology and culture* (pp. 113–120). Needham Heights, MA: Allyn and Bacon.

Rohner, R. P. (2005). Parental acceptance-rejection bibliography [on-line at www.cspar.uconn.edu]

Rohner, R. P., & Khaleque, A. (Eds.). (2005). *Handbook for the study of parental acceptance and rejection.* Storrs, CT: Rohner Research. [order from www.cspar.uconn.edu]

Rohner, R. P., Khaleque, A., & Cournoyer, D. E. (2005). Parental acceptance-rejection theory, methods, evidence, and implications. *Ethos, 33*, 299–334.

Roid, G. (2003). *Stanford-Binet Intelligence Scales* (5th ed.). Chicago: Riverside Publishing.

Roisman, G. I., Madsen, S. D., Hennighausen, K. H., & Collins, W. A. (2001). The coherence of dyadic behavior across parent-child and romantic relationships as mediated by the internalized representation of experience. *Attachment and Human Development, 3*, 156–172.

Rommetveit, R. (1979). On the architecture of intersubjectivity. In R. Rommetveit & R. M. Blakar (Eds.), *Studies of language, thought, and verbal communication.* New York: Academic Press.

Rooks J.P., Weatherby N.L., Ernst E.K., Stapleton S., Rosen D., Rosenfield A. (1989). Outcomes of care in birth centers. The National Birth Center Study. *New England Journal of Medicine, 321*, 180–411.

Roopnarine, J. L. (1984). Sex-typed socialization in mixed-age preschool classrooms. *Child Development, 55*, 1078–1084.

Rose, S. A., Gottfried, A. W., & Bridger, W. H. (1981). Cross-modal transfer and information processing by the sense of touch in infancy. *Developmental Psychology, 17*, 90–98.

Rose, S. A., & Ruff, H. A. (1987). Cross-modal abilities in human infants. In J. D. Osofsky (Ed.), *Handbook of infant development* (2nd ed.). New York: Wiley.

Rose, A., Swenson, L., & Waller, E., (2004). Overt and relational aggression and perceived popularity: Developmental differences in concurrent and prospective relations. *Developmental Psychology, 40*, 378–387.

Rosen, G. D., Galaburda, A. M., & Sherman, G. F. (1990). The ontogeny of anatomic asymmetry: Constraints derived from basic mechanisms. In A. B. Scheibel & A. F. Wechsler (Eds.), *Neurobiology of higher cognitive function.* New York: Guilford.

Rosengren, K. S., & Braswell, G. (2001). Variability in children's reasoning. In H. W. Reese & R. Kail (Eds.), *Advances in child development and behavior* (Vol. 28). San Diego, CA: Academic Press.

Rosenholtz, S. J., & Simpson, C. (1984). The formation of ability conceptions: Developmental trend or social construction? *Review of Educational Research, 64*, 479–530.

Rosenstein, D., & Oster, H. (1988). Differential facial responses to four basic tastes in newborns. *Child Development, 59*, 1555–1568.

Rosenthal, R., & DiMatteo, M. R. (2001). Meta-Analysis: Recent developments in quantitative methods in literature reviews. *Annual Review of Psychology, 52*, 59–82.

Ross, M., Heine, S. J., Wilson, A. E., & Sugimori, S. (2005). Cross-cultural discrepancies in self-appraisals. *Personality & Social Psychology Bulletin, 31*, 1175–1188.

Ross, H. S., & Lollis, S. P. (1989). A social relations analysis of toddler peer relationships. *Child Development, 60*, 1082–1091.

Ross, H. S., & Lollis, S. P. (1987). Communication within infant social games. *Developmental Psychology, 23*, 241–248.

Ross, J., Zinn, A., & McCauley, E. (2000). Neurodevelopmental and psychosocial aspects of Turner syndrome. *Mental Retardation and Developmental Disabilities Research Review, 6*, 135–141.

Rosso P. (1990). *Nutrition and metabolism in pregnancy.* New York: Oxford University Press.

Rothbart, M. K., & Hwang, J. (2005). Temperament and the development of competence and motivation. In A.J. Elliot & C.S. Dweck (eds.), *Handbook of competence and motivation.* New York: Guilford.

Rothbart, M. K., & Posner, M. I. (1985). Temperament and the development of self-regulation. In L. C. Hartledge & C. F. Telzrow (Eds.), *The neuropsychology of individual differences: A developmental perspective.* New York: Plenum.

Rothbart, M. K., & Rueda, M. R. (2005). The development of effortful control. In U. Mayr, E. Awh, & S. Keele (Eds.), *Developing individuality in the human brain: A tribute to Michael I. Posner* (167188). Washington, DC: American Psychological Association.

Rothbaum F., Pott, M., Azuma, H., Miyake, K., & Weisz, J. (2000). The development of close relationships in Japan and the United States: Paths of symbiotic harmony and generative tension. *Child Development, 71*, 1121–1142.

Rovee-Collier, C. K. (1987). Learning and memory in infancy. In J. Osofsky (Ed.), *Handbook of infant development* (2nd ed.). New York: Wiley.

Rovee-Collier, C. K. (1999). The development of infant memory. *Current Directions in Psychological Science, 8*, 80–85.

Rovee-Collier, C. K., Hartshorn, K., & DiRubbo, M. (1999). Long-term maintenance of infant memory. *Developmental Psychobiology, 35*, 91–102.

Rovee-Collier, C. K., & Shyi, G. (1992). A functional and cognitive analysis of infant long-term retention. In M. L. Howe, C. J. Brainerd, & V. F. Reyna (Eds.), *Development of long-term retention.* New York: Springer-Verlag.

Royal, C. W., & Baker, S. B. (2005). Effects of a deliberate moral education program on parents of elementary school students. *Journal of Moral Education, 34*, 215–230.

Royer, J. M., Tronsky, L. N., Chan, Y., Jackson, S. J., & Marchant, H. III (1999). Math-fact retrieval and the cognitive mechanism underlying gender differences in math test performance. *Contemporary Educational Psychology, 24*, 181–266.

Rubenstein, J., & Howes, C. (1976). The effect of peers on toddler interaction with mother and toys. *Child Development, 47*, 597–605.

Rubenstein, A. J., Kalakanis, L., & Langlois, J. H. (1999). Infant preferences for attractive faces: A cognitive explanation. *Developmental Psychology, 35*, 848–855.

Rubin, K. H. (1988). *The social problem-solving test revised.* Waterloo, Ontario: University of Waterloo Press.

Rubin, K. H. (1989). The Play Observation Scale (POS). Unpublished manuscript. University of Waterloo, Waterloo, Ontario.

Rubin, K. H., Burgess, K. B., & Coplan, R. J. (2002). Social withdrawal and shyness. In P. K. Smith & C. H. Hart (Eds.), *Blackwell handbook of childhood social development.* Malden, MA: Blackwell Publishers.

Rubin, K. H., Burgess, K. B., Dwyer, K. M., & Hastings, P. D. (2003). Predicting preschoolers' externalizing behaviors from toddler temperament, conflict, and maternal negativity. *Developmental Psychology, 39*, 164–176.

Rubin, K. H., Bukowski, W., & Parker, J. G. (1998). Peer interactions, relationships, and groups. In W. Damon (Series Ed.) & N.

Eisenberg (Vol. Ed.), *Handbook of child psychology*: Vol. 3. *Social, emotional, and personality development* (5th ed.). New York: Wiley.

Rubin, K. H., Fein, G. G., & Vandenberg, B. (1983). Play. In P. H. Mussen (Series Ed.) & E. M. Hetherington (Vol. Ed.), *Handbook of child psychology*: Vol. 4. *Socialization, personality, and social development* (4th ed.). New York: Wiley.

Rubin, K. H., & Krasnor, L. R. (1986). Social-cognitive and social behavioral perspectives on problem solving. In M. Perlmutter (Ed.), *Minnesota symposia on child psychology*: Vol. 19. *Cognitive perspectives on children's social and behavioral development*. Hillsdale, NJ: Erlbaum.

Rubin, K. H., Lynch, D., Coplan, R., Rose-Krasnor, L., & Booth, C. L. (1994). "Birds of a feather . . .": Behavioral concordances and preferential personal attraction in children. *Child Development, 65*, 1778–1785.

Rubin, J. Z., Provenzano, F. J., & Luria, Z. (1974). The eye of the beholder: Parents' views on sex of newborns. *American Journal of Orthopsychiatry, 44*, 512–519.

Rubin, K. H., & Rose-Krasnor, L. (1992). Interpersonal problem solving and social competence in children. In W. B. Van Hasselt & M. Hersen (Eds.), *Handbook of social development*. New York: Plenum.

Rubin, K. H., Stewart, S. L., & Chen, X. (1995). Parents of aggressive and withdrawn children. In M. H. Bornstein (Ed.), *Handbook of parenting*. Vol. 1. *Children and parenting*. Mahwah, NJ: Erlbaum.

Rubin, K. H., Watson, K. S., & Jambor, T. W. (1978). Free-play behaviors in preschool and kindergarten children. *Child Development, 49*, 534–536.

Rubin, Z. (1980). *Children's friendships*. Cambridge, MA: Harvard University Press.

Ruble, D. N., & Flett, G. L. (1988). Conflicting goals in self-evaluative information seeking: Developmental and ability level analyses. *Child Development, 59*, 97–106.

Ruble, D. N., & Frey, K. S. (1987). Social comparison and outcome evaluation in group contexts. In J. C. Masters & W. P. Smith (Eds.), *Social comparison, social justice, and relative deprivation*. Hillsdale, NJ: Erlbaum.

Ruble, D. N., & Frey, K. S. (1991). Changing patterns of behavior as skills are acquired: A functional model of self-evaluation. In J. Suls & T. A. Wills (Eds.), *Social comparison: Contemporary theory and research*. Hillsdale, NJ: Erlbaum.

Ruble, D. N., & Martin, C. L. (1998). Gender development. In W. Damon (Series Ed.) & N. Eisenberg (Vol. Ed.), *Handbook of child psychology*: Vol. 3. *Social, emotional, and personality development* (5th ed.). New York: Wiley.

Ruble, D. N., & Dweck, C. S. (1995). Self-perceptions, person conceptions, and their development. In N. Eisenberg (Ed.), *Review of personality and social psychology*: Vol. 15. *Development and social psychology: The interface*. Thousand Oaks, CA: Sage.

Ruble, D. N., & Stangor, C. (1986). Stalking the elusive schema: Insights from developmental and social-psychological analyses of gender schemas. *Social Cognition, 4*, 227–261.

Rueda, M. R., Posner, M. I., & Rothbart, M. K. (2005). The development of executive attention: Contributions to the emergence of self-regulation. *Developmental Neuropsychology, 28*, 573–594.

Rueschenberg, E., & Buriel, R. (1989). Mexican American family functioning and acculturation: A family systems perspective. *Hispanic Journal of Behavioral Sciences, 11*, 232–244.

Ruff, H. A., Capozzoli, M., & Weissberg, R. (1998). Age, individuality, and contexts as factors in sustained visual attention during the preschool years. *Developmental Psychology, 34*, 454–464.

Ruff, H. A., & Rothbart, M. K. (1996). *Attention in early development*. New York: Oxford University Press.

Ruffman, T., Perner, J., Naito, M., Parkin, L., & Clements, W. A. (1998). Older (but not younger) siblings facilitate false belief understanding. *Developmental Psychology, 34*, 161–174.

Ruffman, T., Slade, L, & Crowe, E. (2002). The relationship between children's and mothers' mental state language and theory-of-mind understanding. *Child Development, 73*, 734–751.

Rumbaut, R.G. (1994). Origins and destinies: Immigration to the United States since World War II. *Sociological Forum, 9*, 583–621.

Rumbaut, R.G., & Portes, A. (2001), *Ethnicities: Children of immigrants in America*. Berkeley: University of California Press.

Rushton, J. P., Fulker, D. W., Neale, M. C., Nias, D. K. B., & Eysenck, H. J. (1986). Altruism and aggression: The heritability of individual differences. *Journal of Personality and Social Psychology, 50*, 1192–1198.

Rust, J., Golombok, S., Hines, M., & Johnston, K. (2000). The role of brothers and sisters in the gender development of preschool children. *Journal of Experimental Child Psychology, 77*, 292–303.

Russell, G. (1999). Primary caregiving fathers. In M.E. Lamb (Ed.), *Parenting and child development in "nontraditional" families* (pp. 57–82). Mahwah, NJ: Erlbaum.

Russell, A., Mize, J., & Bissaker, K. (2002). Parent-child relationships. In P. K. Smith & C. H. Hart (Eds.), *Blackwell handbook of childhood social development*. Malden, MA: Blackwell Publishers.

Russell, G., & Russell, A. (1987). Mother-child and father-child relationships in middle childhood. *Child Development, 58*, 1573–1585.

Russell, A., & Saebel, J. (1997). Mother-son, mother-daughter, father-son, and father-daughter: Are they distinct relationships? *Developmental Review, 17*, 111–147.

Rutter, M. (1976). Maternal deprivation 1972–1978: New findings, new concepts, new approaches. *Child Development, 50*, 283–305.

Rutter, M. (1987). Continuities and discontinuities from infancy. In J. D. Osofsky (Ed.), *Handbook of infant development* (2nd ed.). New York: Wiley.

Rutter, M., Kreppner, J., & O'Connor, T. (2001). Specificity and heterogeneity in children's responses to profound institutional privation. *British Journal of Psychiatry, 179*, 97–103.

Ryan, K.E., & Ryan, A.M. (2005). Psychological processes underlying stereotype threat and standardized math test performance. *Educational Psychologist, 40*, 53–63.

Rymer, R. (1994). *Genie: A scientific tragedy*. New York: HarperCollins.

Saarni, C. (1989). Children's understanding of strategic control of emotional expression in social transactions. In C. Saarni & P. L. Harris (Eds.), *Children's understanding of emotion*. Cambridge: Cambridge University Press.

Saarni, C. (1990). Emotional competence: How emotions and relationships become integrated. In R. A. Thompson (Ed.), *Nebraska symposium on motivation*: Vol. 36. *Socioemotional development*. Lincoln: University of Nebraska Press.

Saarni, C. (1999). *The development of emotional competence*. Guilford series on social and emotional development. New York: Guilford.

Saarni, C., Mumme, D., & Campos, J. J. (1998). Emotional development: Action, communication, and understanding. In W. Damon (Series Ed.) & N. Eisenberg (Vol. Ed.), *Handbook of child psychology*: Vol. 3. *Social, emotional, and personality development* (5th ed.). New York: Wiley.

Sachs, J. (2001). Communication development in infancy. In J. B. Gleason (Ed.), *The development of language* (5th ed.). Boston: Allyn and Bacon.

Sachs, J., & Devin, J. (1976). Young children's use of age-appropriate speech styles in social interaction and role-playing. *Journal of Child Language, 3*, 81–98.

Sadker, D., & Sadker, M. (1985). Is the classroom OK? *Phi Delta Kappan, 55*, 358–367.

Sadker, M., & Sadker, D. (1994). *Failing at fairness : How America's schools cheat girls*. New York: Scribner.

Sagi, A., & Hoffman, M. L. (1976). Empathic distress in the newborn. *Developmental Psychology, 12*, 175–176.

Sagi, A., Lamb, M. E., Shoham, R., Dvir, R., & Lewko-wicz, K. S. (1985). Parent-infant interaction in families on Israeli kibbutzim. *International Journal of Behavioral Development, 8*, 273–284.

Sagi, A., van IJzendoorn, M. H., Aviezer, O., Donnell, F., Koren-Karie, N., Joels, T., et al. (1995). Attachments in multiple-caregiver and multiple-infant environments: The case of the Israeli kibbutzim. In E. Waters, B. E. Vaughn, G. Posada, & K. Kondo-Ikemura (Eds.), Caregiving, cultural, and cognitive perspectives on secure-base behavior and working models. *Monographs of the Society for Research in Child Development, 60*(23, Serial No. 244).

Sagi, A., van Ijzendoorn, M. H., Aviezer, O., Donnell, F., & Mayseless, O. (1994). Sleeping out of home in a kibbutz communal arrangement: It makes a difference for infant-mother attachment. *Child Development, 65*, 992–1004.

Saigal, S., Hoult, L. A., Streiner, L. L., Stoskopf, F. L., & Rosenbaum, P. L. (2000). School difficulties in adolescence in a regional cohort of children who were extremely low birth weight. *Pediatrics, 105*, 325–331.

Sakuma, M., Endo, T., & Muto, T. (2000). The development of self-understanding in preschoolers and elementary school children: Analysis of self-descriptions and self-evaluations. *Japanese Journal of Developmental Psychology, 11*, 176–187.

Saleh, M., Lazonder, A. W., & De Jong, T. (2005). Effects of within-class ability grouping on social interaction, achievement, and motivation. *Instructional Science, 33*, 105–119.

Sallis, J., Prochaska, J., & Taylor, W. (2000). A review of correlates of physical activity of children and adolescents. *Medicine and Science in Sports and Exercise, 32*, 963–975.

Salmivalli, C. (2001). Group view on victimization: Empirical findings and their implications. In J. Juvonen & S. Graham (Eds.), *Peer harassment in school: The plight of the vulnerable and victimized*. New York: Guilford.

Salomone, R.C. (2003). *Same, different, equal: Rethinking single-sex schooling*. New Haven, CT: Yale University Press.

Sameroff, A. J., Seifer, R., Baldwin, A., & Baldwin, C. (1993). Stability of intelligence from preschool to adolescence: The influence of social and family risk factors. *Child Development, 64*, 80–97.

Sampson, E. E. (1989). The challenge of social change for psychology: Globalization and psychology's theory of the person. *American Psychologist, 44*, 914–921.

Sandberg, S., Rutter, M., Pickles, A., McGuinness, D., & Angold, A. (2001). Do high-threat life events really provoke the onset of psychiatric disorder in children? *Journal of Child Psychology and Psychiatry, 42*, 523–532.

Sanders, M. G., & Herting, J. R. (2000). Gender and the effects of school, family, and church support on the academic achievement of African-American urban adolescents. In M. G. Sanders (Ed.), *Schooling students placed at risk: Research, policy, and practice in the education of poor and minority adolescents* (pp. 141–161). Mahwah, NJ: Erlbaum.

Sanders, J., Koch, J., & Urso, J. (1997). *Gender equity right from the start.* Mahwah, NJ: Erlbaum.

Santos, L.R., & Hauser, M.D. (2000). A non-human primate's understanding of solidity: Dissociations between seeing and acting. *Developmental Science, 5*, F1F7.

Santrock, J.W. (2004). *Educational psychology* (2nd ed.). New York: McGraw-Hill.

Sanvitale, D., Saltzstein, H. D., & Fish, M. C. (1989). Moral judgments by normal and conduct-disordered preadolescent and adolescent boys. *Merrill-Palmer Quarterly, 35*, 463–481.

Sarason, S. B. (2004). *And what do you mean by learning?* Portsmouth, NH: Heinemann.

Sasanuma, S. (1980). Do Japanese show sex differences in brain asymmetry? Supplementary findings. *Behavioral and Brain Sciences, 3*, 247–248.

Saunders, N. (1997). Pregnancy in the 21st century: Back to nature with a little assistance. *Lancet Supplement, 349*(9052), 1720.

Saxe, G. (1990). *Culture and cognitive development.* Hillsdale, NJ: Erlbaum.

Scaife, M., & Bruner, J. (1975). The capacity for joint visual attention in the infant. *Nature, 253*, 265–266.

Scarborough, H., & Wyckoff, J. (1986). Mother, I'd still rather do it myself: Some further non-effects of "motherese." *Journal of Child Language, 13*, 431–437.

Scarr, S. (1981). *Race, social class, and individual differences in IQ: New studies of old problems.* Hillsdale, NJ: Erlbaum.

Scarr, S. (1992). Developmental theories for the 1990s: Development and individual differences. *Child Development, 63*, 119.

Scarr, S. (1993). Biological and cultural diversity: The legacy of Darwin for development. *Child Development, 64*, 1333–1353.

Scarr, S., & Kidd, K. K. (1983). Developmental behavior genetics. In P. H. Mussen (Series Ed.) & M. M. Haith & J. J. Campos (Vol. Eds.), *Handbook of child psychology: Vol. 2. Infancy and developmental psychobiology* (4th ed.). New York: Wiley.

Scarr, S., & McCartney, K. (1983). How people make their own environments: A theory of genotypeenvironment effects. *Child Development, 54*, 424–435.

Scarr, S., Pakstis, A. J., Katz, S. H., & Barker, W. B. (1977). Absence of a relationship between degree of white ancestry and intellectual skills within a black population. *Human Genetics, 39*, 69–86.

Schacter, F. F., Shore, E., Hodapp, R., Chalfin, S., & Bundy, C. (1978). Do girls talk earlier? Mean length of utterance in toddlers. *Developmental Psychology, 14*, 388–392.

Scher, A., Epstein, R., & Tirosh, E. (2004). Stability and changes in sleep regulation: A longitudinal study from 3 months to 3 years. *International Journal of Behavioral Development, 28*(3), 268–274,

Scher, A., Epstein, R., & Tirosh, E. (2004). Stability and changes in sleep regulation: A longitudinal study from 3 months to 3 years. *International Journal of Behavioral Development, 28*(3), 268–274,

Scheven, A. (1981). *Swahili proverbs.* Washington, DC, University Press of America,.

Schunk, D. H. (2000). *Learning theories: An educational perspective.* Upper Saddle Rirar NJ: Merrill.

Schmader, T., Johns, M. (2003). Converging evidence that stereotype threat reduces working memory capacity. *Journal of Personality and Social Psychology, 85*, 440–452.

Schmader, T., Johns, M., & Barquissau, M. (2004). The costs of accepting gender differences: The role of stereotype endorsement in women's experience in the math domain. *Sex Roles, 50*, 835–850.

Schmuckler, M. A. (1995). Self-knowledge of body position: Integration of perceptual and action system information. In P. Rochat (Ed.), *The self in infancy: Theory and research.* Amsterdam: Elsevier.

Schneider, B. H., Atkinson, L., & Tardif, C. (2001). Childparent attachment and children's peer relations: A quantitative review. *Developmental Psychology, 37*, 86–100.

Schneider, B. H., & Byrne, B. M. (1985). Children's social skills training: A meta-analysis. In B. H. Schneider, K. H. Rubin, & J. E. Ledingham (Eds.), *Children's peer relations: Issues in assessment and intervention.* New York: Springer-Verlag.

Schneider, K. H. Rubin, & J. E. Ledingham (Eds.), *Children's peer relations: Issues in assessment and intervention.* New York: Springer-Verlag.

Schneider, W., & Bjorklund, D. F. (1998). Memory. In W. Damon (Series Ed.) & D. Kuhn & R. S. Siegler (Vol. Eds.), *Handbook of child psychology: Vol. 2. Cognition, perception, and language* (5th ed.). New York: Wiley.

Schneider, W., Gruber, H., Gold, A., & Opwis, K. (1993). Chess expertise and memory for chess positions in children and adults. *Journal of Experimental Child Psychology, 56*, 328–349.

Schneider, W., Korkel, J., & Weinert, F. E. (1987). *The knowledge base and memory performance: A comparison of academically successful and unsuccessful learners.* Paper presented at the meeting of the American Educational Research Association, Washington, DC.

Schneider, W., & Pressley, M. (1997). *Memory development between 2 and 20* (2nd ed.). Mahwah, NJ: Erlbaum.

Schofield, J. W. (1995). *Computers and classroom culture.* New York: Cambridge University Press.

Schonert-Reichl, K. A. (1999). Relations of peer acceptance, friendship adjustment, and social behavior to moral reasoning during early adolescence. *Journal of Early Adolescence, 19*, 249–279.

Schonfeld, A. M., Mattson, S. N., Lang, A., Delis, D. C., & Riley, E. P. (2001). Verbal and nonverbal fluency in children with heavy prenatal alcohol exposure. *Journal of Studies on Alcohol, 62*, 239–246.

Schulze, P. A., Harwood, R. L., & Schöelmerich, A. (2001). Feeding practices and expectations among middle-class Anglo and Puerto Rican mothers of 12-months-old infants. *Journal of Cross-Cultural Psychology, 32*(4), 397–406.

Schulze, P. A., Harwood, R. L., Schölmerich, A., & Leyendecker, B. (2002). The cultural structuring of parenting and universal developmental tasks. *Parenting: Science and Practice, 2*(2), 151–178.

Schunk, D. H. (1987). Peer models and children's behavioral change. *Review of Educational Research, 57*, 159–174.

Schunk, D. H., & Miller, S. D. (2002). Self-efficacy and adolescents' motivation. In F. Pajares & T.C., Undan (Eds.), *Academic motivation of adolescents.* Information Age Publishing.

Schwartz, D., Dodge, K. A., Pettit, G. S., & Bates, J. E. (1997). The early socialization of aggressive victims of bullying. *Child Development, 68*, 665–675.

Schwartz, R. G., & Camarata, S. (1985). Examining relationships between input and language development: Some statistical issues. *Journal of Child Language, 12*, 199–207.

Schwartz, S. J., Cote, J. E., & Arnett, J. J. (2005). Identity and agency in emerging adulthood: Two developmental routes in the individualization process. *Youth & Society, 37*, 201–229.

Schwartz, R. G., Leonard, L. B., Frome-Loeb, D. M., & Swanson, L. A. (1987). Attempted sounds are sometimes not: An expanded view of phonological selection and avoidance. *Journal of Child Language, 14*, 411–418.

Schweinhart, L. J. (1994). Lasting benefits of preschool programs, ERIC Digest. ERIC Clearinghouse on Elementary and Early Childhood Education, Urbana, IL, 1994 (ED365478)

Scott, F., Peters, H., Boogert, T., Robertson, R., Anderson, J., McLennan, A., Kesby, G., & Edelman, D. (2002). The loss rates for invasive prenatal testing in a specialised obstetric ultrasound practice. *Aust N Z J Obstet. Gynaecol. 42*(1), 558.

Scott, S. K., Wise, R. J. S. (2003). PET and fMRI studies of the neural basis of speech perception. *Speech Communication, 41*(1), 23–34.

Sears, M., and Sears, W. (2001). *The Breastfeeding Book.* California MD: Little Brown.

Sears, R., Maccoby, E., & Levin, H. (1957). *Patterns of child rearing.* New York: Harper & Row.

Seashore, M. J., Leifer, A. D., Barnett, C. R., & Leiderman, P. H. (1973). The effects of denial of early mother-infant interaction on maternal self-confidence. *Journal of Personality and Social Psychology, 26*, 369–378.

Sebald, H. (1989). Adolescent peer orientation: Changes in the support system during the last three decades. *Adolescence, 24*, 937–945.

Segal, L. B., Oster, H., Cohen, M., Caspi, B., Myers, M., & Brown, D. (1995). Smiling and fussing in seven-month-old preterm and full-term Black infants in the still-face situation. *Child Development, 66*, 1829–1843.

Segal, N. L. (1999). *Entwined lives.* New York: Penguin Putnam.

Seginer, R. (1998). Adolescents' perceptions of relationships with older sibling in the context of other close relationships. *Journal of Research on Adolescence, 8*, 287–308.

Seidman, E., Aber, J. L., & French, S. H. (2004). School transitions during adolescence: Risky situations in need of restructuring. In C. Schellenbach, K. Maton, B. Leadbeater, & A. Solarz (Eds.), *Investing in children, families and communities: Strengths based research and policy.*

Seidman, E., Allen, L., Aber, J. L., Mitchell, C., & Feinman, J. (1994). The impact of school transition in early adolescence on the self-system and perceived social context of poor urban youth. *Child Development, 65*, 507–522.

Selman, R. L. (1980). *The growth of interpersonal understanding: Development and clinical analyses.* New York: Academic Press.

Selman, R. L. (1994). The relation of role taking to the develop-ment of moral judgment in children. In B. Puka (Ed.), *Fundamental research in moral development*, New York: Garland Publishing,

Seong, H., Bauer, S. C., & Sullivan, L. M. (1998). Gender differences among top performing elementary school students in mathematical ability. *Journal of Research and Development in Education, 31*, 133–141.

Serbin, L. A., Connor, J. M., Burchardt, C. J., & Citron, C. C. (1979). Effects of peer presence on sex-typing of children's play behavior. *Journal of Experimental Child Psychology, 27*, 303–309.

Serbin, L. A., Poulin-Dubois, D., Colburne, K. A., Sen, M. G., & Eichstedt, J. A. (2001). Gender stereotyping in infancy: Visual preferences for and knowledge of gender-stereotyped toys in the second year. *International Journal of Behavioral Development, 25*, 715.

Serbin, L. A., Powlishta, K. K., & Gulko, J. (1993). The development of sex-typing in middle childhood. *Monographs of the Society for Research in Child Development, 58*(Serial No. 232).

Serbin, L. A., & Sprafkin, C. (1986). The salience of gender and the process of sex-typing in three- to seven-year-old children. *Child Development, 57*, 1188–1199.

Serbin, L.A., Stack, D. M., Schwartzman, A. E., Cooperman, J., Bentley, V., Saltaris, C., et al. (2002). A longitudinal study of aggressive and withdrawn children into adulthood: Patterns of parenting and risk to offspring. In R. J. & R. D. Peters (Eds.), *The effects of parental dysfunction on children*. New York: Kluwer Academic/Plenum Publishers.

Serbin, L. A., Zelkowitz, P., Doyle, A., & Gold, D. (1990). The socialization of sex-differentiated skills and academic performance: A mediational model. *Sex Roles, 23*, 613–628.

Serpa, M. D. L., Lira, S. D. A., & Stokes, W. (2004). Immersion: What are the implications for teaching & learning before and after question 2. Retrieved May 2, 2005, from http://www.mec.edu/mascd/ docs/serpa.htm

Serbin, L. A., Powlishta, K. K., & Gulko, J. (1993). The development of sex-typing in middle childhood. *Monographs of the Society for Research in Child Development, 58*(Serial No. 232).

Sethi, A., Mischel, W., Aber, J. L., Shoda, Y., & Rodriguez, M. L. (2000). The role of strategic attention deployment in development of self-regulation: Predicting preschoolers' delay of gratification from mother-toddler interactions. *Developmental Psychology, 36*, 767–777.

Shapka, J. D., & Keating, D. (2003). Effects of a girls-only curriculum during adolescence: Performance, persistence, and engagement in mathematics and science. *American Educational Research Journal, 40*, 929–960.

Share, D. L., & Leikin, M. (2004). Language impairment at school entry and later reading disability: Connections at lexical versus supralexical levels of reading. *Scientific Studies of Reading, 8*, 87–110.

Sharpe, R. M., & Skakkebaek, N. E. (1993). Are oestrogens involved in falling sperm counts and disorders of the male reproductive tract? *Lancet, 341*, 1392–1395.

Shantz, C. U. (1987). Conflicts between children. *Child Development, 58*, 283–305.

Shatz, M., & Gelman, R. (1973). The development of communication skills: Modifications in the speech of young children as a function of the listener. *Monographs of the Society for Research in Child Development, 38* (5, Serial No. 152).

Shantz, C. U., & Hartup, W. W. (Eds.). (1995). *Conflict in child and adolescent development*. New York: Cambridge University Press.

Shatz, M., & McCloskey, L. (1984). Answering appropriately: A developmental perspective on conversational knowledge. In S. A. Kuczaj (Ed.), *Discourse development: Progress in cognitive developmental research*. New York: Springer-Verlag.

Shayer, M., Kucheman, D. E., & Wylam, H. (1976). The distribution of Piagetian stages of thinking in British middle and secondary school children. *British Journal of Educational Psychology, 46*, 164–173.

Shayer, M., & Wylam, H. (1978). The distribution of Piagetian stages of thinking in British middle and secondary school children: II. 14 to 16 year old and sex differentials. *British Journal of Educational Psychology, 48*, 62–70.

Shaywitz, S. E., & Shaywitz, B. A. (2005). Dyslexia (Specific reading disability). *Biological Psychiatry, 57*, 1301–1309.

Shaywitz, B. A., Shaywitz, S. E., Pugh, K. R., Constable, R. T., Skudlarski, P., Fulbright, R. K., et al. (1995). Sex differences in the functional organization of the brain for language. *Nature, 373*, 607–609.

She, H-C. (2000). The interplay of a biology teacher's beliefs, teaching practices and gender-based student-teacher classroom interaction *Educational Research, 42*, 100–111.

She, H., & Fisher, D. (2002). Teacher communication behavior and its association with students' cognitive and attitudinal outcomes in science in Taiwan. *Journal of Research in Science Teaching, 39*, 63–78.

Shea, D. L., Lubinski, D., & Benbow, C. P. (2001). Importance of assessing spatial ability in intellectually talented young adolescents: A 20-year longitudinal study. *Journal of Educational Psychology, 93*, 604–614.

Sheldon, A. (1990). Pickle fights: Gendered talk in preschool disputes. *Discourse Processes, 13*, 531.

Sheldon, A. (1992). Conflict talk: Sociolinguist challenges to self-assertion and how young girls meet them. *Merrill-Palmer Quarterly, 38*, 95–117.

Sheldon, S.B., & Epstein, J.L. (2005). Involvement counts: Family and community partnerships and mathematics achievement. *Journal of Educational Research, 98*, 196–206.

Sherif, M., Harvey, O. J., White, B. J., Hood, W. R., & Sherif, C. W. (1961). *Intergroup conflict and cooperation: The Robbers Cave experiment*. Norman: University of Oklahoma Press.

Shigetomi, C. C., Hartmann, D. P., & Gelfand, D. M. (1981). Sex differences in children's altruistic behavior and reputations for helpfulness. *Developmental Psychology, 17*, 434–437.

Shiloh, S. (1996). Genetic counseling: A developing area of interest for psychologists. *Professional Psychology: Research and Practice, 27*, 475–486.

Shirk, S., Burwell, R., & Harter, S. (2003). Strategies to modify low self-esteem in adolescents. In M.A. Reinecke, F.M. Dattilio, & A. Freedman (Eds.), *Cognitive therapy with children and adolescents: A casebook for clinical practice* (2nd ed.). New York: Guilford.

Shisslak, C. M., Crago, M., McKnight, K. M., Estes, L. S., Gray, N., Parnaby, O. G. (1998). Potential risk factors associated with weight control behaviors in elementary and middle school girls. *Journal of Psychosomatic Research, 44*, 301–313.

Shoda, Y., Mischel, W., & Peake, P. K. (1990). Predicting adolescent cognitive and self-regulatory competencies from preschool delay of gratifica-

tion: Identifying diagnostic conditions. *Developmental Psychology, 26*, 978–986.

Shonkoff, J. P., & Phillips, D. A. (2000). *From neurons to neighborhoods: The science of early childhood development*. Washington, DC: National Academy Press.

Shore, C. M. (1995). *Individual differences in language development*. Thousand Oaks, CA: Sage.

Shore, R. (1997). *Rethinking the brain*. New York: Families and Work Institute.

Shu, S. (1999). Grandparents, parents, and children: A study of three-generation family structure and intergenerational relationships in contemporary China. Unpublished doctoral dissertation, University of London.

Shucard, J. L., & Shucard, D. W. (1990). Auditory evoked potentials and hand preference in 6-month-old infants: Possible gender-related differences in cerebral organization. *Developmental Psychology, 26*, 923–930.

Shucard, J. L., Shucard, D. W., Cummins, K. R., & Campos, J. J. (1981). Auditory evoked potentials and sex-related differences in brain development. *Brain and Language, 13*, 91–102.

Shulman, S., & Collins, W. A. (Eds.). (1997). New directions for child development: No. 78. *Romantic relationships in adolescence: Developmental perspectives*. San Francisco: Jossey-Bass.

Shure, M. B. (1989). Interpersonal competence training. In W. Damon (Ed.), *Child development today and tomorrow*. San Francisco: Jossey-Bass.

Shwe, H. I., & Markman, E. M. (1997). Young children's appreciation of the mental impact of their communicative signals. *Developmental Psychology, 33*, 630–636.

Shweder, R. A. (2003). *Why do men barbecue? : Recipes for cultural psychology*. Cambridge, MA: Harvard University Press.

Shweder, R. A., & Bourne, L. (1984). Does the concept of the person vary cross-culturally? In R. Shweder & R. Levine (Eds.), *Culture theory: Essays on mind, self, and emotion* (pp. 158–190). New York: Cambridge University Press.

Shweder, R. A., Goodnow, J., Hatano, G., LeVine, R. A., Markus, H., & Miller, P. (1998). The cultural psychology of development: One mind, many mentalities. In W. Damon (Series Ed.) & R. M. Lerner (Vol. Ed.), *Handbook of child psychology: Vol. 1. Theoretical models of human development* (5th ed.). New York: Wiley.

Shweder, R. A., Jensen, L. A., & Goldstein, W. M. (1995). Who sleeps by whom revisited: A method for extracting the moral goods implicit in practice. In J. J. Goodnow, P. J. Miller, & F. Kessel (Eds.), *New directions for child development*: No. 67. *Cultural practices as contexts for development*. San Francisco: Jossey-Bass.

Shweder, R. A., Mahapatra, M., & Miller, J. (1987). Culture and moral development. In J. Kagan & S. Lamb (Eds.), *The emergence of morality in young children*. Chicago: University of Chicago Press.

Shweder, R. A., & Much, M. C. (1987). Determinations of meaning: Discourse and moral socialization. In W. M. Kurtines & J. L. Gewirtz (Eds.), *Moral development through social interaction*. New York: Wiley.

Sieber, J. E. (1992). *Planning ethically responsible research: A guide for students and internal review boards*. Newbury Park, CA: Sage.

Siegal, M. (1987). Are sons and daughters treated more differently by fathers than by mothers? *Developmental Review, 7*, 183–209.

Siegel, L. S. (1984). Home environment influences on cognitive development in preterm and full-term children during the first 5 years. In A. W.

Gottfried (Ed.), *Home environment and early cognitive development*. New York: Academic Press.

Siegel, J. M. (2001). The REM Sleep-Memory Consolidation Hypothesis. *Science, 294*(5544), 1058–1064.

Siegel, D. J., & Hartzell, M. (2003). *Parenting from the inside out* (Jeremy P. Tarcher: New York).

Siegler, R. S. (1976). Three aspects of cognitive development. *Cognitive Psychology, 8*, 481–520.

Siegler, R. S. (1978). The origins of scientific reasoning. In R. S. Siegler (Ed.), *Children's thinking: What develops?* Hillsdale, NJ: Erlbaum.

Siegler, R. S. (1981). Developmental sequences within and between concepts. *Monographs of the Society for Research in Child Development, 46* (2, Serial No. 189).

Siegler, R. S. (1988). Individual differences in strategy choices: Good students, not-so-good students, and perfectionists. *Child Development, 59*, 833–851.

Siegler, R. S. (1991). *Children's thinking* (2nd ed.). Englewood Cliffs, NJ: Prentice Hall.

Siegler, R. S. (1995). How does change occur?: A microgenetic study of number conservation. *Cognitive Psychology, 28*, 225–273.

Siegler, R. S. (1996). *Emerging minds: The process of change in children's thinking*. New York: Oxford University Press.

Siegler, R. S. (1998). *Children's thinking* (3rd ed.). Upper Saddle River, NJ: Prentice Hall.

Siegler, R. S. (2000). *The rebirth of children's learning*. Child Development, 71, 2635.

Siegler, R. S. (2005). Children's learning, *American Psychologist, 60*, 769–778.

Siegler, R.S. (2006). Mocrogenetic analyses of learning. In W. Damon & R. M Lerner (Series Eds.) & D. Kuhn & R. S. Siegler (Vol. Eds), *Handbook of child psychology*: Volume 2: *Cognition, perception and language* (6th ed., pp. 464–510). Hoboken, NJ: Wiley.

Siegler, R. & Alibali, M. (2005a). Sociocultural theories of development. In *Children's thinking* (pp. 107–140). Upper Saddle, NJ: Prentice Hall.

Siegler, R. S., & Jenkins, E. (1989). *How children discover new strategies*. Hillsdale, NJ: Erlbaum.

Siegler, R. S., & Shipley, C. (1995). Variation, selection, and cognitive change. In T. J. Simon & G. S. Halford (Eds.), *Developing cognitive competence: New approaches to process modeling*. Hillsdale, NJ: Erlbaum.

Siegler, R. S., & Shrager, J. (1984). Strategy choices in addition and subtraction: How do children know what to do? In C. Sophian (Ed.), *Origins of cognitive skills*. Hillsdale, NJ: Erlbaum.

Siegler R. S., & Svetina, M. (2006). What leads children to adopt new strategies? A microgenetic/cross-sectional study of class inclusion. *Child Development, 77*, 997–1015.

Siervogel, R. M., Waynard, L. M., Wisemandle, W. A., Roche, A. F., Guo, S. S., Chumlea, W. C., et al. (2000). Annual changes in total body fat and fat-free mass in children from 8 to 18 years in relation to changes in body mass index: The Fels Longitudinal Study. *Annals of the New York Academy of Science, 904*, 420–423.

Signorella, M., & Liben, L. S. (1984). Recall and reconstruction of gender-related pictures: Effects of attitude, task difficulty, and age. *Child Development, 55*, 393–405.

Signorella, M. L., Bigler, R. S., & Liben, L. S. (1993). Developmental differences in children's gender schemata about others: A meta-analytic review. *Developmental Review, 13*, 147–183.

Signorelli, N. (2001). Television's gender role images and contribution to stereotyping: Past, present, future. In D. G. Singer & J. Singer (Eds.),

Handbook of children and the media. Thousand Oaks, CA: Sage.

Signorelli, N., & Bacue, A. (1999). Recognition and respect: A content analysis of prime-time television characters across three decades. *Sex Roles, 40*, 527–544.

Silver, L. B. (1999). *Attention-deficit hyperactivity disorder* (2nd ed.). Washington, DC: American Psychiatric Press.

Silvera, D. H. & Seger, C. R. (2004). Feeling good about ourselves: Unrealistic self-evaluations and their relation to self-esteem in the United States and Norway. *Journal of Cross-Cultural Psychology, 35*, 571–585.

Simos, P. G., Fletcher, J. M., Foorman, B. R., Francis, D. J., Castillo, E. M., Davis, R. N., Fitzgerald, M., Mathes, P. G., Denton, C., & Papanicolaou, A. C. (2002). Brain activation profiles during the early stages of reading acquisition. *Journal of Child Neurology, 17*(3), 159–164.

Simpkins, S.D., Davis-Kean, P.E., & Eccles, J.S. (2005). Parents' socializing behavior and children's participation in math, science, and computer out-of-school activities. *Applied Developmental Science, 9*, 1430.

Simpson, J. M. (2001). Infant stress and sleep deprivation as an actiological basis for sudden infant death syndrome. *Early Human Development, 61*, 143.

Singer, D., Golinkoff, R. M., & Hirsh-Pasek, K. (Eds.) (2006). Play-Learning: How play motivates and enhances children's cognitive and social-emotional growth. New York; Oxford University Press.

Sirkin, S. R. (2005). Socioeconomic status and academic achievement: A meta-analytic review of the research. *Review of Educational Research, 75*, 417–453.

Sit, C. H. P., Linder, K. J., Koenraad, J., & Sherrill, C. (2002). Sport participation of Hong Kong Chinese children with disabilities in special schools. *Adapted Physical Activity Quarterly, 19*, 453–471.

Skandera, H., & Sousa, R. (2002). Mobility and the achievement gap. *Hoover Digest, 3* (Spring 2002).

Skelton, C. (2001). *Schooling the boys: Masculinities and primary education*. Buckingham, UK: Open University Press.

Skinner, B. F. (1953). *Science and human behavior*. New York: Macmillan.

Skinner, B. F. (1957). *Verbal behavior*. New York: Appleton-Century-Crofts.

Slaby, R. G., & Frey, K. S. (1975). Development of gender constancy and selective attention to same-sex models. *Child Development, 46*, 849–856.

Slater, A., Johnson, S. P., Brown, E., & Badenoch, M. (1996). Newborn infants' perception of partly occluded objects. *Infant Behavior and Development, 19*, 145–148.

Slater, A., Johnson, S. P., Kellman, P. J., & Spelke, E. S. (1994). The role of three-dimensional depth cues in infants' perception of partly occluded objects. *Early Development and Parenting, 3*, 187–191.

Slater, A., Mattock, A., & Brown, E. (1990). Size constancy at birth: Newborn infant's responses to retinal and real size. *Journal of Experimental Child Psychology, 49*, 314–322.

Slater, A., Mattock, A., Brown, E., & Bremner, J. G. (1991). Form perception at birth: Cohen and Younger (1984) revisited. *Journal of Experimental Child Psychology, 51*, 395–406.

Slater, A., von der Schulenburg, C., Brown, E., Badenoch, M., Butterworth, G., Parsons S., et al. (1998). Newborn infants prefer attractive

faces. *Infant Behavior and Development, 21*, 345–354.

Slaughter-DeFoe, D. T., Nakagawa, K., Takanishi, R., & Johnson, D. J. (1990). Toward cultural/ecological perspectives on schooling and achievement in African- and Asian-American children. *Child Development, 61*, 363–383.

Slavin, R. (1990). On making a difference. *Educational Researcher, 19*(13), 30–44.

Slavin, R. E. 1990. *Cooperative learning: Theory, research and practice*. Englewood Cliffs, NJ: Prentice Hall.

Slobin, D. I. (1982). Universal and particular in the acquisition of language. In E. Wanner & L. R. Gleitman (Eds.), *Language acquisition: The state of the art*. Cambridge: Cambridge University Press.

Slobin, D. I. (1985a). Crosslinguistic evidence for the language-making capacity. In D. I. Slobin (Ed.), *The crosslinguistic study of language acquisition*: Vol. 2. *Theoretical issues*. Hillsdale, NJ: Erlbaum.

Slobin, D. I. (Ed.). (1985b). *The crosslinguistic study of language acquisition*: Vol. 2. *Theoretical issues*. Hillsdale, NJ: Erlbaum.

Sloboda, Z. (2002). Changing patterns of "drug abuse" in the United States: Connecting findings from macro- and microepidemiologic studies. *Substance Use & Misuse, 37*(810), 1229–1252.

Slomkowski, C. L., & Dunn, J. (1993). *Conflict in close relationships*. Paper presented at the meeting of the Society for Research in Child Development, New Orleans.

Slomkowski, C. L., & Killen, M. (1992). Young children's conceptions of transgressions with friends and nonfriends. *International Journal of Behavioral Development, 15*, 247–258.

Slotta, J. D., Chi, M. T. H., & Joram, E. (1995). Assessing students' misclassification of physics concepts: An ontological basis for conceptual change. *Cognition and Instruction, 13*(3), 373–400.

Smetana, J. G., & Braeges, J. L. (1990). The development of toddlers' moral and conventional judgments. *Merrill-Palmer Quarterly, 36*, 329–346.

Smetana, J. G., Killen, M., & Turiel, E. (1991). Children's reasoning about interpersonal and moral conflicts. *Child Development, 62*, 629–644.

Smetana, J. G., Schlagman, N., & Adams, P. (1993). Preschoolers' judgments about hypothetical and actual transgressions. *Child Development, 64*, 202–214.

Smilansky, S. (1968). *The effects of sociodramatic play on disadvantaged preschool children*. New York: Wiley.

Smiley, P. A., & Dweck, C. S. (1994). Individual differences in achievement goals among young children. *Child Development, 65*, 1723–1743.

Smiley, P., & Huttenlocher, J. (1989). Young children's acquisition of emotion concepts. In C. Saarni & P. L. Harris (Eds.), *Children's understanding of emotion*. Cambridge: Cambridge University Press.

Smith, B. A., & Blass, E. M. (1996). Taste-mediated calming in premature, preterm, and full-term human infants. *Developmental Psychology, 32*, 1084–1089.

Smith, B. A., Stevens, K., Torgerson, W. S., & Kim, J. H. (1992). Diminished reactivity of postmature human infants to sucrose compared with term infants. *Developmental Psychology, 28*, 811–820.

Smith, C., Carey, S., & Wiser, M., (1985). On differentiation: A case study of the concepts of size, weight, and density. *Cognition, 21*, 177–237.

Smith, E., & Udry, J. (1985). Coital and non-coital sexual behaviors of white and black adolescents.

American Journal of Public Health, 75, 1200–1203.

Smith, P. K. (1978). A longitudinal study of social participation in preschool children: Solitary and parallel play reexamined. *Developmental Psychology, 14,* 517–523.

Smith, P. K., & Drew, L. M. (2002). Grandparenthood. In M. H. Bornstein (Ed.), *Handbook of parenting* (2nd ed., Vol. 3). Mahwah, NJ: Erlbaum.

Snarey, J. R. (1985). Cross-cultural universality of social-moral development: A critical review of Kohlbergian research. *Psychological Bulletin, 97,* 202–232.

Snarey, J. R., & Keljo, K. (1991). In a Gemeinschaft voice: The cross-cultural expansion of moral development theory. In W. M. Kurtines & J. L. Gewirtz (Eds.), *Handbook of moral behavior and development*: Vol. 1. *Theory*. Hillsdale, NJ: Erlbaum.

Snidjers, R. J. M. & Nicolaides, K. H. (1996). Assessment of risks. In: *Ultrasound markers for fetal chromosomal defects*. Canforth, UK, Parthenon Publ.

Snow, C. E. (1983). Saying it again: The role of expanded and deferred imitations in language acquisition. In K. E. Nelson (Ed.), *Children's language* (Vol. 4). Hillsdale, NJ: Erlbaum.

Snow, C. E. (1999). Social perspectives on the emergence of language. In B. MacWhinney (Ed.), *The emergence of language*. Mahwah, NJ: Erlbaum.

Snow, C. E., & Beals, D. (2001). Deciding what to tell: Selecting an elaborative narrative. Topics in family interactions and children's personal experience stories. In S. Blum-Kulka & C. Snow (Eds.), *Talking to adults*. Mahwah, NJ: Erlbaum.

Snow, C. E., & Ferguson, C. (1977). *Talking to children: Language input and acquisition*. Cambridge: Cambridge University Press.

Snow, C. E., & Goldfield, B. A. (1983). Turn the page please: Situation-specific language acquisition. *Journal of Child Language, 10,* 551–569.

Snow, C. E., Perlman, R., & Nathan, D. (1987). Why routines are different: Toward a multiple-factors model of the relation between input and language acquisition. In K. E. Nelson & A. VanKleeck (Eds.), *Children's language* (Vol. 6). Hillsdale, NJ: Erlbaum.

Snow, C. E., Pan, B. E., Imbens-Bailey, A., & Herman, J. (1996). Learning how to say what one means: A longitudinal study of children's speech act use. *Social Development, 5,* 56–84.

Snyder, T. D., & Hoffman, C. M. (2000). Digest of education statistics: 1999. *Education Statistics Quarterly, 2,* 123–126.

Snyder, J. J., & Patterson, G. R. (1995). Individual differences in social aggression: A test of a reinforcement model of socialization in the natural environment. *Behavior Therapy, 26,* 371–391.

Sohlberg, M. E., & Olweus, D. (2003). Prevalence estimation of school bullying with the Olweus bully/victim questionnaire. *Aggressive Behavior, 29,* 239–268.

Sokolov, E. N. (1960). *Perception and the conditioned reflex*. New York: Macmillan.

Soltis, J. (2004). The signal functions of early infant crying. *Behavioral & Brain Sciences, 27*(4), 433–459.

Somary, K., & Stricker, G. (1998). Becoming a grandparent: A longitudinal study of expectations and early experiences as a function of sex and lineage. *Gerontologist, 38,* 53–61.

Sonnenschein, S. (1988). The development of referential communication: Speaking to different listeners. *Child Development, 59,* 694–702.

Sorce, J. F., Emde, R. N., Campos, J. J., & Klinnert, M. D. (1985). Maternal emotional signaling: Its effect on the visual cliff behavior of 1-year-olds. *Developmental Psychology, 21,* 195–200.

Sorkhabi, N. (2005). Applicability of Baumrind's parent typology to collective cultures: Analysis of cultural explanations of parent socialization effects. *International Journal of Behavioral Development, 29*(6), 552–563.

Sostek, A. M., Vietze, P., Zaslow, M., Kreiss, L., van de Waals, F., & Rubenstein, D. (1981). Social context in caregiver-infant interaction. A film study of Fais and the United States. In T. M. Field, A. M. Sostek, P. Vietze, & P. H. Leiderman (Eds.), *Culture and early interactions*. Hillsdale, NJ: Erlbaum.

Spearman, C. (1927). *The abilities of man*. New York: Macmillan.

Speer, J. R., & Flavell, J. H. (1979). Young children's knowledge of the relative difficulty of recognition and recall memory tasks. *Developmental Psychology, 15,* 214–217.

Spelke, E. S. (1976). Infants' intermodal perception of events. *Cognitive Psychology, 8,* 533–560.

Spelke, E. S. (1985). Perception of unity, persistence, and identity: Thoughts on infants' conceptions of objects. In J. Mehler & R. Fox (Eds.), *Neonate cognition: Beyond the blooming buzzing confusion*. Hillsdale, NJ: Erlbaum.

Spelke, E. S. (1988). Where perceiving ends and thinking begins: The apprehension of objects in infancy. In A. Yonas (Ed.), *Minnesota symposia on child psychology*: Vol. 20. *Perceptual development in infancy*. Hillsdale, NJ: Erlbaum.

Spelke, E. S. (2000). Core knowledge. *American Psychologist, 55*(11), 1233–1243.

Spelke, E. S., & Newport, E. L. (1998). Nativism, empiricism, and the development of knowledge. In W. Damon (Series Ed.) & R. M. Lerner (Vol. Ed.), *Handbook of child psychology*: Vol. 1. *Theoretical models of human development* (5th ed.). New York: Wiley.

Spelke, E. S., & Van de Walle, G. (1993). Perceiving and reasoning about objects: insights from infants. In N. Eilan, R. McCarthy, & B. Brewer, *Spatial representation*, Cambridge, MA: Blackwell.

Spencer-Rodgers, J., Peng, K., Wang, L., & Hou, Y. (2004). Dialectical self-esteem and east-west differences in psychological well-being. *Personality and Social Psychology Bulletin, 30,* 1416–1432.

Spinath, B., & Spinath, F. M. (2005). Development of self-perceived ability in elementary school: The role of parents' perceptions, teacher evaluations, and intelligence. *Cognitive Development, 20,* 190–204.

Spinath, B., Spinath, F. M., Riemann, R. (2003). Implicit theories about personality and intelligence and their relationship to actual personality and intelligence. *Personality & Individual Differences, 35,* 939–651.

Spinrad, T. L., Eisenberg, N., Harris, E., Hanish, L., Fabes, R. A., Kupanoff, K., Ringwald, S., & Holmes, J. (2004). The relation of children's everyday nonsocial peer play behavior to emotionality, regulation, and social functioning. *Developmental Psychology, 40,* 67–80.

Spinrad, T. L., Stifter, C. A., Donelson-McCall, N., & Turner, L. (2004). Mothers' regulation strategies in response to toddlers' affect: Links to later emotion self-regulation. *Social Development, 13,* 40–55.

Sprauve, M. E. (1996). Substance abuse and HIV in pregnancy. *Clinical Obstetrics and Gynecology, 39,* 316–332.

Springer, S. P., & Deutsch, G. (1998). *Left brain, right brain* (5th ed.). San Francisco: Freeman.

Sridhar, D., & Vaughn, S. (2002). Bibliotherapy: Practices for improving self-concept and reading comprehension. In B.Y.L. Wong & M.L. Donahue (Eds.), *The social dimensions of learning disabilities: Essays in honor of Tanis Bryan* (pp. 161–185). Mahwah, NJ: Erlbaum.

Sroufe, L. A. (1979). Socioemotional development. In J. Osofsky (Ed.), *Handbook of infant development* (462–516). New York: Wiley.

Sroufe, L. A. (1986). Bowlby's contribution to psychoanalytic theory and developmental psychology: Attachment, separation, loss. *Journal of Child Psychology and Psychiatry, 27,* 841–849.

Sroufe, L. A. (1996). *Emotional development*. New York: Cambridge University Press.

Sroufe, L. A., Bennett, C., Englund, M., Urban, J., & Shulman, S. (1993). The significance of gender boundaries in preadolescence: Contemporary correlates and antecedents of boundary relations and maintenance. *Child Development, 64,* 455–466.

Stack, D., & Muir, D. W. (1992). Adult tactile stimulation during face-to-face interactions modulates 5 month-olds' affect and attention. *Child Development, 63,* 1509–1525.

Stangor, C., & McMillan, D. (1992). Memory for expectancy-congruent and expectancy-incongruent information: A review of the social and social developmental literatures. *Psychological Bulletin, 111,* 42–61.

Stangor, C., & Ruble, D. N. (1987). Development of gender role knowledge and gender constancy. In L. S. Liben & M. L. Signorella (Eds.), New directions for child development: No. 38. *Children's gender schemata*. San Francisco: Jossey-Bass.

Stanovich, K. E. (1986). Matthew effects in reading: Some consequences of individual differences in the acquisition of literacy. *Reading Research Quarterly, 21,* 360–407.

Stanovich, K. E., Cunningham, A. E., & West, R. F. (1998). Literacy experiences and the shaping of cognition. In S. G. Paris & H. M. Wellman (Eds.), *Global prospects for education: Development, culture, and schooling*. Washington, DC: American Psychological Association.

Stanton-Salazar, R. D., & Spina, S. U. (2003). Informal mentors and role models in the lives of urban Mexican-origin adolescents. *Anthropology and Education Quarterly, 34*(3), 231–254.

Stanwood, G. D., & Levitt, P. (2001). The effects of cocaine on the developing nervous system. In C. A. Nelson & M. Luciana (Eds.), *Handbook of developmental cognitive neuroscience*. Cambridge, MA: MIT Press.

State of the World's Children (2006). Executive Summary: Excluded and Invisible. Unicef. Retrieved March 16, 2006. From http://www.unicef.org/publications/files/SOWC_2006_-_English_Executive_Summary.pdf

Stattin, H., & Magnusson, D. (1990). *Pubertal maturation in female development*. Hillsdale, NJ: Erlbaum.

Staub, E. (1971). Helping a person in distress: The influence of implicit and explicit rules of conduct on children and adults. *Journal of Personality and Social Psychology, 17,* 137–145.

Steele, C. M. (2003). Through the back door to theory. *Psychological Inquiry, 14,* 314–317.

Steele, C. M., & Aronson, J. (1995). Stereotype threat and the intellectual test performance of African-Americans. *Journal of Personality and Social Psychology, 69,* 797–811.

Steele, C. M., & Aronson, J. (1998). Stereotype threat and the test performance of academically successful African Americans. In C. Jencks & M. Phillips (Eds.), *The Black-White test score gap*. Washington, DC: Brookings Institution.

Steele, H., Steele, M., & Fonagy, P. (1996). Associations among attachment classifications of mothers, fathers, and their infants. *Child Development, 67*, 541–555.

Steele, C. M., Spencer, S. J., Hummel, M., Carter, K., Harber, K., Schoem, D., & Nisbett, R. (in press). African-American college achievement: A 'wise' intervention. *Harvard Educational Review.*

Steele, L., Stockley, T. L., & Ray, P. N. (2000). The role of molecular genetic testing in fetal health. *Frontiers in Fetal Health, 2*(7).

Stein, A.H., Pohly, S. R., & Mueller, E. (1971). The influence of masculine, feminine, and neutral tasks on children's achievement behavior, expectancies of success, and attainment values. *Child Development, 42*, 195–207.

Stein, M. T., Kennell, J. H., & Fulcher, A. (2004).Benefits of a Doula Present at the Birth of a Child. *Pediatrics, 114*, 1488–1491.

Steinberg, L. (2001). We know some things: Parenta-dolescent relationships in retrospect and prospect. *Journal of Research on Adolescence, 11*, 119.

Steinberg, L., Mounts, N. S., Lamborn, S. D., & Dornbusch, S. M. (1991). Authoritative parenting and adolescent adjustment across varied ecological niches. *Journal of Research on Adolescence, 1*, 19–36.

Steiner, J. E. (1979). Human facial expressions in response to taste and smell stimulation. In H. W. Reese & L. P. Lipsitt (Eds.), *Advances in child development and behavior* (Vol. 13). New York: Academic Press.

Stenberg, C. R., Campos, J. J., & Emde, R. N. (1983). The facial expression of anger in seven-month-old infants. *Child Development, 54*, 178–184.

Stern, E. (2005) Pedagogy meets neuroscience. *Science, 310* (4), 745.

Stern, M., & Karraker, K. (1992). Modifying the prematurity stereotype in matters of premature and ill full-term infants. *Journal of Clinical Child Psychology, 21*, 76–82.

Sternberg, R. (1988). Mental self-government: A theory of intellectual styles and their development. *Human Development, 31*, 197–224.

Sternberg, R. J. (1985). *Beyond IQ: A triarchic theory of human intelligence.* New York: Cambridge University Press.

Sternberg, R. J., & Grigorenko, E. J. (2002a). *Dynamic testing: The nature and measurement of learning potential.* New York: Cambridge University Press.

Sternberg, R. J. (2004). What is wisdom and how can we develop it? *The Annals of the American Academy of Political and Social Science, 591*, 164–174.

Sternberg, R. J., Forsythe, G. B., Hedlund, J., Horvath, J. A., Wagner, R. K., Williams, W. M., et al. (2000). *Practical intelligence in everyday life.* Cambridge: Cambridge University Press.

Sternberg, R. J., Grigorenko E. L. & Bundy, D. A. (2001). The predictive value of IQ. *Merrill Palmer Quarterly, 47*, 141.

Sternberg, R. J., Grigorenko, E. L., & Kidd, K. K. (2005). Intelligence, race, and genetics. *American Psychologist, 60*, 46–59.

Sternberg, R. J., & Lubart, T. I. (1991). An investment theory of creativity and its development. *Human Development, 34*, 131.

Sternberg, R. J., & Lubart, T. I. (1995). *Defying the crowd: Cultivating creativity in a culture of conformity.* New York: Free Press.

Sternberg, R. J., & Lubart, T. I. (1996) Investing in creativity. *American Psychologist, 51*, 677–688.

Stevens, J. H. Jr. (1984). Black grandmothers' and black adolescent mothers' knowledge about parenting. *Developmental Psychology, 20,* 1017–1025.

Stevens, M., Golombok, S., Beveridge, M., & Study Team, ALSPAC (2002). Does father absence influence children's gender development?: Findings from a general population study of preschool children. *Parenting: Science and Practice, 2*, 47–60

Stevenson, H. W., Chen, C., & Lee, S. (1993). Motivation and achievement of gifted children in East Asia and the United States. *Journal for the Education of the Gifted, 16*, 223–250.

Stevenson, H. W., Lee, S., & Chen, C. (1990). Mathematics achievement of children in China and the United States. *Child Development, 61*, 1053–1066.

Stevenson, H. W., Lee, S., & Stigler, J. W. (1986). Mathematics achievement of Chinese, Japanese, and American children. *Science, 231*, 693–699.

Stevenson, M. R., & Black, K. N. (1988). Paternal absence and sex-role development: A meta-analysis. *Child Development, 59*, 793–814.

Stice, E., Presnell, K., & Bearman, S. K. (2001). Relation of early menarche to depression, eating disorders, substance abuse, and comorbid psychopathology among adolescent girls. *Developmental Psychology, 37*, 608–619.

Stifter, C. A., & Braungart, J. M. (1995). The regulation of negative reactivity in infancy: Function and development. *Developmental Psychology, 31*, 448–455.

Stiles, J. (2000). Neural plasticity and cognitive Development. *Developmental Neuropsychology, 18*(2), 237–272.

Stipek, D. J. (1990). Children's use of dispositional attributions in predicting the performance and behavior of classmates. *Journal of Applied Developmental Psychology, 11*, 13–28.

Stipek, D. J. (2002). *Motivation to learn: Integrating theory and practice* (4th ed.). Boston: Allyn & Bacon.

Stipek, D. J., & Gralinski, J. H. (1991). Gender differences in children's achievement-related beliefs and emotional responses to success and failure in mathematics. *Journal of Educational Psychology, 83*, 361–371.

Stipek, D., & Gralinski, J. H. (1996). Children's beliefs about intelligence and school performance. *Journal of Educational Psychology, 88*(3), 397–407.

Stipek, D. J., Recchia, S., & McClintic, S. (1992). Self-evaluation in young children. *Monographs of the Society for Research in Child Development, 57*(1, Serial No. 226).

Stipek, D. J., & Tannatt, L. (1984). Children's judgments of their own and their peers' academic competence. *Journal of Educational Psychology, 76*, 75–84.

Stjernfeldt, M., Berglund, K., Lindsten, J., & Ludvigssonf, J. (1986). Maternal smoking during pregnancy and risk of childhood cancer. *Lancet, 1*, 1350–1352.

Stocker, C., & Dunn, J. (1990). Sibling relationships in childhood: Links with friendships and peer relationships. *British Journal of Developmental Psychology, 8*, 227–244.

Stocker, C. M., & Mantz-Simmons, L. M. (1993). Children's friendship and peer status: Links with family relationships, temperament, and social skills. Unpublished manuscript.

Stoddart, T., & Turiel, E. (1985). Children's concepts of cross-gender activities. *Child Development, 56*, 1241–1252.

Stoll, C., Dott, B., Alembik, Y., & Roth, M. (1993). Evaluation of routine prenatal ultrasound examination in detecting fetal chromosomal abnormalities in a low risk population. *Human Genetics, 91*, 37–41.

Stone, C. A., & Day, M. C. (1978). Levels of availability of a formal operational strategy. *Child Development, 49*, 1054–1065.

Stone, M. R., & Brown, B. B. (1999). Identity claims and projections: Descriptions of self and crowds in secondary school. *New Directions for Child & Adolescent Development, 99* (84), 720.

Stormshak, E. A., Bierman, K. L., McMahon, R. J., Lengua, L. J., & Conduct Problems Prevention Research Group. (2000). Parenting practices and child disruptive behavior problems in early elementary school. *Journal of Clinical Child Psychology, 29*, 17–29.

Straker, G. (1992). *Faces in the revolution.* Cape Town, South Africa: David Philip.

Strapp, C. M. (1999). Mothers', fathers', and siblings' responses to children's language errors: Comparing sources of negative evidence. *Journal of Child Language, 26*, 373–391.

Straughan, R. (1986). Why act on Kohlberg's moral judgments? (Or how to reach Stage 6 and remain a bastard). In S. Modgil & C. Modgil (Eds.), *Lawrence Kohlberg: Consensus and controversy.* Philadelphia: Falmer.

Strayer, F. F., & Noel, J. M. (1986). The prosocial and antisocial functions of preschool aggression: An ethological study of triadic conflict among young children. In C. Zahn-Waxler, E. M. Cummings, & R. Iannotti (Eds.), *Altruism and aggression: Biological and social origins.* Cambridge: Cambridge University Press.

Streissguth, A. P., & Connor, P. D. (2001). Fetal alcohol syndrome and other effects of prenatal alcohol: Developmental cognitive neuroscience implications. In C. A. Nelson & M. Luciana (Eds.), *Handbook of developmental cognitive neuroscience.* Cambridge, MA: MIT Press.

Streri, A., Lhote, M., & Dutilleul, S. (2000). Haptic perception in newborns. *Developmental Science, 3*, 319–327.

Subrahmanyam, K., & Greenfield, P. M. (1994). Effect of video game practice on spatial skills in girls and boys. *Journal of Applied Developmental Psychology, 15*, 13–32.

Subrahmanyam, K., & Greenfield, P. M. (1996). Effect of video game practice on spatial skills in girls and boys (pp. 95–114). In P. M. Greenfield & R. R. Cocking (Eds.), *Interacting with video* (pp. 95–114). Norwood, NJ: Ablex.

Subrahmanyam, K., & Greenfield, P. M. (1998). Computer games for girls: What makes them play? In J. Cassell & H. Jenkins (Eds.), *From Barbie to Mortal Kombat: Gender and computer games.* Cambridge, MA: MIT Press.

Subrahmanyam, K., Greenfield, P. M., Kraut, R., & Gross, E. (2001). The impact of computer use on children's and adolescents' development. *Applied Developmental Psychology, 22*, 730.

Sue, S., & Ozaki, S. (1990). Asian-American educational achievements: A phenomenon in search of an explanation. *American Psychologist, 45*, 913, 920.

Sujan, H., Weitz, B. A., & Sujan, M. (1988). Increasing sales productivity by getting salespeople to work smarter, *Journal of Personnel Selling and Sales Management*, 919.

Sullivan, P. F. (1995). Mortality in anorexia nervosa. *American Journal of Psychiatry, 152*, 1073–1074.

Super, C. M. (1981). Cross-cultural research on infancy. In H. C. Triandis & A. Heron (Eds.), *Handbook of cross-cultural psychology*: Vol. 4. *Developmental psychology.* Boston: Allyn & Bacon.

Super, C. M., & Harkness, S. (1986). The developmental niche: A conceptualization at the interface of child and culture. *International Journal of Behavioral Development* (Special Issue: Cross-cultural human development) 9, 545–569.

Super, C., Harkness, S., van Tijen, N., van der Vlugt, E., Fintelman, M., & Dijkstra, J. (1996) The three R's of Dutch childrearing and the socialization of infant arousal. In S. Harkness & C. Super (Eds.), *Parents' cultural belief systems* (pp. 447–466). New York: Guilford.

Supplee, L. H., Shaw, D. S., Hailstones, K., & Hartman, K. (2004). Family and child influences on early academic and emotion regulatory behaviors. *Journal of School Psychology, 42,* 221–242.

Sussman, E. J., Inoff-Germain, G., Nottelmann, E. D., Loriauz, L., Cutler, G. B., & Chrousos, G. P. (1987). Hormones, emotional dispositions, and aggressive attributes in young adolescents. *Child Development, 58,* 1114–1134.

Sutton P., & Mathews, T. J. (2004). Trends in characteristics of births by state: United States, 1990, 1995, and 2000-2002. *National Vital Statistics Reports, 52*(19). Hyattsville, MD: National Center for Health Statistics.

Sutton-Smith, B., & Roberts, J. M. (1973). The cross-cultural and psychological study of games. In B. Sutton-Smith (Ed.), *The folkgames of children.* Austin: University of Texas Press.

Suzuki, A. (2005). Development of self-regulation in young children in interpersonal situations: An investigation of self-inhibitive and self-assertive behavior using experimental and imaginary tasks. *Japanese Journal of Developmental Psychology, 16,* 202–204.

Suzuki, A., Koyasu, M., & An, N. (2004). Development of understanding of others' intention, social problem solving abilities, and, theory of mind in young children. *Japanese Journal of Developmental Psychology, 15,* 292–301.

Symons, D. K. (2004). Mental state discourse, theory of mind, and the internalisation of self-other understanding. *Developmental Review, 24,* 159–188.

Swain, I. U., Zelazo, P. R., & Clifton, R. K. (1993). Newborn infants' memory for speech sounds retained over 24 hours. *Developmental Psychology, 29,* 313–323.

Swallen, K. C., Reither, E., Haas, S. A., & Meier, A. (2005). Obesity, social background, and quality of life among adolescents. *Pediatrics, 115*(2):340–347.

Sweeney, L. & Rapee, R. (2001) Social phobia in children and adolescents: Psychological treatments. In W. Ray Crozier & Lynne E. Alden (Eds.), *International Handbook of Social Anxiety* (pp. 525–537). New York: Wiley.

Taddio, A., Katz, J., Bersich, A. L., Goren, K. (1997). Effect of neonatal circumcision on pain response during subsequent routine vaccination. *Lancet, 349,* 599–603.

Taddio, A., Shah, V., Gilbert-MacLeod, C., & Katz, J. (2002). Conditioning and hyperalgesia in newborns exposed to repeated heel lances. *Journal of the American Medical Association, 288,* 857–861.

Tafaradi, R. W., Marshall, T. C., & Katsura, H. (2004). Standing out in Canada and Japan. *Journal of Personality, 72,* 785–814.

Tager-Flusberg, H., & Calkins, S. (1990). Does imitation facilitate the acquisition of grammar? Evidence from a study of autistic, Down's syndrome and normal children. *Journal of Child Language, 17,* 591–606.

Takahashi, K. (1990). Are the key assumptions of the "Strange Situation" procedure universal? A view from Japanese research. *Human Development, 33,* 23–30.

Tamis-LeMonda, C. S., & Bornstein, M. H. (1991). Individual variation, correspondence, stability, and change in mother and toddler play. *Infant Behavior and Development, 14,* 143–162.

Tamis-LeMonda, C. S., Uzgiris, I. C., & Bornstein, M. H. (2002). Play in parent-child interactions. In M. H. Bornstein (Ed.), *Handbook of parenting* (2nd ed., Vol. 5). Mahwah, NJ: Erlbaum.

Tamres, L. K., Janicki, D., & Helgeson, V. S. (2002). Sex differences in coping behavior: A meta-analytic review and an examination of relative coping. *Personality and Social Psychology Review, 6,* 2–30.

Tanapat, P., Hastings, N., & Gould, E. (2001). Adult neurogenesis in the hippocampal function. In C.A. Nelson & M. Luciana (Eds.), *Handbook of developmental cognitive neuroscience.* Bradford Books.

Tangney, J. P., Baumeister, R. F., & Boone, A. (2004). High self-control predicts good adjustment, less pathology, better grades, and interpersonal success. *Journal of Personality, 72,* 271–324.

Tangney, J., & Fischer, K. (Eds.). (1995). *Self-conscious emotions: The psychology of shame, guilt, embarrassment, and pride.* New York: Guilford.

Tanner, J. M. (1990). *Fetus into man: Physical growth from conception to maturity* (2nd ed.). Cambridge, MA: Harvard University Press.

Tanner, J. M. (1992). Growth as a measure of the nutritional and hygienic status of a population. (eng; includes abstract). *Hormone Research, 38*(1), 106–121.

Tanner, J. M., Whitehouse, R. H., & Takaishi, M. (1966). Standards for growth and growth velocities. *Archives of Disease in Childhood, 41,* 467.

Tappan, M. B. (1997) Language, culture, and moral development: A Vygotskian perspective. *Developmental Review, 17,* 78–100.

Tarabulsy, G., Bernier, A., Provost, M., Maranda, J., Larose, S., Moss, E., Larose, M., & Tessier, R. (2005). Another look inside the gap: Ecological contributions to the transmission of attachment in a sample of adolescent mother-infant dyads. *Developmental Psychology, 41,* 212–224.

Tardif, T., Gelman, S. A., & Xu, F. (1999). Putting the "noun bias" in context: A comparison of English and Mandarin. *Child Development, 70,* 620–635.

Tasker, F. L., & Golombok, S. (1997). *Growing up in a lesbian family: Effects on child development.* New York: Guilford.

Tatum, B.D. (1997). *Why are all the black kids sitting together in the cafeteria? and other conversations about race.* New York: Basic Books.

Taylor, H. G., Klein, N., Minich, N. M., & Hack, M. (2000). Middle-school-age outcomes in children with very low birthweight. Child Development, 71, 1495–1511.

Taylor, J., Iacono, W. G., & McGue, M. (2001). Evidence for a genetic etiology of early-onset delinquency. *Journal of Abnormal Behavior, 109,* 634–643.

Taylor, M. G. (1996). The development of children's beliefs about social and biological aspects of gender differences. *Child Development, 67,* 1555–1571.

Taylor, M. J., & Baldeweg, T. (2002). Application of EEG, ERP and intracranial recordings to the investigation of cognitive functions in children. *Developmental Science, 5,* 318–334.

Taylor, M., Cartwright, B. S., & Bowden, T. (1991). Perspective taking and theory of mind: Do children predict interpretive diversity as a function of differences in observers' knowledge? *Child Development, 62,* 1334–1351.

Taylor, M., Esbensen, B. M., & Bennett, R. T. (1994). Children's understanding of knowledge acquisition: The tendency for children to report that they have always known what they have just learned. *Child Development, 65,* 1581–1604.

Taylor, R. D., Casten, R., & Flickinger, S. M. (1993). Influence of kinship social support on the parenting experiences and psychosocial adjustment of African-American adolescents. *Developmental Psychology, 29,* 382–388.

Taylor, S. D. (2004). Predictive genetic test decisions for Huntington's disease: context, appraisal and new moral imperatives. *Social Science & Medicine, 58*(1), 137–150.

Teller, D. Y., & Bornstein, M. H. (1987). Infant color vision and color perception. In P. Salapatek & L. Cohen (Eds.), *Handbook of infant perception:* Vol. 1. *From sensation to perception.* New York: Academic Press.

Temple, J. A., Reynolds, A. J., & Miedel, W. T. (2000). Can early intervention prevent high school dropout? Evidence from the Chicago Child-Parent Centers. *Urban Education, 35*(1), 31–56.

Tenenbaum, H. R., & Leaper, C. (2003). Parent-child conversations about science: The socialization of gender inequities? *Developmental Psychology, 39,* 34–47.

Tennant, G. (2004). Differential classroom interactions by ethnicity: A qualitative approach. *Emotional & Behavioral Difficulties, 9,* 191–204.

Terwogt, M. M. (2002). Emotional states in self and others as motives for helping in 10-year-old children. *British Journal of Developmental Psychology, 20,* 131–147.

Tesser, A. (1984). Self-evaluation maintenance processes: Implications for relationships and for development. In J. C. Masters & K. Yarkin-Levin (Eds.), *Boundary areas in social and developmental psychology.* New York: Academic Press.

Teti, D. M. (1992). Sibling interaction. In V. B. Van Hasselt & M. Hersen (Eds.), *Handbook of social development.* New York: Plenum.

Thabet, A., & Vostanis, P. (1999). Post-traumatic stress reactions in children of war. *Journal of Child Psychology and Psychiatry and Allied Disciplines, 40,* 385–391.

Tharp, R. G. (1989). Psychocultural variables and constants: Effects on teaching and learning in schools. *American Psychologist, 44,* 349–359.

Thatcher, R. W., Lyon, G. R., Ramsey, J., & Krasneger, J. (1996). *Developmental neuroimaging.* San Diego, CA: Academic Press.

The State of the World's Children 2002. New York:, United Nations Children's Fund, 2002.

Thelen, E. (1994). Three-month-old infants can learn task-specific patterns of interlimb coordination. *Psychological Science, 5,* 280–285.

Thelen, E. (1995). Motor development: A new synthesis. *American Psychologist, 50,* 79–95.

Thelen, E. (2000). Motor development as foundation and future of developmental psychology. *International Journal of Behavioral Development, 24,* 385–397.

Thelen, E., Corbetta, D., & Spencer, J. (1996). The development of reaching during the first year: The role of movement speed. *Journal of Experimental Psychology: Human Perception and Performance, 22,* 1059–1076.

Thelen, E., & Fisher, D. M. (1983). The organization of spontaneous leg movements in newborn infants. *Journal of Motor Behavior, 15,* 353–377.

Thelen, E., & Smith, L. B. (1998). Dynamic systems theories. In W. Damon (Series Ed.) & R. M. Lerner (Vol. Ed.), *Handbook of child psychology:*

Vol. 1. *Theoretical models of human development* (5th ed.). New York: Wiley.

Thoman, E. B. (1990). Sleeping and waking states in infants: A functional perspective. *Neuroscience and Biobehavioral Reviews, 14,* 93–107.

Thoman, E. B. (1993). Obligation and option in the premature nursery. *Developmental Review, 13,* 1–30.

Thoman, E. B., & McDowell K. (1989). Sleep cyclicity in infants during the earliest postnatal weeks. *Physiology and Behaviour, 45*(3), 51–722.

Thomas, A., & Chess, S. (1977). *Temperament and development.* New York: Bruner/Mazel.

Thomas, A., & Chess, S. (1986). The New York Longitudinal Study: From infancy to early adult life. In R. Plomin & J. Dunn (Eds.), *The study of temperament: Changes, continuities and challenges.* Hillsdale, NJ: Erlbaum.

Thomas, A., Chess, S., & Birch, H. G. (1968). *Temperament and behavior disorders in children.* New York: New York University Press.

Thomas, A., Chess, S., & Birch, H. G. (1970). The origin of personality. *Scientific American, 223,* 102–109.

Thompson, R. A. (1990). Vulnerability in research: A developmental perspective on research risk. *Child Development, 61,* 1–16.

Thompson, R. A. (1999). Early attachment and later development. In J. Cassidy & P. R. Shaver (Eds.), *Handbook of attachment: Theory, research, and clinical applications* (pp. 265–286). New York: Guilford.

Thomson, J. R., & Chapman, R. S. (1977). Who is "Daddy" revisited: The status of two-year-olds' over-extended words in use and comprehension. *Journal of Child Language, 4,* 359–375.

Thompson, R. A., Easterbrooks, M. A., & Padilla-Walker, L. M. (2003). Social and emotional development in infancy. In R.M. Lerner & M.A. Easterbrooks (Eds.), *Handbook of psychology: Developmental psychology* (Vol. 6, pp. 91–112). New York: Wiley.

Thompson, R. A., Flood, M. F., & Lundquist, L. (1995). Emotion regulation: Its relations to attachment and developmental psychopathology. In D. Cicchetti & S. L. Toth (Eds.), *Emotion, cognition, and representation. Rochester Symposium on Developmental Psychopathology* (Vol. 6). Rochester, NY: University of Rochester Press.

Thompson, R. A., & Limber, S. (1991). "Social anxiety" in infancy: Stranger wariness and separation distress. In H. Leitenberg (Ed.), *Handbook of social and evaluation anxiety* (pp. 85–137). New York: Plenum.

Thompson, R. A., & Nelson, C. A. (2001). Developmental science and the media. *American Psychologist, 56*(1), 5–16.

Thompson, T. L., & Zerbinos, E. (1995). Gender roles in animated cartoons: Has the picture changed in 20 years? *Sex Roles, 32,* 651–674.

Thompson, T. L., & Zerbinos, E. (1997). Television cartoons: Do children notice it's a boy's world? *Sex Roles, 37,* 415–432.

Thorne, B. (1993). *Gender play: Girls and boys in school.* New Brunswick, NJ: Rutgers University Press.

Tiedemann, J. (2000). Parents' gender stereotypes and teachers' beliefs as predictors of children's concept of their mathematical ability in elementary school. *Journal of Educational Psychology, 92,* 144–151.

Tiemann-Boege, I., Navidi, W., Grewal, R., Cohn, D., Eskenazi, B., Wyrobek, A., & Arnheim, N. (2002). The observed human sperm mutation frequency cannot explain the achondroplasia paternal age effect. *Proceedings of the National Academy of Sciences of the United States of America. 99*(23), 14952–14957.

Tieso, C. L. (2003). Ability grouping is not just tracking anymore. *Roeper Review, 26,* 29–36.

Tieszen, H. R. (1979). Children's social behavior in a Korean preschool. *Journal of Korean Home Economics Association, 17,* 71–84.

Tisak, M. S., & Turiel, E. (1988). Variation in seriousness of transgressions and children's immoral and conventional concepts. *Developmental Psychology, 24,* 352–357.

Tobey, A. E., & Goodman, G. S. (1992). Children's eyewitness memory: Effects of participation and forensic context. *Child Abuse and Neglect, 16,* 779–796.

Tobin, J. J., Wu, D. Y. H., & Davidson, D. H. (1989). *Preschool in three cultures.* New Haven, CT: Yale University Press.

Toda, S., & Fogel, A. (1993). Infant response to the still-face situation at 3 and 6 months. *Developmental Psychology, 29,* 532–538.

Tomasello, M., & Call, J. (1997). *Primate cognition.* Oxford: Oxford University Press.

Tomasello, M. (2001). Perceiving intentions and learning words in the second year of life. In M. Bowerman & S. C. Levinson (Eds.), *Language acquisition and conceptual development.* New York: Cambridge University Press.

Tomasello, M., Conti-Ramsden, G., & Ewert, B. (1990). Young children's conversations with their mothers and fathers: Differences in breakdown and repair. *Journal of Child Language, 17,* 115–130.

Tomasello, M., & Farrar, M. J. (1986). Joint attention and early language. *Child Development, 57,* 1454–1463.

Tomasello, M., & Haberl, K. (2003). Understanding attention: 12- and 18-month-olds know what is new for other persons. *Developmental Psychology, 39,* 906–912.

Tomasello, M., & Merriman, W. E. (Eds.). (1995). *Beyond names for things: Young children's acquisition of verbs.* Hillsdale, NJ: Erlbaum.

Tomasello, M., Savage-Rumbaugh, S., & Kruger, A. C. (1993). Imitative learning of actions on objects by children, chimpanzees, and enculturated chimpanzees. *Child Development, 64,* 1688–1705.

Tooby, J., & Cosmides, L. (1995). Mapping the evolved functional organization of mind and brain. In M. S. Gazzaniga (Ed.), *The cognitive neurosciences.* Cambridge, MA: MIT Press.

Torgesen, J. K., & Burgess, S. R. (1998). Consistency of reading-related phonological processes throughout early childhood: Evidence from longitudinal-correlational and instructional studies. In J. Metsala & L. Ehri (Eds.), *Word recognition in beginning reading.* Hillsdale, NJ: Erlbaum.

Trainor, L. J., & Heinmiller, B. M. (1998). The development of evaluative responses to music: Infants prefer to listen to consonance over dissonance. *Infant Behavior and Development, 21,* 77–88.

Trautner, H. M. (1992). The development of sex-typing in children: A longitudinal analysis. *German Journal of Psychology, 16,* 183–199.

Trehub, S. E. (1976). The discrimination of foreign speech contrasts by infants and adults. *Child Development, 47,* 466–472.

Trehub, S. E., & Henderson, J. (1994, July). *Caregivers' songs and their effect on infant listeners.* Proceedings of the Meeting of the International Conference for Music Perception and Cognition. Liege, Belgium.

Trehub, S. E., & Schellenberg, E. G. (1995). Music: Its relevance to infants. In R. Vasta (Ed.), *Annals of child development* (Vol. 11). London: Kingsley.

Tremblay, R. E., Japel, C., Perusse, D., McDuff, P., Boivin, M., Zoccolillo, M., et al. (1999). The search for the age of "onset" of physical aggression: Rousseau and Bandura revisited. *Criminal Behaviour and Mental Health, 9,* 8–23.

Tremblay, R. E., Pihl, R. O., Vitaro, F., & Dobkin, P. L. (1994). Predicting early onset of male antisocial behavior from preschool behavior. *Archives of General Psychiatry, 51,* 732–739.

Triandis, H. C., Brislin, R., &. Hui, C. H. (1988). Cross-cultural training across the individualism-collectivism divide. *International Journal of Intercultural Relations, 12,* 3.

Trickett, P. K., & McBride-Chang, C. (1995). The developmental impact of different forms of child abuse and neglect. *Developmental Review, 15,* 311–337.

Trivers, R. L. (1971). The evolution of reciprocal altruism. *Quarterly Review of Biology, 46,* 35–57.

Trivers, R. L. (1983). The evolution of cooperation. In D. L. Bridgeman (Ed.), *The nature of prosocial development.* New York: Academic Press.

Trost, S. G., Pate, R. R., Sallis, J. F., et al. (2002). Age and gender differences in objectively measured physical activity in youth. *Med. Sci. Sports Exerc., 34,* 350–355.

Trzesniewski, K. H., Donnellan, M. B., & Robins, R. W. (2003). Stability of self-esteem across the lifespan. *Journal of Personality and Social Psychology, 84,* 205–220.

Tucker, C. J., McHale, S. M., & Crouter, A. C. (2001). Conditions of sibling support in adolescence. *Journal of Family Psychology, 15,* 254–271.

Tudge, J. R. H. (1989). When collaboration leads to regression: Some negative consequences of socio-cognitive conflict. *European Journal of Social Psychology, 19,* 123–138.

Tudge, J. R. H. (1992). Processes and consequences of peer collaboration: A Vygotskian analysis. *Child Development, 63,* 1364–1379.

Tuladhar, R., Harding, R., Adamson, T. M., & Horne, R. S. C.. Comparison of postnatal development of heart rate responses to trigeminal stimulation in sleeping preterm and term infants. *Journal of Sleep Research, 14*(1) 29–36.

Turati, C., Cassia, V. M. Simion, F., & Leo, I. (2006). Newborns' face recognition: Role of inner and outer facial features. *Child Development, 77,* 297–311.

Turiel, E. (2002). *The culture of morality.* New York: Cambridge University Press.

Turiel, E., Killen, M., & Helwig, C. C. (1987). Morality: Its structure, functions, and vagaries. In J. Kagan & S. Lamb (Eds.), *The emergence of moral concepts in young children.* Chicago: University of Chicago Press.

Turiel, E., & Wainryb, C. (1994). Social reasoning and the varieties of social experiences in cultural contexts. In H. W. Reese (Ed.), *Advances in child development and behavior* (Vol. 25). San Diego, CA: Academic Press.

Turkheimer, E. (2000). Three laws of behavior genetics and what they mean. *Current Directions in Psychological Science, 9,* 160–164.

Turkheimer, E., & Waldron, M. (2000). Nonshared environment: A theoretical, methodological, and quantitative review. *Psychological Bulletin, 126,* 78–108.

Turiel, E. (2002). *The culture of morality.* New York: Cambridge University Press.

Turner, P. J., & Gervai, J. (1995). A multidimensional study of gender typing in preschool children and their parents: Personality, attitudes, preferences, behavior, and cultural differences. *Developmental Psychology, 31,* 759–772.

Turner, L. A., & Johnson, B. (2003). A model of mastery motivation for at-risk preschoolers. *Journal of Educational Psychology, 95*, 495–505.

Twenge, J. M., Catanese, K. R., & Baumeister, R. F. (2002). Social exclusion causes self-defeating behavior. *Journal of Personality and Social Psychology, 83*, 606–615.

Twenge, J. M., Catanese, K. R., & Baumeister, R. F. (2003). Social exclusion and the deconstructed state: Time perception, meaninglessness, lethargy, lack of emotion, and self-awareness. *Journal of Personality and Social Psychology, 85*, 409–423.

Underwood, M. K. (2003). *Social aggression among girls.* New York: Guilford.

Underwood, M. K., Coie, J. D., & Herbsman, C. R. (1992). Display rules for anger and aggression in school-age children. *Child Development, 63*, 366–380.

United Nations Development Programme. (2002). Human Development Report. New York.

Updegraff, K. A., McHale, S. M., & Crouter, A. C. (2000). Adolescents' sex-typed friendship experiences: Does having a sister versus a brother matter? *Child Development, 71*, 1597–1610.

Urbain, E. S., & Kendell, P. C. (1980). Review of social-cognitive problem-solving interventions with children. *Psychological Bulletin, 88*, 109–143.

Urberg, K. A. (1999). Introduction: Some thoughts about studying the influence of peers on children and adolescents. *Merrill-Palmer Quarterly, 45*, 1–12.

Urberg, K. A., Degirmencioglu, S. M., & Pilgrim, C. (1997). Close friend and group influence on adolescent cigarette smoking and alcohol use. *Developmental Psychology, 33*, 834–844.

U.S. Census Bureau. (1992). General population characteristics: United States (Current Population Reports, CP-1-1). Washington, DC: U.S. Department of Commerce.

U.S. Bureau of the Census (2001). *Statistical abstract of the United States* (121st ed.). Washington, DC: U.S. Government Printing Office.

U.S Bureau of the Census (2003). *Language use and English-speaking ability: 2000.* Retrieved December 5, 2005, http://www.census.gov/ Press-Release/www/releases/archives/census_2000/001-4 06.html.

U.S. Department of Education. (2001). *Nation's report card: Mathematics 2000.* http://nces.ed.gov/nationsreportcard/pubs/main20 00/ 2001–517.asp

U.S. Department of Education (2005). State formula grant program. Retrieved March 22, 2005, from http://www.ed.gov/programs/sfgp/ nrgcomp.html

U.S. Department of Health and Human Services. (1999). *Mental Health: A report of the Surgeon General—Executive Summary.* Rockville, MD: U.S. Department of Health and Human Services, Substance Abuse and Mental Health Services Administration, Center for Mental Health Services.

U.S. Department of Health and Human Services. (2000). *Healthy people 2010: Understanding and improving health. 2nd ed.* Washington, DC: U.S. Government Printing Office, Retrieved March 16, 2006 from http://www.healthypeople.gov/ Document/HTML/Volume2/16MICH.htm#_ Toc494699653.

U.S. Department of Health and Human Services (2004). Health Resources and Services Administration, Maternal and Child Health Bureau. *Child Health USA 2004.* Rockville, MD: U.S. Department of Health and Human Services.

U.S. Food & Drug Administration (2004). *Antidepressant use in children, adolescents, and adults.* U.S. Food and Drug Administration (http://www.fda.gov/cder/drug/antidepressants/de fault.htm). Accessed August 7, 2005.

Uttal, D. H. (2000). Seeing the big picture: Map use and the development of spatial cognition. *Developmental Science, 3*, 247–286.

Valian, V. (1996). *Parental replies: Linguistic status and didactic role.* Cambridge, MA: MIT Press.

Valian, V. (1999). Input and language acquisition. In W. C. Ritchie & T. K. Bhatia (Eds.), *Handbook of child language acquisition.* San Diego, CA: Academic Press.

Valsiner, J. (1997). *Culture and the development of children's action: A theory of human development.* New York: Wiley.

Vamvakoussi, X., & Vosniadou, S. (2004). Understanding the structure of the set of rational numbers: A conceptual change approach. *Learning and Instruction 14*, 453–467.

Van Balen, F. (1998). Development of IVF children. *Developmental Review, 18*, 30–46.

Van de gaer, E., Pustjens, H., Van Damme, J., & De Munter, A. (2004). Effects of single-sex versus co-educational classes and schools on gender differences in progress in language and mathematics achievement. *British Journal of Sociology of Education, 25*, 307–322.

Van Den Bergh, B. R. H. (1992). Maternal emotions during pregnancy and fetal and neonatal behavior. In J. G. Nijhuis (Ed.), *Fetal behavior: Developmental and perinatal aspects.* New York: Oxford University Press.

Van den Bergh, B. R., & De Rycke, L. (2003). Measuring the multidimensional self-concept and global self-worth of 6- to 8-year-olds. *Journal of Genetic Psychology, 164*, 201–225.

Van den Bergh, B. R. H., & Marcoen, A. (1999). Harter's self-perception profile for children: Factor structure, reliability, and convergent validity in a Dutch-speaking Belgian sample of fourth, fifth and sixth graders. *Psychologica Belgica, 39*, 29–47.

van den Boom, D. C. (1994). The influence of temperament and mothering on attachment and exploration: An experimental manipulation of sensitive responsiveness among lower-class mothers with irritable infants. *Child Development, 65*, 1457–1477.

van den Boom, D., & Hoeksma, J. B. (1994). The effect of infant irritability on mother-infant interaction: A growth-curve analysis. *Developmental Psychology, 30*, 581–590.

Van der Veer, R., & Valsiner, J. (1988). Lev Vygotsky and Pierre Janet: On the origin of the concept of sociogenesis. *Developmental Review, 8*, 52–65.

van Giffen, K., & Haith, M. M. (1984). Infant visual response to gestalt geometric forms. *Behavior and Development, 7*, 335–346.

van IJzendoorn, M. H. (1992). Intergenerational transmission of parenting: A review of studies in nonclinical populations. *Developmental Review, 12*, 76–99.

van IJzendoorn, M. H. (1995). Associations between adult attachment representations and parent-child attachment, parent responsiveness, and clinical status: A meta-analysis on the predictive validity of the Adult Attachment Interview. *Psychological Bulletin, 117*, 387–403.

van IJzendoorn, M. H., & De Wolff, M. S. (1997). In search of the absent father-meta-analyses of infant-father attachment: A rejoinder to our discussants. *Child Development, 68*, 604–609.

van IJzendoorn, M. H., Goldberg, S., Kroonenberg, P. M., & Frenkel, O. J. (1992). The relative effects of maternal and child problems on the quality of attachment: A meta-analysis of attachment in clinical samples. *Child Development, 63*, 840–858.

van IJzendoorn, M. H., Juffer, F., & Duyvesteyn, M. G. C. (1995). Breaking the intergenerational cycle of insecure attachment: A review of the effects of attachment-based interventions on maternal sensitivity and infant security. *Journal of Child Psychology and Psychiatry and Allied Disciplines, 36*, 225–248.

Van IJzendoorn, M. H., Juffer, F., & Klein Poelhuis, C. W. (2005). Adoption and cognitive development: A meta-analytic comparison of adopted and nonadopted children.s IQ and school performance. *Psychological Bulletin, 131*, 301–316.

van IJzendoorn, M. H., & Kroonenberg, P. M. (1988). Cross-cultural patterns of attachment: A meta-analysis of the Strange Situation. *Child Development, 59*, 147–156.

van IJzendoorn, M., & Sagi, A. (1999). Cross-cultural patterns of attachment: Universal and contextual dimensions. In J. Cassidy & P. Shaver (Eds.), *Handbook of attachment* (pp. 713–734). New York: Guilford.

Van Leeuwen, L., Kaufmann, F., & Walther, D. (2000). Control of action and interaction: Preceiving and producing effects in action and interaction with objects. In W.J. Perrig & G. Alexander (Eds.), *Control of human behaviour, mental processes, and consciousness: Essays in honor of the 60th birthday of August Flammar.* Mahwah, NJ: Erlbaum.

Van Tuinen, I., & Wolfe, S. M. (1993). *Unnecessary cesarean sections: Halting a national epidemic.* Washington, DC: Public Citizens' Health Research Group.

van Wieringen, P. C. W. (1986). Motor coordination: Constraints and cognition. In M.G. Wade and H.T.A. Whiting (Eds.), *Motor development in children: Aspects of coordination and control* (pp. 361–371). Dordrecht: Martinus Nijhoff.

Vandell, D. L., Minnet, A. M., Johnson, B. S., & Santrock, J. W. (1990). Siblings and friends: Experiences of school-aged children. Unpublished manuscript, University of Texas at Dallas.

Vartanian, L. R. (2000). Revisiting the imaginary audience and personal fable constructs of adolescent egocentrism: A conceptual review. *Adolescence, 35*, 639–661.

Vasta, R., Knott, J. A., & Gaze, C. E. (1996). Can spatial training erase the gender differences on the water-level task? *Psychology of Women Quarterly, 20*, 549–567.

Vasta, R., & Liben, L. S. (1996). The water-level task: An intriguing puzzle. *Current Directions in Psychological Science, 5*, 171–177.

Vasta, R., Rosenberg, D., Knott, J. A., & Gaze, C. E. (1997). Experience and the water-level task revisited: Does expertise exact a price? *Psychological Science, 8*, 336–339.

Vaughn, B. E., & Bost, K. K. (1999). Attachment and temperament: Redundant, independent, or interacting influences on interpersonal adaptation and personality development? In J. Cassidy & P. R. Shaver (Eds.), *Handbook of attachment: Theory, research, and clinical applications.* New York: Guilford.

Vellutino, F. R., Fletcher, J. M., Snowling, M. J., & Scanlon, D. M. (2004). Specific reading disability (dyslexia): What have we learned in the past four decades? *Journal of Child Psychology & Psychiatry, 45*, 2–40.

Veneziano, R. & Muller, B. (Eds.) (2005). Theme issue: Cross-cultural research in parental acceptance-rejection theory [Special issue]. *Ethos, 33*, (3).

Verbeek, P., Hartup, W. W., & Collins, W. A. (2000). Conflict management in children and adolescents. In F. Aureli & F. B. M. de Waal (Eds.), *Natural conflict resolution*. Berkeley: University of California Press.

Vierikko, E., Pulkkinen, L., Kaprio, J., Viken, R., & Rose, R. J. (2003). Sex differences in genetic and environmental effects on aggresion. *Aggressive Behavior, 29*, 55–68.

Vietze, P. M., & Vaughan, H. G. (1988). *Early identification of infants with developmental disabilities*. Philadelphia: Grune & Stratton.

Vihman, M. M. (1985). Language differentiation by the bilingual infant. *Journal of Child Language, 12*, 297–324.

Vinden, P. G. (1996). Junin Quechua children's understanding of mind. *Child Development, 67*, 1707–1716.

Volling, B. L., Youngblade, L. M., & Belsky, J. (1997). Young children's social relationships with siblings and friends. *American Journal of Orthopsychiatry, 67*, 102–111.

Volterra, V., Caselli, M. C., & Capirci, O. (2005). Gesture and the emergence and development of language. In M. Tomasello & D.I. Slobin (Eds.), *Beyond nature-nurture: Essays in honor of Elizabeth Bates* (pp. 3–40). Mahwah, NJ: Erlbaum.

Volterra, V., & Taeschner, T. (1978). The acquisition and development of language by bilingual children. *Journal of Child Language, 5*, 311–326.

Vosniadou, S., Skopeliti, I. & Ikospentaki, K. (2004). Modes of knowing and ways of reasoning in elementary astronomy. *Cognitive Development, 19*, 203–222.

Voyer, D., Voyer, S., & Bryden, M. P. (1995). Magnitude of sex differences in spatial abilities: A meta-analysis and consideration of critical variables. *Psychological Bulletin, 117*, 250–270.

Vuchinich, S. (1990). The sequential organization of closing in verbal family conflict. In A. D. Grimshaw (Ed.), *Conflict talk: Sociolinguistic investigations of arguments in conversations*. Cambridge: Cambridge University Press.

Vuchinich, S., Bank, L., & Patterson, G. R. (1992). Parenting, peers, and the stability of antisocial behavior in preadolescent boys. *Developmental Psychology, 28*, 510–521.

Vurpillot, E. (1968). The development of scanning strategies and their relation to visual differentiation. *Journal of Experimental Child Psychology, 6*, 632–650.

Vurpillot, E., & Ball, W. A. (1979). The concept of identity and children's selective attention. In G. A. Hale & M. Lewis (Eds.), *Attention and cognitive development*. New York: Plenum.

Vurpillot, E., Castelo, R., & Renard, C. (1975). Extent of visual exploration and number of elements present around the stimulus in a perceptual differentiation task. *Anné Psychologique, 75*, 362–363.

Vygotsky, L. S. (1934/1962). *Thought and language*. Cambridge, MA: MIT Press.

Vygotksy, L. S. (1978). *The collected works of L. S. Vygotsky: Vol. 1. Problems of general psychology*. New York: Plenum Press.

Vygotsky, L. S. (1981). The genesis of higher mental functions. In J. V. Wertsch (Ed.), *The concept of activity in Soviet psychology*. Armonk, NY: M. E. Sharpe.

Vyt, A. (2001). Processes of visual self-recognition in infants: Experimental induction of "mirror" experience via video self-image presentation. *Infant & child development, 10*, 173–187.

Waas, G. A. (1988). Social attributional biases of peer-rejected and aggressive children. *Child Development, 59*, 969–975.

Wadsworth, S. J., Corley, R. P., Hewitt, J. K., & De-Fries, J. C. (2001). Stability of genetic and environmental influences on reading performance at 7, 12, and 16 years of age in the Colorado Adoption Project. *Behavior Genetics, 31*, 353–359.

Wagner, R. K., Torgesen, J. K., & Rashotte, C. A. (1997). Changing relations between phonological processing abilities and word-level reading as children develop from beginning to skilled readers: a 5-year longitudinal study. *Developmental Psychology, 33*, 468–479.

Wainryb, C. (1993). The application of moral judgments to other cultures: Relativism and universality. *Child Development, 64*, 924–933.

Wakely, A., Rivera, S., & Langer, J. (2000). Can young infants add and subtract? *Child Development, 71*, 1525–1534.

Waksler, F. C. (1996) *The little trials of childhood and children's strategies for dealing with them*, London: Falmer.

Walden, T., & Ogan, T. (1988). The development of social referencing. *Child Development, 59*, 1230–1240.

Waldman, I. D. (1996). Aggressive boys' hostile perceptual and response biases: The role of attention and impulsivity. *Child Development, 67*, 1015–1033.

Waldman, I. D., Weinberg, R. A., & Scarr, S. (1994). Racial-group differences in IQ in the Minnesota Transracial Adoption Study: A reply to Levin and Lynn. *Intelligence, 19*, 29–44.

Walker, L. J. (1989). A longitudinal study of moral reasoning. *Child Development, 60*, 157–166.

Walker, L. J. (1991). Sex differences in moral reasoning. In W. M. Kurtines & J. L. Gewirtz (Eds.), *Handbook of moral behavior and development*: Vol. 2. *Research*. Hillsdale, NJ: Erlbaum.

Walker, L. J. (1995). Sexism in Kohlberg's moral psychology? In W. M. Kurtines & J. L. Gewirtz (Eds.), *Moral development: An introduction*. Needham Heights, MA: Allyn & Bacon.

Walker-Andrews, A. S. (1997). Infants' perception of expressive behaviors: Differentiation of multi-modal information. *Psychological Bulletin, 121*, 437–456.

Walker-Andrews, A. S., Bahrick, L. E., Raglioni, S. S., & Diaz, I. (1991). Infants' bimodal perception of gender. *Ecological Psychology, 3*, 55–75.

Walker, H. M., Colvin, G., & Ramsey, E. (1995). *Anti-social behavior in school: Strategies and best practices*. Pacific Grove, CA: Brooks/Cole.

Walker, L. J., Hennig, K. H., & Krettenauer, T. (2000). Parent and peer contexts for children's moral reasoning development. *Child Development, 71*, 1033–1048.

Walker, K. L. & Satterwhite, T. (2002). Academic performance among African American and European American college students: Is the family still important? *College Student Journal, 36*, 113–128.

Walker, L. J., & Taylor, J. H. (1991). Family interactions and the development of moral reasoning. *Child Development, 62*, 264–283.

Wallach, M. A., & Kogan, N. (1966). *Modes of thinking in young children*. New York: Holt, Rinehart, and Winston.

Wallerstein, J. S., Lewis, J. M., & Blakeslee, S. (2000). *The unexpected legacy of divorce: A 25 year landmark study*. New York: Hyperion.

Walls, T. A., & Little, T. D. (2005). Relations among personal agency, motivation, and school adjustment in early adolescence. *Journal of Educational Psychology, 97*, 23–31.

Walsh, J. A. and Sattes, B. D. (2005). *Quality questioning: Research-based practice to engage every learner*. Thousand Oaks, CA: AEL and Corwin Press.

Walton, G. E., Bower, N. J., & Bower, T. G. (1992). Recognition of familiar faces by newborns. *Infant Behavior and Development, 15*, 265–269.

Wang, D. B. (2004). Family background factors and mathematics success: A comparison of Chinese and US students. *International Journal of Educational Research, 41*, 40–54.

Wang, Q., Leichtman, M. D., & Davies, K. I. (2000). Sharing memories and telling stories: American and Chinese mothers and their 3-year-olds. *Memory, 8*, 159–177.

Wang, Z., & Xu, Y. (2005). Learning style, academic self-concept, and academic achievement. *Chinese Journal of Clinical Psychology, 13*, 203–205.

Ward, M. J., & Carlson, E. A. (1995). Associations among adult attachment representations, maternal sensitivity, and infant-mother attachment in a sample of adolescent mothers. *Child Development, 66*, 69–79.

Wark, G. R., & Krebs, D. L. (1996). Gender and dilemma differences in real-life moral judgment. *Developmental Psychology, 32*, 220–230.

Warikoo, N. (2004). Race and the teacher-student relationship: Interpersonal connections between West Indian students and their teachers in a New York City high school. *Race Ethnicity & Education, 7*, 135–147.

Wasserman, G. A., Liu, X., Pine, D. S., & Graziano, J. H. (2001). Contribution of maternal smoking during pregnancy and lead exposure to early child behavior problems. *Neurotoxicology and Teratology, 23*, 13–21.

Wasz-Hockert, O., Michelsson, K., & Lind, J. (1985). Twenty-five years of Scandinavian cry research. In B. M. Lester & C. Z. Boukydis (Eds.), *Infant crying: Theoretical and research perspectives*. New York: Plenum.

Waterman, A. S. (1999). Identity, the identity statuses, and identity status development: A contemporary statement. *Developmental Review, 19*, 591–621.

Watson, J. D. (1990). The Human Genome Project: Past, present, and future. *Science, 248*, 44–49.

Watson, J. D., & Crick, F. H. C. (1953). Molecular structure of nucleic acid: A structure for deoxyribose nucleic acid. *Nature, 171*, 737–738.

Watt, H.M. (2004). Development of adolescents' self-perceptions, values, and task perceptions according to gender and domain in 7th- through 11th-grade Australian students. *Child Development, 75*, 1556–1574.

Waxman, S. R. (1990). Linguistic biases and the establishment of conceptual hierarchies. *Cognitive Development, 5*, 123–150.

Webb, N. M., & Palinscar, A. S. (1996). Group processes in the classroom. In D. C. Berliner & R. C. Calfee (Eds.), *Handbook of educational psychology*. New York: Simon & Schuster Macmillan.

Weber-Fox, C. M., & Neville, H. J. (1996). Maturational constraints on functional specializations for language processing: ERP and behavioral evidence in bilingual speakers. *Journal of Cognitive Neuroscience, 8*, 231–256.

Wechsler, D. (1967). *Manual for the Wechsler Preschool and Primary Scale of Intelligence*. New York: Psychological Corporation.

Weinberg, M. K., Tronick, E. Z., Cohn, J. F., & Olson, K. L. (1999). Gender differences in emotional expressivity and self-regulation during early infancy. *Developmental Psychology, 35*, 175–188.

Weine, S., Becker, D., McGlashan, T., Vojvoda, D., Hartman, S., & Robbins, J. (1995). Adolescent survivors of "ethnic cleansing" on the first year in America. *Journal of the American Academy of Child and Adolescent Psychiatry, 34*, 1153–1159.

Weinfield, N. S., Sroufe, L. A., Egeland, B., & Carlson, E. A. (1999). The nature of individual differences in infant-caregiver attachment. In J. Cassidy & P.R. Shaver (Eds.), *Handbook of attachment: Theory, research, and clinical applications* (pp. 68–88). New York: Guilford.

Weinfield, N. S., Whaley, G. J. L., & Egeland, B. (2004). Continuity, discontinuity, and coherence in attachment from late infancy to late adolescence: Sequelae of organization and disorganization. *Attachment & Human Development, 61*, 73–97.

Weinraub, M., Clemens, L. P., Sockloff, A., Ethridge, T., Gracely, E., & Myers, B. (1984). The development of sex role stereotypes in the third year: Relationships to gender labeling, gender identity, sex-typed toy preference, and family characteristics. *Child Development, 55*, 1493–1503.

Weinraub, M., Horvath, D. L., & Gringlas, M. B. (2002). Single parenthood. In M.H. Bornstein (Ed.), *Handbook of parenting*, vol 3: *Being and becoming a parent* (pp. 109–140), 2nd ed. Mahwah, NJ: Erlbaum.

Weinstein, R. S. (2002). Achievement cultures for university faculty. In R. S. Weinstein (Ed.), *Reaching higher: The power of expectations in schooling*. Cambridge, MA: Harvard University Press.

Weinstein, R.S., Gregory, A., & Strambler, M.J. (2004). Intractable self-fulfilling prophecies. *American Psychologist, 59*, 511–520.

Weinstein, R. S., Madison, S. M., & Kuklinski, M. R. (1995). Raising expectations in schooling: Obstacles and opportunities for change. *American Educational Research Journal, 32*(1), 121–159.

Weisner, T. S., & Wilson-Mitchell, J. E. (1990). Nonconventional family life styles and sex typing in six-year-olds. *Child Development, 61*, 1915–1933.

Weiss, B., Dodge, K. A., Bates, J. E., & Pettit, G. S. (1992). Some consequences of early harsh discipline: Child aggression and a maladaptive social information processing style. *Child Development, 63*, 1321–1335.

Weiss, M. G., & Miller, P. H. (1983). Young children's understanding of displaced aggression. *Journal of Experimental Child Psychology, 35*, 529–539.

Weizman, Z. O., & Snow, C. E. (2001). Lexical output as related to children's vocabulary acquisition: Effects of sophisticated exposure and support for meaning. *Developmental Psychology, 37*, 265–279.

Wekselman, K., Spiering, K., Hetterberg, C., Kenner, C., & Flandermeyer, A. (1995). Fetal alcohol syndrome from infancy to childhood: A review of the literature. *Journal of Pediatric Nursing, 10*, 296–303.

Welch-Ross, M. K., & Schmidt, C. R. (1996). Gender schema development and children's constructive story memory: Evidence for a developmental model. *Child Development, 67*, 820–835.

Wellman, H. M. (1977). Preschoolers' understanding of memory-relevant variables. *Child Development, 48*, 1720–1723.

Wellman, H. M. (1988). The early development of memory strategies. In F. E. Weinert & M. Perlmutter (Eds.), *Memory development: Universal changes and individual differences*. Hillsdale, NJ: Erlbaum.

Wellman, H. M., Ritter, K., & Flavell, J. H. (1975). Deliberate memory behavior in the delayed reactions of very young children. *Developmental Psychology, 11*, 780–787.

Wenglinsky, H. (2002). How schools matter: The link between teacher classroom practices and student academic performance. *Education Policy Analysis Archives, 10*(12).

Wentworth, N., Haith, M. M., & Hood, R. (2002). Spatiotemporal regularity and interevent contingencies as information for infants' visual expectations. *Infancy, 3*, 303–322.

Wentzel, K. R., & Watkins, D. E. (2002). Peer relationships and collaborative learning as contexts for academic enablers. *School Psychology Review, 31*, 366–377.

Werker, J. F., & Tees, R. C. (1999). Influences on infant speech processing: Toward a new synthesis. *Annual Review of Psychology, 50*, 509–535.

Werker, J. F., & Vouloumanos, A. (2001). Speech and language processing in infancy: a neurocognitive approach. In C. A. Nelson & M. Luciana (Eds.), *Handbook of Developmental Cognitive Neuroscience*, pp. 269–307, Cambridge, MA: MIT Press.

Werner, E. E. (1990). Protective factors and individual resilience. In S.J. Meisels & Shonkoff, J.P. (Eds.), *Handbook of early childhood intervention*. New York: Cambridge University Press.

Werner, E., & Smith, R. (1982). *Vulnerable but invincible: A study of resilient children*. New York: McGraw Hill.

Werner, E. E., & Smith, R. S. (2001). *Journeys from childhood to midlife: Risk, resilience, and recovery*. Ithaca, NY: Cornell University Press.

Wertsch, J. V. (1981). *Voices of the mind*. Cambridge, MA: Harvard University Press.

Wertsch, J. V. (1985). *Vygotsky and the social formation of mind*. Cambridge, MA: Harvard University Press.

Wertsch, J. V., & Kanner, B. G. (1992). A sociocultural approach to intellectual development. In R. J. Sternberg & C. Berg (Eds.), *Intellectual development*. New York: Cambridge University Press.

Wertheimer, M. (1961). Psychomotor coordination of auditory-visual space at birth. *Science, 134*, 16–92.

Wertsch, J. V., & Tulviste, P. (1992). J. S. Vygotsky and contemporary developmental psychology. *Developmental Psychology, 28*, 548–557.

Wettersten, K. B., Guilmino, A., et al. (2005). Predicting educational and vocational attitudes among rural high school students. *Journal of Counseling Psychology, 52*, 658–663.

Wheeler, L., & Suls, J. (2005). Social comparison and self-evaluations of competence. In A. J. Elliot, & C. S. Dweck (Eds.), *Handbook of competence and motivation*. New York: Guilford.

Whelan, T. A., & Kirkby, R. J. (2000). Parent adjustment to a child's hospitalization. *Journal of Family Studies, 6*, 46–64.

White, B. L., Castle, P., & Held, R. (1964). Observations on the development of visually directed reaching. *Child Development, 35*, 349–364.

White, S., & Tharp, R. G. (1988, April). *Questioning and wait-time: A cross-cultural analysis*. Paper presented at the meeting of the American Educational Research Association, New Orleans.

Whitehurst, G. J., Falco, F. L., Lonigan, C. J., Fischel, J. E., DeBaryshe, B. D., Valdez-Menchaca, M. C., & Caulfield, C. (1988). Accelerating language development through picture book reading. *Developmental Psychology, 24*, 552–559.

Whitehurst, G. J., & Lonigan, C. J. (1998). Child development and emergent literacy. *Child Development, 69*, 848–872.

Whitehurst, G. J., & Novak, G. (1973). Modeling, imitation training, and the acquisition of sentence phrases. *Journal of Experimental Child Psychology, 16*, 332–345.

Whitehurst, G. J., & Sonnenschein, S. (1985). The development of communication: A functional analysis. In G. J. Whitehurst (Ed.), *Annals of child development* (Vol. 2). Greenwich, CT: JAI Press.

Whiteside, M. F., & Becker, B. J. (2000). Parental factors and the young child's post-divorce adjustment: A meta-analysis with implications for parenting arrangements. *Journal of Family Psychology, 14*, 5–26.

Whiting, B. B., & Edwards, C. P. (1988). *Children of different worlds: The formation of social behavior*. Cambridge, MA: Harvard University Press.

White, T. L., Leichtman, M. D., & Ceci, S. J. (1997). The good, the bad, and the ugly: Accuracy, inaccuracy, and elaboration in preschoolers' reports about a past event. *Applied Cognitive Psychology, 11*, S37–S54.

Whiting, B. B., & Whiting, J. W. M. (1975). *Children of six cultures: A psycho-cultural analysis*. Cambridge, MA: Harvard University Press.

Whitley, R., & Goldenberg, R. (1990). Infectious disease in the prenatal period and the recommendations for screening. In I. R. Merkatz & J. E. Thompson (Eds.), *New perspectives on prenatal care*. New York: Elsevier.

Whitman, N. (2003). *Learning from Japanese middle school math teachers*. Phi Delta Kappa, Educational Foundation, Bloomington, IN.

Whitney, E. N., & Rolfes, S. R. (2002). *Understanding nutrition* (9th ed.). Belmont, CA: Wadsworth Publishing Company.

Wicherts, J. M., Dolan, C. V., Hessen, D. J., Oosterveld, P., Baal, G. C. M. van, Boomsma, D. I., & Span, M. M. (2004). Are intelligence tests measurement invariant over time? Investigating the nature of the Flynn effect. *Intelligence, 32*, 509–537.

Wichstrom, L. (1995). Harter's Self-Perception Profile for Adolescents: Reliabilty, validity, and evaluation of the question format. *Journal of Personality Assessment, 65*(1), 100–116.

Wiener, J. & Tardif, C. (2004). Social and emotional functioning of children with learning disabilities: Does special education placement make a difference? *Learning Disabilities Research and Practice, 19*, 20–33.

Wigfield, A., Battle, A., Keller, L. B., & Eccles, J. S. (2002). Sex differences in motivation, self-concept, career aspiration and career choice: Implications for cognitive development. In A. V. McGillicuddy-De Lisi & R. De Lisi (Eds.), *Biology, society, and behavior: The development of sex differences in cognition*. Greenwich, CT: Ablex.

Wigfield, A., Eccles, J. S., Yoon, K. S., Harold, R. D., Arbreton, A., Freedman-Doan, K., et al. (1997). Changes in children's competence beliefs and subjective task values across the elementary school years: A three-year-study. *Journal of Educational Psychology, 89*, 451–469.

Wikipedia (2006). Thalidomide. Retrieved March 10, 2006 from http://en.wikipedia.org/wiki/Thalidomide

Wilcox, A. J., Baird, D. D., Weinberg, C. R., Hornsby, P. P., & Herbst, A. L. (1995). Fertility in men exposed prenatally to diethylstilbestrol. *New England Journal of Medicine, 332*, 1411–1416.

Williams, J. (1987). *Psychology of women: Behavior in a biosocial context*. New York: Norton.

Williams, J. E., & Best, D. L. (1990). *Measuring sex stereotypes: A multinational study*. Newbury Park, CA: Sage.

Williams, K., Veronica, W. & Johnson, M. A. (2002). Eliminating Africans-American health disparity via history-based policy. *Features: Equality and Health Care, 3*(2).

Willingham, W. W., & Cole, N. S. (Eds.). (1997). *Gender and fair assessment*. Mahwah, NJ: Erlbaum.

Willingham, W. W., Cole, N. S., Lewis, C., & Leung, S. W. (1997). Test performance. In W. W. Willingham & N. S. Cole (Eds.), *Gender and fair assessment*. Mahwah, NJ: Erlbaum.

Wills, T. A., Gibbons, F. X., Gerrard, M., Murray, V. B., & Brody, G. H. (2003). Family communication and religiosity related to substance use and sexual behavior in early adolescence: A test for pathways through self-control and prototype perceptions. *Psychology of Addictive Behaviors, 17*, 312–323.

Wills, T. A., & Resko, J. A. (2004). Social support and behavior toward others: Some paradoxes and some directions. In A.G. Miller (Ed.), *The social psychology of good and evil*. New York: Guilford.

Wilson, R. S. (1986). Growth and development of human twins. In F. Falkner & J. M. Tanner (Eds.), *Human growth: A comprehensive treatise*. New York: Plenum.

Wilson, M. (Ed.). (1995). *African American family life: Its structural and ecological aspects*. San Francisco: Jossey-Bass.

Wilson, W. J. (1996). *When work disappears : The world of the new urban poor*. New York: Vintage.

Windrim, R. (2005). Vaginal delivery in birth centre after previous caesarean section. *Lancet, 365*, 106–107.

Windsor, J. (1993). The functions of novel word compounds. *Journal of Child Language, 20*, 119–138.

Winner, E. (1996). *Gifted children*. New York: Basic Books.

Winner, E. (2000). The origins and ends of giftedness. *American Psychologist, 55*, 159–169.

Winsler, A., Dias, R. M., McCarthy, E. M., Atencio, D. J., & Chabay, L. (1999). Mother-child interactions, private speech, and task performance in preschool children with behavior problems. *Journal of Child Psychology and Psychiatry, 40*, 891–904.

Winstok, Z., & Enosh, G. (2004). Towards re-conceptualization of global-self-image: Preliminary findings of the validity and reliability of a structured scale. *Individual Differences Research, 2*, 63–80.

Witelson, S. F. (1976). Sex and the single hemisphere: Specialization of the right hemisphere for spatial processing. *Science, 193*, 425–427.

Withnall, A. (2006). Exploring influences on later life learning. *International Journal of Lifelong Education, 25*(1), 29–49.

Wittmer, D. S., & Honig, A. S. (1988). Teacher re-creation of negative interactions with toddlers. *Early Child Development & Care, 33*, 77–88.

Wolchik, S. A., Wilcox, K. L., Tein, J., & Sandler, I. N. (2000). Maternal acceptance and consistency of discipline as buffers of divorce stressors on children's psychological adjustment problems. *Journal of Abnormal Child Psychology, 28*, 87–102.

Wolff, P. H. (1959). Observations on newborn infants. *Psychosomatic Medicine, 21*, 110–118.

Wolff, P.H. (1966). The causes, controls and organization of behavior in the neonate. *Psychological Issues, 5*(17).

Wolff, P.H. (1969). The natural history of crying and other vocalizations in early infancy. In B. Foss (Ed.), *Determinants of infant behavior* (Vol. 4). London: Methuen.

Wolk, S., Zeanah, C., Garcia Coll, C., & Carr, S. (1992). Factors affecting parents' perception of temperament in early infancy. *American Journal of Orthopsychiatry, 62*, 71–82.

Wolters, C.A. (2004). Advancing achievement goal theory: Using goal structures and goal orientations to predict students' motivation, cognition, and achievement. *Journal of Educational Psychology, 96*, 236–250.

Wonacott, M. E. (2003). *Everyone goes to college. Myths and realities*. Office of Educational Research and Improvement, Washington, DC.

Wong, C. A., Eccles, J. S., Sameroff, A. (2003). The influence of ethnic discrimination and ethnic identification on African American adolescents' school and socioemotional adjustment. *Journal of Personality, 71*(6), 1197–1232.

Wood, D., Bruner, J., & Ross, G. (1976). The role of tutoring in problem solving. *Journal of Child Psychology and Psychiatry, 17*, 89–100.

Wood, E., Desmarais, S., & Gugula, S. (2002). The impact of parenting experience on gender stereotyped toy play of children. *Sex Roles, 47*, 39–49.

Woody-Dorning, J., & Miller, P. H. (2001). Children's individual differences in capacity: Effects on strategy production and utilization. *British Journal of Developmental Psychology, 19*, 543–557.

Woodward, A. L. (1998). Infants selectively encode the goal object of an actor's reach. *Cognition, 69*, 1–34.

Woodward, A. L., & Markman, E. M. (1998). Early word learning. In W. Damon (Series Ed.) & D. Kuhn & R. S. Siegler (Vol. Eds.), *Handbook of child psychology:* Vol. 2. *Cognition, perception, and language* (5th ed.). New York: Wiley.

World Education Services. (2005). World education database. Retrieved from www.wes.org. http://nt5.scbbs.com/cgibin/om_isapi.dll?clientID=263528&infobase=iwde.nfo&softpage=PL_frame

World Health Organization. (2005). Retrieved March 17, 2006 from http://www.who.int/mediacentre/factsheets/fs288/en/index.html

World Health Organization (2006). Retrieved March 16, 2006 from http://www.who.int/nutrition/challenges/en/index.html.

The world health report 2005 WHO (2005). *Make every mother and child count*. Geneva, World Health Organization, Retrieved 11 October 2005 from (http://www.who.int/whr/2005/en,).

Worobey J., & Blajda, V. M. (1989). Temperament ratings at 2 weeks, 2 months, and 1 year: Differential stability of activity and emotionality. *Developmental Psychology, 25*, 257–263.

Wright, J. C., Huston, A. C., Vandewater, E. A., Bickham, D. S., Scantlin, R. M., Kotler, J. A., et al. (2001). American children's use of electronic media in 1997: A national survey. *Applied Developmental Psychology, 22*, 31–47.

Wu, X., Hart, C. H., Draper, T. W., & Olsen, J. A. (2001). Peer and teacher sociometrics for preschool children: Cross-information concordance, temporal stability, and reliability. *Merrill-Palmer Quarterly, 47*, 416–443.

Wu, T., Mendola, P., & Buck, G. M. (2002). Ethnic differences in the presence of secondary sex characteristics and menarche among US girls: The

Third National Health and Nutrition Examination Survey, 1988–1994. *Pediatrics, 110*, 752–757.

Wulfert, E., Block, J. A., Santa Ana, E., Rodriguez, M. L., & Colsman, M. (2002). Delay of gratification: Impulsive choices and problem behaviors in early and late adolescence. *Journal of Personality, 70*, 533–552.

Wynn, K. (1992). Addition and subtraction by human infants. *Nature, 358*, 749–750.

Yang, F. (2004). Exploring high school students' use of theory and evidence in an everyday context: The role of scientific thinking in environmental science decision-making. *International Journal of Science Education, 26*, 1345–1364.

Yang, L., & Yu, S. (2002). A research review on the mental mechanisms of children's self-imposed delay of gratification. *Psychological Science (China), 25*, 712–715.

Yarrow, L. J., McQuiston, S., MacTurk, R. H., McCarthy, M. E., Klein, R. P., & Vietze, P. M. (1983). Assessment of mastery motivation during the first year of life: contemporaneous and cross-age relationships. *Developmental Psychology, 19*, 159–171.

Yarrow, L. J., Rubenstein, J. L., & Pedersen, F. A. (1975). *Infant and environment: Early cognitive and motivational development*. Bethesda, MD: NICHD.

Yates, G. C. R., Yates, S. M., & Beasley, C. J. (1987). Young children's knowledge of strategies in delay of gratification. *Merrill-Palmer Quarterly, 33*, 159–169.

Yates, M., & Youniss, J. (1996). A developmental perspective on community service in adolescence. *Social Development, 5*, 85–111.

Yeakey, C. C. & Henderson, R. D. (2003). *Surmounting all odds: Education, opportunity, and society in the new millennium*. Volume 1. A volume in research on african american education. Connecticut: Information Age Publishing.

Yeung, A.S., & McInerney, D.M. (2005). Students' school motivation and aspiration over high school years. *Educational Psychology, 25*, 537–554.

Yeung, W. J., Sandberg, J. F., Davis-Kean, P. E., & Hoffert, S. L. (2001). Children's time with fathers in intact families. *Journal of Marriage and the Family, 63*, 136–154.

Yeung, D. Y. L., So-kum Tang, C., & Lee, A. (2005). Psychosocial and cultural factors influencing expectations of menarche: A Study on Chinese premenarcheal teenage girls. *Journal of Adolescent Research, 20*, 118–135.

Young, L., & Ansell, N. (2003).Young AIDS migrants in Southern Africa: policy implications for empowering children, *AIDS Care, 15*(3): 337–345.

Youngblade, L. M., & Belsky, J. (1992). Parent-child antecedents of 5-year-olds' close friendships: A longitudinal analysis. *Developmental Psychology, 28*, 700–713.

Younger, A., Gentile, C., & Burgess., K. (1993). Children's perceptions of social withdrawal: Changes across age. In K. Rubin & J. Asendorpf (Eds.), *Social withdrawal, inhibition, and shyness in childhood* (pp. 215–236). Hillsdale NJ: Erlbaum

Younger, A., Schneider, B., & Pelley, G. (March, 1993). *Children's behavioral descriptions of their shy, withdrawn peers*. Presented at the Biennial meeting of the Society for Research in Child Development, New Orleans, LA.

Younger, A., Schneider, B., Wadeson, R., Guiguis, M., & Bergeron, B. (2000). A behaviour-based, peer-nomination measure of social withdrawal in children. *Social Development, 9*, 544–564.

Younger, A. J., & Piccinin, A. M. (1989). Children's recall of aggressive and withdrawn behaviors: Recognition memory and likability judgments. *Child Development, 60,* 580–590.

Younger, A. J., Schwartzman, A. E., & Ledingham, J. E. (1985). Age-related changes in children's perceptions of aggression and withdrawal in their peers. *Developmental Psychology, 21,* 70–75.

Youniss, J., McLellan, J. A., & Mazer, B. (2001). Voluntary service, peer group orientation, and civic engagement. *Journal of Adolescent Research, 5,* 456–468.

Youniss, J., & Volpe, J. (1978). A relational analysis of children's friendship. In W. Damon (Ed.), *New directions for child development: No. 1. Social cognition.* San Francisco: Jossey-Bass.

Youth Violence: A Report of the Surgeon General. (2001). http://www.surgeongeneral.gov/library/youthviolence/default.htm) Accessed February 23, 2006

Yowell, C. M. (2000). Possible selves and future-orientation: Exploring hopes and fears of Latino boys and girls. *Journal of Early Adolescence, 20,* 245–280.

Yowell, C. M. (2002). Dreams of the future: The pursuit of educational and career possible selves among ninth grade Latino youth. *Applied Developmental Science, 6,* 62–72.

Yussen, S. R., & Levy, Y. M. (1975). Developmental changes in predicting one's own span of short-term memory. *Journal of Experimental Child Psychology, 19,* 502–508.

Zabriski, A. L., & Coie, J. D. (1996). A comparison of aggressive-rejected and nonaggressive-rejected children's interpretations of self-directed and other-directed rejection. *Child Development, 67,* 1048–1070.

Zahn-Waxler, C., & Radke-Yarrow, M. (1982). The development of altruism: Alternative research strategies. In N. Eisenberg (Ed.), *The development of prosocial behavior.* San Diego, CA: Academic Press.

Zahn-Waxler, C., Radke-Yarrow, M., Wagner, E., & Chapman, M. (1992). Development of concern for others. *Developmental Psychology, 28,* 126–136.

Zahn-Waxler, C., Robinson, J. L., & Emde, R. N. (1992). The development of empathy in twins. *Developmental Psychology, 28,* 1038–1047.

Zahn-Waxler, C., Schiro, K., Robinson, J., Emde, R. N., & Schmitz, S. (2001). Empathy and prosocial patterns in young MZ and DZ twins: Development and genetic and environmental influences. In R. N. Emde & J. K. Hewitt (Eds.), *Infancy to early childhood: Genetic and environmental influences on developmental change.* Oxford: Oxford University Press.

Zametkin, A. J., Nordahl, T. E., Gross, M., King, A. C., Semple, W. E., Rumsey, J., et al. (1990). Cerebral glucose metabolism in adults with hyperac-tivity of childhood onset. *New England Journal of Medicine, 20,* 1361–1366.

Zang, L., & Zang, X. (2003). A study of the relationships among learning strategy-use, self-efficacy, persistence and academic achievement in middle school students. *Psychological Science* (China), *26,* 603–607.

Zarbatany, L., Hartmann, D. P., Elfand, D. M., & Vinciguerra, P. (1985). Gender differences in altruistic reputation: Are they artifactual? *Developmental Psychology, 21,* 97–101.

Zeidner, M. (1990). Does test anxiety bias scholastic aptitude test performance by gender and sociocultural group? *Journal of Personality Assessment, 55,* 145–160.

Zelazo, P. D. (1999). Language, levels of consciousness, and the development of intentional action. In P. D. Zelazo, J. W. Astington, & D. R. Olson (Eds.), *Developing theories of intention.* Mahwah, NJ: Erlbaum.

Zelazo, P. D., & Frye, D. (1998). Cognitive complexity and control: II. The development of executive function in childhood. *Current Directions in Psychological Science, 7,* 121–126.

Zelazo, N. A., Zelazo, P. R., Cohen, K. M., & Zelazo, P.D. (1993). Specificity of practice effects on elementary neuromotor patterns. *Developmental Psychology, 29,* 686–691.

Zelazo, P. R., Weiss, M. J. S., & Tarquino, N. (1991). Habituation and recovery of neonatal orienting to auditory stimuli. In M. J. S. Weiss & P. R. Zelazo (Eds.), *Newborn attention: Biological constraints and the influence of experience.* Norwood, NJ: Ablex.

Zempsky, W. T. & Cravero, J. P. (2004). Committee on Pediatric Emergency Medicine and Section on Anesthesiology and Pain Medicine. Relief of pain and anxiety in pediatric patients in emergency medical systems. *Pediatrics,* 114(5), 1348–1356.

Zentner, M. R., & Kagan, J. (1998). Infants' perception of consonance and dissonance in music. *Infant Behavior and Development, 21,* 483–492.

Zeskind, P. S., & Lester, B. M. (2001). Analysis of infant crying. In L. T. Singer & P. S. Zeskind (Eds.), *Biobehavioral assessment of the infant.* New York: Guilford.

Zeskind, P. S., & Marshall, T. R. (1988). The relation between variations in pitch and maternal perceptions of infant crying. *Child Development, 59,* 193–196.

Zeskind, P. S., & Ramey, C. T. (1981). Preventing intellectual and interactional sequelae of fetal malnutrition: A longitudinal, transactional and synergistic approach to development. *Child Development, 52,* 213–218.

Zhang, D., & Katsiyannis, A. (2002). Minority representation in special education: A persistent challenge. *Remedial & Special Education, 23,* 180–187.

Zhen, Z., & Yousui, L. (2004). The research trend and measuring method on implicit self-esteem. *Psychological Science* (China), *27,* 961–963.

Zhou, Q., Eisenberg, N., Wang, Y., & Reiser, M. (2004). Chinese children's effortful control and dispositional anger/frustration: Relations to parenting styles and children's social functioning. *Developmental Psychology, 40,* 352–366.

Ziegler, A., & Stoeger, H. (2004). Evaluation of an attributional retraining (modeling technique) to reduce gender differences in chemistry instruction. *High Ability Studies, 15,* 63–83.

Zigler, E. (1988). Day care and its effect on children: An overview for pediatric health professionals. *Journal of Developmental & Behavioral Pediatrics, 9,* 38–46.

Zill, N., Collins, M., West, J., & Hausken, E. (1995). Approaching kindergarten: A look at preschoolers in the United States. Public Policy Report. *Young Children, 51,* 35–38.

Zill, N., Morrison, D. R., & Coiro, M. J. (1993). Long-term effects of parental divorce on parent-child relationships, adjustment, and achievement in young adulthood. *Journal of Family Psychology, 7,* 1–13.

Zimbardo, P., & Radl, S. (1999). *The shy child : overcoming and preventing shyness from infancy to adulthood .* Malor Books.

Zimmerman, P., & Becker-Stoll, F. (2002). Stability of attachment representations during adolescence: The influence of ego-identity status. *Journal of Adolescence, 25,* 107–124

Zimmerman, B. J., & Blom, D. E. (1983). Toward an empirical test of the role of cognitive conflict in learning. *Developmental Review, 3,* 18–38.

Zimmerman, F. J., & Christakis, D. A. (2005). Children's television viewing and cognitive outcomes: A longitudinal analysis of national data. *Archives of Pediatrics & Adolescent Medicine, 159,* 687–689.

Zimmerman, B. & Schunk, D. (2001). *Educational psychology: A century of contributions.* Hillsdale, NJ: Erlbaum.

Zirkel, S. (2002). Is there a place for me? Role models and academic identity among white students and students of color. *Teachers College Record, 104,* 357–376.

Zucker, K. J. (2001). Biological influences on psychosexual differentiation. In R. Unger (Ed.), *Handbook of the psychology of women and gender.* New York: Wiley.

Zucker, K. J., Bradley, S. J., Oliver, G., Blake, J., Fleming, S., & Hood, J. (1996). Psychosexual development of women with congenital adrenal hyperplasia. *Hormones and Behavior, 30,* 300–318.

Zucker, K. J., Wilson-Smith, D. N., Kurita, J. A., & Stern, A. (1995). Children's appraisals of sex-typed behavior in their peers. *Sex Roles, 33,* 703–725.

Zukow-Goldring, P. (2002). Sibling caregiving. In M. H. Bornstein (Ed.), *Handbook of parenting* (2nd ed., Vol. 3). Mahwah, NJ: Erlbaum.

Author Index

Subject Index